The Cambridge Handbook of
Violent Behavior and Aggression

This *Handbook* provides a comprehensive, multidisciplinary examination of the most current research and thinking about the complex issue of violence and violent behavior. The volume examines a range of theoretical, policy, and research issues and provides a comprehensive overview of aggressive and violent behavior. The breadth of coverage is impressive, ranging from research on biological factors related to violence and behavior-genetics to research on terrorism and the impact of violence in different cultures. The *Handbook* examines violence from international cross-cultural perspectives, with chapters that present both quantitative and qualitative research. The *Handbook* also examines violence at multiple levels: individual, family, neighborhood, and cultural, and across multiple perspectives and systems, including treatment, justice, education, and public health. The *Handbook* represents the most current and up-to-date research from leading experts around the world.

Dr. Flannery is currently Professor of Justice Studies and Director of the Institute for the Study and Prevention of Violence at Kent State University (KSU). He was named a University Distinguished Scholar at KSU in 2006. He is a licensed clinical psychologist and an Associate Professor of Pediatrics at Case Western Reserve University and University Hospitals of Cleveland. He is co-editor of *Youth Violence: Prevention, Intervention, and Social Policy* (1999) and author of the recently released book *Violence and Mental Health in Everyday Life: Prevention and Intervention for Children and Adolescents* (2006). His primary areas of research are in youth violence prevention, the link between violence and mental health, and program evaluation. He received his PhD in 1991 in Clinical-Child Psychology from Ohio State University. His previous appointments were as Assistant Professor of Family Studies at the University of Arizona and as Associate Professor of Child Psychiatry at Case Western Reserve University. He has published more than 100 empirical articles and book chapters on youth violence prevention, delinquency, and parent-adolescent relations. He has also generated more than $15 million in external support for his research. He has served as a consultant to various local and national organizations, including the U.S. Departments of Justice and Education, the Centers for Disease Control and Prevention, the National Crime Prevention Council, and the National Resource Center for Safe Schools.

Dr. Vazsonyi is currently Professor of Human Development and Family Studies at Auburn University in Alabama. He has been a Fulbright Fellow in Slovenia, currently serves as the editor of the *Journal of Early Adolescence*, and has served as a representative to the United Nations in Geneva and Vienna for the American Society of Criminology. He serves as a panel member and grant reviewer for the National Science Foundation, SAMHSA, and the Department of Education; currently reviews for more than 20 peer-reviewed journals; and is a member of three editorial boards (*International Journal of Comparative and Applied Criminal Justice, Journal of Marriage and Family,* and the *Journal of Youth and Adolescence*). His research interests focus on the etiology of child and adolescent problem behaviors, deviance, and violence, and he has a particular interest in the application of the cross-cultural or cross-national comparative method to the study of human development and behaviors.

Dr. Waldman is currently Professor of Psychology at Emory University in Atlanta. He is a clinical psychologist with developmental interests who examines the genetic and environmental etiology of disruptive behavior disorders in childhood and adolescence. His current research explores the role of candidate genes in the development of externalizing behavior problems, as well as genetic and environmental influences on comorbidity and on the links between normal variation in symptoms and in personality in the general population.

The Cambridge Handbook of
Violent Behavior and Aggression

Edited by

DANIEL J. FLANNERY
Kent State University

ALEXANDER T. VAZSONYI
Auburn University

IRWIN D. WALDMAN
Emory University

CAMBRIDGE
UNIVERSITY PRESS

CAMBRIDGE UNIVERSITY PRESS
Cambridge, New York, Melbourne, Madrid, Cape Town, Singapore, São Paulo, Delhi

Cambridge University Press
32 Avenue of the Americas, New York, NY 10013-2473, USA

www.cambridge.org
Information on this title: www.cambridge.org/9780521845670

First published 2007

Printed in the United States of America

A catalog record for this publication is available from the British Library.

Library of Congress Cataloging in Publication Data
The Cambridge handbook of violent behavior and aggression / edited by
Daniel J. Flannery, Alexander T. Vazsonyi, Irwin D. Waldman.
    p. cm.
Includes bibliographical references and index.
ISBN-13: 978-0-521-84567-0 (hardback)
ISBN-10: 0-521-84567-X (hardback)
ISBN-13: 978-0-521-60785-8 (pbk.)
ISBN-10: 0-521-60785-X (pbk.)
1. Violence.   2. Aggressiveness.   3. Deviant behavior.   4. Antisocial
personality disorders.   I. Flannery, Daniel J., 1962–   II. Vazsonyi,
Alexander T., 1964–   III. Waldman, Irwin D.   IV. Title.

HM1116.C36 2007
303.601—dc22   2006038912

ISBN   978-0-521-84567-0 hardback
ISBN   978-0-521-60785-8 paperback

We dedicate this volume to James J. Flannery (Daniel Flannery), a wonderful father and teacher by example, and to Gabor E. Vazsonyi (Alexander T. Vazsonyi), a tireless pedagogue and visionary—both passed away during the completion of this volume. Irwin Waldman dedicates this volume to his parents, Mel and Barbara, for their encouragement of reaching his career goals and the freedom to pursue his intellectual curiosity wherever it has led. We also dedicate this volume to the work and memory of David C. Rowe.

Contents

Contributors

Robert S. Agnew is a Professor of Sociology at Emory University. His research interests focus on the causes of delinquency, particularly his general strain theory of delinquency. Recent books include *Juvenile Delinquency: Causes and Control* (Roxbury, 2005) and *Why Do Criminals Offend? A General Theory of Crime and Delinquency* (Roxbury, 2005). He is currently completing a book titled *Pressured Into Crime: An Overview of General Strain Theory* (Roxbury, forthcoming).

Lara M. Belliston earned her PhD and MS from Auburn University in human development and family studies and a BS from Brigham Young University. She currently works at the Ohio Department of Mental Health (ODMH), Office of Program Evaluation and Research as an Evaluation Researcher on Ohio's Mental Health Transformation State Incentive Grant (TSIG). Before joining ODMH, Dr. Belliston completed a postdoctoral fellowship with the Institute for the Study and Prevention of Violence at Kent State University. Her research interests and experience include program evaluation, the influence of family relationships on internalizing and externalizing behaviors, violence prevention, and risk and protective factors for adjustment.

Daniel M. Blonigen, MA, is a PhD candidate at the Clinical Science and Psychopathology Research Program at the University of Minnesota, Twin Cities. He attained his bachelor's degree with honors (Summa Cum Laude), and his master's degree at the University of Minnesota, Twin Cities. His research interests involve the use of behavior-genetic and longitudinal methods to understand the etiology and development of psychopathic personality, normal personality, and externalizing psychopathology. He is a former trainee in the NIMH Neurobehavioral Aspects of Personality and Psychopathology Training Program and recipient of the Eva O. Miller Fellowship and Doctoral Dissertation Fellowship from the Graduate School at the University of Minnesota.

Michel Boivin is the Canada Research Chair in Child Social Development and Professor of Psychology at Laval University. Dr. Boivin's main research interests concern children's social behaviors, peer relationships, and school adjustment. He is currently Co-Principal Investigator in three large-scale population-based longitudinal studies investigating the early biological and social antecedents of social and school adjustment, as well as their consequences. He is now a member of the executive commitee and Director at Laval University of the Research Unit on Children's Psycho-Social Maladjustment (GRIP), a multidisciplinary and interuniversity research center investigating risk and protective factors that influence children's development.

Jeanne Brooks-Gunn is the Virginia and Leonard Marx Professor of Child Development at Teachers College and the College of Physicians and Surgeons of Columbia University. She co-directs the Columbia University Institute of Child and Family Policy. She has extensively studied neighborhood and family socioeconomic status and poverty and their impacts on children's behavior problems and academic outcomes. Her publications include *Neighborhood Poverty: Context and Consequences for Children (Vol. 1)* and *Policy Implications in Studying Neighborhoods (Vol. 2)* with G. Duncan and L. Aber, and *Consequences of Growing Up Poor* with G. Duncan.

ANDREW CANASTAR is a Developmental Psychobiology Research Group Postdoctoral Trainee at the University of Colorado Health Sciences Center. Initially he studied the effect of X and Y chromosomes on the development of sex differences in mouse aggressive and mating behavior. Later, he worked on the genetics of intersexually aggressive behaviors in mice. Currently, he is using molecular biology approaches to address the interactions between smoking and schizophrenia on the regulation of nicotine receptors in human postmortem brains.

NOEL A. CARD is an Assistant Professor in Family Studies and Human Development at the University of Arizona. His quantitative interests are in structural equation modeling, longitudinal data analysis, meta-analytic techniques, and methods of analyzing interdependent data. His substantive interests are in child and adolescent social development, especially in peer relations (friendships, antipathetic relationships, group status) and aggressive behavior (aggressors, victims, aggressor-victim relationships).

EMIL F. COCCARO, MD, is Professor and Chairperson of the Department of Psychiatry at the University of Chicago. Over the course of his career, Dr. Coccaro has spearheaded investigations of the serotonergic basis of abnormal impulsive aggression and its clinical correlates. This work has encompassed the identification of a biological risk factor (postsynaptic serotonin receptor subsensitivity), refinement of the psychiatric nosology of impulsive aggression, and the testing of treatments targeted against known biological risk factors. Most recently he has been investigating the neuroscience of impulsive aggression, as well as its behavioral and molecular genetics.

NICKI R. CRICK is the Distinguished McKnight University Professor, the Emma Birkmaier Educational Leadership Professor, and the Director of the Institute of Child Development at the University of Minnesota. Dr. Crick is a clinical and developmental psychologist who studies relational aggression across development, social information-processing capacities in children, and the development of psychopathology. Dr. Crick is a Fellow of the American Psychological Association and serves on the editorial boards of *Development and Psychopathology*, *Journal of Personality and Social Psychology*, and *Social Development*.

LINDA L. DAHLBERG is the Deputy Associate Director for Science in the Division of Violence Prevention at the U.S. Centers for Disease Control and Prevention. She is a senior science and policy advisor and coordinates international research and programmatic activities for the Division. For the past 15 years, she has worked in the area of violence prevention – specifically on the efficacy and effectiveness of interventions to reduce violence. More recently she served as the Executive Scientific Editor of the *World Report on Violence and Health* (2002).

GARTH DAVIES is an Assistant Professor in the School of Criminology at Simon Fraser University. His research interests include the impact of crime on communities. He received his PhD in criminal justice from Rutgers University.

SCOTT H. DECKER is the Director and Professor in the School of Criminology and Criminal Justice at Arizona State University. His main research interests are in the areas of gangs, juvenile justice, criminal justice policy, and the offender's perspective. He is the Research Partner for Project Safe Neighborhoods in the Eastern District of Missouri and the Southern District of Illinois. His books on gangs include *Life in the Gang* (Cambridge), *Confronting Gangs* (Roxbury), *Policing Gangs and Youth Violence* (Wadsworth), *Responding to Gangs* (National Institute of Justice), and *European Street Gangs and Troublesome Youth Groups* (AltaMira Press, 2005).

KENNETH A. DODGE is the William McDougall Professor of Public Policy and Psychology and the Director of the Center for Child and Family Policy at Duke University. He is the recipient of a Senior Scientist Award from NIH. He studies the development and prevention of chronic antisocial behavior in youth.

DOROTHY L. ESPELAGE is an Associate Professor of Counseling Psychology in the Department of Educational Psychology at the University of Illinois, Urbana-Champaign. She earned her PhD in counseling psychology from Indiana University in 1997. She is a Fellow of Division 17 (Counseling Psychology) of the American Psychological Association and was recently named University of Illinois Scholar. She has conducted research on bullying and school violence and is Co-Editor of *Bullying in American Schools: A Social-Ecological Perspective on Prevention and Intervention*, published by Erlbaum (2004). Her research focuses on translating empirical findings into prevention and intervention programming.

JEFFREY FAGAN is a Professor of Law and Public Health at Columbia University. His research and scholarship examine crime, law, and social policy. He is a member of the National Consortium on Violence Research, the MacArthur Foundation's Research Network on Adolescent Development and Juvenile Justice, and the Working Group on Legitimacy and the Criminal Law of the Russell Sage Foundation. He is a Fellow of the American Society of Criminology and is a Soros Senior Justice Fellow.

ALBERT D. FARRELL is Professor of Psychology at Virginia Commonwealth University (VCU), where he directs the VCU Clark-Hill Institute for Positive Youth Development. His research has focused on the application of an action-research model to develop and evaluate the effectiveness of prevention programs directed at high-risk youth. Dr. Farrell has published extensively in the areas of youth violence and drug use, assessment, and research methodology and has served on national task forces on youth violence initiated by the CDC and by the American Psychological Association. He is a licensed clinical psychologist and is a Fellow of the American Psychological Association

DAVID P. FARRINGTON is Professor of Psychological Criminology at the Institute of Criminology, Cambridge University, and Adjunct Professor of Psychiatry at Western Psychiatric Institute and Clinic, University of Pittsburgh. He is a Fellow of the British Academy, of the Academy of Medical Sciences, of the British Psychological Society, and of the American Society of Criminology and is an Honorary Life Member of the British Society of Criminology and of the Division of Forensic Psychology of the British Psychological Society. He is Co-Chair of the Campbell Collaboration Crime and Justice Group, a member of the Board of Directors of the International Society of Criminology, a member of the jury for the Stockholm Prize in Criminology, and a joint Editor of *Cambridge Studies in Criminology* and of the journal *Criminal Behaviour and Mental Health*. His major research interest is in developmental criminology, and he is Director of the Cambridge Study in Delinquent Development and Co-Investigator of the Pittsburgh Youth Study.

DANIEL J. FLANNERY is currently Professor of Justice Studies and Director of the Institute for the Study and Prevention of Violence at Kent State University. He is also a licensed clinical psychologist and an Associate Professor of Pediatrics at Case Western Reserve University and University Hospitals of Cleveland. He is Co-Editor (with C. R. Huff) of *Youth Violence: Prevention, Intervention and Social Policy* (1999) for American Psychiatric Press. He is also author of the recently released book *Violence and Mental Health in Everyday Life: Prevention and Intervention for Children and Adolescents* (2006). His primary areas of research are in youth violence prevention, the link between violence and mental health, and program evaluation. He received his PhD in 1991 in clinical-child psychology from Ohio State University. His previous appointments were as Assistant Professor of Family Studies at the University of Arizona and as Associate Professor of Child Psychiatry at Case Western Reserve University School of Medicine. He has served as consultant to various local and national organizations, including the U.S. Departments of Justice and Education, the Centers for Disease Control and Prevention, the National Crime Prevention Council, and the National Resource Center for Safe Schools.

MARK S. FLEISHER is a Professor at the Mandel School of Applied Social Sciences at Case Western Reserve University. He has conducted anthropological fieldwork in Mexico, Guatemala, and Indonesia and on Northwest Coast Native American reservations and has extensive research experience in federal prisons and among youth gangs. His books include *Warehousing Violence* (Sage, 1988), *Beggars and Thieves: Lives of Urban Street Criminals* (University of Wisconsin Press, 1995), and *Dead End Kids: Gang Girls and the Boys They Know* (University of Wisconsin Press, 1998), as well as the co-edited volume *Crime and Employment: Issues in Crime Reduction for Corrections* (2003, AltaMira).

VANGIE A. FOSHEE is a tenured Associate Professor in the Department of Health Behavior and Health Education in the School of Public Health at the University of North Carolina at Chapel Hill. Her research focus is on adolescent problem behaviors and includes both etiological and evaluation research.

HOLLY FOSTER is an Assistant Professor at Texas A&M University and a Research Affiliate of the National Center for Children and Families, Teachers College. She is conducting research on children's exposure to violence, the impact of parental incarceration on children, and crime and social inequality over the life course.

RICHARD J. GELLES serves as the Dean of the School of Social Policy and Practice and holds the Joanne and Raymond Welsh Chair of Child Welfare and Family Violence in the School of Social Work at the University of Pennsylvania. He is the Director of the Center for Research on Youth and Social Policy and Co-Director of the Field Center for Children's Policy, Practice, and Research. In addition, he directs the Ortner-Unity Program on Family Violence. His book *The Violent Home* was the first systematic empirical investigation of family violence and continues to be highly influential. He is the author or co-author of 24 books and more than 100 articles and chapters on family violence. His latest books are *The Book of David: How Preserving Families Can Cost Children's Lives* (Basic Books, 1996), *Intimate Violence in Families, 3rd Edition* (Sage Publications, 1997), and *Current Controversies on Family Violence, 2nd Edition* (with Donilene Loseke and Mary Cavanaugh – Sage Publications, 2005).

DENISE C. GOTTFREDSON is a Professor in the Department of Criminal Justice and Criminology at the University of Maryland. Her research interests include delinquency and delinquency prevention, and particularly the effects of school environments on youth behavior. Much of her career has been devoted to developing effective collaborations between researchers and practitioners.

GARY D. GOTTFREDSON is a Professor in the Department of Counseling and Personnel Services at the University of Maryland. A Fellow of the American Psychological Association Divisions of Measurement, Evaluation and Statistics and of Counseling Psychology, he pursues research on the prevention of problem behavior, problems of program implementation, program evaluation, and the measurement of individual and organizational differences.

MICHAEL R. GOTTFREDSON is Professor of Criminology, Law, and Society and of Sociology and Executive Vice Chancellor and Provost at the University of California, Irvine. He is the co-author or Editor of *Control Theories of Crime and Delinquency* (2003), *The Generality of Deviance* (1994), *A General Theory of Crime* (1990), *Decisionmaking in Criminal Justice* (1988), and *Victims of Personal Crime* (1978), as well as numerous articles in criminology, sociology, and law.

RICHARD E. HEYMAN is Research Professor in the Department of Psychology at the State University of New York at Stony Brook. He has received support from major U.S. funding agencies on a variety of family topics, from anger escalation in couples to the impact of family violence on children to community-level prevention of family maltreatment, substance problems, and suicidality. He has published more than 60 scientific articles and book chapters focused on couples dysfunction, partner abuse, and child maltreatment. He has researched and written about couples approaches to partner abuse treatment. He is perhaps best known for his work observing the differences in communication among abusive, distressed, and nondistressed couples. Dr. Heyman is a licensed psychologist.

JAMES C. (BUDDY) HOWELL is formerly the Director of Research and Program Development at the federal Office of Juvenile Justice and Delinquency Prevention, U.S. Department of Justice. He is currently a Senior Research Associate with the National Youth Gang Center, Tallahassee, Florida. His recent book is titled *Preventing and Reducing Juvenile Delinquency: A Comprehensive Framework*. He has published other academic contributions in books and professional journals. His current interests include youth gangs, youth violence, evidence-based practice, and juvenile justice system reforms.

MEGAN Q. HOWELL is a Research Associate in the Center for the Prevention of School Violence, North Carolina Department of Juvenile Justice and Delinquency Prevention. She received her MCJ degree from the University of South Carolina, Department of Criminology and Criminal Justice. Her research interests include school violence, juvenile justice, juvenile violence, and juvenile transfers to the criminal justice system.

LI HUANG is a doctoral candidate in the Department of Human Development and Family Study at Auburn University. Her research interests include statistics/methodology and cross-cultural/national contextual research, with a particular focus on deviant behaviors and youth violence.

L. ROWELL HUESMANN is Amos N. Tversky Collegiate Professor of Psychology and Communication Studies at the University of Michigan and Director of the Research Center for Group Dynamics at Michigan's Institute for Social Research. Professor Huesmann's research has focused on the psychological foundations of aggressive and antisocial behavior and in particular on how violence in the mass media and video games influences the long-term development of aggressive and violent behavior. He has authored more than 100 scientific articles and books on this topic. He is editor of the journal *Aggressive Behavior* and was the 2005 recipient of the American Psychological Association's award for Distinguished Lifetime Contributions to Media Psychology. He is a Past President of the International Society for Research on Aggression, a life member of Clare Hall College, Cambridge, and a member of the LIFE faculty at the Max Planck Institute in Berlin. He received his BS at the University of Michigan in 1964 and his PhD at Carnegie-Mellon University in 1969. Prior to being on the faculty at Michigan, he was on the faculty of Yale University and the University of Illinois at Chicago.

CYNTHIA IRVIN is a Senior Social Scientist in the Health Security Program at RTI International and serves on the Board of Directors of the Inter American Center for Human Rights. She also serves as Amnesty International USA Country Specialist for France and Spain, a position she has held since 1996. Her work focuses on international politics dealing with issues of ethnic conflict; terrorism; the political, social, and economic reconstruction of societies coming out of war; and human rights.

GARY F. JENSEN is a Professor of Sociology and Religious Studies and the Joe B. Wyatt Distinguished University Professor at Vanderbilt University. He has authored or co-authored and edited or co-edited 8 books and more than 75 articles and chapters primarily focusing on crime and delinquency. His most recent works include *Social Learning and the Explanations of Crime: A Guide for the New Century*, co-authored with Ronald Akers, and *The Path of the Devil: A Study of Early Modern Witch Hunts* (Rowman and Littlefield, forthcoming). He is working on the fourth edition of *Delinquency and Youth Crime*, co-authored with Dean G. Rojek. He was initiated as a Fellow of the American Society of Criminology in 2001.

YOSHITO KAWABATA is a doctoral student at the Institute of Child Development, University of Minnesota. Mr. Kawabata is interested in examining cultural differences and similarities in childhood aggression, victimization, and social-psychological adjustment. His current research explores the role of culture (i.e., Asian) in relational aggression and adjustment, as well as cultural influences on social information-processing patterns and friendships.

LUCYNA KIRWIL is Associate Professor of Social Psychology at the Warsaw School of Social Psychology and Principal Investigator at the Institute for Social Studies of Warsaw University in Poland. She has been a Visiting Professor in the Department of Communication

Studies at the University of Michigan and a Visiting Scholar at its Institute for Social Research. She has published numerous articles and book chapters on aggression and violence in society and the media, including media violence's impact on the development of aggression in children, perceptions of the TV world by children, and the relation of parents' beliefs about aggression to the development of their children's aggression. Her recent research focuses on emotional reactions and physiological responses to media violence among populations regularly exposed to extreme violence. She is a Fellow of the International Society for Research on Aggression, the Society for Personality and Social Psychology, the Polish Psychological Association, and the Polish Association of Social Psychology. She received her PhD from Warsaw University in 1979.

JEFF M. KRETSCHMAR is a Project Director at Kent State University's Institute for the Study and Prevention of Violence. Dr. Kretschmar received his PhD in Social Psychology from Miami University in 2003. He is presently conducting research on the effectiveness of several juvenile behavioral health programs in Ohio. Current research interests include mental and behavioral health, aggression, substance use, and exposure to violence and victimization.

ROBERT F. KRUEGER, PhD, is the McKnight Presidential Fellow and Associate Professor of Clinical Psychology, and Individual Differences, Personality, and Behavior Genetics in the Department of Psychology, and Adjunct Associate Professor of Child Psychology in the Institute of Child Development, at the University of Minnesota, Twin Cities. Dr. Krueger obtained his PhD from the University of Wisconsin at Madison and completed his clinical internship at Brown University. He is currently an Associate Editor of the *Journal of Abnormal Psychology* and has served on the editorial boards of numerous other journals. Professor Krueger's major interests lie at the intersection of research on personality, psychopathology, disorders of personality, behavior-genetics, and quantitative methods. He was the recipient of a 2003 Early Career Award from the International Society for the Study of Individual Differences, a 2005 American Psychological Association Distinguished Scientific Award for Early Career Contribution to Psychology, and a 2006 Theodore Millon Mid-Career Award from the American Psychological Foundation.

MARKUS J. P. KRUESI is a Professor in the Department of Psychiatry and Behavioral Sciences, Medical University of South Carolina. Dr. Kruesi, MD, is a child and adolescent psychiatrist who serves as Director of the Youth Division and Training Director, Child and Adolescent Psychiatry. His research examines influences on aggression (including suicidal behavior) and disruptive behavior disorders (e.g., conduct disorder, ADHD). His current research uses magnetic resonance imaging to examine brain anatomy and function in conduct disorder. He is a co-author of an emergency department protocol for adolescent suicide/homicide prevention, which was rated effective by the SPRC Registry of Evidence-Based Suicide Prevention Programs.

BENJAMIN B. LAHEY is a Professor at the University of Chicago, Department of Health Studies. His research interests include taxonomy of child and adolescent mental disorders, developmental and genetic epidemiology of youth mental disorders, attention-deficit/hyperactivity disorder, conduct disorder, and juvenile delinquency. Dr. Lahey earned his PhD in psychology from the University of Tennessee in 1970.

ROYCE LEE, MD, is Assistant Professor in the Department of Psychiatry at the University of Chicago. Dr. Lee is a psychiatrist seeking to further our understanding of the neurobiological abnormalities underlying personality disorder (i.e., borderline personality disorder). His current research has examined relationships between developmental risk factors and the neurobiology of emotion and stress reactivity, using such methods as assays of cerebrospinal fluid samples, functional magnetic resonance imaging, and intranasal stress peptide drug challenges.

SCOTT O. LILIENFELD is an Associate Professor of Psychology at Emory University. Dr. Lilienfeld is a clinical psychologist whose work focuses on personality disorders (especially psychopathic and antisocial personality disorders), personality assessment, anxiety disorders, psychiatric classification and diagnosis, and questionable practices in clinical psychology. Much of his current research examines the advantages and disadvantages of alternative approaches to detecting psychopathic and antisocial personality traits, as well as focusing on testing models of the etiology of these traits.

TODD D. LITTLE is director of the Research Design and Analysis Unit of the Schiefelbusch Life Span Institute. He is also Professor in the Department of Psychology where he serves as Director of the quantitative psychology doctoral training program and Co-Director of the developmental psychology doctoral training program. His quantitative research focuses on general latent variable techniques and longitudinal data analysis. His substantive program of research focuses on action-control processes, motivation, aggression/victimization, and self-regulation in children and adolescents.

ANNE MARTIN is a Research Scientist at the National Center for Children and Families at Teachers College. Her interests include adolescent fertility and family formation, the intergenerational transfer of disadvantage, and children's early cognitive development.

REBECCA A. MATTHEW received a master's degree in public health and health behavior and health education from the University of North Carolina at Chapel Hill in 2005. For several years, she has been involved in research related to childhood sexual violence, community-based participatory research, doctor–patient communication, and diabetes regimen adherence.

STEPHEN C. MAXSON is Professor of Psychology and Biobehavioral Sciences at the University of Connecticut. Since 1975, he has been investigating the genetics of aggression and mating in male mice and the role of chromosomes and genes in predicting male mouse aggression. He is currently working with the Tennessee Mouse Genome Consortium to screen for chemically induced and chromosome-specific mutants with effects on aggression. He is also interested in developing the genetic effects on mouse aggression as models for human aggression. He is a Fellow of the International Society for Research on Aggression, and he is an elected member of its governing Council for 2005 to 2008. In 1998, he was the recipient of the Dobzhansky Memorial Award for a Lifetime of Outstanding Scholarship in Behavior Genetics and of the Excellence Award for Research of the University of Connecticut Chapter of the AAUP.

JACQUELYN MIZE is Professor of Human Development and Family Studies at Auburn University. She has served on the editorial boards of *Developmental Psychology*, *Merrill-Palmer Quarterly*, and *Early Childhood Research Quarterly*. Her research focuses on the development of social competence among young children, particularly the roles of social-cognitive processes and parenting.

TERRIE E. MOFFITT researches how nature and nurture interact in the origins of human psychopathology. She is particularly interested in antisocial behaviors. She is a clinical psychologist and professor at the University of Wisconsin and at the Institute of Psychiatry, King's College London. She directs the Medical Research Council–funded Environmental-Risk Longitudinal Twin Study (called "E-risk") and is also associate director of the Dunedin Multidisciplinary Health and Development Study. For her research, she has received the Distinguished Scientific Award for Early Career Contribution from the American Psychological Association (1993) and has been named a Fellow of the Academy of Medical Sciences (1999), the American Society of Criminology (2003), the British Academy (2004), and Academia Europaea (2005). She currently holds a Royal Society-Wolfson Merit Award (2002–2007).

DANIEL S. NAGIN is Teresa and H. John Heinz Professor of Public Policy and Statistics at Carnegie Mellon University and since January 2006 has served as the school's Associate Dean of Faculty. He received his PhD in 1976 from what is now the Heinz School. Dr. Nagin has participated in two MacArthur Foundation Networks – the Network on Adolescent Development and Juvenile Justice and the Network on Economic Inequality and Social Interactions. He is an elected Fellow of the American Society of Criminology and of the American Society for the Advancement of Science and was the 2006 recipient of the American Society of Criminology Edwin H. Sutherland Award. His research focuses on the evolution of criminal and antisocial behaviors over the life course, the deterrent effect of criminal and noncriminal penalties on illegal behaviors, and the development of statistical methods for analyzing longitudinal data.

JAMIE M. OSTROV is an Assistant Professor, Department of Psychology, University at Buffalo, the State University of New York. Dr. Ostrov is a developmental psychologist with a developmental psychopathology orientation who explores the development of relational and physical aggression. His current research uses observational methods to study subtypes of aggression during early childhood. He is the Co-Editor of special issues on relational aggression during early childhood in *Early Education and Development* and the *Journal of Applied Developmental Psychology*. Dr. Ostrov is a Consulting Editor for *Early Childhood Research Quarterly*.

CHRISTOPHER J. PATRICK is Starke R. Hathaway Distinguished Professor and Director of Clinical Training in the Department of Psychology at the University of Minnesota. His current research uses techniques of psychometrics, psychophysiology, and cognitive-affective neuroscience to study problems including psychopathy, antisocial behavior, and substance use/abuse. He is the recipient of Distinguished Early Career awards from the American Psychological Association (1995) and the Society for Psychophysiological Research (1993). He is also Editor of *The Handbook of Psychopathy*, which was published in 2005 by Guilford Press.

BOWEN PAULLE is a lecturer on the Faculty of Social and Behavioural Sciences, Department of Sociology and Anthropology at the University of Amsterdam, as well as an independent researcher, policy advisor, and interventionist. His dissertation, an ethnographic comparison, investigated the mechanisms and meanings that governed the practice and hidden forms of violence in nonselective secondary schools of Amsterdam and New York. His current focus is on the socioeconomic integration of public school systems on both sides of the Atlantic.

GREGORY S. PETTIT is Human Sciences Professor in the Department of Human Development and Family Studies at Auburn University. He is a Fellow of the American Psychological Association and Past Associate Editor of *Developmental Psychology* and the *Journal of Social and Personal Relationships*. His research focuses on the mechanisms through which family and peer experiences exert an impact on important developmental outcomes and on the risk and protective factors that moderate those linkages.

ADRIAN RAINE is the Robert G. Wright Professor of Psychology at the University of Southern California. For the past 23 years, Dr. Raine's research has focused on the biosocial bases of antisocial and violent behavior in both children and adults. He has published three books (including *The Psychopathology of Crime: Criminal Behavior as a Clinical Disorder*, Academic Press, 1993) and more than 100 journal articles and book chapters on brain imaging, psychophysiology, neurochemistry, antisocial behavior, schizotypal personality, and alcoholism.

SOO HYUN RHEE is an Assistant Professor in the Department of Psychology at University of Colorado-Boulder. Dr. Rhee is a clinical psychologist who conducts behavior-genetic studies examining the etiology and development of childhood disruptive disorders and substance use disorders. Her recent research has focused on the causes of comorbidity in psychiatric disorders.

ANGELA SCARPA is Associate Professor of Psychology at Virginia Tech. She has been studying the relationship of physiological reactivity to behavior problems and emotional expression since 1993. Her research interests center on the interaction of biological bases and social experiences in the development of behavioral and emotional problems, such as aggression, anxiety, and depression. Physiological reactivity and the developmental consequences of child physical abuse or other violence exposure are two primary areas of interest.

JEAN R. SÉGUIN is an Associate Research Scientist in the Department of Psychiatry, Université de Montréal. Dr. Séguin is a clinical psychologist who is mainly interested in cognitive approaches to behavior regulation. His current research concerns the joint development of physical aggression, hyperactivity, and executive function and the factors that influence this process, particularly self-regulation. Dr. Séguin also examines risk factors for alcoholism and hypertension.

MICHELLE R. SHERRILL is a doctoral student in social psychology at Duke University. She studies consequences and predictors of self-regulatory failure.

MARK I. SINGER is the Leonard W. Mayo Professor of Family and Child Welfare, Director of the Dual Disorders Research Program, and Co-Director of the Center on Substance Abuse and Mental Illness at the Mandel School of Applied Social Sciences, Case Western Reserve University. He is a recipient of a National Institute of Mental Health Fellowship (1977–1979), a National Research Training Award from the National Institute on Alcoholism and Alcohol Abuse (1980–1981), and a Faculty Development Award from the NIAAA/NIDA/CSAP (1990–1995). Dr. Singer's primary areas of scientific inquiry have been youth violence, adolescent substance abuse, and adolescent mental health.

AMY M. SMITH SLEP is Research Associate Professor in the Department of Psychology at the State University of New York at Stony Brook. She is a licensed clinical psychologist whose research focuses on affect regulation in parent-child and marital dyads, etiology of parental and partner aggression/abuse, and connections between parenting and marital functioning and includes studies of basic processes as well as innovative intervention and prevention approaches.

KEVIN J. STROM is a Criminologist with RTI International, where he directs research on public safety and homeland security issues. This includes a National Institute of Justice (NIJ)–funded study examining interagency coordination and response following the July 2005 terrorist attacks in the United Kingdom. His research interests include the use of information technology to improve domestic preparedness, the structural determinants of community violence, and the measurement of violent crime using alternative data sources.

PATRICK SYLVERS is a doctoral student at Emory University. Mr. Sylvers' research focuses on the etiology of personality disorders (mostly psychopathic and antisocial personality disorders), specifically the psychophysiological and neuropsychological underpinnings of the disorders. Mr. Sylvers is currently researching sex differences in the manifestation of psychopathic traits, as well as relational aggression.

PATRICK H. TOLAN is Director of the Institute for Juvenile Research at the University of Illinois and Professor in the Department of Psychiatry and College of Public Health at the University of Illinois at Chicago. He has conducted research on prevention, developmental-ecological risk models of children's mental health, and the public health problems of antisocial behavior in youth. He is a Fellow of five divisions of the American Psychological Association and the Academy for Experimental Criminology. He has served as Principal Investigator or Co-Investigator on the Chicago Youth Development Study, the Metropolitan Area Child Study, the SAFE Children Prevention Study, and the Multisite Middle School Violence Prevention Project. He is the Editor of 4 books and more than 100 chapters and papers on prevention, family intervention, family assessment, family-school relations, violence, delinquency, and child psychopathology.

ELIZABETH TREJOS-CASTILLO is a doctoral candidate in the Department of Human Development and Family Studies at Auburn University. Her research interests include the etiology of problem behaviors in adolescents, family processes, Hispanic and immigrant populations, and cross-cultural/cross-national methods.

RICHARD E. TREMBLAY is Canada Research Chair in Child Development and Professor of Pediatrics/Psychiatry/Psychology at the University of Montreal. Since the early 1980s, he has conducted a program of longitudinal and experimental studies addressing the physical, cognitive, emotional, and social development of children from conception onward, in order to gain a better understanding of the development and prevention of antisocial and violent behavior. He is director of the Centre of Excellence for Early Childhood Development, a Fellow of the Royal Society of Canada, and the Molson Fellow of the Canadian Institute for Advanced Research.

MANFRED VAN DULMEN is an Assistant Professor of Psychology at Kent State University. His research focuses on understanding behavioral continuity and change from adolescence into young adulthood, as well as methodological issues in developmental psychopathology. His current research program investigates the role of adolescent close relationships as antecedents of continuity and change of antisocial behavior. He is Co-Editor of the *Oxford Handbook of Methods in Positive Psychology* (2006).

JOHAN VAN WILSEM is an Assistant Professor of Criminology at Leiden University, The Netherlands. His research interests include cross-national crime patterns, the distribution of crime across neighborhoods, and the situational analysis of crime. He has published on these issues in the *European Sociological Review*, the *European Journal of Criminology, Social Problems*, and, in his dissertation, *Crime and Context: The Impact of Individual, Neighborhood, City, and Country Characteristics* (2003).

ALEXANDER T. VAZSONYI is Professor of Human Development and Family Studies at Auburn University. His research interests include etiological risk factors in adolescent problem behaviors, deviance, and delinquency; criminological theory; and the comparative approach in the study of human development and behavior. He currently serves as the editor of the *Journal of Early Adolescence* and as an editorial board member of the *Journal of Marriage and Family* and the *International Journal of Comparative and Applied Criminal Justice*.

EDELYN VERONA is an Assistant Professor in the Department of Psychology, University of Illinois at Urbana-Champaign. Her research interests include biological (psychophysiology and genetics), temperamental, and stress risk factors for aggression, antisocial behavior, and impulsive suicide in adults and adolescents, with a particular emphasis on mechanisms underlying gender differences. She was recently appointed Consulting Editor for *Journal of Abnormal Psychology*.

FRANK VITARO is from the Department of Psycho-Education, University of Montreal. Dr. Vitaro is a developmental psychologist whose interests revolve around the role of peers in explaining and preventing deviant behaviors, particularly aggressive and delinquent behaviors, in children and adolescents. He is currently involved in four large-scale longitudinal studies and two large-scale prevention programs to examine these issues. All the studies have a multifactorial and long-term longitudinal perspective starting during the preschool period.

MONIQUE VULIN-REYNOLDS is a PhD candidate in clinical child psychology at Virginia Commonwealth University. She received her BA in psychology from Yale University. Ms. Vulin-Reynolds' research interests include the effects of youth exposure to violence and the development of programs to attenuate these effects and prevent future violence.

IRWIN D. WALDMAN is a Professor in the Department of Psychology at Emory University. Dr. Waldman is a clinical psychologist with developmental interests who examines the genetic and environmental etiology of disruptive behavior disorders (e.g., ADHD, conduct disorder) in childhood and adolescence. His current research explores the role of candidate genes in the development of externalizing behavior problems, as well as genetic and environmental influences on comorbidity and on the links between normal variation in symptoms and in personality in the general population and extreme variants in clinical samples.

MARK WARR is Professor of Sociology at the University of Texas at Austin. His research concentrates on social reactions to crime, peer influence and group delinquency, opportunity and crime, and life-course approaches to crime and deviance. His recent work includes *Companions in Crime* (Cambridge University Press, 2002), "Making Delinquent Friends" (*Criminology*, 2005), and "Rethinking Social Reactions to Crime" (*American Journal of Sociology*, 2000).

STANLEY WASSERMAN is an Applied Statistician and Rudy Professor of Sociology, Psychology, and Statistics at Indiana University. He has appointments in the Departments of Sociology, Psychological and Brain Sciences, and Statistics, in Bloomington. He also has an appointment in the Karl F. Schuessler Institute for Social Research. He is best known for his work on statistical models for social networks and for his text, co-authored with Katherine Faust, *Social Network Analysis: Methods and Applications*. He is a Fellow of the Royal Statistical Society and an Honorary Fellow of the American Statistical Association and the American Association for the Advancement of Science.

DEANNA L. WILKINSON is an Associate Professor in the Department of Human Development and Family Science at Ohio State University. Her primary research interests are youth violence, firearm use, prevention, event perspectives, and urban communities. She is the author of *Guns, Violence, and Identity* (LFB Scholarly Publications, 2003).

Acknowledgments

A volume this complex and far reaching would never have come to fruition without the vision, persistence, and commitment of several individuals who deserve mention. First, we would like to thank Philip Laughlin, Psychology Editor at Cambridge University Press when the handbook project first got off the ground, and the champion of the original idea and effort. Phil, in short, made it all happen. We are also grateful to Armi Macallabug, Senior Editorial Assistant, Social Sciences, at Cambridge, who shepherded us through the many details of getting the initial manuscript completed. Maggie Meitzler at Aptara, Inc., did a splendid job of helping us move through the copy editing and production phases. There are many staff at the Institute for the Study and Prevention of Violence at Kent State University who helped with organizational, administrative, and editing tasks along the way, but we owe a special debt of gratitude to Barbara Fahrny for her patience, organizational skills, and her commitment to getting things right. We thank the initial reviewers of the handbook prospectus, who provided some great ideas that ultimately improved the end product, and our many colleagues who listened to our ideas and provided feedback about topics, potential authors, and the organization of the handbook. Lastly, an effort this comprehensive and multidisciplinary would never have come to fruition without the participation of the chapter authors. We thank them for their patience and persistence, but mostly for their commitment to producing works of high quality. The handbook reflects their work and thinking. We hope you find reading about their work as satisfying and compelling as we found working with each of them.

Introduction

Alexander T. Vazsonyi, Daniel J. Flannery, and
Irwin D. Waldman

The current collection of essays represents a culmination of almost 3 years of intensive work and collaboration among the three editors of this volume, dedicated to compiling what we believe to be the current state of the art and science related to the study of violence and aggression. Rather than providing a preview and map of the volume, we find it more pertinent to provide in this introduction some history about the process leading up to the planning and completion of this book. In trying to develop this edited volume, it became clear that distinct expertise was required to identify interdisciplinary streams of scholarship that focused on the etiology, development, and prevention of violence and violent behaviors. We hope the chapters in this volume provide such an overview and reflect the most current thinking and research about violence.

In early conversations at Kent State University, where Dan Flannery is the Director of the Institute for the Study and Prevention of Violence, we began to discuss how we might develop the volume. One early challenge was how to achieve the provision of

substantial interdisciplinary breadth, which we agreed included behavior genetics, brain imaging, comparative animal studies, criminal justice, criminology, human development, prevention sciences, and psychopharmacology. We also wanted to include perspectives from public health and sociology, as well as reviews of state-of-the-art methods that can be profitably applied to the study of violent and aggressive behaviors.

Ultimately, we decided to focus the handbook primarily on violence and violent behaviors. Of course, this focus does not exclude aggression, but it does lend the volume a clear emphasis. This was one of the few guidelines we provided to the contributors, namely to focus primarily on violence, though not excluding relevant research on aggression and aggressive behavior. We also asked authors to cover issues related to gender and culture as part of their contribution, rather than focusing on these issues as separate substantive chapters. We thus were quite light on guidelines, leaving it to each author or team of authors to present the most important issues in their discipline, rather than superimposing an artificial template on chapter format or substantive content.

Each of the three editors brought to this task different strengths, perspectives, and training, as well as somewhat different substantive foci and areas of scholarship. Each of us, however, shares an interest in studying violence and aggression. In no small measure, this shared interest can be traced to the profound influence of one important scholar, David Rowe, with whom each of us had the pleasure of working. David was a mentor, a departmental colleague, a collaborator, and a friend to each of us in a different way.

David had a profound influence not only on our thinking and scholarship regarding aggression, violence, and deviance but also on our careers as scientists. His controversial style was sometimes revered, and sometimes scorned, not only on campus at the University of Arizona but also throughout social and behavioral science communities within the United States and abroad. David was a true scholar, with limited interest in politics, but with virtually infinite energy and motivation for science and the growth of knowledge. As such, David frequented the sociology/criminology colloquia on campus and co-taught courses and collaborated with colleagues from the department of psychology. He also maintained a vibrant genetics lab, wherein Alex Vazsonyi participated in DNA sample collection and extraction and in the genotyping of candidate gene polymorphisms over a decade ago, well before the current rage. This was typical of David's persona and professional presence, which included attendance at the annual or biennial meetings of the Behavior Genetics Association, the Society for Research in Child Development, as well as the American Society of Criminology. His highly prolific scholarship and publication record closely matched this interdisciplinary approach. At its core this approach embodied the essence of behavior genetic methods in seeking to uncover and understand the contributors to variability in aggression, violence, deviance, or delinquency, regardless of whether these influences were due to inherited differences and propensities *or* to socialization pressures and other experiences – something so many misunderstood about his research.

It would be challenging indeed to identify the most integral examples of David's scholarship. Those of greatest relevance for the current volume would include his theory of crime, published in an edited volume by Thornberry (1997), *Developmental Theories of Crime and Delinquency*; his own books, *The Limits of Family Influence* (1994) and *Biology and Crime* (2002); and several highly influential papers published both in developmental journals (e.g., *Child Development* and *Developmental Psychology*) and in criminology journals (e.g., *Criminology* and *Journal of Research in Crime and Delinquency*). David also published seminal work on developmental processes, including his paper, "No More Than Skin Deep" published in *Psychological Review* (1994), as well as papers that pioneered assessments of the vertical transmission of deviance through the study of sibling resemblance. Finally, David was one of the architects of the National Longitudinal Study of Adolescent Health (Add Health), a research project that includes a twin sample to facilitate behavior genetic inquiry.

In David's spirit of being a multidisciplinary social and behavioral scientist, the current collection represents theoretical advances and quantitative developments, as well as diverse substantive empirical approaches to the study of violence and aggression, broadly construed. Thus, we dedicate this volume to our colleague, mentor, and friend, David C. Rowe, for his lifetime accomplishments and contributions to the study of violence, aggression, deviance, and crime. David was truly a gentle giant who cast a long shadow over these research domains. It is a shadow that will follow us, and the field, for a long time to come. His contribution and dedication will not soon be forgotten.

Part I

GENERAL PERSPECTIVES

CHAPTER 1

Understanding Violence

Patrick H. Tolan

Defining and Understanding Violence

Defining Violence – I Know It When I See It

In defining violence, the oft-quoted statement by Justice Potter Stewart (*Jacobellis v. Ohio*, 378 U.S. 184, 197, [1964]) on what constitutes obscene material or hardcore pornography comes to mind: "I know it when I see it. . . ."

Violence, like obscenity, is generally considered undesirable, yet there is substantial variation in what is included and the features considered critical for defining it (Tolan, Gorman-Smith, & Henry, 2006). Variations that emphasize different aspects of motivation, impact, and action and of psychological, social, and political meaning lead to quite different definitions. These variations carry forward important implications for how violence is understood, how its patterns are identified, how risk factors are related, and which interventions and policies seem most appropriate. In fact, these variations can lead to different conclusions from a given set of data, testimony, and other information (Loseke, Gelles, & Cavanaugh,

2005). The lack of consensus hinders coordination and comparison between studies, programming, and policies designed to address violence, which in turn impedes the impact these interventions have on this serious public health problem. As Justice Stewart's comment alludes, almost everyone can tell whether or not a given act or situation is violent. However, it is more difficult to identify clearly extractable characteristics that can be generalized in determining what is violent and what is not.

This chapter briefly reviews some issues underlying the persistent variations in definitions of violence, including those offered officially by such agencies as the World Health Organization and the Centers for Disease Control, those offered by commissions within professional organizations such as the American Psychological Association or the Institute of Medicine, and those shared by segments of researchers or policy advocates. The intent is to summarize major issues in defining violence, including identifying some commonly recognized categories. This review is followed by a more focused discussion of controversies in defining and understanding family violence, which is arguably the predominant portion of violence. The issues occurring within the family violence arena provide an excellent example of the issues that arise in attempting to define violence. The chapter also focuses on violence during one age period, youth, and suggests differentiating violence into four types for the purpose of furthering and specifying patterns. This review is presented to illustrate how definitional issues can affect our understanding of violence and the ultimate utility of efforts to reduce violence and its harmful impact.

A NOTE ON PERSPECTIVE

As emphasized throughout this chapter, the variations in interest and the perspective of the stakeholders can explain much of the differences in how violence is viewed and defined (Chalk & King, 1998). Accordingly, it is important to note that this review is written from the perspective of a violence research base focused on youth and family violence. The focus is also primarily on violence as it occurs and affects various cultures and groups within the United States. Fit and generalization may decrease as one moves to other settings and targets and to cultures other than Western industrialized societies.

The Challenge of Defining Violence

Violence as a Distinct Form of Morbidity and Mortality

Typically, violence is differentiated from disease and unintentional injuries because it involves the intention to harm self or another. The notion of intent to injure is a common and central feature of what is meant by violence (Krug, Dahlberg, Mercy, Zwi, & Lozano, 2002). Its importance can be seen in the common legal distinction among an accident (no intention), negligence (failure to show due caution or care that results in an injury or harm), recklessness (acting in such a manner as to greatly increase the potential for injury), and such crimes as assault or battery, in which the intention (*mens rea*) is essential to prove that the crime

occurred and that the person charged is responsible or guilty. What is violent and how serious or offensive is that violence depend on how fully formed the intent to harm is.

This distinction is particularly important for public health efforts to reduce violence because it focuses on motivation, suggesting that interventions, whether legal, educational, or behavioral, might be most effective if informed by the motivation of those acting violently or the precipitants that might increase the likelihood of violence. Yet, the perceived role of motivation is a matter of ongoing controversy and often results in countervailing actions and policy advocacy. Some prefer to emphasize personal responsibility and favor legal methods to influence violence, whereas those who view it as a behavioral health issue may prefer training or environmental manipulations that lessen its likelihood. The former view tends to emphasize distinguishing among types of violence with related differentiation of actions and policies as the most effective response. The latter, behavioral view would emphasize actions and policies similar to those promoted for disease and unintentional injury prevention (e.g., reduce environmental precipitants, reduce risk among those most likely to be affected).

The Challenges of Certainty and Agreement in Defining Violence

There is less certainty, as well as substantial disagreement, about how fully intentional the expression to cause physical harm must be for the act to be considered violent. Similarly, it is an unsettled debate whether, for violence to be present, the intention must be to cause physical harm or merely to coerce another (Tolan et al., 2006). For example, most would agree that threatening to hit someone unless he or she did as you demanded is violent. Whether it is still violent if the threat does not include physical aggression remains a question; how clearly must physical harm be threatened for violence to occur? (Chalk & King, 1998). Stakeholders vary widely on where such boundaries should be drawn (Jouriles, McDonald,

Norwood, & Ezell, 2001). Similarly, they vary widely on whether engaging in what is considered oppressive or coercive practices toward another might be considered violent.

A third factor that influences the definition of violence is a recipient or victim's perception of potential harm or threat of injury or the extent of his or her experienced injury. Some would argue that acts, orientations, or statements that intimidate, oppress, or create undue insecurity are violent, even if they do not involve actual physical aggression or specific verbal threats. Others suggest that violence should be differentiated from the victim's perception of threat, even if only to permit more careful empirical testing of the relation between acts and perceptions (Hines & Malley-Morrison, 2004; Johnson, 1995). When should the perception of threat be considered violence, and when is it, although certainly a problem, perhaps better understood as a correlate or related class of behaviors? Further, how are relationship characteristics, such as high levels of conflict, contemptuous attitudes, or neglect of expected care, related to violence? Are these co-occurring problems, adjacent problems that may overlap, or independent forms of violence?

Thus, although the exhibition of physical force with the intent to coerce or harm another is a common and central aspect of most definitions of violence, there are other important features as well, and these features vary in their centrality in such definitions (Jouriles et al., 2001). A fairly typical example is the definition rendered as part of a World Health Organization summit on violence in 1996: "Violence is defined as the intentional use of physical force or power, threatened or actual, against oneself, another person, or against a group or community, that either results in or has a high likelihood of resulting in injury, death, psychological harm, maldevelopment or deprivation" (p. 5).

Although broad, this definition is not among the broadest. A recent review, for example, applied a broad conceptualization of injury in defining violence. Jackman (2002) indicates that violence may include "actions that inflict, threaten, or cause injury. Actions may be corporal, written, or verbal. Injuries may be corporal, psychological, material, or social" (p. 389). This review notes that, without such a broad set of forms of harm, we run the risk of overemphasizing singularly violent acts between individuals, which may not carry as much social and economic importance as do activities broader. This view is found in many attempts to define violence, although they may vary in breadth and the extent to which acts or implied acts other than intentional physical injury are included (see Chalk & King, 1998, for a review of these, and Jouriles et al., 2001, for a cogent discussion of these issues as they pertain to family violence).

Although comprehensive and inclusive, such definitions as Jackman's and those of the WHO may be overly inclusive and not specific enough to allow determining consistently and with confidence whether a given act is violent. Thus, one limitation of such a broad definition is that it becomes difficult to presume what the label of violence means, even if this definition is accepted as the one to use. For example, the WHO definition includes the use of power, not just physical force, as a form of violence. It also includes threats and intimidation along with actual acts of physical aggression. Unlike some definitions, this one does not include acts of omission of care, such as neglect (American Psychological Association Presidential Task Force on Violence and the Family, 1996). However, it does include effects of deprivation and maldevelopment, which implies that neglect is a form of violence. This definition is also typical in broadening potential harm beyond the immediate injury to its impact on subsequent opportunities and functioning. Finally, although not explicitly stated in the definition, the larger document from which it is derived emphasizes that exploitation of differences in physical size, economic capability, and political status and other misuse of power can be equated with violence (Krug et al., 2002).

The interest in not constricting the parameters of violence may have the unintended effect of introducing more variation into what is meant or what can be presumed by the term *violence*. As a result, such definitions may fail to differentiate or calibrate violence by seriousness or potential to injure. In turn, such broad and nonspecific definitions may sacrifice clarity that facilitates scientific advancement, the shared understanding of findings, advocacy arguments, and policy requirements. Thus, we may improve our understanding, communication, and problem solving about the nature of violence and what can be done about it if we strive for less inclusive definitions of violence.

Cultural and Societal Variations in What Is Considered Violence

Another important challenge in defining violence is that cultural differences may affect the meaning of the terms "violence" and "injury" (Walters & Parke, 1964). For example, injury in some cultures extends to attempts to harm or manipulate the well-being of others, whereas in other cultures, injury is reserved for physical harm. Similarly, what is considered very offensive in one culture may be considered acceptable, even expected, behavior in another. Even if the force is clearly physical, such acts may not be seen as violent, or they may not be treated as similar to other acts of violence. Whether cultural acceptability and common occurrence should be considered as criteria for differentiating violence from other physical acts or harmful methods remains controversial. For example, in a state of armed struggle, teaching children to have empathy for and not act violently toward members of the warring faction may seem valuable in reducing violence (or similarly among gangs in an urban community in the United States or other scenarios). Yet, that very training may be considered as harming the children by diminishing their vigilance and risking their safety (Garbarino, 1996).

Cultural considerations in the definition of violence are also evident in how fear and perceived safety are related to actual levels of harm. For example, in the United States, there is a growing belief that schools today are more violent and dangerous, with a corresponding belief that students are less safe, with its negative ramifications for learning. However, this perception is countered by data showing that schools remain one of the safest settings for children and adults (Tolan, 2001). If the perception of violence leads to a harmful impact on felt safety and on developmental progress in learning, is this violence or is it important to differentiate that impact from the effects of actual violent incidents?

Gender and Violence

Related to the cultural and societal variation in the orientation to violence is the understanding of gender in violence. Evidence clearly shows that males experience greater levels of violence than females (Farrington, Langan, & Tonry, 2004). Gender differences, particularly in physical aggression, seem to be present early and remain throughout development (Tremblay et al., 2004). Further, it is widely held that male aggression includes more violence, ability to harm, intimidation, and other threatening aspects than female aggression. Male aggression and violence, it is argued, is more likely to be part of a pattern of coercion, intimidation, or contempt. This difference in social power is considered important in defining violence and in locating concerns about battering, political and economic inequities, and social resources when characterizing gender-based violence (APA Presidential Task Force, 1996; Jouriles et al., 2001). Gaining a better understanding of violence requires due consideration of how engrained and how important violence-related beliefs can influence definitions. The view of gender in relation to violence, as well as other cultural and societal variations in how a given act or perception is related to violence, can be marked through legal codification, traditions, or social structures, and other sanctioning of the behavior is often influential in shaping violence definitions (Chalk & King, 1998; Tolan et al., 2006).

Moreover, there is much controversy about how such cultural variations and gender specifically should be incorporated into violence definitions. For example, even if legal or sanctioned, should actions that diminish the rights or status of others, and by so doing promote violence, be labeled "not violent" in a given culture (Fagan & Browne, 1994)? When an act seriously harms the viability and safety level of a community, even if legal or sanctioned, should it still be considered violent? Is the failure to care for those in pain or to impose prolonged neglect or discomfort an act of violence? Not surprisingly, some argue for culturally based definitions of violence, whereas others argue for absolute definitions, with variations by culture or society to be measured and then interpreted within cultural contexts and other potential influences (Farrington et al., 2004; Krug et al., 2002).

Further, whether culture norms should be considered when defining a given act as violent can vary depending on the act and who is defining it. Finding a level of certainty and specificity that promotes shared understanding of what is meant by violence yet does not ignore cultural variation and the role of social status and power is among the greatest challenges in defining violence.

The Challenge in Attempting to Formulate a Shared Definition of Violence

Although it might be inferred that it is merely narrow-focused constituencies that stubbornly blocks consensus on a clear and encompassing definition of violence, this view is too simplistic and ignores the complex issues vexing the field. In addition, there is a trade-off between a comprehensive, widely acceptable definition and specificity about what is considered violence or how violence should be connoted. Most essentially, what might be crafted so as to not offend any constituency would fail to respect that those engaged in advocacy, research, program development, and policy formulation recognize that what is defined as violence and what is definitely *not* violence carries substantial economic, political, and social ramifications (APA Presidential Task Force, 1996). For example, there is much controversy about whether violence occur-

ring within intimate, marital, or marriage-like relationships should be termed intimate partner violence, domestic violence, one form of violence against women, or battering (Jouriles et al., 2001). Each of these terms carries quite different connotations about the nature of the violence, the extent to which it is assumed to be unidirectional or inherently the responsibility of one partner (in most cases the male), and the prominence that gender-related social and physical power differences should have in framing, measuring, and addressing the problem (Tolan et al., 2006). Further, there is accompanying disagreement, sometimes even among those espousing a given term, about whether relationship violence should be limited to actual acts of physical force or should include other threatening and coercive actions, statements, and practices. Although there has been increasing interest in conceptually and empirically scrutinizing the validity and utility of these competing terms, resolution remains elusive on key conceptual differences and in relating these concepts in an orderly fashion to advance understanding (Daro, Edleson, & Pinderhughes, 2004). As such, progress has been slow toward shared approaches to the study of relationship violence, how to sample the populations, what measures to use, and how to characterize patterns of prevalence, risk factor correlations, and intervention effects (or lack thereof).

Research and Policy Differentiation of Forms of Violence

Although almost always conceptualized as inherently undesirable, violence is not an uncommon human behavior (Krug et al., 2002). In addition, although violent behavior shares common features, it occurs in many forms. One can identify patterns of repeated use of violence by individuals and by certain groups and identify risk markers for violence, but violence is also something that most persons exhibit at some time, albeit infrequently and often without the clear precipitants implied by risk studies

(Tolan, 2001). In addition, there are violent acts, such as physical punishment of children, that are legally sanctioned and conventionally supported. There are times when violence carries virtue, such as in a righteous war or when a policeman subdues a person who is harming others. Moreover, in literature and popular media, the use of violence to resolve conflict, undo injustices, restore order, and redeem characters is very common. Thus, violence is a ubiquitous yet patterned behavior with substantial concentration in a very small portion of most populations and with conflicting views about its inherent undesirability (Jackman, 2002).

Yet, there is little controversy about the need to address the problem of violence and to view violence as problematic. As the volume of publications attest, it is well documented that violence imposes great costs on our societies through increased mortality and morbidity; decreased capability; related legal, health, and welfare costs; and unrealized human potential (Tolan, 2001). For example, along with unintentional injuries, violence is the leading cause of mortality and morbidity for children under age 12 in the United States (CDC, 2004). Violence is widespread and a leading cause of morbidity and mortality across societies, although there is much variation from country to country and across regions in the rates of violence and types of violence that are most prominent (Krug et al., 2002). For example, in 2000, an estimated 1.6 million persons died of violence worldwide, which translates to a rate of 28.8 per 100,000. Of these, 520,000 were homicides, or a rate of 8.8 per 100,000; 815,000 were suicides, or 14.5 per 100,000 people. War-related deaths numbered 310,000, or 5.2 per 100,000.

Violence costs are difficult to estimate. In part this is because the costs are imbued in burdens to health care, criminal justice, and child welfare and education systems, and as such they are estimates of debatable certainty. However, the WHO estimates the cost of violence in 2000 in the United States to be $126 billion annually for gunshot injuries and $51 billion for stab wounds. One study estimated that each suicide imposes approximately $850,000 in costs (Tolan, 2001).

Lethal violence rates are tied to a country's economic status, with a rate of 32.1 per 100,000 in low- to middle-income countries and 14.4 per 100,000 in high-income countries. Across nations, though, 91% of violent deaths occur in low-income areas of the population. Violent deaths, particularly homicides, are also age related, with a rate of 5.4 per 100,000 among those aged 0 to 4, dropping to 2.1 per 100,000 for those aged 5 to 14, and jumping to 19.4 for males and 4.4 for females aged 15 to 24. This gender divergence persists for the remainder of the lifespan. The rate remains at or near this level for females, whereas for males it remains near this level until age 44 to 55, when it drops to 14.8. At each succeeding decade, the rate declines some for males. Suicide shows a different age pattern, climbing for each age period, from negligible rates for those under age 15 to rates of 15.6 for 15- to 29-year-old males. This rate more than doubles, to 44.9 per 100,000, for males older than age 60. Rates for females, although also negligible in childhood and lower across the lifespan than for males, jump from approximately 12 per 100,000 to 22.6 per 100,000 after age 60.

The proportion of violent deaths due to suicide or homicide varies considerably among regions of the world, implying that cultural differences may relate to patterns of violence, particularly lethal violence. Violent deaths are much more likely to be due to suicide than homicide in European, Southeast Asia, and the Western Pacific regions, but much more likely to be homicide in the Americas and Africa. However, within these overall regional differences, there are major variations in relative rates of homicide versus suicide among countries and within and across countries among urban and rural populations, richer and poorer segments, and ethnic groups.

Identifying Categories or Types of Violence

Despite this controversy and considerable challenge in defining violence, there is the recognition that differentiating the many categories of violence may be valuable for epidemiology, risk and causal understanding, intervention, and policy (Elliott & Tolan, 1999). At the broadest level, a distinction is commonly made among collective violence, self-directed violence, and interpersonal violence (WHO Global Consultation on Violence and Health, 1996). Collective violence refers to acts by groups, often perpetrated for political purpose. Most typically this refers to oppressive intent to suppress liberty and economic opportunity of others. This form of violence while emerging as more important, is not the focus of most of the work on youth violence. Self-directed violence includes self-injurious (abuse, mutilation) and suicidal behaviors. Interpersonal violence refers to violence between individuals and is predominantly family violence, which is the most common form of violence to others in the United States. Family violence comprises three broad categories: domestic violence or violence to or between romantic or marital partners, child abuse or violence toward a child, and elder violence (Tolan et al., 2006). For adolescents, acquaintance violence and community violence (violence toward or from a person in the community but not personally known to the other, such as a member of a neighboring gang) are common forms of interpersonal violence. Another form of interpersonal violence is media violence, which is exposure to violence through popular media, such as television shows, movies, video games, music, and print. Another category of violence often included as a component of interpersonal violence is institutional violence or violence that occurs within work, school, prison, nursing homes, or other institutional settings. Implicit in this notion is that something about the setting precipitates, tolerates, or promulgates the violent acts.

Within interpersonal violence, many surveys and much research single out sexual violence from other forms of violence, likely because of its particularly offensive status. It may also be differentiated because of assumptions about differences in causes, responsiveness to treatment, and patterns of that behavior (WHO Global Consultation on Violence and Health, 1996). There is increasing recognition that, although worthy of distinction, sexual violence should not be omitted from violence study or policy, but rather related and differentiated from other forms of violence as is scientifically supported (Fagan & Browne, 1994).

Categories of Family Violence: An Example of Definitional Controversies

These major categories of violence do not constitute all forms of violence, and none is free of effects and uncertainty stemming from the definitional issues raised. Each is encumbered with definitional challenges. However, the designation of types of violence does provide a base for comparing their conceptual differentiation and similarity. Family violence accounts for the largest portion of violence across countries and groups. Yet, it is clear that family violence has several forms, with no consensus about how the forms should be differentiated, characterized, and related. As noted by Jouriles et al. (2001), these are more than semantic disputes: they represent major differences in views about the important features of the problem. In fact, family violence presents a particularly apt example of how the issues involved in defining violence are related to the identification of and relationships among forms of violence.

Family violence is a more recent term used to refer to the three major types of violence among family members: domestic violence; child abuse or neglect or other major failings in parenting; and elder abuse, usually of one's parent or former caregiver (Tolan et al., 2006). As noted in Tolan and colleagues' earlier more extensive review, within each area, but most contentiously within domestic violence, controversy exists about what constitutes family violence and which related terms should be used to describe these categories.

A central controversy is the degree to which the term "family violence" should be synonymous with abuse or substantial mistreatment of family members (Jouriles et al.,

2001). Are all acts of violence abuse, and are all forms of harm or abuse violent, or should family violence refer only to serious or ongoing patterns of violence? Some fear a too-restrictive definition will overlook the harm that accumulates from "minor" examples, whereas others argue that by including such a broad range of behaviors, serious acts and patterns of substantial and repeated harm will be lost amid larger patterns of infrequent, unpatterned acts. The inclusion of minor and more accepted acts would also muddle the meaning of empirical findings and policy discussions (Heise, 1998). In addition, it is frequently noted that actual physical violence is part of a set of behaviors that define abuse, and to separate them is to neglect important contributors to the abusive impact (Jouriles et al., 2001).

Like violence in general, how family violence is defined can affect its rates, meaning, and implications. For example, studies of child abuse often mix neglect cases with abuse cases. Because the prevalence of neglect is about three times that of physical abuse, many samples in studies of child abuse are predominantly made up of children who have been neglected. If the interest is in abuse, this is a minor concern, but if the interest is distinctly about violence, the implications of the results may be misleading (Cicchetti, Rappaport, Sandler, & Weissberg, 2000). Further, without differentiating violence from neglect, we may overlook the different effects of neglect and violence individually, as well as the effects when they overlap (Edleson, 1999).

As in other areas, but perhaps to a greater degree in family violence, a major issue is how to incorporate into the definition of family violence any gender inequities and dependency differences that stem from power differentials within family relationships; specifically, how and whether to differentiate between male violence toward females, and female violence toward males. Some argue for differentiating by gender because of social differences in gender-accorded power in male-female relationships, even when the specific violent acts are the same (APA Presidential Task Force, 1996; Heise, 1998).

Others, in contrast, argue that the failure to equate violence perpetrated by females with that perpetrated by males impedes a full understanding of violence patterns that may harm both genders. This view is predicated on the idea that the circumstances of violent acts should be measured, and meaning should be attached to the acts to formulate understanding. To date, empirical tests do not support the contention that all violence between spouses or couples occurs within the context of such a power differential (Johnson, 1995). Emerging data from community samples suggest that much of the violence between couples, regardless of initiator, is similar in frequency and seriousness and that it is better explained as a relationship factor than as the imposition of power (Magdol, Moffitt, Caspi, Newman, & Fagan, 1997). However, other studies find patterns of serious, quite dangerous violence primarily by men toward women; this finding calls into question the extent to which survey data are sensitive to this type of domestic violence (Hines & Malley-Morrison, 2004).

The definition of family violence is also affected by the extent to which common or socially sanctioned violent behavior should be considered problematic (Hines & Malley-Morrison, 2004). How should definitions address the rather high likelihood that a person will experience violence within an intimate relationship at some point in life or findings that both males and females use violence with no clear pattern of initiation or seriousness (Magdol et al., 1997)? Should the definition be limited to violence that is unusual or lasting or that causes serious harmful effects, so that family violence can be understood as a major health threat? A similar issue arises when considering corporal punishment, a common practice in the United States. Although parenting experts and mental health professionals find little value in spanking as a means of disciplining children (Benjet & Kazdin, 2003), the results from research are inconsistent regarding its negative effects. Similarly, the most prevalent type of family violence is among siblings, yet is least often considered as abusive or in need of intervention (Gelles & Straus,

1988). Thus, from a human rights perspective, sibling violence, the use of corporal punishment, and other common and often accepted forms of violence among family members still constitute an aberration. They are considered like other forms of violence and not to be tolerated. Yet others argue that there is no evidence of specific or consistent harm from these forms of violence, and therefore they should not be included in the family violence problem (Hines & Malley-Morrison, 2004).

These controversies reflect the political ramifications of terminology. In addition, each form arises from a focus on one type of family relationship, which emphasizes only part of the ecology of family relationships, their interdependence, and their overall meaning about violence within families. This has led to the unfortunate and continuing resistance to integrating different forms of family violence into a unified picture and related understanding. Yet, there is growing empirical and theoretical support for a more precise understanding of the commonalities among family violence and how the various forms relate (Daro et al., 2004; Margolin & Gourdis, 2000).

Consensus is growing that threatening verbal behavior and intimidation are components of family violence are especially important when measuring the impact and characterizing patterns of such violence (Chalk & King, 1998; Jouriles et al., 2001). There is a shared recognition that violence in family relationships may have different meanings because of dependency among family members (Johnson, 1995). The evidence suggests that each form is affected by multiple influences but that each shares with the other forms important risk factors and elements of efficacious interventions. Further consensus should emerge as studies that measure violent acts separately also include multiple forms of family violence as simultaneous foci and measure psychological aggression and coercive and intimidating aspects of relationships along with such related components as fear, intention, relation to other relationship qualities, and developmental and functional outcomes. Such studies would explore the competing hypotheses about the nature and heterogeneity of forms of family violence, as well as permit a better understanding of the interrelations among those forms and the relation between violent behavior and abuse.

Differentiating Patterns of Youth Violence: Four Patterns of Adolescent Violence?

The controversies in defining family violence suggest why such definitions have eluded the field. These same controversies also affect other areas of violence, such as youth violence. In addition, the amount of related scientific evidence on such factors as patterns, risk factors, and prevalence and their application to intervention and policy can also limit consensus (Tolan, 2001) . For example, if one examines the epidemiological patterns and applies a developmental-ecological or multifactor, multilevel understanding of population patterns and risk factors, there appears to be utility in differentiating four types of youth violence[1]: situational, relationship, predatory, and pathological. Each of these types can be differentiated by patterns of prevalence, concentration, continuity over the life course, and needed interventions, as well as response to various interventions (Tolan & Guerra, 1994). These types, although consistent with the existing literature, have not been tested for discriminative validity or for robustness in explaining diverse theoretical and policy questions.

Although the specific causal contributors are not yet clear for any one of these four types of violence, the emerging evidence suggests they can exist on a multidimensional continuum within a biopsychosocial model of cause, with differences in prevalence within various populations, the likely causes, the synergy of risk factors, and the likely age of onset (Lipsey & Derzon, 1998; Moffitt, 1993). The four types vary in the extent to which the violence arises or is precipitated by the setting or situation versus by individual differences.

Situational violence, the first of the four types, seems to arise from group contagion and has situational precipitants, such as a contentious football game or a party with substantial alcohol consumption. Police records, emergency room surveys, and other archival sources show increases in violence during extreme heat, on weekends, and during times of nonindividual social stress (Rotton & Frey, 1985). Similarly, frustration in pursuing planned events or the occurrence of unavoidable accidents or events increases the likelihood of aggressive behavior (Averill, 1983). Contextual factors such as poverty and neighborhood disorder (Sampson, Raudenbush, & Earls, 1997) and social factors such as low socioeconomic status are related to the likelihood of violence perpetration and victimization (Tolan et al., 2006). To the extent that these social or contextual factors accompany or are part of patterns of social discrimination and oppression, the elevated rates of violence in lower socioeconomic communities may be situationally driven (Elliott, 1994b). It may be, too, that situations catalyze an individual predisposition toward violence into actual violence, or they may directly provoke violence (Fagan & Wilkinson, 1998) . Two particularly important catalysts for youth violence are the access to handguns and the use of alcohol and drugs (Rosenberg, Mercy, & Annest, 1998).

As noted above, a large portion of violence arises from interpersonal disputes between persons with ongoing relationships. Thus, *relationship violence* or violence among friends and family members is a common type of adolescent violence. For example, dating violence occurs at disturbing rates. Bergman (1992) found that 15.7% of adolescent females and 7.8% of males reported being physically victimized on dates. Similarly, it appears that other forms of youth violence are related to being a victim or a perpetrator of family violence (Tolan et al., 2006). As with other age groups, the prevalence of relationship violence in youth may suggest that more emphasis is needed on building relationship skills and emphasizing the importance of relationships in efforts to prevent, stop, and recover from such violence.

In addition to situational and relationship violence there is *predatory violence*, the third most common form among teens. This type is defined as violence that is perpetrated intentionally to obtain some gain or as part of a pattern of criminal or antisocial behavior. Muggings, robbery, and gang assaults represent common forms of this type of violence. Most estimates indicate that 20 to 30% of adolescents commit an act of predatory violence (Elliott, 1994a), but that a small portion of teens (between 5% and 8% of males and between 3% and 6% of females) are responsible for most of the serious predatory violence. Much of this predatory violence occurs as part of a pattern of serious, chronic, antisocial behavior (Elliot & Tolan, 1999). Notably, even within this subset, a very small percentage commit repeated acts of violence (Tolan & Gorman-Smith, 1998). For example, among the 6% in a community sample of males who were most seriously and persistently criminals, only one third had a violent criminal record, and of those, 88.5% had only one such offense (Weitekamp, Kerner, Schindler, & Schubert, 1995). Notably, 72.7% of aggravated assaults committed by this chronic group of 627 adolescent males were committed by 32 of its members, and 71.4% of the group's homicides (or 50% of all homicides from this cohort sample) were committed by only 10 individuals.

Thus, although predatory violence does seem to occur more often as a pattern of behavior than does interpersonal or situational violence, there is not as much repetition, continuity, or predictability among those exhibiting such violence. Yet, this patterning and the extent to which it represents more patterned or criminal behavior have spurred much research on and extension of knowledge about violence, particularly youth violence; (see Pettit, 2004 and numerous chapters in this volume for such advances).

A fourth type of youth violence that seems to merit differentiation is what we have termed *pathological violence*. Fortunately this form is rare. It represents violence that may be repetitively exhibited by an individual with relatively little provocation or presence of situational precipitants (Cornell, Benedek, & Benedek, 1987). The violence of these individuals seems to arise from neural trauma or dysfunction or from extreme psychological neglect or abuse. As the ability to identify neurochemical markers, individual propensities, and the ecological influences on violence increases, the models of risk and the utility of further specifying subtypes should increase (Tolan & Gorman-Smith, 2002).

There is a tension between comprehensive definitions that address the wide variation in type, scale, and patterning of violent acts and situations and more focused and specific definitions, the latter of which can be criticized for foreclosing or excluding unnecessarily certain forms of violence. The more specific a definition, the more readily it can be identified as occurring. However, specificity often makes it more difficult to translate findings to usable policy.

Measuring Violence

Although it is important to render clear and specific definitions to help advance our understanding of violence, attaining this shared understanding and certainty is hampered by the difficult in accurately measuring the majority of incidents of violence, which are nonlethal, occur often among family members, and are often not reported if recognized as problematic. In addition, as detection interest and capability can vary greatly across jurisdictions and agencies, the comparability of violence data is questionable.[2] After reviewing the issues in defining the four types of youth violence, the challenges in trying to measure violence become more apparent. Our knowledge about violence rests on the clarity and consistency across users in what is understood to be violence. Its measurement or epidemiology depends on this consistency. Yet, settling on a definition is only a first step toward the reliable and comparable estimation of violence levels.

There are vast differences across communities and across issues of violence in data availability and quality and the resources to collect, collate, and analyze that data. The extent to which more visible and clear instances of violence (such as battery, for example) are also present in those more hidden and more speculative forms (such as domestic violence) is difficult to determine, but it is likely that the prevalence varies by setting, resources, and issue at hand. For example, although it may be that the rates of predatory violence that results in battery are fairly similar across jurisdictions in the United States, records of battery stemming from domestic violence are likely to be much more varied; that is, in how a given act is recorded.

In addition, how consistently such matters are recorded may be influenced by presumptions held about various subpopulations. For example, domestic violence in a family of considerable means or status may not be recorded, whereas violence in a working class family may be. Alternatively, in higher income communities, much more attention may be paid to incidents of domestic violence than in those where resources are strained. These differences suggest that care should be taken when making generalizations based on findings from careful research compared with less carefully formulated and managed surveillances for public health reasons. Similarly, findings in one location or with one population may not apply to others, or those from overall patterns may also not fit subpopulations. This lack of applicability may make it difficult to identify appropriate population differentiation and may lead to mischaracterized patterns and implications for subgroups.

Summary and Conclusions

This chapter has briefly summarized the many controversies in defining violence. As noted here, these differences are quite engrained and promote segregation between those interested in one view or one type of violence from others. This segregation also promotes dismissal of views and evidence that challenge currently held views. There is a complex iterative process between how violence is defined and how it manifests in policy. That is, how violence is defined can affect which studies are produced and how violence problems are framed for policy influence. For example, we have argued elsewhere for the value of integrating forms of family violence into a developmental-ecological perspective because viewing through this lens makes the continuity of one form to another more evident and the potential value of relationship-focused interventions more recognizable (Tolen, et al., 2006).

The following chapters each offer an implicit, if not explicit, operational definition of violence that will express assumptions and perspectives about each of the issues highlighted in this chapter. There is richness in the variation, and there are many examples of how a given view is valid and important. Similarly, the continuities across chapters provide more of a general understanding of violence. The challenge for the reader is to understand the continuities and the variations and to extract a comprehensive understanding of violence in its various forms and definitions.

Notes

1. Accepting, of course, the limitations and inconsistencies in the data's availability or how that data may be recorded.
2. This is one reason that homicide data are often used to understand violence trends. Homicide is one of the most regularly detected acts of violence and once detected is among the most easily classified; that is, there has been a death and there is good indication it was not caused by a disease or accident.

Acknowledgments

This work is partially the result of support from the Centers for Disease Control, the National Institute of Child Health and Development, and the University of Illinois Faculty Scholar Award. Correspondence should be sent to Patrick H. Tolan, Institute of Juvenile Research, University of Illinois at Chicago, 1747 W. Roosevelt Rd. Chicago, IL 60608 or Tolan@uic.edu.

References

American Psychological Association Presidential Task Force on Violence and the Family. (1996). *Violence and the family*. Washington, DC.

Averill, J. R. (1983). Studies on anger and aggression: Implications for theories of emotion. *American Psychologist, 38*, 1145–1160.

Benjet, C., & Kazdin, A. E. (2003). Spanking children: The controversies, findings, and new directions. *Clinical Psychology Review, 23*, 197–224.

Bergman, L. (1992). Dating violence among high school students. *Social Work, 37*(1), 21–27.

Centers for Disease Control (CDC). (2004). *Web-based Injury Statistics Query and Reporting System (WISQARS)*. Retrieved January 30, 2005, from www.cdc.gov/ncipc/wisqars.

Chalk, R., & King, P. A. (1998). *Violence in families: Assessing prevention and treatment programs*. Washington, DC: National Academy Press.

Cicchetti, D., Rappaport, J., Sandler, I. N., & Weissberg, R. P. (2000). *The promotion of wellness in children and adolescents*. Washington, DC: Child Welfare League of America Press.

Cornell, D., Benedek, E., & Benedek, D. (1987). Juvenile homicide: Prior adjustment and a proposed typology. *American Journal of Orthopsychiatry, 57*, 383–393.

Daro, D., Edleson, J. L., & Pinderhughes, H. (2004). Finding common ground in the study of child maltreatment, youth violence, and adult domestic violence. *Journal of Interpersonal Violence, 19*(3), 282–298.

Edleson, J. L. (1999). The overlap between child maltreatment and woman battering. *Violence Against Women, 5*, 134–154.

Elliott, D. S. (1994a). Longitudinal research in criminology: Promise and practice. In E. G. Weitekamp & H. J. Kerner (Eds.), *Cross-national longitudinal research on human development and criminal behavior* (pp. 189–201). Netherlands: Kluwer Academic Publishers.

Elliott, D. S. (1994b). Serious violent offenders: Onset, developmental course, and termination—The American Society of Criminology 1993 presidential address. *Criminology, 32*(1), 1–21.

Elliott, D. S., & Tolan, P. H. (1999). Youth, violence prevention, intervention and social policy: An overview. In D. Flannery & R. Huff (Eds.), *Youth violence: Prevention, intervention, and social policy* (pp. 3–46). Washington, DC: American Psychiatric Press.

Fagan, J., & Browne, A. (1994). Violence between spouses and intimates: Physical aggression between women and men in intimate relationships. In A. Reiss & J. Roth (Eds.), *Understanding and preventing violence: Social influences* (Vol. 3, pp. 115–292). Washington, DC: National Academy Press.

Fagan, J., & Wilkinson, D. (1998). Social contexts and functions of adolescent violence. In D. S. Elliott, B. A. Hamburg, & K. R. Williams (Eds.), *Violence in American schools: A new perspective* (pp. 55–93). New York: Cambridge University Press.

Farrington, D. P., Langan, P. A., & Tonry, M. (2004). *Cross-national studies in crime and justice*. Washington, DC: U.S. Department of Justice, Office of Justice Programs.

Garbarino, J. (1996). Youth in dangerous environments: Coping with the consequences. In K. Hurrelmann & S. F. Hamilton (Eds.), *Social problems and social contexts in adolescence: Perspectives across boundaries* (pp. 269–290). New York: Aldine De Gruyter.

Gelles, R. J., & Straus, M. A. (1988). *Intimate violence: The causes and consequences of abuse in the American family*. New York: Simon and Schuster.

Heise, L. L. (1998). Violence against women: An integrated, ecological framework. *Violence Against Women, 4,* 262–290.

Hines, D., & Malley-Morrison, K. (2004). *Family violence in the United States*. Thousand Oaks, CA: Sage.

Jackman, M. R. (2002). Violence in social life. *Annual Review of Sociology, 28,* 387–415.

Johnson, M. P. (1995). Patriarchal terrorism and common couple violence: Two forms of violence against women. *Journal of Marriage and the Family, 57,* 283–294.

Jouriles, E. N., McDonald, R., Norwood, W. D., & Ezell, E. (2001). Issues and controversies in documenting the prevalence of children's exposure to domestic violence. In S. A. Graham-Bermann & J. L. Edleson (Eds.), *Domestic violence in the lives of children: The future of research, intervention, and social policy* (pp. 12–34). Washington, DC: American Psychological Association.

Krug, E. G., Dahlberg, L. L., Mercy, J., Zwi, A. B., & Lozano, R. (2002). *World report on violence and health*. Geneva: World Health Organization.

Lipsey, M. W., & Derzon, J. H. (1998). Predictors of violent and serious delinquency in adolescence and early adulthood: A synthesis of longitudinal research. In R. Loeber & D. P. Farrington (Eds.), *Serious and violent juvenile offenders: Risk factors and successful interventions* (pp. 86–105). Thousand Oaks, CA: Sage.

Loseke, D. R., Gelles, R. J., & Cavanaugh, M. M. (2005). *Current controversies on family violence* (2nd ed.). Thousand Oaks, CA: Sage.

Magdol, L., Moffitt, T. E., Caspi, A., Newman, D. L., & Fagan, J. (1997). Gender differences in partner violence in a birth cohort of 21-year olds: Bridging the gap between clinical and epidemiological approaches. *Journal of Consulting and Clinical Psychology, 65*(1), 68–78.

Margolin, G., & Gourdis, E. (2000). The effect of family and community violence on children. *Annual Review of Psychology, 51,* 445–479.

Moffitt, T. E. (1993). The neuropsychology of conduct disorder. *Development and Psychopathology, 5,* 135–151.

Pettit, G. S. (2004). Violent children in developmental perspective: Risk and protective factors and the mechanisms through which they (may) operate. *Current Directions in Psychological Science, 13*(5), 194–197.

Rosenberg, M. L., Mercy, J. A., & Annest, J. L. (1998). The problem of violence in the United States and globally. In R. Wallace & B. N. Doebbeling (Eds.), *Maxcy-Rosenau-Last Public Health & Preventive Medicine* (14th ed., pp. 1223–1226). Stamford, CT: Appleton & Lange.

Rotton, J., & Frey, J. (1985). Air pollution, weather, and violent crime: Concomitant time-series analysis of archival data. *Journal of Personality and Social Psychology, 49,* 1207–1220.

Sampson, R. J., Raudenbush, S. W., & Earls, F. (1997). Neighborhoods and violent crime: A multilevel study of collective efficacy. *Science, 277,* 918–924.

Tolan, P. (2001). Youth violence and its prevention in the United States: An overview of current knowledge. *Injury Control and Safety Promotion, 8*(1), 1–12.

Tolan, P., & Gorman-Smith, D. (1998). Development of serious and violent offending careers. In R. Loeber & D. Farrington (Eds.), *Serious and violent juvenile offenders* (pp. 68–85). Thousand Oaks, CA: Sage.

Tolan, P., & Gorman-Smith, D. (2002). What violence prevention research can tell us about developmental psychopathology. *Development and Psychopathology, 14,* 713–729.

Tolan, P. H., Gorman-Smith, D., & Henry, D. (2006). Family violence. In S. T. Fiske, A. E. Kazdin, & D. Schacter (Eds.), *Annual Review of Psychology, 57,* 557–583.

Tolan, P., & Guerra, N. (1994). *What works in reducing adolescent violence: An empirical review of the field.* Boulder, CO: Center for the Study and Prevention of Violence, Institute for Behavioral Sciences.

Tremblay, R. E., Nagin, D. S., Seguin, J. R., Zoccolillo, M., Zelaco, P. D., Boivin, M., et al. (2004). Physical aggression during early childhood: Trajectories and predictors. *Pediatrics, 114,* 43–50.

Walters, R. H., & Parke, R. D. (1964). Social motivation, dependency, and susceptibility to social influence. In L. Berkowitz (Ed.), *Advances in experimental social psychology* (Vol. 1, pp. 231–276). New York: Academic Press.

Weitekamp, E., Kerner, H.-J., Schindler, V., & Schubert, A. (1995). On the "dangerousness" of chronic/habitual offenders: A reanalysis of the 1945 Philadelphia birth cohort data. *Journal of Studies on Crime and Crime Prevention: Annual Review, 4*(2), 159–175.

WHO Global Consultation on Violence and Health. (1996). *Violence: A public health priority* (Document WHO/EHA/SPI.POA.2). Geneva: World Health Organization.

CHAPTER 2

Origins of Violent Behavior Over the Life Span

David P. Farrington

Introduction

The most basic definition of violence is behavior that is intended to cause, and that actually causes, physical or psychological injury. The most important violent offenses defined by the criminal law are homicide, assault, robbery, and rape.

This chapter has three main sections. The first section reviews basic knowledge about violence over the life span: its measurement and prevalence, continuity from childhood to adulthood, specialization or versatility, and changes with age. The second section reviews modifiable risk factors for violence (i.e., excluding unchangeable factors, such as gender and race). The third section presents a theory of violence.

Risk factors for violence are defined as variables that predict a high probability of violence. To determine whether a risk factor is a predictor or possible cause of violence, the risk factor needs to be measured before the violence occurs. Hence, longitudinal follow-up studies are needed, and especially longitudinal studies of large com-

munity samples of several hundred persons containing information from several data sources (to maximize validity). This chapter focuses especially on the most important results obtained in such studies (for reviews, see Farrington, 1998; Hawkins, Herrenkohl, Farrington, Brewer, Catalano, & Harachi, 1998). The Appendix in this chapter summarizes some of the most important prospective longitudinal surveys of violence.

The best prospective surveys include both interview and record data and span a follow-up period of at least 5 years. Such surveys are surprisingly rare. For example, Mossman (1994) reviewed 44 studies of the prediction of violence, and only 2 (Farrington, 1989a; Kandel, Brennan, Mednick, & Michelson, 1989) met these criteria.

The main emphasis here is on results obtained in Great Britain and the United States and on stranger or street violence, rather than domestic or within-family violence (cf. Capaldi & Clark, 1998). Most research focuses on male offenders and on the most common offenses of assault and robbery. There are few prospective longitudinal studies of homicide (but see Loeber, Pardini, Homish, Wei, Crawford, Farrington et al., 2005). Within a single chapter, it is impossible to review everything that is known about violence; for more extensive information, see Reiss and Roth (1993), Loeber and Farrington (1998), Tonry and Moore (1998), and Flannery and Huff (1999).

This chapter focuses on results obtained in the Cambridge Study in Delinquent Development, which is a prospective longitudinal survey of 400 London males from age 8 to age 48 (see Farrington, 1995b, 2003b). A summary of the key features of this project follows.

The Cambridge Study

The males in the Cambridge Study were originally assessed in 1961–1962, when they were in six state primary schools and were aged 8 to 9 (West, 1969). Hence the most common year of birth of the males is 1953. The males are not a sample drawn systematically from a population but rather the complete population of boys of that age in those schools at that time. The vast majority of boys were living in two-parent families, had fathers in manual jobs, and were White and of British origin.

The males in the study have been interviewed and assessed nine times between age 8 and age 48. Attrition has been very low; for example, 95% of those still alive were interviewed at age 18, 94% at age 32, and 93% at age 48 (for information about how the males were traced, see Farrington, Gallagher, Morley, St. Ledger, & West, 1990). The assessments in schools measured such factors as intelligence, personality, and impulsiveness, and information was collected in the interviews about such topics as living circumstances, employment histories, relationships with females, leisure activities such as drinking, drug use and fighting, and, of course, offending behavior.

The boys' parents were also interviewed about once a year from when the boys were aged 8 until when they were aged 15. The parents provided details about such matters as family income, family composi-

tion, their employment histories, their child-rearing practices (including discipline and supervision), and the boy's temporary or permanent separations from them. In addition, the boys' teachers completed questionnaires when the boys were aged about 8, 10, 12, and 14. These questionnaires furnished information about such topics as their restlessness or poor concentration, truancy, school attainment, and disruptive behavior in class. Searches were also carried out of the criminal records of the males, of their biological relatives (fathers, mothers, brothers, and sisters), of their wives and co-habitees, and of any person who ever offended with any of our males.

The data collected at age 48 have not yet been fully analyzed. However, the follow-up from age 32 (the previous interview) to age 48 made it possible to assess changes with age in criminal career features and measures of life success (based on housing relationships, employment, violence, drinking, drug use, mental health, and offending behavior). Between ages 32 and 48, the average length of criminal careers and the number of late-onset offenders (starting after age 21) both increased considerably, life success generally increased, and violence decreased. The desisters (males who stopped offending before age 21) were similar to unconvicted men in measures of life success at age 48, whereas they had been deviant (in fighting, drinking, drug use, and offending behavior) at age 32.

About one in five of the males was convicted as a juvenile (under age 17 at the time), whereas 40% were convicted up to age 40. Most convictions were for theft, taking vehicles, burglary, deception, or violence; minor offenses, such as traffic infractions, drunkenness, or common assault, are excluded from these figures. This chapter concentrates on the violent offenders.

Violence Over the Life Span

Measurement and Prevalence

The most common ways of identifying violent offenders are by using police or court records or self-reports of offending. For example, Elliott (1994) in the U.S. National Youth Survey (see Appendix) inquired about aggravated assault (attacking someone with the idea of seriously hurting or killing that person), being involved in a gang fight, and robbery (using force or strong-arm methods to get money or things from people). Prevalences of these behaviors were surprisingly high. In the first wave of the survey (ages 11–17 in 1976), 31% of African American boys and 22% of White boys admitted to felony assault in the previous year (aggravated assault, gang fight, or sexual assault). At the same time, 13% of African American boys and 6% of White boys admitted to robbery (of teachers, students, or others) in the previous year.

The comparison between self-reports and official records gives some indication of the probability of a violent offender being caught and convicted. In the Cambridge Study, 45% of boys admitted starting a physical fight or using a weapon in a fight between ages 15 and 18, but only 3% were convicted of assault between these ages (Farrington, 1989b). Self-reported violence had predictive validity: 10% of those who admitted assault up to age 18 were subsequently convicted of assault, compared with 5% of the remainder.

Up to age 40, 16% of the Cambridge Study males were convicted of a violent offense (assault, robbery, carrying or using carrying weapons); 9% were convicted for violence between ages 10 and 20, and 10% between ages 21 and 40. One fifth of the males (20% of 389 known) were identified as self-reported violent offenders at age 15–18, because they were highest on these measures: number of fights, starting fights, carrying a weapon, and using a weapon in a fight (Farrington, 2000). Between ages 27 and 32, 16% (of 377 males known) were identified as self-reported violent offenders because they had either (a) been involved in four or more physical fights in which blows were struck or (b) hit their wife or female partner without her hitting them (Farrington, 2001a).

This chapter describes childhood risk factors for youthful and adult violence convic-

tions at ages 10–20 and 21–40 and for self-reported violence at ages 15–18 and 27–32. There was a significant overlap between self-reported and official violence in the Cambridge Study. One quarter of young self-reported violent offenders were convicted for violence by age 20, compared with 5% of self-reported nonviolent youth (odds ratio = 6.2, 95% confidence interval = 3.0 to 12.7). Similarly, 26% of adult self-reported violent offenders were convicted for violence as adults, compared with 7% of self-reported nonviolent adults (odds ratio = 4.5, confidence interval = 2.2 to 9.2). Table 2.1 summarizes childhood predictors of youthful violence, and Table 2.2 summarizes childhood predictors of adult violence.

Continuity

In general, there is continuity from juvenile to adult violence and from childhood aggression to youth violence. In Columbus, Ohio, 59% of violent juveniles were arrested as adults in the next 5 to 9 years, and 42% of these adult offenders were charged with at least one Index (serious) violent offense (Hamparian, Davis, Jacobson, & McGraw, 1985). More of those arrested for Index violence as juveniles were rearrested as adults than of those arrested for minor violence (simple assault or molesting) as juveniles.

In the Cambridge Study, 34% of the boys convicted for youthful violence were reconvicted for adult violence, compared with only 8% of those not convicted for youthful violence (odds ratio = 6.1, confidence interval = 2.8 to 13.5). There was also continuity in self-reported violence; 29% of youthful violent offenders were also adult violent offenders, compared with 12% of nonviolent youth (odds ratio = 3.0, confidence interval = 1.7 to 5.4). Although it is possible that part of the continuity in officially recorded violence may be attributable to continuity in police targeting, the continuity in self-reported violence indicates that there is real continuity in violent behavior.

Generally, violent males have an early age of onset of offending of all types (Farrington, 1991b). Both in official records

Table 2.1: Childhood predictors of youthful violence

Age 8–10 Predictors	Convicted OR	Convicted 95% CI	Self-Reported OR	Self-Reported 95% CI
Behavioral				
Troublesome	4.8*	2.4–9.6	3.3*	1.9–5.7
Dishonest	2.4*	1.1–5.1	1.4	0.8–2.5
Antisocial	5.6*	2.7–11.3	2.7*	1.6–4.6
Individual				
High daring	4.4*	2.2–9.0	3.9*	2.3–6.6
Lacks concentration	2.9*	1.4–6.0	1.6	0.9–2.9
Nervous	0.7	0.3–1.7	0.6	0.3–1.2
Few friends	0.5	0.1–2.0	0.3*	0.1–0.9
Unpopular	1.8	0.9–3.7	1.7*	1.0–2.8
Low nonverbal IQ	3.0*	1.5–6.1	1.6	0.9–2.7
Low verbal IQ	1.4	0.7–3.0	1.4	0.8–2.4
Low attainment	2.1*	1.0–4.4	1.6	0.9–2.9
Family				
Convicted parent	3.1*	1.5–6.2	2.2*	1.3–3.7
Delinquent sibling	3.0*	1.3–6.9	1.4	0.7–2.9
Harsh discipline	3.4*	1.7–7.0	1.9*	1.1–3.3
Poor supervision	3.6*	1.7–7.6	2.3*	1.3–4.1
Broken family	3.7*	1.8–7.4	1.9*	1.1–3.2
Parental conflict	2.8*	1.3–5.9	1.4	0.8–2.6
Large family size	2.5*	1.3–5.1	2.6*	1.5–4.4
Young mother	1.4	0.6–2.9	1.9*	1.1–3.4
Socioeconomic				
Low SES	1.5	0.7–3.3	1.5	0.9–2.8
Low family income	2.7*	1.4–5.6	2.6*	1.5–4.4
Poor housing	2.1*	1.0–4.1	2.1*	1.2–3.4
Vulnerable	3.7*	1.8–7.9	2.5*	1.9–6.4

Notes: OR = odds ratio; CI = confidence interval; SES = socioeconomic status

* $p < 0.05$.

and self-reports, an early age of onset of violent offending predicts a relatively large number of violent offenses (Elliott, 1994; Hamparian, Schuster, Dinitz, & Conrad, 1978). Moffitt (1993) suggested that the "life-course-persistent" offenders who started early (around age 10) and had long criminal careers were fundamentally different from the "adolescence-limited" offenders who started later (around age 14) and had short criminal careers lasting no longer than 5 to 6 years (see Chapter 3 in this volume).

Childhood aggression predicts later violence. In the Orebro (Sweden) longitudinal study (Stattin & Magnusson, 1989), two thirds of boys who were officially recorded for violence up to age 26 had high aggressiveness scores at ages 10 and 13 (rated by teachers), compared with 30% of all boys. In the Woodlawn (Chicago) follow-up study of African American children, teacher ratings of aggressiveness at age 6 predicted arrests for violent crimes up to age 32 (McCord & Ensminger, 1997). Similarly, in the Jyvaskyla (Finland) follow-up (Pulkkinen, 1987), peer ratings of aggression at ages 8 and 14 significantly predicted officially recorded violence up to age 20 (see Appendix).

One likely explanation for the continuity in violence over time is that there are

Table 2.2: Childhood predictors of adult violence

Age 8–10 Predictors	Convicted OR	Convicted 95% CI	Self-Reported OR	Self-Reported 95% CI
Behavioral				
Troublesome	1.6	0.8–3.3	1.7	0.9–3.2
Dishonest	2.5*	1.2–5.2	1.7	0.9–3.3
Antisocial	2.1*	1.1–4.2	1.1	0.6–2.2
Individual				
High daring	2.1*	1.1–4.0	1.7	0.9–3.0
Lacks concentration	1.8	0.9–3.7	0.7	0.3–1.5
Nervous	1.2	0.6–2.7	1.8	1.0–3.3
Few friends	0.4	0.1–1.7	0.4	0.1–1.3
Unpopular	1.0	0.5–2.0	1.3	0.7–2.4
Low nonverbal IQ	1.6	0.8–3.3	0.7	0.3–1.4
Low verbal IQ	2.9*	1.5–5.6	1.4	0.8–2.6
Low attainment	2.2*	1.1–4.6	1.7	0.9–3.2
Family				
Convicted parent	3.4*	1.7–6.5	1.8*	1.0–3.3
Delinquent sibling	1.8	0.7–4.2	1.4	0.6–3.2
Harsh discipline	2.3*	1.1–4.5	1.1	0.6–2.0
Poor supervision	2.1*	1.0–4.5	1.2	0.6–2.5
Broken family	2.5*	1.3–5.0	2.3*	1.3–4.2
Parental conflict	1.7	0.8–3.7	1.6	0.8–3.0
Large family size	2.0*	1.0–3.9	2.0*	1.1–3.6
Young mother	1.3	0.6–2.7	2.1*	1.1–3.8
Socioeconomic				
Low SES	2.1*	1.0–4.3	2.3*	1.3–4.3
Low family income	2.8*	1.4–5.4	1.6	0.8–2.9
Poor housing	1.7	0.9–3.3	1.3	0.7–2.2
Vulnerable	3.9*	1.9–7.8	1.9*	1.0–3.8

Notes: OR = odds ratio; CI = confidence interval; SES = socioeconomic status
* $p < 0.05$.

persisting individual differences in an underlying potential to commit aggressive or violent behavior. In any cohort, the people who are relatively more aggressive at one age also tend to be relatively more aggressive at later ages, even though absolute levels of aggressive behavior and behavioral manifestations of violence are different at different ages.

Specialization or Versatility

Generally, violent offenders tend to be versatile rather than specialized. They tend to commit many different types of crimes and also to show other problems, such as heavy drinking, drug use, an unstable job record, and sexual promiscuity (West & Farrington, 1977, p.149). For example, males who assault their female partners are significantly likely to have convictions for other types of violent offenses (Farrington, 1994a). However, there is a small degree of specialization in violence superimposed on this versatility (Brennan, Mednick, & John, 1989).

As an indication of their versatility, violent people typically commit more nonviolent offences than violent offenses. In the Cambridge Study, the convicted violent delinquents up to age 21 had nearly three times as many convictions for nonviolent offenses as for violent offences (Farrington, 1978). The likelihood of committing a violent offense increased steadily with the total number of offenses committed (Farrington, 1991b). In the Oregon Youth Study (see Appendix), the boys arrested for violence had an average of 6.6 arrests of all kinds (Capaldi & Patterson, 1996). Piquero (2000) and Piquero and Buka (2002) also found that violent offenders were versatile, rather than specialized, in the Philadelphia and Providence perinatal cohorts, respectively.

In the Cambridge Study, the best childhood (age 8–10) predictor of youthful convictions for violence was the rating of troublesomeness in class by teachers and peers; 21% of 90 troublesome boys were convicted, compared with 5% of the remaining 319 nontroublesome boys (odds ratio = 4.8, confidence interval 2.4 to 9.6; see Table 2.1). Troublesomeness also significantly predicted youthful self-reported violence, but not adult convictions or self-reported violence (see Table 2.2). Childhood dishonesty (rated by peers) significantly predicted convictions but not self-reported violence, and a combined measure of antisocial personality (Farrington, 1991a) significantly predicted convictions and youthful self-reported violence, but not adult self-reported violence. It might be expected that childhood risk factors would predict youthful violence more strongly than adult violence (because of greater proximity) and would predict convictions more strongly than self-reports (because convicted persons are more extreme and distinctive). These results generally support the idea that continuity in violence from childhood to adulthood largely reflects continuity in general antisocial behavior.

Changes With Age

Violent offending tends to peak in the teenage years in many different countries. In the United States in 2003, the peak age of arrest was 18 for robbery and 18 for forcible rape, 19 for murder, and 21 for aggravated assault (Federal Bureau of Investigation,

2004, p. 280). In England and Wales in 2003, the peak ages for convictions and cautions for indictable offenses were 18 for males and 15 for females (Home Office, 2004, p. 55). Tarling (1993) also found that the peak age for serious assault, robbery, and rape was 17 to 18. In 2003 in England and Wales, there were 10.9 recorded violent offenders per 1,000 males aged 15–17 and 10.0 per 1,000 males aged 18–20; there were 2.6 recorded violent offenders per 1,000 females aged 15–17 and 1.4 per 1,000 females aged 18–20.

Similar results have been obtained in self-report surveys. For example, in the 1992 English national self-report survey, the peak age for violence was 16 for males and females (Graham & Bowling, 1995). For males, the percentage admitting violence in the previous year decreased from 12% at age 14–17 to 9% at age 18–21 and 4% at age 22–25; for females, the figures were 7%, 4%, and less than 1%, respectively. In the most recent 2003 English national self-report survey covering a wider range of ages, the percentage admitting violence in the previous year peaked at 23% of males at age 16–17 and 12% of females at age 14–15 (Budd, Sharp, & Mayhew, 2005). The increased prevalence in the later survey could reflect an increase in violence over time or differences in methodology between the surveys.

Many theories have been proposed to explain why offending (especially by males) peaks in the teenage years. For example, offending (and especially violence) has been linked to testosterone levels in males, which increase during adolescence and early adulthood and decrease thereafter (Archer, 1991; Ramirez, 2003). Other explanations focus on changes with age in physical capabilities and opportunities for crime, linked to changes in "routine activities" (Cohen & Felson, 1979), such as going to bars in the evenings with other males. The most popular explanation emphasizes the importance of social influences (Farrington, 1986). From birth, children are under the influence of their parents, who generally discourage offending. However, during their teenage years, juveniles gradually break away from the control of their parents and become influenced by their peers, who may encourage offending in many cases. After age 20, offending declines again as peer influences give way to a new set of family influences hostile to offending, originating in spouses and female partners.

Risk Factors for Violence

Violent offenses, like other crimes, arise from interactions between offenders and victims in situations. Some violent acts are probably committed by people with relatively stable and enduring violent tendencies, whereas others are committed by more "normal" people who find themselves in situations that are conducive to violence. This chapter summarizes knowledge about the development of violent persons (i.e., persons with a relatively high probability of committing violent acts in any situations) and the occurrence of violent acts.

In the interests of throwing light on possible causes of violence and prevention methods, the emphasis in this chapter is on risk factors that can change over time. Thus, gender, race, and genetic factors that are fixed at birth, such as the XYY chromosome abnormality, are not discussed, but biological factors that can change, such as resting heart rate, are included. Where results differ by gender or race, this difference is noted. The main focus is on individual-level studies as opposed to aggregate-level ones (e.g., of rates of violence in different areas), and on violent offenders rather than victims of violence. However, it should be noted that victims of violence overlap significantly with violent offenders (Farrington, 1995a; Rivara, Shepherd, Farrington, Richmond, & Cannon, 1995).

Biological Risk Factors

According to Raine (1993), one of the most replicable findings in the literature is that antisocial and violent people tend to have low resting heart rates (see also Lorber, 2004). This finding can be easily demonstrated by taking pulse rates. The main theory underlying this finding is that a low heart rate indicates low autonomic arousal and/or fearlessness. Low autonomic arousal, like boredom, leads to sensation-seeking and risk-taking behavior in an attempt to increase stimulation and arousal levels. Conversely, high heart rates, especially in infants and young children, are associated with anxiety, behavioral inhibition, and a fearful temperament (Kagan, 1989), which tend to inhibit violence.

In the British National Survey of Health and Development (see Appendix), heart rate was measured at age 11 (Wadsworth, 1976). A low heart rate predicted convictions for violence and sexual offenses up to age 21: 81% of violent offenders and 67% of sexual offenders had below-average heart rates. There was also an interaction between heart rate and family background. A low heart rate was especially characteristic of boys who had experienced a broken home before age 5, but among these boys it was not related to violence or sexual offenses. However, a low heart rate was significantly related to violence and sexual offenses among boys who came from intact homes.

In the Cambridge Study, resting heart rate was not measured until age 18 and hence is not shown in the tables. However, it was significantly related to convictions for violence and to self-reported violence at age 18, independently of all other variables (Farrington, 1997b). More than twice as many of the boys with low heart rates (65 beats per minute or less) were convicted of violence as of the remainder (25% compared with 11%; odds ratio = 2.8, confidence interval = 1.6 to 5.0).

Perinatal (pregnancy and delivery) complications have been studied, because of the hypothesis that they might lead to neurological damage, which in turn might lead to violence. In the Copenhagen perinatal study, Kandel and Mednick (1991) found that delivery complications predicted arrests for violence up to age 22; 80% of violent offenders scored in the high range of delivery complications, compared with 30% of property offenders and 47% of nonoffenders. However, pregnancy complications did not significantly predict violence. Interestingly, delivery complications especially predicted violence when a parent had a history of psychiatric illness; in this case, 32% of males with high delivery complications were arrested for violence, compared with only 5% of those with low delivery complications (Brennan, Mednick, & Mednick, 1993). Interactions between biological and psychosocial factors are quite common (Raine, 2002; Raine, Brennan, & Farrington, 1997).

Individual Factors

Among the most important personality dimensions that predict violence are hyperactivity, impulsiveness, poor behavioral control, and attention problems. Conversely, nervousness and anxiety tend to be negatively related to violence. In the Dunedin, New Zealand, follow-up (see Appendix), ratings of poor behavioral control (e.g., impulsiveness, lack of persistence) at ages 3 to 5 significantly predicted boys convicted of violence up to age 18, compared to those with no convictions or with nonviolent convictions (Henry, Caspi, Moffitt, & Silva, 1996). In the same study, the personality dimensions of low constraint (e.g., low cautiousness, seeking excitement) and high negative emotionality (e.g., nervousness, alienation) at age 18 were significantly correlated with convictions for violence (Caspi et al., 1994). Impulsiveness is one of the key dimensions of psychopathy, along with an arrogant, deceitful interpersonal style and deficient affective experience (e.g., low empathy, low guilt); all these dimensions are correlated with violence (Cooke, Michie, Hart, & Clark, 2004).

Many other studies show linkages between impulsiveness and violence. In the Copenhagen perinatal project, hyperactivity (restlessness and poor concentration) at age 11–13 significantly predicted arrests for violence up to age 22, especially among boys experiencing delivery complications (Brennan et al., 1993). More than half of those with both hyperactivity and high delivery complications were arrested for violence, compared to less than 10% of the remainder. Similarly, in the Orebro longitudinal study in Sweden, hyperactivity at age 13 predicted police-recorded violence up to age 26. The highest rate of violence was among males with both motor restlessness and concentration difficulties (15%), compared to 3% of the remainder (Klinteberg, Andersson, Magnusson, & Stattin, 1993).

Similar results were obtained in the Cambridge and Pittsburgh studies (Farrington, 1998). High daring or risk-taking behavior at age 8–10 predicted youthful and adult convictions for violence and youthful self-reported violence in the Cambridge Study (see Tables 2.1 and 2.2). Poor concentration and attention difficulties predicted youthful convictions for violence in the Cambridge Study and reported violence (by boys, mothers, and teachers) in Pittsburgh. High anxiety/nervousness was negatively related to youthful violence in both studies, and low guilt significantly predicted court referrals for violence in the Pittsburgh Youth Study. Table 2.1 shows that nervousness was negatively related to youthful violence and positively related to adult violence in the Cambridge Study (but not significantly so). However, social isolation (having few friends) was consistently negatively related to violence. Farrington, Gallagher, Morley, St. Ledger, and West (1988) suggested that shyness and social isolation might act as protective factors against offending for boys from high-risk backgrounds.

There is no doubt that highly aggressive children trend to be rejected by most of their peers (Coie, Dodge, & Kupersmidt, 1990). In the Oregon Youth Study (see Appendix), peer rejection at age 9–10 significantly predicted adult antisocial behavior at age 23–24 (Nelson & Dishion, 2004). However, low popularity at age 8–10 was only a marginal predictor of youthful violence in the Cambridge Study (Table 2.1).

The other main group of individual factors that predict violence comprise low intelligence and low school attainment. In the Philadelphia perinatal cohort (Denno, 1990), low verbal and performance IQ at ages 4 and 7 and low scores on the California Achievement Test at age 13–14 (vocabulary, comprehension, maths, language, spelling) all predicted arrests for violence up to age 22. In the Woodlawn study in Chicago, low IQ at age 6 predicted arrests for violent crimes up to age 32 (McCord & Ensminger, 1997). In Project Metropolitan in Copenhagen, low IQ at age 12 significantly predicted police-recorded violence between ages 15 and 22. The link between low IQ and violence was strongest among lower class boys (Hogh & Wolf, 1983).

Similar results were obtained in the Cambridge and Pittsburgh studies (Tables 2.1 and 2.2; Farrington, 1998). Low nonverbal IQ at age 8–10 predicted youthful official violence in the Cambridge Study, low verbal IQ predicted adult official violence, and low school achievement at age 10 predicted official violence in both studies. The extensive meta-analysis by Lipsey and Derzon (1998) also showed that low IQ, low school attainment, and such psychological factors as hyperactivity, attention deficit, impulsivity, and risk-taking behavior were important predictors of later serious and violent offending.

Impulsiveness, attention problems, low intelligence, and low attainment could all be linked to deficits in the executive functions of the brain, which are located in the frontal lobes. These executive functions include sustaining attention and concentration, abstract reasoning and concept formation, goal formulation, anticipation and planning, programming and initiation of purposive sequences of motor behavior, effective self-monitoring and self-awareness of behavior, and inhibition of inappropriate or impulsive behaviors (Moffitt & Henry, 1991; Morgan & Lilienfeld, 2000). Interestingly, in the Montreal longitudinal-experimental study (see Appendix), a measure of executive functions based on cognitive-neuro-psychological tests at age 14 was the strongest neuropsychological discriminator of violent and nonviolent boys (Seguin, Pihl, Harden, Tremblay, & Boulerice, 1995). This relationship held independently of a measure of family adversity (based on parental age at first birth, parental education level, broken family, and low socioeconomic status).

Family Factors

Numerous family factors predict violence. In the Cambridge Study, the strongest childhood predictor of adult convictions for violence was having a convicted parent by the 10th birthday; 20% of boys with convicted parents were themselves convicted, compared with 7% of the remainder (odds ratio = 3.4, confidence interval = 1.7 to 6.5; Table 2.2). Many other researchers have also found that antisocial parents tend to have aggressive children (e.g., Johnson, Smailes, Cohen, Kasen, & Brook, 2004).

Farrington, Jolliffe, Loeber, Stouthamer-Loeber, and Kalb (2001) reviewed six possible explanations for why antisocial behavior was concentrated in families and transmitted from one generation to the next. First, there may be intergenerational continuities in exposure to multiple risk factors, such as poverty, disrupted families, and living in deprived neighborhoods. Second, assortative mating (the tendency of antisocial females to choose antisocial males as partners) facilitates the intergenerational transmission of antisocial behavior. Third, family members may influence each other (e.g., older siblings may encourage younger ones to be antisocial). Fourth, the effect of an antisocial parent on a child's antisocial behavior may be mediated by environmental mechanisms, such as poor parental supervision and inconsistent discipline. Fifth, intergenerational transmission may be mediated by genetic mechanisms. Sixth, there may be labeling and police bias against known criminal families.

In her classic follow-up of 250 Boston boys in the Cambridge-Somerville Youth Study, McCord (1979) found that the strongest predictors at age 10 of later convictions for violence (up to age 45) were poor parental supervision, parental aggression (including harsh, punitive discipline), and parental conflict. An absent father was almost significant as a predictor, but the mother's lack of affection was not significant. McCord (1977) also demonstrated that fathers convicted for violence tended to have sons convicted for violence. In her later analyses, McCord (1996) showed that violent offenders were less likely than nonviolent offenders to have experienced parental affection and good discipline and supervision, but equally likely to have experienced parental conflict. However, most reviews conclude that parental conflict does predict later antisocial behavior (Buehler et al., 1997).

Similar results have been obtained in other studies (Haapasalo & Pokela, 1999; Smith & Stern, 1997). In the Chicago Youth Development Study (see Appendix), poor parental monitoring and low family cohesion predicted self-reported violent offending (Gorman-Smith, Tolan, Zelli, & Huesmann, 1996). Also, poor parental monitoring and low attachment to parents predicted self-reported violence in the Rochester Youth Development Study (Thornberry, Huizinga, & Loeber, 1995). Living in broken families between birth and age 10 predicted convictions for violence up to age 21 in the British National Survey (Wadsworth, 1978), and single-parent status at age 13 predicted convictions for violence up to age 18 in the Dunedin study (Henry et al., 1996). Parental conflict and a broken family predicted official violence in the Cambridge and Pittsburgh studies, and coming from a single-parent female-headed household predicted official and reported violence in Pittsburgh (Farrington, 1998).

Harsh physical punishment by parents and child physical abuse typically predict violent offending by sons (Malinosky-Rummell & Hansen, 1993). Harsh parental discipline predicted official and self-reported violence in the Cambridge Study (Table 2.1). In the Columbia County Study Eron, Huesmann, and Zelli (1991) reported that parental punishment at age 8 predicted not only arrests for violence up to age 30 but also the severity of the man's punishment of his child at age 30 and his history of spouse assault.

In the Pittsburgh Youth Study, harsh physical punishment predicted violence for White families but not for African Americans (Farrington, Loeber, & Stouthamer-Loeber, 2003). It has been suggested (e.g.,

by Deater-Deckard, Dodge, Bates, & Pettit, 1996; Kelley, Power, & Wimbush, 1992) that this is because physical discipline is associated with neglect and coldness in White families but with concern and warmth in African American families. In the Cambridge-Somerville Youth Study, McCord (1997) found that physical punishment predicted convictions for violence, especially when it was combined with low parental warmth and affection.

In a longitudinal study of over 900 abused children and nearly 700 controls in Indianapolis, Widom (1989) discovered that recorded child physical abuse and neglect predicted later arrests for violence, independently of other predictors, such as gender, ethnicity, and age. Predictability was greater for females than for males (Widom & White, 1997). Child sexual abuse also predicted adult arrests for sex crimes (Widom & Ames, 1994). In the Rochester Youth Development Study, Smith and Thornberry (1995) showed that recorded childhood maltreatment under age 12 predicted self-reported violence between ages 14 and 18, independently of gender, ethnicity, socioeconomic status, and family structure. Similarly, child abuse and neglect predicted later violence in a Swedish longitudinal survey (Lang, Klinteberg, & Alm, 2002). There was a biosocial interaction in the Dunedin study, because child maltreatment predicted a high probability of later violence for males with low monoamine oxidase (MAO) activity, but not for males with high MAO activity (Caspi et al., 2002).

Possible environmental causal mechanisms linking childhood victimization and later violence were reviewed by Widom (1994). First, childhood victimization may have immediate but long-lasting consequences (e.g., shaking may cause brain injury). Second, childhood victimization may cause bodily changes (e.g., desensitization to pain) that encourage later violence. Third, child abuse may lead to impulsive or dissociative coping styles that, in turn, lead to poor problem-solving skills or poor school performance. Fourth, victimization may cause changes in self-esteem or in social information-processing patterns that encourage later violence. Fifth, child abuse may lead to changed family environments (e.g., being placed in foster care) that have deleterious effects. Sixth, juvenile justice practices may label victims, isolate them from prosocial peers, and encourage them to associate with delinquent peers.

Large family size (number of children) predicted youth violence in both the Cambridge and Pittsburgh studies (Tables 2.1 and 2.2; Farrington 1998). In the Oregon Youth Study, large family size at age 10 predicted self-reported violence at age 13–17 (Capaldi & Patterson, 1996). There are many possible reasons why a large number of siblings might increase the risk of a child's delinquency (Brownfield & Sorenson, 1994). Generally, as the number of children in a family increases, the amount of parental attention that can be given to each child decreases. Also, as the number of children increases, the household tends to become more overcrowded, possibly leading to increases in frustration, irritation, and conflict. In the Cambridge Study, large family size did not predict delinquency for boys living in the least crowded conditions, with two or more rooms than there were children (West & Farrington, 1973, p. 33). This finding suggests that household overcrowding might be an important factor mediating the association between large family size and offending.

Young mothers (mothers who had their first child at an early age, typically as a teenager) also tend to have violent sons, as Morash and Rucker (1989) demonstrated in the Cambridge Study for the prediction of self-reported violence at age 16. Interestingly, the relationship between a young mother and a convicted son in this study disappeared after controlling for other variables, notably large family size, a convicted parent, and a broken family (Nagin, Pogarsky, & Farrington, 1997). Tables 2.1 and 2.2 show that having a teenage mother predicted self-reported violence more strongly than convictions for violence in the Cambridge Study. A young mother also predicted official and reported violence in the Pittsburgh Youth Study (Farrington, 1998)

and self-reported violence for males in the Rochester Youth Development Study (Pogarsky, Lizotte, & Thornberry, 2003). In the Dunedin study, Jaffee, Caspi, Moffitt, Belsky, and Silva (2001) concluded that the link between teenage mothers and violent children was mediated by maternal characteristics (e.g., intelligence, criminality) and family factors (e.g., harsh discipline, family size, disrupted families).

Substance use by parents also predicts violence by children, and smoking by the mother during pregnancy is a particularly important risk factor. A large-scale follow-up of a general population cohort in Finland showed that maternal smoking during pregnancy doubled the risk of violent offending by male offspring, after controlling for other biopsychosocial risk factors (Rasanen, Hakko, Isohanni, Hodgins, Jarvelin, & Tiihonen, 1999). Similar results were obtained in a Copenhagen birth cohort study (Brennan, Grekin, & Mednick, 1999).

Peer, Socioeconomic, and Neighborhood Factors

Having delinquent friends is an important predictor of youth violence; peer delinquency and gang membership predicted self-reported violence in the Seattle Social Development Project (Hawkins et al., 1998). What is less clear is to what extent the link between delinquent friends and delinquency is a consequence of co-offending, which is particularly common under age 21 (Reiss & Farrington, 1991). Elliott and Menard (1996) in the U. S. National Youth Survey concluded both that delinquency caused delinquent peer bonding and that delinquent peer bonding caused delinquency. In the Pittsburgh Youth Study, Farrington, Loeber, Yin, and Anderson (2002) found that peer delinquency did not predict a boy's delinquency within individuals (unlike poor parental supervision), suggesting that it was a correlate rather than a cause. In the Cambridge Study, boys particularly tended to offend with their brothers, and a delinquent older sibling predicted youthful convictions for violence (Table 2.1). Sibling resemblance in delinquency held after controlling for numerous family factors in an Australian longitudinal survey (Fagan & Najman, 2003).

In general, coming from a low socioeconomic status (SES) family predicts violence. For example, in the U. S. National Youth Survey, the prevalences of self-reported felony assault and robbery were about twice as high for lower class youth as for middle-class ones (Elliott, Huizinga, & Menard, 1989). Similar results have been obtained for official violence in Project Metropolitan in Stockholm (Wikström, 1985), in Project Metropolitan in Copenhagen (Hogh & Wolf, 1983), and in the Dunedin Study in New Zealand (Henry et al., 1996). Interestingly, all three of these studies compared the SES of the family at the boy's birth, based on the father's occupation, with the boy's later violent crimes. The strongest predictor of official violence in the Pittsburgh Youth Study was family dependence on welfare benefits (Farrington, 1998). Low SES predicted violence more strongly for Whites than for African Americans in this project (Farrington et al., 2003). Several researchers have suggested that the link between a low SES family and antisocial behavior is mediated by family socialization practices. For example, Larzelere and Patterson (1990) in the Oregon Youth Study concluded that the effect of SES on delinquency was entirely mediated by parental management skills.

Tables 2.1 and 2.2 show that, in the Cambridge Study, coming from a low SES family (having a father with an unskilled manual job) did not significantly predict the boy's youthful violence, but did predict his adult violence. Low family income predicted youthful and adult convictions and youthful self-reported violence, whereas poor housing predicted youthful violence. Vulnerability was a combined index, developed at an early stage (West & Farrington, 1973, p. 131), which included low family income, large family size, a convicted parent, low nonverbal IQ, and poor parental child-rearing behavior (harsh or erratic discipline or parental conflict). One quarter (24%) of the vulnerable boys (with three or more risk factors) were convicted as adults, compared with 8% of the remainder (odds ratio = 3.9, confidence interval = 1.9 to 7.8).

Generally, people living in urban areas are more violent than those living in rural ones. In the U.S. National Youth Survey, the prevalence of self-reported felony assault and robbery was considerably higher among urban youth (Elliott et al., 1989). Within urban areas, people living in high-crime neighborhoods are more violent than those living in low-crime neighborhoods. In the Rochester Youth Development Study, living in a high-crime neighborhood significantly predicted self-reported violence (Thornberry et al., 1995). Similarly, in the Pittsburgh Youth Study, living in a bad neighborhood (either as rated by the mother or based on census measures of poverty, unemployment, and female-headed households) significantly predicted official and reported violence (Farrington, 1998). Interestingly, violence in advantaged neighborhoods seemed to be predicted mainly by individual factors, whereas violence in disadvantaged neighborhoods seemed to be predicted mainly by social and contextual factors (Beyers, Loeber, Wikström, & Stouthamer-Loeber, 2001). In this survey, living in a bad neighborhood, low SES, and the family on welfare were among the factors that best predicted homicide offenders out of other offenders (Loeber et al., 2005).

It is clear that offenders disproportionately live in inner-city areas characterized by physical deterioration, neighborhood disorganization, and high residential mobility (Shaw & McKay, 1969). However, it is difficult to determine how much the areas themselves influence antisocial behavior and how much it is merely the case that antisocial people tend to live in deprived areas (e.g., because of their poverty or public housing allocation policies). Interestingly, both neighborhood researchers such as Gottfredson, McNeil, and Gottfredson (1991), and developmental researchers, such as Rutter (1981), have concluded that neighborhoods have only indirect effects on antisocial behavior via their effects on individuals and families. However, Sampson,

Raudenbush, and Earls (1997) argued that a low degree of "collective efficacy" in a neighborhood (a low degree of informal social control) caused high violent crime rates.

Situational Factors

It might be argued that all the risk factors reviewed so far in this section – biological, individual, family, peer, socioeconomic, and neighborhood – essentially influence the development of a long-term individual potential for violence. In other words, they contribute to between-individual differences: why some people are more likely than others, given the same situational opportunity, to commit violence. Another set of influences – situational factors – explain how the potential for violence becomes the actuality in any given situation. Essentially, they explain short-term within-individual differences: why a person is more likely to commit violence in some situations than in others. Situational factors may be specific to particular types of crimes: robberies as opposed to rapes, or even street robberies as opposed to bank robberies. One of the most influential situational theories of offending is routine activities theory (Cohen & Felson, 1979). This theory suggests that, for a predatory crime to occur, the minimum requirement is the convergence in time and place of a motivated offender and a suitable target, in the absence of a capable guardian.

Much work on describing situations leading to violence has been carried out in Great Britain under the heading of crime analysis (Ekblom, 1988). This work begins with a detailed analysis of patterns and circumstances of crimes and then proceeds to devising, implementing, and evaluating crime reduction strategies. For example, Barker, Geraghty, Webb, and Kay (1993) analyzed the nature of street robbery in London. Most of these crimes occurred in predominantly ethnic minority areas, and most offenders were 16- to 19-year-old Afro-Caribbean males. The victims were mostly White females, alone, and on foot. Most offenses occurred at night, near the victim's home. The main motive for robbery was to get money, and the main factor in choosing victims was whether they had a wealthy appearance.

In their Montreal longitudinal study of delinquents, LeBlanc and Frechette (1989) provided detailed information about motives and methods used in different offenses at different ages. For example, for violence committed at age 17, the main motivation was utilitarian or rational. For all crimes, however, the primary motivation changed from hedonistic (searching for excitement, with co-offenders) in the teenage years to utilitarian (with planning, psychological intimidation, and use of instruments such as weapons) in the twenties (LeBlanc, 1996). In the U.S. National Survey of Youth, which was a cross-sectional survey of nearly 1,400 American youth aged 11 to 18, assaults were usually committed for retaliation or revenge or because of provocation or anger (Agnew, 1990).

In the Cambridge Study, motives for physical fights depended on whether the boy fought alone or with others (Farrington, 1993). In individual fights, the boy was usually provoked, became angry, and lashed out to hurt his opponent and to discharge his own internal feelings of tension. In group fights, the boy often said that he became involved to help a friend or because he was attacked, and rarely said that he was angry. The group fights were more serious, occurring in bars or streets, and they were more likely to involve weapons, produce injuries, and lead to police intervention. Fights often occurred when minor incidents escalated, because both sides wanted to demonstrate their toughness and masculinity and were unwilling to react in a conciliatory way.

Many of the boys in the Cambridge Study fought after drinking alcohol, and it is clear that alcohol intoxication is an immediate situational factor that precipitates violence. Heavy drinking at age 18 was one of the best independent predictors of adult convictions (Farrington & West, 1995). In Sweden, Wikström (1985) found that about three quarters of violent offenders and about half of the victims of violence were intoxicated at the time. Conventional wisdom suggests that alcohol consumption has a disinhibiting effect on behavior that encourages both offending and victimization. However, the biological links between alcohol and violence are complex (Miczek et al., 1994).

Much is known about the situations in which violence occurs (Sampson & Lauritsen, 1994). For example, in Sweden, violence preceded by situational arguments typically occurred in streets or restaurants, whereas violence preceded by relationship arguments typically occurred in homes (Wikström, 1985). In Pittsburgh, gang membership, drug selling, and weapon carrying predicted homicide offenders out of all violent offenders (Loeber et al., 2005). In England, stranger assaults typically occurred in streets, bars, or discotheques, nonstranger assaults typically occurred at home or work, and robberies typically occurred in the street or on public transport (Hough & Sheehy, 1986). A more recent study confirmed that most violence occurs on weekend nights around pubs and clubs and involves young males who have been drinking (Allen, Nicholas, Salisbury, & Wood, 2003). Violence in public places could be investigated using systematic observation; for example, recording incidents from closed-circuit television cameras mounted on buildings. More research on situational influences on violent acts needs to be incorporated into prospective longitudinal studies to link up the developmental and situational perspectives.

Risk Mechanisms

It is important to investigate mechanisms linking risk factors and antisocial behavior. As an example, Juby and Farrington (2001) tested different explanations of the relationship between disrupted families and delinquency in the Cambridge Study. Trauma theories suggest that the loss of a parent has a damaging effect of a child, most commonly because of the effect on attachment to the parent. Life course theories focus on separation as a sequence of stressful experiences and on the effects of multiple stressors, such as parental conflict, parental loss, reduced economic circumstances, changes in par-

ent figures, and poor child-rearing methods. Selection theories argue that disrupted families produce delinquent children because of pre-existing differences from other families in risk factors, such as parental conflict, criminal or antisocial parents, low family income, or poor child-rearing methods.

It was concluded that the results favored life course theories rather than trauma or selection theories. Although boys from broken homes (permanently disrupted families) were more delinquent than boys from intact homes, they were not more delinquent than boys from intact high-conflict families. These results were later replicated in Switzerland (Haas, Farrington, Killias, & Sattar, 2004). Generally, broken homes caused by disharmony were more damaging than those caused by death (see also Wells & Rankin, 1991). Overall, the most important factor was the postdisruption trajectory. Boys who remained with their mother after the separation had the same delinquency rate as boys from intact low-conflict families. Boys who remained with their father, with relatives, or with others (e.g., foster parents) had high delinquency rates. The results were similar whether convictions or self-reported delinquency were studied.

Effects of Life Events

It is also important to investigate the effects of life events on the course of development of antisocial behavior. In the Cambridge Study, going to a high delinquency-rate school at age 11 did not seem to amplify the risk of offending because badly behaved boys tended to go to high delinquency-rate schools (Farrington, 1972). However, getting convicted did lead to an increase in offending, according to the boys' self-reports, and a plausible intervening mechanism was increased hostility to the police (Farrington, 1977). Unemployment also caused an increase in offending, but only for crimes leading to financial gain, such as theft, burglary, robbery, and fraud. There was no effect of unemployment on other offenses, such as violence, vandalism or drug use, suggesting that the link between unemployment and offending was mediated by lack of money rather than boredom (Farrington, Gallagher, Morley, St. Ledger, & West, 1986).

It is often believed that marriage to a good woman is one of the most effective treatments for male offending, and indeed Farrington and West (1995) found that getting married led to a decrease in offending compared with staying single. In addition, later separation from a wife led to an increase in offending compared with staying married, and the separated men were particularly likely to be violent. Another protective life event was moving out of London, which led to a decrease in self-reported violence (Osborn, 1980). This move was protective probably because of the effect of the move in breaking up delinquent groups.

Studies of the effects of life events on the course of development usually involve within-individual analyses. A major problem with most research on violence is that knowledge about risk factors is based on between-individual differences. For example, it is demonstrated that children who receive poor parental supervision are more likely to offend than other children who receive good parental supervision, after controlling for other between-individual factors that influence both parental supervision and offending. However, within-individual variations are more relevant to the concept of cause, as well as to prevention or intervention research (which requires within-individual change). For example, if it was demonstrated that children were more likely to offend during time periods when they are receiving poor parental supervision than during time periods when they were receiving good parental supervision, this would be more compelling evidence that poor parental supervision caused offending. More within-individual analyses are needed.

Protective Factors

Most research on violence seeks to identify risk factors: variables associated with an increased probability of violence. It is also important to identify protective factors –

those associated with a decreased probability of violence. Protective factors may have more implications than risk factors for prevention and treatment. However, there are three separate meanings of protective factors.

The first suggests that a protective factor is merely the opposite end of the scale (or the other side of the coin) to a risk factor. For example, if low intelligence is a risk factor, high intelligence may be a protective factor. The usefulness of this statement depends, however, on whether there is a linear relationship between the variable and violence. To the extent that the relationship is linear, little is gained by identifying the protective factor of high intelligence as well as the risk factor of low intelligence.

The second definition specifies protective factors that are free-standing, with no corresponding, symmetrically opposite, risk factor. Protective factors especially tend to be free-standing when variables are nonlinearly related to violence. For example, if high nervousness was associated with a low risk of violence, and medium and low nervousness were associated with a fairly constant average risk, nervousness could be a protective factor but not a risk factor (because the probability of violence was not high at low levels of nervousness). In the Pittsburgh Youth Study, Farrington and Loeber (2000) discovered a number of variables that were nonlinearly related to delinquency, of which the most important was the age of the mother at her first birth. In the Cambridge Study, having few friends seemed to be a protective factor against violence.

The third definition of a protective factor identifies variables that interact with risk factors to minimize or buffer their effects (Farrington, 1994b, 1997a). These protective factors may or may not be associated with violence themselves. To facilitate the exposition here, a risk variable (e.g., family income) is distinguished from a risk factor (e.g., low family income). Interaction effects can be studied in two ways, either by focusing on the effect of a risk variable in the presence of a protective factor or by focusing on the effect of a protective variable in the presence of a risk factor. For example, the effect of family income on violence could be studied in the presence of good parental supervision, or the effect of parental supervision on violence could be studied in the presence of low family income.

Most studies focusing on the interaction of risk and protective factors identify a subsample at risk (with some combination of risk factors) and then search for protective variables that predict successful members of this subsample. In a classic example (see Appendix), Werner and Smith (1982) in Hawaii studied children who possessed four or more risk factors for delinquency before age 2 but who nevertheless did not develop behavioral difficulties during childhood or adolescence. They found that the major protective factors included being first-born, being active and affectionate infants, having a small family size, and receiving a high amount of attention from caretakers.

There has been little research on protective factors for violence. In the Pittsburgh Youth Study, all explanatory variables were divided into a risk category (the worst quarter), a neutral category (the middle half), and a protective category (the best quarter) and their relationships with delinquency (rated by the boy, the mother, and the teacher) were investigated (Stouthamer-Loeber, Loeber, Farrington, Zhang, van Kammen, & Maguin, 1993). The most common finding was that a variable was related to delinquency both at the protective end (versus the middle category) and at the risk end (versus the middle category). A number of variables had risk effects only, but none had protective effects only across all three cohorts. A later analysis showed that the efficiency of prediction of persistent serious delinquency was improved by including both protective factors and risk factors (Stouthamer-Loeber, Loeber, Wei, Farrington, & Wikström, 2002).

More research is needed on protective factors. Several past studies attempted to identify interactions between biological and psychosocial factors (discussed earlier), and a key challenge is to discover environmental protective factors that counteract biological risk factors. It would also be important to establish risk and protective factors in different neighborhoods.

A Theory of Violence

To develop theories of violence, it is important to establish how risk factors have independent, additive, interactive, or sequential effects. Generally, the probability of violence increases with the number of risk factors (Farrington, 2001a). For example, in the Cambridge Study, the percentage of boys convicted for violence between ages 10 and 20 increased from 2% of those with none of the five vulnerability risk factors to 28% of those with four or five. This type of research gives some indication of how accurately violence might be predicted. Interaction effects have been discussed above (see also Raine, Brennan, & Mednick, 1994).

Numerous investigations of independent predictors of violence have been carried out in the Cambridge Study. For example, Farrington (2001a) reported that the most important independent childhood predictors of adult violence convictions were a convicted parent, low family income, dishonesty, and harsh discipline; the most important independent childhood predictors of adult self-reported violence were a broken family, low SES, nervousness, and a young mother. As an example of a study of sequential effects, Johnson et al. (2004), in a longitudinal survey of York State children, concluded that poor parenting mediated the relationship between antisocial parents and violence by the children as adults.

Developmental and life course theories aim to explain development, risk factors, and the effect of life events (Farrington, 2005). Such theories can help explain how and why biological factors such as a low heart rate, individual factors such as impulsivity or a low IQ, family factors such as poor parental supervision, peer factors, socioeconomic factors, and neighborhood factors influence the development of an individual potential for violence. For example, living in a bad neighborhood and suffering socioeconomic deprivation may in some way cause poor parenting, which in some way causes impulsivity and school failure, which in some way causes a high potential for violence. Theories can also help in specifying more general concepts that underlie violence potential, such as low self-control or weak bonding to society. Theories can also help in specifying how a potentially violent person interacts with situational factors to produce violent acts.

Figure 2.1 shows the key elements of my theory (Farrington, 2003a). It was designed to explain offending by lower class males and can easily be modified to explain violence. I call it the Integrated Cognitive Antisocial Potential (ICAP) theory. It integrates ideas from many other theories, including strain, control, learning, labeling, and rational choice approaches; its key construct is antisocial potential (AP); and it assumes that the translation from antisocial potential to antisocial and violent behavior depends on cognitive (thinking and decision-making) processes that take account of opportunities and victims. Figure 2.1 is deliberately simplified in order to show the key elements of the ICAP theory on one page; for example, it does not show how the processes operate differently for onset compared with desistance or at different ages.

The key construct underlying offending is antisocial potential (AP), which refers to the potential to commit antisocial acts, including violence. Long-term persistent between-individual differences in AP are distinguished from short-term within-individual variations in AP. Long-term AP depends on impulsiveness, on strain, modeling and socialization processes, and on life events, whereas short-term variations in AP depend on motivating and situational factors. The ICAP theory suggests that long-term individual, family, peer, school, and neighborhood influences lead to the development of long-term, fairly stable, slowly changing differences between individuals in the potential for violence.

Regarding long-term AP, people can be ordered on a continuum from low to high. The distribution of AP in the population at any age is highly skewed; relatively few people have high levels of AP. People with high AP are more likely to commit many different types of antisocial acts including violence. Hence, offending and antisocial behavior are versatile not specialized. The relative ordering of people on AP (long-term between-individual variation) tends to be consistent over time, but absolute levels of AP vary with age, peaking in the teenage years, because of changes within individuals in the factors that influence long-term AP (e.g., from childhood to adolescence, the increasing importance of peers and decreasing importance of parents).

Following strain theory, the main energizing factors that potentially lead to high long-term AP are desires for material goods, status among intimates, excitement, and sexual satisfaction. However, these motivations only lead to high AP if antisocial methods of satisfying them are habitually chosen. Antisocial methods tend to be chosen by people who find it difficult to satisfy their needs legitimately, such as people with low income, unemployed people, and those who fail at school. However, the methods chosen also depend on physical capabilities and behavioral skills; for example, a 5-year-old child would have difficulty stealing a car. For simplicity, energizing and directing processes and capabilities are shown in one box in Figure 2.1.

Long-term AP also depends on attachment and socialization processes. AP will be low if parents consistently and contingently reward good behavior and punish bad behavior. (Withdrawal of love may be a more effective method of socialization than hitting children.) Children with low anxiety will be less well-socialized, because they care less about parental punishment. AP will be high if children are not attached to (prosocial) parents; for example, if parents are cold and rejecting. Disrupted families (broken homes) may impair both attachment and socialization processes.

Long-term AP will also be high if people are exposed to and influenced by antisocial models, such as criminal parents, delinquent siblings, and delinquent peers; for example, in high-crime schools and neighborhoods.

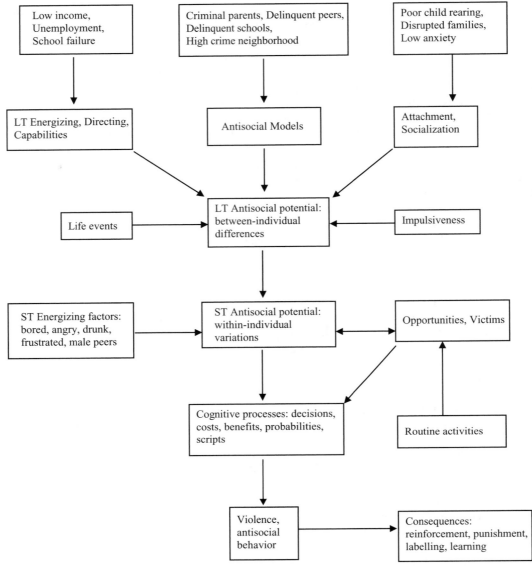

Figure 2.1. The Integrated Cognitive Antisocial Potential (ICAP) Theory. Note: LT = long-term; ST = short-term.

Long-term AP will also be high for impulsive people, because they tend to act without thinking about the consequences. Also, life events affect AP; it decreases after people get married or move out of high-crime areas, and it increases after separation from a partner. There may also be interaction effects between the influences on long-term AP. For example, people who experience strain or poor socialization may be disproportionally antisocial if they are also exposed to antisocial models. In the interests of simplicity, Figure 2.1 does not attempt to show such interactions.

Figure 2.1 attempts to show some of the processes by which risk factors have effects on AP. It does not show biological factors, but these could be incorporated in the theory at various points. For example, the children of criminal parents could have high AP partly because of genetic transmission, excitement-seeking could be driven by low cortical arousal, school failure could depend partly on low intelligence, and high impulsiveness and low anxiety could both reflect biological factors.

According to the ICAP theory, the commission of offenses and other types of antisocial acts depends on the interaction between the individual (with his immediate level of AP) and the social environment (especially criminal opportunities and victims). Superimposed on long-term between-individual differences in violence potential are short-term within-individual variations. Short-term AP varies within individuals according to short-term energizing factors, such as being bored, angry, drunk, or frustrated or being encouraged by male peers. Criminal opportunities and the availability of victims depend on routine activities. Encountering a tempting opportunity or victim may cause a short-term increase in AP, just as a short-term increase in AP may motivate a person to seek out criminal opportunities and victims.

Faced with an opportunity for violence, whether a person with a certain level of AP actually is violent depends on cognitive processes, including considering the subjective benefits, costs, and probabilities of the different outcomes and stored behavioral repertoires or scripts (based on previous experiences). The subjective benefits and costs include immediate situational factors, such as the perceived utility of hurting someone and the likelihood and consequences of being caught by the police. They also include social factors, such as likely disapproval by parents or female partners, and encouragement or reinforcement from peers. In general, people tend to make decisions that seem rational to them, but those with low levels of AP will not commit offenses even

when (on the basis of subjective expected utilities) it appears rational to do so. Equally, high short-term levels of AP (e.g., caused by anger or drunkenness) may induce people to commit offenses when it is not rational for them to do so.

The consequences of violence may, as a result of a learning process, lead to changes in long-term AP and in future cognitive decision-making processes. This effect is especially likely if the consequences are reinforcing (e.g., gaining pleasure or peer approval) or punishing (e.g., receiving legal sanctions or parental disapproval). Also, if the consequences involve labeling or stigmatizing the offender, this effect may make it more difficult for him to achieve his aims legally and hence may lead to an increase in AP. (It is difficult to show these feedback effects in Figure 2.1 without making it very complex.)

This approach is an explicit attempt to integrate developmental and situational theories. The interaction between the individual and the environment is seen in decision making in criminal opportunities, which depends both on the underlying potential for antisocial behavior and on situational factors (costs, benefits, and probabilities). Also, the double-headed arrow shows the possibility that encountering a tempting opportunity may cause a short-term increase in AP, just as a short-term increase in potential may motivate a person to seek out an opportunity for violence. The theory includes cognitive elements (perception, memory, and decision making) as well as the social learning and causal risk factor approaches.

As in most criminological theories, there is insufficient attention to typologies of offenders. Perhaps some people are violent primarily because of their high violence potential (e.g., "life-course-persistent" offenders), whereas others are violent primarily because they happen to be in violent situations. Or perhaps some people are violent primarily because of short-term influences (e.g., getting drunk frequently) and others primarily because of the way they think and make decisions in potentially violent situations. From the point of view of both explanation and prevention, it would be useful to classify people according to their most influential risk factors and most important reasons why they commit violent acts.

Conclusions

The major long-term risk factors for violence are biological (low resting heart rate), individual (high impulsiveness and low intelligence, possibly linked to the executive functions of the brain), family (poor supervision, harsh discipline, child physical abuse, a violent parent, large family size, a young mother, and a broken family), peer delinquency, low socioeconomic status, urban residence, and living in a high-crime neighborhood. These results may be useful in developing risk assessment instruments. Important short-term situational factors include the motives of potential offenders (e.g., anger, a desire to hurt), alcohol consumption, and actions leading to violent events (e.g., the escalation of a trivial altercation). More research is needed that searches specifically for protective factors against violence; for example, by investigating why aggressive children do not become violent adults. The discovery of protective factors could have important policy implications.

To investigate development and risk factors for violence and the effects of life events, longitudinal studies are needed. Such studies should include multiple cohorts in order to draw conclusions about different age groups from birth to the mid-twenties. They should include both males and females and the major racial/ethnic groups, so that results can be compared for different subgroups. Previous research suggests that males and females, and African Americans and Whites, differ in their number of risk factors more than in the relationships between risk factors and violence (Farrington et al., 2003; Moffitt, Caspi, Rutter, & Silva, 2001), but this needs to be investigated further. Longitudinal studies should measure a wide range of risk and especially protective factors, and

seek to discover interaction effects. They should be based on large, high-risk samples, especially in inner-city areas, incorporating screening methods to maximize the yield of violent offenders while simultaneously making it possible to draw conclusions about the total population. They should include long-term follow-ups to permit conclusions about developmental pathways. They should make a special effort to study careers of violence and to link developmental and situational data.

Violence reduction programs should be based on knowledge about risk factors (Farrington, 2002). More systematic reviews and meta-analyses of risk factors and prevention programs are needed. High-quality evaluation research shows that many types of programs are effective, and that in many cases their financial benefits outweigh their financial costs (Welsh & Farrington, 2000). The best programs include general parent education in home visits, parent management training, preschool intellectual enrichment programs, child skills training, peer influence resistance techniques, antibullying programs, improved street lighting, and increased police patrolling of crime "hot spots" (Farrington, 2001b). Risk-focused prevention can not only reduce crime and violence but also improve mental and physical health and life success in such areas as education, employment, relationships, housing, and child rearing.

The most pressing need is to advance knowledge about causes of violence. More tests of alternative causal mechanisms that may intervene between risk factors and violence are needed, and especially more within-individual analyses should be carried out. Virtually all knowledge about risk factors is based on between-individual analyses, but variables that are related to violence between individuals may not be related within individuals. Longitudinal studies with frequent data collection are needed for within-individual analyses. Such analyses may radically alter our conclusions about the causes of violent behavior over the life span. This is the new frontier.

Appendix: Major Prospective Longitudinal Surveys of Violence

Cohen, Brook

(New York State Longitudinal Study): 976 randomly sampled mothers in two upstate New York counties, with a child aged 1–10, interviewed in 1975. Mothers interviewed three times up to 1991 and children interviewed at an average age of 30. Focus on drug use. Children searched in criminal records in 2000 (Johnson et al., 2004).

Denno, Piquero, Buka

(National Collaborative Perinatal Project): National U.S. multisite follow-up of pregnancies in 1959–1966, focusing on perinatal factors. (1) 987 AfricanAmerican children born in Philadelphia in 1959–1962 followed in police records to age 22 (Denno, 1990); (2) 3,828 children born in Providence (Rhode Island) in 1960–1966 followed up in police records to age 33 (Piquero & Buka, 2002).

Dinitz, Conrad, Hamparian

(Dangerous Offender Project): (1) All 811 children born in 1956–1958 and arrested for violence as juveniles (before age 18) in Columbus, Ohio. Followed in adult arrest records to 1983 (Hamparian et al., 1985). (2) 1,591 adult offenders arrested for violence in Columbus, Ohio in 1950–1976. Arrest histories studied (Miller, Dinitz, & Conrad, 1982).

Elliott, Huizinga

(National Youth Survey): Nationally representative U. S. sample of 1,725 adolescents aged 11–17 in 1976. Interviewed in 5 successive years (1977–1981), at 3-year intervals up to 1993, and in 2002–2003. Focus on self-reported delinquency, but arrest records collected (Elliott, 1994).

Eron, Huesmann, Dubow

(Columbia County Study): All 856 third-grade children (age 8) in Columbia County, New York State, first assessed in 1960. Focus on aggressive behavior. Interviewed 10, 22, and 40 years later. Criminal records searched up to age 48 (Eron et al., 1991).

Farrington, West

(Cambridge Study in Delinquent Development): 411 boys aged 8–9 in 1961–1962; all boys of that age in six London (UK) schools. Boys interviewed nine times up to age 48. Information also from parents, teachers and peers. Boys and all biological relatives searched in criminal records at least up to 1994 (Farrington, 2003b).

Hawkins, Catalano

(Seattle Social Development Project): 808 fifth-grade students (age 10) in 18 elementary schools in Seattle in 1985. Also intervention study. Followed annually to age 16 and then every 2–3 years at least to age 27, with interviews and criminal records (Hawkins, Smith, Hill, Kosterman, Catalano, & Abbott, 2003).

Huizinga, Esbensen

(Denver Youth Survey): 1,528 children aged 7, 9, 11, 13, or 15 in high-risk neighborhoods of Denver, first assessed in 1988. Children and parents assessed at yearly intervals up to 1998. Youngest two cohorts assessed in 2002. Focus on self-reported delinquency; criminal record data collected up to 1992 (Huizinga, Weiher, Espiritu, & Esbensen, 2003).

Janson, Wikström

(Stockholm Project Metropolitan) All 15,117 children born in Stockholm (Sweden) in 1953, and living there in 1963. Tested in schools in 1966. Subsample of mothers interviewed in 1968. Followed up in police records to 1983 (Wikström, 1990).

Kellam, Ensminger, McCord

(Woodlawn Project): Information from teachers and mothers of 1,242 children in first grade (age 6) in African American Chicago neighborhood in 1966. Children and mothers interviewed in 1975. Focus on shy and aggressive behaviors and substance use. Follow-up interviews at age 32 (McCord & Ensminger, 1997).

Klinteberg

(Young Lawbreakers as Adults): 192 delinquent and 95 control boys aged 11–14 in Stockholm (Sweden) first examined in 1959–1963 and followed in criminal records to age 38–46 (Lang et al., 2002).

LeBlanc

(Montreal Two-Samples Longitudinal study): (1) Representative sample of 3,070 French-speaking Montreal adolescents. Completed self-report questionnaires in 1974 at age 12–16 and again in 1976. (2) 470 male delinquents seen at age 15 in 1974 and again at ages 17 and 22. Followed in criminal records to age 40. Males interviewed at ages 30 and 40 (LeBlanc, 1996).

Loeber, Stouthamer-Loeber, Farrington

(Pittsburgh Youth Study): 1,517 boys in first, fourth, or seventh grades of Pittsburgh public schools in 1987–1988 (age 7, 10, or 13). Information from boys, parents, and teachers every 6 months for 3 years, and then every year up to age 19 (youngest), 13 (middle), 25 (oldest). Focus on delinquency, substance use, and mental health problems (Loeber, Farrington, Stouthamer-Loeber, Moffitt, Caspi, White, et al. 2003).

Magnusson, Stattin, Bergman, Klinteberg

(Orebro Project): 1,027 children age 10 (all those in third grade) in Orebro (Sweden) in 1965. School follow-up data between ages 13 and 18. Questionnaire and record data up to age 43–45 (Klinteberg et al., 1993).

McCord

(Cambridge-Somerville Youth Study): 650 boys (average age 10) nominated as difficult or average by Cambridge-Somerville (Boston) public schools in 1937–1939. Randomly assigned to treated or control groups. Treated group visited by counselors for an average of 5 years, and followed up in 1975–1980 by interviews, mail questionnaires, and criminal records (McCord, 1991).

Mednick, Moffitt, Brennan, Hodgins

(Danish Birth Cohort Studies): (1) All 358,180 persons born in Denmark in 1944–1947. Followed in police records to age 44 (Brennan, Mednick, & Hodgins, 2000). (2) 4,169 males born in Copenhagen in 1959–1961, with extensive perinatal data. Followed in criminal records to age 34 (Brennan et al., 1999).

Moffitt, Caspi, Poulton

(Dunedin Multidisciplinary Health and Development Study): 1,037 children born in 1972–1973 in Dunedin (New Zealand), and first assessed at age 3. Assessed every 2 to 3 years on health, psychological, education, and family factors up to age 32. Self-reported delinquency measured from age 13. Convictions collected up to age 32 (Moffitt et al., 2001).

Patterson, Dishion, Capaldi

(Oregon Youth Study): 206 fourth-grade boys (age 10) in Eugene/Springfield (Oregon) in 1983–1985. Assessed at yearly intervals, with data from boys, parents, teachers, and peers, at least to age 30. Followed in criminal records at least to age 30 (Capaldi & Patterson, 1996).

Pulkkinen

(Jyvaskyla Longitudinal Study of Personality and Social Development): 369 children aged 8–9 in Jyvaskyla (Finland) in 1968. Peer, teacher, and self-ratings collected.

Followed five times to age 42 with interviews and questionnaires and in criminal records (Pulkkinen & Pitkanen, 1993).

Raine, Venables, Mednick

(Mauritius Joint Child Health Project): 1,795 children age 3 recruited in 1972–1973 from two towns in Mauritius. Focus on psychophysiological measures. Followed at least to age 31 by interviews and up to age 23 in court records (Raine, Reynolds, Venables, Mednick, & Farrington, 1998).

Rasanen

(Northern Finland Birth Cohort Study): 5,636 males born in 1966 and living in Finland at age 16. Followed in criminal records to age 28 (Rasanen et al., 1999).

Thornberry, Lizotte, Krohn

(Rochester Youth Development Study): 1,000 seventh and eighth graders (age 13–14) in Rochester (New York State) public schools, first assessed in 1988, disproportionately sampled from high-crime neighborhoods. Followed up initially every 6 months, then every year, and then at intervals up to age 32. Self-reports and criminal records collected (Thornberry Lizotte, Krohn, Smith, & Porter, 2003).

Tolan, Gorman-Smith, Henry

(Chicago Youth Development Study): 362 African American and Latino boys in fifth or seventh grades (age 11–13) of Chicago public schools in 1991. Followed with data from boys, mothers, and teachers to age 25–28 (Tolan, Gorman-Smith, & Henry, 2003).

Tremblay

(Montreal Longitudinal-Experimental Study): 1,037 French-speaking kindergarten boys (age 6) from poor areas of Montreal assessed by teachers in 1984. Disruptive boys randomly allocated to treatment (parent training plus individual skills training)

or control groups. All boys followed up each year from age 10 to age 26, including self-reported delinquency and aggression (Tremblay, Vitaro, Nagin, Pagani, & Seguin, 2003).

Wadsworth, Douglas

(National Survey of Health and Development): 5,362 children selected from all legitimate single births in England, Scotland, and Wales during one week of March 1946. Followed in criminal records to age 21. Mainly medical and school data collected, but samples were interviewed at ages 26, 36, 43, and 50 (Wadsworth, 1991).

Werner, Smith

(Kauai Longitudinal Study): 698 children born in 1955 in Kauai (Hawaii) assessed at birth and ages 2, 10, 18, 30, and 40. Criminal records up to age 40. Focus on resilience (Werner & Smith, 2001).

Widom, Maxfield

(Longitudinal Study of Abused Children): 908 abused children age under 11 identified in Indianapolis court records in 1967–1971 and 667 matched control children. Followed in arrest records to 1994 (Maxfield & Widom, 1996).

Wolf, Hogh

(Copenhagen Project Metropolitan): All 12,270 boys born in 1953 in Copenhagen (Denmark) and tested in schools in 1965–1966. Sample of mothers interviewed in 1968. Followed in police records to 1976 (Hogh & Wolf, 1983).

Wolfgang, Figlio, Thornberry, Tracy

(Philadelphia Birth Cohort Studies): (1) 9,945 boys born in Philadelphia in 1945 and living there at least from age 10 to 17. Sample interviewed at age 26 and followed in police records to age 30 (Wolfgang, Thornberry, & Figlio, 1987).

(2) 27,160 children born in Philadelphia in 1958 and living there at least from 10–17. Followed in police records to age 26 (Tracy & Kempf-Leonard, 1996).

Acknowledgments

For assistance in completing this Appendix, I am very grateful to Deborah Capaldi, Rowell Huesmann, David Huizinga, Marc Leblanc, Terrie Moffitt, Lea Pulkkinen, Adrian Raine, Hakan Stattin, Patrick Tolan, and Richard Tremblay.

References

Agnew, R. (1990). The origins of delinquent events: An examination of offender accounts. *Journal of Research in Crime and Delinquency, 27,* 267–294.

Allen, J., Nicholas, S., Salisbury, H., & Wood, M. (2003). Nature of burglary, vehicle and violent crime. In C. Flood-Page & J. Taylor (Eds.), *Crime in England and Wales 2001/2002: Supplementary volume* (pp. 41–68). London: Home Office (Statistical Bulletin 01/03).

Archer, J. (1991). The influence of testosterone on human aggression. *British Journal of Psychology, 82,* 1–28.

Barker, M., Geraghty, J., Webb, B., & Kay, T. (1999). *The prevention of street robbery.* London: Home Office Police Department.

Beyers, J. M., Loeber, R., Wikström, P.-O. H., & Stouthamer-Loeber, M. (2001). Predictors of adolescent violence by neighborhood. *Journal of Abnormal Child Psychology, 29,* 369–381.

Brennan, P. A., Grekin, E. R., & Mednick, S. A. (1999). Maternal smoking during pregnancy and adult male criminal outcomes. *Archives of General Psychiatry, 56,* 215–219.

Brennan, P. A., Mednick, S. A., & Hodgins, S. (2000). Major mental disorders and criminal violence in a Danish birth cohort. *Archives of General Psychiatry, 57,* 494–500.

Brennan, P. A., Mednick, S. A., & John, R. (1989). Specialization in violence: Evidence of a criminal subgroup. *Criminology, 27,* 437–453.

Brennan, P. A., Mednick, B. R., & Mednick, S. A. (1993). Parental psychopathology, congenital factors, and violence. In S. Hodgins (Ed.), *Mental disorder and crime* (pp. 244–261). Newbury Park, CA: Sage.

Brownfield, D., & Sorenson, A. M. (1994). Sibship size and sibling delinquency. *Deviant Behavior, 15,* 45–61.

Budd, T., Sharp, C., & Mayhew, P. (2005). *Offending in England and Wales: First results from the 2003 Crime and Justice Survey.* London: Home Office (Research Study No. 275).

Buehler, C., Anthony, C., Krishnakumar, A., Stone, G., Gerard, J., & Pemberton, S. (1997). Interparental conflict and youth problem behaviors: A meta-analysis. *Journal of Child and Family Studies, 6,* 233–247.

Capaldi, D. M., & Clark, S. (1998). Prospective family predictors of aggression toward female partners for at-risk young men. *Developmental Psychology, 34,* 1175–1188.

Capaldi, D. M., & Patterson, G. R. (1996). Can violent offenders be distinguished from frequent offenders? Prediction from childhood to adolescence. *Journal of Research in Crime and Delinquency, 33,* 206–231.

Caspi, A., McClay, J., Moffitt, T. E., Mill, J., Martin, J., Craig, I. W., Taylor, A., & Poulton, R. (2002). Role of genotype in the cycle of violence in maltreated children. *Science, 297,* 851–854.

Caspi, A., Moffitt, T. E., Silva, P. A., Stouthamer-Loeber, M., Krueger, R. F., & Schmutte, P. S. (1994). Are some people crime-prone? Replications of the personality-crime relationship across countries, genders, races, and methods. *Criminology, 32,* 163–195.

Cohen, L. E., & Felson, M. (1979). Social change and crime rate trends: A routine activity approach. *American Sociological Review, 44,* 588–608.

Coie, J. D., Dodge, K. A., & Kupersmidt, J. (1990). Peer group behavior and social status. In S. R. Asher & J. D. Coie (Eds.), *Peer rejection in childhood* (pp. 17–59). Cambridge, UK: Cambridge University Press.

Cooke, D. J., Michie, C., Hart, S. D., & Clark, D. A. (2004). Reconstructing psychopathy: Clarifying the significance of antisocial and socially deviant behavior in the diagnosis of psychopathic personality disorder. *Journal of Personality Disorders, 18,* 337–357.

Deater-Deckard, K., Dodge, K. A., Bates, J. E., & Pettit, G. S. (1996). Physical discipline among African American and European American mothers: Links to children's externalizing behaviors. *Developmental Psychology, 32,* 1065–1072.

Denno, D. W. (1990). *Biology and violence: From birth to adulthood.* Cambridge, UK: Cambridge University Press.

Ekblom, P. (1988). *Getting the best out of crime analysis*. London: Home Office.

Elliott, D. S. (1994). Serious violent offenders: Onset, developmental course, and termination. *Criminology, 32*, 1–21.

Elliott, D. S., Huizinga, D., & Menard, S. (1989). *Multiple problem youth: Delinquency, substance use, and mental health problems*. New York: Springer-Verlag.

Elliott, D. S., & Menard, S. (1996). Delinquent friends and delinquent behavior: Temporal and developmental patterns. In J. D. Hawkins (Ed.), *Delinquency and crime: Current theories* (pp. 28–67). Cambridge, UK: Cambridge University Press.

Eron, L. D., Huesmann, L. R., & Zelli, A. (1991). The role of parental variables in the learning of aggression. In D. J. Pepler & K. J. Rubin (Eds.), *The development and treatment of childhood aggression* (pp. 169–188). Hillsdale, NJ: Erlbaum.

Fagan, A. A., & Najman, J. M. (2003). Sibling influences on adolescent delinquent behavior: An Australian longitudinal study. *Journal of Adolescence, 26*, 547–559.

Farrington, D. P. (1972). Delinquency begins at home. *New Society, 21*, 495–497.

Farrington, D. P. (1977). The effects of public labelling. *British Journal of Criminology, 17*, 112–125.

Farrington, D. P. (1978). The family backgrounds of aggressive youths. In L. Hersov, M. Berger, & D. Shaffer (Eds.), *Aggression and antisocial behavior in childhood and adolescence* (pp. 73–93). Oxford: Pergamon.

Farrington, D. P. (1986). Age and crime. In M. Tonry & N. Morris (Eds.), *Crime and justice* (Vol. 7, pp. 189–250). Chicago: University of Chicago Press.

Farrington, D. P. (1989a). Early predictors of adolescent aggression and adult violence. *Violence and Victims, 4*, 79–100.

Farrington, D. P. (1989b). Self-reported and official offending from adolescence to adulthood. In M. W. Klein (Ed.), *Cross-national research in self-reported crime and delinquency* (pp. 399–423). Dordrecht, The Netherlands: Kluwer.

Farrington, D. P. (1991a). Antisocial personality from childhood to adulthood. *The Psychologist, 4*, 389–394.

Farrington, D. P. (1991b). Childhood aggression and adult violence: Early precursors and later life outcomes. In D. J. Pepler & K. H. Rubin (Eds.), *The development and treatment of childhood aggression* (pp. 5–29). Hillsdale, NJ: Erlbaum.

Farrington, D. P. (1993). Motivations for conduct disorder and delinquency. *Development and Psychopathology, 5*, 225–241.

Farrington, D. P. (1994a). Childhood, adolescent and adult features of violent males. In L. R. Huesmann (Ed.), *Aggressive behavior: Current perspectives* (pp. 215–240). New York: Plenum.

Farrington, D. P. (1994b). Interactions between individual and contextual factors in the development of offending. In R. K. Silbereisen & E. Todt (Eds.), *Adolescence in context: The interplay of family, school, peer and work in adjustment* (pp. 366–389). New York: Springer-Verlag.

Farrington, D. P. (1995a). Crime and physical health: Illnesses, injuries, accidents and offending in the Cambridge Study. *Criminal Behavior and Mental Health, 5*, 261–278.

Farrington, D. P. (1995b). The development of offending and antisocial behavior from childhood: Key findings from the Cambridge Study in Delinquent Development. *Journal of Child Psychology and Psychiatry, 36*, 929–964.

Farrington, D. P. (1997a). Key issues in studying the biosocial bases of violence. In A. Raine, P. A. Brennan, D. P. Farrington, & S. A. Mednick (Eds.), *Biosocial bases of violence* (pp. 293–300). New York: Plenum.

Farrington, D. P. (1997b). The relationship between low resting heart rate and violence. In A. Raine, P. A. Brennan, D. P. Farrington, & S. A. Mednick (Eds.), *Biosocial bases of violence* (pp. 89–105). New York: Plenum.

Farrington, D. P. (1998). Predictors, causes, and correlates of youth violence. In M. Tonry & M. H. Moore (Eds.), *Youth violence* (pp. 421–475). Chicago: University of Chicago Press.

Farrington, D. P. (2000). Adolescent violence: Findings and implications from the Cambridge Study. In G. Boswell (Ed.), *Violent children and adolescents: Asking the question why* (pp. 19–35). London: Whurr.

Farrington, D. P. (2001a). Predicting adult official and self-reported violence. In G.-F. Pinard & L. Pagani (Eds.), *Clinical assessment of dangerousness: Empirical contributions* (pp. 66–88). Cambridge, UK: Cambridge University Press.

Farrington, D. P. (2001b). The causes and prevention of violence. In J. Shepherd (Ed.), *Violence in health care* (2nd ed.) (pp. 1–27). Oxford: Oxford University Press.

Farrington, D. P. (2002). Developmental criminology and risk-focussed prevention. In M. Maguire, R. Morgan, & R. Reiner (Eds.), *The*

Oxford handbook of criminology (3rd ed., pp. 657–701). Oxford: Oxford University Press.

Farrington, D. P. (2003a). Developmental and life-course criminology: Key theoretical and empirical issues. *Criminology, 41*, 221–255.

Farrington, D. P. (2003b). Key results from the first 40 years of the Cambridge Study in Delinquent Development. In T. P. Thornberry & M. D. Krohn (Eds.), *Taking stock of delinquency: An overview of findings from contemporary longitudinal studies* (pp. 137–183). New York: Kluwer/Plenum.

Farrington, D. P. (Ed.). (2005). *Integrated developmental and life-course theories of offending. Vol. 14: Advances in criminological theory.* New Brunswick, NJ: Transaction.

Farrington, D. P., Gallagher, B., Morley, L., St. Ledger, R. J., & West, D. J. (1986). Unemployment, school leaving, and crime. *British Journal of Criminology, 26*, 335–356.

Farrington, D. P., Gallagher, B., Morley, L., St. Ledger, R. J., & West, D. J. (1988). Are there any successful men from criminogenic backgrounds? *Psychiatry, 51*, 116–130.

Farrington, D. P., Gallagher, B., Morley, L., St. Ledger, R. J., & West, D. J. (1990). Minimizing attrition in longitudinal research: Methods of tracing and securing cooperation in a 24-year follow-up. In D. Magnusson & L. Bergman (Eds.), *Data quality in longitudinal research* (pp. 122–147). Cambridge, UK: Cambridge University Press.

Farrington, D. P., Jolliffe, D., Loeber, R., Stouthamer-Loeber, M., & Kalb, L. M. (2001). The concentration of offenders in families, and family criminality in the prediction of boys' delinquency. *Journal of Adolescence, 24*, 579–596.

Farrington, D. P., & Loeber, R. (2000). Some benefits of dichotomization in psychiatric and criminological research. *Criminal Behavior and Mental Health, 10*, 100–122.

Farrington, D. P., Loeber, R., & Stouthamer-Loeber, M. (2003). How can the relationship between race and violence be explained? In D. F. Hawkins (Ed.), *Violent crime: Assessing race and ethnic differences* (pp. 213–237). Cambridge, UK: Cambridge University Press.

Farrington, D. P., Loeber, R., Yin, Y., & Anderson, S. J. (2002). Are within-individual causes of delinquency the same as between-individual causes? *Criminal Behavior and Mental Health, 12*, 53–68.

Farrington, D. P., & West, D. J. (1995). Effects of marriage, separation and children on offending by adult males. In J. Hagan (Ed.), *Current perspectives on aging and the life cycle. Vol. 4: Delinquency and disrepute in the life course* (pp. 249–281). Greenwich, CT: JAI Press.

Federal Bureau of Investigation (2004). *Crime in the United States, 2003.* Washington, DC.

Flannery, D. J., & Huff, C. R. (Eds.). (1999). *Youth violence: Prevention, intervention, and social policy.* Washington, DC: American Psychiatric Press.

Gorman-Smith, D., Tolan, P. H., Zelli, A., & Huesmann, L. R. (1996). The relation of family functioning to violence among inner-city minority youths. *Journal of Family Psychology, 10*, 115–129.

Gottfredson, D. C., McNeil, R. J., & Gottfredson, G. D. (1991). Social area influences on delinquency: A multilevel analysis. *Journal of Research in Crime and Delinquency, 28*, 197–226.

Graham, J., & Bowling, B. (1995). *Young people and crime.* London: Home Office.

Haapasalo, J., & Pokela, E. (1999). Child-rearing and child abuse antecedents of criminality. *Aggression and Violent Behavior, 1*, 107–127.

Haas, H., Farrington, D. P., Killias, M., & Sattar, G. (2004). The impact of different family configurations on delinquency. *British Journal of Criminology, 44*, 520–532.

Hamparian, D. M., Davis, J. M., Jacobson, J. M., & McGraw, R. E. (1985). *The young criminal years of the violent few.* Washington, DC: Office of Juvenile Justice and Delinquency Prevention.

Hamparian, D. M., Schuster, R. Dinitz, S., & Conrad, J. P. (1978). *The violent few: A study of dangerous juvenile offenders.* Lexington, MA: D.C. Heath.

Hawkins, J. D., Herrenkohl, T., Farrington, D. P., Brewer, D., Catalano, R. F., & Harachi, T. W. (1998). A review of predictors of youth violence. In R. Loeber & D. P. Farrington (Eds.), *Serious and violent juvenile offenders: Risk factors and successful interventions* (pp. 106–146). Thousand Oaks, CA: Sage.

Hawkins, J. D., Smith, B. H., Hill, K. G., Kosterman, R., Catalano, R. F., & Abbott, R. D. (2003). Understanding and preventing crime and violence: Findings from the Seattle Social Development Project. In T. P. Thornberry & M. D. Krohn (Eds.), *Taking stock of delinquency: An overview of findings from contemporary longitudinal studies* (pp. 255–312). New York: Kluwer/Plenum.

Henry, B., Caspi, A., Moffitt, T. E., & Silva, P. A. (1996). Temperamental and familial predictors of violent and nonviolent criminal convictions: Age 3 to age 18. *Developmental Psychology, 32*, 614–623.

Hogh, E., & Wolf, P. (1983). Violent crime in a birth cohort: Copenhagen 1953–1977. In K. T. van Dusen & S. A. Mednick (Eds.), *Prospective studies of crime and delinquency* (pp. 249–267). Boston: Kluwer-Nijhoff.

Home Office (2004). *Criminal statistics, England and Wales, 2003.* London: The Stationery Office.

Hough, M., & Sheehy, K. (1986). Incidents of violence: Findings from the British Crime Survey. *Home Office Research Bulletin, 20*, 22–26.

Huizinga, D., Weiher, A. W., Espiritu, R., & Esbensen, F. (2003). Delinquency and crime: Some highlights from the Denver Youth Survey. In T. P. Thornberry & M. D. Krohn (Eds.), *Taking stock of delinquency: An overview of findings from contemporary longitudinal studies* (pp. 47–91). New York: Kluwer/Plenum.

Jaffee, S., Caspi, A., Moffitt, T. E., Belsky, J., & Silva, P. A. (2001). Why are children born to teen mothers at risk for adverse outcomes in young adulthood? Results from a 20-year longitudinal study. *Development and Psychopathology, 13*, 377–397.

Johnson, J. G., Smailes, E., Cohen, P., Kasen, S., & Brook, J. S. (2004). Antisocial parental behavior, problematic parenting, and aggressive offspring behavior during adulthood. *British Journal of Criminology, 44*, 915–930.

Juby, H., & Farrington, D. P. (2001). Disentangling the link between disrupted families and delinquency. *British Journal of Criminology, 41*, 22–40.

Kagan, J. (1989). Temperamental contributions to social behavior. *American Psychologist, 44*, 668–674.

Kandel, E., Brennan, P. A., Mednick, S. A., & Michelson, N. M. (1989). Minor physical anomalies and recidivistic adult violent criminal behavior. *Acta Psychiatrica Scandinavica, 79*, 103–107.

Kandel, E., & Mednick, S. A. (1991). Perinatal complications predict violent offending. *Criminology, 29*, 519–529.

Kelley, M. L., Power, T. G., & Wimbush, D. D. (1992). Determinants of disciplinary practices in low-income black mothers. *Child Development, 63*, 573–582.

Klinteberg, B. A., Andersson, T., Magnusson, D., & Stattin, H. (1993). Hyperactive behavior in childhood as related to subsequent alcohol problems and violent offending: A longitudinal study of male subjects. *Personality and Individual Differences, 15*, 381–388.

Lang, S., Klinteberg, B. A., & Alm, P.-O. (2002). Adult psychopathy and violent behavior in males with early neglect and abuse. *Acta Psychiatrica Scandinavica, 106*, 93–100.

Larzelere, R. E., & Patterson, G. R. (1990). Parental management: Mediator of the effect of socioeconomic status on early delinquency. *Criminology, 28*, 301–324.

LeBlanc, M. (1996). Changing patterns in the perpetration of offenses over time: Trajectories from early adolescence to the early 30's. *Studies on Crime and Crime Prevention, 5*, 151–165.

LeBlanc, M., & Frechette, M. (1989). *Male criminal activity from childhood through youth.* New York: Springer-Verlag.

Lipsey, M. W., & Derzon, J. H. (1998). Predictors of violent or serious delinquency in adolescence and early adulthood: A synthesis of longitudinal research. In R. Loeber & D. P. Farrington (Eds.), *Serious and violent juvenile offenders: Risk factors and successful interventions* (pp. 86–105). Thousand Oaks, CA: Sage.

Loeber, R., & Farrington, D. P. (Eds.). (1998). *Serious and violent juvenile offenders: Risk factors and successful interventions.* Thousand Oaks, CA: Sage.

Loeber, R., Farrington, D. P., Stouthamer-Loeber, M., Moffitt, T. E., Caspi, A., White, H. R., Wei, E., & Beyers, J. M. (2003). The development of male offending: Key findings from 14 years of the Pittsburgh Youth Study. In T. P. Thornberry & M. D. Krohn (Eds.), *Taking stock of delinquency: An overview of findings from contemporary longitudinal studies* (pp. 93–136). New York: Kluwer/Plenum.

Loeber, R., Pardini, D., Homish, D. L., Wei, E. H., Crawford, A. M., Farrington, D. P., et al. (2005). The prediction of violence and homicide in young men. *Journal of Consulting and Clinical Psychology, 73*(6), 1074–1088.

Lorber, M. F. (2004). Psychophysiology of aggression, psychopathy, and conduct problems: A meta-analysis. *Psychological Bulletin, 130*, 531–552.

Malinosky-Rummell, R., & Hansen, D. J. (1993). Long-term consequences of childhood physical abuse. *Psychological Bulletin, 114*, 68–79.

Maxfield, M. G., & Widom, C. S. (1996). The cycle of violence revisited 6 years later.

Archives of Pediatrics and Adolescent Medicine, 150, 390–395.

McCord, J. (1977). A comparative study of two generations of Native Americans. In R. F. Meier (Ed.), *Theory in criminology* (pp. 83–92). Beverly Hills, CA: Sage.

McCord, J. (1979). Some child-rearing antecedents of criminal behavior in adult men. *Journal of Personality and Social Psychology, 37*, 1477–1486.

McCord, J. (1991). Family relationships, juvenile delinquency, and adult criminality. *Criminology, 29*, 397–417.

McCord, J. (1996). Family as crucible for violence: Comment on Gorman-Smith et al. (1996). *Journal of Family Psychology, 10*, 147–152.

McCord, J. (1997). On discipline. *Psychological Inquiry, 8*, 215–217.

McCord, J., & Ensminger, M. E. (1997). Multiple risks and comorbidity in an African-American population. *Criminal Behavior and Mental Health, 7*, 339–352.

Miczek, K. A., DeBold, J. F., Haney, M. Tidey, J. Vivian, J., & Weeris, E. M. (1994). Alcohol, drugs of abuse, aggression and violence. In A. J. Reiss & J. A. Roth (Eds.), *Understanding and preventing violence. Vol. 3: Social influences* (pp. 377–570). Washington, DC: National Academy Press.

Miller, S. J., Dinitz, S., & Conrad, J. P. (1982). *Careers of the violent: The dangerous offender and criminal justice.* Lexington, MA: D. C. Heath.

Moffitt, T. E. (1993). Adolescence-limited and life-course-persistent antisocial behavior: A developmental taxonomy. *Psychological Review, 100*, 674–701.

Moffitt, T. E., Caspi, A., Rutter, M., & Silva, P. A. (2001). *Sex differences in antisocial behavior.* Cambridge, UK: Cambridge University Press.

Moffitt, T. E., & Henry, B. (1991). Neuropsychological studies of juvenile delinquency and juvenile violence. In J. S. Milner (Ed.), *Neuropsychology of aggression* (pp. 131–146). Boston: Kluwer.

Morash, M., & Rucker, L. (1989). An exploratory study of the connection of mother's age at childbearing to her children's delinquency in four data sets. *Crime and Delinquency, 35*, 45–93.

Morgan, A. B., & Lilienfeld, S. O. (2000). A meta-analytic review of the relation between antisocial behavior and neuropsychological measures of executive function. *Clinical Psychology Review, 20*, 113–136.

Mossman, D. (1994). Assessing predictions of violence: Being accurate about accuracy. *Journal of Consulting and Clinical Psychology, 62*, 783–792.

Nagin, D. S., Pogarsky, G., & Farrington, D. P. (1997). Adolescent mothers and the criminal behavior of their children. *Law and Society Review, 31*, 137–162.

Nelson, S. E., & Dishion, T. J. (2004). From boys to men: Predicting adult adaptation from middle childhood sociometric status. *Development and Psychopathology, 16*, 441–459.

Osborn, S. G. (1980). Moving home, leaving London, and delinquent trends. *British Journal of Criminology, 20*, 54–61.

Piquero, A. (2000). Frequency, specialization, and violence in offending careers. *Journal of Research in Crime and Delinquency, 37*, 392–418.

Piquero, A. R., & Buka, S. L. (2002). Linking juvenile and adult patterns of criminal activity in the Providence cohort of the National Collaborative Perinatal Project. *Journal of Criminal Justice, 30*, 259–272.

Pogarsky, G., Lizotte, A. J., & Thornberry, T. P. (2003). The delinquency of children born to young mothers: Results from the Rochester Youth Development Study. *Criminology, 41*, 1249–1286.

Pulkkinen, L. (1987). Offensive and defensive aggression in humans: A longitudinal perspective. *Aggressive Behavior, 13*, 197–212.

Pulkkinen, L., & Pitkanen, T. (1993). Continuities in aggressive behavior from childhood to adulthood. *Aggressive Behavior, 19*, 249–263.

Raine, A. (1993). *The psychopathology of crime: Criminal behavior as a clinical disorder.* San Diego, CA: Academic Press.

Raine, A. (2002). Biosocial studies of antisocial and violent behavior in children and adults: A review. *Journal of Abnormal Child Psychology, 30*, 311–326.

Raine, A., Brennan, P. A., & Farrington, D. P. (1997). Biosocial bases of violence: Conceptual and theoretical issues. In A. Raine, P. A. Brennan, D. P. Farrington, & S. A. Mednick (Eds.), *Biosocial bases of violence* (pp. 1–20). New York: Plenum.

Raine, A., Brennan, P. A., & Mednick, S. A. (1994). Birth complications combined with early maternal rejection at age 1 year predispose to violent crime at age 18 years. *Archives of General Psychiatry, 51*, 984–988.

Raine, A., Reynolds, C., Venables, P. H., Mednick, S. A., & Farrington, D. P. (1998). Fearlessness, stimulation-seeking, and large body size at age 3 years as early predispositions to childhood aggression at age 11 years. *Archives of General Psychiatry, 55*, 745–751.

Ramirez, J. M. (2003). Hormones and aggression in childhood and adolescence. *Aggression and Violent Behavior, 8*, 621–644.

Rasanen, P., Hakko, H., Isohanni, M., Hodgins, S., Jarvelin, M., & Tiihonen, J. (1999). Maternal smoking during pregnancy and risk of criminal behavior among adult male offspring in the Northern Finland 1966 birth cohort. *American Journal of Psychiatry, 156*, 857–862.

Reiss, A. J., & Farrington, D. P. (1991). Advancing knowledge about co-offending: Results from a prospective longitudinal survey of London males. *Journal of Criminal Law and Criminology, 82*, 360–395.

Reiss, A. J., & Roth, J. A. (Eds.). (1993). *Understanding and preventing violence* (4 vols.). Washington, DC: National Academy Press.

Rivara, F. P., Shepherd, J. P., Farrington, D. P., Richmond, P. W., & Cannon, P. (1995). Victim as offender in youth violence. *Annals of Emergency Medicine, 26*, 609–614.

Rutter, M. (1981). The city and the child. *American Journal of Orthopsychiatry, 51*, 610–625.

Sampson, R. J., & Lauritsen, J. L. (1994). Violent victimization and offending: Individual, situational, and community-level risk factors. In A. J. Reiss & J. A. Roth (Eds.), *Understanding and preventing violence. Vol. 3: Social influences* (pp. 1–114). Washington, DC: National Academy Press.

Sampson, R. J., Raudenbush, S. W., & Earls, F. (1997). Neighborhoods and violent crime: A multilevel study of collective efficacy. *Science, 277*, 918–924.

Seguin, J., Pihl, R. O., Harden, P. W., Tremblay, R. F., & Boulerice, B. (1995). Cognitive and neuropsychological characteristics of physically aggressive boys. *Journal of Abnormal Psychology, 104*, 614–624.

Shaw, C. R., & McKay, H. D. (1969). *Juvenile delinquency and urban areas* (rev. ed.). Chicago: University of Chicago Press.

Smith, C. A., & Stern, S. B. (1997). Delinquency and antisocial behavior: A review of family processes and intervention research. *Social Service Review, 71*, 382–420.

Smith, C. A., & Thornberry, T. P. (1995). The relationship between childhood maltreatment and adolescent involvement in delinquency. *Criminology, 33*, 451–481.

Stattin, H., & Magnusson, D. (1989). The role of early aggressive behavior in the frequency, seriousness, and types of later crime. *Journal of Consulting and Clinical Psychology, 57*, 710–718.

Stouthamer-Loeber, M., Loeber, R., Wei, E., Farrington, D. P., & Wikström, P.-O. H. (2002). Risk and promotive effects in the explanation of persistent serious delinquency in boys. *Journal of Consulting and Clinical Psychology, 70*, 111–123.

Stouthamer-Loeber, M., Loeber, R., Farrington, D. P., Zhang, Q., van Kammen, W., & Maguin, E. (1993). The double edge of protective and risk factors for delinquency: Inter-relations and developmental patterns. *Development and Psychopathology, 5*, 683–701.

Tarling, R. (1993). *Analysing offending: Data, models and interpretations*. London: Her Majesty's Stationery Office.

Thornberry, T. P., Huizinga, D., & Loeber, R. (1995). The prevention of serious delinquency and violence: Implications from the program of research on the causes and correlates of delinquency. In J. C. Howell, B. Krisberg, J. D. Hawkins, & J. J. Wilson (Eds.), *Sourcebook on serious, violent and chronic juvenile offenders* (pp. 213–237). Thousand Oaks, CA: Sage.

Thornberry, T. P., Lizotte, A., Krohn, M. D., Smith, C. A., & Porter, P. K. (2003). Causes and consequences of delinquency: Findings from the Rochester Youth Development Study. In T. P. Thornberry & M. D. Krohn (Eds.), *Taking stock of delinquency: An overview of findings from contemporary longitudinal studies* (pp. 11–46). New York: Kluwer/Plenum.

Tolan, P. H., Gorman-Smith, D., & Henry, D. B. (2003). The developmental ecology of urban males' youth violence. *Developmental Psychology, 39*, 274–291.

Tonry, M. & Moore, M. H. (Eds.). (1998). *Youth violence*. Chicago: University of Chicago Press.

Tracy, P. E., & Kempf-Leonard, K. (1996). *Continuity and discontinuity in criminal careers*. New York: Plenum.

Tremblay, R. E., Vitaro, F., Nagin, D., Pagani, L., & Seguin, J. R. (2003). The Montreal Longitudinal and Experimental Study: Rediscovering the power of descriptions. In T. P. Thornberry & M. D. Krohn (Eds.), *Taking stock of delinquency: An overview of findings from contemporary longitudinal studies* (pp. 205–254). New York: Kluwer/Plenum.

Wadsworth, M. E. J. (1976). Delinquency, pulse rates, and early emotional deprivation. *British Journal of Criminology, 16,* 245–256.

Wadsworth, M. E. J. (1978). Delinquency prediction and its uses: The experience of a 21-year follow-up study. *International Journal of Mental Health, 7,* 43–62.

Wadsworth, M. E. J. (1991). *The imprint of time.* Oxford: Clarendon Press.

Wells, L. E., & Rankin, J. H. (1991). Families and delinquency: A meta-analysis of the impact of broken homes. *Social Problems, 38,* 71–93.

Welsh, B. C., & Farrington, D. P. (2000). Monetary costs and benefits of crime prevention programs. In M. Tonry (Ed.), *Crime and justice* (vol. 27, pp. 305–361). Chicago: University of Chicago Press.

Werner, E. E., & Smith, R. S. (1982). *Vulnerable but invincible: A longitudinal study of resilient children and youth.* New York: McGraw-Hill.

Werner, E. E., & Smith, R. S. (2001). *Journeys from childhood to midlife.* Ithaca, NY: Cornell University Press.

West, D. J. (1969). *Present conduct and future delinquency.* London: Heinemann.

West, D. J., & Farrington, D. P. (1973). *Who becomes delinquent?* London: Heinemann.

West, D. J., & Farrington, D. P. (1977). *The delinquent way of life.* London: Heinemann.

Widom, C. S. (1989). The cycle of violence. *Science, 244,* 160–166.

Widom, C. S. (1994). Childhood victimization and adolescent problem behaviors. In R. D. Ketterlinus & M. E. Lamb (Eds.), *Adolescent problem behaviors* (pp. 127–164). Hillsdale, NJ: Erlbaum.

Widom, C. S., & Ames, M. A. (1994). Criminal consequences of childhood sexual victimization. *Child Abuse and Neglect, 18,* 303–318.

Widom, C. S., & White, H. R. (1997). Problem behaviors in abused and neglected children grown up: Prevalence and co-occurrence of substance use, crime, and violence. *Criminal Behavior and Mental Health, 7,* 287–310.

Wikström, P.-O. H. (1985). *Everyday violence in contemporary Sweden.* Stockholm: National Council for Crime Prevention.

Wikström, P.-O. H. (1990). Age and crime in a Stockholm cohort. *Journal of Quantitative Criminology, 6,* 61–84.

Wolfgang, M. E., Thornberry, T. P., & Figlio, R. M. (1987). *From boy to man, from delinquency to crime.* Chicago: University of Chicago Press.

CHAPTER 3

A Review of Research on the Taxonomy of Life-Course Persistent Versus Adolescence-Limited Antisocial Behavior

Terrie E. Moffitt

Introduction

This chapter reviews 10 years of research into a developmental taxonomy of antisocial behavior that proposes two primary hypothetical prototypes: life-course persistent versus adolescence-limited offenders. According to the taxonomic theory, life-course persistent offenders' antisocial behavior has its origins in neurodevelopmental processes, begins in childhood, and continues persistently thereafter. In contrast, adolescence-limited offenders' antisocial behavior has its origins in social processes, begins in adolescence, and desists in young adulthood. According to the theory, life-course persistent antisocial individuals are few, persistent, and pathological. Adolescence-limited antisocial individuals are common, relatively transient, and near normative (Moffitt, 1990, 1993, 1994, 1997, 2003).

Discussions in the literature have pointed out that, if the taxonomic theory is shown to be valid, it could usefully improve classification of subject groups for research

(Nagin, Farrington, & Moffitt, 1995; Silverthorn & Frick, 1999; Zucker, Ellis, Fitzgerald, Bingham, & Sanford, 1996), focus research into antisocial personality and violence toward the most promising causal variables (Brezina, 2000; Lahey, Waldman, & McBurnett, 1999; Laucht, 2001; Osgood, 1998), and guide the timing and strategies of interventions for delinquent types (Howell & Hawkins, 1998; Scott & Grisso, 1997; Vermeiren, 2002). Several writers have extracted implications for intervention from this taxonomy. Howell and Hawkins (1998) observed that preventing life-course persistent versus adolescence-limited antisocial behavior requires interventions that differ in both timing and target. Preventing life-course persistent lifestyles requires early childhood interventions in the family. In contrast, adolescence-limited offending ought to be prevented by treating adolescents individually, to counteract peer influence, instead of in groups that facilitate deviant peer influence (Dishion, McCord, & Poulin, 1999). Scott and Grisso (1997) argued compellingly that the juvenile justice system should identify adolescence-limited delinquents and give them room to reform. Surveys of juvenile court judges and forensic psychologists reveal that the offender characteristics they rely on to recommend a juvenile for transfer to adult court match the characteristics that distinguish life-course persistent from adolescence-limited delinquents (Slaekin, Yff, Neumann, Liestico, & Zalot, 2002). In contrast, Scott and Grisso (1997) argue that waiving life-course persistent delinquents to adult court is wrong because the cognitive deficits typical of these delinquents render them unlikely to meet legal criteria for competency to stand trial.

The taxonomy of childhood- versus adolescent-onset antisocial behavior has been codified in the *DSM-IV* (American Psychiatric Association, 1994), presented in many abnormal psychology and criminology textbooks, and invoked in the NIMH Fact Sheet *Child and Adolescent Violence Research* (2000), the U.S. Surgeon General's report *Youth Violence* (2001), the World Health Organization's *World Report on Violence and Health* (2002), and the National Institutes of Health's *State-of-the-Science Consensus Statement on Preventing Violence* (2004). But is it valid?

The reader is referred to two prior publications that articulate the main hypotheses derived from this taxonomic theory. The first article that proposed the two prototypes and their different etiologies ended with a section headed "Strategies for Research," which described predictions about epidemiology, age, social class, risk correlates, offense types, desistance from crime, abstainers from crime, and the longitudinal stability of antisocial behavior (Moffitt, 1993, pp. 694–696). The article specified which findings would disconfirm the theory. A version published elsewhere specified disconfirmable hypotheses about sex and race (Moffitt, 1994). When these hypotheses from the taxonomy were put forward 10 years ago, none of them had been tested, but since then several have been tested by us and by others. This chapter reviews the results of that research, as of summer 2004, and points out where more research is needed.

A Brief Introduction to the Two Prototypes

In a nutshell, we suggested that life-course persistent antisocial behavior originates early in life, when the difficult behavior of a high-risk young child is exacerbated by a high-risk social environment. According to the theory, the child's risk emerges from inherited or acquired neuropsychological variation, which is initially manifested as subtle cognitive deficits, difficult temperament, or hyperactivity. The environment's risk comprises such factors as inadequate parenting, disrupted family bonds, and poverty. The environmental risk domain expands beyond the family as the child ages to include poor relations with other people, such as peers and teachers. Opportunities to learn prosocial skills are lost. Over the first two decades of development, transactions between the individual and the environment gradually construct a disordered personality with hallmark features of physical aggression and antisocial behavior persisting to midlife. The theory predicts that antisocial behavior will infiltrate multiple adult life domains: illegal activities, problems with employment, and victimization of intimate partners and children. This infiltration diminishes the possibility of reform.

In contrast, we suggested that adolescence-limited antisocial behavior emerges alongside puberty, when otherwise ordinary healthy youngsters experience psychological discomfort during the relatively role-less years between their biological maturation and their access to mature privileges and responsibilities, a period we called the "maturity gap." They experience dissatisfaction with their dependent status as a child and impatience for what they anticipate are the privileges and rights of adulthood. Although young people are in this "gap," it is virtually normative for them to find the delinquent style appealing and to mimic it as a way to demonstrate autonomy from parents, win affiliation with peers, and hasten social maturation. However, because their pre-delinquent development was normal, most adolescence-limited delinquents are able to desist from crime when they age into real adult roles, returning gradually to a more conventional lifestyle. This recovery may be delayed if the antisocial activities of adolescence-limited delinquents attract factors we called "snares," such as a criminal record, incarceration, addiction, or truncated education without credentials. Such snares can compromise the ability to make a successful transition to adulthood.

Research Issues

The Hypothesis That Life-Course Persistent Antisocial Development Emerges From Early Neurodevelopmental and Family-Adversity Risk Factors

The original hypothesis about childhood risk specified that predictors of life-course persistent antisocial behavior should include "health, gender, temperament, cognitive abilities, school achievement, personality traits, mental disorders (e.g., hyperactivity), family attachment bonds, child-rearing practices, parent and sibling deviance, and socioeconomic status, but not age" (Moffitt, 1993, p. 695).

Our own tests of this hypothesis have been carried out in the Dunedin Multidisciplinary Health and Development Study, a 32-year longitudinal study of a birth cohort of 1,000 New Zealanders. A full description of the Dunedin Study and the New Zealand research setting can be found in Moffitt, Caspi, Rutter, and Silva (2001). These tests have examined childhood predictors measured between ages 3 and 13, operationalizing the two prototypes of antisocial behavior using both categorical and continuous statistical approaches. These studies showed that the life-course persistent path was differentially predicted by individual risk characteristics, including undercontrolled temperament measured by observers at age 3, neurological abnormalities and delayed motor development at age 3, low intellectual ability, reading difficulties, poor scores on neuropsychological tests of memory, hyperactivity, and slow heart rate (Jeglum-Bartusch, Lynam, Moffitt, & Silva, 1997; Moffitt, 1990; Moffitt & Caspi, 2001; Mof-

fitt, Lynam, & Silva, 1994). The life-course persistent path was also differentially predicted by parenting risk factors, including teenaged single parents, mothers with poor mental health, mothers who were observed to be harsh or neglectful, as well as by experiences of harsh and inconsistent discipline, much family conflict, many changes of primary caretaker, low family socioeconomic status (SES), and rejection by peers in school.

In contrast, study members on the adolescence-limited path, despite being involved in teen delinquency to the same extent as their counterparts on the life-course persistent path, tended to have backgrounds that were normative or sometimes even better than the average Dunedin child's (Moffitt & Caspi, 2001). A replication of this pattern of differential findings was reported by a study of 800 children followed from birth to age 15 years (Brennan, Hall, Bor, Najman, & Williams, 2003). An early-onset persistent antisocial group, an adolescent-onset antisocial group, and a non-antisocial group were identified. Measured "biological risks" (e.g., neuropsychological test deficits at age 15) and childhood "social risks" (e.g., harsh discipline, maternal hostility), and an interaction between these two risks, predicted membership in the early-onset persistent group, but membership in the adolescent-onset group was unrelated to childhood social risks or biological risks.

The aforementioned Dunedin findings about differential neurodevelopmental and family risk correlates for childhood-onset versus adolescent-onset offenders are generally in keeping with findings reported from other samples in Australia, Canada, England, Mauritius, New Zealand, Norway, Russia, Sweden, and several states within the United States. These studies operationalized the types using a variety of conceptual approaches, many different measures of antisocial behaviors, and very different statistical methods (Aguilar, Sroufe, Egeland & Carlson, 2000; Arseneault, Tremblay, Boulerice, & Saucier, 2002; Brennan et al., 2003; Chung, Hill, Hawkins, Gilchrist, & Nagin, 2002; Dean, Brame, &

Piquero, 1996; Donnellan, Ge, & Wenk, 2000; Fergusson, Horwood, & Nagin, 2000; Kjelsberg, 1999; Kratzer & Hodgins, 1999; Lahey, Loeber, Quay, Applegate, Shaffer, Waldman, & Hart, 1998; Magnusson, Klintberg, & Stattin, 1994; Maughan, Pickles, Rowe, Costello, & Angold, 2001; Mazerolle, Brame, Paternoster, Piquero, & Dean, 2000; McCabe, Hough, Wood, & Yeh, 2001; Nagin et al., 1995; Nagin & Tremblay, 1999, 2001a; Patterson, Forgatch, Yoerger, & Stoolmiller, 1998; Piquero, 2001; Piquero & Brezina, 2001; Raine, Moffitt, Caspi, Loeber, Stouthamer-Loeber, & Lynam, 2005; Raine, Yaralian, Reynolds, Venables, & Mednick, 2002; Roeder, Lynch, & Nagin, 1999; Ruchkin, Koposov, Vermeiren, & Schwab-Stone, 2003; Tibbetts & Piquero, 1999; Tolan & Thomas, 1995; Wiesner & Capaldi, 2003). Each of the above-cited studies added support for the taxonomy's construct validity by reporting differential correlates for early-onset/persistent antisocial behavior versus later onset/temporary antisocial behavior. However, at least one research team found mixed evidence for the taxonomy (cf. Brame, Bushway, & Paternoster, 1999 versus Paternoster & Brame, 1997).

Other studies, although not necessarily presented as a formal test of the two types, have reported findings consonant with our predictions about the types' differential childhood risk. For example, children's hyperactivity interacts with poor parenting skill to predict antisocial behavior that has an early onset and escalates to delinquency (Patterson, De Garmo, & Knutson, 2000), an interaction that fits the hypothesized origins of the life-course persistent path. Other studies have reported that measures reflecting maldevelopment of the infant nervous system interact with poor parenting and social adversity to predict aggression that is chronic from childhood to adolescence (Arseneault et al., 2002). Measures indexing infant nervous system maldevelopment and social adversity also interact to predict early-onset violent crime (Raine, Brennan, & Mednick, 1994; Raine, Brennan, Mednick, & Mednick 1996), but do not predict nonviolent crime (Arseneault, Tremblay, Boulerice, Seguin, & Saucier, 2000; Raine, Brennan, & Mednick, 1997).

Two additional findings are consistent with our prediction that infant nervous system maldevelopment contributes to long-term life-course persistent antisocial outcomes. First, prenatal malnutrition has been found to predict adult antisocial personality disorder (Neugebauer, Hoek, & Susser, 1999). Second, adults with antisocial personality disorder exhibit two nervous system abnormalities attributable to disruption of brain development in early life: enlargement of the corpus callosum assessed by structural magnetic resonance imaging and abnormal corpus callosum connective function assessed by divided visual field tests (Raine, Lencz, Taylor, Hellige, Bihrle, Lacasse et al., 2003).

Our differential-risk prediction encountered a particular challenge from a longitudinal study of a low-SES Minneapolis sample (Aguilar et al., 2000). This research team observed that differences between their childhood-onset and adolescent-onset groups were not significant for neurocognitive and temperament measures taken prior to age 3, although they found that significant differences did emerge later in childhood. The authors inferred that childhood psychosocial adversity is sufficient to account for the origins of life-course persistent antisocial behavior, which is similar to Patterson and Yoerger's (1997) thesis that unskilled parenting is sufficient to account for the early-onset antisocial type. Such exclusive socialization hypotheses are probably not defensible, in view of emerging evidence that the life-course persistent pattern of antisocial behavior appears to have substantial heritable liability (DiLalla & Gottesman, 1989; Eley, Lichtenstein, & Moffitt, 2003; Taylor, Iacono, & McGue, 2000), a finding we revisit later in this chapter. The lack of significant early childhood differences in the Minneapolis study may have arisen from methodological features of the study, including the unrepresentative and homogeneous nature of the sample (all high-risk, low-SES families), irregular sex composition of the groups (more females than males were antisocial), or weak psychometric qualities of the infant measures (unknown predictive validity). Infant measures are known for their poor predictive validity (McCall & Carriger, 1993), and thus it is possible that the failure of the infant measures to predict the life-course persistent path is part of such measures' more general failure to predict outcomes.

One study has reported that difficult temperament assessed at age 5 months distinguished a group of children who showed a trajectory of high rates of physical aggression, as compared to cohort peers, at ages 17, 30, and 42 months (Tremblay, Nagin, Seguin, Zoccolillo, Zelazo, & Boivin, 2004). However, until this cohort of 572 infants is followed beyond age 3.5 years, into adolescence, we cannot be confident that they represent youngsters on the life-course persistent pathway. Other studies have reported a significant relation between life-course persistent-type offending and problems known to be associated with neurocognitive and temperamental difficulties in infancy: perinatal complications, minor physical anomalies, and low birth weight (Arseneault et al., 2000, 2002; Kratzer & Hodgins, 1999; Raine et al., 1994; Tibbetts & Piquero, 1999). These studies have desirable features for testing neurodevelopmental risks from the beginning of infancy for persistent antisocial behavior: large samples, representative samples, infant measures with proven predictive validity, and attention to interactions between neurodevelopmental and social adversity (Cicchetti & Walker, 2003).

What research is needed? Research already documents that life-course persistent antisocial behavior has the predicted neurodevelopmental correlates in the perinatal and middle childhood periods, but the Aguilar et al. (2000) study remains the only one that has reported objective measures of infants' temperament and neurocognitive status prior to age 3 years, and it did not find the associations predicted by the theory. This study constitutes an important challenge that must be taken seriously,

particularly as Brennan et al. (2003) also found no significant connection between temperament or vocabulary assessed in early life and early-onset persistent aggression. Clearly more research is needed to fill in the critical gap between birth and age 3 years. This might be accomplished by following up the antisocial outcomes of infants tested with newer neurocognitive measures having documented predictive validity, such as the infant attention-habituation paradigm (Sigman, Cohen, & Beckwith, 1997).

Another feature of life-course persistent theory that needs testing is the argument that antisocial behavior becomes persistent because a child's early difficult behavior provokes harsh treatment or rejection from parents, teachers, and peers, which in turn promotes more difficult child behavior. Adoption and twin studies have documented an initial "child effect," which is a form of gene-environment correlation. That is, children carrying a genetic liability to antisocial behavior provoke harsh parenting responses from their parents (Ge, Conger, Cadoret, Neiderhauser, Yates, & Troughton, 1996; Jaffee, Caspi, Moffitt, & Taylor, 2004a; O'Connor, Deater-Deckard, Fulker, Rutter, & Plomin, 1998; Riggins-Caspers, Cadoret, Knutson & Langbehn, 2003). Such genetically informative studies should be followed up to ascertain whether this process beginning with a child effect ultimately leads to antisocial behavior that persists on a long-term basis.

Is a Third Group Needed? Childhood-Limited Aggressive Children May Become Low-Level Chronic Criminal Offenders With Personality Disorders

The original theoretical taxonomy asserted that two prototypes, life-course persistent and adolescence-limited offenders, account for the preponderance of the population's antisocial behavior and thus warrant the lion's share of attention by theory and research. However, our analyses revealed a small group of Dunedin study males who had exhibited extreme, pervasive, and persistent antisocial behavior problems during childhood, but who surprisingly engaged in only low to moderate delinquency during adolescence from age 15 to 18, not extreme enough to meet criteria for membership in the life-course persistent group (Moffitt, Caspi, Dickson, Silva, & Stanton, 1996). Like the life-course persistent offenders they had extremely undercontrolled temperaments as 3-year-olds (Moffitt et al., 1996), and in childhood they too suffered family adversity and parental psychopathology and had low intelligence (unpublished analyses). The existence of a small group of boys who exhibit serious aggression in childhood, but are not notably delinquent in adolescence, has been replicated in the Pittsburgh Youth Survey, where they were called "childhood-limited" antisocial children (Raine et al., 2005). In the Pittsburgh cohort too, these boys had many risk factors, including family adversity, parental psychopathology, and severe neuropsychological deficits.

This group was a surprise to the theory, because the theory argued that an early-onset chain of cumulative interactions between aggressive children and high-risk environments will perpetuate disordered behavior. On that basis, we had predicted that "false positive subjects, who meet criteria for a stable and pervasive antisocial childhood history and yet recover (eschew delinquency) after puberty, should be extremely rare" (Moffitt, 1993, p. 694). When we discovered this group, we optimistically labeled it the "recovery group" (Moffitt et al., 1996). Many researchers, we among them, hoped that this group would allow us to identify protective factors that can be harnessed to prevent childhood aggression from persisting and becoming more severe. However, our study of this group has revealed no protective factors.

Researchers testing for the presence of the life-course persistent and adolescence-limited types have since uncovered a third type that replicates across longitudinal studies. It was first identified in trajectory analyses of a British cohort (Nagin et al., 1995). This third group of offenders has been labeled "low-level chronics" because they

have been found to offend persistently but at a low rate from childhood to adolescence (Fergusson et al., 2000) or from adolescence to adulthood (D'Unger, Land, McCall, & Nagin, 1998; Nagin et al., 1995). Persuaded by these findings, we followed up the so-called recovery group in the Dunedin cohort at age 26 to see if they might fit the low-level chronic pattern as adults. We found that recovery was clearly a misnomer, as their modal offending pattern over time fit a pattern referred to by criminologists as "intermittency," in which some offenders are not convicted for a period but then reappear in the courts (Laub & Sampson, 2001). This Dunedin group's long-term offending pattern closely resembles that of the low-level chronic offender.

Anticipating true recoveries from serious childhood conduct disorder to be extremely rare, the taxonomic theory had argued that teens who engage in less delinquency than predicted on the basis of their childhood conduct problems might have off-putting personal characteristics that excluded them from the social peer groups in which most delinquency happens. Consistent with this prediction, a group in the Oregon Youth Study, who showed high levels of antisocial behavior at age 12 that decreased thereafter, scored low as adolescents on a measure of involvement with pro-delinquency peers (Wiesner & Capaldi, 2003). In the Dunedin cohort followed up to age 26, the members of this low-level chronic group, unlike other cohort men, were often social isolates; their informants reported that they had difficulty making friends, none had married, few held jobs, and many had diagnoses of agoraphobia and/or social phobia. Almost all social phobics meet criteria for avoidant, dependent, and/or schizotypal personality disorders (Alnaes & Torgersen, 1988), and we speculate that men in this group may suffer from these isolating personality disorders. As many as one third of this group had diagnosable depression; the personality profile of this subgroup showed elevated neuroticism, and their informants rated them as the most depressed, anxious men in the cohort. This pattern in which formerly antisocial boys develop into depressed, anxious, socially isolated men resembles closely a finding from a British longitudinal study of males followed from aged 8 to 32. In that study, too, at-risk antisocial boys who became adult "false positives" (committing less crime than predicted) had few or no friends, held low-paid jobs, lived in dirty home conditions, and had been described in case records as withdrawn, highly strung, obsessional, nervous, or timid (Farrington, Gallagher, Morley, St. Ledger, & West, 1988).

Robins (1966) is often quoted as having said that one half of conduct-problem boys do not grow up to have antisocial personalities. Such quotations are intended to imply that early conduct problems are fully malleable and need not be a cause for pessimism. However, less often quoted is Robins' (1966) observation that conduct-problem boys who do not develop antisocial personalities generally suffer other forms of maladjustment as adults. This is an assertion of "multifinality" in the poor outcomes of at-risk children (Cicchetti & Cohen, 1995). In the Dunedin birth cohort, 87 boys had childhood conduct problems: 47 in the life-course persistent group and 40 in the so-called recovery group. Of these 87 males, only 15% ($n = 13$) seemed to have truly recovered as adults, escaping all adjustment problems measured in the study at age 26. Taken together, findings from Dunedin and the studies by Farrington and Robins are consistent with our taxonomic theory's original assertion that childhood-onset antisocial behavior is *virtually always* a prognosticator of poor adult adjustment.

What research is needed? Several studies have detected an unexpected group, variously labeled "recoveries," "childhood-limited," or "low-level chronic offenders," depending on how long the cohort was followed. However, few studies have been able to shed any light on the personal characteristics of the members of this group. The characteristics revealed so far are suggestive of avoidant, dependent, schizotypal personality disorders and/or low intelligence, but these outcomes have not been directly measured in adulthood. To test the the-

ory's assertion that serious childhood-onset antisocial behavior reliably predicts long-term maladjustment it is important to know whether this group has adult psychopathology.

Is a Fourth Group Needed? Adult-Onset Antisocial Behavior

Some investigators have suggested, on the basis of examining official data sources, that significant numbers of offenders first begin to offend as adults (Eggleston & Laub, 2002; Farrington, Ohlin, & Wilson, 1986). This claim would appear to challenge our developmental taxonomy's assertion that two groups, life-course persistent and adolescence-limited, suffice to account for the majority of antisocial participation across the life course. However, the observation that many antisocial individuals are adult-onset offendes may be an artifact of official measurement. Estimates of the age at which antisocial behavior begins depend on the source of the data. For example, in the Dunedin Study only 4% of boys had been convicted in court by age 15 years, but 15% had been arrested by police by age 15, and 80% had self-reported the onset of illegal behaviors by age 15 (see Chapter 7 in Moffitt et al., 2001). These findings suggest that official data lag behind the true age of onset by a few years. Similar findings have emerged from other studies in other countries. For example, a Canadian survey showed that self-reported onset antedated conviction by about 3.5 years (Loeber & LeBlanc, 1990), and a U.S. survey showed that self-reported onset of "serious" delinquency antedated the first court contact by 2.5 years, and onset of "moderate" delinquency antedated the first court contact by 5 years (U.S. Office of Juvenile Justice and Delinquency Prevention, 1998). In the Seattle Social Development cohort, the self-reported onset of crime antedated the first court referral by 2.4 years, and the study estimated that the average offender committed 26 crimes before his official crime record began (Farrington, Jolliffe, Hawkins,

Catalano, Hill, & Kosterman, 2003). These comparisons of data sources suggest that investigations relying on official data will ascertain age of onset approximately 3 to 5 years after it has happened. A 3- to 5-year lag is relevant because most studies have defined adult-onset offenders as those whose official crime records began at or after age 18 years (Eggleston & Laub, 2002).

It also is useful to note that whereas the 18th birthday may have demarked adulthood for young people born before 1960, that birthday falls only midway between puberty and adulthood for contemporary generations. This shift has emerged because contemporary generations are experiencing a more protracted adolescence, lasting until the mid-twenties (Arnett, 2000) or even into the early thirties for the cohort born after 1970 (Ferri, Bynner, & Wadsworth, 2003; Furstenberg, Cook, Sampson, & Slap, 2002). Although adult-onset crime begins at age 18 in legal terms, in developmental terms for contemporary cohort samples, it begins some time after age 25.

In contrast to studies using official crime records, self-report cohort studies show that fewer than 4% of males commit their first criminal offense after age 17 (Elliott, Huizinga, & Menard, 1989). Self-report studies of American and European cohorts agree (Junger-Tas, Terlouw, & Klein, 1994). By age 18, virtually all of the Dunedin Study members had already engaged in some form of illegal behavior at some time, according to their self-reports (Moffitt et al., 2001). Only 9% of Dunedin males and 14% of females remained naive to all delinquency by age 18, and only 3% of males and 5% of females first offended as an adult, between ages 18 and 21. These findings carry an important lesson for methodology in developmental research into antisocial behavior. "Adult-onset" offenders cannot be defined for study with any certainty unless self-reported data are available to rule out juvenile onset prior to participants' first official contact with the judicial system. When self-report data are consulted, they reveal that onset of antisocial behavior after adolescence is extremely rare. This conclusion extends to serious and violent offending (Elliott, 1994).

One way to ascertain whether adult-onset offenders constitute a significant group for study is to apply semi-parametic modeling techniques (Nagin, 1999; Nagin & Tremblay, 2001b; Roeder et al., 1999) to identify types or groups of trajectories within a population-representative cohort of individuals whose behavior has been followed into adulthood. Three studies have done so. The Dunedin Study identified no adult-onset trajectory in self-reports of delinquency from ages 7 to 26 years (Moffitt, Arseneault, Taylor, Nagin, Milne, & Harrington, in preparation). The Oregon Youth Study identified no adult-onset trajectory in self-reports of offending from ages 12 to 24 years (Wiesner & Capaldi, 2003). The Cambridge Longitudinal Study identified no adult-onset trajectory in official crime records for a cohort born in the 1950s that was followed to age 32 (Nagin et al., 1995).

The original theoretical taxonomy asserted that two prototypes, life-course persistent and adolescence-limited offenders, can account for the preponderance of the population's antisocial behavior. After more than 10 years of research, this assertion appears to be correct. Some studies of the taxonomy have reported an adult-onset group (e.g., Kratzer & Hodgins, 1999). However, these studies used official crime data, and thus most of their adult-onset offenders would probably be revealed as having adolescent onset if self-report data were available. These so-called adult-onset offenders can probably be accommodated by the adolescence-limited theory because, when studied, the alleged adult-onset group has not differed from ordinary adolescent offenders (Eggleston & Laub, 2002). Moreover, as with adolescence-limited offenders, adult-onset offenders' crime careers tend to be brief and not serious (Farrington, Ohlin, & Wilson, 1986). In our view, the existence of individuals whose official crime record begins after age 18 does not constitute a threat to the taxonomy.

The Hypothesis That Adolescence-Limited Antisocial Behavior Is Influenced by the Maturity Gap and by Social Mimicry of Antisocial Models

The original theory asserted that "individual differences should play little or no role in the prediction of short-term adolescent offending careers. Instead, the strongest predictors of adolescence-limited offending should be peer delinquency, attitudes toward adolescence and adulthood reflecting the maturity gap [such as a desire for autonomy], cultural and historical contexts influencing adolescence, and age" (Moffitt, 1993, p. 695).

Most research on the taxonomy to date has focused on testing hypotheses about the etiology of life-course persistent offenders. Unfortunately, adolescence-limited offenders have been relegated to the status of a contrast group, and the original hypotheses about the distinct etiology of adolescent-onset offending have not captured the research imagination. This is unfortunate because adolescent-onset offenders are quite common (one quarter of both males and females as defined in the Dunedin cohort), and their antisocial activities are not benign. They are found among adjudicated delinquents, as well as in the general population (Scholte, 1999). Moreover, even if adolescence-limited individuals commit fewer violent offenses than life-course persistent individuals, the size of the adolescence-limited group is much larger than the size of the life-course persistent group. As a result the adolescence-limited group can be expected to account for an important share of a society's serious and violent offenses. In Dunedin, life-course persistent men (10% of the cohort) accounted for 53% of the cohort's 554 self-reported violent offenses at age 26, but adolescence-limited men (26% of the cohort) accounted for 29% of the cohort's violent offenses, a nontrivial amount of violence (Moffitt, Caspi, Harrington, & Milne, 2002).

Do adolescents find the maturity gap psychologically aversive, and does this motivate their newfound interest in delinquency? Aguilar et al. (2000) discovered that adolescent-onset delinquents experienced elevated internalizing symptoms and perceptions of stress at age 16, which may be consistent with the taxonomy's assertion that these adolescents experience psychological discomfort during the maturity gap. The theory suggested that this discomfort motivated adolescents to engage in antisocial behavior in order for them to seem older. In a study of the Gluecks' sample, adolescents' concerns about appearing immature increased their likelihood of delinquency (Zebrowitz, Andreoletti, Collins, Lee, & Blumenthal, 1998). One interesting ethnographic study has made use of the maturity gap to explain *korttteliralli*, the street-racing alcohol youth culture of Finland (Vaaranen, 2001). The Victoria Adolescence Project studies 452 adolescents and their parents to examine how young people negotiate the maturity gap (Galambos, Barker, & Tilton-Weaver, 2003). This study identified a group of 25% of adolescents who exhibited a cluster of characteristics they called "pseudo-maturity." These adolescents, relative to their age cohort, were characterized by more advanced biological pubertal status, older subjective age ("I feel a lot older than my age"), elevated perceptions of self-reliance, more wishes to emulate older brothers (but not sisters), more older friends, a greater desire to be older ("I would like to look a lot older than my age"), more involvement in pop culture, and less involvement in school but more involvement with peers. This cluster was not associated with SES level. The study concluded that, for a large proportion of teens, pubertal maturation brings about a poor fit between their developmental stage and their social environment: "they are caught in the maturity gap" (Galambos et al., 2003, p. 262). Parent and self-reports confirmed that this pseudo-mature group of teenagers engaged in elevated rates of problem behaviors, as expected by the theory of adolescence-limited delinquency.

Do adolescence-limited teenagers want to be more like life-course persistent offenders?

The theory of adolescence-limited delinquency borrowed the concept of "social mimicry" from the field of ethology to explain how adolescents might mimic the antisocial behavior of life-course persistent antisocial boys in their midst, in an effort to attain the mature status embodied in the antisocial lifestyle. New developmental research has shown that when ordinary young people age into adolescence they begin to admire good students less and to admire aggressive, antisocial peers more (Bukowski, Sippola, & Newcomb, 2000; Luthar & McMahon, 1996; Rodkin, Farmer, Pearl, & Van Acker, 2000). One sociometric study that followed 905 children from age 10 to 14 reported that the association between physical aggression and being disliked by peers dissolved during this age period; as they grew older, the teenagers came to perceive their aggressive age-mates as having higher social status and more influence (Cillessen & Mayeux, 2004). Moreover, during adolescence, young people who place a high value on conforming to adults' rules become unpopular with their peers (Allen, Weissberg, & Hawkins, 1989).

Our Dunedin studies documented that an increase in young teens' awareness of peers' delinquency antedates and predicts onset of their own later delinquency (Caspi, Lynam, Moffitt, & Silva, 1993). We also showed that the adolescence-limited path is associated more strongly with delinquent peers than the life-course persistent path (Jeglum-Bartusch et al., 1997; Moffitt & Caspi, 2001). However, one study that traced peer-affiliation trajectories concluded that peers were as influential for childhood-onset persistent offenders as for adolescent-onset offenders (LaCourse, Nagin, Tremblay, Vitaro, & Claes, 2003). In contrast, others have shown that delinquent peer influences directly promote increases in delinquency, specifically among young males whose antisocial behavior begins in adolescence (Simons, Wu, Conger, & Lorenz, 1994; Vitaro, Tremblay, Kerr, Pagani, & Bukowski, 1997). In contrast, these same studies suggest that, among males whose

antisocial behavior begins in childhood, the direction of influence runs the other way: the child's own early antisocial behavior promotes increases at adolescence in the number of delinquent peers who selectively affiliate with him. This finding is consistent with our life-course persistent theory's assertion that during adolescence life-course persistent antisocial boys become "magnets" for peers who wish to learn delinquency.

The most direct test of the adolescence-limited etiological hypothesis was carried out in the Youth in Transition Survey of 2,000 males (Piquero & Brezina, 2001). This study was introduced to the literature with lyrics from a song titled "Eighteen" by rocker Alice Cooper that express the ennui of the maturity gap: "I'm in the middle without any plans, I'm a boy and I'm a man." The study tested the hypothesis that desires for autonomy promoted adolescent-onset offending. It found that, as predicted, the offenses committed by adolescence-limited delinquents were primarily rebellious (not physically aggressive) and that this rebellious offending was accounted for by the interaction between maturational timing and aspects of peer activities that were related to personal autonomy. However, one measure of youth autonomy in this study did not predict offending.

It is important to acknowledge that alternative accounts of late-onset delinquency have been put forward. In particular, Patterson and Yoerger (1997) outlined a learning model in which decreases in parents' monitoring and supervision when their children enter adolescence cause adolescents to begin offending. We had argued that, although parents' monitoring and supervision were certainly negatively correlated with adolescent-onset delinquency, the direction of cause and effect was unclear, and our adolescence-limited theory would say that this correlation arises because teens' desires to gain autonomy via delinquency motivate them to evade their parents' supervision (Moffitt, 1993, p. 693). A longitudinal study of 1,000 Swedish 14-year-olds and their parents suggested that our interpretation may be correct (Kerr & Stattin, 2000). Adolescents actively controlled their parents' access to information about their activities, and teens who took part in deviant behavior limited their parents' capacity to monitor them. The study showed that parents' efforts to supervise and monitor were not very effective in controlling their teenagers' activities and could even backfire if teens felt controlled.

What research is needed? Clearly, there is not very much research testing whether measures of the maturity gap and social mimicry can account for adolescence-limited delinquency, so any new studies with this aim would add to our understanding. Agnew (2003) offers a cogent breakdown of maturity gap elements that can be tested. Short-term longitudinal studies of young teens might ask if a developmental increase in attitudes rejecting childhood and favoring autonomy is correlated with a growing interest in and approval of illicit activities. Moreover, there is the curious fact that life-course persistent antisocial individuals are rejected by peers in childhood but later become more popular with peers in adolescence. The theory of social mimicry predicted this shift in popularity, but more longitudinal research following individuals' changes in social standing is needed to understand it fully. Finally, we should consult historical and anthropological work to ascertain if historical periods and cultures characterized by a clearly demarcated transition from childhood dependency to adulthood rights and responsibilities are also characterized by relatively low levels of delinquency and adolescent rebelliousness.

The Hypothesis That Abstainers From Delinquency Are Rare Individuals, Who Are Excluded From Normative Peer Group Activities in Adolescence

If, as the theory says, adolescence-limited delinquency represents normative adaptational social behavior, then the existence of teens who abstain from delinquency requires an explanation. In other words, if ordinary teens take up delinquent behavior, then teens who eschew delinquency must be extraordinary in some way. The origi-

nal theory speculated that teens committing no antisocial behavior would be rare and that they must have either structural barriers that prevent them from learning about delinquency, no maturity gap because of early access to adult roles, or personal characteristics unappealing to other teens that cause them to be excluded from teen social group activities (Moffitt, 1993, pp. 689, 695). As noted above, research has shown that during adolescence, young people who place a high value on conforming to adults' rules become unpopular with their peers (Allen, Weissberg, & Hawkins, 1989).

We have studied male abstainers in the Dunedin cohort. Consistent with the rarity prediction, the Dunedin cohort contained only a very small group of males who avoided virtually any antisocial behavior during childhood and adolescence; abstainers were fewer than 10% of the cohort (Moffitt et al., 1996). The very small size of this group has been confirmed in other samples. Only 13% of 17-year-olds in the National Longitudinal Survey of Youth replied that they had "never" done any of the survey's 13 offense items (Piquero, Brezina, & Turner, 2005). Two longitudinal cohort studies used a theory-free method to characterize heterogeneous trajectories within repeated measures of aggressive behavior. Nagin and Tremblay (1999) detected an abstainer trajectory from childhood to adolescence that contained very few males, and Wiesner and Capaldi (2003) detected an abstainer trajectory from adolescence to adulthood containing even fewer males (5%).

The small group of Dunedin abstainers described themselves at age 18 on personality measures as extremely overcontrolled, fearful, interpersonally timid, and socially inept, and they were latecomers to sexual relationships (i.e., virgins at age 18). Dunedin abstainers fit the profile that Shedler and Block (1990) reported for youth who abstained from drug experimentation in a historical period when it was normative: overcontrolled, not curious, not active, not open to experience, socially isolated, and lacking social skills. Dunedin abstainers were unusually good students, fitting the profile of the compliant good student who during adolescence can become unpopular with peers (Allen et al., 1989; Bukowski et al., 2000). Other studies have suggested that abstention from delinquency and substance use during adolescence is associated with feeling socially isolated from peers (Dunford & Elliott, 1984), having few friends (Farrington & West, 1993), or being a loner (Tolone & Tieman, 1990). Such findings prompted Shedler and Block (1990, p. 627) to comment that abstention is "less the result of moral fiber or successful prevention programs than the result of relative alienation from peers and a characterological overcontrol of needs and impulses."

Dunedin's age-26 follow-up data confirmed that the teenaged abstainers did not become so-called adult-onset offenders (Moffitt et al., 2002). Although their teenage years had been socially awkward for them, their style became more successful in adulthood. As adults they retained their self-constrained personality, had virtually no crime or mental disorder, were likely to have settled into marriage, were delaying children (a desirable strategy for a generation needing prolonged education to succeed), were likely to be college educated, held high-status jobs, and expressed optimism about their own futures.

Another study of abstainers from delinquency was conducted using 1,600 17-year olds from the 1997 National Longitudinal Survey of Youth (Piquero et al., 2005). Consistent with the theoretical prediction, relative to participants in delinquency the abstainers were few in number, monitored more closely by their parents, more attached to teachers, and less physically mature; they reported less autonomy, dated less, and were less involved with friends who drank, smoked, tried drugs, and cut classes. However, an unexpected new finding was that abstainers were not wholly friendless. Rather they reported they had prosocial peers who "go to church regularly," "plan to go to college," and "participate in volunteer work." This study also attempted to test the theory's prediction that abstainers have personalities that make them unattractive to peers, using an item called "sadness/depression,"

intended to assess a morose, uncheerful style unlikely to appeal to peers. However, the study found that sadness/depression was correlated with delinquent participation, not abstention. This test was ambiguous because the depression item probably did not measure the overcontrolled, incurious, timid, socially inept personality style thought to preclude delinquency. Thus, this study provided some modest support for the taxonomy's view of abstainers as a minority existing outside the social scene that creates opportunities for delinquency among the teen majority. Moreover the study suggested the provocative new finding that abstainers do have friends, who are prosocial like themselves.

What research is needed? To our knowledge, our finding that abstainers are social introverts as teens remains to be confirmed or discounted by another study directly designed to test this hypothesis. Adolescent sociometric studies might ask if delinquent abstention is indeed correlated with unpopularity and social isolation. Further study of abstainers is critical for testing the hypothesis that the delinquency of adolescence-limited offenders is normative adaptational behavior by ordinary young people.

The Hypothesis That Life-Course Persistent Development Is Differentially Associated in Adulthood With Serious Offending and Violence

The original theory predicted that life-course persistent offenders, as compared to adolescence-limited offenders, would engage in a wider variety of offense types, including "more of the victim-oriented offenses, such as violence and fraud" (Moffitt, 1993, p. 695).

By the time the Dunedin cohort reached age 18, we reported that the life-course persistent pathway was differentially associated with conviction for violent crimes (Jeglum-Bartusch et al., 1997; Moffitt et al., 1996), whereas the adolescence-limited pathway was differentially associated with nonviolent delinquent offenses (Jeglum-Bartusch et al., 1997). These Dunedin findings are buttressed by reports from other samples that physical aggression usually begins in childhood and seldom in adolescence (e.g., Brame, Nagin, & Tremblay, 2001). Moreover, we had shown that preadolescent antisocial behavior that was accompanied by neuropsychological deficits predicted greater persistence of crime and more violence up to age 18 (Moffitt et al., 1994).

Our follow-up at age 26 confirmed that life-course persistent men as a group particularly differed from adolescence-limited men in the realm of violence, including violence against the women and children in their homes. This finding was corroborated with large effect sizes by data from multiple independent sources, including self-reports, informant reports, and official court conviction records (Moffitt et al., 2002). In a comparison of specific offenses, life-course persistent men tended to specialize in serious offenses (carrying a hidden weapon, assault, robbery, violating court orders), whereas adolescence-limited men specialized in non-serious offenses (theft less than $5, public drunkenness, giving false information on application forms, pirating computer software). Life-course persistent men accounted for five times their share of the cohort's violent convictions. Thus although they were a small group (10% of males), they accounted for 43% of the cohort's officially sanctioned violent crime.

Domestic violence against women and children at home was specifically predicted to be an outcome of the life-course persistent group (Moffitt, 1993). At the age-26 Dunedin follow-up this group's scores were elevated on self-reported and official conviction measures of abuse toward women, both physical abuse (e.g., beating her up, throwing her bodily) and controlling abuse (e.g., stalking her, restricting her access to her friends and family). Because the Dunedin cohort has been interviewed repeatedly about illicit behaviors for many years, study members now trust the Study's guarantee of confidentiality and can be asked questions about hitting children, with the expectation of giving valid responses. Life-course persis-

tent men were the most likely to report that they had hit a child out of anger, not in the course of normal discipline. Our finding that life-course persistent offenders perpetrated more domestic violence was supported by the Christchurch Study's finding that young adults with childhood-onset antisocial behavior engaged in significantly more violence against partners than did those with adolescent-onset antisocial behavior (Woodward, Fergusson, & Horwood, 2002). Similarly, a study of New York parolees reported that those defined as life-course persistent based on a childhood-onset offense record engaged in twice as much domestic violence as parolees with an adolescent-onset offense record (Mazerolle & Maahs, 2002).

In general, a large empirical literature shows that the strongest long-term predictors of violence are the same predictors implicated by our theory of life-course persistent offending: early-onset antisocial behavior, neurodevelopmental risk factors, and family risk factors (for a review, see Farrington, 1998). Moreover, research comparing violent crime with general nonviolent delinquency has shown that violence is differentially predicted by birth complications (Raine et al., 1997), minor physical anomalies (Arseneault et al., 2000), difficult temperament (Henry, Caspi, Moffitt, & Silva, 1996), and cognitive deficits (Piquero, 2001), each of which are hypothetical risks for life-course persistent development (for a review, see Raine, 2002). The Christchurch Study reported that people with serious childhood-onset conduct problems, compared to children without conduct problems, engaged in ten times more violent crime by age 25 (Fergusson, Horwood, & Ridder, 2005). The Patterns of Care Study of 1,715 service-users aged 6 to 17 years also compared childhood-onset versus adolescent-onset conduct disorder cases and reported that the childhood-onset group committed significantly more "bullying," but not more of the other physically aggressive conduct disorder symptoms (McCabe et al., 2001). However, this study did not have an adult follow-up. Lahey and colleagues (1998) reported more physical aggression associated with childhood-onset than with adolescent-onset conduct disorder.

What research is needed? The literature makes it clear that neurodevelopmental and family risks predict violence when it is measured on a continuum, but only a few studies have compared the adult violent outcomes of *groups* defined on the basis of early versus late antisocial onset. In addition, research is needed to clarify why life-course persistent offenders are more violent. Our theory implies that verbal cognitive deficits may limit their options for handling conflict (a neuropsychological explanation), that they may have learned in their families that violence is an effective way to manage conflict (a social-cognition explanation), and that broken attachment bonds lead to alienation from their potential victims (an attachment explanation; Moffitt, 1994; Moffitt & Caspi, 1995). All of these explanations specify early childhood as a critical period influencing adult violence.

But which, if any, of these explanatory processes are correct? Research using designs that control for genetic transmission of a predisposition to aggression in families has now documented that experiences in the family do promote childhood-onset aggression through processes that are environmentally mediated. Environmental effects on children's aggression have now been documented for exposure to parents' domestic violence (Jaffee, Moffitt, Caspi, Taylor, & Arseneault, 2002), being reared by an antisocial father (Jaffee, Moffitt, Caspi, & Taylor, 2003), being reared by a depressed mother (Kim-Cohen, Moffitt, Taylor, Pawlby, & Caspi, 2005), being a recipient of maternal hostility (Caspi et al., 2004), and being a victim of child maltreatment (Jaffee et al., 2004b). These studies controlled for familial liability to psychopathology, suggesting that the risk factors influence children through environmental experience. This information gives fresh impetus for research to uncover how these experiences are mediated via the child's thoughts and emotions to produce persistent aggression. Research is needed on mediating developmental processes, because findings will point to targets for intervention.

The Hypothesis That Childhood-Onset Antisocial Behavior Will Persist Into Middle Adulthood, Whereas Adolescent-Onset Antisocial Behavior Will Desist in Young Adulthood

Inherent in the name "life-course persistent" is the assertion that the antisocial activities of these individuals will persist across the life course. Though the whole population may decrease its antisocial participation as it ages, the life-course persistent individuals should remain at the top of the heap on antisocial behaviors. Thus, the taxonomy accepts that antisocial participation declines markedly in midlife, but nonetheless, it expects rank-order stability, particularly on age-relevant measures of antisocial activity. To test the differential desistance prediction, it is necessary to follow a cohort's antisocial behavior from childhood to adulthood, but only a few studies have done so.

We followed up the Dunedin cohort at age 26 (Moffitt et al., 2002) to test hypotheses critical to this part of the theory: childhood-onset antisocial behavior, but not adolescent-onset antisocial behavior, should be associated in adulthood with antisocial personality and continued serious antisocial behavior that expands into maladjustment in work life and victimization of partners and children (Moffitt, 1993, p. 695). Indeed, the adolescent-onset delinquents at 26 were still engaging in elevated levels of property offending and they had financial problems, but they did not show a pattern of serious offending. Interestingly, the adolescent-onset delinquents self-reported problems with mental health and substance dependence, but these difficulties were not corroborated by informants who knew them well. Consistent with the taxonomy's predictions, the childhood-onset delinquents at age 26 were the most elevated on psychopathic personality traits, mental health problems, substance dependence, numbers of children sired, financial problems, work problems, domestic abuse of women and children, and drug-related and violent crimes.

In a study of 4,000 California Youth Authority inmates followed into their thirties, significantly more early-starters than later-starters continued offending past age 21, past age 25, and past age 31. Moreover, early onset and low cognitive ability significantly predicted which inmates continued to offend past age 31 (Ge, Donnellan, & Wenk, 2001). A different study of California Youth Authority offenders looked in depth at predictors of criminal career duration among 377 parolees released on average at age 24 and followed for 12 years (Piquero, Brame, & Lynam, 2004). This study found that criminal career duration was predicted by low tested cognitive abilities and by the interaction between childhood poverty status and cognitive ability. Similarly, a large Swedish study reported less crime in adulthood among offenders who possessed positive personal characteristics resembling the characteristics of Dunedin adolescence-limited offenders (Stattin, Romelsjo, & Stenbacka, 1997).

The above-mentioned findings were obtained using groups of adolescence-limited and life-course persistent males defined by applying common-sense clinical cut-offs (e.g., Moffitt et al., 1996). However, in the past decade new analytic methods have become available for ascertaining whether distinctive trajectories exist within a population of individuals whose behavior has been measured repeatedly during development (Nagin, 1999; Nagin & Tremblay, 2001b; Roeder et al., 1999). These new semi-parametric methods offer several advantages over the clinical-cut-offs approach. First, the methods are agnostic with respect to taxonomic theories, and thus results are relatively free from investigator bias. Second, the methods can search a longitudinal data set to ask whether there is indeed more than one developmental trajectory in it, as a taxonomy implies. Third, they can ascertain the relative goodness of fit of competing models having one, two, three, four, or more trajectories to ascertain whether the taxonomic theory has specified the right number of developmental subtypes in the population. Fourth, they generate output from the best-fitting model that reveals whether its trajectories rise and fall at ages specified by the theory. Fifth, they generate output about which study participants belong to which trajectory, making it possible to ascertain whether each trajectory group approximates its population prevalence as specified by the theory. It is important to keep in mind that what researchers put into the method determines what they can get out, and therefore testing the taxonomy of life-course persistent and adolescence-limited antisocial behavior calls for representative samples, repeated measures taken at informative ages from childhood to adulthood, and measures of antisocial behavior that capture its heterotypic continuity across developmental periods. In these respects, the Dunedin data set, although not perfect, was pretty good fodder for the semi-parametric method.

We applied this method to counts of conduct disorder symptoms assessed (via self, mother, and teacher reports) for 525 male study members at ages 7, 9, 11, 13, 15, 18, 21, and 26 years (Moffitt et al., in preparation). Conduct disorder symptoms are fighting, bullying, lying, stealing, cruelty to people or animals, vandalism, and disobeying rules; three such symptoms earn a formal diagnosis. The model that best fit the Dunedin data detected the following groups (Figure 3.1). A life-course persistent group, 7% of the cohort, had a fairly stable high trajectory, exhibiting between four and seven antisocial symptoms at every age from 7 years to 26 years. This group had more symptoms than any of the other groups at every age. A group whose trajectory resembled an adolescence-limited pattern began with 2 symptoms at age 7 but increased to a peak of 4.5 symptoms at age 18, and then decreased on a slight downward trajectory to 3.5 symptoms at age 26. A recovery group, 21% of the cohort (similar to the "childhood-limited" or "low-level-chronic" groups described in an earlier section of this chapter), began with six symptoms at age 7, but decreased steadily with age, and had only one symptom by ages 21 and 26. An abstainer group, 11%, had less than one symptom on average at every age. Two further trajectory groups were identified. The first of these took an

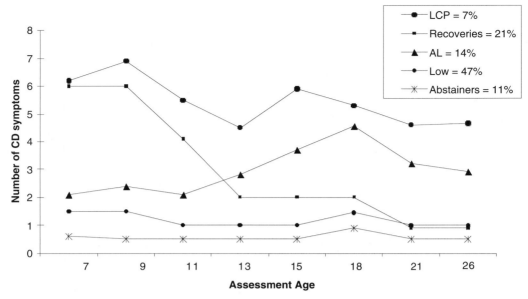

Figure 3.1. Twenty-year trajectories of conduct disorder symptoms among 525 Dunedin males.

adolescence-limited shape, but at a low level, and the second took a recovery shape, but also at a low level. For illustrative purposes in Figure 3.1 these two groups were collapsed into a consistently low group, 47% of the cohort, which had one to two symptoms on average at each age. Thus, the best-fitting model bore a not unreasonable resemblance to the taxonomy. Differential outcomes for the trajectory groups mirrored the outcomes for the clinically defined Dunedin groups (Moffitt et al., 2002). Males on the adolescence-limited trajectory were still engaging in property offending and substance abuse, but not serious offending at age 26. Males on the life-course persistent trajectory were the most elevated at age 26 on mental health problems and substance dependence, numbers of children sired, financial and work problems, domestic abuse of women and children, and drug-related and violent crimes.

Other cohort studies have applied trajectory analysis to repeated measures of antisocial behavior from childhood to adulthood. A British longitudinal study followed official crime records for a 1950s birth cohort of 400 men to age 32, detecting chronic and adolescence-limited trajectories that showed the expected differential desistance (Nagin et al., 1995). Unexpectedly, offenders defined as adolescence-limited had desisted from criminal offending according to their official police records, but according to their self-reports they continued into their thirties to drink heavily and get into fights. The South Holland epidemiological study followed 2,000 Dutch children from age 4 to 30 years (Bongers, Koot, van der Ende, Donker, & Verhulst, in review). This study reported two trajectories of young people with high levels of externalizing problems, as assessed by the Child Behavior Checklist (Achenbach, 1985). One trajectory was normative and distinguished by increasing truancy, alcohol, and drug use, but did not markedly increase the risk of adult offending. The other trajectory was characterized by increasing oppositional behavior and hot temper and was associated with elevated risk of serious and violent adult offending. Low trajectories were also detected.

The Rutgers Health and Human Development Project also followed its longitudinal sample into adulthood and reported a test of the taxonomy using nonparametric mixture modeling to detect trajectory groups (White, Bates, & Buyske, 2001). However, this paper's Figure 3.1, showing delinquency trajectories for the resulting groups, suggests that the group labeled "persistent" in this study was in reality adolescence-limited, because this group's trajectory showed very low levels of offending at ages 12 and 28, but a very pronounced adolescent-offending peak at age 18. This sample may not have contained life-course persistent members, because it was recruited via random telephone dialing with an initial 17% rate of refusal to the phone call and afterward a 52% completion rate for enrollment in data collection. Families with life-course persistent risk characteristics are known to be difficult to engage as research participants (Farrington, Gallagher, Morley, St. Ledger & West, 1990), and therefore they were probably among those who did not take part in the Rutgers Study. Given the strong possibility that groups were mislabeled in this study, it is unclear what to make of it in terms of the taxonomy.

The Oregon Youth Study applied trajectory analysis to 200 males followed from age 12 to 24 (Wiesner & Capaldi, 2003). In addition to the abstainer trajectory and the decreasing trajectory discussed in earlier sections of this chapter, the analysis also yielded a group whose antisocial behavior was chronically at the cohort's highest level (life-course persistent?) and a group whose antisocial behavior increased somewhat from age 12 to a peak at 19 and then decreased from age 20 to 24 (adolescence-limited?). It is not clear that Weisner and Capaldi would agree with our characterization of their groups; indeed, they used different labels for them. In any case, although these two groups seemed fairly similar in late adolescence, they diverged at the study's age 23–26 outcome point, with the chronic group showing much higher levels of alcohol use, drug use, and depression symptoms, as well as more adult antisocial behavior (Wiesner, Kim, & Capaldi, 2005).

One clear shortcoming of the available longitudinal database that has been used to test for the presence of life-course persistent versus adolescence-limited subtypes is that it is "right-hand censored"; in other words, study participants have generally been followed only until their twenties or thirties. What is needed is a cohort that represents the general population and that has been followed through the age period of risk for most criminal offending, up to midlife. Such a cohort does not yet exist. However, in the absence of the ideal representative cohort, there is one important study that warrants our focus. Sampson and Laub (2003) reported a follow-up of half of the Gluecks' sample, those who were adolescent inmates in Massachusetts in the 1940s. The authors constructed a unique database of official criminal records for almost 500 men, covering the period from age 7 years to the end of each offender's life, up to age 70 years. The study was noteworthy for collecting nationwide FBI records and for attending to artifacts in crime records arising from periods of incarceration or the offender's premature death. The authors' analyses were motivated by their skepticism about the idea of prospectively predicting a group of offenders who will account for a disproportionate amount of society's serious crime. Sampson and Laub (2003) reported two findings from the study that they believed challenge this idea. First, they found that almost all of the men in the Gluecks' sample desisted from criminal offending sooner or later. Second, they found heterogeneity in adulthood crime career patterns within the sample of adolescent inmates, and they found that this heterogeneity was not explained by measures of childhood risk.

Because the Sampson and Laub (2003) publication was represented as a challenge to the life-course persistent taxonomy, we must take a closer look at whether or not these two findings discredit the taxonomy. In so doing, it is useful to consider the nature of the sample studied by Sampson and Laub. According to the taxonomy, virtually all of the men studied would have been regarded as candidates for the life-course persistent subtype. They had been incarcerated as young adolescents as inmates in reform schools, a status reserved at that time for a very small fraction of a state's youth, those having established already by adolescence the most serious, persistent records of deviance that could not be controlled by parents or schools. It is well documented that as a group the boys had backgrounds of marked family adversity, social disadvantage, and childhood antisocial conduct. Sampson and Laub note details about the sample that fit the life-course persistent pattern, such as low mean IQ and mean first arrest at 11.9 years. Thus, this sample born in 1924–1932 probably comprised, relative to the much larger population of Boston males their age, a small subgroup who had started on the life-course persistent pathway.

Sampson and Laub's first finding was that the men in the Gluecks's sample desisted from criminal offending sooner or later: "aging out of crime appears to reflect a general process" (p. 577). Unfortunately, Sampson and Laub (2003) misrepresented the taxonomy's prediction. They set up a "straw" prediction: that life-course persistent offenders should carry on committing crimes at the same high rate from adolescence through old age, until their deaths. Clearly this was never implied by the taxonomy, because the original publication acknowledged the population-wide process of aging out of crime. It also explained that the term "life-course persistent antisocial behavior" did not require crime per se in old age; instead "persistent" referred to the persistence of antisocial personality characteristics or antisocial behaviors within the family (Moffitt, 1993, p. 680). The taxonomy's actual prediction was that delinquents like those in the Gluecks's sample would continue offending well beyond the age when most young men in their cohort population desisted. The study followed only reform-school boys, and thus it could not provide comparative data on crime careers for Boston men born 1924–1932. However, it is known that desistance from delinquency in young adulthood was the norm for cohorts such as this one, which came of age in the postwar era of near-full employment. In contrast to that norm, 84% of the Glueck study men were arrested between the ages of 17 and 24, 44% were arrested in their forties, 23% were arrested in their fifties, and 12% were arrested in their sixties. The

reform-school sample's mean crime career length was 25.6 years. It seems reasonable to believe that such remarkable statistics do not also describe the rest of the male population of Boston. Thus, the study's results seem reasonably consistent with the taxonomy's prediction that boys who begin life on the life-course persistent pathway will have unusually extended offending careers, thereby accounting for more than their share of the crime rate.

Sampson and Laub's second finding was that they found heterogeneity in adulthood crime career patterns within the Gluecks's sample. Again, the alternative hypothesis seems like a "straw man." The alternative would be that males who spent their youth and early adulthood on the life-course persistent pathway can show no variation in subsequent offending during midlife and aging, over a span of many years. Such uniformity is implausible, and the taxonomic theory did not make such a prediction. Within the Gluecks's sample six trajectories emerged from a semi-parametric group-based modeling analysis. Thus, the men, all of whom began on the life-course persistent pathway, varied subsequently in their age at desistance from crime and in their rate of offending up to the point of their desistance. Importantly, child and family characteristics did not discriminate among these six trajectories. On the one hand, this failure of discrimination is not surprising given that the cohort members' childhood backgrounds were almost uniformly high risk. On the other hand, this finding suggests that, to the extent that different crime careers emerge during midlife within a group of life-course persistent men, concurrent life experiences must account for the divergence. This would constitute an interesting extension to the taxonomic theory, on a topic it did not originally address: heterogeneity within life-course persistent delinquents in the ways they age out of crime.

This study by Sampson and Laub was well-executed and well-intentioned. The authors were concerned about practitioners who have reified the life-course persistent idea, treating it as if it describes a group having hard boundaries, made up of individual children who are easy to identify in early childhood and who deserve radical interventions to avert their inevitable destiny as predatory criminals. The authors' concern is well placed, and their efforts to dissuade such reification are laudable. To their credit, the authors point out that "the current bandwagon . . . is not consistent with the logic of Moffitt's actual argument" (p. 576). Nonetheless, to make their points, the authors inadvertently had to misrepresent the original taxonomy as having made predictions that it did not make. Here we set the record straight. Life-course persistent delinquents do not have to be arrested for illegal crimes steadily up to age 70, but they do have to maintain a constellation of antisocial attitudes, values, and proclivities that affect their behavior toward others. Life-course persistent delinquents do not have to all live exactly the same crime trajectory as they age out of crime; it is interesting to learn how their lives diverge. Laub and Sampson (2003) are leading the way in researching these new questions using qualitative as well as quantitative methods.

What research is needed? Overall, our theory's prediction that childhood-onset antisocial behavior persists longer into adulthood than adolescent-onset delinquency seems to be on fairly solid empirical footing. It has been known for decades that early onset of offending predicts a longer duration of crime career, and this association was recently affirmed by two careful reviews (Gendreau, Little, & Goggin, 1996; Krohn, Thornberry, Rivera, & LeBlanc, 2001). Nonetheless, the adolescence-limited groups in the Dunedin cohort and other cohorts continued to experience some adjustment problems as adults, and we need research to understand what accounts for this finding. The original taxonomy put forward the hypothesis that we should expect some adolescence-limited delinquents to recover to good adult adjustment later than others and that this age variation might be explained by "snares," such as a conviction record that harms job prospects (Moffitt, 1993, p. 691). The idea is that engaging in even limited delinquency

as a young person can diminish the probability of subsequent good outcomes, particularly if one is caught and sanctioned. Also important is the information emerging from the work of Laub and Sampson (2003) pointing to marked heterogeneity within the life-course persistent group in middle and late life, suggesting research into midlife turning-point experiences is needed. Overall, longitudinal studies are needed that follow the life-course persistent, low-level chronic, abstainer, and adolescence-limited groups to reveal the very long-term implications of their experiences in the first two decades of life.

Conclusions

Before 1993, virtually no research compared delinquent subtypes defined on a developmental basis, but now this research strategy has become almost commonplace. Many research teams have assessed representative samples with prospective measures of antisocial behavior from childhood to adulthood, and this has enabled comparisons based on age of onset and persistence. Now that the requisite databases are available, many hypotheses derived from the original taxonomic theory are being tested. After 10 years of research, what can be stated with some certainty is that the hypothesized life-course persistent antisocial individual exists, at least during the first three decades of life. Consensus about this group has emerged from all studies that have applied trajectory-detection analyses to a representative cohort sample having longitudinal repeated measures of antisocial behavior. Tremblay et al. (2004) detected a "high physical aggression" group constituting 14% of Canadian children followed from age 17 months to 42 months. Broidy et al. (2003) detected a "chronic aggressive" group constituting 3 to 11% of children followed from age 6 to 13 years in six different cohorts from three countries. Maughan et al. (2001) detected a "stable high aggressive" group constituting 12% of North Carolina youth followed from age 9 to 16 years. Brame et al. (2001) detected a "high chronic aggressive" group constituting 3% of Canadian youth followed from age 6 to 17 years. Raine et al. (2005) detected a "life-course persistent path" group that constituted 13% of Pittsburgh youth followed from age 7 to 17 years. Fergusson et al. (2000) detected a "chronic offender" group constituting 6% of Christchurch youth followed from age 12 to 18 years. Chung et al. (2002) detected a "chronic offender" group constituting 7% of Seattle youth followed from age 13 to 21 years. Wiesner and Capaldi (2003) detected a "chronic high-level" group constituting 16% of Oregon youth followed from age 12 to 24 years. Moffitt et al. (in preparation) detected a "high-persistent" group that constituted 7% of Dunedin young people followed from age 7 to 26 years. Nagin et al. (1995) detected a "high-level chronic" group that constituted 12% of London males followed from age 10 to 32 years. So far as we know, no research team that has looked for a persistent antisocial group has failed to find it.

Other studies not reviewed here are now addressing how the life-course persistent versus adolescence-limited types are related to gender, race, genetic risk, and adult personality outcomes. However, in this chapter, page limitations precluded reviewing those literatures. They are reviewed in Moffitt (2006). Some predictions from the taxonomy have not been tested sufficiently, including the following hypotheses: Life-course persistent antisocial individuals will be at high risk in midlife for poor physical health, cardiovascular disease, and early disease morbidity and mortality. Adolescence-limited offenders must rely on peer support for crime, but life-course persistent offenders should be willing to offend alone (although in adolescence they serve as magnets for less expert offenders). "Snares" (such as a criminal record, incarceration, addiction, or truncated education without credentials) should explain variation in the age at desistence from crime during the adult age period, particularly among adolescence-limited offenders. The two groups should react differently to turning-point opportu-

nities: as they enter adulthood, adolescence-limited offenders should get good partners and jobs that help them to desist from crime, whereas life-course persistent offenders should selectively get undesirable partners and jobs and in turn expand their repertoire as young adults into domestic abuse and workplace crime. It is pleasing that the 1993 taxonomy has generated interest and research. Some findings have been faithful to the hypotheses originally formulated. Other findings have pointed to important revisions needed to improve the fit between the taxonomy and nature, and some findings raise serious challenges to aspects of the taxonomy. All three kinds of findings are much appreciated.

References

Achenbach, T. M. (1985). *Assessment and taxonomy of child and adolescent psychopathology.* Newbury Park, CA: Sage.

Agnew, R. (2003). An integrated theory of the adolescent peak in offending. *Youth and Society, 34,* 263–299.

Aguilar, B., Sroufe, L. A., Egeland, B., & Carlson, E. (2000). Distinguishing the early-onset-persistent and adolescent-onset antisocial behavior types: From birth to 16 years. *Development and Psychopathology, 12,* 109–132.

Allen, J. P., Weissberg, R. P., & Hawkins, J. A. (1989). The relation between values and social competence in early adolescence. *Developmental Psychology, 25,* 458–464.

Alnaes, R., & Torgersen, S. (1988). The relationship between DSM-III symptom disorders (Axis I) and personality disorders (Axis II) in an outpatient population. *Acta Psychiatrica Scandinavica, 78,* 485–492.

American Psychiatric Association (1994). *Diagnostic and Statistical Manual of Mental Disorders* (4th ed.). Washington, D.C.: Author.

Arnett, J. J. (2000). Emerging adulthood: A theory of development from the late teens through the twenties. *American Psychologist, 55,* 469–480.

Arseneault, L., Tremblay, R. E., Boulerice, B., & Saucier, J.-F. (2002). Obstetric complications and adolescent violent behaviors: Testing two developmental pathways. *Child Development, 73,* 496–508.

Arseneault, L., Tremblay, R. E., Boulerice, B., Seguin, J. R., & Saucier, J.-F. (2000). Minor physical anomalies and family adversity as risk factors for adolescent violent delinquency. *American Journal of Psychiatry, 157,* 917–923.

Bongers, I. L., Koot, H. M., van der Ende, J., Donker, A., & Verhulst, F. C. (in review). *Predicting delinquency in young adulthood from developmental pathways of externalizing behavior.* Manuscript submitted for publication.

Brame, R., Bushway, S., & Paternoster, R. (1999). *On the use of panel research designs* and random effects models to investigate static and dynamic theories of criminal offending. *Criminology, 37,* 599–642.

Brame, R., Nagin, D. S., & Tremblay, R. E. (2001). Developmental trajectories of physical aggression from school entry to late adolescence. *The Journal of Child Psychology and Psychiatry, 42,* 503–512.

Brennan, P. A., Hall, J., Bor, W., Najman, J. M., & Williams, G. (2003). Integrating biological and social processes in relation to early-onset persistent aggression in boys and girls. *Developmental Psychology, 39,* 309–323.

Brezina, T. (2000). Delinquent problem-solving: An interpretive framework for criminological theory and research. *Journal of Research in Crime and Delinquency, 37,* 3–30.

Broidy, L., Broidy, L. M., Nagin, D. S., Tremblay, R. E., et al. (2003). Developmental trajectories of childhood disruptive behaviour disorders and adolescent delinquency: A six-sample replication. *Developmental Psychology, 39,* 222–245.

Bukowski, W. M., Sippola, L. K., & Newcomb, A. F. (2000). Variations in patterns of attraction to same-and other-sex peers during early adolescence. *Developmental Psychology. 36,* 147–154.

Caspi, A., Lynam, D., Moffitt, T. E., & Silva, P. A. (1993). Unraveling girls' delinquency: Biological, dispositional, and contextual contributions to adolescent misbehavior. *Developmental Psychology, 29,* 19–30.

Caspi, A., Moffitt, T. E., Morgan, J., Rutter, M., Taylor, A., Arseneault, L., Tully, L., Jacobs, C., Kim-Cohen, J., & Polo-Tomas, M. (2004). Maternal expressed emotion predicts children's antisocial behavior problems: Using MZ-twin differences to identify environmental effects on behavioral development. *Developmental Psychology, 40,* 149–161.

Chung, I., Hill, L. D., Hawkins, J. D., Gilchrist, K. G., & Nagin, D. (2002). Childhood predictors of offense trajectories. *Journal of Research in Crime and Delinquency, 39,* 60–90.

Cicchetti, D. & Cohen, D. J. (1995). Perspectives on developmental psychopathology. In D. Cicchetti & D. Cohen (Eds.), *Developmental psychopathology* (Vol. 1, pp. 3–20) New York: Wiley.

Cicchetti, D., & Walker, E. R. (2003). *Neurobiological mechanisms in psychopathology.* New York: Cambridge University Press.

Cillessen, A. H. N., & Mayeux, L. (2004). From censure to reinforcement: Developmental changes in the association between aggression and social status. *Child Development, 75,* 147–163.

Dean, C. W., Brame, R., & Piquero, A. R. (1996). Criminal propensities, discrete groups of offenders, and persistence in crime. *Criminology, 34,* 547–574.

DiLalla, L. F., & Gottesman, I. I. (1989). Heterogeneity of causes for delinquency and criminality: Lifespan perspectives. *Development and Psychopathology, 1,* 339–349.

Dishion, T. J., McCord, J., & Poulin, F. (1999). Iatrogenic effects in interventions that aggregate high-risk youth. *The American Psychologist, 54,* 1–10.

Donnellan, M. B., Ge, X., & Wenk, E. (2000). Cognitive abilities in adolescence-limited and life-course-persistent criminal offenders. *Journal of Abnormal Psychology, 109,* 396–402.

Dunford, F. W., & Elliott, D. S. (1984). Identifying career offenders using self-reported data. *Journal of Research in Crime and Delinquency, 21,* 57–86.

D'Unger, A. V., Land, K. C., McCall, P. L., & Nagin, D. S.,(1998). How many latent classes of delinquent/criminal careers? *American Journal of Sociology, 103,* 1593–1630.

Eggleston, E. P., & Laub, J. H. (2002). The onset of adult offending: A neglected dimension of the criminal career. *Journal of Criminal Justice, 30,* 603–622.

Eley, T. C., Lichtenstein, P., & Moffitt, T. E. (2003). A longitudinal analysis of the etiology of aggressive and non-aggressive antisocial behaviour. *Development and Psychopathology, 15,* 155–168.

Elliott, D. S. (1994). Serious violent offenders: Onset, developmental course, and termination. *Criminology, 32,* 1021.

Elliott, D. S., Huizinga, D., & Menard, S. (1989). *Multiple problem youth: Delinquency, substance use, and mental health problems.* New York: Springer-Verlag.

Farrington, D. P. (1998). Predictors, causes, and correlates of male youth violence. *Crime and Justice: A Review of Research, 24*, 421–476.

Farrington, D. P., Gallagher, B., Morley, L., St. Ledger, R. J., & West, D. (1988). Are there any successful men from criminogenic backgrounds? *Psychiatry, 51*, 116–130.

Farrington, D. P., Gallagher, B., Morley, L., St. Ledger, R. J., & West, D. (1990). Minimizing attrition in longitudinal research. In L. R. Bergman & D. Magnusson (Eds.), *Data quality in longitudinal research* (pp. 122–147). New York: Cambridge University Press.

Farrington, D. P., Jolliffe, D., Hawkins, J. D., Catalano, R. F., Hill, K. G., & Kosterman, R. (2003). Comparing delinquency careers in court records and self-reports. *Criminology, 41*, 933–958.

Farrington, D. P., Ohlin, L., & Wilson, J. Q. (1986). *Understanding and controlling crime.* New York: Springer-Verlag.

Farrington, D. P., & West, D. J. (1993). Criminal, penal and life histories of chronic offenders. *Criminal Behaviour and Mental Health, 3*, 492–523.

Fergusson, D. M., Horwood, L. J., & Nagin, D. S. (2000). Offending trajectories in a New Zealand birth cohort. *Criminology, 38*, 525–552.

Fergusson, D. M., Horwood, L. J., & Ridder, E. M. (2005). Show me the child at seven: The consequences of conduct problems in childhood for psychosocial functioning in adulthood. *Journal of Child Psychology and Psychiatry, 46*(8), 837–849.

Ferri, E., Bynner, J., & Wadsworth, M. (2003). *Changing Britain, changing lives: Three generations at the turn of the century.* London: Institute of Education, University of London.

Furstenberg, F. F. Jr., Cook, T. D., Sampson, R., & Slap, G. (Eds.). (2002). *Early adulthood in cross-national perspective.* London: Sage Publications.

Galambos, N. L., Barker, E. T., & Tilton-Weaver, L. C. (2003). Who gets caught in the maturity gap? A study of pseudomature, immature, and mature adolescents. *International Journal of Behavioral Development, 27*, 253–263.

Ge, X., Conger, R. D., Cadoret, R. J., Neiderhauser, J. M., Yates, W., Troughton, E., et al. (1996). The developmental interface between nature and nurture: A mutual influence model of child antisocial behavior and parent behaviors. *Developmental Psychology, 32*, 574–589.

Ge, X., Donnellan, M. B., & Wenk, E. (2001). The development of persistent criminal offending in males. *Criminal Justice and Behavior, 28*, 731–755.

Gendreau, P., Little, T., & Goggin, C. (1996). A meta-analysis of the predictors of adult offender recidivism: What works! *Criminology, 34*, 575–607.

Henry, B., Caspi, A., Moffitt, T. E., & Silva, P. A. (1996). Temperamental and familial predictors of violent and non-violent criminal convictions: From age 3 to age 18. *Developmental Psychology, 32*, 614–623.

Howell, J. C., & Hawkins, J. D. (1998). Prevention of youth violence. *Crime and Justice: A Review of Research, 24*, 263–316.

Jaffee, S. R., Caspi, A., Moffitt, T. E., Polo-Tomas, M., Price, T., & Taylor, A. (2004a). The limits of child effects: Evidence for genetically mediated child effects on corporal punishment, but on physical maltreatment. *Developmental Psychology, 40*, 1047–1058.

Jaffee, S. R., Caspi, A., Moffitt, T. E., & Taylor, A. (2004b). Physical maltreatment victim to antisocial child: Evidence of an environmentally mediated process. *Journal of Abnormal Psychology, 113*, 44–55.

Jaffee, S. R., Moffitt, T. E., Caspi, A., Taylor, A., & Arseneault, L. (2002). The influence of adult domestic violence on children's internalizing and externalizing problems: An environmentally-informative twin study. *Journal of the American Academy of Child and Adolescent Psychiatry, 41*, 1095–1103.

Jaffee, S. R., Moffitt, T. E., Caspi, A., & Taylor, A. (2003). Life with (or without) father: The benefits of living with two biological parents depend on the father's antisocial behavior. *Child Development, 74*, 109–126.

Jeglum-Bartusch, D., Lynam, D., Moffitt, T. E., & Silva, P. A. (1997). Is age important? Testing general versus developmental theories of antisocial behavior. *Criminology, 35*, 13–47.

Junger-Tas, J., Terlouw, G., & Klein, M. (1994). *Delinquent behaviour among young people in the western world.* Amsterdam: Kugler Publications.

Kerr, M., & Stattin, H. (2000). What parents know, how they know it, and several forms of adolescent adjustment: Further support for reinterpretation of monitoring. *Developmental Psychology, 36*, 366–380.

Kim-Cohen, J., Moffitt, T. E., Taylor, A., Pawlby, S., & Caspi, A. (2005). Maternal depression and child antisocial behavior: Nature and nurture effects. *Archives of General Psychiatry, 62,* 173–181.

Kjelsberg, E. (1999). Adolescent-limited versus life-course persistent criminal behaviour in adolescent psychiatric inpatients. *European Child and Adolescent Psychiatry, 8,* 276–282.

Kratzer, L., & Hodgins, S. (1999). A typology of offenders: A test of Moffitt's theory among males and females from childhood to age 30. *Criminal Behaviour and Mental Health, 9,* 57–73.

Krohn, M. D., Thornberry, T. P., Rivera, C., & LeBlanc, M. (2001). Later delinquency careers of very young offenders. In R. Loeber & D. P. Farrington (Eds.), *Child delinquents* (pp. 67–94). Thousand Oaks, CA: Sage.

LaCourse, E., Nagin, D., Tremblay, R. E., Vitaro, F., & Claes, M. (2003). Developmental trajectories of boys' delinquent group membership and facilitation of violent behaviors during adolescence. *Development & Psychopathology, 15,* 183–197.

Lahey, B. B., Loeber, R., Quay, H. C., Applegate, B., Shaffer, D., Waldman, I., et al. (1998). Validity of DSM-IV subtypes of conduct disorder based on age of onset. *Journal of the American Academy of Child and Adolescent Psychiatry, 37,* 435–442.

Lahey, B. B., Waldman, I. D., & McBurnett, K. (1999). The development of antisocial behavior: An integrative causal model. *Journal of Child Psychology and Psychiatry, 40,* 669–682.

Laub, J. H., & Sampson, R. J. (2001). Understanding desistance from crime. *Crime and Justice: A Review of Research, 28,* 1–69.

Laub, J. H., & Sampson, R. J. (2003). *Shared beginnings, divergent lives: Delinquent boys to age 70.* Cambridge, MA: Harvard University Press.

Laucht, M. (2001). Antisoziales Verhalten im jugendalter: Entstehungsbedingungen und Verlaufsformen. *Zeitschrift fur Kinder-Jugendpsychiatry, 29,* 297–311.

Loeber, R., & LeBlanc, M. (1990). Toward a developmental criminology. *Crime and Justice: A Review of Research, 7,* 29–149.

Luthar, S. S., & McMahon, T. J. (1996). Peer reputation among inner-city adolescents: Structure and correlates. *Journal of Research on Adolescence, 6,* 581–603.

Magnusson, D., Klintberg, B., & Stattin, H. (1994). Juvenile and persistent offenders: Behavioral and physiological characteristics. In R. D. Kettelinus & M. Lamb (Eds.), *Adolescent problem behaviors* (pp. 81–91). Hillsdale, NJ: Erlbaum.

Maughan, B., Pickles, A., Rowe, R., Costello, E. J., & Angold, A. (2001). Developmental trajectories of aggressive and non-aggressive conduct problems. *Journal of Quantitative Criminology, 16,* 199–222.

Mazerolle, P., Brame, R., Paternoster, R., Piquero, A., & Dean, C. (2000). Onset age, persistence, and offending versatility: Comparisons across gender. *Criminology, 38,* 1143–1172.

Mazerolle, P., & Maahs, J. (2002). *Developmental theory and battering incidents: Examining the relationship between discrete offender groups and intimate partner violence.* Washington, DC: U.S. National Institute of Justice, U.S. Dept. of Justice.

McCabe, K. M., Hough, R., Wood, P. A., & Yeh, M. (2001). Childhood and adolescent onset conduct disorder: A test of the developmental taxonomy. *Journal of Abnormal Child Psychology, 29,* 305–316.

McCall, R. B., & Carriger, M. S. (1993). A meta-analysis of infant habituation and recognition memory performance as predictors of later IQ. *Child Development, 64,* 57–79.

Moffitt, T. E. (1990). Juvenile delinquency and attention-deficit disorder: Developmental trajectories from age three to fifteen. *Child Development, 61,* 893–910.

Moffitt, T. E. (1993). "Life-course-persistent" and "adolescence-limited" antisocial behavior: A developmental taxonomy. *Psychological Review, 100,* 674–701.

Moffitt, T. E. (1994). Natural histories of delinquency. In E. Weitekamp & H. J. Kerner (Eds.), *Cross-national longitudinal research on human development and criminal behavior* (pp. 3–61). Dordrecht, The Netherlands: Kluwer Academic Press.

Moffitt, T. E. (1997). Adolescence-limited and life-course-persistent offending: A complementary pair of developmental theories. In T. Thornberry (Ed.), *Advances in criminological theory: Developmental theories of crime and delinquency* (pp. 11–54). London: Transaction Press.

Moffitt, T. E. (2003). Life-course persistent and adolescence-limited antisocial behaviour: A 10-year research review and a research agenda. In B. Lahey, T.E. Moffitt, & A. Caspi (Eds.),

The causes of conduct disorder and serious juvenile delinquency (pp. 49–75). New York: Guilford.

Moffitt, T. E. (2006). Life-course persistent and adolescence-limited antisocial behavior. In D. Cicchetti & D. Cohen (Eds.), *Developmental psychopathology* (2nd ed.). New York: Wiley.

Moffitt, T. E., Arseneault, L., Taylor, A., Nagin, D., Milne, B., & Harrington, H. (in preparation). Life-course persistent and adolescence-limited antisocial trajectories detected in a 26-year longitudinal study using theory-agnostic semiparametric modelling.

Moffitt, T. E., & Caspi, A. (1995). The continuity of maladaptive behavior: From description to explanation in the study of antisocial behavior. In D. Cicchetti & D. Cohen (Eds.), *Developmental psychopathology* (Vol. 2). New York: Wiley.

Moffitt, T. E., & Caspi, A. (2001). Childhood predictors differentiate life-course persistent and adolescence-limited pathways among males and females. *Development and Psychopathology, 13,* 355–375.

Moffitt, T. E., Caspi, A., Dickson, N., Silva, P. A., & Stanton, W. (1996). Childhood-onset versus adolescent-onset antisocial conduct in males: Natural history from age 3 to 18. *Development and Psychopathology, 8,* 399–424.

Moffitt, T. E., Caspi, A., Harrington, H., & Milne, B. (2002). Males on the life-course persistent and adolescence-limited antisocial pathways: Follow-up at age 26. *Development and Psychopathology, 14,* 179–206.

Moffitt, T. E., Caspi, A., Rutter, M., & Silva, P. A. (2001). *Sex differences in antisocial behaviour: Conduct disorder, delinquency, and violence in the Dunedin longitudinal study.* Cambridge, UK: Cambridge University Press.

Moffitt, T. E., Lynam, D., & Silva, P. A. (1994). Neuropsychological tests predict persistent male delinquency. *Criminology, 32,* 101–124.

Nagin, D. S. (1999). Analyzing developmental trajectories: Semi-parametric, group-based approach. *Psychological Methods, 4,* 139–177.

Nagin, D. S., Farrington, D. P., & Moffitt, T. E. (1995). Life-course trajectories of different types of offenders. *Criminology, 33,* 111–139.

Nagin, D. S., & Tremblay, R. E. (1999). Trajectories of boys' physical aggression, opposition, and hyperactivity on the path to physically violent and non-violent juvenile delinquency. *Child Development, 70,* 1181–1196.

Nagin, D. S., & Tremblay, R. E. (2001a). Parental and early childhood predictors of persistent physical aggression in boys from kindergarten to high school. *Archives of General Psychiatry, 58,* 389–394.

Nagin, D. S., & Tremblay, R. E. (2001b). Analyzing developmental trajectories of distinct but related behaviors: A group-based method. *Psychological Medicine, 6,* 18–34.

National Institutes of Health (2004). *State-of-the-science consensus statement on preventing violence and related health-risking social behaviors in adolescents.* Bethesda, MD.

National Institute of Mental Health. (2000). *Child and adolescence violence research* (NIH Publication No. 00–4706). Bethesda, MD.

Neugebauer, R., Hoek, H. W., & Susser, E. (1999). Prenatal exposure to wartime famine and development of antisocial personality disorder in early adulthood. *Journal of the American Medical Association, 282,* 455–462.

O'Connor, T. G., Deater-Deckard, K., Fulker, D., Rutter, M., & Plomin, R. (1998). Genotype-environment correlations in later childhood and early adolescence: Antisocial behavioral problems and coercive parenting. *Developmental Psychology, 34,* 970–981.

Osgood, D. W. (1998). Interdisciplinary integration: Building criminology by stealing from our friends. *The Criminologist, 23,* 1–4.

Paternoster, R., & Brame, R. (1997). Multiple routes to delinquency?: A test of developmental and general theories of crime. *Criminology, 35,* 49–84.

Patterson, G. R., DeGarmo, D. S., & Knutson, N. (2000). Hyperactive and antisocial behaviors: Comorbid or two points in the same process? *Development and Psychopathology, 12,* 91–106.

Patterson, G. R., Forgatch, M. S., Yoerger, K. L., & Stoolmiller, M. (1998). Variables that initiate and maintain an early onset trajectory for juvenile offending. *Development and Psychopathology, 10,* 531–548.

Patterson, G. R., & Yoerger, K. L. (1997). A developmental model for later-onset delinquency. In R. Deinstbier & D.W. Osgood (Eds.), *Motivation and delinquency* (pp. 119–177). Lincoln, NE: University of Nebraska Press.

Piquero, A. R. (2001). Testing Moffitt's neuropsychological variation hypothesis for the prediction of life-course persistent offending. *Psychology, Crime and Law, 7,* 193–216.

Piquero, A. R., Brame, R., & Lynam, D. (2004). Studying the factors related to career length? *Crime and Delinquency, 50,* 412–435.

Piquero, A. R., & Brezina, T. (2001). Testing Moffitt's account of adolescence-limited delinquency. *Criminology, 39,* 353–370.

Piquero, A. R., Brezina, T., & Turner, M. G. (2005). Testing Moffitt's account of delinquency abstinence. *Journal of Research in Crime and Delinquency, 42 (1),* 27–54.

Raine, A.,(2002). Annotation: The role of prefrontal deficits, low autonomic arousal, and early health factors in the development of antisocial and aggressive behaviour in children. *Journal of Child Psychology and Psychiatry, 43,* 417–434.

Raine, A., Brennan, P., & Mednick, S. A. (1994). Birth complications combined with early maternal rejection at age 1 year predispose to violent crime at age 18 years. *Archives of General Psychiatry, 51,* 984–988.

Raine, A., Brennan, P., & Mednick, S. A. (1997). Interaction between birth complications and early maternal rejection in predisposing individuals to adult violence: Specificity to serious, early-onset violence. *American Journal of Psychiatry, 154,* 1265–1271.

Raine, A., Brennan, P., Mednick, B., & Mednick, S. A. (1996). High rates of violence, crime, academic problems, and behavioral problems in males with both early neuromotor deficits and unstable family environments. *Archives of General Psychiatry, 53,* 544–549.

Raine, A., Lencz, T., Taylor, K., Hellige, J. B., Bihrle, S., Lacasse, L., Lee, M., Ishikawa, S. S., & Colletti, P. (2003). Corpus callosum abnormalities in psychopathic antisocial individuals. *Archives of General Psychiatry, 60,* 1134–1142.

Raine, A., Moffitt, T. E., Caspi, A., Loeber, R., Stouthamer-Loeber, M., & Lynam, D. (2005). Neurocognitive impairments in boys on the life-course persistent antisocial path. *Journal of Abnormal Psychology, 114 (1),* 38–49.

Raine, A., Yaralian, P. S., Reynolds, C., Venables, P. H., & Mednick, S. A. (2002). Spatial but not verbal cognitive deficits at age 3 years in persistently antisocial individuals. *Development & Psychopathology, 14,* 25–44.

Riggins-Caspers, K. M., Cadoret, R. J., Knutson, J. F., & Langbehn, D. (2003). Biology-environment interaction and evocative biology-environment correlation: Contributions of harsh discipline and parental psychopathology to problem adolescent behaviors. *Behavior Genetics, 33,* 205–220.

Robins, L. N. (1966). *Deviant children grown up.* Baltimore: Williams & Wilkins.

Rodkin, P. C., Farmer, T. W., Pearl, R., & Van Acker, R. (2000). Heterogeneity of popular boys: Antisocial and prosocial configurations. *Developmental Psychology, 36,* 14–24.

Roeder, K., Lynch, K. G., & Nagin, D. S. (1999). Modeling uncertainty in latent class membership: A case study in criminology. *Journal of the American Statistical Association, 94,* 766–776.

Ruchkin, V., Koposov, R., Vermeiren, R., & Schwab-Stone, M. (2003). Psychopathology and the age of onset of conduct problems in juvenile delinquents. *Journal of Clinical Psychiatry, 64,* 913–920.

Sampson, R. J., & Laub, J. H. (2003). Life-course desisters? Trajectories of crime among delinquent boys followed to age 70. *Criminology, 41,* 555–592.

Scholte, E. M. (1999). Factors predicting continued violence into adulthood. *Journal of Adolescence, 22,* 3–20.

Scott, E. S., & Grisso, T. (1997). The evolution of adolescence: A developmental perspective on juvenile justice reform. *Journal of Criminal Law and Criminology, 88,* 137–189.

Shedler, J., & Block, J. (1990). Adolescent drug use and psychological health. *American Psychologist, 45,* 612–630.

Sigman, M., Cohen, S. E., & Beckwith, L. (1997). Why does infant attention predict adolescent intelligence? *Infant Behavior and Development, 20,* 133–140.

Silverthorn, P., & Frick, P. J. (1999). Developmental pathways to antisocial behavior: The delayed-onset pathway in girls. *Development and Psychopathology, 11,* 101–126.

Simons, R. L., Wu, C. I., Conger, R., & Lorenz, F. O. (1994). Two routes to delinquency: Differences between early and late starters in the impact of parenting and deviant peers. *Criminology, 32,* 247–275.

Salekin, R. T., Yff, R. M., Neumann, C. S., Leistico, A. R., & Zalot, A. A. (2002). Juvenile transfer to adult courts: A look at the prototypes of dangerousness, sophistication-maturity, and amenability to treatment through a legal lens. *Psychology, Public Policy, and Law, 8,* 373–410.

Stattin, H., Romelsjo, A., & Stenbacka, M. (1997). Personal resources as modifiers of the risk for future criminality. *British Journal of Criminology, 37,* 198–223.

Taylor, J., Iacono, W. G., & McGue, M. (2000). Evidence for a genetic etiology for early-onset delinquency. *Journal of Abnormal Psychology*, *109*, 634–643.

Tibbetts, S., & Piquero, A. (1999). The influence of gender, low birth weight and disadvantaged environment on predicting early onset of offending: A test of Moffitt's interactional hypothesis. *Criminology*, *37*, 843–878.

Tolan, P. H., & Thomas, P. (1995). The implications of age of onset for delinquency risk. II: Longitudinal data. *Journal of Abnormal Child Psychology*, *23*, 157–181.

Tolone, W. L., & Tieman, C. R. (1990). Drugs, delinquency, and "nerds": Are loners deviant? *Journal of Drug Education*, *20*, 153–162.

Tremblay, R. E., Nagin, D. S., Seguin, J. R., Zoccolillo, M., Zelazo, P. D., Boivin, M., et al. (2004). Physical aggression during early childhood: Trajectories and predictors. *Pediatrics*, *114*, e43-e50.

U.S. Office of Juvenile Justice and Delinquency Prevention (1998). *Serious and violent juvenile offenders*. Washington, DC: U.S. Department of Justice.

U.S. Surgeon General. (2001). *Youth violence: A report of the surgeon general*. Retrieved from http://www.surgeongeneral.gov/library/youthviolence/.

Vaaranen, H. (2001). The blue-collar boys at leisure: An ethnography on cruising club boys' drinking, driving, and passing time in cars in Helsinki. *Mannsforsking*, *1*, 48–57.

Vermeiren, R. (2002). Psychopathology and delinquency in adolescents: A descriptive and developmental perspective. *Clinical Psychology Review*, *583*, 1–42.

Vitaro, F., Tremblay, R. E., Kerr, M., Pagani, L., & Bukowski, W. M. (1997). Disruptiveness, friends' characteristics, and delinquency in early adolescence: A test of two competing models of development. *Child Development*, *68*, 676–689.

White, H. R., Bates, M. E., & Buyske, S. (2001). Adolescence-limited versus persistent delinquency: Extending Moffitt's hypothesis into adulthood. *Journal of Abnormal Psychology*, *110*, 600–609.

Wiesner, M., & Capaldi, D. M. (2003). Relations of childhood and adolescent factors to offending trajectories of young men. *Journal of Research in Crime and Delinquency*, *40*, 231–262.

Wiesner, M., Kim, H. K., & Capaldi, D. (2005). Developmental trajectories of offending: Validation and prediction to young adult alcohol use, drug use, and depressive symptoms. *Development and Psychopathology*, *17*, 251–270.

Woodward, L. J., Fergusson, D. M., & Horwood, L. J. (2002). Romantic relationships of young people with early and late onset antisocial behavior problems. *Journal of Abnormal Child Psychology*, *30*, 231–243.

World Health Organization (2002). *World report on violence and health*. Geneva: Author.

Zebrowitz, L. A., Andreoletti, C., Collins, M., Lee, S. H., & Blumenthal, J. (1998). Bright, bad, babyfaced boys: Appearance stereotypes do not always yield self-fulfilling prophecy effects. *Journal of Personality and Social Psychology*, *75*, 1300–1320.

Zucker, R. A., Ellis, D. A., Fitzgerald, H. E., Bingham, C. R., & Sanford, K. (1996). Other evidence for at least two alcoholisms: II. Life-course variation in antisociality and heterogeneity of alcoholic outcome. *Development and Psychopathology*, *8*, 831–848.

Part II

BIOLOGICAL BASES
OF VIOLENCE

CHAPTER 4

Behavior-Genetics of Criminality and Aggression

Soo Hyun Rhee and Irwin D. Waldman

More than a hundred twin and adoption studies of antisocial behavior have been published. In contrast, there have been few behavior-genetic studies of violence. With the exception of a few studies that have contrasted the magnitude of genetic influences on violent versus nonviolent criminality (Bohman, Cloninger, Sigvardsson, & von Knorring, 1982; Cloninger & Gottesman, 1987; Mednick, Gabrielli, & Hutchings, 1984), twin and adoption studies have not examined the construct of "violence" per se. However, the behavior-genetic literature has addressed the magnitude of genetic and environmental influences on two phenotypes related to violence: aggression (Carey, 1994) and criminality (DiLalla & Gottesman, 1991). In addition, Rhee and Waldman (2002) have conducted a meta-analysis of twin and adoption studies of antisocial behavior, a broader construct.

Here, we address the specific question of the magnitude of genetic and environmental influences on criminality and aggression. In the twin and adoption studies reviewed here, criminality has been defined as an unlawful act that leads to arrest, conviction, or incarceration, whereas delinquency has been defined as unlawful acts committed as a juvenile. In addition to official records, researchers also have assessed delinquency with anonymous self-reports of criminal activity that has not led to arrest, conviction, or incarceration. Aggression is usually studied as a personality characteristic and assessed with such measures as the Adjective Checklist (Gough & Heilbrun, 1972) and the Multidimensional Personality Questionnaire (Tellegen, 1982 as cited in Tellegen, Lykken, Bouchard, Wilcox, Segal, & Rich, 1988). The operationalization of aggression has been very heterogeneous in the past, ranging from reports of negative affect (Partanen, Bruun, & Markkanen, 1966) to observations of the number of hits to a Bobo doll (Plomin, Foch, & Rowe, 1981). For the present review, the operationalization of aggression was restricted to the type of behavioral aggression described in the *DSM-IV* criteria for conduct disorder (CD) (e.g., bullying, initiating physical fights, and using a weapon that can cause serious physical harm).

The role of familial influences on antisocial behavior has been studied extensively. Dysfunctional familial influences, such as psychopathology in the parents (e.g., Robins, 1966), coercive parenting styles (e.g., Patterson, Reid, & Dishion, 1992), physical abuse (Dodge, Bates, & Pettit, 1990), and family conflict (e.g., Norland, Shover, Thornton, & James, 1979), have been shown to be significantly related to antisocial behavior. Often, these variables are considered environmental influences, and the possibility that they may also reflect genetic influences is not considered. This is unfortunate because disentangling the influences of nature and nurture is the first step toward reaching the eventual goal of explaining the etiology of antisocial behavior. Also, estimating the relative magnitude of genetic and environmental influences on antisocial behavior is an important step toward the search for specific candidate genes and environmental risk factors underlying antisocial behavior. Although it is not possible to disentangle genetic from environmental influences in family studies because genetic and environmental influences are confounded in nuclear families, twin and adoption studies have the unique ability to disentangle genetic and environmental influences and to estimate the magnitude of both simultaneously.

Twin studies can disentangle genetic and environmental influences by comparing the similarity between monozygotic twin pairs – who share 100% of their genes identical by descent – to the similarity between dizygotic twin pairs, who share 50% of their genes, on average. Traits with genetic influences will show greater similarity between monozygotic twins than between dizygotic twins. Adoption studies demonstrate that there are genetic influences on a trait if there is a significant correlation between the adoptees' traits and their biological relatives' traits, and that there are environmental influences on a trait if there is a significant correlation between the adoptees' traits and their adoptive relatives' traits.

Method

Search Strategy

We began our search for twin and adoption studies of criminality and aggression by examining the PsycInfo and Medline databases. The search terms used in this process were aggressive, aggression, crime, criminality, delinquent, or delinquency in combination with the terms twin(s), adoptee(s), adoptive, genetic, genetics, genes, environmental, or environment. We examined the references from the research studies and review papers found through this method for any additional studies that might have been missed or published before the databases were established. After excluding unsuitable studies according to the criteria described below (i.e., construct validity, inability to calculate tetrachoric or intraclass correlations, and assessment of related disorders), and addressing the problem of nonindependence in these studies, 5 studies examining criminality and 14 studies examining aggression remained. Tables 4.1 and 4.2 list the behavior-genetic studies examining criminality and aggression, respectively. They also list the method of assessment and method of zygosity determination (in twin studies) used in the study, the mean or median age, the sex of the sample, the number of pairs, the relationship of the pairs, and the effect sizes.

Inclusion Criteria for Studies in the Meta-Analysis

Construct Validity

CRIMINALITY AND DELINQUENCY
All studies examining criminality used the assessment method of official records of arrests or convictions and were therefore included in the meta-analysis.

AGGRESSION
Studies examining aggression were included if they examined behavioral aggression (e.g., physical fighting, cruelty to animals, and bullying). Studies that examined other related variables, such as anger, hostility, or

Table 4.1: Effect sizes for studies examining criminality

Study	Assessment	Zygosity	Age	Sex	N	Relationship	Effect size
Danish adoptees Baker 89	records	N/A	N/A	fm-fm	7,065	a-bm	.15
				fm-m		a-bf	.12
				fm-both		a-bp	.14
				fm-fm		a-am	-.02
				fm-m		a-af	.05
				fm-both		a-ap	.01
				m-fm	6,129	a-bm	.20
				m-m		a-bf	.14
				m-both		a-bp	.17
				m-fm		a-am	.06
				m-m		a-af	.11
				m-both		a-ap	.09
Swedish adoptees Bohman 78	records	N/A	N/A	m-f	1077	a-bm	.00
				fm-both	1988	a-bp	.12
NAS-NRC twins Centerwall 89	records	blood grouping/ questionnaire/ fingerprinting	36.50	m-m	5933	MZ	.74
					7554	DZ	.29
Maudsley twins Coid 93	records	blood grouping/ questionnaire	45.90	both-both	92	MZ	.70
					109	DZ	.80
Danish twins Carey 92	records	blood grouping/ questionnaire	lifetime	m-m	365	MZ	.74
					700	DZ	.47
				fm-fm	347	MZ	.74
					690	DZ	.46
				m-fm	2073	DZ	.23

Note. Only the first author's name was included in the table. m = male; fm = female; both = both male and female; a-bf = adoptee-biological father; a-bm = adoptee-biological mother; a-bp = adoptee-biological parent; a-af = adoptee-adoptive father; a-am = adoptee-adoptive mother; a-ap = adoptee-adoptive parent; MZ = MZ twin pairs; DZ = DZ twin pairs.

Table 4.2: Effect sizes for studies examining aggression

Study	Assessment	Zygosity	Age	Sex	N	Relationship	Effect size
Midwest twins Cates 93	self report	blood grouping/ questionnaire	42.50	fm-fm	77	MZ	.07 (assault)
					21	DZ	.41 (assault)
					77	MZ	.41 (verbal)
					21	DZ	.06 (verbal)
					77	MZ	.40 (indirect)
					21	DZ	.01 (indirect)
California twins Ghodsian-Carpey 87	parent report	questionnaire	5.20	both-both	21	MZ	.78
					17	DZ	.31
London twins (adults – 70s) Wilson 77	reaction to stimuli		30.50	both-both	49	MZ	.59
					52	DZ	.34
London twins (adults – 80s) Rushton 86	self report	blood grouping/ questionnaire	30.00	m-m	90	MZ	.33
					46	DZ	.16
				fm-fm	206	MZ	.43
					133	DZ	.00
				m-fm	98	DZ	.12
Minnesota twins (reared together – 70s) Tellegen 88	self report	blood grouping	21.65	both-both	217	MZ	.43
					114	DZ	.14
Minnesota twins (90s – adults) Finkel 97	self report	blood grouping/ questionnaire	37.76	m-m	220	MZ	.37
					165	DZ	.12
				fm-fm	406	MZ	.39
					352	DZ	.14
				m-fm	114	DZ	.12
Boston twins (children) Scarr 66	parent report	blood grouping	8.08	fm-fm	24	MZ	.35
					28	DZ	-.08
Philadelphia twins Meininger 88	teacher report	blood grouping	8.50	both-both	61	MZ	.67
					34	DZ	.11

Study	Method	Measure	Value	Pairing	N	Zygosity	r
Missouri twins Owen 70	reaction to stimuli	blood grouping	10.00	m-m	10	MZ	.09
					11	DZ	-.24
				fm-fm	11	MZ	.58
					13	DZ	.22
Colorado twins (80's) Plomin 81	objective test	questionnaire	7.60	both-both	53	MZ	.42
					32	DZ	.42
California twins Rahe 78	self report	blood grouping	48.00	m-m	82	MZ	.31
					79	DZ	.21
British Columbia twins Blanchard 95 (personal communication)	self report		36.18	both-both	96	MZ	.59
					48	DZ	.34
Dutch twins van den Oord 96	parent report	blood grouping/ questionnaire	3.00	m-m	210	MZ	.81
					265	DZ	.49
				fm-fm	236	MZ	.83
					238	DZ	.49
				m-fm	409	DZ	.45
Swedish Twins (adults) Gustavsson 96	self report			both-both	15	MZ ra	.22 (indirect)
					26	MZ	.41 (indirect)
					29	DZ	.27 (indirect)
					15	MZ ra	-.03 (verbal)
					26	MZ	.22 (verbal)
					29	DZ	.23 (verbal)

Note. Only the first author's name was included in the table. Information within the parentheses indicates whether the data were obtained from personal communication or another publication. m = male; fm = female; both = both male and female; MZ = MZ twin pairs; DZ = DZ twin pairs; MZ ra = MZ twin pairs reared apart.

impulsivity, were not included because it was not clear whether they examined aggression or some related but distinct trait. An additional study (Partanen, Brunn, & Markkanen, 1966) was excluded because the aggression items examined (e.g., "Are you readily insulted?" and "Do you easily become unhappy about even small things?") suggest that negative affect or anger, rather than aggression per se, was being assessed.

Inability to Calculate Tetrachoric or Intraclass Correlations

The effect sizes used in this meta-analysis were the Pearson product moment or intraclass correlations that were reported in the studies, or the tetrachoric correlations that were estimated from the concordances or percentages reported in the studies. These effect sizes were analyzed using model-fitting programs that estimate the relative contribution of genetic and environmental influences and test the fit of alternative etiological models.

Nonindependent Samples

Another justification for exclusion from the meta-analysis was nonindependent sampling. Several effect sizes from studies in the original reference list were from nonindependent samples, in which researchers examined more than one dependent measure of antisocial behavior in their sample or published follow-up data of the same sample in separate publications.

Experts on meta-analysis have several suggestions for dealing with nonindependent samples (Mullen, 1989; Rosenthal, 1991). For example, Mullen gives four options for dealing with this problem: choosing the best dependent measure, averaging the effect sizes of the different dependent measures, conducting separate meta-analyses for each of the dependent measures, or using nonindependent samples as if they were independent samples (the least recommended approach). We did not follow the option of choosing the best dependent measure, unless one of the dependent

measures did not fulfill the inclusion criteria described above, making the decision easy. Taking this option would have required making subjective choices, because we were aware of the effect sizes associated with each of the dependent measures. The option of conducting separate meta-analyses for each of the dependent measures was not chosen simply as a practical matter, given that there were a large number of effect sizes from nonindependent samples. Therefore, the most viable option was to average the effect sizes from nonindependent samples.

Model-fitting analyses must indicate the sample size. Therefore, we used the option of averaging multiple effect sizes in cases where the sample size was identical across the nonindependent samples. If the sample size was not identical across the nonindependent samples, we used the effect size from the largest sample. More specifically, in cases of nonindependence where the same dependent measure was used in the same sample multiple times (e.g., in follow-up analyses), we chose the effect size estimated from the largest sample. In cases of nonindependence in which different dependent measures were used in the same sample (e.g., the author of one publication examining more than one dependent measure or authors of different publications examining different dependent measures in one sample), the effect sizes were averaged if the sample size was the same across the nonindependent samples, and the effect size from the largest sample was used if the sample size differed across the nonindependent samples.

Analyses

Determination of the Effect Size

Some adoption and twin studies used a continuous variable to measure antisocial behavior and reported either Pearson product moment or intraclass correlations, which were the effect sizes used from these studies in the meta-analysis. In other studies, a dichotomous variable was used, and concordances, percentages, or a contingency table (including the number of twin pairs with both members affected, one member affected, and neither member affected) were reported. The information from the concordances or percentages was transformed into a contingency table, which was then used to estimate the tetrachoric correlation (i.e., the correlation between the latent continuous variables that are assumed to underlie the observed dichotomous variables). For these studies, the tetrachoric correlation was the effect size used in the meta-analysis.

For some studies, we directly estimated the tetrachoric correlation from the raw data because the tetrachoric correlation had to be estimated from contingency tables. For these studies, we were also able to estimate the weight matrix, (i.e., the asymptotic co-variance matrix of the correlation matrix). If the weight matrix can be estimated, it is possible to use weighted least squares (WLS) estimation in the model-fitting analyses, which is more appropriate for non-normally distributed variables like diagnoses of conduct disorder (CD) or antisocial personality disorder (ASPD), rather than maximum likelihood (ML) estimation.

Model-Fitting Analyses

The magnitude of additive genetic influences (a^2) and the magnitude of nonadditive genetic influences (d^2) constitute the proportion of variance in the liability for antisocial behavior that is due to genetic differences among individuals. If genetic influences are additive, this means that the effects of alleles from different loci are independent and "add up" to influence the liability underlying a trait. If genetic influences are nonadditive, this means that alleles interact with each other to influence the liability for a trait, either at a single genetic locus (i.e., dominance) or at different loci (i.e., epistasis). Shared environmental influences (c^2) represent the proportion of liability variance that is due to environmental influences that are experienced in common and make family members similar to one another, whereas nonshared environmental influences (e^2) represent the amount of liability variance that is due to environmental

influences that are experienced uniquely and make family members different from one another.

It is customary in contemporary behavior-genetic analyses to compare alternative models, which contain different sets of causal influences, for their fit to the observed data (i.e., twin or familial correlations or co-variances). These models posit that anti-social behavior is affected by the types of influences described above: additive genetic influences (A), shared environmental influences (C), nonadditive genetic influences (D), and nonshared environmental influences (E). In the present meta-analysis, we compared the ACE model, the AE model, the CE model, and the ADE model. We assessed the fit of each model, as well as of competing models, using both the χ^2 statistic and the Akaike Information Criterion (AIC), a fit index that reflects both the fit of the model and its parsimony (Loehlin, 1992). The AIC has been used extensively in both the structural equation modeling and behavior-genetics literatures. Among competing models, that with the lowest AIC and the lowest χ^2 relative to its degrees of freedom is considered to be the best-fitting model.

It is not possible to estimate c^2 and d^2 simultaneously or test an ACDE model with data only from twin pairs reared together because the estimation of c^2 and d^2 both rely on the same information (i.e., the difference between the MZ and DZ twin correlations). If the DZ correlation is greater than half the MZ correlation, the ACE model is the correct model, and the estimate of d^2 in the ADE model is always zero. If the DZ correlation is less than half the MZ correlation, the ADE model is the correct model, and the estimate of c^2 in the ACE model is always zero.

Results and Discussion

Table 4.3 shows the model-fitting results for criminality and aggression. The ADE model was the best-fitting model for criminality $(a^2 = .33, d^2 = .42, e^2 = .25)$, whereas the

Table 4.3: Model-fitting results: Standardized parameter estimates and fit statistics

	Parameter estimates				Fit statistics			
	a^2	c^2	e^2	d^2	χ^2	df	p	AIC
Criminality								
ACE model	.36	.22	.42	—	208.20	11	<.01	186.20
AE model	.47	—	.53	—	411.61	12	<.01	387.61
CE model	—	.41	.59	—	669.00	12	<.01	645.00
ADE model	.33	—	.25	.42	116.37	11	<.01	94.37
Aggression								
ACE model	.44	.06	.50	—	333.18	38	<.01	257.18
AE model	.51	—	.49	—	335.84	39	<.01	257.84
CE model	—	.38	.62	—	422.50	39	<.01	344.50
ADE model	.51	—	.49	.00	335.84	38	<.01	259.84

ACE model was the best-fitting model for aggression ($a^2 = .44$, $c^2 = .06$, $e^2 = .50$). The fit of the ACE and the fit of the AE models for aggression were very close, and the magnitude of shared environmental influences on aggression is modest. The evidence for the role of shared environmental influences on aggression is at best tentative pending future studies.

The possible effects of confounding between operationalization and assessment method and between operationalization and age should be considered when interpreting these results (see Tables 4.1 and 4.2). Specifically, all of the behavior-genetic studies of criminality examined adults using the assessment method of official records, whereas a variety of assessment methods (self-report, parent report, teacher report, objective test, and reaction to stimuli) were used to examine aggression in both children and adults.

Although there were not enough studies to examine violent versus nonviolent criminality quantitatively, two adoption studies and one twin study have reported noteworthy results regarding violent vs. nonviolent crimes. Mednick, Gabrielli, and Hutchings (1984) found that, in Danish adopted males, the frequency of property crime was related to the number of convictions of the biological father, whereas the frequency of violent crime was not. Bohman, Cloninger, Sigvardsson, and von Knorring (1982) also found evidence that property crime and violent crime may differ in their etiology. Genetic influences were found to be significant for property crimes, but not for cases of violent crime associated with alcoholism. Cloninger and Gottesman (1987) analyzed the data from the Danish twin sample and found that the heritability for property crimes was .78, whereas the heritability for violent crime was .50. When cross-correlations were examined, they found that there was no genetic overlap between property crime and violent crime, suggesting a distinct and specific etiology for property crime and violent crime. Two limitations in these studies are the assessment of criminality via official records and the definition of criminality as convicted crimes. The sole use of official records fails to assess criminality that escaped detection because of intelligence or high social status (Raine & Venables, 1992). The additional use of self-reports may lessen this problem, but reliance on self-report alone also may be problematic, given respondents' possible reluctance to admit to crimes given concerns regarding stigmatization or confidentiality. Future twin and adoption studies that examine property and violent criminality using both methods would be useful.

We were unable to examine a meaningful distinction between two different kinds of aggression, relational and overt aggression (Crick, Casa, & Mosher, 1997; Crick & Grotpeter, 1995) because there are no published twin or adoption studies of relational aggression. Overt aggression harms others through physical damage or the threat thereof, whereas relational aggression harms others by damaging their peer relationships or reputation (e.g., spreading rumors, excluding from the peer group). Although relational aggression does not lead to physical harm to the victims, it has serious consequences for both the aggressors (e.g., higher levels of loneliness, depression, and negative self-perceptions, as well as concurrent and future peer rejection; Crick & Grotpeter, 1995) and the victims (e.g., depression, anxiety; Crick & Grotpeter, 1996). The distinction between relational and overt aggression is an especially important consideration when examining sex differences in aggression and its causes, given that females are significantly more relationally aggressive and less overtly aggressive than males (Crick & Grotpeter, 1995; Crick et al., 1997). Given the evidence that overt and relational aggression are correlated but distinct (Crick et al., 1997), future behavior-genetic studies of overt and relational aggression should examine the degree of genetic and environmental influences that are common to both types of aggression versus the degree specific to each.

Similarly, past behavior-genetic studies have not distinguished between reactive and proactive aggression (Dodge, Lochman, Harnish, Bates, & Pettit, 1997; Vitaro, Brendgen, & Tremblay, 2002; Waschbusch, Willoughby, & Pelham, 1998). Reactive aggression is characterized by "hot-blooded" anger, appears to be a frustration response, and is associated with a lack of self control, whereas proactive aggression is "cold-blooded," less emotional, and more likely driven by the expectation of reward (Dodge et al., 1997). Evidence suggests that reactively and proactively aggressive children differ in developmental histories, adjustment, and social information-processing patterns and that reactive and proactive aggres-

sion are distinct forms of aggression (Dodge et al., 1997; Vitaro et al., 2002). Behavior-genetic studies examining the degree of common and specific genetic and environmental influences on reactive and proactive aggression are also needed.

Candidate Genes for Aggression, Violence, and Antisocial Behavior

Broadly speaking, there are two general strategies for identifying genes that contribute to the etiology of a disorder or trait. The first is a genome scan, in which linkage is examined between a disorder or trait and evenly spaced DNA markers (e.g., approximately 10,000 base pairs apart) distributed across the entire genome (Haines, 1998). Evidence for linkage between any of these DNA markers and the trait or disorder of interest implicates a broad segment of the genome that may contain hundreds of genes, and lack of evidence for linkage can, in some cases, be used to exclude genomic segments. Subsequent fine-grained linkage analyses can then use a new set of more tightly grouped markers within the implicated genomic region to locate the functional mutation. Thus, genome scans may be thought of as exploratory searches for putative genes that contribute to the etiology of a disorder. The fact that major genes have been found for many medical diseases via genome scans is testament to the usefulness of this method. Unfortunately, the power of linkage analyses in genome scans is typically quite low, making it very difficult, if not impossible, to detect genes that account for less than ~15% of the variance in a disorder. Given this limitation, the promise for genome scans of complex traits remains largely unknown.

The second strategy for finding genes that contribute to the etiology of a disorder is the candidate gene approach. In many ways, candidate gene studies are polar opposites of genome scans. In contrast to the exploratory nature of genome scans, well-conducted candidate gene studies represent a targeted test of the role of specific genes in the etiology of a disorder, as the location, function, and etiological relevance of candidate genes are most often known or strongly hypothesized a priori. Thus, an advantage of well-conducted candidate gene studies in comparison with genome scans is that positive findings are easily interpretable because one already knows the gene's location, function, and etiological relevance, even if the specific polymorphism(s) chosen for study in the candidate gene is not functional and the functional mutation(s) in the candidate gene is as yet unidentified. There are also disadvantages to the candidate gene approach given that only previously identified genes can be studied. Thus, one cannot find genes that one has not looked for or have yet to be discovered, and because there are relatively few strong candidate genes for psychiatric disorders, the same genes are examined as candidates for almost all psychiatric disorders, regardless of how disparate the disorders may be in terms of their symptomatology or conjectured pathophysiology.

In well-designed studies, however, knowledge regarding the biology of the disorder is used to select genes based on the known or hypothesized involvement of their gene product in the etiology of the trait or disorder (i.e., its pathophysiological function and etiological relevance). With respect to aggression, violence, and antisocial behavior, genes underlying various aspects of the dopaminergic and serotonergic neurotransmitter pathways may be conjectured to be involved based on several lines of converging evidence suggesting a role for these neurotransmitter systems in the etiology and pathophysiology of these traits and their relevant disorders. For example, there is considerable overlap between antisocial behavior and childhood ADHD (e.g., Lilienfeld & Waldman, 1990); thus candidate genes for ADHD may also be relevant candidates for aggression, violence, and antisocial behavior. Several genes within the dopamine system appear to be risk factors for ADHD (see Waldman & Gizer, 2006, for a recent review). Dopamine genes are plausible candidates for ADHD, given that the stimulant medications that are the most frequent and effective treatments for ADHD appear to

act primarily by regulating dopamine levels in the brain (Seeman & Madras, 1998; Solanto, 1984) and also affect noradrenergic and serotonergic function (Solanto, 1998). In addition, "knock-out" gene studies in mice, which examine the behavioral effects of the deactivation of specific genes, have further demonstrated the potential relevance of genes within these neurotransmitter systems. Results of such studies have markedly strengthened the consideration as candidate genes for ADHD of genes within the dopaminergic system, such as the dopamine transporter gene (*DAT1*; Giros, Jaber, Jones, Wightman, & Caron, 1996) and the dopamine receptor *D3* and *D4* genes (*DRD3* and *DRD4*; Accili et al., 1996; Dulawa, Grandy, Low, Paulus, & Geyer, 1999; Rubinstein et al., 1997), as well as genes within the serotonergic system, such as the serotonin 1β receptor gene (*HTR1β*; Saudou et al., 1994). Serotonergic genes also are plausible candidates for aggression, violence, and antisocial behavior, given the demonstrated relations between serotonergic function and aggression and violence (Berman, Kavoussi, & Coccaro, 1997).

Although a comprehensive review of molecular genetic studies of aggression and antisocial behavior is beyond the scope of this review, several lines of research have implicated an association between serotonin and antisocial behavior, especially violence and aggression. Several researchers have found lower cerebrospinal fluid levels of 5-hydroxyindoleacetic acid, a serotonin metabolite, in aggressive or violent individuals (e.g., Brown, Goodwin, Ballenger, Goyer, & Major, 1979; Linnoila et al., 1983). Mice lacking the 5-hydroxytryptamine 1β (5-HT1β) receptor show enhanced aggressive behavior (Saudou et al., 1994), and a serotonin transporter (5HTT) polymorphism is associated with aggression in nonhuman primates who experienced insecure early attachment relationships (Suomi, 2003). Human studies examining the association between the 5HTT-linked polymorphic region (5HTT-LPR) and violence or aggression have yielded conflicting results, with some studies finding a positive association with the long allele (e.g., Twitchell et al., 2001; Zalsman et al., 2001), but other studies finding a positive association with the short allele (e.g., Hallikainen et al., 1999, Retz et al., 2004), and still others finding no association (e.g., Beitchman et al., 2003; Davidge et al., 2004; Reist, Mazzani, Vu, Thran, & Goldstein, 2001).

Candidate genes for neurotransmitter systems may include (1) *precursor genes* that affect the rate at which neurotransmitters are produced from precursor amino acids (e.g., tyrosine hydroxylase for dopamine, tryptophan hydroxylase for serotonin); (2) *receptor genes* that are involved in receiving neurotransmitter signals (e.g., genes corresponding to the five dopamine receptors, *DRD1*, *D2*, *D3*, *D4*, and *D5*, and to the serotonin receptors, such as *HTR1b* and *HTR2A*); (3) *transporter genes* that are involved in the reuptake of neurotransmitters back into the presynaptic terminal (e.g., the dopamine and serotonin transporter genes, *DAT1* and *5HTT*); (4) *metabolite genes* that are involved in the metabolism or degradation of these neurotransmitters (e.g., the genes for catechol-o-methyl-transferase [*COMT*] and for monoamine oxidase A and B [i.e., *MAOA* and *MAOB*]); and (5) genes that are responsible for the *conversion* of one neurotransmitter into another (e.g., dopamine beta hydroxylase, or *DbH*, which converts dopamine into norepinephrine). We anticipate that there will be a steep increase in the number of studies of such candidate genes and aggression, violence, and antisocial behavior over the next decade.

In conclusion, the results of a meta-analysis suggest that there are moderate additive genetic influences, nonadditive genetic influences, and nonshared environmental influences on criminality, and moderate additive genetic and nonshared environmental influences and modest shared environmental influences on aggression. Three studies have reported results suggesting that nonviolent criminality is more heritable than violent criminality, and behavior-genetic studies examining relational versus overt aggression and reactive versus proactive aggression need to be conducted. An association between serotonin and violence and aggression has been implicated in candidate gene studies, although human studies examining the association between the serotonin transporter gene and violence or aggression have yielded conflicting results.

Acknowledgments

This work was supported in part by NIDA DA-13956 and NIMH MH-01818. Earlier versions of this chapter were presented at the meeting of the American Society of Criminology in 1996 and the meeting of the Behavior Genetics Association in 1997, and a more extensive version has been published in *Psychological Bulletin*, *128*(3), pp. 490–529.

References

References marked with an asterisk indicate studies included in the meta-analysis.

Accili, D., Fishburn, C. S., Drago, J., Steiner, H., Lachowicz, J. E., Park, B. H., et al. (1996). A targeted mutation of the *D*3 dopamine receptor gene is associated with hyperactivity in mice. *Proceedings of the National Academy of Sciences USA*, 93, 1945–1949.

*Baker, L., Mack, W., Moffitt, T., & Mednick, S. (1989). Sex differences in property crime in a Danish adoption cohort. *Behavior Genetics*, 19, 355–370.

Beitchman, J. H., Davidge, K. M., Kennedy, J. L., Atkinson, L, Lee, V., Shapiro, S., et al. (2003). The serotonin transporter gene in aggressive children with and without ADHD and nonaggressive matched controls. *Annals of the New York Academy of Sciences*, 1008, 248–251.

Berman, M. E., Kavoussi, R. J., & Cocarro, E. F. (1997). Neurotransmitter correlates of human aggression. In D. M. Stoff, J. Breiling, & J. D. Maser (Eds.), *Handbook of antisocial behavior* (pp. 305–313). New York: John Wiley.

*Blanchard, J. M., Vernon, P. A., & Harris, J. A. (1995). A behavior genetic investigation of multiple dimensions of aggression. *Behavior Genetics*, *25*(3), 256.

*Bohman, M. (1978). Some genetic aspects of alcoholism and criminality: A population of adoptees. *Archives of General Psychiatry*, *35*, 269–276.

Bohman, M., Cloninger, C. R., Sigvardsson, S., & von Knorring, A.-L. (1982). Predisposition to petty criminality in Swedish adoptees. I. Genetic and environment heterogeneity. *Archives of General Psychiatry*, *39*, 1233–1241.

Brown, G. L., Goodwin, F. K., Ballenger, J. C., Goyer, P. F., & Major, L. F. (1979). Aggression in humans correlates with cerebrospinal fluid amine metabolites. *Psychiatry Research*, *1*, 131–139.

*Carey, G. (1992). Twin imitation for antisocial behavior: Implications for genetic and family environment research. *Journal of Abnormal Psychology*, *101*(1), 18–25.

Carey, G. (1994). Genetics and violence. In A. J. Reiss, K. A. Miczek, & J. A. Roth (Eds.), *Understanding and preventing violence* (Vol. 2, pp. 21–58). Washington, DC: National Academy Press.

*Cates, D. S., Houston, B. K., Vavak, C. R., Crawford, M. H., & Uttley, M. (1993). Heritability of hostility-related emotions, attitudes, and behaviors. *Journal of Behavioral Medicine*, *16*, 237–256.

*Centerwall, B. S., & Robinette, C. D. (1989). Twin concordance for dishonorable discharge from the military: With a review of genetics of antisocial behavior. *Comprehensive Psychiatry*, *30*, 442–446.

Cloninger, C. R., & Gottesman, I. I. (1987). Genetic and environmental factors in antisocial behavior disorders. In S. A. Mednick, T. E. Moffitt, & S. A. Stack (Eds.), *The causes of crime: New biological approaches* (pp. 92–109). New York: Cambridge University Press.

*Coid, B., Lewis, S. W., & Reveley, A. M. (1993). A twin study of psychosis and criminality. *British Journal of Psychiatry*, *162*, 87–92.

Crick, N. R., Casa, J. F., & Mosher, M. (1997). Relational and overt aggression in preschool. *Developmental Psychology*, *33*(4), 579–588.

Crick, N. R., & Grotpeter, J. K. (1995). Relational aggression, gender, and social-psychological adjustment. *Child Development*, *66*, 710–722.

Crick, N. R., & Grotpeter, J. K. (1996). Children's treatment by peers: Victims of relational and overt aggression. *Development and Psychopathology*, *8*, 367–380.

Davidge, K. M., Atkinson, L., Douglas, L., Lee, V., Shapiro, S., Kennedy, J. L., et al. (2004). Association of the serotonin transporter and 5HT1D beta receptor genes with extreme, persistent and pervasive aggressive behaviour in children. *Psychiatric Genetics*, *14*, 143–146.

DiLalla, L. F., & Gottesman, I. I. (1991). Biological and genetic contributors to violence: Widom's untold tale. *Psychological Bulletin*, *109*, 125–129.

Dodge, K. A., Bates, J., & Pettit, G. S. (1990). Mechanisms in the cycle of violence. *Science*, *250*, 1678–1683.

Dodge, K. A., Lochman, J. E., Harnish, J. D., Bates, J. E., & Pettit, G. S. (1997). Reactive and proactive aggression in school children and psychiatrically impaired chronically assaultive youth. *Journal of Abnormal Psychology*, *106*, 37–51.

Dulawa, S. C., Grandy, D. K., Low, M. J., Paulus, M. P., & Geyer, M. A. (1999). Dopamine D4 receptor-knock-out mice exhibit reduced exploration of novel stimuli. *Journal of Neuroscience*, *19*, 9550–9556.

*Finkel, D., & McGue, M. (1997). Sex differences and nonadditivity in heritability of the multidimensional personality questionnaire scales. *Journal of Personality and Social Psychology*, *72*(4), 929–938.

*Ghodsian-Carpey, J., & Baker, L. A. (1987). Genetic and environmental influences on aggression in 4- to 7-year-old twins. *Aggressive Behavior*, *13*, 173–186.

Giros, B., Jaber, M., Jones, S. R., Wightman, R. M., & Caron, M. G. (1996). Hyperlocomotion and indifference to cocaine and amphetamine in mice lacking the dopamine transporter. *Nature*, *379*, 606–612.

Gough, H. G., & Heilbrun, A. B. (1972). *The adjective checklist manual*. Palo Alto, CA: Consulting Psychologists Press.

*Gustavsson, J. P., Pedersen, N. L., Åsberg, M., & Schalling, D. (1996). Exploration into the sources of individual differences in aggression-, hostility-, and anger-related (AHA) personality traits. *Personality and Individual Differences*, *21*(6), 1067–1071.

Haines, J. L. (1998). Genomic screening. In J. L. Haines & M. A. Pericak-Vance (Eds.), *Approaches to gene mapping in complex human diseases* (pp. 243–252). New York: Wiley.

Hallikainen, T., Saito, T., Lachman, H. M., Volavka, J., Pohjalainen, T., Ryynanen, O. P., et al. (1999). Association between low activity serotonin transporter promoter genotype and early onset alcoholism with habitual impulsive violent behavior. *Molecular Psychiatry*, *4*, 385–388.

Lilienfeld, S. O., & Waldman, I. D. (1990). The relation between childhood Attention-Deficit Hyperactivity Disorder and adult antisocial behavior reexamined: The problem of heterogeneity. *Clinical Psychology Review, 10,* 699–725.

Linnoila, M., Virkkunen, M., Scheinin, M., Nuutila, A., Rimon, R., & Goodwin, F. K. (1983). Low cerebrospinal fluid 5–hydroxyindoleacetic acid concentration differentiates impulsive from nonimpulsive violence behavior. *Life Sciences, 33,* 2609–2614.

Loehlin, J. C. (1992). *Latent variable models: An introduction to factor, path, and structural analysis* (2nd ed.). Hillsdale, NJ: Erlbaum.

Mednick, S. A., Gabrielli, W. F., & Hutchings, B. (1984). Genetic influences in criminal convictions: Evidence from an adoption cohort. *Science, 224,* 891–894.

*Meininger, J. C., Hayman, L. L., Coates, P. M., & Gallagher, P. (1988). Genetics or environment? Type A behavior and cardiovascular risk factors in twin children. *Nursing Research, 37*(6), 341–346.

Mullen, B. (1989). *Advanced BASIC meta-analysis.* Hillsdale, NJ: Erlbaum.

Norland, S., Shover, N., Thornton, W., & James, J. (1979). Intrafamily conflict and delinquency. *Pacific Sociological Review, 22,* 233–237.

*Owen, D., & Sines, J. O. (1970). Heritability of personality in children. *Behavior Genetics 1,* 235–248.

Partanen, J., Bruun, K., & Markkanen, T. (1966). *Inheritance of drinking behavior: A study on intelligence, personality, and use of alcohol of adult twins.* Helsinki: The Finnish Foundation for Alcohol Studies.

Patterson, G. R., Reid, J. B., & Dishion, T. J. (1992). *Antisocial boys.* Eugene, OR: Castalia Publishing.

*Plomin, R., Foch, T. T., & Rowe, D. C. (1981). Bobo clown aggression in childhood: Environment, not genes. *Journal of Research in Personality, 15,* 331–342.

*Rahe, R. H., Hervig, L., & Rosenman, R. H. (1978). Heritability of type A behavior. *Psychosomatic Medicine, 40*(6), 478–486.

Raine, A., & Venables, P. H. (1992). Antisocial behaviour: Evolution, genetics, neuropsychology, and psychophysiology. In A. Gale & M. W. Eysenck (Eds.), *Handbook of individual differences: Biological perspectives* (pp. 287–321). New York: John Wiley & Sons.

Reist, C., Mazzanti, C., Vu, R., Tran, D., & Goldman, D. (2001). Serotonin transporter promoter polymorphism is associated with attenuated prolactin response to fenfluramine. *American Journal of Medical Genetics, 105,* 363–368.

Retz, W., Retz-Junginger, P., Supprian, T., Thome, J., & Rosler, M. (2004). Association of serotonin transporter promoter gene polymorphism with violence: Relation with personality disorders, impulsivity, and childhood ADHD psychopathology. *Behavioral Sciences and the Law, 22,* 415–425.

Rhee, S. H., & Waldman, I. D. (2002). Genetic and environmental influences on antisocial behavior: A meta-analysis of twin and adoption studies. *Psychological Bulletin, 128,* 490–529.

Robins, L. N. (1966). *Deviant children grown up.* Baltimore: Williams & Wilkins.

Rosenthal, R. (1991). *Meta-analytic procedures for social research.* Newbury Park, CA: Sage.

Rubinstein, M., Phillips, T. J., Bunzow, J. R., Falzone, T. L., Dziewczapolski, G., Zhang, G., et al. (1997). Mice lacking dopamine D4 receptors are supersensitive to ethanol, cocaine, and methamphetamine. *Cell, 90,* 991–1001.

*Rushton, J. P., Fulker, D. W., Neale, M. C., Nias, D. K. B., & Eysenck, H. J. (1986). Altruism and aggression: The heritability of individual differences. *Journal of Personality and Social Psychology, 50,* 1192–1198.

Saudou, F., Amara, D. A., Dierich, A., LeMeur, M., Ramboz, S., Segu, L., et al. (1994). Enhanced aggressive behavior in mice lacking 5-HT1B receptor. *Science, 265,* 1875–1878.

*Scarr, S. (1966). Genetic factors in activity motivation. *Child Development, 37,* 663–673.

Seeman, P., & Madras, B. K. (1998). Anti-hyperactivity medication: Methylphenidate and amphetamine. *Molecular Psychiatry, 3,* 386–396.

Solanto, M. V. (1984). Neuropharmacological basis of stimulant drug action in attention deficit disorder with hyperactivity: A review and synthesis. *Psychological Bulletin, 95,* 387–409.

Solanto, M. V. (1998). Neuropsychopharmacological mechanisms of stimulant drug action in attention-deficit hyperactivity disorder: A review and integration. *Behavioural Brain Research, 94,* 127–152.

Suomi, S. J. (2003). Gene-environment interactions and the neurobiology of social conflict. *Annals of the New York Academy of Sciences, 1008,* 132–139.

*Tellegen, A., Lykken, D. T., Bouchard, T. J., Wilcox, K., Segal, N., & Rich, S. (1988). Personality similarity in twins reared apart and together. *Journal of Personality and Social Psychology, 54,* 1031–1039.

Twitchell, G. R., Hanna, G. L., Cook, E. H., Stoltenberg, S. F., Fitzgerald, H. E., & Zucker, R. A. (2001). Serotonin transporter promoter polymorphism genotype is associated with behavioral disinhibition and negative affect in children of alcoholics. *Alcoholism: Clinical and Experimental Research, 25,* 953–959.

*van den Oord, E. J. C. G., Verhulst, F. C., & Boomsma, D. I. (1996). A genetic study of maternal and paternal ratings of problem behaviors in 3-year-old twins. *Journal of Abnormal Psychology, 105*(3), 349–357.

Vitaro, F., Brendgen, M., & Tremblay, R. E. (2002). Reactively and proactively aggressive children: Antecedent and subsequent characteristics. *Journal of Child Psychology and Psychiatry, 43,* 495–505.

Waldman, I. D., & Gizer, I. (2006). The genetics of attention deficit hyperactivity disorder. *Clinical Psychology Review, 26,* 396–432.

Waschbusch, D. A., Willoughby, M. T., & Pelham, W. E. (1998). Criterion validity and utility of reactive and proactive aggression: Comparisons to attention deficit hyperactivity disorder, oppositional defiant disorder, conduct disorder, and other measures of functioning. *Journal of Clinical Child Psychology, 27,* 396–405.

*Wilson, G. D., Rust, J., & Kasriel, J. (1977). Genetic and family origins of humor preferences: A twin study. *Psychological Reports, 41*(2), 659–660.

Zalsman, G., Frisch, A., Bromberg, M., Gelernter, J., Michaelovsky, E., Campino, A., et al. (2001). Family-based association study of serotonin transporter promoter in suicidal adolescents: No association with suicidality but possible role in violence traits. *American Journal of Medical Genetics, 105,* 239–245.

CHAPTER 5

The Genetics of Aggression in Mice

Stephen C. Maxson and Andrew Canastar

Introduction

There are many definitions of aggression and of aggressive behavior. One of these is "overt behavior involving intent to inflict noxious stimulation to or behave destructively toward another organism" (Volavka, 1995). Another is "any form of behavior directed toward the goal of harming or injuring another living being who is motivated to avoid such treatment" (Baron & Richardson, 1994). These definitions specify broadly the behavioral domain considered in this chapter about mice.

It has long been recognized that, at least in animals, there are many types of aggression or aggressive behavior. These types differ in mechanism, eliciting stimuli, development, function, and phylogeny. Consequently, they may also differ in their genetics. That is to say, the same genes may not be causes of differences in each type of aggression or be involved in the development of each type of aggression. In male and female mice, four types of aggression are offense, defense, infanticide, and predation (Maxson,

1992a). There are also female-specific types of aggression that occur during pregnancy or lactation (Bjorkqvist & Niemela, 1992). Offense and defense by males and females (either not pregnant and lactating, or pregnant or lactating) are agonistic behaviors, whereas infanticide and predation by males and females are not. As defined by Scott (1966), agonistic behaviors are adaptations for situations involving physical conflict or contests between members of the same species. Because most of the research on the genetics of aggression in mice is about offense in males, this is the focus of this chapter. It considers the research and findings of several long-term studies on the genetics of offense primarily in male mice. Information on the other types of aggressive behavior in mice can be found in these references (Alleva, 1993; Brain, Haug, & Kamis, 1983; Jones & Brain, 1987; Maxson, 1992a,b).

Since the first studies on the genetics of mouse aggression were conducted by Scott (1942) and Ginsburg and Allee (1943), it has been argued that these studies are relevant, with due caution, to our understanding of one or more types of human aggression. At the end of this chapter we consider the potential role of current research on the genetics of mouse agonistic behavior as a tool in generating hypotheses about the biological and environmental causes of human agonistic behavior.

Offense and Defense in Mice

Offense and defense in mice can be distinguished in three ways.

1. Function: The adaptive function of offense is to obtain and retain resources such as space, food, and mates. The adaptive function of defense is to protect oneself, mates, and progeny from injury by attacks from other conspecifics.
2. Attack or bite target: In offense, the preferred attack or bite targets are the hindquarters and base of tail. In defense, the preferred attack or bite targets are the face and shoulders.
3. Motor patterns: The motor patterns of offense are chase, sideways offensive posture, upright offensive posture, and attack (flank bites or bite-and-kick attacks). The motor patterns of defense are flight, sideways defense posture, upright defense posture, and lung and bite attacks. In addition, tail rattle is an agonistic motor pattern in mice that may be associated with either offense or defense.

In most natural and many experimental encounters, each opponent shows a mix of offense and defense. However, in the resident-intruder test (described below), the resident usually shows offense, and the intruder usually shows defense.

The following are frequently used as dependent variables in tests of mouse agonistic behavior: (1) latency to offensive attack, (2) frequency of one or more motor patterns of offense, and (3) total test duration of one or all motor patterns of offense.

Life History and Test Conditions

There are several aspects of life history and test condition that may vary in research on mouse agonistic behavior. These have been reviewed in detail by Maxson (1992b), and some are considered here.

- Life history: The most important factor is the social environment of the mice after weaning. Two types of housing are often used. One of these is pairing of a male and female together. The other is isolation for a period of time.
- Test conditions: Two types of tests are often used. In the resident-intruder test, the test takes place in the home cage of the mouse being tested. In the neutral cage test, the test takes place in an arena that is not the home cage of either opponent.
- Type of opponent: With mice from isogenic populations (inbred, congenic, or coisogenic strains or F1 hybrids) the opponents can be of the same genotype. This is known as a homogeneous set test. With mice from heterogenic populations, such as F2s, the opponent must be a mouse of a single, defined genotype (inbred, congenic, or coisogenic strains or F1 hybrids). This is a standard opponent test.

The Male-Specific Part of the Y Chromosome and Offense in Mice

The mammalian Y chromosome has two parts. One region is male specific and passed strictly from father to son. The other part, known as the pseudoautosomal region (PAR), is found on both the X and Y chromosomes with recombination occurring between them at meiosis. One or more genes on the male-specific part of the Y can affect variation in the expression of offense of male mice. This effect was first shown for the Y chromosomes of DBA/1 and C57BL/10 inbred mouse strains using a homogeneous set test in a neutral cage, in which the males were isolated from weaning to testing.

Across several measures, DBA/1 males are more aggressive than C57BL/10 males, and F1 males with the DBA/1 Y chromosome are more aggressive than those with the C57BL/10 Y chromosome (Selmanoff, Maxson, & Ginsburg, 1976). The same pattern is seen in mice congenic for the Y chromosome. Y-congenic strains are identical in autosomes, X chromosomes, pseudoautosomal regions of the X and Y chromosomes, mitochondria, prenatal maternal environments, and postnatal maternal environments; they differ only in the male-specific region of the Y chromosome. One congenic pair is DBA/1 and DBA/1.C57BL1/0-Y (Maxson, Didier-Erickson, & Ogawa, 1989). Across several measures male DBA/1 are more aggressive than male DBA/1.C57BL/10-Y. Similar effects on offense have been reported for the male-specific region of four other pairs of mouse Y chromosomes (Maxson, 1996). The effects on offense of the Y chromosomal genes and their variants have not been identified. However, there may be as few as 13 protein coding genes on the mouse Y chromosome (Mitchell, 2000). Seven of these are expressed in brain at one or more stages of development (Lahr, Maxson, Mayer, Just, Pilgrim, & Reisert, 1995; Mayer, Mosler, Just, Pilgrim, & Reisert, 2000; Xu, Burgoyne, & Arnold, 2002).

The expression of one or more of these Y chromosomal genes in the brains of male but not female mice could potentially be involved in the context-dependent sex differences in offensive aggression of mice. This possibility has been investigated with sex-reversed mice (Canastar, Maxson & Bishop, 2004): XY females with ovaries and female genitalia and XX males with testes and male genitalia. In a resident-intruder test, XY males were more aggressive than XY females, whereas XX and XY females were equally pacific. Similarly in a neutral cage test, XY and XX males were equally aggressive. Thus, it does not appear that the presence of the male-specific region of the

Y chromosome in males and its absence in females can account for the sex differences in context-dependent aggression of mice.

There appear to be three limiting but interesting conditions for the differential effects of variants of the male-specific region of the Y chromosome on offense: the genetic background, the maternal environment, and the type of opponent.

Genetic background effects were first seen with reciprocal F1s. Reciprocal F1s of DBA/1 and C57BL/10 mice differ in aggression, whereas those of DBA/1 and C57BL/6 mice do not (Selmanoff et al., 1976). Genetic background effects were also seen with Y chromosomal congenics. C57BL/10 and C57BL/10.DBA/1-Y are another pair of strains that are congenic for the male-specific part of the Y chromosome. This congenic pair does not differ in any measure of aggression. Thus, the male-specific regions of the DBA/1 and C57BL/10 Y chromosomes differ in effects on aggression in the DBA/1 or F1 but not the C57BL/10 genetic background. Similar effects of genetic background have been seen for four other pairs of Y chromosomes (Maxson, 1996).

The maternal environment can also modify the effect of this part of the Y chromosome on offense (Carlier, Roubertoux, & Pastoret 1991). A higher proportion of mice from a cross of CBA/H females to CBA/H x NZB F1 males attack standard opponent A/J males in a neutral cage than those from a cross of CBA/H females to NZB x CBA/H F1 males. Mice of these two backcross populations have different Y chromosomes, but the same CBA/H maternal environments. When the maternal environments are those of F1 females, the effect of these two Y chromosomes on offense is reversed. Here CBA/H ovaries were transplanted into F1 females, and these females were backcrossed to the reciprocal F1 males. These reciprocal backcross populations still have different Y chromosomes, but the maternal environment is that of the F1 rather than CBA/H genotype. Now a higher proportion of mice from a cross of CBA/H females to NZB x CBA/H F1 males attack standard opponent A/J males than those from a cross of CBA/H females to CBA/H x NZB F1 males. Thus, there appears to be an effect of maternal environments on either the direction of the effect of the same alleles of a Y chromosomal gene on offense or on the effect of alleles of different Y chromosomal genes on offense.

Some but not all of the differential effects of the DBA/1 and C57BL/10 Y chromosomes on aggression depend on the type of opponent. The NZB and CBA/H Y chromosomes have differential effects on offense in a homogeneous set test but not in a standard opponent test (Guillot, Carlier, Maxson, & Roubertoux, 1995). Here the standard opponent was a male of the AJ strain. A similar effect has been reported for the DBA/1 and C57BL/10 Y chromosomes. For this pair of Y chromosomes, whether there is an effect and the direction of the effect depend on the genotype of the opponent (Maxson, Didier-Ericson, & Ogawa, 1989; Monahan & Maxson, 1998). In this case, the effect of opponent type appears to be mediated by urinary odor types that are not dependent on testosterone in adults (Schellinick, Monahan, Brown, & Maxson, 1993).

Several aspects of the studies with these variants of the male-specific region of the Y chromosome are worth noting:

- The effects of such Y chromosomal variants on offense can depend on genetic background, the maternal environment, and the test opponent. Such modulating effects of the environment should be considered for other genetic variants that act on offense and other types of aggression not only in mice but also in other species including humans.
- The effects of this region of the Y chromosome on offense are not due to effects on levels of testosterone in adults.
- As is indicated above, the gene or genes on the male-specific part of the Y chromosome with these behavioral effects have not as yet been identified. However, many other genes with effects on offense have been identified. We turn next to some of these.

Genes, Gonadal Steroids, and Offense in Mice

Steroid hormones have long been known to have an effect on offense in male mice (Simon, McKenna, Lu, & Cologer-Clifford, 1996). Adult castration reduces offense, and testosterone replacement restores it. Some of the effects of adult testosterone on male offense may be direct, and some may be due to its conversion to estradiol. The conversion of testosterone to estradiol involves the enzyme aromatase that is coded by the *Cyp19* gene on mouse Chromosome 9. For testosterone, there is an intracellular androgen receptor that is coded by the gene *Ar* on the X chromosome. For estradiol, there are two intracellular receptors. The alpha estrogen receptor is coded by *Esr1* gene on Chromosome 6, and the beta estrogen receptor is coded by the *Esr2* gene on Chromosome 12. When combined with the appropriate hormonal ligand, the androgen, alpha estrogen, and beta estrogen receptors become transcription factors that can bind to the appropriate hormone response elements in one or more genes, thereby regulating gene transcription.

Wild type and *Esr1* knockout mice have been compared for offense (Ogawa, Lubahn, Korach, & Pfaff, 1997). When the males were tested in a resident-intruder paradigm, the intruders were olfactory bulbectomized males of the Swiss-Webster strain. The wild type and knockout males were also tested in a homogenous set test in a neutral cage. Males were individually housed. In both tests, the homozygous *Esr1* knockout mice rarely displayed any offensive attacks. Also, although daily injections of testosterone propionate increased offensive attacks in castrated homozygous wild type mice, they did not do so in castrated homozygous *Esr1* knockout males (Ogawa, Washburn, Taylor, Lubahn, Korach, & Pfaff, 1998). However, homozygous *Esr1* knockout mice could elicit attacks from resident C57BL/6 males.

Recently, it has also been shown that homozygous *Esr1* knockout males not only have fewer attacks than homozygous wild type males with male opponents but also have more attacks than wild type males with female opponents (Scordalakes & Rissman, 2003). This was observed in a resident-intruder test with singly housed males. Both wild type and knockout residents had been castrated and received the same replacement dose of testosterone. Opponent males were either wild types or heterozygotes with intact gonads, and opponent females were wild types or heterozygotes that had been gonadectomized and had received estradiol replacement. The authors suggested that the homozygous *Esr1* knockout males do not discriminate between male and female mice as a result of a failure to process relevant chemosensory cues.

As noted above, when the alpha estrogen receptor is activated by binding estrogens, it becomes a transcription factor that regulates the expression of downstream genes. Some of these genes may code for some aspects of neurotransmitter systems. One of these is the gene for the neuropeptide transmitter, argenine vasopressin (AVP). Brain levels of AVP and its mRNA are reduced in castrated males. These levels are fully restored by testosterone treatment and partially restored by estradiol treatment. Also, a knockout of the AVP 1b receptor reduces offense by male mice in a resident-intruder test (Wersinger, Ginns, O'Carroll, Lolait, & Young III, 2002).

For this reason, both offense and arginine vasporessin immunoreactivity (AVP-ir) in several limbic brain areas were compared in homozygous wild type and *Esr1* knockout mice (Scordalakes & Rissman, 2004). Mice were gonadectomized and treated with estradiol prior to resident-intruder tests of singly housed males. The intruder was an intact C57BL/6 male. As in previous studies, none of the homozygous *Esr1* knockout mice attacked. However, the levels of limbic brain AVP-ir were the same in both homozygous *Esr1* knockout and wild type mice. Thus, the effect of the *Esr1* knockout on male offense does not seem to be mediated by an effect on AVP-ir, at least in limbic structures. It may be that the other neurotransmitter systems are affected in the *Esr1* knockout mouse. For example, estrogen treatment increases mRNA for neurokinin

B in the arcuate nucleus of the hypothalamus in homozygous wild type mice but not in homozygous *Esr1* knockout mice (Dellovade & Merchenthaler, 2004).

Wild type and *Cyp19* knockout males have also been compared for offense (Toda, Sailbara, Okada, Onishi, & Shizuta, 2001). The *Cyp19* gene codes for the aromatase P40 enzyme that converts testosterone to estradiol. In a resident-intruder paradigm, there is a complete absence of offense in homozygous *Cyp19* knockout residents. The intruders were homozygous wild type or knockout males. Males were singly housed. When the knockouts were treated with estradiol from birth to testing, there was a dose-dependent increase in the percentage of mice showing offense. However, the duration of displayed offensive behavior was shorter in the estrogen-treated knockouts than in the wild type mice. These findings imply that there are both prenatal and postnatal roles for the alpha estrogen receptor in the development and expression of male offense.

Wild type and *Esr2* knockout mice have been compared for offense (Ogawa, Chan, Chester, Gustafsson, Korach, & Pfaff, 1999). When the males were tested in a resident-intruder paradigm, the intruders were olfactory bulbectomized males of the Swiss-Webster strain. The wild type and knockout males were also tested in a homogenous set test in a neutral cage. Males were individually housed. In both tests, the homozygous *Esr2* knockout mice, unlike the homozygous *Esr1* knockout mice, displayed offensive attacks. In this study, the mice were tested for 3 days. Over the 3 days, attack latency decreased, and the number of attack bouts increased in wild type mice. There was no change in any of these measures for homozygous *Esr2* knockout males. As a consequence, homozygous *Esr2* knockout males were more aggressive than wild type males on the first but not subsequent days of testing. However, summed across all 3 days, there was no difference in aggression of wild type and *Esr2* knockout homozygotes. This was the pattern in adult mice. Pubertal males and young adults showed a different pattern. When the data were summed across the three tests for these mice, *Esr2* knockout homozygotes had shorter latencies, more aggressive bouts, and longer aggressive bouts than did homozygous wildtypes (Nomura et al., 2002).

When mice were homozygous for both the *Esr1* and *Esr2* knockout, they did not show much if any offensive attacks in both resident-intruder tests and neutral cage tests (Ogawa et al., 2000). In this regard, they were much like males homozygous for just the *Esr1* knockout. However, the double knockout homozygotes showed lunge and bite attacks, which are defensive.

The beta estrogen receptor, coded for by *Esr2*, but not the alpha estrogen receptor, coded for by *Esr1*, is localized in the paraventricular nucleus of the hypothalamus. Estrogens appear to regulate the synthesis of some neuropeptides in the neurons of this nucleus. Males homozygous for the *Esr2* knockout had an increase in oxytocin mRNA and a decrease in AVP mRNA as compared with wild types homozygotes (Nomura, McKenna, Korach, Pfaff, & Ogawa, 2002). There was no effect on mRNAs of corticotrophin-releasing hormone. It may be that the behavioral effects of the *Esr2* knockout are due to these changes in neuropeptide synthesis.

The effects of the *Esr1* and of the *Esr2* knockouts on female aggression have also been studied. Homozygous *Esr1* knockout, resident females were more aggressive toward female intruders than were homozygous wild type females (Ogawa, Eng, Taylor, Lubahn, Korach, & Pfaff, 1998). The residents were gonadally intact, and the female intruders were gonadectomized Swiss-Webster mice with estradiol replacement. Gonadectomy of the resident did not affect this difference in offense by females toward females. However, neither homozygous *Esr2* knockout nor wild type resident females displayed any aggressive behavior at any phase in the estrous cycle toward gonadectomized female CD-1 intruders (Ogawa et al., 1999).

There have been two studies on an androgen receptor mutant and offense of male mice. In one study, intact *Ar* mutants

displayed no offensive behaviors (Ohno, Geller, & Lai, 1974), whereas in the other study, gonadectomized *Ar* mutants with estradiol replacement were as aggressive as similarly treated wild types (Scordalakes & Rissman, 2004).

The studies with the *Esr1* and *Esr2* knockout mice were done on the C57BL/6J genetic background. There is evidence that effects of *Esr1* on mating behaviors are modulated by genetic background (Dominguez-Salazar, Bateman, & Rissman, 2004). The effects of other knockouts and genes on offense are also known to be dependent on genetic background, and this may be the case for the effects of *Esr1* and *Esr2* knockouts on aggression as well.

Several aspects of the studies with these knockouts are worth noting:

- The same effects of the *Esr1* and *Esr2* knockouts were found in resident intruder and neutral cage tests.
- The same effect of the *Esr1* and *Esr2* knockouts were found in the standard opponent (olfactory bulbectomized) and homogeneous set test.
- All males in these studies were individually housed.
- The *Esr1* and *Esr2* knockouts had different effects on male offense, which may reflect the different distribution of their steroid receptors in the brain.
- The effects of the *Esr1* and *Esr2* knockouts were not the same for male and female offense, suggesting that at least in part the mechanisms of male and female offense are different.
- The effects of the *Esr1* and *Esr2* proteins on offense are due to regulation of downstream genes. This may provide a window on other genetic effects on offense.

The Pseudoautosomal Part of the Y and X Chromosomes, Steroid Sulfatase, and Offense in Mice

There is a region of the X and Y chromosomes in mammals that pairs and recombines at meiosis. This is the pseudoautosomal region (PAR). In the mouse, there is a single gene in this region. It is the structural or coding gene for the enzyme steroid sulfatase (STS). The role of this gene and its enzyme in offense has been studied in different behavioral tests and with different genetic methods.

The initial study showed co-segregation of the PAR and offense by males (Roubertoux et al., 1994). The inbred strains used were NZB (N) and CBA/H (H). At weaning, each male was housed with a female until testing at 62 to 70 days of age. Tests were in a neutral cage with bedding from several cages that housed males of the tested group. The opponent was an A/JOrl male. Males of this strain rarely initiate attack. The proportion of males attacking in this test is the index of offense. N males attack more than H males, and males with the N PAR on the Y chromosome attack more than those with the H PAR. In this study, the activity of steroid sulfatase was measured in the liver. There was higher enzymatic activity in those with the N PAR than those with the H PAR.

Steroid sulfatase (STS) occurs in the glial cells of mouse brain. The concentration of STS is higher in the brains of the N than of the H strain. The association between brain concentration and initiation of attacks was further studied in 11 inbred strains of mice (LeRoy et al. (1999). There was a high ($r = 0.89$) correlation across the strains for STS concentration (pmols STS/mg protein) in the brain and proportion of males attacking. This association was only found for males housed with a female from weaning, tested in the neutral cage, and tested with an A/J opponent. It was not found with other kinds or rearing, test situation, and opponent such as isolated males, a resident-intruder test, and same-strain opponents.

In both an F2 and advanced intercross lines derived from crosses of NZB and CBA/H mice, DNA markers on the PAR were associated with the number of attacks in tests with nonisolated males, a neutral arena, and A/J opponents (Roubertoux & Carlier, 2003). Also, in an F2 derived from NZB and C57BL/6 mice, DNA markers on the PAR were associated with number of

attacks in tests with nonisolated males, a neutral arena, and A/J opponents. However, this association was not found for isolated males in a resident-intruder test with A/J opponents.

Pharmacological studies support the genetic evidence for the involvement of STS in attack by males, at least in the experimental conditions described above (Nicolas, Pinoteau, Papot, Routier, Guillaumet, & Mortaud, 2001). CBA/H male mice were injected with varying doses of DHEAS (dihydroepiandrosterone-sulfate) in the presence or absence of Coumate. Coumate is an inhibitor of steroid sulfatase activity. Coumate was administered orally at a dose that maximally inhibits brain steroid sulfatase activity. DHEAS by itself maximally increased the proportion of attacking males at the higher does. The combination of Coumate and DHEAS increased the proportion of attacking males at doses of DHEAS lower than 5 mg/kg but not at higher doses. This finding is consistent with a role for STS in regulating neurosteroid metabolism and thereby offensive aggression.

Neurosteroids can be sulfated or not. This property is regulated by STS. Free or sulfated neurosteroids appear to have opposite effects on neurotransmitters systems. For example, DHEAS and pregnalone sulfate act as antagonists of the GABA receptor, whereas allopregnanalone act as agonists of the GABA receptor. Because knockouts of neurotransmitter systems genes often act on offensive aggression in males (Maxson & Canastar, 2003), it may be that steroid sulfatase exerts its effects on offense by regulating one or more relevant neurotransmitter systems.

Several aspects of the studies with this genetic variant are worth noting:

- The research program systematically varied parameters known to affect offense. These parameters included post-weaning social environment, type of test, and type of opponent. This approach should be incorporated into other studies of the genetics of mouse aggression.

- Regardless of those parameters, the STS variants have effects on male offense in one set of experimental conditions – non-isolated males, a neutral cage test and a A/J standard opponent – but not in others.

- Most genes with effects on offense in mice have been detected with knockouts. One allele codes for a functional protein, whereas the other allele codes for a non-functional protein. Here both alleles code for a functioning STS protein that differ in enzymatic activity. The effect of this type of allelic variation on aggression should be studied with more genes. Variants of 46 other genes have been reported to affect offense in male mice (Maxson & Canastar, 2006b). Most of these have been studied in knockouts. We suggest that effects of functional allelic variants for these and other genes should also be studied.

Genes, Nitric Oxide and Offense in Mice

There are three homologous genes that code for nitric oxide synthase. *nNos* (Chromosome 5) codes for the neuronal enzyme, *eNos* (Chromosome 5) codes for the endothelia enzyme, and *iNos* (Chromosome 11) codes for the macrophage enzyme. All nitric oxide synthase catalyzes the conversion of argenine to nitric oxide (NO) and citrulline. In the nervous system, NO is a retrograde neurotransmitter. Here, this gaseous neurotransmitter is formed in the postsynaptic cell and acts on the presynaptic one. There are knockout mice of *nNos* and *eNos*. Both have effects on offense in males, and *nNos* also has effects on offense in females.

Initially, animal caretakers observed a high incidence of deaths in group-housed male mice homozygous for the *nNos* knockout. These mice had scarring indicative of fighting among the mice. Video observation in the colony of other *nNos* homozygous mice showed that there was indeed a high incidence of fights with potentially lethal attacks.

The offensive aggression of homozygous *nNos* knockout males was compared with that of wildtype homozygous males in two tests (Nelson et al., 1995): a dyadic resident-intruder test and a neutral cage test with a group of four males. The opponent in the resident-intruder test was a wild type male (essentially C57BL/6J). In the neutral cage test, each male was of the same genotype. In the resident-intruder test, the proportion of total attacks and the total number of offensive encounters were higher in the *nNos* homozygous knockouts than in homozygous wild types, but the two groups did not differ in latency to attack. In the neutral cage grouped test, again the proportion of total attacks and the duration of offensive encounters were higher in the *nNos* homozygous knockouts than in homozygous wild types. Also, the latency to first attack was lower in *nNos* homozygous knockouts than in homozygous wild types. These differences only occur in males that have had a period of isolation and do not occur if mice have been group housed. In addition, the differences depend on genetic background. They occur on the C57BL/6J but not the C57BL/6Orl background (LeRoy et al., 2000).

In the *nNos* homozygous knockout, there was also a change in the attack or bite target. The preferred bite target for offensive attacks in mice is the base of the tail and the hindquarters. In contrast, most of the bites in *nNos* homozygotes are directed at the junction of the head and spine. Such bites could sever the brain and spinal cord, which might account for the lethality of attacks in *nNos* males.

In knockouts, the functional gene and its protein are absent from conception in all tissues. Thus, the knockout could have its effects developmentally or physiologically. These alternatives were tested by administering 7-nitoindazole or 7-NI (an inhibitor of nNOS) to adult wild type males (Demas et al., 1997). A resident-intruder and a neutral cage test were used. The intruders were untreated C57BL/6J mice. There were four mice of the same treatment type in the neutral cage test. All mice had been individually housed. In the resident-intruder test, the

7-NI group had more offensive encounters as well as more pursuits, attacks and bites, and in the grouped neutral cage test, the 7-NI group had more offensive encounters and a longer duration of aggressive encounters. It appears that this knockout may have primarily, if not exclusively, physiological effects on offense.

Offensive aggression in male mice is usually testosterone dependent, and the effect on the *nNos* mutant on male offensive aggression is no exception (Kriegsfeld, Dawson, Dawson, Nelson, & Solomon, 1997). As above, both a resident-intruder test and a neutral cage test (involving two rather than four mice) were used. Castration reduced and testosterone replacement restored offensive aggression in both tests for both wild type and *nNos* knockout homozygotes.

Although there is no effect of the *nNos* knockout on the offensive aggression of nonpregnant and nonlactating female mice, offensive aggression in lactating females was reduced in *nNos* homozygous knockout mice (Gammie & Nelson, 1999). An intruder CD1 or C57BL/6 male was introduced into the cage of a lactating female 3 minutes after her pups were removed. The *nNos* homozygous knockout female showed fewer attacks and less time engaging in offensive aggression than homozygous wild type females. As with *Esr1* and *2* knockouts, the effect of *nNos* knockout is not the same in males and females, and the effect in females depends on reproductive state.

The nitric oxide synthase coded by *eNos* also has an effect on offensive aggression in males (Demas et al., 1999). Again there were both resident-intruder tests and neutral cage tests (involving four mice). In the resident-intruder test, the number and duration of offensive encounters were greatly reduced in *eNos* knockout homozygotes. Offensive aggression was also essentially eliminated in the neutral cage test (four mice). The *eNos* knockout mice are hypertensive, but this does not seem to be the cause of the greatly reduced aggression. These mice were still pacific after treatment with an antihyper-

tensive drug (hydralzine). The *eNos* knockout has no effect on the aggressive behavior of lactating females (Gammie, Huang, & Nelson, 2000).

It has been recently proposed that both the *nNos* and *eNos* knockouts alter aspects of the serotonin neurotransmitter system and that this is the intermediate step between loss of the functional enzyme, absence of NO, and offensive aggression (Chiavegatto, Dawson, Mamounas, Koliatsos, Dawson, & Nelson, 2000; Chiavegatto & Nelson, 2003). The levels of 5HT (serotonin) but not its metabolite 5HIAA (5-hydroxyindoleacetic acid) in cerebral cortex, hippocampus, hypothalamus, cerebellum, and midbrain were lower in *nNos* homozygous knockouts than in homozygous wild types. Treating wild type and *nNos* knockout homozygotes with 5HTP (5-hydroxytryptophan) increased 5HT, 5HIAA, and 5HT turnover. After the 5HTP treatment, there was also a dramatic reduction in the offensive aggression of the *nNos* knockout homozygotes in the resident-intruder test. In addition, agonists of the 5-HT1A and 5-HT1B receptors reduced offensive aggression in both wild type and knockout homozygotes but at higher doses for knockouts than for wild types.

Several aspects of the studies with this genetic variant are worth noting:

- The effect of the *nNos* knockout occurs in both resident-intruder and neutral cage tests.
- The effect of the *nNos* knockout occurs in isolated mice, but it does not occur in nonisolated mice.
- In contrast, variants of *Sts* only affect offense when the males are pair housed with a female prior to testing, and when tested in a neutral cage. These opposite findings for effects on *Sts* and *nNos* variants on offense suggest that there may be at least two different mechanisms underlying variation in male offense.
- The effect of the *nNos* variant on aggression is not the same in males and females. A sex difference was also seen for effects of the *Esr1* and *Esr2* on aggression. These

findings suggest that at least some aspects of the mechanisms of offense may not be the same in male and female mice.

- Chiavegatto and Nelson (2001) have proposed that most if not all knockouts with effects on male aggression do so by acting on some aspect of the serotonin neurotransmitter system. If valid, this might be a final common pathway for most if not all knockouts acting on male offense. For example, there was elevated rather than reduced 5HT metabolism in the brains of the *eNos* knockout.

Genes, Monoamines, and Offense in Mice

There is substantial genetic, neurochemical, and pharmacological evidence for a major role of serotonergic and catecholaminergic neurotransmission (dopamine, norepinephrine, epinephrine) in offense of mice and other mammals. Knockouts of four genes and their effects on aggression are relevant to this hypothesis. These genes are *Maoa* (monoamine oxidase A, X chromosome), *Comt* (catechol-o-methyl transferase, Chromosome 16), *Slc6a4* (serotonin transporter, Chromosome 11), and *Slc6a3* (dopamine transporter, Chromosome 13). Also relevant is the knockout for *Maob* (monoamie oxidase B, X chromosome).

The protein coded by each of these is involved in removing one or more of the biogenic amines from the synaptic space or presynaptic neuron. When a transgene was inserted into the *Maoa* gene, the gene and its protein became inactive (Cases et al., 1995). This effect was due to replacement of Exon two and three of the *Maoa* gene by the transgene. The MAOA protein of wild type mice degrades synaptic serotonin and catecholamines. Because the MAOA protein from the null mutant had essentially no enzymatic activity, there was a higher level in brain of serotonin and norepinephrine but not dopamine and a lower level of 5HIAA in the null mutant than in wild type mice. There were many neurological effects of the mutant on pups, such as abnormal postures, violent shaking during sleep, and hyperactive startle responses. The neurological effects in null mutant pups were attenuated by inhibitors of serotonin synthesis but not by inhibitors of catecholamine synthesis. Aggressive behaviors of adult mice were assessed in two tests. The first was between cage mates in the home cage. Here, skin wounds were assessed in 2-, 3-, 4-, and 7-month-old males. Wounds were found in the null mutant cage mates but not in the wild type cage mates. The second was in a resident-intruder test. Prior to the aggression test, the resident had either a long period of breeding or had a long period of isolation. For both conditions, the null mutants had lower latency to first attack than did the wild types.

There are downstream effects of the *Maoa* knockout on neurotransmitter systems that may account for its effect on offense. These effects include downregulation of the serotonin transporter and desensitization of the 5-HT1A receptors in the *Maoa* knockout (Evrard et al., 2002). Also, there are increased expression of the argenine vasopressin (AVP) in the suprachiasmatic nucleus, decreased expression of AVP in the supraoptic nucleus, and no effect on AVP expression in the paraventricular nucleus of *Maoa* knockout males (Vacher, Calas, Maltonti, & Hardin-Pouzet, 2004). A knockout of the AVP1b receptor reduces offense by male mice in a resident-intruder test (Wersinger et al., 2002). Furthermore, the barrel fields in the somotosensory cortex are totally absent in the *Maoa* null mutants (Cases, Vitalis, Seif, De Maeyer, Sotelo, & Gaspar, 1996). This may be due to the disruption of serotonin metabolism. It might also contribute to the effect of the null mutant on attack behavior. The barrel fields receive sensory input from the vibrissae, and successful attacks depend on feedback from the vibrissae.

In contrast, the knockout of *Maob* has no effect on male offense (Shih, Chen, & Ridd, 1999). MAOB primarily metabolizes phenylethylamine rather than serotonin and catecholamines. In this knockout, only phenyethylamine was increased. Thus, it may be that phenylethylamine has no role in male offense of mice.

There is a knockout of *Slc6a4* that codes for the serotonin transporter (Holmes, Murphy & Crawley, 2002). The serotonin transporter regulates the reuptake of serotonin after it is released into the synaptic space. As a consequence, in the knockout mouse, there is an increase in extracellular serotonin levels and compensatory desensitization of the serotonin 1A and 1B receptors. Offensive aggression but not social investigation is eliminated in the *Slc6a4* homozygotes and greatly reduced in the heterozygotes. On the first and second encounter, the homozygous knockouts had longer latency to first attack and fewer attacks than the homozygous wild types. In addition, there was an increase in aggressive behavior from day 1 to 2 for the wild types but not the homozygous knockouts. A resident-intruder test was used in which the residents had been isolated, and DBA/2 males were the intruders.

The *Slc6a4* homozygous knockouts resemble the *Maoa* knockout in two ways. Both have elevated levels of serotonin, and both do not have cortical barrel fields. However, the two knockouts have opposite effects on offensive aggression. For this reason, it may be that neither the elevated serotonin levels nor the absence of cortical barrel fields is in the causal pathway from either null mutant to behavioral effect. However, the *Maoa* mutant is in the C3H strain background, whereas the *Slc6a4* knockout is in the C57BL/6 strain background. Either elevated serotonin levels or absence of cortical barrel fields may interact with respective backgrounds to have opposite phenotypic effects.

Regardless, there is also an opposite effect of the *Maoa* and the *Slc6a4* knockout on expression of the adenosine 2A receptor that may account for the opposite effects of the two knockouts on offense (Mossner et al., 2000) as it is downregulated in the *Maoa* knockout and upregulated in the *Slc6a4* knockout. A knockout of the adenosine 2A gene increases aggression in a resident-intruder test (Ledent et al., 1997).

There is a knockout mutant for *Comt* that codes for catechol-o-methyl transferase (Gogos et al., 1998). COMT degrades synaptic dopamine, norepinephrine, and epinephrine. In brain or liver, this *Comt* knockout mutant produces no detectable mRNA. In the homozygous knockouts, there was an increase in dopamine in the frontal cortex but not other areas, and there were no changes in serotonin, 5HIAA, or norepinephrine levels. The levels of these were not reported for the heterozygote. Male mice that are heterozyous for this knockout mutant were significantly more aggressive than either wild type or knockout homozygotes. The heterozygotes had more aggressive bouts and shorter attack latencies. The males were given a homogenous set test in a neutral arena and had been individually housed.

There is a knockout mutant of *Slc6a3* that codes for the dopamine transporter (Rodriguiz, Chu, Caron, & Wetsel, 2004). The dopamine transporter regulates the reuptake of dopamine after it is released into the synaptic space. As a consequence, extracellular dopamine is increased, and there is reduced expression of the dopamine receptors D1 and D2 in the striatum. In a resident-intruder test, the *Slc6a3* homozygotes had more threat postures but no more attacks than the wild type homozygotes, whereas in a neutral cage test, the *Slc6a3* homozygotes had more threat postures and more attacks than the wild type homozygotes. More social behavior was also initiated in both tests by the knockout homozygotes. The wild type or knockout homozygotes had been isolated for 2 weeks prior to the aggression tests. In the resident-intruder test and neutral cage test, the opponent was a C3H/He male.

Several aspects of these studies are worth noting

- There was an individually housed group for all knockouts. For each, there was an effect on offense.
- All knockouts were given a resident-intruder test. There was an effect on offense in this test for all knockouts except for the dopamine transporter knockout.
- The *Maoa* and the *Slc6a4* knockouts have similar effects on levels of serotonin

and on the development of the cortical barrel fields but opposite effects on offensive aggression. The opposite effects on offense of these two knockouts may be due to opposite effects on the expression of the adenosine 2A receptor.

- Serotonin is thought to be the primary neurotransmitter involved in offense. However, two of the knockouts (*Comt* and *Slc6a3*) provide evidence for a role of dopamine in offensive aggression.
- There are effects of *Maoa* variants on human aggression (Brunner, Nelen M., Breakefield, Ropers, & van Oost, 1993; Caspi et al., 2002). This is significant given that there are only a few examples where the same gene with effects on aggression in mice has been studied with regard to human aggression. Here a gene found to have an effect on mouse aggression also has an effect on human aggression.

Genes, the Hippocampus, and Offense in Mice

In 1971, four male and three female mice (*Mus domesticus*) were trapped in a mansion near Groningen, The Netherlands. Their descendants were the base population for selectively breeding a short attack latency (SAL) and a long attack latency (LAL) line of males (van Oortmerssen & Bakker, 1981) The mice were tested in a cage that had both a home area and a border area where an intruder was encountered. The resident was familiar with both areas. The intruder was a male from an inbred albino strain (MAS-Gro). Prior to the test, the experimental mice were pair housed. Selection was rapid in the SAL line and slow in the LAL line. After 30 generations of selection, the SAL line males attacked almost instantaneously, and the LAL almost never attacked in the 600-second test. Females of both lines never attack in this test.

The genes that differ between SALs and LALs are found on autosomes, the pseudoautosomal region of the heterosomes, and the male-specific region of the Y chromosome. These genetic differences have been related to three mechanisms. The first is variation in *Sts* on the PAR (van Oortmerssen & Sluyter, 1994). The effect of *Sts* variants on offense was discussed in a previous section. The second is an effect of the autosomes on adult testosterone sensitivity and levels (van Oortmerssen, Dijk, & Schuurman, 1987; van Oortmerssen, Benus, & Sluyter, 1992). The effect on adult testosterone sensitivity may be mediated by prenatal testosterone (Compaan, DeRuiter, Koolhaas, van Oortmerssen, & Bohus, 1991). The effects of steroid hormones, their metabolism, and steroid hormone receptors on offense were discussed in a previous section. The third mechanism is an effect on the morphology of the hippocampal mossy fibers that project from the granule cell of the dentate gyrus to the pyramidal cells of the CA3 region. The intra- and infrapyramidal mossy fiber fields (IIPMF) are smaller in SAL males than they are in LALs (Sluyter, Jamot, van Oortmerssen, & Crusio, 1994). Some of this difference is due to one or more genes on autosomes, and some of it is due to one or more genes on the male-specific part of the Y chromosome (Hensbroek, Sluyter, Guillot, van Oortmerssen, & Crusio, 1995).

This association between the size of the IIPMF and offensive aggression has also been shown across seven inbred strains (Guillot, Roubertoux, & Crusio, 1994). The IIPMF and the proportion of mice attacking were measured in each strain. The strain correlation for the two traits was $r = -0.82$. Aggression was assessed in a resident-intruder test with an A/J intruder. The resident had been housed with a female until 13 days before the resident-intruder test. This correlation was not observed when aggression is assessed in a neutral cage, when the resident had NOT been housed with a female and then isolated for 13 days, or when the opponent was of the same strain. We note that the conditions for the strain correlation with *Sts* variants were not the conditions for strain correlation with mossy fiber variation. The strain correlation with *Sts* variants occurred with mice that were housed with a female and then isolated for just 1 day prior to a neutral cage test.

There is a coisogenic pair of C57BL/6 strains that differ in a single gene (Jamot, Bertholet, & Crusio, 1994). The N strain has smaller IIPMF than the K strain. In both a resident-intruder and a neutral cage test, males of the N strain had fewer tail rattles, made fewer attacks, and had a longer attack latency than males of the K strain (Sluyter, Marican, & Crusio, 1999). Also, the K strain had more males attacking than the N strain. From weaning, the males had been housed with a female prior to the neutral cage test, and they had been isolated prior to the resident-intruder test. The opponent in both tests was a DBA/2 male. Interestingly, the substrains may differ in 2-D gel electrophoresis for expression of a single hippocampal-specific protein (Bonnet & Crusio, 1996).

However, there have been some failures to find an association between IIPMF variation and offensive aggression. There is a knockout mutation for the *Fmr1* (X chromosome), which coded for the FMRP protein. In humans, this is involved in fragile X mental retardation syndrome. *Fmr1* knockout males have smaller IIPMF than wild type males, but they did not differ in aggression. This was a neutral cage test with an AJ opponent for which the mice had not been isolated. Also, nonisolated mice of the FVB/N and C57BL/6 strain were tested in a neutral cage with an A/J opponent (Mineur & Crusio, 2002). The IIPMF are larger in C57BL/6 than in FVB/N mice. However, there was only a difference in frequency and latency of tail rattle and in no other measure of aggression. Males of the AB/Gat strain are very pacific, and males of the CS/ag stain are highly aggressive. After 14 days of isolation, the mice were tested in a neutral cage with a C3H strain opponent male. In contrast to the majority of other studies, the more aggressive CS/ag strain has larger IIPMF than the pacific AB/Gat strain (Prior, Schwegler, Marashi, & Sachser, 2004).

Regardless of the conflicting evidence on the association between size of the hippocampal mossy fibers and aggression, there have been recent studies on gene expression in the hippocampus of adult SAL and LAL males (Feldker et al, 2003a,b). These studies used gene chip technology to assess differences in mRNA levels for 30,000 genes. There was differential expression between SALs and LALs for 191 genes. This included differential expression of cytoskeletal and signal transduction genes, which may be related to the structural differences in the hippocampus of SALs and LALs as described above. A similar study has looked at strain correlation in hippocampal gene expression and aggression (Fernades, Paya-Cano, Sluyter, D'Souza, Plomin, & Schalkwyk, 2004). A correlation was found for level of *Comt* expression and aggression.

The following are worth noting:

• The effect of the IIPMF variation on male offense occurs in some life history and testing contexts but not in others. Again, this suggests that there may be more than one mechanism for male offense.
• There are no effects of the genetic variation in IIPMF on female offense. Again, this finding suggests that at least some of the mechanisms of male and female offense are different.
• Some genes with effects on male offense appear to act by altering the development of neural structures.
• Gene chips are a new technology that can screen for phenotypic or genotypic differences in mRNAs of tens of thousands of genes. They can be used not only to find differences in gene expression but also to investigate how one gene or a set of genes influence the expression of other genes, as well as how the environment or experience can do the same. This new technology promises to be a most useful approach for the study of genes, brain, and behavior, including aggressive behavior.

Genes, Environments, Adaptations, and Offense in Mice

Many years ago both Ginsburg (1958) and Benzer (1971) suggested that genetic variants could be used to dissect the brain and other mechanisms of behavior, including aggression. Forty-six genes are now known to influence variation in offense by male mice (Maxson & Canastar, 2006). As indicated above, some of these are being used to systematically study the brain mechanisms involved in offense by male and female mice. However, it is obvious that whether or not a genetic variant has an effect on offense often depends on life history and testing contexts. Among these contexts are genetic background, maternal environment, postweaning social environment, type of test, and type of opponent (Maxson & Canastar, 2003).

For example, males of the selected strains, TA (aggressive) and TNA (nonaggressive), were tested in four paradigms (Nyberg, Sandnabba, Schalkwyk, & Sluyter, 2004): in a neutral cage test, as the resident in a resident-intruder test, as an intruder in a resident-intruder test, and sexual aggression with a male paired with a familiar or unfamiliar female. The opponent in all tests was a mouse of a Swiss strain. Attack latency was measured. The strain difference in each test depended on specific combinations of environmental parameters. In concluding their study, the authors write, "These data suggest that the identification of genes underlying aggressive behavior in mice is by no means straightforward, and that the results of this search will depend on the environmental design of the study (type of paradigm, housing condition)."

It is clear that context is very important for finding and understanding genetic effects on offense in mice and perhaps other animals (Young & Balaban, 2003). Context may provide developmental or encounter information that can influence the decision of the mouse or other animal, including humans, to escalate an encounter to a fight with the potential for injury to self as well as to the opponent. Genotype may then be conceived as a modulator of these context effects. There are two implications of this conception for research on the genetics of offense and other kinds of aggression in mice. The first is methodological. We suggest as we have elsewhere in detail (Maxson & Canastar, 2003) that a standard set of developmental and encounter environments be used with all genetic variants to be tested for offense and other types of aggression and that subsequently they be systematically varied. To some degree this is already being done. This will enable direct comparisons of one variant with another in common contexts, and will also facilitate the successful searches for context-dependent effects of genetic variants. The second implication is substantive. The studies described above imply that there are at least two genetic and neural systems involved in offense by male mice. One of these is seen when pair-housed mice are tested in a neutral cage paradigm with a standard opponent. An example of this is variants of the *Sts* gene. Another of these is seen when isolated mice are tested in a resident-intruder test with a standard opponent. An example of this is the variants of the hippocampal mossy fibers (IIPMF). The differences and similarities between these two genetic and neural systems are much in need of further study.

Of Mice and Humans

More than 60 years ago, the first studies on genetic variants of male mouse offense were published (Ginsburg & Allee, 1942; Scott, 1942). In part, both studies were done not only to investigate the genetics of aggression in mice but also to understand the biology of this and other kinds of aggression in humans. Today, we would speak of this effort as developing mouse models for human aggression. Mouse and other animal models are still sought for adaptive, nonadaptive, pathological, and criminal aggression in humans. Examples of this search for mouse models of human aggression are to be found in Miczek, Fish, & Debold (2003); Sluyter, Arseneault, Moffitt, Veenema, de Boer, and Koolhaas (2003); and Haller and Kruk (2006). All of these essentially propose face validity models based on behavioral similarities between one or more kinds of aggression in mice and extreme aggression or violence in humans. In contrast, we suggest a different approach.

There are inherent problems in applying the term "model" to behavior. A model is usually a scaled-down version of the real. Thus, we have model cars, boats, and planes. These are miniature versions of what they model. As such, these can be used by engineers to study and test some aspect of the design of the real thing. The concept of model can be reasonably extended to biological structures that are similar in some way across related species. For example, all mammals have four-chambered hearts. This structure could be studied in any mammal, and the findings can then be generalized with due caution to humans.

But behavior is a function and not a structure. Behavior in one species, such as mice, is not a scaled-down version of that in another, such as humans. For this reason, the behavior of a mouse or of another animal should not be thought of as a model for human behavior. However, the brain of one animal can be a model for that of another and the functions of the two brains compared. Regrettably, too little is known of the relationship between brain structures and offense or other kinds of aggression in mice as well as humans.

Rather, we suggest that genetic variants with effects on mouse offense or other types of aggression should be viewed as hypothesis generators (Maxson, 2003). They potentially can generate four types of hypotheses for the causes underlying human aggression. First, genetic variants in the mouse with effects on offense or other types of aggression have homologues in the human genome. Currently, 46 genes have been shown to affect male mouse offense (Maxson & Canastar, 2006). Variants of the human homologues could be assessed for effects on one or more types of human aggression. Second, as has been shown in this chapter, genetic variants can be used to dissect the neural and other mechanisms of offense in mice. Some aspects of these gene-based neural mechanisms for offense in mice can potentially generate testable hypotheses about the neural and other mechanisms of one or more types of human aggression. For example, because variants of MAOA have effects on both mouse offense and some types of human aggression, the anatomical, physiological, and biochemical effects on offense of the MAOA variant in mice can be used to generate hypotheses about the mechanisms for the effect of the MAOA variants in humans. Third, the effects of genetic variants in mice are often, if not always, context dependent. Such context dependence should be expected for genes with effects on human aggression. In fact, there is already one example of such genotype-environment interaction in humans. The effect of a variant of the human MAOA gene on antisocial behaviors, including aggression, depends on whether or not the individual has been maltreated as a child (Caspi et al., 2002). The finding that there are at least two genetic and neural systems in mice with different dependence on context may also generate hypotheses about the context dependence for effects of gene variants in humans on one or more types of aggression or violence. Fourth, in mice some genetic variants have the same effects on male and female offense, others have opposite effects in male and females, and others affect only offense in male or only in females. These different kinds of variants may generate hypotheses of the first, second, and third type about genetic effects on male and female aggression and violence in humans.

Elsewhere, we have argued for a comparative genetics of aggression (Maxson & Canastar, 2005). We reviewed there the suitability of fruit flies, honeybees, stickleback fish, zebrafish, chickens and other birds, mice, rats, voles, dogs, cats, and monkeys for this comparative genetics. A goal of such a comparative genetics would be to determine if a gene with effects on a type of aggression in one species has a similar effect in other species and whether the mechanism of its effects were similar in two or more species. This approach has also been suggested recently for other animal behaviors (Enserink, 2005). It was argued there that this would establish a comparative genomics of animal behavior. For example, as discussed in Enserink's review, the gene that codes for cGMP-dependent kinase has a role in the foraging and feeding behaviors of a nematode, the fruit fly, and honeybees. Such a comparative genomics of behavior can and should be extended to include humans. There is already one example for aggression. Variants of the monoamine oxidase gene affect aggression in mice (Cases et al., 1995), monkeys (Newman et al., 2005) and humans (Caspi et al., 2002). In addition, in monkeys and humans, experience similarly influences whether or not the genetic variants have differential effects on aggression.

References

Alleva, E. (1993). Assessment of aggressive behavior in rodents. In P. M. Conn (Ed.), *Methods in neurosciences* (Vol. 14, pp. 111–137). New York: Academic Press.

Baron, R. A., & Richardson, D. R. (1994). *Human aggression* (2nd ed). New York: Plenum Press.

Benzer, S. (1971). From genes to behavior. *Journal of the American Medical Association, 218,* 1015–1022.

Bjorkqvist, K., & Niemela, P. (1992). *Of mice and women: Aspects of female aggression.* New York: Academic Press.

Brain. F., Haug, M., & Kamis, A. (1983) Hormones and different tests for aggression with particular reference to the effects of testosterone metabolites. In J. Balthazart, E. Prove, & R. Gilles (Eds.), *Hormones and behaviour in higher vertebrates* (pp. 290–304). Berlin: Springer-Verlag.

Bonnet, F., & Crusio, W. E. (1996). Bidimensional gel electrophoresis of hippocampal proteins in adult males from different inbred strains. *European Journal of Neuroscience, 9*(Suppl.), 178.

Brunner, H. G., Nelen, M., Breakefield, X. O., Ropers, H. H., & van Oost, B. A. (1993). Abnormal behavior associated with a point mutation in the structural gene for monoamine oxidase A. *Science, 262,* 578–580.

Canastar, A., Maxson, S. C., & Bishop, B. E. (2004, Summer). *Aggressive behavior in two types of sex reversed mice, XY females and XX males.* Paper presented at ISRA XVI Meeting, Santorini, Greece.

Carlier, M., Roubertoux, P. L., & Pastoret, C. (1991). The Y chromosome effect on intermale aggression in mice depends on the maternal environment. *Genetics, 129,* 231–236.

Cases, O., Seif I., Grimsby, J., Gaspar, P., Chen, K., Pournin, S., et al. (1995). Aggressive behavior and altered amounts of brain serotonin and norepinephrine in mice lacking MAOA. *Science, 268,* 1763–1766.

Cases, O., Vitalis, T., Seif, I., De Maeyer, E., Sotelo, C., & Gaspar, P. (1996). Lack of barrels in the somatosensory cortex of monoamine oxidase A-deficient mice: Role of a serotonin excess during the critical period. *Neuron, 16,* 297–307.

Caspi, A., McClay, J., Moffitt, T. E., Mill, J., Martin, J., Craig, I. W., et al. (2002). Role of genotype in the cycle of violence in maltreated children. *Science, 297,* 851–854.

Chiavegatto, S., Dawson, V. L., Mamounas, L. A., Koliatsos, V. E., Dawson, T. M., & Nelson, R. J. (2001). Brain serotonin dysfunction accounts for aggression in male mice lacking neuronal nitric oxide synthase. *Proceedings of the National Academy of Sciences, 98,* 1277–1281.

Chiavegatto, S., & Nelson, R. J. (2001). Molecular basis of aggression. *Trends in Neuroscience, 24,* 713–719.

Chiavegatto, S., & Nelson, R. J. (2003). Interaction of nitric acid and serotonin in aggressive behavior. *Hormones and Behavior, 44,* 233–241.

Compaan, J. C., DeRuiter, A. J. H., Koolhaas, J. M., van Oortmerssen, G. A., & Bohus, B. (1991). Differential effects of neonatal testosterone treatment on aggression in two selection lines of mice. *Physiology and Behavior, 51,* 7–10.

Dellovade, T. L., & Merchenthaler, I. (2004). Estrogen regulation of neurokinin B gene expression in the mouse arcuate nucleus is mediated by estrogen receptor alpha. *Endocrinology, 145,* 736–742.

Demas, G. E., Eliasson M. J. L., Dawson T. M., Dawson V. L., Kriegsfeld, L. J., Nelson, R. J., et al. (1997). Inhibition of neuronal nitric oxide synthase increases aggressive behavior in mice. *Molecular Medicine, 3,* 611–617.

Demas, G. E., Kriegsfeld, L. J., Blackshaw, S., Huang. P., Gammie, S. C., Nelson, R. J., et al. (1999). Elimination of aggressive behavior in male mice lacking endothelial nitric oxide synthase. *Journal of Neuroscience, 19,* 1–5.

Dominguez-Salazar, E., Bateman, H. L., & Rissman, E. F. (2004) Background matters: The effects of estrogen receptor alpha gene disruption on male sexual behavior are modified by background strain. *Hormones and Behavior, 46,* 482–490.

Enserink, M. (2005). A genomic view of animal behavior. *Science, 307,* 30–33.

Evrard, A., Malagie, I., Laporte, A. M., Boni, C., Hanoun, N., Trillat, A. C., et al. (2003).

Altered regulation of the 5-HT system in the brain of MAO-A knock-out mice. *European Journal of Neuroscience*, 15, 841–851.

Feldker, D. E., Datson, N. A., Veenema, A. H., Meulmeester, E., de Kloet, E, R., & Vreugdenhil, E. (2003a). Serial analysis of gene expression predicts structural differences in hippocampus of long attack latency and short attack latency mice. *European Journal of Neuroscience*, 17, 379–387.

Feldker, D. E., Datson, N. A., Veenema, A. H., Proutski, V., Lathouwers, D., De Kloet, E. R., et al. (2003b). Gene chip analysis of hippocampal gene expression profiles of short- and long-attack-latency mice: Technical and biological implications. *Journal of Neuroscience Research*, 74, 701–716.

Fernandes, C., Paya-Cano, J. L., Sluyter, F., D'Souza, U., Plomin, R., & Schalkwyk, L. C. (2004). Hippocampal gene expression profiling across eight mouse inbred strains: Towards understanding the molecular basis for behaviour. *European Journal of Neuroscience*, 19, 2576–2582.

Gammie, S. C., Huang, P. L., & Nelson, R. J. (2000). Maternal aggression in endothelial nitric oxide synthase-deficient mice. *Hormones and Behavior*, 38, 13–20.

Gammie, S. C., & Nelson, R. J. (1999). Maternal aggression is reduced in neuronal nitric oxide synthase-deficient mice. *Journal of Neuroscience*, 19, 8027–8035.

Ginsburg, B. E. (1958). Genetics as a tool in the study of behavior. *Perspectives in Biology and Medicine*, 1, 397–424.

Ginsburg, B. E., & Allee, W. C. (1942). Some effects of conditioning on social dominance and subordination in inbred strains of mice. *Physiology and Zoology*, 15, 485–506.

Gogos, J. A., Morgan, M., Luine, V., Santha, M., Ogawa, S., Pfaff, D., et al. (1998). Catechol-O-methyltransferase-deficient mice exhibit sexually dimorphic changes in catecholamine levels and behavior. *Proceedings of the National Academy of Sciences*, 95, 9991–9996.

Guillot, P.-V., Carlier, M., Maxson, S. C., & Roubertoux, P. L. (1995) Intermale aggression tested in two procedures, using four inbred strains of mice and their reciprocal congenics: Y chromosomal implications. *Behavior Genetics*, 25, 357–360.

Guillot, P.-V., Roubertoux, P. L., & Crusio, W. E. (1994). Hippocampal mossy fiber distribution and intermale aggression in seven inbred mouse strains. *Brain Research*, 660, 167–169.

Haller, J., & Kruk, M. (2006). Normal and abnormal aggression: Human disorders and novel laboratory models. *Neuroscience Biobehavioral Review*, 30(3), 292.

Hensbroek, R. A., Sluyter, F., Guillot, P. V., van Oortmerssen, G. A., & Crusio, W. E. (1995). Y chromosomal effects on hippocampal mossy fiber distributions in mice selected for aggression. *Brain Research*, 682, 203–206.

Holmes, A., Murphy, D. L, & Crawley, J. N. (2002). Reduced aggression in mice lacking the serotonin transporter. *Psychopharmacology*, 161, 160–167.

Jamot, L., Bertholet, J.-Y., & Crusio, W. E. (1994). Genetic analysis of hippocampal mossy fibers and radial-maze learning in two substrains of C57BL/6J inbred mice. *Brain Research*, 644, 352–356.

Jones S. E., & Brain P. F. (1987). Performance of inbred and outbred laboratory mice in putative tests of aggression. *Behavior Genetics*, 17, 87–96.

Kriegsfeld, L. J., Dawson, T. M., Dawson, V. L., Nelson, R. J., & Solomon, H (1997). Aggressive behavior in male mice lacking the gene for neuronal nitric oxide synthase requires testosterone. *Brain Research*, 769, 66–70.

Lahr, G., Maxson, S. C., Mayer A., Just, W., Pilgrim, C., & Reisert, I. (1995). Transcription of the Y chromosomal gene, Sry, in adult mouse brain. *Molecular Brain Research*, 33, 179–182.

Ledent, C., Vaugeois. J. M., Schiffmann, S. N., Pedrazzini, T., El Yacoubi, M., Vanderhaeghen, J, J., et al. (1997). Aggressiveness, hypoalgesia and high blood pressure in mice lacking the adenosine A2a receptor. *Nature*, 388, 674–678.

LeRoy I., Mortaud S., Tordjman S., Donsez-Darcel E., Carlier M., Degrelle H., et al. (1999). Genetic correlation between steroid sulfatase concentration and initiation of attack behavior in mice. *Behavior Genetics*, 29, 131–136.

LeRoy, I., Pothion, S., Mortaud, M., Chabert, C., Nicolas, L., Cherfouh, A., et al. (2000). Loss of aggression after transfer onto a C57BL/6 background in mice carrying a targeted disruption of the neuronal nitric oxide synthase gene. *Behavior Genetics*, 30, 367–373.

Maxson, S. C. (1992a). Potential genetic models of aggression and violence in males. In P. Driscoll (Ed.), *Genetically defined animal* models of neurobehavioral dysfunctions (pp. 174–188). Boston: Birkhauser.

Maxson, S. C. (1992b). Methodological issues in genetic analyses of an agonistic behavior (offense) in male mice. In D. Goldowitz, D. Wahlsten, & R. E. Wimer (Eds.), *Techniques for the genetic analysis of brain and behavior: Focus on the mouse* (pp. 349–373). Amsterdam: Elsevier.

Maxson, S. C. (1996). Searching for candidate genes with effects on an agonistic behavior, offense, in mice. *Behavior Genetics, 26,* 471–476.

Maxson, S. C. (2003). Animal models of human behavior. In D. N. Cooper (Ed.), *Nature encyclopedia of the human genome* (Vol. 1, pp. 136–139). London: Nature Publishing Group.

Maxson, S. C., & Canastar, A. (2003). Conceptual and methodological issues in the genetics of mouse agonistic behavior. *Hormones and Behavior, 44,* 258–262.

Maxson S. C., & Canastar, A. (2005). Genetic aspects of aggression in nonhuman animals. In R. J. Nelson (Ed.), *Biology of aggression.* New York: Oxford University Press.

Maxson, S. C., & Canastar, A. (2006). Aggression: Concepts and methods relevant to genetic analyses in mice and humans. In B. J. Jones & P. Mormede (Eds.), *Neurobehavioral genetics: Methods and applications.* Boca Raton, FL: CRC Press.

Maxson, S. C., Didier-Erickson, A., & Ogawa, S. (1989). The Y chromosome, social signals, and offense in mice. *Behavioral and Neural Biology, 52,* 251–259.

Maxson, S. C., Ginsburg, B. E., & Trattner, A. (1979). Interaction of Y-chromosomal and autosomal gene(s) in the development of intermale aggression in mice. *Behavior Genetics, 9,* 219–226.

Mayer, A., Mosler, G., Just, W., Pilgrim, C., & Reisert, I. (2000). Developmental profile of Sry transcripts in mouse brain. *Neurogenetics, 3,* 25–30.

Miczek, K. A., Fish, E. W., & Debold, J. F. (2003). Neurosteroids, GABAA receptors, and escalated aggressive behavior. *Hormones and Behavior, 44,* 242–257.

Mineur, Y. S., & Crusio, W. E. (2002). Behavioral and neuroanatomical characterization of FVB/N inbred mice. *Brain Research Bulletin, 57,* 41–47.

Mitchell, M. J. (2000). Spermatogenesis and the mouse Y chromosome: Specialization out of decay. *Results and Problems in Cell Differentiation. 28,* 233–270.

Monahan, E. J., & Maxson, S. C. (1998). Y chromosome, urinary chemosignals, and an agonistic behavior (offense) of mice. *Physiology and Behavior, 64,* 123–132.

Mossner, R., Albert, D., Persico, A. M., Hennig, T., Bengel, D., Holtman, B., et al. (2000). Differential regulation of adenosine A(1) and A(2A) receptors in serotonin transporter and monoamine oxidase A-deficient mice. *European Journal of Neuropsychopharmacology, 10,* 489–493.

Nelson, R. J., Demas, G. E., Huang, P. L., Fishman, M. C., Dawson, V. L., Dawson, T. M., et al. (1995). Behavioral abnormalities in male mice lacking neuronal nitric oxide synthase. *Nature, 378,* 383–386.

Newman, T. K., Syagailo, Y. V., Barr, C. S., Wendland, J. R., Champoux, M., Graessle, M., et al. (2005). Monoamine oxidase A gene promoter variation and rearing experience influences aggressive behavior in rhesus monkeys. *Biological Psychiatry, 57,* 167–172.

Nicolas, L. B., Pinoteau, W., Papot, S., Routier, S., Guillaumet, G., & Mortaud, S. (2001). Aggressive behavior induced by the steroid sulfatase inhibitor COUMATE and by DHEAS in CBA/H mice. *Brain Research, 992,* 218–222.

Nomura, M., Durbak, L., Chan, J., Smithies, O., Gustafsson, J. A., Korach. K. S., et al. (2003). Genotype/age interactions on aggressive behavior in gonadally intact estrogen receptor beta knockout (betaERKO) male mice. *Hormones and Behavior, 41,* 288–296.

Nomura, M., McKenna, E., Korach, K. S., Pfaff, D., & Ogawa, S. (2002). Estrogen receptor-β regulates transcript levels for oxytocin and arginine vasopressin in the hypothalamic paraventricular nucleus of male mice. *Molecular Brain Research, 109,* 84–94.

Nyberg, J., Sandnabba, K., Schalkwyk, L., & Sluyter, F. (2004). Genetic and environmental (inter)actions in male mouse lines selected for aggressive and nonaggressive behavior. *Gene, Brain, and Behavior, 3,* 101–109.

Ogawa, S., Chan, J., Chester, A. E., Gustafsson, J. A., Korach, K. S., & Pfaff, D. W. (1999). Survival of reproductive behaviors in estrogen receptor beta gene-deficient (betaERKO) male and female mice. *Proceedings of the National Academy of Sciences USA, 96,* 12887–12892.

Ogawa, S., Chester, A. E., Hewitt, S. C., Walker, V. R., Gustafsson, J. A., Smithies, O., et al. (2000). Abolition of male sexual behaviors in mice lacking estrogen receptors alpha and beta (alpha beta ERKO). *Proceedings of the National Academy of Sciences USA, 97*, 14737–14741.

Ogawa, S., Eng, V., Taylor, J., Lubahn, D. B., Korach, K. S., & Pfaff, D. W. (1998). Roles of estrogen receptor-alpha gene expression in reproduction-related behaviors in female mice. *Endocrinology, 139*, 5070–5081.

Ogawa, S., Lubahn, D. B., Korach, K. S., & Pfaff, D. W. (1997). Behavioral effects of estrogen receptor gene disruption in male mice. *Proceedings of the National Academy of Sciences USA, 94*, 1476–1481.

Ogawa, S., Washburn, T. F., Taylor J., Lubahn, D. B., Korach, K. S., & Pfaff, D. W. (1998). Modifications of testosterone-dependent behaviors by estrogen receptor-a gene disruption in male mice. *Endocrinology, 139*, 5058–5069.

Ohno, S., Geller, L. N., & Lai, E. V. 1974Tfm mutation and masculinization versus feminization of the mouse central nervous system. *Cell. 3*, 235–242.

Prior, H., Schwegler, H., Marashi, V., & Sachser, N. (2004). Exploration, emotionality, and hippocampal mossy fibers in nonaggressive AB/Gat and congenic highly aggressive mice. *Hippocampus, 14*, 135–140.

Rodriguiz, R. M., Chu, R., Caron, M. G., & Wetsel, W. C. (2004). Aberrant responses in social interaction of dopamine transporter knockout mice. *Behavioral Brain Research, 148*, 185–198.

Roubertoux, P. L., & Carlier, M. (2003) Y chromosome and antisocial behavior. In M. P. Mattson (Ed.), *Neurobiology of aggression: Understanding and preventing violence* (pp. 119–134). Totowa, NJ: Humana.

Roubertoux, P. L., Carlier, M., Degrelle, H., Phillips, J., Tordjamn, S., Dupertuis-Haas, M. C., et al. (1994). Co-segregation of intermale aggression with the pseudoautosomal region of the Y chromosome in mice. *Genetics, 135*, 225–230.

Schellinck, H. M., Monahan E., Brown, R. E., & Maxson, S. C. (1993) A comparison of the contribution of the major histocompatibility complex (MHC) and Y chromosomes to the discriminability of individual urine odors of mice by Long-Evans rats. *Behavior Genetics, 23*, 257–263.

Scordalakes, E. M., & Rissman, E. F. (2003). Aggression in male mice lacking functional estrogen receptor alpha. *Behavioral Neuroscience, 117*, 38–45.

Scordalakes, E. M., & Rissman, E. F. (2004). Aggression and arginine vasopressin immunoreactivity regulation by androgen receptor and estrogen receptor alpha. *Genes, Brain, and Behavior, 3*, 20–26.

Scott, J. P. (1942). Genetic differences in the social behavior of inbred strains of mice. *Journal of Heredity, 33*, 11–15.

Scott, J. P. (1966). Agonistic behavior in mice and rats: A review. *American Zoologist, 6*, 683–701.

Selmanoff, M. K., Maxson, S. C., & Ginsburg, B. E. (1976). Chromosomal determinants of intermale aggressive behavior in inbred mice. *Behavior Genetics, 6*, 53–69.

Shih, J. C., Chen, K., & Ridd, M. J. (1999). Monamine oxidase: From gene to behavior. *Annual Review of Neuroscience, 22*, 197–217.

Simon, N. G., McKenna, S. E., Lu, S.-F., & Cologer-Clifford, A. (1996). Development and expression of hormonal systems regulating aggression. *Annals of the New York Academy of Science, 794*, 8–17.

Sluyter, F., Arseneault, L., Moffitt, T. E., Veenema, A. H., de Boer, S., & Koolhaas, J. M. (2003). Toward an animal model for antisocial behavior: Parallels between mice and humans. *Behavior Genetics, 33*, 563–574.

Sluyter, F., Jamot, L., van Oortmerssen, G.A., & Crusio, W. E. (1994). Hippocampal mossy fiber distributions in mice selected for aggression. *Brain Research, 16*, 145–148.

Sluyter, F., Marican, C. C., & Crusio, W. E. (1999). Further phenotypical characterisation of two substrains of C57BL/6J inbred mice differing by a spontaneous single-gene mutation. *Behavioral Brain Research, 98*, 39–43.

Toda, K., Sailbara, T., Okada, T., Onishi, S., & Shizuta, Y. (2001). A loss of aggressive behavior and its reinstatement by oestrogen in mice lacking the aromatase gene (Cyp19). *Journal of Endocrinology, 168*, 217–220.

Vacher, C. M., Calas, A., Maltonti, F., & Hardin-Pouzet. H. (2002). Postnatal regulation by monoamines of vasopressin expression in the neuroendocrine hypothalamus of MAO-A-deficient mice. *European Journal of Neuroscience, 19*, 1110–1114.

van Oortmerssen, G. A. & Bakker, Th. C. M. (1981). Artificial selection for short and long attack latencies in wild *Mus musculus domesticus. Behavior Genetics. 11*, 115–126.

van Oortmerssen, G. A., Benus, R. F., & Sluyter, F. (1992). Studies on wild house mice IV: On the heredity of testosterone and readiness to attack. *Aggressive Behavior, 18.* 143–148.

van Oortmerssen, G. A., Dijk, D. J., & Schuurman, T. (1987). Studies in wild house mice II: Testosterone and aggression. *Hormones and Behavior, 21,* 139–153.

van Oortmerssen, G. A., & Sluyter, F. (1994) Studies on wild house mice. V. Aggression in lines selected for attack latency and their Y-chromosomal congenics. *Behavior Genetics, 24,* 73–78.

Wersinger, S. R., Ginns, E. I., O'Carroll, A. M., Lolait, S. J., & Young, W. S., III. (2002). Vasopressin V1b receptor knockout reduces aggressive behavior in male mice. *Molecular Psychiatry, 7,* 975–984.

Volavka, J. (1995). *Neurobiology of violence.* Washington, DC: American Psychiatric Press.

Xu, J., Burgoyne, P, S., & Arnold, A. P. (2002). Sex differences in sex chromosome gene expression in mouse brain. *Human Molecular Genetics 11,* 1409–1419.

Young, R. M., & Balaban, E. (2003). Aggression, biology, and context: Deja-Vu all over again. In M. P. Mattson (Ed.), *Neurobiology of aggression: Understanding and preventing violence* (pp. 119–134). Totowa, NJ: Humana.

CHAPTER 6

The Psychophysiology of Aggression: Autonomic, Electrocortical, and Neuro-Imaging Findings

Christopher J. Patrick and Edelyn Verona

In this chapter, we review findings from studies that have used psychophysiological measures to investigate aggressive behavior and its neurobiological underpinnings. The domain of psychophysiology has expanded in recent years to encompass brain imaging techniques, in addition to peripheral autonomic and electrocortical (EEG/ERP) measures (Cacioppo, Tassinary, & Berntson, 2000). In this chapter, we consider findings from studies using all of these recording techniques.

A salient challenge in a review of this kind is that, in addition to variations in physiological measurement techniques, the studies to be reviewed vary widely in terms of the nature of questions investigated, procedural strategies (e.g., experimental tasks or conditions of testing), participant populations, and theoretical perspectives according to which findings are interpreted. This wide variation creates major challenges for integrating findings across studies and formulating general conclusions. We have attempted to deal with this complexity in three ways. First, we have aimed to be broad in our coverage of the literature in order to expose readers to the range of available findings and to highlight inconsistencies and unresolved questions. Second, in the closing section of the chapter, we discuss strategies for future research that can help improve our ability to integrate findings across these different areas of psychophysiological research. Third, to provide a basis for thinking in an integrated fashion about existing work, we discuss findings of various studies in relation to two conceptual models: (1) a quantitative model of externalizing syndromes (Krueger, Hicks, Patrick, Carlson, Iacono, & McGue, 2002; Krueger, Markon, Patrick, & Iacono, 2005) that conceives of various types of impulse control problems, including aggressive-antisocial behavior, as manifestations of a common dispositional vulnerability, and (2) a neurobiological model (Davidson, Putnam, & Larson, 2000) that views persistent aggression as arising from dysfunction in a series of interconnected brain systems (including the prefrontal cortex, anterior cingulate cortex, and amygdala) that function to regulate affective states, including anger. We summarize these two models briefly here and refer to each of them again at various points in the review.

An integrative, structural model of the externalizing spectrum – encompassing child and adult antisocial deviance, alcohol and drug dependence, and impulsive personality traits – has recently been developed to account for the systematic co-variation known to exist among these phenomena (Krueger et al., 2002, 2005; see also Kendler, Prescott, Myers, & Neale, 2003; Young, Stallings, Corley, Krauter, & Hewitt, 2000). This model posits that trait dispositions and maladaptive behaviors within the externalizing spectrum can be viewed as arising from a general underlying, largely constitutional trait vulnerability that operates in conjunction with environmental influences to produce specific overt behavioral (phenotypic) manifestations of deficient impulse control. Impulsive aggressive behavior is symptomatic of both child conduct disorder and adult antisocial personality, and recent quantitative modeling work aimed at defining the boundaries of the externalizing spectrum has confirmed that aggression of various types is a key element of this spectrum (Krueger, Markon, Patrick, Benning, & Kramer, in press). With this in mind, we endeavor at various points to reference findings on the psychophysiology of aggression to what is known about externalizing problems more generally.

The other model we consider is the neurobiological model of aggression formulated by Davidson and colleagues (2000). In this model, impulsive aggressive behavior is seen as arising from dysfunction in a coordinated set of brain structures that function to regulate emotional responding. These brain structures include the prefrontal cortex (in particular, its orbitofrontal and ventromedial subdivisions); the anterior cingulate cortex; and subcortical-limbic structures (in particular, the amygdala, hippocampus, and hypothalamus). The subcortical components of this circuit play a primary role in activating emotional states, whereas the anterior cingulate cortex and prefrontal cortex operate to detect circumstances under which affective control is needed and to implement control processes, respectively. From this perspective, repetitive episodes of impulsive aggression reflect a breakdown in the normal ability to recognize and respond to signals of possible provocation as they arise and/or to modulate defensive reactivity in the face of direct provocation or threat. We consider this neurobiological model especially in relation to neuroimaging studies that have directly examined abnormalities in brain structure and function in aggressive individuals.

Autonomic Nervous System Functioning and Antisocial/Aggressive Behaviors

In this section, we review studies that have investigated autonomic nervous system reactivity in relation to antisocial, hostile, and aggressive behavior. We consider findings from varying domains (developmental investigations of antisocial-aggressive behavior, adult psychopathy studies, behavioral medicine research, social psychological studies of aggression) that have differing theoretical orientations according to which findings are interpreted. Separate sections are devoted to each research domain, with some discussion of the conceptual perspective within each area. At the end, an attempt is made to integrate findings and conceptualizations across areas in order to identify consistent patterns that bear on our understanding of aggression and violence.

Autonomic Activity in Child/Adolescent Conduct Problems and Aggression

The literature on childhood conduct problems and aggression is reviewed here, separately from that on aggression in adults, because some research has suggested that there may be distinct psychophysiological correlates of antisocial and aggressive behavior in children compared with adults (Lorber, 2004).

Resting autonomic activity and antisocial behavior. The most reliable finding in this area is that low resting heart rate (HR) in childhood and adolescence is prospectively linked to antisocial behavior in adulthood (see, e.g., Maliphant, Hume, & Furnham, 1990; Raine & Venables, 1984; Wadsworth, 1976). Studies demonstrating this effect have been reviewed by Scarpa and Raine (1997) and by Raine (2002) and were the specific focus of a recent meta-analysis by Ortiz and Raine (2004). The main analysis reported by Ortiz and Raine incorporated 45 separate effect sizes for the association between resting HR and antisocial behavior derived from 40 studies conducted between 1971 and 2002 (total $N = 5,868$ children). A supplementary meta-analysis was performed on studies that examined HR reactivity to phasic stressors. Ortiz and Raine reported effects sizes (d) of $-.44$ and $-.76$ (ps <.0001), respectively, for resting HR and for HR during a stressor. Variables, such as age, gender, recruitment source, basis of antisocial behavior rating, HR recording procedure, inclusion of a psychiatric control group, and whether the association between HR and antisociality was evaluated concurrently or prospectively, failed to emerge as significant moderators of the association. Ortiz and Raine concluded that low resting HR is the most robust biological correlate of antisocial behavior in children and adolescents identified so far. Likewise, in his meta-analysis of autonomic reactivity studies more generally, Lorber (2004) concluded that low resting HR was linked to conduct problems in both children ($d = -.34$) and adolescents ($d = -.35$). Moreover, the relationship between child conduct problems and resting autonomic activity appeared to generalize across physiological measures: Lorber (2004) also reported that low resting skin conductance (SC) was associated primarily with child (although not adolescent) conduct problems ($d = -.30$).

The highly robust association for resting HR in particular has been interpreted as indicating that general physiological hypoarousal represents an underlying risk factor for antisocial behavior, mainly because chronic understimulation promotes a need for thrill- and sensation-seeking (cf. Eysenck, 1967). Raine (2002) suggested that the link between low resting HR (or biological correlates more generally) and antisocial

behavior is particularly strong among more advantaged (higher SES) groups – presumably because a stronger biology-antisociality association can be identified in social contexts in which environmental predispositions (or "pushes") toward crime are minimized (Mednick, 1977; Raine & Venables, 1981). However, other research indicates that it is the combination of physiological risk factors and childhood adversity that leads to more antisocial behavior (Farrington, 1997). In response to this claim, Raine (2002) pointed out that in such research, in which antisocial behavior constitutes the dependent variable, consideration of multiple risk factors (low HR, adverse home environment, etc.) is likely to enhance prediction of antisocial outcomes. On the other hand, in studies in which psychophysiological reactivity is the dependent variable (as in studies of resting HR differences between groups), an effect for the physiological variable can be detected more readily.

Autonomic activity and aggression/violence. Scarpa and Raine (1997) suggested that the HR-antisociality association is strongest between low resting HR and violent/aggressive behavior in particular, although this conclusion is based on a relatively small number of studies. One of these was a study of more than 1,800 British boys, in which low resting HR at age 11 prospectively predicted delinquency at age 21 (Wadsworth, 1976). Moreover, HR differences in this study were largest when the delinquent group was restricted to those who had committed the most violent crimes. Elsewhere, Kindlon, Tremblay, Mezzacappa, Earls, Laurent, and Schaal (1995) reported low resting HR among children exhibiting the greatest amount of fighting behavior in their preteen years (ages 9 to 12). In another study involving children with conduct disorder and/or attention-deficit hyperactivity disorder (ADHD), Zahn and Kruesi (1993) found some evidence that reduced HR was associated with ratings of aggressiveness, although many of the reported associations were not significant. Lorber (2004), in his meta-analysis, reported moderate effect sizes for the relationship between low resting HR and child ($d = -.51$) and adult ($d = -.30$) aggression. On the other hand, resting SC was not found to be associated with aggression in the meta-analysis, although too few studies were included with child/adolescent samples to permit examination of these relationships separately for adults and children.

Other research has investigated autonomic *reactivity* to aversive events (measured either as response change from baseline or as raw reactivity during task presentation), which would presumably tap a different aspect of the physiology-behavior relationship. Whereas resting autonomic activity is associated with tonic levels of arousal (i.e., chronic underarousal among antisocial individuals), autonomic reactivity assesses physiological functioning associated with brain systems that govern fear responses, defensive activation, and negative affect (e.g., amygdala, ventromedial prefrontal cortex). For example, the finding that antisocial behavior or aggression is associated with attenuated reactivity to aversive stimuli would suggest that persons engaging in these behaviors may do so because they are less sensitive to the negative consequences of their behavior, which may mitigate the development of a moral conscience or adherence to social values (cf. Eysenck, 1967). On the other hand, increased reactivity in those with aggressive or antisocial traits would suggest that they experience lower thresholds for defensive activation, which would explain their tendency to engage in violent or destructive behaviors at the most minimal provocation.

However, in contrast with the literature on psychopathy and reactivity to aversive cues (SC response, in particular; see below), findings on physiological reactivity and aggression in children/adolescents are quite mixed. Pelham, Milich, Cummings, Murphy, Schaughency, and Greiner (1991) reported decreased HR reactivity to provocation among aggressive children with ADHD relative to nonaggressive ADHD children. Waschbusch et al. (2002) recently reported greater HR acceleration in children

with conduct problems and ADHD (relative to an ADHD-pure group) after a no-provocation condition in a point-subtraction aggression task. No HR differences between the two groups were observed after a provoking condition. Lorber (2004) reported a positive effect size for the relationship between HR reactivity (increase from baseline) and conduct problems in children ($d = .26$) during exposure to aversive stimuli; however, conduct problems were associated with *low* HR reactivity when participants were exposed to neutral or nonnegative stimuli ($d = -.20$). Unfortunately, effect size estimates for HR reactivity and aggression, in particular, could not be calculated in children because there were not enough studies of this kind, although there was a small positive relationship in adults ($d = .27$). SC reactivity did not show reliable relationships with aggression in this meta-analysis, although not enough of the studies reviewed included child/adolescent participants.

Hubbard and colleagues (2002, 2004) have suggested that mixed findings in the association between child/adolescent aggression and autonomic reactivity may be due to the fact that researchers have not distinguished between reactive (or angry/hostile) and proactive (instrumental) aggression in their analyses. These researchers found that reactive aggression was related to greater overall SC reactivity during play interactions with a provoking child confederate and greater increases in SC reactivity across time. In contrast, children exhibiting proactive aggression showed decreases in HR across time relative to children who were high on reactive aggression.

Parasympathetic and vagal influences on conduct problems and aggression. More recent work has attempted to parse the parasympathetic (PSN) and sympathetic (SNS) nervous system influences on HR in order to clarify how activity in these different branches of the autonomic nervous system relates to antisocial and aggressive behavior. Most of this work has been conducted with child and adolescent samples, using parent or teacher reports of participants' externalizing or aggressive behaviors. Cardiac vagal tone (an index of parasympathetic influence on HR) has been shown to be reduced in antisocial male adolescents (Mezzacappa et al., 1997). Beauchaine, Katkin, Strassberg, and Snarr (2001) have suggested that vagal regulation of cardiac activity is associated with control of fight/flight responses, and thus may be implicated in aggressive behaviors. In line with Fowles (1980), these authors postulated that motivational response dispositions – including defensive activation to punishment cues associated with the Behavioral Inhibition System (BIS; Gray, 1987) and reactivity to rewarding or appetitive stimuli associated with the Behavioral Activation (BAS; Gray, 1987) – both entail activation of the SNS. Because aggressive conduct disorder and ADHD both involve impulsivity and behavioral disinhibition, attenuated BIS and enhanced BAS activity would be implicated in both disorders. On the other hand, aggressive conduct problems but not ADHD involve reduced thresholds for fight/flight response activation. Because vagal control is critical for the regulation of fight/flight responses, parasympathetic activity is expected to be reduced among children with aggressive conduct disorder (CD).

Consistent with these hypotheses, both ADHD and aggressive CD/ADHD adolescent groups in the Beauchaine et al. (2001) study showed lower nonspecific fluctuations of SC at baseline compared to controls, suggesting that diminished BIS activity is associated with impulsivity and disinhibition. However, no group differences were found in SC reactivity during extinction. The hypothesis of greater BAS activity in the aggressive CD/ADHD group was not supported, as this group exhibited longer preejection period (SNS-linked cardiac activity) at baseline and during reward, indicating *attenuated* sympathetic activity in aggressive conduct problems. Finally, the CD/ADHD group showed reduced respiratory-sinus arrhythmia (RSA) at baseline and during a videotaped conflict situation compared to pure-ADHD and control groups, supporting the hypothesis that the former group would show less vagal control implicated in the reg-

ulation of fight/flight responding. Based on these findings, the authors conjectured that aggressive/conduct problems are associated with attenuated BIS *and* BAS activity, which is consistent with theories of sensation-seeking that implicate chronic underarousal (Eysenck, 1967) and with the literature on low resting HR in aggressive/antisocial behavior (Raine, 2002). The reduced RSA activity in the aggressive CD/ADHD group suggested a reduced threshold for fight/flight responding. Taken as a whole, these findings indicate that reduced vagal control, in combination with attenuated BIS and higher sensation-seeking, can lead to enhanced aggression.

El-Sheikh and colleagues (El-Sheikh, 2001; El-Sheikh, Harger, & Whitson, 2001) have also reported that lower vagal control in children from at-risk homes (conflict-ridden or alcoholic) was associated with more internalizing and externalizing outcomes. Thus, vagal control seemed to represent a protective physiological factor for the development of emotional and conduct problems in at-risk children. In addition, reminiscent of the study reported in Beauchaine et al. (2001), the children in El-Sheikh (2001) with the lowest expressed fear (associated with BIS activity) and low vagal control were the ones at highest risk for externalizing problems. Elsewhere, Iacono, Carlson, Taylor, Elkins, and McGue (1999) reported a failure to effectively modulate autonomic reactivity during anticipation of a warned stressor among adolescents generally at risk for externalizing problems. In line with the formulation of Davidson et al. (2000), these authors interpreted this finding as evidence of a general impairment in cortico-frontal regulatory capacity in individuals disposed to disorders of impulse control.

However, at least two studies have not replicated the association between reduced vagal control and aggressive/conduct problems. Burgess, Marshall, Rubin, and Fox (2003) recently reported that HR and RSA activity in 4-year-old children during social activity with unfamiliar peers were unrelated to externalizing problems assessed at the same age. Additionally, Scarpa,

Fikretoglu, and Luscher (2000) found that self-reported aggressive behavior, as assessed by the Aggression Questionnaire (Buss & Perry, 1992), was related to low resting HR and to *increased* heart rate variability (HRV), which is associated with parasympathetic (vagal) activity. Scarpa et al. (2000) suggested that the combination of low HR and increased HRV may reflect *increased* parasympathetic influence or increased vagal tone associated with aggression in this study of student volunteers. However, this study by Scarpa and colleagues tested young adults, and not children or adolescents, and employed a self-report measure of aggression, which may account for the discrepant findings.

Summary of child/adolescent literature. In summary, this literature provides fairly strong evidence for low resting autonomic activity (both HR and SC) in connection with general antisocial behavior, and potentially to aggression in particular, among children and adolescents. Associations between autonomic reactivity to aversive stimuli and aggression are more mixed, but recent evidence suggests that higher autonomic reactivity (HR and SC) may be associated specifically with reactive aggression in children (with the opposite possibly the case for proactive aggression). Finally, some newer work has investigated parasympathetic versus sympathetic mediation of cardiovascular activity to clarify HR associations with aggression and conduct problems. Some of the best-conducted studies of this kind have revealed lower vagal (parasympathetic) involvement in children/adolescents with aggressive conduct problems and have provided evidence that this lack of vagal regulation, in combination with reduced BIS activity (indexed by SC) and chronic underarousal (indexed by resting HR), may directly relate to lower thresholds for aggression and violence.

Relevant to this finding, other research has implicated vagal influences in the development of emotional dysregulation problems in children (Porges & Doussard-Roosevelt, 1997). Thus, studies showing lower vagal regulation in aggressive children are fairly consistent with the idea that aggression in children at least partly involves difficulties regulating anger experiences. Additionally, this literature also does not provide strong evidence for the idea of heightened BAS activity in conduct problems and aggression, which has been confirmed in more recent work by Beauchaine (2004) in which various autonomic responses are indexed while children are responding to reward. Nonetheless, findings related to lower vagal control in aggressive children, purportedly indexing a lower threshold for fight/flight responding, suggest that such children (in contrast with adult psychopaths; see the next section) may exhibit enhanced rather than reduced physiological mobilization for defensive action under conditions of threat.

Autonomic Activity in Adults With Psychopathy

Given the well-established association between psychopathy and risk for violence and violent recidivism (Douglas, Vincent, & Edens, 2006; Porter & Woodworth, 2006), we briefly consider the literature on the psychophysiology of psychopathy. It should be noted that the construct of psychopathy as it has been studied in adults differs importantly from the sorts of constructs that have been emphasized in the child/adolescent literature just reviewed – delinquency, conduct disorder, antisocial behavior, aggression, and other variants of "externalizing" psychopathology; cf. Achenbach & Edelbrock, 1984; Krueger et al., 2002). The crucial difference is that a diagnosis of psychopathy requires the presence of characteristic emotional-interpersonal features – such as the absence of remorse or empathy or the presence of shallow affect. as well as glibness, grandiosity, and manipulativeness – in addition to impulsive antisocial tendencies (Hare, 1991, 2003; Harpur, Hare, & Hakstian, 1989). For this reason, the construct of psychopathy has been viewed as distinct from antisocial personality or externalizing (Hart & Hare, 1996; Patrick, Hicks, Krueger, & Lang, 2005), and a prominent emphasis in theories of psychopathy has been on deficits in emotional reactivity, in particular fear (Fowles, 1980; Hare, 1965; Lykken, 1957, 1995; Patrick, 1994, 2007).

The most commonly noted autonomic response finding for psychopathy is SC hyporeactivity. In addition, heightened heart rate (HR) acceleration during anticipation of aversive stimuli has also been noted in some studies. The best-known studies of psychopathy and autonomic response were conducted in the 1960s and 1970s; in these studies, psychopathy was typically assessed using the criteria set forth by Cleckley (1941). In a classic review of this work, Hare (1978) concluded that psychopathy was characterized by (a) enhanced anticipatory HR responses suggestive of active coping that served to reduce the impact of the aversive stimulus (see also Fowles, 1980), and (b) reduced fear reactivity as measured by tonic SC level and reduced SC response to aversive stimuli and in conditioning or quasi-conditioning paradigms.

More recent studies including measures of autonomic response have focused on psychopathy as indexed by the Psychopathy Checklist (PCL; Hare, 1980) and its revised version (PCL-R; Hare, 1991, 2003). Arnett (1997) reviewed this more recent work on autonomic responsivity in psychopaths and reached conclusions similar to those of Hare (1978). He postulated that psychopathy is characterized by a "motivational imbalance," with increased responding to reward (as evidenced by HR acceleration) and attenuated reactivity to punishment or negative cues (as evidenced by SC hyporesponsivity). However, psychopathy-related differences in HR response have not been found consistently, and other research suggests that properties of the cueing stimulus or situation can influence the magnitude of group differences in autonomic reactivity reported in different studies. For example, adult psychopaths showed reduced SC response during imagery of fearful scenes (Patrick, Cuthbert, & Lang, 1994) and to phasic emotional sounds (Verona, Patrick, Curtin, Bradley, & Lang, 2004) but not to emotional pictures (Levenston, Patrick, Bradley, & Lang, 2000; Patrick, Bradley, & Lang, 1993).

Lorber (2004) conducted a meta-analysis of relations reported between autonomic (HR, SC) reactivity and psychopathic and antisocial traits/behaviors in studies conducted since the 1960s. He found that psychopathy/sociopathy (notably, some of the studies did not differentiate between Cleckley-defined psychopathy and antisocial behavior more generally) was associated with lower SC responding at rest ($d = -.30$) and during experimental tasks ($ds = -.25$ to $-.31$), but the latter effect size was strongest when participants were responding to negative ($d = -.47$) as opposed to neutral stimuli ($d = -.11$). However, Lorber (2004) found no consistent relationship between HR (either at rest or in response to test stimuli) and psychopathy/sociopathy across the studies reviewed.

In summary, this literature is generally consistent in reporting decreased SC activity in anticipation of punishment or aversive cues in adults diagnosed as psychopathic, which suggests an insensitivity to punishment or a lower threshold for defensive (fear) activation (Lykken, 1957; Patrick, 1994). This result is somewhat at odds with work on reactivity in aggressive individuals reviewed below; in some of these studies aggressive individuals have demonstrated increased SC response to stressors. With regard to HR, some evidence was found in earlier studies for increased HR acceleration in psychopaths during anticipation of stressors, but such findings have been less consistent. Especially notable, in view of the highly consistent finding of lower resting heart in antisocial youth (cf. Ortiz & Raine, 2004), is the absence of resting HR differences for adults diagnosed as psychopathic. This finding may be due to the aforementioned differences in the diagnostic criteria for psychopathy as opposed to antisociality or externalizing; in particular, the emphasis on emotional-interpersonal features in psychopathy may lead to the selection of a fundamentally different type of individual. Notable in this regard is that psychopathy (its emotional-interpersonal features in particular) is associated more strongly with proactive than with reactive aggression

(Patrick, Zempolich, & Levenston, 1997; Woodworth & Porter, 2002), whereas impulsive-angry aggression has been the focus of most physiological studies of violence per se. However, another factor that must also be considered is that patterns of physiological reactivity may change as a function of age, perhaps in connection with general personality changes known to occur across time (Roberts, Walton, & Viechtbauer, 2006).

Autonomic Reactivity and Trait Aggression in Adults

History of violence and autonomic activity. Some studies in this domain have examined autonomic activity among participants who have a history of engaging in assaultive or violent behavior. One area in which this has been extensively studied is the domestic violence literature, with the best-known work conducted by Gottman and colleagues (1995). These authors proposed a typology involving two distinct subgroups of male batterers who could be distinguished on the basis of autonomic reactivity. Type 1 batterers displayed reductions in HR during a conflictual marital interaction, whereas Type 2 batterers showed increases.

Gottman et al. (1995) reported that husbands classified into these two groups differed on a variety of relevant criterion variables. Type 1 batterers exhibited more emotional aggression (i.e., expressions of contempt and belligerence toward a partner), had a greater history of assaultive behaviors toward others (although both batterer subtypes were equally violent toward their partner), and scored higher on antisocial traits and lower on interpersonal dependency than Type 2 batterers; in addition, the partners of these individuals exhibited more sadness and defensiveness and less anger than Type 2 partners. During a 2-year follow up, none of the Type 1 couples were divorced or separated, whereas about 27% of Type 2 couples were either separated or divorced. Both types of batterers exhibited increases in cardiac vagal activity after the conflictual marital interaction. Gottman et al. (1995) suggested that the

HR deceleration exhibited by Type 1 men may serve to focus their attention on controlling and intimidating the partners, which may explain why the partners of these men tended to show more sadness than anger and were less likely to leave the marriage than Type 2 partners.

Although the typology proposed by Gottman et al. (1995) seemed promising in identifying distinct etiological factors underlying domestic violence, at least two studies by different research groups have failed to replicate these results (Babcock, Green, Webb, & Graham, 2004; Meehan, Holtzworth-Munroe, & Herron, 2001). Additionally, studies that have compared batterers and nonbatterers have not reported any significant differences in physiological activity, including HR or finger pulse transit or amplitude during a marital interaction (Jacobson et al., 1994), or in RSA to a postural challenge (Umhau et al, 2002) – although in the latter study the batterers did not show the typical strong correlation between change in heart period and change in RSA. Thus, a history of interpersonal violence toward a romantic partner does not seem to be associated consistently with differences in physiological reactivity.

Autonomic reactivity in persons who are violent toward their own children has also been examined in at least one study by Frodi and Lamb (1980). In this study, mothers with a documented history of physically abusing their children were compared to a matched group of nonabusing mothers in terms of their physiological responses to videotapes of infants smiling or crying. The abusers showed smaller increases from baseline in diastolic blood pressure (DBP) and larger increases in HR and SC than did nonabusers in response to the crying infant videotape. More important, the abusers also showed HR acceleration, increases in DBP, and larger increases in SC to the smiling baby, whereas the nonabusers showed a drop in DBP and a HR deceleratory response to the smiling baby. The abusers also provided higher ratings of annoyance and less sympathy when the baby cried and reported significantly less attentiveness, happiness, or pleasure when the baby smiled. In general, this pattern of findings suggests that abusers responded to baby crying and smiling in a similar fashion (with greater HR and SC arousal), whereas the nonabusers had differential responses to the two types of infant behavior. The implication is that abusers may experience any form of social elicitation by the child as aversive, so that a wider range of child behaviors may prompt aggressive responses from abusive parents.

A few studies have also been conducted with persons who have engaged in suicidal acts, frequently involving violence. Wolfersdorf, Straub, Barg, Keller, and Kaschka (1999) assessed SC reactivity among inpatients and examined suicidal outcomes in these patients. They found that patients who committed suicide using violent methods (e.g., guns, knives) showed reduced SC activity to simple auditory stimuli compared with depressed age- and sex-matched nonsuicidal controls and depressed suicide ideators. SC habituation rates did not differentiate between violent and nonviolent suicide attempters. In a separate study, Doron, Karis, Bashore, Coles, and Gratton (1998) compared the physiological responses of attempters, ideators, and nonsuicidal control inpatients to a film about two teenagers who commit suicide. The only significant difference in physiological response was that the suicide attempters exhibited significantly lower HR after viewing the film and less overall change in heart and respiration rates than the other two groups. Additionally, the suicide attempters revealed an increase in psychomotor agitation (according to behavioral coding) until the discovery of the suicide and a decrease thereafter, whereas the agitation of the nonsuicidal patients continued to increase from the start to the end of the film. This study provides preliminary evidence that suicidal tendencies, particularly of a violent nature, may be associated with attenuated SNS reactivity.

In summary, two points that emerge from the limited research conducted to date on individuals with and without violence histories is that (1) few studies exist that have compared persons who are generally assaultive with nonassaultive controls, and (2) clearly interpretable differences in physiological response have not typically been reported in such studies. A further point is that interpretation of the findings of these studies needs to consider the sorts of stimulus cues used to elicit physiological activity and how these cues relate to the particular characteristics of the violent groups (e.g., infant social elicitation among child abusers).

Aggression-relevant trait measures and autonomic reactivity. In other work, researchers have examined associations between trait measures relevant to aggression or violence (such as hostility, Type A personality, and trait aggression) and physiological responses to relevant cues (provocation, conflict, etc). The largest literature of this kind comes from the behavioral medicine/health psychology area. Health psychologists have hypothesized that frequent overactivation of the autonomic system in the form of flight/fight responses that exhaust cardiovascular biomechanisms may be the moderating link between personality factors (such as Type A, increased hostility, and anger expression) and risk for the development of cardiovascular disease (Krantz & Manuck, 1984).

A number of studies have yielded evidence that persons who experience more intense feelings of hostility tend to exhibit increased blood pressure and/or HR reactivity during a stressor or during provocation (Suarez, Harlan, Peoples, & Williams, 1993). However, Suls and Wan (1993) conducted a systematic meta-analysis of the relationship between trait hostility and cardiovascular reactivity and reported that most effect sizes were small in nature and nonsignificant across cardiovascular measures (HR, systolic blood pressure [SBP], DBP) and trait measures (hostility, anger expression, Type A). On the other hand, robust positive effect sizes were found for the association between trait hostility (particularly antagonistic hostility – involving outward expressions of anger, such as verbal and physical aggression) and cardiovascular reactivity (particularly SBP or DBP) in studies that included affectively arousing and interpersonally provocative stressors (as opposed to noninterpersonal stressors). Suls and Wan (1993) concluded that low or null effect sizes may be due to the fact that interpersonal provocation stressors were not used in many of these studies. Thus, physiological reactivity in angry or hostile persons may be specific to contexts in which they experience threat to esteem or unjust treatment from others.

Some additional studies have been conducted on this topic since publication of the Suls and Wan (1993) meta-analysis. Gallo, Smith, and Kircher (2000) reported that women's scores on Buss and Perry's (1992) Aggression Questionnaire (AQ) were associated significantly with increases in SBP while giving a speech; however, AQ scores did not predict greater physiological reactivity during interpersonal provocation compared with no-provocation. AQ scores were also uncorrelated with HR, SC, or DBP. More recently, Peters, Godaert, Ballieux, and Heijnen (2003) found no association between trait hostility (measured using the Buss-Durkee Hostility Inventory [BDHI] – the predecessor to the AQ) and baseline cardiovascular (SBP, DBP, HR) response or endocrine or immunological function. However, trait hostility was significantly related to increased immune function during a high-effort stressor (mental arithmetic) and to reduced immune function during a low-effort stressor (reaction time task). Keltikangas-Jarvinen and Keinonen (1988) also failed to find a relationship between pulse frequency change during the performance of challenging cognitive tasks (e.g., color-word Stroop) and aggression scores assessed using a Type A interview in a sample of 15-year-old Finnish adolescents.

Smith and Gallo (1999) examined trait hostility (measured via the AQ) and physiological reactivity among married couples who were asked to engage in a discussion under low or high evaluative threat, in which they either agreed or disagreed with each other. In the evaluative threat condition (participants were told that their discussion would be evaluated for level of verbal intelligence), blood pressure (particularly SBP) responses were positively correlated with husband's AQ scores, although there was no significant relationship between men's HR and AQ scores. Additionally, cardiovascular responses were unrelated to AQ scores in the wives, although in a previous study by this research group (Gallo et al., 2000, reviewed above), hostility and cardiovascular reactivity were related in women interacting with strangers. Interestingly, the husbands' AQ scores were significantly related to the wives' HR reactivity in the disagreement condition, and to wives' reports of their husband's increased dominance in the discussion. These results provide some insight not only into relationships between trait hostility and men's own cardiovascular functioning but also into the impact of trait hostility in men on their wives' cardiovascular functioning. Specifically, the authors concluded that the increased SBP in hostile men under evaluative threat reflected increased active coping techniques that served to maintain interpersonal dominance and control over their wives during marital interaction. Additionally, the results indicate that, along with interpersonal stimuli involving conflict and provocation, situations involving perceived threats to status or control can heighten cardiovascular reactivity in hostile persons.

Interestingly, Edguer and Janisse (1994) reported similar associations between Type A personality (marked by high levels of hostility and time urgency) and SBP while participants administered loud noises to a fictional partner in a Buss-aggression procedure. However, these effects were evident only in a condition in which the participants believed that the partner would have an opportunity to retaliate against them in the future. These authors also interpreted the increased SBP in Type A individuals as indicating an increased need to control their environment and their responses. Gerra and colleagues (1997) also reported that participants rated as high and low on aggressiveness (defined using a number of measures including the BDHI and impressions from psychiatrists) did not differ on resting

HR and blood pressure. However, after engagement in a point-subtraction aggression paradigm, HR and SBP (but not DBP) increased more in the aggressive compared to the nonaggressive participants. Participants classified as aggressive also exhibited higher overt aggressiveness in the form of subtracting more points from the putative competitor.

Consistent with the conclusion advanced by Suls and Wan (1993) in their meta-analytic review, the literature on trait hostility/aggression and physiological response demonstrates that cardiovascular reactivity is observed when hostile participants are exposed to interpersonal threat. More recent studies are also consistent with this perspective: trait hostility and aggression are unrelated to cardiovascular reactivity to noninterpersonal stressors (Keltikangas-Jarvinen & Keinonen, 1988; Peters et al., 2003), but a relationship is evident when participants are engaged in stressful interpersonal interactions (Edguer & Janisse, 1994; Gallo et al., 2000; Smith & Gallo, 1999). This perspective is also consistent with Lorber's (2004) meta-analysis, which found that positive associations between aggression (variously measured as self-report and laboratory indices) and autonomic reactivity (SC and HR) were observed only in studies in which participants were exposed to negative or aversive stimuli (although Lorber did not distinguish between interpersonal and other negative contexts).

On the other hand, the health psychology literature has generally reported robust blood pressure reactivity differences in hostile/aggressive individuals compared with nonaggressive individuals, and this result has been interpreted as suggesting increased arousal in the service of active coping techniques to effect control and dominance over their environment. This interpretation would be consistent with the idea that physiological reactivity in hostile/aggressive individuals serves to prime these individuals for action, which is in turn reminiscent of the work by Beauchaine et al. (2001) indicating lower thresholds for flight/flight responding in aggressive conduct disorder.

Autonomic Reactivity During Laboratory-Induced Aggression

Autonomic arousal and behavioral indices of aggression. Studies conducted from the perspective of social psychology over the last few decades have examined the emotional and physiological precipitants to aggressive behavior measured in controlled laboratory contexts. Some of this early work was based on the assumption that unpleasant levels of physiological arousal from one source can increase the potential for aggression on minimal provocation, a phenomenon that Zillman (1983) described as excitation-transfer. Zillman further suggested that the initial arousal need not be associated with the target of aggression and showed in numerous studies that arousal associated with physical exercise or exertion could increase the aggressive behavior of nonselected participants. He also suggested that high levels of arousal can interrupt adequate problem solving and cognitive regulation, which further enhances the probability of aggression under provocation.

More recently, Berkowitz (1990) advanced a cognitive neo-associationist model of aggressive behavior in which unpleasant events of *all* kinds (including interpersonal provocation, frustration, and physical discomfort) are presumed to be capable of priming the initiation of escape and attack behaviors. In this model, the elicitation of negative affect is seen as automatically priming aggressive behavior because the two are connected within a common associative network involving adaptive mobilization for defensive action. This view emphasizes the importance of assessing multiple channels of activation in studies of aggression, including subjective evaluations, physiological responses, and motor impulses after exposure to an aversive event, in order to fully evaluate the individual's motivational state (cf. P. J. Lang, 1979).

However, unlike Zillman (1983), Berkowitz (1990; Berkowitz & Harmon-Jones, 2004) has postulated that provocation need not be present for seemingly impersonal stressors to activate hostile and aggressive responses directed toward an innocent target. Consistent with this claim, there is evidence that hostile judgments of a stranger or delivery of electric shock to a confederate within a laboratory paradigm can be facilitated by physical stressors, such as foul odors (Rotton, 1979), hot rooms (Bell & Baron, 1976), painful cold-water immersion (Berkowitz, Cochran, & Embree, 1981), and exposure to an air blast stressor (Verona, Patrick, & Lang, 2002). Berkowitz (1989) provided an explanation for these effects in his reformulation of the frustration-aggression hypothesis. He suggested that it is the resulting negative affect, and not the aversive event per se, that leads to increases in the probability of aggression. This perspective highlights the importance of directly examining relationships among negative affective states during a stressor, using physiological measures, and aggression after the stressor.

Some studies have examined direct relationships between physiological activation and behavioral indices of aggression assessed in the laboratory. The findings of these studies have been mixed. Johnson and Rule (1986) reported a positive association between HR arousal and delivery of aversive noise blasts to a provoking confederate, although this relationship was eliminated if participants learned of mitigating circumstances that explained the confederate's rude behavior prior to being provoked. Thomas (1982) reported that men who were subjected to an interpersonal provocation (insult) after having viewed an aggressive film showed more aggression toward a confederate (i.e., delivered higher levels of shock), but exhibited lower pulse rates before and after shock delivery relative to unprovoked men and those who watched a nonviolent control film. The association between aggressive behavior and pulse rate was generally negative across conditions. The author interpreted these findings as suggesting that exposure to violent media may predispose to aggressive behavior via a desensitization effect (lower responsivity to violence), in opposition to the idea that exposure to violent media increases aggression via increasing arousal (Zillman, 1983).

More recently, Panee and Ballard (2002) failed to find any significant relationship between HR and blood pressure reactivity during video game play and the frequency of aggressive actions or hostility displayed in the video game. On the other hand, Gerra and colleagues (2001, 2004) reported positive relationships (rs in the .40s—.50s) between cardiac (HR, blood pressure) reactivity and aggressive responding (i.e., subtraction of points from a confederate) in a point-subtraction aggression paradigm in two related studies, one involving normal participants and the other involving heroin-dependent individuals. The magnitude of the correlations between physiological indicators and aggressive response was similar across the two samples.

In summary, there is substantial evidence that exposure to emotionally evocative contexts that presumably increase arousal leads to higher levels of aggression in the laboratory as indexed by various behavioral measures (e.g., delivery of shocks or loud noises to a confederate; removal of points that reduce the confederate's monetary winnings). On the other hand, few studies have directly examined the relationship between physiological arousal and aggressive behavior. Existing studies of this kind report mixed findings. This is surprising, given that most of these studies included some form of interpersonal provocation, which reliably increased aggression. However, one potential reason for the discrepancy may be that links between physiological arousal and aggressive behavior are moderated by individual difference factors. This topic is addressed in the next section.

Trait and gender differences in the negative emotional priming of aggression. Mixed findings regarding the link between physiological arousal and aggression may be clarified to some extent by considering individual differences in the emotional priming of aggression. Hokanson (1970) conducted some of the earliest work of this kind. Based on Freud's (1959) hydraulic model of aggressive behavior, Hokanson focused on the potentially cathartic effects of aggressive behavior in reducing physiological arousal brought on by provocation. Across a series of studies, Hokanson and colleagues (Hokanson & Burgess, 1962a,b; Hokanson, Burgess, & Cohen, 1963; Hokanson & Shetler, 1961) found that the receipt of electric shocks from a confederate led to increases in autonomic reactivity (primarily HR and SBP) in participants; however, if participants were allowed to subsequently retaliate using physical or verbal means, dramatic decreases in SBP were observed after an aggressive counter-response. These results were most robust when the provocateur was of equal (as opposed to higher) status and when retaliation was directed at the provocateur (versus other substitute targets).

However, these initial studies included only male participants. In other studies that included female participants, Hokanson and colleagues (Hokanson & Edelman, 1966; Hokanson, Willers, & Koropsak, 1968) observed the usual vascular arousal on receipt of aggression, but arousal reduction following an aggressive counter-response (versus other responses, including a friendly response) was not observed in female participants. Female participants showed slow cardiovascular recovery after aggressive or ignore responses, although recovery rates were faster in these conditions than for women who were not allowed to counter-respond at all. More robust arousal reduction was observed in women when they were allowed to make a friendly counter-response.

Hokanson (1970) interpreted these results as indicating that the successful removal of the noxious arousal actually reinforced the behavioral responses that were instrumental in producing this reduction. Thus, among men, the fact that they experienced arousal reduction following aggression would serve to reinforce this behavior. Gender differences in aggression may be due to the differential cathartic effects of aggression on arousal reduction. Consistent with this learning-theory model, Hokanson et al. (1968) showed that when women were reinforced for aggressive responding during an initial learning phase

of the experiment (i.e., the confederate countered with a friendly response following women's aggressive responses), women's aggressive responses showed significant increases in frequency, and by the end of the learning phase, women showed cathartic-like SBP reduction when they made aggressive counter-responses to their partner's aggression and slow recovery when they made friendly responses.

Recently, Verona and Sullivan (2004) replicated Hokanson's basic finding of HR reduction following aggressive versus nonaggressive responding in a sample of young adults. However, no gender difference in arousal reduction was observed in this study – possibly because participants had no other choice but to respond with aggression (whereas various alternative responses were available in Hokanson's studies). Verona and Sullivan also reported that the degree of HR reduction was correlated positively with the intensity of accompanying aggression, as well as with increases in aggression across blocks. This is the first study to have reported relationships between physiological (HR) reductions following aggression and actual aggressive responding.

Other more recent work has also emphasized the importance of examining individual differences in the relationship between emotional arousal and aggression. For example, Taylor et al. (2000) postulated that, although fight/flight responding could characterize physiological activation to stress in males and females, behaviorally females may show more of a tendency toward "tend-and-befriend" than fight/flight. These authors cited evidence from extensive animal and human literatures showing that, because of differential parental investment between the genders, female stress responses have evolved to reinforce affiliation in social groups as a way of maximizing the survival of the female and of her offspring. Neuroendocrine and sex hormone responses are considered to be particularly important in mediating these differential responses in men and women.

Other research has postulated that gender differences in the emotion-aggression association are more robust in certain contexts than others. Knight, Guthrie, Page, and Fabes (2002) concluded from their meta-analysis that gender differences in aggression were smaller in interpersonal contexts that were rated as very low or very high in emotional evocativeness (no or extreme provocation, respectively), whereas gender differences were most robust under slightly or moderately evocative situations. Although not discussed by Knight and colleagues, this last finding may relate to the fact that moderate levels of instigation allow for greater ambiguity in the likely behavioral response, and thus gender differences are most observable in such ambiguous contexts. As an illustration, Bettencourt and Miller (1996) reported in their meta-analysis that gender differences in laboratory-assessed aggression were reduced under interpersonal provocation, presumably the most direct and unambiguous context in eliciting aggression.

Based on these prior findings, Verona and Curtin (2006) hypothesized that stress reactivity and physiological activation would be related more strongly to laboratory-assessed aggressive behavior in men than in women. These investigators used startle reactivity to unwarned noise probes rather than autonomic measures to directly index emotional activation during periods of unpredictable exposure to a physical stressor (air blast administrations to the throat) and during periods of frustration (monetary goal-blocking by confederate). The main results were that men exposed to the physical stressor exhibited significant increases in aggression, whereas women did not show this effect. On the other hand, frustration produced increases in aggression in both men and women. Despite equivalent increases in startle reactivity associated with the occurrence of the physical stressor across genders, increases in startle activation were related to increases in aggression in men and to decreases in aggression in women. Thus, consistent with the model of Taylor et al. (2000), this study provided evidence that women's physiological responses to general stress were not associated with a fight response.

Other research by Verona and colleagues has identified further examples of individual differences in the emotional priming of aggression. Verona et al. (2002) showed that trait negative emotionality in men was associated with increases in aggression and in tonic levels of startle reactivity during periods of unpredictable exposure to the same physical stressor. Additionally, the association between tonic startle reactivity and laboratory-assessed aggression (i.e., delivery of electric shocks to an innocent confederate) during stress was only present in the men who were high (as opposed to low) in trait negative emotionality. In a follow-up to this study, Verona (2005) found that trait negative emotionality was positively related to stress-induced aggression in men but not in women. In addition, replicating Verona and Curtin (2006), tonic startle reactivity was found to be associated with increases in aggression among men but not women. In a further study, Verona, Joiner, Johnson, and Bender (2006) assessed the moderating effects of gender and of differences in the serotonin transporter genotype, which has been implicated in the development of a number of syndromes associated with emotional dysregulation, on stress-induced aggression and startle reactivity. The authors found that men carrying the homozygous short (s/s) genotype showed increased aggression specifically under conditions of stress, compared with other groups of men. However, there was no gene-by-stress interaction for women. Additionally, tonic startle reactivity was related to slight increases in aggression in s/s men, but was associated with significant decreases in aggression among men carrying the long allele.

This combination of findings suggests that certain individuals possess temperamental and genetic predispositions to react with aggression under stress and that the physiological responses of these individuals seem to serve a preparatory function in the initiation of stress-related aggressive activity. In addition, the available evidence suggests that both state (startle reflex) and trait (temperament, serotonin transporter gene) facets of negative emotionality are associated more strongly with the elicitation of aggressive behavior in men than in women. More research should be conducted to examine individual differences in affective-physiological priming of aggression using multiple measures of physiological activation, including blood pressure, HR, and SC.

Summary and Discussion

The foregoing major section reviewed studies that have examined links between various measures of aggression (parent-reported conduct problems in children, self-report aggression and hostility, history of violence, and behavioral indices in the laboratory) and autonomic physiological activity and reactivity. One highly consistent finding in this literature is that low resting HR is associated with the presence and development of aggression and conduct problems. One interpretation of this finding is that individuals who are generally low in autonomic arousal may seek out extreme levels of stimulation to compensate for chronic understimulation (e.g., Raine, 2002). This conceptualization appears consistent with results from studies indicating that increased levels of boredom-susceptibility and thrill-seeking are observed in aggressive populations.

However, with regard to autonomic *reactivity* to aversive stimuli and events, the picture is more mixed. This could be because most studies do not make key distinctions in terms of (1) different subgroups of aggressive and antisocial populations and (2) particular contexts that may promote stronger associations between aggressiveness and physiological reactivity. As described by Hubbard et al. (2002, 2004), increased autonomic reactivity may be associated specifically with reactive aggression, whereas autonomic nervous system hypoactivity may be more characteristic of individuals who engage in proactive aggression. This conclusion would be consistent with the literature showing blunted SC reactivity to aversive stimulation among psychopaths, who tend to engage more in instrumental/proactive

aggression than in reactive aggression (Porter & Woodworth, 2006). Additionally, other recent evidence from laboratory studies suggests that the association between physiological arousal and aggression is more robust in men than women (Taylor et al., 2000; Verona & Curtin, 2006) and among individuals who are temperamentally predisposed (i.e., high negative emotional traits, short allele of serotonin transporter gene) to react to stress with greater behavioral activation (Verona et al., 2002, 2006).

In addition, studies in the health psychology literature have consistently indicated that trait hostility and aggression are associated more strongly with autonomic arousal (particularly SBP) under conditions involving interpersonal as opposed to noninterpersonal stress. These data have been interpreted as indicating that individuals high on hostility and aggression respond to interpersonal conflict by activating physiological responses that prepare them to actively cope with these situations. This coping activity is typically in the form of controlling and dominant behavior. Together with other findings reviewed here, the implication is that physiological responses in individuals who engage in reactive forms of aggression and hostility serve to prepare these individuals for action under stressful or conflict situations.

Electrocortical (EEG/ERP) Studies

Electroencephalographic (EEG) Studies

Early work on the psychophysiology of violence focused on "abnormal" electroencephalographic (EEG) activity in violent individuals; these studies have been extensively reviewed by Milstein (1988) and Volavka (1990). The interest in EEG was partly fueled by evidence of histories of head injury and trauma (Lewis, Pincus, Feldman, Jackson, & Bard, 1986) and of deficient performance on standard neuropsychological tests (Yeudall, Fromm-Auch, & Davies, 1982) among violent and homicidal inmates. Some early work even investigated links between epilepsy (or history of seizures) and violent behavior; however, the majority of the evidence failed to confirm this putative association (Milstein, 1988).

As a whole, the findings of this early research on EEG brain activity and aggression/violence suggested higher levels of slow-wave (particularly delta, < 4 Hz) activity in violent or aggressive individuals (Milstein, 1988), although there have been some negative findings (see Volavka, 1990). Various EEG abnormalities were observed in violent individuals, but these were not consistently tied to particular scalp regions (see Milstein, 1988 for a review), even though some investigators focused specifically on frontal (Fishbein, Herning, Pickworth, Haertzen, Hickey, & Jaffe, 1989) or temporal regions (Williams, 1969).

Some of this early literature was plagued by subject selection bias, including factors that favored the inclusion of participants with known neurological abnormalities, and by qualitative analysis of EEG chart tracings before the advent of computerized, recording and quantitative analysis of EEG. More recently, using quantitative EEG analyses, Convit, Czobor, and Volavka (1991) found significant correlations between EEG delta activity and the number of violent incidents among psychiatrically hospitalized patients, even after controlling for the use of neuroleptic medications and length of stay. Interestingly, these investigators found evidence for lateralization of these effects, with an excess of delta band waves most prominent over the left frontotemporal area relative to the right. The authors interpreted findings of enhanced slow-wave EEG activity as indicating cortical immaturity and/or brain damage among those who exhibit violent behaviors.

Elsewhere, Raine, Venables, and Williams (1990) reported prospective evidence that lower resting HR, lower SCR, and slower frequency EEG activity at 15 years old predicted antisocial behavior at age 24. These data were collectively interpreted as reflecting general cortical hypoarousal among antisocial and aggressive individuals, which according to the authors tends to promote increased thrill-seeking to compensate for a presumably noxious state of underarousal.

A recent, intriguing line of research on the association between electrocortical activation and aggression is one by Harmon-Jones and colleagues that has focused on anterior EEG asymmetry in relation to induced states of anger and trait differences in anger proneness (for a review of this work, see Harmon-Jones, 2003). This research has challenged the prevailing notion that relative left frontal brain activation reflects the presence of positively valenced emotion (e.g., Ahern & Schwartz, 1985; Davidson, 1998; Heller, 1990). Harmon-Jones's work instead suggests that left frontal brain activation reflects mobilization for approach behavior, whether positive-appetitive or negative-defensive. This conclusion is based on data from EEG investigations of anger, which can be viewed as an approach-related negative emotion. States of anger provoked by insults or circumstances of perceived unfairness elicit relative increases in left frontal EEG activity compared with neutral baseline states, particularly when subjects anticipate being able to cope actively with the provoking situation (Harmon-Jones & Sigelman, 2001; Harmon-Jones, Sigelman, Bohlig, & Harmon-Jones, 2003). In addition, individuals high in trait anger show greater relative left frontal brain activation at rest than individuals who are low in trait anger (Harmon-Jones & Allen, 1998). In addition to challenging the positive valence perspective on left frontal asymmetry, this work is important because it suggests that the disposition to actively confront challenges and opportunities is at least somewhat distinct from general tendencies to experience positive and negative affect. A strong bias to respond actively to challenge or provocation may be characteristic of individuals who are prone to aggression.

Event-Related Potential (ERP) Studies

Reviews of existing studies on antisociality/aggression and brain event-related potential (ERP) response have been provided by Raine (1989, 1993), Volavka (1990), and Garza-Trevino (1994). Compared with the large number of studies that have examined EEG activity in aggressive individuals, the ERP literature focusing specifically on aggressive behavior is fairly limited. In his 1989 review, Raine noted that most of the available ERP studies in this area had focused on psychopathy, rather than on antisociality or aggression. Notably, the findings for psychopathy were quite mixed, with some studies yielding effects opposite to those of others and some yielding null effects. This inconsistency could in part reflect the fact that the psychopathy construct comprises distinctive components that show differing relations with a variety of criterion measures (Hare, 2003; Harpur et al., 1989; Patrick, 2001; Verona, Patrick, & Joiner, 2001; see also below).

Among the ERP studies that have focused specifically on aggression and antisociality, the most consistent finding has been reduced amplitude of the P300 component of the ERP in "oddball" tasks in which participants respond to infrequent target stimuli intermingled with frequent, nontarget stimuli (Barratt, Stanford, Kent, & Felthous, 1997; Branchey, Buydens-Branchey, & Lieber, 1988; Gerstle, Mathias, Stanford, 1998; Harmon-Jones, Barratt, & Wigg, 1997; Mathias & Stanford, 1999; but see Drake, Pakalnis, Brown, & Hietter, 1988). Reduced P300 has also been shown to be associated with antisocial personality, a disorder often marked by impulsive aggressive behavior (Bauer, Hesselbrock, O'Connor, & Roberts, 1994; Bauer, O'Connor, & Hesselbrock, 1994; Costa et al., 2000; Iacono, Carlson, Malone, & McGue, 2002). The P300, a positive scalp potential that is maximal at parietal sites, has been theorized to reflect the updating of information in working memory (Donchin, 1981; Donchin & Coles, 1988). Thus, a reduction in P300 amplitude implies a deficit in higher level cognitive functioning in antisocial-aggressive individuals.

Notably, Stanford, Houston, Villemarette-Pittman, and Greve (2003) found no difference in P300 amplitude response in an auditory oddball task for a group of psychiatric outpatients characterized as "premeditated aggressors" in comparison with a normal, nonaggressive control group. Similar results were reported by Barratt et al. (1997). The findings of these studies indicate that the relationship between reduced P300 brain response and aggression may be specific to individuals who manifest aggression of an impulsive nature.

Reduced P300 response amplitude has also been found for a variety of other impulse control problems, most notably alcohol dependence (cf. Polich, Pollock, & Bloom, 1994) – but also drug dependence (Attou, Figiel, & Timsit-Berthier, 2001; Biggins, MacKay, Clark, & Fein, 1997; Branchey, Buydens-Branchey, & Horvath, 1993), nicotine dependence (Anokhin et al., 2000; Iacono et al., 2002), child conduct disorder (Bauer & Hesselbrock, 1999a,b, 2002; Kim, Kim, & Kwon, 2001), and ADHD (Johnstone & Barry, 1996; Klorman, 1991; Strandburg et al., 1996). These findings suggest that P300 amplitude reduction might reflect something that these disorders have in common, rather than what is unique to any one of them. Specifically, reduced P300 amplitude could be an indicator of the general "externalizing" factor (Krueger, 1999) that these disorders share. This general factor appears to be substantially heritable (Kendler et al., 2003; Krueger et al., 2002; Young et al., 2000) and has been conceptualized as a trait vulnerability to disorders of this type (Krueger et al., 2002).

We (Patrick, Bernat, Malone, Iacono, Krueger, & McGue, 2006) evaluated this possibility in a sample of 968 males recruited from the community. We examined the association between reduced P300 amplitude and scores on this general externalizing factor, defined as the primary component derived from a principal components analysis of symptoms of various DSM-IIIR impulse control disorders (i.e., conduct disorder; adult antisocial behavior; and alcohol, drug, and nicotine dependence). We found a highly significant negative relationship between scores on the externalizing factor and P300 brain response amplitude (i.e., higher externalizing scores, reflecting more severe symptoms of a greater number of impulse problems, were associated with smaller P300 amplitude). Moreover, we found that significant univariate associations between each individual diagnostic variable and P300 amplitude were accounted for entirely by the externalizing factor – that is, after controlling for scores on this common factor, all associations for individual disorders dropped to nonsignificance. These results suggest that the relationship that has been demonstrated between impulsive aggression and P300 response may reflect the presence of this broad externalizing factor as a contributor to impulsive aggressive behavior (but not premeditated aggression; cf. Barrett et al., 1997; Stanford et al., 2003). Elsewhere, it has been suggested that general externalizing vulnerability may in turn reflect variations in the functioning of anterior brain systems, including the prefrontal cortex (Iacono, Carlson, & Malone, 2000; Patrick & Bernat, 2006).

It should be noted that associations with aggression have been reported for other components of the ERP aside from P300. For example, Fishbein et al. (1989) reported longer latencies of brainstem auditory evoked potentials in male drug abusers with self-reported histories of aggression compared with nonaggressive drug abusers. However, in a subsequent study of this kind that focused on impulsive-aggressive individuals meeting criteria for "episodic-dyscontrol" syndrome, Drake, Hietter, and Pakalnis (1992) found no difference in brainstem evoked potential latencies. In a study of brain responses to rapidly changing visual displays in a large sample of treatment-seeking youth, Bars, Heyrend, Simpson, and Munger (2001) found a higher occurrence of high-amplitude early positive (P100) potentials in the ERPs of those exhibiting episodes of explosive aggressive behavior compared with those not exhibiting aggressive behavior. Tarkka et al. (2001), using ERP source localization to examine brain regions mediating reactions to familiar "alerting" tones and novel tone stimuli, found interesting differences between a violent alcoholic group and two other groups tested (nonviolent alcoholics, controls). Whereas processing of the familiar alerting tones was localized to medial temporal brain regions in the two nonviolent groups, processing of these tones was localized to frontal brain regions in the violent alcoholic group. In addition, violent subjects showed simultaneous activation in frontal and temporal areas to the novel tones, whereas these two brain regions showed sequential activation to novel tones in the nonviolent groups. Although the findings of these particular ERP studies are intriguing, the effects are basically isolated ones and thus should be treated with caution.

Neuro-Imaging Studies

A variety of neuro-imaging techniques have been applied to the study of aggression, including CT (computerized tomography), SPECT (single photon emission computerized tomography), PET (positron emission tomography), and MRI (magnetic resonance imaging). To index brain structure, CT relies on variations in the attenuation of x-ray beams passed through the brain, associated with regional differences in the density of tissues encountered on the way through. SPECT and PET both rely on the injection of radioactive tracer isotopes into the blood in small amounts; particles emitted by the isotope from brain regions of interest (i.e., photons in the case of SPECT and positrons in the case of PET) can be used to index either neuronal activity or neurotransmitter function in those regions. MRI detects variations in the alignment of endogenous subatomic particles within a magnetic field to index anatomic details of the brain (structural MRI) or variations in blood flow associated with neuronal activity in specific brain regions (functional MRI).

CT Studies

Findings from the few available studies of aggressive behavior that have included CT scans have mainly implicated the temporal lobes of the brain. Tonkonogy (1991) reported results from clinical CT and structural MRI scans performed on 14 violent patients diagnosed with "organic" mental disorders. Lesions in the anterior-inferior temporal lobe were evident in five (37.5%) of these cases. In a sample of hospitalized offenders with mental disorders, Wong, Lumsden, Fenton, and Fenwick (1994) reported a positive association between the number of CT and EEG abnormalities localized to the temporal lobes and ratings of the severity of violent behavior prior to admission. Blake, Pincus, and Buckner (1995) summarized results of "neurological examinations" (involving EEG, MRI or CT scans, and neuropsychological testing) on 31 individuals charged or convicted of murder. Evidence of frontal dysfunction was evident in 20 (64.5%) of cases, whereas evidence of temporal lobe abnormality was evident in only 9 (29%) of cases. However, these findings must be interpreted with caution given the small sample sizes and, in two of the studies, the diversity of brain assessment methods used – and also because of the basic limitations of CT as an imaging technique (i.e., CT provides relatively poor spatial resolution compared with either PET or MRI).

SPECT Studies

SPECT imaging studies that have examined brain activity differences in violent or aggressive individuals have consistently revealed evidence of reduced blood flow (hypoperfusion) both in the prefrontal cortex and in the temporal lobes. The earliest of these studies (Amen, Stubblefield, Carmichael, & Thisted, 1996) compared 40 aggressive psychiatric patients (i.e., adolescents or adults who engaged in physical attack or destruction of property within 6 months of the study evaluation) with 40 psychiatric control patients who had no recorded episodes of aggression. Resting SPECT data revealed significantly reduced activity in the prefrontal cortex for the aggressive group versus the controls, along with focal abnormalities in the left temporal lobe. In addition, aggressive participants showed increased activity in antero-medial regions of the frontal lobes bilaterally and increased left-lateralized activity in the basal ganglia, and in some cases in subcortical

(limbic) regions. Subsequently, Soderstrom, Tullberg, Wikkelsoe, Ekholm, and Forsman (2000) used SPECT to examine 21 individuals convicted of impulsive violent offenses and again found reduced blood flow in both frontal and temporal lobe sites. This study also found reduced bilateral hippocampal functioning and reduced functioning in the right (but not left) angular gyrus in the violent offenders.

Hirono, Mega, Dinov, Mishkin, and Cummings (2000) compared 10 patients exhibiting both dementia and aggressive behavior with 10 nonaggressive dementia patients using resting SPECT, and found reduced blood flow for the aggressive patients bilaterally in dorsofrontal cortex (but not in orbitofrontal cortex), as well as reduced blood flow in the left anterior temporal lobe. One other SPECT study by Kuruoglu, Arikan, Vural, and Karatas (1996) showed significantly reduced frontal regional cerebral blood flow (rCBF) in 15 alcoholic individuals with comorbid antisocial personality disorder compared to 10 nonalcoholic controls. Although aggressive behavior is a characteristic feature of antisocial personality disorder, it should be noted that participants in this study were not selected specifically for a history of aggression.

Three other published studies, drawing on essentially the same sample of participants, employed single-photon emission tomography (with iodine-123-labeled 2 beta-carbomethoxy-3 beta[4-iodophenyl]tropane [beta-CIT] as the tracer) to examine neurotransmitter function rather than regional blood flow in individuals with a history of impulsive violence. Two of these studies examined indices of dopamine transporter density in the region of the striatum, based on animal and human findings pointing to increased dopaminergic transmission as a factor in aggressive behavior. In the first, Tiihonen et al. (1995) examined 48 subjects – 19 habitually impulsive violent alcoholics, 10 nonviolent alcoholics, and 19 healthy controls – and found striatal dopamine transporter density to be substantially lower in nonviolent alcoholics than in healthy controls, whereas the violent alcoholics had slightly higher (approaching significance) dopamine transporter densities than controls. In other words, the two alcoholic subtypes appeared to show differences in the striatal dopamine system in opposing directions. Kuikka et al. (1998) examined two other parameters of striatal dopamine density (heterogeneity and asymmetry) in a slightly expanded version of this sample comprising 21 violent offenders, 10 nonviolent alcoholic individuals, and 21 age-matched control subjects. This analysis revealed, for the violent offender group, a greater heterogeneity of dopamine transporter density in the right striatum compared with healthy controls and an absence of the left-to-right asymmetry in density observed in the control group. Taken together, these findings provide some evidence of abnormalities in the striatal dopaminergic system in violent individuals.

A later study by Tiihonen et al. (1997) used the full sample of Kuikka et al. (1998) to examine serotonin-transporter-specific binding of the tracer in the region of the midbrain. A blind quantitative analysis of the data revealed that serotonin-specific binding in the region of the midbrain was lower in violent offenders ($n = 21$) than in either the healthy control subjects ($n = 21$) or the nonviolent alcoholics ($n = 10$). Consistent with the postmortem studies revealing deficits in central serotonin in impulsively violent individuals, the findings of this study suggest an association between persistent impulsive aggressive behavior and decreased serotonin transporter density.

PET Studies

Evidence for prefrontal dysfunction. By far the largest number of neuro-imaging studies of aggression have used PET methodology, and the majority of these studies have yielded evidence of prefrontal dysfunction in violent individuals. In an early investigation, Volkow and Tancredi (1987) used PET to compare resting brain activity in two groups: forensic psychiatric patients with histories of impulsive violence ($n = 4$)

and nonpatient controls ($n = 4$). Two of the four violent patients showed evidence of abnormal activity in the frontal cortex. Another early PET study that demonstrated a relationship between aggression and prefrontal activity was conducted by Goyer, Andreason, Semple, and Clayton (1994). This study included 17 subjects diagnosed with personality disorders according to DSM-III criteria along with 43 controls. Scanning took place during a continuous performance task designed to activate the prefrontal cortex. Within the personality disorder group, a significant inverse association was found between aggression and prefrontal brain activity: specifically, a higher number of impulsive aggressive acts (as indexed by higher scores on a self-report scale) were associated with reduced glucose metabolism in orbitofrontal cortex. Another PET study by Volkow et al. (1995) compared eight psychiatric patients with past histories of repeated violence (three of whom were diagnosed as schizophrenic) against eight normal controls on a nonactivation, eyes open, resting procedure. The violent group in this study evidenced a significant reduction in glucose metabolism in bilateral prefrontal regions compared with controls.

In an oft-cited study, the first of its kind, Raine et al. (1994) compared local cerebral uptake of glucose using PET in 22 subjects accused of murder and 22 control participants matched for age and gender. A continuous performance task was used to activate the prefrontal cortex. Subjects in the murderer group showed reduced glucose metabolism in both lateral and medial regions of prefrontal cortex compared with controls. This difference appeared to be quite site-specific: no group differences were found in glucose metabolism for posterior frontal, temporal, or parietal regions. A follow-up investigation by Raine, Buchsbaum, and LaCasse (1997) used an expanded version of this sample, consisting of 41 convicted murderers and an equivalent number of control participants matched for age and gender, and diagnosis of schizophrenia (if present in the homicide offender with whom the control participant was matched). They assessed brain activity using [18]fluorodeoxyglucose (FDG) PET in a visual continuous performance task designed to activate the prefrontal cortex. As in the initial (1994) study, the murderer group showed significantly reduced glucose metabolism in bilateral prefrontal cortex compared with controls. In addition, decreased metabolic activity was found in other brain regions, along with abnormal asymmetry in subcortical structures (described below).

Two other papers by this research group further elucidated these basic findings. In a reanalysis of data for the full sample reported on by Raine et al. (1997), Raine, Stoddard, Bihrle, and Buchsbaum (1998) reported that the reduced prefrontal activity for murderers versus controls was attributable to the subgroup of murderers in the sample who were blindly rated as *lacking* a significant history of psychosocial impoverishment. This finding is important because it suggests that prefrontal differences are particularly evident in individuals without a strong environmental push toward deviancy. In a further reanalysis of data from this sample, Raine et al. (1998) parsed the murderer group into "predatory" and "affective" subgroups, using a classification scheme that distinguished between deliberate, instrumental aggression directed at achieving a desired goal and aggression characterized by impulsiveness and strong emotion. Subtype ratings were assigned by personnel who were blind to the imaging data. This analysis revealed that prefrontal dysfunction was specific to affective, impulsive murderers: murderers in this subgroup evidenced significantly lower prefrontal glucose metabolism than controls, whereas frontal metabolism in the predatory subgroup did not differ from controls. Another interesting finding of this study was that, in contrast to the prefrontal findings, both murderer subgroups showed *increased activity* in subcortical regions (including midbrain, amygdala, hippocampus, and thalamus) compared to controls.

A number of other studies, inspired by the well-documented association between reduced serotonergic functioning and impulsive aggressive behavior, have used PET methodology to investigate brain reactivity to drugs that activate the serotonin system in aggressive and nonaggressive individuals. Siever et al. (1999) compared changes in regional glucose metabolism in six impulsive aggressive patients and five healthy control subjects after administration of either a serotonergic-releasing agent (d,l-fenfluramine) or a placebo. Within the control group, increased glucose metabolism was found after fenfluramine administration in orbitofrontal and ventromedial regions of prefrontal cortex and in the cingulate and inferior parietal cortex. In contrast, impulsive aggressive patients did not show significant increases in glucose metabolism in any region after administration of fenfluramine. Compared with the control group, the aggressive group evidenced significantly reduced metabolic reactivity in regions of orbitofrontal, ventromedial, and cingulate cortex, although not in inferior parietal cortex. Similar findings were reported by Soloff, Meltzer, Greer, Constantine, and Kelly (2000) in an [18]fluorodeoxyglucose (FDG) PET fenfluramine challenge study. This study differed from the one by Siever et al. in that the test group consisted of patients ($n = 5$) diagnosed with borderline personality (which includes impulsiveness and proneness to anger as features), rather than patients selected specifically as aggressive. Nevertheless, this study also found reduced brain reactivity (as indexed by uptake of FDG) after fenfluramine administration in patients compared to controls ($n = 8$), particularly in medial and orbital regions of right prefrontal cortex, the left middle and superior temporal gyri, left parietal lobe, and left caudate body.

In another PET study of this sort, New et al. (2002) examined regional glucose metabolism in response to a postsynaptic serotonin receptor agonist, meta-chlorophenylpiperazine (m-CPP), in 13 individuals with impulsive aggression and 13 healthy controls. Compared with controls, the aggressive patients showed reduced glucose metabolism specifically in the left anteromedial orbital cortex and in anterior cingulate cortex after administration of m-CPP. On the other hand, aggressive patients showed *enhanced* activation of the posterior cingulate gyrus compared with controls. Two other PET studies examined regional serotonin transporter distribution in the brains of individuals with impulsive aggression using radiotracers to assess serotonin-binding potential. Parsey et al. (2002) examined relations between aggression and binding potential of serotonin-1A receptors in a PET procedure that used [carbonyl-C-11] WAY-100635, a radioligand that binds selectively to 1A type receptors. Participants were 25 individuals from the community (12 female) assessed for lifetime episodes of aggression using a self-report inventory. A significant negative association was found between reported lifetime aggression and serotonin receptor binding (i.e., higher aggression was associated with reduced binding) in several brain regions, including medial and orbital regions of prefrontal cortex. In contrast with this finding, Frankle et al. (2005) did not find differences in binding within prefrontal regions for impulsive aggressive individuals versus controls in a study that employed a different radiotracer – although differences were evident in the cingulate cortex (see below).

Along these same lines, a particularly innovative study was conducted by New et al. (2004). The question addressed in this study was whether administration of a selective serotonin reuptake inhibitor drug (fluoxetine) known to improve the behavior of impulsive aggressive individuals would produce changes in brain regions that have previously been linked to aggression. Ten impulsive aggressive patients diagnosed with borderline personality disorder were assessed with PET both before and after receiving fluoxetine at 20 mg/day for 12 weeks. The major findings were that (1) significant increases in glucose metabolism within specific regions of orbitofrontal cortex were found following treatment with fluoxetine, and (2) significant improvement was evident on an observer-rated index

of aggressive behavior. These findings are important because they point to a mechanism of action of anti-aggression drugs in specific brain regions (i.e., orbitofrontal cortex) that have been found to be dysfunctional in aggressive individuals.

In addition, a small number of studies have examined brain reactivity during states of induced anger using PET. Two of these have involved imagery manipulations. Pietrini, Guazzelli, Basso, Jaffe, and Grafman (2000) examined brain activity in 15 healthy nonpatients selected to be high in imagery ability during processing of an imaginal scenario in which they expressed unrestrained aggressive behavior. Compared with imagery of a neutral emotional scene, significant decreases in blood flow were observed in the prefrontal cortex, specifically the ventromedial region, during aggressive imagery. In contrast with this finding, Drexler et al. (2000) reported increased activation of inferior frontal cortex during imagery of a personal anger scene (compared with a neutral scene) in a group of nicotine-dependent men who were included as controls in a study of anger in cocaine-dependent men. Although on the face of it, this result seems at odds with that of Pietrini et al. (2000), the difference may lie in the fact that, in the Pietrini study, participants imagined themselves actively aggressing; ventromedial prefrontal cortex may show activation mainly during anger states in which overt aggression is suppressed (cf. Davidson et al., 2000). Interestingly, cocaine-dependent men in the study by Drexler et al. (2000) showed relative decreases in frontal brain activation during anger imagery. The authors' intriguing interpretation was that cocaine dependence may be associated with deficits in anger regulation that dispose such individuals toward aggressive behavior and relapse under circumstances of stress.

More recently, Dougherty et al. (2004) examined brain reactivity during anger imagery in two unmedicated patient groups and a control group. One of the patient groups consisted of individuals diagnosed with major depression who also exhibited "anger attacks"; the other consisted of individuals with depression but not anger. All participants imagined four scenes drawn from personal experience, two in which they had experienced anger and two involving neutral experiences. Patients exhibiting both depression and anger evidenced smaller increases in regional cerebral blood flow in the left ventromedial prefrontal cortex during anger imagery (cf. Drexler et al., 2000) than control participants, whereas depression-only patients did not differ from controls. Dougherty et al. (2004) also found an inverse association between blood flow changes in the left ventromedial prefrontal cortex and left amygdala (cf. Ochsner, Bunge, Gross, & Gabrielli, 2002) in the control group during imagery of anger scenes, whereas angry-depressed patients showed a positive association between activity in these brain regions during anger imagery.

Of course, there are studies that have examined prefrontal activity using PET that have not found differences between violent and nonviolent individuals. As noted earlier, Frankle et al. (2005) failed to replicate findings of reduced serotonin receptor binding in prefrontal areas in aggressive individuals. Wong et al. (1997) tested for differences in frontal as well as temporal regions in an FDG PET study comparing violent forensic patients with nonviolent patients and controls; they obtained significant group effects only for the latter. George et al. (2004) compared individuals exhibiting domestic violence as well as alcoholism ($n = 8$) with nonviolent alcoholic ($n = 11$) and control groups ($n = 10$) for glucose metabolism in various brain regions and found no group differences for frontal regions. The authors speculated that this null finding might be attributable to small sample sizes. However, the sample sizes in this study exceeded those of some other studies that have reported frontal differences, and domestic abusers did show significant glucose metabolism differences in other brain regions and in relations between activity across regions (see below).

Evidence for temporal lobe dysfunction. As noted earlier, studies comparing aggressive

and nonaggressive individuals using SPECT methodology have found differences in temporal as well as prefrontal cortex. A number of PET studies (including some cited in the preceding subsection) have also reported differences in temporal cortex, but these are far fewer in number than those reporting differences in prefrontal regions. Volkow and Tancredi (1987), cited above, found significantly decreased left temporal blood flow and glucose metabolism in all four repetitively violent patients whom they tested against controls. Volkow et al. (1995), cited above, reported significant reductions bilaterally in medial temporal regions as well as prefrontal cortex in a group of eight psychiatric patients with histories of repeated violence. Using FDG PET, Wong et al. (1997), cited above, compared brain activity in violent and nonviolent forensic patients ($n = 17$ and 14, respectively) against that of normal control subjects ($n = 6$). They examined FDG uptake for a range of brain regions covering frontal and temporal areas. The subgroup of patients with a history of repetitive violent offending evidenced significantly reduced FDG uptake in both right and left anterior inferior temporal regions compared with the nonviolent patient group and the control group. Seidenwurm, Pounds, Globus, and Valk (1997) compared seven subjects with histories of severe violence with nine nonviolent control subjects. Analyses of FDG PET data revealed decreased glucose metabolism in the temporal lobes (medial region in particular) for the violent group as compared to the control group. In another relevant study, Gatzke-Kopp, Raine, Buchsbaum, and LaCasse (2001) examined resting EEG in a subsample of murderers included in the study by Raine et al. (1997), cited above, and found abnormalities in the region of the temporal lobes, even though PET imaging had not revealed dysfunction in this region.

Evidence for dysfunction in anterior cingulate cortex. Evidence of anterior cingulate cortex dysfunction has been reported mainly in studies that have assessed serotonergic function in relation to aggression. In a study that compared changes in glucose metabolism after administration of a serotonergic-releasing agent (fenfluramine) in impulsive-aggressive patients and healthy controls, Siever et al. (1999), cited above, found attenuated metabolic reactivity in cingulate cortex among other regions. In a study that assessed changes in glucose metabolism to a different serotonin agonist (m-CPP), New et al. (2002), cited above, reported that patients with impulsive aggression showed deactivation of the anterior cingulate to the pharmacologic manipulation in contrast with the increased activation exhibited by nonaggressive controls. An opposite pattern was found in the posterior cingulate gyrus: aggressive subjects showed activation in this region, whereas controls showed deactivation. Likewise, in a study assessing serotonin-binding potential, Parsey et al. (2002), cited above, found evidence of a significant negative association between lifetime aggression and binding in various brain regions including anterior cingulate cortex. Finally, Frankle et al. (2005) compared 10 individuals with impulsive aggression against 10 normal controls matched for age and gender in a PET procedure that employed [^{11}C]McN 5652 as the serotonin transporter radiotracer. Compared to controls, subjects with impulsive aggression showed reduced serotonin transporter density (indexed by reduced binding potential) in the anterior cingulate cortex, but similar density in other regions examined. Taken together, these findings suggest that impulsive aggressive behavior may be associated with reduced serotonergic innervation in the anterior cingulate cortex, a region that plays important roles in affect regulation and decision making.

Evidence for dysfunction in the amygdala and hippocampus. As in the case of the temporal cortex, some PET studies have revealed evidence of abnormalities in amygdala and hippocampal regions. However, these reports have been fewer than those reporting prefrontal abnormalities. Raine et al. (1997), cited above, found evidence of abnormal asymmetry of functioning in the amygdala and hippocampus in murderers compared to controls (i.e., decreased functioning on the left side and increased functioning on the right in both the amygdala and hippocampus). In their study of serotonin-binding potential, Parsey et al. (2002), cited above, reported a significant negative relationship between lifetime aggression and binding in brain regions including the amygdala (but not hippocampus). George et al. (2004), cited above, in a study of domestic abusers with comorbid alcoholism, reported decreased correlations between glucose activity in the amygdala and glucose activity in various cortical structures compared with nonviolent controls. The authors postulated that these decreased associations reflect a lack of cortical input to the amygdala that is related to increased sensitivity to environmental stressors among impulsively violent individuals.

Dysfunction in other brain regions. Evidence of abnormalities in other brain regions has been inconsistent, emerging only in isolated PET studies. For example, in their study of murderers, Raine et al. (1997) reported decreased metabolic activity in the corpus callosum along with decreased activity bilaterally in the prefrontal cortex. A key finding in the aforementioned study by George et al. (2004) was that domestic abusers showed significantly reduced glucose uptake in the right hypothalamus compared to control participants; indeed, this was the only brain region in this study for which glucose metabolism differentiated the groups.

Structural MRI Studies

Fewer studies have been reported using structural MRI techniques. These studies have yielded generally less consistent results than PET studies. Woermann et al. (2000) used structural MRI to examine gray matter density in two groups of temporal lobe epilepsy patients, an aggressive group ($n = 24$) and a nonaggressive group ($n = 24$), along with a group of nonpatient controls ($n = 35$). Compared with the two nonaggressive groups, aggressive patients showed reduced gray matter volume in the left prefrontal cortex. Van Elst et al. (2003) used structural MRI to examine limbic and prefrontal brain volumes in eight unmedicated female patients diagnosed with borderline personality disorder (a disorder marked by impulsivity and anger control problems) and eight female nonpatient controls. The specific structures targeted for volumetric analysis were the orbitofrontal and dorsolateral prefrontal cortex, the anterior cingulate cortex, and the hippocampus and amygdala. The patient group showed a significant (24%) reduction in the volume of left orbitofrontal cortex (but not dorsolateral frontal cortex) and a similar (26%) reduction in the right anterior cingulate cortex. Significant reductions in hippocampal and amygdala volumes were also found.

However, other structural MRI studies have yielded conflicting results. Dolan, Deakins, Roberts, and Anderson (2002) compared frontal and temporal lobe regions in 18 male personality disorder patients exhibiting impulsive aggressive behavior versus 19 healthy controls and found a significant (20%) reduction in temporal lobe volume in the patients versus the controls. However, no significant reduction in frontal lobe volume was found – despite the fact that patients evidenced deficits in performance on neuropsychological tests of executive function in relation to controls. Furthermore with regard to subcortical structures, van Elst, Woermann, Lemieux, Thompson, and Trimble (2000) did not find differences between aggressive and nonaggressive temporal-lobe epilepsy patients (defined by presence versus absence of a history of intermittent explosive disorder; $n = 25$ per group) in amygdala volume or amygdala pathology. In a structural MRI study that specifically compared volumes of the hippocampus in early-onset (type 2) alcoholics with comorbid antisocial personality and violence versus late-onset, non-antisocial (type 1) alcoholics and normal controls, Laakso et al. (2000) failed to find differences

between the violent and nonviolent alcoholic groups – although both of these groups showed a significant reduction in right (but not left) hippocampal volume in relation to the controls.

Other Neuro-Imaging Studies

The remaining three aggression/neuro-imaging studies of which we are aware each used a different imaging technique. Critchley et al. (2000) used magnetic resonance (MR) spectroscopy to examine concentrations and ratios of N-acetyl aspartate (NAA) and creatine phosphocreatine (Cr+PCr) – reflecting neuronal density and high-energy phosphate metabolism, respectively – within prefrontal and subcortical ("amygdala-hippocampal complex") regions in 10 mildly retarded repetitively violent offenders compared with 8 control subjects. The violent patient group showed lower concentrations of NAA and Cr+PCr in prefrontal cortex and a lower ratio of NAA/Cr+PCr in the amygdala-hippocampal complex than the control group, implying reduced neuronal density and abnormal phosphate metabolism in these brain regions, respectively. (A different MR spectroscopy study by van Elst et al., [2001] also yielded evidence of reduced NAA concentration in [dorsolateral] prefrontal cortex, but the index group in this study was borderline personality disorder patients rather than individuals selected specifically as violent.)

Hoptman et al. (2002) used the MR technique of diffusion tensor imaging to test for associations between the density and integrity of white matter in frontal brain regions and trait variations in aggression and impulsivity assessed by self-report in a sample of male schizophrenia patients ($n = 14$). Two indices of white matter microstructure were examined: trace, an index of white matter density, and fractional anisotropy, an index of the orientational coherence (structural organization) of fibers. The major findings were that (1) higher trace in frontal regions (reflecting lower white matter density) was associated with aggressiveness and (2) reduced fractional anisotropy in right inferior frontal white matter (reflecting poor fiber organization) was associated with higher impulsiveness. These findings, which must be interpreted with caution due to the small sample size and lack of pre-selection for low versus high aggressiveness, are nonetheless consistent with other imaging data indicating a key role of frontal brain regions in impulsive aggressive behavior.

One further study by Raine et al. (2001) used functional MRI (fMRI) to examine differences in brain activation during performance of a visual/verbal working memory task in groups differentiated on the basis of serious violent behavior and history of early abuse. Participants were recruited from community employment agencies to form four groups: violence + abuse ($n = 5$); violence only ($n = 4$); abuse only ($n = 5$); and no violence or abuse (controls; $n = 9$). Major findings were (1) reduced right hemisphere activation, particularly within right temporal cortex, in violent individuals who had been abused as children; (2) relatively lower left, but higher right, activation of the superior temporal gyrus in abused individuals without violence; and (3) reduced cortical activation during task processing, especially in the left hemisphere, in abused individuals regardless of violence status. The authors interpreted these results as indicating a unique role of right hemisphere dysfunction, when combined with exposure to early abuse, in violent behavior. Once again, however, the findings of this study must be interpreted with caution due to the small sample sizes. (Another fMRI study by Schneider et al. [2000] that examined brain activation during an aversive conditioning procedure in which faces served as conditioned stimuli and a foul odor served as the unconditioned stimulus found signal increases in the amygdala and dorsolateral prefrontal cortex during acquisition for individuals with antisocial personality disorder [versus signal decreases for control subjects]; however, the index group in this study consisted of individuals diagnosed as antisocial

as opposed to individuals identified specifically as violent.)

Neuro-Imaging Studies of Individuals Diagnosed as Psychopathic

A number of neuro-imaging studies have also been conducted to examine brain differences in individuals diagnosed as psychopathic according to the criteria of the Psychopathy-Checklist Revised (PCL-R; Hare, 1991, 2003). These include studies by Intrator, Hare, Stritzke, and Brichtswein (1997); Kiehl et al. (2001, 2004); Laakso et al. (2001, 2002); Muller et al. (2003); Raine et al. (2000, 2003, 2004); Soderstrom et al. (2002); Tiihonen, Hodgins, and Vaurio (2000); Veit et al. (2002); and Yang et al. (2005). Because these studies have recently been reviewed in detail elsewhere (Raine & Yang, 2006) and because these studies did not specifically target violent-aggressive behavior (although psychopathy does tend to be strongly predictive of aggression; Porter & Woodworth, 2006), these studies are not reviewed here.

However, it should be noted that, in addition to the lack of specific focus on aggressive behavior, the findings of these neuro-imaging studies are difficult to compare with those already reviewed because of important differences between the construct of psychopathy embodied in the PCL-R and that of impulsive aggressiveness or externalization. The PCL-R psychopathy construct includes affective-interpersonal features (shallow affect, lack of remorse or empathy, glibness, grandiosity, manipulativeness, etc.) in addition to impulsive-antisocial features, and these affective-interpersonal features show unique associations with diagnostic, personality, behavioral, and physiological variables (Fowles & Dindo, 2006; Hare, 1991, 2003; Patrick, 2001, 2007). Because the PCL-R includes these affective-interpersonal features, psychopathy as indexed by this instrument tends to be associated more with predatory-instrumental aggression than with angry-impulsive aggression (Porter & Woodworth, 2006; Woodworth & Porter,

2002; see also Patrick et al., 1997) – and as noted earlier, there is evidence that these forms of aggression are associated with different patterns of brain activity (Raine et al., 1998).

Summary and Conclusions

The most consistent finding to emerge from neuro-imaging studies of aggression is evidence of abnormalities in the prefrontal cortex. In particular, most available PET imaging studies that have compared aggressive individuals with controls have yielded indications of prefrontal deviations in the form of reduced glucose metabolism at rest or during performance of continuous performance tasks, reduced metabolic reactivity to serotonin agonist agents, decreased serotonin-receptor binding, or reduced neural activation during imagery of anger-evoking situations. PET imaging studies that have differentiated among subregions of prefrontal cortex have more often demonstrated abnormalities in orbital and medial/ventromedial regions than in dorsolateral prefrontal cortex. SPECT imaging studies have also consistently yielded evidence of prefrontal deficits, although such studies have also tended to demonstrate abnormalities in temporal brain regions (a pattern observed even more so in CT studies).

The findings of structural MRI studies have been somewhat more mixed. Two of these studies revealed evidence of decreased brain volume in prefrontal cortex – one of them specifically in left orbitofrontal cortex (along with reductions in anterior cingulate cortex, hippocampus, and amygdala). However, a third study found evidence of reduced temporal lobe volume with no difference in frontal lobe volume, even though the aggressive group in this study showed significant impairments in performance on neuropsychological tests of executive function. Two other MR studies that employed techniques of MR spectroscopy and diffusion tensor imaging also revealed evidence of neuronal abnormalities in frontal brain regions. One study that used functional MRI to compare brain activation in aggressive

and nonaggressive individuals during performance of a working memory task did not find abnormalities specifically in prefrontal brain regions; instead, it found a general reduction in right hemisphere activation, particularly within right temporal cortex.

In addition to deviations in prefrontal cortex and to a lesser degree temporal cortex, other brain structures that have been implicated with some consistency in neuro-imaging studies of aggression are anterior cingulate cortex and limbic structures, in particular the amygdala and hippocampus. The strongest evidence for abnormalities in anterior cingulate cortex has emerged from pharmacological challenge studies focusing on serotonin system reactivity and studies of serotonin-binding potential. Four recent (since 1999) studies of this kind have revealed indications of reduced serotonergic function in the anterior cingulate cortex – an important finding considering the role that this brain region is known to play in the regulation of motivated behavior and the extensive evidence for a link between reduced serotonergic function and aggression.

With regard to amygdala and hippocampus, PET research by Raine and colleagues (1997, 1998) revealed evidence of *increased* activation in these brain regions in murderers versus controls, concurrently with decreased prefrontal activation, during performance of a visual continuous performance task. Related to these findings, Dougherty et al. (2004), also using PET, reported an anomalous positive association between ventromedial prefrontal and amygdala activation during imagery of anger-evoking situations in depressed patients with a history of angry outbursts (i.e., healthy controls and depressed patients without angry episodes showed a contrasting inverse association between activity in these brain regions during anger imagery). Another PET study by George et al. (2004) found decreased associations between glucose activity in the amygdala and activity in other brain regions, which the authors interpreted as reflecting a lack of cortico-limbic downregulation. One other study (Parsey et al., 2002) reported poorer serotonin-receptor binding in the amygdala among individuals high in aggression, a finding that could also be interpreted as symptomatic of weaker limbic regulatory capacity.

Based on a review of some of the studies in this area (along with research on serotonin system function in aggressive individuals and findings from studies of patients with lesions to distinct regions of the prefrontal cortex), Davidson et al. (2000) postulated that persistent impulsive aggressive behavior arises from dysfunction in an interrelated set of brain structures including the prefrontal cortex (the orbitofrontal and ventromedial [collectively orbitomedial; cf. Blumer & Benson, 1975] regions, in particular), the anterior cingulate cortex, and subcortical-limbic structures (the amygdala, in particular). According to these authors, the orbitomedial prefrontal cortex, which connects directly with limbic structures along with other regions of frontal cortex, plays a crucial direct role in emotion regulation – defined as the capacity to enhance, inhibit, or maintain affective states instigated by subcortical motive systems (e.g., amygdala). Related to this role, the anterior cingulate cortex functions to signal the need for regulatory control on the part of the prefrontal cortex by detecting conflict among competing goals and response dispositions.

The consistent evidence from neuroimaging studies for reduced activity in prefrontal brain regions (including orbitomedial cortex) in aggressive individuals, together with the somewhat less consistent evidence for reduced anterior cingulate activity and enhanced or otherwise dysregulated amygdala activity, is largely consistent with this formulation. Of course, much work remains to be done to elucidate the functions of these distinct subsystems and the precise nature of their interactions, as they pertain to an understanding of aggressive behavior.

Conclusions and Future Directions

A number of consistent findings have emerged from psychophysiological studies of aggression and aggressive individuals. One of these is the finding of a robust association between low levels of resting HR and antisocial-aggressive behavior. Work by Raine and colleagues has shown that low resting HR prospectively predicts the emergence of antisocial deviance in at-risk individuals, suggesting that this variable could represent a biological marker (endophenotype) for antisociality. Data indicating a stronger association of this kind for individuals from high versus low socioeconomic backgrounds have been interpreted as providing further support for this possibility (Raine, 2002). With regard to underlying processes, reduced baseline HR in antisocial-aggressive individuals has been interpreted as reflecting low dispositional arousal, which is assumed to promote stimulation seeking and disinhibited behavior (Ortiz & Raine, 2004; Raine, 1993, 2002).

Two other findings of related interest from the electrocortical literature are those of enhanced EEG slow wave activity and reduced P300 brain potential response in antisocial-aggressive individuals. Enhanced EEG slow wave, like low resting HR, has been interpreted as reflecting low dispositional arousal and an affiliated need for stimulation (Eysenck, 1967; Zuckerman, 1979). Various interpretations have been attached to the finding of reduced P300 response amplitude in individuals with externalizing problems (e.g., Begleiter & Porjesz, 1999; Iacono, 1998). One interpretation that could fit with the findings of low resting HR and enhanced EEG slow wave, and also with evidence for diminished nonspecific electrodermal actvity (cf. Raine, 1993), is that the processing style of antisocial-aggressive individuals is less proactive and more stimulus-driven (i.e., anticipatory and preparatory activities are reduced in such individuals). Relevant to this interpretation, there is evidence that such individuals show differential vigilance (as indexed by alpha-band EEG activity) prior to the occurrence of stimuli in a standard oddball task in which reduced P300 was observed (Malone, Bernat, Patrick, & Iacono, 2002).

Although findings indicating reduced P300 amplitude in antisocial-aggressive individuals have been emphasized in this review, it should be noted that, historically, reduced P300 has been studied more extensively as an indicator of risk for alcohol problems (cf. Polich et al., 1994). Studies demonstrating reductions in P300 amplitude in connection with other externalizing syndromes have appeared more recently. These more recent findings raise the possibility that P300 amplitude reduction may reflect a disposition toward externalizing problems generally, rather than to specific problem(s) within this spectrum – and support for this hypothesis has indeed emerged (Patrick et al., 2006). This raises the question of whether reduced HR level and enhanced EEG slow wave are unique to antisocial-aggressive individuals or if these physiological indicators are also associated with externalizing problems more generally. To address this question, it will be valuable in future research to systematically investigate relations between these physiological indicators and other problems that fall within the externalizing spectrum (e.g., alcohol, drug, and nicotine dependence).

In contrast with the data indicating reduced cardiac, electrodermal, and electrocortical activation at rest and in simple stimulus-processing tasks, data from studies examining phasic reactivity to stressful or aversive stimuli have demonstrated *enhanced* reactivity to such stimuli in hostile, aggressive, and abusive individuals. Relevant findings include heightened cardiac and electrodermal reactivity in response to stressors, poorer regulation of autonomic activity during stressor anticipation, and reduced cardiac vagal tone. Moreover, there is some evidence that this pattern of enhanced reactivity to phasic stressors, like reduced P300 amplitude, may be generally characteristic of individuals with externalizing problems, rather than specific to one manifestation of externalizing (Iacono et al., 1999; Taylor, Carlson, Iacono, Lykken, & McGue, 1999). Although at first glance heightened reactivity to phasic stressors might seem to be at odds with data indicating lower levels of resting activation, this overall pattern of results is potentially understandable in terms of the aforementioned hypothesis of externalizing (including impulsive-aggressive tendencies)

as entailing a stimulus-driven response style marked by lack of normal preparatory processing. From this standpoint, high externalizing individuals tend to react more to situational challenges because they anticipate and prepare for them less effectively (cf. Iacono et al., 1999; Taylor et al., 1999). This pattern of results is also interpretable from the standpoint of Davidson et al.'s (2000) neurobiological model of impulsive aggression: aggressive individuals are impaired in terms of normal conflict detection and/or affect-modulating systems that mediate normal anticipatory processing and proactive coping; consequently, they exhibit reduced levels of activation until challenges/stressors are actually encountered.

It should be noted that these findings for impulsive aggression (and externalizing more generally) are clearly at odds with findings for the construct of psychopathy. For example, Raine (1993) noted that adult psychopaths do not show consistent reductions in resting HR level or P300 response amplitude. Also, psychopathy has consistently been associated with reduced phasic reactivity to aversive cues, including attenuated electrodermal response (cf. Arnett, 1997; Hare, 1978) and deficient startle reflex potentiation (e.g., Levenston et al., 2000; Patrick, 1994). The explanation for this apparent anomaly almost certainly lies in the distinction between the core affective-interpersonal features of psychopathy and the antisocial deviance features: it is the latter features that are associated most strongly with heightened externalizing tendencies, including impulsivity and aggression (Patrick et al., 2005). Most electrocortical and neuro-imaging studies of psychopathy to date have not examined effects separately for the affective-interpersonal and antisocial deviance (externalizing) components. This is an important issue that needs to be addressed directly and systematically in future research.

More broadly, the differences in findings for psychopathy versus externalizing signal a need to delineate more precisely the trait dispositions associated with persistent aggressive behavior. For example, traits, such as glibness, grandiosity, and manipulativeness, which are central to psychopathy, appear to be relatively unimportant in predicting aggression (Hall, Benning, & Patrick, 2004; Patrick et al., 1997). Related to this, it will be important in future research to distinguish among alternative forms of aggression (e.g., instrumental-proactive versus impulsive-reactive) that may reflect different underlying motives. In particular, it is the impulsive-reactive form that appears to be most related to externalizing and to impairments in brain systems that govern emotion regulation. It will also be useful in future research to employ multiple measures of physiological reactivity (peripheral autonomic and electrocortical) within common task procedures so that results for different measures can be directly compared.

The findings of neuro-imaging studies to date have been consistent for the most part with Davidson et al.'s (2000) model of aggression as involving dysfunction in fronto-cortical and limbic brain regions that mediate emotional activation and emotional control. Key questions for future research include the following: (1) What are the unique functional roles of each of these brain regions, and how do they interact to achieve regulatory control over emotional states? Basic cognitive and affective neuroscience research is needed to address this issue. (2) What specific impairments in the functioning of these brain systems predispose toward aggression, and how do such impairments arise? To address the first part of this question, it will be necessary to conduct functional neuro-imaging studies that examine online processing and brain reactivity within ecologically valid tasks, such as interpersonal provocation paradigms. Addressing the latter issue will require the coordinated efforts of cognitive and affective neuroscience researchers together with longitudinal-developmental investigators and behavioral and molecular geneticists. (3) Is dysfunction in these systems characteristic of externalizing psychopathology generally (i.e., does it represent a substrate for the predominantly

constitutional factor that these disorders share), or is it characteristic more specifically of aggressive manifestations of externalizing vulnerability? Relevant to this issue, Krueger et al. (in press) reported evidence that aggressive manifestations of externalizing likely involve distinct trait dispositions in addition to those that confer general risk for externalizing problems. Thus, an important challenge for future research will be to delineate the nature of impairments within particular brain systems that confer specific vulnerability to impulsive aggression versus general vulnerability to externalizing problems.

A final key point to emerge from brain imaging studies on aggression is evidence for the role of specific neurotransmitter systems in aggressive behavior. For example, perhaps the most consistent finding in studies of this kind to date has been that of deficient serotonin transporter density in the region of the anterior cingulate cortex. Some indications have also emerged of abnormalities in ventral striatal (DA) system function in aggressive individuals. Increased understanding of differences in neurotransmitter function in aggressive individuals using brain-imaging methods is potentially of great value for designing and evaluating new interventions. As an example, New et al. (2004) demonstrated increases in glucose metabolism within specific regions of orbitofrontal cortex following treatment with an anti-aggression medication (fluoxetine) coincident with improvements in the incidence of aggressive behavior in a patient sample. Continued work along these lines should enhance our understanding of the mechanisms underlying aggressive behavior while also contributing to improved methods of intervention.

References

Achenbach, T. M., & Edelbrock, C. S. (1984). Psychopathology of childhood. *Annual Review of Psychology, 35*, 227–256.

Ahern, G. L., & Schwartz, G. E. (1985). Differential lateralization for positive and negative emotion in the human brain: EEG spectral analysis. *Neuropsychologia, 23,* 745–755.

Amen, D. G., Stubblefield, M., Carmichael, B., & Thisted, R. (1996). Brain SPECT findings and aggressiveness. *Annals of Clinical Psychiatry, 8,* 129–137.

Anokhin, A. P., Vedeniapin, A. B., Sirevaag, E. J., Bauer, L. O., O'Connor, S. J., Kuperman, S., et al. (2000). The P300 brain potential is reduced in smokers. *Psychopharmacology, 149,* 409–413.

Arnett, P. A. (1997). Autonomic responsivity in psychopaths: A critical review and theoretical proposal. *Clinical Psychology Review, 17,* 903–936.

Attou, A., Figiel, C., & Timsit-Berthier, M. (2001). ERP assessment of heroin detoxification and methadone treatment in chronic heroin users. *Clinical Neurophysiology, 31,* 171–180.

Babcock, J. C., Green, C. E., Webb, S. A., & Graham, K. H. (2004). A second failure to replicate the Gottman et al. (1995) typology of men who abuse intimate partners . . . and possible reasons why. *Journal of Family Psychology, 18,* 396–400.

Barratt, E. S., Stanford, M. S., Kent, T. A., & Felthous, A. R. (1997). Neuropsychological and cognitive psychophysiological substrates of impulsive aggression. *Biological Psychiatry, 41,* 1045–1061.

Bars, D. R., Heyrend, F. L., Simpson, C. D., & Munger, J. C. (2001). Use of visual evoked-potential studies and EEG data to classify aggressive, explosive behavior of youths. *Psychiatric Services, 52,* 81–86.

Bauer L. O., & Hesselbrock, V. M. (1999a). P300 decrements in teenagers with conduct problems: Implications for substance abuse risk and brain development. *Biological Psychiatry, 46,* 263–272.

Bauer L. O., & Hesselbrock, V. M. (1999b). Subtypes of family history and conduct disorder: Effects on P300 during the Stroop test. *Neuropsychopharmacology, 21,* 51–62.

Bauer, L. O., & Hesselbrock, V. M. (2002). Brain maturation and subtypes of Conduct Disorder: Interactive effects on P300 amplitude and topography in male adolescents. *Journal of the American Academy of Child and Adolescent Psychiatry, 42,* 106–115.

Bauer, L. O., Hesselbrock, V. M., O'Connor, S., & Roberts, L. (1994). P300 differences between non-alcoholic young men at average and above-average risk for alcoholism: Effects

of distraction and task modality. *Progress in Neuro-Psychopharmacology and Biological Psychiatry, 18,* 263–277.

Bauer, L. O., O'Connor, S. & Hesselbrock, V. M. (1994). Frontal P300 decrements in antisocial personality disorder. *Alcoholism: Clinical and Experimental Research, 18,* 1300–1305.

Beauchaine, T. P. (2004). BAS motivation, affect regulation, and externalizing psychopathology: Three studies spanning preschool to adolescence [Abstract]. *Psychophysiology, 41,* S10.

Beauchaine, T. P., Katkin, E. S., Strassberg, Z, & Snarr, J. (2001). Disinhibitory psychopathology in male adolescents: Discriminating conduct disorder from attention-deficit/hyperactivity disorder through concurrent assessment of multiple autonomic states. *Journal of Abnormal Psychology, 110,* 610–624.

Begleiter, H., & Porjesz, B. (1999). What is inherited in the predisposition toward alcoholism? A proposed model. *Alcoholism: Clinical and Experimental Research, 23,* 1125–1135.

Bell, P. A., & Baron, R. A. (1976). Aggression and heat: The mediating role of negative affect. *Journal of Applied Social Psychology, 6,* 18–30.

Berkowitz, L. (1989). Frustration-aggression hypothesis: Examination and reformulation. *Psychological Bulletin, 106,* 59–73.

Berkowitz, L. (1990). On the formation and regulation of anger and aggression: A cognitive-neoassociationistic analysis. *American Psychologist, 45,* 494–503.

Berkowitz, L., Cochran, S., & Embree, M. (1981). Physical pain and the goal of aversively stimulated aggression. *Journal of Personality and Social Psychology, 40,* 687–700.

Berkowitz, L., & Harmon-Jones, E. (2004). Toward an understanding of the determinants of anger. *Emotion, 4,* 107–130.

Bettencourt, B. A., & Miller, N. (1996). Gender differences in aggression as a function of provocation: A meta-analysis. *Psychological Bulletin, 119,* 422–447.

Biggins, C. A., MacKay, S., Clark, W., & Fein, G. (1997). Event-related potential evidence for frontal cortex effects of chronic cocaine dependence. *Biological Psychiatry, 42,* 472–485.

Blake, P. Y., Pincus, J. H., & Buckner, C. (1995). Neurological abnormalities in murderers. *Neurology, 45,* 1641–1647.

Blumer, D., & Benson, D. F. (1975). Personality changes with frontal and temporal lobe lesions. In D. F. Benson & D. Blumer (Eds.),

Psychiatric aspects of neurological disease (pp. 151–169). New York: Grune & Stratton.

Branchey, M. H., Buydens-Branchey, L., & Horvath, T. B. (1993). Event-related potentials in substance-abusing individuals after long-term abstinence. *American Journal of Addictions, 2,* 141–148.

Branchey, M. H., Buydens-Branchey, L., & Lieber, C. S. (1988). P3 in alcoholics with disordered regulation of aggression. *Psychiatry Research, 25,* 49–58.

Burgess, K. B., Marshall, P. J., Rubin, K. H., & Fox, N. (2003). Infant attachment and temperament as predictors of subsequent externalizing problems and cardiac physiology. *Journal of Child Psychology and Psychiatry, 44,* 819–831.

Buss, A. H., & Perry, M. (1992). The Aggression Questionnaire. *Journal of Personality and Social Psychology, 63,* 452–459.

Cacioppo, J. T., Tassinary, L. G., & Berntson, G. G. (2000). *Handbook of psychophysiology* (2nd ed.). Cambridge, UK: Cambridge University Press.

Carlson, S. R., Katsanis, J., Iacono, W. G., & Mertz, A. K. (1999). Substance dependence and externalizing psychopathology in adolescent boys with small, average, or large P300 event-related potential amplitude. *Psychophysiology, 36,* 583–590.

Cleckley, H. (1941). *The mask of sanity.* St. Louis, MO: Mosby.

Convit, A, Czobor, P., Volavka, J. (1991). Lateralized abnormality in the EEG of persistently violent psychiatric inpatients. *Biological Psychiatry, 30,* 363–370.

Costa, L., Bauer, L., Kuperman, S., Porjesz, B., O'Connor, S., Hesselbrock, V., et al. (2000). Frontal P300 decrements, alcohol dependence, and antisocial personality disorder. *Biological Psychiatry, 47,* 1064–1071.

Critchley, H. D., Simmons, A., Daly, E. M., Russell, A., van Amelsvoort, T., & Robertson, D. M. (2000). Prefrontal and medial temporal correlates of repetitive violence to self and others. *Biological Psychiatry, 47,* 928–934.

Davidson, R. J. (1998). Anterior electrophysiological asymmetries, emotion, and depression: Conceptual and methodological conundrums. *Psychophysiology, 35,* 607–614.

Davidson, R. J., Putnam, K. M., & Larson, C. L. (2000). Dysfunction in the neural circuitry of emotion regulation – a possible prelude to violence. *Science, 289,* 591–594.

Dolan, M. C., Deakin, J. F. W., Roberts, N., & Anderson, I. M. (2002). Quantitative frontal and temporal structural MRI studies in personality-disordered offenders and control subjects. *Psychiatry Research Neuroimaging, 116,* 133–149.

Donchin, E. (1981). Surprise! . . . Surprise? *Psychophysiology, 18,* 493–513.

Donchin, E., & Coles, M. G. H. (1988). Is the P300 a manifestation of context updating? *Behavioral and Brain Sciences, 11,* 355–372.

Doron, A., Stein, D., Levine, Y., Abramovitch, Y., Eilat, E., & Neuman, M. (1998). Physiological reactions to a suicide film: Suicide attempters, suicide ideators, and nonsuicidal patients. *Suicide and Life-Threatening Behavior, 28,* 309–314.

Dougherty, D. D., Rauch, S. L., Deckersbach, T., Marci, C., Loh, R., Shin, L. M., et al. (2004). Ventromedial prefrontal cortex and amygdala dysfunction during an anger induction Positron Emission Tomography Study in patients with major depressive disorder with anger attacks. *Archives of General Psychiatry, 61,* 795–804.

Douglas, K. S., Vincent, G. M., & Edens, J. F. (2006). Risk for criminal recidivism: The role of psychopathy. In C. J. Patrick (Ed.), *Handbook of psychopathy* (pp. 533–554). New York: Guilford Press.

Drake, M. E., Hietter, S. A., & Pakalnis, A. (1992). EEG and evoked potentials in episodic-dyscontrol syndrome. *Neuropsychobiology, 26,* 125–128.

Drake, M. E., Pakalnis, A., Brown, M. E., & Hietter, S. A. (1988). Auditory event related potentials in violent and nonviolent prisoners. *European Archives of Psychiatry and Clinical Neuroscience, 238,* 7–10.

Drexler, K., Schweitzer, J. B., Quinn, C. K., Gross, R., Ely, T. D., Muhammad, F., et al. (2000). Neural activity related to anger in cocaine-dependent men: A possible link to violence and relapse. *American Journal of Addictions, 9,* 331–339.

Edguer, N., & Janisse, M. P. (1994). Type A behaviour and aggression: Provocation, conflict and cardiovascular responsivity in the Buss teacher-learner paradigm. *Personality and Individual Differences, 17,* 377–393.

El-Sheikh, M. (2001). Parental drinking problems and children's adjustment: Vagal regulation and emotional reactivity as pathways and moderators of risk. *Journal of Abnormal Psychology, 110,* 499–515.

El-Sheikh, M., Harger, J., & Whitson, S. M. (2001). Exposure to interparental conflict and children's adjustment and physical health: The moderating role of vagal tone. *Child Development, 72*, 1617–1636.

Eysenck, H. J. (1967). *The biological basis of personality.* Springfield, IL: Charles C. Thomas.

Farrington, D. P. (1997). The relationship between low resting heart rate and violence. In A. Raine, P. A. Brennan, D. Farrington, & S. A. Mednick (Eds.), *Biosocial bases of violence* (pp. 89–105). New York: Plenum.

Fishbein, D. H., Herning, R. I., Pickworth, W. B., Haertzen, C. A., Hickey, J. E., & Jaffe, J. H. (1989). EEG and brainstem auditory evoked response potentials in adult male drug abusers with self reported histories of aggressive behavior. *Biological Psychiatry, 26*, 595–611.

Fowles, D. C. (1980). The three arousal model: Implication of Gray's two-factor learning theory for heart rate, electrodermal activity, and psychopathy. *Psychophysiology, 17*, 87–104.

Fowles, D. C., & Dindo, L. (2006). A dual deficit model of psychopathy. In C. J. Patrick (Ed.), *Handbook of psychopathy* (pp. 14–34). New York: Guilford Press.

Frankle, W. G., Lombardo, I., New, A. S., Goodman, M., Talbot, P. S., Huang, Y., et al. (2005). Brain serotonin transporter distribution in subjects with impulsive aggressivity: A positron emission study with [11C]McN 5652. *American Journal of Psychiatry, 162*, 915–923.

Freud, S. (1959). *Collected papers.* New York: Basic Books.

Frodi, A. M., & Lamb, M. E. (1980). Child abusers' responses to infant smiles and cries. *Child Development, 51*, 238–241.

Gallo, L. C., Smith, T. W., & Kircher, J. C. (2000). Cardiovascular and electrodermal responses to support and provocation: Interpersonal methods in the study of psychophysiological reactivity. *Psychophysiology, 37*, 289–301.

Garza-Trevino, E. S. (1994). Neurobiological factors in aggressive behavior. *Hospital and Community Psychiatry, 45*, 690–699.

Gatzke-Kopp, L. M., Raine, A., Buchsbaum, M. S., & LaCasse, L. (2001). Temporal lobe deficits in murderers: EEG findings undetected by PET. *Journal of Neuropsychiatry & Clinical Neurosciences, 13*, 486–491.

George, D. T., Rawlings, R. R., Williams, W. A., Phillips, M. J., Fong, G., Kerich, M., et al. (2004). A select group of perpetrators of domestic violence: Evidence of decreased metabolism in the right hypothalamus and reduced relationships between cortical/subcortical brain structures in position emission tomography. *Psychiatry Research: Neuroimaging, 130*, 11–25.

Gerra, G., Zaimovic, A., Avanzini, P. Chittolini, B., Giucastro, G., et al. (1997). Neurotransmitter-neuroendocrine responses to experimentally induced aggression in humans: Influence of personality variable. *Psychiatry Research, 66*, 33–43.

Gerra, G., Zaimovic, A., Moi, G., Bussandri, M., Bubici, C., Mossini, M., et al. (2004). Aggressive responding of abstinent heroin addicts: Neuroendocrine and personality correlates. *Progress in Neuro-Psychopharmacology and Biological Psychiatry, 28*, 129–139.

Gerra, G., Zaimovic, A., Raggi, M. A., Giusti, F., Delsignore, R., Bertacca, S., et al. (2001). Aggressive responding of male heroin addicts under methadone treatment: Psychometric and neuroendocrine correlates. *Drug and Alcohol Dependence, 65*, 85–95.

Gerstle, J. E., Mathias, C. W., & Stanford, M. S. (1998). Auditory P300 and self-reported impulsive aggression. *Progress in Neuro-Psychopharmacology and Biological Psychiatry, 22*, 575–583.

Gottman, J. M., Jacobson, N. S., Rushe, R. H., Shortt, J. W., Babcock, J., et al. (1995). The relationship between heart rate reactivity, emotionally aggressive behavior, and general violence in batterers. *Journal of Family Psychology, 9*, 227–248.

Goyer, P. F., Andreason, P. J., Semple, W. E., & Clayton, A. H. (1994). Positron-emission tomography and personality disorders. *Neuropsychopharmacology, 10*, 21–28.

Gray, J. A. (1987). *The psychology of fear and stress* (2nd ed.). Cambridge, UK: Cambridge University Press.

Hall, J., Benning, S. D., & Patrick, C. J. (2004). Criterion-related validity of the three-factor model of psychopathy: Personality, behavior, and adaptive functioning. *Assessment, 11*, 4–16.

Hare, R. D. (1965) Temporal gradient of fear arousal in psychopaths. *Journal of Abnormal Psychology, 70*, 442–445.

Hare, R. D. (1978). Electrodermal and cardiovascular correlates of psychopathy. In R. D. Hare & D. Schalling (Eds.), *Psychopathic behavior: Approaches to research* (pp. 107–143). Chichester: Wiley.

Hare, R. D. (1980). A research scale for the assessment of psychopathy in criminal populations. *Personality and Individual Differences*, *1*, 111–119.

Hare, R. D. (1991). *The Hare Psychopathy Checklist-Revised*. Toronto: Multi-Health Systems.

Hare, R. D. (1999). Psychopathy as a risk factor for violence. *Psychiatric Quarterly*, *70*, 191–197.

Hare, R. D. (2003). *Manual for the Hare Psychopathy Checklist-Revised* (2nd ed.). Toronto: Multi-Health Systems.

Hart, S. D., & Hare, R. D. (1996). Psychopathy and antisocial personality disorder. *Current Opinion in Psychiatry*, *9*, 120–132.

Harmon-Jones, E. (2003). Clarifying the emotive functions of asymmetrical frontal cortical activity. *Psychophysiology*, *40*, 838–848.

Harmon-Jones, E., & Allen, J. J. B. (1998). Anger and prefrontal brain activity: EEG asymmetry consistent with approach motivation despite negative affective valence. *Journal of Personality and Social Psychology*, *74*, 1310–1316.

Harmon-Jones, E., Barratt, E. S., & Wigg, C. (1997). Impulsiveness, aggression, reading and the P300 component of the event-related potential. *Personality and Individual Differences*, *22*, 439–445.

Harmon-Jones, E., & Sigelman, J. (2001). State anger and prefrontal brain activity: Evidence that insult-related relative left-prefrontal activation is associated with experienced anger and aggression. *Journal of Personality and Social Psychology*, *80*, 797–803.

Harmon-Jones, E., Sigelman, J. D., Bohlig, A., & Harmon-Jones, C. (2003). Anger, coping, and frontal cortical activity: The effect of coping potential on anger-induced left frontal activity. *Cognition and Emotion*, *17*, 1–24.

Harpur, T. J., Hare, R. D., & Hakstian, A. R. (1989). Two-factor conceptualization of psychopathy: Construct validity and assessment implications. *Psychological Assessment: A Journal of Consulting and Clinical Psychology*, *1*, 6–17.

Heller, W. (1990). The neuropsychology of emotion: Developmental patterns and implications for psychopathology. In N. L. Stein, B. Leventhal, & T. Trabasso (Eds.), *Psychological and biological approaches to emotion* (pp. 167–211). Hillsdale, NJ: Erlbaum.

Hirono, N., Mega, M. S., Dinov, I. D., Mishkin, F., & Cummings, J. L. (2000). Left fronto-temporal hypoperfusion is associated with aggression in patients with dementia. *Archives of Neurology*, *57*, 861–866.

Hokanson, J. E. (1970). Psychophysiological evaluation of the catharsis hypothesis. In E. I. Megargee & J. E. Hokanson (Eds.), *The dynamics of aggression* (pp. 74–86). New York: Harper-Collins.

Hokanson, J. E. (1974). An escape-avoidance view of catharsis. *Criminal Justice and Behavior*, *1*, 195–223.

Hokanson, J. E., & Burgess, M. (1962a). The effects of status, type of frustration and aggression on vascular processes. *Journal of Abnormal and Social Psychology*, *65*, 232–237.

Hokanson, J. E., & Burgess, M. (1962b). The effects of three types of aggression on vascular processes. *Journal of Abnormal and Social Psychology*, *64*, 446–449.

Hokanson, J. E., Burgess, M., & Cohen, M. F. (1963). Effects of displaced aggression on systolic blood pressure. *Journal of Abnormal and Social Psychology*, *67*, 214–218.

Hokanson, J. E., & Edelman, R. (1966). Effects of three social responses on vascular processes. *Journal of Personality and Social Psychology*, *3*, 442–447.

Hokanson, J. E., & Shetler, S. (1961). The effect of overt aggression on physiological arousal. *Journal of Abnormal and Social Psychology*, *63*, 446–448.

Hokanson, J. E., Willers, K. R., & Koropsak, E. (1968). The modification of autonomic responses during aggressive interchange. *Journal of Personality*, *36*, 386–404.

Hoptman, M. J., Volavka, J., Johnson, G., Weiss, E., Bildera, R. M., & Lim, K. O. (2002). Frontal white matter microstructure, aggression, and impulsivity in men with schizophrenia: A preliminary study. *Biological Psychiatry*, *52*, 9–14.

Houston, R. J., Stanford, M. S., Villemarette-Pittman, N. R., Conklin, S. M., & Helfritz, L. E. (2003). Neurobiological correlates and clinical implications of aggressive subtypes. *Journal of Forensic Neuropsychology*, *3*, 67–87.

Hubbard, J. A., Parker, E. H., Ramsden, S. R., Flanagan, K. D., Relyea, N., Dearing, K. F., et al. (2004). The relations among observational, physiological, and self-report measures of children's anger. *Social Development*, *13*, 14–39.

Hubbard, J. A., Smithmyer, C. M., Ramsden, S. R., Parker, E. H., Flanagan, K. D., Dearing, K. F., et al. (2002). Observational, physiological, and self-report measures of children's anger: Relations to reactive versus proactive aggression. *Child Development*, *73*, 1101–1118.

Iacono, W. G. (1998). Identifying psychophysiological risk for psychopathology: Examples from substance abuse and schizophrenia research. *Psychophysiology, 35,* 621–637.

Iacono, W. G., Carlson, S. R., & Malone, S. M. (2000). Identifying a multivariate endophenotype for substance use disorders using psychophysiological measures. *International Journal of Psychophysiology, 38,* 81–96.

Iacono, W. G., Carlson, S. R., Malone, S. M., & McGue, M. (2002). P3 event-related potential amplitude and risk for disinhibitory disorders in adolescent boys. *Archives of General Psychiatry, 59,* 750–757.

Iacono, W. G., Carlson, S. R., Taylor, J., Elkins, I. J., & McGue, M. (1999). Behavioral disinhibition and the development of substance use disorders: Findings from the Minnesota Twin Family Study. *Development and Psychopathology, 11,* 869–900.

Intrator, J., Hare, R., Stritzke, P., & Brichtswein, K. (1997). A brain imaging (single photon emission computerized tomography) study of semantic and affective processing in psychopaths. *Biological Psychiatry, 42,* 96–103.

Jacobson, N. S., Gottman, J. M., Waltz, J., Rushe, R., Babcock, J., & Holtzworth-Munroe, A. (1994). Affect, verbal content, and psychophysiology in the arguments of couples with a violent husband. *Journal of Consulting and Clinical Psychology, 62,* 982–988.

Johnson, T. E., & Rule, B. G. (1986). Mitigating circumstance information, censure, and aggression. *Journal of Personality and Social Psychology, 50,* 537–542.

Johnstone, S. J., & Barry, R. J. (1996). Auditory event-related potentials to a two-tone auditory discrimination paradigm in attention deficit hyperactivity disorder. *Psychiatry Research, 64,* 179–192.

Keltikangas-Jarvinen, L., & Keinonen, M. (1988). Aggression, self-confidence, and cardiovascular reactions in competitive performance in adolescent boys. *Aggressive Behavior, 14,* 245–254.

Kendler, K. S., Prescott, C. A., Myers, J., & Neale, M. C. (2003). The structure of genetic and environmental risk factors for common psychiatric and substance use disorders in men and women. *Archives of General Psychiatry, 60,* 929–937.

Kiehl, K. A., Smith, A. M., Hare, R. D., Mendrek, A., Forster, B. B., & Brink, J. (2001). Limbic abnormalities in affective processing by criminal psychopaths as revealed by functional magnetic resonance imaging. *Biological Psychiatry, 50,* 677–684.

Kiehl, K. A., Smith, A. M., Mendrek, A., Forster, B. B., Hare, R. D., & Liddle, P. F. (2004). Temporal lobe abnormalities in semantic processing by criminal psychopaths as revealed by functional magnetic resonance imaging. *Psychiatry Research: Neuroimaging, 130,* 27–42.

Kim, M. S., Kim, J. J., & Kwon, J. S. (2001). Frontal P300 decrement and executive dysfunction in adolescents with conduct problems. *Child Psychiatry and Human Development, 32,* 93–106.

Kindlon, D. J., Tremblay, R. E., Mezzacappa, E., Earls, F., Laurent, D., & Schaal, B. (1995). Longitudinal patterns of heart rate and fighting behavior in 9- through 12-year-old boys. *Journal of the American Academy of Child and Adolescent Psychiatry, 34,* 371–377.

Klorman, R. (1991). Cognitive event-related potentials and in attention deficit disorder. *Journal of Learning Disabilities, 24,* 130–140.

Knight, G. P., Guthrie, I. K., Page, M. C., & Fabes, R. A. (2002). Emotional arousal and gender differences in aggression: A meta-analysis. *Aggressive Behavior, 28,* 366–393.

Krantz, D. S., & Manuck, S. B. (1984). Acute psychophysiologic reactivity and risk of cardiovascular disease: A review and methodologic critique. *Psychological Bulletin, 96,* 435–464.

Krueger, R. F. (1999). The structure of common mental disorders. *Archives of General Psychiatry, 56,* 921–926.

Krueger, R. F., Hicks, B., Patrick, C. J., Carlson, S., Iacono, W. G., & McGue, M. (2002). Etiologic connections among substance dependence, antisocial behavior, and personality: Modeling the externalizing spectrum. *Journal of Abnormal Psychology, 111,* 411–424.

Krueger, R. F., Markon, C. M., Patrick, C. J., Benning, S. D., & Kramer, M. (in press). Linking antisocial behavior, substance use, and personality: An integrative quantitative model of the adult externalizing spectrum. *Journal of Abnormal Psychology.*

Krueger, R. F., Markon, C. M., Patrick, C. J., & Iacono, W. G. (2005). Externalizing psychopathology in adulthood: A dimensional-spectrum conceptualization and its implications for DSM-V. *Journal of Abnormal Psychology, 114*(4), 537–550.

Kuikka, J. T., Tiihonen, J., Bergstrom, K. A., Karhu, J., Rasanen, P., & Eronen, M. (1998). Abnormal structure of human striatal dopamine re-uptake sites in habitually violent alcoholic offenders: A fractal analysis. *Neuroscience Letters, 253*, 195–197.

Kuruoglu, A. C., Arikan, Z., Vural, G., & Karatas, M. (1996). Single photon emission computerised tomography in chronic alcoholism: Antisocial personality disorder may be associated with decreased frontal perfusion. *British Journal of Psychiatry, 169*, 348–354.

Laakso, M. P., Gunning-Dixon, F., Vaurio, O., Repo-Tiihonen, E., Soininen, H., & Tiihonen, J. (2002). Prefrontal volumes in habitually violent subjects with antisocial personality disorder and type 2 alcoholism. *Psychiatry Research: Neuroimaging, 114*, 95–102.

Laakso, M. P., Vaurio, O., Koivisto, E., Savolainen, L., Eronen, M., & Aronen, H. J. (2001). Psychopathy and the posterior hippocampus. *Behavioural Brain Research, 118*, 187–193.

Laakso, M. P., Vaurio, O., Savolainen, L., Repo, E., Soininen, H., Aronen, H. J., & Tiihonen, J. (2000). A volumetric MRI study of the hippocampus in type 1 and 2 alcoholism. *Behavioural and Brain Research, 109*, 177–186.

Lang, P. J. (1979). A bio-informational theory of emotional imagery. *Psychophysiology, 16*, 495–512.

Levenston, G. K., Patrick, C. J., Bradley, M. M., & Lang, P. J. (2000). The psychopath as observer: Emotion and attention in picture processing. *Journal of Abnormal Psychology, 109*, 373–385.

Lewis, D. O., Pincus, J. H., Feldman, M., Jackson, L., & Bard, B. (1986). Psychiatric, neurological and psychoeducational characteristics of 15 death row inmates in the United States. *American Journal of Psychiatry, 143*, 838–845.

Lorber, M. F. (2004). Psychophysiology of aggression, psychopathy, and conduct problems: A meta-analysis. *Psychological Bulletin, 130*, 531–552.

Lykken, D. T. (1957). A study of anxiety in the sociopathic personality. *Journal of Abnormal and Social Psychology, 55*, 6–10.

Lykken, D. T. (1995). *The antisocial personalities.* Hillsdale, NJ: Erlbaum.

Maliphant, R., Hume, F., & Furnham, A. (1990). Autonomic nervous system (ANS) activity, personality characteristics, and disruptive behaviour in girls. *Journal of Child Psychology and Psychiatry and Allied Disciplines, 31*, 619–628.

Malone, S. M., Bernat, E., Patrick, C. J., & Iacono, W. G. (2002). P300 and prestimulus EEG power: Relationship to externalizing psychopathology in adolescent males. *Psychophysiology, 39*, S54.

Mathias, C. W., & Stanford, M. S. (1999). P300 under standard and surprise conditions in self-reported impulsive aggression. *Progress in Neuro-Psychopharmacology and Biological Psychiatry, 23*, 1037–1051.

Mednick, S. A. (1977). A bio-social theory of the learning of law-abiding behavior. In S. A. Mednick & K. O. Christianson (Eds.), *Biosocial bases of criminal behavior* (pp. 1–8). New York: Gardner Press.

Meehan, J. C., Holtzworth-Munroe, A., & Herron, K. (2001). Maritally violent men's heart rate reactivity to marital interactions: A failure to replicate the Gottman et al. (1995) typology. *Journal of Family Psychology, 15*, 394–408.

Mezzacappa, E., Tremblay, R. E., Kindlon, D., Saul, J. P., Arseneault, L., Seguin, J., et al. (1997). Anxiety, antisocial behavior and heart rate regulation in adolescent males. *Journal of Child Psychology and Psychiatry, 38*, 457–469.

Milstein, V. (1988). EEG topography in patients with aggressive violent behavior. In T. E. Moffitt & S. A. Mednick (Eds.), *Biological contributions to crime causation* (pp. 40–54). Dordrecht, North Holland: Martinus Nijhoff.

Muller, J. L., Sommer, M., Wagner, V., Lange, K., Taschler, H., Roder, C. H., et al. (2003). Abnormalities in emotion processing within cortical and subcortical regions in criminal psychopaths: Evidence from a functional magnetic resonance imaging study using pictures with emotional content. *Biological Psychiatry, 54*, 152–162.

New, A. S., Buchsbaum, M. S., Hazlett, E. A., Goodman, M., Koenigsberg, H. W., Lo, J., et al. (2004). Fluoxetine increases relative metabolic rate in prefrontal cortex in impulsive aggression. *Psychopharmacology, 176*, 451–458.

New, A. S., Hazlett, E. A., Buchsbaum, M. S., Goodman, M., Reynolds, D., Mitropoulou, V., et al. (2002). Blunted prefrontal cortical [18] fluorodeoxyglucose positron emission tomography response to meta-chlorophenylpiperazine in impulsive aggression. *Archives of General Psychiatry, 59*, 621–629.

Ochsner, K., Bunge, S. A., Gross, J., & Gabrieli, J. D. (2002). Rethinking feelings: An fMRI study of the cognitive regulation of emotion. *Journal of Cognitive Neuroscience, 14,* 1215–1229.

Ortiz, J., & Raine, A. (2004). Heart rate level and antisocial behavior in children and adolescents: A meta-analysis. *Journal of the American Academy of Child and Adolescent Psychiatry, 43,* 154–162.

Panee, C. D., & Ballard, M. E. (2002). High versus low aggressive priming during video-game training: Effects on violent action during game play, hostility, heart rate, and blood pressure. *Journal of Applied Social Psychology, 32,* 2458–2474.

Parsey, R. V., Oquendo, M. A., Simpson, N. R., Ogden, R. T., Van Heertum, R., Arango, V., et al. (2002). Effects of sex, age, and aggressive traits in man on brain serotonin 5-HT-sub(1A) receptor binding potential measured by PET using [C-11]WAY-100635. *Brain Research, 954,* 173–182.

Patrick, C. J. (1994). Emotion and psychopathy: Startling new insights. *Psychophysiology, 31,* 319–330.

Patrick, C. J. (2001). Emotional processes in psychopathy. In A. Raine & J. Sanmartin (Eds.), *Violence and psychopathy* (pp. 57–77). New York: Kluwer Academic Publishers.

Patrick, C. J. (2007). Getting to the heart of psychopathy. In H. Herve & J. C. Yuille (Eds.), *Psychopathy: Theory, research, and social implications* (pp. 207–252). Hillsdale, NJ: Erlbaum.

Patrick, C. J., & Bernat, E. (2006). The construct of emotion as a bridge between personality and psychopathology. In R. F. Krueger & J. Tackett (Eds.), *Personality and psychopathology* (pp. 174–209). New York: Guilford Press.

Patrick, C. J., Bernat, E., Malone, S. M., Iacono, W. G., Krueger, R. F., & McGue, M. K. (2006). P300 amplitude as an indicator of externalizing in adolescent males. *Psychophysiology, 43*(1), 84–92.

Patrick, C. J., Bradley, M. M., & Lang, P. J. (1993). Emotion in the criminal psychopath: Startle reflex modulation. *Journal of Abnormal Psychology, 102,* 82–92.

Patrick, C. J., Cuthbert, B. N., & Lang, P. J. (1994) Emotion in the criminal psychopath: Fear image processing. *Journal of Abnormal Psychology, 103,* 523–534.

Patrick, C. J., Hicks, B. M., Krueger, R. F., & Lang, A. R. (2005). Relations between psychopathy facets and externalizing in a criminal offender sample. *Journal of Personality Disorders, 19*(4), 339–356.

Patrick, C. J., Zempolich, K. A., & Levenston, G. K. (1997). Emotionality and violent behavior in psychopaths: A biosocial analysis. In A. Raine, P. Brennan, D. P. Farrington, & S. A. Mednick (Eds.), *Biosocial bases of violence* (pp. 145–161). New York: Plenum.

Pelham, W. E., Milich, R., Cummings, E. M., Murphy, D. A., Schaughency, E. A., & Greiner, A. R. (1991). Effects of background anger, provocation, and methylphenidate on emotional arousal and aggressive responding in attention-deficit hyperactivity disorders boys with and without concurrent aggressiveness. *Journal of Abnormal Child Psychology, 19,* 407–426.

Peters, M. L., Godaert, G. L. R., Ballieux, R. E., & Heijnen, C. J. (2003). Moderation of physiological stress responses by personality traits and daily hassles: Less flexibility of immune system responses. *Biological Psychology, 65,* 21–48.

Pietrini, P., Guazzelli, M., Basso, G., Jaffe, K., & Grafman, J. (2000). Neural correlates of imaginal aggressive behavior assessed by positron emission tomography in healthy subjects. *American Journal of Psychiatry, 157,* 1772–1781.

Polich, J., Pollock, V. E., & Bloom, F. E. (1994). Meta-analysis of P300 amplitude from males at risk for alcoholism. *Psychological Bulletin, 115,* 55–73.

Porges, S. W., & Doussard-Roosevelt, J. A. (1997). Early physiological response patterns and later psychological development. In H. W. Reese & M. D. Franzen (Eds.), *Life-span developmental psychology: Biological and neuropsychological mechanisms* (pp. 163–179). Hillsdale, NJ: Erlbaum.

Porter, S., & Woodworth, M. (2006). Psychopathy and aggression. In C. J. Patrick (Ed.), *Handbook of psychopathy* (pp. 481–494). New York: Guilford Press.

Raine, A. (1989). Evoked potentials and psychopathy. *International Journal of Psychophysiology, 8,* 1–16.

Raine, A. (1993). *The psychopathology of crime.* San Diego: Academic Press.

Raine, A. (1996). Autonomic nervous system activity and violence. In D. M. Stoff & R. B. Cairns (Eds.), *Aggression and violence: Genetic, neurobiological, and biosocial perspectives* (pp. 145–168). Mahwah, NJ: Erlbaum.

Raine, A. (2002). Biosocial studies of antisocial and violent behavior in children and adults: A review. *Journal of Abnormal Child Psychology*, *30*, 311–326.

Raine, A., Buchsbaum, M., & LaCasse, L. (1997). Brain abnormalities in murderers indicated by positron emission tomography. *Biological Psychiatry*, *42*, 495–508.

Raine, A., Buchsbaum, M. S., Stanley, J., Lottenberg, S., Abel, L., & Stoddard, J. (1994). Selective reductions in pre-frontal glucose metabolism in murderers. *Biological Psychiatry*, *36*, 365–73.

Raine, A., Ishikawa, S. S., Arce, E., Lencz, T., Knuth, K. H., Bihrle, S., et al. (2004). Hippocampal structural asymmetry in unsuccessful psychopaths. *Biological Psychiatry*, *55*, 185–91.

Raine, A., Lencz, T., Bihrle, S., LaCasse, L., & Colletti, P. (2000). Reduced prefrontal gray matter volume and reduced autonomic activity in antisocial personality disorder. *Archives of General Psychiatry*, *57*, 119–127.

Raine, A., Lencz, T., Taylor, K., Hellige, J. B., Bihrle S., Lacasse L., et al. (2003). Corpus callosum abnormalities in psychopathic antisocial individuals. *Archives of General Psychiatry*, *60*, 1134–42.

Raine, A., Meloy, J. R., Bihrle, S., Stoddard, J., LaCasse, L., & Buchsbaum, M. S. (1998). Reduced prefrontal and increased subcortical brain functioning assessed using positron emission tomography in predatory and affective murderers. *Behavioral Sciences and the Law*, *16*, 319–332.

Raine, A., Park, S., Lencz, T., Bihrle, S., LaCasse, L., Widom, C. S., et al. (2001). Reduced right hemisphere activation in severely abused violent offenders during a working memory task: An fMRI study. *Aggressive Behavior*, *27*, 111–129.

Raine, A., Stoddard, J., Bihrle, S., & Buchsbaum, M. (1998). Prefrontal glucose deficits in murderers lacking psychosocial deprivation. *Neuropsychiatry, Neuropsychology, and Behavioral Neurology*, *11*, 1–7.

Raine, A., & Venables, P. H. (1981). Classical conditioning and socialization – A biosocial interaction. *Personality and Individual Differences*, *2*, 273–283.

Raine, A., & Venables, P. H. (1984). Tonic heart rate level, social class, and antisocial behaviour in adolescents. *Biological Psychology*, *18*, 123–132.

Raine, A., Venables, P. H., & Williams, M. (1990). Relationships between N1, P300 and CNV recorded at age 15 and criminal behavior at age 24. *Psychophysiology*, *27*, 567–575.

Raine, A., & Yang, Y. (2006). The neuroanatomical bases of psychopathy: A review of brain imaging findings. In C. J. Patrick (Ed.), *Handbook of psychopathy* (pp. 278–295). New York: Guilford Press.

Roberts, B. W., Walton, K., & Viechtbauer, W. (2006). Patterns of mean-level change in personality traits across the life course: A meta-analysis of longitudinal studies. *Psychological Bulletin*, *132*(1), 1–25.

Rotton, J. (1979). The air pollution experience and physical aggression. *Journal of Applied Social Psychology*, *9*, 397–412.

Scarpa, A., Fikretoglu, D., & Luscher, K. (2000). Community violence exposure in a young adult sample: II. Psychophysiology and aggressive behavior. *Journal of Community Psychology*, *28*, 417–425.

Scarpa, A., & Raine, A. (1997). Psychophysiology of anger and violent behavior. *The Psychiatric Clinics of North America*, *20*, 375–394.

Schneider, F., Habel, U., Kessler, C., Posse, S., Grodd, W., & Muller-Gartner, H. W. (2000). Functional imaging of conditioned aversive emotional responses in antisocial personality disorder. *Neuropsychobiology*, *42*, 192–201.

Seidenwurm, D., Pounds, T. R., Globus, A., & Valk, P. E. (1997). Abnormal temporal lobe metabolism in violent subjects: Correlation of imaging and neuropsychiatric findings. *American Journal of Neuroradiology*, *18*, 625–631.

Siever, L. J., Buchsbaum, M. S., New, A. S., Spiegel-Cohen, J., Wei, T., Hazlett, E. A., et al. (1999). d,l-Fenfluramine response in impulsive personality disorder assessed with [18F]flurodeoxyglucose positron emission tomography. *Neuropsychopharmacology*, *20*, 413–423.

Smith, T. W., & Gallo, L. C. (1999). Hostility and cardiovascular reactivity during marital interaction. *Psychosomatic Medicine*, *61*, 436–445.

Soderstrom, H., Hultin, L., Tullberg, M., Wikkelso, C., Ekholm, S., & Forsman, A. (2002). Reduced frontotemporal perfusion in psychopathic personality. *Psychiatry Research: Neuroimaging*, *114*, 81–94.

Soderstrom, H., Tullberg, M., Wikkelsoe, C., Ekholm, S., & Forsman, A. (2000). Reduced regional cerebral blood flow in non-psychotic violent offenders. *Psychiatry Research: Neuroimaging*, *98*, 29–41.

Soloff, P. H., Meltzer, C. C., Greer, P. J., Constantine, D, & Kelly, T. M. (2000). Fenfluramine-activated FDG-PET study of borderline personality disorder. *Biological Psychiatry, 47*, 540–547.

Stanford, M. S., Houston, R. J., Villemarette-Pittman, N. R., & Greve, K. W. (2003). Premeditated aggression: Clinical assessment and cognitive psychophysiology. *Personality and Individual Differences, 34*, 773–781.

Strandburg, R. J., Marsh, J. T., Brown, W. S., Asarnow, R. F., Higa, J., Harper, R., & Guthrie, D. (1996). Continuous-processing related event-related potentials in children with attention deficit hyperactivity disorder. *Biological Psychiatry, 40*, 964–980.

Suarez, E. C., Harlan, E., Peoples, M. C., & Williams, R. B. (1993). Cardiovascular and emotional responses in women: The role of hostility and harassment. *Health Psychology, 12*, 459–468.

Suls, J., & Wan, C. K. (1993). The relationship between trait hostility and cardiovascular reactivity: A quantitative review and analysis. *Psychophysiology, 30*, 615–626.

Tarkka, I. M., Karhu, J., Kuikka, J., Pääkkönen, A., Bergström, K., Partanen, J., et al. (2001). Altered frontal lobe function suggested by source analysis of event-related potentials in impulsive violent alcoholics *Alcohol and Alcoholism, 36*, 323–328.

Taylor, J., Carlson, S. R., Iacono, W. G., Lykken, D. T., & McGue, M. (1999). Individual differences in electrodermal responsivity to predictable aversive stimuli and substance dependence. *Psychophysiology, 36*, 193–198.

Taylor, S. E., Klein, L. C., Lewis, B. P., Gruenewald, T. L., Gurung, R. A. R., & Updgraff, J. A. (2000). Biobehavioral responses to stress in females: Tend-and-befriend, not fight-or-flight. *Psychological Review, 107*, 411–429.

Thomas, M. H. (1982). Physiological arousal, exposure to a relatively lengthy aggressive film, and aggressive behavior. *Journal of Research in Personality, 16*, 72–81.

Tiihonen, J., Hodgins, S., & Vaurio, O. (2000). Amygdaloid volume loss in psychopathy. *Society for Neuroscience Abstracts*, 2017.

Tiihonen, J., Kuikka, J., Bergstrom, K., Hakola, P., Karhu, J., Ryynanen, O. P., et al. (1995). Altered striatal dopamine re-uptake site densities in habitually violent and non-violent alcoholics. *Nature Medicine, 1*, 654–657.

Tiihonen, J., Kuikka, J. T., Bergstrom, K. A., Karhu, J., Viinamaki, H., Lehtonen, J., et al. (1997). Single-photon emission tomography imaging of monoamine transporters in impulsive violent behaviour. *European Journal of Nuclear Medicine and Molecular Imaging, 24*, 1253–1260.

Tonkonogy, J. M. (1991). Violence and temporal lobe lesion: Head CT and MRI data. *Journal of Neuropsychiatry and Clinical Neurosciences, 3*, 189–196.

Umhau, J. C., George, D. T., Reed, S., Petrulis, S. G., Rawlings, R., & Porges, S. W. (2002). Atypical autonomic regulation in perpetrators of violent domestic abuse. *Psychophysiology, 39*, 117–123.

van Elst, L. T., Hesslinger, B., Thiel, T., Geiger, E., Haegele, K., Lemieux, L., et al. (2003). Frontolimbic brain abnormalities in patients with borderline personality disorder: A volumetric magnetic resonance imaging study. *Biological Psychiatry, 54*, 163–171.

van Elst, L. T., Thiel, T., Hesslinger, B., Lieb, K., Bohus, M., Hennig, J., et al. (2001). Subtle prefrontal neuropathology in a pilot magnetic resonance spectroscopy study in patients with borderline personality disorder. *Journal of Neuropsychiatry and Clinical Neurosciences, 13*, 511–514.

van Elst, L. T. Woermann, F. G., Lemieux, L., Thompson, P. J., & Trimble, M. R. (2000). Affective aggression in patients with temporal lobe epilepsy: A quantitative MRI study of the amygdala. *Brain, 123*, 234–243.

Veit, R., Flor, H., Erb, M., Hermann, C., Lotze, M., Grodd, W., et al. (2002). Brain circuits involved in emotional learning in antisocial behavior and social phobia in humans. *Neuroscience Letters, 328*, 233–236.

Verona, E. (2005). State and trait negative emotionality links to aggressive behavior in men and women. *Psychophysiology, 42*, S24.

Verona, E., & Curtin, J. J. (2006). Gender differences in the negative affective priming of aggression. *Emotion, 6*, 115–124.

Verona, E., Joiner, T. E., Johnson, F., & Bender, T. (2006). Gender specific gene-environment interactions on laboratory-assessed aggression. *Biological Psychology, 71*, 33–41.

Verona, E., Patrick, C. J., Curtin, J. J., Lang, P. J., & Bradley, M. M. (2004). Psychopathy and physiological response to emotionally evocative sounds. *Journal of Abnormal Psychology, 113*, 99–108.

Verona, E., Patrick, C. J., & Joiner, T. E. (2001). Psychopathy, antisocial personality, and suicide risk. *Journal of Abnormal Psychology*, *110*, 462–470.

Verona, E., Patrick, C. J., & Lang, A. R. (2002). A direct assessment of the role of state and trait negative emotion in aggressive behavior. *Journal of Abnormal Psychology*, *111*, 249–258.

Verona, E., & Sullivan, E. S. (2004). Catharsis hypothesis revisited: Autonomic recovery following aggressive responses [Abstract]. *Psychophysiology*, *41*, S31.

Volavka, J. (1990). Aggression, electroencephalography, and evoked potentials: A critical review. *Neuropsychiatry, Neuropsychology, and Behavioral Neurology*, *3*, 249–259.

Volkow, N. D., & Tancredi, L. (1987). Neural substrates of violent behaviour: A preliminary study with positron emission tomography. *British Journal of Psychiatry*, *151*, 668–673.

Volkow, N. D., Tancredi, L. R., Grant, C., Gillespie, H., Valentine, A., Mullani, N., et al. (1995). Brain glucose metabolism in violent psychiatric patients: A preliminary study. *Psychiatry Research: Neuroimaging*, *61*, 243–253.

Wadsworth, M. E. J. (1976). Delinquency, pulse rate and early emotional deprivation. *British Journal of Criminology*, *16*, 245–256.

Waschbusch, D. A., Pelham, W. E., Jennings, J. R., Greiner, A. R., Tarter, R. E., & Moss, H. B. (2002). Reactive aggression in boys with disruptive behavior disorders: Behavior, physiology, and affect. *Journal of Abnormal Child Psychology*, *30*, 641–656.

Williams, D. (1969). Neural factors related to habitual aggression: Consideration of differences between those habitual aggressives and others who have committed crimes of violence. *Brain*, *92*, 503–520.

Woermann, F. G., Van Elst, L. T., Koepp, M. J., Free, S. L., Thompson, P. J., Trimble, M. R., et al. (2000). Reduction of frontal neocortical grey matter associated with affective aggression in patients with temporal lobe epilepsy: An objective voxel by voxel analysis of automatically segmented MRI. *Journal of Neurology, Neurosurgery, and Psychiatry*, *68*, 162–169.

Wolfersdorf, M., Straub, R., Barg, T., Keller, F., & Kaschka, W. P. (1999). Depressed inpatients, electrodermal reactivity, and suicide – A study about psychophysiology of suicidal behavior. *Archives of Suicide Research*, *5*, 1–10.

Woodworth, M., & Porter, S. (2002). In cold blood: Characteristics of criminal homicides as a function of psychopathy. *Journal of Abnormal Psychology*, *111*, 436–445.

Wong, M. T., Fenwick, P. B., Lumsden, J., Fenton, G. W., Maisey, M. N., Lewis, P., et al. (1997). Positron emission tomography in male violent offenders with schizophrenia. *Psychiatry Research*, *68*, 111–123.

Wong, M. T. H., Lumsden, J., Fenton, G. W., & Fenwick, P. B. C. (1994). Electroencephalography, computed tomography and violence ratings of male patients in a maximum-security mental hospital. *Acta Psychiatrica Scandinavica*, *90*, 97–101.

Yang, Y., Raine, A., Lencz, T., Bihrle, S., Lacasse, L., & Colletti, P. (2005). Volume reduction in prefrontal gray matter in unsuccessful criminal psychopaths. *Biological Psychiatry*, *57*, 1103–1108.

Yeudall, L. T., Fromm-Auch, D., & Davies, P. (1982). Neuropsychological impairment of persistent delinquency. *Journal of Nervous and Mental Disease*, *170*, 257–265.

Young, S. E., Stallings, M. C., Corley, R. P., Krauter, K. S., & Hewitt, J. K. (2000). Genetic and environmental influences on behavioral disinhibition. *American Journal of Medical Genetics (Neuropsychiatric Genetics)*, *96*, 684–695.

Zahn, T. P., & Kruesi, M. J. P. (1993). Autonomic activity in boys with disruptive behavior disorders. *Psychophysiology*, *30*, 605–614.

Zillman, D. (1983). Transfer of excitation in emotional behavior. In J. T. Cacioppo & R. E. Petty (Eds.), *Social psychophysiology: A sourcebook* (pp. 215–240). New York: Guilford.

Zuckerman, M. (1979). *Sensation seeking: Beyond the optimal level of arousal*. Hillsdale, NJ: Erlbaum.

CHAPTER 7

Biosocial Bases of Violence

Angela Scarpa and Adrian Raine

Introduction

The early works of Cesare Lombroso (1895) in Italy and Earnest Hooton (1939) in the United States formed the foundation of biological criminology in which researchers attempted to understand the biological underpinnings of the criminal. Unfortunately, at that time, racist overtones plagued this line of research, and it was used to support such public policies as eugenics and euthanasia. Historically, in an attempt to divorce themselves from these negative connotations, sociologists and criminologists began to take an extreme environmentalist position. From this stance, crime and violence were viewed as legal constructions that were completely based in societal factors, such as poverty and lack of social control. Even today, surveys indicate that about 85% of American criminologists consider themselves to be strict environmentalists (Ellis & Hoffman, 1990; Ellis & Walsh, 1999). Now stripped of its political agendas, however, biological criminology has made a resurgence, and there is a growing body of literature showing that violence is associated with genetic, neurobiological, psychophysiological, hormonal, and other health-related factors (e.g., see Scarpa & Raine, 1997, and Volavka, 1995, for reviews). In fact, this literature has become so strong that Raine (2002a) concluded, "It is now beyond doubt that brain deficits contribute in some way to antisocial and aggressive behavior" (p. 425).

More recently, biosocial theories of violence have emerged in an attempt to reunite these two seemingly disparate camps from the biological and environmental traditions. That is, biosocial explanations of violence clearly acknowledge the role of both biological and psychosocial factors in the etiology of violence and suggest that the interaction of these variables provides the most accurate and comprehensive understanding of this often tragic phenomenon (e.g., Raine, Brennan, Farrington, & Mednick, 1997; Walsh & Ellis, 2003). The goal of this chapter is to review the best, most current work in this area, with a focus on psychosocial interactions with low autonomic functioning, prefrontal deficits, and early health factors in relation to violence (see Raine, 2002a, for a review of the main effects of these biological variables). This chapter updates prior reviews by Raine (2002b) and Scarpa and Raine (2003). The terms "aggression" and "violence" are used interchangeably here to reflect acts that cause, or threaten to cause, bodily harm to another (Quadagno, 2003). Though obviously relevant, gene-environment interactions are not covered here because they are reviewed in Chapter 10, "The Interaction of Nature and Nurture in Antisocial Behavior" (Dodge & Sherrill; see Caspi et al., 2002, for an example).

Autonomic Underarousal

Of the many psychophysiological processes studied, low autonomic functioning has been found most repeatedly in relation to antisocial, criminal, and violent behavior in both children and adults (see Raine, 2002a, for a review). In a recent meta-analysis of 40 studies of antisocial behavior in children and adolescents, for example, the average effect size for heart rate (HR) was -0.44 at rest and -0.76 during a stressor (Ortiz & Raine, 2004), leading the authors to conclude that low resting heart rate is the best-replicated biological correlate of antisocial behavior to date. In support of this conclusion for violence in particular, another recent meta-analysis of 19 studies found that both child and adult aggression was related to low resting heart rate with an average effect size of -0.38 ($d = -0.51$ in child samples and -0.30 in adults; Lorber, 2004). Moreover, Raine (2002a) notes that (1) this relationship is not artifactual, with studies repeatedly ruling out potential confounds, such as height, weight, drug/alcohol use, physical exercise, and psychosocial adversity; (2) no other psychiatric or behavioral condition has been linked to low heart rate, suggesting that it is diagnostically specific; (3) findings have been replicated in at least six different countries, suggesting it is a robust marker across cultural contexts; and (4) it seems to particularly characterize life-course persistent antisocial offenders (Moffitt & Caspi, 2001).

Thus, there is a strong case for the importance of autonomic underarousal, and specifically low heart rate, in relation to aggressive behavior. Biosocial findings suggest that heart rate also interacts with psychosocial risk factors in increasing violence (see Scarpa & Raine, 2003). For example, Farrington (1997) reports that boys with low resting heart rates are more likely to become adult violent criminals if they also have a poor relationship with their parents and come from a large family. He also reports that boys with low heart rate are more likely to be rated as aggressive by their teachers if their mother was pregnant as a teenager, they come from a low social class family, or they were separated from a parent before age 10.

The biosocial interaction with low heart rate may also be specific to certain forms of aggression. In a recent study of community children, for example, community violence victimization was positively related to proactive (i.e., instrumental, goal-directed) aggression only in those with low heart rate, whereas heart rate level did not moderate the effect for reactive (i.e., impulsive, provoked) aggression (Scarpa, Tanaka, & Haden, 2006). These findings would be consistent with transactional models of development, also referred to as ecological or biopsychosocial, which suggest that aggressive behavioral problems arise when there is a mismatch between intrinsic childhood characteristics and family or environmental conditions (Rothbart & Ahadi, 1994; Sameroff, 1995; Sanson, Smart, Prior, & Oberklaid, 1993; Thomas & Chess, 1977). This perspective emphasizes the sensitivity of children with certain vulnerabilities to adverse social environments and also suggests that it is the interaction of adverse social environments with child vulnerabilities that increases the risk for later aggressive antisocial behavior. However, it must also be remembered that there is significant heritability for heart rate (Boomsma & Plomin, 1986; Ditto, 1993), and consequently the link between low heart rate and antisocial behavior may be explained by genetic processes.

By the same token, some findings seem to support a social push hypothesis, which posits that psychophysiological relationships to antisocial behavior are stronger when coupled with benign and not adverse backgrounds. The social push hypothesis suggests that, in people who lack social factors that "push" or predispose them to violent behavior, biological factors may more likely explain the behavior (Raine & Venables, 1981). Conversely, when criminogenic social factors exist, the social causes of violence camouflage the biological contribution. For example, in a prospective study (in which measures taken early in life are used to predict later outcome), low heart rate at age 3 years predicted aggression at age 11 years in children from high but not low social classes (Raine, Venables, & Mednick, 1997). In addition, in a study of young adults, low heart rate was related to increased aggression in both victims and nonvictims of violence, but increased heart rate variability (increased parasympathetic dominance related to reduced HR level) was positively related to aggression only in the nonvictims (Scarpa & Ollendick, 2003). These authors suggested that high vagal tone, which reflects increased parasympathetic functioning, might be the mediating cardiovascular mechanism that explains the low heart rate in aggressive individuals who do not have a history of violence exposure.

The research clearly shows that violence is related to an interaction between autonomic underarousal, in terms of low resting heart rate, with psychosocial experiences and background. Low resting heart rate theoretically may reflect a predisposition to such traits as fearlessness, callousness/unemotionality, disinhibited temperament, and sensation-seeking that increase the likelihood of engaging in violence (Frick, Cornell, Bodin, Dane, Barry, & Loney, 2003; Raine, 1993; Scarpa & Raine, 2004). Indeed, in a sample of 199 second- and third-grade children, ineffective parenting was related to aggressive behavior and other conduct problems only in children who were rated as callous and unemotional (Oxford, Cavell, & Hughes, 2003). The authors suggested that the biogenetic makeup of this group predisposed them to be less amenable to parental influences (akin to the social push hypothesis described above). In addition, low heart rate may be mediated by neural mechanisms, such as reduced noradrenergic functioning, right hemisphere dysfunction, or prefrontal deficits (Raine, 2002a).

Deficits in Prefrontal Functioning

Although neuropsychological and brain imaging results have not been entirely consistent, and brain dysfunction is not a necessary precursor to violent behavior, research findings are providing evidence for individual differences in the quality of functioning of different parts of the brain that mediate and control behavior. These subtle individual differences may exist in the absence of any clear structural brain damage and may predispose an individual to violent behavior. Many brain areas and structures have been studied in relation to antisocial behavior. The frontal lobes and prefrontal cortex in particular seem to be especially important in the regulation of aggressive impulses. Studies examining damage to the frontal cortex in noncriminal samples, for example, have shown a pattern of personality changes, including argumentativeness, lack of concern for consequences of behavior, loss of social graces, impulsivity, distractibility, shallowness, lability, violence, and reduced ability to use symbols (termed frontal lobe syndrome; Silver & Yudofsky, 1987). Though variability in findings do occur, reviews of brain imaging studies of violent and psychopathic populations generally concur that violent offenders have functional deficits to the anterior regions of the brain, particularly the frontal region (Henry & Moffitt, 1997; Raine, 1993, 2002a; Raine & Buchsbaum, 1996). Furthermore, these deficits seem to especially characterize violent offenders whose act of murder was impulsive rather than planned or instrumental in nature (Raine et al., 1998a).

To our knowledge, there are no brain imaging studies of violent youth, so it is unclear whether the relationship between prefrontal deficits and aggression occurs across the life span. Studies of children with head injuries, however, clearly show increased rates of conduct disorder and externalizing behavior problems following head trauma (Butler, Rourke, Fuerst, & Fisk, 1997; Hux, Bond, Skinner, Belau, & Sanger, 1998; Max et al., 1998; Mittenbereg, Wittner, & Miller, 1997). Moreover, several case studies have indicated that children with lesions specifically to the prefrontal cortex showed antisocial behavior after their injuries that included impulsive aggressive as well as nonaggressive antisocial acts (Bechara, Damasio, Tranel, & Damasio, 1997; Pennington & Bennetto, 1993). These studies suggest that prefrontal deficits may reflect a neurodevelopmental risk for violence.

Raine (2002a,b) suggests that immature frontal lobes may lead to violent behavior by resulting in deficient executive cognitive functioning, including problems in the following areas: sustained attention, behavioral flexibility to changing contingencies, working memory, self-regulation and inhibitory control, abstract decision making, planning, and organization. These difficulties may lead to a "processing overload" in response to stressors in children, especially adolescents, who have either pre-existing prefrontal deficits or a developmental delay in prefrontal maturation. Aggressive behavior would also persist into adulthood in those who suffered head trauma or any other condition that would prevent the prefrontal cortex from maturing to normal levels over time. Similarly, other mechanisms that have been proposed to explain the relationship between prefrontal deficits and violence include: (1) an inability to reason and make appropriate decisions in risky situations (Bechara et al., 1997), leading to impulsivity and reckless behavior; (2) poor fear conditioning and stress responsivity (Damasio, 1994; Hugdahl, 1998), leading to poor conscience development; and (3) poor regulation of arousal (Dahl, 1998), leading to stimulation-seeking associated with underarousal of the central nervous system. A recent study by Leon-Carrion & Ramos (2003) found some limited support for the processing overload hypothesis. In this study, both violent and

nonviolent prisoners reported academic difficulties in high school. The violent group, however, also suffered head injuries that were never treated, suggesting that neurological damage may have lessened the ability to handle school demands during adolescence, which increased the likelihood of entering a violent developmental trajectory.

The executive cognitive functions subserved by the prefrontal cortex seem primed for helping the individual adapt to changing environmental circumstances and thus would naturally predict interactions between prefrontal dysfunction and psychosocial adversity. The evidence indeed supports such biosocial interactions, though few studies specifically assess prefrontal deficits. For example, one prospective study of juvenile delinquents found that a combination of child abuse plus three neurocognitive indicators was associated with an average of 5.4 violent offenses in adulthood. This was in comparison to an average of 2.1 adult violent offenses in those having only neurocognitive deficits and 1.9 offenses in those having only a history of child abuse (Lewis, Lovely, Yeager, & Della Femina, 1989). Another study found that the highest rates of adult violent and criminal offending occurred in those with both early neuromotor deficits and an unstable home environment, compared to those who had only the social or only the biological risks (Raine, Brennan, Mednick, & Mednick, 1996). Similarly, Moffitt (1990) found that boys with both neuropsychological deficits and family adversity had the highest levels of aggression, and this relationship seems especially characteristic of life-course persistent offenders (Moffitt & Caspi, 2001). Consistent with this finding, a recent study of 370 high-risk adolescents in Australia found that the interaction of biological and social risks from age 5 to 15 was related specifically to early-onset persistent aggression and not to adolescent-onset aggression, and only for boys (Brennan, Hall, Bor, Najman, & Williams, 2003). In addition to the assessment of neuropsychological functioning (i.e., low receptive vocabulary scores at age 5, low vocabulary IQ at age

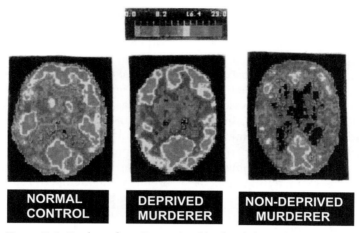

Figure 7.1. Findings from Raine, Stoddard, Bihrle, and Buchsbaum (1998b), indicating relatively good prefrontal functioning in deprived murderers, but significantly reduced prefrontal functioning in non-deprived murderers compared to a normal control group.

15, and deficits in executive cognitive functioning at age 15), biological risks in this study also included perinatal risks and birth complications, maternal illness during pregnancy, and infant temperament. Thus, the authors argue that it is the accumulation of biological and social risks and their transaction during development that maintains a persistent aggressive trajectory. Lastly, in a study using functional magnetic resonance imaging to assess brain activity, violent offenders who had suffered severe child abuse showed reduced functioning in the right hemisphere, particularly in the right temporal lobe (Raine et al., 2001). Raine interpreted this finding to suggest that right hemisphere dysfunction, when combined with a history of severe child physical abuse, predisposes one to serious violence.

In support of the social push hypothesis, which suggests that biological bases of antisocial behavior are most clear in the absence of the criminogenic push from psychosocial risks (Raine, 2002b; Raine & Venables, 1981), a sample of murderers was divided into those with deprived or nondeprived home backgrounds. They were then compared to noncriminal controls on frontal lobe brain activity that was assessed using positron

emission tomography (Raine, Stoddard, Bihrle, & Buchsbaum, 1998b). In this study, deprivation scores took into account various adverse experiences, such as early physical and sexual abuse, neglect, extreme poverty, foster home placement, family conflict, a broken home, and having a criminal parent. Results indicated that the deprived murderers showed relatively good prefrontal functioning, whereas the nondeprived murderers showed significantly reduced prefrontal functioning compared to the normal control group (see Figure 7.1). This finding is consistent with the brain imaging studies noted above that generally find reduced functioning of the prefrontal cortex in violent offenders, but suggests that reduced prefrontal functioning may be a particularly strong characteristic of violent offenders from relatively good home environments.

These biosocial studies suggest that rates of antisocial behavior appear to be highest when abnormalities of the central nervous system are combined with a history of adverse environmental experiences. They also suggest that central nervous system dysfunction appears stronger in antisocial individuals from relatively good home backgrounds in comparison to those with a history of psychosocial deprivation. With the exception of Raine et al. (1998b), however, these biosocial studies do not directly assess prefrontal functioning. Thus, although the biosocial role of deficient prefrontal functioning is implicated by the very nature of that brain region to facilitate adaptation to external demands, further research evidence is warranted and is especially lacking in children. Nonetheless, it is clear that some interaction between environmental experiences and central nervous system functioning, possibly even multisite brain dysfunction, is involved in violence.

Early Health-Related Factors

If brain functioning is related to aggressive behavior, it becomes critical to understand what early factors might increase the probability of brain impairment during development. Another critical question involves what factors might increase the negative impact of pre-existing brain deficits. As such, biological and social factors may play bidirectional roles, in that social factors such as poverty might influence neurological health through malnutrition or lack of access to good health care, but neurological dysfunction might also influence the ability to appropriately respond to stressful situations in a flexible manner. In a related manner, diathesis-stress models posit that stressors in the environment can trigger the expression of pre-existing vulnerabilities. Some early health factors that may be involved in these complex biosocial interactions include birth complications, fetal neural maldevelopment, nicotine exposure during pregnancy, and malnutrition.

Birth complications. Several studies have shown that babies who suffer birth complications are more likely to develop conduct disorder, engage in delinquency, and commit impulsive crime and violence in adulthood when other psychosocial risk factors are present. Birth complications in these studies included low gestational age (i.e., premature birth), low birth weight, low Apgar score, placement in a neonatal intensive care unit, forceps delivery, Cesarean section, resuscitation required after delivery, anoxia (i.e.,

lack of oxygen during delivery), and pre-eclampsia in the mother (i.e., hypertension leading to anoxia). Specifically, obstetric factors have been shown to *interact* with psychosocial risk factors in relation to adult violence. Werner (1987) found that birth complications interacted with a disruptive family environment (maternal separation, illegitimate child, marital discord, parental mental health problems, paternal absence) in predisposing to delinquency. Similarly, Raine, Brennan, and Mednick (1994) prospectively assessed birth complications and maternal rejection at age 1 year in 4,269 live male births in Copenhagen, Denmark. Birth complications significantly interacted with maternal rejection of the child in predicting to violent offending at age 18 years (see Figure 7.2, upper half). Only 4% of the sample had both birth complications and maternal rejection, but this small group accounted for 18% of all the violent crimes committed by the entire sample.

In a later study, the 4,269 babies were followed up to age 34 at which time outcome for violent crime was reassessed (Raine, Brennan, & Mednick, 1997). The biosocial interaction that was previously observed held for violent but not nonviolent criminal offending. Furthermore, the interaction was specific to more serious forms of violence and not threats of violence. The interaction held for early onset but not late-onset violence and was not accounted for by psychiatric illness in the mothers. Rearing in a public care institution in the first year of life and attempt to abort the fetus were the key aspects of maternal rejection found to interact with birth complications in predisposing to violence, suggesting that early maternal attachment experiences may play a key role.

Another study from Denmark also showed that birth complications interacted with parental mental illness in predicting violent crime in male offspring (see Figure 7.3; Brennan, Mednick, & Mednick, 1993). These findings from Denmark have recently been replicated in four other countries (Sweden, Finland, Canada, and the United States) in the context of a variety of psychosocial risk factors. Piquero and Tibbetts

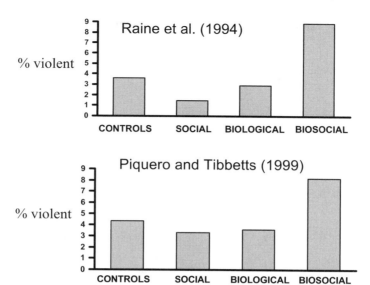

Figure 7.2. Birth complications significantly interacted with maternal rejection of the child in predicting violent offending at age 18 years (Raine, Brennan, and Mednick, 1994; upper half of figure). Piquero & Tibbetts, (1999) replicated these results, finding that those with both pre/perinatal disturbances and a disadvantaged familial environment were much more likely to become adult violent offenders (lower half of figure).

(1999) in a prospective longitudinal study of 867 males and females from the Philadelphia Collaborative Perinatal Project found that those with both pre/peri-natal disturbances and a disadvantaged familial environment were much more likely to become adult violent offenders (see Figure 7.2, lower half).

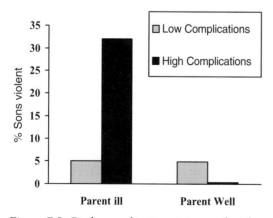

Figure 7.3. Birth complications interacted with parental mental illness in predicting violent crime in male offspring (Brennan, Mednick, & Mednick, 1993).

Similarly, pregnancy complications interacted with poor parenting in predicting adult violence in a large Swedish sample of 7,101 men (Hodgins, Kratzer, & McNeil, 2001). In a Canadian sample of 849 boys, Arsenault, Tremblay, Boulerice, and Saucier (2002) found that infant nervous system maldevelopment resulting from serious obstetric complications interacted with poor parenting and social adversity to raise the likelihood of chronic aggression and violent offending from childhood to age 17 years. In a Finnish sample, perinatal risk interacted with being an only child in raising the odds of adult violent offending by a factor of 4.4 in a sample of 5,587 males (Kemppainen, Jokelainen, Jaervelin, Isohanni, & Raesaenen, 2001). In this final study, being an only child is not obviously linked to psychosocial adversity, and so the meaning of this interaction needs clarification.

In contrast, two studies found no interaction between perinatal insult and social class (Cannon, Huttenen, Tanskanen, Arsenault, Jones, & Murray, 2002) or family adversity

(Laucht et al., 2000). The first of these failures to find an interaction occurred in a sample of 601 individuals with schizophrenia spectrum disorders in Helsinki, in which the outcome was a record of either serious criminal offending or violence by adulthood. Perhaps the risks for schizophrenia in this sample obscured findings for criminality. The second failure occurred for a smaller sample of 322 German children where outcome was restricted to follow-up at age 8 years. This latter failure may be due to the fact that neurological deficits stemming from birth complications may particularly influence the more severe outcome of life-course persistent antisocial behavior, rather than the more common outcome of child antisocial behavior (Moffitt, 1993; Moffitt & Caspi, 2001). Indeed, several of the aforementioned studies found that interaction effects involving birth complications and family factors show evidence of linkage to what may be broadly termed life-course persistent violent behavior, rather than adolescent-limited antisocial behavior. This linkage was recently replicated by Brennan et al. (2003) who found that cumulative biosocial risks, including perinatal risks and birth complications, were particularly related to early-onset persistent aggression. In addition to these interactions with psychosocial variables, low Apgar scores at birth have been found to interact with maternal smoking in the prediction of adult violent offending (Gibson & Tibbetts, 1998).

Birth complications, such as anoxia (i.e., lack of oxygen), forceps delivery, and preeclampsia (i.e., hypertension leading to anoxia) are thought to contribute to brain damage, and they may be just one of a number of early sources of brain dysfunction observed in child and adult antisocial groups. However, as indicated above, birth complications may not by themselves predispose to crime, but instead may require the presence of negative environmental circumstance to trigger later adult crime and violence. Furthermore, although birth complications are likely to contribute to prefrontal damage, their effects would not be specific to this brain area but would affect multiple brain sites, including the hippocampus. In light of the fact that the hippocampus is particularly susceptible to anoxia, it is interesting to note that some brain imaging studies have shown abnormal hippocampal functioning in murderers (Raine, Buchsbaum, & LaCasse, 1997) and structural abnormalities in psychopaths (Laakso et al., 2001).

Fetal neural maldevelopment. At least six studies have found an association between increased minor physical anomalies (MPAs) and increased antisocial behavior in children (Raine, 1993). MPAs have been associated with disorders of pregnancy and are thought to be a marker for fetal neural maldevelopment toward the end of the first 3 months of pregnancy. As such, they may be viewed as an indirect marker of abnormal brain development. MPAs are relatively minor physical abnormalities consisting of such features as low-seated ears, adherent ear lobes, and a furrowed tongue. Although MPAs may have a genetic basis, they may also be caused by environmental factors acting on the fetus, such as anoxia, bleeding, and infection (Guy, Majorski, Wallace, & Guy, 1983).

At least three studies have found that MPAs interact with social factors in predicting antisocial and violent behavior. Mednick and Kandel (1988) assessed MPAs in a sample of 129 12-year-old boys seen by an experienced pediatrician. MPAs were found to be related to violent offending, although not to property offenses without violence, as assessed 9 years later when the subjects were aged 21 years. However, as illustrated in Figure 7.4, when subjects were divided into those from unstable, nonintact homes and those from stable homes, a biosocial interaction was observed. MPAs only predicted violence in those individuals raised in unstable home environments. Similarly, in a sample of 72 male offspring of psychiatrically ill parents, those with both MPAs and family adversity had especially high rates of adult violent offending (Brennan, Mednick, & Raine, 1997). This interaction was again confirmed by Pine, Shaffer, Schonfeld, and Davies (1997) who found that MPAs in 7-year-old boys and girls combined with environmental risk in predisposing to

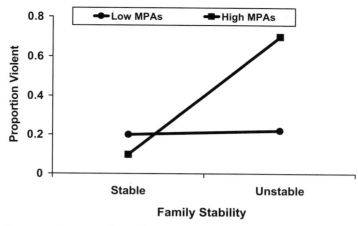

Figure 7.4. Minor physical anomalies predicted violence in those individuals raised in unstable home environments (Mednick and Kandel, 1988).

conduct disorder at age 17. These findings are similar to those on birth complications reported above; in both cases the presence of a negative psychosocial factor is required to "trigger" the biological risk factor, and in both cases the effects are specific to violent offending. In a study confirming specificity of MPAs to violence, MPAs assessed at age 14 in 170 males predicted violent, but not nonviolent, delinquency at age 17 (Arseneault, Tremblay, Boulerice, Seguin, & Saucier, 2000); however, in this study, effects were independent of family adversity.

Prenatal nicotine exposure. The effect of fetal exposure to alcohol in increasing risk for conduct disorders is well known (e.g., Fast, Conry, & Loock, 1999; Olson, Streissguth, Sampson, Barr, Bookstein, & Thiede, 1997; Streissguth, Barr, Bookstein, Sampson, & Olson, 1999), but a recent wave of studies have established beyond reasonable doubt a significant link between smoking during pregnancy and later conduct disorder and violent offending (e.g., Rantakallio, Laara, Isohanni, & Moilanen, 1992). Three of these studies have also observed interactions between nicotine exposure and psychosocial variables in the prediction of later violent offending and are impressive in terms of their size, the prospective nature of data collection, long-term outcome, and control for potential

confounds, such as antisocial behavior in the parents, other drug use, and low social class. For example, in a birth cohort of 4,169 males, there was a two-fold increase in adult violent offending in the offspring of mothers who smoked 20 cigarettes a day, as well as a dose-response relationship between increased number of cigarettes smoked and increased violence (Brennan, Grekin, & Mednick, 1999). However, a *fivefold* increase in adult violence was found when nicotine exposure was combined with exposure to delivery complications – there was no increase in violence in those who were nicotine-exposed but lacking delivery complications. Moreover, the effects were specific to persistent offending and did not apply to adolescent-limited offending. Similarly, Rasanen, Hakko, Isohanni, Hodgins, Jaervelin, and Tiihonen (1999) found a two-fold increase of violent criminal offending at age 26 in the offspring of women who smoked during pregnancy. In addition, nicotine exposure led to an 11.9-fold increase in recidivistic violence when combined with single-parent family, and a 14.2-fold increase when combined with teenage pregnancy, single-parent family, unwanted pregnancy, and developmental motor lags. Again, odds-ratios were stronger for recidivistic violence than for violence in general or property offending. Lastly, Gibson and

Tibbetts (2000) also found that maternal smoking interacted with parental absence in predicting early onset of offending in a U.S. sample.

Maternal smoking during pregnancy may be an important contributory factor to the aforementioned brain deficits that have been found in adult offenders. Animal research has clearly demonstrated the neurotoxic effects of two constituents of cigarette smoke – carbon monoxide (CO) and nicotine (see Olds, 1997, for a detailed review). In addition, prenatal nicotine exposure, even at relatively low levels, disrupts the development of the noradrenergic neurotransmitter system and disrupts cognitive functions (Levin, Wilkerson, Jones, Christopher, & Briggs, 1996). Reduction of noradrenergic functioning caused by smoking would be expected to disrupt sympathetic nervous system activity; this effect is consistent with evidence for reduced sympathetic arousal in antisocial individuals (Raine, 1996). Moreover, pregnant rats exposed to nicotine have offspring with an enhancement of cardiac M2-muscarinic cholinergic receptors that *inhibit* autonomic functions (Slotkin, Epps, Stenger, Sawyer, & Seidler, 1999). This finding would help explain the well-replicated finding of *low* resting heart rate in antisocial individuals outlined above (Raine, 1993). Lastly, it is clear that other social and biological factors are related to chronic smoking of mothers during pregnancy, such as teenage pregnancy, maternal aggression and delinquency, and lower maternal education, highlighting the dynamic biosocial relationships inherent in this risk factor (Cornelius, Leech, & Goldschmidt, 2004). In other words, prenatal nicotine exposure may represent a proxy variable that encompasses multiple biosocial risks.

Malnutrition. Although deficiency in nutrition has been rarely studied in relation to externalizing behavior problems in children, several studies have demonstrated the effects of related processes, including food additives, hypoglycemia, and cholesterol on behavior (Fishbein & Pease, 1994; Raine, 1993; Rutter, Giller, & Hagell, 1998). In addition, epidemiological studies have shown associations between increased aggressive behavior and vitamin and mineral deficiency (Breakey, 1997; Werbach, 1995). There is also some evidence in animal studies of a link between zinc and protein deficiency and aggression (Halas, Reynolds, & Sandstead, 1977; Tikal, Benesova, & Frankova, 1976). In humans, zinc deficiency during pregnancy is related to impaired DNA, RNA, and protein synthesis during brain development and to congenital brain abnormalities (King, 2000; Pfeiffer & Braverman, 1992). King (2000) also noted that smoking during pregnancy, which is associated with violence in offspring, can impair the transportation of zinc from the mother to the fetus. Interestingly, males with a history of assaultive behavior have been found to have lower zinc-copper ratios in their blood compared to a control group with no assaultive behavior.

These findings offer a tentative suggestion that malnutrition in the developing fetus or in young children can affect later violent behavior. Some support for this link comes from a study of the children of women who were pregnant during a food blockade in Holland that occurred toward the end of World War II (Neugebauer, Hoek, & Susser, 1999). These women were exposed to malnutrition at different stages of pregnancy. The male offspring of these nutritionally deprived pregnant women were found to have 2.5 times the normal rate of antisocial personality disorder in adulthood compared to controls. Furthermore, effects were found for severe malnutrition during the first and second trimesters of pregnancy, but not the third trimester. Findings from a recent study of over 1,500 Mauritian children indicated that children with signs of malnutrition at age 3 years were more aggressive/ hyperactive at age 8 years, had higher externalizing problems at age 11, and a higher incidence of conduct disorder and motor excess at age 17 compared to controls (Liu, Raine, Venables, & Mednick, 2004; see Figure 7.5). These results were independent of psychosocial adversity and were not moderated by gender or ethnicity. A dose-response relationship was observed between degree

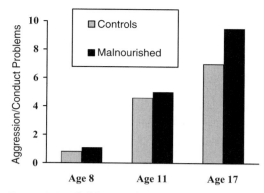

Figure 7.5. Children with signs of malnutrition at age 3 years were more aggressive/hyperactive at age 8 years, had higher externalizing problems at age 11, and higher conduct disorder and motor excess at age 17 compared to controls (Liu, Raine, Venables, and Mednick, 2004).

of malnutrition and degree of externalizing behavior at ages 8 and 17, and low IQ was found to mediate the link between malnutrition and externalizing behavior at ages 8 and 11. Based on these findings, the authors suggested that malnutrition predisposes to neurocognitive deficits, which in turn predispose to persistent externalizing behavior problems throughout childhood and adolescence.

To our knowledge, no studies to date have specifically examined the interactive effects of malnutrition with other biological or social factors. Nonetheless, these findings are intriguing and suggest that malnutrition may be a risk factor for impairments in the developing brain that, in turn, could interact with psychosocial adversity. Malnutrition also seems to represent a variable that itself is at the interface of biological and social influences. Social variables clearly affect the availability and access to adequate nutrition, as exemplified in the study of near-starved pregnant women resulting from a war-related food blockade (Neugebauer et al., 1999). Yet, malnutrition can also clearly impair neurological functioning (King, 2000) and then further interact with future psychosocial adversity. As such, the study of biosocial interactions in this regard would seem a ripe area of future research.

Biosocial Protective Influences

One nice advantage to understanding crime and violence from a biosocial perspective is that it suggests several pathways by which protection from a negative outcome can be offered. For example, biosocial explanations would suggest that the negative effects of biological risk factors in predisposing to antisocial behavior may be ameliorated by the benefits of a positive home environment. There appear to be few tests of this hypothesis. In support of this notion, Streissguth, Barr, Kogan, and Bookstein (1996) found that a stable home environment protected children with fetal alcohol syndrome from an antisocial outcome. Additional support comes from an intriguing case study of a Spanish man who had an iron spike pass through his head, selectively destroying the prefrontal cortex. Unlike the infamous case of Phineas Gage, this individual did not have an outcome over the next 60 years of antisocial or criminal behavior (Mataro, Jurado, Garcia-Sanchez, Barraquer, Costa-Jussa, & Junque, 2001), leading the authors to conclude that prefrontal damage can be followed by stable psychosocial functioning. Another interpretation, however, is that the external support and structure provided by his family buffered him from an outcome of antisocial behavior and psychosocial dysfunction. It is noteworthy that this man had wealthy parents who owned a family business in which he would be employed for the rest of his life, and that his fianc (a childhood sweetheart) stood by him after the accident and married him, producing two good children and a family that, in the words of one of the children, "protected" him throughout his life. Without such psychosocial support, a very different outcome may have resulted.

Stable and supportive environments, therefore, may minimize the negative effects of a biological vulnerability for antisocial outcome. By the same token, biosocial theories would suggest that biological factors can minimize the negative antisocial outcome brought on from social risks. There is now some evidence that heightened autonomic arousal may play such a role. For example, adolescent antisocial behavior is a risk factor for later criminal behavior, but some antisocial adolescents desist from further antisocial behavior. These "desistors," compared to both antisocial boys who become criminal and controls who were never antisocial, show increased electrodermal and cardiovascular arousal and orienting in an English sample (Raine, Venables, & Williams, 1995, 1996). In an independent extension of these findings, Brennan et al. (1997) found that Danish boys who had a criminal father but who did not become criminal themselves were characterized by increased electrodermal and cardiovascular orienting compared to both non-antisocial offspring of noncriminal controls, and criminal offspring with criminal fathers. This latter study is particularly interesting because it illustrates how the social risk factor for crime of having a criminal father may be moderated by the protective role of heightened autonomic functioning.

Implications for Prevention and Intervention

The early works in biological criminology openly used findings to support such practices as eugenics and euthanasia, believing that attempts to reform criminals were futile due to their biological inferiority (Rafter, 2004). This interpretation is clearly misguided and heavily influenced by the false notion of determinism, which would conclude that a biological vulnerability for antisocial behavior will necessarily and always result in that outcome. The biosocial research on protective influences noted above provides compelling evidence to refute such a fatalistic view. None of these studies specifically measured violent antisocial outcome, and so it is not known if the findings apply to general antisocial behavior or more specific violent forms of antisociality. Regardless, they are worthy of note in that they suggest some potential and fruitful avenues for prevention or intervention.

First, environmental manipulations can be used to alter biological risk factors. For example, an environmental enrichment at ages 3 to 5 years using a randomized, stratified design resulted in significant increases in psychophysiological arousal and attention 8 years later at age 11 years (Raine, Venables, Dalais, Mellingen, Reynolds, & Mednick, 2001). The enrichment consisted of programs providing nutritional, physical exercise, and educational enhancement. This study suggests that early environmental manipulations can produce long-term shifts in autonomic and cognitive functioning. Second, such biological shifts can moderate responsivity to interventions. In a school-based program for delinquency, for example, children with concentration problems did not respond as favorably as those without such problems (Rebok, Hawkins, Krener, Mayer, & Kellam, 1996). Third, psychosocial influences may moderate the effects of prevention and intervention programs on antisocial behavior. As one example, Olds et al. (1998) demonstrated that a prevention program targeting prenatal and early postnatal health was more successful in reducing delinquency at age 15 years in the offspring of unmarried, low SES mothers than in the offspring of less disadvantaged mothers. This health program included improving the quality of the mother's prenatal diet and reducing smoking during pregnancy over an average of nine nurse home visitations during pregnancy.

In addition, prevention and intervention programs for antisocial behavior may be more effective if they incorporate strategies that can reduce brain deficits or help these individuals develop alternative strategies to successfully adapt to their deficits and to their environments. For example, Lally, Mangione, and Honig (1988) showed that advising pregnant women on good nutrition, health, and child rearing led to a reduction in their offspring's delinquency 15 years later, presumably because good prenatal health and postnatal parenting promote the infant's neurological well-being. Other programs that could potentially reduce brain deficits or injury might incorporate stress management during pregnancy and physical abuse prevention during childhood. Intervention programs that might buffer the effects of prefrontal dysfunction might include cognitive remediation focusing on executive functions. For example, Fishbein (2003) recommends cognitive rehabilitation programs for inmates that focus on improving prefrontal executive cognitive functioning, specifically problem-solving ability, social skills, independence, impulse control, self-monitoring, and goal setting. Biosocial research on risk and protective factors themselves should clearly be a priority for establishing a new generation of more biosocially informed prevention and intervention programs.

Summary and Conclusions

In summary, the evidence provides strong support for autonomic underarousal (particularly low heart rate), central nervous system dysfunction (probably related to prefrontal deficits), and early health factors (including obstetric complications, malnourishment, and prenatal nicotine exposure) in relation to violence. Low resting heart rate, in particular, is one of the best-replicated psychophysiological measures that characterize antisocial behavior and theoretically may index a fearless/disinhibited temperament and/or a tendency toward stimulation-seeking, characteristics that have both been found to be predictive of antisocial outcomes (Raine, Reynolds, Venables, Mednick, & Farrington, 1998c). Damage to the prefrontal area of the brain has been associated with personality and behavioral characteristics that are similar to what is observed in psychopathic individuals, thus leading Damasio (1994) to coin the term "acquired sociopathy" in people who suffer these sorts of injuries. Even in the absence of visible lesions, there may exist some subtle impairment in frontal lobe functioning, which can lead to antisocial behavior by interrupting fear conditioning, regulation of autonomic arousal, emotional control, and executive cognitive functioning (i.e., planning, decision making, consideration of future consequences to guide behavior, reasoning, etc.). Lastly, birth complications, fetal neural maldevelopment, prenatal exposure to toxins, and poor nutrition are early health factors that may contribute to the central nervous system deficits observed in violent individuals.

There is increasing evidence that these biological factors interact with psychosocial risk factors in relation to violence. In other words, physiological relationships to aggressive behavior seem to differ depending on one's history of environmental experiences. Overall, there appear to be two primary findings in regard to biosocial interactions. One finding shows stronger biology-violence relationships in antisocial populations with a history of relatively benign or "good" home backgrounds, such as high social class and absence of exposure to violence or parental conflict (e.g., Raine, et al., 1998b). In other words, violent individuals from good versus bad backgrounds can be distinguished by their physiological functioning, with greater deficits found in those from good backgrounds. These findings lend support to the social push hypothesis that suggests that biological bases of antisocial behavior are most clear in the absence of the criminogenic push toward antisociality typically received from psychosocial risks (Raine, 2002b; Raine & Venables, 1981).

The second primary finding, and arguably the stronger one, is that the violent outcome seems greatest when biological risks are combined with psychosocial risks relative to having either set of risks alone. This finding is consistent with transactional models of development, which posit that behavior problems arise out of contributions from both intrinsic and extrinsic risk factors that cannot be readily separated from each other (Sameroff, 1995). These findings also converge with biosocial interactions involving many other biological systems, including genes, hormones, and neurotransmitters (see Raine, 2002b, for a review). A corollary of this finding is that the combination of biosocial risks seems to be relevant primarily for lifelong persistent offending, rather than time-limited adolescent offending. Several studies reviewed above noted that individuals with a life-course persistent trajectory of antisocial behavior were more likely to evidence both biological and social risks relative to people in adolescent-limited trajectories (e.g., Brennan et al., 1999, 2003; Liu et al., 2004; Moffitt & Caspi, 2001). Thus, the accumulation and interaction of biological vulnerabilities with social adversity may be most pertinent to the development of early and chronic behavior problems.

What implications do these findings on biosocial interactions have for both clinical and research practice? Regarding research implications, these findings form the basis for more sophisticated research on interactive effects. For example, research needs to move toward specifying the processes in benign and adverse environments that might influence biological structure and function and why or how such social or biological changes are related to violent antisocial outcomes. Some researchers have suggested, for instance, that continued exposure to violence in one's home or community can lead to a desensitization process whereby violence becomes viewed as normal and autonomic arousal to such behavior is reduced (Cooley-Quille & Lorion, 1999). Others have suggested that developmental stressors can overload an already vulnerable biological system, for example in the adolescent overload hypothesis posited by Raine (2002a,b). Still others have found that early factors, such as malnutrition, which can clearly be influenced by social factors, such as poverty, may increase aggression via impaired neurological and cognitive development (Liu et al., 2004). Future research might also consider the role of additional factors, such as hyperactivity or alcoholism, in clarifying the relationship of biology and environmental experience to violence.

The role of gender and ethnicity/culture must also be examined. Though the findings from Raine and colleagues on underarousal, malnutrition, and prevention apply to both genders and across ethnic groups (Liu et al.

2004; Raine, Venables, & Mednick, 1997; Raine, Venables, et al., 2001), others apply only to boys (Brennan et al., 2003). Currently, there have not been sufficient tests of the moderating effects of gender/ethnicity on biosocial influences to warrant clear conclusions.

Perhaps the most important research implication from biosocial findings is that they should encourage researchers to consider both biological and social variables in their work. Biological effects do not occur in a social vacuum nor do psychosocial effects occur in a biological vacuum, yet little research in the field considers both sets of risk factors simultaneously. Indeed, researchers who study these variables in isolation and find no significant main effects might conclude that they have no etiological significance when a study of their interactive effect would lead to a much different conclusion.

Regarding clinical implications, findings on biosocial interactions suggest some avenues for prevention and intervention. These findings would suggest, for example, that treatment to reduce conflict in the home or create a more stable environment could have a protective influence on children who have biological deficits. Other programs that aim to improve parenting skills, promote stronger parent-infant attachments, eliminate child maltreatment, or redirect stimulation-seeking to more prosocial activities may similarly suppress a biological predisposition toward violence. Alternatively, early intervention might also benefit children who experience psychosocial hardship but do not yet show behavioral difficulties by changing their psychophysiological and cognitive functioning. Directly altering biological functioning through interventions like good prenatal care, nutrition and health programs, biofeedback training, or psychotropic medication may also have some utility. It is clear that the most effective prevention and treatment programs and the greatest understanding of violent antisocial development will include multiple modes of treatment and information from both biological and psychosocial perspectives.

References

Arseneault, L., Tremblay, R. E., Boulerice, B., & Saucier, J-F. (2002). Obstetric complications and adolescent violent behaviors: Testing two developmental pathways. *Child Development, 73*, 496–508.

Arseneault, L., Tremblay, R. E., Boulerice, B., Seguin, J. R., & Saucier, J. F. (2000). Minor physical anomalies and family adversity as risk factors for violent delinquency in adolescence. *American Journal of Psychiatry, 157*, 917–923.

Bechara, A., Damasio, H., Tranel, D., & Damasio, A. R. (1997). Deciding advantageously before knowing the advantageous strategy. *Science, 275*, 1293–1294.

Boomsma, D. I., & Plomin, R. (1986). Heart rate and behavior in twins. *Merrill Palmer Quarterly, 32*, 141–151.

Breakey, J. (1997). The role of diet and behavior in childhood. *Journal of Pediatric Child Health, 33*, 190–194.

Brennan, P. A., Grekin, E. R., & Mednick, S. A. (1999). Maternal smoking during pregnancy and adult male criminal outcomes. *Archives of General Psychiatry, 56*, 215–219.

Brennan, P. A., Hall, J., Bor, W., Najman, J. K., & Williams, G. (2003). Integrating biological and social processes in relation to early-onset persistent aggression in boys and girls. *Developmental Psychology, 39*, 309–323.

Brennan, P. A., Mednick, B. R., & Mednick, S. A. (1993). Parental psychopathology, congenital factors, and violence. *Mental Disorder and Crime*, 244–261.

Brennan, P. A., Mednick, S. A., & Raine, A. (1997). Biosocial interactions and violence: A focus on perinatal factors. In A. Raine, P. A. Brennan, D. P. Farrington, & S. A. Mednick (Eds.), *Biosocial bases of violence* (pp. 163–174). New York: Plenum Press.

Brennan, P. A., Raine, A., Schulsinger, F., Kirkegaard-Sorensen, L., Knop, J., Hutchings, B., et al. (1997). Psychophysiological protective factors for male subjects at high risk for criminal behavior. *American Journal of Psychiatry, 154*, 853–855.

Butler, K., Rourke, B. P., Fuerst, D. R., & Fisk, J. L. (1997). A typology of psychosocial functioning in pediatric closed-head injury. *Child Neuropsychology, 3*, 98–133.

Cannon, M., Huttenen, M. O., Tanskanen, A. J., Arseneault, L., Jones, P. B., & Murray, R. M. (2002). Perinatal and childhood risk factors for later criminality and violence in schizophrenia. *British Journal of Psychiatry, 180*, 496–501.

Caspi, A., McClay, J., Moffitt, T., Mill, J., Martin, J., Craig, I., et al. (2002). Evidence that the cycle of violence in maltreated children depends on genotype. *Science, 297*, 851–854.

Cooley-Quille, M., & Lorion, R. (1999). Adolescents' exposure to community violence: Sleep and psychophysiological functioning. *Journal of Community Psychology, 27*, 367–375.

Cornelius, M. D., Leech, S. L., & Goldschmidt, L. (2004). Characteristics of persistent smoking among pregnant teenagers followed to young adulthood. *Nicotine and Tobacco Research, 6*, 159–169.

Dahl, R. E. (1998). The regulation of sleep and arousal: Development and psychopathology. In E. A. Farber, & M. Hertzig (Eds.), *Annual progress in child psychiatry and child development* (pp. 3–28). Bristol, PA: Bruner/Mazel.

Damasio, A. R. (1994). *Descartes' error: Emotion, reason, and the human brain*. New York: Avon Books.

Ditto, B. (1993). Familial influences on heart rate, blood pressure, and self-report anxiety responses to stress: Results from 100 twin pairs. *Psychophysiology, 30*, 635–645.

Ellis, L., & Hoffman, H. (1990). Views of contemporary criminologists on causes and theories of crime. In L. Ellis & H. Hoffman (Eds.), *Crime in biological, social, and moral contexts* (pp. 50–58). New York: Praeger.

Ellis, L. & Walsh, A. (1999). Criminologists' opinions about causes and theories of crime and delinquency. *The Criminologist, 24*, 3–6.

Farrington, D. P. (1997). The relationship between low resting heart rate and violence. In A. Raine, P. A. Brennan, D. P. Farrington, & S. A. Mednick (Eds.), *Biosocial bases of violence* (pp. 89–106). New York: Plenum Press.

Fast, D. K., Conry, J., & Loock, C. A. (1999). Identifying Fetal Alcohol Syndrome among youth in the criminal justice system. *Journal of Developmental & Behavioral Pediatrics, 20*, 370–372.

Fishbein, D. (2003). Neuropsychological and emotional regulatory processes in antisocial behavior. In A. Walsh & L. Ellis (Eds.), *Biosocial criminology: Challenging environmentalism's supremacy* (pp. 185–208). New York: Nova Science.

Fishbein, D., & Pease, S. (1994). Diet, nutrition, and aggression. *Offender Rehabilitation, 21*, 117–144.

Frick, P. J., Cornell, A. H., Bodin, S. D., Dane, H. E., Barry, C. T., & Loney, B. R. (2003). Callous-unemotional traits and developmental pathways to severe conduct problems in children. *Developmental Psychology, 39,* 246–260.

Gibson, C. L., & Tibbetts, S. G. (1998). Interaction between maternal cigarette smoking and Apgar scores in predicting offending behavior. *Psychological Reports, 83,* 579–586.

Gibson, C. L., & Tibbetts, S. G. (2000). A biosocial interaction in predicting early onset of offending. *Psychological Reports, 86,* 509–518.

Guy, J. D., Majorski, L. V., Wallace, C. J., & Guy, M. P. (1983). The incidence of minor physical anomalies in adult male schizophrenics. *Schizophrenia Bulletin, 9,* 571–582.

Halas, E. S., Reynolds, G. M., & Sandstead, H. H. (1977). Intra-uterine nutrition and its effects on aggression. *Physiology and Behavior, 19,* 653–661.

Henry, B., & Moffitt, T. E. (1997). Neuropsychological and neuroimaging studies of juvenile delinquency and adult criminal behavior. In J. Breiling, D. M. Stoff, & J. D. Maser (Eds.), *Handbook of antisocial behavior* (pp. 280–288). New York: Wiley.

Hodgins, S., Kratzer, L., & McNeil, T. F. (2001). Obstetric complications, parenting, and risk of criminal behavior. *Archives of General Psychiatry, 58,* 746–752.

Hooton, E. A. (1939). *Crime and the man.* Cambridge, MA: Harvard University Press.

Hugdahl, K. (1998). Cortical control of human classical conditioning: Autonomic and positron emission tomography data. *Psychophysiology, 35,* 170–178.

Hux, K., Bond, V., Skinner, S., Belau, D., & Sanger, D. (1998). Parental report of occurrences and consequences of traumatic brain injury among delinquent and non-delinquent youth. *Brain Injury, 12,* 667–681.

Kemppainen, L., Jokelainen, J., Jaervelin, M. R., Isohanni, M., & Raesaenen, P. (2001). The one-child family and violent criminality: A 31-year follow-up study of the Northern Finland 1966 birth cohort. *American Journal of Psychiatry, 158,* 960–962.

King, J. C. (2000). Determinants of maternal zinc status during pregnancy. *American Journal of Clinical Nutrition, 71,* 1334–1343.

Laakso, M. P., Vaurio, O., Koivisto, E., Savolainen, L., Eronen, M., Aronen, H. J., et al. (2001). Psychopathy and the posterior hippocampus. *Behavioural Brain Research, 118,* 187–193.

Lally, J. R., Mangione, P. L., & Honig, A. S. (1988). Long-range impact of an early intervention with low income children and their families. In D. R. Powell (Ed.), *Parent education as early childhood intervention* (pp. 79–104). Norwood, NJ: Ablex.

Laucht, M., Esser, G., Baving, L., Gerhold, M., Hoesch, I., Ihle, W., et al. (2000). Behavioral sequelae of perinatal insults and early family adversity at 8 years of age. *Journal of the American Academy of Child and Adolescent Psychiatry, 39,* 1229–1237.

Leon-Carrion, J., & Ramos, F. J. C. (2003). Blows to the head during development can predispose to violent criminal behaviour: Rehabilitation of consequences of head injury is a measure for crime prevention. *Brain Injury, 17,* 207–216.

Levin, E. D., Wilkerson A., Jones, J. P., Christopher, N. C., & Briggs, S. J. (1996). Prenatal nicotine effects on memory in rats: Pharmacological and behavioral challenges. *Developmental Brain Research, 97,* 207–215.

Lewis, D. O., Lovely, R., Yeager, C., & Della Femina, D. (1989). Toward a theory of the genesis of violence: A follow-up study of delinquents. *Journal of the American Academy of Child and Adolescent Psychiatry, 28,* 431–436.

Liu, J., Raine, A., Venables, P. H., & Mednick, S. A. (2004). Malnutrition at age 3 years and externalizing behavior problems at ages 8, 11, and 17 years. *American Journal of Psychiatry, 161,* 2005–2013.

Lombroso, C. (1895). *L'homme criminal.* Paris: F. Alcan.

Lorber, M. F. (2004). Psychophysiology of aggression, psychopathy, and conduct problems: A meta-analysis. *Psychological Bulletin, 130,* 531–552.

Mataro, M., Jurado, M. A., Garcia-Sanchez, C., Barraquer, L., Costa-Jussa, F. R., & Junque, C. (2001). Long-term effects of bilateral frontal brain lesion 60 years after injury with an iron bar. *Archives of Neurology, 58,* 1139–1142.

Max, J. E., Koele, S. L., Smith, W. L., Sato, Y., Lindgren, S. D., Robin, D. A., & Arndt, S. (1998). Psychiatric disorders in children and adolescents after severe traumatic brain injury: A controlled study. *Journal of the American Academy of Child and Adolescent Psychiatry, 37,* 832–840.

Mednick, S. A., & Kandel, E. S. (1988). Congenital determinants of violence. *Bulletin of the*

American Academy of Psychiatry & the Law, 16, 101–109.

Mittenberg, W., Wittner, M. S., & Miller, L. J. (1997). Postconcussion syndrome occurs in children. *Neuropsychology, 11*, 447–452.

Moffitt, T. E. (1990). Juvenile delinquency and attention deficit disorder: Boys' developmental trajectories from age 3 to age 15. *Child Development, 61*, 893–910.

Moffitt, T. E. (1993). Adolescence-limited and life-course-persistent antisocial behavior: A developmental taxonomy. *Psychological Review, 100*, 674–701.

Moffitt, T. E., & Caspi, A. (2001). Childhood predictors differentiate life-course persistent and adolescent limited pathways among males and females. *Development and Psychopathology, 13*, 355–375.

Neugebauer, R., Hoek, H. W., & Susser, E. (1999). Prenatal exposure to wartime famine and development of antisocial personality disorder in early adulthood. *Journal of the American Medical Association, 4*, 479–481.

Olds, D. (1997). Tobacco exposure and impaired development: A review of the evidence. *Mental Retardation and Developmental Disabilities Research Reviews, 3*, 257–269.

Olds, D., Henderson, C. R. J., Cole, R., Eckenrode, J., Kitzman, H., Luckey, D., et al. (1998). Long-term effects of nurse home visitation on children's criminal and antisocial behavior: 15-year follow-up of a randomized controlled trial. *Journal of the American Medical Association, 280*, 1238–1244.

Olson, H. C., Streissguth, A. P., Sampson, P. D., Barr, H. M., Bookstein, F. L., & Thiede, K. (1997). Association of prenatal alcohol exposure with behavioral and learning problems in early adolescence. *Journal of the American Academy of Child and Adolescent Psychiatry, 36*, 1187–1194.

Ortiz, J., & Raine, A. (2004). Heart rate level and antisocial behavior in children and adolescents: A meta-analysis. *Journal of the American Academy of Child and Adolescent Psychiatry, 43*, 154–162.

Oxford, M., Cavell, T. A., & Hughes, J. N. (2003). Callous/unemotional traits moderate the relation between ineffective parenting and child externalizing problems: A partial replication and extension. *Journal of Clinical Child and Adolescent Psychology, 32*, 577–585.

Pennington, B. F., & Bennetto, L. (1993). Main effects or transactions in the neuropsychology of conduct disorder? Commentary on the "The neuropsychology of conduct disorder."

Development and Psychopathology, 5, 153–164.

Pfeiffer, C. C., & Braverman, E. R. (1992). Zinc, the brain and behavior. *Biological Psychiatry, 17*, 513–532.

Pine, D. S., Shaffer, D., Schonfeld, I. S., & Davies, M. (1997). Minor physical anomalies: Modifiers of environmental risks for psychiatric impairment? *Journal of the American Academy of Child and Adolescent Psychiatry, 36*, 395–403.

Piquero, A., & Tibbetts, S. (1999). The impact of pre/perinatal disturbances and disadvantaged familial environment in predicting criminal offending. *Studies on Crime and Crime Prevention, 8*, 52–70.

Quadagno, D. (2003). Genes, brains, hormones, and violence interactions within complex environments. In A. Walsh & L. Ellis (Eds.), *Biosocial criminology: Challenging environmentalism's supremacy* (pp. 167–184). New York: Nova Science.

Rafter, N. (2004). Earnest A. Hooton and the biological tradition in American criminology. *Criminology, 42*, 735–772.

Raine A. (1993). *The psychopathology of crime: Criminal behavior as a clinical disorder.* San Diego: Academic Press.

Raine, A. (1996). Autonomic nervous system activity and violence. *Aggression and Violence: Genetic, Neurobiological, and Biosocial Perspectives*, 145–168.

Raine, A. (2002a). Annotation: The role of prefrontal deficits, low autonomic arousal, and early health factors in the development of antisocial and aggressive behavior in children. *Journal of Child Psychology and Psychiatry, 43*, 417–434.

Raine, A. (2002b). Biosocial studies of antisocial and violent behavior in children and adults: A review. *Journal of Abnormal Child Psychology, 30*, 311–326.

Raine, A., Brennan, P. A., Farrington, D. P., & Mednick, S. A. (Eds.). (1997). *Biosocial bases of violence.* New York: Plenum Press.

Raine, A., Brennan, P., & Mednick, S. A. (1994). Birth complications combined with early maternal rejection at age 1 year predispose to violent crime at age 18 years. *Archives of General Psychiatry, 51*, 984–988.

Raine, A., Brennan, P., & Mednick, S. A. (1997). Interaction between birth complications and early maternal rejection in predisposing individuals to adult violence: Specificity to serious, early-onset violence. *American Journal of Psychiatry, 154*, 1265–1271.

Raine, A., Brennan, P., Mednick, B., & Mednick, S. A. (1996). High rates of violence, crime, academic problems, and behavioral problems in males with both early neuromotor deficits and unstable family environments. *Archives of General Psychiatry, 53,* 544–549.

Raine, A., & Buchsbaum, M. S. (1996). Violence and brain imaging. In D. M. Stoff & R. B. Cairns (Eds.), *Neurobiological approaches to clinical aggression research* (pp. 195–218). Mahwah, NJ: Erlbaum.

Raine, A., Buchsbaum, M., & LaCasse, L. (1997). Brain abnormalities in murderers indicated by positron emission tomography. *Biological Psychiatry, 42,* 495–508.

Raine, A., Meloy, J. R., Bihrle, S., Stoddard, J., Lacasse, L., & Buchsbaum, M. S. (1998a). Reduced prefrontal and increased subcortical brain functioning assessed using positron emission tomography in predatory and affective murderers. *Behavioral Sciences and the Law, 16,* 319–332.

Raine, A., Park, S., Lencz, T., Bihrle, S., LaCasse, L., Widom, C. S., et al. (2001). Reduced right hemisphere activation in severely abused violent offenders during a working memory task: An fMRI study. *Aggressive Behavior, 27,* 111–129.

Raine, A., Reynolds, C., Venables, P. H., Mednick, S. A., & Farrington, D. P. (1998c). Fearlessness, stimulation-seeking, and large body size at age 3 years as early predispositions to childhood aggression at age 11 years. *Archives of General Psychiatry, 55,* 745–751.

Raine, A., Stoddard, J., Bihrle, S., & Buchsbaum, M. (1998b). Prefrontal glucose deficits in murderers lacking psychosocial deprivation. *Neuropsychiatry, Neuropsychology, and Behavioral Neurology, 11,* 1–7.

Raine, A., & Venables, P. H. (1981). Classical conditioning and socialization – a biosocial interaction. *Personality and Individual Differences, 2,* 273–283.

Raine, A., Venables, P. H., Dalais, C., Mellingen, K., Reynolds, C., & Mednick, S. A. (2001). Early educational and health enrichment at age 3–5 years is associated with increased autonomic and central nervous system arousal and orienting at age 11 years: Evidence from the Mauritius Child Health Project. *Psychophysiology, 38,* 254–266.

Raine, A., Venables, P. H., & Mednick, S. A. (1997). Low resting heart rate at age 3 years predisposes to aggression at age 11 years: Findings from the Mauritius Joint Child Health Project. *Journal of the American Academy of Child and Adolescent Psychiatry, 36,* 1457–1464.

Raine, A., Venables, P. H., & Williams, M. (1995). High autonomic arousal and electrodermal orienting at age 15 years as protective factors against criminal behavior at age 29 years. *American Journal of Psychiatry, 152,* 1595–1600.

Raine, A., Venables, P. H., & Williams, M. (1996). Better autonomic conditioning and faster electrodermal half-recovery time at age 15 years as possible protective factors against crime at age 29 years. *Developmental Psychology, 32,* 624–630.

Rantakallio, P., Laara, E., Isohanni, M., & Moilanen, I. (1992). Maternal smoking during pregnancy and delinquency of the offspring: An association without causation? *International Journal of Epidemiology, 21,* 1106–1113.

Rasanen, P., Hakko, H., Isohanni, M., Hodgins, S., Jarvelin, M. R., & Tiihonen, J. (1999). Maternal smoking during pregnancy and risk of criminal behavior among adult male offspring in the northern Finland 1996 birth cohort. *American Journal of Psychiatry, 156,* 857–862.

Rebok, G. W., Hawkins, W. E., Krener, P., Mayer, L. S., & Kellam, S. G. (1996). The effect of concentration problems on the malleability of aggressive and shy behaviors in an epidemiologically-based preventive trial. *Journal of the American Academy of Child and Adolescent Psychiatry, 35,* 193–203.

Rothbart, M. K., & Ahadi, S. A. (1994). Temperament and the development of personality. *Journal of Abnormal Psychology, 103,* 55–66.

Rutter, M., Giller, H., & Hagell, A. (1998). *Antisocial behavior by young people.* Cambridge, UK: Cambridge University Press.

Sameroff, A. J. (1995). General systems theories and developmental psychopathology. In D. Cicchetti & D. J. Cohen (Eds.), *Developmental psychopathology. Vol. 1: Theory and methods* (pp. 659–695). New York: Wiley.

Sanson, A., Smart, D., Prior, M., & Oberklaid, F. (1993). Precursors of hyperactivity and aggression. *Journal of the American Academy of Child and Adolescent Psychiatry, 32,* 1207–1216.

Scarpa, A., & Ollendick, T. H. (2003). Community violence exposure in a young adult sample: III. Psychophysiology and victimization interact to affect risk for aggression. *Journal of Community Psychology, 31,* 321–338.

Scarpa, A., & Raine, A. (1997). Biology of wickedness. *Psychiatric Annals, 27*, 624–629.

Scarpa, A., & Raine, A. (2003). The psychophysiology of antisocial behavior: Interactions with environmental experiences. In A. Walsh & L. Ellis (Eds.), *Biosocial criminology: Challenging environmentalism's supremacy* (pp. 209–226). New York: Nova Science.

Scarpa, A., & Raine, A. (2004). The psychophysiology of child misconduct. *Pediatric Annals, 33*, 296–304.

Scarpa, A., Tanaka, A., & Haden, S. C. (2006). *Biosocial bases of reactive and proactive aggression: The roles of community violence exposure and heart rate.* Manuscript submitted for publication.

Silver, J. M., & Yudofsky, S. C. (1987). Aggressive behavior in patients with neuropsychiatric disorders. *Psychiatric Annals, 17*, 367–370.

Slotkin, T. A., Epps T. A., Stenger, M. L., Sawyer, K. J., & Seidler, F. J. (1999). Cholinergic receptors in heart and brainstem of rats exposed to nicotine during development: Implications for hypoxia tolerance and perinatal mortality. *Brain Research, 113*, 1–12.

Streissguth, A. P., Barr, H. H., Bookstein, F. L., Sampson, P. D., & Olson, H. C. (1999). The long-term neurocognitive consequences of prenatal alcohol exposure: A 14-year study. *Psychological Science, 10*, 186–190.

Streissguth, A. P., Barr, H. H., Kogan, J., & Bookstein, F. L. (1996). *Understanding the occurrence of secondary disabilities in clients with Fetal Alcohol Syndrome (FAS) and Fetal Alcohol Effects (FAE).* Seattle: Washington Publication Services.

Thomas, A., & Chess, S. (1977). *Temperament and development.* New York: Bruner/Mazel.

Tikal, K., Benesova, O., & Frankova, S. (1976). The effect of pyrithioxine and pyridoxine on individual behavior, social interactions, and learning in rats malnourished in early postnatal life. *Psychopharmacologia, 46*, 325–332.

Volavka, J. (1995). *Neurobiology of violence.* Washington, DC: American Psychiatric Press.

Walsh, A., & Ellis, L. (2003). *Biosocial criminology: Challenging environmentalism's supremacy.* New York: Nova Science.

Werbach, M. (1995). Nutritional influences on aggressive behavior. *Journal of Orthomolecular Medicine, 7*, 45–51.

Werner, E. E. (1987). Vulnerability and resiliency in children at risk for delinquency: A longitudinal study from birth to young adulthood. In J. D. Burchard & S. N. Burchard (Eds.), *Primary prevention of psychopathology* (pp. 16–43). Newbury Park, CA: Sage.

CHAPTER 8

Neurobiology of Impulsive Aggression:

Focus on Serotonin and the Orbitofrontal Cortex

Royce Lee and Emil F. Coccaro

Introduction

Behavioral aggression can be examined from political, social, psychological, and neurobiological perspectives. The evolutionary preservation of behavioral aggression over time and across phylogenies reflects its adaptive value in hostile natural and social environments and is one indication of the validity of a neurobiological perspective. In humans, when aggression is directed against other humans, without clear gain and in a recurrent pattern, it is a clinical problem that has been described variously as impulsive, affective, or reactive aggression. Idiopathic impulsive aggression, exemplified by the DSM-IV diagnostic category, Intermittent Explosive Disorder (IED), is thought to affect between 5% and 7% of the population (Kessler et al., 2006). IED categorizes the extreme aspect of dimensionally measured impulsive aggression, also referred to as affective or reactive aggression, which does not have as a causative factor gross neurological lesion, substance intoxication, mood disorder, or psychotic disorder. Although current DSM-IV criteria do not permit,

in most cases, a simultaneous diagnosis of IED with borderline and antisocial personality disorder, revised research criteria as set forth by Coccaro and associates (Coccaro et al., 1998a) do permit the simultaneous diagnosis; the rationale for this is based on empirical studies demonstrating that aggression and anger are important facets of these personality disorders (Raine, 1993; Stevenson, Meares, & Comerford, 2003) and may represent the more commonly encountered clinical manifestations of impulsive aggression.

Impulsive aggression is a concatenation of individual behaviors from several different domains, including social information processing, emotion, and impulse control. Important characteristics of impulsive aggression include its dependence on a social provocation and the resulting intense affects of anger, shame, disgust, or fear; the importance of contextual social, emotional, and biological factors; and its impulsive, rather than instrumental, nature. In simple terms, this means that impulsive aggression occurs in response to a perceived social threat, is often marked by intensely negative emotions, and has negative consequences for the aggressor.

It is hypothesized that dysfunction of brain circuits mediating and regulating normal behavioral aggression is an underlying biological risk factor for IED. These circuits include the interconnected structures of the amygdala and orbitofrontal cortex (OFC), as well as associated prefrontal and limbic structures. Refinements in the last decade of the ability to study in vivo brain activity and biology, particularly limbic and prefrontal cortex function, have permitted a brain-based model of emotional behavior that incorporates data from the previous decade of investigations into the serotonergic, molecular biology of impulsive aggression. Given the phenomenological and biological complexity of impulsive aggression, other biological factors are sure to have importance. In this chapter, we review (a) the recently expanded understanding of the role of frontal-limbic circuits and serotonin function in normative anger and aggression; (b) evidence of serotonergic and prefrontal cortex abnormalities in impulsive aggression; and (c) evidence for the relevance of other neurobiological factors to impulsive aggression.

The Role of the Orbitofrontal Cortex in Emotion and Impulsivity

An understanding of the role of the orbitofrontal cortex (OFC) in normative emotional and impulsive behaviors provides a foundation for and understanding of its role in impulsive aggression. The OFC is mapped across the orbital surface of the frontal lobe. In humans its medial section stretches caudally from area 25, through area 10, to the frontal pole. Its lateral section stretches caudally from area 47/12 and includes areas 11 and parts of 10 (Petrides & Pandya, 1994). The OFC receives visual, gustatory, olfactory, auditory, and somatosensory information from primary and secondary association cortices (Rolls, 2004). It is extensively interconnected with the amygdala (Ongur & Price, 2000), which processes sensory information to create emotionally valenced,

or conditioned, object memories (Cahill, Babinsky, Markowitsch, & McGaugh, 1995), which are available to bias decision-making processes of the OFC (Bechara, Damasio, & Damasion, 2000). Much of the early work delineating the function of the OFC focused on relatively simple reinforcers, such as the olfactory or gustatory reinforcing qualities of food and how their reinforcement value is altered by motivational states, such as hunger. However, it is important to emphasize that contemporary, biologically based conceptions of emotion include both conventionally included "emotional" states, such as sadness and anger, and more basic motivational states, such as hunger and thirst.

Three processes which rely on intact OFC function, and which when dysregulated contribute to impulsive aggression, are emotion, social information processing, and impulsivity. These processes all involve the processing of representations of reward and punishment. In the case of emotion, these representations are of internal motivational states, such as the states of hunger or anger. In the case of social information processing, these are representations of the reinforcing or punishing attributes of social interactions. In the case of impulsivity, these are representations of time-delayed reinforcers and punishments, such as the cost and benefits of using a resource immediately versus saving it for more beneficial use in the future.

Both the medial and lateral sections of the OFC are relevant to aggression with preliminary evidence of abnormal medial and lateral OFC function during processing of angry face stimuli in adults with IED (Coccaro et al., 2000). The medial OFC is involved in the mental representation of object reward associations (reviewed in Elliott, Dolan, & Frith, 2000), particularly when they change or reverse over time, and for this function it is dependent on interconnections with the amygdala (Ongur & Price, 2000). As with other prefrontal cortex structures, so-called delay neurons of the OFC assume a working-memory-like task in the sustained representation of anticipated reward during a time delay between stimulus perception and a behavioral response (Hikosaka & Wanatabe,

2000). These medial OFC processes would be expected to be relevant to the processing of both emotional and social information (Iversen & Mishkin, 1970). Indeed, lesions of the medial OFC are associated with deficits in processing the reward value of stimuli and with disinhibited social behaviors (Damasio, 1994).

Evidence from human studies indicates that the role of the medial OFC (and related structures) in processing reward associations is relevant to complex mental representations, including the subjective experience of such emotions as sadness, anger, happiness, and fear (Damasio et al., 2000). Because anger is an emotional mental operation, it follows then that the medial OFC is involved in the processing of anger. Indeed, experimentally evoked anger has been found to result in metabolic activation of the medial OFC (Kimbrell et al., 1999). The OFC may play a regulating role in the outward expression of anger, as imagined unrestrained physical aggression against another human is associated with decreased medial OFC metabolic activity (Pietrini, Guazzelli, Basso, Jaffe, & Grafman, 2000). These findings are consistent with reports of the effect of OFC lesions on increased behavioral aggression (Grafman et al., 1996, Zald & Kim, 1996). The medial OFC thus may play a role in the regulation of emotional states, such as anger, subject experience of anger, control of behavioral aggression, evaluation of the social milieu, and cognitive impulsivity.

The best understood functions of the lateral OFC are reversal learning and response inhibition. Although some studies have found results suggesting that the lateral OFC is involved in processing of emotion-valence specific stimuli, such as negative versus positive emotions (Northoff et al., 2000), anger induction (Doughtery et al., 1999), and angry faces (Blair, Morris, Frith, Perret, & Dolan, 1999), the apparent valence specificity of these stimuli may be due to invocation of a reversal learning and response inhibition functions. For example, angry faces may signal the punishment value of continuing a provocative behavior, but so may other

facial expressions, as evidenced by a recent fMRI study using a visual reversal learning task (Kringelbach & Rolls, 2003). In addition to a role in processing emotionally salient stimuli, the lateral OFC also plays a role in the cortical inhibition of motoric impulsivity, which may serve to suppress impulsive aggressive behavior in response to provocation (Bechara et al., 2000).

In summary, both the medial and lateral sections of the OFC play key roles in processing of anger and behavioral impulsivity.

Serotonergic Function in the Prefrontal-Limbic "Emotion" Circuit

Serotonin, or 5-hydroxytryptamine (5-HT), is a neurotransmitter that regulates the flow of information processing in pyramidal inhibitory interneurons of prefrontal (i.e., OFC) cortex. This fact establishes the biological plausibility of 5-HT dysfunction as a risk factor for impulsive aggression. Serotonergic neurons in the prefrontal cortex arise from the rostral 5-HT system, whose cell bodies in the midbrain and rostral pons ascend to the forebrain (Pineyro & Blier, 1999). In the prefrontal cortex, the majority of neurons, even nonserotonergic neurons, contain 5-HT receptors. 5-HT$_{1A}$ and 5-HT$_{2A}$ receptor mRNA is found in approximately 60% of prefrontal cortical cells, including pyramidal cell neurons. Although the two receptor subtypes are highly co-localized (Amargòs-Bosch et al., 2004), 5-HT$_{1}$A receptors are predominantly inhibitory whereas 5-HT$_{2A}$ receptors are predominantly excitatory. Activation of 5-HT$_{2A}$ receptors has been found to increase the frequency of pyramidal cell excitatory postsynaptic potentials, whereas activation of 5-HT$_{1A}$ receptors leads to hyperpolarization. Thus these two receptors exert opposing influences on the transmission of neural information in the prefrontal cortex (Marek & Aghajanian, 1997). 5-HT$_{2A}$ receptors are also found in GABAergic interneurons, which are extensively networked in the prefrontal cortex. By inhibiting other pyramidal cell neurons, these GABAergic interneurons play an important role in focusing neuronal activity and permitting the efficient and effective transmission of information (Jakab & Goldman-Rakic, 1998).

Disruptions of 5-HT spare some prefrontal cortex functions, such as working memory and attention, while leading to selective impairments in OFC-related functions, such as preference for immediate versus time-delayed reinforcers (a behavioral analogue of impulsivity; Mobini, Chiang, Ho, Bradshaw, & Szabadi, 2000), and reward-reversal learning (Clarke, Dalley, Crofts, Robbins, & Roberts, 2004; Clarke, Walker, Dalley, Robbins, & Roberts, 2005). Perhaps because of altered OFC function, emotion processing in humans is also altered by serotonergic manipulations. Depletion of the molecular precursor to serotonin, tryptophan, which causes a precipitous fall in brain serotonin availability, leads to enhanced amygdala activation to fearful face stimuli in subjects with higher levels of anxiety (Cools et al., 2005), enhanced recognition of fearful faces in healthy controls (Harmer, Rogers, Tunbridge, Cowen, & Goodwin, 2003), and greater negative mood induction following a stressor (Richell, Deakin, & Anderson, 2005). Tryptophan depletion results in decreased OFC activation during a task of behavioral inhibition, providing functional evidence for the role of serotonin in allowing the OFC to respond metabolically to task demands (Rubia et al., 2005). These alterations in emotion processing and behavioral inhibition could explain the ability of tryptophan depletion to increase behavioral aggression in response to simulated social provocations (Bjork, Dougherty, Moeller, & Swann, 2000; Bond, Windgrove, & Critchlow, 2001; Cleare & Bond, 1995, Marsh, Dougherty, Moeller, & Swann, 2002).

Developmental Considerations

The ontogeny of 5-HT and OFC function is not completely understood. Although traumatic lesions of the OFC with associated changes in personality have been described, less extreme variation in OFC and/or 5-HT system integrity may be caused by more common developmental factors, such as early maternal separation in primates (Bennett et al., 2002; Poeggel, Nowicki, & Braun, 2003) and early-life parental neglect and environmental deprivation in humans (Chugani et al., 2001; Goodman, New, & Siever, 2004). Genetic polymorphisms of the 5-HT transporter molecule, although not necessarily pathogenic, alter the rate of 5-HT transport out of the neuronal synapse. The less active form of the transporter is associated with greater activation of the amygdala to aversive images (Hairi et al., 2005) and greater coupling of the amygdala and OFC (Heinz et al., 2005). How transporter variations interact with other risk factors to lead to pathological states is unknown. In the next decade, it is likely that our understanding of the genetic and environmental determinants of 5-HT and OFC function will expand greatly to provide a mechanistic understanding of their role in the development of prefrontal and limbic cortical function.

5-HT and Impulsive Aggression

Cross-sectional, human data linking serotonin to aggression were first published by Brown et al. (1979, 1982), who found that levels of the cerebrospinal fluid (CSF) metabolite of 5-HT, 5-hydroxyindoleacetic acid, were inversely related to life history of aggression in personality-disordered Navy recruits. Impulsive aggression (Virkkunen et al., 1987, 1989, 1994), but not premeditated aggression (Linnoila et al., 1983), has been linked to low levels of CSF 5-HIAA. Failure to replicate these results (Castellanos et al., 1994; Coccaro et al., 1997c) Gardner, Lucas, & Cowdry, 1990; Gardner et al., 1990; Moller et al., 1996), questions about their validity (Balaban, Alpor, & Kasamon, 1996), and uncertainty about the degree to which CSF 5-HIAA reflects neural 5-HT activity led to the exploration of alternative measures of brain 5-HT function.

When 5-HT is measured intracellularly in awake, aggressing mice, 15% decreases in prefrontal, cortical, extracellular 5-HT levels are found (Van Erp & Miczek, 2000), suggesting that regionally and temporally specific alterations in 5-HT function may facilitate aggression. In humans, such invasive studies are not possible for ethical and safety reasons. Administration of serotonergic challenge agents, such as d-fenfluramine, and measurement of their impact on peripheral neurohormone secretion, have been used to study 5-HT receptor function in impulsive aggressive and nonaggressive humans. Fenfluramine administration leads to relase of newly formed 5-HT into the synapse, stimulation of hypothalamic 5-HT receptors, stimulation of a prolactin-releasing factor (Coccaro, Klar, & Siever, 1994), and release of peripheral prolactin (Quattrone et al., 1983). Although several 5-HT receptor subtypes may mediate the release of prolactin by d-fenfluramine, experimental studies indicate that 5-HT_{2A} and/or 5-HT_{2C} receptors are likely to be involved (Albinsson, Palazidou, Stephenson, & Andersson, 1994; Coccaro et al., 1996, 1997; Park & Cowen, 1995). The first such study by Coccaro and colleagues (Coccaro et al., 1989) found that in patients diagnosed either with a personality disorder or affective disorder, prolactin response to d l-fenfluramine was inversely correlated with the lifetime history of impulsive aggression. These results have been replicated in personality disorder (New et al., 1997; Siever & Trestman 1983; Stein, Trestman, & Mitropoulou, 1996), violent offenders (O'Keane et al., 1992), and depressed subjects with anger attacks (Fava et al., 2000) and with primates (Botchin, Kaplan, Manuck, & Mann, 1993). Further neuropsychopharmacological work has probed the stereoselectivity of the fenfluramine/prolactin finding in impulsive aggression using the more stereoselective enantionmer of d-fenfluramine (Coccaro et al., 1996a; Park & Cowen, 1995) and the 5-HT_{1A} and 5-HT_{2C} agonist m-CPP (Coccaro et al., 1997a; Handlesman et al., 1996; Moss, Yao, & Panzak, 1990). Failure to replicate these findings have been reported in substance abusers (Bernstein & Handlesman, 1995; Fishbein, Lozofsky, & Jaffe,

1989) and children (Halperin et al., 1997; Pine et al., 1997; Stoff et al., 1992), perhaps due to specific sample characteristics, such as effects of past psychoactive drugs or developmental discontinuities in 5-HT function. Blunted 5-HT receptor sensitivity has also been found to be related to aggressive behavior in human volunteers behaving aggressively in the laboratory using the Taylor and Point-Subtraction Aggression paradigms, which simulate social antagonistic encounters (Moller et al., 1996; Quattrone et al., 1983; Strous, Bark, Parsia, Volavka, & Lachman, 1997). This finding provides cross-validation of the association of 5-HT receptor subsensitivity with aggression, even in relatively healthy subject samples.

Because of homology between the DNA sequence of the platelet and the brain 5-HT_{2A} receptor, platelet 5-HT function has been investigated as a peripheral biomarker of trait impulsive aggression. Inverse relationships have been found between impulsive aggressive behavior and 5-HT_{2A} receptor binding (Coccaro et al., 1997; Stoff 1987), platelet serotonin content (Goveas et al., 2004), and 5-HT-stimulated ionic calcium release (Reist, Vu, Coccaro, & Fujimoto, 2000).

5-HT Function in Prefrontal and Limbic Cortex Represents a Pathophysiological Mechanism of Impulsive Aggression

Recent work using in vivo neuroimaging techniques have localized 5-HT dysfunction to brain regions relevant to aggressive behavior, validating the work using peripheral neuroendocrine measures of 5-HT function. Because 5-HT is synthesized in the brain, reduced brain synthesis could theoretically alter brain 5-HT activity and hence lead to impulsive or impulsive aggressive behavior. Leyton and others (2001), using a PET radioligand for the 5-HT precursor tryptophan, found reduced 5-HT synthesis in corticostriatal pathways to be inversely correlated with impulsivity in a sample of borderline personality disorder subjects.

5-HT receptor function in the brain can be examined using pharmacological challenge techniques in combination with neuroimaging. Fenfluramine administration, in addition to causing a peripheral release of prolactin, has been found to result in activation of prefrontal cortex, probably via agnostic effects on the 5-HT receptor (Mann et al., 1996). Siever and colleagues (1999) found that impulsive aggressive personality disorder subjects have blunted cortical metabolic response to fenfluramine challenge in orbitofrontal, adjacent medial frontal, and cingulate cortex, as measured by PET. Soloff and co-workers (2000) found comparable findings using a similar paradigm. Using the 5-HT2 receptor agonist m-CPP, New and colleagues (2002) found blunted prefrontal cortex activation in impulsive aggressive personality disorder subjects (2002). Evidence has also been found for an inverse relationship between orbitofrontal cortex 5-HT1A receptor binding and impulsive aggression, as measured using PET imaging of the radioactive 5-HT1A agonist, [c-11]WAY-100635 (Parsey et al., 2002). These pharmacological/neuroimaging studies have provided as direct evidence as is possible, given current technological limitations, of in vivo relationships between prefrontal cortex 5-HT function and impulsive aggression. Given the role of the prefrontal cortex in regulating amygdala activity, it is of interest that a recent fMRI study has found that patients with IED compared to healthy controls exhibited greater left amygdala and OFC activation in response to faces displaying social threat (fearful, angry, and disgusted; Coccaro, McCloskey, Fitzgerald, & Phan, 2005).

Genetic polymorphisms affecting serotonergic function have been linked to aggression (for a recent review, see Noblett & Coccaro, 2005). Not surprisingly, subtypes of aggressive behavior may have separate genetic determinants (Hennig et al., 2005). Further work in this area will be needed to understand how polymorphisms of serotonin-related molecules, in combination with environmental risk factors, affect the risk of impulsive aggression.

Augmenting Serotonergic Function Alters Frontal-Limbic Brain Metabolism and Decreases Impulsive Aggression

Increasing brain 5-HT function by administration of 5-HT-augmenting pharmacological agents has been investigated as a therapeutic intervention for impulsive aggression. In support of this concept, chronic administration of the serotonin precursor molecule, tryptophan, has been found to decrease aggressive behavior in healthy controls (Moskowitz et al., 2003). Interfering with the degradation of synaptic 5-HT by blockade of its transport protein (5-HT transporter) with selective serotonergic reuptake inhibitors (SSRI) has been a mainstay of depression treatment for the past two decades. The mechanism of action is complex, but it is known that chronic SSRI administration leads to OFC 5-HT terminal autoreceptor desensitization in the rat, which would permit an increase in OFC 5-HT activity (Mansari, Bouchard, & Blier, 1995). In humans, administration of a norepinephrine and serotonin transporter inhibitor reduces identifications of angry and fearful facial expressions, as well as negative-emotion-modulated acoustic startle, providing a plausible physiological mechanism for the efficacy of norepinephrine and serotonin reuptake blockers in emotion-related psychopathololgy (Harmer, Shelley, Cowen, & Goodwin, 2004). Further fMRI studies of the effect of selective serotonergic agents on the neural circuitry of emotion processing are warranted.

Randomized, double-blind, placebo-controlled trials of SSRIs for the treatment of impulsive aggression in personality disordered subjects have been conducted, validating the role of serotonergic augmentation for clinical treatment of trait aggression. Coccaro and others (1997) found that fluoxetine was significantly more effective than placebo in reducing verbal aggression. The effective dose appeared to be higher, and the time needed to separate from placebo appeared to be longer, in comparison to treatment studies of major depressive disorder, suggesting parallels between the treatment of aggression and treatment of anxiety. Rates of physical aggression were not high enough to detect differences between fluoxetine treatment and placebo. Analysis of the results of this trial suggested that more severely aggressive subjects, who were also more likely to have blunted 5-HT receptor sensitivity to d-fenfluramine, were less likely to improve with fluoxetine treatment (Lee & Coccaro, 2003). Unpublished analysis of a larger group of randomized subjects replicated the finding of fluoxetine's superiority over placebo in reducing impulsive aggression, but did not replicate the interaction of severity and improvement. Double-blind, placebo-controlled studies of fluoxetine have demonstrated efficacy in the treatment of impulsive aggression in other patient groups, including depressives with anger attacks (Fava et al., 1993) and adults with autism (McDougle et al., 1996), although it is unknown whether similar mechanisms of action are occurring across the three subject groups. A randomized, placebo-controlled study of fluvoxamine for the treatment of affective and impulsive symptoms in females with borderline personality disorder did not find that it was superior to placebo in reducing impulsive aggression (Rinne et al., 2002), although the too-short, 6-week duration of the trial precludes conclusions about the efficacy of fluvoxamine, given prior evidence that improvement in impulsive aggression may take longer than 8 weeks to separate from placebo (Lee & Coccaro, 2003).

New and colleagues (2004), in an innovative PET-imaging/treatment study, probed the serotonergic, brain-mediated mechanism of SSRI treatment of impulsive aggression, using pre- and post-treatment PET assessments of brain metabolic activity. In a group of 10 borderline personality disorder subjects with histories of impulsive aggression, treatment with fluoxetine resulted in an increase in OFC metabolism as measured by PET imaging (New et al., 2004). Improvement in aggression was correlated with an increase in OFC and anterior cingulate metabolic activity, suggesting that the therapeutic effect of SSRI treatment on impulsive aggression is mediated by increased OFC function. Consistent with this finding, treatment of borderline personality disorder patients with olanzapine, which antagonizes at the 5-HT2A receptor in the prefrontal cortex, has been found to reduce impulsive aggression more than placebo (Zanarini, Frankenburg, & Parachini, 2004).

In summary, preclinical and clinical studies have found important links between brain 5-HT function and impulsive aggressive behavior. These links are compatible with our understanding of the brain-mediated, frontal-limbic modulation of aggression. This modulation maximizes the likelihood that behavioral aggression occurs in response to provocation in a context-appropriate, advantageous way. Dysfunction of 5-HT may lead to frontal-limbic failure to restrain behavioral aggression in response to provocation, leading to poor social function or even injury and death. Understanding this mechanism has provided the basis for a pharmacological treatment for aggression that is superior to placebo.

Other Neurobiological Factors

Although this review has focused on the relevance of the 5-HT function in the OFC to impulsive aggression, the OFC is networked with other frontal-limbic brain structures with known roles in emotion processing, such as the insula, amygdala, hypothalamus, bed nucleus of the stria terminalis, and cingulate cortex. Dysfunction in these structures would also be expected to affect impulsive aggressive behavior, and the extent of their contribution to both pathological and normal aggression is under investigation. Neurobiological factors other than 5-HT also play important roles in aggressive behavior. Some of these factors are briefly reviewed below.

Catecholamines

Catecholamine neurotransmitters, which include epinephrine, norepinephrine, and dopamine, are formed from the precursor molecules, phenylalanine and tyrosine. They play both inhibitory and excitatory roles in the brain. Some preliminary human data support a relationship between genetic variations in catecholamine metabolism and aggression (Volavka, Bilder, & Nolan, 2004). Although catecholaminergic function is undoubtedly involved in all of the behavioral processes relevant to impulsive aggression (emotion, social information processing, and impulsivity), a fully developed, mechanistic understanding is not yet available.

Norepinephrine (NE) function, as measured by assay of CSF metabolite levels, has been inconsistently linked with impulsive aggression (Virkkunen et al., 1987, 1994). A single study has found that plasma concentrations of the NE metabolite, 3-methoxy-5-hydroxyphenylglycol (MHPG), are inversely correlated with a lifetime history of aggression (Coccaro, Lee, & McCloskey, 2003). Postsynaptic receptor function, as measured by growth hormone response to the alpha-2-agonist clonidine, was positively correlated with self-reported irritability (Coccaro et al., 1991), which would be consistent with norepinephrine's role in activation of the fight/flight response.

Limited data support dopaminergic mechanisms in aggressive behavior. The role of dopamine in borderline personality disorder has been recently reviewed by Friedel (2004). Studies to date have found that aggression is associated with both reduced and increased indices of dopamine function, as assessed by CSF dopamine metabolite levels (homovanillic acid [HVA]; Linnoila et al., 1983), and SPECT imaging of striatal dopamine transporter density (Kuikka et al., 1998). Although the nonspecific behavioral effects of blocking dopaminergic function with dopamine receptor antagonists limit the usefulness of neuroleptic treatments for impulsive aggression (Miczek et al., 2004), newer dopaminergic antagonists may have useful therapeutic effects on impulsive aggression (Zanarini & Frankenburg, 2001; Zanarini et al., 2004), via either activity at different dopamine receptor subtypes or serotonin receptor blockade. The side effect profile of these agents, including diabetes and obesity, has not yet been adequately assessed in patients with known, severe problems with impulse control.

Testosterone

Testosterone facilitates aggression when administered to adults (Kouri, Lukas, Pope, & Olivia, 1995; Pope, Kouri, & Hudson, 2000), perhaps by increasing anger and hostility (O'Connor, Archer, & Wu, 2004). It may also play a role in the development of aggression (Sanchez et al., 2000). Several studies have found evidence of higher plasma/saliva testosterone levels in males with criminal aggression (Banks & Dabbs, 1996; Bergman & Brismar, 1994) and in volunteers with higher levels of behavioral aggression (Gerra et al., 1996, 1997). Further studies of testosterone are warranted.

Cholesterol/Fatty Acids

Low peripheral levels of cholesterol have been linked to aggression for more than three decades (Virkkunen, 1983). There has been some evidence that cholesterol-lowering drugs may increase deaths caused by violence, suicide, and accidents (Goier, Marzuk, Leon, Weiner, & Tardiff, 1993; Kunugi, Takei, Aoki, & Nanko, 1997; Maes et al., 1987; Muldoon et al., 1990, 1993; Neaton et al., 1992; Zureik, Courbon, & Ducimetiere, 1996), but these findings have not always been replicated, and a definitive neural mechanism has yet to be specified.

Decreased intake of omega-3 fatty acids has been linked to suicide and mood disorders. This mechanism is also not well understood but is biologically plausible given the role of fatty acids in constituting the neural lipid bilayer membrane. A recent double-blind, placebo-controlled study examining the efficacy of omega-3 fatty acids in the treatment of anger and depressive symptoms in borderline personality disorder found that omega-3 fatty acids were superior to placebo in leading to reductions in anger and depressive symptoms (Zanarini & Frankenburg, 2003). This interesting work is currently being retested in a different sample.

GABA

The inhibitory neurotransmitter GABA is found in approximately 40% of cortical neurons and is expressed heavily in frontal and limbic cortex. Although its role in behavior is not limited to the facilitation or control of aggression, it plays an important role in impulsivity, anger, and aggression (Bond, Curran, Bruce, O'Sullivan, & Shine, 1995; Coccaro et al., in preparation; Dimascio, 1973; Weisman, Berman, & Taylor, 1998). Because GABA acts on both inhibitory-inhibitory synapses and inhibitory-excitatory synapses, alteration of GABA activity may have both inhibitory or excitatory consequences. Biphasic effects on aggression have been documented with administration of benzodiazepines, which act as positive allosteric modulators of the GABA-A receptor, with higher doses appearing to inhibit (Itil & Seaman, 1978; Lion, Ascarate, & Koepke, 1975; Sheard, 1984) and lower doses increasing aggression and arousal (Bond et al., 1975; Dimascio, 1973; Weisman et al., 1998). Administration of benzodiazepines may lead to clinically significant increases in aggression in a subset of personality disordered patients with prior histories of behavioral dyscontrol (Cowdry & Gardner 1988). Alcohol, one substance consistently associated with violence and aggression, has similar biphasic effects on aggression in humans (Cherek, Spiga, & Egli, 1992). Among its actions on ligand-gated ion channels, alcohol, at low concentrations, is more specific for the GABA-A receptor complex (Grant, 1994; Grobin, Mathews, Devaud, & Morrow, 1998).

Neuropeptides

The neuropeptides, oxytocin and vasopressin, play important roles in the neurobiology of social interaction (for a recent review, see Winslow, 2005). Vasopressin receptors are found in the amygdala and bed nuclei stria terminalis (Fliers, Guldenaar, van de Wal, & Swaab, 1986; Loup, Tribollet, Dubois-Dauphin, & Dreifuss, 1991), whereas both oxytocin and vasopressin receptors are found in the brainstem and hypothalamus (Loup et al., 1991). Intranasal administration of vasopressin, with presumed CNS penetration, has been found to alter the physiological response to neutral emotional facial expression presentation, suggesting that frontal-limbic circuits processing emotional facial expression may be altered by vasopressin (Thompson, Gupta, Miller, Mills, & Orr, 2004). A previous study found that intranasal vasopressin administration causes an increase in CSF levels of vasopressin, providing evidence that intranasal application does penetrate the blood-brain barrier (Riekkinen et al., 1987). Consistent with a pathophysiological role for vasopressin in impulsive aggression, the CSF level of vasopressin correlates positively with life history of aggression in a sample of personality disordered subjects (Coccaro et al., 1998c). The interaction of neuropeptides with other neurobiological factors, such as serotonin, should also be investigated. It is known that 5-HT neurons can stimulate release of neuropeptides such as oxytocin (Lee & Coccaro, 2003) and that increased aggression as a result of mouse neuropeptide Y gene knockout can be abolished by serotonergic agonist administration (Karl et al., 2004).

Conclusion

Expanded knowledge of the role of 5-HT receptors in prefrontal cortical neural circuit has permitted a more mechanistic understanding of the neurobiology of impulsive aggression. It is hypothesized that genetic or environmental influences on 5-HT function lead to altered neural development and altered frontal-limbic emotional and social information processing in the context of increased behavioral impulsivity. In response to provocation, impulsive aggressive individuals are less able to regulate their emotional reaction and their behavioral response because of abnormal orbitofrontal cortex function. This hypothesized mechanism needs further testing, and how it interacts with other neurobiological factors needs to be probed. It is likely that over the next two decades, further information will come from genetic, preclinical, brain imaging, and clinical research studies. Neurobiological factors of heightened interest include neuropeptide hormones, the benzodiazepine/GABA receptor complex, serotonin-related genetic polymorphisms, and perhaps other relatively new areas of biological understanding, such as dosage-sensitive X-linked polymorphisms (Good et al., 2003).

Therapeutic interventions that increase 5-HT function in the brain are able to decrease impulsive aggression in most patients, given a treatment trial of adequate duration and high enough dosage. However, not all patients improve meaningfully, with some evidence suggesting that the more severe cases benefit the least. Therefore, although our understanding of the neurobiology of impulsive aggression has provided the rationale for a therapeutic intervention that has some efficacy, it is apparent that work remains on developing other treatments, perhaps with different neurobiological targets.

References

Albinsson, A., Palazidou, E., Stephenson, J., & Andersson, G. (1994). Involvement of the 5-HT-2 receptor in the 5-hT receptor mediated stimulation of prolactin release. *European Journal of Pharmacology, 251*, 61.

Amargós-Bosch, M., Bortolozzi, A., Puig, M. V., Serrats, J., Adell, A., Celada, P., et al. (2004). Co-expression and in vivo interaction of serotonin1A and serotonin 2A receptors in pyramidal neurons of prefrontal cortex. *Cerebral Cortex, 14*, 281–299.

Balaban, E., Alpor, J. S., & Kasamon, Y. L. (1996). Mean genes and the biology of aggression: A critical review of recent animal and human research. *Journal of Neurogenetics, 11*, 1–43.

Banks, T., & Dabbs, J. M. (1996). Salivary testosterone and cortisol in a delinquent and violent urban subculture. *Journal of Social Psychology, 136*, 49–56.

Bechara, A., Damasio, H., & Damasio, A. R. (2000). Emotion, decision making, and the orbitofrontal cortex. *Cerebral Cortex, 10*, 295–307.

Bechara, A., Damasio, H., Damasio, A. R., & Lee, G. P. (1999). Different contributions of the human amygdala and ventromedial prefrontal cortex to decision-making. *Journal of Neuroscience, 19*, 5473–5481.

Bennett, A. J., Lesch, K. P., Heils, A., Long, J. C., Lorenz, J. G., Shoaf, S. E., et al. (2002). Early experience and serotonin transporter gene variation interact to influence primate CNS function. *Molecular Psychiatry, 7*, 118–122.

Bergman, B., & Brismar, B. (1994). Characteristics of imprisoned wife-beaters. *Forensic Science International, 65*, 157–167.

Berman, M. E., Jones, G. D., & McCloskey, M. S. (2004). The effects of diazepam on human self-aggressive behavior. *Psychopharmacology, 10*, 1–14.

Bernstein, D. P., & Handlesman, L. (1995). The neurobiology of substance abuse and personality disorders. In J. J. Ratey (Ed.), *Neuropsychiatry of behavior disorders* (pp. 120–148). Cambridge, MA: Blackwell Scientific Publications.

Bjork, J. M., Dougherty, D. M., Moeller, F. G., & Swann, A. C. (2000). Differential behavioral effects of plasma tryptophan depletion and loading in aggressive and nonaggressive men. *Neuropsychopharmacology, 22*, 357–369.

Blair, R. J. R., Morris, J. S., Frith, C. D., Perret, D. I., & Dolan, R. J. (1999). Dissociable neural responses to facial expressions of sadness and anger. *Brain, 122*, 883–893.

Bond, A. J., Curran, H. V., Bruce, M. S., O'Sullivan, G., & Shine, P. (1995). Behavioral aggression in panic disorder after 8 weeks' treatment with alprazolam. *Journal of Affective Disorders, 35*, 17–23.

Bond, A. J., Windgrove, J., & Critchlow, D. G. (2001). Trytophan depletion increases aggression in women during the premenstrual phase. *Psychopharmacology, 156*, 477–480.

Botchin, M. B., Kaplan, J. R., Manuck, S. B., & Mann, J. J. (1993). Low versus high prolactin responders to fenfluramine challenge: Marker of behavioral differences in adult male cynomolgus macaques. *Neuropsychopharmacology, 9,* 93–99.

Brown, G. L., Goodwin, F. K., Ballenger, J. C., Goyer, P. F., & Major, L. F. (1979). Aggression in human correlates with cerebrospinal fluid amine metabolites. *Psychiatry Research, 1,* 131–139.

Brown, G. L., Ebert, M. H., Goyer, P. F., Jimerson, D. C., Klein, W. J., Bunney, W. E., et al. (1982). Aggression, suicide, and serotonin: Relationships to CSF amine metabolites. *American Journal of Psychiatry, 139,* 741–746.

Cahill, L., Babinsky, R., Markowitsch, H. J., & McGaugh, J. L. (1995). The amygdala and emotional memory. *Nature, 377,* 295–296.

Castellanos, F. X., Elia, J., Kruesi, M. J., Gulorta, C. S., Mefford, I. N., Potter, W. Z., et al. (1994). Cerebrospinal fluid monoamine metabolites in boys with attention-deficit hyperactivity disorder. *Psychiatry Research, 52,* 305–316.

Cherek, D. R., Spiga, R., & Egli, M. (1992). Effects of response requirement and alcohol on human aggressive responding. *Journal of Experimental and Analytic Behavior, 58,* 577–587.

Chugani, H. T., Behen, M. E., Muzik, O., Juha, C., Nagy, F., & Chugani, D. C. (2001). Local brain functional activity following early deprivation: A study of postinstitutionalized Romanian orphans. *Neuroimage, 14,* 1290–1301.

Clarke, H. F., Dalley, J. W., Crofts, H. S., Robbins, T. W., & Roberts, A. C. (2004). Cognitive inflexibility after prefrontal serotonin depletion. *Science, 304,* 878–880.

Clarke, H. F., Walker, S. C., Dalley, J. W., Robbins, T. W., & Roberts, A. C. (2005). Prefrontal serotonin depletion affects reversal learning but not attentional set shifting. *Journal of Neuroscience, 25,* 532–538.

Cleare, A. J., & Bond, A. J. (1995). The effect of tryptophan depletion and enhancement on subjective and behavioral aggression in normal male subjects. *Psychopharmacology, 118,* 72–81.

Coccaro, E. F., McCloskey, M. S., Fitzgerald, D. A., Phan, K. L. (in press). Amygdala orbitofrontal reactivity to social threat in individuals with impulsive aggression. *Biological Psychiatry.*

Coccaro, E. F. (2000). Intermittent explosive disorder. *Current Psychiatry Reports, 2,* 67–71.

Coccaro, E. F. (in preparation).

Coccaro, E. F., Berman, M. E., Kavoussi, R. J., & Hauger, R. L. (1996). Relationship of prolactin response to d-fenfluramine to behavioral and questionnaire assessments of aggression in personality-disordered men [see comments]. *Biological Psychiatry, 40,* 157–164.

Coccaro, E. F., Kavoussi, R. J., Berman, M. E., & Lish, J. D. (1998). Intermittent explosive disorder-revised: Development, reliability, and validity of research criteria. *Comprehensive Psychiatry, 39,* 368–376.

Coccaro, E. F., Kavoussi, R. J., Cooper, T. B., & Hauger, R. L. (1997). Central serotonin activity and aggression: Inverse relationship with prolactin response to d-fenfluramine, but not CSF 5-HIAA concentrations in human subjects. *American Journal of Psychiatry, 154,* 1430–1435.

Coccaro, E. F., Kavoussi, R. J., Cooper, T. B., & Hauger, R. (1998). Acute tryptophan depletion attenuates the prolactin response to d-fenfluramine challenge in healthy human subjects. *Psychopharmacology, 138,* 9–15.

Coccaro, E. F., Kavoussi, R. J., Hauger, R. L., Cooper, T. B., & Ferris, C. F. (1998). Cerebrospinal fluid vasopressin levels: Correlates with aggression and serotonin function in personality disordered subjects. *Archives of General Psychiatry, 55,* 708–714.

Coccaro, E. F., Kavoussi, R. J., Oakes, M., Cooper, T. B., & Hauger, R. (1996). 5-HT2a/2c receptor blockatde by amesergide fully attenuates prolactin response to d-fenfluramine challenge in physically healthy human subjects. *Psychopharmacology (Berl), 126,* 24–30.

Coccaro, E. F., Kavoussi, R. J., Sheline, Y. I., Berman, M. E., & Csernansky, J. G. (1997). Impulsive aggression in personality disorder correlates with platelet 5-hT2A receptor binding. *Neuropsychopharmacology, 16,* 211–216.

Coccaro, E. F., Kavoussi, R. J. (1997). Fluoxetine and impulsive aggressive behavior in personality-disordered subjects. *Arch Gen Psychiatry* 1997, 54: 1081–1088.

Coccaro, E. F., Kavoussi, R. J., Trestman, R. L., Gabriel, S. M., Cooper, T. B., & Siever, L. J. (1997). Serotonin function in human subjects: Intercorrelations among central 5-HT indices and aggressiveness. *Psychiatry Research, 73,* 1–14.

Coccaro, E. F., Klar, H., & Siever, L. J. (1994). Reduced prolactin response to fenfluramine challenge in personality disorder patients is not due to deficiency of pituitary lactotrophs. *Biological Psychiatry, 36*, 344–346.

Coccaro, E. F., Lawrence, T., Trestman, R., Gabriel, S., Klar, H. M., & Siever, L. (1991). Growth hormone responses to intravenous clonidine challenge correlates with behavioral irritability in psychiatric patients and in healthy volunteers. *Psychiatry Research, 39*, 129–139.

Coccaro, E. F., Lee, R., & McCloskey, M. (2003). Norepinephrine function in personality disorder: Plasma MHPG correlates with life history of aggression. *European Journal of Neuroscience, 23*(2), 552–560.

Coccaro, E. F., Lee, R., & Petty, F. (2005). *Cerebrospinal fluid GABA concentration: Relationship with impulsivity, but not aggression in human subjects.* Manuscript under review.

Coccaro, E. F., McCloskey, M. S., Fitzgerald, D. A., & Phan, K. L. (2005). *Cortico-limbic responses to harsh faces in patients with impulsive aggression.* Abstract presented at the American Psychiatric Association, Atlanta.

Coccaro, E. F., Schmidt, C. S., Samuels, J., & Nestadt, G. (2004). Lifetime and one-month prevalence rates of Intermittent Explosive Disorder in a community sample. *Journal of Clinical Psychiatry, 65*, 820–824.

Coccaro, E. F., Siever, L. J., Klar, H. M., Maurer, G., Cochrane, K., Cooper, T. B., et al. (1989). Serotonergic studies in patients with affective and personality disorders. Correlates with suicideal and impulsive aggressive behavior. *Archives of General Psychiatry, 46*, 587–599.

Cools, C., Calder, A. J., Lawrence, A. D., Clark, L., Bullmore, E., & Robbins, T. W. (2005). Individual differences in threat sensitivity predict serotonergic modulation of amygdala response to fearful faces. *Psychopharmacology (Berl), 180*(4), 670–679.

Cowdry, R. W., & Gardner, D. L. (1988). Pharmacotherapy of borderline personality disorder. Alprazolam, carbamazepine, trifluoperazine, and tranylcypromine. *Archives of General Psychiatry, 45*, 111–119.

Damasio, A. R. (1994). *Descartes' error.* New York: Putnam.

Damasio, A. R., Brabowski, T., Bechara, A., Damasio, H., Ponto, L. L. B., Parvazi, J., et al. (2000). Subcortical and cortical brain activity during the feeling of self-generated emotions. *Nature Neuroscience, 10*, 1049–1056.

Dimascio, A. (1973). The effects of benzodiazepines on aggression: Reduced or increased. *Psychopharmacologia, 30*, 95–102.

Dougherty, D. D., Shin, L. M., Alpert, N. M., Pitman, R. K., Orr, S. P., Lasko, M., Macklin, M. L., Fishman, A. J., Rauch, S. L. (1999). Anger in healthy men: A PET study using script-driven imagery. *Biol. Psychiatry* 1999; 46: 466–724.

Elliott, R., Dolan, R. J., & Frith, C. D. (2000). Dissociable functions in the medial and lateral orbitofrontal cortex: Evidence from human neuroimaging studies. *Cerebral Cortex, 10*, 308–317.

Fava, M., Rosenbaum, J. F., Pava, J. A., McCarthy, M. K., Steingard R. J., & Bouffides, E. (1993). Anger attacks in unipolar depression, part 1: Clinical correlates and response to fluoxetine treatment. *American Journal of Psychiatry, 150*, 1158–1163.

Fava, M., Vuolo, R. D., Wright, E. C., Nierenberg, A. A., Alpert, J. E., & Rosenbaum, J. F. (2000). Fenfluramine challenge in unipolar depression with and without anger attacks. *Psychiatry Research 94*, 9–18.

Fishbein, D. H., Lozovsky, D., & Jaffe, J. H. (1989). Impulsivity, aggression, and neuroendocrine responses to serotonergic stimulation in substance abusers. *Biological Psychiatry, 25*, 1049–1066.

Fliers, E., Guldenaar, S. E., van de Wal, N., & Swaab, D. F. (1986). Extrahypothalamic vasopressin and oxytocin in the human brain: Presence of vasopressin cells in the bed nucleus of the stria terminalis. *Brain Research, 375*, 363–367.

Frick et al. 1987.

Friedel, R. O. (2004). Dopamine dysfunction in borderline personality disorder: A hypothesis. *Neuropsychopharmacology, 29*, 1029–1039.

Gardner, D. L., Lucas, P. B., & Cowdry, R. W. (1990) SF metabolites in borderline personality disorder compared with normal controls. *Biological Psychiatry, 28*, 247–254.

Gerra, G., Avanzini, P., Zaimovic, A., Fertonani, G., Caccavari, R., Delsignore, R., et al. (1996). Neurotransmitter and endocrine modulation of aggressive behavior and its components in normal humans. *Behavioral Brain Research, 81*, 19–24.

Gerra, G., Zaimovic, A., Avanzini, P., Chittolini, B., Giucastro, G., Caccavari, R., et al. (1997). Neurotransmitter-neuroendocrine responses to experimentally induced aggression in humans: Influence of personality variable. *Psychiatry Research, 66*, 33–43.

Goier, J. A., Marzuk, P. M., Leon, A. C., Weiner, C., & Tardiff, K. (1993). Low serum cholesterol and attempted suicide. *American Journal of Psychiatry, 152,* 419–423.

Good, C. D., Lawrence, K., Thomas, N. S., Price, C. J., Ashburner, J., Friston, K. J., et al. (2003). Dosage sensitive X-linked locus influences the development of amygdala and orbitofrontal cortex, and fear recognition in humans. *Brain, 126* (Pt 11), 2431–2446.

Goodman, M., New, A., & Siever, L. (2004). Trauma, genes, and the neurobiology of personality disorders. *Annals of the New York Academy of Science, 1032,* 105–116.

Goveas, J. S., Csernansky, J.G,, & Coccaro, E. F. (2004). Platelet serotonin content correlates inversely with life history of aggression in personality-disordered subjects. *Psychiatry Research, 126,* 23–32.

Goyer, P. F., Andreason, P. J., Semple, W. E., Clayton, A. H., King, A. C., Compton-Toth, B. A., et al. (1994). Positron-emission tomography and personality disorders. *Neuropsychopharmacology, 10*(1), 21–28.

Grafman, J., Schwab, K., Warden, D., Pridgen, A., Brown, H. R., & Salazar, A. M. (1996). Frontal lobe injuries, violence, and aggression: A report of the Vietnam Head Injury Study. *Neurology, 46,* 1231–1238.

Grant, K. A. (1994). Mmerging neurochemical concepts in the actions of ethanol at ligand-gated ion channels. *Behavioral Pharmacology, 5,* 383–404.

Grobin, A. C., Mathews, D. B., Devaud, L. L., & Morrow, A. L. (1998). The role of GABAa receptors in the acute and chronic effects of ethanol. *Psychopharmacology, 139,* 2–19.

Halperin, J. M., Newcorn, J. H., Schwartz, S. T., Sharma, V., Siever, L. J., Koda, V. H., et al. (1997). Age-related changes in the association between serotonergic function and aggression in boys with ADHD. *Biological Psychiatry, 41,* 682–689.

Handlesman, L., Holoway, K., Kahn, R. S., Sturiano, C., Rinaldi, P. J., Bernstein, D. P., et al. (1996). Hostility is associated with a low prolactin response to meta-chlorophenylpiperazine in abstinent alcoholics. *Alcoholism: Clinical and Experimental Research, 5,* 824–829.

Hariri, A. R., Drabant, E. M., Munoz, K. E., Kolachana, B. S., Mattay, V. S., Egan, M.F, et al. (2005). A susceptibility gene for affective disorders and the response of the human amygdala. *Archives of General Psychiatry, 62,* 146–152.

Harmer, C. J., Rogers, R. D., Tunbridge, E., Cowen, P. G., & Goodwin, G. M. (2003). Tryptophan depletion decreases the recognition of fear in female volunteers. *Psychopharmacology, 167,* 411–417.

Harmer, C. J., Shelley, N. C., Cowen, P. J., & Goodwin, G. M. (2004). Increased positive versus negative affective perception and memory in healthy volunteers following selective serotonin and norepinephrine reuptake inhibition. *American Journal of Psychiatry, 161,* 1256–1263.

Heinz, A., Braus, D., Smolka, M. N., Wrase, J., Puls, I., Hermann, D., et al. (2005). Amygdala-prefrontal coupling depends on a genetic variation of the serotonin transporter. *Nature Neuroscience, 8,* 20–21.

Hennig, J., Reuter, M., Netter, P., Burk, C., & Landt, O. (2005). Two types of aggression are differentially related to serotonergic activity and the A779C TPH polymorphism. *Behavioral Neuroscience, 119,* 16–25.

Hikosaka, K., & Watanabe, M. (2000). Delay activity of orbital and lateral prefrontal neurons of the monkey varying with different rewards. *Cerebral Cortex, 10,* 263–271.

Huber, R. (2005). Amines and motivated behaviors: A simpler systems approach to complex behavioral phenomena. *Journal of Comparative Physiology A, 191,* 231–239.

Itil, T. M., & Seaman, P. (1978). Drug treatment of human aggression. *Progress in Neuropsychopharmacology, 2,* 659.

Iversen, S., & Mishkin, M. (1970). Perseverative interference in monkey following selective lesions of the inferior prefrontal convexity. *Experimental Brain Research, 11,* 376–386.

Jacobs, B. L., & Fornal, C. A. (1999). Activity of serotonergic neurons in behaving animals. *Neuropsychopharmacology, 21,* 9S.

Jakab, R. L., & Goldman-Rakic, P. S. (1998). 5-hydroxytryptamine (2A) serotonin receptors in the primate cerebral cortex: Possible site of action of hallucinogenic and antipsychotic drugs in pyramidal cell apical dendrites. *Proceedings of the National Academy of Sciences USA, 95,* 735–740.

Jolas, T., Haj-Dahmane, S., Kidd, E. J., Langlois, X., Lanfumery, L., & Fattaccini, C. M. (1994). Central pre- and post-syntaptic 5-HT1A receptors in rats treated chronically with a novel antidepressant, cericlamine. *Journal of Pharmacology and Experimental Therapeutics, 268,* 1432–1443.

Karl, T., Lin, S., Schwarzer, C., Sainsbury, A., Couzens, M., Wittman, W., et al. (2004).

Y1 receptors regulate aggressive behavior by modulating serotonin pathways. *Proceedings of the National Academy of Sciences USA, 101,* 12742–12747.

Kessler, R. C., Coccaro, E. F., Fava, M., Jaeger, S., Jin, R., & Walter, E. (2006). The prevalence and correlates of DSM-IV intermittent explosive disorder in the National Comorbidity Survey Replication. *Arch Gen Psychiatry, 63,* 669–678.

Kimbrell, T. A., George, M. S., Parekh, P. I., Ketter, T. A., Podell, D. M., Danielson, A. L., et al. (1999). Regional brain activity during transient self-induced anxiety and anger in healthy adults. *Biological Psychiatry, 46,* 454–465.

Kouri, E. M., Lukas, S. E., Pope, H. G., Jr., & Oliva, P. S. (1995). Increased aggressive responding in male volunteers following the administration of gradually increasing doses of testosterone cypionate. *Drug and Alcohol Dependence, 40,* 73–79.

Kringelbach, M. L., Rolls E.T (2003). Neural correlates of rapid reversal learning in a simple model of human social interaction. *Neuroimage,* 2003; 1371–1383.

Kuikka, J. T., Tiihonen, J., Bergstrom, K. A., Karhu, J., Rasanen, P., & Eronen, M. (1998). Abnormal structure of human striatal dopamine re-uptake sites in habitually violent alcoholic offenders: A fractal analysis. *Neuroscience Letters, 253,* 195–197.

Kunugi, H., Takei, N., Aoki, H., & Nanko, S. (1997). Low serum cholesterol in suicide attempters. *Biological Psychiatry, 41,* 196–200.

Lee, R. J., & Coccaro, E. F. (2003). Treatment of aggression: Serotonergic agents. In E. F. Coccaro (Ed.), *Aggression: Psychiatric assessment and treatment* (pp. 351–367). New York: Marcel Dekker.

Lee, R., Garcia, F., van de Kar, L. D., Hauger, R. D., & Coccaro, E. F. (2003). Plasma oxytocin in response to pharmaco-challenge to D-fenfluramine and placebo in healthy men. *Psychiatry Research, 118,* 129–136.

Leyton, M., Okazawa, H., Diksic, M., Paris, J., Rosa, P., Mzengeza, S., Young, S. N., Blier, P., Benkelfat, C. (2001). Brain regional alpha-[11C]methyl-L-tryptophan trapping in impulsive subjects with borderline personality disorder. *Am J Psychiatry,* 158: 774–82.

Linnoila, M., Virkkunen, M., Scheinin, M., Nuutila, A., Rimon, R., & Goodwin, F. K. (1983). Low cerebrospinal fluid 5-hydroxylndolacetic acid concentration differentiates impulsive from nonimpulsive violent behavior. *Life Sciences, 33,* 2609–2614.

Lion, J. R., Ascarate, C., & Koepke, H. (1975). Paradoxical rage reactions during psychotropic medication. *Diseases of the Nervous System, 36,* 557–558.

Loup, F., Tribollet, E., Dubois-Dauphin, M., & Dreifuss, J. J. (1991). Localization of high affinity binding sites for oxytocin and vasopressin in the human brain. An autoradiographic study. *Brain Research, 555,* 220–232.

Maes, M., Sharpe, P., D'Hondt, P., Peeters, D., Wauters, A., Neels, H., et al. (1996). Biochemical metabolic and immune correlates of seasonal variation in violent suicide: A chronoepidemiologic study. *European Psychiatry, 11,* 21–33.

Maes, M., Smith, R., Christophe, A., Vandoolaeghe, E., Van Gastel, A., Neels, H., et al. (1997). Lower serum high density lipoprotein cholesterol (HDL-C) in major depression and in depressed men with serious suicidal attempts: Relationship with immune-inflammatory markers. *Acta Psychiatrica Scandinavica, 95,* 212–221.

Mann, J., Malone, K., Diehl, D., Perel, J., Nichols, T. E., & Mintun, M. A. (1996). Positron emission tomographic imaging of serotonin activation effects on prefrontal cortex in healthy volunteers. *Journal of Cerebral Blood Flow and Metabolism, 16,* 418–426.

Mansari, M. E., Bouchard, C., & Blier, P. (1995). Alteration of serotonin release in the guinea pig orbito-frontal cortex by selective serotonin reuptake inhibitors. *Neuropsychopharmacology, 13,* 17–127.

Marek, G. J., & Aghajanian, G. K. (1997). Serotonin induces excitatory postsynaptic potentials in apical dendrites of neocortical pyramidal cells. *Neuropharmacology, 36,* 589–599.

Markovitz, J. H., Smith, D., Raczynski, J. M., Oberman, A., Williams, O. D., Knox, S., et al. (1997). Lack of relations of hostility, negative affect and high risk behavior with low plasma lipid levels in the Coronary Artery Risk Development in Young Adults Study. *Archives of Internal Medicine, 157,* 1953–1959,

Marsh, D. M., Dougherty, D. M., Moeller, G., Swann, A. C., & Spiga, R. (2002). Laboratory measured aggressive behavior of women: Acute tryptophan depletion and augmentation. *Neuropsychopharmacology, 26,* 660–671.

McDougle, C. J., Naylor, S. T., Cohen, D. J., Volkmar, F. R., Heninger, G. R., & Price, L. H. (1996). A double-blind, placebo-controlled study of fluvoxamine in adults with autistic disorder. *Archives of General Psychiatry, 53,* 1001–1008.

Miczek, K. A., Faccidomo, S., Almeida, R. M. M., Bannai, M., Fish, E. W., & DeBold, J. F. (2004). Escalated aggressive behavior: New pharmacotherapeutic approaches and opportunities. *Annals of the New York Academy of Sciences, 1036*, 336–355.

Mobini, S., Chiang, T. J., Ho, M. Y., Bradshaw, C. M., & Szabadi, E, (2000). Effects of central 5-hydroxytryptamine depletion on sensitivity to delayed and probabilistic reinforcement. *Psychopharmacology, 152*, 390–397.

Moller, S. E., Mortensen, E. L., Breum, L., Alling, C., Larsen, O. G., Boge-Rasmussen T., et al. (1996). Aggression and personality: Association with amino acids and monoamine metabolites. *Psychological Medicine, 26*, 323–331.

Moskowitz, D. S., Pinard, G., Zuroff, D. C., Annable, L., & Young, S. N. (2003). Tryptophan, serotonin and human social behavior. *Advances in Experimental Medicine and Biology, 527*, 215–224.

Moss, H. B., Yao, J. K., & Panzak, G. L. (1990). Serotonergic responsivity and behavioral dimensions in antisocial personality disorder with substance abuse. *Biological Psychiatry, 28*, 325–338.

Muldoon, M. F., Manuck, S. B., & Matthews, K. A. (1990). Lowering cholesterol concentration and mortality: A quantitative review of primary prevention trials. *British Medical Journal, 301*, 309–314.

Muldoon, M. F., Rossouw, J. E., Manuck, S. B., Glueck, C. J., Kaplan, J. R., & Kaufmann, P. G. (1993). Low or lowered cholesterol and risk of death from suicide and trauma. *Metabolism, 42*(Suppl. 1), 45–56.

Neaton, J. D., Blackburn, H., Jacobs, D., Kuller, L., Lee, D. J., Sherwin, R., et al. (1992). Serum cholesterol level and mortality findings for men screened in the Multiple Risk Factor Intervention Trial Research Group. *Archives of Internal Medicine, 152*, 1490–1500.

New, A. S., Buchsbaum, M. S., Hazlett, E. A., Goodman, M., Koenigsberg, H. W., Lo, J., et al. (2004). Fluoxetine increases relative metabolic rate in prefrontal cortex in impulsive aggression. *Psychopharmacology, 176*, 451–458.

New, A. S., Hazlett, E. A., Buchsbaum, M. S., Goodman, M., Reynolds, D., Mitropoulou, V., et al. (2002). Blunted prefrontal cortical 18 fluorodeoxyglucose positron emission tomography response to meta-chlorophenylpiperazine in impulsive aggression. *Archives of General Psychiatry, 59*, 621–629.

New, A. S., Trestman, R. L., Mitropoulou, V., Benishay, D. S., Coccaro, E., Silverman, J., et al. (1997). Serotonergic function and self-injurious behavior in personality disorder patients. *Psychiatry Research, 69*, 17–26.

Newmark, R., Brand, J., O'Flynn, K., & Siever, L. J. (2004). Fluoxetine increases relative metabolic rate in prefrontal cortex in impulsive aggression. *Psychopharmacology, 176*, 451–458.

Noblett, K. L., & Coccaro, E. F. (2005). Molecular genetics of personality. *Current Psychiatry Reports, 1*, 73–80.

Northoff, G., Richter, A., Gessner, M., Schlagenhauf, F., Fell, J., Baumgart, F., et al. (2000). Functional dissociation between medial and lateral prefrontal cortical spatiotemporal activation in negative and positive emotions: A combined fMRI/MEG study. *Cerebral Cortex, 10*, 93–107.

O'Connor, D. B., Archer, J., & Wu, F. C. (2004). Effects of testosterone on mood, aggression, and sexual behavior in young men: A double-blind, placebo-controlled, cross-over study. *Journal of Clinical Endocrinology and Metabolism, 89*, 2837–2845.

O'Keane, V., Loloney, E., O'Neil, H., O'Connor, A., Smith, C., & Dinam, T. B. (1992). Blunted prolactin responses to d-fenfluramine challenge in sociopathy: Evidence for subsensitivity of central serotonergic function., 643–646.

Ongur, D., & Price, J. L. (2000). The organization of networks within the orbital and medial prefrontal cortex of rats, monkeys, and humans. 206–219.

Oquendo, M. A., Krunic, A., Parsey, R. V., Milak, M., Malone, K. M., Anderson, A., et al. (2005). Positron emission tomography of regional brain metabolic responses to a serotonergic challenge in major depressive disorder with and without borderline personality disorder. *Neuropsychopharmacology, 30*(6), 1163–1172.

Parsey, R. V., Oquendo, M. A., Simpson, N. R., Ogden, R. T., Van Heertum, R., Arango, V., et al. (2002). Effects of sex, age, and aggressive traits in man on brain serotonin 5-HT$_{1A}$ receptor binding potential measured by PET using [C-11]WAY – 100635. *Brain Research, 954*, 173–182.

Park, S. B., & Cowen, P. J. (1995). Effect of pindolol on the prolactin response to d-fenfluramine. *Psychopharmacology (Berl), 118*, 471–474.

Petrides, M., & Pandya, D. N. (1994). Comparative architechtonic analysis of the human and macaque frontal cortex. In F. Boller & J.

Grafman (Eds.), *Handbook of neuropsychology* (Vol. 9, pp. 17–58). Amsterdam: Elsevier.

Pietrini, P., Guazzelli, M., Basso, G., Jaffe, K., & Grafman, J. (2000). Neural correlates of imaginal aggressive behavior assessed by positron emission tomography in healthy subjects. *American Journal of Psychiatry, 157,* 1772–1781.

Pine, D. S., Coplan, J. D., Wasserman, G. A., Miller, L. S., Fried, J. E., Davies, M., et al. (1997). Neuroendocrine response to fenfluramine challenge in boys. Associations with aggressive behavior and adverse rearing [see comments]. *Archives of General Psychiatry, 54,* 839–846.

Pineyro, G., & Blier, P. (1999). Autoregulation of serotonin neurons: Role in antidepressant drug action. *Pharmacological Reviews, 51,* 533–591.

Poeggel, G., Nowicki, L., & Braun, K. (2003). Early social deprivation alters monoaminergic afferents in the orbital prefrontal cortex of octodon degus. *Neuroscience, 116,* 617–620.

Pope, H. G., Jr., Kouri, E. M., & Hudson, J. I. (2000). Effects of supraphysiologic doses of testosterone on mood and aggression in normal men: A randomized controlled trial. *Archives of General Psychiatry, 57,* 133–140.

Posternak, M. A., & Zimmerman, M. (2002). Anger and aggression in psychiatric outpatients. *Journal of Clinical Psychiatry, 63,* 665–672.

Quattrone, A., Tedeschi, G., Aguglia, U., Scopacasa, F., Direnzo, G. F., & Annunziato, L. (1983). Prolactin secretion in man: A useful tool to evaluate the activity of drugs on central 5-hydroxytryptaminergic neurones. Studies with fenfluramine. *British Journal of Clinical Pharmacology, 16,* 471–475.

Raine, A. (1993). Features of borderline personality disorder and violence. *Journal of Clinical Psychology, 49,* 277–281.

Reist, C., Vu, R., Coccaro, E. F., & Fujimoto, K. (2000). Serotonin-stimulated calcium release is decreased in platelets from high impulsivity patients. *International Journal of Neuropsychopharmacology, 3,* 315–320.

Richell, R. A., Deakin, J. F. W., & Anderson, I. M. (2005). Effect of acute tryptophan depletion on the response to controllable and uncontrollable noise stress. *Biological Psychiatry, 57,* 295–300.

Riekkinen, P., Legros, J. J., Sennef, C., Jolkkonen, J., Smitz, S., & Soininen, H. (1987). Penetration of DGAVP (Org 5667) across the blood-brain barrier in human subjects. *Peptides, 8,* 261–265.

Rinne, T., van den Brink, W., Wouters, L., van Dyck, R. (2002). SSRI treatment of borderline personality disorder: A randomized, placebo-controlled.

Roberts, A. C., & Wallis, J. D. (2000). Inhibitory control and affective processing in the prefrontal cortex: Neuropsychological studies in the common marmoset. *Cerebral Cortex, 10,* 252–262.

Rolls, E. T. (2004). The functions of the orbitofrontal cortex. *Brain Cogn., 55:* 11–29

Rubia, K., Lee, F., Cleare, A. J., Tunstall, N., Fu, C. H. Y., Brammer, M., et al. (2005). Tryptophan depletion reduces right inferior prefrontal activation during response inhibition in fast, event-related fMRI. *Psychopharmacology (Berl), 179*(4), 791–803.

Sanchez, J. R., Martin, E., Fano, L., Ahedo, J., Cardas, J., Brain, P. F., et al. (2000). Rating testosterone levels and free play social behavior in male and female preschool children. *Psychoendocrinology, 8,* 773–783.

Sheard, M. H. (1984). Clinical pharmacology of aggressive behavior. *Clinical Neuropharmacology, 7,* 173–183.

Siever, L. J., Buchsbaum, M.S,. New, A. S., Hazlett, E. A., Grossman, R., & Reynolds, D. (2000). Serotonergic responsiveness in impulsive/aggressive personality disorders. *Biological Psychiatry, 47,* 1S–173S.

Siever, L. J., Buchsbaum, M. S., New, A. S., Spiegel-Cohen, J., Wei, T., Hazlett, E. A., et al. (1999). d,l-Fenfluramine response in impulsive personality disorder assessed with [18F]fluorodeoxyglucose positron emission tomography. *Neuropsychopharmacology, 20,* 413–423.

Siever, L. J., & Trestman, R. L. (1998). The serotonin system and aggressive personality disorder. *International Clinical Psychopharmacology, 8,* 33–39.

Soloff, P. H., Meltzer, C. C., Greer, P. J., Constantine, D., & Kelly, T. M. (2000). A fenfluramine-activated FDG-PET study of borderline personality disorder. *Biological Psychiatry, 47,* 540–547.

Stanford, M. S., Helfritz, L. E., Villemarette-Pittman, N. R., Greve, K. W., Adams, D., & Houston, R. J. (2005). A comparison of anticonvulsants in the treatment of impulsive aggression. *Experimental and Clinical Psychopharmacology, 13,* 72–77.

Stein, D., Trestman, R. L., & Mitropoulou, V. (1996). Impulsivity and serontonergic vunction in obsessive compulsive personality disorder. *Journal of Neuropsychiatry and Clinical Neuroscience, 8,* 393–398.

Stevenson. J., Meares, R., & Comerford, A. (2003). Diminished impulsivity in older patients with borderline personality disorder. *American Journal of Psychiatry, 160,* 165–166.

Stoff, D. M., Pollock, L., Vitiello, B., Behar, D., Bridger, W. H. (1987). Reduction of (3H) imipramine binding in blood platelets of conduct-disordered children. Neuropsychopharmacology 1: 55–62

Stoff, D. M., Pastiempo, A. P., Yeung, J. H., Cooper, T. B., Bridger, W. H., & Rabinovich, H. (1992). Neuroendocrine responses to challenge with d,1-fenfluramine and aggression in disruptive behavior disorders of children and adolescents. *Psychiatry Research, 43,* 263–276.

Strous, R. D., Bark, N., Parsia, S. S., Volavka, J., & Lachman, H. M. (1997). Analysis of a functional catechol-O-methyltransferase gene polymorphism in schizophrenia: Evidence for association with aggressive and antisocial behavior. *Psychiatry Research, 69,* 71–77.

Thompson, R., Gupta, S., Miller, K., Mills, S., & Orr, S. (2004). The effects of vasopressin on human facial responses related to social communication. *Psychoneuroendocrinology, 29,* 35–48.

Van Der Vegt, B. J., Lieuwes, N., & Cremers, T. I. F. H. (2003). Cerebrospinal fluid monoamines and metabolite concentrations and aggression in rats. *Hormones and Behavior, 44,* 199–208.

Van Erp, A. M. M., & Miczek, K. A. (2000). Aggressive behavior, increased accumbal dopamine and decreased cortical serotonin in rats. *Journal of Neuroscience, 15,* 9320–9325.

Virkkunen. M. (1983). Serum cholesterol in levels in homicidal offenders. A low cholesterol level is connected with a habitually violent tendency under the influence of alcohol. *Neuropsychobiology, 10,* 65–69.

Virkkunen, M., DeJong, J., Bartko, J., Goodwin, F. K., & Linnoila, M. (1989). Relationship of psychobiological variables to recidivism in violent offenders and impulsive fire setters. *Archives of General Psychiatry, 46,* 600–603.

Virkkunen, M., Nuutila, A., Goodwin, F. K., & Linnoila, M. (1987). Cerebrospinal fluid monoamine metabolite levels in male arsonists. *Archives of General Psychiatry, 44,* 241–247.

Virkkunen, M., Rawlings, R., Tokola, R. P. P., Poland, R. E., Guidotti, A., Nemeroff, C., et al. (1994). CSF biochemistries, glucose metabolism, and diurnal activity rhythms in alcoholic, violent offenders, fire setters, and

healthy volunteers. *Archives of General Psychiatry, 51,* 20–27.

Volavka, J., Bilder, R., & Nolan, K. (2004). Catecholamines and aggression: The role of COMT and MAO polymorphisms. *Annals of the NY Academy of Sciences, 1036,* 393–398.

Weisman, A. M., Berman, M. E., & Taylor, S. P. (1998). Effects of clorazepate, diazepam, and oxazepam on a laboratory measurement of aggression in men. *International Clinical Psychopharmacology, 13,* 183–188.

Westergaard, G. C., Suomi, S. J., Chavanne, T. J., Houser, L., Hurley, A., Cleveland, A., et al. (2003). Physiological correlates of aggression and impulsivity in free-ranging female primates. *Neuropsychopharmacology, 28,* 1045–1055.

Windle, R. C., & Windle, M. (1995). Longitudinal patterns of physical aggression: Associations with adult social, psychiatric, and personality functioning and testosterone levels. *Development and Psychopathology, 7,* 563–585.

Winslow, J. T. (2005). Neuropeptides and non-human primate social deficits associated with pathogenic rearing experience. *International Journal of Developmental Neurosciences, 23,* 245–251.

Zald, D. H., & Kim, S. W. (1996). The anatomy and function of the orbital frontal cortex, II. Function and relevance to obsessive compulsive disorder. *Journal of Neuropsychiatry and Clinical Neuroscience, 8,* 249–261.

Zanarini, M. C., & Frankenburg, F. R. (2001). Olanzapine treatment of female borderline personality disorder patients: A double-blind, placebo-controlled study. *Journal of Clinical Psychiatry, 62,* 849–854.

Zanarini, M. C., & Frankenburg, F. R. (2003). Omega-3 fatty acid treatment of women with borderline personality disorder: A double-blind placebo-controlled study. *American Journal of Psychiatry, 160,* 167–169.

Zanarini, M. C., Frankenburg, F. R., & Parachini, E. A. (2004). A preliminary, randomized trial of fluoxetine, olanzapine, and the olanzapine-fluoxetine combination in women with borderline personality disorder. *Journal of Clinical Psychiatry, 65,* 903–907.

Zureik, M., Courbon, D., & Ducimetiere, P. (1996). Serum cholesterol concentration and death from suicide in men: Paris prospective study I. *British Medical Journal, 313,* 649–651.

CHAPTER 9

The Neuropsychology of Violence

Jean R. Séguin, Patrick Sylvers, and Scott O. Lilienfeld

Introduction

Neuropsychology has typically sought to assess the often subtle, yet dramatic effects of brain lesions on information processing and behavior. Following certain brain lesions, a well-adapted individual can become irritable, impulsive, incapable of sustaining concentration, and neglectful of social rules. In such cases, the individual's ability to process information in a socially adaptive way becomes severely impaired. The observation of these profound changes prompted the development of neuropsychological accounts for the deficits, seen in a broad range of behavior problems, including violent behavior.

These *deficit models* emphasize fundamental processing difficulties that are tied more closely to brain anatomy or physiology. In contrast, other accounts of violent behavior, such as social information-processing models, provide several complementary angles of analysis to a neuropsychological model. Social information-processing models (see Chapter 15, "Social-Cognitive Processes in the Development of Antisocial and

Violent Behavior") can be described as *distortion models*, as they emphasize the role of biases, beliefs, attributions, appraisals, and schemas, such as those targeted by cognitive-behavioral therapies. Deficits and distortions influence behavior either through interpretive biases or limits in the capacity to process information. In fact, deficits can sometimes be manifested as distortions. Thus, cognitive therapies may prove less effective when a fundamental neuropsychological deficit is at the core of an information-processing difficulty. Conversely, individuals with hostile attributional biases but without neuropsychological deficits may be more amenable to cognitive therapies. Finally, these systems may combine additively or interact statistically with individual motivational predispositions and situations.

Chapter Overview

In this chapter, we review the neuropsychological approach to cognitive deficits associated with violent behavior. In Part I, we examine issues pertaining to the assessment of neuropsychological function and the assessment of clinical syndromes, which include delinquency and criminality, associated with violence. In Part II, we provide an overview of developmental issues affecting brain maturation and behavioral regulation. We integrate the aforementioned issues in Part III, where we review studies that help us understand violence from a neuropsychological perspective. As we note there, because a key method in neuropsychology has been the use of lesion analyses, we examine the extent to which violence is a consequence of brain lesions. We then turn to the few neuropsychological studies of violence and examine the larger body of literature on clinical syndromes associated with violence. In that section, we examine the extent to which neuropsychological problems have been identified in violence-prone individuals. Finally, we summarize and integrate the key observations derived from this review, address limitations in the extant body of research, and offer suggestions for further research on in this important and still growing area.

Part I: Assessment

Neuropsychological Assessment

Classic neuropsychological testing involves the administration of a battery of tests. These tests are designed to assess a variety of brain functions, ranging from basic perception to more complex neocortical problem solving, and require either verbal or motor responses. The stimuli used for these tests may be visual or auditory. Visual stimuli include pictures, abstract designs, and combinations of these stimuli, such as those found in various forms of puzzles, mazes, assortments of objects, pictorial depictions of story lines, printed colors, words, and numbers. Auditory stimuli may involve spoken words, numbers, problems, or stories. Computerized batteries are usually limited to motor responses performed through the click of a mouse or by means of a touch screen interface, although voice-onset recording, eye tracking devices, electrophysiology, and functional

brain imaging are also used, albeit more rarely. Many of these tests qualify as neuropsychological because they were developed to test theories of brain function and were typically validated with lesion analysis studies, brain electrophysiological studies, or, more recently, with brain imaging studies. In other words, individuals with relatively well-circumscribed brain lesions were found to perform poorly on such tests, or these tests were found to engage specific areas of the brain. Thus, these batteries provide a profile of strengths and weaknesses that presumably vary as a function of the location and extent of lesions. Because location may correspond to some aspect of function, neuropsychological tests, in addition to being used to test individuals with documented lesions, are used to infer localization of brain lesions. For example, a frontal lobe hypothesis of violence emerged because violent individuals often perform poorly on tests of frontal lobe functioning.

The brain is a highly complex organ of interrelated areas that function as networks. Functioning in one area may depend on the functioning of others. This phenomenon refers to hierarchy of function and is called single (or simple) dissociation. Functioning in two areas may also occur independently from one another, referred to as double dissociation (Shallice, 2003). These notions are essential for testing specificity of deficits. Thus, tests are typically sensitive to certain functions, but not to others. However, pure tests of specific functions are rare. The interpretation of performance on such tests must be conducted in the context of other discriminating tests, in part because "lesions" can be diffuse or circumscribed, subtle or gross. Neuropsychological testing often complements a more basic but equally important neurological examination (which involves testing of snout, suck, and grasp reflexes; abnormal smooth pursuit eye movements; reciprocal hand movement coordination; and other capacities).

Neuropsychological lesions can be the outcome of pregnancy or birth complications, various illnesses, aging, head injury, intracranial tumors, cerebrovascular disorders, exposure to toxic substances, or corrective surgical procedures. They can also be temporary and reversible, such as those observed under the acute effects of drugs and alcohol or certain illnesses, although some of these conditions can cause irreversible damage. Finally, results on neuropsychological tests are often assumed to represent the actual competence of the individual. However, there may be a gap between competence and actual performance. Thus, interpretation of test results should take into account the individual's motivation, attention, capacity to remember the sometimes complex rules required for optimal performance, language of administration, and cultural background. We refer the reader to more specialized sources for additional information (Kolb & Wishaw, 2003; Lezak, Howieson & Loring, 2004).

Clinical Syndromes Associated With Violence

Although physical violence is relatively easy to identify because of its overt nature, there is a paucity of studies examining the neuropsychology of violence. Much of what we know about the neuropsychology of violence derives from research on conditions that are associated with violence rather than violence per se. Thus, to appreciate the strengths and limitations of this body of literature, we first discuss the clinical syndromes most commonly associated with violence.

Violence research is conducted within two broad and overlapping nomenclatures, legal/judicial and clinical. In the legal/judicial areas, researchers have studied delinquency and criminal behavior. In the clinical arena, physical violence as a symptom is found under such conditions as conduct disorder (CD; 312.xx), antisocial personality disorder (ASPD; 301.7), Personality Change due to a General Medical Condition, Aggressive Type (310.1), and the differential disorder Intermittent Explosive Disorder (IED; 312.34) in the *Diagnostic and Statistical Manual of Mental Disorders – Text Revision* (DSM-IV-TR; American Psychiatric Association, 2000). In addition, it is sometimes found in psychopathy (Hare, 1999). Although the DSM-IV-TR regards ASPD as essentially synonymous with psychopathy, research strongly suggests otherwise, as we discuss later in this chapter (Hare, 2003).

One major limitation to studying violence by examining these disorders is that violent behavior is not necessary for their diagnosis. Only 6 of 15 CD symptoms and 1 of 7 of the adult ASPD symptoms qualify as explicitly violent if we define violence as physical aggression toward other people or threats of physical force. None of the criteria for IED meets this strict definition because a diagnosis can also be made in cases of property destruction alone. Three symptoms are necessary to obtain a diagnosis of CD (at least one of them before age 10 years) and ASPD, although ASPD also requires a history of CD before age 15 years (provided that symptoms are not due primarily to schizophrenia or a bipolar episode). IED can only be diagnosed when its symptoms are not attributable to CD, ASPD, other impulse control disorders, or a medical condition. The table of contents of the DSM–IV-TR does not include the words "violence" or "aggression." However, physical abuse of children (995.54 or V61.21) or adults (995.81 or V62.83), Adult Antisocial Behavior (V71.01), and Child or Adolescent Antisocial Behavior (V71.02) are additional nondisorder categories that may be the focus of clinical attention and in which violence may be present. Finally, aggression may also be secondary to "persecutory or grandiose delusions with anger" in Schizophrenia, Paranoid Type (295.30), and child or spouse abuse, as well as violent behavior, may occur during the course of an acute manic phase of Bipolar Disorder with psychotic features (296.xx) although none of these behaviors constitute official symptoms of these conditions.

Psychopathy can be considered a clinical syndrome, although it is not listed officially in the DSM-IV-TR. It has been investigated most commonly in criminals. Psychopathy is most often assessed with the Psychopathy Checklist-revised (PCL-R score > 30), which involves both a standardized interview and a thorough review of official records (Hare, Hart, & Harpur, 1991). Other methods of assessing psychopathy have been developed. For example, self-report instruments exist (Levenson, Kiehl, & Fitzpatrick, 1995; Lilienfeld & Andrews, 1996; Lynam, Whiteside, & Jones, 1999), and children with psychopathic tendencies have been studied using various behavior rating systems (Frick, O'Brien, Wootton, & McBurnett, 1994; Lynam, 1998). In prisons, the overlap between psychopathy and ASPD is substantial but asymmetrical: most incarcerated psychopaths meet criteria for ASPD but not vice versa. Approximately 70 to 80% of prisoners meet criteria for ASPD, whereas only about 15 to 25% meet PCL-R criteria for psychopathy (Hare, 2003). Higher rates of violence are found in criminal psychopaths than in other criminals (Hare,), but not all psychopaths are violent. Psychopathy is also a potent risk factor for criminal and sexual recidivism (Salekin, Rogers, & Sewell, 1996).

Physical violence has also been studied developmentally. The most relevant studies focus on physical aggression. However, in most developmental studies, aggression scales often fail to distinguish physical from other forms of aggression. For example, the Child Behavior Checklist (CBCL; Achenbach, Edelbrock, & Howell, 1987) yields an aggression scale comprising 23 items, 3 of which refer explicitly to physical aggression, but more studies are extracting physical aggression items from that scale to study its development (Bongers, Koot, van der Ende, & Verhulst, 2004; National Institute of Child Health and Human Development Early Child Care Research Network, 2004). A similar problem plagues research on proactive and reactive aggression; most items of either scale do not refer specifically to physical aggression.

Given these limitations, it is therefore possible for neuropsychological studies in this literature to include nonphysically violent forms of CD, ASPD, psychopathy,

or aggression. Nevertheless, investigators have not always made this distinction, as all of these behavior problems are often subsumed under the broad banner of antisocial problems. Further, the clinical syndromes in which physical violence is present, in addition to being comorbid with each other, are often comorbid with other conditions characterized by impulsivity, drug and alcohol abuse (DSM codes 303.xx, 304.xx, or 305.xx), and gambling (312.31) and with attention-deficit hyperactivity disorder (ADHD; 314.xx) and oppositional defiant disorder (ODD; 313.81) in developmental studies with childhood externalizing disorders. As we see later, several studies find or fail to find neuropsychological impairments in these associated conditions but without having taken violence into account. Conversely, several studies of violence have not taken these comorbid conditions into account. Thus, questions of specificity remain largely unresolved, although there have been notable improvements along these lines in the recent literature.

Part II: Developmental Issues

Developmental Patterns of Behavior

Moffitt (1993a) emphasized a brain-behavior account for the *development* of antisocial behavior. Historically, evidence supporting such an approach became clearer in the mid-19th century (Damasio, Grabowski, Frank, Galaburda, & Damasio, 1994; Mataro et al., 2001; Weiger & Bear, 1988). Moffitt built on this existing literature and her own longitudinal studies to bring this model to the forefront of research on antisocial behavior.

An initial classification as a function of developmental history of behavior gave rise to a flurry of studies. Research on the etiology and trajectory of CD suggests that "early-onset/persistent" (a.k.a. as "life-course-persistent;" Moffitt, 1993a) and "adolescent-limited" CD are actually distinct types (Kivlahan, Marlatt, Fromme, Coppel, & Williams, 1990). This finding underscores a key methodological point; namely, that comparing or contrasting groups of adolescents or adults without knowing their natural history can be fraught with problems. "Early-onset/persistent" CD is presumably a more heritable condition likely to persist into adulthood, whereas "late-onset CD" is presumably less severe and usually limited to adolescence (Moffitt, 2003). Individuals with "early-onset/persistent" CD appear to be more likely to engage in physically aggressive behavior than individuals with "late-onset" CD (Lahey et al., 1998). This finding suggests that what may be driving "late onset" CD is not physical aggression but other antisocial behaviors. The identification of a "childhood-only/recovery/childhood-limited" group that displays antisocial behavior uniquely in childhood (Lahey, Waldman, & McBurnett, 1999; Moffitt, Caspi, Harrington, & Milne, 2002; Raine et al., 2005; Raine, Yaralian, Reynolds, Venables, & Mednick, 2002) suggests an additional problem behavior group. In one study, this group remained significantly impaired in adult life, as it displayed symptoms of internalizing disorders and continued to partake in less severe antisocial behaviors (Moffitt et al., 2002).

Although the concept of age of "onset" has sparked controversy (Tremblay, 2000) it has spawned valuable research into the development of antisocial behavior. Research into developmental trajectories suggests that the "early-onset/persistent" versus "late-onset" CD distinction is less clear than proposed by the DSM-IV-TR (Bongers et al., 2004; Broidy et al., 2003; National Institute of Child Health and Human Development Early Child Care Research Network, 2004). The typical developmental trends are for declines over time (Tremblay, 2000; Tremblay et al., 1996), a few children (about 5% of community samples) maintain relatively high levels of antisocial behavior across development (Bongers et al., 2004; National Institute of Child Health and Human Development Early Child Care Research Network, 2004), with an "onset" at around 2 years of age, although children may begin hitting, pushing, and kicking as soon as their limbs have enough strength. Moreover, in a few samples, an increase from low-level childhood physical aggression can be observed until pre-adolescence (Broidy et al., 2003). But the absence of adolescence data in these samples limits their usefulness for understanding trajectories of physical aggression across childhood and adolescence. We also note that developmental patterns may differ as a function of the delinquent behavior of interest (i.e., physical aggression versus theft or vandalism; Barker et al., in press; Lacourse et al., 2002).

In sum, moderate levels of physical aggression are normative in preschoolers, and most children exhibit a decline over time. This may correspond to a "childhood-only" pattern, that is, an "early onset" (or "early starter") group that is not persistent. For a few children, initial levels of antisocial behavior remain high across development, corresponding to the "early-onset/persistent" pattern. In very few samples, we observe increases in physical aggression over time, but no evidence of sudden "late onset," and lack of adolescent data in those samples precludes a full appreciation of their trajectory. Nonetheless, the labels "late-onset/late starter/adolescent limited" may reflect less violence than "early onset/persistent" when global measures of behavior, such as CD, antisocial behavior, or delinquency, are used.

Risk Factors That May Affect Brain Development

As developmental patterns have been studied with longitudinal designs, there has been increasing interest in conditions that can contribute both to those patterns and to poor neuropsychological function, such as a history of exposure during or after pregnancy to brain-altering psychopharmacological agents (e.g., cigarette smoke, alcohol, drugs), other perinatal or birth complications, poor nutrition, traumatic experiences (e.g., abuse), chronic stress, or behavior problems that heighten the risk of head trauma through accidents or fights (i.e., ADHD, ODD).

Cigarettes may exert early effects in the intrauterine environment and later in the home environment. For example, exposure to environmental tobacco smoke appears related to poor cognitive performance in children aged 6 to 16 years (Yolton, Dietrich, Auinger, Lanphear, & Hornung, 2005). These effects were not due to exposure during pregnancy. Cigarette use during pregnancy has been extensively studied in recent years because it appears to remain relatively widespread, affecting 20 to 25% of mothers (Huijbregts et al., 2006), and could constitute one important target for preventative measures. Although there are sustained efforts to encourage pregnant women to stop smoking, the mechanisms by which smoking during pregnancy could affect behavior or neuropsychological development remain poorly understood. These effects may vary as a function of age. For example, early cognitive problems are related to poor behavioral adjustment in the preschool years (Séguin, 2004; Séguin & Zelazo, 2005), and maternal smoking during pregnancy was related to early physical aggression (Tremblay et al., 2004) and multiple problem behavior (Huijbregts, Séguin, Zoccolillo, Boivin, & Tremblay, in press). However, maternal smoking during pregnancy was not related to early cognitive problems once parental education was taken into account (Huijbregts et al., 2006). This finding suggests that the neurotoxic effects of cigarette smoke during pregnancy may more specifically affect preschool behavior regulation, but not necessarily through a cognitive regulation pathway.

Low birthweight is one consequence of maternal smoking during pregnancy (Huijbregts et al., 2006), but other conditions, such as perinatal and birth complications, may also affect neuropsychological and behavioral development (Raine, 2002a). For example, one study found that obstetrical complications interacted statistically with early family adversity in predicting later violent delinquency (Arseneault, Tremblay, Boulerice, & Saucier, 2002). As a complication, hypoxia at birth is associated with poor

cognitive development (Hopkins-Golightly, Raz, & Sandler, 2003). In another study, minor physical anomalies of the mouth, which are thought to correspond to in utero neural development, were markers of later violent delinquency even after statistically controlling for familial adversity (Arseneault, Tremblay, Boulerice, Séguin, & Saucier, 2000).

Several chronically stressful developmental conditions have been associated with the development of smaller hippocampal volumes, at least in animals (Meaney, Aitken, van Berkell, Bhatnagar, & Sapolsky, 1988), which in turn may increase vulnerability to stress (Gilbertson et al., 2002). Although hypotheses positing a neurotoxic effect of cortisol have yet to be fully tested, early traumatic experiences have been implicated in the poor development of executive function (Mezzacappa, Kindlon, & Earls, 2001), even though the potential causal role of third variables (e.g., parental aggression or impulsivity) is difficult to exclude. In other studies, duration and quality of early care were associated with cognitive development (Castle et al., 2000). Malnutrition at age 3 years, one aspect of the early environment, was found to be related to later externalizing problems, a link that was mediated by IQ (Liu, Raine, Venables, & Mednick, 2004). Conversely, the duration of breastfeeding was found to be related to higher IQ even after statistical control for key confounds (Mortensen, Fleischer Michaelsen, Sanders, & Machover Reinish, 2002). Another risk factor that may be even more direct is family history of antisocial behavior, \ vspace*{pt} although the effect of this risk factor may be genetic, shared environmental, or both. We now know that maternal smoking during pregnancy is correlated with parental antisocial behavior (Huijbregts et al., in press). Finally, early head injury is sometimes thought to be an important risk factor. One might expect early lesions to increase the risk of physical aggression. However, there is little support for that hypothesis as follow-up studies of children with early documented lesions rarely report physical aggression (Eslinger, Flaherty-Craig, & Benton, 2004).

Part III

Given the background considerations reviewed thus far, we now address two complementary questions: (1) Do some brain lesions dependably increase the risk for violent behavior? and (2) Do violence-prone individuals exhibit specific neuropsychological deficits?

The Effects of Brain Lesions on the Risk for Violence

Brain lesions in various areas can affect social behavior. However, interest in the cognitive aspects of the brain-violence relation has centered largely on the role of the frontal lobe because of its centrality to the regulation of antisocial behavior. Anatomically, the frontal lobe represents 20% of the neocortex and is located above the eyes and behind the forehead. Nomenclatures for describing the frontal lobe and its functions vary. Areas are typically distinguished by cytoarchitectonic analysis; that is, the architecture of the cells and their connections. Briefly, three major areas are typically designated: motor (area 4), premotor (areas 6 and 8, although area 8 is also referred to as posterior dorsolateral; Petrides, Alivisatos, Evans, & Meyer, 1993a), and prefrontal. The prefrontal cortex is further divided into dorsolateral (areas 9 & 46; both may be referred to as mid-dorsolateral; Petrides et al., 1993a), inferior (or ventral or orbitofrontal; areas 10 through 14), and medial (areas 25 and 32) regions.

One of the major cognitive functions of the prefrontal cortex is the temporal organization of behavior in memory (Milner, Petrides, & Smith, 1985), which is also one of the core aspects of executive functioning. In contrast, the premotor cortex is involved in movement selection and the motor cortex in movement execution. Frontal patients have difficulty regulating their behavior in response to external stimuli, as well as organizing it. One set of functions relates to the concept of working memory, which involves not only the online maintenance of information and control of interference but also the active processing of that information as an individual engages in action. Poor working memory affects all stages of executive function (Séguin & Zelazo, 2005); hostile biases in appraising a problem could be difficult to reconsider, plans could be difficult to carry out, rules (even if they are otherwise well-known) could be difficult to apply in real time, and monitoring of a plan (detection and error correction) could be difficult to achieve.

In terms of emotional regulation, individuals with lesions involving the orbitofrontal lobe have been shown to be disinhibited, socially inappropriate, susceptible to misinterpreting others' moods, impulsive, unconcerned with the consequences of their actions, irresponsible in everyday life, lacking in insight into the seriousness of their condition, and prone to weak initiative (Damasio et al., 1994; Rolls, Hornak, Wade, & McGrath, 1994). Primate studies also show that individuals with orbitofrontal lesions may be insensitive to social dominance hierarchies. The main consequence of such lesions has also been described as impairments in self-reflective awareness (Stuss, Gow, & Hetherington, 1992), perspective taking (Stuss, Gallup, & Alexander, 2001), social schema knowledge (Grafman et al., 1996), the ability to respond appropriately to social reinforcement (Rolls et al., 1994), the ability to make inferences about the mental states of others (or a Theory of Mind; Stone, Baron-Cohen, & Knight, 1998), and processing of social cues (Brothers, 2001). Some of these problems may also reflect malfunction of the amygdala (Bechara, Damasio, & Damasio, 2003), which is involved in processing of cues of fear (Whalen et al., 2004) and sadness (Blair, Morris, Frith, Perrett, & Dolan, 2000). In this way, all of these functions are less cognitive in nature and require more than straightforward neuropsychological testing to be evaluated. Individuals with such acquired conditions may lead a relatively stable life when provided with good post-trauma care, support, and considerable external structure. Nonetheless, their behavior may remain difficult to manage, and they may not recover any sense of autonomy (Mataro et al., 2001).

The ensuing syndrome has often been labeled as either acquired sociopathy (Damasio, 2000; Damasio, Tranel, & Damasio, 1991), acquired ASPD (Meyers, Berman, Scheibel, & Hayman, 1992), or pseudopsychopathy. Because these lesions appear to lead to psychopathic-like behavior, they were often thought to underlie physical violence. However, there is limited support for this hypothesis. Studies of war veterans, for example, support the hypothesis that orbitofrontal and mediofrontal damage increase the risk for aggressive and violent attitudes (Grafman et al., 1996), but not necessarily physical violence. Thus, physical violence is rare in acquired forms of antisocial behavior, which may in part be due to the fact that individuals with acquired brain lesions do not necessarily possess the many premorbid risk factors associated with physical violence. In fact, aggression (including physical aggression) appears to be associated with acquired frontal lesions only when there is a premorbid history of major depression, poor social functioning, and alcohol and drug abuse (Tateno, Jorge, & Robinson, 2004).

Other cortical abnormalities associated with aggressive outbursts include acute episodes of temporal lobe (temporolimbic) epilepsy (also known as interictal violence), which are similar in manifestation to IED (for a critical review, see Filley et al., 2001). Epilepsy is often an exclusion criterion in brain studies of violence (Critchley et al., 2000). Otherwise, violence in epilepsy is very rare, and a temporal lobe hypothesis of violence must be treated with caution (Teichner & Golden, 2000). Similarly, a limbic psychotic trigger reaction is a second type of seizure thought to underlie certain forms of sudden and unplanned violence. Consciousness may be severely clouded, resulting in amnesia, in the epileptic forms of seizures. By contrast, in the psychotic trigger reaction the individual typically remembers violent and bizarre acts, which are committed with flat affect and are totally – uncharacteristic (Pontius & Lemay, 2003). Such a psychotic reaction also appears to be distinct from violence related to schizophrenia (Pontius, 2003).

Neuropsychological Studies of Physically Violent Behavior

The other main approach to the neuropsychology of violence is to study physically violent individuals. This approach is probably the one most familiar to readers of this book. We begin with the most severe form, murder, and move on to less severe forms of physical aggression. We then follow with disorders and antisocial behavior problems in which physical violence is sometimes present. One of the first issues in research on such individuals involves determining whether they suffered head trauma at any point in their lives. Because of the limitations inherent in retrospective recall, most of the studies reviewed are not able to control for this variable. Moreover, defining the extent and types of injuries that qualify as head traumas is difficult. Prospective studies are better equipped to handle this issue. Nonetheless, retrospective studies of physically violent individuals have been informative.

Murderers

Several studies of murderers appear to support a dysfunctional frontal lobe hypothesis. For example, "frontal dysfunctions" were found in 65% of murderers (Blake, Pincus, & Buckner, 1995). This study used a multimethod approach including EEG and brain imaging, both complementing neuropsychological test results (although results for all tests were not available for all participants). However, far from deriving from a random sample, these individuals had been assessed at the request of their defense attorney. Further, the sample included individuals with poor general intellectual abilities, and it was not compared with a nonviolent offender group. Moreover, the use of multiple methods may have increased the risk of erroneously inferring the presence of frontal dysfunction. As a consequence of these methodological limitations, these findings are difficult to interpret.

In another study, violent adolescent and adult psychiatric patients, compared with nonviolent controls, were shown to exhibit reduced overall prefrontal activity and increased anterior medial prefrontal activity (Amen, Stubblefield, Carmichael, & Thisted, 1996). However, neuropsychological testing does not complement many such brain imaging studies. It is therefore unclear whether these functional findings correspond to neuropsychological performance. Moreover, the correspondence between brain imaging and neuropsychology may also be elusive. For example, a series of brain imaging studies carried out by Raine and colleagues support a frontal deficit hypothesis (see also Chapter 7 in this volume). However, some of these studies used the Continuous Performance Task, a measure of sustained attention, and found brain processing differences in the absence of test performance differences between individuals who had committed impulsive murders as opposed to planned murders (Raine et al., 1994). The authors speculated that the visual cortex might have compensated for the frontal impairments. This study illustrates a key methodological point for interpreting neuropsychological test results; namely, that even under the best performance conditions, different strategies or brain networks may be employed by different individuals to achieve the same level of performance.

Although the frontal lobe has been implicated in these and other studies, they may account for only one portion of the explanation. Models that consider frontal dysfunction in murderers are broader and include developmental psychosocial factors (Blake et al., 1995; Raine, 2002b) and other factors reviewed in this book.

Physical Aggression

Although murder is the most severe form of violence, investigators have also examined whether neuropsychological problems are evident in milder forms of violence, such as in physical aggression. Physical aggression can be defined as hitting, kicking, biting, use of a weapon, and getting into fights. In some cases, this definition is broadened to include bullying and threats of violence. There are surprisingly few neuropsychological studies of physical aggression per se.

As a consequence, Séguin, Pihl, Harden, Tremblay, and Boulerice (1995) sought to develop a neuropsychological test battery on the basis of the frontal lobe and memory work of Petrides and Milner (1985). We complemented the battery on the basis of reviews of the neuropsychology of delinquency and conduct disorder. In her review of this literature, Moffitt (1990b) identified deficits in three areas: language abilities, executive function, and cerebral dominance. However, most studies did not assess these dimensions simultaneously. In a series of studies that contrasted executive function, verbal and spatial abilities, and tests of cerebral dominance, we first found that working memory, a basic ability involved in executive functions, was poorest in boys from a community sample with a history of physical aggression even after controlling for nonexecutive abilities relevant to executive function (Séguin et al., 1995).

To assess working memory we used the Self-Ordered Pointing (SOP) test, a number of randomization test (mid-dorsolateral frontal lobe), and conditional association tests (posterior dorsolateral frontal lobe; Petrides, Alivisatos, Meyer, & Evans, 1993b; Petrides et al., 1993a). We used the abstract and concrete versions of the SOP. Briefly, one trial consists of the selection of one of 12 different images in a 3 × 4 array by pointing at it. The images are repeated in varying positions on 12 such arrays. All 12 different images need to be chosen to obtain a perfect score. To succeed, the individual must monitor these self-ordered selections. To increase interference, two additional trials with the same set of images follow the first one. Errors can be computed within trials (and summed across trials). For the conditional association tasks, the individual must identify the underlying rule that associates each of six pairs of stimuli. Feedback is provided, which also makes this an inductive learning task. At the behavioral level, a concurrent history of early hyperactivity is thought to increase the risk for "early-onset persistent" antisocial behavior (Lynam, 1998; Moffitt, 1990a). However, several studies fail to support this hypothesis (see, Farrington & Loeber, 2000; Lahey, Loeber, Burke, & Rathouz, 2002; Lilienfeld & Waldman, 1990; Loeber, Burke, & Lahey, 2002; Nagin & Tremblay, 1999; Stouthamer-Loeber, Loeber, Wei, Farrington, & Wikström, 2002).

Nonetheless, hyperactivity should be concurrently assessed in studies of violence because it co-occurs frequently with antisocial behavior problems, and there is considerable evidence linking executive function problems to hyperactivity in children (Nigg, 2005; Nigg et al., 2004). Studies examining the neuropsychology of hyperactivity, inattention, impulsivity, or conduct problems typically measure one behavioral dimension while controlling statistically for the others. In a follow-up to our first study, we controlled statistically for ADHD or teacher-rated hyperactivity and still found working memory impairments after also controlling for IQ (Séguin, Boulerice, Harden, Tremblay, & Pihl, 1999). However, we learned little about the neuropsychology of hyperactivity, and it remained possible that physical aggression and hyperactivity combined in additive or synergistic ways (Waschbusch, 2002). Moreover, by controlling for "comorbid" psychopathology, one may inadvertently be controlling statistically for important variance relevant to the disorder in question (Meehl, 1971).

Therefore, in a third study, we selected young adult males on the basis not only of having a physically aggressive history (teacher-rated from kindergarten to age 15), but also of having a history of hyperactivity (without a focus on inattention or impulsivity; Séguin, Nagin, Assaad, & Tremblay, 2004). We found no statistical interaction, but we did find clear additive effects, even after controlling for test motivation. Although the impairments observed

included IQ and short-term memory, working memory remained significantly impaired even after statistical control for these other cognitive abilities. In other words, both physical aggression and hyperactivity exhibited significant independent associations with neuropsychological function and working memory. However, more of the tests in this battery were associated significantly and independently with physical aggression than they were with hyperactivity. Other studies of girls have also found a negative association between executive control and physical aggression after controlling for ADHD (Giancola, Mezzich, & Tarter, 1998). Studies of bullying (which includes threats of physical aggression) have revealed similar results, although they have not always controlled statistically for comorbid externalizing problems (Coolidge, DenBoer, & Segal, 2004).

In summary poor neuropsychological function is often found in adolescents and young adults from the community with a history of physical aggression. These deficits appear to be independent from other externalizing behavior problems. Developmentally, these associations can be detected as early as the preschool years (Séguin, 2003). Work on physical aggression is consistent with that position: the children who showed the greatest neuropsychological impairment had already been identified as physically aggressive and hyperactive in kindergarten (Séguin et al., 2004), and preschool physical aggression and hyperactivity trajectories were associated synergistically with cognitive performance at age 3½ years (Séguin, Zelazo, & Tremblay, 2005). Séguin and Zelazo (2005) recently reviewed the literature on preschool cognitive function in early physical aggression. They noted that this literature was characterized by similar problems to those we are reviewing here (i.e., use of global measures of behavior problems without specific focus on physical violence, history of problem behavior not necessarily taken into account, and use of global measures of cognitive function instead of specific measures sensitive to frontal function). Nonetheless, they also noted that poor cognitive function was often but not always associated with problem behavior in several studies of preschoolers.

Neuropsychological Studies of Antisocial Disorders in Which Physical Violence May Be Present

The bulk of research on the neuropsychology of violence derives from clinically oriented studies of disorders and antisocial behavior problems that may include physical violence.

ANTISOCIAL BEHAVIORS

Several of the behavioral problems listed here have been grouped under the global label of "antisocial behaviors." These behaviors, among others, were examined in a meta-analysis of studies of executive function by Morgan and Lilienfeld (2000). Although executive function is one narrow type of neuropsychological deficit, this study provides a global view of that literature. We then complement this global view with a more specific focus on each key antisocial behavior problem. This meta-analysis comprised 39 studies, yielding 4,589 subjects total. To be included in the meta-analysis, tests of executive functioning must have attempted to measure volition, planning, purposive action, or effective performance and either differentiated patients with frontal lesions from other patients or preferentially activated the frontal cortex in previous studies. To investigate whether antisocial behavior was related to executive functioning deficits per se rather than neuropsychological deficits in general, three neuropsychological tests that do not rely heavily on executive functioning were analyzed as "control" measures. The antisocial behavior groups used in the meta-analysis included individuals meeting criteria for one or more of the following antisocial behavior problems: ASPD, CD, psychopathic personality disorder, criminality, or delinquency.

The results of the meta-analysis indicated that the antisocial behavior groups performed significantly worse than comparison groups, with a combined and weighted effect size Cohen's d (Cohen, 1992) of 0.62 standard deviations. Two of the three neuropsychological tests that did not measure executive functioning also produced significant, albeit weaker, differences between groups, with the antisocial behavior groups performing significantly worse (effect sizes of $d = 0.34$ and $d = 0.39$ standard deviations). However, tests of the homogeneity of variance across samples yielded significant results, indicating that the effect sizes were heterogeneous. When considering the type of antisocial grouping used in the studies, the heterogeneity of effect sizes was reduced within each group, and all group effect sizes remained significantly different than zero. Moreover, criminality ($d = 1.09$, weighted $d = 0.94$) and delinquency ($d = 0.86$, weighted $d = 0.78$) were found to be associated most strongly with executive functioning deficits. Potential moderators, including age, sex, ethnicity, and IQ, were not associated with the magnitude of the observed effect sizes, although scores on some of these moderators (e.g., sex, ethnicity) were not reported in all studies.

Morgan and Lilienfeld (2000) identified several limitations to this research. First, they were not able to examine the potential influence of substance abuse or ADHD on the results because these potential confounds were not assessed systematically in most studies. Second, the executive functioning measures were not subdivided by the frontal brain regions (e.g., dorsolateral, orbitofrontal) with which they are believed to be primarily associated. Third, the finding that criminality and delinquency were associated with more pronounced executive functioning deficits than other conditions is difficult to interpret given the differences in comparison groups used across studies. For example, executive functioning studies frequently compared criminals or delinquents with normal or unselected samples, whereas psychopaths were frequently compared with nonpsychopathic criminals. The latter studies may have yielded lower effect sizes because they used more stringent comparison samples.

This meta-analysis provides an interesting backdrop against which to compare studies with a focus on history of physical aggression. With a focus on physical aggression trajectories between ages 6 and 15 years as originally defined by Nagin and Tremblay (1999), we found that the standardized mean difference for a contrast between extreme groups (chronic versus never) was 0.66 for a number randomization task, 1.52 for Self-Ordered Pointing, and 1.12 for conditional association tasks (Séguin et al., 2004). For the current review we examined the two most severe groups (chronic physical aggression versus high desistance physical aggression) and found our standardized mean differences for those three tests to be, respectively, 0.33, 0.65, and 0.53. This finding supports the notion that clear neuropsychological impairments can be observed when we take into account the history and type of behavior (physical aggression).

At a developmental level, one prospective longitudinal study using behavioral assessments at ages 8 and 17 years suggests that poor spatial abilities at age 3 may be characteristic of "early-onset/persistent" antisocial behavior even after controlling statistically for hyperactivity, an effect that had largely disappeared by age 11 once social adversity had been controlled statistically (Raine et al., 2002). Although frontal tasks had not been administered and physical aggression was not specifically used to classify children, this finding is consistent with others (Séguin & Zelazo, 2005) and brings an additional prospective longitudinal component to this research. However, in another study based on ages 7–17 years antisocial behavior ratings, "child-limited" antisocial children were as impaired neuropsychologically as an "early-onset/persistent" group when tested in late adolescence (Raine et al., 2005).

PSYCHOPATHY

Psychopaths are more violent than other criminals (Hare, 1999) and consequently have received considerable research attention in the past 25 years. Initial reports of neuropsychological, especially frontal lobe, impairments in psychopaths (Gorenstein, 1982) have not been consistently replicated (Hare, 1984; Hart, Forth, & Hare, 1990;

Hoffman, Hall, & Bartsch, 1987; Sutker & Allain, 1987). Possible exceptions are studies in which psychopaths' anxiety levels were taken into account (Smith, Arnett, & Newman, 1992) or when life adjustment was taken into account. In the latter case, the more successful psychopaths (not defined by the PCL-R) showed better dorsolateral frontal lobe function than less successful psychopaths (Ishikawa, Raine, Lencz, Bihrle, & LaCasse, 2001). Smith et al. (1992) found two significant effects (out of six expected) for the Block Design subtest of the Wechsler Adult Intelligence Scale (Wechsler, 1981) and for the Trail Making Test-B (TMT-B) after controlling for IQ and substance abuse, but only in a contrast between low-anxious psychopaths and low-anxious nonpsychopaths. Marginally significant effects of psychopathy were found in two studies conducted on inmates, one using the TMT-B ($p < 0.06$; Hart et al., 1990), the other using the Wisconsin Card Sorting Task (WCST; Lapierre, Braun, & Hodgins, 1995). The latter test is a relatively global and nonspecific measure of executive function (Heaton, 1981), in which the perseverative error score was significant at $p < 0.08$, and categories achieved (out of six) at $p < 0.07$. However, all effect sizes were in the moderate range. For Hart et al. (1990) we computed weighted effect sizes of $d = 0.40$ for comparing high versus moderate psychopaths, and of $d = 0.64$ for comparing high versus low psychopaths. And in Lapierre et al. (1995) we computed weighted effect sizes of $d = 0.48$ and $d = -0.49$ for errors and categories achieved, respectively. In that latter study, psychopaths performed significantly poorly on tasks purported to measure orbitofrontal lobe function. Because the evidence remained unclear, we agree with Lynam (1998) that it is still reasonable to consider neuropsychological factors in studies of psychopathy.

In support of that possibility, Morgan and Lilienfeld's (2000) table examining PCL-R and non-PCL-R defined psychopathy indicates that the average effect size of neuropsychological (executive functioning) deficits was $d = 0.29$ ($d = 0.25$

weighted) in both cases (see Table 2 in Morgan & Lilienfeld, 2000). These analyses included a wide variety of tests showing heterogeneous effect sizes ranging up to $d = 1.41$. Because these studies frequently compared psychopaths with nonpsychopathic criminals, as in the two studies with results approaching significance and for which we calculated effect sizes, any effects of neuropsychological function that are correlates of criminality could be attenuated when criminals are subdivided as a function of psychopathy. Finally, one complementary account for inconsistent findings suggests that psychopaths may experience greater difficulty with left- than right-hemisphere tasks, especially when heavy information processing demands are placed on the left hemisphere (Suchy & Kosson, 2005).

In addition to studies using more classic neuropsychological tests, psychopaths appear to experience greater difficulty in shifting a dominant behavior when contingencies are changed and reversed. Newman and colleagues have proposed two pathways to account for that impairment: (1) a difficulty in regulation of affect and (2) a more fundamental information-processing deficit related to attention; that is, a difficulty in shifting attention to peripheral but potentially meaningful information from the environment (Newman & Lorenz, 2002). We found that physically aggressive boys perseverate on such "emotion regulation" tasks even after controlling for neuropsychological function and that stability/instability of physical aggression may vary as a function of both pathways proposed by Newman and colleagues (Séguin, Arseneault, Boulerice, Harden, & Tremblay, 2002). Psychopaths typically perform better than nonpsychopaths on some Stroop interference type tasks when stimuli are not totally embedded into one another, such as for standard color-word Stroop on which they show the expected interference effects (Hiatt, Schmitt, & Newman, 2004). According to the authors of that study psychopaths can focus (if not perseverate) better on a dominant rule and ignore potentially interfering information. Interference from such

peripheral information is often adaptive for most individuals and helps them adjust their course of action or modulate their response.

Psychopathy has also received attention from neuroscientists who observed the psychopathic-like behavior that we described earlier following brain lesions involving the orbitofrontal or ventromedial frontal lobes. Studies of the effects of these lesions on behavior offer particularly interesting results, because lesions are often relatively circumscribed with an absence of typical neuropsychological impairment. Such lesions were thought to be associated with problems on the Iowa Gambling Task (Bechara, Damasio, Damasio, & Anderson, 1994) and the Intradimensional/Extradimensional Shift Task from the Cambridge Neuropsychological Test Automated Battery (CANTAB; Downes et al., 1989). The Intradimensional/Extradimensional Shift Task breaks down confounded stages of the WCST, is also essentially inductive, and consists of up to 10 progressive stages that involve visual discrimination within and between dimensions (using the dimensions of color, shapes-lines, and number), as well as shifts of reward contingencies (or underlying correct rule). These tasks are clearly described by Mitchell, Colledge, Leonard, and Blair (2002).

The Iowa Gambling Task requires participants to choose a card from one of four decks. After choosing, the participant receives either a financial reward or punishment. There are two "good" decks that offer small to moderate rewards and are associated with little chance of punishment, and two "bad" decks that offer large rewards but are much more likely to result in punishment. Healthy controls often choose the "good" decks, whereas lesioned patients more often choose the "bad" decks. Patients with such lesions are said to be insensitive to future consequences of their decisions. The "somatic marker hypothesis," which is consistent with these observations, suggests that ventromedial frontal lobe lesions impair the capacity to consider emotions when making decisions (Damasio, 1996; Damasio et al., 1991). Despite an initial failing to extend the Iowa Gambling Task to adult psychopaths (Schmitt, Brinkley, & Newman, 1999), PCL-R psychopaths (Mitchell et al., 2002) and boys with psychopathic tendencies (Blair, Colledge, & Mitchell, 2001) did show poor performance on that task when the original methodology was applied. Nonetheless, there remain profound differences between psychopaths and individuals with these acquired conditions. For example, the aggression of brain-injured patients is typically reactive/hostile as opposed to the aggression of psychopaths, which is likely to be proactive/instrumental (Blair & Cipolotti, 2000; Cornell et al., 1996). Moreover, poor performance on the Iowa Gambling Task may be attributable to mechanisms other than insufficient somatic marking. For example, individuals may perform poorly on this task as a consequence of inadequate impulse control or reward dominance, or of poor working memory.

Recent reviews have also questioned the orbitofrontal account of psychopathy (Blair, 2004; Séguin, 2004). Although impairments on the Iowa Gambling Task (Bechara et al., 1994) and the Intradimensional/Extradimensional Shift Task (Mitchell et al., 2002) may be similar in psychopathy and in acquired psychopathy, it now appears that neither task is sensitive to *focal* orbitofrontal lesions (Manes et al., 2002). Earlier conclusions about the relevance of the OFC on these tasks relied on cases with lesions extending to the orbitofrontal cortex, but specific orbitofrontal lesions actually appear to increase deliberation and reduce impulsivity, quite the opposite of what was initially expected. Thus, the specific role of the orbitofrontal cortex in antisocial behavior may need to be re-examined.

Much research now focuses on the amygdala, which assigns motivational value to stimuli. Both psychopaths and individuals with amygdala lesions appear to exhibit poor recognition of fear and sadness (Blair et al., 2002), although their own experience of fear and sadness may be unimpaired (Anderson & Phelps, 2002). This finding constitutes an interesting dissociation between percep-

tion and subjective experience. The amygdala may be involved in the reactive aggression of psychopaths, because it is considered to be a key component in the regulation of such aggression in a complex circuit that involves the orbital frontal lobe and the anterior cingulate cortex (Davidson, Putnam, & Larson, 2000). It is important to reiterate, however, that instrumental aggression appears to be more central to psychopathy (Cornell et al., 1996). This line of research gave rise to the violence inhibition mechanism model of psychopathy, which posits that psychopaths exhibit deficiencies in a system that preferentially responds to sad, and more specifically fearful, emotional displays (Blair et al., 2004). From a developmental perspective, Blair and colleagues suggested that amygdala dysfunction may predate OFC impairments, as only amygdala function seems impaired in children with psychopathic tendencies, whereas both amygdala and OFC functions appear impaired in adult psychopaths (Mitchell et al., 2002).

Criminality and Delinquency

Physical violence is considered to be a violent offense from a legal/judicial point of view. It is rarely officially sanctioned in children, but is part of official delinquency in adolescence and criminal behavior in adulthood. Thus, violence present in any of the disorders reviewed here is also likely to be legally sanctioned. However, there are cases in which violence occurs that are not necessarily in the context of a mental disorder. Such is the case when we study physical aggression and violent criminals in childhood and adolescence (reviewed above). Morgan and Lilienfeld (2000) found their strongest effect sizes on executive function for criminals and delinquents. One recent study of incarcerated youth found them to perform more poorly than nonoffenders attending public schools on spatial span (a spatial analogue to the digit span task), a measure of short-term memory from the CANTAB tests, but not on such frontal tasks as the Intradimensional/Extradimensional

Shift Task, Tower of London, or spatial working memory task (Cauffman, Steinberg, & Piquero, 2005).

Some of the important theoretical work developed by Moffitt centered around delinquency initially (Moffitt, 1990b; Moffitt & Henry, 1989, 1991; Moffitt, Lynam, & Silva, 1994; Moffitt & Silva, 1988a,b). In one study, "early-onset/persistent" delinquents performed more poorly than "late-onset" delinquents on IQ and other neuropsychological tests (Taylor, Iacono, & McGue, 2000), as predicted by Moffitt's (1993a) developmental theory of antisocial behavior. In this study, however, IQ was not used as a co-variate, rendering it difficult to make conclusions regarding the specificity of cognitive deficits.

The use of global scales of delinquency or criminality may obscure key relations between specific behaviors and neuropsychological function. For example, one study found that among juvenile delinquents, IQ was positively related to theft, but negatively related to violence (Walsh, 1987). Presumably, this finding reflects the requirement for planning for theft, but an impulsive problem-solving style for violence. Intrigued by this isolated report, we recently analyzed data from the Rutgers longitudinal study (White, Bates, & Buyske, 2001). In that study, theft and violence were initially combined within a global index of delinquency. Neuropsychological function had failed to separate "persistent" from "adolescence-limited" delinquents. Following the lead from Lacourse et al. (2002) and our own work with physical aggression and hyperactivity (Séguin et al., 2004), we identified trajectories for theft and for physical violence. Using the same tests as the original study, we replicated Walsh's (1987) finding and found poorest neuropsychological function in highly violent individuals who were low on theft (Barker et al., in press). This replication requires further study, but suggests the need for a finer parsing of the relation between neuropsychological function and global indices of antisocial behavior.

Much research in the neuropsychology of violence may also bear implications for the justice system. Decisions to try adolescents who committed violent crimes in adult courts hinge on research on brain development and maturation. Beckman (2004; see also Sommers & Satel, 2005) recently reviewed that issue. However, the bulk of the literature reviewed by Beckman ignored the brain/violence literature, including that reviewed here. From a brain maturation perspective, some claim that adolescent brains are not sufficiently mature to justify trying violent adolescents in adult courts. However, research shows that the overwhelming majority of adolescents are not violent. Further, impaired brain function has been found in many violent (and nonviolent) adults. These data raise the question of why legal decision making should use age per se as a criterion. Moreover, neuropsychological function (and possibly brain maturation) may account only for a relatively small amount of variance in physical violence, although it could be an important influence in some cases. Thus the sensitive issue of trying violent adolescents in adult courts should probably rest on broader grounds, and evidence reviewed herein to inform the legal decision-making system should be used with caution.

Intermittent Explosive Disorder

The DSM-IV (American Psychiatric Association, 2000) places intermittent explosive disorder (IED) under the category of impulse control disorders not elsewhere classified. The primary feature of IED is the experience of discrete episodes of aggressive behavior resulting in personal injuries or property damage. The course, onset, and prevalence of IED are poorly understood, although this condition appears to be more common in males than females. Not surprisingly, there is a dearth of studies on the neuropsychological correlates of IED. In the only published controlled study, Best, Williams, and Coccaro (2002) show that the IED participants performed poorly on the Iowa Gambling Task compared with controls. However, there were no group differences on the Self-Ordered Pointing test, a working memory test most sensitive to physical aggression (Séguin et al., 2004).

Conduct Disorder

As mentioned earlier, Moffitt (1993b) has reviewed the literature on the neuropsychology of CD and identified deficits in three major areas: language, executive function and cerebral dominance. Several studies supported that distinction (Lueger & Gill, 1990). However, except for our early work on physical aggression (see Séguin et al., 1995), the evidence for the specific involvement of executive function in CD per se was weak, partly because ADHD was rarely controlled (Pennington & Ozonoff, 1996). It seems that not much has changed since Pennington and Ozonoff's (1996) review (Nigg, Willcutt, Doyle, & Sonuga-Barke, 2005). Several studies find neuropsychological impairment in ADHD even after statistical control for CD. However, authors of these studies often recognize that CD is not an object of study in itself (see, e.g., Nigg, Hinshaw, Carte, & Treuting, 1998). In other words, it is possible that there might have been unique variance related to CD as well after controlling for ADHD. Indeed, a few additional studies have examined CD and contrasted it with ADHD, also in the hopes of addressing the issues of specificity and comorbidity. When Morgan and Lilienfeld (2000) reviewed the CD literature they found an effect size of $d = 0.4$ (weighted $d = 0.36$) for poor performance on executive functioning tasks. Not included in that review was one study of explicitly violent CD females that found poor executive function even after controlling statistically for ADHD (Giancola et al., 1998). Otherwise, when physical violence and ADHD have not been examined, mixed results have been typical, even from the same investigative team. For example, one group of researchers failed to find executive function problems but found verbal problems in CD adolescents (mean age 15.4 years) after controlling statistically for ADHD (Déry, Toupin, Pauzé, Mercier, & Fortin, 1999). However, this research group found an executive func-

tioning deficit after controlling statistically for ADHD in a subsequent study of children (age range of 7 to 12 years; Toupin, Déry, Pauzé, Mercier, & Fortin, 2000). We note that the level of participants' physical violence was not clear in these two studies. The authors also speculated that differences between studies may be explained by (a) a lack of sensitivity of verbal measures in the child study; (b) the possibility that the CD adolescent group could have contained a mixture of "life-course persistent" and "adolescent-limited" delinquents (theoretically less physically aggressive); and (c) the possibility that the discrepancy between groups may increase with development (J. Toupin, personal communication, February 14, 2006). With regards to this last proposition, Blair and colleagues formulated a similar hypothesis in their developmental model of psychopathy to account for discrepancies between their child and adult data (Mitchell et al., 2002). The most relevant demonstration of a need to account for physical aggression are the findings that within CD, violence and theft are related in an opposite direction (violence positively, and theft negatively) with neurocognitive dysfunction (Barker et al. in press).

We provide an example to illustrate further the potential importance of accounting for physical aggression in studies of the neuropsychology of antisocial behavior. In one study that focused on physical aggression and hyperactivity, 67% of boys classified as CD and 72% of boys classified as ADHD between the ages of 14 and 16 years were in the high physical aggression and high hyperactivity trajectories, respectively, on the basis of teacher ratings from ages 6 to 15 years (Séguin et al., 2004). High trajectories in this case were a combination of the two highest ("chronic" and "high desistor") versus the two lowest ("low desistor" and "never") trajectories identified by Nagin and Tremblay (1999) for both physical aggression and hyperactivity. However, across the entire sample only 5% and 6.7% of boys met criteria for CD or ADHD, respectively. This finding suggests that if one is high in physical aggression (or hyperactivity) one is more likely to meet criteria for CD (or ADHD). But that study was different from the typical studies selecting for CD and ADHD in that it selected children on the basis of physical aggression and hyperactivity instead. A selection based on CD and ADHD may not necessarily have included either physical aggression or hyperactivity, or these specific behaviors may have contributed only a low weight to the diagnoses. Thus, a focus on physical aggression and hyperactivity yielded a greater number of study participants, most of whom did not meet criteria for CD or ADHD, and those more specific behaviors were sensitive to neuropsychological function and executive function in particular (Séguin et al., 2004).

A Note on CD/ODD

There has been considerable literature contrasting ODD/CD with ADHD. A problem arises mainly when this literature is used to make claims that there are no neuropsychological impairments in CD when ADHD is taken into account. ODD/CD is a loose combination of either ODD or CD symptoms, not CD per se. As we mentioned earlier, the diagnosis of ODD does not contain physical aggression symptoms and CD children may or may not show such symptoms. Neuropsychological impairments might be found in CD when physical aggression is present, as some studies have shown. It is not surprising to find that most of these studies report that poor neuropsychological function is found mainly in ADHD (or when ADHD is combined with ODD/CD; see Clark, Prior, & Kinsella, 2000; Geurts, Verté, Oosterlaan, Roeyers, & Sergeant, 2004; Kalff et al., 2002; Nigg et al., 1998; Oosterlaan, Scheres, & Sergeant, 2005) although issues of statistical power plague these studies (Clark et al., 2002). Conclusions from these studies are also consistent with those that compared ADHD with ODD (Speltz, DeKlyen, Calderon, Greenberg, & Fisher, 1999) when it is not necessarily combined with CD. Further, these studies, as well as studies contrasting conduct problems (CP) and

hyperactivity/impulsivity/attention (HIA), typically compare groups using one-factor designs (e.g., lowCP-lowHIA, lowCP-highHIA, highCP-lowHIA, highCP-highHIA) instead of considering the two behavioral dimensions (e.g., CP high & low and HIA high and low) as independent factors. The latter designs are required to determine if the effects are additive or synergistic (Waschbusch, 2002).

CD Summary

In summary, results from CD research have been mixed. Several reasons may account for this unclear picture. At the behavioral level, there is often no specific inclusion of physical aggression and no control for ADHD or hyperactivity. Moreover, many of these studies combine CD with ODD, equate delinquency or antisocial behavior with CD, derive estimates of CD from behavior scales not necessarily designed for such a purpose, and fail to take the history of problem behavior into account. At the neuropsychological level, there is often no statistical control for IQ or verbal ability in studies examining constructs related to executive function. Moreover, many studies are possibly overinclusive in describing some tasks as assessing executive function, as such studies sometimes make the questionable assumption that one task of executive function represents the entire construct.

Antisocial Personality Disorder

ASPD is diagnosed only in individuals over the age of 18 with a history of CD. As we mentioned above, psychopathy is often found among individuals with ASPD. We also note that PCL-R scores >20 but <30 (the PCL-R cut-off point for psychopathy) may reflect ASPD also and that many ASPD individuals have a criminal record. There are few neuropsychological studies of ASPD. Morgan and Lilienfeld (2000) had noted two studies that examined executive function (Deckel, Hesselbrock, & Bauer, 1996; Malloy, Noel, Rogers, Longabaugh, & Beattie, 1989). Overall, they found that

ASPD associations with executive function are weak (effect size $d = 0.10$, weighted $d = 0.08$; Morgan & Lilienfeld, 2000), as was also found in subsequent studies of neuropsychological function (Crowell, Kieffer, Kugeares, & Vanderploeg, 2003; Dinn & Harris, 2000; Stevens, Kaplan, & Hesselbrock, 2003). For example, in one study that controlled for concurrent alcohol and substance abuse, ASPD symptoms were negatively and significantly correlated with WAIS similarities scores but no other intelligence nor executive functioning variables (Stevens et al., 2003). In that study, the strongest correlate of executive function was family history of alcoholism. Finally, one brain imaging study had noted an 11% reduction in frontal gray matter in ASPD even after control for psychosocial factors, but with unclear neuropsychological significance (Raine, Lencz, Bihrle, LaCasse, & Coletti, 2000).

Other Disorders in Which Violence May be Present

Although violence is likely to be found in the more explicitly antisocial disorders that have already been reviewed, violence is often associated as well with alcohol and substance use disorders, schizophrenia, and bipolar disorder. Hence, we briefly review their relation to neuropsychological function.

ALCOHOL AND SUBSTANCE USE

A considerable limitation to the literature investigating neuropsychological function in violent problem behaviors and associated disorders is a potential confound with alcohol and substance abuse. In fact, it is possible that most violent acts occur under the influence of substances. This is relatively well documented in the case of alcohol (Murdoch, Pihl, & Ross, 1990), where there is a clear relation between per-capita alcohol consumption and homicide (studies effect size $d = 0.22$; Rossow, 2001), although the relation may not be causal (Room, Babor, & Rehm, 2005). The culture of illegal drugs is also associated with violence, but that is not dispositive evidence for the violence potential of the drugs themselves. As part of the

mechanisms, we note that alcohol increases the heart rate of nonalcoholic young men with a family history of alcoholism and who also show a history of aggressive behavior (Assaad et al., 2003). These individuals tend to consume more alcohol and make more commission errors (i.e., pressing a button when a "No-go" signal is presented) on a Go/No-go task when intoxicated as opposed to sober, and as opposed to low heart rate responders (whether they were intoxicated or sober, Assaad et al., 2006). Although performance on Go/No-go tasks may not be entirely under frontal lobe control, a family history of alcoholism may be associated more strongly with poor neuropsychological function than ASPD (Stevens et al., 2003).

Our central question, however, concerns the role of neuropsychological factors in this equation. This issue may be best summarized by the work of Giancola (Giancola, 2000) and Pihl (Hoaken, Giancola, & Pihl, 1998). Giancola (2004) showed that aggression in reaction to provocation (using a shock paradigm) was possibly more a function of executive function than of alcohol. However, synergistic mechanisms may be at play, as alcohol preferentially increased aggression in men with lower levels of executive function. In this way, executive function could act both as a mediator and moderator of the alcohol-aggression relationship. However, alcohol could also moderate the quality of executive function on a state (temporary) basis. Indeed, alcohol impairs executive function, mostly on the descending limb of the blood alcohol curve (Pihl, Paylan, Gentes-Hawn, & Hoaken, 2004). Finally, a similar literature exists for substance abuse (Fishbein, 2000).

Schizophrenia

In a recent review, Pontius (2003)noted that less than 10% of violence can be attributed to psychosis, but that the odds of violence in schizophrenia as opposed to no mental disorder is about 4:1. She also pointed out that violence in schizophrenia is often intentional and planned, but that it derives from seriously distorted thinking, delusions, or hallucinations. Such violence occurs typically in paranoid schizophrenia, and neuropsychological function may be otherwise intact. One study of paranoid schizophrenia noted that violence was associated with poor theory of mind (Abu-Akel & Abushua'leh, 2004). Theory of mind is a key social ability to attribute mental states to self and others and requires a broad network including the frontal cortex and cingulate (Calarge, Andreasen, & O'Leary, 2003). A separate neural system underlying belief attribution would complement systems underlying inhibitory control (Saxe, Carey, & Kanwisher, 2004). Although violence was also associated with a history of alcohol and drug abuse (Abu-Akel & Abushua'leh, 2004), another study of murderers showed increased risk for schizophrenia and delusional disorder even after controlling for a history of alcoholism (Schanda et al., 2004). Nevertheless, neuropsychological problems in schizophrenia can be broad and manifold and include attention, memory, executive control, language, and reasoning (Barch, 2005; Heinrichs, 2005), but none of these has yet been specifically related to violence.

Bipolar Disorder

Bipolar disorder is associated with several reckless behaviors characterized by impulsivity, poor judgment, and poor planning (Moeller, Barratt, Dougherty, Schmitz, & Swann, 2001). Bipolar disorder may be associated with violence when it is comorbid with alcohol disorders (Schanda et al., 2004) or substance use disorders (Quanbeck et al., 2005). It is sometimes comorbid with CD. However, preliminary studies of this comorbidity suggest that bipolar disorder does not appear to add to the neuropsychological impairment found in CD (Olvera, Semrud-Clikeman, Pliszka, & O'Donnell, 2005). This finding is consistent with other studies of acute mania in which neuropsychological deficits were stronger in sustained attention and verbal learning than on typical neuropsychological tests associated with CD, such as tests of executive function and the Iowa Gambling Task (Clark, Iversen, &

Goodwin, 2001). However, other studies report executive function impairments even in the nonacute phase, although bipolar patients in either manic or euthymic phase did not differ much from depressed patients (Martinez-Arán et al., 2004).

Chapter Summary and Concluding Comments

The neuropsychology of antisocial behavior has a rich history dating back at least to the mid-19th century. Unfortunately, as our review shows, not as much can be said about the neuropsychology of physical violence. The main problem is that the specificity of neuropsychological deficits to physically violent behavior has been difficult to establish. The bulk of our knowledge regarding the neuropsychology of violence derives from studies of clinical syndromes in which the presence of violence is plausible, but rarely confirmed. Global measures of antisocial, disruptive, externalizing, delinquent, or criminal behavior are also often used. This state of affairs reflects the heterogeneity of processes underlying those conditions, although some factors may be common to all of these conditions. For example, we recently found that the relation between IQ and externalizing behavior problems was moderated by a variation in the dopamine D4 receptor (DeYoung et al., 2006); there was no relation between IQ and externalizing behavior in those who had the 7 repeat allele. We replicated this finding in one community sample and two clinical samples. This moderating effect held across and, in some cases within, externalizing behavior problems. Thus, global measures do have their utility.

Nonetheless, as this book shows, violence is a common outcome in a wide variety of heterogeneous conditions. Violence is present in many disorders for which there may be a neuropsychological basis, although that neuropsychological basis may not necessarily be for violence per se. To advance a research agenda in the study of the neuropsychology of violence, we recommend testing for the specificity of behavior problems, such as identifying physical aggression and isolating it from other co-occurring behavior problems. More explicit assessment of violence or physical aggression is needed with key contrasts to such disorders as ADHD, alcoholism, and nonviolent forms of antisocial behavior. Although this approach should reduce the heterogeneity of behavior of interest, it may not reduce the heterogeneity of underlying processes as much as one hopes; subtypes of physical violence also need to be addressed. The few studies that included a focus on physical aggression or violence did find clear and large effects. But more of these studies are required to investigate the value of this research strategy. A well-documented history of behavior problems should also help reduce heterogeneity. The study of the process of desistance from violence would be informative in this regard.

Our review shows that neuropsychological impairments, even in executive function, are not necessarily specific to physical aggression. We first observed that lesions among frontal lobe patients, despite their poor executive function, rarely lead to physical violence even when acquired at very young ages. Moreover, there is considerable literature on other problems, such as ADHD, and their relation to executive function. However, we note that studies in the ADHD literature rarely control for co-occurring physical aggression. Further, neuropsychological factors tend to explain at most 10% of the variance in measures of violence. Therefore, future studies need to examine potential moderators that may increase our ability to predict violence risk from neuropsychological dysfunction. Such factors could include a history of abuse or neglect, malnutrition, abilities to process and regulate emotions (including autonomic arousal), capacities to cope with stress and perceived provocation, perinatal factors, and genetic factors such as those we referred to earlier (see, e.g., DeYoung et al., 2006). Although many of these variables have been widely studied, few have been examined in conjunction with neuropsychological func-

tion. In this context, poor neuropsychological function will probably comprise only one element of an exceedingly complex model of violent behavior. As this chapter illustrates, however, it may provide one essential piece of a still unsolved puzzle.

References

Abu-Akel, A., & Abushua'leh, K. (2004). 'Theory of mind' in violent and nonviolent patients with paranoid schizophrenia. *Schizophrenia Research*, 69, 45–53.

Achenbach, T. M., Edelbrock, C. S., & Howell, C. T. (1987). Empirically based assessment of the behavioral/emotional problems of 2- and 3-year-old children. *Journal of Abnormal Child Psychology*, 15, 629–650.

Amen, D. G., Stubblefield, M., Carmichael, B., & Thisted, R. (1996). Brain SPECT findings and aggressiveness. *Annals of Clinical Psychiatry*, 8, 129–137.

American Psychiatric Association (2000). *Diagnostic and statistical manual of mental disorders – Text revision (DSM-IV-TR)*. (4th ed.) Washington, DC.

Anderson, A. K. & Phelps, E. A. (2002). Is the human amygdala critical for the subjective experience of emotion? Evidence of intact dispositional affect in patients with amygdala lesions. *Journal of Cognitive Neuroscience*, 14, 709–720.

Arseneault, L., Tremblay, R. E., Boulerice, B., & Saucier, J. F. (2002). Obstetrical complications and violent delinquency: Testing two developmental pathways. *Child Development*, 73, 496–508.

Arseneault, L., Tremblay, R. E., Boulerice, B., Séguin, J. R., & Saucier, J. F. (2000). Minor physical anomalies and family adversity as risk factors for adolescent violent delinquency. *American Journal of Psychiatry*, 157, 917–923.

Assaad, J.-M., Pihl, R. O., Séguin, J. R., Nagin, D. S., Vitaro, F., Carbonneau, R., et al. (2003). Aggressiveness, family history of alcoholism, and the heart rate response to alcohol intoxication. *Experimental and Clinical Psychopharmacology*, 11, 158–166.

Assaad, J.-M., Pihl, R. O., Séguin, J. R., Nagin, D. S., Vitaro, F., & Tremblay, R. E. (2006). Intoxicated behavioral disinhibition and the heart rate response to alcohol. *Experimental and Clinical Psychopharmacology*, 14(3), 377–388.

Barch, D. M. (2005). The cognitive neuroscience of schizophrenia. *Annual Review of Clinical Psychology, 1,* 321–353.

Barker, E. D., Séguin, J. R., White, H. R., Bates, M. E., Lacourse, É., Carbonneau, R., & Tremblay, R. E. (in press). Developmental trajectories of physical violence and theft: Relation to neuro-cognitive performance. *Archives of General Psychiatry.*

Bechara, A., Damasio, A. R., Damasio, H., & Anderson, S. W. (1994). Insensitivity to future consequences following damage to human prefrontal cortex. *Cognition, 50,* 7–15.

Bechara, A., Damasio, H., & Damasio, A. R. (2003). Role of the amygdala in decision-making. *Annals of the New York Academy of Sciences, 985,* 356.

Beckman, M. (2004). Crime, culpability, and the adolescent brain. *Science, 305,* 596–599.

Best, M., Williams, J. M., & Coccaro, E. F. (2002). Evidence for a dysfunctional prefrontal circuit in patients with an impulsive aggressive disorder. *Proceedings of the National Academy of Sciences, 99,* 8448–8453.

Blair, R. J. R. (2004). The roles of orbital frontal cortex in the modulation of antisocial behavior. *Brain and Cognition, 55,* 198–208.

Blair, R. J. R., & Cipolotti, L. (2000). Impaired social response reversal: A case of "acquired sociopathy." *Brain, 123,* 1122–1141.

Blair, R. J. R., Colledge, E., & Mitchell, D. G. V. (2001). Somatic markers and response reversal: Is there orbitofrontal cortex dysfunction in boys with psychopathic tendencies? *Journal of Abnormal Child Psychology, 29,* 499–511.

Blair, R. J. R., Mitchell, D. G. V., Peschardt, K. S., Colledge, E., Leonard, R. A., Shine, J. H., et al. (2004). Reduced sensitivity to others' fearful expressions in psychopathic individuals. *Personality and Individual Differences, 37,* 1111–1122.

Blair, R. J. R., Mitchell, D. G. V., Richell, R. A., Kelly, S., Leonard, A., Newman, C., et al. (2002). Turning a deaf ear to fear: Impaired recognition of vocal affect in psychopathic individuals. *Journal of Abnormal Psychology, 111,* 682–686.

Blair, R. J. R., Morris, J. S., Frith, C. D., Perrett, D. I., & Dolan, R. J. (2000). Dissociable neural responses to facial expressions of sadness and anger. *Brain, 122,* 883–893.

Blake, P. Y., Pincus, J. H., & Buckner, C. (1995). Neurologic abnormalities in murderers. *Neurology, 45,* 1641–1647.

Bongers, I. L., Koot, H. M., van der Ende, J., & Verhulst, F. C. (2004). Developmental trajectories of externalizing behaviors in childhood and adolescence. *Child Development, 75,* 1523–1537.

Broidy, L., Nagin, D. S., Tremblay, R. E., Bates, J. E., Brame, R., Dodge, K. A., et al. (2003). Developmental trajectories of childhood disruptive behaviors and adolescent delinquency: A six site, cross-national study. *Developmental Psychology, 39,* 222–245.

Brothers, L. (2001). *Friday's footprint: How society shapes the human mind.* London: Oxford University Press.

Calarge, C., Andreasen, N. C., & O'Leary, D. S. (2003). Visualizing how one brain understands another: A PET study of theory of mind. *American Journal of Psychiatry, 160,* 1954–1964.

Castle, J., Groothues, C., Bredenkamp, D., Beckett, C., O'Connor, T. G., Rutter, M., et al. (2000). Effects of qualities of early institutional care on cognitive attainment. *American Journal of Orthopsychiatry, 69,* 424–437.

Cauffman, E., Steinberg, L., & Piquero, A. R. (2005). Psychological, neuropsychological and physiological correlates of serious antisocial behavior in adolescence: The role of self-control. *Criminology, 43,* 133–175.

Clark, C., Prior, M., & Kinsella, G. J. (2000). Do executive function deficits differentiate between adolescents with ADHD and Oppositional Defiant/Conduct Disorder? A neuropsychological study using the Six Elements Test and Halying Sentence Completion Test. *Journal of Abnormal Child Psychology, 28,* 404–414.

Clark, C., Prior, M., & Kinsella, G. J. (2002). The relationship between executive function abilities, adaptive behaviour, and academic achievement in children with externalising behaviour problems. *Journal of Child Psychology and Psychiatry, 43,* 785–796.

Clark, L., Iversen, S. D., & Goodwin, G. M. (2001). A neuropsychological investigation of prefrontal cortex involvement in acute mania. *American Journal of Psychiatry, 158,* 1605–1611.

Cohen, J. (1992). A power primer. *Psychological Bulletin, 112,* 155–159.

Coolidge, F. L., DenBoer, J. W., & Segal, D. L. (2004). Personality and neuropsychological correlates of bullying behavior. *Personality and Individual Differences, 36,* 1559–1569.

Cornell, D. G., Warren, J., Hawk, G., Stafford, E., Oram, G., & Pine, D. (1996). Psychopathy in instrumental and reactive violent offenders. *Journal of Consulting and Clinical Psychology*, *64*, 783–790.

Critchley, H. D., Simmons, A., Daly, E. M., Russell, A., van Amelsvoort, T., Robertson, D. M., et al. (2000). Prefrontal and medial temporal correlates of repetitive violence to self and others. *Biological Psychiatry*, *47*, 928–934.

Crowell, T. A., Kieffer, K. M., Kugeares, S., & Vanderploeg, R. D. (2003). Executive and nonexecutive neuropsychological functioning in antisocial personality disorder. *Cognitive and Behavioral Neurology*, *16*, 100–109.

Damasio, A. R. (1996). The somatic marker hypothesis and the possible functions of the prefrontal cortex. *Philosophical Transactions of the Royal Society of London*, *351*, 1413–1420.

Damasio, A. R. (2000). A neural basis for sociopathy. *Archives of General Psychiatry*, *57*, 128–129.

Damasio, A. R., Tranel, D. T., & Damasio, H. C. (1991). Somatic markers and the guidance of behavior: Theory and preliminary testing. In H. S. Levin, H. M. Eisenberg, & A. L. Benton (Eds.), *Frontal lobe function and dysfunction* (pp. 217–229). New York: Oxford University Press.

Damasio, H., Grabowski, T., Frank, R., Galaburda, A. M., & Damasio, A. R. (1994). The return of Phineas Gage: Clues about the brain from the skull of a famous patient. *Science*, *264*, 1102–1105.

Davidson, R. J., Putnam, K. M., & Larson, C. L. (2000). Dysfunction in the neural circuitry of emotion regulation: A possible prelude to violence. *Science*, *289*, 591–594.

Deckel, W. A., Hesselbrock, V., & Bauer, L. O. (1996). Antisocial personality disorder, childhood delinquency, and frontal brain functioning: EEG and neuropsychological findings. *Journal of Clinical Psychology*, *52*, 639–650.

Déry, M., Toupin, J., Pauzé, R., Mercier, H., & Fortin, L. (1999). Neuropsychological characteristics of adolescents with conduct disorder: Association with Attention-Deficit-Hyperactivity and aggression. *Journal of Abnormal Child Psychology*, *27*, 225– 236.

DeYoung, C. G., Peterson, J. B., Séguin, J. R., Mejia, J. M., Pihl, R. O., Beitchman, J. H. et al. (2006). Variation in the dopamine d4 receptor gene moderates the association between externalizing behavior and IQ. *Archives of General Psychiatry*, *63*, 1410–1416.

Dinn, W. M., & Harris, C. L. (2000). Neurocognitive function in antisocial personality disorder. *Psychiatry Research*, *97*, 173–190.

Downes, J. J., Roberts, A. C., Sahakian, B. J., Evenden, J. L., Robbins, R. G., & Robbins, T. W. (1989). Impaired extradimensional shift performance in medicated and unmedicated Parkinson's disease: Evidence for a specific attentional dysfunction. *Neuropsychologia*, *27*, 1329–1343.

Eslinger, P. J., Flaherty-Craig, C. V., & Benton, A. L. (2004). Developmental outcomes after early prefrontal cortex damage. *Brain and Cognition*, *55*, 84–103.

Farrington, D. P., & Loeber, R. (2000). Epidemiology of juvenile violence. *Child and Adolescent Psychiatric Clinics of North America*, *9*, 733.

Filley, C. M., Price, B. H., Nell, V. D., Antoinette, T., Morgan, A. S., Bresnahan, J. F., et al. (2001). Toward an understanding of violence: Neurobehavioral aspects of unwarranted physical aggression: Aspen Neurobehavioral Conference Consensus Statement. *Neuropsychiatry, Neuropsychology, and Behavioral Neurology*, *14*, 1–14.

Fishbein, D. H. (2000). Neuropsychological function, drug abuse, and violence – A conceptual framework. *Criminal Justice and Behavior*, *27*, 139–159.

Frick, P. J., O'Brien, B. S., Wootton, J. M., & McBurnett, K. (1994). Psychopathy and conduct disorder problems in children. *Journal of Abnormal Psychology*, *103*, 700–707.

Geurts, H. M., Verté, S., Oosterlaan, J., Roeyers, H., & Sergeant, J. A. (2004). How specific are executive functioning deficits in attention deficit hyperactivity disorder and autism? *Journal of Child Psychology and Psychiatry*, *45*, 836–854.

Giancola, P. R. (2000). Executive functioning: A conceptual framework for alcohol-related aggression. *Volkow Experimental and Clinical Psychopharmacology*, *8*, 576–597.

Giancola, P. R. (2004). Executive functioning and alcohol-related aggression. *Journal of Abnormal Psychology*, *113*, 541–555.

Giancola, P. R., Mezzich, A. C., & Tarter, R. E. (1998). Executive cognitive functioning, temperament, and antisocial behavior in conduct-disordered adolescent females. *Journal of Abnormal Psychology*, *107*, 629–641.

Gilbertson, M. W., Shenton, M. E., Ciszewski, A., Kasai, K., Lasko, N. B., Orr, S. P., et al. (2002). Smaller hippocampal volume predicts pathologic vulnerability to psychological trauma. *Nature Neuroscience, 5,* 1242–1247.

Gorenstein, E. E. (1982). Frontal lobe functions in psychopaths. *Journal of Abnormal Psychology, 91,* 368–379.

Grafman, J., Schwab, K., Warden, D., Pridgen, A., Brown, H. R., & Salazar, A. M. (1996). Frontal lobe injuries, violence, and aggression: A report of the Vietnam Head Injury Study. *Neurology, 46,* 1231–1238.

Hare, R. D. (1984). Performance of psychopaths on cognitive tasks related to frontal lobe function. *Journal of Abnormal Psychology, 93,* 133–140.

Hare, R. D. (1999). Psychopathy as a risk factor for violence. *Psychiatric Quarterly, 70,* 181–197.

Hare, R. D. (2003). *Manual for the Revised Psychopathy Checklist* (2nd ed.). Toronto: Multi-Health Systems.

Hare, R. D., Hart, S. D., & Harpur, T. J. (1991). Psychopathy and the DSM-IV criteria for antisocial personality disorder. *Journal of Abnormal Psychology, 100,* 391–398.

Hart, S. D., Forth, A. E., & Hare, R. D. (1990). Performance of criminal psychopaths on selected neuropsychological tests. *Journal of Abnormal Psychology, 99,* 374–379.

Heaton, R. K. (1981). *A manual for the Wisconsin Card Sorting Test.* Odessa, FL: Psychological Assessment Resources.

Heinrichs, R. W. (2005). The primacy of cognition in schizophrenia. *American Psychologist, 60,* 229–242.

Hiatt, K. D., Schmitt, W. A., & Newman, J. P. (2004). Stroop tasks reveal abnormal selective attention among psychopathic offenders. *Neuropsychology, 18,* 50–59.

Hoaken, P. N. S., Giancola, P. R., & Pihl, R. O. (1998). Executive cognitive functions as mediators of alcohol-related aggression. *Alcohol and Alcoholism, 33,* 47–54.

Hoffman, J. J., Hall, R. W., & Bartsch, T. W. (1987). On the relative importance of "psychopathic" personality and alcoholism on neuropsychological measures of frontal lobe dysfunction. *Journal of Abnormal Psychology, 96,* 158–160.

Hopkins-Golightly, T., Raz, S., & Sandler, C. J. (2003). Influence of slight to moderate risk for birth hypoxia on acquisition of cognitive and language function in the preterm infant: A cross-sectional comparison with preterm-birth controls. *Neuropsychology, 17,* 3–13.

Huijbregts, S. C. J., Séguin, J. R., Zelazo, P. D., Parent, S., Japel, C., & Tremblay, R. E. (2006). Interrelations between pregnancy smoking, birth weight and sociodemographic factors in the prediction of early cognitive outcome. *Infant and Child Development, 15,* 593–606.

Huijbregts, S. C. J., Séguin, J. R., Zoccolillo, M., Boivin, M., & Tremblay, R. E. (in press). Maternal smoking during pregnancy and externalizing behavior problems during early childhood. *Journal of Abnormal Child Psychology.*

Ishikawa, S. S., Raine, A., Lencz, T., Bihrle, S., & LaCasse, L. (2001). Autonomic stress reactivity and executive function in successful and unsuccessful criminal psychopaths from the community. *Journal of Abnormal Psychology, 110,* 423–432.

Kalff, A. C., Hendriksen, J. G. M., Kroes, M., Vles, J. S. H., Steyaert, J., Feron, F. J. M., et al. (2002). Neurocognitive performance of 5- and 6-year-old children who met criteria for attention deficit/hyperactivity disorder at 18 months follow-up: Results from a prospective population study. *Journal of Abnormal Child Psychology, 30,* 589–598.

Kivlahan, D. R., Marlatt, G. A., Fromme, K., Coppel, D. B., & Williams, E. (1990). Secondary prevention with college drinkers: Evaluation of an alcohol skills training program. *Journal of Consulting and Clinical Psychology, 58,* 805–810.

Kolb, B., & Wishaw, I. Q. (2003). Fundamentals of human neuropsychology (5th ed.). New York: Freeman.

Lacourse, É., Côté, S., Nagin, D. S., Vitaro, F., Brendgen, M., & Tremblay, R. E. (2002). A longitudinal-experimental approach to testing theories of antisocial behavior development. *Development and Psychopathology, 14,* 911–926.

Lahey, B. B., Loeber, R., Burke, J. D., & Rathouz, P. J. (2002). Adolescent outcomes of childhood conduct disorder among clinic-referred boys: Predictors of improvement. *Journal of Abnormal Child Psychology, 30,* 333–348.

Lahey, B. B., Loeber, R., Quay, H., Applegate, B., Shaffer, D., Waldman, I. D., et al. (1998). Validity of DSM-IV subtypes of conduct disorder based on age of onset. *Journal of the American Academy of Child and Adolescent Psychiatry, 37,* 435–442.

Lahey, B. B., Waldman, I. D., & McBurnett, K. (1999). Annotation: The development of antisocial behavior: An integrative causal model. *Journal of Child Psychology and Psychiatry, 40,* 669–682.

Lapierre, D., Braun, M. J., & Hodgins, S. (1995). Ventral frontal deficits in psychopathy: Neuropsychological test findings. *Neuropsychologia, 33,* 139–151.

Levenson, M. R., Kiehl, K. A., & Fitzpatrick, C. M. (1995). Assessing psychopathic attributes in a noninstitutionalized population. *Journal of Personality and Social Psychology, 68,* 151–158.

Lezak, M. D., Howieson, D. B., & Loring, D. W. (2004). *Neuropsychological Assessment.* (4th ed.). New York: Oxford University Press.

Lilienfeld, S. O., & Andrews, B. P. (1996). Development and preliminary validation of psychopathic personality traits in noncriminal populations. *Journal of Personality Assessment, 66,* 488–524.

Lilienfeld, S. O., & Waldman, I. D. (1990). The relation between childhood attention-deficit hyperactivity disorder and adult antisocial behavior reexamined: The problem of heterogeneity. *Clinical Psychology Review, 10,* 699–725.

Liu, J., Raine, A., Venables, P. H., & Mednick, S. A. (2004). Malnutrition at age 3 years and externalizing behavior problems at ages 8, 11, and 17 years. *American Journal of Psychiatry, 161,* 2005–2013.

Loeber, R., Burke, J. D., & Lahey, B. B. (2002). What are adolescent antecedents to antisocial personality disorder? *Criminal Behaviour and Mental Health, 12,* 24–36.

Lueger, R. J., & Gill, K. J. (1990). Frontal-lobe cognitive dysfunction in conduct disorder adolescents. *Journal of Clinical Psychology, 46,* 696–705.

Lynam, D. R. (1998). Early identification of the fledgling psychopath: Locating the psychopathic child in the current nomenclature. *Journal of Abnormal Psychology, 107,* 566–575.

Lynam, D. R., Whiteside, S., & Jones, S. (1999). Self-reported psychopathy: A validation study. *Journal of Personality Assessment, 73,* 110–132.

Malloy, P., Noel, N., Rogers, S., Longabaugh, R., & Beattie, M. C. (1989). Risk factors for neuropsychological impairment in alcoholics: Antisocial personality, age, years of drinking and gender. *Journal of Studies on Alcohol, 50,* 422–426.

Manes, F., Sahakian, B., Clark, L., Rogers, R. D., Antoun, N., Aitken, M., et al. (2002). Decision-making processes following damage to the prefrontal cortex. *Brain, 125,* 624–639.

Martinez-Arän, A., Vieta, E., Reinares, M., Colom, F., Torrent, C., Sanchez-Moreno, J., et al. (2004). Cognitive function across manic or hypomanic, depressed, and euthymic states in bipolar disorder. *American Journal of Psychiatry, 161,* 262–270.

Mataro, M., Jurado, M. A., Garcia-Sanchez, C., Barraquer, L., Costa-Jussa, F. R., & Junque, C. (2001). Long-term effects of bilateral frontal brain lesion: 60 years after injury with an iron bar. *Archives of Neurology, 58,* 1139–1142.

Meaney, M. J., Aitken, D. H., van Berkell, C., Bhatnagar, S., & Sapolsky, R. M. (1988). Effect of neonatal handling on age-related impairments associated with the hippocampus. *Science, 239,* 766–768.

Meehl, P. E. (1971). High school yearbooks: A reply to Schwarz. *Journal of Abnormal Psychology, 77,* 143–148.

Meyers, C. A., Berman, S. A., Scheibel, R. S., & Hayman, A. (1992). Case report: Acquired antisocial personality disorder associated with unilateral left orbital frontal lobe damage. *Journal of Psychiatry and Neuroscience, 17,* 121–125.

Mezzacappa, E., Kindlon, D., & Earls, F. J. (2001). Child abuse and performance task assessments of executive functions in boys. *Journal of Child Psychology and Psychiatry, 42,* 1041–1048.

Milner, B., Petrides, M., & Smith, M. L. (1985). Frontal lobes and the temporal organization of memory. *Human Neurobiology, 4,* 137–142.

Mitchell, D. G. V., Colledge, E., Leonard, A., & Blair, R. J. R. (2002). Risky decision and response reversal: Is there evidence of orbitofrontal cortex dysfunction in psychopathic individuals? *Neuropsychologia, 1423,* 1–10.

Moeller, F. G., Barratt, E. S., Dougherty, D. M., Schmitz, J. M., & Swann, A. C. (2001). Psychiatric aspects of impulsivity. *American Journal of Psychiatry, 158,* 1783–1793.

Moffitt, T. E. (1990a). Juvenile delinquency and attention deficit disorder: Boy's developmental trajectories from age 3 to age 15. *Child Development, 61,* 893–910.

Moffitt, T. E. (1990b). The neuropsychology of juvenile delinquency: A critical review. In M. Tonry & N. Morris (Eds.), *Crime and justice: A review of research* (12th ed., pp. 99–169). Chicago: University of Chicago Press.

Moffitt, T. E. (1993a). Adolescence-limited and life-course-persistent antisocial behavior: A developmental taxonomy. *Psychological Review, 100,* 674–701.

Moffitt, T. E. (1993b). The neuropsychology of conduct disorder. *Development and Psychopathology, 5,* 135–151.

Moffitt, T. E. (2003). Life-course-persistent and adolescence-limited antisocial behavior: A 10-year research review. In B. B. Lahey, T. E. Moffitt, & A. Caspi (Eds.), *Causes of conduct disorder and juvenile delinquency.* New York: Guilford.

Moffitt, T. E., Caspi, A., Harrington, H. L., & Milne, B. J. (2002). Males on the life-course-persistent and adolescence-limited antisocial pathways: Follow-up at age 26 years. *Development and Psychopathology, 14,* 179–207.

Moffitt, T. E., & Henry, B. (1989). Neuropsychological assessment of executive functions in self-reported delinquents. *Development and Psychopathology, 1,* 105–118.

Moffitt, T. E., & Henry, B. (1991). Neuropsychological studies of juvenile delinquency and juvenile violence. In J. S. Milner (Ed.), *Neuropsychology of aggression* (pp. 67–91). Boston: Kluwer.

Moffitt, T. E., Lynam, D. R., & Silva, P. A. (1994). Neuropsychological tests predicting persistent male delinquency. *Criminology, 32,* 277–300.

Moffitt, T. E., & Silva, P. A. (1988a). Neuropsychological deficit and self-reported delinquency in an unselected birth cohort. *Journal of the American Academy of Child and Adolescent Psychiatry, 27,* 233–240.

Moffitt, T. E., & Silva, P. A. (1988b). Self-reported delinquency, neuropsychological deficit, and history of attention deficit disorder. *Journal of Abnormal Child Psychology, 16,* 553–569.

Morgan, A. B., & Lilienfeld, S. O. (2000). A meta-analytic review of the relation between antisocial behavior and neuropsychological measures of executive function. *Clinical Psychology Review, 20,* 113–136.

Mortensen, E. L., Fleischer Michaelsen, K., Sanders, S. A., & Machover Reinish, J. (2002). The association between duration of breast-feeding and adult intelligence. *Journal of the American Medical Association, 287,* 2365–2371.

Murdoch, D. D., Pihl, R. O., & Ross, D. F. (1990). Alcohol and crimes of violence: Present issues. *International Journal of the Addictions, 25,* 1065–1081.

Nagin, D. S., & Tremblay, R. E. (1999). Trajectories of boys' physical aggression, opposition, and hyperactivity on the path to physically violent and nonviolent juvenile delinquency. *Child Development, 70,* 1181–1196.

National Institute of Child Health and Human Development Early Child Care Research Network (2004). Trajectories of physical aggression from toddlerhood to middle childhood: Predictors, correlates, and outcomes. *Monographs of the Society for Research in Child Development, 69*(4), vii–128.

Newman, J. P., & Lorenz, A. R. (2002). Response modulation and emotion processing: Implications for psychopathy and other dysregulatory psychopathology. In R. J. Davidson, K. Scherer, & H. H. Goldsmith (Eds.), *Handbook of affective sciences* (pp. 1043–1067). Oxford: Oxford University Press.

Nigg, J. T. (2005). Neuropsychologic theory and findings in attention-deficit/hyperactivity disorder: The state of the field and salient challenges for the coming decade. *Biological Psychiatry, 57,* 1424–1435.

Nigg, J. T., Glass, J. M., Wong, M. M., Poon, E., Jester, J. M., Fitzgerald, H. E., et al. (2004). Neuropsychological executive functioning in children at elevated risk for alcoholism: Findings in early adolescence. *Journal of Abnormal Psychology, 113,* 302–314.

Nigg, J. T., Hinshaw, S. P., Carte, E. T., & Treuting, J. J. (1998). Neuropsychological correlates of childhood Attention-Deficit/Hyperactivity Disorder explainable by comorbid disruptive behavior or reading problems? *Journal of Abnormal Psychology, 107,* 468–480.

Nigg, J. T., Willcutt, E. G., Doyle, A. E., & Sonuga-Barke, E. J. S. (2005). Causal heterogeneity in attention-deficit/hyperactivity disorder: Do we need neuropsychologically impaired subtypes? *Biological Psychiatry, 57,* 1224–1230.

Olvera, R. L., Semrud-Clikeman, M., Pliszka, S. R., & O'Donnell, L. (2005). Neuropsychological deficits in adolescents with conduct disorder and comorbid bipolar disorder: A pilot study. *Bipolar Disorders, 7,* 57–67.

Oosterlaan, J., Scheres, A., & Sergeant, J. A. (2005). Which executive functioning deficits are associated with AD/HD, ODD/CD and comorbid AD/HD plus ODD/CD? *Journal of Abnormal Child Psychology, 33,* 69–85.

Pennington, B. F., & Ozonoff, S. (1996). Executive functions and developmental psychopathology. *Journal of Child Psychology and Psychiatry, 37*, 51–87.

Petrides, M., Alivisatos, B., Evans, A. C., & Meyer, E. (1993a). Dissociation of human mid-dorsolateral from posterior dorsolateral frontal cortex in memory processing. *Proceedings of the National Academy of Sciences USA, 90*, 873–877.

Petrides, M., Alivisatos, B., Meyer, E., & Evans, A. C. (1993b). Functional activation of the human frontal cortex during the performance of verbal working memory tasks. *Proceedings of the National Academy of Sciences USA, 90*, 878–882.

Pihl, R. O., Paylan, S. S., Gentes-Hawn, A., & Hoaken, P. N. S. (2004). Alcohol affects executive cognitive functioning differentially on the ascending versus descending limb of the blood alcohol concentration curve. *Alcoholism: Clinical and Experimental Research, 27*, 773–779.

Pontius, A. A. (2003). Violence in schizophrenia versus limbic psychotic trigger reaction: Prefrontal aspects of volitional action. *Aggression and Violent Behavior, 9*, 503–521.

Pontius, A. A., & Lemay, M. (2003). Aggression in temporal lobe epilepsy and limbic psychotic trigger reaction implicating vagus kindling of hippocampus/amygdala (in sinus abnormalites on MRIs). *Aggression and Violent Behavior, 8*, 245–257.

Quanbeck, C. D., Stone, D. C., Scott, C. L., McDermott, B. E., Altshuler, L. L., & Frye, M. A. (2005). Clinical and legal correlates of inmates with bipolar disorder at time of criminal arrest. *Journal of Clinical Psychiatry, 65*, 198–203.

Raine, A. (2002a). Annotation: The role of prefrontal deficits, low autonomic arousal, and early health factors in the development of antisocial and aggressive behavior in children. *Journal of Child Psychology and Psychiatry, 43*, 417–434.

Raine, A. (2002b). Biosocial studies of antisocial and violent behavior in children and adults: A review. *Journal of Abnormal Child Psychology, 30*, 311–326.

Raine, A., Buchsbaum, M. S., Stanley, J., Lottenberg, S., Abel, L., & Stoddard, J. (1994). Selective reductions in prefrontal glucose metabolism in murderers. *Biological Psychiatry, 36*, 365–373.

Raine, A., Lencz, T., Bihrle, S., LaCasse, L., & Coletti, P. (2000). Reduced prefrontal gray matter volume and reduced autonomic activity in antisocial personality disorder. *Archives of General Psychiatry, 57*, 119–127.

Raine, A., Moffitt, T. E., Caspi, A., Loeber, R., Stouthamer-Loeber, M., & Lynam, D. R. (2005). Neurocognitive impairments in boys on the life-course persistent antisocial path. *Journal of Abnormal Psychology, 114*, 38–49.

Raine, A., Yaralian, P. S., Reynolds, C., Venables, P. H., & Mednick, S. A. (2002). Spatial but not verbal cognitive deficits at age 3 years in persistently antisocial individuals. *Development and Psychopathology, 14*, 25–44.

Rolls, E. T., Hornak, J., Wade, D., & McGrath, J. (1994). Emotion-related learning in patients with social and emotional changes associated with frontal lobe damage. *Journal of Neurology, Neurosurgery, and Psychiatry, 57*, 1518–1524.

Room, R., Babor, T., & Rehm, J. (2005). Alcohol and public health. *The Lancet, 365*, 519–530.

Rossow, I. (2001). Alcohol and homicide: A cross-cultural comparison of the relationship in 14 European countries. *Addiction, 96*, S77–S92.

Salekin, R. T., Rogers, R., & Sewell, K. (1996). A review and meta-analysis of the psychopathy checklist and psychopathy checklist-revised: Predictive validity of dangerousness. *Clinical Psychology Science and Practice, 3*, 203–215.

Saxe, R., Carey, S., & Kanwisher, N. (2004). Understanding other minds: Linking developmental psychology and functional neuroimaging. *Annual Review of Psychology, 55*, 87–124.

Schanda, H., Knecht, G., Schreinzer, D., Stompe, T., Ortwein-Swoboda, G., & Waldhoer, T. (2004). Homicide and major mental disorders: A 25-year study. *Acta Psychiatrica Scandinavica, 110*, 98–107.

Schmitt, W. A., Brinkley, C. A., & Newman, J. P. (1999). Testing Damasio's somatic marker hypothesis with psychopathic individuals: Risk takers or risk averse? *Journal of Abnormal Psychology, 108*, 538–543.

Séguin, J. R. (2003, April). *Executive function in early physical aggression: Longitudinal data from ages 17 to 60 months.* Paper presented at the Society for Research in Child Development Biennial Meeting.

Séguin, J. R. (2004). Neurocognitive elements of antisocial behaviour: Relevance of an orbitofrontal cortex account. *Brain and Cognition, 55*, 185–197.

Séguin, J. R., Arseneault, L., Boulerice, B., Harden, P. W., & Tremblay, R. E. (2002). Response perseveration in adolescent boys with stable and unstable histories of physical aggression: The role of underlying processes. *Journal of Child Psychology and Psychiatry, 43,* 481–494.

Séguin, J. R., Boulerice, B., Harden, P., Tremblay, R. E., & Pihl, R. O. (1999). Executive functions and physical aggression after controlling for attention deficit hyperactivity disorder, general memory, and IQ. *Journal of Child Psychology and Psychiatry, 40,* 1197–1208.

Séguin, J. R., Nagin, D. S., Assaad, J.-M., & Tremblay, R. E. (2004). Cognitive-neuropsychological function in chronic physical aggression and hyperactivity. *Journal of Abnormal Psychology, 113,* 603–613.

Séguin, J. R., Pihl, R. O., Harden, P. W., Tremblay, R. E., & Boulerice, B. (1995). Cognitive and neuropsychological characteristics of physically aggressive boys. *Journal of Abnormal Psychology, 104,* 614–624.

Séguin, J. R., & Zelazo, P. D. (2005). Executive function in early physical aggression. In R. E. Tremblay, W. W. Hartup, & J. Archer (Eds.), *Developmental origins of aggression* (pp. 307–329). New York: Guilford.

Séguin, J. R., Zelazo, P. D., & Tremblay, R. E. (2005, April). *Early cognitive function in physical aggression and hyperactivity trajectories from ages 17–42 months.* Paper presented at the biennial meeting of the Society for Research in Child Development, Atlanta.

Shallice, T. (2003). Functional imaging and neuropsychology findings: How can they be linked? *Neuroimage, 20,* S146–S154.

Smith, S. S., Arnett, P. A., & Newman, J. P. (1992). Neuropsychological differentiation of psychopathic and nonpsychopathic criminal offenders. *Personality and Individual Differences, 13,* 1233–1243.

Sommers, C. H., & Satel, S. (2005). *One nation under therapy: How the helping culture is eroding self-reliance.* New York: St. Martin's Press.

Speltz, M. L., DeKlyen, M., Calderon, R., Greenberg, M. T., & Fisher, P. A. (1999). Neuropsychological characteristics and test behaviors of boys with early onset conduct problems. *Journal of Abnormal Psychology, 108,* 315–325.

Stevens, M., Kaplan, R., & Hesselbrock, V. (2003). Executive-cognitive functioning in the development of antisocial personality disorder. *Addictive Behaviors, 28,* 285–300.

Stone, V. E., Baron-Cohen, S., & Knight, R. T. (1998). Frontal lobe contributions to theory of mind. *Journal of Cognitive Neuroscience, 10,* 640–656.

Stouthamer-Loeber, M., Loeber, R., Wei, E., Farrington, D. P., & Wikström, P.-O. H. (2002). Risk and promotive effects in the explanation of persistent serious delinquency in boys. *Journal of Consulting and Clinical Psychology, 70,* 111–123.

Stuss, D. T., Gallup, G. G., & Alexander, M. P. (2001). The frontal lobes are necessary for "theory of mind." *Brain, 124,* 279–286.

Stuss, D. T., Gow, C. A., & Hetherington, C. R. (1992). "No longer Gage": Frontal lobe dysfunction and emotional changes. *Journal of Consulting and Clinical Psychology, 60,* 349–359.

Suchy, Y., & Kosson, D. S. (2005). State-dependent executive deficits among psychopathic offenders. *Journal of the International Neuropsychological Society, 11,* 311–321.

Sutker, P. B., & Allain, A. N. (1987). Cognitive abstraction, shifting, and control: Clinical sample comparisons of psychopaths and nonpsychopaths. *Journal of Abnormal Psychology, 96,* 73–75.

Tateno, A., Jorge, R. E., & Robinson, R. G. (2004). Clinical correlates of aggressive behavior after traumatic brain injury. *Journal of Neuropsychiatry and Clinical Neurosciences, 15,* 155–160.

Taylor, J., Iacono, W. G., & McGue, M. (2000). Evidence for a genetic etiology of early-onset delinquency. *Journal of Abnormal Psychology, 109,* 634–643.

Teichner, G., & Golden, C. J. (2000). The relationship of neuropsychological impairment to conduct disorder in adolescence: A conceptual review. *Aggression and Violent Behavior, 5,* 509–528.

Toupin, J., Déry, M., Pauzé, R., Mercier, H., & Fortin, L. (2000). Cognitive and familial contributions to conduct disorder in children. *Journal of Child Psychology and Psychiatry, 41,* 333–344.

Tremblay, R. E. (2000). The development of aggressive behaviour during childhood: What have we learned in the past century? *International Journal of Behavioral Development, 24,* 129–141.

Tremblay, R. E., Boulerice, B., Harden, P. W., McDuff, P., Pérusse, D., Pihl, R. O., et al. (1996). Do children in Canada become more aggressive as they approach adolescence? In *Growing up in Canada* (pp. 127–137). Ottawa: Statistics Canada.

Tremblay, R. E., Nagin, D. S., Séguin, J. R., Zoccolillo, M., Zelazo, P. D., Boivin, M., et al. (2004). Physical aggression during early childhood: Trajectories and predictors. *Pediatrics, 114,* e43–e50.

Walsh, A. (1987). Cognitive functioning and delinquency: Property versus violent offenses. *International Journal of Offender Therapy and Comparative Criminology, 31,* 285–289.

Waschbusch, D. A. (2002). A meta-analytic examination of comorbid hyperactive – impulsive – attention problems and conduct problems. *Psychological Bulletin, 128,* 118–150.

Wechsler, D. (1981). *Manual for the Wechsler Adult Intelligence Scale-Revised.* San Antonio, TX: The Psychological Corporation.

Weiger, W. A., & Bear, D. M. (1988). An approach to the neurology of aggression. *Journal of Psychiatry Research, 22,* 85–98.

Whalen, P. J., Kagan, J., Cook, R. G., Davis, F. C., Kim, H., Polis, S., et al. (2004). Human amygdala responsivity to masked fearful eye whites. *Science, 306,* 2061.

White, H. R., Bates, M. E., & Buyske, S. (2001). Adolescence-limited versus persistent delinquency: Extending Moffitt's hypothesis into adulthood. *Journal of Abnormal Psychology, 110,* 600–609.

Yolton, K., Dietrich, K., Auinger, P., Lanphear, B. P., & Hornung, R. (2005). Exposure to environmental tobacco smoke and cognitive abilities among U.S. children and adolescents. *Environmental Health Perspectives, 113,* 98–103.

CHAPTER 10

The Interaction of Nature and Nurture in Antisocial Behavior

Kenneth A. Dodge and Michelle R. Sherrill

Perhaps the most important discovery in developmental psychopathology over the past two decades has been the interaction (i.e., moderation, not coaction) effect between genes and the social-rearing environment in predicting individual differences in antisocial behavior outcomes (e.g., Caspi et al., 2002). This finding has the potential to resolve long-standing disputes regarding the primacy of genetic versus social-environmental influences by highlighting the fact that each factor is significant but the magnitude of its effect depends on levels of the other factor. The dispute itself has roots in philosophical arguments about the nature of the human species as a tabula rasa (Locke, 1690/1913) to be shaped by the environment versus the material determinism and biological destiny in Hobbes's *Leviathan* (1651/1969) and Rousseau's (1762) noble savage. Parties on both sides of the contentious debate have found solace in the interaction effect. However, merely concluding that nature and nurture interact tells us nothing about the shape and meaning of the effect. The goals of this chapter are to propose a general hypothesis regarding the shape of the interaction effect, to review published evidence, and to interpret the findings for future research, practice, and public policy.

Biosocial interactions have been posited since Mednick and Christiansen's (1977) studies of 1,800 3-year-olds in Mauritius. Most investigators of interaction-effect findings have examined the effect in terms of the magnitude of the genetic effect at different levels of the environment. For example, Foley et al. (2004) interpreted their interaction effect between a functional polymorphism in the promoter of the monoamine oxidase A (MAO-A) gene and the environmental experience of physical maltreatment as indicating that "variation in exposure to environmental risks reorders genotypic effects" (p. 742). Raine, Brennan, and Mednick (1994) interpreted their biosocial interaction as predominantly a main effect of biological factors that is evidenced under certain conditions: "It is possible that such (birth) complications result in brain dysfunction and associated neurological and neuropsychological deficits that in turn directly and indirectly predispose to violence"

(p. 987). This interpretation of accelerating, synergistic, or exacerbating effects of an environmental factor has been viewed simply as providing a clearer window on the predominant biological main effect. The most likely reason for emphasizing the genotypic effect is that most of these researchers are primarily studying genetic influences.

For clinical practice and public policy, however, these same findings need to be interpreted from the perspective of the environmental effect. That is, for which kinds of children are environmental influences the strongest? Which kinds of children should receive the most public resources? In proposing policies to prevent crime, Herrnstein and Murray (1994) wrote, "Much of public policy toward the disadvantaged starts from the premise that interventions can make up for genetic or environmental disadvantages, and *that premise is overly optimistic.*... Much can and should be done... for those who have the *greatest* potential" (p. 550). They clearly imply that the environmental impact will be weakest for those children at highest genetic risk for crime and that therefore public dollars should not be devoted to those children because they are beyond hope of protection through intervention. This perspective reflects the prevailing public policy and opinion toward violent youth today. As Elliott, Hamburg, and Williams (1998) concluded, "The nation is investing far more resources in building and maintaining prisons than in primary prevention programs. Such investments imply an emphasis on reacting to violent offenders after the fact and removing them from the community, rather than preventing children from becoming violent offenders in the first place" (p. 11). This perspective holds that some children are destined to become "super predators" and that public resources and environmental factors will have little effect on their outcomes.

The Shape of the Interaction Effect

One of the challenges in investigating interaction effects is that person (*P*) risk variables and environmental (*E*) risk variables tend to be positively correlated, resulting in relatively few individuals in the asymmetric cells (i.e., low *P* risk but high *E* risk, and high *P* risk but low *E* risk) that are necessary to test interaction effects. This *P–E* correlation occurs through both evocative processes (i.e., person factors cause certain environments to occur) and passive processes (i.e., both person factors and environmental factors are caused by a common third factor, such as genes). This P–E correlation results in low statistical power in testing interaction effects in most studies (McClelland & Judd, 1993) and sometimes leads to the false-negative conclusion that interaction effects are not present. It can also disguise one type of main effect for the other main effect, if appropriate controls are not included in statistical models. Fortunately, recent studies have employed large samples that include sufficient statistical power to detect moderate-sized interaction effects or have taken advantage of natural experiments that de-confound genes and environments (e.g., twin studies, adoption studies, and intervention experiments). With these innovations, interactions have now been robustly identified.

The shape of the interaction effect has received surprisingly little debate. Given that most theories, logic, plausibility, and findings to date suggest that the high *P*-risk/high *E*-risk group will be the most likely to become antisocial over time and that the low *P*-risk/low *E*-risk group will be least likely to become antisocial, interaction-effect hypotheses must focus on the two asymmetric cells; that is, the high *P*-risk and low *E*-risk group and the low *P*-risk and high *E*-risk group. Four hypotheses are plausible. First, strict biological hegemonists would argue that environmental effects are not independent causal effects, but that they simply mask unexamined genetic variables. When genetic factors are crossed with environmental factors, the *E* effects would disappear. This hypothesis is not an interaction hypothesis at all; rather, it posits that the high *P*-risk/low *E*-risk group will be identical to the high *P*-risk/high *E*-risk group and the low P-risk/high E-risk group will be identical to the low P-risk/low E-risk group (i.e., a P-risk main effect). A second plausible alternative is that environmental effects mediate, account for, and even cause biological risk factors. Thus, this hypothesis is again not an interaction effect, but instead merely a main effect of E-risk and no effect of P-risk.

Two true interaction effect hypotheses are also plausible. The first was advocated by Mednick and Christiansen (1977), who proposed a pattern "in terms of the interaction of early family training and individual physiological characteristics. If there are lacks in either of these spheres, the learning of law-abidance will be incomplete, retarded and/or unsuccessful" (p. 1). Mednick was suggesting that *either P* risk or *E* risk is sufficient to lead to antisocial outcomes; thus, both asymmetric cell groups should display antisocial outcomes as high as those for the combined high P-risk/high E-risk group. A corollary of Mednick's hypothesis is that the magnitude of the E effect will be zero at high levels of P risk and large at low levels of P risk.

The hypothesis posed in this chapter is the exact opposite. It is hypothesized that, perhaps paradoxically, children who are at *highest* genetic risk for violent behavior are the *most* susceptible to environmental influence, the *most* plastic with regard to life-course outcomes, and the *most* likely to benefit from public resources. The hypothesis that some children might be more susceptible to environmental influence than other children was offered by Wachs and Gandour (1983) as the "organismic-specificity" hypothesis. Boyce and Ellis (2004) called this variation "biological sensitivity to context." Belsky (2005) offered an evolutionary theory to account for this within-species diversity in environmental susceptibility as a way to protect the species under unforeseen and heterogeneous environmental conditions. Furthermore, he suggested that variation in environmental susceptibility is a function of the genotype. He did not specify parameters of the genotype, however. In this chapter, we posit that environmental susceptibility is greatest at high levels of genetic risk.

One source of this hypothesis comes from selective breeding studies of mice. Gottlieb (2003) reported Hood's (2005) study in which mice were bred across 39 generations to be extremely aggressive or nonaggressive, and then offspring were randomly assigned to receive an environment of normal group-rearing or adverse isolation-rearing (akin to neglect). Among the low genetic-risk group of mice, the environmental effect of group- versus isolation-rearing was nil (group-rearing $M = 5$ aggressive behaviors per unit of time, isolation-rearing $M = 0$ aggressive behaviors, E effect $= -5$). Among the high genetic-risk group of mice, however, the E effect was quite large (group-rearing $M = 0$ aggressive behaviors, isolation-rearing $M = 53$ aggressive behaviors, E effect $= 53$). Only among the high genetic-risk group did the rearing environment make a difference in aggressive behavior outcomes. In genetic theory terms, the "range of reaction" was greater for high genetic-risk mice than for low genetic-risk mice.

A similar effect has been observed by Suomi (1997) with rhesus macaques selectively bred for high versus low fearfulness/anxiety and then cross-fostered to rearing by highly nourishing or average foster mothers. Dramatic environmental rearing effects on behavioral disturbance occurred, but only among the high genetic-risk macaques. In a second study, Bennett et al. (2002) selected 132 rhesus macaques for variation in serotonin transporter genes and randomly assigned them to nourishing rearing by mothers or deprived rearing by peers. They found that parent-rearing led to normal CSF 5-HIAA concentrations for both high- and low-genetic risk groups, and only under problematic rearing conditions did the genetic risk become expressed in deficient 5-HIAA concentrations (which have been associated with antisocial behavior outcomes).

This chapter evaluates the differential susceptibility to environmental rearing hypothesis in studies of aggressive behavior in children, first by reviewing briefly the literature on genetic and environmental main effects on antisocial behavior, then by reviewing person-by-environment inter-action studies, and finally by formulating the implications of these findings for theory, research, practice, and policy.

"Nature" Main Effects on the Development of Antisocial Behavior

Temperament and Personality

Numerous longitudinal studies from diverse cultures have identified early tempera-mental and personality characteristics that predispose children to later antisocial out-comes through main effects. Shaw, Gilliom, Ingoldsby, and Nagin (2003) found that observed fearlessness among Americans at age 2 distinguished a chronically high anti-social group from all other trajectory groups. Raine, Reynolds, Venables, Mednick, and Farrington (1998) found that measures of fearlessness and stimulation-seeking among Mauritians at age 3 predicted aggression at age 11. Tremblay, Pihl, Vitaro, and Dobkin (1994) found that teacher-rated impulsivity among Canadian boys in kindergarten predicted self-reported delinquency at age 13. Finally, Caspi et al. (1995) found that lack-of-control temperament ratings among New Zealanders at age 3 predicted antisocial behavior at ages 9 and 11, conduct disorder at ages 13 and 15, and violent convictions at age 18 (Henry, Caspi, Moffitt, & Silva, 1996).

Miller and Lynam (2001) conducted a meta-analysis of 59 studies of the relation between personality characteristics and anti-social behavior and found that dimensions of disagreeableness and lack of conscientious-ness consistently predicted antisocial out-comes, albeit modestly. At the extreme, the construct of psychopathy has been found to predict aggressive and violent behavior (Murrie, Cornell, Kaplan, McConville, & Levy-Elkon, 2004). For example, Lynam (1997) found that psychopathy was mod-erately correlated (r's range from 0.19 to 0.39) with past and current delinquency, and Kosson, Cyterski, Steuerwald, Neumann, and Walker-Matthews (2002) found that psychopathy scores correlated with the

number of violent charges ($r = 0.27$) in a sample of adolescents on probation.

Of course, these findings are tempered by the fact that measures of temperament and personality are, at best, indirect measures of "nature" and are themselves subject to influ-ence by environmental factors.

Biological Characteristics

A variety of biological characteristics of chil-dren have been correlated with antisocial behavior. Raine (2002) found six studies that report a main-effect association between minor physical anomalies, presumed to be markers for fetal maldevelopment, and anti-social behavior in children. Raine et al. (1994) found that complications at birth (e.g., pre-eclampsia, loss of oxygen) pre-dicted violent offending at age 18 in a sample of over 4,200 men from Copenhagen. Bren-nan, Grekin, and Mednick (1999) found a two-fold increase in adult violent offend-ing in the offspring of mothers who smoked in a birth cohort of over 4,000 men. Raine (2002) has called low resting heart rate "the best-replicated biological correlate of anti-social behavior in child and adolescent sam-ples" (p. 418). Lorber's (2004) meta-analysis confirmed the robustness of this relationship and identified high heart rate reactivity as a second major autonomic correlate of anti-social behavior. A meta-analysis by Brook, Starzyk, and Quinsey (2001) revealed a modest but robust relation between testos-terone levels and aggressive behavior. Lower concentrations of cerebrospinal fluid (CSF) 5-HIAA, the major metabolite of sero-tonin, have been found among violent offenders, individuals with personality dis-orders characterized by aggression, and vio-lent alcoholics (e.g., Tuinier, Verhoeven, & van Praag, 1995; Virkunnen, Eggert, Rawl-ings, & Linnoila, 1996). Other researchers have indexed platelet levels of monoamine oxidase (MAO), which is responsible for metabolizing both serotonin and dopamine. Although MAO activity is an indirect mea-sure, results from such studies are consis-tent with other studies that have examined serotonin more directly in that low-platelet

MAO activity has been shown to be associated with impulsivity, violent crime, and persistent criminality (e.g., Alm et al., 1994; Belfrage, Lidberg, & Oreland, 1992).

Heritability

Over 100 studies have examined the heritability of antisocial behavior. A meta-analysis by Rhee and Waldman (2002) involving 42 independent twin samples and 10 adoption samples revealed heritability estimates of 0.44 for a clinical diagnosis of antisocial disorder, 0.44 for continuous measures of aggression, and 0.47 for measures of antisocial behavior. One of the largest studies, the Environmental Risk (E-Risk) Longitudinal Twin Study (Arseneault et al., 2003), followed 1,116 families from a national registry of twins born in England and Wales; it revealed heritability estimates of 0.42 for self-reports and 0.76 for teacher reports of aggressive behavior. O'Connor et al. (1998), drawing on the Nonshared Environment and Adolescent Development (NEAD) project of 720 monozygotic and dyzogotic twins, full siblings, half-siblings, and unrelated siblings, found a heritability estimate of 0.56 for aggressive behavior.

Genes

The most direct measure of "nature" is the gene itself. Until recently, methods were not available to measure genes, and theory was not available to identify candidate genes to consider. The monoamine oxidase-A (MAO-A) gene, located on the X chromosome, encodes the MAO-A enzyme, which metabolizes the neurotransmitter serotonin (5-HT), rendering it inactive. Genetic deficiencies in MAO-A have been correlated with aggression in both mice and humans. In humans, a null allele at the MAO-A locus was found in five members of a Dutch family lineage characterized by antisocial behavior (Brunner, Nelen, Breakefield, & Ropers, 1993). In mice, cross-generational breeding of a strain for which the gene that encodes MAO-A had been deleted produced increased levels of 5-HT and increased aggressive behavior (Cases et al., 1995). Fur-

thermore, aggressive behavior was reduced when MAO-A was normalized (Shih et al., 1999). Nonetheless, the correlation between MAO-A and aggressive behavior in humans remains controversial (Parsian & Cloninger, 2001).

"Nurture" Main Effects on the Development of Antisocial Behavior

Numerous environmental factors have been associated with individual differences in aggressive behavior in children (Dodge, Coie, & Lynam, 2006). The most robust factors that predict angry aggressive behavior are those that pose a personal threat to the developing child, including adversity, abuse, and rejection.

Poverty

Being born into a neighborhood context of relative disadvantage has been associated with later antisocial behavior and crime. Sampson, Raudenbush, and Earls (1997) used multilevel analyses of adolescents to find structural characteristics of neighborhoods that are associated with individual variation in violent behavior among the 10,000 participants in the Chicago Neighborhood Study. Beyers, Bates, Pettit, and Dodge (2003) followed 585 boys and girls across time to find that neighborhood-level scores (based on census tract information) for the proportions of families characterized by poverty, unemployment, marital divorce, and low income represent significant overlapping risk factors for individual-level conduct problems.

Poverty within the family increases the probability of peer-directed aggressive behavior by both children (Bradley & Corwyn, 2002) and adolescents (Spencer, Dobbs, & Swanson, 1988), as well as adult crime (Sampson & Laub, 1994), even when neighborhood levels of poverty have been controlled.

Domestic Violence

Observing parents assault each other is a stressful and threatening experience that has been correlated with increases in aggressive behavior. Fergusson and Horwood (1998) found robust correlations between observing domestic violence and later antisocial behavior. Jaffee, Moffitt, Caspi, Taylor, and Arseneault (2002) employed a twin research design to find that adult domestic violence accounted for 5% of the variance in child antisocial behavior, even when genetic factors are controlled.

Parental Rejection

Rejection by a parent, especially early in life, presents threat that has been linked to later aggressive behavior. Shaw and Vondra (1995) found that insecure attachment, particularly disorganized attachment, predicted aggression scores on the Child Behavior Checklist at age 5. Caspi et al. (2004) used a monozygotic twin study that controls for genetic differences to find that maternal expressed emotion (that is, verbal statements of negative affect about a child) predicted children's antisocial behavior problems. Deater-Deckard (2000) used identical and fraternal twin pairs to reach the same conclusion.

Harsh Discipline and Maltreatment

Gershoff's (2002) meta-analysis has revealed a consistent correlation between the experience of corporal punishment and increases in childhood aggressive behavior. McCord's (1991) analyses of the Cambridge-Somerville Youth Study revealed that the experience of physical punishment by one's father predicted a boy's adult record of criminality, even when paternal criminality was controlled. Farrington and Hawkins (1991) found that the experience of harsh discipline at age 8 predicted later onset of delinquency among the 411 London males of the Cambridge Longitudinal Study.

Experiencing extreme levels of physical assault have been correlated even more robustly with later antisocial behavior. Luntz and Widom (1994) found that, compared with matched controls, children who had been reported as physically abused prior

to age 11 had twice the probability of being diagnosed as having an adult antisocial personality disorder 20 years later, even when controlling for race, sex, and family socioeconomic status. One of the problems with studies using children who have been identified as abused by child protective services (CPS) is that the experience of physical abuse is confounded with the actions taken by CPS, including being removed from the home, publicly labeled as abused, and grouped with deviant children in foster and group home settings. Dodge, Bates, and Pettit (1990) used extended clinical interviews to assess the experience of physical maltreatment in a community sample of preschool children and then followed this sample through childhood. They found short-term effects of physical maltreatment on aggressive behavior in kindergarten, as well as long-term effects through late adolescence that included school suspensions for misbehavior and physical violence (Lansford et al., 2002).

As a check on genetically based selection biases in the experience of maltreatment, Jaffee, Caspi, Moffitt, and Taylor (2004) found that physical maltreatment was associated with higher mothers' and teachers' reports of aggressive behavior at ages 5 and 7 among 1,116 twin pairs in Great Britain, controlling for genetic and other factors.

Peer Rejection

Dodge et al. (2003) have found that the experience of chronic social rejection by peers increases aggressive behavior among children who are aggressive initially. Similar findings that peer rejection predicts growth in aggression above and beyond the level of aggression that might have led to that rejection have now been reported by Bierman and Wargo (1995), Coie (2004), Patterson and Bank (1989), and Kupersmidt and Coie (1990).

A common factor among these environmental predictors of aggressive behavior is the phenomenological experience of personal threat, relative disadvantage, harsh treatment, and rejection. These experiences may ignite a defensive reaction that is characterized by anger (as in reactive aggression) or the instrumental use of aggressive behavior to harm others because of reduced caring about the harm being caused to others (as in proactive aggression).

The Nature–Nurture Interaction Effect

The findings reviewed above illustrate that both person and environmental main effects predict antisocial outcomes, but only at modest to moderate levels of magnitude. The interaction of these factors has been found to add to the strength of this prediction in the studies that are reviewed next. We conducted an informal literature search, seeking studies reporting a significant interaction between person variables and adverse environmental experiences in predicting antisocial behavior. For each study, we calculated the environmental effect (E effect) at each level of the person variable (P risk level) to test the hypothesis that the E effect is largest at the highest P risk level. The findings are summarized in Table 10.1. Because not all studies reported standard errors or even group means, the E effect size could not be computed on the same metric; therefore, contrasts of E effects across studies are unwarranted. The studies are categorized into five groups: the first four groups are differentiated by the type of person factor (personality/temperament, biological characteristics, heritability, and genes), and the last group consists of experimental manipulations of the environment through intervention.

Temperament by Environment

Lynam et al. (2000) examined the interaction between impulsivity and adverse neighborhood context on antisocial behavior in 425 12- to 13-year-old boys in the Pittsburgh Youth Study. They measured the P factor impulsivity through average performance on 11 laboratory tasks and ratings by the self, parents, and teachers. They measured the E factor through four census-defined gradations of economic disadvan-

tage in the boys' residential neighborhoods. They measured violent offending through self-reports using the National Youth Survey Self-Report Delinquency Instrument (Elliott, Huizinga, & Morse, 1986). Controlling for family socioeconomic status, and ethnicity, the P and E factors each exerted main effects on violent offending, and the interaction between P and E was significant. As hypothesized here, the E effect (expressed as Cohen's d) at the highest level of P risk (0.6) was stronger than at the lowest level of P risk (−0.2).

Kochanska (1997) found a significant interaction between temperamental fearlessness (P risk, as observed in laboratory tasks) and maternal behavior (E risk, measured by mother-child attachment security) in predicting later conscience development and antisocial themes in response to story stimuli in 99 toddlers followed from age 33 months to 46 months. Again, the effect of E at the high level of P risk (scored as a simple beta of 0.42) was stronger than at the low level of P risk (beta of −0.01).

Belsky, Hsieh, and Crnic (1998) examined the interaction between infant negative emotionality (P risk) and hostile parenting (E risk) in a sample of 125 first-born 3-year-old boys. They found significantly greater effects of hostile (versus positive) parenting on externalizing behavior problems among boys who had high levels of P risk than among boys at low levels of P risk (E effect size of 14% vs. 4%, respectively).

Lengua, Wolchik, Sandler, and West (2000) examined the interaction between P risk factors (impulsivity and lack of positive emotionality, measured by mother and child reports on standardized instruments) and E risk factors (maternal rejection and inconsistent discipline, measured by mother and child reports on standardized instruments) in predicting conduct problems (again measured by mother and child reports on standardized instruments) in a sample of 231 9- to 12-year-old children in divorced families. Both impulsivity and inconsistent discipline exerted significant main effects on conduct problems, and the interaction effect was marginally significant. The simple effect

Table 10.1: Person-by-environment interaction effects

Study		Environmental Risk		Biological Risk	Outcome
Hi E/Hi P	*Lo E/Hi* P	*Hi E/Lo* P	*Lo E/Lo* P	E *Effect/Hi* P	E *Effect/Lo* P

Temperament by Environment

Study		Environmental Risk		Biological Risk	Outcome
Belsky et al. (1998)		Maternal Sensitivity		Negativity	Behavior Problems
				Beta = −0.38	Beta = −0.19
Dodge et al. (2003)		Social Rejection		Dispositional Agg	Aggressive Behavior
				Diff = 17	Diff = 1
Lengua et al. (2000)		Parental Rejection		Positive Emotionality	Conduct Problems
0.25	−0.7	−0.65	−0.7	ES = 0.9	ES = 0.1
Inconsistent Discipline		Impulsivity		Conduct Problems	
0.8	−0.2	−0.6	−0.85	ES = 1	ES = 0.3
Lynam et al. (2000)		Census SES		Impulsivity	Variety of Crimes
4.3	2.5	0.5	1.25	ES = 0.6	ES = −0.2
Maziade et al. (1985)		Adverse Family		Difficult Temperament	Behavior Problems

Biological Factor by Environment

Study		Environmental Risk		Biological Risk	Outcome
Brennan et al. (2003)		Adverse Family		Birth Complications	% Childhood Aggression
65	16	24	12	Diff = 49	Diff = 12
El-Sheikh et al. (2001)		Verbal Marital Conflict		Vagal Tone	% Childhood Anxiety
98	5	1	10	Diff = 94	Diff = −9
Hodgins et al. (2001)		Inadequate Parenting		Pregnancy Complicated	Criminal Offending
8.2	2.2	5.7	2.7	Diff = 6	Diff = 3
Kemppainen et al. (2001)		Only Child		Prenatal/Perinatal Risk	Violent Crime
4.4		1.8	1		
Pine et al. (1997)		Composite Risk		Minor Phys Anomalies	Disruptive Behavior
				Beta = 1.24	Beta = 0.33
Piquero & Tibbetts (1999)		Familial Risk		Prenatal/Perinatal Risk	Violent Crime
0.0842	0.0333	0.0358	0.0435	Diff = 0.0484	Diff = −0.0102
Raine et al. (1994)		Maternal Rejection		Birth Complications	% Violent Crime
8.3	3	1.7	3.6	Diff = 5.3	Diff = −1.9

Study		Environmental Risk		Biological Risk	Outcome
Hi E/Hi P	*Lo E/Hi P*	*Hi E/Lo P*	*Lo E/Lo P*	*E Effect/Hi P*	*E Effect/Lo P*

Heritability by Environment

Cadoret et al. (1983)		Adoptive Parent Risk		Biological Parent Risk Diff = 2.3	Antisocial behaviors Diff = 0.2
Cadoret et al. (1995)		Adverse Home Env		Antisocial Personality	Childhood Aggression
3	0.5	0.9	0.9	Diff = 2.5	Diff = 0
		Adverse Home Env		Antisocial Personality	Adolescent Aggression
3.8	2.2	2.3	2.5	Diff = 1.6	Diff = −0.2
Cloninger et al. (1982)		Adoptive Par Criminal		Bio Par Criminal	% Criminality
40	12.1	6.7	2.9	Diff = 27.9	Diff = 3.8
Hutchings & Mednick (1973)		Adoptive Par Criminal		Bio Par Criminal	% Criminality
36	21	12	10	Diff = 15	Diff = 2
Jaffee et al. (2005)		Childhood Maltreatment		Twin Status of CD	% Conduct Problems
50	33	21	17	Diff = 17	Diff = 4
Kendler et al. (1995)		Stressful Life Events		Twin Status of Depress	% Depression
14	1	6	0.5	Diff = 13	Diff = 5.5
Riggins-Casper et al. (2003)		Adoptive Harsh Disc		Parent CD	% Conduct Disorder
				r = 0.45	r = 0.01

Gene by Environment

Caspi et al. (2002)		Childhood Maltreat		MAOA Activity	Antisocial Behavior
1	−0.26	0.4	−0.1	Diff = 1.26	Diff = 0.5
Caspi et al. (2003)		Stressful Life Events		ShortAllele5-HTTLPR	Depressive Symptoms
12	2	5	2.75	Diff = 10	Diff = 2.25
		Stressful Life Events		ShortAllele5-HTTLPR	Suicide Ideation
0.145	0.005	0.04	0.03	Diff = 0.14	Diff = 0.01
		Childhood Maltreat		ShortAllele5-HTTLPR	Major DepressEpisode
24.5	18.6	20	20.5	Diff = 5.9%	Diff = −0.5%
Foley et al. (2004)		Childhood Adversities		MAOA Activity	Conduct Problems
0.62	0.3	0.3	0.3	Diff = 0.32	Diff = 0

continued

Table 10.1 *continued*

Study		Environmental Risk		Biological Risk	Outcome
Hi E/Hi P	*Lo E/Hi P*	*Hi E/Lo P*	*Lo E/Lo P*	*E Effect/Hi P*	*E Effect/Lo P*

Personality by Intervention

Study		Outcome		Int Effect/Hi P	Int Effect/Lo P
Intervention High P	Control High P	Intervention Low P	Control Low P		
Blair (2002)		Internalizing Behavior			
54.3	56.9	52.8	53.0	diff $= 1.5$	diff $= 3.9$
Stoolmiller et al. (2000)		Aggressive Behaviors			
				$ES = 0.82$	$ES = -0.07$
van Lier et. al. (2004)		Grade 1 Conduct Problems			
2.1	2.8	0.3	0.3	$ES = 0.55$	$ES =$ nil
Weiss et. al. (2003)					
-5	0.4	-0.8	-0.6	$ES = 0.50$	$ES = 0.03$

of the E risk factor of inconsistent discipline was stronger at a high level of impulsivity (E effect size, calculated as Cohen's $d, = 1.0$, $p < 0.01$) than at a low level of impulsivity (Cohen's $d = 0.3$, *n.s.*). In a second analysis, main effects of maternal rejection and lack of positive emotionality significantly predicted conduct problems, and their interaction effect was marginally significant. Again, the simple effect of the E risk factor of maternal rejection was stronger at a high P-risk level of lack of positive emotionality (Cohen's $d = 0.9$, $p < 0.01$) than at a low P-risk level (Cohen's $d = 0.1$, *n.s.*).

Belsky (2004) drew on the data of the NICHD Study of Early Child Care to find that the environmental effect of maternal lack of sensitivity (as measured by direct observation at 6, 15, 24, and 36 months of age) on child disruptive behavior problems at age 36 months was significantly greater among children who had been rated as high in negative emotionality (P risk) at age 6 months than among children rated as low in negative emotionality (E effects, expressed as β, were 0.38 for high P risk and 0.19 for low P-risk groups).

Dodge et al. (2003) examined the interaction between early dispositional aggression and the experience of chronic social rejection by peers in predicting later aggressive behavior problems in a sample of 585 boys and girls followed from preschool through age 8. The main effects of early disposition and peer rejection were significant, as was the interaction effect. Comparisons of the means in Figure 10.1 reveals that the effect of being rejected by peers was greater among children initially high in dispositional problems (E effect, by difference in behavior scores, of 17 points) than among children initially low in dispositional problems (E effect of 1 point).

Similar findings have been reported by Maziade et al. (1985), who found that difficult temperament and adverse family conditions at age 7 interacted to predict psychiatric diagnoses of behavior problems at age 12, with the effect of adverse family conditions being stronger for children with difficult temperament. Sanson, Oberklaid, Pelow, and Prior (1991) found that the effect of a poor mother-infant relationship on the incidence of preschool behavior adjustment problems was stronger among children with difficult infancy-temperament than among children with average infancy-temperament. Morris et al. (2002) found that maternal

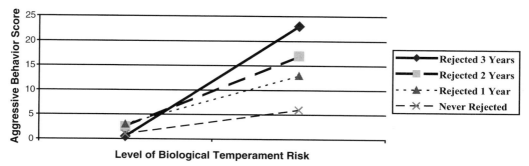

Figure 10.1. Mean aggressive behavior scores as a function of temperament and years of peer social ejection (from Dodge et al., 2003).

harsh discipline predicted teacher-rated externalizing problems to a greater degree among high irritable-distress children (high P risk) than low irritable children (E effects of 0.31 vs. 0.06). Finally, Deater-Deckard and Dodge (1997) found that the correlation between preschool maternal harsh discipline and externalizing problems during each of the next 6 years was greater among children who had been rated as having persistent difficult temperaments (i.e., high P risk) as infants than those as having average temperaments (low P risk).

Thus, consistent with the hypothesis advanced here, in all studies reviewed, the environmental effect was found to be *stronger* among children at relatively *high* dispositional risk than among children low in dispositional risk. In fact, the effect of different environmental experiences was close to nil among children at low dispositional risk, indicating that dispositional factors can act as protective buffers against the adverse effects of threatening environments. Undoubtedly, dispositionally based protection has a limit; very severe trauma is likely to yield adverse outcomes in almost all children. However, some children appear to be protected against the adverse impact of most environmental stressors. This finding has important implications for clinical prognoses for some children following trauma.

In contrast, among children who are high in dispositional risk, environmental effects are particularly strong. It is these children for whom the environment matters most. For these children, long-term outcomes depend on the environment in which they are placed and the treatments to which they are exposed. Finally, these findings indicate that certain environments can protect a child from the ill effects of a high-risk disposition or genetic loading. It is these children who merit the most environmental investment; unfortunately, because dispositional risk factors are often positively correlated with environmental risk factors, these children are not likely to receive the environment that would protect them. The children who need a supportive environment most are the least likely to receive it.

Biological Characteristics by Environment

Numerous biological characteristics, acquired through presumed heredity or in utero experience, have been identified as person-level risk factors for antisocial behavior (reviewed by Dodge, Coie, & Lynam, 2006). Several of these characteristics, particularly ones that render the person less able to resist stress and threat, have been found to interact with environmental experiences in predicting antisocial outcomes.

Brennan, Hall, Bor, Najman, and Williams (2003) tested the effects of biological and social risk factors in predicting early-onset persistent aggression measured by maternal ratings on the Child Behavior Checklist at ages 5 and 15. They scored biological risk factors as the cumulative sum of

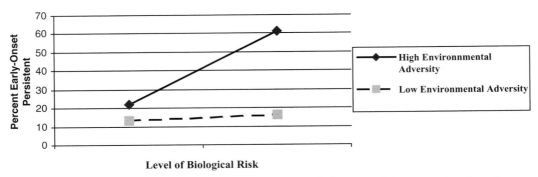

Figure 10.2. Percent of children with persistent aggressive behavior problems as a function of biological and social risks (from Brennan et al., 2003).

such problems as perinatal and birth complications, maternal illness during pregnancy, low birthweight, low Apgar score, maternal prenatal alcohol consumption, infant temperament, and executive function deficits. They scored social risk factors as the cumulative sum of such problems as family poverty, family instability, mother's negative attitude toward the infant at 6 months of age, maternal harsh discipline at age 5, and child's perceptions of parental hostility and lack of acceptance. Biological and social risk scores were dichotomized, forming a two-by-two factorial that was tested through logistic regressions predicting incidence of early-onset persistent aggression. The interaction term was significant. As indicated in Figure 10.2, among those children who were at the low level of biological risk, the predictive difference between low and high number of social risk factors was negligible, whereas among children at high biological risk, there was a three-fold difference between low and high number of social risk factors in predicting the incidence of early-onset persistent aggression.

Raine et al. (1994) tested the biosocial interaction between birth complications (e.g., pre-eclampsia, prolonged cord prolapse) and the early experience of extreme rejection by the mother (e.g., institutional care of infant, unwanted pregnancy) in predicting violent crime recorded by police at age 18 in a sample of 4,269 males born in Copenhagen, Denmark, in 1959 to 1961. The interaction term was highly significant.

Among the low biological-risk group (i.e., no birth complications), the experience of maternal rejection had no effect on later violent crime (E difference $= -1.9\%$). Among the high biological-risk group, the experience of maternal rejection had a larger effect (E difference $= 5.3\%$). The same authors (Raine et al., 1997) later followed up the same sample to age 34 and replicated the interaction pattern with violent crimes (robbery, rape, and murder). At age 34, the E difference among the low biological-risk group was -4%, whereas the E difference among the high biological-risk group was 8%.

Arsenault, Tremblay, Boulerice, Seguin, and Saucier (2000) replicated this finding with an independent sample of 849 boys from Montreal, Canada. Life-threatening obstetrical complications (pre-eclampsia, umbilical cord prolapse, and induced labor, scored from hospital records) significantly interacted with early experience of family adversity (e.g., not living with biological parents, low socioeconomic status) to predict teacher-rated physical aggression at age 6 and self-reported delinquency at age 17. Unfortunately, the actual group means and E effect sizes are not reported, but the authors state that the shape of the interaction effect replicated that of Raine et al. (1994) indicated that family adversity "plays an important role in the development of early chronic physical aggression for boys who were subjected to pre-eclampsia, umbilical cord prolapse, or induced labor during delivery"

(p. 505). The same pattern was replicated by Piquero and Tibbetts (1999).

Hodgins, Kratzer, and McNeil (2001) examined the interaction between obstetrical complications (e.g., pre-eclampsia, toxemia) and the experience of child maltreatment (i.e., a Child Welfare Committee record of intervening because of inadequate parenting) in predicting official records of crimes by all 15,117 persons born in Stockholm in 1953 and still residing there in 1963. The effect of child maltreatment on later crimes (and, especially, violent crimes) was stronger among those males at high biological risk (that is, with obstetrical complications; means = 8.2 and 2.2, for maltreated and nonmaltreated groups, respectively, yielding an E difference of 6.0) than among those males at low biological risk (that is, no obstetrical complications; means = 5.7 and 2.7, for maltreated and nonmaltreated groups, respectively, yielding an E difference of 3.0). The E effect was twice as large among boys at high biological risk than among boys at low biological risk. The same pattern was observed for less common violent crimes.

Another biological risk factor is the presence of minor physical anomalies (MPAs, e.g., abnormally large gap between toes, high-arched palate, asymmetrical eyes), which are indicators of disruption in fetal central nervous system development. Pine, Saffer, Schonfeld, and Davies (1997) tested the interaction of MPAs and environmental risk factors (e.g., low income, spousal conflict, marital disruption) in predicting psychiatrically diagnosed disruptive behavior disorder at age 17 in a sample of 126 African American males from the 1962–1963 Columbia Presbyterian Medical Center birth cohort. The interaction term was significant, and the E effect was larger among the group with high MPAs (beta = 1.24) than among the group without MPAs (beta = 0.33). Additionally, Breslau (1995) found that low birthweight predicts disruptive behavior disorders among children who had experienced disadvantaged early environments but not among children raised under less adverse circumstances.

El-Sheikh, Harger, and Whitson (2001) found that psychophysiological vagal tone and experience of marital conflict interact significantly to predict mother-reported externalizing behavior scores in a sample of 75 10-year-olds, such that among children with high (healthy) vagal tone, marital conflict had no effect on externalizing outcomes, whereas among children with problematic vagal tone, the experience of marital conflict was positively related to externalizing behavior problems.

In summary, a variety of biological characteristics that may represent genetic or prenatal/perinatal processes have been identified as risk factors for later aggressive behavior problems, but the mechanisms through which these markers operate have not yet been identified. The studies reviewed here indicate that several of these biological risk factors (including obstetrical complications, minor physical anomalies, and poor vagal tone) interact with adverse early environmental experiences such that the harsh environment leads to antisocial outcomes more strongly (and sometimes only) among children with high biological risk. These findings suggest that biological risk reduces the child's ability to cope with adversity and threat.

Heritability by Environment

In these studies, a variety of behavior-genetic designs (e.g., twin studies, adoption studies) have been used to test heritable and environmental risk factors. Mednick, Cloninger, Cadoret, and Kendler each independently pioneered the use of adoption studies to parse the effects of heritable factors (based on biological parents' status) and environmental factors (based on adoptive parents' status) in predicting antisocial crime outcomes. The design of these studies is simply a two (biological parents' antisocial behavior as no or yes) by two (adoptive parents' antisocial behavior as no or yes) factorial, with the child's antisocial behavior or crime record as the outcome.

Hutchings and Mednick (1973) tested the effects of criminal backgrounds of biological and adoptive parents on offspring criminality in a sample of 662 males adopted at birth. Among sons with no criminal biological parent, the effect of adoptive parents' criminality on the son's criminality was nil (10% for adoptive parents with no criminality vs. 12% for adoptive parents with criminality, E difference = 2%). Among sons with a criminal biological parent, however, the effect of adoptive parents' criminality on the son's criminality was substantially greater (21% for adoptive parents with no criminality vs. 36% for adoptive parents with criminality, E difference = 15%).

Cloninger, Sigvardsson, Bohman, and von Knorring (1982) tested the interaction between biological parents' characteristics and adoptive parents' characteristics in a sample of all 862 males born in Stockholm between 1930 and 1949 who were adopted at an early age by nonrelatives. Among those males whose biological parents were not criminals, adoptive parents' characteristics had little effect on sons' criminality (E difference of 3.8%). Among those males whose biological parents were criminals, however, adoptive parents' characteristics had a large effect on sons' criminality (E difference of 27.9%). The contrast in group mean probabilities is staggering: low E risk/low P risk = 0.03, low E risk/high P risk = 0.12, high E risk/low P risk = 0.07, and high E risk/high P risk = 0.40. These findings illustrate that either low biological risk or low environmental risk is sufficient to keep a child from having a probability of crime from rising beyond 12%, whereas the synergistic effects rise over three-fold to 40%.

Cadoret and Cain (1981) found a significant interaction effect in a sample of 367 adoptees in Des Moines, Iowa, such that among children with low biological-family risk, the adoptive (environmental) family's risk had no effect on the number of antisocial behaviors by the child (E difference = 0.2 behaviors), whereas among children with high biological-family risk, the adoptive (environmental) family's risk had a large effect on the number of antisocial behaviors by the child (E difference = 2.3 behaviors). Cadoret, Cain, and Crowe (1983) reported

similar shapes of interaction effects in each of two additional samples, 75 adoptees who had been born either to an incarcerated female offender or to a nonoffender, and 108 adoptees from St. Louis, Missouri. In both studies, the E effect was large among those children with an antisocial biological parent and negligible among those children without an antisocial biological parent. Cadoret (1985) reported an identical interaction shape in a fourth sample of adoptees from a different agency.

Cadoret, Yates, Troughton, Woodworth, and Stewart (1995) reported results of a fifth sample of 197 adoptees followed into early adulthood. For number of childhood aggressive behaviors, the adoptive home environment had no effect among those children at low heritable risk (E difference = 0 behaviors), whereas the adoptive home environment had a large effect among those children at high heritable risk (E difference = 2.5 behaviors). For number of adolescent aggressive behaviors, the adoptive home environment again had no effect among those children at low heritable risk (E difference = −0.4 behaviors), whereas the adoptive home environment had a large effect among those children at high heritable risk (E difference = 2.8 behaviors). Finally, for number of conduct disorder symptoms, the adoptive home environment again had no effect among those children at low heritable risk (E difference = 0.2 symptoms), whereas the adoptive home environment had a large effect among those children at high heritable risk (E difference = 2.7 symptoms). Riggins-Caspers, Cadoret, Knutson, and Langbehn (2003) examined reports of adoptive family harsh discipline practices and found that this variable also interacted significantly with biological parent status to predict offspring adolescent conduct disorder symptoms.

Finally, Jaffee et al. (2005) used monozygotic and dizygotic twin pairs to test the interaction of heritable risk and the experience of physical maltreatment to predict psychiatric conduct disorder (CD) in a sample of 1,116 5-year-old twin pairs in Great Britain. They identified four rank-ordered

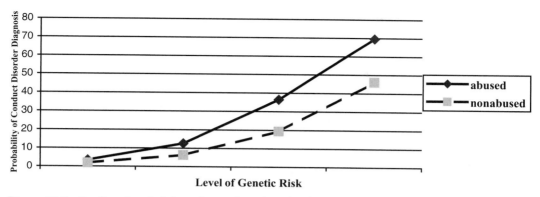

Figure 10.3. Predicted probability of a conduct disorder diagnosis as a function of genetic risk and physical maltreatment (from Jaffee et al., 2005).

groups of increasing heritable risk, following a procedure used by Kendler et al. (1995), with the lowest heritable-risk group being children whose monozygotic twin is not CD, the next lowest group being children whose dizygotic twin is not CD, the next highest group being children whose dizygotic twin is CD, and the highest group being children whose monozygotic twin is CD. The experience of child physical maltreatment was determined by clinical interview with the mother, following procedures by Dodge et al. (1990). The findings are depicted in Figure 10.3. Among the children at lowest heritable risk, the experience of physical maltreatment had no effect on conduct disorder outcomes (E difference $= 1.6\%$). Among the next highest level of heritable risk, the effect of maltreatment was small (E difference $= 6.3\%$). Among the next highest level, the effect of maltreatment grew larger (E difference $= 17.1\%$). Finally, among the highest level, the effect of maltreatment was largest (E difference $= 33.5\%$).

Genes by Environment

The most direct tests of gene-by-environment interactions involve measurement of genes. Two studies have tested the interaction between a functional polymorphism in the promoter of the monoamine oxidase A (MAO-A) gene and child physical maltreatment in predicting conduct disorder in children. The MAO-A gene is located on the X chromosome. It encodes the MAO-A enzyme, which metabolizes serotonin and dopamine, thus rendering them inactive, and is thought to be critical in the regulation of neurotransmitter systems in response to trauma and major threatening stressors. It has been hypothesized that low MAO-A activity (that is, a problem in metabolizing neurotransmitters) presents a genetic risk for antisocial behavior in response to environmental threat.

Caspi et al. (2002) tested the hypothesis of a gene-environment interaction effect in the Dunedin Multidisciplinary Health and Development Study of 1,037 children and found a significant interaction effect, with the effect of maltreatment larger among youth with low MAO-A activity (Cohen's $d = 1.25$) than among youth with high MAO-A activity (Cohen's $d = 0.41$; see Figure 10.4).

Foley et al. (2004) replicated this pattern in their community-based sample of 514 male twins aged 8 to 17 years. Instead of physical maltreatment, their measure of environmental risk was a composite score of parental neglect, exposure to interparental conflict, and inconsistent parental discipline. They found a significant interaction effect, with the effect of childhood adversity on conduct disorder (CD) being larger among youth with low MAO-A activity (E difference $= 96\%$) than among youth with high MAO-A activity (E difference $= -10\%$).

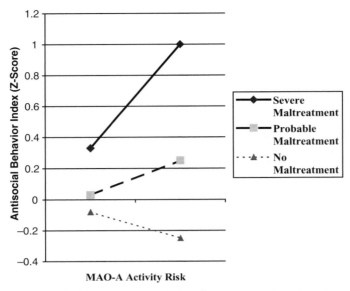

Figure 10.4. Mean aggressive behavior scores as a function of MAO-A activity and physical maltreatment (from Caspi et al., 2002).

Person by Experimental Manipulation of Environment

The final type of relevant study is the intervention experiment, in which the environmental experience of the child is manipulated systematically. Because all of the studies reviewed above involve naturally occurring environmental variation, it is possible that the interaction effects reflect a gene-by-gene interaction (although numerous studies indicate that very harsh environments are not significantly correlated with heritable factors; Jaffee et al., 2004). Thus, experimental manipulation of the environment offers a stronger test of the person-by-environment interaction effect. Because all interventions are intended to be positive experiences, these studies do not test the effect of a harsh or threatening environment; rather, they test the malleability of children to nurturing experiences.

Based on the findings above, it was hypothesized that children who are *highest* in person-level risk would display the *largest* response to environmental intervention. This hypothesis is counterintuitive to those scholars and clinicians who have

argued that the highest biological-risk youth, including psychopaths, are less "treatable" than lower risk youth (Andrews & Bonta, 1994; Heilbrun et al., 1998).

Universal interventions that treat a wide range of risk-status children offer the broadest opportunity to test this hypothesis. van Lier, Muthen, van der Sar, and Crijne (2004) randomly assigned (by classroom) 744 second-grade children in 31 classrooms in the Netherlands either to a universal preventive intervention called the Good Behavior Game (GBG) or a non-treated control group. GBG is a widely used behavior-management strategy that trains teachers to promote prosocial behavior and reduce aggressive behavior through group-level contingencies and rewards. The intervention relies on children to socialize each other in positive ways. The intervention lasted 2 years, and conduct problems were assessed at baseline, 12 months, 18 months, and the end of the 24-month period. Based on preintervention scores, children were classified into high-risk (14% of sample), moderate-risk (26% of sample), or low-risk (60% of sample) groups. Assignment to intervention significantly interacted with risk level to predict trajectories of conduct problem development over time. Consistent with the hypothesis, the intervention-control difference effect size was 0.55 standard deviations for the high-risk group, .42 standard deviations for the moderate-risk group, and nonsignificant (≈0.00 standard deviations) for the low-risk group.

Kellam, Rebok, Ialongo, and Mayer (1994) found a similar interaction effect. They randomly assigned 714 first-grade children to classrooms and then randomly assigned classrooms either to receive the Good Behavior Game or serve as nontreated controls. Teacher ratings of aggressive behavior prior to intervention classified individual children into high- and low-risk groups. Outcome analyses in middle school revealed that assignment to intervention had a positive effect on aggressive behavior, but only among the high-risk males and not among the low-risk males.

Blair (2002) examined the data of the Infant Health and Development intervention experiment, designed to prevent maladaptation among low-birthweight infants from economically disadvantaged homes. Infants who were high or low in negative emotionality (P risk) were randomly assigned to receive 2 years of enriched rearing through home visiting and parent support (or not; experimentally manipulated E risk). The effect of treatment was significant and positive in the group of infants with high negative emotionality, but not significant among the group with low negative emotionality.

Finally, Weiss, Harris, Catron, and Han (2003) reported a significant interaction in the opposite direction, among a narrow-range group of 93 fourth-grade children with initially high levels of externalizing and comorbid internalizing problems. Children were randomly assigned to the RECAP multimodal skills development intervention. The treatment effect size was larger among the less high-risk group than among the highest risk group, contrary to the hypothesis. It must be noted that all children were at high risk; thus, the findings of this study in combination with those from the universal intervention studies suggest a possible curvilinear effect of person risk-status on treatment effect size.

Implications for Theory

The findings reviewed here provide robust support for a person-environment interaction effect in predicting antisocial behavior outcomes. However, few theorists have speculated about the shape of that interaction, which has been interpreted here as indicating that the magnitude of environmental effect is stronger among children at high person-level risk than at low person-level risk. Even fewer scholars have offered a theoretical perspective to account for this pattern of findings. Bronfenbrenner and Ceci (1994) anticipated interaction effects and offered a "first approximation" (their term) account of interactions among genes, distal environmental contexts, and proximal social processes; however, their speculation focused mainly on how distal environmental contexts interact with proximal environmental social processes. Instead, the studies reviewed here indicate that some children are more susceptible to adverse environmental influences than others, and this difference in susceptibility to adverse environments appears to be associated with specific temperamental, biological, inherited, and genetic factors. The authors of most of these studies have abdicated theory and have merely described the nonlinear acceleration effect that sometimes occurs when independent risk factors accumulate. No explanation has been offered for when and why interaction effects will or will not occur.

We offer a hypothesis that focuses on the "hand-in-glove fit" between the environmental risk factors and the person risk factors that seem to characterize the interaction findings. In physical health domains, this kind of synergistic interaction has been described in terms of a host-pathogen model (Evans & Relling 1999; Hill, 1999). That is, without implying a statistical correlation between the presence of a host and infiltration by a pathogen, such models note the specific vulnerability of one type of host to a particular type of pathogen that attacks that host's idiosyncratic weakness. In the psychopathology of depressive disorder, such a model has been termed a diathesis-stress model (Monroe & Simons, 1991), which implies that individuals with a particular biologically based vulnerability, called a diathesis, are acutely affected by a matching environmental stressor.

Most environmental risk factors for antisocial behavior involve social threat, either through harsh treatment or comparative disadvantage (Dodge et al., 2006). Mere poverty does not invoke an antisocial reaction as much as relative adversity, especially if perceived as unfair (Bradley & Corwyn, 2002). Threats to life that are nonsocial in origin (e.g., natural disasters, hunger) do not invoke antisocial reactions as much as do direct provocations. Maternal rejection is a risk factor; maternal loss (through death) is not. Physical harm does not elicit aggressive reactions; physical maltreatment does (Lansford et al., 2002). It is the socially threatening quality of an environmental risk factor that is most potent in producing aggressive outcomes.

On the person side, the pattern of risk factors suggests that it is individuals who are highly reactive and sensitive to such threats who are at greatest risk. "Difficult" temperament infants, described as "prickly" and "touchy," are at risk for antisocial behavior (Caspi et al., 1995). Youth demonstrating psychophysiological hyperreactivity to threats are likely to be aggressive (Pitts, 1996; van Goozen et al., 1998). The gene MAO-A has been implicated in reactive aggression, both in mice and human studies (Brunner et al., 1993).

Why might low levels of MAO-A induce risk for aggressive behavior? It has been hypothesized that MAO-A might protect the organism from stress reactions to threat. Low levels of MAO-A may dispose an organism to respond to threat with hypervigilance and hyperreactivity (Morell, 1993). These patterns are consistent with psychophysiological findings that autonomic

hyperreactivity (Lorber, 2004) and difficult ("prickly") temperament (Bates et al., 1991) characterize aggressive individuals. Studies of social information-processing patterns in children reveal that hypervigilance to hostile cues and hostile attributional biases predict growth in aggressive behavior (Dodge & Pettit, 2003). Thus, stable differences in how a person responds neurologically, psychophysiologically, emotionally, and cognitively to threat may provide a general mechanism for understanding aggressive behavior patterns in humans. Thus, we offer the hypothesis that, because of inherited genes or biological characteristics acquired early in life through acute insult, some individuals become hypersensitive to threat.

The essential hypotheses offered in our model are the following: (1) the primary proximal mechanism for aggressive behavior in humans is a sociobiologically evolved defensive response to severe social threat to personal intregrity; (2) chronic aggressive behavior develops largely as a function of chronic or acute severe social threat; (3) most humans are equipped biologically to withstand, or cope with, social threat in a manner that does not lead to debilitating aggressive reactions; and (4) because of individual differences in the biologically based capacity to cope with social threat, some children are unable to regulate their response to threat and instead respond with chronic aggressive behavior.

Analogies to human skin and immune deficiencies provide insight. Ordinarily, our skin provides healthy protection against bacteria that would otherwise penetrate the body and induce infection. Deficiencies in the thickness of our skin lead to high risk for bacterial infection. Likewise, deficiencies in immunological function are associated with risk for asthma and bacterial and viral illnesses, and they have been posited as an explanation for why some individuals readily acquire particular illnesses at a greater rate than others. Immunological deficiencies paradoxically involve two types of responses: (1) a lack of resistance to threatening bacteria and (2) hyperreactive response to allergens, in which case the response is more debilitating than the external agent. Of course, "skin deficiencies" lead to illness only if exposed to a pathogen that attacks through the skin. Even severely immunologically compromised infants have been saved from illness by engineering a safe environment, through sterilizing procedures like the hypothetical baby who survives in a plastic bubble.

We propose that the salient characteristic of person-risk factors for antisocial behavior is analogous to "psychologically thin skin" in response to interpersonal threat. Most humans are relatively protected from the adverse effects of social rejection, physical maltreatment, and interpersonal threat (except, perhaps, at the most extreme levels). Some individuals are described as "thin-skinned" and hypersensitive. Under normal (that is, safe) environmental conditions, these persons may have modest interpersonal difficulty, but are able to function. Under severe socially threatening environmental conditions, though, these persons hyperrespond with high levels of aggressive behavior.

Studies of the phenomenological experiences of aggressive and nonaggressive children are consistent with this notion. In response to the presentation of video-recorded social stimuli that vary in threat level, aggressive children have been found to be hypervigilant to threatening cues relative to nonaggressive children (Dodge, Pettit, McClasky, & Brown, 1986). Dodge et al. (2003) found that aggressive children are less able than nonaggressive children to recall relevant and mitigating social cues presented via videotape. Instead, aggressive children have been found to attend selectively to threatening social cues in a stimulus array more than their nonaggressive peers do, and to have difficulty diverting attention away from threat cues (Gouze, 1987). Aggressive children also display a particular readiness to infer hostile intent to peers. Hostile attributional biases have been reported in many aggressive school-based samples, including aggressive 8- to 12-year-old children (Guerra & Slaby,

1989; Lochman, 1987), aggressive African American middle-school boys (Graham & Hudley, 1994), aggressive Latino children (Graham, Hudley, & Williams, 1992), and rejected British 8- to 10-year-old children (Aydin & Markova, 1979). Hostile attributional biases have also been found in aggressive clinical samples, including children with diagnosed disruptive behavior disorders (MacBrayer, Milich, & Hundley, 2003), hyperactive-aggressive children from an outpatient psychiatric clinic (Milich & Dodge, 1984), incarcerated violent offenders (Slaby & Guerra, 1988), and aggressive boys in residential treatment (Nasby, Hayden, & DePaulo, 1979).

Because maltreatment of children also alters biological processes in neural brain development (De Bellis, 2001), biology and the environment do not merely interact; they transact across development. A comprehensive theory of antisocial development must go beyond interaction effects to account for person-environment transactions in a more dynamic model (Dodge & Pettit, 2003).

Implications for Research

The admittedly awkward analogy to psychological thin skin suggests the need for more refined theory that can come from future empirical studies. The interaction-effect findings reviewed in this chapter suggest a direction for that inquiry.

The first recommendation is that studies of environmental effects should incorporate measures of individual-difference variables that are likely to interact with the environment. Measures of person factors should focus on variables that imply susceptibility to stress and the regulation of emotional reactions. At the temperament and personality level, these variables involve rejection-sensitivity, hypersensitivity, and disagreeableness. At the psychophysiological level, they involve regulatory capacity, such as vagal tone and latency to return to baseline following stress. At the neurotransmitter level, they involve the degradation of serotonin and "serotonin-like immunoreactivity" (Cases et al., 1995). Direct measurement of inheritance is optimal, through research designs that include twins, siblings, or adoptees, but these designs are not essential. Finally, the examination of genes will undoubtedly proliferate in the next decade, with the decreasing cost of obtaining and assaying DNA samples. The challenge will be to select the "right" genes for analysis of an interaction with the environmental factors under study.

Studies of person-factor effects on aggressive behavior would be enhanced by reliable and valid measurement of the environment. Behavior-genetic studies historically have not measured the environment directly; instead, they have apportioned leftover variance (after inherited effects) to within-family and between-family environments. More precise measurement of the environment is necessary to understand the interaction of dispositions and the environment. Measurement of environmental risk factors for aggressive behavior should focus on variables that are likely to be socially threatening. Although socioeconomic disadvantage is an obvious variable, we hypothesize that poverty is a less-specific risk factor than is comparative (relative) economic disadvantage, especially if it occurs through unfair practices such as discrimination. Maternal rejection is a known risk factor, but it is likely to be a stronger predictor if it occurs maliciously. Physical maltreatment is the prototypic environmental risk factor for further inquiry.

By measuring biological risk factors, power will be increased to identify environmental risk factors, and by measuring environmental risk factors, power will be increased to identify biological risk factors. Thus, future studies will yield larger returns to the extent that they incorporate both kinds of variables and test for hypothesized interaction effects.

Finally, the findings reviewed here have important implications for research in clinical trials for antisocial behavior. Early trials tested the efficacy of a single intervention (e.g., a drug or a parent-training therapy) versus a no-treatment control on a clinical outcome of interest. More recent trials have packaged interventions with multiple diverse components (e.g., Conduct Problems Prevention Research Group, 2004). Some trials have tested whether the addition of component B to an intervention with component A brings a more favorable outcome than component A alone (e.g., Metropolitan Areas Community Study Research Group, 2002), but this design does not test the interaction effect between component A and component B. The findings reviewed here suggest that interaction effects might occur and should be tested whenever a theoretical reason warrants it.

Implications for Practice and Policy

The findings reviewed here have paradigm-shifting implications for treatment, prevention, and policy. Public policies should be implemented to reallocate resources toward children at high risk for antisocial behavior, because circumstances have been identified under which these children could enjoy positive outcomes, even to the level enjoyed by low-risk children. Analyses of the huge aggregate economic burden of antisocial behavior (Anderson, 1999) and the lifetime costs to society of chronic antisocial behavior (i.e., $2 million per chronic criminal; Cohen, 1998) suggest that reallocating resources to prevent these outcomes could prove cost beneficial. Currently, an inordinate proportion of public resources are directed toward children who are at low risk for antisocial behavior. For example, because funding for public education in the United States occurs predominantly at the local level, children in wealthier school districts receive more expenditures for public schooling than do children in poorer districts. College-tuition loan programs support that segment of the population that is most likely to be successful even without loans, whereas loans for high-risk adolescents would be considered heresy. Of course, reallocation is politically risky and would be foolish in the absence of evidence of the likely payoffs. The findings in this chapter suggest targets of emphasis that are most likely to yield returns, such as the following.

First, "it is a widely held belief that psychopathic individuals are extremely difficult to treat, if not immune to treatment" (Salekin, 2002, p. 79), but the findings of this review suggest that the opposite may actually prove true. Rather than withhold treatments and resources from aggressive youth, the findings suggest that treatments may be particularly effective with aggressive youth because they are highly reactive to environmental conditions. Effective treatments have not yet been discovered for all kinds of aggressive children, but the search should continue because the payoff is likely to be high.

The implications for prevention are even more striking, especially for the matching of environmental interventions with particular high-risk children. On the person-risk side, it may be possible to identify individuals who are vulnerable to adverse environments, and on the environment-risk side, it may be possible to engineer environments or alter rearing conditions for these vulnerable children. For example, at particularly high biological risk are those boys whose mothers had experienced serious prenatal or perinatal complications, such as pre-eclampsia, umbilical cord prolapse, and induced labor. Evidence strongly supports the importance of early environmental experience for this group in determining whether their risk for later violent crime is realized. A secure attachment between mother and child, maternal acceptance of the infant, and early maternal warmth may mitigate risk in this group. Public policies that support the development of a warm parent-infant relationship in this high-risk group may prove particularly valuable. These policies could include publicly supported (or health insurance-covered) extended parental leave (Clark, Hyde, Essex, & Klein, 1997) and nurse-practitioner home visiting (Olds, Kitzman, Cole, & Robinson, 1997).

Another high biological-risk group is that set of children whose biological parents have histories of violent criminal behavior (e.g., children of prisoners). Unfortunately, these children are likely to become wards of the state and moved into foster care, thus increasing their likelihood of becoming physically maltreated or neglected. Ironically, the children who are most vulnerable to the adverse effects of physical maltreatment are the ones who are most likely to experience maltreatment through child welfare practices. Public policies could be implemented to take especially benevolent care of these children, rather than indiscriminant care.

A particularly controversial policy, but one that could prove enormously valuable, is the genetic screening of children, especially those who are at high environmental risk. Although group statistics are robust, the state of the science is not yet mature enough to warrant clinical practice to identify individual children who are at high genetic risk. However, we are near the point of being able to identify which children will respond most poorly to adverse environments. One could imagine a day when screening identifies these children so that resources can be directed to preventing the environmental events that would potentiate their risk.

Caveats

Numerous caveats temper the conclusions reached in this chapter. First, because the environmental effects involve natural variations in environmental conditions (except for the intervention experiments), the findings are correlational. A plausible alternative interpretation is that the gene-by-environment interaction effects reflect a hidden gene-by-gene interaction, with the environmental variable serving as a proxy for an unknown genetic process. We believe that this alternative is unlikely because the studies that control for heritability still find a main effect of physical maltreatment on child antisocial outcomes (Jaffee et al., 2004).

A second caveat is that the most powerful interaction findings, those involving a true gene-by-environment interaction (Caspi et al., 2002), require more replication before they can be fully accepted. Because there are thousands of possible interaction effects that could be tested, the gene-by-environment interactions that are reported might be spurious. Counteracting this possibility is the elegance of the theory supporting the empirical finding.

Yet, another caveat is that all of the outcomes studied are at one end of a continuum that might include prosocial outcomes at the other end. It is plausible that the appearance of an interaction effect merely reflects a truncation of measurement at the positive end, which would be evidenced as an environmental effect on prosocial outcomes that is seen even in low biological-risk children. It is not at all clear whether the higher susceptibility to environmental influences found for high person-risk children will generalize to environmental influences at both ends of this continuum or only the adverse end. It is plausible that these high genetic-risk children are truly more susceptible to all environmental influences, as Belsky (2004) would hypothesize; it is also plausible that their susceptibility is specific to adverse threats. Likewise, it is not known whether their hypersusceptibility extends to other domains of environmental influence, including other psychosocial stimuli as well as environmental toxins.

The contrasts examined here have assumed only linear effects of genes and of the environment. It is plausible, even likely, that limits in these effects, and therefore in the interaction effects, would be reached at the extremes. For example, some unfortunate children might well suffer extreme biological impairments that cannot be overcome through any environmental intervention. The findings that we do report cover a fairly broad range of populations and influences, however, and so if limits are reached they probably affect only very small proportions of the population. Likewise, the horror of extreme physical maltreatment might render even the most genetically invulnerable child antisocial.

Yet, another caveat is that these findings apply particularly to angry, reactive aggressive behavior, but might not hold for other kinds of aggressive behavior. Instrumental proactive aggression, for example, might follow main effects of social learning without interaction with genes.

Conclusion

Despite the caveats noted, the consistent and robust findings in the literature regarding the shape of the interaction effect between dispositions and environments in predicting aggressive behavior require immediate transformation of the way that research, clinical practice, and public policy are conducted on aggressive behavior.

References

Alm, P. O., Alm, M., Humble, K., Leppeter, J., et al. (1994). Criminality and platelet monoamine oxidase activity in former juvenile delinquents as adults. *Acta Psychiatrica Scandinavica, 89,* 41–45.

Anderson, D. A. (1999). The aggregate burden of crime. *Journal of Law and Economics, 42,* 611–642.

Andrews, D. A., & Bonta, J. (1994). *The psychology of criminal conduct.* Cincinnati, OH: Anderson Publishing.

Arseneault, L., Moffitt, T. E., Caspi, A., Taylor, A., et al. (2003). Strong genetic effects on cross-situational antisocial behaviour among 5-year-old children according to mothers, teachers, examiner-observers, and twins' self-reports. *Journal of Child Psychology and Psychiatry and Allied Disciplines, 44,* 832–848.

Arsenault, L., Tremblay, R. E., Boulerice, B., Seguin, J. R., & Saucier, J. (2000). Minor physical anomalies and family adversity as risk factors for violent delinquency in adolescence. *American Journal of Psychiatry, 157,* 917–923.

Aydin, O., & Markova, I. (1979). Attribution tendencies of popular and unpopular children. *British Journal of Social and Clinical Psychology, 18,* 291–298.

Belfrage, H., Lidberg, L., & Oreland, L. (1992). Platelet monoamine oxidase activity in mentally disordered violent offenders. *Acta Psychiatrica Scandinavica, 85,* 218–221.

Belsky, J. (2004). Differential susceptibility to rearing influence: An evolutionary hypothesis and some evidence. In B. Ellis & D. D. Bjorklund (Eds.), *Origins of the social mind:*

Evolutionary psychology and child development (pp. 139–163). New York: Guilford.

Belsky, J., Hsieh, K. H., & Crnic, K. (1998). Mothering, fathering and infant negativity as antecedents of boys' externalizing problems and inhibition at age 3 years: Differential susceptibility to rearing experience? *Development and Psychopathology, 10,* 301–319.

Bennett, A. J., Lesch, K. P., Heils, A., Long, J. C., Lorenz, J. G., Shoaf, S. E., et al. (2002). Early experience and serotonin transporter gene variation interact to influence primate CNS function. *Molecular Psychiatry, 7,* 118–122.

Beyers, J. M., Bates, J. E., Pettit, G. S., & Dodge, K. A. (2003). Neighborhood structure, parenting processes, and the development of youths' externalizing behaviors: A multilevel analysis. *American Journal of Community Psychology, 31,* 35–53.

Bierman, K. L., & Wargo, J. B. (1995). Predicting the longitudinal course associated with aggressive-rejected, aggressive (nonrejected), and rejected (nonaggressive) status. *Development and Psychopathology, 7,* 669–682.

Blair, C. (2002). Early intervention for low birth weight, preterm infants: The role of negative emotionality in the specification of effects. *Development and Psychopathology, 14,* 311–332.

Brook, A. S., Starzyk, K. B., & Quinsey, V. L. (2001). The relationship between testosterone and aggression: A meta-analysis. *Aggression and Violent Behavior, 6,* 579–599.

Boxer, P., Guerra, N. G., Huesmann, L. R., & Morales, J. (2005). Proximal peer-level effects of a small-group selected prevention on aggression in elementary school children: An investigation of the peer contagion hypothesis. *Journal of Abnormal Child Psychology, 33*(3), 325–338.

Boyce, W. T., & Ellis, B. J. (2005). Biological sensitivity to context: I. An evolutionary-developmental theory of the origins and functions of stress reactivity. *Development and Psychopathology, 17,* 271–301.

Bradley, R. H., & Corwyn, R. F. (2002). Socioeconomic status and child development. *Annual Review of Psychology, 53,* 371–399.

Brennan, P. A., Grekin, E. R., & Mednick. S. A. (1999). Maternal smoking during pregnancy and adult male criminal outcomes. *Archives of General Psychiatry, 56,* 215–219.

Brennan, P. A., Hall, J., Bor, W., Najman, J. M., & Williams, G. (2003). Integrating biological and social processes in relation to early-onset persistent aggression in boys and girls. *Developmental Psychology, 39,* 309–323.

Breslau, N. (1995). Psychiatric sequelae of low birth weight. *Epidemiological Review, 17,* 96–106.

Bronfenbrenner, U., & Ceci, S. J. (1994). Nature nurture reconceptualized in developmental perspective: A bioecological model. *Psychological Review, 101,* 568–586.

Brunner, H. G. Nelen, M., Breakefield, X. O., & Ropers, H. H. (1993). Abnormal behavior associated with a point mutation in the structural gene for monoamine oxidase A. *Science, 262,* 578–580.

Cadoret, R. J. (1985). Genes, environment and their interaction in the development of psychopathology. In T. Sakai & T. Tsuboi (Eds.), *Genetic aspects of human behavior* (pp. 165–175). Tokyo: Igaku-Shoin.

Cadoret, R. J., & Cain, C. (1981). Environmental and genetic factors in predicting adolescent antisocial behavior in adoptees. *Psychiatric Journal of the University of Ottowa, 6,* 220–225.

Cadoret, R. J., Cain, C. A., & Crowe, R. R. (1983). Evidence for gene-environment interaction in the development of adolescent antisocial behavior. *Behavior Genetics, 13,* 301–310.

Cadoret, R. J., Yates, W. R., Troughton, E., Woodworth, G., & Stewart, M. A. (1995). Genetic-environmental interaction in the genesis of aggressivity and conduct disorders. *Archives of General Psychiatry, 52,* 916–924.

Cases, O., Seif, I., Grimsby, J., Gaspar, P., et al. (1995). Aggressive behavior and altered amounts of brain serotonin and norepinephrine in mice lacking MAOA. *Science, 268,* 1763–1766.

Caspi, A., Henry, B., McGee, R. O., Moffitt, T. E., et al. (1995). Temperamental origins of child and adolescent behavior problems: From age three to fifteen. *Child Development, 66,* 55–68.

Caspi, A., McClay, J., Moffitt, T. E., Mill, J., Martin, J., Craig, I., et al. (2002). Role of genotype in the cycle of violence in maltreated children. *Science, 297,* 851–854.

Caspi, A., Snugden, K., Moffitt, T. E., Taylor, A., Craig, I. W., Harrington, H., et al. (2003). Influence of life stress on depression: Moderation by a polymorphism in the 5-HTT gene. *Science, 301,* 386–389.

Caspi, A., Moffitt, T. E., Morgan, J., Rutter, M., Taylor, A., Arseneault, L., Tully, L., Jacobs, C., Kim-Cohen, J., & Polo-Tomas, M. (2004). Maternal expressed emotion predicts children's antisocial behavior: Using MZ-twin differences to identify environmental effects on behavioral development. *Development Psychology, 40,* 149–161.

Clark, R., Hyde, J. S., Essex, M. J., & Klein, M. H. (1997). Length of maternity leave and quality of mother-infant interactions. *Child Development, 68,* 364–383.

Cloninger, R., Sigvardsson, S., Bohman, M., & von Knorring, A. (1982). Predisposition to petty criminality in Swedish adoptees. *Archives of General Psychiatry, 39,* 1242–1247.

Cohen, M. A. (1998). The monetary value of saving a high-risk youth. *Journal of Quantitative Criminology, 14,* 5–33.

Coie, J. D. (2004). The impact of negative social experiences on the development of antisocial behavior. In J. B. Kupersmidt & K. A. Dodge (Eds.), *Children's peer relations: From development to intervention* (pp. 243–268). Washington, DC: American Psychological Association.

Conduct Problems Prevention Research Group. (2004). The effects of the Fast Track Program on serious problem outcomes at the end of elementary school. *Journal of Clinical Child and Adolescent Psychology, 33,* 650–661.

De Bellis, M. D. (2001). Developmental traumatology: The psychobiological development of maltreated children and its implications for research, treatment, and policy. *Development and Psychopathology, 13,* 539–564.

Deater-Deckard, K. (2000). Parenting and child behavioral adjustment in early childhood: A quantitative genetic approach to studying family processes. *Child Development, 71,* 468–484.

Deater-Deckard, K., & Dodge, K. A. (1997). Externalizing behavior problems and discipline revisited: Nonlinear effects and variation by culture, context, and gender. *Psychological Inquiry, 8,* 161–175.

Dodge, K. A., Bates, J. E., & Pettit, G. S. (1990). Mechanisms in the cycle of violence. *Science, 250,* 1678–1683.

Dodge, K. A., Coie, J., & Lynam, D. R. (2006). Aggression and antisocial behavior in youth. In W. Damon (Ed.), *Handbook of child psychology. Vol. 3: Social, emotional, and personality development* (6th ed., pp. 719–788). New York: Wiley.

Dodge, K. A., Lansford, J. E., Burks, V. S., Bates, J. E., Pettit, G. S., Fontaine, R., et al. (2003). Peer rejection and social information-processing factors in the development of aggressive behavior problems in children. *Child Development, 74,* 374–393.

Dodge, K. A., & Pettit, G. S. (2003). A biopsychosocial model of the development of chronic conduct problems in adolescence. *Developmental Psychology, 39*(2), 349–371.

Dodge, K. A., Pettit, G. S., McClaskey, C. L., & Brown, M. (1986). Social competence in children. *Monographs of the Society for Research in Child Development* (Serial No. 213, Vol. 51, No. 2).

Elliott, D. S., Hamburg, B. A., & Williams, K. R. (Eds.). (1998). *Violence in American schools: A new perspective.* New York: Cambridge University Press.

Elliott, D. S., Huizinga, D., & Morse, B. (1986). Self-reported violent offending: A descriptive analysis of juvenile violent offenders and their offending careers. *Journal of Interpersonal Violence, 1,* 472–514.

El-Sheikh, M., Harger, J., & Whitson, S. M. (2001). Exposure to interparental conflict and children's adjustment and physical health: The moderating role of vagal tone. *Child Development, 72,* 1617–1636.

Evans, W. E., & Relling, M. V. (1999). Pharmacogenetics: Translating functional genomics into rational therapeutics. *Science, 286,* 487–491.

Farrington, D. P., & Hawkins, J. D. (1991). Predicting participation, early onset and later persistence in officially recorded offending. *Criminal Behaviour and Mental Health, 1,* 1–33.

Fergusson, D. M., & Horwood, J. L. (1998). Exposure to interparental violence in childhood and psychosocial adjustment in young adulthood. *Child Abuse and Neglect, 22,* 339–357.

Foley, D. L., Eaves, L. J., Wormley, B., Silberg, J. L., Maes, H. H., Kuhn, J., et al. (2004). Childhood adversity, monoamine oxidase A genotype, and risk for conduct disorder. *Archives of General Psychiatry, 61,* 738–744.

Gershoff, E. T. (2002). Corporal punishment by parents and associated child behaviors and experiences: A meta-analytic and theoretical review. *Psychological Bulletin, 128,* 539–579.

Gottlieb, G. (2003). On making behavioral genetics truly developmental. *Human Development, 46,* 337–355.

Gouze, K. R. (1987). Attention and social problem solving as correlates of aggression in preschool males. *Journal of Abnormal Child Psychology, 15,* 181–197.

Graham, S., & Hudley, C. (1994). Attributions of aggressive and nonaggressive African-American male early adolescents: A study of construct accessibility. *Developmental Psychology, 30,* 365–373.

Graham, S., Hudley, C., & Williams, E. (1992). Attributional and emotional determinants of aggression among African-American and Latino young adolescents. *Developmental Psychology, 28,* 731–740.

Guerra, N. G., & Slaby, R. G. (1989). Evaluative factors in social problem solving by aggressive boys. *Journal of Abnormal Child Psychology, 17,* 277–289.

Heilbrun, K., Hart, S. D., Hare, R. D., Gustafson, D., Nunez, C., & White, A. J. (1998). Inpatient and postdischarge aggression in mentally disordered offenders: The role of psychopathy. *Journal of Interpersonal Violence, 13,* 514–527.

Henry, B., Caspi, A., Moffitt, T. E., & Silva, P. A. (1996). Temperamental and familial predictors of violent and nonviolent criminal convictions: Age 3 to age 18. *Developmental Psychology, 32,* 614–623.

Herrnstein, R. J., & Murray, C. A. (1994). *The bell curve: Intelligence and class structure in American life.* New York: Free Press.

Hill, A. V. S. (1999). Genetics and genomics of infectious disease susceptibility. *British Medical Bulletin, 55,* 401–413.

Hobbes, T. (1969). *Leviathan.* Cambridge, UK: Cambridge University Press. (Original work published 1651.)

Hodgins, S., Kratzer, L., & McNeil, T. F. (2001). Obstetric complications, parenting, and risk of criminal behavior. *Archives of General Psychiatry, 58,* 746–752.

Hood, K. (2005). Development as a dependent variable: Robert B. Cairns on the psychobiology of aggression. In D. M. Stoff & E. J. Susman (Eds.), *Developmental psychobiology of aggression* (pp. 29–45). New York: Cambridge University Press.

Hutchings, B., & Mednick, S. A. (1973). Genetic and environmental influences on criminality in Denmark. In B. S. Brown & E. F. Torrey (Eds.), *International collaboration in mental health* (pp. 113–123). Rockville, MD: National Institute of Mental Health.

Jaffee, S. R., Caspi, A., Moffitt, T. E., Dodge, K. A., Rutter, M., Taylor, A., et al. (2005). Nature x nurture: Genetic vulnerabilities interact with physical maltreatment to promote conduct problems. *Development and Psychopathology, 17,* 67–84.

Jaffee, S. R., Caspi, A., Moffitt, T. E., & Taylor, A. (2004). Physical maltreatment victim to antisocial child: Evidence of an environmentally mediated process. *Journal of Abnormal Psychology, 113,* 44–55.

Jaffee, S. R., Moffitt, T. E., Caspi, A., Taylor, A., & Arseneault, L. (2002). Influence of adult domestic violence on children's internalizing and externalizing problems: An environmentally informative twin study. *Journal of the American Academy of Child and Adolescent Psychiatry, 41,* 1095–1103.

Kellam, S. G., Rebok, G. W., Ialongo, N., & Mayer, L. S. (1994). The course and malleability of aggressive behavior from early first grade into middle school: Results of a developmental epidemiology-based preventive trial. *Journal of Child Psychology and Psychiatry and Allied Disciplines, 35,* 259–281.

Kemppainen, L., Jokelainen, J., Jarvelin, M., Isohanni, M., & Rasanen, P. (2001). The one-child family and violent criminality: A 31-year follow-up study of the Northern Finland 1966 birth cohort. *American Journal of Psychiatry, 158,* 960–962.

Kendler, K. S., Kessler, R. C., Walters, E. E., MacLean, C., Neale, M. C., Heath, A. C., et al. (1995). Stressful life events, genetic liability and onset of an episode of major depression in women. *American Journal of Psychiatry, 152,* 833–842.

Kochanska, G. (1997). Multiple pathways to conscience for children with different temperaments: From toddlerhood to age 5. *Developmental Psychology, 33,* 228–240.

Kosson, D. S., Cyterski, T. S., Steuerwald, B. L., Neumann, C. S., & Walker-Matthews, S. (1999). The reliability and validity of the Psychopathy Checklist: Youth Version (PCL: YV) in nonincarcerated adolescent males. *Psychological Assessment, 14,* 97–109.

Kupersmidt, J. B., & Coie, J. D. (1990). Preadolescent peer status, aggression, and school adjustment as predictors of externalizing problems in adolescence. *Child Development, 61,* 1350–1362.

Lansford, J. E., Dodge, K. A., Pettit, G. S., Bates, J. E., Crozier, J., & Kaplow, J. (2002). A 12-year prospective study of the long-term effects of early child physical maltreatment on psychological, behavioral, and academic problems in adolescence. *Archives of Pediatrics and Adolescent Medicine, 156,* 824–830.

Lengua, L. J., Wolchik, S. A., Sandler, I. N., & West, S. G. (2000). The additive and interactive effects of parenting and temperament in predicting adjustment problems of children of divorce. *Journal of Clinical Child Psychology, 29,* 232–244.

Lochman, J. E. (1987). Self and peer perceptions and attributional biases of aggressive and nonaggressive boys. *Journal of Consulting Clinical Psychology, 55,* 4404–4410.

Locke, J. (1913). *Some thoughts concerning education.* London: Cambridge University Press. (Original work published 1690.)

Lorber, M. F. (2004). Psychophysiology of aggression, psychopathy, and conduct problems: A meta-analysis. *Psychological Bulletin, 130,* 531–552.

Luntz, B. K., & Widom, C. S. (1994). Antisocial personality disorder in abused and neglected children grown up. *American Journal of Psychiatry, 151,* 670–674.

Lynam, D. R. (1997). Pursuing the psychopath: Capturing the fledgling psychopath in a nomological net. *Journal of Abnormal Psychology, 106,* 425–438.

Lynam, D. R., Caspi, A., Moffitt, T. E., Wilkstroem, P. O., Loeber, R., & Novak, S. (2000). The interaction between impulsivity and neighborhood context on offending: The effects of impulsivity are stronger in poorer neighborhoods. *Journal of Abnormal Psychology, 109,* 563–574.

MacBrayer, E. K., Milich, R., & Hundley, M. (2003). Attributional biases in aggressive children and their mothers. *Journal of Abnormal Psychology, 112,* 698–708.

Maziade, M., Caperaa, P. Laplante, M., Boudreault, M., Thivierge, T., Cote, R., et al. (1985). Value of difficult temperament among 7-year-olds in the general population for predicting psychiatric diagnosis at age 12. *American Journal of Psychiatry, 142,* 943–946.

McClelland, G. H., & Judd, C. M. (1993). Statistical difficulties of detecting interactions and moderator effects. *Psychological Bulletin, 114,* 376–390.

McCord, J. (1991). Questioning the value of punishment. *Social Problems, 38,* 167–179.

Mednick, S. A., & Christiansen, K. O. (1977). *Biosocial bases of criminal behavior.* Oxford: Gardner Press.

Metropolitan Area Child Study Research Group. (2002). A cognitive-ecological approach to preventing aggression in urban settings: Initial outcomes for high-risk children. *Journal of Consulting and Clinical Psychology, 70,* 179–194.

Milich, R., & Dodge, K. A. (1984). Social information processing patterns in child psychiatric populations. *Journal of Abnormal Child Psychology, 12,* 471–490.

Miller, J. D., & Lynam, D. R. (2001). Structural models of personality and their relation to antisocial behavior: A meta-analytic review. *Criminology, 39,* 765–792.

Monroe, S. M., & Simons, A. D. (1991). Diathesis stress theories in the context of life stress research: Implications for the depressive disorders. *Psychological Bulletin, 110,* 406–425.

Morell, V. (1993). Evidence found for a possible "aggression gene." *Science, 260,* 1722–1723.

Morris, A. S., Silk, J. S., Steinberg, L., Sessa, F. M., Avenevoli, S., & Essex, M. J. (2002). Temperamental vulnerability and negative parenting as interacting predictors of child adjustment. *Journal of Marriage and Family, 64,* 461–471.

Murrie, D. C., Cornell, D. G., Kaplan, S., McConville, D., & Levy-Elkon, A. (2004). Psychopathy scores and violence among juvenile offenders: A multi-measure study. *Behavioral Sciences and the Law, 22,* 49–67.

Nasby, W., Hayden, B., & DePaulo, B. M. (1979). Attributional bias among aggressive boys to interpret unambiguous social stimuli as displays of hostility. *Journal of Abnormal Psychology, 89,* 459–468.

O'Connor, T. G., McGuire, S., Reiss, D., Hetherington, E., & Plomin, R. (1998). Co-occurrence of depressive symptoms and antisocial behavior in adolescence: A common genetic liability. *Journal of Abnormal Psychology, 107*(1), 27–37.

Olds, D., Kitzman, H., Cole, R., & Robinson, J. (1997). Theoretical foundations of a program of home visitation for pregnant women and parents of young children. *Journal of Community Psychology, 25,* 9–25.

Parsian, A., & Cloninger, C. R. (2001). Serotonergic pathway genes and subtypes of alcoholism: Association studies. *Psychiatric Genetics, 11,* 89–94.

Patterson, G. R., & Bank, C. L. (1989). Some amplifying mechanisms for pathologic processes in families. In E. Thelen & M. Gunnar (Eds.), *The Minnesota Symposia in Child*

Psychology, Vol. 22 (pp. 69–99). Hillsdale, NJ: Erlbaum.

Pine, D. S., Saffer, D., Schonfeld, I. S., & Davies, M. (1997). Minor physical anomalies: Modifiers of environmental risks for psychiatric impairment? *Journal of the American Academy of Child and Adolescent Psychiatry, 36,* 395–403.

Piquero, A., & Tibbetts, S. (1999). The impact of pre/perinatal disturbances and disadvantaged familial environment in predicting criminal offending. *Studies on Crime and Crime Prevention, 8,* 52–70.

Pitts, T. B. (1996). Reduced heart rate levels in aggressive children. In A. Raine, P. A. Brennan, D. P. Farrington, & S. A. Mednick (Eds.), *Biosocial bases of violence* (pp. 317–320). New York: Plenum.

Raine, A. (2002). Annotation: The role of prefrontal deficits, low autonomic arousal and early health factors in the development of antisocial and aggressive behavior in children. *Journal of Child Psychology and Psychiatry and Allied Disciplines, 43,* 417–434.

Raine, A., Brennan, P., & Mednick, S. A. (1994). Birth complications combined with early maternal rejection at age 1 year predispose to violent crime at age 18 years. *Archives of General Psychiatry, 51,* 984–988.

Raine, A., Brennan, P., & Mednick, S. (1997). Interaction between birth complications and early maternal rejection in predisposing individuals to adult violence: Specificity to serious, early-onset violence. *American Journal of Psychiatry, 154,* 1265–1271.

Raine, A., Reynolds, C., Venables, P. H., Mednick, S. A., & Farrington, D. P. (1998). Fearlessness, stimulation-seeking, and large body size at age 3 years as early dispositions to childhood aggression at age 11 years. *Archives of General Psychiatry, 55,* 745–751.

Rhee, S. H., & Waldman, I. D. (2002). Genetic and environmental influences on antisocial behavior: A meta-analysis of twin and adoption studies. *Psychological Bulletin, 128,* 490–529.

Riggins-Casper, K. M., Cadoret, R. J., Knutson, J. F., & Langbehn, D. (2003). Biology-environment interaction and evocative biology-environment correlation: Contributions of harsh discipline and parental psychopathology to problem adolescent behaviors. *Behavior Genetics, 33,* 205–220.

Rousseau, J. J. (1762). *The social contract: Or principles of political right* (G. D. H. Cole, Trans.).

Salekin, R. T. (2002). Psychopathy and therapeutic pessimism: Clinical lore or clinical reality? *Clinical Psychology Review, 22,* 79–112.

Sampson, R. J., & Laub, J. H. (1994). Urban poverty and the family context of delinquency: A new look at structure and process in a classic study. *Child Development, 65,* 523–540.

Sampson, R. J., Raudenbush, S. W., & Earls, F. (1997). Neighborhoods and violent crime: A multilevel study of collective efficacy. *Science, 277,* 918–924.

Sanson, A., Oberklaid, F., Pedlow, R., & Prior, M. (1991). Risk indicators: Assessment of infancy predictors of preschool behavioral maladjustment. *Journal of Child Psychology and Psychiatry, 32,* 609–626.

Shaw, D. S., Gilliom, M., Ingoldsby, E. M., & Nagin, D. S. (2003). Trajectories leading to school-age conduct problems. *Developmental Psychology, 39,* 189–200.

Shaw, D. S., & Vondra, J. I. (1995). Infant attachment security and maternal predictors of early behavioral problems: A longitudinal study of low-income families. *Journal of Abnormal Child Psychology, 23,* 335–357.

Shih, J. C., Ridd., M. J., Chen, K., Meehan, P. W., Kung, M., Seif, I., et al. (1999). Ketanserin and tetrabenazine abolish aggression in mice lacking monoamine oxidase A. *Brain Research, 835,* 104–112.

Shih, J. C., & Thompson, R. F. (1999). Monoamine oxidase in neuropsychiatry and behavior. *American Journal of Human Genetics, 65,* 593–598.

Slaby, R. G., & Guerra, N. G. (1988). Cognitive mediators of aggression in adolescent offenders: 1. Assessment. *Developmental Psychology, 24,* 580–588.

Spencer, M. B., Dobbs, B., & Swanson, D. P. (1988). African American adolescents: Adaptational processes and socioeconomic diversity in behavioural outcomes. *Journal of Adolescence, 11,* 117–137.

Stoolmiller, M., Eddy, J. M., & Reid, J. B. (2000). Detecting and describing preventive intervention effects in a universal school-based randomized trial targeting delinquent and violent behavior. *Journal of Consulting and Clinical Psychology, 68,* 296–306.

Suomi, S. J. (1997). Nonverbal communication in nonhuman primates: Implications for the emergence of culture. In P. Molnar & C. U. Segerstrale (Eds.), *Where nature meets culture* (pp. 112–132). Hillsdale, NJ: Erlbaum.

Tremblay, R. E., Pihl, R. O., Vitaro, F., & Dobkin, P. L. (1994). Predicting early onset of male antisocial behavior from preschool behavior. *Archives of General Psychiatry, 51,* 732–739.

Tuinier, S., Verhoeven, W. M. A., & van Praag, H. M. (1995). Cerebrospinal fluid 5 hydroxyindolacetic acid and aggression: A critical reappraisal of the clinical data. *International Clinical Psychopharmacology, 10,* 147–156.

van Goozen, S. H. M., Matthys, W., Cohen-Kettenis, P. T., Gispen-de Wied, C., Wiegant, V. M., & van Engeland. (1998). Salivary cortisol and cardiovascular activity during stress in oppositional-defiant disorder boys and normal controls. *Biological Psychiatry, 43,* 531–539.

van Lier, P. A. C., Muthen, B. O., van der Sar, R. M., & Crijne, A. A. M. (2004). Preventing disruptive behavior in elementary schoolchildren: Impact of a universal classroom-based intervention. *Journal of Consulting and Clinical Psychology, 72,* 467–478.

Virkkunen, M., Eggert, M., Rawlings, R., & Linnoila, M. (1996). A prospective follow-up study of alcoholic violent offenders and fire setters. *Archives of General Psychiatry, 53,* 523–529.

Wachs, T. D., & Gandour, M. J. (1983). Temperament, environment, and six-month cognitive intellectual development: A test of the organismic specificity hypothesis. *International Journal of Behavioral Development, 6,* 135–152.

Weiss, B., Harris, V., Catron, T., & Han, S. S. (2003). Efficacy of the RECAP intervention program for children with concurrent internalizing and externalizing problems. *Journal of Consulting and Clinical Psychology, 71,* 364–374.

Part III

INDIVIDUAL FACTORS
AND VIOLENCE

CHAPTER 11

Relational Aggression and Gender: An Overview

Nicki R. Crick, Jamie M. Ostrov, and Yoshito Kawabata

Introduction

Childhood aggression has been one of the most widely studied topics in psychology during the past several decades because of its empirically demonstrated, detrimental consequences for children, for families, for schools, and for society in general (for a review see Coie & Dodge, 1998). Despite impressive and significant progress in this area, the majority of past investigations have failed to consider aggression as exhibited by girls (Crick & Dodge, 1994; Robins, 1986). This lack of attention to aggressive girls has taken several forms. In some studies, girls have been excluded from relevant studies altogether. In others, the forms of aggression studied (e.g., physical aggression) have been relatively uncharacteristic of girls, and thus any outcomes obtained were most applicable for boys.

One of the challenges for researchers in recent years has been to rectify the gender imbalance in our knowledge of childhood aggression, and increased attention to the behavioral problems of girls has ensued. In one attempt to address this problem, a relational form of aggression has been identified that has been shown to have significant promise for increasing our understanding of the aggressive interpersonal exchanges of girls (Crick & Grotpeter, 1995). The purpose of this chapter is to provide an overview of recent studies of relational aggression and gender with a particular focus on the following: (1) the definition of relational aggression and how it differs from other forms of aggression; (2) assessment of relational aggression; (3) developmental manifestations of relational aggression from early childhood to adulthood; (4) gender differences; (5) risk and harm associated with relational aggression; (6) the role of culture; (7) intervention efforts, and (8) contributions, conclusions, and suggestions for future research directions.

What is Relational Aggression?

Relational aggression has been defined as behaviors that employ damage to relationships, or the threat of damage to relationships, as the vehicle of harm (Crick et al.,

1999). These behaviors may be direct or indirect in nature. For example, a direct relationally aggressive act might involve telling a peer that she can't come to your birthday party unless she does what you tell her to do. In contrast, an indirect relationally aggressive act might involve withdrawing one's attention or friendship by giving a peer the "silent treatment," or it may use nasty rumor spreading as a way to encourage others to reject the peer. Direct relationally aggressive acts appear to be more common than indirect relationally aggressive acts during early childhood; however, both types seem to be common during middle childhood and adolescence (Crick et al., 1999).

The specific focus on the potentially harmful manipulation of relationships as the weapon of harm distinguishes relational aggression from other forms of aggression. For example, the most commonly studied aggressive acts, physically aggressive behaviors, involve the use of physical damage (or the threat of physical damage) as the vehicle of harm (e.g., hitting, threatening to beat a peer up unless she does what you tell her to do). Relational aggression can also be distinguished from verbal aggression. Verbally aggressive acts include hostile, mean behaviors that are verbally delivered (e.g., verbal insults), but that do not necessarily involve the use of relationships. Thus, some, but certainly not all, of relationally aggressive behaviors could be considered verbal aggression and vice versa by some researchers (we prefer to consider verbal aggression to be limited to verbal insults that do not specifically involve relationship damage). Relational aggression can also be differentiated from indirect forms of aggression. Indirect aggression involves hostile behaviors in which the perpetrator does not confront the target. Similar to verbal aggression, these behaviors do not necessarily involve the use of relationships to harm others. Thus, indirect aggressive acts could include such behaviors as putting sugar in someone's gas tank or sending anonymous, nasty e-mails. They also could include behaviors that target relationships as the focus of harm, and

thus, some exemplars of indirect aggression overlap with indirect types of relationally aggressive behaviors (e.g., spreading harmful rumors to encourage peers to reject a classmate).

Study of relational aggression has contributed significantly to our understanding of the role of gender in the development of aggression. Traditionally, studies of childhood aggression have targeted forms of aggression that are more typical of boys than girls. The most widely studied form has been physical aggression. Research on physical aggression has resulted in a significant empirical knowledge base of the development and consequences of aggressive behavior for boys; however, it has not yielded nearly as great an understanding of the role of hostile, aggressive behaviors in the lives of girls. In sharp contrast, studies of relational aggression (as well as those of related forms of aggression, such as indirect aggression) have vastly increased our understanding of aggressive girls, in addition to aggressive boys (Crick & Zahn-Waxler, 2003). These studies have demonstrated that, despite theoretical formulations of the development of aggression among girls in which aggressive behavior has been posited to be almost nonexistent during early and middle childhood (Keenan & Shaw, 1997; Moffitt, 1993; Silverthorn & Frick, 1999), relational aggression can be reliably observed among girls (and boys) as early as the preschool years (Crick, Ostrov, Burr et al., 2006; Ostrov & Keating, 2004; Ostrov, Woods, Jansen, Casas, & Crick, 2004; Stauffacher & DeHart, 2005; for a review see Crick, Ostrov, Appleyard, Jansen, & Casas, 2004). Thus, research on relational aggression counters the "myth of the benign childhoods of girls" (Zahn-Waxler, 1993) and provides unique insight into antisocial, aggressive behavior patterns, particularly for girls.

Assessment of Relational and Physical Aggression

Scholars have successfully used a number of measurement techniques (e.g., field observations, lab-based analogue and playgroup designs, peer assessments, structured interviews, responses to hypothetical scenarios, and standard reports from various informants) to document aggressive behavior among children and adolescents across development (see Coie & Dodge, 1998). Recent advances in the study of relational aggression rely on these past methodological traditions, but continually adapt and introduce innovative, developmentally appropriate, psychometrically sound methods to better reflect the nuances of this relationship-based subtype of aggression. More specifically, the study of relational aggression was the impetus for the development of focal child observational procedures used over longer periods of time to capture these relatively more subtle aggressive behaviors during free play sessions in the classroom and on the playground. The use of focal child observational procedures, which requires the observer to stay within earshot of the participant, allows the researcher to assess the unfolding of the interaction and to monitor the nature of the interaction for proper assessment of harmful intent (see Ostrov & Keating, 2004). In addition, these types of methods allow the observer to rule out more benign and adaptive forms of social behavior and play (e.g., rough and tumble play, see Pellegrini, 1989). In some developmental periods (e.g., early and middle childhood) teachers are privy to instances of relationally aggressive behavior and have been used successfully as reliable informants. Self-report methods may not be as reliable for assessing relational aggression within peer relationships, especially during earlier developmental periods; however, peer nomination and peer rating procedures have been used successfully to study both relational and physical aggression during these age periods (see Crick, Casas, & Mosher, 1997; Crick & Grotpeter, 1995). A brief overview of these methods follows; it further underscores the importance of generating unique as well as developmentally appropriate assessment instruments for the study of relational aggression.

Observations. Naturalistic and semi-structured observational designs have successfully captured relationally aggressive behavior at home (Stauffacher & DeHart, 2005), school (i.e., classroom and playground), and in the lab during early childhood (see Crick, Ostrov, Burr et al., 2006; McEvoy, Estrem, Rodriguez, & Olson, 2003; McNeilly-Choque, Hart, Robinson, Nelson, & Olsen, 1996; Ostrov, 2006; Ostrov & Keating, 2004; Ostrov et al., 2004). The focal child approach (Fagot & Hagan, 1985) and associated procedures, in which one child is observed for a continuous period of time (e.g., 10 minutes) for a number of sessions (e.g., five to eight sessions over a 2- to 3-month period), provides a reliable and valid method for assessing relational and physical aggression (Ostrov & Keating, 2004) during early childhood and the transition into kindergarten (for further description see Crick et al., 2004). Additional methods, including scan sampling observations (McNeilly-Choque et al., 1996) and ethnographic observational analysis, have been conducted with young children on the playground as well (Goodwin, 2002).

Teacher reports. Standard teacher report methods (i.e., Preschool Social Behavior Scale-Teacher Form; Children's Social Behavior Scale – Teacher Form) are increasingly used by aggression scholars to assess relational and physical aggression and victimization (e.g., Bonica, Yeshova, Arnold, Fisher, & Zeljo, 2003; Crick, 1996; Crick et al., 1997; Crick, Ostrov, Burr et al., 2006; Dettling, Gunnar, & Donzella, 1999; Hart, Nelson, Robinson, Olsen, & McNeilly-Choque, 1998; Hawley, 2003; Sebanc, 2003). These methods have been shown to be reliable and valid (e.g., Bonica et al., 2003; Crick et al., 1997), even demonstrating significant concurrent (e.g., Ostrov & Keating, 2004) and predictive associations with observational methods (see Crick, Ostrov, Burr et al., 2006). These findings suggest that teachers can reliably detect relationally aggressive behaviors, especially during early and middle childhood, when these behaviors may be less covert and sophisticated than in the adolescent period. In recent years, additional teacher report measures with acceptable psychometric properties have also been developed and used by researchers (Macgowan, Nash, & Fraser, 2002).

Peer reports. Peer assessment techniques are often used to obtain a reliable index of social behavior (i.e., relational and physical aggression) in classrooms from early childhood (e.g., Crick et al., 1997; Crick, Ostrov, Burr et al., 2006; McNeilly-Choque et al., 1996), middle childhood (e.g., Crick & Grotpeter, 1995; Henington, Hughes, Cavell, & Thompson, 1998; Rose, Swenson, & Waller, 2004; Rys & Bear, 1997), early adolescence (e.g., Cillessen & Mayeux, 2004; Pellegrini & Long, 2003), and late adolescence/early adulthood (e.g., Werner & Crick, 1999). These methods often demonstrate the ability to provide unique variance in the identification of relationally aggressive behaviors and may be most useful during the late middle childhood and adolescent period, when observations are increasingly more difficult to conduct in a nonreactive and ecologically valid manner and when teachers no longer have as much access to the covert aspects of their students' peer relationships.

Additional methods. A myriad of additional reporting instruments have been developed in studies of relational aggression (see Crick et al., 2004). These include: self-report instruments (e.g., Little, Jones, Henrich, & Hawley, 2003); open-ended free response interviews concerning disliked peers (e.g., French, Jansen, & Pidada, 2002); assessments of relationally aggressive children's social cognitions (e.g., Leff, Kupersmidt, & Power, 2003); and hostile attribution biases for relational and instrumental provocation in peer situations (e.g., Crick & Dodge, 1996; Crick, Grotpeter, & Bigbee, 2002). As the field continues to explore the development of relational aggression, specificity in our selection of research instruments may be based on the particular age of the participants and the developmental manifestations of the aggressive behavior.

Developmental Manifestations of Relational Aggression

Studies of relational aggression during early childhood show that these behaviors tend to be direct; displayed in clear view of the victim, bystanders, and adult observers; and based in the present situational context (e.g., "I won't be your friend anymore unless you give me that toy," "You can't come to my house because you are mean," covering ears to signal ignoring; see Crick et al., 1999; Crick, Ostrov, Burr et al., 2006). Recent evidence indicates that relatively sophisticated forms of relational aggression (e.g., malicious secret spreading) may also be reliably detected among 3-year-old girls (Ostrov et al., 2004). However, these more complex behaviors appear to be less frequent and more direct (e.g., secret spreading may be done right in front of and within hearing range of the intended target) than those exhibited by older children. There is corroborating evidence to suggest that the first signs of relational aggression emerge no later than 30 months and continue to become more sophisticated (i.e., more covert and involving third parties) throughout the early childhood period (Bonica et al., 2003; Crick et al., 1997, 1999; Crick, Ostrov, Burr et al., 2006; Hawley, 2003; McNeilly-Choque et al., 1996; Ostrov, 2006; Ostrov & Keating, 2004; Ostrov et al., 2004; Sebanc, 2003). Finally, recent evidence suggests that young children may learn and be socialized by older siblings (i.e., sisters) to display relationally aggressive behavior in the home context, which might serve as a training ground prior to the transition to subsequent peer relationships at school (Stauffacher & DeHart, 2005).

The majority of studies investigating relational aggression have focused on middle childhood. Relative to early childhood, relational aggression during this developmental period appears to be more covert and sophisticated (e.g., use of malicious gossip, rumors, or secrets to damage relationships via third parties and beyond the purview of the intended target). However, the behaviors may still manifest in rather direct ways where the victim is clearly aware of the identity of the perpetrator (e.g., peer exclusion: "You can't sit here at our table"; Crick et al., 1999). Evidence indicates that, in addition to the general peer group, friendships become an important context in which relational aggression is exhibited during middle childhood (Grotpeter & Crick, 1996). Relational aggression within friendships may serve a number of purposes, including maintaining control over the friend, keeping the friend from establishing other close relationships, or as a way to express anger.

During adolescence and adulthood, the nature of relationally aggressive acts continues to grow in complexity. At the same time, these behaviors also maintain many of the same themes as demonstrated at younger ages (e.g., social exclusion, withdrawal of love and friendship). One unique feature of relational aggression during these older developmental periods is that, as the establishment of romantic relationships becomes an important focus of development, this context provides an important "opportunity" for the exhibition of relational aggression. Romantic partners sometimes become the targets of relationally aggressive behaviors, and they also may serve as pawns in relationally aggressive tactics (e.g., a relationally aggressive female may flirt with a friend's romantic partner because she wants to damage the relationship between the friend and the friend's romantic partner).

Gender Differences

In contrast to physical aggression, which has been shown to be more typical of boys than girls starting at about age 4 (for reviews, see Coie & Dodge, 1998; Keenan & Shaw, 1997), relational aggression has been hypothesized to be more prevalent among girls (Crick & Grotpeter, 1995). This prediction is based, in part, on evidence that girls are more likely than boys to exhibit relational orientations, or the tendency to focus on, invest in, and to derive self- and psychologically

relevant information from interpersonal relationships (for reviews, see Crick & Zahn-Waxler, 2003; Cross & Madsen, 1997; Geary, 1998; Leadbeater, Blatt, & Quinlan, 1995; Maccoby, 1990). Because of these orientations, it has been proposed that using relationships as a vehicle of harm (i.e., relational aggression) is an effective means for aggressing among females because it involves damage to something that they particularly value (for a review, see Crick et al., 1999). Further, in contrast to physical aggression, relational aggression involves behaviors that are consistent with female stereotypes and thus are less likely to elicit sanctions from significant others.

A number of studies have examined the issue of gender differences in relational aggression. These studies have varied widely in terms of the type of assessment tools used to measure relational aggression and in the ages of the participants evaluated. The vast majority of studies have used teacher- or peer-report measures, and a few have employed observational techniques. During the preschool years, observational studies have consistently demonstrated that girls are more relationally aggressive than boys (McNeilly-Choque et al., 1996; Ostrov, 2006; Ostrov & Keating, 2004; Ostrov et al., 2004). Studies employing teachers as informants have tended to yield similar results (Crick et al., 1997; Crick, Casas, & Ku, 1999; McNeilly-Choque et al., 1996). In contrast, research based on peer informants has yielded mixed results, with some studies showing that girls are more relationally aggressive than boys and others indicating no gender differences (e.g., Crick et al., 1997, 1999; McNeilly-Choque et al., 1996).

During middle childhood, evaluations of gender differences in relational aggression have relied on teacher, peer, and self-reports. Although the majority of studies have shown that girls are more relationally aggressive than boys, some studies have yielded no gender differences, and others have shown boys to be more relationally aggressive than girls (e.g., Crick, 1997; Crick & Grotpeter, 1995; David & Kistner, 2000; Henington et al., 1998; Rys & Bear, 1997; Tomada &

Schneider, 1997). Although relatively fewer studies have examined gender differences in relational aggression during adolescence and early adulthood, evidence is also mixed with some studies, indicating that girls are significantly more relationally aggressive than boys (e.g., MacDonald & O'Laughlin, 1997) and other studies showing the opposite finding or no gender difference (e.g., Loudin, Loukis, & Robinson, 2003). It is important to note that, at these older developmental periods, self-reports of relational aggression have typically been the assessment tool employed.

Although evidence is mixed in some instances, the majority of studies have yielded gender differences in relational aggression that favor girls. This finding has been most apparent in studies that have employed observational methods, assessment techniques that are less prone to biases due to gender stereotypes than those based on self-, peer, and teacher reports. Additional research is needed to clarify the degree of gender differences in relational aggression across development, ethnic groups, geographic regions, and assessment procedures (see David & Kistner, 2000). Another important issue for future studies, in addition to gender differences in relational aggression, concerns the salience of relational aggression for boys versus girls. Given that relational aggression has been posited to be more hurtful and salient for girls (for evidence that supports this hypothesis, see Crick, 1995; Crick, Grotpeter, & Bigbee, 2002), it will be particularly important in future studies to evaluate individual differences in the meaning of relational aggression for both perpetrators and targets.

Developmental Risk and Harm Associated With Relational Aggression

A number of recent investigations have examined the impact of relational aggression on those who serve as the frequent targets. This research was initiated as a way to evaluate whether, similar to physical aggression, relational aggression is indeed hurtful and "aggressive." This issue has been addressed in two ways. In the first, children's or adolescents' perceptions of the harmfulness of relational aggression have typically been assessed via open-ended interviews or hypothetical-situation questionnaires. Findings from these studies have consistently shown that preschoolers, grade-schoolers, and adolescents view relationally aggressive behaviors as hurtful, hostile, emotionally distressing, and aggressive, especially for girls (e.g., Crick, 1995; Crick, Bigbee, & Howes, 1996; Crick, Grotpeter, & Bigbee, 2002; Crick et al., 2004; French et al, 2002; Goldstein, Tisak, & Boxer, 2002; Roecker-Phelps, 2001). Further, initial evidence indicates that relationally aggressive behaviors that are delivered directly are viewed by grade-school children as particularly hostile (Sumrall, Ray, & Tidwell, 2000).

In the second type of studies designed to examine the hurtfulness of relational aggression, researchers have directly examined the association between the experience of relational aggression (i.e., relational victimization) and indexes of social-psychological adjustment. Findings from these investigations have consistently demonstrated significant links between relational victimization and a host of adjustment difficulties, including internalizing difficulties, externalizing problems, peer rejection, and problematic friendships (Crick & Bigbee, 1998; Crick et al., 1999; Grotpeter & Crick, 1996; Crick & Nelson, 2002; Hipwell, Loeber, Stouthamer-Loeber, Keenan, White, & Krone-Man, 2002; Prinstein, Boergers, & Vernberg, 2001; Putallaz, Kupersmidt, Grimes, & DeNero, 1999; Schafer, Werner, & Crick, 2002).

Taken together, these sets of studies provide relatively robust evidence for the harmful nature of relational aggression for those who experience it. Another line of research has been devoted to the examination of the consequences of relational aggression for those who perpetrate it. These studies have clearly demonstrated that relational aggression is associated with a variety of adverse adjustment outcomes, both concurrent and future, for children from the preschool to the adolescent years (e.g.,

Crick, 1996; 1997; Crick & Grotpeter, 1995; Crick, Ostrov, & Werner, 2006; Grotpeter & Crick, 1996; Foster, 2005; Werner & Crick, 1999; Zimmer-Gembeck, Geiger, & Crick, 2005). For example, relational aggression has been shown to significantly predict future peer rejection, depressive/anxious symptoms, and delinquent behavior (Crick, Ostrov, & Werner, 2006; Murray-Close, Ostrov, & Crick, 2007; Zimmer-Gembeck et al., 2005). Additionally, two studies have demonstrated a link between ADHD, specifically the combined subtype, and relational aggression (Blachman & Hinshaw, 2002; Zalecki & Hinshaw, 2004), a finding that has been replicated elsewhere with independent samples (Leff, Costigan, Eiraldi, & Power, 2000). Other studies with school-aged children have documented a link between relational aggression and disruptive behavioral disorder symptoms (Prinstein et al., 2001). Recent preliminary findings also suggest a link between personality disorders and relational aggression. That is, a time-dependent link between relational aggression and features of borderline personality disorder has been empirically supported (Crick, Murray-Close, & Woods, 2006) in recent longitudinal research with a large group of young adolescents.

It is noteworthy, that, when boys engage in high levels of relational aggression, which is a gender non-normative practice, they are at greater risk of adjustment problems than girls who are relationally aggressive or even boys who display gender-normative physically aggressive behaviors (Crick, 1997). Similarly, when girls display extreme levels of physical aggression relative to their peers they are at greater risk for developing problematic social-psychological adjustment outcomes. Thus, it is crucial that both boys and girls are included in future studies of physical and relational aggression in order to determine those most at risk for maladaptive outcomes.

Studies of the close relationships of relationally aggressive children have provided additional information about their adjustment difficulties. The friendships of relationally aggressive children have been shown to

be characterized by aversive features, such as relatively high levels of jealousy and preferences for exclusivity (Grotpeter & Crick, 1996; Sebanc, 2003). Further, the romantic relationships of relationally aggressive young adults have been demonstrated to be associated with problematic behaviors, such as anxious clinging to the partner, frustration, lack of trust, and jealousy (Linder, Crick, & Collins, 2002).

In addition to their risk for adjustment problems and problematic relationships, relationally aggressive children may also be at risk for continued behavioral problems. Recent evidence from longitudinal studies indicate that relational aggression is moderately stable across 18- to 24-month periods during early childhood (see Crick, Ostrov, Burr et al., 2006; Ostrov et al., 2004) and over a 36-month period in middle childhood (Zimmer-Gembeck et al., 2005). Moreover, across a 12-month period, girls increase in their use of relational aggression at a faster rate than boys (i.e., as indicated by significant slope differences; Murray-Close et al., 2007). Thus, if left untreated relationally aggressive behaviors may continue across different peer groups and developmental periods.

These findings indicate that, similar to physically aggressive children, relationally aggressive children may be at serious risk for social-psychological maladjustment. Combined with the findings demonstrating a significant association between relational victimization and maladjustment, these results provide substantial evidence for the importance of a research focus on relational aggression, in addition to physical aggression.

Relational Aggression and Culture

Although a myriad of studies exploring relational aggression and victimization have been conducted in the United States, a relatively smaller literature exists exploring these important developmental questions with children from other cultures. Investigating the role of culture in aggression, particularly relational aggression, is essential because the meaning and functions of relational aggression might differ across cultures and contexts.

A few studies have been conducted in other Western cultures. For example, Russell, Hart, Robinson, and Olsen (2003) conducted a study of American and Australian preschool children, and the results of their factor analysis demonstrated that Australian preschool teachers reliably distinguished between relational and physical aggression. In terms of gender differences, the teachers perceived that girls were significantly more relationally aggressive, whereas boys were significantly more physically aggressive. Research in Germany with children in middle childhood has demonstrated that girls were more relationally victimized and boys were more physically victimized (Schafer et al., 2002).

To test important questions related to the role of relational aggression in societies that place comparably greater emphasis on the salience of relationships, recent attention has also turned to cultures that may be more collectivistic or interdependent in nature. In a Russian study with preschool children (Hart et al., 1998), teachers and peers reliably distinguished among relational and physical forms of aggression. In contrast to previous findings with U.S. children, no gender differences were found in physical and relational aggression, a finding that the authors believe was attributable to the collectivistic-oriented society in which children's socialization was potentially highly influenced by the former Soviet Union. Similarly, research with Italian children revealed that, as expected, separate factors for relational and physical forms of aggression as well as prosocial behavior emerged from teacher and peer reports. In contrast to a priori expectations, results indicated that boys were both more physically and relationally aggressive than girls. The gender differences favoring boys, according to the investigators, may be due to cultural differences in family and kin networks in rural village contexts. Interestingly, not all interdependent cultures demonstrate these effects, and

given the range of variability in cultures it should not be surprising that some findings do not generalize across these groups. For example, results from a school-aged sample of Indonesian children, using culturally specific qualitative interviews and quantitative methods, demonstrated that boys exhibited higher frequencies of physical aggression, whereas girls were significantly more involved in relational aggression (French et al., 2002).

Members of collectivistic/interdependent-oriented cultures (e.g., Japan, China) place high value on relationships with others and groups (Markus & Kitayama, 1991). Therefore, cultural differences in the social-cognitive processes in the formation of the self may be particularly important to the etiology of relational aggression and the relative influence of these behaviors on social and emotional adjustment problems (e.g., loneliness, depression). Preliminary analysis of a recent cross-cultural study showed that, regardless of gender, Japanese children who were relationally aggressive and/or relationally victimized by peers displayed more depressive symptoms than American children involved with these behaviors (Kawabata, Crick, & Hamaguchi, 2006a, b). This finding suggests that relational aggression and victimization may be more detrimental to children's social and emotional adjustment in interdependent-oriented cultures (e.g., Japan) than those in independent-oriented cultures (e.g., United States) that may place less emphasis on interpersonal close relationships with peers. Additional cross-cultural research is warranted to fully understand the mechanism by which relational aggression and victimization relate to adjustment problems. Research is especially needed in Asian and African cultures because they have been neglected or understudied in the past.

Finally, it is important to highlight that, in contrast to most of existing cross-cultural research on relational aggression, the aforementioned French et al. (2002) study made an effort to replicate their findings among different cultural groups (i.e., American and

Indonesian youth) using culturally derived and defined methods and constructs (i.e., the emic or culturally specific conceptual and methodological approach) and compared their findings across the two cultures to test for the possibility of cultural diversity or universality of relational aggression (i.e., the etic or universal approach to studying human behavior; Berry, 1999; Pike, 1967). In future studies it will be important not to simply assume that measures developed in the United States or other Western cultures are directly transferable to and valid in other cultures, even if the best cross-cultural practices (e.g., back translation) are implemented. Accordingly, both emic and etic approaches are necessary to fully understand the nature of relational aggression around the world.

Intervention for Relationally Aggressive Children

Despite the fact that school administrators report they are more likely to intervene for incidents involving physical aggression than relational aggression (Xie, Swift, Cairns, & Cairns, 2002), a few attempts to conduct school-based interventions (e.g., "Second Step" program) have been successful during this developmental period (Van Schoiack-Edstrom, Frey, & Beland, 2002). Preliminary empirical evidence demonstrates that intervention efforts within inner-city urban schools are feasible and successfully reduce relationally aggressive social cognitions and relationally aggressive behaviors among at-risk girls (see Leff, Goldstein, Angelucci, Cardaciotto, & Grossman, in press). Group-based interventions with relationally aggressive adolescent girls may also offer some promise at reducing positive attitudes about these behaviors (see Cummings, Hoffman, & Leschied, 2004). Finally, initial attempts during the early childhood period offer some possible points of intervention for simple classroom-based approaches (e.g., implementation of the "You can't say you can't play" rule) with kindergarten children

(Harrist & Bradley, 2003). Although the state of knowledge regarding relational aggression is limited with respect to information that is needed to develop empirically based intervention and prevention programs (Geiger, Zimmer-Gembeck, & Crick, 2004), this should be a high-priority goal for the immediate future. To increase the effectiveness and viability of these efforts, additional research is needed that targets mechanisms and factors that contribute to the development and maintenance of relational aggression (e.g., family and peer factors that increase the risk for engagement in relational aggression).

Contributions, Conclusions, and Future Directions

In addition to enhancing the gender-balanced nature of the types of aggressive behaviors considered by researchers and other professionals, the study of relational aggression has contributed in a number of ways to the broader study of childhood aggression. One important theoretical contribution has been the recognition that a substantial number of girls experience serious behavioral problems during the early and middle childhood years in the form of relational aggression. This finding stands in stark contrast to existing theories of the development of aggression. These models typically posit that behavioral difficulties do not tend to emerge for girls until adolescence (e.g., Keenan & Shaw, 1997; Silverthorn & Frick, 1999).

A second contribution that has emerged because of the recent focus on relational aggression is the identification of adjustment outcomes associated with aggression that have not previously been included in aggression research. For example, although it has not been examined in past studies of aggression, as already discussed, recent research on relational aggression has shown that it is significantly associated with borderline personality features (Crick, Murray-Close et al., 2006; Werner & Crick, 1999).

Research on the family factors associated with relational aggression has also resulted in new innovations for aggression researchers. Specifically, these investigations have involved the assessment and study of family factors that have not been considered in past research. For instance, evidence indicates that relational aggression is associated with family relationships that are enmeshed, jealous, and exclusive (for a review, see Crick et al., 1999), relationship features that have not been a focus of past studies of aggression and that stand in sharp contrast to those assessed in traditional studies of aggression (e.g., conflict, lack of intimacy and warmth). These studies have also highlighted the importance of studying fathers, in addition to mothers, particularly when attempting to understand the aggressive behavior of girls (Crick, 2003; Nelson & Crick, 2002). The role of fathers has often been neglected in past research.

Another addition that research on relational aggression has made to the broader study of aggression concerns the contexts in which aggression has been examined. The majority of past studies have focused on children's engagement in aggressive behaviors toward peers within group settings such as classrooms or playgroups. However, recent studies of relational aggression have demonstrated the importance of also assessing aggressive behaviors and their consequences within the context of close, dyadic relationships, such as friendships or romantic relationships (Crick & Nelson, 2002; Linder, Crick, & Collins, 2002).

Efforts to develop observational procedures for assessing relational aggression have also resulted in new innovations in aggression research. Because of the relatively subtle and verbal nature of some relationally aggressive acts, observational methods used in past research to measure physical aggression have largely proved inadequate. Thus, to address this issue, researchers have begun to generate creative, new observational approaches that appear to reliably and validly assess physical and relational forms of aggression, as well as other types of social behaviors (Ostrov & Keating, 2004; Ostrov

et al., 2004; Putallaz et al., 1999). These approaches have involved both naturalistic observations and laboratory analog tasks. The methods that have been developed tend to differ from past approaches in their use of longer time intervals per observation and in their ability to capture all verbalizations.

Although a great deal of progress has been made in our understanding of relational aggression during the past decade, our knowledge in this area lags far behind that of more traditionally studied forms of aggression such as physical aggression. As a result, a number of exciting challenges remain for future research on relational aggression. One of the most serious limitations of existing relational aggression research concerns the lack of longitudinal studies. Only a few prospective studies have been published and, although they have contributed significant information to existing knowledge, a number of shortcomings should be rectified in future empirical efforts. Long-term longitudinal studies are needed that include comprehensive assessments of the antecedents, correlates, and consequences of relational aggression and that examine changes, as well as continuities, in the prevalence of relational aggression across multiple developmental periods.

An additional challenge for the future will be to systematically examine the role of gender in the development of relational aggression and its consequences. Given that gender differences have been proposed with respect to the meaning, prevalence, and perceived hurtfulness of relational aggression, studies are needed that explore the role of relational aggression in the lives of boys versus girls. Another important avenue for future empirical efforts will be to further develop and refine observational methods for assessing relational aggression and to expand the range of ages and contexts in which observations can be applied. Thus far, observational studies have focused on preschool and grade-school children in peer and sibling contexts. It will be important in future studies to consider additional age groups (e.g., adolescents, adults) and settings (e.g., sports teams, school dances, neighborhoods, work contexts). Further, it will be of value to include children or adolescents of both genders in these investigations so that gender differences can be evaluated with observational techniques (existing observational studies with middle childhood samples have neglected boys thus far). In summary, we are excited by the recent increase in empirical research exploring developmental questions related to physical and relational aggression, and we strongly encourage further quality investigations in this burgeoning area.

Acknowledgments

Preparation of this chapter was facilitated, in part, by grants from NIMH (MH63684), NSF (BCS-0126521), and NICHD (HD046629) to the first author. We appreciate the support of the parents, children, teachers and directors involved in our ongoing research endeavors. Finally, we acknowledge our many past and present collaborators who have assisted us in refining our understanding of relational aggression in our own research projects.

References

Berry, J. W. (1999). Emics and etics: A symbiotic conception. *Culture and Psychology, 5,* 165–171.

Blachman, D. R., & Hinshaw, S. P. (2002). Patterns of friendship among girls with and without attention-deficit/hyperactivity disorder. *Journal of Abnormal Child Psychology, 30,* 625–640.

Bonica, C., Yeshova, K., Arnold, D. H., Fisher, P. H., & Zeljo, A. (2003). Relational aggression and language development in preschoolers. *Social Development, 12,* 551–562.

Cillessen, A. H. N., & Mayeux, L. (2004). From censure to reinforcement: Developmental changes in the association between aggression and social status. *Child Development, 75,* 147–163.

Coie J. D., & Dodge, K. A. (1998). Aggression and antisocial behavior. In N. Eisenberg (Ed.), *Handbook of child psychology: Vol. 3.*

Social, emotional, and personality development (pp. 779–862). New York: John Wiley.

Crick, N. R. (1995). Relational aggression: The role of intent attributions, feelings of distress, and provocation type. *Development and Psychopathology, 7,* 313–322

Crick, N. R. (1996). The role of overt aggression, relational aggression, and prosocial behavior in the prediction of children's future social adjustment. *Child Development, 67,* 2317–2327.

Crick, N. R. (1997). Engagement in gender normative versus non-normative forms of aggression: Links to social-psychological adjustment. *Developmental Psychology, 33,* 610–617.

Crick, N. R. (2003). A gender-balanced approach to the study of childhood aggression and reciprocal family influences. In A. C. Crouter & A. Booth (Eds.), *Children's influence on family dynamics: The neglected side of family relationships.* (pp. 229–235). Mahwah, NJ: Lawrence Erlbaum.

Crick, N. R., & Bigbee, M. A. (1998). Relational and overt forms of peer victimization: A multi-informant approach. *Journal of Consulting and Clinical Psychology, 66,* 337–347.

Crick, N. R., Bigbee, M. A., & Howes, C. (1996). Gender differences in children's normative beliefs about aggression: How do I hurt thee? Let me count the ways. *Child Development, 67,* 1003–1014.

Crick, N. R., Casas, J. F., & Ku, H. C. (1999). Relational and physical forms of peer victimization in preschool. *Developmental Psychology, 35,* 376–385

Crick, N. R., Casas, J. F., & Mosher, M. (1997). Relational and overt aggression in preschool. *Developmental Psychology, 33,* 579–587.

Crick, N. R., & Dodge, K. A. (1994). A review and reformulation of social information processing mechanisms in children's social adjustment. *Psychological Bulletin, 115,* 74–101.

Crick, N. R., &. Dodge, K. A. (1996). Social information-processing mechanisms in reactive and proactive aggression. *Child Development 67,* 993–1002.

Crick, N. R., & Grotpeter, J. K. (1995). Relational aggression, gender, and social-psychological adjustment. *Child Development, 66,* 710–722.

Crick, N. R., Grotpeter, J. K., & Bigbee, M. A. (2002). Relationally and physically aggressive children's intent attributions and feelings of distress for relational and instrumental peer conflicts. *Child Development, 73,* 1134–1142.

Crick, N. R., Murray-Close, D., & Woods, K. A. (2006). Borderline personality features in childhood: A shorter-term longitudinal study. *Development and Psychopathology, 17,* 1051–1070.

Crick, N. R., & Nelson, D. A. (2002). Relational and physical victimization within friendships: Nobody told me there'd be friends like these. *Journal of Abnormal Child Psychology, 30,* 599–607.

Crick, N. R., Ostrov, J. M., Appleyard, K., Jansen, E. A., & Casas, J. F. (2004). Relational aggression in early childhood: "You can't come to my birthday party unless..." In M. Putallaz, & K. L. Bierman (Eds.), *Aggression, antisocial behavior, and violence among girls: A developmental perspective.* New York: Guilford Press.

Crick, N. R., Ostrov, J. M., Burr, J. E., Jansen-Yeh, E. A., Cullerton-Sen, C., & Ralston, P. (2006). A longitudinal study of relational and physical aggression in preschool. *Journal of Applied Developmental Psychology, 27,* 254–268.

Crick, N. R., Ostrov, J. M., & Werner, N. E. (2006). A longitudinal study of relational aggression, physical aggression and children's social-psychological adjustment. *Journal of Abnormal Child Psychology, 34*(2), 127–138.

Crick, N. R., Werner, N. E., Casas, J. F., O'Brien, K. M., Nelson, D. A., Grotpeter, J. K., et al. (1999). Childhood aggression and gender: A new look at an old problem. In D. Bernstein (Ed.), *Gender and motivation. Nebraska symposium on motivation* (Vol. 45, pp. 75–141). Lincoln, NE: University of Nebraska Press.

Crick, N. R., & Zahn-Waxler, C. (2003). The development of psychopathology in females and males: Current progress and future challenges. *Development and Psychopathology, 15,* 719–742.

Cross, S. E. & Madsen, L. (1997). Models of the self: Self-construals and gender. *Psychological Bulletin, 122,* 5–37.

Cummings, A. L., Hoffman, S., & Leschied, A. W. (2004). A psychoeducational group for aggressive adolescent girls. *Journal for Specialists in Group Work, 29,* 285–299.

David, C. F., & Kistner, J. A. (2000). Do positive self-perceptions have a "dark side"? Examination of the link between perceptual bias and aggression. *Journal of Abnormal Child Psychology, 28,* 327–337.

Dettling, A. C., Gunnar, M. R., & Donzella, B. (1999). Cortisol levels of young children in full-day childcare centers: Relations with age and temperament. *Psychoneuroendocrinology, 24,* 519–536.

Fagot, B. T., & Hagan, R. (1985). Aggression in toddlers: Responses to the assertive acts of boys and girls. *Sex Roles, 12,* 341–351.

Foster, S. L. (2005). Aggression and antisocial behavior in girls. In D. J. Bell, J. Debora, S. L. Foster, & E. J. Mash (Eds.), *Handbook of behavioral and emotional problems in girls.* (pp. 149–180). New York, NY: Kluwer Academic/Plenum Publishers

French, D. C., Jansen, E. A., & Pidada, S. (2002). United States and Indonesian children's and adolescents' reports of relational aggression by disliked peers. *Child Development, 73,* 1143–1150.

Geary, D. C. (1998). *Male, female: The evolution of human sex differences.* Washington, DC: American Psychological Association

Geiger, T., Zimmer-Gembeck, M., & Crick, N. R. (2004). The science of relational aggression: Can we guide intervention? In M. Morretti & C. Feiring (Eds.), *Girls and aggression: Contributing factors and intervention principles.* New York: Springer.

Goldstein, S. E., Tisak, M. S., & Boxer, P. (2002). Preschoolers' normative and prescriptive judgments about relational and overt aggression. *Early Education and Development, 13,* 23–39.

Goodwin, M. H. (2002). Exclusion in girls' peer groups: Ethnographic analysis of language practices on the playground. *Human Development, 45,* 392–415.

Grotpeter, J. K., & Crick, N. R. (1996). Relational aggression, overt aggression, and friendship. *Child Development, 67,* 2328–2338.

Harrist, A. W., & Bradley, K. D. (2003). You can't say you can't play: Intervening in the process of social exclusion in the kindergarten classroom. *Early Childhood Research Quarterly, 18,* 185–205.

Hart, C. H., Nelson, D. A., Robinson, C. C., Olsen, S. F., & McNeilly-Choque, M. K. (1998). Overt and relational aggression in Russian nursery-school-age children: Parenting style and marital linkages. *Developmental Psychology, 34,* 687–697.

Hawley, P. H. (2003). Strategies of control, aggression, and morality in preschoolers: An evolutionary perspective. *Journal of Experimental Child Psychology, 85,* 213–235.

Henington, C., Hughes, J. N., Cavell, T. A., & Thompson, B. (1998).The role of relational aggression in identifying aggressive boys and girls. *Journal of School Psychology, 36,* 457–477.

Hipwell, A. E., Loeber, R., Stouthamer-Loeber, M., Keenan, K., White, H. R., & Krone-Man, L. (2002). Characteristics of girls with early onset disruptive and antisocial behaviour. *Criminal Behaviour and Mental Health, 12,* 99–118.

Kawabata, Y., Crick, N. R., & Hamaguchi, Y. (2006a). *Relational victimization and culture: Links to social information-processing patterns and social-psychological adjustment.* Manuscript submitted for publication.

Kawabata, Y., Crick, N. R., & Hamaguchi, Y. (2006b). *The role of culture in relational aggression: Links to social-psychological adjustment problems among Japanese and U.S. school children.* Manuscript submitted for publication.

Keenan, K., & Shaw, D. (1997). Developmental and social influences on young girls' early problem behavior. *Psychological Bulletin, 121,* 95–113.

Leadbeater, B. J., Blatt, S. J., Quinlan, D. M. (1995). Gender-linked vulnerabilities to depressive symptoms, stress, and problem behaviors in adolescents. *Journal of Research on Adolescence, 5,* 1–29.

Leff, S. S., Costigan, T. E., Eiraldi, R., & Power, T. J. (2000, April). *An examination of children's aggressive behaviors and social skills as a function of ADHD subtype and gender.* Poster presented at the biennial meeting of the Society of Research in Child Development, *Minneapolis,* MN.

Leff, S. S., Goldstein, A. B., Angelucci, J., Cardaciotto, L., & Grossman, M. (in press). Using a participatory action research model to create a school-based intervention program for relationally aggressive girls: The Friend to Friend Program. In J. Zins, M. Elias, & C. Maher (Eds.), *Handbook of prevention and intervention in peer harassment, victimization, and bullying.* New York: Haworth Press.

Leff, S. S., Kupersmidt, J. B., & Power, T. J. (2003). An initial examination of girls' cognitions of their relationally aggressive peers as a function of their own social standing. *Merrill-Palmer Quarterly, 49,* 28–53.

Linder, J. R., Crick, N. R., & Collins, W. A. (2002). Relational aggression and victimization in young adults' romantic relationships: Associations with perceptions of parent, peer, and romantic relationship quality. *Social Development, 11,* 69–86.

Little, T. D., Jones, S. M., Henrich, C. C., & Hawley, P. H. (2003). Disentangling the "whys" from the "whats" of aggressive behavior. *International Journal of Behavioral Development, 27,* 122–183.

Loudin, J. L., Loukas, A., & Robinson, S. (2003). Relational aggression in college students: Examining the roles of social anxiety and empathy. *Aggressive Behavior, 29,* 430–439.

Maccoby, E. E. (1990). Gender and relationships: A developmental account. *American Psychologist, 45,* 513–520.

MacDonald, C., & O'Laughlin, E. (1997, April). Relational aggression and risk behaviors in middle school students. Poster presented at the biennial meeting of the Society for Research in Child Development, Washington, DC.

Macgowan, M. J., Nash, J. K., & Fraser, M. W. (2002). The Carolina Child Checklist of risk and protective factors for aggression. *Research on Social Work Practice, 12,* 253–276

Markus, H. R., & Kitayama, S. (1991). Culture and the self: Implications for cognition, emotion, and motivation. *Psychological Review, 98,* 224–253.

McEvoy, M. A., Estrem, T. L., Rodriguez, M. C., & Olson, M. L. (2003). Assessing relational and physical aggression among preschool children: Inter-method agreement. *Topics in Early Childhood Special Education, 23,* 53–63.

McNeilly-Choque, M. K., Hart, C. H., Robinson, C. C., Nelson, L., & Olsen, S. F. (1996). Overt and relational aggression on the playground: Correspondence among different informants. *Journal of Research in Childhood Education, 11,* 47–67.

Moffitt, T. E. (1993). Adolescence-limited and life-course-persistent antisocial behavior: A developmental taxonomy. *Psychological Review, 100,* 674–701.

Murray-Close, D., Ostrov, J. M., & Crick, N. R. (2007). Growth of relational aggression during middle childhood: Associations with gender and internalizing problems. *Development and Psychopathology, 19,* 187–203.

Nelson, D. A., & Crick, N. R. (2002). Parental psychological control: Implications for childhood physical and relational aggression. In B. K. Barber (Ed). *Intrusive parenting: How psychological control affects children and adolescents.* (pp. 161–189). Washington, DC: American Psychological Association.

Ostrov, J. M. (2006). Deception and subtypes of aggression during early childhood. *Journal of Experimental Child Psychology, 93,* 322–336.

Ostrov, J. M., & Keating, C. F. (2004). Gender differences in preschool aggression during free play and structured interactions: An observational study. *Social Development, 13,* 255–277.

Ostrov, J. M., Woods, K. E., Jansen, E. A., Casas, J. F., & Crick, N. R. (2004). An observational study of delivered and received aggression and social psychological adjustment in preschool: "This white crayon doesn't work." *Early Childhood Research Quarterly, 19,* 355–371.

Pellegrini, A. D. (1989). Categorizing children's rough-and-tumble play. *Play and Culture, 2,* 48–51.

Pellegrini, A. D., & Long, J. D. (2003) A sexual selection theory longitudinal analysis of sexual segregation and integration in early adolescence. *Journal of Experimental Child Psychology, 85,* 257–278.

Pike, K. L. (1967). *Language in relation to a unified theory of the structure of human behavior.* The Hague: Motion.

Prinstein, M. J., Boergers, J., & Vernberg, E. M. (2001). Overt and relational aggression in adolescents: Social-psychological adjustment of aggressors and victims. *Journal of Clinical Child Psychology, 30,* 479–491.

Putallaz, M., Kupersmidt, J., Grimes, C. L., & DeNero, K. (1999, April). Overt and relational aggressors, victims, and gender. Paper presented at the biennial meeting of the Society for Research in Child Development, Albuquerque, NM.

Robins, L. (1986). The consequences of conduct disorder in girls. In D. Olweus, J. Block, & M. Radke-Yarrow (Eds.), *Development of antisocial and prosocial behavior: Research, theories, and issues.* (pp. 385–414). New York: Academic Press.

Roecker-Phelps, C. E. (2001). Children's responses to overt and relational aggression. *Journal of Clinical Child Psychology, 31,* 240–252.

Rose, A. J., Swenson, L. P., & Waller, E. M. (2004). Overt and relational aggression and perceived popularity: Developmental differ-ences in concurrent and prospective relations. *Developmental Psychology, 40,* 378–387.

Russell, A., Hart, C. H., Robinson, C., & Olsen, S. F. (2003). Children's sociable and aggressive behavior with peers: A comparison of the U.S. and Australia, and contributions of temperament and parenting styles. *International Journal of Behavioral Development, 27,* 74–86.

Rys, G. S., & Bear, G. G., (1997). Relational aggression and peer relations: Gender and developmental issues. *Merrill-Palmer Quarterly, 43,* 87–106.

Schafer, M., Werner, N. E., & Crick, N. R. (2002). A comparison of two approaches to the study of negative peer treatment: General victimization and bully/victim problems among German schoolchildren. *British Journal of Developmental Psychology, 20,* 281–306.

Sebanc, A. M. (2003). The friendship features of preschool children: Links with prosocial behavior and aggression. *Social Development, 12,* 249–268.

Silverthorn, P., & Frick, P. J. (1999). Developmental pathways to antisocial behavior: The delayed-onset pathway in girls. *Development and Psychopathology, 11,* 101–126.

Stauffacher, K., & DeHart, G. (2005). Preschoolers' relational aggression with siblings and friends. *Early Education and Development, 16,* 185–206.

Sumrall, S. G., Ray, G. E., & Tidwell, P. S. (2000). Evaluations of relational aggression as a function of relationship type and conflict setting. *Aggressive Behavior, 26,* 179–191.

Tomada, G., & Schneider, B. H., (1997). Relational aggression, gender, and peer acceptance: Invariance across culture, stability over time, and concordance among informants. *Developmental Psychology, 33,* 601–609.

Van Schoiack-Edstrom, L., Frey, K. S., & Beland, K. (2002). Changing adolescents' attitudes about relational and physical aggression: An early evaluation of a school-based intervention. *School Psychology Review, 31,* 201–216.

Werner, N. E., & Crick, N. R. (1999). Relational aggression and social-psychological adjustment in a college sample. *Journal of Abnormal Psychology, 108,* 615–623.

Xie, H., Swift, D., Cairns, B. D., & Cairns, R. B. (2002). Aggressive behaviors in social interaction and developmental adaptation: A narrative analysis of interpersonal conflicts during early adolescence. *Social Development,* *11,* 205–224.

Zahn-Waxler, C. (1993). Warriors and worriers: Gender and psychopathology. *Development and Psychopathology, 5,* 79–89.

Zalecki, C. A., & Hinshaw, S. P. (2004). Overt and relational aggression in girls with attention deficit hyperactivity disorder. *Journal of* *Clinical Child and Adolescent Psychology, 33,* *125–137*

Zimmer-Gembeck, M., Geiger, T., & Crick, N. R. (2005). Relational aggression, physical aggression, prosocial behavior, and peer relations: Gender moderation and bidirectional associations. *Journal of Early Adolescence, 25,* 421–452.

CHAPTER 12

Personality Dispositions and the Development of Violence and Conduct Problems

Benjamin B. Lahey and Irwin D. Waldman

The goal of our psychological model of youth violence and conduct problems (Lahey & Waldman, 2003) is to provide a set of testable causal hypotheses that attempt to explain the development of violence and related mental health problems. Our causal model is developmental in two ways. First, it describes causal processes that begin in early childhood and continue at least through adolescence. Second, our model highlights the importance of distinguishing among differing developmental trajectories of child and adolescent offending for the purpose of identifying causal influences on offending.

The focus of this chapter is on the development of violence, but we believe that violence cannot be understood fully without viewing it as part of a broader syndrome of dysfunctional antisocial behavior. In this chapter, we thus use the term "conduct problems" to refer to a constellation of correlated antisocial behaviors that includes crimes against persons and property offenses (aggression, forced sex, theft, robbery, vandalism, etc.), status offenses (running away from home and truancy), and behaviors that are considered to be symptoms of conduct

disorder in DSM-IV and ICD-10 that typically do not result in arrest (lying, bullying, fighting, cruelty to animals, violating family curfew, etc.). Moreover, this broad syndrome of conduct problems is only one part of a broader spectrum of correlated antisocial behaviors, which includes substance abuse and risky behavior (reckless driving, high-risk sexual behavior, etc.). In addition, youth who engage in the most serious and persistent forms of violence and other antisocial behaviors tend to meet diagnostic criteria for a range of mental health problems, including attention-deficit/hyperactivity disorder, oppositional defiant disorder, depression, and anxiety disorders. Because the diagnosis of conduct disorder (CD) is defined by engaging in a variety of conduct problems, many youth who engage in serious and persistent violence also meet diagnostic criteria for CD.

For two reasons, we believe that it is not possible to develop an adequate development model of juvenile violence without considering the full range of antisocial behavior. First, the critically important early development of juvenile violence is seen in conduct problems that are less serious than arrestable criminal offenses or manifest acts of violence. Not considering these conduct problems to be part of the same syndrome would make it impossible to study the earliest components of developmental trajectories. Second, minor conduct problems, juvenile offenses, violent behaviors, substance abuse, risky behavior, and several types of mental health problems are correlated because they *share some of their causal influences*. In this chapter, we focus on the subset of antisocial behaviors that we have defined as conduct problems. We briefly address substance abuse, risky behaviors, and mental health problems to advance hypotheses for why they tend to co-occur in the same youth (i.e., hypotheses regarding their shared causal influences).

Overview of the Developmental Model

Our primary goal is to advance testable hypotheses regarding the causal processes that link risk factors to youth violence and other antisocial behaviors. In this section, we provide a brief overview of the structure of our causal model. In the sections that follow, we provide more detailed causal hypotheses.

Social Learning and Child Characteristics

One overarching goal of our model is to integrate the most useful constructs from previous causal models. We attempt to build on this integrated foundation by elaborating key concepts that have not been developed fully and by adding new elements to the model. In general terms, our model is as an extension of the social learning model (Patterson, 1982; Patterson, Reid, & Dishion, 1992). That is, we view reinforcement, modeling, persuasion, and other forms of social influence as fundamental causal processes. Our model is also a developmental model of violence and antisocial behavior (Loeber, 1988; Loeber & LeBlanc, 1990; Moffitt, 1993) in its emphases on both processes of change in behavior over time and the importance of

heterogeneity among differing developmental trajectories of antisocial behavior.

Like Moffitt (1993), we place special emphasis on the characteristics of the child that are associated with differing trajectories of conduct problems. We adopt Gottfredson and Hirschi's (1990) term "antisocial propensity" to refer to individual differences in a youth's net predisposition to offend that derive from characteristics of the youth that transact over developmental time with social and situational influences. Antisocial propensity is often simply inferred from antisocial behavior, but to avoid circularity, it must be defined independently of the behavior that it explains (Farrington, 1991, 1995). In our model, the child's dispositions and cognitive abilities are the key elements of antisocial propensity.

Recent statements of the social learning model have acknowledged the importance of child characteristics in the development of conduct problems (Snyder, Reid, & Patterson, 2003). Our model offers more detailed hypotheses regarding the child characteristics that play a profoundly important role in the social learning process. In addition, because our model also reflects important influences from the fields of developmental psychopathology (e.g., Keenan & Shaw, 2003; Olson, Bates, Sandy, & Lanthier, 2000; Rutter, 1988; Sanson & Prior, 1999), developmental epidemiology (Rutter, 1997), and behavior genetics (Plomin, DeFries, & Loehlin, 1977; Rutter et al., 1997), we offer hypotheses regarding both environmental and genetic influences on antisocial propensity.

Cairns (1979) borrowed the concept of "epigenesis" from developmental biology to describe behavioral development. Just as simple cells develop into complex organs over time, behavior develops from the simple and undifferentiated into the complex. This development occurs through a process of interactions between behavior and the environment. Likewise, we hypothesize a developmental sequence from the undifferentiated dimensions of dispositions that have substantial genetic influences into complex behaviors, including antisocial behaviors, through transactions with the environment.

Children enter the world with a wide range of dispositional characteristics and capacities to develop complex cognitive skills. At birth, these individual differences are the product of genetic influences and any prenatal environmental influences. From the moment of birth on, however, the child engages in reciprocal interactions (transactions) with his or her postnatal environment that shape their abilities, dispositions, and adaptive or maladaptive behavior. In some cases, the nonspecific behaviors that we refer to as dispositions are literally shaped into conduct problems. In other cases, individual differences in dispositions influence the likelihood that the child will develop conduct problems by altering the social learning environment and by influencing the child's reaction to it.

Developmental Trajectories of Conduct Problems

It is now clear that youth who commit juvenile offenses do not all follow the same developmental trajectory (Farrington, 1991; Loeber, 1988). Developmental trajectories of conduct problems are defined both by the youth's intercept (e.g., the level of conduct problems at the youngest age at which conduct problems are measured) and by the youth's slope (increases or decreases in conduct problems over time). Like others, we take the position that variations in developmental trajectories are central to understanding the causes of juvenile offending (Hinshaw, Lahey, & Hart, 1993; Moffitt, 1993; Patterson, Reid, & Dishion, 1992). In contrast to Moffitt's (1993) "developmental taxonomy," however, we hypothesize that there is a continuum of developmental trajectories, rather than two distinct trajectories with qualitatively different causes. The continuum of developmental trajectories results from variations across the full continua of each element of antisocial propensity and social influence.

Developmental types of conduct problems. To understand developmental trajectories,

we believe that it is necessary to distinguish between two types of conduct problems based on their individual developmental trajectories in the general population. *Developmentally early* conduct problems are behaviors like lying and minor aggression (bullying, fighting, and hurting animals) that are highly prevalent in children at the time of school entry, but become less prevalent in most youth with increasing age through adolescence. In contrast, *developmentally late* conduct problems are nonaggressive conduct problems (e.g., stealing, running away from home, truancy, breaking and entering) and serious forms of aggression (e.g., robbery, use of a weapon, and forced sex) that are very uncommon during early childhood, but become more prevalent with increasing age, reaching a peak during adolescence.

Most theorists have differentiated among developmental trajectories at least partly in terms of the age of onset of antisocial behavior. We agree that it is meaningful to measure the age of onset of some developmentally late conduct problems that never occur in early childhood (e.g., automobile theft) or the age of the youth's first criminal conviction. In contrast, as noted by Tremblay (Tremblay et al., 1996), attempting to measure the age of onset of developmentally early conduct problems is problematic. He has shown that nearly half of all toddlers hit, kick, intentionally break things, take other children's toys, state untruths, and resist the authority of adults from the time they can walk and talk (Tremblay et al., 1999). Over the course of development, most children become less likely to engage in these problem behaviors, but others do not. Thus, although it may be meaningful to think of youth learning new behaviors, such as drug sales or burglary, it may be more accurate to think of children as sometimes failing to "unlearn" developmentally early behaviors such as fighting when it is normative for them to do so (Tremblay, 2000). This formulation implies differences in the mix of causal influences on developmentally early and developmentally late conduct problems. We offer detailed hypotheses regarding this point later in this chapter.

Varying developmental trajectories. At school entry, levels of developmentally early conduct problems vary tremendously. A small group of children already exhibit high levels of conduct problems that seriously impair their social and academic functioning, another small group exhibits no conduct problems at school entry, and most children fall between these extremes. Slopes of conduct problems vary in every possible direction from these varying starting points at school entry through adolescence. In general, however, it is possible to predict future trajectories of conduct problems from school entry through late adolescence reasonably well from the level of developmentally early conduct problems at school entry (Lahey & Loeber, 1994). Children with higher levels of developmentally early conduct problems at school entry are more likely than other children to show high levels of conduct problems that persist (at least) through adolescence (Brame, Nagin, & Tremblay, 2001; Nagin & Tremblay, 1999). On the other hand, nearly half of all children who engage in high levels of conduct problems at school entry show considerable improvement by early adolescence (Fergusson, Lynskey, & Horwood, 1996; Moffitt, Caspi, Dickson, Silva, & Stanton, 1996; Nagin & Tremblay, 1999). Thus, a comprehensive model of conduct problems must not only explain why some children have high initial levels of conduct problems at school entry but also why some children persist (or worsen) when other children desist.

Over time, the youth whose high initial levels of developmentally early conduct problems do not desist are more likely than other youth to add developmentally late conduct problems to their repertoires during late childhood and adolescence (Brame et al., 2001; Sampson & Laub, 1992). These developmentally late conduct problems are likely to include serious and violent behaviors (Haemaelaeinen & Pulkkinen, 1996). In addition, some youth with histories of low to moderate levels of developmentally early conduct problems during childhood show increasing levels of developmentally late conduct problems during late childhood or adolescence. They mostly (but not always) engage in less serious and nonviolent offenses, such as truancy and theft (Brame et al., 2001).

Components of Antisocial Propensity

The focus of our model is on the individual components of antisocial propensity. Our goal is to describe them, give them independent operationalizations, and advance hypotheses regarding how they contribute to the development of conduct problems.

Dimensions of Dispositions That Contribute to Antisocial Propensity

We hypothesize that three independent dimensions of dispositions each contribute to the risk for conduct problems in our developmental model. Like others (Buss & Plomin, 1984; Goldsmith, Losoya, Bradshaw, & Campos, 1994), we define dispositions as broad aspects of socioemotional functioning. Some variations in dispositions are evident in infancy, whereas others emerge later in early childhood. Individual differences in dispositions tend to persist into adolescence and adulthood and constitute the socioemotional core of "personality traits" across the life span (Caspi, 1998, 2000; Clark & Watson, 1999; Rothbart & Ahadi, 1994; Rutter, 1987).

Our measurement-based model differs from existing models of dispositions and personality in two ways. First, we developed a new measure of child and adolescent dispositions, termed the Child and Adolescent Dispositions Scale (CADS; (Waldman, Van Hulle, Applegate, Pardini, Frick, & Lahey, 2007)) by searching the existing literature for disposition-like characteristics that had been shown to be related to conduct problems. Second, because our goal was to use the CADS in studies that examined relations between dispositions and conduct problems (and other mental health problems), we were careful to exclude items from the CADS if they could be considered to be synonyms or antonyms of conduct problems or symptoms of mental health problems. If the

CADS had not been constructed in this way, any correlations of dispositions with conduct problems or mental health problems could reflect the overlapping items (Sanson, Prior, & Kyrios, 1990). This is important as all existing dispositions and personality scales are contaminated by items such as "angry," "aggressive," "impulsive," "untrustworthy," "anxious," "nervous," "fearful," and "depressed." Recent studies that "purified" existing dispositional measures by eliminating common items (Lemery, Essex, & Smider, 2002; Lengua, West, & Sandler, 1998) suggest that not all of the association between dispositions and conduct problems is an artifact of overlapping items, however, supporting our decision to develop a model and measure of dispositions that does not include such items.

In an earlier statements (Lahey & Waldman, 2003), we provided a detailed discussion of the similarities among these three putative dispositional dimensions and two of the three dimensions consistently identified in three-factor models of personality (Clark & Watson, 1999; Eysenck, 1947; Tellegen, 1982) and three of the factors in the robust five-factor model of personality (Costa & McCrae, 1987, 1995; Goldberg & Rosolack, 1994). We do not repeat this detailed discussion in the present chapter, but we briefly summarize it to place our model of dispositions in the context of contemporary models of dispositions and personality.

The CADS was developed by first conducting exploratory factor analyses of a pool of relevant items in a population-based sample to refine the hypothesized factor structure. Then, the CADS model was tested against alternative models using confirmatory factor analysis in a second population-based sample. The model was strongly supported in these stringent tests (Waldman et al., 2007). The three CADS dimensions of dispositions are termed *prosociality, daring,* and *negative emotionality.*

Prosociality. Based in part on Eisenberg and Mussen's (1991) construct of "dispositional sympathy," a hypothesized dimension of prosociality is defined in the CADS by

frequent manifestations of concern for the feelings of others, such as spontaneous sharing and helping. Several concurrent and longitudinal studies suggest that sympathy and concern for others are inversely correlated with youth conduct problems (e.g., Cohen & Strayer, 1996; Eisenberg, Fabes, Murphy, Karbon, Smith, & Maszk, 1996; Graziano, 1994; Graziano & Ward, 1992; Haemaelaeinen & Pulkkinen, 1996; Hastings, Zahn-Waxler, Robinson, Usher, & Bridges, 2000; Hughes, White, Sharpen, & Dunn, 2000; John, Caspi, Robins, Moffitt, & Stouthamer-Loeber, 1994; Luengo, Otero, Carrillo-de-la-Pena, & Miron, 1994) .

Daring. The second hypothesized dimension distinguished in the CADS is defined by daring, adventurousness, and enjoyment of loud, rough, and risky activities (Lahey & Waldman, 2003). We labeled this hypothesized dimension as *daring* based on Farrington and West's (1993) finding that children rated on the single item of "daring" were markedly more likely to be chronic criminal offenders during adolescence and adulthood. This dimension bears a strong resemblance to aspects of "sensation seeking" (Zuckerman, 1996) and "novelty seeking" (Cloninger, 1987), which have been found to be positively correlated with conduct problems (Arnett, 1996; Daderman, 1999; Daderman, Wirsen, & Hallman, 2001; Goma-I-Freixnet, 1995; Greene, Krcmar, Walters, Rubin, & Hale, 2000; Luengo et al., 1994; Newcomb & McGee, 1991; Schmeck & Poustka, 2001). For this reason, some items that were included in the CADS to reflect daring were based on our earlier measure of sensation-seeking in children (Russo et al., 1993).

It is also seems likely that daring represents the inverse of Kagan, Reznick, and Snidman's (1988) construct of "behavioral inhibition." In a series of studies, young children were classified as "behaviorally inhibited" if they were fretful, slow to respond to persons and objects, and slow to vocalize when exposed to challenging laboratory situations, (e.g., meeting an unfamiliar adult and having a robot emerge from behind a curtain and speak to them; Garcia-Coll,

Kagan, & Reznick, 1984; Kagan, Reznick, Snidman, Schwartz, Snidman, & Kagan, 1999). Children who displayed the opposite pattern in these situations were classified as "behaviorally disinhibited." Behavioral disinhibition has been found to predict behavior problems (Biederman et al., 2001; Hirshfeld et al., 1992; Kerr, Tremblay, Pagani-Kurtz, & Vitaro, 1997; Raine, Reynolds, Venables, Mednick, & Farrington, 1998; Schwartz, Snidman, & Kagan, 1996; Shaw, Gilliom, Ingoldsby, & Nagin, 2003). Other studies suggest that behavioral inhibition predicts anxiety disorders (Biederman et al., 2001; Muris, Merckelbach, Schmidt, Gadet, & Bogie, 2001). These findings suggest the hypothesis that the CADS dimension of daring will be positively related to conduct problems and inversely related to anxiety disorders.

Negative emotionality. Youth who are given high ratings on the CADS dimension of negative emotionality experience negative emotions frequently, intensely, and out of proportion to the circumstances. The items that define this dimension in the CADS mostly do not refer to specific emotions, but to negative emotions in general. The only specificity in the CADS *negative emotionality* dimension is that the items of "jealous" and "easily bored" loaded uniquely on this dimension. Based on the nonspecific nature of the negative emotionality dimension, we hypothesize that it measures a general tendency to react to situations with negative emotions, similar to Gray and McNaughton's (1996) conceptualization of the "fight-or-flight" system. A dimension similar to CADS negative emotionality has been identified in all major dispositions and personality measures, variously termed neuroticism (Bouchard & Loehlin, 2001; Digman & Inouye, 1986; Eysenck, 1947; Goldberg, 1993), negative affectivity, or negative emotionality (Rothbart, Ahadi, Hersey, & Fisher, 2001; Watson, Clark, & Tellegen, 1988; Zuckerman, Kuhlman, Joireman, Teta, & Kraft, 1993).

Consistent with our view of negative emotionality as a nonspecific tendency to respond to provocations with any of a range of negative emotions, previous studies have found similar negative affect dimensions to be related to a wide range of mental health problems, including anxiety disorders, depression, and antisocial behavior across the life span (Eysenck & Eysenck, 1970; Goma-I-Freixnet, 1995; Krueger, 1999; Moffitt et al., 1996; Roberts, & Kendler, 1999; Shiner, Masten, & Tellegen, 2002). Not all previous studies of children and adolescents found negative emotionality to be significantly correlated with conduct problems, however (e.g., Heaven, 1996; John et al., 1994; Powell & Stewart, 1983; Tranah, Harnett, & Yule, 1998). These studies raise important empirical questions about the conditions under which negative emotionality is and is not associated with antisocial behavior.

Note on "difficult dispositions." Other developmental theorists have used the construct of "difficult dispositions." Prospective studies have shown that children who are classified as exhibiting difficult dispositions during infancy and toddlerhood are at increased risk for serious conduct problems (Kingston & Prior, 1995; Olson et al., 2000; Sanson & Prior, 1999). The relation between the construct of difficult dispositions and the CADS model, if any, has not yet been defined. It seems likely, however, that young children who are classified as difficult exhibit deviant levels of one or more of the CADS dimensions of dispositions, particularly negative emotionality.

Contribution of Cognitive Abilities to Antisocial Propensity

Based on evidence that cognitive abilities, particularly verbal abilities, inversely predict the development of conduct problems (Elkins, Iacono, Doyle, & McGue, 1997; Ge, Donnellan, & Wenk, 2000; Giancola, Martin, Tarter, Pelham, & Moss, 1996; Kratzer & Hodgins, 1999; Lynam, Moffitt, & Stouthamer-Loeber, 1993; Moffitt & Silva, 1988; Seguin, Boulerice, Harden, Tremblay, & Pihl, 1999; Stattin & Klackenberg-Larsson, 1993), we hypothesize that lower cognitive ability and slow language development also increase risk for conduct problems. A series of studies have provided evidence that this inverse correlation cannot be explained by differences in SES associated with cognitive abilities, the greater likelihood that more intelligent delinquent youth will avoid detection, or differences in motivation to perform well on cognitive tests (Lynam et al., 1993; Moffitt & Silva, 1988). A range of constructs has been used to refer to the cognitive deficits associated with conduct problems, including verbal intelligence, language delays, neuropsychological dysfunction, and executive functioning. It is not presently clear which construct or constructs are most defensible, but this is an area of active inquiry (e.g., Nigg & Huang-Pollock, 2003).

Genetic and Environmental Influences on Antisocial Propensity

In this section, we summarize existing evidence for genetic and environmental influences on the development of conduct problems. We first address evidence for these causal influences on conduct problems per se. Second, we discuss evidence for causal influences on dispositions and cognitive abilities. Third, we discuss the complex interplay between genetic and environmental influences in general terms. Finally, we integrate these topics in the context of our causal model.

Rhee and Waldman (2002) recently reviewed the body of evidence from twin and adoption studies and concluded that there is convincing evidence of both substantial genetic and substantial environmental influences on child and adolescent conduct problems (see also Lahey & Waldman, 2003). Other evidence suggests that this includes genetic influences on both the origins of child conduct problems and on their persistence over time (O'Connor, Neiderhiser, Reiss, Hetherington, & Plomin, 1998; Robinson, Kagan, Reznick, & Corley, 1992; Saudino, Plomin, & DeFries, 1996).

There is also strong and consistent evidence that dimensions of dispositions and personality that appear to be simi-

lar to the three CADS dimensions have both genetic and environmental influences. Studies of traits like negative emotionality using other measures have found evidence of both moderate genetic and environmental influences from toddlerhood through adulthood (Cyphers, Phillips, Fulker, & Mrazek, 1990; Emde et al., 1992; Gjone & Stevenson, 1997; Goldsmith, Buss, & Lemery, 1997; McGue, Bacon, & Lykken, 1993; Pedersen, Plomin, McClearn, & Friberg, 1988; Phillips & Matheny, 1997; Saudino et al., 1996; Tellegen et al., 1988). Similarly, studies of sympathy and prosocial behavior have shown modest to moderate genetic influences across the life span (Davis, Luce, & Kraus, 1994; Emde et al., 1992; Matthews, Batson, Horn, & Rosenman, 1981; Zahn-Waxler, Robinson, & Emde, 1992). The same has been found for the construct of behavioral inhibition in toddlers and children (Cyphers et al., 1990; DiLalla, Kagan, & Reznick, 1994; Emde et al., 1992; Goldsmith et al., 1997; Phillips & Matheny, 1997; Robinson et al., 1992), which we believe to be related to *daring* in our model. It is also very clear that there are both genetic and environmental influences on cognitive ability and language development from toddlerhood on (Eley, Dale, & Bishop, 2001; Emde et al., 1992; Petrill et al., 1997; Plomin & Petrill, 1997). Based on this evidence, we hypothesize that the four elements of antisocial propensity in the CADS model (cognitive ability and the three dimensions of dispositions) will each have substantial genetic and environmental influences.

Interplay of Genetic and Environmental Influences

There are genetic and environmental influences on conduct problems. Because genetic and environmental influences are ubiquitous on all significant aspects of human behavior, this information is of little importance by itself. It is the nature of the complex *interplay* between genetic and environmental influences that is important. In this section, we discuss this interplay in general terms to lay a foundation for more specific hypotheses. In particular, it is essential to consider environmental influences in the context of their interplay with genetic influences to understand them fully and to harness their power in prevention and treatment. This is partly because the child's transactions with the environment that shape dispositions and behavior operate largely through both genotype-environment correlations and genotype-environment interactions (Rutter, 1997; Rutter et al., 1997).

Genotype-environment correlations. In many cases, genetic and environmental influences on the origins of conduct problems are correlated, rather than independent of one another. There are three types of genotype-environment correlations that appear to be relevant to the development of conduct problems: passive, evocative, and active (Plomin et al., 1977; Rutter, 1997; Rutter et al., 1997).

The interplay of genetic and environmental influences takes the form of *passive genotype-environment correlations* when characteristics of the child and the causally significant aspects of the family environment share the same genetic influences. Because parents and children share genetic influences, children with the most serious conduct problems tend to have antisocial fathers and tend to be raised by younger antisocial mothers with mental health problems (Klerman, 1993; Lahey et al., 1988, 1989; Nagin, Pogarsky, & Farrington, 1997; Wahler & Hann, 1987; Wakschlag et al., 2000). Because such families are poorly prepared to provide the kinds of skilled child rearing that could prevent the development of conduct problems, this genotype-environment correlation fosters the development of conduct problems.

In the case of *evocative genotype-environment* correlations, the child's genetically influenced dispositions and cognitive characteristics evoke aspects of the social environment that foster the development of conduct problems. Consistent with the social learning model (Patterson, 1982), we hypothesize that parenting plays the key role in the developmental transformation of anti-

social predisposition into conduct problems. Cognitively and dispositionally predisposed children are less likely to develop conduct problems if they receive adaptive parenting. Unfortunately, we hypothesize that such predisposing child characteristics evoke exactly the kinds of coercive, harsh, nonresponsive, inconsistent, and negative parenting behaviors that foster conduct problems (Anderson, Lytton, & Romney, 1986; Ge et al., 1996; Loeber & Tengs, 1986; Patterson, 1982; Sanson & Prior, 1999).

In other cases, *active genotype-environment correlations* operate because genetic influences lead some children to actively seek out social environments that foster their development of conduct problems. For example, there is evidence that children with conduct problems tend to associate with delinquent peers (Fergusson & Horwood, 1999) and that associating with delinquent peers fosters the future development of delinquent behavior (Fergusson, Swain-Campbell, & Horwood, 2002; Keenan, Loeber, & Zhang, 1995). Furthermore, there is evidence of genetic influences on associating with delinquent peers and that these genetic influences are shared in common with those on antisocial behavior itself (Rowe & Osgood, 1984). Thus, we hypothesize that there is an active genotype-environment correlation reflecting genetic influences on characteristics of children that lead to the selection of social environments that foster violence and antisocial behavior.

Genotype-environment interactions. These interactions occur when the effects of genetic and environmental influences on a trait depend on one another (i.e., are not simply additive). For example, a number of adoption studies indicate that conduct problems in the adopted-away offspring of antisocial parents are less common when they are raised by well-adjusted adoptive parents than by adoptive parents with problems similar to those of their biological parents (Bohman, 1996; Cadoret, Yates, Troughton, Woodward, & Stewart, 1995). This finding suggests that genetic influences on conduct problems are muted by the favorable social learning environments of well-functioning adoptive families. Similarly, there is emerging evidence that individuals respond in different ways to social factors that encourage conduct problems partly because of genetic differences. For example, Caspi et al. (2002) provided striking evidence that maltreated children who have one particular version (allele) of the gene that controls levels of monoamine oxidase (MAO), which is an enzyme that inactivates the neurotransmitters serotonin, dopamine, and norepinephrine in the brain, are more likely to engage in antisocial behavior than maltreated children without this allele. The allele confers little increased risk for conduct problems in the absence of physical abuse. We expect that many such gene-environment interactions will need to be examined to understand the role of both genes and the environment. For example, we hypothesize that genetic influences are one factor that increase or decrease the likelihood that youth will respond to the social influences on delinquent behavior.

Antisocial Propensity and the Mediation Hypothesis

It is likely that genetic influences (and any prenatal environmental influences) on conduct problems are *mediated* by the dispositional and cognitive components of antisocial propensity (Lahey, Waldman, & McBurnett, 1999; Rutter, 2003). That is, we hypothesize that there are genetic influences and possibly prenatal environmental influences on dispositions and cognitive ability, but there is little (if any) direct genetic or environmental influence on complex behaviors, such as violence, stealing, and vandalism. In contrast, we hypothesize that genetic and environmental influences on conduct problems are *indirect*, operating through the four dimensions of antisocial propensity.

The mediation hypothesis is based in part on evidence that the genetic influences on conduct problems, ODD, and ADHD overlap substantially (Coolidge, Thede, & Young, 2000; Eaves et al., 2000; Thapar, Harrington, & McGuffin, 2001; Waldman, Rhee, Levy, & Hay, 2001). In terms of the CADS

model, we hypothesize that the dispositional and cognitive-verbal components of antisocial propensity (a) each have unique genetic influences and (b) these components of propensity mediate the genetic influences on conduct problems (Lahey & Waldman, 2003).

A number of behavior-genetic studies provide preliminary support for the mediation hypothesis. Schmitz et al. (1999) found that maternal ratings of negative emotionality measured at the ages of 14, 20, 24, and 36 months predicted a composite rating of oppositional, aggressive, and nonaggressive conduct problems at age 4 years. Consistent with the mediation hypothesis, 96% of the correlation between negative emotionality and conduct problems was explained by genetic influences common to both variables. In 270 pairs of twins, Lemery et al. (2002) found that dispositional ratings at 5 years of age predicted conduct problems at age 7. Consistent with the mediation hypothesis, genetic influences on conduct problems were substantial and were entirely mediated by the dispositions. Although Lemery and colleagues did not use the CADS, two of the dispositional dimensions in their measure (negative affectivity and surgency) resemble negative emotionality and daring enough to lend plausibility to our mediation hypothesis.

Gjone and Stevenson (1997) followed a sample of 759 twin pairs who were 5 to 15 years old when first assessed. Parent ratings of negative emotionality in the first assessment predicted both aggressive and nonaggressive conduct problems 2 years later. Genetic influences on *aggressive* conduct problems were mediated by *negative emotionality*. In contrast, neither common genetic nor shared environmental influences explained the prospective association between dispositions and nonaggressive conduct problems. Although the CADS model would have predicted some shared causal influences on negative emotionality and nonaggressive conduct problems, this finding is consistent with our hypothesis that the conduct problems of youth who follow a trajectory of high and persistent conduct problems beginning at school entry, which include aggressive conduct problems, have stronger genetic influences that are mediated by the components of antisocial propensity than the conduct problems of youth with later ages of onset (whose conduct problems tend to be nonaggressive). In addition, there is preliminary evidence that executive functions mediate a substantial proportion of the genetic influences on conduct problems (Coolidge et al., 2000). This finding is consistent with our hypothesis that genetic influences on conduct problems are mediated partly by deficits in cognitive ability.

Developmental Trajectories and Causal Influences

We hypothesize that the same set of child characteristics and social factors influence conduct problems in children who follow all developmental trajectories, but that differences in developmental trajectories result from different combinations of the same set of causal influences. Note that we speak of different developmental trajectories in this section as if they are discrete categories for the sake of simplicity and clarity. We view them, however, as points along the two continua of trajectories: (1) the continuum of initial levels of conduct problems (intercepts) and (2) the continuum of slopes from these initial levels.

When young children show increased risk on one or more component of antisocial propensity, their deviant dispositions and/or slow verbal development foster high levels of developmentally early conduct problems prior to school entry. The stronger the child's net propensity early in life, the more likely the child is to show a developmental trajectory characterized by high levels of developmentally early conduct problems at school entry, little or no decline in these behaviors, and the rapid learning of developmentally late conduct problems. Therefore, children with high levels of antisocial propensity tend to develop versatile repertoires of conduct problems, which tend to endure and sometimes worsen over time. Only a small pro-

portion of children in the general population have extreme levels of antisocial propensity in early childhood, but these children commit a high proportion of crimes because they start early, are versatile, commit serious offenses, offend frequently, and persist in their offending over long periods of time.

Some children exhibit high levels of developmentally early conduct problems at school entry, but improve over the course of childhood. Compared to children who exhibit persistent conduct problems, several studies suggest that children who improve have less extreme initial levels of childhood conduct problems, are more intelligent, have fewer delinquent friends, and come from families with higher socioeconomic status (SES) and fewer antisocial and mental health problems (Fergusson et al., 1996; Lahey, Loeber, Burke, & Rathouz, 2002; Nagin & Tremblay, 2001). Thus, we hypothesize that children who exhibit deviant but decreasing levels of early conduct problems at school entry improve both because they have less maladaptive dispositions and higher intelligence and because they live in more adaptive social environments. It seems likely that their social environments are more adaptive partly because of passive, evocative, and active genotype-environment correlations that are driven by genetic influences. In either case, we hypothesize that these youth who improve during childhood are not at high risk for adding developmentally late conduct problems to their repertoires during adolescence, given that they lack both the extreme antisocial propensity and social environments that would place them at risk.

Youth whose dispositions and cognitive abilities are in the average range during childhood are not likely to develop serious conduct problems. They can, and often do, become offenders, however, if social influences to offend are sufficiently strong. Such youth tend to show normative levels of developmentally early conduct problems at school entry, but show increasing levels of developmentally late conduct problems in late childhood or adolescence. They never exhibit high levels of developmentally early conduct problems because they lack the dispositional and cognitive basis for acquiring them early in life. When peer influences become more powerful during late childhood and early adolescence, they may acquire developmentally late conduct problems. Because they lack the dispositional basis for the development of aggression, however, they mostly acquire less serious nonaggressive conduct problems (e.g., truancy and stealing).

Youth with little antisocial propensity (i.e., highly adaptive dispositions and cognitive abilities) are unlikely to engage in conduct problems. This is because they lack the dispositional and cognitive basis for developmentally early conduct problems and their adaptive traits protect them from social pressures to engage in delinquent acts during adolescence.

Specific Causal Mechanisms in the Development of Conduct Problems

Through what causal mechanisms do individual differences in antisocial propensity influence the social learning of conduct problems? The answer lies in the interplay between child characteristics (propensity) and the social environment (Keenan & Shaw, 1995, 2003; Lahey & Waldman, 2003). Social learning plays the key role for youth on all developmental trajectories, but in ways that reflect the characteristics of the child. In this section, we explicate our causal model in greater detail.

From dispositions to conduct problems. Deviant levels of dispositions influence how children and adolescents respond to the environmental demands that are placed on them, how they relate to peers and adults, and what activities are perceived as desirable. The three putative dimensions of dispositions are hypothesized to operate in somewhat different ways.

Toddlers who are high in negative emotionality often become highly upset when they are frustrated or annoyed in even minor ways. The rules that adults place on children at home, in day care, and at school are a prime source of frustration. As a result, higher *negative emotionality* creates a press

to oppose and circumvent adult rules by lying and acting covertly. In addition, the inevitable frustrations of daily social life in the home or preschool (e.g., having a sibling or classmate take away the toy they were playing with or bump into them) cause children who are higher in negative emotionality to react with intense, global negative affect. Very little is required from the social environment to shape these affective reactions into the more specific behaviors of hitting, shoving, biting, and destroying property. Because of the frequency and intensity of their negative affective responses, toddlers who are high in negative emotionality are more likely to push a child down or land a flailing blow that is reinforced by removing the frustration.

High levels of negative emotionality in children may also strain parent-child relationships (Rothbart & Ahadi, 1994) and lead to peer rejection (Maszk, Eisenberg, & Guthrie, 1999). These consequences may contribute to the development of conduct problems by disrupting parenting and isolating the child from well-behaved peers early in life. Likewise, high negative emotionality would be expected to promote the increasingly aversive parent-child exchanges that Patterson (1982) refers to as the "coercive cycle." Thus, negative emotionality contributes to the development of conduct problems largely through genotype-environment correlations.

In contrast, we hypothesize that prosociality and daring primarily contribute to the social learning of conduct problems mostly by influencing how different children respond to the same environmental influences (i.e., genotype-environment interactions). Consider, for example, a toddler who accidentally pushes another child onto the floor during an argument over a toy. For a child who is low in prosociality, the victim's crying and acquiescence would tend to positively reinforce the aggression; in contrast, the victim's crying would tend to punish the same behavior in a child who is high in prosociality. That is, the same event would influence the likelihood of future aggression in opposite directions in toddlers who are high or low on prosociality. Similarly, if a child covertly took a toy from a classmate who became upset over its loss, the child's sadness would punish the act of stealing in a highly prosocial child, but not in a less prosocial child.

The dispositional dimension of daring alters the child's response to the social environment in similar ways. To a child who is high on daring, leaving the school building without permission would be exciting and positively reinforcing, but to a child who is low on daring, the same event would be punishing. Similarly, children high on daring would tend to enjoy being in physical fights and be more likely to fight in the future because of it. In contrast, children who are low on daring would be frightened by being in a fight and would be less likely to fight again. In addition, peers quickly learn who is game for risky ventures, such as shoplifting or vandalism, and seek them out for joint delinquent activities. In many such ways, the dimensions of dispositions both influence the social environment (genotype-environment correlation) and influence the child's reaction to it (genotype-environment interaction).

Role of cognitive skills. Although much remains to be learned, we suspect that variations in cognitive abilities influence the development of conduct problems in multiple ways. For example, the extent to which children understand rules, appreciate the potential consequences of their behavior, and have adaptive options for success available to them is related to their cognitive ability. In addition, particularly in early childhood, individual differences in intelligence are manifested partly as differences in the development of communication skills (Sparks, Ganschow, & Thomas, 1996; Stattin & Klackenberg-Larsson, 1993). A number of cross-sectional and prospective studies have shown that children with slow language development in early childhood are more likely to develop conduct problems (Baker & Cantwell, 1987; Beitchman et al., 2001; Cohen et al., 1998; Dery, Toupin, Pauze, Mercier, & Fortin, 1999; Pennington & Ozonoff, 1996). Following Keenan and

Shaw (1997, 2003), we hypothesize that it is easier for parents and other caregivers to socialize young children who have better developed communication skills. This is both because they can understand parental instructions better and because they can communicate their needs better (and hence are less likely to be frustrated during interactions with adults and peers).

Interactions among the components of antisocial propensity. We believe that it is likely that the dispositional and cognitive components of antisocial propensity operate both additively and interactively. This means that (1) deviance in the direction of increased risk on any component of antisocial propensity increases the risk of conduct problems; and (2) some combinations of deviance on the components of antisocial propensity contribute to the likelihood of conduct problems in more than an additive manner. At this point, there is tentative evidence that the CADS dimensions of dispositions may contribute to the likelihood of conduct problems interactively, rather than additively (Waldman et al., 2007), but this will be an important topic for future studies.

It also seems likely that interactions will be found between cognitive ability and at least some dimensions of dispositions. For example, it is likely that children with lower cognitive abilities and delayed language will often experience failure in tasks and games. If they were also high on negative emotionality, these frustrations would elicit a high rate of the kinds of negative affective reactions that promote the development of aggression and alienate both peers and adults (Hughes, Cutting, & Dunn, 2001). In addition, during elementary school, children with less well-developed cognitive skills are at increased risk for grade retention. A longitudinal study (Pagani, Tremblay, Vitaro, Boulerice, & McDuff, 2001) has shown that grade retention does not improve academic performance, but increases future conduct problems, particularly in boys. This effect might occur both because grade retention is frustrating and because it places children with a dispositional predisposition to aggression with younger and weaker classmates who are more likely to reinforce their aggression by cowering and complying. Because lower intelligence is the major reason for grade retention, lower intelligence also can contribute to this social opportunity for becoming more aggressive.

Dispositions and the Construct of Psychopathy

The construct of psychopathy is defined by callous disregard for others, irresponsibility, lack of guilt, sensation-seeking, and impulsivity. Adults with psychopathic characteristics are known to be at greatly increased risk for serious and persistent offending and violence (Hare, 1970). Studies using measures of psychopathy developed for children and adolescents have similarly found psychopathy to be correlated with conduct problems (Frick, Bodin, & Barry, 2000; Frick, O'Brien, Wootton, & McBurnett, 1994; Lynam, 1998). It is important that psychopathic characteristics have been found to be related to the five-factor model personality dimensions of low agreeableness and low conscientiousness in adults (Miller & Lynam, 2001). Because these are two of the dimensions of the five-factor model that appear to be similar to the CADS dimensions, we will test the hypothesis that youth with psychopathic characteristics tend to exhibit high levels of daring and low levels of prosociality in the CADS model. If so, this would integrate the CADS model with a large and important literature.

Note on Situational Influences

We have not addressed the important topic of situational influences on offending, both because of lack of space and because this topic has been treated well by Wikström and Sampson (2003) and others. This is an exceptionally important topic for the prevention of violence and offending. If we are correct that the most serious offenders are characterized by persistent maladaptive dispositions and cognitive abilities, it will be very difficult to control offending until methods of changing antisocial propensity

have been developed. This is because we hypothesize a propensity-by-situation interaction, in which opportunities for offending and violence will more often lead to actual offending in high-propensity than in low-propensity youth. Until the field learns how to reduce antisocial propensity in youth, however, the most effective solutions would seem to lie in reducing opportunities for offending through increased adult supervision, such as by providing well-supervised and engaging after-school programs.

Explaining the Co-Occurrence of Conduct Problems and other Disorders

Youth who engage in conduct problems are very likely to meet diagnostic criteria for a wide range of mental health problems, including attention-deficit/hyperactivity disorder (ADHD), oppositional defiant disorder (ODD), anxiety disorders, and depression (Angold, Costello, & Erkanli, 1999; Lahey, Miller, Gordon, & Riley, 1999). This high degree of co-occurrence is found primarily, but not exclusively, among youth who follow trajectories of high and stable levels of conduct problems from school entry through adolescence (Henry, Caspi, Moffitt, & Silva, 1996; Hinshaw et al., 1993; Lahey et al., 1998; Loeber, Green, Keenan, & Lahey, 1995; Lynam, 1998; Moffitt, 1990; Moffitt et al., 1996). This means that most youth who engage in serious and persistent juvenile offending also have serious mental health problems. Therefore, a satisfactory model of juvenile offending should be able to explain such frequent co-occurrence.

Co-occurrence with ADHD, ODD, Substance Abuse, and Risky Behavior

There is recent evidence that ADHD and ODD share dispositional and cognitive profiles that are similar to conduct problems (Waldman et al., 2007). We have hypothesized that variations in the child's social environment are the primary determinants of which children with high-risk levels of dispositions and cognitive ability exhibit which combination of ADHD behaviors, ODD behaviors, and conduct problems (Waldman et al., 2007). In addition, there may be somewhat different dispositions and ability profiles when these disorders occur separately or co-occur. Consistent with the latter possibility, children in the Australian Dispositions Project with co-occurring conduct problems and ADHD were more likely to receive high ratings on a trait similar to negative emotionality from infancy onward than children with only conduct problems, only ADHD, or neither disorder (Sanson & Prior, 1999). In addition, there is consistent evidence from many studies (reviewed by Hinshaw, 1992; Hogan, 1999; and Waschbusch, 2002) that children with both conduct problems and ADHD tend to have lower verbal intelligence scores than children with only conduct problems, only ADHD, or neither disorder. Indeed, youth who exhibited only conduct problems and not ADHD did not differ from nondisordered control children in verbal intelligence (Waschbusch, 2002).

Studies of adolescents and adults also suggest that three of the five-factor model dimensions of personality (agreeableness, conscientiousness, and negative emotionality) that appear to be related to the three CADS dimensions are correlated with alcohol and drug abuse (Flory, Lynam, Milich, Leukefeld, & Clayton, 2002; McCormick, Dowd, Quirk, & Zegarra, 1998; Wills, Sandy, & Yaeger, 2000) and with high-risk behavior (Gullone & Moore, 2000). This finding suggests the possibility that juvenile offenders often abuse drugs and alcohol and engage in risky behavior partly because the same dimensions of dispositions that increase the likelihood of the development of conduct problems also increase the likelihood of substance abuse and risky behavior. This hypothesis could be tested by determining if youth who engage in conduct problems and also abuse substances and engage in high-risk behaviors are lower in prosociality and higher in negative emotionality and daring than youth who only engage in conduct problems. It should be noted that there is some evidence that substance use also increases the risk of offending over time

(e.g., Van Kammen & Loeber, 1994). This could be because substance use creates a need for money to buy drugs, because intoxication temporarily increases antisocial personality, or both. Much more research from longitudinal studies is needed on the possibility of bidirectional influences.

Co-occurrence With Anxiety and Depression

We have hypothesized that persistent conduct problems often co-occur with emotional disorders primarily because these mental health problems are also more common in youth with high levels of negative emotionality (Lahey et al., 2002; Lahey & Waldman, 2003). For example, as noted earlier, many studies suggest that negative emotionality is positively correlated with conduct problems, ADHD, ODD, anxiety, and depression. This suggests that negative emotionality is a nonspecific dispositional dimension that fosters the development of many types of problems and, therefore, increases the likelihood of co-occurring disorders.

In addition, there is strong evidence from longitudinal studies that childhood conduct problems predict the later emergence of depression, but not vice versa (Capaldi, 1992; Lahey et al., 2002; Patterson & Stoolmiller, 1991). There is evidence that some of this prospective association is mediated by the adverse effect of the youth's conduct problems on aspects of his or her social environment (e.g., rejection by peers and adults) that foster depression (Burke, Loeber, Lahey, & Rathouz 2005; Capaldi, 2002).

The CADS model may be able to explain three well-established, but seemingly paradoxical findings regarding the relation between conduct problems and anxiety. First, it is clear that anxiety disorders co-occur with conduct problems at greater-than-chance rates across the life span (Loeber & Keenan, 1994; Zoccolillo, 1992). Second, children with conduct problems who are characterized as "socially withdrawn" are at increased risk for persistent and serious conduct problems (Blumstein, Farrington, &

Moitra, 1985; Kerr et al., 1997; Serbin, Moskowitz, Schwartzman, & Ledingham, 1991). Third, shyness and anxiety in young children without early conduct problems *protect* against the development of later conduct problems (Graham & Rutter, 1973; Kohlberg, Ricks, & Snarey, 1984; Mitchell & Rosa, 1981; Sanson, Pedlow, Cann, Prior, & Oberklaid, 1996), and juvenile offenders with high levels of anxiety have lower recidivism rates than other juvenile offenders (Quay & Love, 1977).

Thus, anxiety and shyness are sometimes associated with increased risk for conduct problems and are sometimes associated with decreased risk. We hypothesize that the difference depends on the profile of dispositions associated with the shyness, anxiety, or social withdrawal. Specifically, we hypothesize that anxiety protects against serious conduct problems if it reflects low daring (i.e., high timidity). When anxiety reflects greater negative emotionality, however, anxiety will be positively correlated with conduct problems (because negative emotionality is also positively correlated with conduct problems). When children are socially withdrawn because they have little interest in other children due to low prosociality, their social withdrawal will be positively correlated with conduct problems because prosociality is inversely related to conduct problems. These hypotheses can be tested easily, shedding important light on this confusing pattern of associations among conduct and emotional problems.

Explaining Demographic Differences in Conduct Problems and Violence

Because there are large demographic differences in the prevalence of conduct problems (Lahey, Miller et al., 1999), a comprehensive causal model of conduct problems must be able to explain these differences.

Sex Differences

By school entry, boys are more likely than girls to engage in conduct problems

(Keenan & Shaw, 1997; Lahey, Schwab-Stone et al., 2000; Lahey et al., 2001; Moffitt et al., 2001; Tremblay et al., 1996). We hypothesize that the causes of conduct problems are the same for girls and boys, with sex differences in conduct problems arising from a combination of sex differences in the *levels* of the components of antisocial propensity (Moffit et al., 2001; Rhee & Waldman, 2002; Rowe, Vazsonyi, & Flannery, 1995) and sex differences in socialization (Keenan & Shaw, 1997). For example, boys lag behind girls on average in the development of language communication during the crucial toddler years (Sanson, Smart, Prior, & Oberklaid, 1993). Keenan and Shaw (1997) suggested that girls are easier to socialize for this reason and that the resulting differences in socialization help create sex differences in conduct problems. To take a second example, girls show higher levels of empathy and guilt than males from toddlerhood through adolescence (Keenan, Loeber, & Green, 1999; Keenan & Shaw, 1997; Zahn-Waxler et al., 1992). We hypothesize that prosociality plays the same role in the development of conduct problems in girls and boys, but from an early age, boys are less prosocial. This difference may reflect inherent sex differences in prosociality, early sex differences in socialization that create differences in prosociality, or both. For this explanation of sex differences in conduct problems to be meaningful, however, it will be necessary to eventually explain why there are sex differences in the levels of dispositions, language development, and socialization.

It should be noted that there is some evidence that there could be more fundamental sex differences in genetic and environmental influences on conduct problems. Two studies suggest that genetic and environmental influences are similar for girls and boys on developmentally early conduct problems, but are more distinct on developmentally late conduct problems (Eley, Lichtenstein, & Stevenson, 1999; Silberg et al., 1996). This finding could reflect sex differences in the magnitude of genetic influences, but it also raises the possibility of unique causal influences on girls' conduct problems that are not included in the present model, such as genetic influences on pubertal timing. This seems plausible, as some evidence suggests that early-maturing girls show an earlier and higher peak in conduct problems (Moffitt et al., 2001) and that pubertal timing has strong genetic influences in girls (Pickles, Pickering, Simonoff, Silberg, Meyer, & Maes, 1998).

Socioeconomic and Race-Ethnic Differences

An inverse relation between SES and conduct problems has been found in many population-based studies (Lahey, Miller et al., 1999). Important tasks for any general model of conduct problems are to explain why this is the case and why the great majority of children from low SES families do *not* engage in serious conduct problems. We hypothesize that multiple environmental factors associated with lower SES influence the developmental transition from antisocial propensity to conduct problems. These SES-linked environmental factors include living in high-crime neighborhoods, attending schools with delinquent peers, and the family's lack of economic resources – which affect access to day care, after-school care, mental health services, and the like (Harnish, Dodge, & Valente, 1995; Kilgore, Snyder, & Lentz, 2000). We hypothesize that these environmental circumstances foster the social learning of conduct problems (Caspi, Taylor, Moffitt, & Plomin, 2000). On the other hand, it seems likely that part of the correlation of lower SES with conduct problems reflects selection effects. There is evidence of downward socioeconomic mobility (or staying at the low SES of their family of origin) among parents who are antisocial and/or have mental health and substance abuse problems (Dohrenwend & Dohrenwend, 1974; Miech, Caspi, Moffitt, Wright, & Silva, 1999). In some instances, then, characteristics of persons lead them to live in adverse socioeconomic circumstances, and these circumstances, in turn, influence their children.

Why do most children living in low-SES circumstances not engage in serious antisocial behavior? Consistent with our general model, we hypothesize that children who are dispositionally and cognitively predisposed to develop conduct problems will be more influenced by the environmental factors associated with lower SES than other children. Because there are genetic influences on antisocial propensity, this means that the environmental influences associated with SES influence the child largely through genotype-environment interactions.

After controlling for SES and neighborhood factors, there is little or no difference in the prevalence of most conduct problems among African American, Hispanic, and non-Hispanic White youth (Bird et al., 2001; Loeber, Farrington, Stouthamer-Loeber, & Van Kammen, 1998). It is likely that there are race-ethnic differences in the rates of some specific crimes, however, such as drug selling and assault with a deadly weapon (Blum et al., 2000). We hypothesize that these differences are mostly attributable to a marked difference in the tendency of youth in different race-ethnic groups to join antisocial gangs. Evidence is sparse for girls, but there is substantial evidence that the boys from all race-ethnic groups who join gangs had high and escalating levels of aggressive and nonaggressive conduct problems prior to gang entrance (Esbensen, Huizinga, & Weiher, 1993; Lahey, Gordon, Loeber, Stouthamer-Loeber, & Farrington, 1999). Different race-ethnic groups have been more or less likely to join antisocial gangs at different times during the last 100 years. For example, Irish immigrant youth were most likely to join gangs around the turn of the 20th century. Presently, however, misbehaving non-Hispanic White boys are much less likely to join gangs than misbehaving African American and Hispanic boys (Lahey, Gordon et al., 1999). There is also clear evidence from longitudinal studies that, during the period of gang membership, gang members show marked increases in the frequency of drug-related and violent offenses (so that they account for 10 times more assaults and drug sales than nongang members), which declines after their period of gang membership ends (Esbensen et al., 1993; Gordon et al., 2004; Thornberry, Krohn, Lizotte, & Chard-Wierschem, 1993). We hypothesize that the powerful social influence of gang membership accounts for the race-ethnic difference in serious adolescent antisocial behavior.

Evaluating and Testing the CADS Model

Nothing Is New Under the Sun – William Shakespeare

In general terms, our hypothesis that antisocial propensity is related to multiple dimensions of dispositions is not original. The conceptual framework for our model was spelled out by Hippocrates around 400 B.C. and revived by Pavlov in the 1920s. More than 40 years ago, Eysenck (1964) proposed that persons who commit crimes are high in neuroticism, psychoticism, and extraversion. In time, it became clear that there were both genetic and environmental influences on Eysenck's dimensions of personality (Eysenck, 1990). Thus, if the present model has value, it must derive from its specific hypotheses.

Potential Strengths and Weaknesses of the CADS Model

The measurement-based CADS model posits dimensions of dispositions that appear to be similar to dimensions identified in the five-factor model of personality, but they are operationalized in a way that is independent of conduct and mental health problems. Thus, the CADS will facilitate research on the dispositional foundations of juvenile offending, violence, and mental health problems. In addition, the CADS model includes cognitive deficits, which have been ignored in previous dispositional/personality models. Our model also places antisocial propensity in developmental context, integrates the propensity model with the social learning model, and uses the concepts and methods of epidemiology and behavior genetics to frame and test our hypotheses regarding environmental and genetic influences.

The CADS model shares with other dispositional models an important threat to its internal validity, however. The correlations between dispositions and conduct problems that appear to support their validity may be circular. If a mother is asked if her child "gets upset easily," "cares about the feelings of others," and "likes risky activities," her responses may be influenced by her knowledge of her child's frequent fighting. Even if there is evidence to the contrary, the salience of the fighting may lead the mother to *infer* that her child is easily upset, unconcerned about others, and likes risky activities.

Therefore, it will be necessary to test the CADS model within a multi-method approach that avoids this potential circularity. There are two key ways in which this could be done. First, it would be useful to test the model using measures of dispositions that are not obtained from the person who rates the youth's conduct problems. For example, studies using independent observers have found that preschoolers with conduct problems engage in less prosocial behavior and display more negative emotion during play (Hughes et al., 2000) and react more emotionally to failure in a competitive task (Hughes et al., 2001). Second, it would be possible to test the CADS model using laboratory tasks. For example, Canli et al. (2001) found striking correlations (in the $r = .70–.85$ range) between Eysenck's dimension of neuroticism and activity in frontal and limbic structures in response to negatively valenced stimuli using functional magnetic resonance imaging. If the CADS negative emotionality dimension showed similar physiological correlates, but the other two CADS dimensions did not, that would support the model.

The most important tests of any model, however, are assessments of its scientific and practical utility. The scientific utility of the CADS model will depend primarily on its ability to organize data and generate empirically supported hypotheses. The CADS model can be evaluated by testing specific model-based a priori hypotheses.

For example, we will test the hypothesis that the dispositional and cognitive-linguistic components of propensity mediate genetic influences on conduct problems. In addition, contemporary behavior-genetic designs offer innovative and powerful ways of testing hypotheses about environmental influences and their interplay with genetic influences that have been very difficult to test in the past (e.g., Rose et al., 2003: Rutter, Pickles, Murray, & Eaves, 2001).

The practical utility of the CADS model should be evaluated in at least two ways. First, the CADS model must be able to predict the future development of conduct problems. If preschool children with deviant levels of parent-rated dispositions and tested cognitive ability in early childhood fail to show high and persistent levels of youth-reported conduct problems through adolescence, the model would be disconfirmed. Second, the CADS model must eventually be able to inform prevention and perhaps intervention research. For example, the CADS model implies that one potentially successful method of prevention would be to modify the dispositional and cognitive elements of predisposition in early childhood. For example, it may be possible to influence prosociality and negative emotionality by teaching parents more adaptive methods of parenting (Eisenberg, Fabes, & Murphy, 1996; Eisenberg & Mussen, 1991; Grusec, 1991; Keenan & Shaw, 2003). Another potentially useful preventive strategy might be to identify high-risk children based on their dispositions and ability profiles and to design school- and home-based social learning interventions to reduce the likelihood that their antisocial propensity will lead to violence or offending. This might include increased adult supervision to limit such opportunities.

References

Anderson, K. E., Lytton, H., & Romney, D. M. (1986). Mothers' interactions with normal and conduct-disordered boys: Who affects whom? *Developmental Psychology, 22,* 604–609.

Angold, A., Costello, E. J., & Erkanli, A. (1999). Comorbidity. *Journal of Child Psychology and Psychiatry, 40,* 57–87.

Arnett, J. J. (1996). Sensation seeking, aggressiveness, and adolescent reckless behavior. *Personality and Individual Differences, 20,* 693–702.

Baker, L., & Cantwell, D. P. (1987). A prospective psychiatric follow-up of children with speech/language disorders. *Journal of the American Academy of Child and Adolescent Psychiatry, 26,* 546–553.

Beitchman, J. H., Wilson, B., Johnson, C. J., Atkinson, L., Young, A. Adlaf, E., et al. (2001). Fourteen-year follow-up of speech/language-impaired and control children: Psychiatric outcome. *Journal of the American Academy of Child and Adolescent Psychiatry, 40,* 75–82.

Biederman, J., Hirshfeld-Becker, D. R., Rosenbaum, J. F., Herot, C., Friedman, D., Snidman, N., et al. (2001). Further evidence of association between behavioral inhibition and social anxiety in children. *American Journal of Psychiatry, 158,* 1673–1679.

Bird, H. R., Canino, G. J., Davies, M., Zhang, H., Ramirez, R., & Lahey, B. B. (2001). Prevalence and correlates of antisocial behaviors among three ethnic groups. *Journal of Abnormal Child Psychology, 29,* 465–478.

Blair, C. (2002). School readiness: Integrating cognition and emotion in a neurobiological conceptualization of children's functioning at school entry. *American Psychologist, 57,* 111–127.

Blum, R., W., Beuhring, T., Shew, M. L., Bearinger, L. H., Sieving, R. E., & Resnick, M. D. (2000). The effects of race/ethnicity, income, and family structure on adolescent risk behaviors. *American Journal of Public Health, 90,* 1879–1884.

Blumstein, A., Farrington, D. P., & Moitra, S. (1985), Delinquency careers: Innocents, desisters, and persisters. In M. Tonry & N. Morris (Eds.), *Crime and justice.* Chicago: University of Chicago Press.

Bohman, M. (1996). Predispositions to criminality: Swedish adoption studies in retrospect. In G. R. Bock & J. A. Goode (Eds.), *Genetics of criminal and antisocial behavior.* Chichester, England: Wiley.

Bouchard, T. J., & Loehlin, J. C. (2001). Genes, evolution, and personality. *Behavior Genetics, 31,* 243–273.

Brame, B., Nagin, D. S., & Tremblay, R. E. (2001). Developmental trajectories of physical

aggression from school entry to late adolescence. *Journal of Child Psychology and
Psychiatry, 42*, 503–512.

Burke, J. D., Loeber, R., Lahey, B. B., & Rathouz,
P. J. (2005). Developmental transitions among
affective and behavioral disorders in adolescent boys. *Journal of Child Psychology and Psychiatry, 46*, 1200–1210.

Buss, A. H., & Plomin, R. (1984). *Dispositions:
Early developing personality traits*. Hillsdale,
NJ: Erlbaum.

Cadoret, R. J., Yates, W. R., Troughton, E., Woodward, G., & Stewart, M. A. (1995). Genetic-
environmental interaction in the genesis of
aggressivity and conduct disorders. *Archives of
General Psychiatry, 52*, 916–924.

Cairns, R. B. (1979). *Social development: The
origins and plasticity of social interchanges*. San
Francisco: Freeman.

Canli, T., Zhao, Z., Desmond, J. E., Kang, E.,
Gross, J., & Gabrieli, J. D. E. (2001). An fMRI
study of personality influences on brain reactivity to emotional stimuli. *Behavioral Neuroscience, 115*, 33–42.

Capaldi, D. M. (1992). Co-occurrence of conduct problems and depressive symptoms in
early adolescent boys: II. A 2-year follow-up
at grade 8. *Development and Psychopathology,
4*, 125–144.

Caspi, A. (1998). Personality development across
the life course. In N. Eisenberg (Ed.), *Handbook of child psychology* (5th ed.) (Vol. 3, pp.
311–388). New York: Wiley.

Caspi, A. (2000). The child is father of the
man: Personality continuities from childhood
to adulthood. *Journal of Personality and Social
Psychology, 78*, 158–172.

Caspi, A., Lynam, D., Moffitt, T. E., & Silva, P.
A. (1993). Unraveling girls' delinquency: Biological, dispositional, and contextual contributions to adolescent misbehavior. *Developmental Psychology, 29*, 19–30.

Caspi, A., McClay, J., Moffitt, T., Mill, J., Martin,
J., Craig, I. W., et al. (2002). Role of genotype
in the cycle of violence in maltreated children.
Science, 297, 851–854.

Caspi, A., Moffitt, T. E., Silva, P. A., Stouthamer-
Loeber, M., Schmutte, P. S., & Krueger, R.
(1994). Are some people crime-prone? Replications of the personality-crime relation across
nation, gender, race and method. *Criminology,
32*, 301–333.

Caspi, A., & Roberts, B. W. (2001). Personality
development across the life course: The argument for change and continuity. *Psychological
Inquiry, 12*, 49–66.

Caspi, A., Taylor, A. L., Moffitt, T. E., & Plomin,
R. (2000). Neighborhood deprivation affects
children's mental health: Environmental risks
identified in a genetic design. *Psychological Science, 11*, 338–342.

Clark, L. A., & Watson, D. (1999). Temperament:
A new paradigm for trait psychology. In L.
A. Pervin & O. P. John (Eds.), *Handbook of
personality: Theory and research* (2nd ed.) (pp.
399–423). New York: Guilford Press.

Cloninger, C. R. (1987). A systematic method for
clinical description and classification of personality variants: A proposal. *Archives of General Psychiatry, 44*, 573–588.

Cohen, D. C., & Strayer, J. (1996). Empathy
in conduct-disordered and comparison youth.
Developmental Psychology, 32, 988–998.

Cohen, N. J., Menna, R., Vallance, D. D., Bar-
wick, M. A., Im, N., & Horodezky, N. B.
(1998). Language, social cognitive processing,
and behavioral characteristics of psychiatrically disturbed children with previously identified and unsuspected language impairments.
Journal of Child Psychology and Psychiatry, 39,
853–864.

Coolidge, F. L., Thede, L. L., & Young, S. E.
(2000). Heritability and the comorbidity of
attention deficit hyperactivity disorder with
behavioral disorders and executive function
deficits: A preliminary investigation. *Developmental Neuropsychology, 17*, 273–287.

Costa, P. T., & McCrae, R. R. (1987).
NEO. Odessa, FL: Psychological Assessment
Resources.

Costa, P. T., & McCrae, R. R. (1995). Primary
traits of Eysenck's P-E-N system: Three and
five-factor solutions. *Journal of Personality and
Social Psychology, 69*, 308–317.

Cyphers, L. H., Phillips, K., Fulker, D. W., &
Mrazek, D. A. (1990). Twin dispositions during the transition from infancy to early childhood. *Journal of the American Academy of
Child and Adolescent Psychiatry, 29*, 392–397.

Daderman, A. M. (1999). Differences between
severely conduct-disordered juvenile males
and normal juvenile males: The study of personality traits. *Personality and Individual Differences, 26*, 827–845.

Daderman, A. M., Wirsen M. A., & Hallman, J.
(2001). Different personality patterns in non-
socialized (juvenile delinquents) and socialized (Air Force pilot recruits) sensation seek-
ers. *European Journal of Personality, 15*, 239–
252.

Davidson, R. J., Putnam, K. M., & Larson, C. L.
(2000). Dysfunction in the neural circuitry of

emotion regulation – a possible prelude to violence. *Science, 289,* 591–594.

Davis, M. H., Luce, C., & Kraus, S. J. (1994). The heritability of characteristics associated with dispositional empathy. *Journal of Personality, 62,* 369–391.

Depue, R. A., & Collins, P. F. (1999). Neurobiology of the structure of personality: Dopamine facilitation of incentive motivation and extraversion. *Behavioral and Brain Sciences, 22,* 491–569.

Dery, M., Toupin, J., Pauze, R., Mercier, H., & Fortin, L. (1999). Neuropsychological characteristics of adolescents with conduct disorder: Association with attention-deficit-hyperactivity and aggression. *Journal of Abnormal Child Psychology, 27,* 225–236.

Digman, J. M., & Inouye, J. (1986). Further specification of the five robust factors of personality. *Journal of Personality and Social Psychology, 50,* 116–123.

DiLalla, L. F., Kagan, J., & Reznick, J. S. (1994). Genetic etiology of behavioral inhibition among 2-year-old children. *Infant Behavior and Development, 17,* 405–412.

Dohrenwend, B. P., & Dohrenwend, B. S. (1974). Social and cultural influences on psychopathology. *Annual Review of Psychology, 25,* 417–452.

Eaves, L., Rutter, M., Silberg, J. L., Shillady, L., Maes, H., & Pickles, A. (2000). Genetic and environmental causes of covariation in interview assessments of disruptive behavior in child and adolescent twins. *Behavior Genetics, 30,* 321–334.

Eisenberg, N., Fabes, R. A., & Murphy, B. C. (1996). Parents' reactions to children's negative emotions: Relations to children's social competence and comforting behavior. *Child Development, 67,* 2227–2247.

Eisenberg, N., Fabes, R. A., Murphy, B., Karbon, M., Smith, M., & Maszk, P. (1996). The relations of children's dispositional empathy-related responding to their emotionality, regulation, and social functioning. *Developmental Psychology, 32,* 195–209.

Eisenberg, N., & Mussen, P. H. (1991). *The roots of prosocial behavior in children.* New York: Cambridge University Press.

Eley, T. C., Dale, P., & Bishop, D. (2001). Longitudinal analysis of the genetic and environmental influences on components of cognitive delay in preschoolers. *Journal of Educational Psychology, 93,* 698–707.

Eley, T. C., Lichtenstein, P., & Stevenson, J. (1999). Sex differences in the etiology of aggressive and nonaggressive antisocial behavior: Results from two twin studies. *Child Development, 70,* 155–168.

Elkins, I., Iacono, W., Doyle, A., & McGue, M. (1997). Characteristics associated with the persistence of antisocial behavior: Results from recent longitudinal research. *Aggression and Violent Behavior, 2,* 101–124.

Emde, R. N., Plomin, R., Robinson, J., Corley, R., et al. (1992). Dispositions, emotion, and cognition at fourteen months: The MacArthur Longitudinal Twin Study. *Child Development, 63,* 1437–1455.

Eron, L. D., & Huesmann, L. R. (1984). The relation of prosocial behavior to the development of aggression and psychopathology. *Aggressive Behavior, 10,* 201–211.

Esbensen, F.-A., Huizinga, D., & Weiher, A. W. (1993). Gang and non-gang youth: Differences in explanatory factors. *Journal of Contemporary Criminal Justice, 9,* 94–116.

Eysenck, H. J. (1947). *Dimensions of personality.* New York: Praeger.

Eysenck, H. J. (1964). *Crime and personality.* New York: Houghton Mifflin.

Eysenck, H. J. (1990). Genetic and environmental contributions to individual differences: The three major dimensions of personality. *Journal of Personality, 58,* 245–261.

Eysenck, S. G., & Eysenck, H. J. (1970). Crime and personality: An empirical study of the three-factor theory. *British Journal of Criminology, 10,* 225–239.

Eysenck, S. G. B., & Eysenck, H. J. (1977). Personality differences between prisoners and controls. *Psychological Reports, 40,* 1023–1028.

Farrington, D. P. (1991). Antisocial personality from childhood to adulthood. *The Psychologist, 4,* 389–394.

Farrington, D. P. (1995). The development of offending and antisocial behaviour from childhood: Key findings from the Cambridge Study in Delinquent Development. *Journal of Child Psychology and Psychiatry, 6,* 929–964.

Farrington, D. P. (2003). Developmental and life-course criminology: Key theoretical and empirical issues. *Criminology, 41*(2), 221–255.

Farrington, D. P., & West, D. J. (1993). Criminal, penal and life histories of chronic offenders: Risk and protective factors and early identification. *Criminal Behaviour and Mental Health, 3,* 492–523.

Fergusson, D. M., & Horwood, L. J. (1999). Prospective childhood predictors of deviant peer affiliations in adolescence. *Journal of Child Psychology and Psychiatry, 40*, 581–592.

Fergusson, D. M., Lynskey, M. T., & Horwood, L. J. (1996). Factors associated with continuity and change in disruptive behavior patters between childhood and adolescence. *Journal of Abnormal Child Psychology, 24*, 533–553.

Fergusson, D. M., Swain-Campbell, N. R., & Horwood, L. J. (2002). Deviant peer affiliations, crime and substance use: A fixed effects regression analysis. *Journal of Abnormal Child Psychology, 30*, 419–430.

Flory, K., Lynam, D., Milich, R., Leukefeld, C., & Clayton, R. (2002). The relations among personality, symptoms of alcohol and marijuana abuse, and symptoms of comorbid psychopathology: Results from a community sample. *Experimental and Clinical Psychopharmacology, 10*, 425–434.

Frick, P. J., O'Brien, B. S., Wootton, J. M., & McBurnett, K. (1994). Psychopathy and conduct problems in children. *Journal of Abnormal Psychology, 103*, 700–707.

Frick, P. J., Bodin, S. D., Barry, C. T. (2000). Psychopathic traits and conduct problems in community and clinic-referred samples of children: Further development of the Psychopathy Screening Device. *Psychological Assessment, 12*, 382–393.

Garcia-Coll, C., Kagan, J., & Reznick, J. S. (1984). Behavioral inhibition in young children. *Child Development, 55*, 1005–1019.

Ge, X., Donnellan, M. B., & Wenk, E. (2001). The development of persistent criminal offending in males. *Criminal Justice and Behavior, 26*, 731–755.

Gershuny, B. S., & Sher, K. J. (1998). The relation between personality and anxiety: Findings from a 3-year prospective study. *Journal of Abnormal Psychology, 107*, 252–262.

Giancola, P. R., Martin, C. S., Tarter, R. E., Pelham, W. E., & Moss, H. B. (1996). Executive cognitive functioning and aggressive behavior in preadolescent boys at high risk for substance abuse/dependence. *Journal of Studies on Alcohol, 57*, 352–359.

Gjone, H., & Stevenson, J. (1997). A longitudinal twin study of dispositions and behavior problems: Common genetic or environmental influences? *Journal of the American Academy of Child and Adolescent Psychiatry, 36*, 1997, 1448–1456.

Goldberg, L. R. (1993). The structure of phenotypic personality traits. *American Psychologist, 48*, 26–34.

Goldberg, L. R., & Rosolack, T. K. (1994). The big five factor structure as an integrative framework: An empirical comparison with Eysenck's P-E-N model. In C. F. Halverson, G. A. Kohnstamm, & R. P. Martin (Eds.), *The developing structure of dispositions and personality from infancy to adulthood* (pp. 7–35). Hillsdale, NJ: Erlbaum.

Goldsmith, H. H., Buss, K. A., & Lemery, K. S. (1997). Toddler and childhood dispositions: Expanded content, stronger genetic evidence, new evidence for the importance of environment. *Developmental Psychology, 33*, 891–905.

Goldsmith, H. H., Losoya, S. H., Bradshaw, D, L,., & Campos, J. J. (1994). Genetics of personality: A twin study of the five-factor model and parent-offspring analyses. In C. F. Halverson, G. A. Kohnstamm, & R. P. Martin (Eds.), *The developing structure of temperament and personality from infancy to adulthood* (pp. 241–265). Hillsdale, NJ: Lawrence Erlbaum.

Goma-I-Freixnet, M. (1995). Prosocial and antisocial aspects of personality. *Personality and Individual Differences, 19*, 125–134.

Goodman, R. (2001). Psychometric properties of the Strengths and Difficulties Questionnaire. *Journal of the American Academy of Child and Adolescent Psychiatry, 40*, 1337–1345.

Gordon, R. A., Lahey, B. B., Kawai, E., Loeber, R., Stouthamer-Loeber, M., & Farrington, D. P. (2004). Antisocial behavior and youth gang membership: Selection and socialization. *Criminology, 42*, 55–87.

Gottfredson, M. R., & Hirschi, T. (1990). *A general theory of crime.* Stanford, CA: Stanford University Press.

Graham P., & Rutter, M. (1973). Psychiatric disorders in the young adolescent: A follow-up study. *Proceedings of the Royal Society of Medicine, 66*, 1226–1229.

Gray, J. A., & McNaughton, N. (1996). The neuropsychology of anxiety: Reprise. (pp. 61–134). In D. A. Hope (Ed.), *Nebraska symposium on motivation, 1995: Perspectives on anxiety, panic, and fear.* Lincoln, NE: University of Nebraska Press.

Graziano, W. G. (1994). The development of agreeableness as a dimension of personality. In C. F. Halverson, G. A. Kohnstamm, & R. P. Martin (Eds.), *The developing structure of dispositions and personality from infancy to adulthood* (pp. 339–354) Hillsdale, NJ: Erlbaum.

Graziano, W. G., & Ward, D. (1992). Probing the Big Five in adolescence: Personality and adjustment during a developmental transition. *Journal of Personality, 60,* 425–439.

Greene, K., Krcmar, M., Walters, L. H., Rubin, D. L., & Hale, J. L. (2000). Targeting adolescent risk-taking behaviors: The contribution of egocentrism and sensation-seeking. *Journal of Adolescence, 23,* 439–461.

Grusec, J. E. (1991). Socializing concern for others in the home. *Developmental Psychology, 27,* 338–342.

Gullone, E., & Moore, S. (2000). Adolescent risk-taking and the five-factor model of personality. *Journal of Adolescence, 23,* 393–407.

Haemaelaeinen, M., & Pulkkinen, L. (1996). Problem behavior as a precursor of male criminality. *Development and Psychopathology, 8,* 443–455.

Hare, R. D. (1970). *Psychopathy: Theory and research.* New York: John Wiley.

Harnish, J. D., Dodge, K. A., & Valente, E. (1995). Mother-child interaction quality as a partial mediator of the roles of maternal depressive symptomatology and socioeconomic status in the development of child conduct problems. *Child Development, 66,* 739–753.

Hastings, P. D., Zahn-Waxler, C., Robinson, J., Usher, B., & Bridges, D. (2000). The development of concern for others in children with behavior problems. *Developmental Psychology, 36,* 531–546.

Heaven, P. C. L. (1996). Personality and self-reported delinquency: A longitudinal analysis. *Journal of Child Psychology and Psychiatry, 37,* 747–751.

Henry, B., Caspi, A., Moffitt, T. E., & Silva, P. A. (1996). Dispositional and familial predictors of violent and nonviolent criminal convictions: Age 3 to age 18. *Developmental Psychology, 32,* 614–623.

Hinshaw, S. P. (1992). Externalizing behavior problems and academic underachievement in childhood and adolescence: Causal relationships and underlying mechanisms. *Psychological Bulletin, 111,* 127–155.

Hinshaw, S. P., Lahey, B. B., & Hart, E. L. (1993). Issues of taxonomy and comorbidity in the development of conduct disorder. *Development and Psychopathology, 5,* 31–50.

Hirshfeld, D. R., Rosenbaum, J. F., Biederman, J., Bolduc, E. A., Faraone, S. V., Snidman, N., et al. (1992). Stable behavioral inhibition and its association with anxiety disorder. *Journal of the American Academy of Child and Adolescent Psychiatry, 31,* 103–111.

Hogan, A. (1999). Cognitive functioning in children with oppositional defiant disorder and conduct disorder. In H. C. Quay & A. E. Hogan (Eds.), *Handbook of disruptive behavior disorders* (pp. 317–335). New York: Kluwer Academic/Plenum.

Hughes, C., Cutting, A. L., & Dunn, J. (2001). Acting nasty in the face of failure? Longitudinal observations of "hard-to-manage" children playing a rigged competitive game with a friend. *Journal of Abnormal Child Psychology, 29,* 403–416.

Hughes, C., White, A., Sharpen, J., & Dunn, J. (2000). Antisocial, angry, and unsympathetic: "Hard-to-manage" preschoolers' peer problems and possible cognitive influences. *Journal of Child Psychology and Psychiatry, 41,* 169–179.

John, O. P., Caspi, A., Robins, R. W., Moffitt, T. E., & Stouthamer-Loeber, M. (1994). The "little five": Exploring the nomological network of the five-factor model of personality in adolescent boys. *Child Development, 65,* 160–178.

Kagan, J. (1992). Stable behavioral inhibition and its association with anxiety disorder. *Journal of the American Academy of Child and Adolescent Psychiatry, 31,* 103–111.

Kagan, J., Reznick, J. S., & Snidman, N. (1988). Biological bases of childhood shyness. *Science, 240,* 167–171.

Kagan, J., Reznick, J. S., Snidman, N., Gibbons, J., & Johnson, M. O. (1988). Childhood derivatives of inhibition and lack of inhibition to the unfamiliar. *Child Development, 59,* 1580–1589.

Keenan, K., Loeber, R., & Green, S. (1999). Conduct disorder in girls: A review of the literature. *Clinical Child and Family Psychology Review, 2,* 3–19.

Keenan, K., Loeber, R., & Zhang, Q. (1995). The influence of deviant peers on the development of boys' disruptive and delinquent behavior: A temporal analysis. *Development and Psychopathology, 7,* 715–726.

Keenan, K., & Shaw, D. (1995). The development of coercive family processes: The interaction between aversive toddler behavior and parenting factors. In J. McCord (Ed.), *Coercion and punishment in long-term perspectives* (pp. 165–180). New York: Cambridge University Press.

Keenan, K., & Shaw, D. (1997). Developmental and social influences on young girls' early problem behavior. *Psychological Bulletin, 121*, 95–113.

Keenan, K., & Shaw, D. (2003). Starting at the beginning: Exploring etiological factors of later antisocial behavior in the first years of life. In B. B. Lahey, T. E. Moffitt, & A. Caspi (Eds.), *Causes of conduct disorder and juvenile delinquency* (pp. 153–181). New York: Guilford Press.

Kerr, M., Tremblay, R. E., Pagani-Kurtz, L., & Vitaro, F. (1997). Boy's behavioral inhibition and the risk of later delinquency. *Archives of General Psychiatry, 54*, 809–816.

Kilgore, K., Snyder, J., & Lentz, C. (2000). The contribution of parental discipline, parental monitoring, and school risk to early-onset conduct problems in African American boys and girls. *Developmental Psychology, 36*, 835–845.

Kingston, L., & Prior, M. (1995). The development of patterns of stable, transient, and school-age onset aggressive behavior in young children. *Journal of the American Academy of Child and Adolescent Psychiatry, 34*, 348–358.

Klerman, L. V. (1993). The relationship between adolescent parenthood and inadequate parenting. *Children and Youth Services Review, 15*, 309–320.

Kohlberg, L., Ricks, D., & Snarey, J. (1984). Childhood development as a predictor of adaptation in adulthood. *Genetic Psychology Monographs, 110*, 91–172.

Kratzer, L., & Hodgins, S. (1999). A typology of offenders: A test of Moffitt's theory among males and females from childhood to age 30. *Criminal Behaviour and Mental Health, 9*, 57–73.

Krueger, R. F. (1999). Personality traits in late adolescence predict mental disorders in early adulthood: A prospective-epidemiologic study. *Journal of Personality, 67*, 39–65.

Lahey, B. B., Gordon, R. A., Loeber, R., Stouthamer-Loeber, M., & Farrington, D. P. (1999a). Boys who join gangs: A prospective study of predictors of first gang entry. *Journal of Abnormal Child Psychology, 27*, 261–276.

Lahey, B. B., & Loeber, R. (1994). Framework for a developmental model of oppositional defiant disorder and conduct disorder. In D. K. Routh (Ed.), *Disruptive behavior disorders in childhood*. New York: Plenum.

Lahey, B. B., Loeber, R., Burke, J., & Rathouz, P. J. (2002a). Adolescent outcomes of childhood conduct disorder among clinic-referred boys: Predictors of improvement. *Journal of Abnormal Child Psychology, 30*, 333–348.

Lahey, B. B., Loeber, R., Burke, J. D., Rathouz, P., & McBurnett, K. (2002b). Waxing and waning in concert: Dynamic comorbidity of conduct disorder with other disruptive and emotional problems over seven years among clinic-referred boys. *Journal of Abnormal Psychology, 111*, 556–567.

Lahey, B. B., Loeber, R., Quay, H. C., Applegate, B., Shaffer, D., Waldman, I., et al. (1998). Validity of DSM-IV subtypes of conduct disorder based on age of onset. *Journal of the American Academy of Child and Adolescent Psychiatry, 37*, 435–442.

Lahey, B. B., McBurnett, K., & Loeber, R. (2000). Are attention-deficit hyperactivity disorder and oppositional defiant disorder developmental precursors to conduct disorder? In A. Sameroff, M. Lewis, & S. Miller (Eds.), *Handbook of developmental psychopathology* (2nd ed.) (pp. 431–446). New York: Plenum.

Lahey, B. B., Miller, T. L., Gordon, R. A., & Riley, A. (1999b). Developmental epidemiology of the disruptive behavior disorders. In H. Quay & A. Hogan (Eds.), *Handbook of the disruptive behavior disorders* (pp. 23–48). San Antonio: Academic Press.

Lahey, B. B. Russo, M. F., Walker, J. L., & Piacentini, J. C. (1989). Personality characteristics of the mothers of children with disruptive behavior disorders. *Journal of Consulting and Clinical Psychology, 57*, 512–515.

Lahey, B. B., Schwab-Stone, M., Goodman, S. H., Waldman, I. D., Canino, G., Rathouz, P. J., et al. (2000). Age and gender differences in oppositional behavior and conduct problems: A cross-sectional household study of middle childhood and adolescence. *Journal of Abnormal Psychology, 109*, 488–503.

Lahey, B. B., Van Hulle, C. A., Waldman, I. D., Rodgers, J. L., D'Onofrio, B. M., Pedlow, S., Rathouz, P. J., Keenan, K. (2006). Testing descriptive hypotheses regarding sex differences in the development of conduct problems and delinquency. *Journal of Abnormal Child Psychology, 34*, 737–755.

Lahey, B. B., & Waldman, I. D. (2003). A developmental propensity model of the origins of conduct problems during childhood and adolescence. In B. B. Lahey, T. E. Moffitt, & A. Caspi (Eds.), *Causes of conduct disorder and juvenile delinquency* (pp. 76–117). New York: Guilford Press.

Lahey, B. B., Waldman, I. D., & McBurnett, K. (1999). The development of antisocial behavior: An integrative causal model. *Journal of Child Psychology and Psychiatry, 40,* 669–682.

Lemery, K. S., Essex, M. J., & Smider, N. A. (2002). Revealing the relationship between dispositions and behavior problems by eliminating measurement confounding: Expert ratings and factor analysis. *Child Development, 73,* 867–882.

Lengua, L. J., West, S. G., & Sandler, I. N. (1998). Temperament as a predictor of symptomatology in children: Addressing contamination of measures. *Child Development, 69,* 164–181.

Loeber, R. (1988). Natural histories of conduct problems, delinquency, and associated substance abuse: Evidence for developmental progressions. In B. B. Lahey & A. E. Kazdin (Eds.), *Advances in clinical child psychology, Vol. 11.* New York: Plenum.

Loeber, R., Farrington, D. P., Stouthamer-Loeber, M., & Van Kammen, W. (1998). *Antisocial behavior and mental health problems: Explanatory factors in childhood and adolescence.* Mahwah, NJ: Erlbaum.

Loeber, R., Green, S. M., Keenan, K., & Lahey, B. B. (1995). Which boys will fare worse? Early predictors of the onset of conduct disorder in a six-year longitudinal study. *Journal of the American Academy of Child and Adolescent Psychiatry, 34,* 499–509.

Loeber, R., & Keenan, K. (1994). Interaction between conduct disorder and its comorbid conditions: Effects of age and gender. *Clinical Psychology Review, 14,* 497–523.

Loeber, R., & LeBlanc, M. (1990). Toward a developmental criminology, In M. Tonry & N. Morris (Eds.), *Crime and justice* (Vol. 12, pp. 375–473). Chicago: University of Chicago Press.

Loeber, R., & Tengs, T. (1986). The analysis of coercive chains between children, mothers, and siblings. *Journal of Family Violence, 1,* 51–70.

Luengo, M. A., Otero, J. M., Carrillo-de-la-Pena, M. T., & Miron, L. (1994). Dimensions of antisocial behaviour in juvenile delinquency: A study of personality variables. *Psychology Crime and Law, 1,* 27–37.

Lynam, D. R. (1998). Early identification of the fledgling psychopath: Locating the psychopathic child in the current nomenclature. *Journal of Abnormal Psychology, 107,* 566–575.

Lynam, D., Moffitt, T., & Stouthamer-Loeber, M. (1993). Explaining the relation between IQ and delinquency: Class, race, test motivation, school failure or self-control? *Journal of Abnormal Psychology, 102,* 187–196.

Maszk, P., Eisenberg, N., & Guthrie, I. K. (1999). Relations of children's social status to their emotionality and regulation: A short-term longitudinal study. *Merrill-Palmer Quarterly, 45,* 468–492.

Matthews, K. A., Batson, C. D., Horn, J., & Rosenman, R. H. (1981). "Principles in his nature which interest him in the fortune of others . . .": The heritability of empathic concern for others. *Journal of Personality, 49,* 237–247.

McCormick, R. A., Dowd, E. T., Quirk, S., & Zegarra, J. H. (1998). The relationship of NEO-PI performance to coping styles, patterns of use, and triggers for use among substance abusers. *Addictive Behaviors, 23,* 497–507.

McGue, M., Bacon, S., & Lykken, D. T. (1993). Personality stability and change in early adulthood: A behavioral genetic analysis. *Developmental Psychology, 29,* 96–109.

Miech, R. A., Caspi, A., Moffitt, T. E., Wright, B. R. E., & Silva, P. A. (1999). Low socioeconomic status and mental disorders: A longitudinal study of selection and causation during young adulthood. *American Journal of Sociology, 104,* 1096–1131.

Miller, J. D., & Lynam, D. R. (2001). Structural models of personality and their relation to antisocial behavior: A meta-analytic review. *Criminology, 39,* 765–792.

Mitchell, S., & Rosa, P. (1981). Boyhood behaviour problems as precursors of criminality: A fifteen year study. *Journal of Child Psychology and Psychiatry, 22,* 19–33.

Moffitt, T. E. (1990). Juvenile delinquency and attention deficit disorder: Boys' developmental trajectories from age 3 to 15. *Child Development, 61,* 893–910.

Moffitt, T. E. (1993). Adolescence-limited and life-course-persistent antisocial behavior: A developmental taxonomy. *Psychological Review, 100,* 674–701.

Moffitt, T. E., Caspi, A., Dickson, N., Silva, P., & Stanton, W. (1996). Childhood-onset versus adolescent-onset antisocial conduct problems in males: Natural history from ages 3 to 18 years. *Development and Psychopathology, 8,* 399–424.

Moffitt, T. E., Caspi, A., Harrington, H., & Milne, B. J. (2002). Males on the life-course-persistent and adolescence-limited antisocial pathways: Follow-up at age 26 years. *Development and Psychopathology, 14*, 179–207.

Moffitt, T. E., Caspi, A., Rutter, M., & Silva, P. A. (2001). Sex differences in antisocial behaviour. Cambridge, UK: Cambridge University Press.

Moffitt, T. E., & Silva, P. A. (1988). IQ and delinquency: A direct test of the differential detection hypothesis. *Journal of Abnormal Psychology, 97*, 330–333.

Muris, P., Merckelbach, H., Schmidt, H., Gadet, B., & Bogie, N. (2001). Anxiety and depression as correlates of self-reported behavioural inhibition in normal adolescents. *Behaviour Research and Therapy, 39*, 1051–1061.

Nagin, D. S., Pogarsky, G., & Farrington, D. P. (1997). Adolescent mothers and the criminal behavior of their children. *Law and Society Review, 31*, 137–162.

Nagin D. S., & Tremblay, R. E. (1999). Trajectories of boys' physical aggression, opposition, and hyperactivity on the path to physically violent and non-violent delinquency. *Child Development, 70*, 1181–1196.

Nagin, D. S., & Tremblay, R. E. (2001). Parental and early childhood predictors of persistent physical aggression in boys from kindergarten to high school. *Archives of General Psychiatry, 58*, 389–394.

Newcomb, M. D., & McGee, L. (1991). Influence of sensation seeking on general deviance and specific problem behaviors from adolescence to young adulthood. *Journal of Personality and Social Psychology, 61*, 614–628.

Nigg, J. T., & Huang-Pollock, C. L. (2003). An early onset model of the role of executive functions and intelligence in conduct disorder/delinquency. In B. B. Lahey, T. Moffitt, & A. Caspi (Eds.), *Causes of conduct disorder and juvenile delinquency* (pp. 227–253). New York: Guilford Press.

O'Connor, T. G., Neiderhiser, J. M., Reiss, D., Hetherington, E. M., & Plomin, R. (1998). Genetic contributions to continuity, change, and co-occurrence of antisocial and depressive symptoms in adolescence. *Journal of Child Psychology and Psychiatry, 39*, 323–336.

Olson, S. L., Bates, J. E., Sandy, J. M., & Lanthier, R. (2000). Early developmental precursors of externalizing behavior in middle childhood and adolescence. *Journal of Abnormal Child Psychology, 28*, 119–133.

Pagani, L., Tremblay, R. E., Vitaro, F., Boulerice, B., & McDuff, P. (2001). Effects of grade retention on academic performance and behavioral development. *Development and Psychopathology, 13*, 297–315.

Patterson, G. R. (1982). *Coercive family interactions*. Eugene, OR: Castalia.

Patterson, G. R., Reid, J. B., & Dishion, T. J. (1992). *Antisocial boys*. Eugene, OR: Castalia.

Patterson, G. R., & Stoolmiller, M. (1991). Replications of a dual failure model for boys' depressed mood. *Journal of Consulting and Clinical Psychology, 59*, 491–498.

Pennington, B. F., & Ozonoff, S. (1996). Executive functions and developmental psychopathology. *Journal of Child Psychology and Psychiatry, 37*, 51–87.

Pedersen, N. L., Plomin, R., McClearn, G. E., & Friberg, L. (1988). Neuroticism, extraversion, and related traits in adult twins reared apart and reared together. *Journal of Personality and Social Psychology, 55*, 950–957.

Petrill, S. A., Saudino, K., Cherny, S. S., Emde, R. N., Hewitt, J. K., Fulker, D. W., et al. (1997). Exploring the genetic etiology of low general cognitive ability from 14 to 36 months. *Developmental Psychology, 33*, 544–548.

Phillips, K., & Matheny, A. P. (1997). Evidence for genetic influence on both cross-situation and situation-specific components of behavior. *Journal of Personality and Social Psychology, 73*, 129–138.

Pickles, A., Pickering, K., Simonoff, E., Silberg, J., Meyer, J., & Maes, H. (1998). Genetic "clocks" and "soft" events: A twin model for pubertal development and other recalled sequences of developmental milestones, transitions, or ages at onset. *Behavior Genetics, 28*, 243–253.

Plomin, R., DeFries, J. C., & Loehlin, J. C. (1977). Genotype-environment interaction and correlation in the analysis of human behavior. *Psychological Bulletin, 84*, 309–322.

Plomin, R., & Petrill, S. A. (1997). Genetics and intelligence: What's new? *Intelligence, 24*, 53–77.

Powell, G. E., & Stewart, R. A. (1983). The relationship of personality to antisocial and neurotic behaviours as observed by teachers. *Personality and Individual Differences, 4*, 97–100.

Presley, R., & Martin, R. P. (1994). Toward a structure of preschool dispositions: Factor structure of the Dispositions Assessment Battery for Children. *Journal of Personality, 62,* 415–448.

Quay, H. C., & Love, C. T. (1977). The effect of a juvenile diversion program on rearrests. *Criminal Justice and Behavior, 4,* 377–396.

Raine, A., Reynolds, C., Venables, P. H., Mednick, S. A., & Farrington, D. P. (1998). Fearlessness, stimulation-seeking, and large body size at age 3 years as early predispositions to childhood aggression at age 11 years. *Archives of General Psychiatry, 55,* 745–751.

Rhee, S. H. & Waldman, I. D. (2002). Genetic and environmental influences on antisocial behavior: A meta-analysis of twin and adoption studies. *Psychological Bulletin, 128,* 490–529.

Roberts, S., & Kendler, K. S. (1999). Neuroticism and self-esteem as indices of the vulnerability to major depression in women. *Psychological Medicine, 29,* 1101–1109.

Robinson, J. L., Kagan, J., Reznick, J. S., & Corley, R. (1992). The heritability of inhibited and uninhibited behavior: A twin study. *Developmental Psychology, 28,* 1030–1037.

Rose, R. J., Viken, R., J., Dick, D. M., Bates, J. E., Pulkkinen, L., & Kaprio, J. (2003). It does take a village: Nonfamilial environments and children's behavior. *Psychological Science, 14,* 273–277.

Rothbart, M. K., & Ahadi, S. A. (1994). Dispositions and the development of personality. *Journal of Abnormal Psychology, 103,* 55–66.

Rothbart, M. K., Ahadi, S. A., Hershey, K. L., & Fisher, P. (2001). Investigations of dispositions at three to seven years: The Children's Behavior Questionnaire. *Child Development, 72,* 1394–1408.

Rowe, D. C., & Osgood, D. W. (1984). Heredity and sociology theories of delinquency: A reconsideration. *American Sociological Review, 49,* 526–540.

Rowe, D. C., Vazsonyi, A. T., & Flannery, D. J. (1995). Sex differences in crime: Do means and within-sex variation have similar causes? *Journal of Research in Crime and Delinquency, 32,* 84–100.

Russo, M. F., Stokes, G. S., Lahey, B. B., Christ, M. A. G., McBurnett, K., Loeber, R., et al. (1993). A sensation seeking scale for children: Further refinement and psychometric development. *Journal of Psychopathology and Behavioral Assessment, 15,* 69–86.

Rutter, M. (1987). Dispositions, personality, and personality disorder. *British Journal of Psychiatry, 150,* 443–458.

Rutter, M. (1988). Epidemiological approaches to developmental psychopathology. *Archives of General Psychiatry, 45,* 486–495.

Rutter, M. L. (1997). Nature-nurture integration: The example of antisocial behavior. *American Psychologist, 52,* 390–398.

Rutter, M. (2003). Crucial paths from risk indicator to causal mechanism. In B. B. Lahey, T. E. Moffitt, & A. Caspi (Eds.), *Causes of conduct disorder and juvenile delinquency* (pp. 3–24). New York: Guilford Press.

Rutter, M., Dunn, J., Plomin, R., Siminoff, E., Pickles, A., Maughan, B., et al. (1997). Integrating nature and nuture: Implications of person-environment correlations and interactions for developmental psychopathology. *Development and Psychopathology, 9,* 335–364.

Rutter, M., Pickles, A., Murray, R., & Eaves, L. (2001). Testing hypotheses on specific environmental causal effects on behavior. *Psychological Bulletin, 127,* 291–324.

Sampson, R. J., & Laub, J. H. (1992). Crime and deviance. *Annual Review of Sociology, 18,* 63–84.

Sanson, A., Pedlow, R., Cann, W., Prior, M., & Oberklaid, F. (1996). Shyness ratings: Stability and correlates in early childhood. *International Journal of Behavioral Development, 19,* 705–724.

Sanson, A., & Prior, M. (1999). Dispositions and behavioral precursors to oppositional defiant disorder and conduct disorder. In H. Quay & A. Hogan (Eds.), *Handbook of the disruptive behavior disorders* (pp. 397–417). New York: Kluwer Academic/Plenum.

Sanson, A., Prior, M., & Kyrios, M. (1990). Contamination of measures in temperament research. *Merrill-Palmer Quarterly, 36,* 179–192.

Sanson, A., Smart, D., Prior, M., & Oberklaid, F. (1993). Precursors of hyperactivity and aggression. *Journal of the American Academy of Child and Adolescent Psychiatry, 32,* 1207–1216.

Saudino, K. J., Plomin, R., & DeFries, J. C. (1996). Tester-rated dispositions at 14, 20 and 24 months: Environmental change and genetic continuity. *British Journal of Developmental Psychology, 14,* 129–144.

Schmeck, K., & Poustka, F. (2001). Dispositions and disruptive behavior disorders. *Psychopathology, 4,* 159–163.

Schmitz, S., Fulker, D. W., Plomin, R., Zahn-Waxler, C., Emde, R. N., & DeFries, J. C. (1999). Dispositions and problem behavior during early childhood. *International Journal of Behavioral Development, 23,* 333–355.

Schwartz, C. E., Snidman, N., & Kagan, J. (1996). Early childhood dispositions as a determinant of externalizing behavior in adolescence. *Development and Psychopathology, 8,* 527–537.

Schwartz, C. E., Snidman, N., & Kagan, J. (1999). Adolescent social anxiety as an outcome of inhibited temperament in childhood. *Journal of the American Academy of Child and Adolescent Psychiatry, 38,* 1008–1015.

Seguin, J. R., Boulerice, B., Harden, P. W., Tremblay, R. E., & Pihl, R. O. (1999). Executive functions and physical aggression after controlling for attention deficit hyperactivity disorder, general memory and IQ. *Journal of Child Psychology and Psychiatry, 40,* 1197–1208.

Serbin, L. A., Moskowitz, D. S., Schwartzman, A. E., & Ledingham, J. E. (1991). Aggressive, withdrawn, and aggressive/withdrawn children in adolescence: Into the next generation. In D. J. Pepler & K. H. Rubin (Eds.), *The development and treatment of childhood aggression.* Hillsdale, NJ: Erlbaum.

Shaw, D. S., Gilliom, M., Ingoldsby, E. M., & Nagin, D. S. (2003). Trajectories leading to school-age conduct problems. *Developmental Psychology, 39,* 189–200.

Shiner, R. L., Masten, A. S., & Tellegen, A. (2002). A developmental perspective on personality in emerging adulthood: Childhood antecedents and concurrent adaptation. *Journal of Personality and Social Psychology, 83,* 1165–1177.

Silberg, J. L., Rutter, M., Meyer, J., Maes, H., Hewitt, J., Siminoff, E., et al. (1996). Genetic and environmental influences on the covariation between hyperactivity and conduct disturbance in juvenile twins. *Journal of Child Psychology and Psychiatry, 37,* 803–816.

Silverthorn, P., & Frick, P. J. (1999). Developmental pathways to antisocial behavior: The delayed-onset pathway in girls. *Development and Psychopathology, 11,* 101–126.

Silverthorn, P., Frick, P. J., & Reynolds, R. (2001). Timing of onset and correlates of severe conduct problems in adjudicated girls and boys. *Journal of Psychopathology and Behavioral Assessment, 23,* 171–181.

Snyder, J., Reid, J., & Patterson, G. (2003). A social learning model of child and adolescent antisocial behavior. In B. B. Lahey, T. Moffitt, & A. Caspi (Eds.), *Causes of conduct disorder and juvenile delinquency.* New York: Guilford Press.

Sparks, R., Ganschow, L., & Thomas, A. (1996). Role of intelligence tests in speech/language referrals. *Perceptual and Motor Skills, 83,* 195–204.

Stattin, H. & Klackenberg-Larsson, I. (1993). Early language and intelligence development and their relationship to future criminal behavior. *Journal of Abnormal Psychology 102,* 369–378.

Tellegen, A. (1982). *Brief manual for the Multidimensional Personality Questionnaire.* Minneapolis: University of Minnesota.

Tellegen, A., Lykken, D. T., Bouchard, T. J., Wilcox, K. J., Segal, N. L. & Rich, S. (1988). Personality similarity in twins reared apart and together. *Journal of Personality and Social Psychology, 54,* 1031–1039.

Thapar, A., Harrington, R., & McGuffin, P. (2001). Examining the comorbidity of ADHD-related behaviours and conduct problems using a twin study design. *British Journal of Psychiatry, 179,* 224–229.

Thornberry, T. P., Krohn, M. D., Lizotte, A. J., & Chard-Wierschem, D. (1993). The role of juvenile gangs in facilitating delinquent behavior. *Journal of Research in Crime and Delinquency, 30,* 55–87.

Tranah, T., Harnett, P., & Yule, W. (1998). Conduct disorder and personality. *Personality and Individual Differences, 24,* 741–745.

Tremblay, R. E. (2000). The development of aggressive behaviour during childhood: What have we learned in the past century? *International Journal of Behavioral Development, 24,* 129–141.

Tremblay, R. E., Boulerice, B., Harden, P. W., McDuff, P., Perusse, D., Pihl, R. O., et al. (1996). Do children in Canada become more aggressive as they approach adolescence? In M. Cappe & I. Fellegi (Eds.), *Growing up in Canada.* Ottawa: Statistics Canada.

Tremblay, R. E., Pihl, R. O., Vitaro, F., & Dobkin, P. L. (1994). Predicting early onset of male antisocial behavior from preschool behavior. *Archives of General Psychiatry, 51,* 732–739.

Van Kammen, W.. & Loeber, R. (1994). Are fluctuations in delinquent activities related to the onset and offset in juvenile illegal drug use and drug dealing? *Journal of Drug Issues, 24,* 9–24.

Wahler, R. G., & Hann, D. M. (1987). An interbehavioral approach to clinical child psychology: Toward an understanding of troubled families. In D. H. Ruben & D. J. Delpratto (Eds.), *New ideas in therapy: Introduction to an interdisciplinary approach*. New York: Greenwood Press.

Wakschlag, L. S., Gordon, R. A., Lahey, B. B., Loeber, R., Green, S. M., & Leventhal, B. L. (2000). Maternal age at first birth and boys' risk for conduct disorder. *Journal of Research on Adolescence, 10*, 417–441.

Waldman, I. D., Rhee, S. H., Levy, F., & Hay, D. A. (2001). Genetic and environmental influences on the covariation among symptoms of attention deficit hyperactivity disorder, oppositional defiant disorder, and conduct disorder. In D. A. Hay & F. Levy (Eds.), *Attention, genes, and ADHD*. Hilsdale, NJ: Erlbaum.

Waldman, I. D., Van Hulle, C. A., Applegate, B., Pardini, D., Frick, P. J., & Lahey, B. B. (2007). Genetic influences on youth conduct disorder are mediated largely through socioemotional dispositions relevant to callous-unemotional traits. Manuscript under review.

Waschbusch, D. A. (2002). A meta-analytic examination of comorbid hyperactive-impulsive-attention problems and conduct problems. *Psychological Bulletin, 128*, 118–150.

Watson, D., Clark, L. A., & Tellegen, A. (1988). Development and validation of brief measures of positive and negative affect: The PANAS scales. *Journal of Personality and Social Psychology, 54*, 1063–1070.

Wikström, P.-O. H., & Sampson, R. J. (2003). Social mechanisms of community influences on crime and pathways in criminality. In B. B. Lahey, T. E. Moffitt, & A. Caspi (Eds.), *Causes of conduct disorder and juvenile delinquency* (pp. 118–148). New York: Guilford Press.

Wills, T. A., Sandy, J. M., & Yaeger, A. (2000). Dispositions and adolescent substance use: An epigenetic approach to risk and protection. *Journal of Personality, 68*, 1127–1151.

Zahn-Waxler, C., Robinson, J. L., & Emde, R. N. (1992). The development of empathy in twins. *Developmental Psychology, 28*, 1038–1047.

Zoccolillo, M. (1992). Co-occurrence of conduct disorder and its adult outcomes with depressive and anxiety disorders: A review. *Journal of the American Academy of Child and Adolescent Psychiatry, 31*, 547–556.

Zuckerman, M. (1996). The psychobiological model for impulsive unsocialized sensation seeking: A comparative approach. *Neuropsychobiology, 34*, 125–129.

Zuckerman, M., Kuhlman, D. M., Joireman, J., Teta, P., & Kraft, M. (1993). A comparison of three structural models for personality: The big three, the big five, and the alternative five. *Journal of Personality and Social Psychology, 65*, 757–768.

CHAPTER 13

Personality and Violence: The Unifying Role of Structural Models of Personality

Daniel M. Blonigen and Robert F. Krueger

Introduction

Since the rejuvenation of personality research in the 1980s, a compelling body of evidence has emerged to suggest that personality traits represent important psychological constructs that have implications for a host of problematic behaviors with high cost to society (e.g., Caspi et al., 1997; Krueger, Caspi, & Moffitt, 2000). Violence is a compelling example of such behavior. Most investigations in the personality-violence literature, however, have tended to focus on the role of personality disorders in this relationship. Such studies have typically sampled from clinical or forensic populations and have largely concluded that personality disorders represent significant clinical risk factors for violent and aggressive behavior (e.g., Egan, Austin, Elliot, Patel, & Charlesworth, 2003; Hart, Dutton, & Newlove, 1993; Krakowski, Volavka, & Brizer, 1986; Litwack & Schlesinger, 1987; Yarvis, 1990). Despite the significance of these findings, studies based on such extreme populations are not suited to document the general relationship between personality and violence in the population at large. More importantly, the categorical model of personality disorders as defined by the *Diagnostic and Statistical Manual of Mental Disorders* (DSM; American Psychiatric Association [APA], 1980, 1987, 1994) has been heavily criticized over the last few decades because of its lack of validity relative to dimensional models of personality (cf. Grove & Tellegen, 1991; Trull & Durrett, 2005; Widiger, 1993). In accordance with Widiger and Trull (1994), we advocate for more systematic investigations of personality and violence using theoretically and empirically validated structural models of personality. Structural models represent hierarchically organized systems of quantitatively distributed personality traits. Personality traits, inferred from the systematic co-variation among sets of behaviors, form the building blocks of structural models that comprise empirically derived nomological networks (see Watson, Clark, & Harkness, 1994, for a review of personality traits and structural models).

There are several advantages to linking violence and aggression within an established structural framework of individual differences (cf. Watson et al., 1994). Broadly, placing violent behavior within this framework can help organize and interpret the range of findings that surface across disparate lines of research. As such, the use of structural models may improve communication among researchers who likely employ a variety of personality measures in their research on violence. Moreover, it can be argued that locating violence within a structural framework of normal-range personality allows scholars to link violent behavior within an established nomological network. For example, a body of research has been conducted on both the etiology (e.g., Tellegen et al., 1988) and development (e.g., Roberts, Caspi, & Moffitt, 2001) of normal personality. Findings from this literature could, in theory, be extended to the literature on violence and aggression, thereby providing an empirical guide to research on the etiology and development of such destructive behavior. In other words, structural models offer a broader and more clearly delineated theoretical framework with which to interpret the current body of knowledge on violence and aggression.

In this chapter, we review the research literature on personality and violence from the standpoint of both personality disorders and structural models of personality. We begin with a brief review of the empirical literature on personality disorders and violence. In this section we note some of the more salient findings from this literature as well as highlight inconsistent findings requiring further exploration. Additionally, we discuss a classification system recently proposed in this literature (Nestor, 2002), which specifies key dimensions of personality that may underlie associations between certain mental disorders and violent behavior. From there, we attempt to place these previous findings within a broader context by addressing the importance of studying violence within a structural framework of normal-range personality and through the use of community-epidemiological samples. Two issues are highlighted in this section.

First, we emphasize how an examination of violence within a structural framework reveals both common and unique associations with other problem behaviors and disinhibitory forms of psychopathology (cf. Krueger, 2002). Second, using the example of psychopathic personality (psychopathy), we discuss the utility of structural models to help disentangle the key personality dimensions underlying relationships between certain personality disorders and violence. Finally, we end by discussing some broader issues and future directions with respect to this approach.

Personality Disorders and Violence: Findings and Critique

To date, psychological inquiry on aggression and violence has been primarily investigated from the standpoint of which DSM-defined mental disorders are related to – or can predict most strongly – violent behavior (Arsenault, Moffitt, Caspi, Taylor, & Silva, 2000; Hodgins, Mednick, Brennan, Schulsinger, & Engberg, 1996; Link, Andrews, & Cullen, 1992; Swanson, Borum, Swartz, & Monahan, 1996; Tiihonen, Isohanni, Rasanen, Koiranen, & Moring, 1997). Given this emphasis on DSM-defined mental disorders, it is perhaps not surprising that associations between personality and violence have typically been examined at the pathological level (i.e., with reference to the presence versus the absence of personality disorder diagnoses). Although a variety of definitions, conceptual approaches, and classification schemes have been proposed for abnormal or disordered personality (see Livesley & Jang, 2000, for a review), the DSM categorical model of personality disorders has received the most attention and investigation in the prediction of violence. In this model, personality disorders are represented by sets of diagnostic criteria that are rationally divided into categorical diagnoses and organized into three non-empirically based clusters: Cluster A (Odd or Eccentric), Cluster B (Dramatic, Emotional, or Erratic), and Cluster C (Anxious or Fearful).

The preponderance of evidence suggests that personality disorders represent clinical risk factors for violent behavior among mentally disordered individuals (e.g., Krakowski et al., 1986; Litwack & Schlesinger, 1987), domestic batterers (Hart et al., 1993), and criminal offenders (Egan et al., 2003; Yarvis, 1990). In spite of these findings, some scholars (e.g., Widiger & Trull, 1994) have raised concerns that such investigations typically fail to control for other comorbid psychopathological syndromes associated with violence. In other words, aggression may not be specific to personality pathology per se, but may be characteristic of psychopathology in general. Despite this methodological criticism, many of these relations between personality disorders and violence remain even after controlling for other comorbid conditions (e.g., Berman, Fallon, & Coccaro, 1998; Johnson et al., 2000; Skeem & Mulvey, 2001).

Although many personality disorders have been linked to violence and aggression (see Ekselius, Hetta, & von Knorring, 1994), the two disorders receiving the most attention are Antisocial Personality Disorder (APD) and Borderline Personality Disorder (BPD). Associations between APD and violence are well documented (e.g., Brownstone & Swaminath, 1989; Eronen, Hakola, & Tiihonen, 1997; Porter & Woodworth, 2006; Robins, Tipp, & Przybeck, 1991). Moreover, this link does not appear to be limited to forensic or psychiatric populations as several epidemiological studies have reported a diagnosis of APD to be a strong risk factor for violence toward both family members and strangers (e.g., Berman et al., 1998; Bland & Orn, 1986; Robins et al., 1991). This notwithstanding, one could argue that these findings are tautological (cf. Krakowski et al., 1986), given that the diagnostic criteria for APD include a history of repeated physical fights and assaults (APA, 1980, 1987, 1994).

BPD represents another focal construct in the study of the relationship between personality disorders and violence. Fits of intense and impulsive rage have been identified in the clinical literature describing this disorder (Kernberg, 1984) and also represent one of the criteria of the diagnosis itself (APA, 1980, 1987, 1994). Studies investigating the relationship between BPD and violence directed toward one's self (e.g., suicide) typically observe greater symptoms of BPD among suicide victims than controls, as well as an increased tendency toward impulsive violence in borderline individuals (Brent et al., 1994; Brodsky et al., 1997; Edwards et al., 2003). Research on the relationship between BPD and violence directed toward others, however, has been less consistent. Studies of psychiatric populations (Coccaro, Berman, & Kavoussi, 1997; Else, Wonderlich, Beatty, Christie, & Staton, 1993; Snyder, Pitts, & Pokorny, 1986; Windle & Windle, 1995) have found significant associations between borderline symptomatology and physical violence. Similarly, Raine (1993) found a strong linear association between dimensional ratings of borderline personality traits and extreme forms of violence (i.e., murder) in a sample of prisoners. In contrast, two community-epidemiological studies (Berman et al., 1998; Johnson et al., 2000) failed to find any relationship between BPD and violence after controlling for other personality disorder symptoms. Thus, prior findings of a specific relationship between BPD and violence may instead be due to other co-occurring personality disorders. Alternatively, as Berman et al. (1993) and Johnson et al. (2000) point out, a link between BPD and violence may only manifest in extremely pathological populations (i.e., clinical and forensic populations) and, therefore, may not be as evident in their investigations with community samples.

Despite the wealth of evidence linking personality disorders and violence, this literature has not been without significant criticisms (see Berman et al., 1998; Widiger & Trull, 1994). One of the more salient issues is that most studies have predominantly used clinical and forensic samples. An emphasis on these populations may be somewhat misleading, given that such samples are likely unrepresentative of the general population with respect to several important risk factors (e.g., socioeconomic status [SES], IQ, legal problems) and may differ substantially from community samples in terms of their variance on relevant dimensions of personality. Two recent investigations addressed this issue by investigating personality disorders and violence within community-epidemiological samples.

Berman and colleagues (1998) used research volunteers from the community to examine relations between personality disorders and violence in the general population. After controlling for several confounding variables (i.e., gender, substance use, mood disorders), seven personality disorders – APD, BPD, histrionic, narcissistic, paranoid, passive-aggressive, schizoid (negatively) – were predictive of violent behavior. Moreover, after controlling for coexisting symptoms of APD and BPD, which are often comorbid with other personality disorders and contain specific diagnostic criteria pertaining to aggression, only paranoid and passive-aggressive personality disorders remained uniquely predictive of violent behavior. Thus, paranoid and passive-aggressive symptoms appear to provide additional information above and beyond other known predictors of violence. Because of weak evidence regarding its validity, passive-aggressive personality disorder has since been removed from the most recent edition of the DSM (APA, 1994). However, paranoid personality disorder and its associated cognitive style of suspiciousness and heightened sensitivity to perceived threats and provocation remain intriguing areas of future investigation with respect to violence – an issue we return to later.

In a similar investigation, Johnson and colleagues (2000) used a longitudinal-community sample to examine the degree to which personality disorders in adolescence are associated with elevated risk for violent behavior in later adulthood. Similar to Berman et al. (1998), these investigators controlled for several confounding variables (i.e., age, gender, SES, co-occurring Axis I and II disorders, parental psychopathology). In terms of specific personality disorders, symptoms of paranoid and passive-aggressive personality disorders, as well as

symptoms of narcissistic personality disorder, were uniquely predictive of violence in adulthood. These results are fairly consistent with Berman and colleagues (1998) and illustrate the importance of a paranoid cognitive style to violent and aggressive behavior.

Another important criticism in the personality disorder and violence literature is the lack of an empirically derived classification scheme or structural model in which to interpret the relevant findings. Since the inception of DSM-III (APA, 1980), several reviews have cogently documented the extensive limitations inherent in the categorical and rationally derived diagnostic system of the DSM personality disorders (Costa & McCrae, 2002; Widiger, 1993; see also Widiger & Trull, 1994, for relevant criticisms in the personality-violence literature). Briefly, the DSM model imposes categorical dichotomies between the presence and absence of a personality disorder, an approach incompatible with extensive research suggesting that a dimensional model better accounts for variation in both normal and abnormal personality (cf. Trull & Durrett, 2005). As well, DSM personality disorder diagnoses demonstrate extremely high comorbidity (e.g., Trull & McCrae, 2002), reflecting in part the fact that these disorders are underpinned by multiple dimensions that cut across many of these putatively distinct categories (Tellegen, 1993; Trull & Durrett, 2005).

Nestor (2002) recently provided an alternative model in his review of the literature on mental disorders and violence. Specifically, Nestor identifies four fundamental personality dimensions, which he describes as underlying associations between certain mental disorders and violence: *impulse control, affect regulation, threatened egotism (narcissism)*, and a *paranoid cognitive personality style*.

Broadly, Nestor comments that personality dimensions of impulse control and affect regulation play a role in virtually all mental disorders associated with violence, particularly substance use disorders and several of the Cluster B personality disorders, such as APD and BPD. Thus, at a broad level and across a range of psychopathology, violent and aggressive behavior is, to a certain degree, a reflection of underlying personality dimensions marked by an inability to modulate or inhibit one's emotions and/or actions.

In contrast to these first two personality dimensions, Nestor posits that threatened egotism may have a more specific role in associations between personality disorders and violence. In a series of studies by Baumeister and colleagues (see Baumeister, Smart, & Boden, 1996 for a review), subjects scoring highest on the Narcissistic Personality Inventory (Raskin & Terry, 1988) responded with the strongest levels of aggression in a laboratory paradigm after having received negative evaluations on essays they wrote prior to the laboratory design. The implication is that negative evaluations represent a form of narcissistic injury that, in turn, may result in an increased likelihood of aggression.

Last, Nestor proposes that a paranoid cognitive personality style may be an important clinical risk factor for violence among individuals with schizophrenia-spectrum disorders. A paranoid cognitive style may be described as a tendency to feel particularly alienated from and suspicious of others and to view the world as especially hostile and threatening. Among the studies cited, an investigation by Arsenault et al. (2000) suggests that a tendency to perceive threat, as measured via the Alienation scale of the Multidimensional Personality Questionnaire (MPQ; Tellegen, in press), at 18 was highly predictive of violent behavior among schizophrenia-spectrum patients at age 21. Such findings are remarkably consistent with the aforementioned studies by Berman et al. (1998) and Johnson et al. (2000) in which paranoid personality disorder symptoms were uniquely predictive of violent behavior even after controlling for comorbid psychopathology. Collectively, such studies imply that a heightened sensitivity to expect threat and to feel alienated from those around you may represent a quantitatively distributed personality trait with strong ties to violence and aggression.

Nestor's efforts to delineate the fundamental personality dimensions underlying associations between mental disorders and violence offer a substantial improvement over the categorical diagnoses from the DSM. Moreover, this armchair taxonomy establishes a link between the aforementioned personality disorders and violence literature by specifying key individual differences dimensions most relevant to violence. Nevertheless, Nestor's (2002) review was primarily focused on personality and violence within the context of mental disorders and, therefore, did not explicitly address the place of violence and aggression within a structural framework of personality or in the population at large. Building on the aforementioned literature, we now turn to structural models as a means of examining links between normal-range personality and violence within community-epidemiological samples.

Structural Models of Personality Traits: Definition and Organization

Structural models of personality have undergone extensive empirical delineation and comprise a rich nomological network that can help organize, interpret, and integrate the range of research findings on the study of personality and violence. For example, although such measures as the Buss-Durkee Hostility Inventory (Buss & Durkee, 1957), the State-Trait Anger Scale (Spielberger et al., 1985), or the Cook-Medley Hostility Inventory (Cook & Medley, 1954) are all reported to be indices of aggression, given that they all are derived from distinct theoretical frameworks, it is somewhat unclear as to how the findings from one measure relate to the findings from another measure. A structural approach would aid in the translation of findings from one study to the next and can ultimately help guide theories and hypotheses on the relationship between personality and violence.

In contrast to the categorical disorders within DSM-Axis II, structural models of personality are based largely on the concept of a trait. Personality traits are character-ized as internal dispositions and tenden-cies to behave, think, and feel in certain consistent ways (Kenrick & Funder, 1988; Tellegen, 1991). Although the notion of traits as real and important was once hotly debated (cf. Mischel, 1968), a wealth of evidence has since demonstrated that argu-ments against their existence or basis in real-ity are unfounded given the data (Kenrick & Funder, 1988). Our conceptual framework regarding personality derives from the writ-ings of Tellegen (1991) and Watson et al. (1994). The overarching premise underlying the theoretical conceptualizations of these scholars is the notion that personality traits are *real* and represent "inferred, relatively enduring psychobiological structures under-lying an extended family of behavioral dis-positions" (Tellegen, 1991, p. 13). In his explication of the nature of personality, Tellegen echoes the sentiments of Paul Meehl (1986) in asserting that traits are structures whose existence is inferred from *systematic co-variation* among observed mea-sures. In essence, personality traits represent a latent entity (source trait) that can explain why certain observable behaviors co-vary. Watson et al. (1994) approach these con-cepts from the standpoint of constructive realism in asserting that traits are not merely "convenient summary labels for observed consistencies in behavior" (p. 19), but instead represent the fundamental causal processes that can explain observed consis-tencies inferred under this trait structure. Furthermore, traits are inherently explana-tory and, thus, can provide surplus meaning by predicting behaviors above and beyond the inferred structure of the trait itself. In contrast to the categorical model of the DSM personality disorders, structural mod-els are posited as consisting of continuously distributed *dimensions* of personality traits. That is, variation with respect to certain trait constructs is conceptualized as lying along a continuum such that individual differences in personality are a matter of degree rather than kind.

Related to the concept of systematic co-variation and central to the conceptual basis of a structural model is the notion that per-sonality traits are organized hierarchically and relate to one another in a system-atic fashion (cf. Harkness, 1992). Specif-ically, latent traits, inferred from correla-tions among observed measures, co-vary with other similar traits to form broader, high-order trait constructs (i.e., global fac-tors). Moreover, this hierarchical structure provides a comprehensive assessment of per-sonality by providing both breadth of cover-age (bandwidth) at a higher-order level, as well as detailed coverage (fidelity) via lower-order primary traits. This represents a key advantage of structural models in that they allow for the investigation of personality in relation to other psychologically relevant phenomena (e.g., violence) at both broad and fine-grained levels of analysis. Although several hierarchical models have been pro-posed within the personality literature (i.e., the Big 3, 4, or 5 models), structural mod-els of both normal and abnormal personality are essentially integrated and appear to be distinct only in terms of their emphasis with respect to certain levels of the trait hierarchy (Markon, Krueger, & Watson, 2005).

In the remainder of this chapter, we high-light contemporary findings using structural models to investigate links between person-ality and violence. Two issues are empha-sized. First, through the comprehensive coverage afforded by structural models, we discuss consistent patterns arising from epi-demiological research that suggests that vio-lence is linked to a broad dimension of exter-nalizing psychopathology, but that this link may be especially strong with alienation, a specific facet of the externalizing dimension. Second, previous studies have established links between several personality disorders and violent tendencies. We propose that the specific mechanisms underlying these associ-ations can be disentangled and better under-stood through the use of structural trait models. For example, psychopathy is a per-sonality disorder reflecting a deviant and manipulative interpersonal style and lack of emotional depth that has been consistently linked to violent and aggressive behavior (see Hare, 1996; Salekin, Rogers, & Sewell,

1996). However, some disagreement exists as to which aspects of the syndrome are most important in this relationship. We outline a recent line of research investigating psychopathy via structural models of personality and illustrate how this approach can help explicate the underlying trait dimensions in the relationship between psychopathy and violence.

Personality and Violence Within a Structural Framework: Broad Relations With the Externalizing Spectrum

Over the past decade or so, several studies have sought to identify the personological (i.e., personality) correlates of a host of problematic and deviant behaviors (e.g., violence) that exact a heavy burden on society. Krueger and colleagues (1994) investigated relationships between personality and crime and delinquency in an 18-year-old cohort of men and women drawn from the Dunedin (New Zealand) Multidisciplinary Health and Development Study (DMHDS) – a longitudinal- epidemiological study. They assessed criminal behavior using several independent data sources including self- and informant reports as well as official records based on police contacts and court convictions. Personality was assessed via the Multidimensional Personality Questionnaire (MPQ; Tellegen, in press), a comprehensive assessment of normal personality that embodies a structural model of individual differences. The MPQ consists of 11 primary scales that cohere into three relatively independent higher-order factors: Positive Emotionality (PEM), a tendency to experience positive emotions resulting from achievement and active engagement in one's social environment; Negative Emotionality (NEM), a propensity to experience aversive emotional states related to anxiety, anger, and alienation; and Constraint (CON), a propensity for cautious and restrained behavior reflected in the avoidance of dangerous activities and endorsement of social norms. Across all measures

of crime and delinquency, and for both men and women, NEM and its respective lower-order subfacets revealed positive relations with crime and delinquency, whereas CON and its lower-order subfacets were negatively related to these indices. Thus, individuals who exhibit criminal and delinquent behavior tend to be more aggressive and reactive to stress, feel alienated from others, and are likely to have difficulty demonstrating impulse control. Notably, this MPQ profile has emerged as a robust predictor of criminal and antisocial behavior across other large epidemiological investigations (e.g., Elkins, Iacono, Doyle, & McGue, 1997; Krueger, Hicks, & McGue, 2001; Moffitt, Caspi, Silva, & Stouthamer-Loeber, 1995). For example, Elkins et al. (1997) report high NEM and low CON as personality correlates of *persistent* antisocial behavior; a developmental form of deviance characterized by disproportionately higher rates of violent offending (Elliot, Huizinga, & Morse, 1986; Moffitt, Mednick, & Gabrielli, 1989).

Although the studies by Krueger et al. (1994) and Elkins et al. (1997) did not directly investigate the personality correlates of violent or aggressive behavior per se, other studies have observed a similar personality profile with respect to violent crime. Using the longitudinal design of the DMHDS, Henry, Caspi, Moffitt, and Silva (1996) examined the degree to which childhood temperament at age 3 could predict convictions for violent and nonviolent criminal offenses at age 18. Results revealed that individuals convicted for violent (but not nonviolent) offenses were significantly predicted by higher scores on *Lack of Control*, a temperamental dimension reflecting impulse control deficits and a reduced threshold for experiencing unpleasant negative emotions. Although Lack of Control was not explicitly derived from a structural model, it is linked descriptively and empirically to the personality profile in the aforementioned studies of crime and delinquency (i.e., high NEM, low CON).

In a related vein, yet geared toward public-health-related concerns, Caspi and colleagues (1997) sought to identify the personality profiles associated with a host of heath-risk behaviors including alcohol abuse, violent crime (operationalized via court convictions), unsafe sexual behavior, and dangerous driving habits. Using the MPQ to locate these health-risk behaviors within a structural model of personality, results revealed a substantial convergence across the personality profiles of these behaviors. Specifically, all behaviors including violent crime were marked consistently and significantly by lower scores on control, traditionalism, and harm avoidance (primary subfacets of CON); lower social closeness (a subfacet of PEM); and elevated scores on aggression (a subfacet of NEM). Thus, individuals who engage in a host of problem behaviors ranging from alcohol use and unsafe sexual practices to antisocial behavior and violent crime can be described in similar personological terms as lacking in impulse control and traditional values, as well as having a heightened propensity to negative affect.

In sum, the aforementioned studies on crime, delinquency, and a range of health-risk behaviors all converge on the same personality profile marked by a heightened sensitivity to experience unpleasant emotional states (i.e., high NEM) and a tendency toward impulsive and disinhibited behavior (i.e., low CON). Interestingly, this profile mirrors the personality correlates of the externalizing dimension of psychopathology (Krueger, 1999), a broad dimension of systematic co-variation among child and adult antisocial behavior and substance abuse. This broad factor has been validated and replicated in both the child (Achenbach & Edelbrock, 1984) and adult psychopathology literatures (Krueger, 1999; Krueger, Caspi, Moffitt, & Silva, 1998) and has been posited to explain the high degree of comorbidity among common forms of disinhibitory psychopathology. In essence, rather than representing discrete, categorical phenomena, common DSM disorders defined by antisocial behavior and substance abuse represent indicators of a latent psychopathological dimension marked by disinhibition. Recent direct comparisons of dimensional and categorical accounts of the co-occurrence of these disorders show a better fit for a dimensional as opposed to a categorical model (Krueger, Markon, Patrick, & Iacono, 2005; Markon & Krueger, 2005). In terms of its personality correlates, several investigations (Krueger, 1999, 2002; Krueger, McGue, & Iacono, 2000; Krueger et al., 2002) have established CON and NEM as broad personality constructs linked to this dimension of disinhibition. In light of this finding, the observed convergence in personality profiles across violence, general crime, substance dependence, and other problem behaviors suggests that violence may be construed as an indicator of this latent externalizing vulnerability. In other words, violent behavior on a broad level represents a manifestation of a core psychopathological vulnerability to a spectrum of disorders marked by disinhibition.

Personality and Violence: The Specificity of Negative Emotionality and Alienation

With respect to this broad association with externalizing, other findings based on structural models suggest that violence per se (as opposed to antisocial behavior in the broad sense) may be selectively linked to only certain personality correlates of the externalizing spectrum. Moffitt, Krueger, Caspi, and Fagan (2000) used members from the DMHDS to investigate whether violence (i.e., domestic abuse) can be differentiated from general crime on the basis of personality. Using MPQ data at age 18 and self-reported partner abuse and general criminal offending data at age 21, they found high NEM as a risk factor for both domestic violence and general crime, whereas low self-control (i.e., low CON) was only related to general crime. These findings reveal important personological links between violence and the externalizing dimension in that violence (specifically domestic abuse) may be defined more prominently by high negative affect, rather than impulse control deficits per se.

Verona, Patrick, and Lang (2002) employed a laboratory paradigm involving manipulations of stress and frustration to examine whether individual differences in negative affect moderate aggressive behavior. Using threat of aversive air blasts as a means of priming aggressive behavior, the authors examined whether individuals in the upper versus the lower quartile on the NEM factor of the MPQ would demonstrate increased aggressive responses during periods of threat. As predicted, high NEM participants were observed as being more aggressive throughout the testing session in terms of delivering longer and more intense shocks during both threat and safe conditions. In conjunction with various physiological indices, the results from this investigation suggest that individuals high on NEM display a heightened sensitivity to stress and provocation, which manifests as an increased probability of more intense acts of aggression. Moreover, the results broadly tie together research from cognitive neuroscience that posits that emotional states of fear, anxiety, and anger are undergirded by a common defensive system (Lang, Bradley, & Cuthbert, 1990) and are related to connections among individual differences in hostility, stress reactivity, and sensitivity to threat cues. In combination with the work of Moffitt and colleagues (2000), these findings highlight the prominence of NEM as a component of externalizing with specific relations to aggression and violence.

In delving further into the role of NEM, several studies point toward alienation as a key subfacet of NEM with the most specific association with violence. Returning to the investigation by Caspi et al. (1997) on the personality correlates of health-risk behaviors, a closer inspection of each of these behaviors reveals that alienation ($d = 1.01$) and aggression ($d = 1.44$) were the subfacets of NEM associated most strongly with violent crime. However, in contrast to aggression, which was highly predictive of all health-risk behaviors measured in this study, alienation was selectively linked to violent crime, while relating to the other health-risk behaviors either negligibly or

to a significantly smaller degree. Thus, the general convergence across the personality profiles of these health-risk behaviors is not entirely uniform, as violence may be uniquely marked by a tendency to be suspicious, distrustful, and hypersensitive to threat cues.

Other investigations further highlight this unique relationship between alienation and violence, which may exist above and beyond other known correlates of violent behavior. Jockin, Arvey, and McGue (2001) examined several predictors of an increasingly common phenomenon described as workplace aggression and conflict. In their review of the literature, the authors highlight the role of perceived victimization (i.e., a suspicion of hostile intent or threat from others) as an important psychological factor associated with violence and aggression. Although they acknowledge past antisocial behavior, alcohol abuse, and personality traits, such as low agreeableness (e.g., aggression) and high neuroticism, as established predictors of violence, Jockin and colleagues hypothesize that these relationships would be stronger among individuals high on perceived victimization, operationalized as scores on MPQ-Alienation. The findings were largely consistent with this moderational hypothesis. Although antisocial behavior, substance abuse, and several personality scales were all predictive of workplace aggression, these relationships were strengthened when accompanied by high scores on alienation. Interestingly, these findings are consistent with those of Arsenault and colleagues (2000) in which MPQ-Alienation was found to be highly predictive of violent behavior among a community sample of psychotic patients. Moreover, both studies are in accordance with previously noted findings in which symptoms of paranoid personality disorder were uniquely predictive of violence (e.g., Berman et al., 1998; Johnson et al., 2000). Thus, when examined within a structural framework of personality, alienation may represent an individual differences dimension that links violence across both the normal and abnormal range of personality variation.

On the whole, the comprehensive assessment afforded by structural models of personality yields several intriguing findings with respect to the relationship between personality and violence. Specifically, the personological convergence across a range of deviant and health-risk behaviors (i.e., high NEM and low CON) suggests that violence is to some degree an indicator of a broad spectrum of psychopathology defined by disinhibition (i.e., externalizing). However, further examination of the lower-order primary scales of these structural models reveals that violence is personologically distinct from other externalizing behavior in that it may be uniquely driven by individual differences in alienation. That is, alienation may represent a specific facet of externalizing with a unique relationship to violence over and above the general influence of the broad externalizing factor. These personality dimensions described in our review of structural models of personality and violence bear a striking resemblance to several theories in the literature. In particular, a personality profile marked by high NEM and low CON is congruent with the personality dimensions of *affect regulation* and *impulse control* described by Nestor (2002). As well, findings regarding the specificity of alienation to violence align closely with Nestor's assertion that a *paranoid cognitive personality style* may underlie relations between violence and psychotic-spectrum disorders. Furthermore, the specificity of alienation in the present context echoes the work of Dodge and colleagues (e.g., Dodge, Pettit, Bates, & Valente, 1995) in which it is hypothesized that aggressive behavior in childhood manifests in part from a hostile attributional bias regarding the intentions of others. Despite these similarities, such theories were not delineated within a structural model. Therefore, it is not entirely clear how these personality styles relate to one another or operate in concert to influence violence and aggression.

The structural approach espoused in this chapter offers a means of explicitly testing the unique role of alienation and hostile attribution in violent and aggressive behav-

ior. For example, given the ability of structural models to capture both bandwidth and fidelity in their assessment of personality, one may assess whether individual differences in alienation or hostile attribution account for unique variance in violent and aggressive behavior after accounting for the broad or general influence of externalizing on violence and aggression (defined by high NEM and low CON). In a sense, such an approach may help unify the array of theories put forth in the personality and violence literature by determining how different factors operate at different levels of analysis to influence violence and aggression.

Psychopathic Personality and Violence

One of the overarching goals of the present discussion is to suggest that a reframing of the associations between certain personality disorders and violence can be better understood using structural models of personality. Psychopathic personality (psychopathy) is among the personality disorders that are linked most consistently to violence and aggression (Hare, 1996; Porter & Woodworth, 2006). Though not formally operationalized in Axis II of the DSM, psychopathy is typically conceptualized as a personality disorder marked by an egocentric and manipulative personality style within the context of an affective deficit (Cleckley, 1941/1976). Although related to APD in some respects, the classic clinical descriptions of psychopathy (Cleckley, 1941/1976; Karpman, 1941) are distinct in that they emphasize a constellation of maladaptive *personality* traits, in contrast to the more behavior-based criteria of APD (Lilienfeld, 1994, 1998). Although the classic clinical conceptions of psychopathy are not characterized by violent or aggressive tendencies per se, extensive empirical research has repeatedly suggested that psychopathy is a strong predictor of future violence among incarcerated offenders (e.g., Salekin, Rogers, & Sewell, 1996). The majority of this research is based on the Psychopathy Checklist-Revised (PCL-R; Hare, 1991, 2003), a semi-structured interview consisting of an oblique two-factor structure (Harpur, Hare, & Hakstian, 1989) that was designed to operationalize the clinical conceptions of psychopathy within incarcerated settings. Factor 1 of the PCL-R is marked by the core interpersonal-affective features described in the clinical literature (e.g., superficial charm, grandiosity, manipulativeness, lack of remorse; e.g., Cleckley, 1941/1976), whereas Factor 2 describes behavioral aspects of a chronic and unstable antisocial lifestyle. Despite evidence suggesting a link between psychopathy and violence, some scholars (e.g., Widiger & Trull, 1994) contend that this association may be inflated given that these forensic-based studies use prisoners who have extensive histories of criminal and violent behavior. Fundamentally, these authors question both the degree to which these findings may generalize to non-incarcerated populations and the degree to which the relationship between psychopathy and violence can be attributable to other co-varying aspects of psychopathy known to be strong predictors of violence (e.g., coexistent mental disorders, SES, verbal intelligence, education, substance abuse).

In response to these issues, Skeem and Mulvey (2001) investigated the extent to which psychopathy as measured by the screening version of the PCL (PCL-SV; Hart et al., 1995) can uniquely predict violence among a sample of civil psychiatric patients. After controlling for an array of co-variates (i.e., criminal history, substance abuse, other personality disorders, demographic variables), the PCL-SV remained significant in its prediction of violence, although the relationship was substantially attenuated. Furthermore, after controlling for the shared variance between Factor 1 and 2, only Factor 2 (antisocial deviance) remained predictive of violence. Moreover, neither the main effect of Factor 1 nor the interaction of these factors provided any substantial prediction of violence in this sample, consistent with a trend previously observed in the PCL-R literature (e.g., Rogers, 1995; Salekin et al., 1996). Although the findings address the issues

raised by Widiger and Trull (1994), the scoring of the PCL-SV takes into account a history of specific antisocial and criminal behaviors. Therefore, it may not explicitly tap the personality-based conceptions of psychopathy described in the clinical literature (e.g., Cleckley, 1941/1976; Karpman, 1941). As well, given the nature of their sample (i.e., civil psychiatric patients), it is still unclear whether the findings of Skeem and Mulvey (2001) are applicable to the general population. Thus, a fundamental question remains: what is the extent of the association between psychopathy and violence in community-epidemiological samples using personality-based measures of psychopathy? This question can be most informed by an examination of psychopathy within a structural framework.

To date, there is compelling evidence to suggest that psychopathy may be sufficiently captured within structural models of personality (e.g., Hicks, Markon, Patrick, Krueger, & Newman, 2004; Miller, Lynam, Widiger, & Leukefeld, 2001; Patrick, 1994; Widiger & Lynam, 1998). Our own program of research has sought to identify and cultivate a normal-range personality proxy to measure psychopathy within community-epidemiological populations. Our initial exploration began with the Psychopathic Personality Inventory (PPI; Lilienfeld & Andrews, 1996), a self-report measure designed to index personality traits related to psychopathy, rather than antisocial or criminal behaviors per se. Factor analytic work (Benning, Patrick, Hicks, Blonigen, & Krueger, 2003) has established that the PPI is underpinned by two uncorrelated factors. The first factor (*Fearless Dominance*) reflects the interpersonal-affective traits of psychopathy and is marked by social dominance, stress immunity, and fearlessness. The second factor (*Impulsive Antisociality*) may be characterized more in terms of high negative emotionality (i.e., alienation and aggression) and low constraint (i.e., self-control and traditionalism).

In addition to the factor analytic findings, multiple regression analyses by Benning and colleagues (2003) revealed that the MPQ captures a substantial portion of variance in the PPI factors. Moreover, subsequent analyses have shown construct validity for the use of the MPQ to index psychopathy across gender and in both community and incarcerated samples (Benning, Patrick, Blonigen, Hicks, & Iacono, 2005). For example, MPQ-Fearless Dominance demonstrates inverse relations with indices of internalizing, such as fear, anxiety, and depression (Blonigen, Hicks, Krueger, Patrick, & Iacono, 2005), while correlating positively with narcissism, thrill-seeking, and Factor 1 of the PCL-R (Benning et al., 2005). MPQ-estimated Impulsive Antisociality, on the other hand, exhibits positive relations with measures of antisocial behavior and substance abuse (Blonigen et al., 2005), as well as anxiety, disinhibition, and Factor 2 of the PCL-R (Benning et al., 2005). Given that these patterns of relations with external criteria strongly mirror the external correlates of the PCL-R factors (e.g., Harpur et al., 1989; Smith & Newman, 1990), these findings provide evidence for construct validity and support for the measurement of psychopathy within a structural framework of normal personality.

Although the MPQ psychopathy constructs have not been directly examined in relation to indices of violence, the personality correlates and external relations of these traits offer some compelling insights. Most notably, Impulsive Antisociality is significantly predicted by NEM (+) and CON (−) from the MPQ, with the alienation subfacet of NEM representing its strongest primary scale correlate (Benning et al., 2003). As previously illustrated, NEM (specifically alienation) and CON demonstrate the most consistent and robust associations with violence in community samples using structural models of personality. Given this, an examination of psychopathy within a structural framework provides a means of articulating more clearly the manner in which psychopathy is related to violence. That is, associations between psychopathy and violence may reflect broad underlying relations with NEM and CON, as well as a specific association with individual differences in alien-

ation. Although converging in some respects with research on the PCL-R and violence, this structural approach extends this literature by addressing associations between psychopathy and violence through a *personality*-based model using a general population sample. Thus, the relationship between psychopathy and violence can be understood more clearly when reframed within a structural model of personality, as opposed to a model based on a history of antisocial or criminal acts.

Summary and Integration

It is patently clear that personality has significant implications for understanding the nature of violence and aggression. Although this association has typically been examined in terms of which personality disorders are most strongly predictive of violence, a compelling body of evidence calls for a more comprehensive examination of this association via structural models of personality. As noted earlier, structural models of personality consist of hierarchically organized systems of quantitatively distributed personality traits and entail a comprehensive assessment of personality in terms of balancing both bandwidth and fidelity. Thus, associations between various personality disorder symptomatology and violent behavior can be disentangled at both broad and fine-grained levels of analysis, thereby providing a more complete picture of the underlying relationship between personality and violence. Using this structural approach, violence and aggression appear to be linked to the externalizing spectrum of psychopathology via broad personality correlates of negative emotionality and constraint. Thus, violence may be conceptualized, in part, as an indicator of a spectrum of disinhibitory psychopathology involving the co-variance of antisocial behavior, substance abuse, and a range of problematic, health-risk behaviors. Nonetheless, an exclusive focus on the common personological relations between externalizing and violence reveals only part of the story. A closer inspection at the lower-order level of the trait hierarchy reveals that alienation may represent a unique aspect of externalizing with specific relations to violence and aggression above and beyond the general influence of externalizing.

A second goal of the present discussion was to illustrate the utility of unpacking or reframing relations between certain personality disorders and violence within a structural framework of personality. As noted in our précis of psychopathy and violence, although psychopathy has been found repeatedly to be a strong predictor of future violence, the reliance on a history of specific criminal or antisocial acts in the assessment of psychopathy and the use of incarcerated or clinical populations creates an ambiguity as to which personality traits of psychopathy are driving the association with violence. Similar criticisms could also be raised with respect to other personality disorders linked to violence (e.g., APD, BPD, paranoid personality disorder). As was illustrated with psychopathy, examining the personality dimensions underlying certain DSM-defined personality disorders may help disentangle which specific individual differences dimensions within and across Axis II disorders are most important in the general association between personality and violence.

In closing, it is worth speculating on some of the broader implications of examining personality and violence using structural models of personality traits. In reviewing the literature it is clear that personality traits have relevance to a range of social problems including violent behavior. However, other disciplines such as criminology that are similarly invested in understanding and preventing violence are often dismissive of the extent to which personality can help address this universal social burden (cf. Gottfredson & Hirschi, 1990). Some of the aforementioned findings from structural analyses of personality and violence, however, highlight some interesting similarities and differences across criminological and personality research. Whereas low self-control and low constraint appear to be largely synonymous concepts deriving from the criminological and personological literatures, respectively, personological research

further notes the importance of negative emotionality and alienation as unique personality correlates of violence. It should be mentioned, however, that negative emotionality and alienation are not altogether novel to the socio-criminological literature, as elements of these personality constructs can be found in several theories on partner violence (e.g., Fagan & Browne, 1994; Holtzworth-Munroe & Stuart, 1994). Nonetheless, personality research may have great utility in helping understand violence by identifying individual differences that may operate in concert with broader social forces to engender or sustain violence and aggression. Thus, we envision structural models as a comprehensive and compelling framework that can help bridge the range of eclectic disciplines invested in understanding violence and aggression.

Finally, it should be noted that placing violence within a structural framework of personality has the added advantage of situating violence within an established nomological network, which may in turn yield insights into the etiological, developmental, and neurobiological underpinnings of this behavior. For example, violence appears to be personologically similar to externalizing psychopathology in that both are defined by high negative emotionality and low constraint. Given this association, findings and theories regarding the genetic (Krueger et al., 2002) and neurobiological bases of externalizing (cf. Iacono, Carlson, Taylor, Elkins, & McGue, 1999; Patrick, 2001) may help elucidate related issues with respect to violence. Along these lines, future studies may be well served to investigate the etiology, development, and underlying neurobiology of alienation and related constructs in order to further delineate the manner in which this unique personality correlate of violence is distinct from the broader psychopathological process of externalizing.

Acknowledgments

Preparation of this chapter was supported in part by USPHS grant MH65137. Daniel M.

Blonigen was supported by NIMH training grant MH17069.

References

Achenbach, T. M., & Edelbrock, C. S. (1984). Psychopathology of childhood. *Annual Review of Psychology*, *35*, 227–256.

American Psychiatric Association. (1980). *Diagnostic and statistical manual of mental disorders* (3rd ed.). Washington, DC.

American Psychiatric Association. (1987). *Diagnostic and statistical manual of mental disorders* (3rd ed., rev.). Washington, DC.

American Psychiatric Association. (1994). *Diagnostic and statistical manual of mental disorders* (4th ed.). Washington, DC.

Arsenault, L., Moffitt, T. E., Caspi, A., Taylor, P. J., & Silva, P. A. (2000). Mental disorders and violence in a total birth cohort: Results from the Dunedin study. *Archives of General Psychiatry*, *57*, 979–986.

Baumeister, R. F., Smart, L., & Boden, J. M. (1996). Relation of threatened egotism to violence and aggression: The dark side of high self-esteem. *Psychological Review*, *103*(1), 533.

Benning, S. D., Patrick, C. J., Blonigen, D. M., Hicks, B. M., & Iacono, W. G. (2005). Estimating facets of psychopathy from normal personality traits: A step toward community-epidemiological investigations. *Assessment*, *12*(1), 3–18.

Benning, S. D., Patrick, C. J., Hicks, B. M., Blonigen, D. M., & Krueger, R. F. (2003). Factor structure of the Psychopathic Personality Inventory: Validity and implications for clinical assessment. *Psychological Assessment*, *15*(3), 340–350.

Berman, M. E., Fallon, A. E., & Coccaro, E. F. (1998). The relationship between personality psychopathology and aggressive behavior in research volunteers. *Journal of Abnormal Psychology*, *107*, 651–658.

Bland, R., & Orn, H. (1986). Family violence and psychiatric disorder. *Canadian Journal of Psychiatry*, *31*, 129–137.

Blonigen, D. M., Hicks, B. M., Krueger, R. F., Patrick, C. J., & Iacono, W. G. (2005). Psychopathic personality traits: Heritability and genetic overlap with internalizing and externalizing psychopathology. *Psychological Medicine*, *25*, 637–648.

Brent, D. A., Johnson, B. A., Perper, J., Connolly, J., Bridge, J., et al. (1994). Personality disorder, personality traits, impulsive violence, and completed suicide in adolescents. *Journal of the American Academy of Child and Adolescent Psychiatry*, *33*(8), 1080–1086.

Brodsky, B. S., Malone, K. M., Ellis, S. P., Dulit, R. A., & Mann, J. J. (1997). Characteristics of borderline personality disorder associated with suicidal behavior. *American Journal of Psychiatry*, *154*(12), 1715–1719.

Brownstone, D. Y., & Swaminath, R. S. (1989). Violent behavior and psychiatric diagnosis in female offenders. *Canadian Journal of Psychiatry*, *34*, 190–194.

Buss, A. H., & Durkee, A. (1957). An inventory for assessing different types of hostility. *Journal of Consulting and Clinical Psychology*, *21*, 343–349.

Caspi, A., Begg, D., Dickson, N., Harrington, H., Langley, J., Moffitt, T. E., et al. (1997). Personality differences predict health-risk behaviors in young adulthood: Evidence from a longitudinal study. *Journal of Personality and Social Psychology*, *73*, 1052–1063.

Cleckley, H. M. (1941/1976). *The mask of sanity*. St. Louis, MO: Mosby.

Coccaro, E. F., Berman, M. E., & Kavoussi, R. J. (1997). Assessment of life-history of aggression: Development and psychometric characteristics. *Psychiatry Research*, *73*, 147–157.

Cook, W. W., & Medley, D. M. (1954). Proposed hostility and Pharisaic-virtue scales for the MMPI. *Journal of Applied Psychology*, *38*, 414–418.

Costa, P. T., & Widiger, T. A. (2002). *Personality disorders and the five-factor model of personality* (2nd ed.). Washington, DC: American Psychological Association.

Dodge, K. A., Pettit, G. S., Bates, J. E., & Valente, E. (1995). Social information-processing patterns partially mediate the effect of early physical abuse on later conduct problems. *Journal of Abnormal Psychology*, *104*(4), 632–643.

Edwards, D. W., Scott, C. L., Yarvis, R. M., Paizis, C. L., & Panizzon, M. S. (2003). Impulsiveness, impulsive aggression, personality disorder, and spousal violence. *Violence and Victims*, *18*(1), 3–14.

Egan, V., Austin, E., Elliot, D., Patel, D., & Charlesworth, P. (2003). Personality traits, personality disorders and sensational interests in mentally disordered offenders. *Legal and Criminological Psychology*, *8*(1), 51–62.

Ekselius, L., Hetta, J., & von Knorring, L. (1994). Relationship between personality traits as determined by means of Karolinska Scales of Personality (KSP) and personality disorders according to DSM-III-R. *Personality and Individual Differences, 16,* 589–595.

Elkins, I. J., Iacono, W. G., Doyle, A. E., & McGue, M. (1997). Characteristics associated with the persistence of antisocial behavior: Results from recent longitudinal research. *Aggression and Violent Behavior, 2,* 101–124.

Elliott, D., Huizinga, D., & Morse, B. (1986). Self-reported violent offending. *Journal of Interpersonal Violence, 1,* 472–514.

Else, L. T., Wonderlich, S. A., Beatty, W. W., Christie, D. W., & Staton, R. D. (1993). Personality characteristics of men who physically abuse women. *Hospital Community Psychiatry, 44,* 54–58.

Eronen, M., Hakola, P., & Tiihonen, J. (1996). Mental disorders and homicidal behavior in Finland. *Archives of General Psychiatry, 53,* 497–501.

Fagan, J., & Browne, A. (1994). Violence between spouses and intimates: Physical aggression between women and men in intimate relationships. In A. J. Reiss, Jr. & J. A. Roth (Eds.), *Understanding and preventing violence. Vol. 3: Social influences* (pp. 115–292). Washington, DC: National Academy of Science Press.

Gottfredson, M. G., & Hirschi, T. (1990). A general theory of crime. Palo Alto, CA: Stanford University Press.

Grove, W. M., & Tellegen, A. (1991). Problems in the classification of personality disorders. *Journal of Personality Disorders, 5,* 31–41.

Hare, R. D. (1991). *The Hare Psychopathy Checklist-Revised.* Toronto: Multi-Health Systems.

Hare, R. D. (1996). Psychopathy: A clinical construct whose time has come. *Criminal Justice and Behavior, 23,* 25–54.

Hare, R. D. (2003). *The Hare Psychopathy Checklist-Revised:* (2nd ed.). Toronto: Multi-Health Systems.

Harkness, A. R. (1992). Fundamental topics in the personality disorders: Candidate trait dimensions from lower regions of the hierarchy. *Psychological Assessment, 4*(2), 251–259.

Harpur, T. J., Hare, R. D., & Hakstian, A. R. (1989). Two-factor conceptualization of psychopathy: Construct validity and assessment implications. *Psychological Assessment, 1,* 6–17.

Hart, S. D., Cox, D., & Hare, R. (1995). Manual for the Psychopathy Checklist: Screening Version (PCL: SV). Toronto: Multi-health Systems.

Hart, S. D., Dutton, D. G., & Newlove, T. (1993). The prevalence of personality disorder among wife assaulters. *Journal of Personality Disorders, 7,* 329–341.

Henry, B., Caspi, A., Moffitt, T. E., & Silva, P. A. (1996). Temperamental and familial factors of violent and nonviolent criminal convictions: Age 3 to age 18. *Developmental Psychology, 32*(4), 614–623.

Hicks, B. M., Markon, K. E., Patrick, C. J., Krueger, R. F., & Newman, J. P. (2004). Identifying psychopathy subtypes on the basis of personality structure. *Psychological Assessment, 16*(3), 276–288.

Hodgins, S., Mednick, S. A., Brennan, P. A., Schulsinger, F., & Engberg, M. (1996). Mental disorder and crime: Evidence from a Danish birth cohort. *Archives of General Psychiatry, 53,* 489–496.

Holtzworth-Monroe, A., & Stuart, G. L. (1994). Typologies of male batterers: Three subtypes and the differences among them. *Psychological Bulletin, 116,* 476–497.

Iacono, W. G., Carlson, S. R., Taylor, J., Elkins, I. J., & McGue, M. (1999). Behavioral disinhibition and the development of substance use disorders: Findings from the Minnesota Twin Family Study. *Development and Psychopathology, 11,* 869–900.

Jockin, V., Arvey, R. D., & McGue, M. (2001). Perceived victimization moderates self-reports of workplace aggression and conflict. *Journal of Applied Psychology, 86*(6), 1262–1269.

Johnson, J. G., Cohen, P., Smailes, E., Kasen, S., Oldham, J. M., Skodol, A. E., et al. (2000). Adolescent personality disorders associated with violence and criminal behavior during adolescence and early adulthood. *American Journal of Psychiatry, 157,* 1406–1412.

Karpman, B. (1941). On the need for separating psychopathy into two distinct clinical types: Symptomatic and idiopathic. *Journal of Criminology and Psychopathology, 3,* 112–137.

Kenrick, D. T., & Funder, D. C. (1988). Profiting from controversy: Lessons from the person-situation debate. *American Psychologist, 43* (1), 23–34.

Kernberg, O. F. (1984). *Severe personality disorders.* New Haven: Yale University Press.

Krakowski, M., Volavka, J., & Brizer, D. (1986). Psychopathology and violence: A review of the literature. *Comprehensive Psychiatry*, *27*, 131–148.

Krueger, R. F. (1999). The structure of common mental disorders. *Archives of General Psychiatry*, *56*, 921–926.

Krueger, R. F. (2002). Personality from a realist's perspective: Personality traits, criminal behaviors, and the externalizing spectrum. *Journal of Research in Personality*, *36*, 564–572.

Krueger, R. F., Caspi, A., & Moffitt, T. E. (2000). Epidemiological personology: The unifying role of personality in population-based research on problem behaviors. *Journal of Personality*, *68*(6), 967–998.

Krueger, R. F., Caspi, A., Moffitt, T. E., & Silva, P. A. (1998). The structure and stability of common mental disorders (DSM-III-R): A longitudinal-epidemiological study. *Journal of Abnormal Psychology*, *107*, 216–227.

Krueger, R. F., Hicks, B. M, & McGue, M. (2001). Altruism and antisocial behavior: Independent tendencies, unique personality correlates, distinct etiologies. *Psychological Science*, *12*, 397–402.

Krueger, R. F., Hicks, B. M., Patrick, C. J., Carlson, S. R., Iacono, W. G., & McGue, M. (2002). Etiologic connections among substance dependence, antisocial behavior, and personality: Modeling the externalizing spectrum. *Journal of Abnormal Psychology*, *111*, 411–424.

Krueger, R. F., Markon, K. E., Patrick, C. J., & Iacono, W. G. (2005). Externalizing psychopathology in adulthood: A dimensional-spectrum conceptualization and its implications for DSM-V. *Journal of Abnormal Psychology*, *114*(4), 537–550.

Krueger, R. F., McGue, M., & Iacono, W. G. (2001). The higher-order structure of common DSM mental disorders: Internalization, externalization, and their connections to personality. *Personality and Individual Differences*, *30*, 1245–1259.

Krueger, R. F., Schmutte, P. S., Caspi, A., Moffitt, T. E., Campbell, K., & Silva, P. A. (1994). Personality traits are linked to crime among men and women: Evidence from a birth cohort. *Journal of Abnormal Psychology*, *103*(2), 328–338.

Lang, P. J., Bradley, M. M., & Cuthbert, B. N. (1990). Emotion, attention, and the startle reflex. *Psychological Review*, *97*, 377–398.

Lilienfeld, S. O. (1994). Conceptual problems in the assessment of psychopathy. *Clinical Psychology Review*, *14*, 17–38.

Lilienfeld, S. O. (1998). Methodological advances and developments in the assessment of psychopathy. *Behaviour Research and Therapy*, *36*, 99–125.

Lilienfeld, S. O., & Andrews, B. P. (1996). Development and preliminary validation of a self-report measure of psychopathic personality traits in noncriminal populations. *Journal of Personality Assessment*, *66*, 488–524.

Link, B. G., Andrews, H., & Cullen, F. (1992). The violent and illegal behavior of mental patients reconsidered. *American Sociological Review*, *57*, 275–292.

Litwack, T. R., & Schlesinger, L. B. (1987). Assessing and predicting violence: Research, law, and applications. In I. B. Weiner & A. K. Hess (Eds.), *Handbook of forensic psychology* (pp. 205–257). New York: Wiley.

Livesley, W. J., & Jang, K. L. (2000). Toward an empirically based classification of personality disorder. *Journal of Personality Disorders*, *14*(2), 137–151.

Lynam, D. R. (2002). Psychopathy from the perspective of the five-factor model of personality. In P. T. Costa & T. A. Widiger (Eds.), *Personality disorders and the five-factor model of personality* (2nd ed., pp. 325–348). Washington, DC: American Psychological Association.

Markon, K. E., & Krueger, R. F. (2005). Categorical and continuous models of liability to externalizing disorders: A direct comparison in NESARC. *Archives of General Psychiatry*, *62*(12), 1352–1359.

Markon, K. E., Krueger, R. F., & Watson, D. (2005). Delineating the structure of normal and abnormal personality: An integrative hierarchical approach. *Journal of Personality and Social Psychology*, *88*, 139–157.

Meehl, P. E. (1986). Trait language and behaviorese. In T. Thompson & M. D. Zeiler (Eds.), *Analysis and integration of behavioral units* (pp. 315–334). Hillsdale, NJ: Erlbaum.

Miller, J. D., Lynam, D. R., Widiger, T. A., & Leukefeld, C. (2001). Personality disorders as extreme variants of common personality dimensions: Can the five-factor model adequately represent psychopathy? *Journal of Personality*, *69*(2), 253–276.

Mischel, W. (1968). *Personality and assessment*. New York: Wiley.

Moffitt, T. E., Caspi, A., Silva, P. A., & Stouthamer-Loeber, M. (1995). Individual differences in personality and intelligence are linked to crime: Cross context evidence from nations, neighborhoods, genders, races, and age-cohorts. In J. Hagan (Ed.), *Current perspectives on aging and the life cycle* (pp. 1–34). Greenwich, CT: JAI Press.

Moffitt, T. E., Krueger, R. F., Caspi, A., & Fagan, J. (2000). Partner abuse and general crime: How are they the same? How are they different? *Criminology, 38*(1), 199–232.

Moffitt, T. E., Mednick, S., & Gabrielli, W. (1989). Predicting careers of criminal violence: Descriptive data and predispositional factors. In D. Brizer & M. Crowner (Eds.), *Current approaches to the prediction of violence* (pp. 13–34). Washington, DC: American Psychiatric Press.

Nestor, P. G. (2002). Mental disorder and violence: Personality dimensions and clinical features. *American Journal of Psychiatry, 159* (12), 1973–1978.

Patrick, C. J. (1994). Emotion and psychopathy: Startling new insights. *Psychophysiology, 31*, 319–330.

Patrick, C. J. (2001). Emotional processes in psychopathy. In A. Raine & J. Sanmartin (Eds.), *Violence and psychopathy* (pp. 57–77). New York: Kluwer Academic.

Porter, S., & Woodworth, M. (2006). Psychopathy and aggression. In C. J. Patrick (Ed.), *Handbook of psychopathy* (pp. 481–494). New York: Guilford Press.

Raine, A. (1993). Features of borderline personality and violence. *Journal of Clinical Psychology, 49*(2), 277–281.

Raskin, R., & Terry, H. (1988). A principal-components analysis of the Narcissistic Personality Inventory and further evidence of its construct validation. *Journal of Personality and Social Psychology, 54*, 890–902.

Roberts, B. W., Caspi, A., & Moffitt, T. E. (2001). The kids are alright: Growth and stability in personality development from adolescence to adulthood. *Journal of Personality and Social Psychology, 81*(4), 670–683.

Robins, L. N., Tipp, J., & Przybeck, T. (1991). Antisocial personality. In L. N. Robins & D. Regier (Eds.), *Psychiatric disorders in America* (pp. 258–290). New York: Free Press.

Rogers, R. (1995). *Diagnostic and structured interviewing. A handbook for psychologists.* Odessa, FL: Psychological Assessment Resources.

Salekin, R., Rogers, R., & Sewell, K. (1996). A review and meta-analysis of the Psychopathy Checklist-Revised: Predictive validity of dangerousness. *Clinical Psychology: Science and Practice, 3*, 203–215.

Skeem, J. L., & Mulvey, E. P. (2001). Psychopathy and community violence among civil psychiatric patients: Results from the MacArthur Violence Risk Assessment Study. *Journal of Consulting and Clinical Psychology, 69*(3), 358–374.

Smith, S. S., & Newman, J. P. (1990). Alcohol and drug abuse-dependence disorders in psychopathic and nonpsychopathic criminal offenders. *Journal of Abnormal Personality, 99*, 430–439.

Snyder, S., Pitts, W. M., & Pokorny, A. D. (1986). Selected behavioral features of patients with borderline personality traits. *Suicide and Life-Threatening Behavior, 16*, 28–39.

Spielberger, C. D., Johnson, E. H., Russell, S. F., Crane, R. J., Jacobs, G. A., & Worden, T. J. (1985). The experience and expression of anger: Construction and validation of an anger expression scale. In M. A. Chesney & R. H. Rosenman (Eds.), *Anger and hostility in cardiovascular and behavioral disorders* (pp. 5–30). New York: Hemisphere/McGraw-Hill.

Swanson, J. W., Borum, R., Swartz, M. S., & Monahan, J. (1996). Psychotic symptoms and disorders and the risk of violent behaviour in the community. *Criminal Behavior and Mental Health, 6*, 317–338.

Tellegen, A. (1991). Personality traits: Issues of definition, evidence, and assessment. In W. M. Grove & D. Cicchetti (Eds.), *Thinking clearly about psychology* (pp. 10–35). Minneapolis: University of Minnesota Press.

Tellegen, A. (1993). Folk concepts and psychological concepts of personality and personality disorder. *Psychological Inquiry, 4*(2), 122–130.

Tellegen, A. (in press). *Manual for the Multidimensional Personality Questionnaire.* Minneapolis, MN: University of Minnesota Press.

Tellegen, A., Lykken, D. T., Bouchard, Jr., T. J., Wilcox, K. J., Segal, N. L., & Rich, S. (1988). Personality similarity in twins reared apart and together. *Journal of Personality & Social Psychology, 54*(6), 1031–1039.

Tiihonen, J., Isohanni, M., Rasanen, P., Koiranen, M., & Moring, J. (1997). Specific major mental disorders and criminality: A 26-year prospective study of the 1996 Northern Finland birth cohort. *American Journal of Psychiatry, 154*, 840–845.

Trull, T. J., & Durrett, C. A. (2005). Categorical and dimensional models of personality disorder. *Annual Review of Clinical Psychology, 1*, 355–380.

Trull, T. J., & McCrae, R. R. (2002). A five-factor perspective on personality disorder research. In P. T. Costa & T. A. Widiger (Eds.), *Personality disorders and the five-factor model of personality* (pp. 45–57). Washington, DC: American Psychological Association.

Verona, E., Patrick, C. J., & Lang, A. R. (2002). A direct assessment of the role of state and trait negative emotion in aggressive behavior. *Journal of Abnormal Psychology, 111*(2), 249–258.

Watson, D., Clark, L. A., & Harkness, A. R. (1994). Structures of personality and their relevance to psychopathology. *Journal of Abnormal Psychology, 103*(1), 18–31.

Widiger, T. A. (1993). The DSM-III-R categorical personality disorder diagnoses: A critique and an alternative. *Psychological Inquiry, 4*(2), 75–90.

Widiger, T. A., & Lynam, D. R. (1998). Psychopathy as a variant of common personality traits: Implications for diagnosis, etiology, and pathology. In T. Millon (Ed.), *Psychopathy: Antisocial, criminal, and violent behavior* (pp. 171–187). New York: Guilford Press.

Widiger, T. A., & Trull, T. J. (1994). Personality disorders and violence. In J. Monahan & H. J. Steadman (Eds.), *Violence and mental disorder: Developments in risk assessment* (pp. 203–226). Chicago: University of Chicago Press.

Windle, R. C., & Windle, M. (1995). Longitudinal patterns of physical aggression: Associations with adult social, psychiatric, and personality functioning and testosterone levels. *Developmental Psychopathology, 7,* 563–585.

Yarvis, R. M. (1990). Axis I and Axis II diagnostic parameters of homicide. *Bulletin of the American Academy of Psychiatry and Law, 18,* 249–269.

CHAPTER 14

Exposure to Violence, Mental Health, and Violent Behavior

Daniel J. Flannery, Mark I. Singer, Manfred van Dulmen, Jeff M. Kretschmar, and Lara M. Belliston

Introduction

The incidence of violence in the lives of children has been a concern for some time, and studies showing high rates of child and adolescent exposure to violence have led to a growing interest in the impact of violence exposure on child development (Buka, Stichick, Birdthistle, & Earls, 2001; Farrell & Sullivan, 2004; Finkelhor, 1995; Flannery, 1996; Gorman-Smith & Tolan, 1998; Osofsky, 1995, 1997, 1999; Pynoos, 1993). The focus of this chapter is on the relationship among violence exposure, mental health, and violent behavior for children and adolescents. Overall, studies have shown a strong association between child and adolescent exposure to violence and mental health symptoms, as well as a relationship between exposure to violence and behavior problem outcomes, including increased risk for aggression, delinquent behavior, and the perpetration of violence (Cooley-Quille, Boyd, Frantz, & Walsh, 2001; Dodge, Bates, & Pettit, 1990; Fitzpatrick & Boldizar, 1993; Lorion & Salzman, 1993; Maxfield & Widom, 1996; Singer, Anglin, Song, &

Lunghofer, 1995; Widom, 1989). Some research has also examined the specific relationship among all three factors, and it suggests that high rates of exposure contribute to increased risk for mental health problems, which, in turn, puts children and adolescents at risk of perpetrating interpersonal (and intrapersonal) violence (Farrell & Bruce, 1997; Flannery, Singer, & Wester, 2001; Song, Singer, & Anglin, 1998).

Violence exposure includes being a witness to violence or being victimized by violence (Singer et al., 1995; Singer, Miller, Guo, Flannery, Frierson, & Slovak, 1999). Exposure to violence can also occur across settings (e.g., home, neighborhood, and school). Research generally differentiates between exposure to violence at home (e.g., family violence or victimization from violence at home via abuse or neglect) and violence exposure in other settings, commonly referred to as community violence exposure. Although this chapter includes a review of research on exposure to violence at home when it has been assessed in a particular study, the chapter does not focus specifically on child abuse or neglect. Further, where appropriate, we clarify whether data on exposure, mental health, and violent behavior have been gathered from a community sample or a targeted sample of youth in treatment or in a restricted setting (e.g., youth detention). Lastly, studies that have examined exposure to violence have assessed either recent exposure to violence (e.g., in the past year) or lifetime exposure to violence (Dodge et al., 1990; Widom, 1989). Most of our work has been on assessing recent (past year) violence exposure, mental health, and violent behavior for children and adolescents in community samples, so that is our focus in this chapter.

Victimization from violence occurs on a continuum, from very rare events of victimization, such as being the victim of a homicide, to more common occurrences of victimization, such as being the victim of assault from a sibling (Finkelhor & Dziuba-Leatherman, 1994). In the same vein, violent behavior must be examined in a developmental context, with violence among very young children being operationalized most typically as aggressive behavior, including shoving, fighting, or name calling. Among older children, aggressive behavior can increase in seriousness and include fighting that results in physical injury, physical assault, or attacks with a weapon and homicide.

For purposes of this chapter, we discuss mental health primarily in the context of internalizing symptoms related to child and adolescent development, including post-traumatic stress disorder symptoms. The most commonly assessed mental health symptoms are anxiety, depression, dissociation, and anger. Where appropriate, we also discuss the relationship between violence exposure and externalizing behavior problems categorized as mental health issues, including conduct disorder and attention-deficit hyperactivity disorder.

Rates of Violence Exposure and Victimization by Setting

Violence exposing victimization and perpetration are inextricably linked. Homicide rates provide the starkest testimony to the risk of victimization for children and youth. In 1998, the murder rate for youth under the age of 18 was seven per day, making homicide the second leading cause of death for adolescents in the United States and one of the leading causes of child mortality (Office of Juvenile Justice and Delinquency Prevention, 2001a,b). Of all the major causes of child deaths in the United States, homicide is the only one to have increased in frequency over the past 30 years (Fox & Zawitz, 2001). It is particularly disturbing that about half the cases of violent victimization go unreported to authorities (Office of Juvenile Justice and Delinquency Prevention, 2000). When one takes into account the combination of fatal and nonfatal victimization, as well as high rates of witnessing violent acts, the number of children and adolescents exposed to violence is substantial. Not only are the overall numbers of youth exposed to high levels of violence increasing but also the nature of the exposure is more immediate and more intense than it has ever been (Flannery, 2006). The Internet and other media outlets have provided immediate, frequent, and intense exposure to violent incidents that occur daily all over the world.

For at least the past decade research has illustrated the high rates of exposure to community violence among children and adolescents (Lorion & Saltzman, 1993; Richters & Martinez, 1993). Numerous studies of both children and adolescents have documented exposure to a variety of violent acts in schools and neighborhoods, ranging from threats of physical harm to knifings and shootings (Boney-McCoy & Finkelhor, 1995; Fehon, Griol, & Lipschitz, 2001a,b; Fitzpatrick & Boldizar, 1993; Jones, Ajirotutu, & Johnson, 1996; Schwab-Stone et al., 1995; Weist, Acosta, & Youngstrom, 2001). Although exposure to more extreme forms of violence, such as beatings and weapons-related violence, is most prevalent in highly populated, low-income neighborhoods, children and adolescents in rural and smaller city settings also experience these forms of violence (Singer et al., 1995, 1999).

The home is the setting in which most children first experience violence exposure, as either a witness to or victim of violence. Data on family violence in the United States indicate there were about 3 million reports of alleged maltreatment to child protective services in 1999, with 28% of those reports being substantiated (Osofsky, 2001). About 40% of all murder victims under the age of 18 are killed by a family member (Office of Juvenile Justice, 2001b). In addition to these statistics, reported levels of sibling assault are as high as 800 per 1,000, yet such assaults tend to go unreported, except in the most severe cases (Finkelhor & Dziuba- Leatherman, 1994; Office of Juvenile Justice, 2000).

In a large community-based survey of exposure to violence among adolescents, nearly 40% of boys and 50% of girls reported seeing someone else being slapped, hit, or punched at home, and nearly 20% of adolescents reported witnessing a beating at home in the past year. Rates of adolescent self-reported victimization were also high, with 1 in 10 girls reporting they had been beaten at home and nearly half of all girls reported witnessing someone else being slapped, hit, or punched at home in the past year (Flannery, Singer, Williams & Castro, 1998).

Because youth spend a considerable amount of time at school, violence in and around schools has gained widespread attention in the media. A nationally representative survey of over 6,500 6th through 12th grade students indicated that nearly three fourths of the students were aware of incidents of physical attack, robbery, or bullying, and more than half had witnessed such events since the beginning of the school year (Nolin, Davies, & Chandler, 1995). Being a victim of a crime at school appears to be a less frequent occurrence than in other settings (Small & Tetrick, 2001), but the incidence of violence experienced by students at school remains disconcerting. In 1998, youth aged 12 through 18 were victimized by 1.2 million nonfatal violent crimes at school. The rate of violent crime (rape, theft, sexual assault, and aggravated assault) experienced by this age group at school has remained rel-atively stable over the last 15 years (Small & Tetrick, 2001).

The percentage of children and adolescents exposed to violence at school remains high, despite drops in the overall levels of violence that occurs in schools (Kingery, Coggeshall, & Alford, 1998). In a recent study, 56 to 87% of adolescents reported they had witnessed at least one violent incident at school, whereas up to 44% of students reported they had been a victim of violence at school (Flannery, Wester, & Singer, 2004).

A particular case of victimization from violence at school is bullying (Nansel, Over-peck, Pilla, Ruan, Simons-Morton, B., & Scheidt, 2001; Olweus, 1993). Some studies have estimated that 70 to 90% of youth will experience ongoing psychological or physical harassment at some point during their school years, characterized by exposure to bullying or being threatened with violence at school (Hazler, 1996; Hoover & Juul, 1993; Hoover & Oliver, 1996; Oliver, Young, & LaSalle, 1994; Singer & Flannery, 2000). In one study, 8% of students reported being bullied one or more times per week (Hoover & Oliver, 1996), and another study found an average of one bullying incident occurred at school every 7 $\frac{1}{2}$ minutes (Ross, 1996).

About 8% of children report that bullying affects their lives so much that they have attempted suicide, run away, or refused to go to school (Cullingford & Morrison, 1995). Adolescents who bully other youth tend to be aggressive, hostile, and less cooperative toward peers (Haynie et al., 2001). Bullies also exhibit higher levels of related behavior problems like conduct disorder and ADHD (Kumpulainen, Rasanen, Hentto-nen, Almqvist, Kresanov, & Linna, 1998). They report more significant mental health problems, including being depressed, having severe suicidal ideation, and having more physical and emotional symptoms compared to their nonbullying peers (Kaltiala-Heino, Rimpela, Marttunen, Rimpela, & Ranta-nen, 1999; Salmon & West, 2000). Victims of bullies also report significant mental health problems, including being more depressed, anxious, insecure, lonely, and unhappy. These associations hold up for youth in the United States, as well as in surveys of youth in other countries (Ando, Asakura & Simons-Morton, 2005; Nansel, Craig, Overpeck, Saluja, & Ruan, 2004).

Bullying and threatening behavior can also lead to more serious violence or consequences. In a 2-year period (1992 to 1994), 105 school-associated violent deaths were identified, with an equal number of deaths occurring in classes or other school-related activities (44%; Kachur et al., 1996). Between 1994 and 1999, 220 violent incidents at school resulted in 172 homicides, 30 suicides, 11 homicide-suicides, 5 legal intervention deaths, and 2 unintentional firearm deaths, with students accounting for 68% of these deaths (Anderson et al., 2001). In 2000, students between the ages of 12 and 18 were victims of 1.9 million total crimes of violence or theft, and about 128,000 were victims of serious violent crimes at school (e.g. rape, sexual assault, or aggravated assault; U.S. Department of Education, 2002). According to the 1999 Youth Risk Behavior Survey, 17% of youth reported that they had carried a weapon in the past 30 days, with 7% of youth reporting they brought the weapon to school (Centers for Disease Control, 2000). Between 1993 and 2001, nearly 10% of students in grades 9 through 12 reported they had been threatened or injured by a weapon on school property within the last 12 months (U.S. Department of Education, 2002). Despite a great deal of media attention, the rate of school-associated student homicides (and the chance of being the victim of a homicide at school) has remained relatively constant from 1994 to the present.

Data on the Relationship Among Violence Exposure, Mental Health, and Violent Behavior

Research over the past 15 years has consistently shown a strong association among exposure to violence and mental health symptoms and aggressive, violent behavior. Exposure to violence, as a witness or a victim, is related to several emotional and behavior problem outcomes, including mental health symptoms, such as anxiety, anger, depression, and dissociation, and aggressive, delinquent, and violent behavior (Breslau, Davis, Andreski, & Peterson, 1991; Flannery, 1999; Flannery, Singer, & Wester, 2001, 2003; Overstreet & Braun, 2000; Schwab-Stone et al., 1995; Singer et al., 1995, 1999).

Over the past decade, we have completed several large-scale studies of community violence exposure in diverse samples of children and adolescents. These studies used self-administered questionnaires that were distributed to subjects during regular school hours. In addition to investigating the overall sample in each study, we also explored subsamples of subjects, such as students who reported committing serious acts of violence (i.e., stabbing and/or shooting/shooting at someone) and students who had threatened others with violence. Some of the important findings of these studies are summarized in this section.

We investigated the relationship among adolescents' exposure to violence, symptoms of psychological trauma, violent behaviors, and coping strategies in 3,724 high-school students from Northeast Ohio and Denver (Singer, et al., 1995). Overall, high percentages of students, particularly those living in large cities (i.e., Denver and Cleveland), were either victims or witnesses of recent community violence. For example, within the past year, about one in two students had witnessed someone being beaten up in their neighborhood, and more than one in three males had reported being slapped/hit/punched at school. Not surprisingly, being a witness or victim of violence was reliably associated with symptoms of psychological trauma, including depression, anxiety, post-traumatic stress, dissociation, and anger. Given the considerable levels of violence exposure and the reliable association between such exposure and psychological distress, youth-serving professionals should routinely screen for violence exposure, and mental health and counseling services for violence-exposed youth should be made readily available.

This study also examined the students' self-reported violent behaviors and coping strategies (Flannery, Singer, & Wester, 2003). Adolescents who reported higher levels of perpetrating violent acts reliably reported high levels of exposure to violence, either as a witness or victim. Furthermore, the most violent adolescents (top 10%) reported higher rates of clinically significant levels of all trauma symptoms. Compared to their peers, the most violent adolescents were also more likely to employ maladaptive coping strategies, such as getting angry and yelling at people, saying something mean, and using alcohol or drugs. These violent adolescents who experience high levels of trauma symptoms and whose coping strategies when under stress are maladaptive are at high risk for social isolation, involvement with antisocial activities, and continued violent behaviors. These youth would benefit from interventions that increase prosocial coping skills to help them build and maintain supportive relationships and to enhance their self-efficacy.

Community samples of violent adolescents are an understudied population. Within the parent study of adolescent high-school students, we identified and explored a subset of students who were dangerously violent (Flannery, Singer, & Wester, 2001). Dangerously violent students were those who self-reported stabbing and/or shooting at/shooting someone within the past year. We identified 349 males and 135 females. Compared with matched controls, these dangerously violent adolescents were witnesses and victims of higher levels of violence in the home, neighborhood, and school. Dangerously violent males were more likely than controls to exhibit clinical levels of anger, post-traumatic stress, and dissociation. Dangerously violent females were more likely to demonstrate clinical levels of all trauma symptoms than controls. These violent females had notably high levels of clinical depression and anger.

Having observed such high levels of depression and anger, we became concerned about suicide risk. The Trauma Symptom Checklist used in the study (Briere, 1996) contained critical questions used to assess suicide potential. Dangerously violent females scored at significantly elevated levels on these critical questions, with about one in five being at high risk for suicide. This high potential for self-harm among these violent adolescent females should be recognized by mental health professionals, and appropriate assessment and treatment should be available.

In another large study, 2,245 students in grades 3 to 8 living in Northeast Ohio were assessed in relation to their exposure to violence, violent behaviors, and psychological trauma (Singer, Flannery, Guo, Miller, & Liebrandt, 2004; Singer et. al, 1999). As in the high-school sample, students in this study reported being exposed to considerable levels of violence both as victims and witnesses. Violence exposure was again reliably related to symptoms of psychological trauma, and violence exposure and lower parental monitoring were significantly related to higher levels of self-reported violent behaviors.

Samples of students in the studies cited above were combined with a sample of 3,518 elementary-school students in Tucson, Arizona, to examine the relationship between children's threats of violence and violent behaviors ($N = 9,487$; Singer & Flannery, 2000). Children's reports of threatening others were significantly associated with self-reported violent behaviors. This relationship was particularly powerful among children who frequently threatened others. These finding suggest that children's threats of violence should be taken seriously, and as with children who threaten self-harm, those who threaten others should receive immediate attention and clinical evaluation. Additionally, students who are aware of such threats should be encouraged to report them to a responsible adult and to understand that protecting someone who is threatening to harm another is not appropriate. We should take threats of interpersonal harm as seriously as we have come to take threats of self-injury.

Recent violence exposure has also been associated with violent behavior. In this same sample, recent and past exposure to violence together explained 26% of the variation on violent behavior for males and 22% for females. Recent exposure in terms of witnessing or victimization of a shooting or knife attack was the strongest predictor of violence for males; for females, witnessing or victimization of a shooting or knife attack, witnessing or victimization at home, and victimization at school were equally associated with violent behaviors (Flannery et al., 1998; Song et al., 1998).

Elementary- and middle-school students are also exposed to high levels of violence. Across sites and gender, between 16.0 and 54.5% had been threatened; between 14.1 and 50.2% had been slapped, hit, or punched; between 2.7 and 18.1% had bean beaten or mugged; and between 2.8% and 10.6% had been attacked with a knife or shot at in the past year. A greater percentage of boys reported being beaten up than girls, across contexts. Students at central city schools reported more serious forms of violence (e.g., beatings, knife attacks, and shootings; Singer et al., 1999). Regression analyses indicated that demographic variables, parental monitoring, television habits, and exposure to violence together explained 45% of the variation in violent behavior; recent exposure to violence was the best single predictor, explaining 24.2% of the variance. Witnessing or victimization of a shooting or knife attack was the strongest predictor, followed by victimization and witnessing violence at home, and witnessing violence at school or in the neighborhood (Singer et al., 1999).

We can conclude from these investigations that regardless of location (urban, suburban, or rural) children and adolescents experience high levels of witnessing violence and victimization from violence. Exposure to recent violence in the past year is related to trauma symptoms and violent behavior across age groups. In particular witnessing and victimization of the most serious violence, a shooting or knife attack, is the strongest predictor of trauma-related symptoms and violent behavior. Victimization and witnessing violence at school are also

problematic, particularly for females. Future research will continue to investigate the psychometric properties of the measures across groups and will establish norms of victimization and witnessing violence across location, context, and type of violence witnessed and how these norms are related to violence and mental health.

Gender, Age, and Ethnicity

Data on victimization from violence and crime have long shown that young people (children and adolescents) are at higher risk of victimization from violence than adults (Finkelhor & Dziuba-Leatherman, 1994). Hashima and Finkelhor (1999) using data from the National Crime Victimization Survey showed that the rate for simple assault among youth aged 12 to 17 was 2.9 times higher than the rate for adults. Higher rates of victimization from violence among 12- to 17-year-olds compared to adults held for almost every type of crime assessed, and youth were almost three times more likely than adults to suffer a crime-related injury (Hashima & Finkelhor, 1999).

Studies of rates of victimization from violence consistently show boys to be victimized by violence at higher overall rates than girls (Finkelhor & Dziuba-Leatherman, 1994; Hashima & Finkelhor, 1999), although girls report significantly higher rates of sexual victimization and assault from a family member (Finkelhor & Dziuba-Leatherman, 1994b). Our recent work with juvenile offenders who present with comorbid mental health and substance abuse issues supports the findings for female victimization. Specifically, we have found that nearly three of four female offenders report being previously victimized by a family member compared to one of four male offenders, with females reporting significantly higher rates of sexual victimization and emotional abuse (Hussey, Drinkard, & Flannery, in press).

Consistent with data on rates of victimization, boys also report higher levels of overall exposure to violence and perpetrating more violence than girls (DuRant,

Cadenhead, Pendergrast, Slavens, & Linder, 1994; Farrell & Bruce, 1997; Fitzpatrick & Boldizar, 1993; Singer et al., 1995, 1999, 2001). This high level of exposure to violence comes with some significant behavior and mental health consequences. For example, youth (both males and females) exposed to high levels of violence report perpetrating higher rates of aggression and violence. High exposure to violence is also related to high levels of clinically significant mental health symptoms like anger, anxiety, depression, and dissociation. Adolescent females in high violence exposure groups are at particular risk of reporting clinically significant anger, depression, and suicide ideation compared to even the most violent males (Flannery et al., 2001).

We have also found some significant developmental changes in the relationship between exposure to violence and youth self-reported mental health symptoms. To illustrate these differences, we put together data from our combined samples of youth in elementary school (grades 3 through 5), middle school (grades 6 through 8), and high school (grades 9 through 12) gathered from three separate studies and including youth from urban and nonurban locations and youth of various backgrounds and economic status (see Table 14.1). Using the Recent Exposure to Violence Scale, we calculated a sum score for exposure and then split the sample into the highest and lowest 10% for low and high violence exposure. Once these two extreme groups were identified, we took the mean score for the entire sample on each subscale of the Trauma Symptom Checklist for Children (Briere, 1996), adjusted by gender. An individual's self-reported score on any scale was considered to be clinically significant if it was greater than 1.5 standard deviations above the mean scale score for that scale. Table 14.1 illustrates the percentage of youth exposed to high and low violence who report clinically significant mental health symptoms, separated by grade level and gender.

A few trends are worth noting. First, as expected, the percentage of youth who report clinically significant mental health symptoms is consistently greater for youth in the high violence exposure group compared to the low violence exposure group, and with few exceptions (e.g., anxiety was always higher for girls), the rates are not very different between males and females. In grades three to five, high exposed males report higher rates of mental health symptoms than females, but this trend reverses in middle school and high school, favoring females. Rates of clinically significant anger increase for high exposure girls from 21% in grades 3 to 5 to 36% for girls in high school, whereas rates for boys decrease from 34 to 29% across the same age groups. Across most mental health symptoms, it is most important to note that rates of clinically significant symptoms in the high violence exposure group are highest among youth in grades three to five and steadily decline through adolescence. This may be a trend that has important implications for preventive interventions because they need to take into account our understanding of the developmental impact of violence exposure on child mental health and behavior.

The question of ethnic similarities and differences in rates of exposure to violence is a bit more complicated than assessing age or gender differences. Some studies have shown that African American youth witness more community violence than Hispanic youth (Crouch, Hanson, Saunders, Kilpatrick, & Resnick, 2000) and more than White youth (Kuo, Mohler, Raudenbush, & Earls, 2000; Selner-O'Hagan, Kindlon, Buka, Raudenbush, & Earls, 1998), but other studies have found no ethnic group differences in levels of exposure (Schwab-Stone et al., 1995; Sheley, McGee, & Wright, 1992). Some studies look more at contextual effects on exposure to violence than at child ethnicity per se; they argue that these contextual factors, such as living in a urban environment, SES, and parent level of education completed, may be more important in determining the child's overall level of exposure to violence (e.g., Crouch et al., 2000; Salzinger, Feldman, Stockhammer, & Hood, 2002).

Table 14.1: Percent of Students in the Clinically Significant Range of Trauma Symptoms

Grades 3–5

Trauma Symptoms	Females n = 113		Males n = 117	
	Low Violence Exposure	High Violence Exposure	Low Violence Exposure	High Violence Exposure
Anger	0	21.2	0	34.4
Anxiety	0	42.2	1.9	34.4
Depression	0	39.4	5.7	37.5
Dissociation	1.2	27.3	0	31.3
PTSD	0	24.2	3.8	37.5
Total Trauma	0	21.2	1.9	39.1

Grades 6–8

Trauma Symptoms	Females n = 117		Males n = 124	
	Low Violence Exposure	High Violence Exposure	Low Violence Exposure	High Violence Exposure
Anger	0	25.0	0	33.8
Anxiety	1.6	32.9	2.3	23.8
Depression	0	30.4	2.3	27.5
Dissociation	3.3	32.1	2.3	26.3
PTSD	1.6	30.4	0	26.3
Total Trauma	1.6	32.1	0	28.8

Grades 9–12

Trauma Symptoms	Females n = 365		Males n = 366	
	Low Violence Exposure	High Violence Exposure	Low Violence Exposure	High Violence Exposure
Anger	0.9	36.1	0	29.7
Anxiety	0.9	26.5	0.6	18.9
Depression	0.9	22.4	0.6	19.3
Dissociation	1.4	25.9	0	21.2
PTSD	0.9	25.9	0	19.3
Total Trauma	0.4	31.3	0	23.6

The Recent Exposure to Violence Scale

In most of our work assessing exposure to violence we have used a child/adolescent self-report survey called the Recent Exposure to Violence Scale (REVS; Singer et al., 1995). The REVS is a 22-item scale that measures five specific acts of violence (either experienced or personally witnessed) at home, at school, or in the neighborhood during the past year: threats, slapping/hitting/punching, beatings, knife attacks, and shootings; reports on knife attacks and shootings were not context specific. The REVS has several advantages over other measures of violence exposure. First, as a youth self-report instrument, it is quick and easy to administer. The items are written to be understandable to a child as young as 8 years old. It measures exposure to violence as both witness and victim, and it assesses exposure across multiple contexts. The REVS asks about violence exposure in the past year, which helps minimize any recall bias inherent in surveys about lifetime exposure to violence, and the items do not ask a child to report the identity of specific perpetrators of violence against them. We have found the REVS to be a reliable and valid instrument that is completed by youth without causing emotional distress. We have used a 26-item measure in some studies, with four additional questions assessing whether children have been (or witnessed someone else being) shot at or shot with a real gun, or if they have been (or witnessed someone else being) touched in a private place on their body where they did not want to be touched (measuring abuse). With elementary school samples these four questions are often removed from the scale as developmentally inappropriate (being shot) or because schools find them overly sensitive (abuse). The analyses presented here are for the shorter, 22-item version that is common across all studies.

The measure was originally tested with students from six public high schools ($n = 3,735$). We performed a principal component analysis with a Varimax rotation, which resulted in five factors: (1) witnessed in neighborhood (3 items); (2) victimized or witnessed at home (6 items); (3) witnessed at school (3 items); (4) victimized at school or in neighborhood (6 items); and (5) shooting/knife attack (4 items). Scale reliability for the five factors ranged from $\alpha = 0.68$ to $\alpha = 0.87$ (Singer et al., 1995). The adequate internal consistency of the factors was confirmed in samples of public school elementary- and middle-school children from third through eighth grades ($n = 2,245$; Singer et al., 1999). To further examine the psychometric properties of the measure, confirmatory factor analyses were conducted on a sample of school children in grades three through six ($n = 2,963$; Flannery et al., 2003). Results indicated that the five-factor solution fit the data moderately well (χ^2/df $= 6.88$, CFI $= 0.92$, RMSEA $= 0.05$). However, the marginal fit of the five-factor solution suggested that alternative models be tested. We found that a seven-factor model that separates out witnessing violence from victimization in each of the three settings examined (home, school, and neighborhood), as well as a severe violence factor, fit the data significantly better than the five-factor model (χ^2/df $=$ 5.98, CFI $= 0.93$, RMSEA $= 0.036$). Multigroup confirmatory factor analyses for the original high-school sample, the elementary-school sample, and a third elementary/middle-school sample showed the seven-factor model was invariant across different samples ($n = 8,695$; CFI $= 0.91$, RMSEA $= 0.057$, RMSEA C. I. $= 0.056$ to 0.058, SRMR $= 0.044$). Additional analyses are being conducted to further investigate the scale's factorial invariance across age, gender, and ethnicity (Van Dulmen, Belliston, Flannery, & Singer, 2005).

Implications for Preventive Interventions

Early and chronic exposure to violence, either through high rates of witnessing violence or via victimization from violence, has reached critically high levels among youth today. Exposure to violence is a significant problem for youth mental health, places them at increased risk for subsequent behavior problems such as delinquency and violence, and is related to a host of other related problem outcomes in relationships with families and peers, academic achievement, and potential involvement with child and family-serving, justice, and treatment systems. The severity, complexity, and chronicity of these outcomes also lead to significant social, economic, and political costs to society. The reactionary strategy of waiting until a youth is exhibiting significant mental health, academic or behavior problem outcomes or is deeply involved in multiple systems (e.g., substance use and legal) is neither efficient nor effective.

All of the research to date on violence exposure and its related mental health and behavior outcomes points to the need for early identification and preventive interventions. The problems are too complex and too difficult to ameliorate to wait until a child is a late adolescent or young adult. School is a logical setting to focus our efforts in this arena, as most children are still attending preschool or early elementary school (grades K through three). Waiting until middle school may even be too late for the most high-risk youth, who may also have 10 or so years of exposure to violence behind them, academic and mental health problems before them, and significant adjustment and behavior problems ahead of them.

Several points about early identification and preventive intervention regarding violence exposure deserve mention here. Of course, there are many other factors to consider, (e.g., Osofsky & Osofsky, 2001).

First, given that schools are a primary context of identification and prevention, we need a concerted effort to place mental health professionals in schools. These individuals should be trained to identify youth in need of additional services and to work closely with community-based providers to get youth and families the help they need early on and quickly.

Second, interventions need to include families and peer groups (i.e., their social networks). There are a myriad of factors related to mental health problems and violence perpetration, but focusing only on an individual child's risk factors or protective qualities will not sustain behavior change over time. As children grow older, peers gain influence, (mostly at the expense of parents), over families, and youth spend increasingly more time with peers than with family members.

Third, our preventive interventions need to address risk and protection at multiple levels and across multiple systems. Individuals grow up in families who live in neighborhoods that contain schools and churches and are characterized by other factors that affect mental health and violence.

Last, our interventions must continue to focus on the development of positive coping skills, competencies, and problem-solving skills that will help young people deal effectively with high levels of exposure to violence. Interventions that rely only on risk reduction miss the other side of the coin (Embry & Flannery, 1999) and will fail over the long-term to achieve the desired outcome of a reduction in mental health symptoms and rates of violent behavior.

Looking Toward the Future

Over the last 15 years or so, ever since the ground-breaking research on violence exposure and victimization by Widom (1989) and Richters and Martinez (1993), the field has experienced a significant increase in research on the prevalence of violence exposure and its association with various mental health and behavior outcomes. The most recent research has begun to examine the factors that may mediate or moderate the relationship between violence exposure and those outcomes as a next step toward prevention and effective intervention. The evidence is consistent and clear regarding several issues:

- Youth in community samples report high rates of exposure to violence, with rates of witnessing various forms of violence generally higher than rates of victimization from violence.
- There is a strong association between violence exposure and increased risk for the perpetration of aggression and violence, even after controlling for demographic and contextual factors.
- Being exposed to violence contributes to higher levels of reported mental health symptoms in both community and clinical samples of youth.
- Rates of exposure to violence (both witnessing and victimization) are generally higher for boys, with the exception of sexual victimization, which is higher for girls.
- Despite overall differences in average rates of exposure, girls who report high levels of exposure to violence are at just as much risk of experiencing clinically significant mental health symptoms and perpetrating aggression and violence as boys who report high levels of violence exposure.
- Younger children report higher levels of victimization from violence than older youth, and similar levels of witnessing violence.

Although these consistent findings in the extant literature have already contributed significantly to our understanding of how exposure to violence affects youth mental health and behavior, including risk for perpetrating violence, we have a long way to go. For example, most of the studies in this arena have been cross-sectional or limited to relatively small, targeted samples of youth in high-risk settings. Although these studies have provided valuable insight into the levels of violence exposure that youth experience and the role of certain contextual factors (e.g., SES, neighborhood disorganization), it is only through longitudinal studies that we will discover the lasting impact of early exposure to violence (e.g., in childhood) on later mental health and behavior outcomes (e.g., risk for perpetrating violence in adolescence). Some short-term longitudinal studies have shown, for example, that previous exposure to violence over one's lifetime has little impact on risk for later aggression and delinquency, whereas many other studies have shown that recent exposure to violence (i.e., in the past year) is the strongest predictor of concurrent mental health symptomatology and risk for perpetrating violence even after controlling for multiple demographic factors (Singer et al., 1999).

Related to the need for studies that examine the effects of exposure to violence longitudinally at different points in development is the need to examine issues of developmental process compared to behavioral outcomes. Assessing developmental processes versus mean group differences on behavior outcomes was first discussed by Rowe, Vazsonyi, and Flannery (1994). They showed that despite differences between groups on mean levels of outcome behaviors (e.g., delinquency, substance use) there existed a high degree of similarity in the development processes that predicted those outcomes between members of different ethnic groups. In other words, although there may be consistent differences in the mean levels of delinquent behavior reported between members of two different ethnic groups, the factors that predict which individuals will become delinquent are the same for members of both groups.

To transfer the analogy, research has consistently shown differences in the levels of exposure to violence for youth who live in certain contexts (e.g., urban vs. nonurban settings) or youth who are exposed to violence in different settings (e.g., home vs. school) or youth who are members of different ethnic groups (although this is sometimes confounded with SES). However, even if youth live in different settings where levels of violence exposure are significantly different, cross-sectional studies have shown that any youth who is exposed to high levels of violence is at significantly increased risk of perpetrating violence and experiencing clinically significant levels of mental health symptoms. Our hypothesis would be that, although contextual and demographic factors may contribute to differences, on average, in *levels* of violence exposure, youth in any of those settings exposed to high levels of violence would be at high risk of clinically significant mental health problems and for perpetrating violent behavior. In other words, it is the high level of exposure to violence that contributes to mental health and behavior problems, even when context and demographic factors are taken into account. More work is needed to examine the issue of developmental processes as they relate to behavior outcomes like violence, particularly given the influence of contextual and demographic factors. Findings may be different depending on the outcomes examined, the type of analyses employed, the number and types of groups compared (e.g., members of different ethnic groups), and the developmental process variables considered (different mediators and moderators; Flannery et al., 2003; Foshee, Ennett, Bauman, Benefield, & Suchindran, 2005; Rosario, Salzinger, Feldman, & Ng-Mak, 2003).

Lastly, future research must continue to examine the factors that may protect a young person from the effects of high exposure to violence. We have come to know a great deal about the risk factors associated with high exposure to violence (witnessing and victimization), but we still know relatively little about what makes some youth resilient and able to cope with violence compared to youth who are emotionally and behaviorally fragile (Christiansen & Evans, 2005). The answers may not lie in our traditional examination of individual-level factors. Instead, we may need to look more at social networks of family members, peers and adult mentors, or to youth and family involvement in different systems, such as education, juvenile justice, and mental health. The answer may lie in examinations of differential and interactive effects studied over longer periods of time as opposed to main effect models assessing relationships at one point in time. For example, Rosario et al. (2003) recently demonstrated how confrontational coping increased the risk for perpetration of delinquent behavior among both boys and girls who witness violence in the community, but having a supportive guardian buffered the association between violence exposure and delinquency for girls. The answer may lie in more integrative, intensive examinations of the roles of genetics and biology as they affect and are in turn affected by environmental and behavioral influences. As we learn more about the relationship between violence and mental health, we seem to raise as many questions as we answer. It will take a concerted, long-term collaborative effort by researchers, practitioners, and policymakers from many different disciplines to understand this complex phenomenon more fully. Only then can we hope to significantly reduce levels of child exposure to violence and its negative impact on mental health and violent behavior.

Appendix

* To be read aloud with students in grades three to five.

Recent Exposure to Violence Scale

Sometimes young people see, hear about, or experience scary, frightening, or violent events. We would like to know about the experiences you have had with these events *over the past year*.

Circle the answer that best describes your experiences. *Do not include things you may have seen or heard about from other people or from TV, radio, the news, or the movies.*

THREATS

(Over the past year)

1. How often over the past year did anyone **at home** tell you they were going to hurt *you*?
Never Sometimes Often Almost every day

2. How often over the past year did anyone **at school** tell you they were going to hurt *you*?
Never Sometimes Often Almost every day

3. How often over the past year did anyone **in your neighborhood** tell you they were going to hurt *you*?
Never Sometimes Often Almost every day

4. How often over the past year did you see *someone else* **at home** being told they were going to be hurt?
Never Sometimes Often Almost every day

5. How often over the past year did you see *someone else* **at school** being told they were going to be hurt?
Never Sometimes Often Almost every day

6. How often over the past year did you see *someone else* **in your neighborhood** being told they were going to be hurt?
Never Sometimes Often Almost every day

SLAPPING, HITTING, PUNCHING

(Over the past year)

7. How often over the past year have you *yourself* been slapped, punched, or hit by someone **at home**?
Never Sometimes Often Almost every day

8. How often over the past year have you *yourself* been slapped, punched, or hit by someone **in school**?
Never Sometimes Often Almost every day

9. How often over the past year have you *yourself* been slapped, punched, or hit by someone **in your neighborhood**?
Never Sometimes Often Almost every day

10. How often over the past year have you seen *someone else* being slapped, punched, or hit by someone **at home**?

Never Sometimes Often Almost every day

11. How often over the past year have you seen *someone else* being slapped, punched, or hit by someone **in school**?

Never Sometimes Often Almost every day

12. How often over the past year have you seen *someone else* being slapped, punched, or hit by someone **in your neighborhood**?

Never Sometimes Often Almost every day

BEATINGS

(Over the past year)

13. How often over the past year have *you* been beaten up **at home**?

Never Sometimes Often Almost every day

14. How often over the past year have *you* been beaten up **in school**?

Never Sometimes Often Almost every day

15. How often over the past year have *you* been beaten up **in your neighborhood**?

Never Sometimes Often Almost every day

16. How often over the past year have you seen *someone else* getting beaten up **at home**?

Never Sometimes Often Almost every day

17. How often over the past year have you seen *someone else* getting beaten up **at school**?

Never Sometimes Often Almost every day

18. How often over the past year have you seen *someone else* getting beaten up **in your neighborhood**?

Never Sometimes Often Almost every day

KNIFE ATTACKS

(Over the past year)

19. How often over the past year have you *yourself* been attacked or stabbed with a knife?

Never Sometimes Often Almost every day

20. How often over the past year have you seen *someone else* being attacked or stabbed with a knife?

Never Sometimes Often Almost every day

GUNS/SHOOTINGS

(Over the past year)

21. How often over the past year has someone pointed a **real** gun at *you*?

Never Sometimes Often Almost every day

22. How often over the past year have you seen someone pointing a **real** gun at *someone else*?

Never Sometimes Often Almost every day

References

Anderson, M., Kaufman, J., Simon, T., Barrios, L., Paulozzi, L., Ryan, G., et al., & the School-Associated Violent Deaths Study Group, (2001). School-associated violent deaths in the United States, 1994–1999. *Journal of the American Medical Association, 286,* 2695–2702.

Ando, M., Asakura, T., & Simons-Morton, B. (2005). Psychosocial influences on physical, verbal and indirect bullying among Japanese early adolescents. *Journal of Early Adolescence, 25,* 268–297.

Belliston, L., Van Dulmen, M., Flannery, D. J., & Singer, M. I. (2005). *Revalidation of the Recent Exposure to Violence Scale across three samples from middle childhood through adolescence.* Unpublished manuscript.

Boney-McCoy, S., & Finkelhor, D. (1995). Psychological sequelae of violence victimization in a national youth sample. *Journal of Consulting and Clinical Psychology, 63,* 726–736.

Breslau, N., Davis, G. C., Andreski, P., & Peterson, E. (1991). Traumatic events and posttraumatic stress disorder in an urban population of young girls. *Archives of General Psychiatry, 48,* 216–222.

Briere, J. (1996). *Professional manual for the Trauma Symptom Checklist for Children (TSC-C).* Odessa, FL: Psychological Assessment Resources.

Buka, S., Stichick, T., Birdthistle, I., & Earls, F. (2001). Youth exposure to violence: Prevalence, risks, and consequences. *American Journal of Orthopsychiatry, 71,* 298–310.

Centers for Disease Control and Prevention (2000). Youth risk behavior surveillance—United States, 1999. *Morbidity and Mortality Weekly Report, 49*, SS-5.

Christiansen, E. J., & Evans, W. P. (2005). Adolescent victimization: Testing models of resiliency by gender. *Journal of Early Adolescence, 25*, 298–316.

Cooley-Quille, M., Boyd, R., Frantz, E., & Walsh, J. (2001). Emotional and behavioral impact of exposure to community violence in inner-city adolescents. *Journal of Clinical Child Psychology, 30*, 199–206.

Crouch, J. L., Hanson, R. F., Saunders, B. E., Kilpatrick, D. G., & Resnick, H. S. (2000). Income, race/ethnicity, and exposure to violence in youth: Results from the National Survey of Adolescents. *Journal of Community Psychology, 28*, 625–641.

Cullingford, C., & Morrison, J. (1995). Bullying as a formative influence: The relationship between the experience of school and criminality. *British Educational Research Journal, 21*, 547–561.

Dodge, K., Bates, J., & Pettit, G. (1990). Mechanisms in the cycle of violence. *Science, 250*, 1678–1683.

DuRant, R. H., Cadenhead, C., Pendergrast, R. A., Slavens, G., & Linder, C. W. (1994). Factors associated with the use of violence among urban black adolescents. *American Journal of Public Health, 84*, 612–617.

Embry, D., & Flannery, D. J. (1999). Two sides of the coin: Multi-level prevention and intervention to reduce youth violent behavior. In D. J. Flannery & C. R. Huff (Eds.), *Youth violence: Prevention, intervention, and social policy* (pp. 47–72). Washington, DC: American Psychiatric Press.

Farrell, A. D., & Bruce, S. E. (1997). Impact of exposure to community violence on violent behavior and emotional distress among urban adolescents. *Journal of Clinical Child Psychology, 26*, 2–14.

Farrell, A. D., & Sullivan, T. N. (2004). Impact of witnessing violence on growth curves for problem behaviors among early adolescents in urban and rural settings. *Journal of Community Psychology, 32*, 505–525.

Fehon, D., Grilo, C., & Lipschitz, D. (2001a). Correlates of community violence exposure in hospitalized adolescents. *Comprehensive Psychiatry, 42*, 283–290.

Fehon, D., Grilo, C., & Lipschitz, D. (2001b). Gender differences in violence exposure and violence risk among adolescent inpatients. *Journal of Nervous and Mental Disease, 189*, 532–540.

Finkelhor, D. (1995). The victimization of children: A developmental perspective. *American Journal of Orthopsychiatry, 65*, 177–193.

Finkelhor, D., & Dziuba-Leatherman, J. (1994a). Children as victims of violence: A national survey. *Pediatrics, 94*, 413–420.

Finkelhor, D., & Dziuba-Leatherman, J. (1994b). Victimization of children. *American Psychologist, 49*, 173–183.

Fitzpatrick, K., & Boldizar, J. (1993). The prevalence and consequences of exposure to violence among African-American youth. *Journal of the American Academy of Child and Adolescent Psychiatry, 32*, 424–430.

Flannery, D. J. (1996). A developmental perspective on the effects of violent environments on children. In W. Reed (Ed.), *Violence and trauma: Understanding and responding to the effects of violence on young children* (pp. 17–26). Cleveland: Urban Child Research Center, Cleveland State University.

Flannery, D. J. (1999). *Exposure to violence and victimization at school* (Choices Briefs, no. 4). New York: Columbia University Institute for Urban and Minority Education.

Flannery, D. J. (2006). *Violence and mental health in everyday life: Prevention and intervention strategies for children and adolescents.* New York: Altamira Press.

Flannery, D. J., Singer, M. I., & Wester, K. (2001). Violence exposure, psychological trauma and suicide risk in a community sample of dangerously violent adolescents. *Journal of the American Academy of Child and Adolescent Psychiatry, 40*, 435–442.

Flannery, D. J., Singer, M. I., & Wester, K. (2003). Violence, coping, and mental health in a community sample of adolescents. *Violence and victims, 18*, 403–418.

Flannery, D. J., Singer, M. I., Williams, L., & Castro, P. (1998). Adolescent violence exposure and victimization at home: Coping and psychological trauma symptoms. *International Review of Victimology, 6*, 63–82.

Flannery, D. J., Vazsonyi, A., Liau, A., Guo, S., Powell, K., Atha, H., et al. (2003). Initial behavior outcomes for Peacebuilders universal school-based violence prevention program. *Developmental Psychology, 39*, 292–308.

Flannery, D. J., Wester, K., & Singer, M. I. (2004). Impact of exposure to violence in school on child and adolescent mental health and behavior. *Journal of Community Psychology, 32,* 559–573.

Foshee, V. A., Ennett, S. T., Bauman, K. E., Benefield, T., & Suchindran, C. (2005). The association between family violence and adolescent dating violence onset: Does it vary by race, socioeconomic status, and family structure? *Journal of Early Adolescence, 25,* 317–344.

Fox, D., & Zawitz, M. (2001). *Homicide trends in the United States.* Washington, DC: U.S. Department of Justice, Office of Justice Programs, Bureau of Justice Statistics. Retrieved from *http//:www.ojp.usdoj.gov/bjs/.*

Gorman-Smith, D., & Tolan, P. (1998). The role of exposure to community violence and developmental problems among inner-city youth. *Development and Psychopathology, 10,* 101–116.

Hashima, P. Y., & Finkelhor, D. (1999). Violent victimization of youth versus adults in the National Crime Victimization Survey. *Journal of Interpersonal Violence, 14,* 799–820.

Haynie, D. L., Nansel, T., Eitel, P., Crump, A. D., Saylor, K., Yu, K., et al. (2001). Bullies, victims, and bully/victims: Distinct groups of at-risk youth. *Journal of Early Adolescence, 21,* 29–49.

Hazler, R. J. (1996). *Breaking the cycle of violence: Interventions for bullying and victimization.* Washington, DC: Accelerated Development.

Hoover, J. H., & Juul, K. (1993). Bullying in Europe and the United States. *Journal of Emotional and Behavioral Problems, 2,* 25–29.

Hoover, J. H., & Oliver, R. (1996). *The bullying prevention handbook: A guide for principals, teachers and counselors.* Bloomington, IN: National Educational Services.

Hussey, D., Drinkard, A., & Flannery, D. J. (in press). Comorbid mental health and substance use issues among offending youth. *Journal of Social Work Practice in the Addictions.*

Jones, F., Ajirotutu, C., & Johnson, J. (1996). African American children and adolescents exposure to community violence: A pilot study. *Journal of Cultural Diversity, 3,* 48–52.

Kachur, S., Stennies, G., Kenneth, E., Modzeleski, W., Stephenson, R., Murphy, R., et al. (1996). School associated violent deaths in the United States, 1992 to 1994. *Journal of the American Medical Association, 275,* 1729–1733.

Kaltiala-Heino, R., Rimpela, M., Marttunen, M., Rimpela, A., & Rantanen, P. (1999). Bullying, depression, and suicidal ideation in Finnish adolescents: School survey. *British Medical Journal, 319,* 348–351.

Kingery, P. M., Coggeshall, M. B., & Alford, A. A. (1998). Violence at school: Recent evidence from four national surveys. *Psychology in the Schools, 35,* 247–258.

Kumpulainen, K., Rasanen, E., Henttonen, I., Almqvist, F., Kresanov, K., & Linna, S. L. (1998). Bullying and psychiatric symptoms among elementary school-aged children. *Child Abuse and Neglect, 22,* 705–717.

Kuo, M., Mohler, B., Raudenbush, S. L., & Earls, F. J. (2000). Assessing exposure to violence using multiple informants: Application of Hierarchical Linear Model. *Journal of Child Psychology and Psychiatry, 41,* 1049–1056.

Lorion, R., & Salzman, W. (1993). Children's exposure to community violence: Following a path from concern to research to action. *Psychiatry, 56,* 55–65.

Maxfield, M. G., & Widom, C. S. (1996). The cycle of violence revisited 6 years later. *Archives of Pediatrics and Adolescent Medicine, 150,* 390–395.

Nansel, T. R., Craig, W., Overpeck, M. D., Saluja, G., & Ruan, W. J. (2004). Cross-national consistency in the relationship between bullying behaviors and psychosocial adjustment. *Archives of Pediatrics and Adolescent Medicine, 158,* 730–736.

Nansel, T. R., Overpeck, M., Pilla, R. S., Ruan, W. J., Simons-Morton, B., & Scheidt, P. (2001). Bullying behaviors among U.S. youth: Prevalence and association with psychosocial adjustment. *Journal of the American Medical Association, 25,* 2094–2100.

Nolin, M., Davies, E., & Chandler, K. (1995). *Student victimization at school. Statistics in brief.* Washington, DC: National Center for Education Statistics, U.S. Department of Education.

Office of Juvenile Justice and Delinquency Prevention (2000). *Children as victims.* (Bulletin). Washington, DC: U.S. Department of Justice, Office of Justice Programs.

Office of Juvenile Justice and Delinquency Prevention (2001a). *Addressing youth victimization* (Bulletin). Washington, DC: U.S. Department of Justice, Office of Justice Programs.

Office of Juvenile Justice and Delinquency Prevention (2001b). *Homicides of children and youth* (Bulletin). Washington, DC: U.S. Department of Justice, Office of Justice Programs.

Oliver, R. L., Young, T. A., & LaSalle, S. M. (1994). Early lessons in bullying and victimization: The help and hindrance of children's literature. *School Counselor, 42,* 137–146.

Olweus, D. (1993). *Bullying at school: What we know and what we can do*. Cambridge, MA: Blackwell Publishers.

Osofsky, H. J., & Osofsky, J. D. (2001). Violent and aggressive behaviors in youth: A mental health and prevention perspective. *Psychiatry, 64*, 285–295.

Osofsky, J. D. (1995). The effects of violence exposure on children. *American Psychologist, 50*, 782–788.

Osofsky, J. D. (1997). *Children in a violent society*. New York: Guilford.

Osofsky, J. D. (1999). The impact of violence on children. *Future of Children, 9*, 33–49.

Osofsky, J. D. (2001, October). *Addressing youth victimization* (Action Plan Bulletin). Washington, DC: U.S. Department of Education, U.S. Department of Justice.

Overstreet, S., & Braun, S. (2000). Exposure to community violence and post-traumatic stress symptoms: Mediating factors. *American Journal of Orthopsychiatry, 70*, 263–271.

Pynoos, R. S. (1993). Traumatic stress and developmental psychopathology in children and adolescents. In J. M. Oldham, M. B. Riba, & A. Tasman (Eds.), *American Psychiatric Press Review of Psychiatry* (pp. 205–238). Washington, DC: American Psychiatric Press.

Richters, J., & Martinez, P. (1993). The NIMH community violence project: Children as victims and witnesses to violence. *Psychiatry, 56*, 7–21.

Rosario, M., Salzinger, S., Feldman, R. S., & Ng-Mak, D. S. (2003). Community violence exposure and delinquent behaviors among youth: The moderating role of coping. *Journal of Community Psychology, 31*, 489–512.

Ross, D. M. (1996). *Childhood bullying and teasing: What school personnel, other professionals, and parents can do*. Alexandria, VA: American Counseling Association.

Rowe, D. C., Vazsonyi, A., & Flannery, D. J. (1994). No more than skin deep: Ethnic and racial similarity in developmental process. *Psychological Review, 101*, 396–413.

Salmon, G., & West, A. (2000). Physical and mental health issues related to bullying in schools. *Current Opinion in Psychiatry, 13*, 375–380.

Salzinger, S., Feldman, R., Stockhammer, T., & Hood, J. (2002). An ecological framework for understanding risk for exposure to community violence and the effects of exposure on children and adolescents. *Aggression and Violent Behavior, 7*, 423–451.

Schwab-Stone, M., Ayers, T., Kasprow, W., Voyce, C., Barone, C., Shriver, T., et al. (1995). No safe haven: A study of violence exposure in an urban community. *Journal of the American Academy of Child and Adolescent Psychiatry, 34*, 1343–1352.

Selner-O'Hagan, M. B., Kindlon, D. J., Buka, S. L., Raudenbush, S. W., & Earls, F. J. (1998). Assessing exposure to violence in urban youth. *Journal of Child Psychology and Psychiatry and Allied Disciplines, 39*, 215–224.

Sheley, J. F., McGee, Z. T., & Wright, J. D. (1992). Gun-related violence in and around inner-city schools. *American Journal of Diseases of Children, 146*, 677–682.

Singer, M. I., Anglin, T. M., Song, L., & Lunghofer, L. (1995). Adolescents' exposure to violence and associated symptoms of psychological trauma. *Journal of the American Medical Association, 273*, 477–482.

Singer, M. I., & Flannery, D. J. (2000). The relationship between children's threats of violence and violent behavior. *Archives of Pediatrics and Adolescent Medicine, 154*, 785–790.

Singer, M. I., Flannery, D. J., Guo, S., Miller, D., & Liebrandt, S. (2004). Exposure to violence, parental monitoring, and television viewing as contributors to children's psychological trauma. *Journal of Community Psychology, 32*, 489–504.

Singer, M. I., Miller, D., Guo, S., Flannery, D. J., Frierson, T., & Slovak, K. (1999). Contributors to violence behavior among elementary and middle school children. *Pediatrics, 104*, 878–884.

Small, M., & Tetrick, K. (2001). School violence: An overview. *Juvenile Justice Bulletin, 8*(1), 3–12.

Song, L, Singer, M. I., & Anglin, T. M. (1998). Violence exposure and emotional trauma as contributors to adolescents' violent behaviors. *Archives of Pediatrics and Adolescent Medicine, 152*, 531–536.

U.S. Department of Education (2002). *Indicators of school crime and safety: 2002*. Washington, DC: U.S. Department of Justice, Office of Justice Programs.

Weist, M., Acosta, O., & Youngstrom, E. (2001). Predictors of violence exposure among inner-city youth. *Journal of Clinical Child Psychology, 30*, 187–198.

Widom, C. (1989). The cycle of violence. *Science, 244*, 160–166.

CHAPTER 15

Social-Cognitive Processes in the Development of Antisocial and Violent Behavior

Gregory S. Pettit and Jacquelyn Mize

Introduction

Research linking social-cognitive processes with child and adolescent behavior and adjustment has increased at a major clip in the past couple of decades. Although a range of social-cognitive perspectives have been brought to bear on the topic, those that focus on the sequential steps in processing social information have engendered the greatest research attention (e.g., Huesmann, 1988; Rubin & Krasnor, 1986), and of these, the social information-processing (SIP) model articulated by Dodge (1986, 1993), and refined and elaborated by Dodge and colleagues (e.g., Crick & Dodge, 1994; Dodge & Pettit, 2003; Dodge & Rabiner, 2004) has been especially fertile.

The basic elements of the model, as they relate to the development of chronic conduct problems, are as follows: (a) In the context of a specific social situation, such as a provocation by a peer, individual differences in encoding, interpretation, and response generation and evaluation distinguish children high versus low in aggression and antisocial behavior; (b) the social-cognitive steps

or components are nonredundantly predictive of aggression and antisocial behavior; (c) individual differences in social-cognitive processes stem in part from aggressogenic life experiences, such as harsh treatment by parents and rejection by classroom peers; (d) such experiences contribute to the development of generalized expectations about self and others (also known as knowledge structures, latent structures, schemas, and scripts) that both guide and constrain the online processing of social information; and (e) these generalized expectations and the social information-processing patterns that flow from them at least partially account for the link between aggressogenic experience and subsequent antisocial and violent behavior (Pettit, 2004). Although these conclusions are not so firm as to be without skeptics or critics (e.g., Patterson, 1994), they reasonably summarize a substantial body of empirical work.

The SIP model now has a certain degree of maturity. It has provided a foundation for a large number of studies of proximal mechanisms in antisocial behavioral development, and elements of it have been incorporated into widely known and disseminated preventive intervention programs. This large body of work has been the subject of a number of recent narrative and quantitative reviews (Orobio de Castro, Veerman, Koops, Bosch, & Monshouwer, 2002; Gifford-Smith & Rabiner, 2004; Yoon, Hughes, Gaur, & Thompson, 1999). The focus of this chapter is on selected elements of this broader matrix of theory and findings. There are two principal aims. The first aim is to consider existing literature in light of a developmental perspective on links between SIP and antisocial behavior, and on links between family and peer experiences and SIP. To foreshadow a subsequent conclusion, the search for antecedents and correlates of SIP patterns by and large has not been conducted within a developmental context. Age-related considerations have been addressed in refinements of the SIP model (Crick & Dodge, 1994), and empirically driven speculations about age effects have been presented (e.g., Dodge & Price, 1994). However, as yet there have been no formal tests, in the context of long-term prospective inquiry, of several key developmental issues, including whether (a) with advancing age children's SIP skill improves, (b) there is individual stability in SIP skill across development, and (c) links between SIP (and its components) and antisocial behavior are stronger in some developmental periods than in others. For example, it is reasonable to expect skill increases in perspective-taking across the middle childhood years, and deficits in perspective-taking may play a more pronounced role in social behavior (e.g., aggression toward peers) concomitant with these developmental changes.

The second aim is to take a closer look at existing literature in terms of the specificity of predictions and findings. Original SIP formulations (Dodge, 1986; Dodge, Pettit, McClaskey, & Brown, 1986) proposed that social information processing was situation-specific; that is, processing of information about events in particular kinds of situations would be more strongly predictive of behavior in similar situations than of behavior in other kinds of situations. The original situations of interest were those identified by teachers as especially problematic for children experiencing difficulties in their peer relations; namely, responding to rebuff when seeking to enter into an ongoing peer activity and responding to physical and verbal provocations (Dodge, McClaskey, & Feldman, 1985). This kind of specificity might be referred to as setting- or instigating-condition specificity, whereby a particular kind of perceived slight or provocation sets into motion a chain of cognitive and emotional processes (e.g., by triggering memories of prior experiences) that lead to scripted, overlearned patterns of interpreting and reacting to such experiences.

Processing specificity also has been theorized to occur with respect to particular types of antisocial behavior and particular types of social experience. Thus, Crick (e.g., Crick & Werner, 1998) suggested that individual differences in social-relational aggression stem in part from processing biases and deficits that are specific to relational aggression, and Dodge and colleagues (Dodge & Coie, 1987; Dodge & Price, 1994) speculated that underlying SIP patterns should differ for children high in angry-reactive aggression compared to children high in proactive-instrumental aggression. Specificity with respect to social experience has received little empirical study, although theory (Crick & Dodge, 1994) suggests that early-step (encoding and interpretation) processing problems might have developmental antecedents that are different from later-step (response generation and evaluation) processing problems (e.g., harsh treatment by parents and peer rejection might be expected to forecast early-step processing problems, whereas exposure to aggressive role models could be associated more strongly with later-step processing deficits; see Dodge, Lochman, Harnish, Bates, & Pettit, 1997). Likewise, specificity with respect to knowledge structures and their links with SIP patterns has received little study (Burks, Laird, Dodge, Pettit, & Bates, 1999).

Before turning to a more detailed consideration of developmental and situational factors in the relation between SIP and violence, we present an overview of the SIP model and its organizing principles. The emphasis in this section, which draws from Dodge and Pettit (2003), is on how SIP can been construed as bridge – a mechanism of transmission – between aggressogenic life experiences and subsequent antisocial behavior and violence. This is followed by a more detailed analysis of current research and thinking with respect to developmental patterns and with respect to specificity versus generality in processing. The chapter concludes with recommendations for future study of the origins and sequelae of SIP.

Given that the focus of the present volume is on violent behavior, we would be remiss if we did not draw attention to the fact that researchers examining the link between SIP and antisocial behavior generally have been concerned with aggressive behavior rather than violence per se. This is not surprising given that the theoretical models that spawned this research focused on social-cognitive processes that might help explain aggressive behavior in children and adolescents (Dodge, 2003; Huesmann, 1998). In our view, violence and aggression overlap in that both refer to behavioral acts leading to harm and injury to the victim that are perpetrated with the aim of inflicting such harm (Pettit, 2004). The severity of such acts might be construed along a continuum, but few studies have explicitly contrasted "severely" violent youth and more "moderately" aggressive youth (Lochman & Dodge, 1994). Such comparisons may prove useful in future research, but for now we must rely on work that has tended to emphasize the development of aggressive behavior.

Social Information Processing as a Mechanism of Social Transmission

The findings from numerous studies implicate social-cognitive processes during social events as crucial factors that mediate the relation between risk factors and antisocial behavior. Building on existing formulations and accumulating empirical findings, Dodge and Pettit (2003) sought to organize these findings in terms of a multilevel social-transmission model. First, they hypothesized that personal characteristics and dispositions, social context, and life experiences lead children to develop particular kinds of social knowledge about their world. Such knowledge, represented in memory, provides the link between past life experiences and future behavioral tendencies. Second, it was posited that, on presentation of a social stimulus (such as a provocation by a peer or adult authority figure), social knowledge guides the child's characteristic pattern of processing social information. Third, the child's pattern of processing social information was hypothesized to lead directly to specific social (or antisocial) behaviors and to mediate the effect of early life experiences on later antisocial behavior problems.

This conceptual model also can accommodate the interaction between dispositional/biological factors and life experiences in the development of antisocial behavior (Moffitt, 2005). Even given a genetic predisposition for aggressive behavior or a disposition that might be exacerbated (or triggered) by a particular kind of social experience (e.g., maltreatment; see Caspi et al., 2002), it is posited that the expression of this risk in elevated levels of antisocial behavior is predicated on the emergence of maladaptive knowledge structures and patterns of SIP. That is, whereas genetic and environmental risk factors and their interaction increase the likelihood that a child will display antisocial and violent behavior, SIP and related social-cognitive processes are thought to serve as a proximal mechanism through which such factors operate (Pettit, 2004).

The notion of "knowledge structure" has a rich history in social, cognitive, clinical, and developmental psychology. Attachment researchers describe such structures in terms of working models; social psychologists describe relational schemes and scripts. Dodge and Pettit (2003) suggest that such structures interface with discrete social information-processing components to guide behavior during social exchanges. Consider the adolescent boy who is being teased in the school parking lot by a group of peers. Does this boy laugh with the crowd, walk away, or retaliate aggressively? Processing models posit that this boy's immediate response occurs as a function of a sequential set of emotional and mental processes, which include the following: (a) attending to and encoding relevant cues into working memory (e.g., are the others laughing or sneering?); (b) mentally representing and interpreting encoded cues in a meaningful way (perhaps either as a provocation by peers or as a harmless prank); (c) accessing one or more potential responses to this situation from one's long-term memorial repertoire (such as getting angry, laughing, or walking away); (d) evaluating accessed responses, perhaps by anticipating whether they lead to desired outcomes or not or by some moral code; and, finally, (e) enactment of a selected response through motor and verbal behavior. Processing at each step adds to the probability of aggressive behavior in a particular situation. For example, selective attention to hostile peer cues, an attribution that others are being hostile toward the self, rapid accessing of aggressive responses, and positive evaluations of aggressive responses all increase the likelihood of aggressive behavior.

There is empirical evidence that processing patterns are associated with harsh parenting and rejecting peer experiences and that processing patterns partially account for the association between early life experiences and later conduct problems (Dodge & Pettit, 2003). This social-transmission process suggests one avenue through which experience exerts an impact on subsequent antisocial and violent behavior, but it is not the only possible avenue of influence. It remains for future theorizing – and empirical study – to specify which kinds of processes will be linked with which kinds of life experiences for which kinds of outcomes. This will need to be done within a developmental framework because it is likely that different processes become operative at different ages (e.g., perspective-taking skills must develop before individual differences in social-cue interpretation become meaningful). It will need to be done in a manner that is sen-

sitive to the contexts within which social-cognitive processes are triggered and serve to guide and constrain behavior. And it will need to be done using well-designed, ecologically valid measures, the use of which across multiple studies may provide a better indication of the generalizability and replicability of the observed relations (Pettit, 2004).

Before turning to a more extended discussion of developmental considerations and context-specificity in the relation between SIP and antisocial behavior, we believe it is useful to examine evidence supporting (a) the existence of separate components of SIP and (b) the theoretical and empirical overlap of knowledge structures and online processing steps.

Multiple Steps or Multiple Indicators?

It is worth noting at the outset that the typical SIP assessment scheme, in which children reflect on and then respond to written or visually depicted (via cartoon line drawings or video vignettes) hypothetical events, may exaggerate the overlap among some processing components. For example, a standard procedure (e.g., Dodge, Pettit, Bates, & Valente, 1995) is to ask children to first make a judgment of peers' intentions in a hypothetical peer conflict and then to ask children what they would do (i.e., behavioral response) if they found themselves in this kind of situation. The proximity of the two questions may yield linked hostile-aggressive or benign-nonaggressive responses. In light of this assessment constraint, evidence of the empirical distinctiveness of the processing components would be especially noteworthy.

In some studies SIP components have been treated as indicators of a common construct (Burks et al., 1999; Weiss, Dodge, Bates, & Pettit, 1992). Such studies typically have investigated the role of SIP, broadly construed, as a factor underlying antisocial and violent behavior and as a mediator of linkages between social experiences (or representations of those experiences) and such behavior. The uniqueness of individual processing steps is not of interest in such inquiries. But other research has been concerned more explicitly with whether SIP is multidimensional or can be explained by a single underlying construct. Fontaine, Burks, and Dodge (2002) found that assessments of two aspects of decision-making processes, response evaluation and outcome expectancy, loaded on two separate factors in a factor analysis, and Hubbard, Dodge, Cillessen, Coie, and Schwartz (2001) reported that measures of attributional bias and response evaluation loaded on distinct factors. A more sophisticated test was conducted by Dodge, Laird, Lochman, Zelli, and the Conduct Problems Prevention Research Group (2002), who used multidimensional latent-construct analysis (i.e., confirmatory factor analyses) to test the hypothesis that the between-construct variance in measurement would be greater than the within-construct measurement variance. Using data from the Fast Track project, they created multi-item measures of intent attribution, goal orientation, response generation, and response evaluation. A structural model with four latent constructs provided a significantly better fit to the data than did a model that included only one latent construct; the model with four latent constructs provided a better fit than did other plausible alternative models.

There are trade-offs in the use of either the multiple-indicator approach or the separate-factors approach. If the goal is to conduct a general test of SIP-behavior linkages, then collapsing across SIP steps is reasonable. If the goal is to conduct tests of links between specific kinds of SIP biases and deficits (e.g., perceptual and attributional biases) and specific aspects of antisocial behavior (e.g., hostile-reactive aggression), then analyzing the SIP steps separately is necessary. Future inquiry also might profitably be directed to an examination of whether one processing step moderates or "conditions" the impact of other steps, as would be the case, for example, if generating aggressive response alternatives were found to be associated with antisocial behavior only when it was accompanied by an expectation

that aggressive behavior would lead to positive instrumental outcomes.

SIP and Latent Knowledge: Distinct or Overlapping?

Although the dominant SIP models hypothesize the existence of enduring latent structures that guide processing, there is considerable variation in how these structures are described and conceptualized. As noted earlier, the Dodge formulation (Dodge, 2003; Dodge & Pettit, 2003) posits that latent knowledge structures serve as memory stores and as organizers of experience that serve to guide or constrain more downstream (and presumably more "online") SIP steps that are activated when children confront specific social situations. An alternative perspective, espoused by Huesmann (1998), is that cue search and interpretation in specific situations lead to a search in memory for a script (i.e., a latent knowledge structure that might be manifested as a normative belief) that is then evaluated and used as a guide for behavior.

Zelli, Dodge, Lochman, Laird, and the Conduct Problems Prevention Research Group (1999) found that processing patterns provide a significant increment in the prediction of children's aggressive behavior, even after controlling for Huesmann and Guerra's (1997) measure of beliefs legitimizing aggression. Dodge et al. (2002) found that processing patterns provide a significant increment after controlling for children's knowledge about emotions. These findings are consistent with the premise that SIP patterns operate within situations in a manner that is distinct from children's beliefs and knowledge. The Zelli et al. (1999) findings also show that the link between beliefs about aggression and subsequent aggressive behavior is partially mediated by hostile processing (i.e., hostile attributional bias, aggressive response selection, positive evaluation of aggressive response), consistent with the social-transmission hypothesis outlined by Dodge and Pettit (2003). However, Zelli et al. (1999) did not examine a mediational model with the direction of effects between normative beliefs and hostile processing reversed, which is the sequence proposed by the Huesmann (1998) model.

Burks et al. (1999) evaluated both types of sequences, using knowledge-structure indices drawn from basic work in traditional cognitive psychology (the "Sentence Completion Task," and the "Assessment of Schema Typicality") that were thought to tap children's generalized expectations of hostility manifested by important persons in their lives. Standard measures of SIP (hostile intent and aggressive response generation to hypothetical conflict situations) were created and both SIP and knowledge structures were examined in relation to children's externalizing behavior problems as reported by parents and teachers. Contrary to expectation, processing was not directly related to externalizing. However, consistent with the Huesmann (1998) formulation, processing was associated with hostile knowledge structures, which in turn were linked with higher levels of externalizing problems. Collectively, these findings suggest that whereas online SIP and more generalized knowledge structures may be empirically distinct, their roles in the development of antisocial and violence behavior are not yet understood fully. As noted by Boxer and Dubow (2002), more research is needed that examines the interplay of knowledge structures and discrete social information-processing components, through the use of longitudinal and experimental designs.

Developmental Patterns in Social Information Processing

In 1994, Lochman and Dodge lamented the lack of information concerning violence- and aggression-relevant aspects of SIP. Although in the past decade a number of studies have addressed developmental questions in SIP, it could be argued that a coherent account of developmental changes in SIP still does not exist. In one sense this lack is understandable; the intent of SIP theory (Crick & Dodge, 1994; Huesmann, 1988; Vasey, Dalgleish, & Silverman, 2003) has

been to explain individual differences in social behavior. In this section we identify three sets of developmental questions in the study of SIP and antisocial behavior. After we summarize research bearing on these developmental issues we propose a research agenda for refining models of the role of SIP in aggression and violence.

The first set of issues involves normative developmental changes in SIP. Perhaps because the SIP framework proposed by Dodge and colleagues is concerned largely with aberrant or deficient SIP and the correlates thereof, less attention has been paid to normative changes. The lack of attention to developmental issues is unfortunate in that a key principle of the emerging field of developmental psychopathology is that understanding normative development is the first step toward understanding deviancy (Sroufe, 1990). Normative patterns and deviations that might mark or presage psychopathology are important to document if SIP assessments are to be of practical use. That is, an understanding of normative developmental patterns is necessary to identify deviations from the norm and advance theory and research on SIP deficits and biases and their impact on antisocial behavior across childhood and adolescence.

The second set of issues concerns whether there is stability in SIP patterns across childhood. Continuity (i.e., absolute similarity across time; Bornstein & Suess, 2000) is unlikely, given expected developmental changes. If, as has been proposed (Dodge, 2003), social information-processing patterns constitute one set of building blocks of personality, they should show cross-time stability. Stability may be examined in specific processes: do kindergarteners who over-attribute hostile intent to peers continue to do so in middle childhood and adolescence? Or stability in SIP may be examined more generally: do problems at one age predict problems later, but in nonspecific ways? This would be the case if problems in SIP (irrespective of SIP step[s]) early on predict problems in any SIP step at a subsequent age.

A closely related issue is whether patterns of association between SIP and aggressive/violent behavior are consistent across development. In particular, do some steps in the SIP chain discriminate more sensitively between aggressive/violent children and children without aggression problems during some developmental stage(s) than do others? In simple terms, are different SIP steps more important at different ages?

Normative Developmental Changes in Social Information Processing

As noted earlier, the goal of most SIP formulations is to explain individual differences in social behavior, not to explain developmental changes. However, a few studies have systematically examined developmental changes (longitudinally) or age differences (cross-sectionally) in SIP.

It is not surprising that some aspects of SIP consistently show improvements over childhood. As children progress from early to middle childhood, they encode more social cues accurately (Dodge, Murphy, & Buchsbaum, 1984; Dodge & Price, 1994), and become better at correctly identifying both hostile (Dodge & Price, 1994) and prosocial intentions (Dodge et al., 1984). Between early and late adolescence, youth become increasingly likely to attribute deviant behaviors to internal characteristics of the actor, such as being antisocial (Boxer & Tisak, 2003). Understanding of others' motivations and judgments of others' behavior as meeting or not meeting standards increase over childhood and into and beyond adolescence (Coie & Pennington, 1976). Over the elementary to middle-school years, children generate more strategies (Dodge & Price, 1994; Mayeux & Cillessen, 2003), more competent strategies (Feldman & Dodge, 1987), and more active social strategies (Mayeux & Cillessen, 2003), and they become more skilled at enacting competent strategies when asked to do so (Dodge & Price, 1994).

Many improvements in SIP skills over childhood that consistently have been observed probably reflect growth in basic attentional and information-processing capacity, knowledge of cultural norms, and understanding of persons. Children's increasing thoroughness and accuracy in encoding relevant social information may be a function, at least partially, of their growing ability to strategically direct attention (Posner & Rothbart, 2000), particularly from about age 3 to age 8 (DeMarie-Dreblow & Miller, 1988; Vurpillot, 1968), and of increasing processing speed or capacity (Kail, 1984). Generation of more and more socially appropriate strategies may reflect increasing cognitive capacity coupled with a growing knowledge base as a result of accumulating peer experience, including disapproval of non-normative behavior, and exposure to adult expectations and teaching. Increases in children's causal attributions to internal factors probably reflect the well-documented developmental trend in studies of social cognition for children increasingly to think beyond superficial qualities of persons.

The direction of change in other aspects of SIP is less consistent across different studies, and whether such changes constitute improvement is not always clear. This seems to be particularly true in regard to hostile attributions and the generation or approval of aggressive strategies to solve social problems. For instance, in one study (Dodge & Price, 1994), older children (third graders) were more likely than were younger children (first graders) to show hostile bias in interpreting peers' behavior, but in another study (Crick & Dodge, 1996) it was the younger children (third and fourth graders) who were more likely, compared to older children (fifth and sixth graders), to attribute hostile intent to others. Apparently contradictory patterns also have been found with regard to endorsement of and efficacy for aggression. In some studies, older children were more likely than younger ones to endorse aggression as a problem-solving strategy (Huesmann & Guerra, 1997, studying second through fifth graders; Keltikangas-Järvinen, 2001, studying children from age 10 to age 17; and Egan, Monson, & Perry, 1998, studying third through seventh graders), even though older children have more awareness of the suffering that aggression can cause the victim

(Egan et al., 1998). But other studies have found that it is the younger children who evaluate aggression more positively (Crick & Dodge, 1996, comparing third and fourth graders with fifth and sixth graders; Dodge & Price, 1994, comparing first and third graders).

These apparent developmental inconsistencies in interpreting and approving aggressive acts could reflect nonlinear developmental trends. Thus, in early elementary school, where children tend to identify with their teachers and where there is a relatively strong focus on learning appropriate behavior, children may become convinced that aggression is inappropriate. Later, as peer culture becomes more salient, and children observe and experience the power of aggression, children may come to view aggression in a more positive light (Cillessen & Mayeux, 2004). Alternatively, some apparent contradictions could reflect methodological variations among studies. Children in the Dodge and Price (1994) study were asked to judge how effective aggression would be were they to use it, whereas children in the Huesmann and Guerra (1997) study were asked how justified aggression would be under certain conditions. Older children may see aggression as being justified on occasion, but, even if justified, not necessarily effective. A third possibility is that some apparent inconsistencies may reflect children's growing sensitivity to situational demands and norms. Findings from the Dodge and Price (1994) study provide a suitable illustration. Fifth graders were more likely than first graders to endorse aggressive responses in a hypothetical teasing situation, whereas first graders were more likely than fifth graders to endorse aggression in peer group entry. The former (aggression in response to being teased) could be considered a reasonable, adaptive, or at least pardonable response, justified in order to maintain the respect of peers, whereas the latter (being aggressive while trying to join others' play) is rarely, if ever, appropriate. We may conclude that, as children mature, they demonstrate more sensitivity and skill in tailoring responses to specific situations.

Stability

The crux of SIP models is that aggressogenic social cognitions (hostile interpretation of social cues, generation of aggressive strategies, beliefs that aggression is effective) are proximal causes of aggressive behavior. Given the considerable intraindividual stability of aggressive and violent behavior over childhood, moderate stability in SIP patterns has been presumed (Dodge et al., 2002). Yet, cross-sectional and short-term longitudinal studies are used more commonly than longitudinal designs in SIP research, and consequently, data on stability and change in SIP patterns are sparse.

There are a number of published studies with assessments of short-term stability (a few months to a year or so) for a limited subset of SIP, or SIP-relevant, constructs. Egan et al. (1998) report moderate stability from fall to spring of an academic year (mdn correlation $= .47$) for third to seventh graders' evaluations of aggression, including efficacy for aggressive acts and expectations that aggression would achieve instrumental goals, that the victim of aggression would suffer, and that the child would take pleasure in or not be concerned about the victims' suffering. Other aspects of social cognition relevant to SIP may become stable later. Huesmann and Guerra (1997), in assessing a similar set of beliefs about aggression, found no stability over 1 year among first and second graders ($mdn = .11$), but moderate stability for fourth graders ($mdn = .38$). Others have reported a comparable degree of stability across 1-year periods among early elementary children for generation of antisocial strategies ($mdn = .39$; Mayeux & Cillessen, 2003).

To our knowledge only three longitudinal studies have published data with assessments of SIP stability over more than a year or so. Keltikangas-Järvinen (2001) and colleagues followed a cohort of children from age 10 or 11 to age 17, examining social problem solving and aggression at each of three ages (10–11, 13–14, and 17). These authors report little stability for social problem solving, even though aggressive behavior was stable. Investigators with the Social Development Project (SDP) report significant modest-to-moderate stability coefficients ($mdn = .34$) for each processing step over a 3-year period for children who were in first, second, and third grades at the beginning of the study (Dodge et al., 2003). The CDP, described earlier, assessed SIP over an even longer period. An initial analysis, reported in Dodge, Pettit, Bates, and Valente (1995), showed generally modest-to-moderate and significant adjacent-year correlations among SIP measures of encoding errors, hostile attributions, accessing aggressive responses, and positive evaluation of aggressive responses ($mdn = .36$), with cross-year internal consistencies ranging from .70 (encoding) to .79 (accessing aggressive responses; see also Harrist, Zaia, Bates, Dodge, & Pettit 1997).

A more comprehensive analysis of SIP stability in the CDP was recently undertaken by Lansford et al. (2006). Encoding and interpretation steps were combined to index cognitions about input; response generation and evaluation were combined to create an index of cognitions about output. Children were classified as high or low (one standard deviation above or below the mean, respectively) on each index in kindergarten and grades 3, 8, and 11. Chi-square analyses revealed no significant continuity in group membership from kindergarten to grade 3 or 8, or from grade 3 to grade 8. Some continuity in group membership was found between grades 8 and 11, mainly involving the no-problem group. That is, children who were not deviant in either early-step or later-step processing in grade 8 tended to show a similar profile in grade 11. Little continuity was observed in terms of early-step versus later-step processing problems.

It therefore appears that stability in SIP patterns is most likely to be observed across relatively short periods of time (from a few months to 2 or 3 years), rather than over more extended periods of time, and among older rather than younger (under age 8) children. These findings generally are consistent with theoretical formulations (Crick & Dodge, 1994; Dodge 2003) that posit that

latent structures and processing patterns attain moderate stability by middle childhood. From a psychological perspective, the increasing stability of SIP across childhood may reflect the increasing coherence of cognitive processes (Crick & Dodge, 1994) or, from a neuroscience perspective, the "fire to wire" principle of neural connectivity (LeDoux, 2002). Alternatively, the greater stability of SIP among older children may reflect growing rigidity of group processes that make it increasingly difficult to change peers' reactions. Later we speculate on ecological factors, including peer group processes, which may affect the stability of SIP patterns.

Future Directions in Developmental Studies of SIP

There is a rich conceptual and empirical literature on developmental changes in cognitive and emotional processing. A good bit is known about how children's attentional skills, learning, information-processing, language, problem-solving, perspective-taking (Sigler, 1998), and emotion-regulation (Saarni, Mumme, & Campos, 1998) capabilities change as they mature. Each of these domains of development is relevant for understanding developmental changes in SIP (Crick & Dodge, 1994), yet little has been done to integrate this knowledge into SIP frameworks and research. Such work is necessary, however, to advance understanding of the role of SIP in the development of antisocial behavior.

Among the more obvious issues are those regarding the extent to which developmental changes in SIP do more than mirror changes in basic nonsocial-cognitive processes, such as language development and working memory capacity. Is older children's tendency to generate more solutions to social problems a function only of more advanced language development? Is older children's ability to encode a greater number of social cues accurately more than a function of growing attentional skills, and would encoding predict adjustment if attentional skills were adequately controlled? Similar questions have been raised previously, particularly regarding whether developmental lags are responsible for apparent links between SIP and antisocial behavior (Orobio de Castro, Slot, Bosch, Koops, & Veerman, 2003). Developmental delay is a risk factor for antisocial behavior (Berkowitz, 1993) and presumably would impair performance on many SIP tasks. In one of the few attempts to control for developmental status or nonsocial information-processing skills, Dodge and colleagues (1984) found that elementary-school children's intention-cue detection errors predicted sociometric neglect and rejection, even after controlling for the ability to discriminate geometric figures. Meece, Mize, and Pettit (1995) found that all SIP steps continued to significantly (attributions, generation of competent strategies) or near-significantly (encoding) predict social competence after controlling for receptive vocabulary. And Waldman (1996) showed that, even after controlling for measures of inattention and impulsivity, measures from two SIP domains – hostile perceptual bias and generation of aggressive responses to nonhostile cues – significantly discriminated between aggressive and nonaggressive boys. Studies that conduct careful assessments of both SIP and other cognitive processes, such as language, attention, and memory capacity, are needed to more conclusively answer questions about the convergence (and divergence) between measures of SIP and measures of neurological and cognitive functioning. Ideally, longitudinal studies would chart potential parallel changes across SIP and basic cognitive domains. Evidence that aggressive children's performance is deficient on social information-processing tasks relative to their performance on nonsocial tasks of comparable complexity would provide evidence for the uniqueness of specifically social information processing.

A related issue is whether the salience of SIP steps for aggressive behavior changes with development. That is, does the strength of association between an individual SIP step and aggression vary as a function of age? There are remarkably little empirical data

relevant to this question. There is some evidence that in early childhood, generation of few and antisocial strategies (as opposed to numerous, prosocial strategies) is linked strongly to social behavior problems (Mize & Ladd, 1988; Pettit, Dodge, & Brown, 1988), whereas attributions of intent do not discriminate well between aggressive and nonaggressive children (Keane, Brown, & Crenshaw, 1990; Pettit et al., 1988), perhaps because of young children's tendency to see all harmful acts as blameworthy (Damon, 1983). There are few speculations about developmental changes in the salience of various SIP steps for social behavior, and even fewer empirical examinations of such issues (but see our description of Huesmann & Guerra, 1997, for an exception).

Additional work on the stability of SIP patterns is also needed. However, in terms of advancing understanding of the role of SIP in aggression and violence, it may be more productive to ask, rather than whether SIP patterns are stable, about conditions that contribute to SIP stability and conditions that promote changes in SIP patterns. The latter is a more complex question, requiring the development of models about how SIP is influenced across childhood and adolescence, as well as multifactorial examinations of stability issues. We propose that stability estimates of SIP can be influenced by recent experiences and by changes in more enduring conditions. Measures of SIP may be especially susceptible to recent experiences because they typically are assessed at a single time point, often in one session; in contrast, measures of aggression usually reflect the child's typical behavior over an extended period of time (e.g., ratings of how aggressive the child usually is, or a summative index of observations over several days). From a measurement perspective, then, assessments of aggressive behavior would be expected to be more stable than assessments of SIP.

A small but growing body of research demonstrates the susceptibility to recent experiences of children's responses during SIP assessments, and the greater vulnerability of aggressive boys to negative influences. Aggressive boys are more likely to make hostile attributions immediately after negative feelings have been induced by unjust loss of a game (Orobio de Castro et al., 2003) or anticipation of peer conflict (Dodge & Somberg, 1987), after exposure to stories in which harm occurred as a result of selfish or thoughtless behavior (Graham & Hudley, 1994), and after exposure to violent video games (Kirsh, 1998). The commonality among these experiences may be that all prime, or make more accessible, constructs or schemas compatible with pessimistic or hostile interpretations of others' behavior. Certainly, children in real-life interactions with peers, teachers, and parents daily experience situations that prime hostility-consistent constructs and situations that prime benevolence-consistent constructs. Greater stability in SIP patterns might be apparent if efforts were made to standardize children's experiences immediately before SIP assessments.

More permanent changes in circumstances and experiences also affect SIP. Although most research has focused on early family experiences as the source of individual differences in SIP, some recent research demonstrates that negative peer relationships can exacerbate SIP problems. Using CDP and SDP data, Dodge and colleagues (2003) found that peer dislike in kindergarten predicted increasing SIP problems in second grade, which, in turn, predicted increased aggression in fourth grade. Considering both data sets, kindergarten peer dislike predicted future problems in encoding, making hostile attributions, generating competent solutions, and competent enactment of strategies. Although not testing the hypothesis directly, other published reports are consistent with Dodge et al.'s (2003) interpretation that treatment by peers can exacerbate SIP problems. Early aggressive behavior is associated in subsequent months and years with increasing endorsement of aggression as a problem-solving approach (Egan et al., 1998; Huesmann & Guerra, 1997), with increasing self-efficacy for aggressive behavior (Egan et al., 1998), and with increasingly negative views of peers (MacKinnon-Lewis, Rabiner, &

Starnes, 1999), whereas early victimization is associated with a decrease in expectations for positive outcomes for aggression (Egan et al., 1998). Having aggressive friends also seems to increase the generation of aggressive responses to hypothetical social problems (Brendgen, Bowen, Rondeau, & Vitaro, 1999). The common (though sometimes unmeasured) factor in these studies may well be the child's experiences in the peer group, experiences that may alter latent structures and SIP for better or for worse (Dodge et al., 2003).

Few other aspects of experience have been examined as potential instigators of change in SIP patterns. However, research and theory outside the SIP framework suggest that changes in family relationships (Crockenberg, 1981), relationships with teachers (Howes, Hamilton, & Phillipsen, 1998; Hughes, Cavell, & Jackson, 1999; Pianta, Steinberg, & Rollins, 1995), and classroom ecology (Hoglund & Leadbeater, 2004) may be powerful forces in altering how children think about and process social information. These influences need not be negative, of course. A supportive teacher who (perhaps in the context of an intervention program) promotes classroom harmony, who does not tolerate aggression or teasing, and who explicitly teaches skills for positive peer relationships may be able to change an at-risk child's beliefs and thinking about peers.

Specificity vs. Generality of Processing Biases and Deficits across Situations and Contexts

Specificity in SIP Across Types of Problematic Social Situations

A central tenet of the SIP framework is that biases and deficits in processing with respect to a given situation or context more strongly predict behavioral competence (or problems) in that situation relative to other situations (Crick & Dodge, 1994; Dodge, 1986). What constitutes a "situation" has varied across studies, however. Dodge et al. (1985) identified problematic social situations on the basis of teacher reports about the social contexts that seemed to be most challenging for socially maladjusted children. Two such contexts were the focus of an early study (Dodge et al., 1986), and support generally was found for the hypothesis that processing about peer rebuff situations (i.e., in which a hypothetical target child was attempting to enter into play with peers) would predict actual performance in a contrived peer rebuff situation and that processing about peer provocation (i.e., in which a hypothetical peer behaves toward the target in a provocative and potentially hostile manner) would predict performance in a contrived peer-provocation situation. The corollary prediction, that cross-situational linkages between processing and performance would be lower in magnitude than within-situational linkages, likewise received support. These were important findings that helped draw attention to the possibility that particular kinds of experiences may engender particular kinds of SIP patterns and that these patterns themselves may be tied to difficulties in particular kinds of interpersonal contexts.

Though promising as a testable and intervention-relevant extension of SIP models, replication of SIP specificity across problematic situations has been elusive. Dodge and Price (1994), in a study of a community sample of elementary-school-aged children, found specificity in processing problems with respect to distinctions between response to authority directive (another of the problematic situations identified by teachers in Dodge et al., 1985) versus peer problems (group entry and response to provocation), but not between the two peer situations. On the other hand, Dodge et al. (2002), employing confirmatory factor analysis, found support both for a four-factor model of processing steps (intent attributions, goal orientation, response generation, and response evaluation) and for an additional two-dimensional structure in which these processing constructs were evaluated within peer provocation and peer-group entry situational contexts. Dodge et al. (2002) conclude that children's processing

patterns vary systematically across component processing steps and across specific situations.

Still, there are comparatively few studies that have examined concordance in SIP across situations. The far more common approaches are to relate maladaptive processing *within* situations to antisocial and violent behavior, or, when multiple situations are considered in the same study, to collapse across them, presumably to increase measurement reliability. Such aggregation across diverse situations and contexts may have the unintended and undesired effect of masking what might be theoretically important variations in the processing patterns of at-risk children and youth.

A variant of the "problematic situation" specificity issue has been to consider the type of provocation behavior that is directed to the child in terms of its instrumental versus relational qualities. Building on earlier work by Bjorkqvist (e.g., Bjorkqvist, 1994; Lagerspetz & Bjorkqvist, 1994; also see Underwood, 2003), Crick and Grotpeter (1995) sought to identify an aspect of aggression that might occur more frequently in girls' peer groups and that might stem from a desire to harm others through the manipulation of relationships and reputations (e.g., through gossip, disparagement, and exclusion) rather than through the more direct (or overt) use of verbal and physically aggression. Aggression based on the manipulation of relationships – termed "relational" aggression by Crick and colleagues – indeed was found to be empirically distinct from overt aggression, to be associated with a range of social and psychological problems, even after controlling for overt aggression, and to be used more commonly by girls than by boys (Crick & Grotpeter, 1995). But more pertinent to the issue here, in later studies of the social-cognitive underpinnings of relational aggression, SIP specificity was found in children's intent attributions in response to relational versus instrumental provocation contexts (Crick, Grotpeter, & Bigbee, 2002). That is, physically aggressive grade-school-aged children displayed a hostile attributional bias in instrumentally provocative contexts (e.g., situations in which the protagonist sought to obtain a desired object), whereas relationally aggressive children exhibited hostile biases in relational provocation contexts (e.g., situations in which the protagonist excluded or gossiped about others). These findings suggest the possibility that girls (especially relationally aggressive girls) may be more prone to making erroneous attributions when confronted with a social-relational provocation (such as being rebuffed by peers), whereas boys (especially physically aggressive boys) may be more prone to misjudging peers' intent in instrumental, physically provocative contexts.

Specificity in Links Between SIP and Types of Antisocial Behavior

Appreciation among violence researchers of the heterogeneity of antisocial behavior is now ubiquitous, and many subtypes of aggressive behavior have been compared and contrasted, such as the overt-relational distinction described in the preceding paragraph and the early-starter (life-course persistent) versus adolescent-limited distinction described by Moffitt (1993) and by Patterson (e.g., Patterson & Yoerger, 2002). Another theory-driven distinction that has gained currency in recent years, and one that has been the focus of considerable SIP research, is that between reactive aggression and proactive aggression (e.g., Atkins & Stoff, 1993; Crick & Dodge, 1996; Dodge & Coie, 1987; Dodge et al., 1997; Vitaro & Brendgen, 2005).

Aggression that is a response to antecedent conditions, especially if the response is hostile in nature, can be described as reactive aggression. Aggression that is outcome-oriented can be described as proactive aggression. Reactive aggression is thought to be "pushed" from within by a child's perception of threat, experience of anger, or frustration at having personal goals blocked (Berkowitz, 1993), whereas proactive aggression is "pulled" by anticipated rewards and positive outcomes (Bandura, 1983). One of the first and still most comprehensive efforts to validate measures of the two forms of aggression was undertaken by Dodge and Coie (1987). A short teacher rating scale was developed, and a factor analysis of the items yielded factors that were consistent with the theoretical notions underlying the two aggression constructs. The proactive aggression score and the reactive aggression score were highly correlated, but small groups of children high on one type of aggression but not the other could be reliably identified. These findings since have been replicated across a number of studies that have employed the reactive-proactive teacher rating scale (e.g., Vitaro, Brendgen, & Tremblay, 2002).

Two of the SIP steps in Dodge's model have particular relevance for the proactive-reactive distinction. In line with the formulations guiding the distinction, proactively aggressive children would be expected to evaluate aggression and its consequences in relatively positive ways, whereas reactively aggressive children should be more inclined to misinterpret peers' intentions in ambiguous provocation situations in the direction of presumed hostility. Data presented by Crick and Dodge (1996) generally are supportive of these hypotheses. On the basis of teacher ratings, several hundred school-aged children were classified as proactively aggressive, reactively aggressive, both proactively and reactively aggressive, or nonaggressive. Comparisons across a range of SIP measures showed that older reactively aggressive children made significantly more hostile attributions than did the nonaggressive group, but not more than the proactively aggressive group. Proactively aggressive children reported significantly more positive outcome expectations and greater efficacy for enacting aggression than did nonproactively aggressive children.

This general pattern – weaker support for links between "early-stage" processing (encoding and attributions) and reactive aggression, stronger support for links between "later-stage" processing (response generation and evaluation) – has been demonstrated across several studies. Dodge and colleagues (1997), in two separate studies, one using data generated as part of the CDP, the other involving a large sample of psychiatrically impaired and chronically violent boys, found that reactively aggressive children made more encoding errors, but were not more hostile in their attributions, compared to their proactively aggressive and nonaggressive peers. Schwartz et al. (1998) examined the attributions and behavior of boys participating in a series of experimental play groups and found only a marginally significant relation between hostile attribution bias and reactive aggression. On the other hand, proactive aggression has been linked more consistently with positive outcome expectations for behaving aggressively (Dodge et al., 1997; Schwartz et al., 1998; Smithmeyer, Hubbard, & Simons, 2000) and greater self-efficacy for enacting aggressive solutions (Dodge et al., 1997). Reactively aggressive children tend not to show these later-stage processing deficits.

Specificity in SIP Across Type of Relationship Partner

Maladaptive SIP may be expressed only with known others (i.e., partners with whom the child has an ongoing relationships, such as a parent, teacher, or classmate), or it may reflect a generalized way of processing and responding to social cues irrespective of partner. The extent to which these processing problems are specific to partner would potentially be revealing about the role of prior experience in the development of these problems (discussed below) and the interpersonal contexts within which antisocial behavior may be more likely to occur. As is seen later in this chapter, there has been little empirical examination of this issue. It also should be noted that specificity at the level of knowledge structure likewise has received scant attention. The slowly accumulating evidence largely has not provided compelling support for specificity, however. As noted by Crick and Dodge (1994), "it is not clear whether children's latent mental structures are organized with situational constraints or whether they are organized at a more global level." The same might also be

said for SIP and its specificity across relationship contexts.

Because theories of the development of individual differences in SIP stress the role of early social experiences with caregivers (e.g., Dodge, Bates, & Pettit, 1990; Huesmann, 1998), it is of interest to trace commonalities in SIP across parents and their children. Thus, it might be that, by observing and listening to what their parents do in social situations, children's SIP orientation begins to mirror that of their parents. It also is possible that parents' ways of mentally representing and responding to social situations are related only indirectly to children's processing, with parents' coaching and instruction in how to respond in social contexts serving as a connecting link (Mize & Pettit, 1997).

MacKinnon-Lewis, Lamb, Arbuckle, Baradaran, and Volling (1992) assessed school-aged boys' attributions about their mothers' intentions and mothers' attributions about their sons' intentions in hypothetical ambiguous provocation situations. Children's and mothers' attributions were not significantly correlated, but boys' aggressiveness with their mothers was predicted by the hostility of the children's attributions about their mothers, and mothers' aggressiveness with their sons likewise was predicted by the hostility of mothers' attributions about their sons.

Keane, Brown, and Crenshaw (1990) also examined associations between children's and mothers' intent attributions in a sample of sociometrically popular and rejected first-grade children and their mothers. Contrary to expectation, rejected children did not have higher hostile attribution scores, compared to popular children; the mothers of the children in the two groups also did not differ on these scores. In contrast, Bickett, Milich, and Brown (1996) found that aggressive boys and their mothers differed from nonaggressive boys and their mothers on various indexes of hostile attribution bias. Aggressive boys' attributions of peers' intent were more hostile than those of nonaggressive boys only in ambiguous provocation situations. Aggressive boys' attributions of teachers' and mothers' intent were more hostile than those of nonaggressive boys irrespective of whether the context was ambiguous or clearly hostile. Mothers of aggressive boys, compared to mothers of nonaggressive boys, likewise were more likely to attribute hostile intent to their child irrespective of situational context. Mothers of aggressive and nonaggressive boys did not differ in hostile attributions of adult peers. Bickett et al. (1996) did not examine associations between mothers' tendencies to make hostile attributions and their children's tendencies to make such attributions.

This line of inquiry was extended by MacBrayer, Milich, and Hundley (2003), who considered hostile attributions and hostile behavioral responses of mothers and their aggressive versus nonaggressive boys and girls in both overt-conflict provocation situations and relational-conflict provocations situations. Findings for child attributions were complex, differing as a function of child sex and provocation type. In the overt-provocation condition, there were no differences between aggressive and nonaggressive boys, but aggressive girls had significantly higher hostile attributions scores compared to nonaggressive girls. In the relational-provocation context, aggressive boys and girls were more hostile in their attributions than nonaggressive boys and girls. Aggressive boys and girls also generated more aggressive behavioral responses compared to nonaggressive boys and girls in the overt-provocation context and (boys only) in the relational-provocation context. Mothers of aggressive children showed a heightened tendency to attribute hostility to their own child, their child's classmate, and their child's teacher, compared to mothers of nonaggressive children. As a whole, mothers made more hostile attributions in relationally provocative situations (compared to overt-provocation situations), and in regard to their own child (compared to any other interpersonal context). Similar patterns were found for mothers' hostile behavioral reactions. As a more direct test of the "transmission" hypothesis, correlations were computed between children's and mothers' scores. None of the correla-

tions were significant for boys, but mothers' and girls' attributions were significantly correlated in the overtly provocative context, and mothers' and girls' attributions and behavioral response were significantly correlated in both the overtly provocative and relationally provocative situational contexts.

Taken together, these findings provide only very modest support for the hypothesis that children and their parents share a common social information-processing style, at least in terms of attributions for others' behavior. It is possible that greater similarity in SIP would be found in more gender-specific contexts (i.e., mothers with daughters and fathers with sons). The hypothesis has not yet been tested, however, as there are no data on fathers' SIP in relation to their children's SIP and behavior. It remains a possibility that aggressive children's SIP about peers stems not from exposure to (and training in) their parents' SIP, but from experiences they have had with specific peers. And, indeed, there is some evidence that, at the dyadic level, relationship history with specific peers has an impact on the attributions made by aggressive children. Coie et al. (1999), for example, found that boys in mutually aggressive dyadic relationships were more likely than boys in nonaggressive dyadic relationships to attribute hostile intentions to their partners.

Specificity in Links Between Life Experiences and SIP Patterns

A considerable body of literature has provided evidence of links between life experiences – and particularly qualities of relationships with parents – and variations in children's SIP. Many of the same experiential factors that have been found to predict antisocial and violent behavior also have been found to be associated with SIP biases and deficits. These include harsh and abusive treatment by parents (e.g., Dodge et al., 1990; Price & Glad, 2003), exposure to family aggression and a hostile family climate (e.g., Dodge et al., 1997; Schultz & Shaw, 2003), and peer rejection (Dodge et al., 2003). When SIP has been studied in these contexts it usually is with the intent of testing whether SIP serves as a mediator – and, theoretically, at least, as transmission mechanism – of the link between aggressogenic family experience and subsequent antisocial and violent behavior. As we have noted elsewhere (Mize, Pettit, & Meece, 2000; Pettit, Polaha, & Mize, 2001), evidence consistent with the mediating-process hypothesis is mixed. At the theoretical level, however, one would expect SIP to serve as one linking process, but one that should be tied both to specific kinds of experience and to specific kinds of outcome.

A detailed specific process model was suggested by Dodge and colleagues (1997) in relation to proactive aggression and reactive aggression. Using data from two separate samples (including the CDP), the hypothesis was tested that a family history of maltreatment would characterize reactively aggressive children, but not proactively aggressive children, whereas exposure to aggressive role models would characterize proactively aggressive children, but not reactively aggressive children. Moreover, "early-stage" processing problems (i.e., encoding relevant cues in social situations and making attributions about others' intentions in those situations) were expected to be associated more strongly with reactive aggression, and "later-stage" processing problems (i.e., generating and evaluating possible behavioral responses) with proactive aggression. Findings were partially consistent with these expectations, but the overall pattern suggested that both experiential antecedents and SIP problems overlapped to a considerable degree in the two aggression groups.

No tests of statistical mediation by SIP were conducted in Dodge et al. (1997), but the general model guiding the research is consistent with a differentiated socialization perspective in which certain kinds of early experience lead to certain kinds of outcome, with specific and unique intervening social-cognitive processes (i.e., that early parental maltreatment and rejection underlie poor attention to and encoding of relevant social cues and interpretation of

peers' intentions as hostile, which, in turn, contribute to the development of angry-reactive aggression, and that exposure to aggressive role models leads to expectations that aggression works and is easy to employ, and that such cognitions pave the way for the development of proactive aggression). Though conceptually compelling, evidence to date has provided only mixed support for the model. As noted earlier, "early-stage" processing problems have not been found to distinguish reliably between reactively aggressive children and proactively aggressive children, and links between harsh and physically abusive parenting and hostile attributional bias have been reported in some studies (Price & Glad, 2003) but not in others (Heidgerken, Hughes, Cavell, & Willson, 2004). Tests of specific-process models may prove too challenging for current methods and modes of analysis. The model requires that a particular aspect of life experience contributes to some aspect of SIP (or other sociocognitive-affective process), but not to others, and to an associated antisocial behavioral outcome (and, depending on theory, perhaps not to others), while ruling out the possibility that the link can be explained equally well by joint correlations with other factors (Mize et al., 2000). Controlling for alternative predictors and mediators, while focusing on a specific outcome, may pose measurement problems that are difficult to overcome.

Conclusions

Research focusing on social-cognitive factors that may underlie antisocial and violent behavior in childhood and adolescence has contributed important insights into how such maladaptive behaviors develop and are maintained over time. The sequential-step model outlined by Dodge and colleagues (Crick & Dodge, 1994; Dodge, 1986; Dodge & Pettit, 2003) has proved to be an especially powerful and useful tool for describing how biases and deficits in social information processing may increase the risk for interpersonal violence and aggression.

How these biases and deficits arise, how they change across development and in response to social experience, and how they express themselves in specific social situations constitute core issues in the evolution of the framework and have served as organizing themes in the current chapter.

The social transmission process outlined by Dodge and Pettit (2003) hypothesizes a developmental sequence in which sociocultural factors and child characteristics interface with the child's proximal social environment to form latent knowledge structures (i.e., memories and schematic representations of experience). The knowledge structures, in turn, are hypothesized to guide the processing of social information, including encoding, interpretation, and response access and evaluation, in specific social situations. These processing patterns serve as proximal triggers for aggressive behavior. The literature summarized earlier suggests that it is too early in the development and testing of this formulation to come to firm conclusions regarding the interplay of latent knowledge structures and SIP, whether SIP is best represented as a set of discrete processes or as an overarching style, or whether the magnitude of associations between SIP and aggressive behavior varies as a function of situational cue (e.g., nature of the provoking stimulus), relationship with the target to whom the aggression is directed, and type of aggression behavior displayed. Further study is needed that integrates these various parameters, with independent measurement of knowledge structure and SIP, across a range of situations, relationships, and antisocial behavioral outcomes.

Understanding the role of SIP in the ontogeny of antisocial and violent behavior also will require the more explicit incorporation of a developmental perspective. This will entail charting normative developmental changes in SIP across the years from preschool through adolescence through the use of longitudinal designs. A chief unanswered question is whether individual differences in SIP can be explained by variation in developmental status on nonsocial-cognitive and information-processing abilities. Limited data suggest that nonsocial cognition cannot account completely for associations between SIP and social behavior, but existing studies have incorporated only a very limited set of nonsocial-cognitive processes (e.g., language ability and ability to distinguish among geometric shapes).

As noted earlier, SIP components have been found to be moderately stable over the short term (a few months to a year or two), but limited stability has been observed when SIP has been examined across multiple years. We suggest that a more fruitful perspective on the issue of whether SIP is stable is to seek to identify moderators of SIP stability. Drawing from research that has focused on factors associated with change in attachment security and trajectories of aggressive behavior, we suggest that likely moderators of SIP stability include changing family circumstances, relationships with teachers and classroom ecology, and peer group membership and processes.

A developmental perspective also leads to questions about the relative salience (in terms of predictive links with antisocial behavior) of different SIP components at differing ages. As was noted, it is possible, even likely, that some aspects of SIP strongly discriminate between aggressive and nonaggressive children at some ages, but have little power to do so at other stages in development.

Each of these issues has implications for understanding the pathways leading to antisocial and violent behavior and for altering the developmental trajectories of children who are at risk for developing long-term problems with violence and aggression. Future research directed at shedding light on the specificity of SIP biases and deficits across situations and types of aggression, the shaping and modifiability of individual differences in SIP through early and continuing social experience, and the salience of SIP components at different points in development should lead to refinements in the SIP model that significantly enhance its utility as a guide for interventions with at-risk youth.

References

Atkins, M.S., & Stoff, D.M. (1993). Instrumental and hostile aggression in childhood disruptive behavior disorders. *Journal of Abnormal Child Psychology*, 21, 165–178.

Bandura, A. (1983). Psychological mechanisms of aggression. In R. Geen & E. Donnerstein (Eds.), *Aggression: Theoretical and empirical reviews. Vol. 1: Theoretical and methodological issues* (pp. 1–40). New York: Academic Press.

Berkowitz, L. (1993). *Aggression: Its causes, consequences, and control*. Philadelphia: Temple University Press.

Bickett, L. R., Milich, R., & Brown, R. T. (1996). Attributional styles of aggressive boys and their mothers. *Journal of Abnormal Child Psychology*, 24, 457–472.

Bjorkqvist, K. (1994). Differences in physical, verbal, and indirect aggression: A review of recent research. *Sex Roles, 30*, 177–188.

Bornstein, M. H., & Suess, P. E. (2000). Child and mother cardiac vagal tone: Continuity, stability, and concordance across the first 5 years. *Developmental Psychology, 36*, 54–65.

Boxer, P., & Dubow, E. F. (2002). A social-cognitive information-processing model for school-based aggression reduction and prevention programs: Issues for research and practice. *Applied and Preventive Psychology, 10*, 177–192.

Boxer, P., & Tisak, M. S. (2003). Adolescents' attributions about aggression: An initial investigation. *Journal of Adolescence, 26*, 559–573.

Brendgen, M., Bowen, F., Rondeau, N., & Vitary, F. (1999). Effects of friends' characteristics on children's social cognitions. *Social Development, 8*, 41–51.

Burks, V. S., Laird, R. D., Dodge, K. A., Pettit, G. S., & Bates, J. E. (1999). Knowledge structures, social information processing and children's aggressive behavior. *Social Development, 8*, 220–236.

Caspi, A., McClay, J., Moffitt, T. E., Mill, J., Martin, J., Craig, I. W., et al. (2002). Role of genotype in the cycle of violence in maltreated children. *Science, 297*, 851–854.

Cillessen, A. H. N., & Mayeux, L. (2004). From censure to reinforcement: Developmental changes in the association between aggression and social status. *Child Development, 75*, 147–163.

Coie, J. D., Cillessen, A., Dodge, K. A., Hubbard, J., Schwartz, D., Lemerise, E., et al. (1999). It takes two to fight: A test of relational factors and a method for assessing aggressive dyads. *Developmental Psychology, 35*, 1179–1185.

Coie, J. D., & Pennington, B. F. (1976). Children's perceptions of deviance and disorder. *Child Development, 47*, 407–413.

Crick, N. R., & Dodge, K. A. (1994). A review and reformulation of social information-processing mechanisms in children's social adjustment. *Psychological Bulletin, 115*, 74–101.

Crick, N. R., & Dodge, K. A. (1996). Social information-processing mechanisms on reactive and proactive aggression. *Child Development, 67*, 993–1002.

Crick, N., & Grotpeter (1995). Relational aggression, gender, and social-psychological adjustment. *Child Development, 66*, 710–722.

Crick, N. R., Grotpeter, J. K., & Bigbee, M. A. (2002). Relationally and physically aggressive children's intent attributions and feelings of distress for relational and instrumental peer provocations. *Child Development, 73*, 1134–1142.

Crick, N. R., & Werner, N. E. (1998). Response decision processes in relational and overt aggression. *Child Development, 69*, 1630–1639.

Crockenberg, S. B. (1981). Infant irritability, mother responsiveness, and social support influences on the security of infant-mother attachment. *Child Development, 52*, 857–865.

Damon, W. (1983). The nature of social-cognitive change in the developing child. In W. F. Overton (Ed.), *The relationship between social and cognitive development* (pp. 103–142). Hillsdale, NJ: Erlbaum.

DeMarie-Dreblow, D., & Miller, P. H. (1988). The development of children's strategies for selective attention: Evidence for a transitional period. *Child Development, 59*, 1504–1514.

Dodge, K. A. (1986). A social information processing model of social competence in children. In M. Perlmutter (Ed.), *Minnesota Symposium On Child Psychology* (pp. 77–125). Hillsdale, NJ: Erlbaum.

Dodge, K. A. (1993). Social-cognitive mechanisms in the development of conduct disorder and depression. *Annual Review of Psychology, 44*, 559–584.

Dodge, K. A. (2003). Do social information-processing patterns mediate aggressive behavior? In B. B. Lahey, T. E. Moffitt, & A. Caspi (Eds.), *Causes of conduct disorder and juvenile delinquency* (pp. 254–274). New York: Guilford.

Dodge, K. A., Bates, J. E., & Pettit, G. S. (1990). Mechanisms in the cycle of violence. *Science, 250,* 1678–1683.

Dodge, K. A., & Coie, J. D. (1987). Social-information-processing factors in reactive and proactive aggression in children's peer groups. *Journal of Personality and Social Psychology, 53,* 1146–1158.

Dodge, K. A., Laird, R., Lochman, J. E., Zelli, A., and the Conduct Problems Prevention Research Group. (2002). Multidimensional latent-construct analysis of children's social information processing patterns: Correlations with aggressive behavior problems. *Psychological Assessment, 14,* 60–73.

Dodge, K. A., Lansford, J. E., Burks, V. S., Bates, J. E., Pettit, G. S., Fontaine, R., et al. (2003). Peer rejection and social information-processing factors in the development of aggressive behavior problems in children. *Child Development, 74,* 374–393.

Dodge, K. A., Lochman, J. E., Harnish, J. D., Bates, J. E., & Pettit, G. S. (1997). Reactive and proactive aggression in school children and psychiatrically impaired chronically assaultive youth. *Journal of Abnormal Psychology, 106,* 37–51.

Dodge, K. A., McClaskey, C. L., & Feldman, E. (1985). Situational approach to the assessment of social competence in children. *Journal of Consulting and Clinical Psychology, 53,* 344–353.

Dodge, K. A., Murphy, R. R., & Buchsbaum, K. (1984). The assessment of intention-cue detection skills in children: Implications for developmental psychopathology. *Child Development, 55,* 163–173.

Dodge, K. A., & Pettit, G. S. (2003). A biopsychosocial model of the development of chronic conduct problems in adolescence. *Developmental Psychology, 39,* 349–371.

Dodge, K. A., Pettit, G. S., Bates, J. E., & Valente, E. (1995). Social information-processing patterns partially mediate the effect of early physical abuse on later conduct problems. *Journal of Abnormal Psychology, 104,* 632–643.

Dodge, K. A., Pettit, G. S., McClaskey, C. L., & Brown, M. M. (1986). Social competence in children. *Monographs of the Society for Research in Child Development, 51,* 1–85.

Dodge, K. A., & Price, J. M. (1994). On the relation between social information processing and socially competent behavior in early school-aged children. *Child Development, 65,* 1385–1397.

Dodge, K. A., & Rabiner, D. L., (2004). Returning to roots: On social information processing and moral development. *Child Development, 75,* 1003–1008.

Dodge, K. A., & Somberg, D. R. (1987). Hostile attributional biases among aggressive boys are exacerbated under conditions of threat to the self. *Child Development, 58,* 213–224.

Egan, S. K., Monson, T. C., & Perry, D. G. (1998). Social-cognitive influences on change in aggression over time. *Developmental Psychology, 34,* 996–1006.

Feldman, E., & Dodge, K. A. (1987). Social information processing and sociometric status: Sex, age, and situational effects. *Journal of Abnormal Child Psychology, 15,* 211–227.

Fontaine, R. G., Burks, V. S., & Dodge, K. A., (2002). Response decision processes and externalizing behavior problems in adolescents. *Development and Psychopathology, 14,* 107–122.

Gifford-Smith, M. E., & Rabiner, D. L. (2004). Social information processing and children's social adjustment. In J. B. Kupersmidt & K. A. Dodge (Eds.), *Children's peer relations: From development to intervention* (pp. 61–79). Washington, DC: American Psychological Association.

Graham, S., & Hudley, C. (1994). Attributions of aggressive and nonaggressive African-American male early adolescents: A study of construct accessibility. *Developmental Psychology, 28,* 731–740.

Harrist, A. W., Zaia, A., Bates, J. E., Dodge, K. A., & Pettit, G. S. (1997). Subtypes of social withdrawal in early and middle childhood: Behavioral and social-cognitive profiles across four years. *Child Development, 68,* 332–348.

Heidgerken, A. D., Hughes, J. N., Cavell, T. A., & Willson, V. L. (2004). Direct and indirect effects of parenting and children's goals on child aggression. *Journal of Clinical Child and Adolescent Psychology, 33,* 684–693.

Hoglund, W. L., & Leadbeater, B. J. (2004). The effects of family, school, and classroom ecologies on changes in children's social competence and emotional and behavioral problems in first grade. *Developmental Psychology, 40,* 533–544.

Howes, C., Hamilton, C. E., & Phillipsen, L. C. (1998). Stability and continuity of child-caregiver and child-peer relationships. *Child Development, 65,* 264–273.

Hubbard, J. A., Dodge, K. A., Cillessen, A. H. N., Coie, J. D., & Schwartz, D. (2001). The dyadic nature of social information processing in boys' reactive and proactive aggression. *Journal of Personality and Social Psychology, 80,* 268–280.

Huesmann, L. R. (1988). An information processing model for the development of aggression. *Aggressive Behavior, 14,* 13–24.

Huesmann, L. R. (1998). The role of social information processing and cognitive schema in the acquisition and maintenance of habitual aggressive behavior. In R. G. Geen & E. Donnerstein (Eds.), *Human aggression: Theories, research, and implications for social policy* (pp. 73–109). San Diego: Academic Press.

Huesmann, L. R., & Guerra, N. G. (1997). Children's normative beliefs about aggression and aggressive behavior. *Journal of Personality and Social Psychology, 72,* 408–419.

Hughes, J. N., Cavell, T. A., & Jackson, T. (1999). Influence of the teacher-student relationship on childhood conduct problems: A prospective study. *Journal of Clinical Child Psychology, 28,* 173–184.

Kail, R. (1984). *The development of memory in children* (2nd ed.). New York: Freeman.

Keane, S. P., Brown, K. P., & Crenshaw, T. M. (1990). Children's intention-cue detection as a function of maternal social behavior: Pathways to social rejection. *Developmental Psychology, 26,* 1004–1009.

Keltikangas-Jarvinen, L. (2001). Aggressive behavior and social problem-solving strategies: A review of the findings of a seven-year follow-up from childhood to late adolescence. *Criminal Behavior and Mental Health, 11,* 236–250.

Kirsh, S. J. (1998). Seeing the world through Mortal Combat colored glasses: Violent video games and the development of a short-term hostile attribution bias. *Childhood, 5,* 177–184.

Lagerspetz, K., & Bjorkqvist, K. (1994). Indirect aggression in boys and girls. In L. R. Huesmann (Ed.), *Aggressive behavior: Current perspectives* (pp. 131–150). New York: Plenum Press.

Lansford, J. E., Malone, P. S., Dodge, K. A., Crozier, J. C., Pettit, G. S., & Bates, J. E. (2006). A 12-year prospective study of patterns of social information processing problems and externalizing behaviors. *Journal of Abnormal Child Psychology, 34*(5), 709–718.

LeDoux, J. E. (2002). *The synaptic self: How our brains become who we are.* New York: Penguin.

Lochman, J. E., & Dodge, K. A. (1994). Social-cognitive processes of severely violent, moderately aggressive, and nonaggressive boys. *Journal of Consulting and Clinical Psychology, 62,* 366–374.

MacBrayer, E. K., Milich, R., & Hundley, M. (2003). Attributional biases in aggressive children and their mothers. *Journal of Abnormal Psychology, 112,* 698–708.

MacKinnon-Lewis, C., Lamb, M. E., Arbuckle, B., Baradaran, L. P., & Volling, B. L. (1992). The relationship between biased maternal and filial attributions and the aggressiveness of their interactions. *Development and Psychopathology, 4,* 403–416.

MacKinnon-Lewis, C., Rabiner, D., & Starnes, R. (1999). Predicting boys' social acceptance and aggression: The role of mother-child interactions and boys' beliefs about peers. *Developmental Psychology, 35,* 632–639.

Mayeux, L., & Cillessen, A. (2003). Development of social problem solving in early childhood: Stability, change, and associations with social competence. *Journal of Genetic Psychology, 164,* 153–173.

Meece, D. W., Mize, J., & Pettit, G. S. (1995, March). Preschoolers' cognitive representations of peer relationships: Family origins and behavioral correlates. In J. A. Cassidy (Chair), *Cognitive representations of family and peer relationships.* Symposium presented at the biennial meeting of the Society for Research in Child Development, Indianapolis.

Mize, J., & Ladd, G. W. (1988). Predicting preschoolers' peer behavior and status from their interpersonal strategies: A comparison of verbal and enactive responses to hypothetical social dilemmas. *Developmental Psychology, 26,* 782–788.

Mize, J., & Pettit, G. S. (1997). Mothers' social coaching, mother-child relationship style, and children's peer competence: Is the medium the message? *Child Development, 68,* 312–332.

Mize, J., Pettit, G. S., & Meece, D. W. (2000). Explaining the link between parenting behavior and children's peer competence: A critical examination of the "mediating process" hypothesis. In K. Kerns, J. Contreras, & A. M. Neal-Barnett (Eds.), *Family and peers: Linking two social worlds* (pp. 137–168). New York: Greenwood/Praeger.

Moffitt, T. E. (1993). Adolescence-limited and life-course persistent antisocial behavior: A developmental taxonomy. *Psychological Review, 100,* 674–701.

Moffitt, T. E. (2005). The new look of behavioral genetics in developmental psychopathology: Gene-environment interplay in antisocial behaviors. *Psychological Bulletin, 131,* 533–554.

Orobio de Castro, B. O., Slot, N. W., Bosch, J. D., Koops, W., & Veerman, J. W. (2003). Negative feelings exacerbate hostile attributions of intent in highly aggressive boys. *Journal of Clinical Child and Adolescent Psychology, 32,* 56–65.

Orobio de Castro, B. O., Veerman, J. W., Koops, W., Bosch, J. D., & Monshouwer, H. J. (2002). Hostile attribution of intent and aggressive behavior: A meta-analysis. *Child Development, 73,* 916–934.

Patterson, G. R. (1994). Some alternatives to seven myths about treating families of antisocial children. In C. Henricson (Ed.), *Crime and the family: Conference report: Proceedings of an international conference. Occasional Paper 20* (pp. 26–49). London: Family Policy Studies Centre.

Patterson, G. R., & Yoerger, K. (2002). A developmental model for early- and late-onset delinquency. In J. Reid & G. R. Patterson (Eds.), *Antisocial behavior in children and adolescents: A developmental analysis and model for intervention.* (pp. 147–172). Washington, DC: American Psychological Association.

Pettit, G. S. (2004). Violent children in developmental perspective: Risk and protective factors and the mechanisms through which they (may) operate. *Current Directions in Psychological Science, 13,* 194–197.

Pettit, G. S. Dodge, K. A., & Brown, M. M. (1988). Early family experience, social problem solving patterns, and children's social competence. *Child Development, 59,* 107–120.

Pettit, G. S., Polaha, J. A., & Mize, J. (2001). Perceptual and attributional processes in aggression and conduct problems. In B. Maughan & J. Hill (Eds.), *Cambridge monographs in child and adolescent psychiatry: Conduct disorders* (pp. 292–319). Cambridge, UK: Cambridge University Press.

Pianta, R. C., Steinberg, M., & Rollins, K. B. (1995). The first two years of school: Teacher-child relationships and deflections in children's classroom adjustment. *Development and Psychopathology, 7,* 295–312.

Posner, M. I., & Rothbart, M. K. (2000). Developing mechanisms of self-regulation. *Development and Psychopathology, 12,* 427–441.

Price, J. M., & Glad, K. (2003). Hostile attributional tendencies in maltreated children. *Journal of Abnormal Child Psychology, 31,* 329–343.

Rubin, K. H., & Krasnor, L. R. (1983). Age and gender differences in solutions to hypothetical social problems. *Journal of Applied Developmental Psychology, 4,* 263–275.

Rubin, K. H., & Krasnor, L. R. (1986). Social-cognitive and social behavioral perspectives on problem solving. In M. Perlmutter (Ed.), *Minnesota Symposium on Child Psychology* (Vol. 18, pp. 1–68). Hillsdale, NJ: Erlbaum.

Saarni, C., Mumme, D., & Campos, J. (1998). Emotional development: Action, communication, and understanding. In W. Damon (Series Ed.) & N. Eisenberg (Vol. Ed.), *Handbook of child psychology* (pp. 237–309). New York: Wiley.

Schwartz, D., Dodge, K. A., Coie, J. D., Hubbard, J. A., Cillessen, A. H. N., Lemerise, E. A., et al. (1998). Social-cognitive and behavioral correlates of subtypes of aggression and victimization in boys' play groups. *Journal of Abnormal Child Psychology, 26,* 431–440.

Schultz, D., & Shaw, D. S. (2003). Boys' maladaptive social information processing, family emotional climate, and pathways to early conduct problems. *Social Development, 12,* 440–460.

Sigler, R. S. (1998). *Children's thinking* (3rd ed.). Upper Saddle River, NJ: Prentice Hall.

Smithmeyer, C. M., Hubbard, J. A., & Simons, R. F. (2000). Proactive and reactive aggression in delinquent adolescents: Relations to aggression outcome expectancies. *Journal of Clinical Child Psychology, 29,* 86–93.

Sroufe, L. A. (1990). Considering normal and abnormal together: The essence of developmental psychopathology. *Development and Psychopathology, 2,* 335–347.

Underwood, M. K. (2003). *Social aggression among girls.* New York: Guilford Press.

Vasey, M. S., Dalgleish, T., & Silverman, W. K. (2003). Research on information-processing factors in child and adolescent psychopathology: A critical commentary. *Journal of Clinical Child and Adolescent Psychology, 32,* 81–93.

Vitaro, F., & Brendgen, M. (2005). Proactive and reactive aggression: A developmental perspective. In R. E. Tremblay, W. W. Hartup, & J. Archer (Eds.), *Developmental origins of aggression* (pp. 178–201). New York: Guilford.

Vitaro, F., Brendgen, M., & Tremblay, R. E. (2002). Reactively and proactively aggressive children: Antecedent and subsequent characteristics. *Journal of Child Psychology and Psychiatry*, 43, 495–506.

Vurpillot, E. (1968). The development of scanning strategies and their relation to visual differentiation. *Journal of Experimental Child Psychology*, 6, 632–650.

Waldman, I. D. (1996). Aggressive boys' hostile perceptual and response biases: The role of attention and impulsivity. *Child Development*, 67, 1015–1033.

Weiss, B., Dodge, K. A., Bates, J. E., & Pettit, G. S. (1992). Some consequences of early harsh discipline: Child aggression and a maladaptive social information processing style. *Child Development*, 63, 1321–1335.

Yoon, J., Hughes, J., Gaur, A., & Thompson, B. (1999). Social cognition in aggressive children: A meta-analytic review. *Cognitive and Behavioral Practice*, 6, 320–331.

Zelli, A., Dodge, K. A., Lochman, J. E., Laird, R. D., and the Conduct Problems Prevention Research Group. (1999). The distinction between beliefs legitimizing aggression and deviant processing of social cues: Testing measurement validity and the hypothesis that biased processing mediates the effects of beliefs on aggression. *Journal of Personality and Social Psychology*, 77, 150–166.

CHAPTER 16

School Violence

Gary D. Gottfredson and Denise C. Gottfredson

The public is naturally concerned about the safety of children attending school, and opinion polls have long shown this concern. Gallup polls show the percentage of parents fearing for their children's safety in school increased from 24% in 1977 to 55% in April 1999 immediately following the Columbine High School shootings and decreased to 21% by 2005 (Jones, 2005). Dramatic instances of shooting violence involving multiple fatalities in Columbine, Paducah, Red Lake, and elsewhere have periodically heightened this concern. Data indicate, however, that although schools are often the venue for a great deal of incivility they are only rarely the locus of extreme violence. Between the 1992–1993 and 2004–2005 school years, 415 school-associated violent deaths occurred (National School Safety Center, 2005), and the average annual incidence of school-associated violent deaths per 100,000 students between 1994 and 1999 was .068 (Anderson et. al. 2001). In contrast, the Centers for Disease Control and Prevention (2004) data show 15.4 deaths due to unintentional injury per 100,000 persons aged 5 to 19 years in 2001.

Estimates of the extent of violence and disorder in schools come from reports from several sources – student victimization surveys, student self-reports of their own violent behavior, teacher surveys, and principal reports. These sources provide disparate estimates.

In a 2001 national household survey (National Crime Victimization Survey [NCVS]; Devoe et al., 2003), 36% of all *serious* violent victimizations of 12- to 18-year-olds (e.g., rape, sexual assault, robbery, or aggravated assault) occurred in school or on the way to and from school. About half of violent victimizations reported in this household survey (defined as those crimes included in serious violent victimization plus simple assault) occur in school.

Less serious forms of crime have been relatively common in and around schools for at least the past 30 years. Considering *all* forms of crime measured in the NCVS for the 2001 school year, more crime victimization occurs in school than out of school. In all, 55% of crimes against students aged 12 to 18 occurred at school or on the way to and from school despite their spending only about 18% of their waking hours in school. The proportion is highest for theft (58%), but also substantial for violent crimes (50%). These data mirror findings from two national studies of victimization in schools (G. D. Gottfredson & Gottfredson, 1985; G. D. Gottfredson, Gottfredson, Czeh, Cantor, Cross, & Hantman, 2000), which found that, although serious victimization in schools was rare, minor victimizations and indignities were common in schools. In the more recent survey, 18% of secondary students reported having been threatened with a beating, 13% reported having been attacked, and 5% reported having been threatened with a knife or gun. Schools are by no means havens against crimes. On the contrary, when all criminal victimizations, rather than only the most serious are considered, youths are at elevated risk for victimization when they are in school or on the way to and from school.

School Characteristics and School Violence: Evidence From Survey Research

Research implies that certain school characteristics are robustly related to school disorder. Different forms of school disorder including rates of violence are related (Gottfredson et al., 2000). Schools experiencing high levels of theft from teachers, for example, are also likely to experience high levels of student attacks. We therefore review the broader literature on school disorder in this section.

In an early examination of the effects of school characteristics on rates of victimization in schools (G. Gottfredson & Gottfredson, 1985), we analyzed the National Institute of Education's (1978) Safe School Study data from a national sample of over 600 U.S. secondary schools. In this sample, community and school demographic characteristics explained 54 and 44% of the variance in teacher victimization rates for middle/junior and senior high schools, respectively. Specifically, community poverty and disorganization (including racial composition and socioeconomic

status), urban (versus rural) location, community crime, and total school enrollment (junior high schools only) were significantly related to teacher victimization rates. We also found that malleable school characteristics accounted for an additional 12 and 18% of the variance in teacher victimization net of community and school demographic characteristics in middle/junior and senior high schools, respectively. Several potentially manipulatable school characteristics were associated with high rates of teacher victimization net of statistical controls: schools in which teachers teach a large number of students and have punitive attitudes, schools in which the rules are not perceived by students as fair and firmly enforced and students had low levels of belief in conventional rules and laws governing behavior, and schools with few teaching resources and low levels of cooperation between teachers and administrators.

Results from other school-level studies of school organization and climate dimensions and student misbehavior have been mixed. Galloway, Martin and Wilcox, (1985) and Hellman and Beaton (1986) found no evidence for school effects on student absenteeism or suspension once community characteristics were controlled. In these studies, the school characteristics examined were limited to features of the school building (e.g., age of building) and aspects of formal school organization commonly found in archival records. Welsh, Stokes, and Greene (2000) found that "school culture" reduced disciplinary incidents in a study of 43 Philadelphia middle schools. However, they measured "school culture" using archival measures of student absence and dropout – indicators commonly used as dependent measures in other studies. In a study that used more appropriate measures of school social organization and included more schools as well, Ostroff (1992) showed that teacher satisfaction and commitment predict student dropout, attendance rates, and disciplinary problems.

In a recent study of hypotheses about school-level predictors of school violence in a nationally representative sample of

254 secondary schools (G. Gottfredson, Gottfredson, Payne, & Gottfredson, 2005), we found that measures of school climate explained substantial variance in teacher victimization, student self-reported delinquency, and student victimization, controlling for the effects of community characteristics and school student composition. Schools with better discipline management (students perceived greater fairness and clarity of rules) had less delinquent behavior and less student victimization, although discipline management did not influence teacher victimization. Schools with more positive psychosocial climates had less teacher victimization, but climate did not influence student victimization or delinquent behavior. Using the same sample, Payne, Gottfredson, and Gottfredson (2003) found that communally organized schools experience less disorder and that the relation between communal school organization and school disorder is partially mediated by student bonding.

Several studies have estimated school effects while controlling for individual-level processes. Felson, Liska, South, and McNulty (1994) examined the effects of normative school values regarding violence on individual interpersonal violence, theft and vandalism, and school delinquency. They found that school norms about violence predicted individual involvement in all three forms of delinquent behavior. The authors concluded that normative values characterizing a school provide additional social control beyond the social control due to individually held values. Similarly, Brezina, Piquero, and Mazerolle (2001), studying a male high-school sample, found that school-average approval of aggression, but not school-average anger, predicted individual-level aggressive behavior. They also found that students in larger schools experienced less aggression than students in smaller schools.

Bryk and colleagues (Bryk & Driscoll, 1988; see also chapter 11 in Bryk, Lee, & Holland, 1993) examined a subset of schools from the national High School and Beyond study to explore the effects of school sense of community on student

learning and behavior. Their study separated the effects of school composition (e.g., the average academic and social class background of the students, minority concentration, and ethnic and social class heterogeneity) from the effects of individual-level demographic characteristics. According to their model, larger school size increased behavioral problems (absenteeism, class cutting, classroom disorder, and dropping out). Communal organization reduced problem behaviors after controlling for school composition, size, parental cooperation, and student selectivity. In addition, communal organization mediated the effects of composition and school size. The authors interpret their results to imply that school composition and size influence problem behavior indirectly via communal organization.

Lee and Croninger (1996) conducted a multilevel study of perceptions of safety among high-school students using data from 5,486 students in 377 schools. They found that 17% of the variability in individual perceptions of safety lies between schools, about 29% of this between-school variance is accounted for by student-level demographics, and school-level variables explain an additional 42% of the between-school variance. The compositional characteristics of the school (percentage minority and average school SES) explained the most variance in student-characteristic-adjusted school average perceptions of safety, followed by positive student-teacher relations. In their models, school size and urban location did not predict perceptions of safety.

Other recent studies have also used hierarchical modeling to examine school climate effects on school disorder as measured by student reports of fighting and being punished in school. Using a sample from 11 schools from a single urban district, Welsh, Greene, and Jenkins (1999) found that individual student characteristics (including school effort, rewards, positive peer associations, involvement, belief in rules, as well as demographic characteristics) accounted for 16% of the variance in school disorder and school and community characteristics accounted for an additional

4.1 to 4.5%; however, among the community and school climate measures, only community poverty significantly predicted the level of school disorder. Stewart (2003) also predicted school misbehavior as measured by school punishments and fighting in a large national sample of 10,578 students from 528 schools. Stewart's measures of school climate were based on administrator and student reports of school social problems (many of which have been treated as dependent measures in other studies) and on teacher and student reports of school cohesion. Stewart found that, although larger schools in urban areas experienced more disorder, the other school characteristics did not explain a significant amount of variation in student misbehavior.

Wilcox and Clayton (2001) found that weapon carrying was explained by school-level as well as individual-level factors in a multilevel examination of a sample of 21 schools, although the school-level variables explained far less of the variance in weapon carrying than did the individual-level factors. School-level SES was the only contextual variable to affect weapon carrying in their analysis. The SES effect was mediated by "school capital" (a scale based on mean levels of protective factors for students in the school) and "school deficits" (a scale based on mean levels of risk factors for students in the school).

In short, prior studies have examined a wide array of measures of school characteristics to predict a variety of measures of problem behavior, but heterogeneity across studies, sample variability, and flawed measures make them difficult to summarize. Nevertheless, these studies have documented several clusters of school characteristics that appear robustly related to school disorder. Many but not all studies have shown that community characteristics and school characteristics that are largely outside the control of individual schools account for much of the between-school variance in disorder. These school and community characteristics include racial heterogeneity, size of school, auspices (public vs. private), urban location, community poverty and disorga-

nization, residential crowding, community crime, and characteristics of the students in the school, including their percentage male and average student age. The level of prior problem behavior of students attending a school also influences the level of disorder experienced in the school.

Research has also shown that school characteristics that can potentially be manipulated predict the level of school disorder beyond the influences of difficult-to-manipulate determinants. Schools that establish and maintain rules, effectively communicate clear expectations for behavior, consistently enforce rules, and provide rewards for rule compliance and punishments for rule infractions experience lower levels of victimization (G. Gottfredson & Gottfredson, 1985; G. Gottfredson et al., 2005). Schools with lower levels of crime are also characterized by more positive psychosocial climates (Bryk & Driscoll, 1988): a sense of community and a network of caring adults who interact regularly with the students and who share norms and expectations about their students seem to produce lower levels of problem behavior. Payne et al. (2003) also documented a relationship between communal school organization and school disorder. Felson et al. (1994) and Brezina et al. (2001) showed that school normative beliefs influence violence or aggressive behavior. Lee and Croninger (1996) demonstrated that positive student-teacher relations are associated with lower levels of fear among students, and Ostroff (1992) showed that teacher satisfaction and commitment predict student dropout rates, attendance, and disciplinary problems. These school effects have generally been small, and not all studies find effects of school manipulatable features of school organization.

What Schools Can Do About Violence: Evidence From Intervention Research

This section shifts attention to research on interventions to reduce or prevent youth violence, including interpersonal aggression, bullying, and (for younger students) biting and throwing things at others. The aggressive acts of younger children have been shown to be precursors of later violent behavior (Tolan & Gorman-Smith, 1998). The section describes a range of school-based violence-prevention interventions that have been studied, including brief descriptions of the most effective approaches. The interventions fall into two classes: (1) interventions that manipulate school or classroom environment or practices and (2) interventions that influence characteristics of individuals. For example, an intervention that seeks to reduce violence by manipulating the fairness and clarity of school rules is an environmental intervention, and a program that seeks primarily to alter features of individual behaviors, beliefs, and attitudes is an individual intervention.

The dependent variables examined in research summarized here include measures of youth violence or aggression, associated outcomes, or both. Associated outcomes include problem behaviors correlated with violence and aggression, including delinquent behavior, other problem behavior, and low self-control. Studies reporting outcome measures that included items measuring violence or aggression combined with items measuring other forms of problem behavior were classified as associated outcomes. If we were uncertain whether or not a study actually demonstrated effects on violence or aggression, we classified it as targeting associated outcomes.

Environmental Interventions

Environmental interventions manipulate school or classroom characteristics or practices. These interventions range from the use of metal detectors to screen entrants into schools for weapons to broad efforts to alter the ways in which schools organize themselves to signal desired behavior and respond to behavior. Table 16.1, based mainly on a meta-analytic review of school-based programs (D. Gottfredson, Wilson, & Najaka, 2002), provides a succinct summary of the range of environmental interventions and state of the evidence about their effectiveness. The following section characterizes each category and provides illustrations of interventions that appear on the basis of the evidence to be effective in reducing

Table 16.1: School-wide or classroom environmental interventions

Type of intervention and examples	Status of knowledge
Security or surveillance procedures (e.g., metal detectors, closed-circuit monitoring, limiting access by intruders)	Little persuasive research is available. Metal detectors appear to reduce carrying of weapons in school.
School resource officer (SRO) programs	Insufficient evidence.
Discipline management processes & procedures	Well-implemented interventions have been shown to reduce problem behavior, but little evidence about violence per se.
Establish clear norms or expectations regarding "bullying" or other interpersonal aggression	Can be effective in reducing aggression.
Classroom or instructional management to improve student engagement, bonding, and school performance	May be effective, but mixed and inconsistent results in different studies of this heterogeneous category of interventions.
Reorganizing scheduling, classes, or grades to create smaller units, continuing interaction, different mixes of students, or provide greater flexibility in instruction	Insufficient evidence.
Architectural arrangements	Insufficient evidence.

aggression, violence, or related problem behavior when well-implemented.

Security or surveillance procedures. Many schools employ approaches to preventing violence by attempting to limit access to schools by intruders or prevent weapons from coming into the schools, and one form or another of such approach has been recommended in one way or another from time to time (Aleem & Moles, 1993; Butterfield & Turner, 1989). Among the techniques in use are controlled entry and identification systems, metal detectors, security personnel or volunteers who challenge intruders, and doors fitted with electromagnetic locks. Over half of schools in the United States employ one or more such procedure (G. Gottfredson & Gottfredson, 2001). With the exception of a survey research, there is little research on the effects of the use of metal detectors or other security procedures in schools. In a sample of high-school students in New York City studied to compare the frequency of weapon carrying in schools with and without metal detectors, Ginsberg and Loffredo (1993) found that students in schools with metal detectors were half as likely to carry a weapon to school as students in schools without metal detectors, but G. Gottfredson and D. Gottfredson (1985) found that extensiveness of school security procedures was positively associated with school disorder. More and better research is required to examine the effectiveness of these approaches to promoting school safety, particularly in view of the practical difficulties involved in putting many of these approaches into use on a consistent basis.

Police or school resource officers in schools. Since the mid-1990s, in part in response to a spate of multivictim violent events in schools, school resource officers (SROs) have been somewhat popular in secondary schools (Girouard, 2001) as a way to prevent violence – with a large program sponsored by an agency of the U.S. Department of Justice. One evaluation of SROs (Johnson, 1999) was insufficiently rigorous to provide evidence of effectiveness of this practice. In view of the cost of deploying uniformed officers in schools, better evidence should be developed about their usefulness in preventing violence.

Discipline management processes and procedures. School and discipline management interventions include decision-making processes or authority structures to enhance the organizational capacity of the school to regulate the behavior of students. These interventions may involve collaboration among staff and sometimes parents, students, and community members to identify problems within the school, develop potential solutions, and design activities to improve the school.

One example of such an intervention, Project PATHE (D. Gottfredson, 1986), altered the organization and management structures in seven secondary schools. School teams used a structured organizational development method (Program Development Evaluation; G. Gottfredson, 1984) to plan, initiate, and sustain needed changes. The intervention schools planned and implemented activities to increase the clarity of school rules, consistency of rule enforcement, and students' experiences of success and feelings of belonging in the school. The students in the intervention schools reported less delinquent behavior and drug use and fewer punishments in school relative to the students in the comparison schools. Evaluations of a number of programs that alter school management or discipline management (summarized in D. Gottfredson et al., 2002) imply that this type of intervention can be effective for reducing problem behaviors, but there is insufficient evidence about the effects of such interventions on youth violence or aggression per se.

Interventions to establish clear norms or expectations regarding "bullying" or other interpersonal aggression. These interventions make school-wide efforts to signal appropriate behavior through such vehicles as newsletters, posters, ceremonies during which students publicly declare their behavioral intentions, and displays of symbols or reminders of appropriate behavior. Two examples are a Bullying Prevention Program (Olweus, Limber, & Mihalic,

1999), and the Safe Dates Program (Foshee et al., 1996, 1998).

Olweus's anti-bullying program targets students in elementary, middle, and high schools and has school-wide, classroom, and individual components. School-wide components include increased adult supervision at bullying "hot spots" and school-wide discussions of bullying. Classrooms develop and enforce rules against bullying. Individual children identified as bullies and victims are counseled. Olweus et al. (1999) summarized evidence that the program can lead to reductions in student bullying and victimization and decreases in the incidence of vandalism, fighting, and theft.

The Safe Dates Program aimed at changing norms for dating violence among adolescents. Within the school, intervention components include a theater production performed by peers; a 10-session curriculum addressing dating violence norms, gender stereotyping, and conflict management skills; and a poster contest. In the community, intervention components include services for adolescents experiencing abuse and training for community service providers. An evaluation of the program for students in eighth and ninth grades (Foshee et al., 1998) found that the students in intervention schools reported less psychological abuse and violence against dating partners than did students in control schools. Based largely on a relatively rigorous evaluation of these two programs, D. Gottfredson et al. (2002) concluded that interventions to establish norms or expectations for behavior can be effective in preventing aggression and other problem behavior.

Classroom or instructional management. These interventions use practices intended to fully engage students in learning, improve their achievement, and increase their attachment to school. These practices are varied, differing in the extent to which they have a basis in research on instructional effectiveness. They range from well-studied cooperative learning techniques to less well-defined "experiential learning" strategies. This heterogeneous category of interventions also includes classroom management strategies, such as avoiding wasting instructional time in transitions between activities in the classroom, establishing and enforcing classroom rules, applying rewards and punishments, and using external resources including parent volunteers and police officers. Taken together, the studies reviewed by D. Gottfredson et al. (2002) suggest that classroom instructional and management strategies can reduce problem behavior. However, when only studies with reasonable scientific rigor are examined, the results are mixed. Although some reasonably rigorous studies have found significant positive effects on measures of antisocial behavior, violence, and aggression (Hawkins, Catalano, Kosterman, Abbott, & Hill, 1999; Hawkins, Von Cleve, & Catalona, 1991), the inconsistency of the findings across studies makes it impossible to draw firm conclusions about the category of interventions as a whole. The programs with the most positive effects tended to be of longer duration and to combine classroom and instructional management strategies with some other major ingredient (e.g., parent training or social skills instruction).

Reorganizing scheduling, classes, or grades. These interventions involve school reorganization to create smaller units, allow continuity in the interaction of students with teachers who know them well, create homogeneity or heterogeneity in student groupings, or provide flexibility in arrangements for instruction. These interventions may involve the school schedule (e.g., introduction of block scheduling) or the formation of grade-level "teams" or "houses."

Project STATUS (D. Gottfredson & Gottfredson, 1992) is one example of this type of intervention. STATUS regrouped seventh- and eighth-grade students at elevated risk of problem behavior into extended 2-hour daily classes to receive an integrated social studies and English program. Instruction included law-related curriculum and emphasized active student participation. The evaluation found positive effects on crime and drug use. The D. Gottfredson et al. (2002) meta-analytic review identified only two evaluations of programs involving the reorganization of grades or classes that measured violence, aggression, or associated outcomes; it concluded that there is insufficient evidence on the effectiveness of this category of interventions, but that this is a promising area for further inquiry.

Architectural arrangements. These arrangements include features of school design that allow for the observation of activities in all parts of the school or particularly of entrances and hallways, the physical design of cafeterias and pathways for ingress and egress, arrangements to regulate the flow of persons throughout the school (e.g., separate stairwells for students in different grades or up-only and down-only stairways), or the construction of obstacles that prevent access to unoccupied portions of a school building. Schools differ considerably in these architectural arrangements. New buildings are sometimes constructed to allow surveillance of many parts of the school from a central office, and old buildings in urban areas of declining enrollment are sometimes altered to block off areas of excess capacity. Most school principals report arrangements to promote safety and orderliness in cafeterias, and two thirds report using physical arrangements to regulate traffic flow within the building (G. Gottfredson & Gottfredson, 2001). Despite the widespread use of these architectural strategies, almost no systematic research on their effects on violence or school safety seems to have been conducted. This type of intervention, described in materials related to the Crime Prevention through Environmental Design approach (CPTED; Schneider, Walker, & Sprague, 2000) is clearly an area deserving of further study.

Interventions to Influence the Characteristics of Individuals

Interventions to influence characteristics of individual students may be directed at knowledge, skills, attitudes or beliefs, expectations, and so on. They may be universal interventions intended to reduce the risk of violence or problem behavior for all students in a school, selective interventions to reduce risk for individuals at elevated risk of violence or problem behavior, or indicated interventions to ameliorate problem behavior for individuals who are displaying it. Table 16.2, based mainly on a meta-analytic review of school-based programs (D. Gottfredson et al., 2002) provides a summary of the range of individual interventions and state of the evidence about their effectiveness. This section characterizes each category and provides illustrations of interventions that appear on the basis of the evidence to be effective in reducing aggression, violence, or related problem behavior when well implemented.

Cognitive-behavioral social competency instruction. This category of instructional interventions seeks to develop students' skills in (1) recognizing situations in which they are likely to get into trouble; (2) controlling or managing their impulses, anticipating the consequences of their actions; (3) perceiving accurately the feelings or intentions of others; or (4) coping with peer influence that may lead to trouble – hence the term "social competency" instruction. These interventions use cognitive-behavioral methods, so called because they use cognitive techniques: they explicitly teach principles for self-regulation and recognizing antecedents of problem behavior, provide cues to help young people remember and apply the principles, use modeling to demonstrate the principles and associated behavior, involve goal setting, provide opportunities for rehearsal and practice of the behavior in social situations (role-playing), provide feedback on student performance, and promote self-monitoring and self-regulation. The instruction generally has roots in cognitive social learning theory (Bandura, 1986) and cognitive-behavioral intervention research more generally (Kaslow & Thompson, 1998; Kazdin & Weisz, 1998).

Interpersonal Problem-Solving Skills (ICPS; Shure & Spivak, 1979, 1980, 1982) provides an example of cognitive-behavioral instruction for preschool students. Teachers use cognitive training to help small groups of 4-year-old children learn to find

Table 16.2: Interventions directed at individuals' skills, knowledge, attitudes, or other individual characteristics

Type of intervention and examples	Status of knowledge
Cognitive-behavioral social competency instruction	Interventions of this kind have been shown to be effective for both violence/aggression and other problem behavior for elementary-school children to high-school youths.
Other instructional interventions	Despite occasional positive results, the preponderance of evidence is that these are usually ineffective.
Behavior modification or cognitive-behavioral interventions to change behavior or cognitive skills directed at individuals or groups	Effective interventions for reducing violence/aggression and other problem behavior for elementary-school children to high-school youth.
Counseling, social work, and other therapeutic interventions (other than behavioral or cognitive-behavioral)	No consistent positive evidence of effectiveness and some negative evidence.
Mentoring, tutoring, and work-study interventions	Mixed evidence with some positive instances of effectiveness failing to replicate.
Recreation, community service, enrichment, and leisure activities without behavioral or cognitive-behavioral instructional components	No evidence of effectiveness.

alternative solutions to problems, become aware of steps required to reach a goal, and consider consequences of their behavior. ICPS has been shown to improve children's problem-solving skills and the ratings of their conduct.

FAST Track (Conduct Problems Prevention Research Group, 1999a,b) is a more recent and more comprehensive example of instruction with cognitive-behavioral methods for elementary-aged children. This program integrates five components to promote competence in the family, child, and school to prevent conduct problems and school failure and to improve interpersonal relations. The program trains parents in family management, and it makes home visits to reinforce skills learned in the training and to promote parental feelings of efficacy. Intervention components directed at the children include social skills coaching, tutoring, and a classroom instruction focusing on social competencies. Teachers are trained to employ specific classroom management strategies. The program combines

several school-based strategies. An experimental evaluation showed that the FAST Track interventions had positive effects on child social cognitive skills and several measures of problem behavior, including aggression. Its evaluation attests to the value of comprehensive, theory-based, and well-implemented preventive interventions.

Anger Control Training (Feindler, Marriott, & Iwata, 1984) illustrates an indicated cognitive-behavioral instruction for early adolescent boys. The intervention involves 10 sessions in which students were taught to analyze the components of the provocation cycle – its antecedent anger cues, aggressive responses, and consequent events – and it teaches adolescents self-monitoring using written logs. Students learn to replace aggressive responses with more appropriate responses, problem-solving techniques, and specific cognitive behaviors, such as self-instruction. Feindler et al. (1984) found experimental students improved more than controls on an interview measure of problem-solving skills and on teacher ratings of self-control. The program also reduced mild verbal and physical misbehaviors (cursing, arguing, and shoving).

We have provided multiple examples of cognitive-behavioral instruction, because this class of interventions can clearly be effective in reducing problem behavior and aggression for children in a broad range of ages.

Other instructional interventions. Schools engage in a large number of other instructional interventions intended to prevent violence or problem behavior (G. Gottfredson & Gottfredson, 2001), but many of them do not meet the criteria for the cognitive-behavioral category. These other instructional programs depend more on traditional methods of instruction, such as workbooks, lecture, and class discussion. These interventions may provide factual information, seek to increase student awareness of social influences to engage in misbehavior, teach about risky or potentially harmful behaviors or situations, or provide instruction on moral virtues, and so forth. In contrast to cognitive-behavioral instructional interventions, two meta-analyses have concluded that these programs are ineffective for reducing youth violence, aggression, or other problem behavior (D. Gottfredson et al., 2002; Lipsey & Wilson, 1998), although a few specific studies have found positive effects.

Behavior modification or cognitive-behavioral interventions to change behavior directed at high-risk individuals or groups. Behavior-modification interventions focus directly on changing behaviors by targeting specific behaviors to change, analyzing environmental antecedents and rewards for undesirable behavior, and applying contingent rewards for desired behavior or punishment for undesired behavior. Some behavioral interventions for delinquent individuals or groups of individuals at elevated risk of problem behavior also involve cognitions. These cognitive-behavioral extensions of behavioral interventions are based in part on a substantial body of research indicating that aggressive or delinquent children and youths tend to be impulsive, tend not

to make self-attributions for negative personal outcomes, tend to have hostile attributional bias in interpreting ambiguous social cues, fail to consider alternative solutions to problems, and lack effective communication skills (Dodge, Bates, & Pettit, 1990).

The Good Behavior Game (GBG; Barrish, Saunders, & Wolf, 1969) is an example of a group-based behavior management program for elementary-aged children. Small student teams are formed within each classroom, and the teams are rewarded for achieving behavioral standards. Because the team reward depends on the behavior of each member of the team, peer pressure is used to promote desired behavior. Dolan et al. (1993) used a randomized control group design to assess the effectiveness of GBG in inner-city schools, finding that GBG males were rated by their peers (but not by their teachers) as significantly less aggressive at the end of first grade. For females, teacher ratings (but not peer ratings) of aggression were significantly lower for GBG students. D. Gottfredson et al. (2002) pooled data across sexes and raters and found an overall significant effect of GBG on aggressive behavior in the Dolan et al. results.

The D. Gottfredson et al. (2002) meta-analytic review concluded that behavioral and cognitive-behavioral interventions can be effective for reducing youth violence, aggression, and problem behavior. A meta-analytic review by Lipsey and Wilson (1998) also found this type of intervention to be effective for youthful criminal offenders.

Counseling, social work, and other therapeutic interventions (other than behavioral or cognitive-behavioral). Counseling activities to prevent problem behavior or promote a safe school environment are almost as common in schools as are instructional programs (G. Gottfredson & Gottfredson, 2001), with 75% of schools employing some sort of counseling, social work, or therapeutic intervention. To merely say that an intervention involves "counseling" is to say very little, however. Counseling involving behavioral or cognitive-behavioral interventions would be classified in the previous category. Perhaps greater clarification about specific techniques and their effectiveness may at some point become available, but at present only the behavioral and cognitive-behavioral variety described earlier has been regularly found effective in reducing aggression or other problem behavior. However, convincing evidence of the efficacy of garden-variety counseling is lacking, and at least one evaluation implies that harmful effects are possible (G. Gottfredson, 1987).

Mentoring, tutoring, and work-study interventions. These interventions usually involve one-on-one interaction with an older, more experienced person who provides advice or assistance. The older adult is generally not a professional counselor, and the interaction is generally not focused on the individuals' problem behavior. There exists evidence of positive effects on several outcomes, including self-reports of trouble with the police, in a randomized efficacy study of one program providing in- and out-of-school services to high-school students (Hahn, Leavitt, & Aaron, 1994; Taggart, 1995). However, a more recent randomized trial failed to find an effect on problem behavior (Maxfield, Schirm, & Rodriguez-Planas, 2002). Two recent reviews (D. Gottfredson et al., 2002; Welsh & Hoshi, 2002) concluded that there is insufficient evidence on the effectiveness of mentoring programs for reducing youth violence, aggression, or other problem behavior.

Recreation, community service, enrichment, and leisure activities without behavioral or cognitive-behavioral instructional components. These interventions include wilderness challenge programs and "ropes" courses, drop-in recreation centers, after-school and weekend programs, dances, community service activities, and other activities often seen as having the potential for keeping young people out of trouble. Two meta-analytic reviews (D. Gottfredson et al., 2002; Lipsey & Wilson, 1998) concluded that there is insufficient evidence to determine the effectiveness of these interventions on violence, aggression, or other problem behavior. Naturally, there is the potential for recreational or after-school programs that incorporate well-implemented interventions of other

kinds – such as cognitive-behavioral treatment or instruction – to prevent violence or other problem behaviors (see, for example, D. Gottfredson et al., 2004). Despite this potential, there is little in the available evidence to lead to the expectation that enrichment or recreational activities not supplemented by effective components will be helpful in preventing violence.

The Special Case of School Multiple Victim Shootings

Multiple victim shootings in schools have had a special place in focusing the public's attention on violence and safety in schools. A number of episodes that might be characterized as rampage violence are chronicled and analyzed in a recent National Research Council Report (Moore, Petrie, Braga, & McLaughlin, 2003). These rampages are rare, making the identification of statistical regularities difficult. The result is that these incidents are a source of tentative hypotheses (at best) about the possible causes and remedies. Among the apparent regularities in these cases are the following: the perpetrators in some sense felt aggrieved, events evidently spiked in the late 1990s, rampages were *not* characteristically inner-city phenomena, all involved boys and firearms, informal peer groups (differing in nature in urban from suburban or rural schools) may have been related in some way to the school experiences of the shooters, and adults in the schools and communities seem to have been mostly unaware of the grievances felt by the perpetrators.

The dramatic nature of these rampages naturally stimulates the impulse to identify either potential shooters or schools in which an incident is likely. But one feature of these events renders the effort to identify or predict essentially futile: these events are rare. Even if well-validated predictors were available – and they are not – the practical application of prediction devices would result mostly in classification errors. Identification of potential school shooters is thwarted by the low base rate for these events (Meehl &

Rosen, 1955). In contrast, the prediction rates of violence and disorder in schools and the search for interventions that will reduce violence and other problem behavior are more tractable problems. Most of the survey and intervention research reviewed earlier in this chapter are directed at these problems. Much remains to be done, and the following section briefly suggests productive directions for research.

Future Directions

At present only a few intervention strategies have persuasive evidence of effectiveness. Many plausible strategies remain untested in sound research, and most of what schools currently do (G. Gottfredson & Gottfredson, 2001) to prevent violence and problem behavior is not only untested in research but also appears to be of low quality (D. Gottfredson & Gottfredson, 2002). The intervention approaches that have been well evaluated tend to focus on changing the characteristics of individuals and involve interventions that can be tested in small-scale research. Despite evidence from survey research that characteristics of school environments are related to a variety of measures of school disorder, environmentally focused interventions are unstudied or understudied: school security arrangements, school architecture, and school management, for example. Rigorous studies of environmental interventions are difficult and expensive to carry out, but examples of rigorous evaluations of organizational and environmental interventions to reduce youth violence can be found (e.g., Sherman & Berk's (1984) random assignment of alternative police practices and Wagenaar, Murray, & Toomey's (2000) random assignment of communities to community mobilization). Rigorous evaluations of a broader range of school violence prevention strategies are required.

The evaluations of these interventions should have stronger designs than characterizes most currently available research. More studies should use randomized experimental research designs. Now, the use of

this or other designs allowing for confident inferences is rare (D. Gottfredson, et al., 2002. Furthermore, few studies of school-based or other youth violence prevention interventions measure long-term program effectiveness, and many studies of school programs addressing problem behavior fail to measure violent behavior directly. These limitations of outcome measurement leave ambiguity about the effectiveness of interventions in preventing violence. Finally, greater attention should be given in conducting and reporting school-based intervention research to the measurement of and reporting on strength of implementation. In the long run, this will be as important in learning about what works as are increasing the range of what is tested and the quality of outcome evaluation designs.

References

Aleem, D., & Moles, O. (1993). *Review of research on ways to attain Goal Six: Creating safe, disciplined, and drug-free schools*. Washington, DC: Office for Education Research and Improvement.

Anderson, M., Kaufman, J., Simon, T., Barrios, L., Paulozzi, L., Ryan, G., et al., & the School-Associated Violent Deaths Study Group. (2001). School-associated violent deaths in the United States, 1994–1999. *Journal of the American Medical Association, 286*, 2695–2702.

Bandura, A. (1986). *Social foundations of thought and action*. Englewood Cliffs, NJ: Prentice Hall.

Barrish, H. H., Saunders, M., & Wolf, M. M. (1969). Good behavior game: Effects of individual contingencies for group consequences on disruptive behavior in a classroom. *Journal of Applied Behavior Analysis, 2*, 119–124.

Brezina, T., Piquero, A. R., & Mazerolle, P. (2001). Student anger and aggressive behavior in school: An initial test of Agnew's macro-level strain theory. *Journal of Research in Crime and Delinquency, 38*, 362–386.

Bryk, A. S., & Driscoll, M. E. (1988). *The school as community: Theoretical foundations, contextual influences, and consequences for students and teachers*. Madison, WI: University of Wisconsin, National Center on Effective Secondary Schools.

Bryk, A. S., Lee, V. E., & Holland, P. B. (1993). *Catholic schools and the common good.* Cambridge, MA: Harvard University Press.

Butterfield, G., & Turner, B. (1989). *Weapons in schools: NSSC resource paper.* Malibu, CA: Pepperdine University, National School Safety Center.

Centers for Disease Control and Prevention. (2004). *National Center for Injury Prevention and Control Web-Based Injury Statistics Query and Reporting System.* Retrieved from http://www.cdc.gov/ncipc/wisqrs/default.htm.

Conduct Problems Prevention Research Group. (1999a). Initial impact of the Fast Track prevention trial for conduct problems: I. The high risk sample. *Journal of Consulting and Clinical Psychology, 67,* 631–647.

Conduct Problems Prevention Research Group. (1999b). Initial impact of the Fast Track prevention trial for conduct problems: II. Classroom effects. *Journal of Consulting and Clinical Psychology, 67,* 648–657.

Devoe, J. F., Peter, K., Kaufman, P., Ruddy, S. A., Miller, A. K., Planty, M., et al. (2003). *Indicators of school crime and safety: 2003* (NCJ 201257). Washington, DC: National Center for Education Statistics and Bureau of Justice Statistics.

Dodge, K. A., Bates, J. E., & Pettit, G. S. (1990). Mechanisms in the cycle of violence. *Science, 250,* 1678–1683.

Dolan, L. J., Kellam, S. G., Brown, C. H., Werthamer-Larsson, L., Rebok, G. W., Mayer, L. S., et al. (1993). The short-term impact of two classroom-based preventive interventions on aggressive and shy behaviors and poor achievement. *Journal of Applied Developmental Psychology, 14,* 317–345.

Felson, R. B., Liska, A. E., South, S. J., & McNulty, T. L. (1994). The subculture of violence and delinquency: Individual vs. school context effects. *Social Forces, 73,* 155–173.

Feindler, E. L., Marriott, S. A., & Iwata, M. (1984). Group anger control training for junior high school delinquents. *Cognitive Therapy and Research, 8,* 299–311.

Foshee, V. A., Bauman, K. E., Arriaga, X. B., Helms, R. W., Koch, G. G., & Linder, G. F. (1998). An evaluation of Safe Dates, an adolescent dating violence prevention program. *American Journal of Public Health, 88,* 45–50.

Foshee, V. A., Linder, G. F., Bauman, K. E., Langwick, S. A., Arriaga, X. B., Heath, J. L., et al. (1996). The Safe Dates project: Theoretical basis, evaluation design, and selected baseline findings. *American Journal of Preventive Medicine, 12,* 39–47.

Galloway, D., Martin, R., & Wilcox, B. (1985). Persistent absence from school and exclusion from school: The predictive power of school and community variables. *British Educational Research Journal, 11,* 51–61.

Ginsberg, C., & Loffredo, L. (1993). Violence-related attitudes and behaviors of high school students – New York City 1992. *Journal of School Health, 63,* 438–439.

Girouard, C. (2001). *OJJDP fact sheet: School resource officer training program.* Washington, DC: U.S. Department of Justice.

Gottfredson, D. C. (1986). An empirical test of school-based environmental and individual interventions to reduce the risk of delinquent behavior. *Criminology, 24,* 705–731.

Gottfredson, D. C., & Bauer, E. L. (2005). Youth violence. In L. Doll, S. Bonzo, J. Mercy, & D. Sleet (Eds.), *Handbook on injury and violence prevention interventions.* New York: Kluwer.

Gottfredson, D. C., & Gottfredson, G. D. (1992). Theory-guided investigation: Three field experiments. In J. McCord & R. Tremblay (Eds.), *The prevention of antisocial behavior in children* (pp. 311–329). New York: Guilford Press.

Gottfredson, D. C., & Gottfredson, G. D. (2002). Quality of school-based prevention programs: Results from a national survey. *Journal of Research in Crime and Delinquency, 39,* 3–35.

Gottfredson, D. C. Weisman, S. A., Soulé, D. A., Womer, S. C., & Lu, S. (2004). Do after school programs reduce delinquency? *Prevention Science, 5*(4), 253–266.

Gottfredson, D. C., Wilson, D. B., & Najaka, S. S. (2002). School based crime prevention. In L. W. Sherman, D. P. Farrington, B. C. Welsh, & D. L. MacKenzie (Eds.), *Evidence-based crime prevention* (pp. 56–164). London: Routledge.

Gottfredson, G. D. (1984). A theory-ridden approach to program evaluation: A method for stimulating researcher implementer collaboration. *American Psychologist, 39,* 1101–1112.

Gottfredson, G. D. (1987). Peer group interventions to reduce the risk of delinquent behavior: A selective review and a new evaluation. *Criminology, 25,* 671–714.

Gottfredson, G. D., & Gottfredson, D. C. (1985). *Victimization in schools.* New York: Plenum.

Gottfredson, G. D., & Gottfredson, D. C. (2001). What schools do to prevent problem behavior and promote safe environments. *Journal* of *Educational and Psychological Consultation*, *12*, 313–344.

Gottfredson, G. D. Gottfredson, D. C., Czeh, E. R., Cantor, D., Crosse, S. B., & Hantman, I. (2000). *National Study of Delinquency Prevention in Schools: Final report*. Ellicott City, MD: Gottfredson Associates, Inc. Retrieved from http://www.gottfredson.com/national.htm.

Gottfredson, G. D., Gottfredson, D. C., Payne, A. A., & Gottfredson, N. C. (2005). School climate predictors of school disorder: Results from the National Study of Delinquency Prevention in Schools. *Journal of Research in Crime and Delinquency*, *42*, 412–444.

Hahn, A., Leavitt, T., & Aaron, P. (1994). *Evaluation of the Quantum Opportunities Program (QOP): Did the program work? A report on the post secondary outcomes and cost-effectiveness of the QOP Program*. Unpublished manuscript, Brandeis University, Waltham, MA.

Hawkins, J. D., Catalano, R. F., Kosterman, R., Abbott, R., & Hill, K. G. (1999). Preventing adolescent health risk behaviors by strengthening protection during childhood. *Archives of Pediatrics & Adolescent Medicine*, *153*, 226–234.

Hawkins, J. D., Von Cleve, E., & Catalano, R. F. (1991). Reducing early childhood aggression: Results of a primary prevention program. *Journal of the American Academy of Child and Adolescent Psychiatry*, *30*, 208–217.

Hellman, D. A., & Beaton, S. (1986). The pattern of violence in urban public schools: The influence of school and community. *Journal of Research in Crime and Delinquency*, *23*, 102–127.

Johnson, I. M. (1999). School violence: The effectiveness of a school resource officer program in a southern city. *Journal of Criminal Justice, 27(2)*, 173–192.

Jones, J. M. (2005). *Fear of children's safety at school remains low: Environment a big fear factor*. Princeton, NJ: Gallup Organization. Retrieved October 31, 2005, from http://institution.gallup.com.proxy-um.researchport.umd.edu/content/ default.aspx?ci = 18694.

Kaslow, N. J., & Thompson, M. (1998). Applying the criteria for empirically supported treatments to studies of psychosocial interventions for child and adolescent depression. *Journal of Clinical Child Psychology*, *27*, 146–155.

Kazdin, A. E., & Weisz, J. R. (1998). Identifying and developing empirically supported child and adolescent treatments. *Journal of Consulting and Clinical Psychology*, *66*, 19–36.

Lee, V. E., & Croninger, R. G. (1996). The social organization of safe high schools. In K. M. Borman, P. W. Cookson, Jr., & J. Z. Spade (Eds.), *Implementing educational reform: Sociological perspectives on educational policy* (pp. 359–392). Norwood, NJ: Ablex Publishing.

Lipsey, M. W., & Wilson, D. B. (1998). Effective intervention for serious juvenile offenders. In R. Loeber & D. P. Farrington (Eds.), *Serious and violent juvenile offenders: Risk factors and successful intervention* (pp. 248–283). Thousand Oaks, CA: Sage.

Maxfield, M., Schirm, A., & Rodriguez-Planas, N. (2002). *The Quantum Opportunity Program demonstration: Implementation and short-term impacts*. Washington, DC: U.S. Department of Labor.

Meehl, P. E., & Rosen, A. (1955). Antecedent probability and the efficiency of psychometric signs, patterns, or cutting scores. *Psychological Bulletin*, *52*, 194–216.

Moore, M. H., Petrie, C. V., Braga, A. A., & McLaughlin, B. L. (Eds.). (2003). *Deadly lessons: Understanding lethal school violence*. Washington, DC: National Academies Press.

National Institute of Education. (1978). *Violent schools – safe schools: The Safe School Study report to Congress*. Washington, DC.

National School Safety Center. (2005, April). *School associated violent deaths*. Westlake Village, CA: Author. Retrieved October 31, 2005, from http://www.nssc1.org.

Olweus, D., Limber, S., & Mihalic, S. F. (1999). *Blueprints for violence prevention: Bullying prevention program*. Boulder, CO: Center for the Study and Prevention of Violence.

Ostroff, C. (1992). The relationship between satisfaction, attitudes, and performance: An organizational level analysis. *Journal of Applied Psychology*, *77*, 963–974.

Payne, A. A., Gottfredson, D. C., & Gottfredson, G. D. (2003). Schools as communities: The relationships among communal school organization, student bonding, and school disorder. *Criminology*, *41*, 749–778.

Schneider, T., Walker, H. & Sprague, J. (2000). *Safe school design: A handbook for educational leaders applying the principles of crime prevention through environmental design*. Eugene, OR: ERIC Clearinghouse on Educational Management, University of Oregon.

Sherman, L. W., & Berk, R. A. (1984). The specific deterrent effects of arrest for domestic assault. *American Sociological Review, 49,* 261–272.

Shure, M. B., & Spivak, G. (1979). Interpersonal cognitive problem solving and primary prevention: Programming for preschool and kindergarten children. *Journal of Clinical Child Psychology, 8,* 89–94.

Shure, M. B., & Spivak, G. (1980). Interpersonal problem solving as a mediator of behavioral adjustment in preschool and kindergarten children. *Journal of Applied Developmental Psychology, 1,* 29–44.

Shure, M. B., & Spivak, G. (1982). Interpersonal problem-solving in young children: A cognitive approach to prevention. *American Journal of Community Psychology, 10,* 341–356.

Stewart, E. A. (2003). School social bonds, school climate, and school misbehavior: A multilevel analysis. *Justice Quarterly, 20,* 575–601.

Taggart, R. (1995). *Quantum Opportunity Program.* Philadelphia: Opportunities Industrialization Centers of America.

Tolan, P. H., & Gorman-Smith, D. (1998). Development of serious and violent offending careers. In R. Loeber & D. P. Farrington (Eds.), *Serious and violent juvenile offenders: Risk factors and successful interventions* (pp. 68–85). Thousand Oaks, CA: Sage.

Wagenaar, A. C., Murray, D. M., & Toomey, T. L. (2000). Communities mobilizing for change on alcohol (CMCA): Effects of a randomized trial on arrests and traffic crashes. *Addiction, 95*(2), 209–217.

Welsh, W. N., Greene, J. R., & Jenkins, P. H. (1999). School disorder: The influence of individual, institutional, and community factors. *Criminology, 37,* 73–116.

Welsh, B. C., & Hoshi, A. (2002). Communities and crime prevention. In L. W. Sherman, D. P. Farrington, B. C. Welsh, & D. L. MacKenzie, D. L. (Eds.), *Evidence-based crime prevention* (pp. 165–197). New York: Routledge.

Welsh, W. N., Stokes, R., & Greene, J. R. (2000). A macro-level model of school disorder. *Journal of Research in Crime and Delinquency, 37,* 243–283.

Wilcox, P., & Clayton, R. R. (2001). A multilevel analysis of school-based weapon possession. *Justice Quarterly, 18,* 509–541.

Part IV

INTERPERSONAL FACTORS AND VIOLENT BEHAVIOR

CHAPTER 17

Peers and Violence: A Two-Sided Developmental Perspective

Frank Vitaro, Michel Boivin, and Richard E. Tremblay

Introduction

The development of youth violence and antisocial behavior is determined by the combined effects of a host of factors (i.e., genetic, temperamental, familial, socioeconomic, school related, social, and community-wide). This chapter focuses on peers as one important contributing factor. Specifically, it covers two types of peer experiences that are linked in different but equally important ways to the development of violent (i.e., aggressive) behaviors in children and adolescents. First, peers may *inflict* psychological or physical violence in the form of rejection or victimization, which may accentuate aggressive behaviors in some children, thus contributing to the cycle of violence. Second, peers may *instigate and support* violence in others by providing a social context in which violence is expressed and valued.

The first two sections of this chapter address each type of peer experience separately. The first section examines theoretical models and empirical evidence linking negative peer experiences, specifically

rejection and victimization by normative peers, to increases in children's aggressive behavior. The second section of the chapter is devoted to theoretical models and empirical evidence that address the contribution of aggressive peers to the development of aggressive and violent behaviors in children and adolescents. Throughout these sections, we distinguish between different subtypes of aggressive behavior to reflect more accurately current theoretical models and recent empirical findings. These distinctions in aggressive behaviors are typically based on form (i.e., physical versus psychological/relational aggression) or function (i.e., reactive versus proactive aggression; Dodge, 1991; Vitaro & Brendgen, 2005). Studies addressing broader measures of antisocial behaviors, externalizing problems, conduct disorders, or delinquency are also considered because these global measures often include several aggression- or violence-related items. The terms "aggression" and "violence" are used interchangeably in this chapter, although we acknowledge that violence may cover more serious physically aggressive acts than aggression.

Finally, these terms primarily reflect acts perpetrated against persons, although they may occasionally include aggressive acts toward objects (i.e., vandalism) or animals. It is also important to note that most of the research reviewed in this chapter concerns school-aged children and adolescents. Although the frequency of physical aggression among humans peaks during the preschool years, hardly any research has attempted to study the role of peers at this crucial developmental period or the long term effects of preschool peer relations on developmental trajectories (Tremblay, 2000).

The third and final section of the chapter presents an integrated model linking peer rejection, deviant peer involvement, and initiation or aggravation of aggressive/antisocial behaviors. Throughout the chapter, the developmental perspective is the guiding principle: longitudinal studies take precedence over cross-sectional studies whenever possible. Longitudinal studies are especially useful in disentangling the directionality of the links between peer experiences and aggressive/antisocial behaviors. Experimental studies that used a prevention/treatment program involving peers and studies that examined the peer processes accounting for the program's distal effects on aggression/antisociality also receive attention.

Part One: Peer Rejection

Rejection by normative peers is typically assessed through peer nominations: classmates nominate or rate each other according to their degree of liking and disliking. Categorical (i.e., sociometric groups, such as rejected, popular, average, neglected, or controversial) or continuous scores (i.e., popularity, unpopularity, social preference, social impact) can be derived from these nominations. Children receiving many "disliking" nominations and few "liking" nominations (i.e., low social preference, see Coie & Dodge, 1983) are typically referred to as being rejected by their peers. Peer rejection is assumed to reflect difficulties in the

social integration within the peer group. Behaviorally, rejected children are an heterogeneous group; they tend to be more aggressive, less sociable, less cognitively skilled, but also more withdrawn than their more accepted peers (Newcomb, Bukowski, & Pattee, 1993). Aggressive behaviors, however, have been identified as the prime behavioral correlate of peer rejection (Coie & Dodge, 1998; Rubin, Bukowski, & Parker, 1998).

Aggressive Behaviors as Determinants of Peer Rejection

Aggressive behaviors may be correlated with peer rejection because they are a cause or a consequence of this negative peer experience. Alternately, they may be related to peer rejection due to a third variable. To establish more clearly that aggressive behaviors cause peer rejection, Coie and Kupersmidt (1983) and Dodge (1983) ran a series of experimental play-group studies in which they assembled unacquainted children and assessed their emerging peer status. Verbal and physical aggressive behaviors were shown to precede and predict the emergence of peer rejection in these new groups, which suggested that aggressive behaviors could be considered a proximal determinant of peer rejection (see Coie, 1990). Other studies with normative samples that distinguished stable from transient peer rejection during childhood also concluded that externalizing problems (especially aggression and low prosociality) predicted stable peer rejection (Parke et al., 1997; Vitaro, Tremblay, Gagnon, & Boivin, 1992) or chronic low peer acceptance (Brendgen, Vitaro, Bukowski, Doyle, & Markiewicz, 2001). Finally, some authors showed that negative qualities in parent-child relationships during the preschool years predicted peer rejection in the early years of elementary school (Cowan & Cowan, 2004).

Hence, socially unskilled/aggressive children who have behavior problems at home are quickly rejected by their normative peers during the formation of a new peer group. Some aggressive children may even become frequent targets of counter-coercive harassment and victimization by peers (Price & Dodge, 1989; Schwartz, Proctor, & Chen, 2001). The association between various forms of aggression and negative peer experiences, however, appears to be moderated by age and group norms. For example, there is a sharp decline in the association between aggression and peer harassment or rejection between third grade and sixth grade (Boivin, Hymel, & Hodges, 2001). As we discuss below, this decreasing association could reflect an increasing mutual affiliation among aggressive children, which shields them from negative behaviors from the peer group (see Boivin & Vitaro, 1995). In addition, the association between aggressive behaviors and peer rejection is not found in groups in which the norms regarding the use of aggression are more positive (Boivin, Dodge, & Coie, 1995). This finding also points to the role of group dynamics in children's adjustment.

Specific forms of aggressive behaviors are differentially associated with peer rejection. For example, bullying (defined as verbal teasing, rumor spreading, and social exclusion) has been found to be positively related to popularity, whereas physical aggression has not (Pellegrini, Bartini, & Brooks, 1999; Rodkin, Farmer, Pearl, & Van Acker, 2000). Similarly, proactive aggressive behaviors have been positively associated with popularity and clique inclusion, and negatively associated with peer victimization, whereas reactive aggression has been linked to peer rejection, peer victimization, and friendlessness (Poulin & Boivin, 2000). Proactive aggression is calculated aggression designed to achieve a self-interested goal (either physically or socially) and is not generally motivated by anger. In contrast, reactive aggression is an impulsive form of aggression driven by anger toward a factual or imagined threatening or unpleasant stimulus, with the aim of harming its author (Dodge, 1991; Vitaro & Brendgen, 2005).

The link between specific types of aggressive behaviors and peer rejection, however, may vary depending on the child's age. One study that looked at the play-group behav-

iors of first-grade children and those of third-grade children found that angry reactive aggression and instrumental aggression (one form of proactive aggressive behavior), but not rough play, were associated with negative peer status at both ages (Dodge, Coie, Pettit, & Price, 1990). Bullying (another form of proactive behavior) was negatively related to status, but only in third-grade groups, as if children had already established their dominance in first grade. Thus, there is substantial evidence indicating that aggressive behaviors, especially of the angry-reactive type, lead to negative peer status and peer experiences during childhood. The evidence concerning proactive aggression is mixed, with the association between proactive aggression and negative peer experiences likely to change with age, often in complex, nonlinear ways.

Aggression as a Consequence of Peer Rejection

THEORETICAL MODELS

There is substantial evidence suggesting that peer rejection is associated with later aggressive/antisocial behaviors, as well as with other forms of maladjustment (see Deater-Deckard, 2001; Kupersmidt, Coie, & Dodge, 1990; Parker & Asher, 1987; Rubin et al., 1998, for reviews). However, theorists and researchers continue to disagree on the precise role of peer rejection in the developmental course of these problems. At least three theoretical models have been proposed to account for the possible role of peer rejection with respect to later aggressive/antisocial behaviors. For the purpose of discussion, we refer to these as the incidental model, the causal model, and the interaction model.

According to the *incidental model* (also labeled the "common cause" model or the behavior-continuity model, Caspi, Elder, & Bem, 1987; Dunn & McGuire, 1992; Parker & Asher, 1987), peer rejection is a byproduct of children's behavior problems, which are the true determinants of later adjustment problems. Accordingly, both peer rejection and later adjustment problems stem from the same underlying personal vulnerabilities. In other words, rejection by peers is seen as an indicator of children's behavior problems, but does not contribute to later adjustment per se.

According to the *causal model*, peer rejection uniquely contributes to the development of aggressive/antisocial behaviors above and beyond children's behavioral dispositions. One version of this model actually views peer rejection as completely mediating the predictive association between children's behavior problems and later adjustment problems (Patterson, DeBaryshe, & Ramsey, 1989). This first version of the causal model can be termed the *mediation-causal model* and posits a chain of causality in which peer rejection plays a central role. Another version views peer rejection as contributing uniquely to later externalizing problems, above and beyond early behavior problems. This second version can be viewed as the *additive-causal model*. The causal model may also be expanded into a *bidirectional causal model* whereby aggressive/antisocial behaviors and peer rejection mutually influence each other over time. Finally, the third model (i.e., the *interaction model*, Bierman & Wargo, 1995; Parker, Rubin, Price, & DeRosier, 1995) posits that peer rejection moderates the link between children's aggressive/antisocial behaviors and later adjustment problems.

These models should not be viewed as mutually exclusive. For instance, peer rejection could partly mediate the contribution of early aggressive behaviors to later antisocial behaviors while increasing, perhaps conditionally (e.g., interactively with early aggressive behaviors), the probability of later antisocial behaviors. The purpose of these models is simply to illustrate the possible roles of peer rejection in the developmental course of aggressive and antisocial behaviors. Indeed, there is empirical evidence to support each of these models.

EMPIRICAL EVIDENCE
As suggested by the incidental model, underlying behavior problems have been found to partly account for the association between peer rejection and later aggressive/antisocial behaviors (Fergusson, Woodward, & Horwood, 1999; Hartup, 1983; Parker & Asher, 1987). In support of the additive-causal model, peer rejection – and, especially, stable peer rejection (i.e., over 1 year or longer) – was found to uniquely predict later adjustment problems after controlling for concurrent externalizing problems (Brendgen et al., 2001; DeRosier, Kupersmidt, & Patterson, 1994; Dodge et al., 2003; Ladd & Troop-Gordon, 2003; Miller-Johnson, Coie, Maumary-Gremaud, Bierman, & Conduct Problems Prevention Research Group, 2002). For example, Ladd and Troop-Gordon (2003) showed that the number of years during which children were rejected by their peers during the first 3 years of primary school predicted later teacher-rated aggression and delinquency above and beyond previous aggressive behaviors, concurrent peer victimization, and involvement in mutual friendships. Interestingly, in this study, both peer rejection and victimization by peers uniquely contributed to variance in later externalizing problems. Another illustrative example comes from a study by Miller-Johnson et al. (2002) that showed that low social preference scores averaged across second and third grade marginally predicted fourth-grade antisocial behavior, despite controlling for grade one aggression and attention-hyperactivity. Although marginal, the additive contribution of low peer status to the predictive equation is impressive given that the study controlled for such factors as aggression and attention-hyperactivity problems. This second example may also be used to illustrate the mediational-causal model because low peer acceptance mediated the link between grade-one attention-hyperactivity problems and grade-four antisocial behaviors (but not the link between early aggression and later antisocial behaviors).

Other studies also support the mediational-causal role of peer rejection between early aggressive/disruptive behaviors and later delinquency-related violence or conduct problems. For example, Laird, Jordan, Dodge, Pettit, and

Bates (2001) showed that rejection by normative peers during the first years of elementary school partially mediated the link between preschool aggressiveness and delinquent/violent behaviors by mid-adolescence. Similarly, Snyder, Prichard, Schrepferman, Patrick, and Stoolmiller (2004) found that the link between disruptiveness problems in kindergarten and the growth of conduct problems over the following 2 years was partly mediated by peer rejection, but for boys only. For girls, peer rejection significantly added to the prediction of later conduct problems above and beyond early disruptiveness. In addition, negative peer experiences (i.e., coercive exchanges) on the playground also contributed uniquely (i.e., independent of classroom peer rejection) to the prediction of later conduct problems. As for classroom peer rejection, these coercive exchanges also partly mediated the link between early disruptiveness and later conduct problems for boys, but not for girls. Again, for girls, classroom peer rejection had an additive effect. Thus, although negative peer experiences seem to predict later conduct problems for boys and girls, the developmental process seems to differ as a function of gender. For boys, there appears to be a spiraling bidirectional process linking behavior problems and problematic peer relationships. There is no evidence for such a bidirectional process among girls, as early aggressive behaviors do not seem to escalate into more serious antisocial behaviors through negative peer status. The fact that this study only examined overt aggressive behaviors, but not the relational forms of aggression that are more characteristic of girls, may account for the gender difference observed.

In line with the additive-causal model, research has documented a link between peer rejection in first grade and antisocial behavior in fourth grade, over and above concurrent rejection and over and above concurrent or earlier aggressive behavior (Cowan & Cowan, 2004). Other researchers found a predictive association between mid- or late-childhood peer rejection and elevated delinquency-related violence or antisociality in early adulthood, above and beyond the contribution of initial behavior problems and school difficulties (Nelson & Dishion, 2004; Reinherz, Giaconia, Hauf, Wasserman, & Paradis, 2000; Woodward & Fergusson, 1999). However, by pre-adolescence, the predictive power of peer rejection could be accounted for by the absence of friendships with normative peers or the presence of deviant friends, both of which are linked to peer rejection and are discussed in greater detail later in this chapter (Bagwell, Newcomb, & Bukowski, 1998; Patterson et al., 1989).

Finally, many studies yielded results that are in line with the interactional model's view. For example, the predictive association between personal dispositions (i.e., aggression) and later violence is exacerbated for individuals who are also rejected by their peers (Bierman & Wargo, 1995; DeRosier et al., 1994). Another example in support of the interactional model comes from a study by Dodge et al. (2003) that revealed a behavior-specific interaction effect between peer rejection and aggressive behaviors. Specifically, cumulative peer rejection, starting in kindergarten, predicted growth in reactive aggression (and not in proactive aggression), but only for children who were initially high on reactive aggression. However, there are also studies that did not find support for peer rejection as a moderator of the link between childhood aggression and later externalizing problems (Miller-Johnson et al., 2002; Woodward & Fergusson, 1999).

Possible Moderators of the Associations Between Peer Rejection and Aggressive/Antisocial Behaviors

The link between peer rejection, or low peer acceptance, and increases in aggressive/antisocial behaviors may depend on the child's age, awareness of his or her rejected status, orientation toward peers, and ethnicity, as well as on local norms for aggressive-antisocial behaviors (MacDougall, Hymel, Vaillancourt, & Mercer, 2001). With respect to gender, the evidence seems to suggest that, for both boys and girls, peer rejection acts as a stressor leading to further aggressive/antisocial behaviors (Coie, Lochman, Terry, & Hyman, 1992; Dodge et al., 2003; Hymel, Wagner, & Butler, 1990; Kupersmidt & Patterson, 1991; Ladd & Troop-Gordon, 2003; Laird et al., 2001). However, there are gender differences. For example, negative peer rejection/experiences seem to mediate the link between early disruptiveness and later conduct problems for boys but not for girls (Snyder et al., 2004). This gender difference may reflect a difference in the mean levels at which boys and girls display particular forms of aggressive/antisocial behaviors (Ladd & Troop-Gordon, 2003). It could also reflect an artifact due to measures that applied more to males than to females (Deater-Deckard, 2001).

The stability of peer rejection and temporal proximity of peer rejection are possible moderators of rejection's impact on aggressive/antisocial behaviors. For example, DeRosier et al. (1994) reported that children rejected over several years had more externalizing (and internalizing) problems than children rejected over just 1 year, even after controlling for early behavior problems. Children who had been rejected during the recent past, however, also experienced more negative outcomes, even if they were not chronically rejected. Similar results have been reported by Brendgen et al. (2001).

Finally, the degree and severity of rejection should also be taken into account when assessing the possible impact of rejection on socio-behavioral adjustment (DeRosier & Thomas, 2003). For example, in the case of highly rejected children, the risk for victimization is extreme; hence, increases in their aggressive behavior, mostly of the reactive type, may reflect their tendency to retaliate against actual or perceived offenses from bullies. As already indicated, aggressive-rejected children are more prone to the use of impulsive aggressive behavior with outbursts of anger than aggressive-nonrejected peers. In contrast, children who are less rejected by their peers, such as controversial children (i.e., those who are disliked by many children, but also liked by others), are not victimized and seem mostly at risk of developing bullying and proactive, relationally aggressive behaviors (DeRosier & Thomas, 2003; Schwartz et al., 2001). For controversial children, the social support provided by peers (i.e., friends or clique members) may actually encourage proactive aggressive behaviors. In sum, the impact of peer rejection on reactive aggression may be exacerbated by the severity of rejection and the absence of friends, whereas proactive aggressive behaviors may be exacerbated by a lower level of rejection and the presence of friends, but only if these friends are also aggressively oriented.

Possible Processes Behind the Contribution of Peer Rejection to Aggressive/Antisocial Behavior

Despite suggestions by Parker and Asher (1987) almost two decades ago, few researchers have examined the processes through which difficult peer relationships contribute to the development of aggressive/antisocial behaviors or the mechanisms though which peer rejection serves as a catalyst for childhood aggression. Peer rejection and victimization may trigger an escalating cycle of negative mutual coercive exchanges between rejected children and peers, thus maintaining and amplifying rejected children's aggressive dispositions (Bierman & Wargo, 1995; Coie, 2004; Coie & Lenox, 1994; Miller-Johnson et al, 2002; Snyder et al., 2004). This cycle of negative exchanges is particularly likely to occur if the rejected or victimized children are already aggressive because they are then more likely than nonaggressive counterparts to reciprocate aggression (Patterson, Littman, & Bricker, 1967; Snyder & Brown, 1983). As suggested by Reid, Patterson, and Snyder (2002), the occasional favorable termination of these rejection/victimization episodes operates as a negative reinforcement of the use of aggression by rejected/victimized children. In fact, this explanation is another version of the coercion process identified by Patterson and his colleagues to explain escalation in aggressive behavior for children who are successful in resisting their parents' incompetent attempts to control their behavior (Patterson et al., 1967). A similar model based on the escalating use of reciprocal aggression to avoid being dominated by aggressive neighborhood peers has been proposed by Anderson (1999) to explain inner-city adolescents' willingness to resort to more and more violence as a mean of gaining and maintaining respect.

Peer rejection and victimization episodes may also alter the way in which rejected children process information during peer interactions, particularly by increasing their tendency to make hostile attributions about peers' behavioral intentions. In turn, distorted social-cognitive processes could foster negative perceptions of peers and increase the probability of escalation in aggressive behaviors (Dodge et al., 2003; Melnick & Hinshaw, 2000). These social-cognitive processes could even mediate the relation between earlier peer rejection and increases in aggressive behavior (Dodge, 1993). As expected, hostile attributions toward peers seem to be related to reactively, but not proactively, aggressive acts (Hubbard, Dodge, Cillessen, Coie, & Schwartz, 2001).

Peer rejection may also alter self-perceptions and perceived capabilities for achieving positive outcomes (Boivin & Hymel, 1997; MacDougall et al., 2001; Rabiner & Coie, 1989). To illustrate, Rabiner and Coie (1989) experimentally manipulated rejected children's expectations about the way they would be treated by unfamiliar peers. As expected, the rejected children who were not led to expect a positive reception from the peers behaved less competently and were less well accepted by the peers than those in the positive induction condition.

Finally, peer rejection may reduce rejected children's opportunities to interact and learn normative values from conventional peers (DeRosier et al., 1994; Kupersmidt & DeRosier, 2004). Rejected children may then model the aggressive behaviors of other rejected and aggressive children who may be the only social partners available, as described in the second part of this chapter.

Positive Effects of Peer Acceptance for Aggressive/Antisocial Children

If peer rejection is a risk factor for later externalizing problems or a catalyst for aggressive behavior, it follows that peer acceptance should be seen as a protective factor with respect to aggression. In theory, aggressive children who are well accepted in their peer group may have more opportunities than rejected-aggressive children to learn normative values and self-governing behaviors and to remedy hostile cognitions and other cognitive biases toward normative peers (Bierman, 2004; Bierman & Wargo, 1995). Peer acceptance would also provide opportunities for aggressive children to establish friendships with normative peers (Ladd & Burgess, 2001). There is indeed evidence showing that aggressive-rejected boys who are brought to believe they are well accepted by newly acquainted peers tend to achieve positive adjustments in their behavioral profile (Coie & Koeppl, 1990).

However, given that peer rejection fosters reactive aggression rather than proactive aggression (Dodge et al., 2003), reducing peer rejection for aggressive children should mostly reduce children's reactive aggression. It is not clear whether reducing peer rejection should also reduce proactive aggression. This is particularly important given that friendships and inclusion in a peer group may actually foster proactive aggression in children who are already proactively aggressive (DeRosier & Thomas, 2003; Poulin & Boivin, 2000). Alternatively, peer rejection/victimization may persuade some aggressive children to reduce their aggressive behavior, provided they are not part of a clique (Boivin & Vitaro, 1995). Recent findings from Snyder et al. (2004) showing that impulsive-inattentive children who are not victimized by their kindergarten peers are particularly at risk for early and persistent conduct problems support this view.

These findings may indicate that negative peer treatment mitigates these children's trajectories toward conduct problems. Alternately, aggressive children who are rejected and actively victimized may have fewer or less deviant friends. Hence, the apparent mitigating effect of rejection/victimization by the peer group may in fact have resulted from associated social experiences at the dyadic level. These alternate interpretations clearly underline the need to examine aggressive children's friendships to better understand the potential contributions of peers to their developmental trajectories.

Part Two: Deviant Friends and Deviant Cliques

Variables and Processes Leading to Affiliation With Aggressive/Antisocial Peers

Although generally rejected by conventional peers, many aggressive/antisocial preadolescents and early adolescents have friends, and most of them participate in cliques (Boivin & Vitaro, 1995; Cairns, Perrin, & Cairns, 1985). Dyadic friendships refer to mutual relationships between two children based on affection, reciprocity, and intimacy (Bukowski & Hoza, 1989). Peer cliques are cohesive groups of children or adolescents who spend time together (Hallinan, 1980/1995). Gangs can be conceptualized as cliques of children and adolescents involved in antisocial behaviors. In contrast to peer rejection/victimization, children's and adolescents' affiliations with specific friends and clique members are voluntary and selective (Cairns, Cairns, Neckerman, Gest, & Gariépy, 1988; Poulin & Boivin, 2000), although this aspect may vary with age.

PREDICTORS AND EVOLUTION OF
AFFILIATION WITH DEVIANT PEERS
DURING CHILDHOOD AND ADOLESCENCE
Rejection by normative peers has been found to predict deviant peer involvement above and beyond children's personal dispositions (Brendgen, Vitaro, & Bukowski, 1998;

Dishion, Patterson, Stoolmiller, & Skinner, 1991; Fergusson et al., 1999). However, affiliation with aggressive/antisocial peers also appears to result from an active selection process based on behavioral homophily. In other words, aggressive/antisocial adolescents select friends and clique members who are similar to themselves with respect to aggression and antisociality (Cairns, Xie, & Leung, 1998; Hektner, August, & Realmuto, 2000; Lahey, Gordon, Loeber, Stouthamer-Loeber, & Farrington, 1999; Poulin & Boivin, 2000; Urberg, Degirmencioglu, & Tolson, 1998). Some studies showed that the tendency for aggressive children to associate with other aggressive peers is already present during the preschool years (Estell, Cairns, Farmer, & Cairns, 2002; Farver, 1996; Snyder, Horsch, & Childs, 1997; Snyder et al., 2005). The friendships and clique membership involving young aggressive children may, however, not be as stable and as exclusive as those involving adolescents.

The notion of a developmental trend in the affiliations of aggressive children with aggressive peers on the basis of their similarities in behavioral norms is compatible with the *confluence model* (Dishion, Patterson, & Griesler, 1994). According to this model, the mutual active selection of friends among deviant children begins by mid-childhood (or possibly earlier), accelerates thereafter, and peaks by early adolescence. Although intuitively appealing, the confluence model does not rest on solid empirical ground because few researchers have examined the affiliation pattern of deviant children over more than two points in time. There are, however, some exceptions. For example, Vitaro, Brendgen, and Wanner (2005) identified four groups, each with distinct profiles of affiliation with delinquent friends, from age 10 through age 13 years: (1) an early affiliative group who already had delinquent friends by age 10; (2) a late affiliative group who started to affiliate with deviant friends by age 12 (i.e., after the transition to high school in this sample); (3) a desistor group who affiliated with deviant friends early on and desisted by age 12; and (4) a large group of children who never affiliated with delinquent friends. Interestingly, more boys than girls followed the early affiliative group compared to the late group. These results reveal a more complex set of patterns of affiliation than initially suggested by Dishion et al. (1994).

Other forces have been found to predict affiliation with deviant peers, either directly or indirectly. These forces include ineffective parenting, school tracking, involvement with the justice system, and neighborhood disadvantage (Ary, Duncan, Duncan, & Hops, 1999; Dodge, Dishion, & Lansford, 2006).

Consequences of Affiliating With Aggressive/Antisocial Peers

Several groups of researchers have documented the association between having deviant peers at the dyadic and the clique level and later externalizing problems (Elliott, Huizinga, & Ageton, 1985; Kim, Hetherington, & Reiss, 1999; Patterson, Dishion, & Yoerger, 2000; Scaramella, Conger, Spoth, & Simons, 2002; Simons, Chao, Conger, & Elder, Jr., 2001). For example, Patterson et al. (2000) showed that early involvement with deviant peers (i.e., by age 10 years) predicted growth in different forms of antisocial behavior throughout adolescence. Using a longitudinal person-centered approach, Lacourse, Nagin, Tremblay, Vitaro, and Claes (2003) found that involvement in a delinquent group at any time during adolescence was associated with an increase in violent behaviors and that leaving the group resulted in a decrease in violent behaviors.

Results from two short-term studies suggest that the consequences of exposure to deviant friends during early childhood may already be detrimental. In one study, Snyder et al. (1997) found that the amount of time preschoolers spent with aggressive peers predicted an increase in observed and teacher-rated aggressive behavior over a 3-month interval. Conversely, children who spent minimal time (less than 15%) with aggressive peers showed a decrease in aggression over the subsequent 3-month period.

More recently, Snyder et al. (2005) reported that association with deviant peers in kindergarten predicted growth in overt conduct problems (e.g., aggressiveness), as well as in covert conduct problems (e.g., lying, stealing, running away from home) on the playground and in the classroom during the following 2 years.

THEORETICAL MODELS WITH RESPECT TO THE ROLE OF DEVIANT PEERS

The above findings are congruent with the *peer influence model*, which posits deviant friends as a cause of violent delinquency. The peer influence model has been referred to as the social facilitation, cultural deviance, differential association, or socialization model, depending on whether one reads the psychological, sociological, or criminological literature (Akers, Krohn, Lanza-Kaduce, & Radosevich, 1979; Cohen, 1977; Elliott et al., 1985; Johnson, Marcos, & Bahr, 1987; Sutherland, 1947). According to this model, both behaviors and attitudes favorable to aggression can be learned from association with deviant friends, a position that is congruent with social learning principles. Two versions of the peer influence model are possible. According to one version, deviant peers are a necessary starting point for aggressive behaviors to emerge or evolve. In this version, deviant peers have a main effect on behavior. In the other version of the peer influence model, affiliation with deviant peers is viewed as a mediator of the link between exposure to such contexts as coercive families (Kim et al., 1999), neighborhood disadvantage (Brody et al., 2001), or involvement with the criminal justice system (Johnson, Simons, & Conger, 2004) and an increase in delinquent behavior.

Strong additional evidence for the peer influence model comes from iatrogenic effects observed in prevention or intervention programs intended to help antisocial youth overcome their problems. For example, Dishion and Andrews (1995) randomly assigned young at-risk adolescents to four conditions: (1) a peer group program that aggregated at-risk participants, (2) a parent group program, (3) a combined program, and (4) a no-program control group. At 1-, 2-, and 3-year follow-ups, teachers reported more conduct problems and students reported more substance use in the two conditions in which the peer group program was used (Poulin, Dishion, & Burraston, 2001). Similarly, Warren, Schoppelrey, Moberg, and McDonald (2005) showed that tracking elementary-school children into homogeneous classrooms amplified their aggressive behaviors. Finally, Leve and Chamberlain (2005) showed that aggregating delinquent adolescents in group care centers increased their involvement with delinquent peers over the course of 1 year in comparison to a foster care alternative treatment. Several more examples of iatrogenic or nonoptimal interventions that aggregate aggressive youth are found in Ang and Hugues (2002), Dishion, McCord, and Poulin (1999), and Dodge et al. (2006).

There is also empirical evidence that does not support the peer influence model. At least two studies indicate that deviant peer association does not predict later delinquency after accounting for prior deviance. Coie, Terry, Akriski, and Lochman (1995) found that early adolescent aggressiveness predicted later delinquency (police arrests), with no influence of associations with deviant peers. Similarly, Tremblay, Mâsse, Vitaro, and Dobkin (1995) found that friends' characteristics did not mediate the association between antisocial behaviors during childhood and delinquency during mid-adolescence; instead, affiliation with deviant peers and delinquency were related because of their common association with early antisocial behavior. Once early antisocial behavior was controlled statistically, the relation disappeared.

The studies showing that deviant friends or deviant clique members do not contribute to later deviant behavior are in line with the *individual characteristics model* (e.g., Cairns et al., 1988; Gottfredson & Hirschi, 1990), which is also referred to as the social control or selection model. This model rests on a process of peer selection and views deviant friends as an epiphenomenona.

In other words, deviant friends play no (causal) role in the development of antisocial behavior and delinquency. Instead, antisocial or aggressive behaviors (which may result from ineffective parenting or difficult temperament) are hypothesized to lead independently both to subsequent delinquency and to involvement with deviant peers.

A perspective that integrates aspects of the individual characteristics model and the peer influence model is offered by the *social interactional (also called the enhancement) model* (Dishion, 1990a,b; Patterson et al., 1989). The social interactional model posits a statistical interaction between personal attributes (i.e., aggression) and peers' deviancy in predicting later antisocial or delinquent behaviors. One version of this model views antisocial peers as the moderator of the link between the child's personal dispositions and later problems. To illustrate, antisocial youths who affiliate with deviant peers have been shown to become even more deviant than antisocial youths who do not affiliate with deviant peers (Dishion, Capaldi, Spracklen, & Li, 1995). Another version views the children's personal dispositions as a moderator of the link between exposure to deviant peers and later problems (Vitaro, Tremblay, Kerr, Pagani, & Bukowski, 1997). For example, van Lier, Wanner, and Vitaro (2007) presented data supporting this version of the model by showing that adolescents who followed a childhood-onset trajectory of delinquent behaviors were mostly characterized by early behavior problems, but did not tend to affiliate with deviant friends. In contrast, the adolescent-onset trajectory was associated with increases in friends' antisocial behavior, but not with behavior problems.

CONCLUDING REMARKS

Overall, the findings we have reviewed so far suggest that the different theoretical perspectives and their underlying process mechanisms (i.e., peer influence, peer selection, or peer enhancement) may all be relevant. It is possible, however, that these models do not all apply to the same individuals.

In line with Moffitt's developmental model of antisocial-delinquent behavior (Moffitt, 1993), the peer influence model seems to apply to "late starters," whereas the individual characteristics or social interactional models seem to apply to "early starters."

Other evidence that partially supports each theoretical model comes from studies on gang membership. For example, different groups of researchers showed that, in accordance with the individual characteristics model, youth who were gang members were already more antisocial than others prior to such affiliation (Gatti, Tremblay, Vitaro, & McDuff, 2005; Gordon et al., 2004; Thornberry, 1998; Thornberry, Krohn, Lizotte, & Chard-Wierschem, 1993; Zhang, Welte, & Wieczorek, 1999). However, behavior problems did not persist after the break-up of the gang membership. Instead, in accordance with the peer influence model, adjustment problems, particularly violent crimes, disappeared after the end of exposure to deviant cliques, suggesting an influence of the deviant clique members. Finally, in accordance with the social interactional model, adjustment problems that preceded exposure to delinquent friends increased further during the period of time in which youngsters were part of a gang.

Variables That Moderate the Link Between Affiliation With Deviant Peers and Increases in Aggressive/Antisocial Behavior

A number of studies suggest that several variables may mitigate or exacerbate the influence of deviant peers/deviant cliques. These variables include children's sex, age, and behavioral dispositions, family and sociodemographic variables, children's social status, peers' social status, and features of friendship.

PERSONAL CHARACTERISTICS

Both girls' and boys' antisocial behavior has been shown to be influenced by deviant peers (Elliott et al., 1985; Laird et al., 2001; Urberg, Degirmencioglu, & Pilgrim, 1997).

However, as suggested by Hartup (1983, 2005), girls may exert more influence over girls than over boys with respect to some forms of aggressive behavior that are normative for girls (i.e., relational aggression), whereas boys may influence other boys more than girls with respect to the use of aggressive behaviors that are more normative for boys (i.e., physical aggression).

Age can also play an important role in determining the consequences of affiliation with or exposure to deviant peers. Anecdotal evidence suggests that younger children are less sensitive to friends' influence than older children (Hartup, 1999); they are also supervised more closely than older children and adolescents. However, clear empirical data are still missing with respect to this issue.

As shown by Fergusson, Vitaro, Wanner, and Brendgen (in press), biological changes, such as early physical maturation, could exacerbate the link between exposure to deviant friends and later delinquency, in addition to showing a main effect. Both the moderating and the main effects of early maturation may be explained by the tendency of early maturing youth (especially girls) to associate with deviant and older peers from outside the school (Stattin & Magnusson, 1990).

As already shown when describing the social interactional model, child and adolescent behavior profiles can moderate the effect of affiliating with deviant peers, although it is not yet clear whether peer influence is strongest for the most aggressive/antisocial individuals (Dishion, Capaldi et al., 1995; Simons, Wu, Conger, & Lorenz, 1994; Warren et al., 2005) or the moderately aggressive/antisocial (van Lier et al., 2007; Vitaro et al., 1997). Finally, negative attitudes toward deviancy or bonding to conventional norms may reduce adolescents' susceptibility to negative peer influence (Elliott et al., 1985; Vitaro, Brendgen, & Tremblay, 2000).

SOCIO-FAMILY FACTORS

Attachment to parents has been reported to moderate the link between exposure to deviant friends and participants' delinquent behaviors (Mason, Cauce, Gonzales, & Hiraga, 1994; Vitaro et al., 2000). However, whether other aspects of parenting (i.e., low supervision/monitoring, harsh/inconsistent discipline) also have a moderating effect is unclear. For example, Vitaro et al. (2000) found no interaction between parental supervision and exposure to deviant friends in predicting later delinquency, although parental supervision had a positive main effect that compensated for the presence of deviant friends. Conversely, Galambos, Barker, and Almeida (2003) found that parents' behavioral control (i.e., regulation of the child's behavior through firm and consistent discipline) moderated the link between exposure to deviant friends and increases in externalizing problems during early adolescence, whereas parents' psychological control (i.e., control of the child's behavior through psychological means, such as withdrawal of love and guilt induction) and support (i.e., responsiveness and connectedness to the child) did not. Obviously, the final word is still to come with respect to the moderating/protective role of diverse aspects of parent-child relationships.

In addition to parental practices, low SES and socio-family adversity have also been shown to increase delinquent behaviors and association with deviant friends (Farrington & West, 1993; Kolvin, Miller, Fletting, & Kolvin, 1988).

CHILD/ADOLESCENT SOCIAL STATUS

Studies that examined whether acceptance by conventional peers or popularity moderated the link between deviant friend involvement and delinquency found contradictory results. On one hand, Fergusson et al. (in press), who used a peer acceptance measure (i.e., a preference-based measure derived from positive and negative nomination) collected during pre-adolescence, found no interaction between social acceptance and exposure to deviant friends in predicting aggressive behavior. Alternatively, Allen, Porter, McFarland, Marsh, and McElhaney (2005) and Haynie (2001) found that

popularity (i.e., a reputation-based measure) increased the link between affiliating with deviant friends and increases in delinquency and drug use during adolescence. These results have been interpreted in the context that some deviant behaviors (i.e., drug use, truancy) become more accepted during adolescence, and popular adolescents are more likely to endorse them than their less socially involved peers (Allen et al., 2005). However, violent behavior does not seem to be part of the behaviors that gain popularity with age, which, in addition to age and type of popularity measures used, may help explain the contradictory findings. Finally, self-perceptions of low peer acceptance have been found to exacerbate the influence of deviant peers on delinquent behaviors (i.e., weapon carrying and physical fighting; Prinstein, Boergers, & Spirito, 2001). This last finding is in line with speculations by Coie (2004) about the increased susceptibility of rejected individuals to peer pressure because of their peripheral position in the peer group, especially for those who are already aggressive and likely to affiliate with other aggressive peers. Coie suggested that, in deviant peer groups in which the norms for aggression and delinquent behavior are high, members who are less well integrated may feel insecure and may be more motivated to endorse the group norms than more integrated members in an effort improve their standing within the group and prove their loyalty. However, at the clique level, this process does not seem to apply because Terry and Coie (1993) found that adolescents who were more central members of deviant cliques reported a greater increase in their antisocial behavior than those who were less central.

PEERS' SOCIAL STATUS

In line with social learning theory, Prinstein (2005) found that average-status adolescents conformed more to peers' manifestations of aggressive behaviors, both at the attitudinal and at the behavioral levels, when the peers appeared high in social status than when they appeared low in status. One innovative feature of this study was the use of an experimental design to illustrate the moderating role of peers' status with respect to peer contagion.[1]

FEATURES OF FRIENDSHIP

Aspects of friendships such as stability or mutuality should, in principle, increase the influence of deviant friends on deviant behaviors. Indeed, Berndt, Hawkins, and Jiao (1999) found that those children who had stable friendships with deviant peers tended to exhibit increases in their own delinquent behavior. In a similar study, Brendgen, Vitaro, and Bukowski (2000) found that stability of friendships with deviant peers predicted increases in antisocial behavior over a 1-year period. However, friendships among aggressive/antisocial children are usually poor in quality (Marcus, 1996; Poulin, Dishion, & Haas, 1999) and deteriorate over the course of a few months (Poulin & Boivin, 2000), although some researchers have found that aggressive children (i.e., boys) know their friends for a longer period of time than nonaggressive children (Bagwell, Schmidt, Newcomb, & Bukowski, 2001).

DEVIANT PEER NETWORK

Children with deviant friends may or may not be involved in cliques, and these cliques may or may not be deviant. Thus, it is possible that the characteristics of the members of the larger peer network moderate the influence of close or best friends. The only study that examined this issue did not find a moderating effect of the extended peer network with respect to the influence of best friends' deviancy on increases in delinquent behaviors (Vitaro et al., 2000).

Proximal Processes (i.e., Mechanisms) That Might Help Explain the Influence of Deviant Friends on Externalizing Behaviors

If one assumes that deviant peers actually play an influential role with respect to violence and delinquency, in accordance with the peer influence or the social interactional model, then it is important to consider the mechanisms through which deviant peer influence could operate. Five possible mechanisms have been proposed.

DIFFERENTIAL REINFORCEMENT THROUGH DEVIANCY TRAINING

Positive verbal reinforcement by peers for deviant behaviors is an important factor with respect to subsequent deviant behavior. This process, labeled "deviancy training" by Dishion and his colleagues (Dishion, Spracklen, Andrews, & Patterson, 1996), has received substantial empirical support. Specifically, deviant peers tend to reinforce (through laughter or positive nonverbal feedback) rule-breaking talk or deviant acts and ignore or punish normative behaviors (Buehler, Patterson, & Furniss, 1966). In turn, this differential reinforcement of deviant behaviors has been found to result in an increase in youngsters' subsequent delinquent behavior and substance use (Dishion, Burraston, & Poulin, 2001; Poulin et al., 2001). It has also been found to mediate the exposure to deviant peers by age 10 and increases in arrests, substance use, and sexual intercourse throughout adolescence (Patterson et al., 2000).

Snyder et al. (2005) have recently reported that deviancy training may occur among kindergarten children. Specifically, engaging in deviant talk and imitative play of deviant behaviors with same-gender peers predicted an increase in overt and covert conduct problems on the playground, at school, and at home. Interestingly and most importantly, this effect was positive even after accounting for deviant peer involvement. Results from Lavallee, Bierman, Nix, and the Conduct Problems Prevention Research Group (2005) with first-grade children support the notion that deviancy training is underway long before adolescence. More specifically, these authors found that ratings of deviancy training within intervention groups targeting high-risk first-grade children predicted an increase in aggression for some children.

COERCION AND LOW-QUALITY FRIENDSHIPS

Antisocial boys have been found to be more bossy with their friends and more frequently involved in coercive and conflictual exchanges than conventional children (Deptula & Cohen, 2004; Dishion, Andrews, & Crosby, 1995; Dishion, Duncan, Eddy, Fagot, & Fetrow, 1994; Windle, 1994). It is possible that the negative features of children's friendships with their deviant friends directly influence these children's problematic behavioral profile through a coercive interactional process similar to the one identified by Patterson and colleagues in regard to parent-child interactions (Patterson et al., 1967). In line with this notion, Kupersmidt, Burchinal, and Patterson (1995) showed that conflict with a best friend predicted delinquency beyond what is already predicted by peer rejection and the best friend's aggressiveness.

PEER PRESSURE TO CONFORM TO NORM-BREAKING BEHAVIOR

There is evidence indicating that pressure to conform to norm-breaking behaviors may serve as a mechanism for deviancy training in the context of friendships or gangs. For example, Bagwell and Coie (2004) reported that 10-year-old aggressive boys and their friends provided more enticement for rule violations in situations that provided opportunities for rule-breaking behavior than nonaggressive boys and their friends. As expected, aggressive boys and their friends also engaged in more rule-breaking behavior than did nonaggressive boys and their friends. Interestingly, however, nonaggressive dyads also engaged in what Bagwell and Coie (2004) called "temptation talk" (i.e., exploration of potential rule violations), but they seldom escalated from temptation talk to actual norm-breaking behaviors. As suggested by Bagwell and Coie (2004), temptation talk is a salient developmental process within friendships during late childhood and early adolescence, as it serves as a way for children to explore limits for behavior (i.e., norms) within the peer group. Temptation talk is not coercive, but the resulting peer enticements may provide the needed push for action in dyads in which the children are prone to antisocial behaviors.

ENTROPY

In the social relationship context, entropy is a measure of the degree of disorganization and lack of consistency in the series of interactions between two or more individuals. A high entropy score represents a disorganized, unfocused, and unpredictable pattern of interactions, whereas a low entropy score reflects the opposite pattern. Recently, Dishion, Nelson, Winter, and Bullock (2004) reported that entropy in deviancy training could play a role in the prediction of antisocial behavior, in addition to the content of the interactions and the accompanying differential reinforcement between the social partners. Using the same videotapes depicting early-onset antisocial boys interacting with their best friends, the authors reported that, by age 14 years, antisocial dyads with well-organized interactions (i.e., low entropy) but high levels of deviant talk were most likely to manifest antisocial behaviors by early adulthood even after controlling for current and past delinquency. In other words, exclusive focus on rule-breaking behaviors exacerbated the risk for continued antisociality. This focus on rule breaking did not, however, have a main effect over and above deviancy training and personal characteristics.

MODELING

Modeling through demonstration of rule-breaking or aggressive behaviors may also partly explain how deviant peers support the maintenance or escalation of aggressive-antisocial acts (Prinstein, 2005) Modeling, however, need not be direct. As suggested by Jussim and Osgood (1989), group norms that are favorable to deviant behavior may be sufficient to encourage some youth to display behaviors compatible with these perceived norms. The indirect modeling effect resulting from perceived group norms is facilitated when members of the group are positively reinforced for displaying behaviors that are in line with these norms.

CONCLUDING REMARKS

The perpetration of aggressive acts by peers may trigger the active learning of new reprehensible acts. Peers' aggressive acts may also lower the threshold of appropriate behavior, encouraging an aggressive child or adolescent to commit similar acts that are already part of his or her repertoire. The current terminology (i.e., "peer contagion," "peer influence") does not allow for a clear distinction in this respect. The distinction between the learning of new acts and lowering of norms is, however, important because the mechanisms involved in these two processes may be totally different.

Clinical Use of Nondeviant Peers With Aggressive/Antisocial Children

Some prevention- or intervention-oriented investigators have exposed deviant children to nondeviant peers in the hope of positive outcomes. These efforts and their results may prove useful in unraveling the role of peers in the development of aggressive behavior.

USE OF NONDEVIANT PEERS IN PREVENTION/INTERVENTION STUDIES

Any discussion of the role of deviant peers for children's further developmental adjustment is hampered by the lack of evidence for a causal relationship. Most of the available evidence is correlational in nature. Prevention/intervention studies using experimental designs can help overcome this important limitation by creating opportunities to experimentally manipulate putative causal factors (i.e., exposure to deviant or nondeviant peers). Although their main goal is the improvement of youngsters' developmental outcomes, these research designs also allow for the examination of the pathways through which the prevention/intervention programs achieve their impact on distal outcomes and whether these pathways are compatible with established theoretical models, thus increasing the plausibility of causal inferences (Cicchetti & Hinshaw, 2002).

In line with the idea of harvesting the positive power of nondeviant peers

and ultimately testing the role of peers, some researchers created "mixed groups" by exposing aggressive children to nonaggressive peers in structured (i.e., social skills training sessions) or unstructured (i.e., social activities or sports) settings (August, Hektner, Egan, Realmuto, & Bloomquist, 2002; Chamberlain & Reid, 1998; Feldman, Caplinger, & Wodarski, 1983; Vitaro, Brendgen, Pagani, Tremblay, & McDuff, 1999). In most cases, these mixed-group prevention programs resulted in less delinquency and violence than control conditions or equivalent programs that aggregated aggressive participants into homogeneous groups (see Ang & Hugues, 2002; and Dodge et al., 2006). Moreover, affiliation with nondeviant peers was found to mediate, in part, the impact of the prevention programs on later violent and delinquent behaviors assessed either through self-reports or criminal records (Eddy & Chamberlain, 2000; Leve & Chamberlain, 2005; Vitaro et al., 1999). A discordant note, however, comes from a recent study by Mager, Milich, Harris, and Howard (2005) who found that a mixed problem-solving training group consisting of early adolescents with and without problems resulted in more externalizing problems than a homogeneous group in which all members had conduct problems. Interestingly, these authors collected process data during the training sessions and noticed more deviancy training in the mixed-group condition than in the homogenous-group condition. Mediation analyses showed that the deviancy training that occurred during the training sessions in the mixed-group condition accounted for the worse postintervention scores. Deviancy training is a process, and it may or may not occur depending on the group dynamics created by the interaction between the participants' characteristics, the context of the intervention, and the skills of the group leader (Dishion & Dodge, 2005).

In conclusion, as proposed by Sullivan (1953) and as shown by many authors (see Bukowski, Newcomb, & Hartup, 1996 for a review), having friends and being part of a peer group can have a very positive impact on children's social and emotional development. Youngsters with deviant friends, however, risk being deprived of these important benefits and, in addition, risk the aggravation of their externalizing problems. Continued research on the predictors and consequences of deviant friendship affiliation, as well as on the underlying mechanisms and the best strategies for preventing or reducing its impact, whether based on an experimental prevention project or a less complex quasi-experimental/longitudinal design, is essential if we want all youngsters to enjoy the positive sides of friendship.

Part Three: Future Directions

Despite all the accumulated evidence regarding the role of peers with respect to the learning or aggravation of aggressive behaviors in children and adolescents, there are still many methodological and conceptual issues that need to be addressed to gain a more complete image of the situation. These issues are examined in the next and final section.

Interplay Between Peer Rejection and Deviant Friends

Despite the potential interplay between rejection by normative peers and exposure to deviant friends, only three studies have examined more than one type of peer experience at the same time with respect to aggressive/violent behaviors. First, Laird et al. (2001) used a model proposed by Patterson et al. (1989) a decade earlier (see Figure 17.1a) to test whether peer rejection during the early grades and the association with antisocial peers in early adolescence could sequentially mediate the link between early disruptiveness and a global score of adolescent delinquency that included violence, theft, vandalism, and substance use. The results of Laird et al. (2001), however, were inconclusive. First, they found no link between early disruptiveness and later antisocial peer involvement for peer rejection to mediate; second, the relation between child-hood peer rejection and a global score of behavior problems during adolescence was not mediated by antisocial peer involvement by early adolescence. In contrast to Laird et al. (2001), two recent studies reported data congruent with Patterson's mediational model, as amended by Hay et al. (2001, see Figure 17.1b), but only when violence was the outcome (see Chapple, 2005; Vitaro, Pedersen, & Brendgen, in press). In these studies, childhood peer rejection and affiliation with deviant peers during early adolescence played a mediating role between early disruptiveness and later violence. Notably, however, individual dispositions remained a significant direct predictor in both studies. Studies examining the dynamic interplay among children's behaviors, peers' reactions, and exposure to deviant friends or other socializing agents as it unfolds across time are most in need.

Different Categories of Peer Experiences

A majority of the existing research has examined the effect of peers at school and often in the classroom. This is a valid strategy because classroom-based and school-based studies capture most of the peer experiences, both at the group and the dyadic levels, during childhood and early adolescence (Ennett & Bauman, 1994). Nonetheless, there is growing evidence that, relative to well-accepted classmates, unpopular adolescents tend to have more friends outside of school (George & Hartmann, 1996). There is also evidence that the proportion of members in a child's clique who do not attend the same school as the child increases with age from middle childhood to late adolescence (Kerr, Stattin, & Kiesner, 2004). Finally, there is evidence that throughout adolescence deviant peers outside the school seem to play important roles not well captured in school-based studies. For example, attending unstructured and unsupervised youth recreation centers is related to an increase in antisocial behavior, over and above personal and socio-family characteristics (Mahoney, Stattin, & Magnusson, 2001; Stattin, Gustafson, & Magnusson, 1989). The effects for girls

A

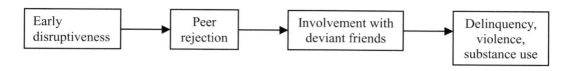

B

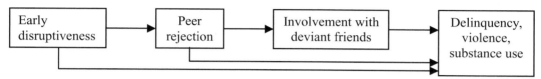

Figure 17.1. Illustration of two versions of the sequential mediational model linking early disruptiveness to later antisocial/delinquent behavior through the mediating role of two types of peer experiences: peer rejection and deviant friend involvement. A. Pattersons et al.'s (1989) sequential mediation model. B. Hays et al.'s (2004) variant of a sequential mediation model.

are especially striking, particularly for those who both attend the centers and are heavily involved with peers or boyfriends outside the centers (Persson, Kerr, & Stattin, 2004; Stattin et al., 1989). Other researchers have also reported that unsupervised wandering in conjunction with deviant peer association predicted both early onset and increased frequency of arrests as measured by official court records (Stoolmiller, 1994).

There is also evidence that many peers who are considered important by the adolescents themselves (i.e., romantic partners, siblings) are not found in their classrooms (Kerr et al., 2004). Moreover, the trend to nominate romantic partners over friends as the most important persons outside the family increases throughout adolescence, suggesting that the contribution of romantic partners may become relatively more important from early through late adolescence (Kerr et al., 2004). Similarly, siblings could also be added as a special category of peers. For example, children with antisocial siblings have recently been reported to be at risk for antisocial behavior, even accounting for their personal dispositions and sociofamilial characteristics (Haynie & McHugh, 2003).

Two additional categories of peers could also be added as possible sources of influence: social crowds and enemies. Social crowds are defined by Brown and Klute (2003) as group clusters that include individuals who have established the same basic image or identity among peers. However, little is known about the influence of social crowds on violent behavior. Finally, as suggested by Hartup and Abecassis (2002) the existence of enemies, enemies' behavioral characteristics, and the type of interactions with them may also help explain increases in deviant behaviors, over and above peers with whom children and adolescents have established positive relationships. Future studies should clarify the role of these different categories of additional peer experiences and their potential interplay with respect to the acquisition or evolution of aggressive behaviors at different periods of development.

More Longitudinal/Experimental Studies That Start Early

One important developmental period that has been ignored almost totally with respect to the role of peer experiences is the period during the preschool years. Human physical aggression is most frequent between 17 and 48 months of age (NICHD, 2004; Tremblay & Nagin, 2005; Tremblay et al., 2004). Children also appear to be learning most from their social environment during the preschool years (e.g., Dionne, 2005; Paus, 2005). If negative peer experiences, such as rejection and victimization by peers, have an impact on short- and long-term development, most of the action may be happening before children enter kindergarten, both because most of the aggressive behaviors occur then and because children learn more quickly during that period. Furthermore, later peer interactions are most likely perceived, processed, and felt in light of the early experiences. Exposure to aggressive peers probably starts very early in life, either as a result of early rejection by the normative peer group or as a consequence of parent selection of children's social environments (i.e., high-quality vs. low-quality day care or structured/supervised settings vs. unstructured/unsupervised settings; see Boivin, Vitaro, & Poulin, 2005, for more details on this issue).

A Closer Focus on Processes and Contextual Factors

There is also a need for studies that examine the micro-social processes between aggressive children and their friends, clique members, romantic partners, siblings, enemies, or normative peers that may help explain peer influence from birth to adulthood. As recently suggested by Dishion and Snyder (2004), assessing micro-social processes may require increasingly sophisticated theoretical models and measurement strategies to capture all relevant aspects of the social interactions (e.g., entropy through the use of dynamic systems analyses or conditional reinforcement through sequential analysis). It may also require a focus on multiple aspects of social interactions, such as coercion in low-quality friendships and deviancy training between friends or clique members. As already suggested, the examina-

tion of these processes should not be limited to adolescents. In fact, it should start with young children if we are to understand what happens during adolescence in light of previous development. Finally, different contexts would need to be considered because the interactions between children/adolescents and their peers seem to vary depending on the amount of structure or supervision provided by adults and whether the interactions occur inside or outside the school, the family, and probably the day care context.

Distinction Among Subtypes of Aggressive Behaviors

The study of violence and peers also needs to distinguish among different subtypes of aggressive behavior based on form (i.e., physical versus psychological/relational aggression) and function (i.e., reactive vs. proactive aggression). There is good evidence that all forms and functions of aggression are present in early childhood (Dionne, 2005; Hay, 2005; Peterson & Flanders, 2005; Tremblay & Nagin, 2005; Vaillancourt, 2005). However, there is very little knowledge regarding the role of peers in the development of these forms and functions of aggression or their consequences for short- and long-term social, emotional, and physical development.

In one study examining this issue, Brendgen, Vitaro, Tremblay, and Wanner (2002) showed that friends' aggression predicted both delinquency-related violence (i.e., mostly proactive) and violence in romantic relationships (i.e., mostly reactive) during adolescence. In contrast, peer rejection predicted only violence in romantic relationships, through the mediating role of rejection sensitivity. In another study, aggregation in deviant cliques was driven by proactive aggression but not by reactive aggression (Poulin & Boivin, 2000). As we stressed throughout the chapter, the role of peer rejection and friends' aggression may vary according to the forms or functions of aggressive behaviors, as further indicated by these results.

Conclusion

Much has been learned to date regarding the role of peers in the learning, maintenance, or escalation of violent behavior. Despite the wealth of this accumulated knowledge, many important gaps remain. Thus, more studies are necessary to fill these gaps. These studies should simultaneously examine different types of peer experiences in an effort to establish their relative, additive, interactive, mediational, or transactional (i.e., bidirectional) links over time. At the same time, the studies should distinguish among different subtypes of aggressive and violent behaviors because the pathways and micro-social processes linking the different types of peer experiences to specific subtypes of aggressive and violent behaviors may vary. Finally, as stressed throughout this chapter, a developmental perspective is necessary to better understand the role of peers. Such a developmental perspective should include the preschool years in order to capture the early role of peers. Studies addressing preschool peer interactions should examine whether and how these early peer experiences play a role in fostering or mitigating children's attitudes and behaviors toward aggression and, possibly, in setting the stage for later peer experiences. The reasons to adopt an early perspective are threefold. First, some peer experiences are already important during the preschool years. Second, it is important to distinguish peer experiences that are persistent from those that are transitory, as their consequences for children's development may differ. Third, peer experiences during the preschool years may be easier to manipulate for prevention purposes than similar peer experiences later on. This new knowledge may pave the way to more pertinent and, it is hoped, more effective preventive/curative programs for aggressive children and adolescents. Such knowledge could also allow interventionists to make more and better use of peers as intervention agents or crucial proximal or intermediate targets. In return, these prevention/intervention programs should help clarify the precise role of peer experiences with respect to the development of aggressive and violent behaviors.

Note

1. We use the expression "peer contagion" because it has been used by the author of the study we reported and because it is becoming increasingly popular (see the special issue of the *Journal of Abnormal Child Psychology*, vol. 33, no. 3). However, it is not clear how it differs from similar terms such as "peer influence." We propose that the term "peer influence" or, for that matter, "peer effect" be reserved when behaviors are learned or expressed under the *direct* exposure to peers. In contrast, the expression "peer contagion" or "peer emulation," for that matter, should be reserved when behaviors are learned or are used, under the *indirect* influence of peers.

References

Akers, R. K., Krohn, M. D., Lanza-Kaduce, L., & Radosevich, M. (1979). Social learning and deviant behavior. A specific test of a general theory. *American Sociological Review, 44*, 636–655.

Allen, J. P., Porter, M. R., McFarland, F. C., Marsh, P., & McElhaney, K. (2005). The two faces of adolescents' success with peers: Adolescent popularity, social adaptation, and deviant behavior. *Child Development, 76*, 747–760.

Anderson, C. A. (1999). Attributional style, depression, and loneliness: A cross-cultural comparison of American and Chinese students. *Personality and Social Psychology Bulletin, 25*, 482–499.

Ang, R. P., & Hugues, J. N. (2002). Differential benefits of skills training with antisocial youth based on group composition: A meta-analytic investigation. *School Psychology Review, 31*, 164–185.

Ary, D. V., Duncan, T. E., Duncan, S. C., & Hops, H. (1999). Adolescent problem behavior: The influence of parents and peers. *Behaviour Research and Therapy, 37*, 217–230.

August, G. L., Hektner, J. M., Egan, E. E., Realmuto, G. M., & Bloomquist, M. L. (2002). The Early Risers longitudinal prevention trial: Examination of three year outcomes in aggressive children with intent-to-treat and as-intended analyses. *Psychology of Addictive Behaviors, 16,* 27–39.

Bagwell, C. L., & Coie, J. D. (2004). The best friendships of aggressive boys: Relationship quality, conflict management, and rule-breaking behavior. *Journal of Experimental Child Psychology, 88,* 5–24.

Bagwell, C. L., Newcomb, A. F., & Bukowski, W. M. (1998). Preadolescent friendship and peer rejection as predictors of adult adjustment. *Child Development, 69,* 140–153.

Bagwell, C. L., Schmidt, M. E., Newcomb, A. F., & Bukowski, W. M. (2001). Friendship and peer rejection as predictors of adult adjustment. *New Directions for Child and Adolescent Development, 91,* 25–49.

Berndt, T. J., Hawkins, J. A., & Jiao, Z. (1999). Influence of friends and friendships on adjustment to junior high school. *Merrill-Palmer Quarterly, 45,* 13–41.

Bierman, K. L. (2004). *Peer rejection: Developmental processes and intervention strategies.* New York: Guilford Press.

Bierman, K. L., & Wargo, J. B. (1995). Predicting the longitudinal course associated with aggressive-rejected, aggressive (nonrejected), and rejected (nonaggressive) status. *Development and Psychopathology, 7,* 669–682.

Boivin, M., Dodge, K. A., & Coie, J. D. (1995). Individual-group behavioral similarity and peer status in experimental play groups: The social misfit revisited. *Journal of Personality and Social Psychology, 69,* 269–279.

Boivin, M., & Hymel, S. (1997). Peer experiences and social self-perceptions: A two-stage mediational model. *Developmental Psychology, 33,* 135–145.

Boivin, M., Hymel, S., & Hodges, E. (2001). Toward a process view of peer rejection and harassment. In J. Jojoven & S. Graham (Eds.), *Peer harassment in school: The plight of the vulnerable and victimized children.* New York: Guilford Press.

Boivin, M., & Vitaro, F. (1995). The impact of peer relationships on aggression in childhood: Inhibition through coercion or promotion through peer support. In J. McCord (Ed.), *Coercion and punishment in long-term perspectives* (pp. 183–197). New York: Cambridge University Press.

Boivin, M., Vitaro, F., & Poulin, F. (2005). Peer relationships and the development of aggressive behavior in early childhood. In R. E. Tremblay, W. W. Hartup, & J. Archer (Eds.), *Devel-opmental origins of aggression* (pp. 376–397). New York: Guilford Press.

Brendgen, M., Vitaro, F., & Bukowski, W. M. (1998). Affiliation with delinquent friends: Contributions of parents, self-esteem, delinquent behavior, and peer rejection. *Journal of Early Adolescence, 18,* 244–265.

Brendgen, M., Vitaro, F., & Bukowski, W. M. (2000). Deviant friends and early adolescents' emotional and behavioral adjustment. *Journal of Research on Adolescence, 10*(2), 173–189.

Brendgen, M., Vitaro, F., Bukowski, W. M., Doyle, A. B., & Markiewicz, D. (2001). Developmental profiles of peer social preference over the course of elementary school: Associations with externalizing and internalizing behavior. *Developmental Psychology, 37,* 308–320.

Brendgen, M., Vitaro, F., Tremblay, R. E., & Wanner, B. (2002). Parent and peer effects on delinquency-related violence and dating violence. *Social Development, 11,* 225–244.

Brody, G. H., Ge, X., Conger, R. D., Gibbons, F. X., Murry, V. M., Gerrard, M., et al. (2001). The influence of neighborhood disadvantage, collective socialization, and parenting on African American children's affiliation with deviant peers. *Child Development, 72,* 1231–1246.

Brown, B. B., & Klute, C. (2003). Friendships, cliques, and crowds. In G. R. Adams & M. D. Berzonsky (Eds.), *Blackwell handbook of adolescence* (pp. 330–348). Oxford: Blackwell.

Buehler, R. E., Patterson, G. R., & Furniss, J. M. (1966). The reinforcement of behavior in institutional settings. *Behaviour Research and Therapy, 4,* 157–167.

Bukowski, W. M., & Hoza, B. (1989). Popularity and friendship: Issues in theory, measurement, and outcome. In T. Berndt & G. Ladd (Eds.), *Peer relationships in child development* (pp. 15–45). New York: Wiley.

Bukowski, W. M., Newcomb, A. F., & Hartup, W. W. (1996). *The company they keep: Friendship in childhood and adolescence.* Cambridge, UK: Cambridge University Press.

Cairns, R., Xie, H., & Leung, M. (1998). The popularity of friendship and the neglect of social networks: Toward a new balance. In W. M. Bukowski & A. H. Cillessen (Eds.), *Sociometry then and now: Building on six decades of measuring children's experiences with the paper group: No. 80. New directions for child development* (pp. 5–24). San Francisco: Jossey-Bass.

Cairns, R. B., Cairns, B. D., Neckerman, H. J., Gest, S. D., & Gariépy, J.-L. (1988). Peer networks and aggressive behavior: Social support or social rejection? *Developmental Psychology, 24,* 815–823.

Cairns, R. B., Perrin, J. E., & Cairns, B. D. (1985). Social structure and social cognition in early adolescence: Affiliative patterns. *Journal of Early Adolescence, 5,* 339–355.

Caspi, A., Elder, G. H., & Bem, D. J. (1987). Moving against the world: Life-course patterns of explosive children. *Developmental Psychology, 23,* 308–313.

Chamberlain, P., & Reid, J. B. (1998). Comparison of two community alternatives to incarceration for chronic juvenile offenders. *Journal of Consulting and Clinical Psychology, 66,* 624–633.

Chapple, C. L. (2005). Self-control, peer relations, and delinquency. *Justice Quarterly, 22,* 89–106.

Cicchetti, D., & Hinshaw, S. P. (2002). Editorial: Prevention and intervention science: Contributions to developmental theory. *Development and Psychopathology, 14,* 667–671.

Cohen, J. (1977). *Statistical power analysis for the behavioral sciences.* New York: Academic Press.

Coie, J. D. (1990). Toward a theory of peer rejection. In S. R. Asher & J. D. Coie (Eds.), *Peer rejection in childhood* (pp. 365–402). New York: Cambridge University Press.

Coie, J. D. (2004). The impact of negative social experiences on the development of antisocial behavior. In J. B. Kupersmidt & K. A. Dodge (Eds.), *Children's peer relations* (pp. 243–267). Washington, DC: American Psychological Association.

Coie, J. D., & Dodge, K. A. (1983). Continuities and changes in children's social status: A five-year longitudinal study. *Merrill-Palmer Quarterly, 29,* 261–282.

Coie, J. D., & Dodge, K. A. (1998). Aggression and antisocial behavior. In W. Damon & N. Eisenberg (Eds.), *Handbook of child psychology: Social, emotional, and personality development* (5th ed.) (Vol. 3, pp. 779–862). New York: Wiley.

Coie, J. D., & Koeppl, G. (1990). Adapting intervention to the problems of aggressive and disruptive rejected children. In S. R. Asher & J. D. Coie (Eds.), *Peer rejection in childhood* (pp. 309–337). New York: Cambridge University Press.

Coie, J. D., & Kupersmidt, J. B. (1983). A behavioral analysis of emerging social status in boys' groups. *Child Development, 54,* 1400–1416.

Coie, J. D., & Lenox, K. F. (1994). The development of antisocial individuals. *Progress in Experimental Personality and Psychopathology Research,* 45–72.

Coie, J. D., Lochman, J. E., Terry, R., & Hyman, C. (1992). Predicting early adolescent disorder from childhood aggression and peer rejection. *Journal of Consulting and Clinical Psychology, 60,* 783–792.

Coie, J. D., Terry, R., Akriski, A., & Lochman, J. (1995). Early adolescent social influences on delinquent behavior. In J. McCord (Ed.), *Coercion and punishment in long-term perspectives* (pp. 229–244). New York: Cambridge University Press.

Cowan, P. A., & Cowan, C. P. (2004). From family relationships to peer rejection to antisocial behavior in middle childhood. In J. B. Kupersmidt & K. A. Dodge (Eds.), *Children's peer relations* (pp. 159–177). Washington, DC: American Psychological Association.

Deater-Deckard, K. (2001). Annotation: Recent research examining the role of peer relationships in the development of psychopathology. *Journal of Child Psychology and Psychiatry, and Allied Disciplines, 42,* 565–579.

Deptula, D. P., & Cohen, R. (2004). Aggressive, rejected, and delinquent children and adolescents: A comparison of their friendships. *Aggression and Violent Behavior, 9,* 75–104.

DeRosier, M. E., Kupersmidt, J. B., & Patterson, C. J. (1994). Children's academic and behavioral adjustment as a function of the chronicity and proximity of peer rejection. *Child Development, 65,* 1799–1813.

DeRosier, M. E., & Thomas, J. M. (2003). Strengthening sociometric prediction: Scientific advances in the assessment of children's peer relations. *Child Development, 75,* 1379–1392.

Dionne, G. (2005). Language development and aggressive behavior. In R. E. Tremblay, W. W. Hartup, & J. Archer (Eds.), *Developmental origins of aggression* (pp. 330–352). New York: Guilford Press.

Dishion, T. J. (1990a). The family ecology for boys' peer relations in middle childhood. *Child Development, 61,* 874–892.

Dishion, T. J. (1990b). Peer context of troublesome behavior in children and adolescents.

In P. Leone (Ed.), *Understanding troubled and troublesome youth* (pp. 128–153). Beverly Hills, CA: Sage.

Dishion, T. J., & Andrews, D. W. (1995). Preventing escalation in problem behaviors with high-risk young adolescents: Immediate and 1-year outcomes. *Journal of Consulting and Clinical Psychology, 63,* 538–548.

Dishion, T. J., Andrews, D. W., & Crosby, L. (1995). Antisocial boys and their friends in early adolescence: Relationship characteristics, quality, and interactional processes. *Child Development, 66,* 139–151.

Dishion, T. J., Burraston, B., & Poulin, F. (2001). Peer group dynamics associated with iatrogenic effects in group interventions with high-risk young adolescents. In C. Erdley & D. W. Nangle (Eds.), *New directions in child development: The role of friendship in psychological adjustment* (pp. 79–92). San Francisco: Jossey-Bass.

Dishion, T. J., Capaldi, D. M., Spracklen, K. M., & Li, F. (1995). Peer ecology of male adolescent drug use. *Development and Psychopathology, 7,* 803–824.

Dishion, T. J., & Dodge, K. A. (2005). Peer contagion in interventions for children and adolescents: Moving towards an understanding of the ecology and dynamics of change. *Journal of Abnormal Child Psychology, 33,* 395–400.

Dishion, T. J., Duncan, T. E., Eddy, J. M., Fagot, B. I., & Fetrow, R. (1994). The world of parents and peers: Coercive exchanges and children's social adaptation. *Social Development, 3,* 255–268.

Dishion, T. J., McCord, J., & Poulin, F. (1999). When interventions harm: Peer groups and problem behavior. *American Psychologist, 54,* 755–764.

Dishion, T. J., Nelson, S. E., Winter, C. E., & Bullock, B. M. (2004). Adolescent friendship as a dynamic system: Entropy and deviance in the etiology and course of male antisocial behavior. *Journal of Abnormal Child Psychology, 32,* 651–663.

Dishion, T. J., Patterson, G. R., & Griesler, P. C. (1994). Peer adaptations in the development of antisocial behavior: A confluence model. In L. R. Huesmann (Ed.), *Aggressive behavior: Current perspectives* (pp. 61–95). New York: Plenum Press.

Dishion, T. J., Patterson, G. R., Stoolmiller, M., & Skinner, M. L. (1991). Family, school, and behavioral antecedents to early adolescent involvement with antisocial peers. *Developmental Psychology, 27,* 172–180.

Dishion, T. J., & Snyder, J. (2004). An introduction to the special issue on advances in process and dynamic system analysis of social interaction and the development of antisocial behavior. *Journal of Abnormal Child Psychology, 32,* 575–578.

Dishion, T. J., Spracklen, K. M., Andrews, D. W., & Patterson, G. R. (1996). Deviancy training in male adolescent friendships. *Behavior Therapy, 27,* 373–390.

Dodge, K. A. (1983). Behavioral antecedents of peer social status. *Child Development, 54,* 1386–1399.

Dodge, K. A. (1991). The structure and function of reactive and proactive aggression. In D. J. Pepler & K. H. Rubin (Eds.), *The development and treatment of childhood aggression* (pp. 201–218). Hillsdale, NJ: Erlbaum.

Dodge, K. A. (1993). Social-cognitive mechanism in the development of conduct disorder and depression. *Annual Review of Psychology, 44,* 559–584.

Dodge, K. A., Coie, J. D., Pettit, G. S., & Price, J. M. (1990). Peer status and aggression in boys' groups: Developmental and contextual analyses. *Child Development, 61,* 1289–1309.

Dodge, K. A., Dishion, T. J., & Lansford, J. E. (2006). *Deviant peer influences in programs for youth: Problems and solutions.* New York: Guilford Press.

Dodge, K. A., Lansford, J. E., Burks, V. S., Bates, J. E., Pettit, G. S., Fontaine, R., et al. (2003). Peer rejection and social information-processing factors in the development of aggressive behavior problems in children. *Child Development, 74,* 374–393.

Dunn, J., & McGuire, S. (1992). Sibling and peer relationships in childhood. *Journal of Child Psychology and Psychiatry, and Allied Disciplines, 33,* 67–105.

Eddy, J. M., & Chamberlain, P. (2000). Family management and deviant peer association as mediator of the impact of treatment condition on youth antisocial behavior. *Journal of Consulting and Clinical Psychology, 68,* 857–863.

Elliott, D. S., Huizinga, D., & Ageton, S. S. (1985). *Explaining delinquency and drug use.* Beverly Hills, CA: Sage.

Ennett, S. T., & Bauman, K. E. (1994). The contribution of influence and selection to adolescent peer group homogeneity: The case of adolescent cigarette smoking. *Journal of Personality and Social Psychology, 67,* 653–663.

Estell, D. B., Cairns, R. B., Farmer, T. W., & Cairns, B. D. (2002). Aggression in inner-city early elementary classroom: Individual and peer-group configurations. *Merrill-Palmer Quarterly, 48,* 52–76.

Farrington, D. P., & West, D. J. (1993). Criminal, penal and life histories of chronic offenders: Risk and protective factors and early identification. *Criminal Behavior and Mental Health, 3,* 492–523.

Farver, J. A. M. (1996). Aggressive behavior in preschoolers' social networks: Do birds of a feather flock together? *Early Childhood Research Quarterly, 11,* 333–350.

Feldman, R. A., Caplinger, T. E., & Wodarski, J. S. (1983). *The St. Louis conundrum: The effective treatment of antisocial youths.* Englewood Cliffs, NJ: Prentice-Hall.

Fergusson, D. M., Vitaro, F., Wanner, B., & Brendgen, M. (in press). Protective and compensatory factors mitigating the influence of deviant friends on delinquent behaviors during early adolescence. *Journal of Adolescence.*

Fergusson, D. M., Woodward, L. J., & Horwood, L. J. (1999). Childhood peer relationship problems and young people's involvement with deviant peers in adolescence. *Journal of Abnormal Child Psychology, 27,* 357–370.

Galambos, N. L., Barker, E. T., & Almeida, D. M. (2003). Parents do matter: Trajectories of change in externalizing and internalizing problems in early adolescence. *Child Development, 74,* 578–594.

Gatti, U., Tremblay, R. E., Vitaro, F., & McDuff, P. (2005). Youth gangs, delinquency and drug use: A test of the selection, facilitation, and enhancement hypotheses. *Journal of Child Psychology and Psychiatry and Allied Disciplines, 46,* 1178–1190.

George, T. P., & Hartmann, D. P. (1996). Friendship networks of unpopular, average, and popular children. *Child Development, 67,* 2301–2316.

Gordon, R. A., Lahey, B. B., Kawai, E., Loeber, R., Stouthamer-Loeber, M., & Farrington, D. P. (2004). Antisocial behavior and gang membership: Selection and socialization. *Criminology, 42*(1), 55–87.

Gottfredson, M. R., & Hirschi, T. (1990). *A general theory of crime.* Palo Alto, CA: Stanford University Press.

Hallinan, M. T. (1995). Patterns of cliquing among youth. In H. Foot & A. T. Chapman (Eds.), *Friendship and social relations in children* (pp. 321–341). New Brunswick, NJ: Transaction Publishers. (Original work published 1980.)

Hartup, W. W. (1983). Peer relations. In P. H. Mussen & E. M. Hetherington (Eds.), *Handbook of child psychology: Vol. 4. Socialization, personality, and social development* (4th ed.). New York: Wiley.

Hartup, W. W. (1999). Constraints on peer socialization: Let me count the ways. *Merrill-Palmer Quarterly, 45,* 172–183.

Hartup, W. W. (2005). Peer interaction: What causes what? *Journal of Abnormal Child Psychology, 33,* 387–394.

Hartup, W. W., & Abecassis, M. (2002). Friends and enemies. In P. K. Smith & C. H. Hart (Eds.), *Blackwell handbook of childhood social development* (pp. 285–306). Oxford: Blackwell.

Hay, D. F. (2005). The beginnings of aggression in infancy. In R. E. Tremblay, W. W. Hartup, & J. Archer (Eds.), *The developmental origins of aggression* (pp. 107–132). New York: Guilford Press.

Hay, D. F., Pawlby, S., Sharp, D., Asten, P., Mills, A., & Kumar, R. (2001). Intellectual problems shown by 11-year-old children whose mothers had postnatal depression. *Journal of Child Psychology and Psychiatry and Allied Disciplines, 42*(7), 871–889.

Hay, D. F., Payne, A., & Chadwick, A. (2004). Peer relations in childhood. *Journal of Child Psychology and Psychiatry, and Allied Disciplines, 45,* 84–108.

Haynie, D. L. (2001). Delinquent peers revisited: Does network structure matter? *American Journal of Sociology, 106,* 1013–1057.

Haynie, D. L., & McHugh, S. (2003). Sibling deviance: In the shadows of mutual and unique friendship effects? *Criminology, 41*(2), 355–391.

Hektner, J. M., August, G. J., & Realmuto, G. M. (2000). Patterns and temporal changes in peer affiliation among aggressive and nonaggressive children participating in a summer school program. *Journal of Clinical Child Psychology, 29,* 603–614.

Hubbard, J. A., Dodge, K. A., Cillessen, A. H. N., Coie, J. D., & Schwartz, D. (2001). The dyadic nature of social information processing in boys' reactive and proactive aggression.

Journal of Personality and Social Psychology, 80, 268–280.

Hymel, S., Wagner, E., & Butler, L. J. (1990). Reputational bias: View from the peer group. In S. R. Asher & J. D. Coie (Eds.), *Peer rejection in childhood* (pp. 156–186). New York: Cambridge University Press.

Johnson, L. M., Simons, R. L., & Conger, R. D. (2004). Criminal justice system involvement and continuity of youth crime: A longitudinal analysis. *Youth and Society, 36,* 3–29.

Johnson, R. E., Marcos, A. C., & Bahr, S. (1987). The role of peers in the complex etiology of drug use. *Criminology,* 323–340.

Jussim, L., & Osgood, D. W. (1989). Influence and similarity among friends: An integrative model applied to incarcerated adolescents. *Social Psychology Quarterly, 52,* 98–112.

Kerr, M., Stattin, H., & Kiesner, J. (2004, February). *Peers and problem behavior: Have we missed something?* Paper presented at the Hot Topics in Developmental Research: Peer Relationships in Adolescence, Nijmegan, The Netherlands.

Kim, J. E., Hetherington, E. M., & Reiss, D. (1999). Associations among family relationships, antisocial peers, and adolescents' externalizing behaviors: Gender and family type differences. *Child Development, 70,* 1209–1230.

Kolvin, I., Miller, F. J., Fletting, M., & Kolvin, P. A. (1988). Social and parenting factors affecting criminal offense rates: Finding from the Newcastle Thousand Family Study (1947–1980). *British Journal of Psychiatry, 152,* 80–90.

Kupersmidt, J. B., Burchinal, M., & Patterson, C. J. (1995). Developmental patterns of childhood peer relations as predictors of externalizing behavior problems. *Development and Psychopathology, 7,* 825–843.

Kupersmidt, J. B., Coie, J. D., & Dodge, K. A. (1990). The role of poor peer relationships in the development of disorder. In S. R. Asher & J. D. Coie (Eds.), *Peer rejection in childhood* (pp. 274–305). New York: Cambridge University Press.

Kupersmidt, J. B., & DeRosier, M. E. (2004). How peer problems lead to negative outcomes: An integrative mediational model. In J. B. Kupersmidt & K. A. Dodge (Eds.), *Children's peer relations* (pp. 119–138). Washington, DC: American Psychological Association.

Kupersmidt, J. B., & Patterson, G. R. (1991). Childhood peer rejection, aggression, withdrawal, and perceived competence as pre-

dictors of self-reported behavior problems in preadolescence. *Journal of Abnormal Child Psychology, 19*(4), 427–449.

Lacourse, E., Nagin, D. S., Tremblay, R. E., Vitaro, F., & Claes, M. (2003). Developmental trajectories of boys delinquent group membership and facilitation of violent behaviors during adolescence. *Development and Psychopathology, 15,* 183–197.

Lacourse, E., Nagin, D. S., Vitaro, F., Côté, S., Arseneault, L., & Tremblay, R. E. (2006). Prediction of early onset deviant peer group affiliation: A 12-year longitudinal study. *Archives of General Psychiatry, 63*(5), 562–568.

Ladd, G. W., & Burgess, K. B. (2001). Do relational risks and protective factors moderate the linkages between childhood aggression and early psychological and school adjustment? *Child Development, 72,* 1579–1601.

Ladd, G. W., & Troop-Gordon, W. (2003). The role of chronic peer difficulties in the development of children's psychological adjustment problems. *Child Development, 74,* 1344–1367.

Lahey, B. B., Gordon, R. A., Loeber, R., Stouthamer-Loeber, M., & Farrington, D. P. (1999). Boys who join gangs: A prospective study of predictors of first gang entry. *Journal of Abnormal Child Psychology, 27,* 261–276.

Laird, R. D., Jordan, K. Y., Dodge, K. A., Pettit, G. S., & Bates, J. E. (2001). Peer rejection in childhood, involvement with antisocial peers in early adolescence, and the development of externalizing behavior problems. *Development and Psychopathology, 13,* 337–354.

Lavallee, K. L., Bierman, K. L., Nix, R. L., & Conduct Problems Prevention Research Group. (2005). The impact of first-grade "Friendship Group" experiences on child social outcomes in the Fast Track Program. *Journal of Abnormal Child Psychology, 33,* 307–324.

Leve, L. D., & Chamberlain, P. (2005). Association with delinquent peers: Intervention effects for youth in the juvenile justice system. *Journal of Abnormal Child Psychology, 33,* 339–347.

MacDougall, P., Hymel, S., Vaillancourt, T., & Mercer, L. (2001). The consequences of childhood peer rejection. In M. R. Leary (Ed.), *Interpersonal rejection* (pp. 213–247). Oxford: Oxford University Press.

Mager, W., Milich, R., Harris, M. J., & Howard, A. (2005). Intervention groups for adolescents with conduct problems: Is aggregation harmful of helpful? *Journal of Abnormal Child Psychology, 33*, 349–362.

Mahoney, J. L., Stattin, H., & Magnusson, D. (2001). Youth recreation centre participation and criminal offending: A 20-year longitudinal study of Swedish boys. *International Journal of Behavioral Development, 25*, 509–520.

Marcus, R. F. (1996). The friendships of delinquents. *Adolescence, 21*, 145–158.

Mason, C. A., Cauce, A. M., Gonzales, N., & Hiraga, Y. (1994). Adolescent problem behavior: The effect of peers and the moderating role of father absence and the mother-child relationship. *American Journal of Community Psychology, 22*, 723–743.

Melnick, S. M., & Hinshaw, S. P. (2000). Emotion regulation and parenting in AD/HD and comparison boys: Linkages with social behaviors and peer preference. *Journal of Abnormal Child Psychology, 28*, 73–86.

Miller-Johnson, S., Coie, J. D., Maumary-Gremaud, A., Bierman, K., & Conduct Problems Prevention Research Group. (2002). Peer rejection and aggression and early starter models of conduct disorder. *Journal of Abnormal Child Psychology, 30*, 217–230.

Moffitt, T. E. (1993). Adolescence-limited and life-course persistent antisocial behavior: A developmental taxonomy. *Psychological Review, 100*, 674–701.

Nelson, S. E., & Dishion, T. J. (2004). From boys to men: Predicting adult adaptation from middle childhood sociometric status. *Development and Psychopathology, 16*, 441–459.

Newcomb, A. F., Bukowski, W. M., & Pattee, L. (1993). Children's peer relations: A meta-analytic review of popular, rejected, neglected, controversial and average sociometric status. *113*(1), 99–128.

NICHD. (2004). Trajectories of physical aggression from toddlerhood to middle school. *Monographs of the Society for Research in Child Development*, (Serial no. 278, 69–4).

Parke, R. D., O'Neil, R., Spitzer, S., Isley, S., Welsh, M., Wang, S., et al. (1997). A longitudinal assessment of sociometric stability and the behavioral correlates of children's social acceptance. *Merrill-Palmer Quarterly – Journal of Developmental Psychology, 43*(4), 635–662.

Parker, J. G., & Asher, S. R. (1987). Peer relations and later personal adjustment: Are low-accepted children at risk? *Psychological Bulletin, 102*, 357–389.

Parker, J. G., Rubin, K. H., Price, J. M., & DeRosier, M. E. (1995). Peer relationships, child development, and adjustment: A developmental psychopathology perspective. In D. Cicchetti & D. J. Cohen (Eds.), *Developmental psychology. Vol. 2: Risk disorder, and adaptation* (pp. 96–161). New York,: Wiley.

Patterson, G. R., DeBaryshe, B. D., & Ramsey, E. (1989). A developmental perspective on antisocial behavior. *American Psychologist, 44*(2), 329–335.

Patterson, G. R., Dishion, T. J., & Yoerger, K. (2000). Adolescent growth in new forms of problem behavior: Macro- and micro-peer dynamics. *Prevention Science, 1*, 3–13.

Patterson, G. R., Littman, R. A., & Bricker, W. (1967). Assertive behavior in children: A step toward a theory of aggression. *Monographs of the Society for Research in Child Development, 32*, 1–43.

Paus, T. (2005). Mapping brain development and aggression. In R. E. Tremblay, W. W. Hartup, & J. Archer (Eds.), *Developmental origins of aggression* (pp. 242–260). New York: Guilford Press.

Pellegrini, A. D., Bartini, M., & Brooks, F. (1999). School bullies, victims, and aggressive victims: Factors relating to group affiliation and victimization in early adolescence. *Journal of Educational Psychology, 91*, 216–224.

Persson, A., Kerr, M., & Stattin, H. (2004). Why a leisure context is linked to normbreaking for some girls and not others: Personality characteristics and parent-child relations as explanations. *Journal of Adolescence, 27*(5), 583–598.

Peterson, J. B., & Flanders, J. L. (2005). Play and the regulation of aggression. In R. E. Tremblay, W. Hartup, & J. Archer (Eds.), *Developmental origins of aggression* (pp. 133–157). New York: Guilford Press.

Poulin, F., & Boivin, M. (2000). The role of proactive aggression and reactive aggression in the formation and development of boys' friendships. *Developmental Psychology, 36*, 233–240.

Poulin, F., Dishion, T. J., & Burraston, B. (2001). 3-year iatrogenic effects associated with aggregating high-risk adolescents in cognitive-behavioral preventive interventions. *Applied Developmental Science, 5*, 214–224.

Poulin, F., Dishion, T. J., & Haas, E. (1999). The peer influence paradox: Friendship quality and deviancy training within male adolescent friendships. *Merrill-Palmer Quarterly, 45*, 42–61.

Price, J. M., & Dodge, K. A. (1989). Reactive and proactive aggression in childhood: Relations to peer status and social context dimensions.

Journal of Abnormal Child Psychology, 17, 455–471.

Prinstein, M. J. (2005, April). *Peer contagion of aggression and health-risk behavior among adolescent males: An experimental investigation of effects on public conduct and private attitudes.* Paper presented at the Bi-annual Conference of the Society for Research on Child Development, Atlanta.

Prinstein, M. J., Boergers, J., & Spirito, A. (2001). Adolescents' and their friends' health-risk behavior: Factors that alter or add to peer influence. *Journal of Pediatric Psychology, 26,* 287–298.

Rabiner, D. L., & Coie, J. D. (1989). Effect of expectancy inductions on rejected children' acceptance by unfamiliar peers. *Developmental Psychology, 25,* 450–457.

Reid, J. B., Patterson, G. R., & Snyder, J. (2002). *Antisocial behavior in children and adolescents: A developmental analysis and model for intervention.* Washington, DC: American Psychological Association.

Reinherz, H. Z., Giaconia, R. M., Hauf, A. M. C., Wasserman, M. S., & Paradis, A. D. (2000). General and specific childhood risk factors for depression and drug disorders by early adulthood. *Journal of the American Academy of Child and Adolescent Psychiatry, 39,* 223–231.

Rodkin, P. C., Farmer, T. W., Pearl, R., & Van Acker, R. (2000). Heterogeneity of popular boys: Antisocial and prosocial configurations. *Developmental Psychology, 36,* 14–24.

Rubin, K. H., Bukowski, W. M., & Parker, J. G. (1998). Peer interactions, relationships, and groups. In W. Damon & N. Eisenberg (Eds.), *Handbook of child psychology. Vol. 3: Social, emotional, and personality development* (5th ed.) (pp. 610–700). New York,: Wiley.

Scaramella, L. V., Conger, R. D., Spoth, R., & Simons, R. L. (2002). Evaluation of a social contextual model of delinquency: A cross-study replication. *Child Development, 73*(1), 175–195.

Schwartz, D., Proctor, L. J., & Chen, D. H. (2001). The aggressive victim of bullying: Emotional and behavioral dysregulation as a pathway to victimization by peers. In J. Juvonen & S. Graham (Eds.), *Peer harassment in the school: The plight of the vulnerable and the victimized* (pp. 147–174). New York: Guilford.

Simons, R. L., Chao, W., Conger, R. D., & Elder, G. H., Jr. (2001). Quality of parenting as medi-ator of the effect of childhood defiance on adolescent friendship choices and delinquency: A growth curve analysis. *Journal of Marriage and the Family, 63,* 63–79.

Simons, R. L., Wu, C., Conger, R. D., & Lorenz, F. O. (1994). Two routes to delinquency: Differences between early and late starters in the impact of parenting and deviant peers. *Criminology, 32,* 247–275.

Snyder, J., & Brown, K. (1983). Oppositional behavior and noncompliance in preschool children: Environmental correlates and skills deficits. *Behavioral Assessment, 5,* 333–348.

Snyder, J., Horsch, E., & Childs, J. (1997). Peer relationships of young children: Affiliative choices and the shaping of aggressive behavior. *Journal of Clinical Child Psychology, 26,* 145–156.

Snyder, J., Prichard, J., Schrepferman, L., Patrick, M. R., & Stoolmiller, M. (2004). Child impulsiveness-inattention, early peer experiences, and the development of early onset conduct problems. *Journal of Abnormal Child Psychology, 32,* 579–594.

Snyder, J., Schrepferman, L., Oeser, J., Patterson, G., Stoolmiller, M., Johnson, K., et al. (2005). Deviancy training and association with deviant peers in young children: Occurrence and contribution to early-onset conduct problems. *Development and Psychopathology, 17,* 397–413.

Stattin, H., Gustafson, S. B., & Magnusson, D. (1989). Peer influences on adolescent drinking: A social transition perspective. *Journal of Early Adolescence, 3,* 227–246.

Stattin, H., & Magnusson, D. (1990). *Pubertal maturation in female development.* Hillsdale, NJ: Erlbaum.

Stoolmiller, M. (1994). Antisocial behavior, delinquent peer association and unsupervised wandering for boys: Growth and change from childhood to early adolescence. *Multivariate Behavioral Research, 29,* 263–288.

Sullivan, H. S. (1953). *The interpersonal theory of psychiatry.* New York: Norton.

Sutherland, E. (1947). *Principles of criminology* (3rd ed.). Philadelphia: Lippincott.

Terry, R., & Coie, J. D. (1993, November). *Changing social networks and its impact on juvenile delinquency.* Paper presented at the Annual Meeting of the American Society for Criminology, Phoenix.

Thornberry, T. P. (1998). Membership in youth gangs and involvement in serious and violent offending. In R. Loeber & D. P. Farrington (Eds.), *Serious and violent juvenile offenders: Risk factors and successful interventions* (pp. 147–166). Thousand Oaks, CA:Sage.

Thornberry, T. P., Krohn, M. D., Lizotte, A. J., & Chard-Wierschem, D. (1993). The role of juvenile gangs in facilitating delinquent behavior. *Journal of Research in Crime and Delinquency, 30*, 55–87.

Tremblay, R. E. (2000). The development of aggressive behavior during childhood: What have we learned in the past century? *International Journal of Behavioral Development, 24*, 129–141.

Tremblay, R. E., Mâsse, L. C., Vitaro, F., & Dobkin, P. L. (1995). The impact of friends' deviant behavior on early onset of delinquency: Longitudinal data from 6 to 13 years of age. *Development and Psychopathology, 7*, 649–667.

Tremblay, R. E., & Nagin, D. S. (2005). The developmental origins of physical aggression in humans. In R. E. Tremblay, W. W. Hartup, & J. Archer (Eds.), *Developmental origins of aggression* (pp. 83–106). New York: Guilford Press.

Tremblay, R. E., Nagin, D. S., Séguin, J. R., Zoccolillo, M., Zelazo, P. D., Boivin, M., et al. (2004). Physical aggression during early childhood: Trajectories and predictors. *Pediatrics, 114*(1), e43–50.

Urberg, K. A., Degirmencioglu, S. M., & Pilgrim, C. (1997). Close friend and group influence on adolescent cigarette smoking and alcohol use. *Developmental Psychology, 33*(5), 834–844.

Urberg, K. A., Degirmencioglu, S. M., & Tolson, J. M. (1998). Adolescent friendship selection and termination: The role of similarity. *Journal of Social and Personal Relationships, 15*, 703–710.

Vaillancourt, T. (2005). Indirect aggression among humans: Social construct or evolutionary adaptation? In R. E. Tremblay, W. Hartup, & J. Archer (Eds.), *Developmental origins of aggression* (pp. 158–177). New York: Guilford Press.

van Lier, P. A. C., Wanner, B., & Vitaro, F. (2007). Onset of antisocial behavior, affiliation with deviant friends and childhood maladjustment: A direct test of the childhood versus adolescent onset model. *Development and Psychopathology, 19*, 167–185.

Vitaro, F., & Brendgen, M. (2005). Proactive and reactive aggression: A developmental perspective. In R. E. Tremblay, W. W. Hartup & J. Archer (Eds.), *Developmental origins of aggression* (pp. 178–201). New York, NY: Guilford Press.

Vitaro, F., Brendgen, M., Pagani, L. S., Tremblay, R. E., & McDuff, P. (1999). Disruptive behavior, peer association, and conduct disorder: Testing the developmental links through early intervention. *Development and Psychopathology, 11*, 287–304.

Vitaro, F., Brendgen, M., & Tremblay, R. E. (2000). Influence of deviant friends on delinquency: Searching for moderator variables. *Journal of Abnormal Child Psychology, 28*, 313–325.

Vitaro, F., Brendgen, M., & Wanner, B. (2005). Patterns of affiliation with deviant friends during late childhood and early adolescence: Correlates and consequences. *Social Development, 14*, 82–106.

Vitaro, F., Pedersen, S., & Brendgen, M. (in press). Children's disruptiveness, peer rejection, friends' deviancy and delinquency: A process-oriented approach. *Development and Psychopathology.*

Vitaro, F., Tremblay, R. E., Gagnon, C., & Boivin, M. (1992). Peer rejection from kindergarten to grade 2: Outcomes, correlates, and prediction. *Merrill-Palmer Quarterly, 38*, 382–400.

Vitaro, F., Tremblay, R. E., Kerr, M., Pagani, L. S., & Bukowski, W. M. (1997). Disruptiveness, friends' characteristics, and delinquency: A test of two competing models of development. *Child Development, 68*, 676–689.

Warren, K., Schoppelrey, S., Moberg, D. P., & McDonald, M. (2005). A model of contagion through competition in the aggressive behaviors of elementary school students. *Journal of Abnormal Child Psychology, 33*, 283–292.

Windle, M. (1994). A study of friendship characteristics and problem behavior among middle adolescents. *Child Development, 65*, 1764–1777.

Woodward, L. J., & Fergusson, D. M. (1999). Childhood, peer relationship problems and psychosocial adjustment in late adolescence. *Journal of Abnormal Child Psychology, 27*, 87–104.

Zhang, L., Welte, J. W., & Wieczorek, W. (1999). Youth gangs, drug use, and delinquency. *Journal of Criminal Justice, 27*, 101–109.

CHAPTER 18

Youth Gangs and Violent Behavior

Scott H. Decker

Introduction

Gangs and violence have become interchangeable terms in the past decade. The dramatic increase in youth homicide in the early 1990s led several commentators to conclude that gangs could be implicated in that increase. Indeed, when the term "gangs" is mentioned in the media or among public audiences, the context typically includes a violent event. However, this relationship between youth gangs and violent behavior is far more complex than it might appear. Although the focus in gang violence is often on homicide and gangs are disproportionately involved in homicide compared to other groups, there is more to gang violence than homicide, much more.

This chapter reviews what is known about youth gangs and violent behavior. It begins by considering the definitions of gang violence, a key to understanding the problem. This section of the chapter pays particular attention to the differentiation between gang and nongang violence, noting the salience of who does the defining of such incidents, as well as the impact of such defi-

nitions for problem identification and interventions. The next section of the chapter is devoted to a consideration of gang homicide. Here we present data from both national surveys of law enforcement the Uniform Crime Reports. This discussion leads naturally to the next section of the chapter, instrumentalities associated with gang violence. Here we consider the role that guns and drugs specifically play in gang violence. We then assess what is known about gang violence from the perspective of the medical setting. This is followed by a review of theories of youth gang violence, specifically the role of structural and social process variables. We then move to an examination of the nature of gang violence in non-American settings in order to isolate the factors that are common and unique to the U.S. context. We conclude this chapter with a set of observations about the future of gang violence.

Definition

The key to understanding youth gangs and violent behavior lies in an appreciation of the difficulty of defining the problem. Like many topics in the study of violence, the definitional issues are complicated and engender many debates. The study of gangs has been replete with dilemmas about definition since Thrasher's seminal work in 1927. One of the key methodological issues in the study of gangs has been whether the unit of analysis is the gang, the gang member, or the act (crime) committed by the gang member or members. As Short (1985, 1989) has ably demonstrated, the unit of analysis issue has important implications for what is learned about gangs.

In analyzing youth gangs and violent behavior, the key issue is whether an act of violence was that of a youth gang. The issue sounds simpler than it is, and surprisingly, there is no consensus on what the definition of a gang crime is or should be. At the federal level, the FBI (1999) has offered a sweeping definition of a gang:

> *The Federal Bureau of Investigation defines a Violent Street Gang/Drug Enterprise As: A criminal enterprise having an organizational structure, acting as a continuing criminal conspiracy, which employs violence and any other criminal activity to sustain the enterprise. From the FBI's perspective a gang is a group of individuals involved in continuing criminal activity. A gang DOES NOT have to have similar clothing (colors), tattoos, hand signs, initiation rituals, or even have a specific name such as Crips or Bloods.*

This definition focuses heavily on the organizational aspects of the gang and is inconsistent with what most local law enforcement agencies and researchers understand about gangs.

Local law enforcement agencies define gangs and gang crimes differently. Their definitions fall roughly into two groups. The first approach defines a gang crime based on the participation of a gang member in the act, either as a victim or an offender. This is the definition used by the city of Los Angeles and many other cities in Southern California. This is a broad and inclusive definition that depends only on the ability of an officer or investigator to determine whether

a victim or offender is a documented gang member. Other cities, such as Chicago, use a much more restrictive definition, relying instead on the motive for an offense. These definitions are referred to as "motive-based" definitions. Thus an offense that may involve a gang member, both as victim and offender, may only be classified as gang related if the motive has something to do with the intentions or desires of the gang or furthers its interests. Such acts often include battles over gang turf, retaliation against rival gangs or gang members, or crimes committed to generate economic gain for the gang.

The use of a motive-based definition requires considerably more information and investigation than the use of a member-based definition of gang crime. There are other consequences to the choice of definition of gang crime as well. Klein and Maxson (Klein, Maxson, & Cunningham, 1991; Maxson & Klein, 1990, 1996) have examined homicides in Los Angeles using both the Los Angeles gang member definition and the Chicago gang motive definition. Their findings are instructive. The member-based definition yields nearly twice as many gang-related homicides as the narrower gang motive definition. This finding underscores the dramatic difference that definition makes in the study of gang violence. Equally important, however was the finding that, regardless of the definition that was used, the substantive characteristics of each group of homicides did not differ. Thus they found that the demographic characteristics of the individuals involved (race, age, and gender) and the situational characteristics (guns, location, victim offender relationship) of the events for motive and member-based definitions were the same.

Homicide

There are several sources of data to assess the magnitude of gang homicide, though all of them have some basis in police reports. It is important to note that, because there is no national source of gang crime reporting, the picture regarding gang crime and violence must be constructed by compiling a variety of sources. Maxson (1999) credits Walter Miller (1982) with the first attempt to bring data on gang homicide together in a single source. Based on a limited sample of nine gang cities, his work demonstrated that gang homicides represented a significant part of the homicide problem in these cities. A number of other researchers (Curry, Ball, & Decker, 1996; Maxson et al., 1995) also have surveyed cities to determine the number of gang homicides and gang members reported by law enforcement. This task was formalized by the National Youth Gang Center (NYGC) beginning in 1995. Their work builds on the foundation provided by Curry and Maxson, who serve as consultants to the NYGC in its annual survey of law enforcement.

The Office of Juvenile Justice and Delinquency Prevention (OJJDP) funds the National Youth Gang Center. Looking across these studies of gang homicide, several patterns are evident. First the *pattern* of gang homicide appears similar to that for youth homicide in the United States, experiencing a dramatic increase in the early 1990s and leveling off by the end of the 1990s. Despite this pattern, the overall *level* of gang homicide is considerably higher than for other subcategories of homicide, including domestics and robbery, reinforcing the consistent finding that gang membership is a significant risk factor for involvement in violence, both as a perpetrator and a victim (Decker & Van Winkle, 1996; Thornberry et al., 2001). Finally, the individual and situational *characteristics* of gang homicides are distinctive from those of homicides in general. Gang homicides are far more likely to involve males, racial or ethnic group minority members, and guns and to occur outside and with multiple participants than are other homicides. This distinctive character is the key thesis for this chapter.

The NYGC survey data on gang homicide begin with the year 1996, when 1,330 gang homicides were reported by cities with populations over 100,000 (Curry, Egley, & Howell, 2004). This figure declined steadily to its level of 1,082 in 1999 and 1,080 in 2000.

However a dramatic increase was observed over the next 3 years, with the number of gang homicides increasing to 1,451 for 2003 (again in cities with a population over 100,000), the highest level recorded by the NYGC survey methodology. This is an increase of 34% over 1999, the nadir in the trend. It is important to note that this increase occurred during a time when national homicide levels were falling since their peaks in the early 1990s, making the increase in gang homicides more troubling and more significant and reinforcing the distinctive character of gang homicides.

Historically, Chicago and Los Angeles have stood out for their exceptionally high levels of gang violence, particularly gang homicide. To a large extent, changes in gang homicide figures for cities over 100,000 population are driven by changes in gang homicide in Chicago and Los Angeles. In 2003, Los Angeles and Chicago accounted for 39% of all gang homicides reported nationally for cities over 100,000 population, and in 2002 they accounted for 53% of all gang homicides, the largest proportion in the eight years that the NYGC has counted gang homicides (Curry et al., 2004). However, the dramatic increase between 1999 and 2003 in gang homicides cannot be attributed wholly to Los Angeles and Chicago, as there was an increase in gang homicides in all other jurisdictions as well.

Because of their prominent role in gang homicide, Los Angeles and Chicago have been the site of a considerable number of studies of gang homicide. Maxson (1999) provides a comparison in trends in gang homicides for these two cities that documents a dramatic increase in both the number of gang homicides and percent of all homicides represented by gang homicides since 1980. The last year in the time series for both cities, 1995, also represents the peak year for the proportion of all homicides classified as gang homicides in these two cities. Forty-five percent of all homicides in Los Angeles County could be classified as gang related, whereas in Chicago, roughly one quarter of all homicides were classified as gang related. These comparisons illustrate the magnitude of the gang problem for these municipal areas, as well as the impact of using ways of defining whether an offense is related to gang involvement. Tita and Abrahamse (2004) examined gang homicide in Los Angeles County for the period 1981–2001. They document small declines in the percent of all homicides represented by gang homicides since 1995, until the years 2000 and 2001 when the percentages jumped to 41 and 48%, respectively. In an interesting analysis, they calculate what the expected gang homicide rate should be based on the demographic characteristics of the population in Los Angeles County and contrast that with the State of California. Their results show that the state of California has about one third the number of homicides that would be expected, but that Los Angeles County has more than twice that number when controlling for age and race characteristics of county residents. Tita and Abrahamse (2004) also show that some forms of homicide, specifically homicides involving rape and nongun felony homicides, have declined during the period of increasing gang homicides and that other forms of homicides, such as "arguments with a stranger, gun involved" (p. 15) have leveled off.

It is important to underscore that gang members are overrepresented both as offenders and victims in homicides. Gang membership has been identified as a risk factor for violent victimization, a fact that in turn leads to a large volume of retaliatory violence. Indeed, an ethnographic study of gang members in St. Louis (Decker & Van Winkle, 1996) found that nearly one quarter of the 99 members of the initial sample had been murdered within a 3-year period following the conclusion of the study.

These results suggest that gangs represent something different when it comes to violence; that is, gangs make a dramatic difference in the level and nature of violence, particularly lethal violence. This chapter examines that distinctive character of gang violence, specifically considering the role of instrumentalities, social structure, and social processes.

Instrumentalities

This chapter has documented a number of correlates that distinguish gang from nongang homicide, including a prior relationship between the victim and the offender, the occurrence of the event out doors, the involvement of multiple suspects, and the presence of firearms and drugs.

Firearms

The disproportionate role of firearms in gang-related homicides and gang violence has been well documented in criminological research. In their 11-city study of arrestees, Decker, Pennell, and Caldwell (1996) found that self-reported gang members were more likely than other subgroups to report wanting, owning, using, and being victimized by firearms. Similarly, Bjerregaard and Lizotte (1995) and Lizotte, Tesoriero, Thornberry, and Krohn (1994) report that gun ownership remains one of the strongest correlates of gang membership and gang violence. Lizotte et al. (1994) report that youth who carry guns for protection are five times more likely to be in a gang than youth who own guns for sporting purposes. Youth who carry guns are also more attractive gang members for recruitment purposes, and gang members are more likely to carry guns outside their homes compared to other youth with similar backgrounds from comparable neighborhoods (Bjerregaard & Lizotte, 1995). Firearms are the weapon of choice among gang members, a preference for ownership that has increased over the course of the past four decades (Howell, 1998). This fact appears to be linked closely to the increased lethality of gang assaults (Block & Block, 1993).

Firearms are intimately linked to a particular and highly publicized form of gang violence, drive-by shootings. Firearms capable of firing multiple projectiles (typically semi-automatic pistols or rifles) are integral to the execution of such violent activities by gang members. In Los Angeles (Hutson, Anglin, & Eckstein, 1996) one estimate is that during a 5-year period one third of gang homicides occurred during a drive-by shooting. Drive-by shootings exemplify many features of gang violence as described by Sanders (1994). He characterizes gang life as one in which "the violent aspects of gang life are always there – either defensively or as an offensive option" (p. 146), a view echoed for St. Louis gang members whose lives are characterized by "threat" from rival gangs, one's own gang, and the police (Decker & Van Winkle, 1996). What makes the drive-by shooting the quintessential gang crime is that it is unpredictable, generates considerable fear among gang and nongang members in communities, and creates intimidation among gang and community residents alike (Howell, 1998).

Drugs

The involvement of youth gang members in drug sales increased dramatically, coinciding with the widespread availability of crack cocaine in the late 1980s. This dramatic increase occurred at a time when the urban underclass also deepened in many large American cities. There is considerable overlap among drug use, drug trafficking, and involvement in violent crime among gang members. Howell and Decker (1999) document the considerable overlap between involvement in drug markets and the use of violence. Block and Block (1993) identify disputes over drug turf as being at the heart of a considerable amount of gang violence. Similarly, Klein, Maxson, and Cunningham (1991) document the substantial involvement of gang members in drug sales. A host of ethnographic studies (Decker & Van Winkle, 1996; Hagedorn, 1998, 1994; Vigil, 1988) have documented that gang members are extensively involved in the sale of drugs. Drug use among gang members has also been reported in a host of studies (Decker & Van Winkle, 1994; Hagedorn, 1989; Howell & Decker, 1999). Despite this involvement a causal relationship between gangs and drugs sales is not supported by the empirical literature.

There are two competing views about the role of gangs and gang members in street drug sales. The first view is that street gangs are well-organized and effective mechanisms for the distribution of illegal drugs and invest drug sales profits into their gang. An alternative explanation posits that gang and gang member drug sales are seldom well organized, with gang members operating independently of their gangs in drug sales.

Two issues that are critical to understanding the link between gangs and drugs and that have implications for gang violence are the organizational aspects of gangs and the nature of the street drug market. Skolnick (1990) and Sanchez-Jankowski (1991) describe gangs as formal-rational organizations with a leadership structure, roles, rules, common goals, and control over members. On the other hand, Klein, Maxson, and Cunningham (1991), Klein and Maxson (1994), and Decker and Van Winkle (1994, 1996) all describe gangs as loosely confederated groups that lack much internal cohesion or formal characteristics of organization.

To control drug sales effectively, gangs must possess several characteristics. First, gangs must have an organizational structure, with a hierarchy of leaders, roles, and rules. Second, gangs must have group goals that are widely shared among members. Third, gangs must promote stronger allegiance to the larger organization than to subgroups within it. Finally, gangs must possess the means to control and discipline their members to produce compliance with group goals.

Most gang members sell drugs, though the level at which they sell may not be increased by gang membership alone. It is clear that involvement in drug trafficking is a risk factor for becoming the victim or, for that matter, the perpetrator of violence. Despite that involvement, conflict between gangs accounts for more gang violence, including homicide than does involvement in the drug trade. The work of Maxson, Gordon, and Klein (1985); Klein, Maxson, and Cunningham (1988, 1991); and Maxson (1995, 1998) documents that the relationship between drug trafficking and gang homicide is not causal and generally not strong. This finding has been supported in research from

Boston, St. Louis, and Chicago (Howell & Decker, 1999). That said, increased involvement in entrepreneurial activities (Coughlin & Venkatesh, 2003) appears to be related to increased involvement in violence, particularly in cities with more organized gangs.

Theories of Gang Violence

Theories of gang violence have either emphasized community-level explanations or approaches that emphasize the role of social processes. The former theories underscore the role of community structure and other social variables, including measures of community social control, in the generation of patterns and trends in homicide. Such explanations typically include measures of racial composition, concentrated poverty, gun availability, and the presence of drug markets and drug use in the neighborhood or city as the unit of analysis (Rosenfeld, Bray, & Egley, 1999). Such approaches often use spatial analysis (Blumstein, Cohen, Cork, Engberg, & Tita, 2002; Cohen & Tita, 1999). Explanations that emphasize collective behavior point to the role of social processes, such as contagion and retaliation, and depend more often on ethnographic or case study materials. The former approach emphasizes the spatial distribution of individual and neighborhood characteristics, whereas the latter highlights dynamic social processes.

Structural Explanations

Curry and Spergel (1988) examined homicide and gang delinquency among both Latinos and African-Americans in Chicago. They conclude that gang homicides have a significantly different ecological pattern than do nongang homicides and conform to classic models of social disorganization and poverty. They argue that conceptualizing gang groups as a function of mobility patterns is a productive conceptual means of understanding gang homicides. Thus in neighborhoods in the process of undergoing shifts in population composition, overall mobility, and

economic change, social disorganization was likely to be found. This disorganization was subsequently linked to gang homicide and other forms of gang crime, particularly violence. This conclusion was reached by examining a host of structural variables, including race/ethnicity and poverty.

The strong spatial concentration of gang homicides in neighborhoods characterized by poverty and social change is a consistent theme throughout the literature (Block, 1991; Block & Block, 1993; Kennedy, Braga, & Piehl, 1998; Rosenfeld et al., 1999; Wilson, 1987). In Chicago, a chronic gang city, Block and Block (1993) found very strong spatial concentrations of gang homicide. They conclude that "the rate of street-gang motivated crime in the 2 most dangerous areas was 76 times that of the 2 safest" (p. 1). Gang rivalries were at the core of the primary motivation in most of the gang homicides recorded in this study. Blumstein et al. (2002) conducted national, cross-city, and within-city analyses of youth homicide from the late 1980s into the mid-1990s. They documented a process of structural diffusion of youth and gang violence across and within cities that involved the growth of street-level crack cocaine sales, which in turn produced a heightened need for firearms to protect the product, profit, and purveyors of this drug. The need for firearms protection for this illicit industry fueled an escalation of armed youth, many of whom were involved in gangs.

The spatial concentration of gang violence has been documented in a number of other cities, particularly Boston (Kennedy et al., 1998). Findings from Boston for gang homicide correspond with those reported by Block for Chicago and by Maxson (1999) for Los Angeles. In Boston, Kennedy et al. (1998) report an especially strong spatial concentration among gang homicides and document that with a very useful sociogram depicting the conflict between gangs. Similarly, Tita, Riley, and Greenwood (2002) have documented the strong spatial concentration of gang violence in the South Central neighborhoods of Los Angeles and the role of intergang conflict. Such events disproportionately involve gun assaults, firearms, and drugs. This finding is similar to that reported by Rosenfeld, Bray, and Egley (1999) for St. Louis, as well as by Cohen and Tita (1999) and Cohen, Cork, Engberg and Tita (1998).

Social Processes

Studies of violence have increasingly focused on the social processes involved in the generation of such violence (Loftin, 1984). This type of analysis is concerned with the dynamics of interactions that lead to initial and, perhaps more important, retaliatory acts of gang violence. This level of analysis is consistent with the middle-range explanation encouraged by Short (1985, 1989), who underscored the role of group process and social-psychological variables in the understanding of gangs and gang activities. In the context of understanding violence, such variables are particularly important as much gang violence has a retaliatory character. It is often difficult to determine the initial incident that motivated a specific act of violence. Although protecting neighborhood turf, drug turf, or both (Block & Block, 1993; Decker & Van Winkle, 1996; Sanchez-Jankowski, 1991; Sanders, 1994) is associated with a large fraction of gang violence, this correlation does not shed light on the motivations for specific incidents of gang violence. Recently, such explanations have looked to patterns of interaction in an effort to better account for the underlying mechanisms involved in the escalation and decline of incidents of gang violence (see Howell, 1998, for a useful summary of this research).

Decker (1996) identified collective behavior processes in gang violence among St. Louis gang members. He observed spikes in violence in gang violence over time that were often quite dramatic in magnitude. Such spikes are not consistent with a "smooth" process of increase or decline. He argued for the role of "threat" in the explanation of gang homicides, especially the retaliatory character of many gang homicides. The emphasis on retaliation in such approaches is important, as it has been identified as a common feature in much gang violence. Such a view emanates from Short's (1989) emphasis on identifying the group aspects of gang violence, rather than isolating the individual characteristics of such acts. This approach better accounts for the observation that gang violence can escalate rapidly, as one event precipitates another. Such an approach emphasizes the dynamic social processes that resemble collective behavior among informal groups and lead to retaliatory violence between gangs and gang members. Decker (1996) and Decker and Curry (2002) argue that such explanations are consistent with both the organizational and normative features of youth gangs.

Vigil (2004) provides an explanation for some of the social psychological processes by which individuals come to participate in "senseless" acts of gang violence. The characteristics of these acts are such that the participants often refer to them as "loco." Vigil argues that in the most marginalized communities – whether that marginalization is a product of economic, cultural, or racial and ethnic marginalization (or all three) – community and social norms lose their potency for the control of behavior. Many individuals in marginalized communities also may experience a series of personal tragedies, including the violent or premature death of a family member or loved one, and the accumulation of such experiences takes a psychological toll on these individuals (Pynoos & Nader, 1988). This is particularly true for individuals who have experienced such personal trauma and who are gang members, as the gang is an effective vehicle for encouraging and supporting involvement in extreme acts of seemingly senseless violence. Thus from the perspective of a marginalized individual living in a marginalized community who has suffered considerable personal trauma, the gang can be an effective mechanism for supporting violent aggression in what appear to be irrational ways.

Support for the "violence escalation hypothesis" can also be found in Klein and Maxson (1987, p. 219) and in Maxson (1999). Their research documents that gang violence can best be understood as a series of reciprocal actions between rival gangs, each of which draws another, often sharper reaction. This reciprocity is reflected in gang rivalries. Such rivalries can be the consequence of a number of factors (drug turf, neighborhood dominance, symbolic ascendance, etc.) that over time are sublimated to the more immediate need to dominate turf, a rival, or both. Klein and Maxson also report that gangs have weak internal structures and generate little cohesion among their members. As such, they are generally ineffective mechanisms for generating compliance among members, thus failing to control acts of violence.

Further support for the role of collective behavior as an explanation for gang homicide comes from the work of Pizzaro and McGloin (2004). They examined homicide incidents occurring over 5 years in Newark, New Jersey. Using the Los Angeles definition of gang homicide as "gang related" they compared the explanatory power of social disorganization and escalation variables to assess the relative importance of each in the explanation of gang homicides. Consistent with much prior research on gang violence, they found that the use of firearms, the event taking place outside, the involvement of multiple suspects, and an acquaintance relationship between victims and offenders statistically distinguished gang from nongang homicides. Measures of the escalation/social process hypothesis included a threat against the group (gang) or status of the group that led to retaliatory function. Their logistic regression models documented the superiority of measures of social process compared to structural variables in explaining the difference between gang and nongang homicides.

Theories emphasizing the social processes involved in gang violence typically underscore the lack of structural control in gangs (Decker & Curry, 2002), particularly the weak control that gangs have over their members, and the role that rivalries can play in leading to violence within and between gangs. In addition, these studies document the role that the transitory nature of gang membership plays in such rivalries, reinforcing the notion that gangs may not be organizations capable of controlling the behavior of their members.

Prison Gang Violence

Imprisonment often follows involvement in violent acts by gang members. The increased use of zero tolerance policies regarding firearms violence, the subsequent dramatic rise in imprisonment during the 1990s and the proliferation of street gang violence resulted in a large number of gang members going to prison or juvenile detention and correctional facilities. One national estimate places the proportion of confined juveniles who claim gang membership at 40% (Parent, Leiter, Livens, Wentworth, & Stephen, 1994), and another placed the figure at 78% (Knox & Tromanhauser, 1991). The Sheley and Wright (1995) survey of inner-city high-school students and residents of juvenile correctional facilities concluded that just over two thirds (68%) of residents were gang members. Adult gang members also constitute an important part of the prison population (Camp & Camp, 1985; Ralph & Marquart, 1991) with dramatic increases in the 1990s.

Prison gangs are more structured than street gangs and have much stronger leadership. The rank-and-file membership often has several gradations, making prison gangs look much like organized crime groups. Research on street gangs shows that where profits are at stake, violence is often the outcome. Inside prisons, the same pattern appears, as prison gangs are heavily involved in prison violence (Ingraham & Wellford, 1987). Camp and Camp (1985) noted that prison gang members comprised 3% of the prison population, but caused 50% or more of the prison violence. In prison, gangs can have a virtual monopoly on drug sales and other gang-related services, such as gambling and prostitution (Fleisher, 1989), which often leads to competition between gangs for illegal markets (Fong, Vogel, & Buentello, 1992).

Prison also appears to compel many young men toward gang membership. Imprisonment may strengthen ties between gang members and their gangs, as gang affiliation is one of the few remaining sources of identification that may remain for incarcerated gang members. Prison plays an increasingly important role in gang violence. As gang members become more involved in crime, their likelihood of going to prison increases. Street gangs may come to be directed by and influenced by prison gang culture. Going to prison also provides gang members with additional status when they return to the street.

Medical Settings

The volume of gang violence, particularly in Los Angeles, has had repercussions for the medical profession. Not surprisingly, a large number of the victims of gang violence require medical attention and end up in trauma facilities. This outcome has provided another opportunity to differentiate gang violence from other forms of violence.

Dealing with gunshot wounds is not new to the medical profession or to trauma centers. However, gunshot wounds caused by gang violence appear to be different both qualitatively and quantitatively from other gunshot wounds. A 29-month investigation of gang shootings in Los Angeles County (Song, Naude, Gilmore, & Bongard, 1996) revealed several important patterns in gang violence that help differentiate it from other forms of violence. Trauma registry records were used to identify the population, with links to law enforcement data regarding gang membership. Gang members were the victims in 272 of the 856 gunshot (32%) injuries during this time. Fifty-five of the gang victims were pediatric, and the rest were adults. The overwhelming majority of these gunshot victims (89%) were males, and less than 5% were classified as Whites. Trauma and Injury severity scores were extremely high for this group, and 9% of the gunshot victims died of their wounds. Forty-three percent of the gunshot wound victims

underwent emergency surgery, and interestingly the vast majority (86%) entered the hospital during hours when staffing was low, causing considerable stress to patient care. The financial toll of the gunshot wounds suffered by gang members was high as well. The cost of providing medical services to these 272 gang-related gunshot victims was just under $5 million ($4,828,828), and 55% of the victims had no third-party health insurance reimbursement. Ninety-one percent of these individuals suffered some form of disability. Together these data present some estimate of the toll placed on trauma centers by gang violence, at least in Los Angeles.

Additional research on gang violence from a medical perspective also comes from Los Angeles. Hutson, Anglin, and Pratts (1994) examined drive-by shootings. Using police data, they examined the universe of victims in drive-by shootings involving someone under the age of 18 for the nature and extent of their injuries, as well as to establish prevalence estimates for such incidents. During calendar year 1991, 673 juveniles were shot at in drive-by shootings; of these, 63% had a gunshot wound, and 5% died from their injuries. These juveniles represent 38% of the total victims (1,548) in drive-by shootings in Los Angeles during 1991. Consistent with the work by Song et al., (1996), the vast majority of victims were either Black or Hispanic (97%, combined). Nearly three quarters (71%) of the drive-by victims were gang members. The three most prevalent situational characteristics of gang shootings were the location (the inner city on public streets), time of day (night), and the type of firearm used (handguns in 71% of the cases). Hutson and his colleagues report that gang-related homicides among adolescents in Los Angeles represent over half (53%) of all adolescent murders, and between 1 and 2 children in 10 in Los Angeles have witnessed a homicide.

Hutson, Anglin, and Mallon (1992) found that drive-by shootings are not random and that many aspects of this form of youth gang violence are highly patterned. Specifically, the location (outside on inner-city streets), gender and race representations

(Hispanic and African American males), choice of weapon (handguns), and ages (highly concentrated among teenagers) are all consistent features across the majority of drive-by shootings. As such, they argue that interventions that are culturally specific and address specific risk factors are needed. In addition, they argue (Hutson et al., 1992) that such injuries can be prevented through effective use of public health strategies. A similar perspective has been endorsed by Hixon (1999), who argues for the use of screening questions in emergency rooms to assess the level of gang involvement and subsequent risk for violent victimization. Such information, from Hixon's perspective can profitably be used for crafting emergency room interventions that involve counseling.

The European Situation

Until recently, the academic and policy focus on gangs has been almost exclusively on the United States. Indeed, the United States has the longest history of youth gangs, and violence among American youth gangs dwarfs the levels in other countries. But that focus has changed dramatically over the past decade. Klein, Kerner, Maxson, and Weitekamp (2001) edited a recent book that documented gangs with similar characteristics to American youth gangs in nearly a dozen countries. Similarly, Covey (2003) reports the presence of gangs in North America, Europe, Central and South America, Russia and Asia, Africa, the Middle East, and Australia and the Pacific Islands. These studies note the role that globalization, modernization, and immigration have played in the transmission of American cultural images and institutional practices around the world. However, early studies indicate that although gangs in Europe (about which we know the most with the best sources of information) resemble American youth gangs in many ways, they participate in violence at much lower levels.

Despite this difference, the migration of American gang styles and cultural symbols to Europe, South American, Asia and Africa

has grown dramatically in the past decade. Many studies of gangs in the international context have underscored the role of popular culture and the media in spreading and popularizing gangs and gang membership, though clearly the growth of immigrant groups in large cities can also be linked to these trends. It is clear that the same sorts of youth culture and affiliational processes at work in the United States occur in many European contexts. However, we generally lack the same sort of police surveys in Europe that would serve to better document levels of street gang violence and make comparisons with the United States more appropriate.

Violence plays a central role in creating solidarity within American youth gangs. It appears that, in the European setting, ethnic identity can be substituted to a large extent for the role of violence. This is not to say, however, that gangs in Europe do not engage in violence. The work of Van Gemert and Fleisher (2005) in The Hague and Amsterdam underscores the instrumental role that violent thefts play in gang solidarity among Dutch gangs. Similarly, Lien (2005a,b) documents the prevalence and role of violence by gangs comprised largely of ethnic minorities in Oslo. She reports that one gang member describes the gang as "hard men, like iron" (2005a, p. 35), and that fighting and robbery are more common among youth gangs than other Norwegian youth. Fighting is reported to be common among street gangs in Genoa, Italy (Gatti, Angelini, Marengo, Melchiorre, & Sasso, 2005), Russians of German descent in Germany (Weitekamp, Reich, & Kerner, 2005), and particularly among Russian youth gangs (Shashkin & Salagaev, 2005; Shashkin, Salagaev, Sherbakova, & Touryanskiy, 2005).

The emergence of youth gangs in Russia provides perhaps the closest parallels to the American situation, with the use of guns, armed robbery and fighting being more common than in other European settings, particularly among gangs of older individuals. Distinguishing between adult and youth gangs in the Russian context is important. Although turf is not as important a source of rivalry among Russian gangs as in many American cities, it does play an important role in many gangs. In addition, masculinity plays a critical role in the generation and maintenance of gang violence. Groups of men with a history of fighting often evolve into gangs in the Russian context. Shashkin and his colleagues (2005) have documented extensive involvement in violence among Russian gangs, particularly in Moscow and Kazan. Indeed, their work has documented a particular form of gangs that has come to be known as "gangs of the Kazan type," which regularly engage in violence. They describe in detail the predatory activities of Russian youth gangs that are active in the Middle Volga region of Russia. the majority of illegal activity conducted by these groups is predatory – selling drugs, organizing small prostitution rings, and robbery – youth gangs do engage in violence. Shashkin et al. (2005) note the impact of several economic changes in Russia in creating a market for illegal goods and the consequent need for groups of young men to provide protection and enforcement for shopowners who dealt in those illegal goods. It is clear from these emerging descriptions of Russian gangs that the links between adult and youth gangs, the involvement in organized crime, and the penetration of organized crime into youth street gang culture provide a rapidly changing – and increasingly violent – context for Russian youth gangs.

What appears to set European gangs apart from American youth gangs with regards to violence, at least at this point in time, is their access to guns, extensive involvement in drug sales, and defense of turf. Levels of European youth gang violence are considerably lower than in the United States. Clearly, the absence of an established history of gangs, reduced access to guns, lower levels of overall violence, and lower social disparities between social classes are important aspects of the explanation for this reduced level of violence. However, there are signs of increasing street gang violence in Europe, particularly as immigration and globalization pressures increase.

Conclusions

This chapter has documented the involvement of youth gangs in violent behavior. Regardless of how a gang is defined and of how gang-related crime is defined a large proportion of violence is related to gang activity. It appears that this pattern of involvement has increased since the turn of the 21st century. It is no longer possible to argue that the more extreme forms of gang violence are confined largely to the Los Angeles and Chicago areas, as cities across the country report a substantial part of their homicide problem as being related to gangs. Gang violence embodies several distinctive characteristics that make it distinguishable from other forms of violence. First, the participants in gang violence share in common a large number of demographic and situational characteristics. Males, inner-city residents and Hispanics and African Americans are disproportionately involved in gang violence, both as victims and as perpetrators. Firearms are used in gang violence more than in other types of violence, and there seems to be a preference for handguns in such violent crimes. Gang violence is most likely to take place out of doors, where it can be observed and felt by a large circle of individuals beyond the perpetrator and their intended victim. Gang violence, more than other forms of violence is likely to involve multiple victims and multiple suspects.

Although structural variables, such as concentrated economic and social disadvantage, are associated with the presence of gang violence, social processes also play an important role in such events. Because a large proportion of gang violence involves retaliation between individuals with an ongoing feud of some sort, understanding the processes that create and perpetuate gang violence is an important task. Much gang violence appears to have a contagious character, spreading from one neighborhood to another and outliving the initial source of the problem. These characteristics of gang violence have consequences for the increase in and spread of prison gang violence. The links between street gangs and prison gangs is most important in this regard, with many incidents in prison linked to the street and many incidents of street violence linked to prison gangs. The role of prison gangs has especially important consequences for current re-entry initiatives. Involvement in prison gangs may thwart community re-integration and make transition to the community more difficult for such individuals. Gang violence has had increasingly important consequences for the medical profession, particularly those who work in trauma or emergency settings. In these settings the costs and volume of cases have become excessive in some jurisdictions. Finally, the problems of youth gangs and violent behavior are no longer confined to the United States. Youth gang violence, particularly in the form of assault and robbery, can be found throughout western and eastern Europe, and increasingly in Central and South America. The prospects for youth gangs becoming an entrenched part of global youth culture is enhanced by this spread of gangs.

References

Bjerregaard, B., & Lizotte, L. (1995). Gun ownership and gang membership. *Journal of Criminal Law and Criminology*, 86, 37–58.

Block, C. R. (1991). Gang homicide in Chicago: Patterns over time, area of city, and type of victim. Presented to the Midwestern Criminal Justice Association. Chicago, Illinois.

Block, C. & R. Block. (1993). Street gang crime in Chicago. Research in Brief. National Institute of Justice. Washington, DC.

Blumstein, A., Cohen, J., Cork, D., Engberg, J., & Tita, G. (2002). *Diffusion processes in homicide*. Washington, DC: National Institute of Justice.

Camp, G. M., & Camp, C. G. (1985). *Prison gangs: Their extent, nature, and impact on prisons*. Washington, DC: U.S. Government Printing Office.

Cohen, J., Cork, D., Engberg, J., & Tita, G. (1998). The role of drug markets and gangs in local homicide rates. *Journal of Homicide Studies*, 2, 241–262.

Cohen, J. & Tita, G. E. (1999). Spatial Diffusion in Homicide: An Exploratory Analysis. *Journal of Quantitative Criminology*, 15, 451–493.

Coughlin, B. C., & Venkatesh, S. A. (2003). The urban street gang after 1970. *Annual Review of Sociology*, 29, 41–64.

Covey, H. C. (2003). *Street gangs throughout the world*. Springfield, IL: Charles C. Thomas.

Curry, G. D., Ball, R. A. & S. H. Decker. (1996). *Update on gang crime and law enforcement recordkeeping: Report of the 1994 NIJ extended national assessment survey of law enforcement anti-gang information resources. Research Report. National Criminal Justice Reference Service*. Washington, DC: US Department of Justice.

Curry, G. D., Egley, H., & Howell, J. C. (2004). *Youth gang homicide trends in the National Youth Gang Survey*. Paper Presented at the American Society of Criminology Meetings. Nashville, TN.

Curry, G. D. & Spergel, I. (1988). Gang homicide, delinquency, and community. *Criminology*, 26, 381–405.

Decker, S. H. (1996). Collective and normative features of gang violence. *Justice Quarterly*, 13(2), 243–264.

Decker, S. H., & Curry, G. D. (2002). Gangs, gang homicides and gang loyalty: Organized crimes or disorganized criminals? *Journal of Criminal Justice*, 30, 343–352.

Decker, S. H., S. P. Pennel, & A. Caldwell (1996). Arrestees and Firearms. Final Report National Institute of Justice. Washington, DC.

Decker, S. H., & Van Winkle, B. (1994). Slingin' dope: The role of gangs and gang members in drug sales. *Justice Quarterly*, 11, 583–684.

Decker, S. H., & Van Winkle, B. (1996). *Life in the gang; Family, friends and violence*. New York: Cambridge University Press.

Federal Bureau of Investigation. (1999). *FBI gang alert*. Washington, DC.

Fleisher, M. S. (1989). *Warehousing violence*. Newbury Park, CA: Sage.

Fong, R. S., Vogel, R. E., & Buentello, S. (1992). Prison gang dynamics: A look inside the Texas Department of Corrections. In P. J. Benekos & A. V. Merlo (Eds.), *Corrections: Dilemmas and directions* (pp. 57–77). Cincinnati: Anderson Publishing.

Gatti, U., Angelini, F., Marengo, G., Melchiorre, N., & Sasso, M. (2005). An old fashioned gang in Genoa. In S. Decker & F. Weerman (Eds.), *European street gangs and troublesome youth groups* (pp. 63–102). Walnut Creek, CA: Alta Mira.

Hagedorn, J. M. (1988). *People and folks: Gangs, crime and the underclass in a Rust Belt city.* Chicago: Lakeview Press.

Hagedorn, J. M. (1994). Homeboys, dope fiends, legits and new jacks. *Criminology, 32,* 197–217.

Hixon, A. L. (1999). Preventing street gang violence. *American Family Physician, 125,* 1–7.

Howell, J. C. (1998). *Youth gangs: An overview.* Washington, DC: U.S. Department of Justice, Office of Juvenile Justice and Delinquency Prevention.

Howell, J. C., & Decker, S. H. (1999). *The youth gangs, drugs, and violence connection.* Washington, DC: U.S. Department of Justice, Office of Juvenile Justice and Delinquency Prevention.

Howell, J. C., & Lynch, J. P. (2000). *Youth gangs in schools.* Washington, DC: U.S. Department of Justice, Office of Juvenile Justice and Delinquency Prevention.

Hutson, H. R., Anglin, D., & Eckstein, M. (1996). Drive-by shootings by violent street gangs in Los Angeles: A five-year review from 1989 to 1993. *Academic Emergency Medicine, 3,* 300–303.

Hutson, H. R., Anglin, D., & Mallon, W. (1992). Injuries and deaths from gang violence: They are preventable. *Annals of Emergency Medicine, 21,* 1234–1236.

Hutson, H. R., Anglin, D., & Pratts, M. J. (1994, February 3). Adolescents and children injured or killed in drive-by shootings in Los Angeles. *New England Journal of Medicine,* 324–327.

Ingraham, B. L., & Wellford, C. F. (1987). The totality of conditions test in eighth-amendment litigation. In S. D. Gottfredson & S. McConville (Eds.), *America's correctional crisis: Prison populations and public policy* (pp. 13–36). New York: Greenwood Press.

Kennedy, D. M., Braga, A. A., & Piehl, A. M. (1998). The (un)known universe: Mapping gangs and gang violence in Boston. In D. Weisburd & J. T. McEwen (Eds.), *Crime mapping and crime prevention* (pp. 219–262). New York: Criminal Justice Press.

Klein, M. W., Kerner, H.-J., Maxson, C. L., & Weitekamp, E. G. M. (2001). *The eurogang paradox: Street gangs and youth groups in the U.S. and Europe.* Dordrecht: Kluwer.

Klein, M. W., & Maxson, C. L. (1989). Street gang violence. In N. A. Weiner & M. E. Wolfgang (Eds.), *Violent crime, violent criminals* (pp. 198–234). Newbury Park, CA: Sage.

Klein, M. W. & C. L. Maxson. (1994). Gangs and Cocaine Trafficking. In D. MacKenzie and C. Uchida (eds.), *Drugs and the Criminal Justice System.* Newbury Park, CA: Sage Publications, 1994.

Klein, M. W., Maxson, C. L., & Cunningham, L. C. (1991). Crack, street gangs, and violence. *Criminology, 29*(4), 623–650.

Knox, G. W., & Tromanhauser, E. D. (1991). Gangs and their control in adult correctional institutions. *Prison Journal, 71,* 15–22.

Lien, I.-L. (2005a). Criminal gangs and their connections: Metaphors, definitions, and structures. In S. Decker & F. Weerman (Eds.), *European street gangs and troublesome youth groups* (pp. 35–62). Walnut Creek, CA: Alta Mira.

Lien, I.-L. (2005b). The role of crime acts in constituting the gang's mentality. In S. Decker & F. Weerman (Eds.), *European street gangs and troublesome youth groups* (pp. 137–164). Walnut Creek, CA: Alta Mira.

Lizotte, A., Tesoriero, J. M., Thornberry, T. P., & Krohn, M. D. (1994). Patterns of adolescent firearms ownership and use. *Justice Quarterly, 11,* 51–73.

Loftin, C. (1984). Assaultive violence as contagious process. *Bulletin of the New York Academy of Medicine, 62,* 550–555.

Maxson, C. L. (2002). Play groups no longer: Urban street gangs in the Los Angeles region. In M. J. Dear (Ed.), *From Chicago to L.A.: Making sense of theory* (pp. 235–266). Thousand Oaks, CA: Sage.

Maxson, C. L. (1999). Gang homicide: A review and extension of the literature. In D. Smith & M. A. Zahn (Eds.), *Homicide: A sourcebook of social research* (pp. 239–236). Newbury Park, CA: Sage.

Maxson, C. L. (1998). Gang homicide: A review and extension of the literature. In M. Dwayne Smith and Margaret A. Zahn (Eds.), *Homicide studies: A sourcebook of social research* (pp. 197–220). Newbury Park, CA: Sage.

Maxson, C. L. & M. W. Klein (1995). Investigating Gang Structures. *Journal of Gang Research, 31,* 33–40.

Maxson, C. L. & M. W. Klein (1990). "Street Gang Violence: Twice as Great, or Half as Great." In. C. Ronald Huff (ed.), *Gangs in America.* Newbury Park, CA: Sage. 71–100.

Maxson, C. L. & M. W. Klein (1996). "Defining gang homicide: An updated look at member and motive mpproaches." In C. R. Huff (ed.),

Gangs in America (2nd ed.) Newbury Park, CA: Sage Publications.

Maxson, C. L., M. Gordon, and M. W. Klein. (1985). "Differences between gang and non-gang homicides." *Criminology*, 23 (2).

Maxson, C. L., Whitlock, M. L., & Klein, M. W. (1998, March). Vulnerability to street gang membership: Implications for practice. *Social Service Review*, 70–91.

Miller, W. B. (1982). *Crime by youth gangs and groups in the United States.* Washington, DC: Office of Juvenile Justice and Delinquency Prevention. U.S. Department of Justice.

Office of Juvenile Justice and Delinquency Prevention. (1996). *Victims of gang violence: A new frontier in victim services.* Washington, DC.

Parent, D., Leiter, V., Livens, L., Wentworth, D., & Stephen, K. (1994). *Conditions of confinement: Juvenile detention and corrections facilities.* Washington, DC: U.S. Department of Justice, Office of Juvenile Justice and Delinquency Prevention.

Pizzaro, J. M., & McGloin, J. M. (2004). Explaining gang homicides in Newark: Collective behavior or social disorganization? Paper presented at the 2004 Meeting of the American Society of Criminology, Nashville, TN.

Pynoos, R. S., & Nader, K. (1988). Psychological first aid and treatment approach to children exposed to community violence: Research implications. *Journal of Traumatic Stress, 1,* 445–473.

Ralph, P. H., & Marquart, J. W. (1991). Gang violence in Texas prisons. *Prison Journal, 71,* 38–49.

Rosenfeld, R. B., T. Bray, & H. Egley. (1999). Facilitating violence: a comparison of gang-motivated, gang-affiliated, and non-gang youth homicides. *Journal of Quantitative Criminology*, 15:495–516.

Sanchez-Jankowski. M. (1991). *Islands in the Street.* Berkeley: University of California Press.

Sanders, W. B. (1994). *Gangbangs and drive-bys: Grounded culture and juvenile gang violence.* New York: Aldine.

Shashkin, A., & Salagaev, A. (2005). Violence and victimisation on the street: Power struggle and masculine hierarchies in Russia. In T. Hoikkala & L. Suurpaa (Eds.), *Finnish Youth Research Network* (pp. 11–45). Helsinki.

Shashkin, A., Salagaev, A., Sherbakova, I., & Touryanskiy, E. (2005). Contemporary Russian gangs: History, membership and crime

involvement. In. S. Decker & F. Weerman (Eds.), *European street gangs and troublesome youth groups* (pp. 209–240). Walnut Creek, CA: Alta Mira.

Sheley, J. F., & Wright, J. D. (1995). *In the line of fire: Youth, guns, and violence in urban America.* New York: Aldine de Gruyter.

Short, J. F., Jr. (1985). The level of explanation problem in criminology. In R. F. Meier (Ed.), *Theoretical models in criminology* (pp. 51–72). Beverly Hills, CA: Sage.

Short, J. F., Jr. (1989). Exploring integration of theoretical levels of explanation: Notes on gang delinquency. In A. E. Liska, M. Krohn, & S. F. Messner (Eds.), *Theoretical integration in the study of deviance and crime* (pp. 243–259). Albany, NY: SUNY Press.

Skolnick, J. (1990). The social structure of street drug dealing. *American Journal of Police, 9,* 1–41.

Song, D. H., Naude, G. P., Gilmore, D. A., & Bongard, F. (1996). Gang warfare: The medical repercussions. *Journal of Trauma, Injury, Infection and Critical Care, 40*(5), 810–815.

Thornberry, T. P., & Burch, J. H. II. (1997). *Gang members and delinquent behavior.* Washington, DC: U.S. Department of Justice, Office of Juvenile Justice and Delinquency Prevention.

Thornberry, T., M. D. Krohn, A. J. Lizotte, C. A. Smith, & K. Tobin. (2001).Gangs in developmental perspective: The origins and consequences of gang membership. New York: Cambridge University Press.

Thrasher, F. (1927). *The gang.* Chicago: University of Chicago Press.

Tita, G., & Abrahamse, A. (2004). *Gang homicide in LA, 1981–2001. Perspectives on violence prevention.* Sacramento: California Attorney General's Office.

Tita, G., Riley, J., & Greenwood, P. (2002). From Boston to Boyle Heights: The process and prospects of a "pulling levers" strategy in a Los Angeles barrio. In S. Decker (Ed.), *Policing gangs and youth violence* (pp. 102–130). Belmont, CA: Wadsworth.

Van Gemert, F., & Fleisher, M. (2005). In the grip of the group: Ethnography of a Moroccan street gang in the Netherlands. In S. Decker & F. Weerman (Eds.), *European street gangs and troublesome youth groups* (pp. 11–34). Walnut Creek, CA: Alta Mira.

Vigil, J. D. (1988). *Barrio gangs: Street life and identity in Southern California.* Austin, TX: University of Texas Press.

Vigil, J. D. (2003). Urban violence and street gangs. *Annual Review of Anthropology, 32,* 225–242.

Vigil, J. D. (2004). The gang subculture and locura: Variations in acts and actors. In R. Martinez, Jr. (Ed.), *Beyond racial dichotomies of violence: Immigrants, ethnicity, and race.* New York: Routledge.

Weitekamp, E., Reich, K., & Kerner, H.-J. (2005). Why do young male Russians of German descent (Aussiedlers) tend to join or form gangs where violence plays a major role? In S. Decker & F. Weerman (Eds.), *European street gangs and troublesome youth groups* (pp. 103–136). Walnut Creek, CA: Alta Mira.

Wilson, W. J. (1987). *The truly disadvantaged: The inner city, the underclass and public policy.* Chicago: University of Chicago Press.

CHAPTER 19

Family Violence

Richard J. Gelles

During the last quarter of the 20th century, violence between intimates and family members was transformed from a private trouble to a social problem that has received increasing professional, public, and policy attention. We now know that family violence is extensive; occurs across societies, cultures, and historical time; and is not limited to one social, economic, or demographic group. We recognize the social, emotional, economic, and societal costs of family violence. We have come to understand the constraints on the victims that limit their ability to protect themselves and their dependents. Although there are numerous controversies among researchers, practitioners, and policymakers about how to best conceptualize and respond to the problem of violence in the family, one consensus has been reached: there is evidence that virtually every type and form of family and intimate relationship have the potential of being violent. Thus, although the title of this chapter is "Family Violence," it examines violence and abuse in intimate as well as family relationships.

The Nature and Scope of Family Violence

Until the early 1960s, violence between family members and/or intimates was considered rare and committed mainly by mentally ill or otherwise disturbed individuals. Only the most sensational and lurid cases received public attention, and there was a general belief that, even though family violence was a significant problem, it was not widespread.

The question of the extent of family violence has not been easy to answer and still leads to contentious debates over the scientific adequacy and rigor of incidence and prevalence estimates (see, e.g., Saltzman, 2004; Sommers, 1994; Tjaden, 2004). The answer to the question, "How big is the problem?" depends, in part, on two factors: (1) the definition of family violence, and (2) how the incidence and prevalence of family violence is measured.

Defining Family Violence

The definitional question has been debated for more than three decades and has been

contentious. On the one hand, one definition is that family violence is "*any* act that
is harmful to the victim." This broad definition of family violence includes physical
attacks, threatened physical attacks, psychological or emotional aggression and abuse,
sexual assaults or threatened sexual assaults,
neglectful behavior, or behaviors intended to
control the other. On the other hand, there
are narrower definitions of violence that are
confined to acts of physical violence.

There is no consensus on how broad
or narrow the definition of family violence
should be or on how to define the specific
components of any definition (e.g. violence,
neglect, rape, psychological abuse, or even
the terms "family" or "intimate"). In addition, there is debate about the boundaries
of relationships that should be captured by
the term – is it family violence, domestic
violence, intimate violence, or intimate relationship violence? The U.S. Census Bureau
defines a family as a group of two or more
persons related by birth, marriage, or adoption residing together in a household (U.S.
Bureau of the Census, 1992). Although such
a definition is useful for enumerating the
number of families, it limits the examination
and analysis of violence to only those related
individuals who share a residence. Violence
in courtship, violence between couples that
are divorced, and violence between gay and
lesbian couples fall outside this definition.

The National Academy of Sciences panel
on "Assessing Family Violence Interventions"
defined family violence as follows:

> Family violence includes child and adult
> abuse that occurs between family members
> or adult intimate partners. For children,
> this includes acts by others that are physi-
> cally or emotionally harmful or that carry
> the potential to cause physical harm. Abuse
> of children may include sexual exploitation
> or molestation, threats to kill or abandon,
> or lack of emotional or physical support nec-
> essary for normal development. For adults,
> family or intimate violence may include
> acts that are physically and emotionally
> harmful or that carry the potential to cause
> physical harm. Abuse of adult partners
> may include sexual coercion or assaults,
> physical intimidation, threats to kill or
> harm, restraint of normal activities or free-
> dom, and denial of access to resources.
> (National Research Council, 1998, p. 19)

Child maltreatment. Child abuse and
neglect, or child maltreatment, are terms
that cover a wide range of acts of commission
and omission, either carried out by a perpetrator or allowed to happen, which result in
a range of injuries ranging from death to serious disabling injury to emotional distress to
malnutrition and illness.

There are six major types of child abuse
and neglect (see National Center on Child
Abuse and Neglect [NCAAN], 1988):

1. *Physical abuse*: Acts of commission that
   result in physical harm, including death,
   to a child
2. *Sexual abuse*: Acts of commission
   including intrusion or penetration,
   molestation with genital contact, or
   other forms of sexual acts in which
   children are used to provide sexual
   gratification for a perpetrator
3. *Emotional abuse*: Acts of commission
   that include confinement, verbal or
   emotional abuse, or other types of abuse,
   such as withholding sleep, food, or shel-
   ter
4. *Physical neglect*: Acts of omission that
   involve refusal to provide health care,
   delay in providing health care, abandon-
   ment, expulsion of a child from a home,
   inadequate supervision, failure to meet
   food and clothing needs, and conspicu-
   ous failure to protect a child from haz-
   ards or danger
5. *Educational neglect*: Acts of omission
   and commission that include permitting
   chronic truancy, failure to enroll a child
   in school, and inattention to the child's
   specific education needs
6. *Emotional neglect*: Acts of omission that
   involve failing to meet the nurturing
   and affection needs of a child, exposing a child to chronic or severe spouse
   abuse, allowing or permitting a child
   to use alcohol or controlled substances,
   encouraging the child to engage in maladaptive behavior, refusal to provide

psychological care, delays in providing psychological care, and other inattention to the child's developmental needs

The Extent of Family Violence

The following section briefly reviews some of the data for each of the major forms of family and intimate violence in the United States.

Child Maltreatment. Various techniques have been used in attempts to achieve an accurate estimate of child abuse and neglect. The Office of Child Abuse and Neglect has conducted three surveys designed to measure the national incidence of reported and recognized child maltreatment (Burgdorf, 1980; NCCAN, 1988; 1996). A total of 2.9 million maltreated children were known by the agencies surveyed in 1993.[1]

A second source of data on the extent of child maltreatment comes from the National Child Abuse and Neglect Data System (NCANDS). NCANDs is a national data collection and analysis project carried out by the U.S. Department of Health and Human Services, Office of Child Abuse and Neglect. In 2003, states received 2.9 million reports of child maltreatment, representing 5.5 million individual child victims. Of these reports, 906,000 children were indicated or substantiated for maltreatment. Data on type of maltreatment were available for 49 states and the District of Columbia (California did not report data on types of abuse). Of 787,156 victims of maltreatment, 148,877 experienced physical abuse; 479,567 experienced neglect; 78,188 experienced sexual abuse; 38,603 experienced psychological maltreatment; and the remainder experienced medical neglect or other forms of maltreatment (U.S. Department of Health and Human Services, 2005).

The National Family Violence Surveys interviewed two nationally representative samples of families –2,146 family members in 1976 and 6,002 family members in 1985 (Gelles & Straus, 1987; 1988; Straus

& Gelles, 1986; Straus, Gelles, & Steinmetz, 1980). Violence and abuse were measured by asking respondents to report on their own behavior toward their children in the previous 12 months. Milder forms of violence, violence that most people think of as physical punishment, were of course, the most common. However, rates of the severe forms of violence were surprisingly high. Abusive violence was defined as acts that had a high probability of injuring the child and included kicking, biting, punching, hitting or trying to hit a child with an object; beating up a child; burning or scalding; and threatening or using a gun or a knife. Slightly more than 2 parents in 100 (2.3%) admitted to engaging in one act of abusive violence during the year prior to the 1985 survey. Seven children in 1,000 were hurt as a result of an act of violence directed at them by a parent in the previous year. Projecting the rate of abusive violence to all children under 18 years of age, who live with one or both parents, means that 1.5 million children experience acts of abusive physical violence each year and 450,000 children are injured each year as a result of parental violence.

A more recent survey of children's experience with violence in the home was conducted by telephone with a representative sample of 900 parents. Straus and Stewart (1999) report that 28.4% of parents of 2- to 4-year-old children and 28.5% of parents of 5- to 8-year-old children reported using an object to spank their child's bottom. Overall, the survey found that 74% of children younger than 5 years old were hit or slapped by their parents (Gallup Organization, 1995).

Finkelhor and his colleagues conducted a national survey of child victimization in 2002–2003 (Finkehor, Ormrod, Turner, & Hamby, 2005). The survey collected data on children aged 2 to 17 years of age. Interviews were conducted with parents and youth. Slightly more than one in seven children (138 per 1,000) experienced child maltreatment. Emotional abuse was the most frequent type of maltreatment. The rate of physical abuse (meaning that children experienced physical harm) was 15, per 1,000,

---

[1]   A fourth study is underway but results are not available as of February, 2006.

whereas the rate of neglect was 11 per 1,000. The overall projected extent of maltreatment was 8,755,000 child victims (Finkehor et al., 2005).

Sexual abuse of children. Among the most dramatic changes taking place over the last few decades has been the increased attention to child sexual abuse. In a comprehensive review of studies on the incidence and prevalence of child sexual abuse, Peters, Wyatt, and Finkelhor (1986) reported that estimates of the prevalence range from 6 to 62% for females and from 3 to 31% for males. They point out that this variation may be accounted for by a number of methodological factors, such as differences in definitions of abuse, sample characteristics, interview format (e.g., in-person vs. phone interview) and number of questions used to elicit information about abuse experiences. Whatever the number, it is clear that sexual abuse is a problem that affects large numbers of children.

An examination of NCAND'S data on reports of child maltreatment reveals that the number of substantiated reports of sexual abuse cases has declined 40% from 1992 to 2000 – from 150,000 cases to 89,500 cases (Finkelhor & Jones, 2004). There are a number of plausible explanations for this drop, and in fact, there are probably many factors that led to the decline. However, Finkelhor and Jones conclude that at least part of the decline is due to a true overall decline in the occurrence of child sexual abuse.

Child homicide. The National Child Abuse and Neglect Data System estimated that 1,500 children were killed by parents or caregivers in 2003 (U.S. Department of Health & Human Services, 2005). Expressed in rates, 2.0 per 100,000 children younger than 18 years of age are victims of fatal child abuse and neglect. This rate is slightly higher than the rate of 1.84 in 2000. Nearly 44% of child maltreatment fatalities were under the age of 1 year, whereas 35% of the victims were from 1 to 3 years of age. Seventy-eight percent of the perpetrators were one or both parents.

Dating and courtship violence. The virtues of romantic love – a phenomenon considered synonymous with American dating patterns – have been extolled in poems, songs, romance novels, television soap operas, and folklore. Sadly, along with the romance is the fact that violence is very much a part of modern dating patterns. Overall, studies indicate that the prevalence of nonsexual courtship violence ranges from 9 to 65%, depending on the definitions and research methods used (Silverman, Raj, Mucci, & Hathaway, 2001).

Intimate Partner Violence. Although there is no official reporting system for partner violence, there are a number of sources of data on the extent of violence between spouses or intimate partners. The National Institute of Justice, an agency of the U.S. Department of Justice, collects data on victims of violent crime using the National Crime Victims Survey (NCVS).

According to data from the NCVS, 578,350 women were victims of intimate partner violence in 2004 (Catalano, 2005). This figure represents a decline from 1.1 million female victims in 1993. In 2004, men were victims of 111,750 violent acts at the hands of their intimate partners, down from 162,870 in 1993.

Straus and Gelles and their colleagues have carried out three national surveys of domestic violence – in-person interviews with a nationally representative sample of 2,143 respondents in 1976 (Straus, Gelles, & Steinmetz, 1980), telephone interviews with a nationally representative sample of 6,002 respondents in 1985 (Gelles & Straus, 1988; Straus & Gelles, 1986), and telephone interviews with a nationally representative sample of 1,970 respondents in 1992 (Straus & Kaufman-Kantor, 1994). The rate of "minor violence" (violence that had a low probability of causing a physical injury) declined from 100 per 1,000 women in 1975 to about 80 per 1,000 in 1985, and then rose to nearly 90 per 1,000 in 1992. More serious or severe acts of violence toward women (acts labeled "severe assaults" or "wife beating" by the investigators) declined from 3.8 per 1,000 in 1975 to 1.9 per 1,000 in 1992.

The National Violence Against Women Survey (NVAW) involved telephone interviews with a nationally representative sample of 8,000 women and 8,000 men (Tjaden & Thoennes, 1998). The survey was conducted between November 1995 and May 1996. The NVAW survey assessed lifetime prevalence and annual prevalence (violence experienced in the previous 12 months) using a "modified" version of the Conflict Tactics Scales to measure violence victimization. Nearly 52% of women surveyed (519 per 1,000 or 52,261,743 women) reported experiencing a physical assault as a child or adult. Nearly 56% percent of women surveyed (559 per 1,000 or 56,289,623 women) reported experiencing any form of violence, including stalking, rape, or physical assault. The rate of lifetime assault at the hands of an intimate partner was 221 per 1,000 for physical violence and 254 per 1,000 for any form of violence-victimization. The rates of forms of violence less likely to cause an injury, such as pushing, grabbing, shoving, or slapping, were the highest (between 160 and 181 per 1,000), whereas the rates of the most severe forms of violence (used a gun, knife, or "beat up") were the lowest (85 per 1,000 for "beat up"; 7 per 1,000 for used a gun).

The annual prevalence or incidence of violence was 19 per 1,000 for physical assault (1,913,243 women) and 30 per 1,000 for any form of violence victimization (3,020,910 women). The annual prevalence of women victimized by intimate partners was 13 per 1,000 for physical assault (1,309,061) and 18 per 1,000 (1,812,546 women) for all forms of victimization.

Homicide of intimates. Approximately 440 husbands and boyfriends were killed by their wives and girlfriends in 2000, whereas 1,247 wives and girlfriends were slain by their husbands or boyfriends. (Rennison, 2003).

Elder abuse. The National Elder Abuse Incidence Survey found that approximately 450,000 elderly persons living in domestic settings were abused and/or neglected in 1996 (National Center on Elder Abuse, 1998).

Siblings, parents, gays, lesbians, and transgendered couples. Although parent-to-child and partner violence have received the most public attention, physical fights between brothers and sisters are by far the most common form of family violence. It is, however, rare that parents, physicians, or social workers consider sibling fighting as problematic forms of family violence, even though violence between siblings often goes far beyond so-called normal violence. A national survey of 2,030 children living in the contiguous states in the United States found that 35% of children experienced a physical assault at the hands of a sibling in the previous year (Finkehor et al., 2005). Boys and girls were nearly equally likely to be a victim of sibling violence. The rate of assault was highest for children 6 to 12 years of age (Finkehor et al., 2005). At least 109,000 children use guns or knives in fights with siblings each year (Straus, Gelles, & Steinmetz, 1980). According to the U.S. Bureau of Justice Statistics, 119 murders in 2002 involved perpetrators and victims who were siblings (Durose et al., 2005). Nearly three quarters (72%) of sibling murders were brother on brother, whereas 14% were brothers killing sisters.

Parents are also hidden victims of family violence. Each year, according to Straus and Gelles's national surveys, between 750,000 to 1 million parents have violent acts committed against them by their teenaged children (Cornell & Gelles, 1982).

Lastly, intimate partner violence is not exclusive to heterosexual relationships. Although there are no national statistics or official reports that tabulate the rates of partner violence in gay, lesbian, and transgendered couples, descriptive research consistently uncovers intimate violence among nonheterosexual couples (see Greenwood et al., 2002; Lockhart, White, Causby, & Isaac, 1994; Tjaden & Thonnes, 2000; Turrell, 2000).

Witnessing Domestic Violence

Witnessing is at the intersection of child abuse and neglect and domestic violence. Children who witness domestic violence are a unique population warranting research and clinical attention (Rosenberg & Rossman, 1990). Researchers and clinicians report that children who witness acts of domestic violence experience negative behavioral and developmental outcomes, independent of any direct abuse or neglect that they may also experience from their caretakers

(Jaffe, Wolfe, & Wilson, 1990; Osofsky, 1990 Rosenberg & Rossman, 1990).

Estimates from the two National Family Violence Surveys are that between 1.5 and 3.3 million children 3 to 17 years of age are exposed to domestic violence each year (Gelles & Straus, 1988; Straus, Gelles & Steinmetz, 1980).

Factors Associated With Family Violence

The early thinking and writing on family violence was dominated by a mental illness model (Gelles, 1973). Violence, abuse, and neglect were thought to be caused by specific personality factors, such as immaturity, impulsiveness, or psychopathology. The assumption was that no psychologically "normal" person would physically abuse a wife or child. However, there are several problems with the psychopathological, or mental illness model, of family violence and abuse. First, most of the conclusions about the causes of family violence are based on studies of a limited number of cases, typically without comparison groups, and that draw conclusions after the data are collected, rather than testing hypotheses developed prior to data collection. Second, such an explanation confuses the cause with the consequence. People who abuse their children or partners are mentally ill, we are told; we know they are mentally ill because they have committed an outrageous act of violence or abuse. A third problem is that the psychopathological model ignores the fact that certain societal factors are also related to family violence. The remainder of this section examines those societal factors.

Sex and Gender Differences

Outside the home, violent men clearly outnumber violent women. However, in the home, women are frequently as or even more violent than men. Research on child abuse finds that mothers were slightly more likely than fathers to abuse or kill their children (National Research Council, 1998; U.S. Department of Health and Human Services, 2005; Wolfner & Gelles, 1993). Abusive females are typically younger than abusive men. Mothers are the perpetrators of 30.5% of child fatalities, whereas fathers are perpetrators in 18% (U.S. Department of Health and Human Services, 2005). However, Margolin (1992) asserted that when one controls for the amount of responsibility that mothers and fathers have for child care, males are more likely to be abusive. More recently, Black, Heyman, and Slep's (2001) review of existing studies that investigated the relationship between sex of the parent and the likelihood of parent-to-child physical aggression, in nationally representative samples and not just cases of abuse reported to child protective services, found that parent sex is not associated with parent-to-child physical abuse.

There is considerable debate about the comparative rates of husband and wife violence. Although some investigators report that the rate of wife-to-husband violence is about the same as the rate of husband-to-wife violence (Moffitt, Caspi, Rutter, & Silva, 2001; Straus & Gelles, 1986; Straus, 1998, 2005), others find that women are the disproportionate victims of family violence (Dobash & Dobash, 1979; Dobash, Dobash, Wilson, & Daly, 1992; Kurz; 2005; Tjaden & Thoennes, 1998). If one goes by how much harm is done, who initiates the violence, and how easy it is for a victim to escape violence, women clearly are the disproportionate victims of domestic violence.

Boys are the more violent siblings and offspring (Durose et al., 2005). Mothers and sisters are the more frequent targets of the young or adolescent boys' family violence (Cornell & Gelles, 1982).

Social Characteristics

There are two conflicting positions regarding the relationship between social class and family violence: (1) Violence cuts across all socioeconomic groups and is not a function of social class or income, and (2) violence is caused by low social class and poverty. Although there appears to be an association between lower income and increased risk for family violence (Cunradi, Caetano, & Schafer, 2002; Rennison, 2003 Schumacher, Feldbau-Kohn, Slep, & Heyman, 2001: U.S.

Department of Justice, 2004), it is not singularly *confined* to lower class families. Victims from lower socioeconomic levels are more likely to go to emergency rooms or clinics, and they are more likely to come to the attention of the authorities if their child is bruised or battered. Similarly, clinics or emergency rooms are the most likely source of medical aid for lower-class battered women. Therefore, family violence is a more observable phenomenon among this social group. Nonetheless, the rates of virtually all forms of family violence are higher among those with low income or who live in disadvantaged neighborhoods (National Research Council, 1998)

Rates of family violence also vary by race. Both official report and self-report survey data suggest that the rates of intimate violence are higher in minority families (National Research Council, 1998; Rennison, 2001). American-Indian women report intimate partner victimization at rates higher than women in other racial or ethnic groups (Rennison, 2001). The rates of violence toward children and between husbands and wives are highest among Hispanics compared to Blacks and Whites, and higher among Blacks compared to Whites (Hampton & Gelles, 1991; Hampton, Gelles, & Harrop, 1989; Straus & Smith, 1990). For partner abuse, the higher rates in Hispanic families reflect the economic deprivation, youthfulness, and urban residence of Hispanics because, when these factors are controlled, there is no statistically significant difference between Hispanics and non-Hispanic Whites. Kantor, Jasinski, and Aldaronodo (1994) report that Hispanic ethnicity may not be a risk factor itself, but may be a marker for other sociodemographic variables that are risk factors for family violence. However, with regard to violence toward children, the differences among Hispanics, Blacks, and Whites persist even when demographic and socioeconomic factors are controlled.

Stress

Career and life stressors have a medium effect on the likelihood of intimate partner violence (Stith, Smith, Penn, Ward, & Tritt, 2004). The prevalence of post-traumatic stress in women victims is high, ranging from approximately 33 to 85% (Astin, Lawrence, & Foy, 1993). Kantor and Straus (1987) suggest that men employed in blue-collar occupations reported higher rates of family violence than did men with white-collar employment. Financial difficulties, as well as other factors, such as being a single parent, being a teenage mother, and sexual problems, are related to heightened stress that may precipitate violent episodes (Cano & Vivian, 2001; Gelles, 1989; Gelles & Straus, 1988). However, overall life experiences that are perceived as stressful appear to have a more significant connection to physical abuse in families than do daily life stressors (MacEwen & Barling, 1988; McKenry, Julian, & Gavazzi, 1994).

Social Isolation

People who are socially isolated from neighbors and relatives are more likely to be violent in the home. One major source of stress reduction, and an insulator to family violence, is being able to call on friends and family for help, aid, and assistance. The more a family is integrated into the community and the more groups and associations it belongs to, the less likely it is to be violent (Milner & Chilamkurti, 1991; Straus et al., 1980). Data from the 1992 National Survey of Families suggest that experiencing satisfaction with social relationships was associated with less intimate partner violence (Rodriquez, Lasch, Chandra, & Lee, 2001). Social connections do not preclude, however, the possibility of physical violence. In fact, some research suggests that receiving little social support is not associated with an increased risk of partner abuse (Barnett, Martinez, & Keyson, 1996; Zlotnick, Kohn, Peterson, & Pearlstein, 1998).

Intergenerational Transmission

The notion that abused children grow up to be abusive parents and violent adults has been widely expressed in the child abuse and family violence literature, and a history of victimization is indeed a major risk factor for family violence offending (Stith et al., 2004). Kaufman and Zigler (1987) reviewed the literature that tested the intergenerational transmission of violence hypothesis and concluded that the best estimate of the rate of intergenerational transmission appears to be 30% (plus or minus 5%). Although a rate of 30% intergenerational transmission is substantially less than a majority of abused children, it is considerably higher than the between 2% and 4% rate of abuse found in the general population (Straus & Gelles, 1986). Barnett and Fagan (1993) found that witnessing parental verbal and psychological aggression was also significantly related to later abusive behavior.

Evidence from studies of parental and partner violence indicate that, although experiencing violence in one's family of origin is often correlated with later violent behavior, such experience is not the sole determining factor. When the cycle of violence occurs, it is likely the result of a complex set of social, psychological, and interpersonal processes.

Factors Associated With Sexual Abuse of Children

There has been a great deal of research on the characteristics of sexual abusers; however, current research has failed to isolate characteristics, especially demographic, social, or psychological factors, that discriminate between sexual abusers and nonabusers (Black et al., 2001; Quinsey, 1984).

One of the key questions raised in discussions about sexual abuse is whether all children are at risk for sexual abuse or whether some children, because of some specific characteristic (e.g., age, sex, or poverty status), are at greater risk than others. Current research is unclear as to definitive factors that can predict future sexual abuse. Finkelhor, Moore, Hamby, and Straus (1997) found that a child's sex does not necessarily predict later victimization. However, Sedlak (1997) asserts that female children are at an increased risk for sexual abuse, and the relationship between a child's sexual victimiza-

tion and age is also associated with family structure and race.

Theoretical Perspectives

A number of sociological and psychological theories may help explain the causes and processes of family violence. They include the following theories described in this section.

Social Learning Theory

Social learning theorists (e.g., Bandura, 1977) posit that most behavior is learned through both the experience and observation of one's own and other's behaviors. According to this theory, individuals who have experienced or witnessed violence are more likely to use violence than those who have experienced little or no violence. Social learning theory provides support for the belief that family violence is learned. The family is the institution and social group in which people learn the roles of husband and wife, parent, and child. The home is the prime location where people learn how to deal with various stressors, crises, and frustrations. In many instances, the home is also the place where an individual first experiences violence. Not only do people learn violent behavior but they also learn how to justify being violent. For example, hearing a father say, "This will hurt me more than it will hurt you," or a mother say, "You have been bad, so you deserve to be spanked," contributes to how children learn to justify violent behavior.

Social Situational/Stress and Coping Theory

Social situational/stress and coping theory explains why violence is used in some situations and not others. The theory proposes that abuse and violence occur because of two main factors. The first is structural stress and the lack of coping resources in a family. For instance, the association between low income and family violence indicates that an important factor in violence is inadequate financial resources. The second factor is the cultural norm concerning the use of force and violence. In contemporary American society, as well as in many societies, violence in general and violence toward children in particular are normative (Straus et al., 1980). Thus, individuals learn to use violence both expressively and instrumentally as a means of coping with stressful events.

Resource Theory

Another explanation of family violence is resource theory (Goode, 1971). This model assumes that all social systems (including the family) rely to some degree on force or the threat of force. The more resources – social, personal, and economic – a person can command, the more force he or she can muster. However, the fewer resources a person has, the more he or she will actually use force in an open manner. Thus, a husband who wants to be the dominant person in the family but has little education, has a job low in prestige and income, and lacks interpersonal skills may choose to use violence to maintain the dominant position. In addition, family members (including children) may use violence to redress a grievance when they have few alternative resources available. Thus, wives who have few social resources or social contacts may use violence toward their husbands in order to protect themselves (Kurz, 2005).

Ecological Theory

Garbarino (1977) and Belsky (1980, 1993) proposed an ecological model to explain the complex nature of child maltreatment. It proposes that violence and abuse arise out of a mismatch of parent to child or family to neighborhood and community. For example, parents who are under a great deal of social stress and have poor coping skills may have a difficult time meeting the needs of a child who is hyperactive. The risk of abuse and violence increases when the functioning of the children and parents is constrained by developmental problems, such as children with learning disabilities and social or emotional handicaps, and when parents are under considerable stress or have personality problems, such as immaturity or impulsiveness. Finally, if there are few institutions and agencies in the community to support troubled families, then the risk of abuse is increased further.

Social Exchange Theory

Exchange theory has been used to explain the complex dynamics inherent in family violence (Gelles, 1983, 1997). It proposes that partner abuse and child abuse are governed by the principle of costs and benefits. Abuse is used when the rewards are greater than the costs (Gelles, 1983). Exchange theorists (Homans, 1967) assert that it is rewarding to inflict costs on someone who has hurt you. The notion of "sweet revenge" is useful in examining why victims may respond with extreme forms of violence after having been victimized. There is a gain to using violence, and that gain is achieving dominance and control over another. The private nature of the family, the reluctance of social institutions and agencies to intervene – in spite of mandatory child abuse reporting laws and arrest laws for partner violence – and the low risk that there will be other interventions reduce the costs of abuse and violence. The cultural approval of violence as both expressive and instrumental behavior raises the potential rewards for violence – the most significant reward being social and interpersonal control and power.

Sociobiological Theory

A sociobiological or evolutionary perspective of family violence suggests that violence toward human or nonhuman primate offspring is the result of diminished reproductive success potential of children and parental investment. The theory's central assumption is that natural selection is the process of differential reproduction and reproductive success (Daly & Wilson, 1980). Males can be expected to invest in offspring when there is some degree of parental certainty (how confident the parent is that the child is his own genetic offspring); females are also inclined to invest under conditions of parental certainty. Parents recognize their offspring and avoid squandering valuable reproductive effort on someone else's offspring. Thus, Daly and Wilson (1985) conclude that parental feelings are established more readily and more profoundly with one's own offspring than in cases where the parent-offspring relationship is artificial. Children not genetically related to the parent (e.g., stepchildren, adopted, or foster children) or children with low reproductive potential (e.g., handicapped or retarded children) are at the highest risk for infanticide and abuse (Burgess & Garbarino, 1983; Daly & Wilson, 1980; Hrdy, 1979). Large families can dilute parental energy and lower attachment to children thus increasing the risk of child abuse and neglect (Burgess & Drais-Parrillo, 2004).

Smuts (1992) applied an evolutionary perspective to male aggression against females. Smuts (1992), Daly, and Wilson (1988) and Burgess and Draper (1989) argue that male aggression against females often reflects male reproductive striving. Both human and nonhuman male primates are postulated to use aggression against females to intimidate them so that they will not resist future male efforts to mate and to reduce the likelihood that they will mate with other males. Thus, males use aggression to control female sexuality to males' reproductive advantage. The frequency of male aggression varies across societies and situations depending on the strength of female alliances, the support women can receive from their families, the strength and importance of male alliances, the degree of equality in male-female relationships, and the degree to which males control the economic resources within a society. Male aggression toward females, expressed in both physical violence and rape, is high when female alliances are weak, when females lack kin support, when male alliances are strong, when male-female relationships are unbalanced, and when males control societal resources.

General Strain Theory

Sociologist Robert Agnew (1992) asserts that violent behavior may be related to the frustration and anger that result as a consequence of being treated poorly in social relationships. Agnew outlines types of strains that increase an individual's feelings of anger and fear. The first source of strain is that associated with a failure to achieve positively valued goals. As a result of this type of strain individuals may use illegitimate means to get what they want. Another source of strain is caused by the presentation of negative stimuli. These stressful life situations may include such adverse events as criminal victimization, child maltreatment, or interpersonal violence. Individuals confronted with such stressors may engage in criminal acts in order to seek revenge. Lastly, another type of strain an individual may encounter is caused by the anticipated or actual loss of positively valued stimuli, such as a loved one or the experience of a major life transition. Difficulties arise when an individual attempts to seek revenge for a loss or tries to prevent major life changes through illegal methods. According to Agnew, the most critical response to strain is anger, which can result in increased aggressive and possibly violent criminal behavior.

Pro-Feminist Theory

Pro-feminist theory is the dominant ideological perspective in the field of relational violence. It uses a gendered lens through which women are viewed as being controlled by an oppressive, patriarchal social system (Gelles, 1993b). Feminist theorists (e.g., Dobash & Dobash, 1979; Loseke, 2005; Pagelow, 1984; Yllo, 1983, 1988) assert that women are the victims of culturally sanctioned, male coercive control. The central thesis of this perspective is that economic, social, and cultural processes operate directly and indirectly to support a patriarchal (male-dominated) social order and family structure. Patriarchy is seen as leading to the subordination of women and causes the historical pattern of systematic violence directed against women. Although the pro-feminist approach is the most widely used among batterer programs, there exists virtually no scientific support for its efficacy (Babcock, Green, & Robie, 2004).

Attachment Theory

Attachment theory describes the propensity of individuals to form a strong emotional bond with a primary caregiver who functions as a source of security and safety (Bowlby, 1973). The theory proposes that there is a clear association between early attachment experiences and the pattern of affectionate bonds one makes throughout one's lifetime. If an individual has formed strong and secure attachments with early caregivers, later adult relationships will also have secure attachments. On the other hand, if an individual has formed insecure, anxious, or ambivalent attachments early on, later adult attachments will be replicated similarly. Therefore, according to the theory, attachment difficulties underlie adulthood relational problems. Bowlby (1988) posits that anxiety and anger go hand in hand as responses to the risk of loss – and that anger is often functional. For certain individuals, with weak and insecure attachments, the functional reaction to anger becomes distorted and is manifested by violent acts against one's partner.

Conclusion

One overriding factor that influences the study and consideration of intimate and family violence is the emotional nature of both research and practice. Few other areas of inquiry in the field of violence studies generate the strong feelings and reactions that child abuse, child sexual abuse, violence against women, elder abuse, and courtship violence generate. Even the most grotesque case examples fail to adequately capture the devastating physical and psychological consequences of physical abuse at the hands of a loved one or caretaker. Those in the field of violence studies not only must face difficult and complex cases but they often are also frustrated by the inadequate conceptual and practical resources they can bring to bear on behalf of victims, offenders, and families.

There are no simple answers or "silver bullets." The relative newness of family and intimate violence as an area of study and the fact that the first decade of research was dominated by a psychopathology model of causation have resulted in a limited level of theoretical development of the field. Moreover, the emotional nature of family and intimate violence has generated deep and heated controversies over estimates of extent, risk and protective factors, and causal models.

Yet, despite the controversies and limited theoretical development, one conclusion is inescapable: no one factor can explain the presence or absence of family and intimate violence. Characteristics of the child, parent, partners, family, social situation, community, and society are related to which family members are abused and under what conditions. Individual and emotional characteristics, psychological characteristics, and community factors, such as cultural attitudes regarding violence, are moderated and influenced by family structure and family situations. In addition, power and control are common features of nearly all forms of family and intimate violence. Thus, interventions and prevention efforts need to be aimed at the importance of power and control and the functions of the family system if family and intimate violence is to be treated and prevented effectively.

References

Agnew, R. (1992). Foundation for a General Strain Theory of crime and delinquency. *Criminology*, 47–87.

Astin, M. Lawrence, C. K. J., & Fox, D. W. (1993). Post-traumatic stress disorder among battered women: Risk and resiliency factors. *Violence & Victims, 8*, 17–28.

Babcock, J. C., Green, C. E., & Robie, C. (2004). Does batterers' treatment work? A meta-analytic review of domestic violence treatment. *Clinical Psychology Review, 23*, 1023–1053.

Bandura, A. (1973). *Aggression: A social learning analysis*. Englewood Cliff, NJ: Prentice Hall.

Barnett, O. W. & Fagan, R. W. (1993). Alcohol use in male spousal abusers and their female partners. *Journal of Family Violence, 8*, 1–25.

Barnett, O. W., Martinez, T. E. & Keyson, M. (1996). The relationship between violence, social support, and self-blame in battered women. *Journal of Interpersonal Violence, 2*, 221–233.

Belsky, J. (1980). Child maltreatment: An ecological integration. *American Psychologist, 35*, 320–335.

Belsky, J. (1993). Etiology of child maltreatment: A developmental-ecological approach. *Psychological Bulletin, 114*, 413–434.

Black, D. A., Heyman, R. E., & Slep, A. M. (2001). Risk factors for child physical abuse. *Aggression and Violent Behavior, 6*, 121–188.

Bowker, L. H. (1983). *Beating wife beating*. Lexington, MA: Lexington Books.

Bowlby, J. (1973). *Attachment and loss. Vol.2: Separation*. London: Hogarth Press.

Bowlby, J. (1988). *A secure base*. London: Hogarth Press.

Burgdorf, K. (1980). *Recognition and reporting of child maltreatment*. Rockville, MD: Westat.

Burgess, R. L., & Drais-Parrillo, A. A. (2004). An analysis of child maltreatment: From behavioral psychology to behavioral ecology. In R. L. Burgess & K. MacDonald (Eds.), *Evolutionary perspectives on human development* (2nd ed.) (pp. 305–330). Thousand Oaks, CA: Sage Publications.

Burgess, R. L., & Draper, P. (1989). The explanation of family violence: The role of biological, behavioral, and cultural selection. In L. Ohlin & M. Tonry (Eds.), *Family violence: Crime and justice: A review of research* (Vol. 11, pp. 59–116). Chicago: University of Chicago Press.

Burgess, R. L., & Garbarino, J. (1983). Doing what comes naturally? An evolutionary perspective on child abuse. In D. Finkelhor, R. Gelles, M. Straus, & G. Hotaling (Eds.), *The dark side of families: Current family violence research* (pp. 88–101). Beverly Hills, CA: Sage.

Cano, A., & Vivian, D. (2001). Life stressors and husband-to-wife violence. *Aggression and Violent Behavior, 6*, 481–497.

Catalano, S. (2005). *Criminal victimization 2004*. Washington, DC: Bureau of Justice Statistics.

Cavanaugh, M. & Gelles, R. J. (2005). The utility of male domestic violence offender typologies: New directions for research, policy, and practice. *Journal of Interpersonal Violence, 20*, 155–166.

Cornell, C. P., & Gelles, R. J. (1982). Adolescent to parent violence. *Urban Social Change Review, 15*, 8–14.

Cunradi, C. B., Caetano, R., & Schafer, J. (2002). Socioeconomic predictors of intimate partner violence among white, Black, and Hispanic couples in the United States. *Journal of Family Violence, 17*, 377–389.

Daly, M., & Wilson, M. (1980). Discriminative parental solicitude: A biosocial perspective. *Journal of Marriage and the Family, 42*, 277–288.

Daly, M., & Wilson, M. (1985). Child abuse and other risks of not living with both parents. *Ethology and Sociobiology, 6*, 197–210.

Daly, M., & Wilson, M. (1988). *Homicide*. New York: Aldine DeGruyter.

Dobash, R. E., & Dobash, R. (1979). *Violence against wives*. New York: Free Press.

Dobash, R. P., Dobash, R. E., Wilson, M. & Daly, M. (1992). The myth of sexual symmetry in marital violence. *Social Problems, 39*, 71–91.

Durose, M. R., Harlow, C. W., Langan, P. A., Motivans, M., Rantala, R. R., & Smith, E. L. (2005). *Family violence statistics: Including statistics on strangers and acquaintances*. Washington, DC: U.S. Department of Justice, Office of Justice Programs.

Finkelhor, D., & Jones, L. (2004). Sexual abuse decline in the 1990s: Evidence for possible causes. *Juvenile Justice Bulletin* (NCJ199298), 1–12.

Finkelhor, D., Moore, D., Hamby, S. H., & Straus, M. A. (1997). Sexually abused children in a national survey of parents: Methodological issues. *Child Abuse and Neglect: The International Journal, 21*, 1–9.

Finkehor, D., Ormrod, R., Turner, H., & Hamby, S. H. (2005). The victimization of children and youth: A comprehensive national survey. *Child Maltreatment, 10*, 5–25.

Gallup Organization. (1995). *Disciplining children in America: A Gallup Poll report*. Princeton, NJ.

Garbarino, J. (1977). The human ecology of child maltreatment. *Journal of Marriage and the Family, 39*, 721–735.

Gelles, R. J. (1973). Child abuse as psychopathology: A sociological critique and reformulation. *American Journal of Orthopsychiatry, 43*, 611–621.

Gelles, R. J. (1983). An exchange/social control theory. In D. Finkelhor, R. Gelles, M. Straus,

& G. Hotaling (Eds.), *The dark side of families: Current family violence research* (pp. 151–165). Beverly Hills, CA: Sage.

Gelles, R. J. (1989). Child abuse and violence in single-parent families: Parent-absence and economic deprivation. *American Journal of Orthopsychiatry, 59*, 492–501.

Gelles, R. J. (1992). Poverty and violence toward children. *American Behavioral Scientist, 35*, 258–274.

Gelles, R. J. (1993). Through a sociological lens. In R. J. Gelles & D. Loseke (Eds.), *Current controversies on family violence* (pp. 31–46). Thousand Oaks, CA: Sage.

Gelles, R. J. (1997). *Intimate violence in families* (3rd ed.). Thousand Oaks, CA: Sage.

Gelles, R. J., & Straus, M. A. (1987). Is violence towards children increasing? A comparison of 1975 and 1985 national survey rates. *Journal of Interpersonal Violence, 2*, 212–222.

Gelles, R. J., & Straus, M. A. (1988). *Intimate violence.* New York: Simon and Schuster.

Goode, W. (1971). Force and violence in the family. *Journal of Marriage and the Family, 33*, 624–636.

Greenwood, G. L., Relf, M. V., Huang, B., Pollack, L. M., Canchola, J. A., & Catania, J. A. (2002). Battering victimization among a probability-based sample of men who have sex with men. *American Journal of Public Health, 92*, 1964–1969.

Hampton, R. L., & Gelles, R. J. (1991). A profile of violence toward Black children. In R. L. Hampton, (Ed.), *Black Family Violence: Current Research and Theory* (pp. 21–34). Lexington, Massachusetts: Lexington Books.

Hampton, R. L., Gelles, R. J. Harop, J. W. (1989). Is violence in Black families increasing? A comparison of 1975 and 1985 national survey rates. *Journal of Marriage and the Family, 51*, 969–980.

Homans, G. (1967). Fundamental social processes. In N. Smelser (Ed.), *Sociology.* New York: John Wiley.

Hrdy, S. B. (1979). Infanticide among animals: A review classification, and examination of the implications for reproductive strategies of females. *Ethology and Sociobiology, 1*, 13–40.

Jaffe, P. G., Wolfe, D. A., & Wilson, S. K. (1990). *Children of battered women.* Newbury Park, CA: Sage.

Kantor, G. K., Jasinski, J., & Aldaronodo, E. (1994). Sociocultural status and incidence of marital violence in Hispanic families. *Violence and Victims, 9*, 207–222.

Kantor, G. K., & Straus, M. A. (1987). The "drunken bum" theory of wife beating. *Social Problems, 34*, 212–230.

Kaufman, J., & Zigler, E. (1987). Do abused children become abusive parents? *American Journal of Orthopsychiatry, 57*, 186–192.

Kurz, D. (2005). Men's violence toward women is a serious social problem. In D. Loseke, R. J. Gelles, & M. Cavanaugh (Eds.), *Current controversies on family violence* (2nd ed.) (pp. 79–96). Thousand Oaks, CA: Sage Publications.

Lockhart, L. L., White, B. W., Causby, V., & Isa (1992/1994). Letting out the secret: Violence in lesbian relationships. *Journal of Interpersonal Violence, 9*, 469–492.

Loseke, D. (2005). Through a sociological lens: Complexities of family violence. In D. Loseke, R. J. Gelles, & M. Cavanaugh (Eds.), *Current controversies on family violence* (2nd ed.) (pp. 35–53). Thousand Oaks, CA: Sage Publications.

MacEwen, K. E., & Barling, J. (1988). Multiple stressors, violence in the family of origin and marital aggression: A longitudinal investigation. *Journal of Family Violence, 3*, 73–87.

Margolin, L. (1992). Beyond maternal blame: Physical child abuse as a phenomenon of gender. *Journal of Family Issues, 13*, 410–423.

McKenry, P. C., Julian, T. W., & Gavazzi, S. W. (1995). Toward a biopsychosocial model of domestic violence. *Journal of Marriage and the Family, 57*, 307–320.

Milner, J. S., & Chilamkurti, C. (1991). Physical child abuse perpetrator characteristics: A review of the literature. *Journal of Interpersonal Violence, 6*, 345–366.

Moffitt, T. E., Caspi, A., Rutter, M., & Silva, P. A. (2001). *Sex differences in anti-social behavior.* Cambridge, UK: Cambridge University Press.

National Center on Child Abuse and Neglect. (1988). *Study findings: Study of national incidence and prevalence of child abuse and neglect: 1988.* Washington, DC: U.S. Department of Health and Human Services.

National Center on Child Abuse and Neglect. (1996). *Study findings: Study of national incidence and prevalence of child abuse and neglect: 1993.* Washington, DC: U.S. Department of Health and Human Services.

National Center on Elder Abuse. (1998). *The national elder abuse incidence study.* Washington, DC: American Public Human Services Association.

National Research Council. (1998). *Violence in families: Assessing prevention and treatment programs*. Washington, DC: National Academy Press.

Osofsky, J. (1990). The effects of exposure to violence on young children. *American Psychologist, 50*, 782–788.

Pagelow, M. (1984). *Family violence*. New York: Praeger.

Pan, H. S. Neidig, P. H., & O'Leary, K. D. (1994). Predicting mild and severe husband-to-wife physical aggression. *Journal of Consulting and Clinical Psychology, 62*, 975–81.

Peters, S. D., Wyatt, G. E., & Finkelhor, D. (1986). Prevalence. In D. Finkelhor (Ed.), *A sourcebook on child sexual abuse* (pp. 15–59). Beverly Hills, CA: Sage.

Quinsey, V. L. (1984). Sexual aggression: Studies of offenders against women. In D. N. Weisstub (Ed.), *Law and mental health: International perspectives* (Vol. 1, pp. 84–121). New York: Pergamon Press.

Rennison, C. (2003). *Intimate partner violence: 1993–2001*. Washington, DC: U.S. Department of Justice, Office of Justice Programs.

Rodriguez, E., Lasch, K. E., Chandra, P., & Lee, J. (2001). Family violence, employment status, welfare benefits, and alcohol drinking in the United States: What is the relation? *Journal of Epidemiology and Community Health, 55*, 172–178.

Rosenberg, M., & Rossman, R. (1990). The child witness to marital violence. In R. T. Ammerman & M. Hersen (Eds.), *Treatment of family violence: A sourcebook* (pp. 183–210). New York: John Wiley & Sons.

Saltzman, L. (2004). Issues related to defining and measuring violence against women: Response to Kilpatrick. *Journal of Interpersonal Violence, 19*, 1235–1243.

Schumacher, J. A., Feldbau-Kohn, S., Slep, A. M., & Heyman, R. E. (2001). Risk factors for male-to-female partner physical violence. *Aggression and Violent Behavior, 6*, 281–352.

Sedlak, A. J. (1997). Risk factors for the occurrence of child abuse and neglect. *Journal of Aggression, Maltreatment, and Trauma, 1*, 149–187.

Silverman, J., Raj, A., Mucci, L., & Hathaway, J. (2001). Dating violence against adolescent girls and associated substance use, unhealthy weight control, sexual risk behavior, pregnancy and suicidality. *Journal of the American Medical Association, 286*, 572–579.

Smuts, B. (1992). Male aggression against women: An evolutionary perspective. *Human Nature, 3*, 1–44.

Sommers, C. H. (1994). *Who stole feminism? How women have betrayed women*. New York: Simon and Schuster.

Stith, S. M., Smith, D. B., Penn, C. E., Ward. D. B., & Tritt, D. (2004). Intimate partner physical abuse perpetration and victimization risk factors: A meta-analytic review. *Aggression and Violent Behavior, 10*, 65–98.

Straus, M. A. (1998). The controversy over domestic violence by women: A methodological, theoretical, and sociology of science analysis. In X. B. Arriaga & S. Oskamp (Eds.), *Violence in intimate relationships*. Thousand Oaks, CA: Sage.

Straus, M. A. (2005). Physical assault by wives: A major social problem. In D. Loseke, R. J. Gelles, & M. Cavanaugh (Eds.), *Current controversies on family violence* (2nd ed., pp. 55–78). Thousand Oaks, CA: Sage.

Straus, M. A., & Gelles, R. J. (1986). Societal change and change in family violence from 1975 to 1985 as revealed in two national surveys. *Journal of Marriage and the Family, 48*, 465–479.

Straus, M. A., Gelles, R. J., & Steinmetz, S. K. (1980). *Behind closed doors: Violence in the American family*. New York: Doubleday/Anchor.

Straus, M. A., & Kaufman Kantor, G. (1994). *Change in spouse assault rates from 1975 to 1992: A comparison of three national surveys in the United States*. Paper presented at the 13th World Congress of Sociology, Bielefeld, Germany.

Straus, M. A., & Smith, C. (1990). Violence in Hispanic families in the United States: Incidence rates and structural interpretations. In M. A. Straus & R. J. Gelles (Eds.), *Physical violence in American families: Risk factors and adaptations in 8,145 families* (pp. 341–367). New Brunswick, NJ: Transaction Books.

Straus, M. A., & Stewart, J. (1999). Corporal punishment by American parents: National data on prevalence, chronicity, severity, and duration in relation to child and family characteristics. *Clinical Child and Family Psychology Review, 2*, 55–70.

Tjaden, P. (2004). What is violence against women? Defining and measuring the problem: A response to Dean Kilpatrick. *Journal of Interpersonal Violence, 19*, 1244–1251.

Tjaden, P. & Thoennes, N. (1998). *Prevalence, incidence and consequences of violence against women: Findings from the National Violence Against Women Survey.* Denver, CO: Center for Policy Research.

Tjaden, P. & Thoennes, N. (2000). *Extent, nature and consequences of intimate partner violence.* (NCJ Publication No. 181867). Washington, DC: U.S. Department of Justice.

Turrell, S. C. (2000). A descriptive analysis of same-sex relationship violence for a diverse sample. *Journal of Family Violence, 15,* 281–294.

U.S. Bureau of the Census. (1992). *Statistical abstract of the United States.* Washington, DC: U.S. Government Printing Office.

U.S. Department of Health and Human Services, Administration on Children, Youth and Families. (2005). *Child maltreatment: 2003.* Washington, DC: U.S. Government Printing Office.

Wolfner, G., & Gelles, R. J. (1993). A profile of violence toward children. *Child Abuse and Neglect: The International Journal, 17,* 197–212.

Yllo, K. (1983). Using a feminist approach in quantitative research. In D. Finkelhor, R. Gelles, M. Straus, & G. Hotaling (Eds.), *The dark side of families: Current family violence research* (pp. 277–288). Beverly Hills, CA: Sage.

Yllo, K. (1988). Political and methodological debates in wife abuse research. In K. Yllo & M. Bograd (Eds.), *Feminist perspectives on wife abuse* (pp. 28–50). Newbury Park, CA: Sage.

Zlotnick, C. K., Kohn, R., Peterson, J., & Pearlstein, T. (1998). Partner physical victimization in a national sample of American families. *Journal of Interpersonal Violence, 13,* 156–166.

CHAPTER 20

Youth Violence Across Ethnic and National Groups: Comparisons of Rates and Developmental Processes

Alexander T. Vazsonyi, Elizabeth Trejos-Castillo, and Li Huang

Introduction

Since the late 1980s, violence among youth in the United State has been a serious public health problem. Crime statistics in the United States show that in 2002 law enforcement agencies in the United States made an estimated 2.3 million arrests of persons under the age of 18. According to the Federal Bureau of Investigation (FBI, 2003), juveniles accounted for 17% of total arrests and for 15% of all violent crime arrests in 2002. Similarly, Snyder (2004) reports that arrests of juveniles accounted for 12% of all violent crimes cleared by arrest – specifically, 5% of murders, 12% of forcible rapes, 14% of robberies, and 12% of aggravated assaults. According to the Centers for Disease Control and Prevention (CDC), more than 877,700 youth in United States between the ages of 10 to 24 years were injured as a result of violent acts during 2002, and approximately 1 in 13 required hospitalization (CDC, 2004). In fact, homicide is the second leading cause of death among youth aged 10 to 24 (Anderson, Kaufman, Simon, Barrios, Paulozzi, & Ryan, 2001). Although

crime rates have decreased during recent years in the United States, based on youth violence statistics, they remain the highest among developed nations (Snyder, 2004). Interestingly, crime rates in the United States based on victimization data appear much less dramatic in comparison to data from other developed countries (Van Kesteren, Mayhew, & Nieuwbeerta, 2000).

In response to the observed differences in rates of crime, particularly violent crime, researchers have become increasingly interested in studying these differences through both cross-cultural and cross-national comparative methods. The need for comparative scholarship on violence and crime seems acute because national differences, in particular, are of such remarkable magnitude. The importance of comparative work is that it can provide new insights and answers to the apparently large differences in rates of violent crime across groups; in addition, it can also inform theoretical work on the etiology of youth violence and guide prevention and intervention efforts that seek to address this issue. In this chapter, based on a cross-cultural and cross-national comparative method, we examine both rates of violence and developmental processes – namely, the relationships between key family processes and measures of violence – across 11 groups of adolescents in five different countries.

The Importance of Comparative Studies on Violence

Comparative research is for the most part a "natural extension of earlier, usually intracultural work" (van de Vijver & Leung, 1997, p. xii). Rohner (1977) identified three reasons for completing comparative research: (1) to test for the level of generalizability of a theory or a proposition, (2) to test for the effects of more extreme behavior that can be found normally within any single society, and (3) to be able to systematically vary factors that cannot be varied within a single population or cultural system. By definition, generalizability studies attempt to establish the generalizability of research findings obtained in one group. Such studies make little or no reference to cultural elements other than the target variables on which cultures are compared. On the other hand, theory-driven studies examine specific aspects of a culture, such as its ecology, ways of raising children, or particular cultural habits that are part of a theoretical framework. Cultural and national variation on these specific aspects is deliberately examined as a way to validate a theoretical model. Thus, specific a priori predictions are tested in these studies. The aims of comparative studies are to explore and to explain potential cross-cultural similarities or differences in levels of violence as well as etiological factors known to be important in violence. These aims can only be accomplished by sampling cultural or national groups known to vary in rates of youth violence (van de Vijver & Leung, 1997). Thus, in a way comparative research is simply an important methodological tool.

Van de Vijver and Leung (1997) have argued that comparative studies are quasi-experiments; they suggest that recent comparative work has been more consistent with a focus on processes or the relationships between variables of interest in contrast with earlier comparative work. They point out that the comparative approach has "become part and parcel of the scientific enterprise in the social and behavioral sciences" (p. 146). From this point of view, there is a great need to conduct comparative research on youth violence to examine potential similarities or differences in the known etiological factors of violence, such as family processes. The comparative method is a sound and rigorous methodological tool useful in establishing the validity, reliability, and generalizability of assessment tools, developmental ideas, as well as explanatory concepts and constructs (Vazsonyi, 2003; Vazsonyi, Hibbert, & Snider, 2003). In the end, without rigorous comparative research, context specificity or the generality of explanatory constructs of violence remains unknown (Archer & Gartner, 1984).

Rates of Violence Across Countries: Official Data, Victimization Data, and Self-Report Studies

There are three principal methods to assess rates of violence in different developmental contexts: official data based on public health databases or crime statistics, victimization using within-country efforts, and "local" efforts based on self-report studies. Official rates of crime and violence indicate that there are large differences among countries, perhaps implicating unique cultural factors in both the etiology and observed rates of violence. Krug, Mercy, Dahlberg, and Powell (1998) conducted an international comparison of firearm and non-firearm-related homicides among children in 27 countries. These countries included both high-income countries (e.g., Japan, The Netherlands, Switzerland, and the United States) and ones characterized by more modest income levels (e.g., Hungary, Mexico, and Slovenia). Findings from this study showed that homicide rates for children under the age of 15 years were five times higher in the United States than in the 26 other countries combined (2.57 vs. 0.51). Lim, Bond, and Bond (2005) recently investigated how society-level homicide data from official sources were associated with "psychological" factors across 56 different nations. The novel characteristic of this study was its use of both society-level measures (e.g., GNP per capita, total unemployment, sex ratio, divorce rate) and psychological measures (e.g., trust, social axioms, emotionality) to develop an understanding of the associations among factors that predict national homicide rates. The study illustrates the importance of combining known etiological constructs with society-level data to develop a more nuanced understanding of the phenomenon. A pressing question that remains is to determine what contributes to observed differences across cultural and national groups. Is there something unique about the United States that could explain the unusually high rates of violence, or alternatively, are there characteristics found in other cultures or countries that can account for observed differences?

A second source for comparative data on violence is victimization data. In part because of the inadequacies associated with comparing official data, the International Crime Victimization Survey (ICVS) examines self-reported rates of victimization, thereby allowing an estimation of "true" levels of violence and crime. To date, surveys have been carried out in 24 industrialized countries since 1989. Interestingly, according to the ICVS conducted in 1999, individuals from the United States reported victimization rates ranging between 20% and 24, which are lower than rates observed in Australia, England, the Netherlands, and Sweden, where victimization rates exceeded 24%. In addition, compared to European countries, crime trends in North America showed substantial declines over time. In the case of personal crimes (robbery, sexual assault, and assault with force), the United States ranked among the lowest: aggressive interpersonal conduct was 1.9% in the United States compared to 2.4% in Australia, 3.6% in England and Wales, and 3.4% in Canada. Similarly, the average violent victimization rate across all study countries was about 3.5% in 1999. This figure was only markedly higher in Australia, Scotland, England, and Wales (about 6%), as well as Canada (5%), whereas it was lower in Japan and Portugal (under 1%; Van Kesteren et al., 2000). The ICVS data also provide evidence that crime increased between 1988 and 1991, stabilized or declined by 1995, and then decreased further by 1999 in most countries. In contrast, victimization data from the United States have shown consistent drops in crime since 1988.

Compared with official data, the major advantage of the ICVS data is that questions and response categories are worded in an identical manner across countries, thereby optimizing cross-national comparability. Official figures based on police reports suffer from major definitional inconsistencies (e.g., van Wilsem, Dirk de Graaf, & Wittebrood, 2003), as well as differences in how offenses are coded and handled or recorded by law enforcement across contexts. In this sense, the ICVS aims to address inadequacies of other crime or violence measures across countries. Studies using the ICVS data set have provided some preliminary evidence of country-level effects based on multilevel analyses of victimization rates across 18 countries (van Wilsem et al., 2003). More specifically, based on data collected between 1992 and 1997, the authors found evidence that theft and violent victimization were associated with national levels of income inequality. They also found that countries with predominantly urban residents had overall higher crime rates. Though the ICVS data are an improvement over official data from different countries, they still do not allow for more rigorous comparative tests of the importance of known predictors of violence across groups, such as family processes. These tests can only be addressed with identical "local" self-report studies that include more extensive measurement of key variables of interest, which then allows for comparative analysis.

Family Processes and Violence

Research has consistently identified relationships between parenting or family process variables and measures of crime, deviance, and violence. Independent of a particular theoretical orientation, it has been shown that effective parenting – namely an affectively close relationship, consistent supervision and monitoring of behaviors, as well as consistent disciplinary practices by parents or caregivers – is associated with positive developmental outcomes in children and youth, whereas missing closeness, supervision, or discipline is associated with negative outcomes, such as antisocial, aggressive, or violent behaviors (e.g., Florsheim, Tolan, & Gorman-Smith, 1996; Gottfredson & Hirschi, 1990; Loeber & Stouthamer-Loeber, 1986; Patterson, Capaldi, & Bank, 1991). Only a relatively small number of studies in this literature have been comparative in nature, mostly focusing on parenting practices and youth violence across different ethnic groups.

Henry, Tolan, and Gorman-Smith (2001) examined the longitudinal associations between (1) family relationships, violence, and nonviolent delinquency of peers and (2) individual delinquency and violence in samples of African American and Latino male youth. Their study provided evidence that youth from families characterized by warm interpersonal relationships and effective parenting were less likely to affiliate with violent peers and to engage in violent and delinquent behaviors, whereas youth from families characterized by low emotional closeness and ineffective parenting skills were more likely to engage in violent behaviors. The study provided some evidence of ethnic/racial differences, as peer violence was only predictive of violence in Hispanic youth, but not African American adolescents. On the other hand, in a study by Forehand, Miller, Dutra, and Chance (1997), the authors tested the importance of parenting processes in adolescent deviant behavior across populations of African American and Hispanic youth. Their findings provided evidence that parental monitoring was the most important predictor and furthermore that this predictor was of equal salience across groups. In general, these findings suggest that the protective effect of parental monitoring is similar by sex, race, ethnicity, and context.

Over the past decade, there has been an increase in scholarship not only on cross-ethnic or racial comparisons (e.g., Knight, Tein, Shell, & Roosa, 1992) but also on cross-national studies of developmental processes that seek to examine whether variability in family processes is associated with youth violence, crime, and delinquency in a similar or dissimilar manner. For instance, Barber and Harmon (2001) conducted a study on the importance of psychological control in antisocial behaviors across nine cultures (or groups): the United States (White), United States (Cheyenne), Colombia, India, Gaza, South Africa (White), South Africa (Black), South African (Colored), and Australia. Psychological control was positively associated with antisocial behaviors across all groups except Colombia. More specifically, standardized regression coefficients ranged from .20 (for United States Cheyenne sample) to .29 (Gaza sample), with an average of .24 across all nine cultures. Thus, the literature provides some evidence that family relationship characteristics or parenting practices may be associated with measures of violence, crime, and deviance in a similar manner across racial, ethnic, or national groups. This means that despite observed mean-level differences in ethnic, racial, or national groups, developmental processes might be similar. Because of the scarcity of studies that have tested this question cross-culturally and cross-nationally, thus limiting the scope of our knowledge base and inhibiting the development of generalizable violence prevention and intervention programs, this chapter also examines developmental processes. In particular, it tests whether developmental processes, namely the associations between family processes and measures of violence, are similar or different in youth across 11 racial and national groups.

The Current Study

The current study aims to fill this gap in the literature of cross-cultural and cross-national comparative studies on youth violence by assessing rates of violence and by comparing developmental processes. It focuses on the potential similarities or differences in the patterns of association between family processes and measures of violence across 11 samples collected in five countries (Hungary, Japan, The Netherlands, Switzerland, and the United States). Data on 9,244 middle and late adolescents (mean age = 17.8 years) were collected as part of the International Study of Adolescent Development (ISAD). The purpose of ISAD was to examine the etiology of adolescent problem behaviors and deviance and to use large, locally representative samples from different countries. All study locations followed a standard data collection protocol, which was approved by a university Institutional Review Board. The protocol consisted of a self-report data collection instrument, which included instructions on how to complete the survey, a description of the ISAD project, and assurances of anonymity. Project staff or teachers who had received extensive verbal and written instructions administered the questionnaires in classrooms, thereby maintaining a standardized protocol across all study locations. Students had a 1- to 2-hour period during which to complete the survey.

Much attention was given to the development of the ISAD survey instrument, particularly by developing new or employing existing measures that could be used cross-culturally without losing nuances or changing meanings. The survey was translated from English into the target languages (Dutch, German, Hungarian, and Japanese) and back-translated by bilingual translators. Surveys were examined by additional bilingual translators; when translation was difficult or ambiguous, consensus was used to produce the final translation.

Method

Samples. Data were collected from 9,244 middle and late adolescents (high school and college age) in five countries (Hungary, $n = 871$; Japan, $n = 355$; The Netherlands, $n = 1,315$; Switzerland, $n = 4,018$; and the United States, $n = 2,685$). In most loca-

tions, schools located in medium-sized cities of similar size were selected for participation. For the Swiss samples, this included a school for university-bound students (Gymnasium), one for teacher's training, and one specializing in vocational/technical training for students in apprenticeships. In the United States, the samples included both rural (African American) and nonrural (African American and Caucasian White) high-school students and university students (both African American and Caucasian; for additional sample details, see Vazsonyi & Crosswhite, 2004; Vazsonyi et al., 2001, 2004).

Measures. Individuals in each country (region) were asked to fill out an identical questionnaire including demographic and background variables (age, sex, family structure, and socioeconomic indicators), measures of family processes, and measures of crime and deviance (details available from the first author). *Family processes* were assessed by three subscales of the Adolescent Family Process (AFP) measure (Vazsonyi et al., 2003) which consisted of 14 items that assessed maternal parenting (closeness, monitoring, support); items were rated on two different 5-point Likert-type scales (1 = *strongly disagree* to 5 = *strongly agree* and 1 = *never* to 5 = *very often*) and averaged for three scale scores. Reliability coefficients ($\alpha = .62$ to $\alpha = 89$) indicated adequate internal consistency across sample subscales and samples. *Assault* was measured by four items (e.g., "Used force or threatened to beat someone up if they didn't give you money or something else you wanted?" or "Beaten someone up so badly they required medical attention?"). Items were rated on a 5-point Likert-type scale and identified the lifetime frequency of behaviors (1 = *never* to 5 = *more than six times*) and averaged. Reliability estimates indicated good internal consistency across samples (see Table 20.2), except for ratings by Japanese adolescents and youth from the Swiss teacher's college. Four items measured *violence witnessing/victimization* (e.g., "Witnessed a crime against property [e.g., theft, vandalism, etc.]?" or "Been a victim of crime against your property [e.g., assault, rape, robbery, etc.]?"). The four items were averaged to form a single score. Reliability coefficients for this scale ranged from $\alpha = .60$ to $\alpha = .93$ across groups.

Results

In an initial step, descriptive statistics and scale reliabilities were computed for each sample and are shown in Table 20.1. With some exceptions (e.g., the assault measure in the Japanese sample and the sample of adolescents attending the teacher's college), scales were internally consistent. Next, in an effort to compare rates of violence across samples, and due to sample differences in key demographic variables, mean assault and witnessing/victimization violence scores were residualized by age, sex, family structure, and SES. These residualized scores were then compared in a one-way ANOVA with post hoc contrasts, where the alpha level was adjusted to reflect the large number of pair-wise tests; more specifically, the critical value was changed from 1.96 to 2.81 ($p = .05/11 = .005$). Figure 20.1A and B includes two plots of standardized residual scores by sample, one for assault and one for violence witnessing/victimization. To simplify discussion of these comparisons by sample, standardized mean difference effect sizes (d) were also computed based on each pair-wise contrast. In total, 110 contrasts were completed and 110 effect sizes computed, 55 for each measure of violence. Most differences were related to the rural African American sample of youth; more specifically, of 16 observed differences on the assault measure, 10 were due to significantly higher levels of assault in rural African American youth in comparison to all other samples, where effect sizes ranged from $d = .31$ to $d = .78$. The remaining six differences were due to significantly higher levels of assault reported by Swiss apprentices (effect size range: $d = .24$ to $d = .47$) in comparison not only to Dutch, Hungarian, and Japanese youth but also to Swiss Gymnasium students as well as Caucasian youth attending high school and college in the United States.

Similar differences were observed in the second measure of violence; of only 13 statistically significant differences, which were generally more modest in size than for the assault measure, 6 were due to higher levels in rural African American youth in comparison to Dutch, Japanese, Hungarian, and all three Swiss samples (effect size range: $d = .28$ to $d = .60$), and 5 were due to significantly lower levels of violence in the Japanese sample in comparison to Dutch youth, Swiss apprentices, both Caucasian and African American high-school students and Caucasian college students (effect size range: $d = .43$ to $d = .58$). The remaining two differences were related to higher levels in Caucasian college students as compared to Hungarian youth and Swiss Gymnasium students ($d = .24$ and $d = .26$, respectively). In summary, only about one quarter of all comparisons (29 of 110, or 26%) indicated statistically significant differences across samples.

The second set of analyses examined developmental processes, namely the patterns of associations between family processes and violence measures. Based on the total sample, Table 20.2 includes partial correlations, where age, sex, family structure, and SES were entered as controls. Consistent with expectations, family processes were negatively associated with the two violence measures. Closeness, support, and monitoring were modestly associated with assault, namely $r = -.21$, $r = -.21$, and $r = -.14$ ($p < .001$), respectively. Similar findings were also made for violence witnessing/victimization. Table 20.3 repeated the same analysis by sample. Findings provided preliminary evidence of great similarities in the associations between family process measures and both violence measures across samples.

Finally, to test this preliminary evidence of similarities in developmental processes, the final analytic step included a comparison of eleven 5 × 5 matrices of partial correlations (three family processes and two measures of violence) using a model-free LISREL analytic approach as pioneered by

Table 20.1: Descriptive statistics and reliabilities of scales

	Items	U.S. HS (AA) N = 180			U.S. HS (C) N = 620			U.S. Rural HS (AA) N = 689			U.S. Univ. (AA) N = 114			U.S. Univ. (C) N = 1,082		
		α	M	SD	α	M	SD	α	M	SD	α	M	SD	α	M	SD
Closeness	6	.82	3.91	.91	.84	3.97	.85	.88	3.64	.99	.87	4.12	.85	.87	4.30	.74
Support	4	.83	3.58	1.23	.88	3.89	1.19	.89	3.36	1.30	.84	4.14	1.03	.85	4.16	.99
Monitoring	4	.81	3.87	1.00	.76	3.81	.89	.84	3.64	1.03	.69	3.40	.92	.79	3.60	.92
Assault	4	.84	1.43	.79	.81	1.24	.63	.93	1.80	1.14	.85	1.19	.54	.75	1.13	.39
Wit/Vict.	4	.84	1.60	.91	.79	1.58	.80	.93	1.84	1.17	.81	1.57	.80	.75	1.54	.70

	Items	Hungary N = 871			Japan N = 355			Netherlands N = 1,315			Swiss Apprentices N = 2,735			Swiss Gymnasium N = 988			Swiss Teacher's College N = 295		
		α	M	SD	α	M	SD	α	M	SD	α	M	SD	α	M	SD	α	M	SD
Closeness	6	.80	3.91	.70	.75	3.91	.68	.73	3.72	.65	.75	3.85	.72	.74	3.91	.66	.67	4.00	.58
Support	4	.76	3.79	.93	.79	4.01	.89	.78	3.84	1.02	.77	4.09	.97	.69	4.30	.78	.62	4.30	.74
Monitoring	4	.75	3.65	.83	.69	2.94	.88	.72	3.55	.84	.78	3.46	.99	.79	3.70	.86	.80	3.90	.81
Assault	4	.73	1.23	.55	.47	1.10	.29	.69	1.22	.49	.75	1.38	.68	.64	1.19	.42	.48	1.12	.29
Wit/Vict.	4	.75	1.47	.67	.67	1.20	.47	.67	1.44	.63	.71	1.51	.71	.64	1.41	.56	.60	1.30	.46

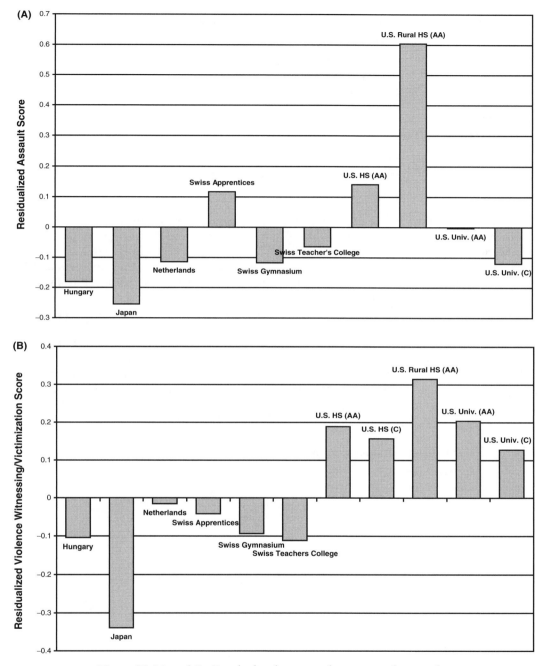

Figure 20.1A and B. Residualized mean violence scores by sample.

Rowe, Vazsonyi, and Flannery (1994). This efficient analytic technique in effect requests an evaluation of whether patterns of associations between the five key constructs vary across the 11 samples; the approach is effi-

cient because avoids the potential problems associated with completing a very large number of pair-wise comparisons necessary to assess similarity or difference, thus also reducing the chances of Type I errors.

Table 20.2: Partial correlations of total sample

	1	2	3	4
1. Closeness				
2. Support	.43			
3. Monitoring	.37	.07		
4. Assault	−.21	−.21	−.14	
5. Witnessing/Victimization Violence	−.16	−.19	−.12	.54

Note: Correlations are statistically significant at $p < .001$. Controls include age, sex, family structure, and SES.

Standard SEM fit statistics are used to assess whether the matrices are similar or different. Standardized measures of association (partial correlations) were used as they are more appropriate, especially when comparing different samples from different cultures (Loehlin, 1992). Model fit was good based on this analysis: $X^2 = 477.35$ ($df = 150$), $CFI = .95$, $RMSEA = .05$. Because of the large sample size, and consistent with expectations, the X^2 was statistically significant, though alternative assessments of fit provided additional evidence of good fit (X^2/df ratio: 3.18).

Program output also allowed an inspection of "by sample" fit, and thus, percentage contribution to the chi square statistic. Figure 20.2 summarizes these percentages by sample. These numbers provided some indication of potential differences in developmental processes, especially for rural African American youth, where the value exceeded 30%. This difference was also confirmed by individual fit measures, as well as through an inspection of plotted standardized residuals, which were quite large. As a simple check of how much these data affected fit across all samples, the test was repeated without

Table 20.3: Partial correlations by sample

	Hungary	Japan	Netherlands	Swiss Apprentices	Swiss Gymnasium	Swiss Teachers College	U.S. HS (AA)	U.S. HS (C)	U.S. Rural HS (AA)	U.S. Univ. (AA)	U.S. Univ. (C)
Assault											
Closeness	−.18**	−.09+	−.20**	−.23**	−.15**	−.15*	−.21*	−.32**	−.25**	−.18+	−.19**
Support	−.11**	−.15**	−.19**	−.25**	−.22**	−.26**	−.05	−.28**	−.30**	−.19+	−.19**
Monitoring	−.23**	.02	−.15**	−.16**	−.11**	−.05	−.25**	−.27**	−.19**	−.05	−.08**
Witnessing/ Victimization											
Closeness	−.18**	−.08	−.18**	−.20**	−.09**	−.17**	−.10	−.32**	−.17**	−.05	−.12**
Support	−.16**	−.07	−.16**	−.21**	−.14**	−.08	−.11	−.33**	−.23**	−.02	−.16**
Monitoring	−.14**	−.01	−.09**	−.17**	−.15**	−.08	−.26**	−.23**	−.10	−.01	−.10

Note: * $p < .05$, ** $p < .01$, + $p < .1$. Controls include age, sex, family structure, and SES. Sample size varied by analysis due to missing data. AA: African American; C: Caucasian.

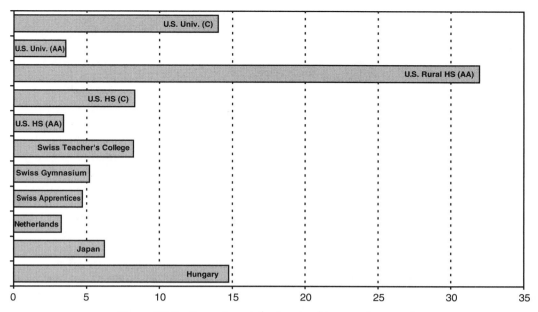

Figure 20.2. Percent contribution to chi square by sample.

the rural African American sample included. Fit only improved slightly, namely $X^2 = 320.77$ ($df = 135$), $CFI = .97$, $RMSEA = .04$, which provided further evidence that though this sample fit the poorest, developmental processes across the 11 samples tested were highly similar.

Discussion

In this chapter, we applied a cross-cultural and cross-national comparative framework to the study of adolescent violence. Based on youth self-reports, our study tested two main questions: whether rates of violence differed by cultural and national groups of adolescents and whether developmental processes are similar or different across cultural and national groups of youth. These questions were addressed because evidence based on official data indicates that the United States has far more violence than other Western countries, though these differences appear to be less dramatic based on international victimization data. "Local" self-report studies are proposed as viable alternatives to both official data and victimization data as

they can not only provide more nuanced information about rates of violence but they also allow tests of known etiological factors.

With some exceptions (e.g., rural African American youth, Japanese late adolescents, and Swiss apprentices), rates of both multi-item indicators of violence, namely assault and witnessing/victimization of violence, were largely invariant across cultural and national groups. Rural African American youth reported significantly higher levels of violence than youth in all other samples and significantly higher levels of witnessing/victimization of violence than a number of samples. Interestingly, Swiss apprentices also exceeded over half of all groups in rates of violence, whereas Japanese late adolescents reported lower levels of witnessing/victimization of violence than a number of their peers. On the question of etiological differences with a focus on key family process measures, the study provides strong evidence of highly similar developmental processes, again with the exception of rural African American youth. Inspection of partial correlation coefficients in this latter group does not provide substantial evidence of differences in comparison to the other samples, even though monitoring is unexpectedly unrelated to witnessing/victimization of violence. In general, the results provide evidence that closeness and support appear to be key family processes across samples in the etiology of violence.

In this sense, findings are inconsistent with Gorman-Smith, Tolan, and Henry's (1999) findings. The authors found that in inner-city communities, the amount of stress experienced by youth and their families appears to overwhelm the impact of family functioning, whereas in urban poor communities, the emotional closeness of the family, beliefs about the importance of family, and effective discipline appear to mediate the effects of stress experienced. These results provided some evidence that previous intervention programs that focused on discipline or monitoring may not be as effective with families living in the inner city as compared to families living in other settings. This finding may also apply to the rural African American sample in the current study.

On the other hand, findings are also consistent with Forehand et al. (1997) and Barber and Harmon's (2001) work in showing a great amount of similarities across groups. Forehand et al. (1997) found that parental monitoring was of primary importance in terms of reducing adolescent problem behaviors in four separate samples from New York, Puerto Rico, and Montgomery, Alabama. Similarly, Barber and Harmon (2001) found that psychological control was positively associated with externalizing behaviors across nine cultural groups they tested: United States (White, Cheyenne), Colombia, India, Gaza, South Africa (White, Black, and Colored), and Australia.

Findings from this study provide some evidence that employing alternative "local" methods in a cross-cultural and cross-national comparative framework appears to be informative in the study of youth violence. Evidence of great similarities in both rates and etiology of violence provides an impetus to consider more broad sweeping, coordinated approaches to the study and prevention of violence; violence appears to be similarly prevalent in a number of cultural and national settings and also consistently associated with the primary socialization mechanism, namely the family. Though comparisons based on official data and descriptive victimization studies are informative, they may also build obstacles in the sense of emphasizing idiosyncratic, contextual explanations, when in fact, violence seems ubiquitous, perhaps a quasi-universal behavioral manifestation and problem. Hamburg and Hamburg (2004) recently provided not only a succinct analysis of what leads to interpersonal violence but also of what socialization mechanisms, such as the family, school, and society as a whole, can do to prevent these behaviors. It appears that some of the propensity to commit violence is largely biological in origin, and certainly the great human need to belong and to differentiate the self from others – the "us versus them" phenomenon – plays prominently into what leads to interpersonal violent conduct. We have shown that some adolescents engage in violent behaviors across cultures and nations to a largely similar extent. We believe that the comparative approach to studying human development as well as to studying the etiology and specific manifestations of behaviors shows good promise of providing important insights into violent behavior, the etiology of violence, and prevention and intervention efforts. We look forward to additional empirical investigations in this area.

Appendix

Assault

Used force or threatened to beat someone up if they didn't give you money or something else you wanted?

Beaten someone up so badly they required medical attention?

Hit or threatened to hit your parent(s)?

Been involved in gang fights or other gang activities?

Violence Witnessing/Victimization

Witnessed a crime against property (e.g., theft, vandalism, etc.)?

Been a victim of crime against your property (e.g., assault, rape, robbery, etc.)?

Witnessed a crime against a person (e.g., assault, rape, robbery, etc.)?

Been a victim of a crime against your person (e.g., assault, rape, robbery, etc.)

References

Anderson, M. A., Kaufman, J., Simon, T. R., Barrios, L., Paulozzi, L., & Ryan, G. (2001). School-associated violent deaths in the United States, 1994–1999. *Journal of the American Medical Association, 286*, 2695–2702.

Archer, D., & Gartner, R. (1984). *Violence and crime in cross-national perspective.* New Haven, CT: Yale University Press.

Barber, B. K., & Harmon, E. L. (2001). Violating the self: Parental psychological control of children and adolescents. In B. K. Barber (Ed.), *Intrusive parenting: How psychological control affects children and adolescent* (pp. 15–52). Washington, DC: American Psychological Association.

Centers for Disease Control (2004). *Web-based Injury Statistics Query and Reporting System (WISQARS).* Retrieved May 17, 2004, from www.cdc.gov/ncipc/wisqars.

Federal Bureau of Investigation (2003). *Uniform crime reports 2002.* Retrieved December 28, 2004, from www.fbi.gov/ucr/cius/02/pdf/02crime.pdf.

Florsheim, P., Tolan, P. H., & Gorman-Smith, D. (1996). Family processes and risk for externalizing behavior problems among African American and Hispanic boys. *Journal of Consulting and Clinical Psychology, 64*(6), 1222–1230.

Forehand, R., Miller, K. S., Dutra, R., & Chance, M. W. (1997). Role of parenting in adolescent deviant behavior: Replication across and within two ethnic groups. *Journal of Consulting and Clinical Psychology, 65*(6), 1036–1041.

Gorman-Smith, D., Tolan, P. H., & Henry, D. (1999). The relation of community and family to risk among urban-poor adolescents. In C. Cohen, C. Slomkowski, & L. N. Robins (Eds.), *Historical and geographical influences on psychopathology* (pp. 349–367). Mahwah, NJ: Erlbaum.

Gottfredson, M. R., & Hirschi, T. (1990). *A general theory of crime.* Palo Alto, CA: Stanford University Press.

Hamburg, D. A., & Hamburg, B. A. (2004). *Learning to live together: Preventing hatred and violence in child and adolescent development.* New York: Oxford University Press.

Henry, D. B., Tolan, P. H., & Gorman-Smith, D. (2001). Longitudinal family and peer group effects on violence and nonviolent delinquency. *Journal of Clinical Child Psychology, 30*(2), 172–186.

Knight, G. P., Tein, J., Shell, R., & Roosa, M. (1992). The cross ethnic equivalence of parenting and family interaction measures among Hispanic and Anglo-American families. *Child Development, 63*, 1392–1403.

Krug, E. G., Mercy, J. A., Dahlberg, L. L., & Powell, K. E. (1998). Firearm- and non-firearm related homicide among children: An international comparison. *Homicide Studies, 2*(1), 83–95.

Lim, F., Bond, M. H., & Bond, M. K. (2005). Linking societal and psychological factors to homicide rates across nations. *Journal of Cross-Cultural Psychology, 36*(5), 515–536.

Loeber, R., & Stouthamer-Loeber, M. (1986). Family factors as correlates and predictors of juvenile conduct problems and delinquency. In M. Tonry & N. Morris (Eds.), *Crime and justice: An annual review of research* (Vol. 7). Chicago: University of Chicago Press.

Loehlin, J. (1992). *Latent variable models: An introduction to factor, path and structural analysis.* Hillsdale, NJ: Erlbaum.

Patterson, G. R., Capaldi, D., & Bank, L. (1991). An early starter model of predicting delinquency. In D. J. Pepler & K. H. Rubin (Eds.), *The development and treatment of childhood aggression* (pp. 139–168). Hillsdale, NJ: Erlbaum.

Rohner, R. P. (1977). Why cross-cultural research? In L. L. Adler (Ed.), *Issues in cross-cultural research* (pp. 3–12). New York: New York Academy of Sciences.

Rowe, D. C., Vazsonyi, A. T., & Flannery, D. J. (1994). No more than skin deep: Ethnic and racial similarity in developmental process. *Psychological Review, 101*(3), 396–413.

Snyder, H. N. (2004). Juvenile arrests. *Juvenile Justice Bulletin.* Washington, DC: Office of Juvenile Justice and Delinquency Prevention.

Van de Vijver, F., & Leung, K. (1997). *Methods and data analysis for cross-cultural research.* Thousand Oaks, CA: Sage.

Van Kesteren, J. N., Mayhew, P., & Nieuwbeerta, P. (2000). *Criminal victimization in seventeen industrialized countries: Key findings from the 2000 international Crime Victims Survey.* The Hague: Ministry of Justice, WODC.

van Wilsem, J., Dirk de Graaf, N. D., & Wittebrood, K. (2003). Cross-national differences in victimization. Disentangling the impact of composition and context. *European Sociological Review, 19,* 125–142.

Vazsonyi, A. T. (2003). Cross-national comparative research in criminology: Content or simply methodology? In C. Britt & M. R. Gottfredson (Eds.), *Control theories of crime and delinquency* (Vol. 12, pp. 179–211). New Brunswick, NJ: Transaction Publishers.

Vazsonyi, A. T., & Crosswhite, J. M. (2004). A test of Gottfredson and Hirschi's General Theory of Crime in African American adolescents.

Journal of Research in Crime and Delinquency, 41(4), 407–432.

Vazsonyi, A. T., Hibbert, J. R., & Snider, J. B. (2003). Exotic enterprise no more? Adolescent reports of family and parenting processes from youth in four countries. *Journal of Research on Adolescence, 13*(2), 129–160.

Vazsonyi, A. T., Pickering, L. E., Junger, M., & Hessing, D. (2001). An empirical test of general theory of crime: A four-nation comparative study of self-control and the prediction of deviance. *Journal of Research in Crime and Delinquency, 38*(2), 91–131.

Vazsonyi, A. T., Wittekind, J. E., Belliston, L. M., & Van Loh, T. (2004). Extending the General Theory of Crime to "The East": Low self-control in Japanese late adolescents. *Journal of Quantitative Criminology, 20*(3), 189–216.

CHAPTER 21

Adolescent Dating Abuse Perpetration: A Review of Findings, Methodological Limitations, and Suggestions for Future Research

Vangie A. Foshee and Rebecca A. Matthew

Abuse in adolescent dating relationships first came to the attention of researchers and practitioners through seminal articles and books published by June Henton (Henton, Cate, Koval, Lloyd, & Christopher, 1983) and Barrie Levy (1990, 1991). Recently, adolescent dating abuse was described as a nascent field of study (Wolfe, Wekerle, Scott, Straatman, & Grasley, 2004). Indeed, the growth of research on adolescent dating abuse has been tremendous in the last few years (see Figure 21.1). In the introduction to one of our adolescent dating abuse papers, written in 1997, we noted that there were no published reports on adolescent dating abuse using longitudinal data. Now, 15 papers have reported findings using longitudinal data. Recent studies have been more theoretically informed and methodologically rigorous than the earlier studies. Even so, we have much work to do to understand the most basic aspects of adolescent dating abuse, including its prevalence, its causes, and how it can be prevented.

This chapter synthesizes the results from research on adolescent dating abuse perpe-tration and points out the methodological limitations of the research. We review findings from studies that examined psychological, physical, or sexual dating abuse perpetration among adolescents who ranged in age from 12 to 20 years old, not including studies conducted with college or other adult samples. We describe how dating abuse perpetration is typically measured and synthesize findings and methodological issues related to determining the extent of the problem. We then describe the associations between demographic characteristics and dating abuse perpetration, with special emphasis on gender-stratified prevalence estimates of dating abuse perpetration and issues related to those estimates, which are among the most controversial issues in the literature. We present results from correlational and etiological studies, as well as studies evaluating the effectiveness of dating abuse prevention programs, and conclude with recommendations for future research on adolescent dating abuse perpetration.

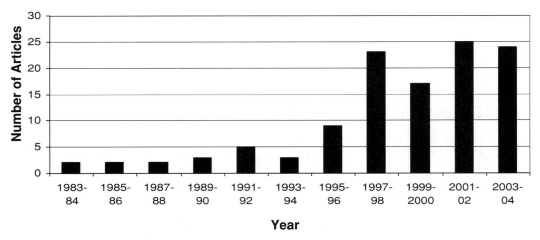

Figure 21.1. Number of adolescent dating abuse articles published in peer-reviewed journals, by year.

Measurement of Adolescent Dating Abuse

Most studies of adolescent dating abuse perpetration measure abuse with an acts scale. On these scales, study respondents indicate whether or how often they have used a specific violent act (e.g., hit, push, assault with a weapon) against a partner. Respondents are categorized as perpetrators or as nonperpetrators based on whether they have done any of the acts listed, or they are given a numerical score based on the number and/or frequency of acts committed. The Conflict Tactics Scale (Straus, 1979) and the Conflict Tactics Scale 2 (Straus, Hamby, Boney-McCoy, & Sugarman, 1996) are the most commonly used acts scales for measuring dating abuse, but others abound (Foshee, 1996; Wolfe, Wekerle, Reitzel-Jaffe, & Lefebvre, 1998; Wolfe, Scott, Reitzel-Jaffe, et al., 2001).

Because of their tendency to flatten the complexity of human social interaction, acts scales have been criticized for being too simplistic. They do not take into consideration the motivations or circumstances surrounding violent acts. Further, kicks to the leg and face are considered to be the same, as are offensive hits and hits in self-defense. In addition, the severity of the violence is difficult to determine from an acts scale, because severity is determined without consideration of the outcome. For example, "twisted my

partner's arm or hair" is listed as a "minor act" on the Conflict Tactics Scale (CTS), but it would not be minor if the arm were broken. Consequently, several researchers have suggested that acts scales do not capture the true nature of partner violence (Bograd, 1990; Breines & Gordon, 1983; Dobash & Dobash, 1988). Dobash and associates (1992) suggest that these types of measures lead to interpretations that "exaggerate, misinterpret, and ultimately trivialize the genuine problem of violence" (p. 79).

Despite these limitations, acts scales continue to be used widely because they are easy to administer and code, they lend themselves well to creating abuse variables that can be used in quantitative analyses, and no alternative measurement technique has been developed that allows for the creation of such variables. Indeed, all of the studies in this review measured dating abuse perpetration with acts scales, and their findings should be considered in light of this limitation.

Extent of the Problem

Point Prevalence Estimates and Methodological Issues

Tremendous variation exists in prevalence estimates of adolescent dating abuse perpetration, making it difficult to ascertain the true extent of the problem. The large variation in prevalence estimates across studies is due to inconsistencies in a number of factors, including (a) the cases that are and are not included in the denominator when calculating estimates (some include daters only, whereas others include the total sample); (b) the time frames assessed (some assess ever perpetration, whereas others assess perpetration only within the past 6 months or only with the current partner); (c) the types of abuse assessed (some estimate psychological, physical, and sexual dating violence perpetration separately, whereas others combine multiple types of abuse into composite measures); (d) the specific behaviors included in composite scores (some composite scores of perpetration include only behaviors that are considered "mild" [e.g., slapped, scratched], some include only "severe" behaviors [e.g., assault with a weapon and beating up], and others include both); (e) the ages studied (some studies look only at middle-school students, others include only high-school students, and some include both); and finally (f) the characteristics of the sample (some are probability samples from localized areas, and some are volunteers in localized areas). Surprisingly, the only nationally representative studies that include dating abuse – the Youth Risk Behavior Survey, the National Longitudinal Study of Adolescent Health (Add Health), and the National Crime Victimization Survey – measure only victimization. Thus, prevalence estimates for dating abuse perpetration by adolescents only come from local samples.

Prevalence estimates of psychological abuse perpetration range from 14 (Wolfe, Scott, Wekerle, & Pittman, 2001) to 82% (Gorman-Smith, Tolan, Sheidow, & Henry, 2001). Between 11 and 41% of adolescents report using some form of physical violence against their dating partners (Avery-Leaf, Cascardi, O'Leary, & Cano, 1997; Bennett & Fineran, 1998; Brendgen, Vitaro, Tremblay, & Lavoie, 2001; Cascardi, Avery-Leaf, O'Leary, & Slep, 1999; Foshee, 1996; Gorman-Smith et al., 2001; Malik, Sorenson, & Aneshensel, 1997; O'Keefe, 1997; O'Keeffe, Brockopp, & Chew, 1986; O'Leary & Slep, 2003; Ozer, Tschann, Pasch, & Flores, 2004; Schwartz, O'Leary,

& Kendziora, 1997; Simons, Lin, & Gordon, 1998; Wolfe, Scott, Wekerle, et al., 2001). Between 4 and 14% of adolescents report using forms of violence against dating partners that are likely to result in serious physical injury, such as hitting a partner with an object, beating up a partner, and using a knife or gun against a partner (Coker et al., 2000; Foshee, 1996; Gorman-Smith et al., 2001; Smith & Williams, 1992). Between 3 and 10% of adolescents report perpetrating sexual violence against a date (Foshee, 1996; O'Keefe, 1997; Poitras & Lavoie, 1995; Schwartz et al., 1997; Smith & Williams, 1992; Wolfe, Scott, Wekerle et al., 2001).

Despite the broad range of prevalence estimates, it is clear that a substantial number of adolescents are perpetrators of dating abuse. Additionally, the studies indicate a high probability that an adolescent who uses violence against a dating partner once will use violence against a dating partner again (Cano, Avery-Leaf, Cascardi, & O'Leary, 1998; Chase, Treboux, O'Leary, & Strassberg, 1998; Foshee, Benefield, Ennett, Bauman, & Suchindran, 2004; O'Leary & Slep, 2003). For example, O'Leary and Slep (2003) found that boys who reported using physical violence against their partner at baseline had a 50% chance of using it again with that same partner within the following 3 months; female perpetrators had a 75% chance. Also, perpetration of one form of dating abuse (psychological, physical, or sexual) correlates with (Cano et al., 1998; Capaldi & Crosby, 1997) and predicts (O'Leary & Slep, 2003; Ozer et al., 2004) perpetration of other forms of dating abuse, and being a perpetrator of dating abuse correlates with being a victim of dating abuse (Bennett & Fineran, 1998; Cano et al., 1998; Gaertner & Foshee, 1999; Gray & Foshee, 1997; Henton et al., 1983; Johnson-Reid & Bivens, 1999; O'Keefe, 1997; O'Keeffe et al., 1986).

The Development of Dating Abuse Perpetration Over Time

Because adolescent dating abuse is still a fairly new area of research, only two multi-wave longitudinal studies have assessed growth trajectories for dating violence perpetration outcomes (Foshee, Bauman et al., 2005; Wolfe et al., 2003). Thus, we have very little information on the development of dating abuse perpetration over the course of adolescence. In a randomized trial of a dating violence prevention program, seven waves of data were collected from adolescents with a history of maltreatment (Wolfe et al., 2003). The data showed a steady decrease in reports of physical and emotional abuse perpetration from ages 14 to 18. Threatening behaviors remained steady across the same time period. One limitation of this analysis was that treatment and control groups were combined when analyzing the growth curves, making it impossible to determine the pattern of growth in dating abuse perpetration for adolescents who were not exposed to a prevention program. In addition to limitations arising from the nonrepresentative sample, another concern is that attrition after the baseline survey could have produced the downward trend observed in the trajectories. Thus, the findings may not be generalizable to the general population of adolescents.

Our Safe Dates Study was a randomized controlled trial testing the effects of a school-based intervention on the prevention of adolescent dating abuse (Foshee et al., 1998, 2000; Foshee, Bauman et al., 2004, 2005). For the trial, the 14 public schools with eighth- or ninth-grade students in one North Carolina county were stratified by grade and matched by school size. One member of each matched pair was randomly assigned to receive the Safe Dates school-based intervention, and the other served as a control. Adolescents in the treatment and control groups completed questionnaires in school at baseline ($n = 1,965$; 81% of all eighth and ninth graders in the county) and then again 1 month and 1, 2, 3, and 4 years after the program was completed.

Using Safe Dates data, we computed random coefficient models to determine the pattern of growth of four types of perpetration (psychological, moderate physical, severe physical, and sexual dating abuse) from 8th to 12th grade. Unlike the Wolfe et al. (2003) study, we used only control group data for the growth modeling, we dealt with attrition by imputing data for missing values using multiple imputation procedures (Rubin, 1987), and the sample was drawn from a general population of adolescents. The results are presented in Figure 21.2.

The quadratic effect of time is associated with moderate physical perpetration ($b = -0.16$, $p = .02$), suggesting that moderate physical perpetration peaks after wave 3, when the adolescents are in grades nine and ten (ages 14 to 15), and then decreases at waves 4 and 5. This is similar to Wolfe et al.'s (2003) finding that physical dating abuse perpetration peaks between 14 and 16 years of age. These conclusions, however, are not consistent with a hypothetical trend in dating abuse perpetration proposed by O'Leary (1999). Based on cross-sectional studies conducted with various age groups, O'Leary proposed that dating abuse increases steadily from ages 10 to 25, where it peaks, and then declines over time. Further, our findings and those of Wolfe and colleagues (2003) suggest that physical dating abuse perpetration may peak earlier than other forms of youth aggression, which have been found to be highest around age 17 (Elliott, Huizinga, & Menard, 1989; Moffitt, 1993). For the other three perpetration outcomes, neither linear nor quadratic effects of time were significant, suggesting that the amount of severe physical, psychological, and sexual abuse perpetration remained constant over time.

Demographic Characteristics and Dating Abuse Perpetration

Almost all of the studies that assessed the association between socioeconomic status and adolescent dating violence perpetration have reported no statistical association (Chapple, 2003; Foshee, Linder, Mac-Dougall, & Bangdiwala, 2001; Lavoie et al., 2002; Malik et al., 1997; O'Keefe, 1997; O'Keeffe et al., 1986; Simons et al., 1998),

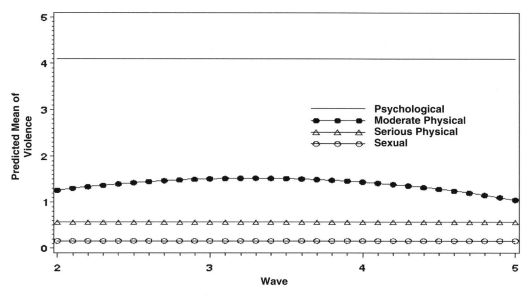

Figure 21.2. Trajectories of four types of dating abuse perpetration over time.

although there was very little variation in socioeconomic status in several of those studies (Chapple, 2003; Lavoie et al., 2002; Simons et al., 1998). An exception was a study conducted in Britain: working-class adolescents reported more dating abuse perpetration than middle- or upper-class adolescents (Hird, 2000). Findings generally suggest that dating violence perpetration is greatest among African American adolescents, followed by Latino and White adolescents, and finally by Asian adolescents (Chapple, 2003; Foshee, Ennett et al., 2005; Malik et al., 1997; O'Keefe, 1997; O'Keeffe et al., 1986; Plass & Gessner, 1983).

Sex-stratified prevalence estimates of adolescent dating abuse perpetration are among the most controversial findings in the adolescent dating abuse area. Most studies that have used acts scales have found that the prevalence of perpetration was either nearly the same for males and females (Bennett & Fineran, 1998; Capaldi & Crosby, 1997; Johnson-Reid & Bivens, 1999; O'Keeffe et al., 1986; Symons, Groër, Kepler-Youngblood, & Slater, 1994; Wolfe et al., 1998) or greater for females than males (Avery-Leaf et al., 1997; Carlson,

1990; Cascardi et al., 1999; Chapple, 2003; Chase et al., 1998; Foshee, 1996; Hird, 2000; Malik et al., 1997; McCloskey & Lichter, 2003; O'Keefe, 1997; O'Leary & Slep, 2003; Ozer et al., 2004; Plass & Gessner, 1983; Schwartz et al., 1997; Wekerle et al., 2001). These findings, however, run counter to societal images of males as the primary perpetrators of partner violence and to the experiences of service providers (McLeod, 1984; Schwartz, 1987) and police officers (Berk, Berk, Loseke, & Rauma, 1983; Dobash & Dobash, 1979; McLeod, 1984), who see almost exclusively female victims and male perpetrators.

Explanations offered for this discrepancy are that (1) many of the acts of perpetration reported by females are probably perpetrated in self-defense, but acts scales usually do not distinguish offensive from self-defense perpetration; (2) women sense impending violence from their partners and strike out pre-emptively to avoid being hurt (Gelles, 1974; Walker, 1984), but that motive typically is not captured on an acts scale; and (3) the severity of the violence used differs by gender, with males perpetrating more serious violence

(Lane & Gwartney-Gibbs, 1985; Make-peace, 1986). In addition, Johnson (1995) notes that surveys do not capture one type of abuse, which he calls patriarchal terror-ism. This abuse involves acts of violence that are embedded in a larger context of control and that are a product of patriarchal tradi-tions within which men control women and women are considered innately inferior to men or as the property of men (Johnson, 1995). According to Johnson, this form of partner violence is perpetrated exclusively by males and is the type of partner vio-lence most often observed in clinical set-tings. Patriarchal terrorists, however, may be unlikely to participate in dating abuse sur-veys, thus biasing sex-stratified prevalence estimates of perpetration. For reviews of other issues associated with sex-stratified prevalence estimates of dating abuse perpe-tration, see Archer (2000), O'Leary (2000), and White, Smith, Koss, and Figueredo (2000).

To learn more about female perpetration, we interviewed a random sample of 63 girls who had reported on at least one of the six Safe Dates surveys that they had per-petrated violence against a dating partner (Foshee, Linder, Bauman, Rice, & Wilcher, in press). These girls were asked to describe in narrative form the first time and the worst time they had used violence against a dating partner. For each act described, we probed (a) relationship characteristics, (b) precipitating events and emotions, (c) motives for using the violence, (d) outcomes of the violence, and (e) situational character-istics surrounding the use of violence. From these narratives, we identified four types of female perpetration that were distinguished by motives, precipitating events, and the abuse history of the partners. Approximately 58% of the acts described were in response to male violence and were described as being enacted as self-defense, for retaliation, or to let the boy know that she was fed up with the violence and was not going to take it anymore. Approximately 44% of the acts represented purely offensive strikes by the girl, acts not precipitated by violence or aggression by the boy. These findings sug-

gest that some female perpetration is in self-defense and some female perpetration is purely offensive.

The Etiology of Adolescent Dating Abuse

Numerous studies have examined corre-lates of adolescent dating abuse perpetra-tion using cross-sectional designs that cannot distinguish predictors from consequences of dating abuse perpetration. This distinction, which is necessary for developing preven-tion programs, is possible with longitudinal study designs. To date, 12 longitudinal stud-ies have examined predictors of adolescent dating abuse perpetration (Arriaga & Foshee, 2004; Bank & Burraston, 2001; Brendgen et al., 2001; Capaldi & Clark, 1998; Capaldi, Dishion, Stoolmiller, & Yoerger, 2001; Fos-hee et al., 2001; Foshee, Ennett et al., 2005; Gorman-Smith et al., 2001; Lavoie et al., 2002; Ozer et al., 2004; Simons et al., 1998; Wolfe et al., 2004). Half of them have studied boys only (Brendgen et al., 2001; Capaldi & Clark, 1998; Capaldi et al., 2001; Gorman-Smith et al., 2001; Lavoie et al., 2002; Simons et al., 1998), despite the fact that research indicates that both males and females perpetrate dating abuse. In this sec-tion, we review the findings from studies that examined correlates and predictors of dating abuse perpetration, emphasizing the studies that used longitudinal data. We use the term "correlate" to indicate an associ-ation found using cross-sectional data and the term "predictor" to indicate an associ-ation found using longitudinal data where the predictor was measured before the dat-ing abuse perpetration outcome and baseline dating abuse was controlled in the analyses.

Social ecological models, which direct attention to the role of both individual and environmental, or macro-level, factors in the development of individual behavior (Bronfenbrenner, 1979; McLeroy, Bibeau, Steckler, & Glanz, 1988), have been used to identify predictors of adolescent problem behaviors, such as peer aggression and vio-lence, substance use, and teen pregnancy. We categorize the variables examined as correlates or predictors of dating abuse perpetration into seven domains that move progressively toward more macro-level factors: psychological attributes, competencies and skills, involvement in other problem behaviors, perceptions of norms, the peer environment, and the family environment. Unfortunately, studies of adolescent dating abuse lag behind those of other adolescent problem behaviors in examining the influence of macro-level factors. All of the correlates and predictors of dating abuse perpetration that have been examined to date, even at more macro-levels such as the peer and family environment, have been measured at the individual level. Thus, the measures are of perceptions of social environments, rather than measures of actual social environments.

Psychological Attributes

Psychological attributes examined include hostility, self-esteem, depression, ability to empathize, suicide attempts, life satisfaction, a variety of trauma-associated symptoms (such as anger, anxiety, hyperactivity, post-traumatic stress, dissociation, and sexual dysfunction), and a variety of motives for the abuse. Hostility has been found to correlate with physical and psychological dating abuse perpetration by both boys and girls (Wolfe et al., 1998). Self-esteem has been negatively correlated with dating abuse perpetration by boys (O'Keefe, 1998) and girls (Capaldi & Crosby, 1997); however, we found that self-esteem was not a correlate or predictor of dating abuse perpetration by males or females (Foshee et al., 2001). Several studies found that depression was positively correlated with dating abuse perpetration by girls but not boys (Capaldi & Crosby, 1997; Foshee et al., 2001; McCloskey & Lichter, 2003). However, we found that it did not predict perpetration by boys or girls (Foshee et al., 2001). Ability to empathize (McCloskey & Lichter, 2003) and life satisfaction (Coker et al., 2000) have been found to correlate negatively with dating abuse perpetration, and attempted suicide has been found to correlate positively with dating abuse perpetration (Coker et al., 2000). Frequency of trauma symptoms when adolescents were in the ninth to eleventh grades predicted emotional abuse perpetration by boys and physical abuse perpetration by girls 1 year later (Wolfe et al., 2004). For girls, it was primarily anger that predicted dating abuse perpetration (Wolfe et al., 2004). Anger is a commonly reported motive for dating abuse perpetration (Henton et al., 1983; O'Keefe, 1997), along with need for control (for males only) and jealousy (O'Keefe, 1997).

Competencies and Skills

Aggressive children tend to have poor conflict management (Carlson, Lahey, & Neeper, 1984) and problem-solving (Richard & Dodge, 1982; Slaby & Guerra, 1988) skills. Adolescents with poor conflict management skills may experience discord in dating relationships, which then increases the likelihood of dating abuse (O'Keefe & Treister, 1998). The few studies that have examined the association between conflict management skills and adolescent dating abuse perpetration found that skills in responding to anger and settling disagreements, ability to empathize with dating partners, and self-efficacy in coping with difficult and sensitive relationship issues were negatively correlated with dating abuse perpetration (Foshee et al., 2001; Wolfe et al., 2004), but that they did not predict perpetration in longitudinal analyses (Foshee et al., 2001; Wolfe et al., 2004). In general, these findings suggest that conflict management and problem-solving skills may not be as important in the etiology of dating abuse as they are in the development of other forms of youth aggression.

Involvement in Other Problem Behaviors

Many studies have found a correlation between involvement in other types of antisocial and delinquent behavior and dating abuse perpetration. For example, using violence against peers has been correlated with using sexual and physical violence against dates, with stronger correlations for boys than girls (Ozer et al., 2004). Antisocial and delinquent behaviors have been found to correlate with dating abuse perpetration by males in some studies (Capaldi & Crosby, 1997), but not in others (O'Keefe, 1997). Involvement in street violence has been associated with violence against partners in a high-risk male sample (Gorman-Smith et al., 2001), and being a bully has been correlated with dating abuse perpetration by both males and females (Connolly, Pepler, Craig, & Taradash, 2000).

In most longitudinal analyses, early antisocial behavior, aggression, and delinquency predicted later use of violence against dating partners. For example, all three longitudinal studies that examined the influence of antisocial behaviors (disobedience to parents, arrest records, damaging of family property, delinquent behavior, and substance use) found that involvement in those behaviors during childhood or early adolescence predicted dating violence perpetration in later adolescence (Capaldi & Clark, 1998; Lavoie et al., 2002; Simons et al., 1998). Brendgen et al. (2001) determined whether "proactive" or "reactive" aggressive behavior perpetrated by young adolescent boys predicted their use of violence against dating partners when they were 16 and 17 years old. Reactive aggression, defined as "affective, defensive, and 'hot-blooded,' involving angry outbursts in response to actual or perceived provocation or threats" (Brendgen et al., 2001, p. 293) predicted dating violence perpetration 4 years later. Proactive aggression, defined as "instrumental, offensive, and 'cold blooded,' [requiring] neither provocation nor anger," did not (Brendgen et al., 2001, p. 293). The association between reactive anger and using violence against a dating partner was moderated by the degree of warmth expressed by the mother: The association was strongest when the boy's mother was low on a warmth scale, and no association existed between reactive anger and dating abuse for adolescents whose mothers scored high on the warmth scale (Brendgen et al., 2001). In the Safe Dates data, we found that carrying a weapon to school predicted use of violence by boys against a dating partner 1 $\frac{1}{2}$ years later, but that

association was reduced to nonsignificance in models controlling for maternal supervision, dating abuse norms, anger management skills, and friends' perpetration of dating abuse (Foshee et al., 2001).

Few studies have assessed the frequency with which alcohol was involved in specific dating abuse events. Most studies have simply assessed the association between ever use of alcohol and dating abuse perpetration, or alcohol and drug use have been included in composite variables for delinquent and antisocial behavior that predicted dating abuse perpetration. Several cross-sectional studies have reported associations between ever use of alcohol or drugs and dating violence perpetration (Malik et al., 1997; O'Keefe, 1997; O'Keeffe et al., 1986), and Foshee et al. (2001) found that alcohol use predicted perpetration of dating abuse by females, but not by males.

Perceptions of Norms

Many cross-sectional analyses have found that attitudes about the acceptability of dating abuse were correlated with adolescent dating abuse perpetration (Cascardi et al., 1999; Chapple, 2003; Chase et al., 1998; Foshee et al., 2001; Malik et al., 1997; O'Keefe, 1997; Slep, Cascardi, Avery-Leaf, & O'Leary, 2001), especially male perpetration (Schwartz et al., 1997; Wolfe et al., 2004). However, Cano et al. (1998) found no association. Perceived prevalence of dating abuse also has been positively correlated with dating abuse perpetration by males (Foshee et al., 2001), and perceptions of negative sanctions for dating abuse have been negatively correlated with dating abuse perpetration by both males and females (Foshee et al., 2001). Based on these findings, dating abuse prevention programs often work to change perceptions of dating abuse norms as a way of preventing dating abuse perpetration. Perceived norms, however, could be a predictor of dating abuse perpetration (i.e., attempts to bring behavior in line with perceived norms), a consequence of dating abuse perpetration (i.e., attempts to relieve cognitive dissonance by justifying violence once it had been used), or both. Making this distinction, which is possible only with longitudinal data, is important for prevention programming.

The two longitudinal studies that examined perceived norms found limited evidence that perceptions of norms predict dating abuse perpetration, even though in both studies the perceived norms variables were correlated with dating abuse perpetration in cross-sectional analyses. In the Safe Dates study (Foshee et al., 2001), attitudes about the acceptability of dating abuse significantly predicted the onset of dating abuse perpetration by boys, but not by girls. Perceived normalcy and negative sanctions did not predict dating abuse perpetration for either boys or girls (Foshee et al., 2001). Wolfe and associates (2004) found that attitudes about dating abuse when adolescents were in the ninth to eleventh grades did not predict abuse perpetration by boys or by girls a year later. Together these findings suggest that the associations observed in cross-sectional studies may reflect efforts to bring attitudes in line with behavior.

Numerous studies have found positive associations between the degree of acceptance of traditional gender-role stereotypes and adult male dating violence (Burke, Stets, Pirog-Good, 1988; Stets & Pirog-Good, 1987), domestic violence (Briere, 1987; Finn, 1986) and rape (Burt, 1980; Check & Malamuth, 1983; Koss, Leonard, Beazley, & Oros, 1985). However, gender stereotyping has rarely been examined in studies of adolescent dating abuse perpetration. In the Safe Dates study, adherence to traditional gender stereotypes did not predict dating abuse perpetration by males or females (Foshee et al., 2001).

The Peer Environment

Despite evidence of the influence of the peer environment on other adolescent problem behaviors, little attention has been given to the role of the peer environment in adolescent dating abuse perpetration. Only the Safe Dates study (Arriaga & Foshee, 2004; Foshee et al., 2001; Foshee, Benefield et al.,

2004) and the Oregon Youth Study (Capaldi et al., 2001) included examination of the role of the peer environment in adolescent dating abuse. Using longitudinal data, we found that having a friend involved in an abusive dating relationship, either as a victim or a perpetrator, predicted later dating violence perpetration by boys (Arriaga & Foshee, 2004) and girls (Arriaga & Foshee, 2004; Foshee et al., 2001). However, the association for males decreased to nonsignificance in models that included measures of acceptance of dating abuse and perceived normalcy, suggesting that those variables may mediate the peer behavior and perpetration relationship (Foshee et al., 2001). The models for females did not include those variables because they were not associated with dating abuse perpetrated by females in bivariate analyses (Foshee et al., 2001). Capaldi et al. (2001) found that having deviant peers in the eighth grade predicted hostile talk about women with peers in the twelfth grade, which predicted use of violence against a dating partner at ages 19 to 24. However, the temporality of associations in that study is difficult to determine because dating abuse was not measured during the eighth and twelfth grades.

The Family Environment

The most frequently examined correlates and predictors of adolescent dating abuse perpetration are measures of exposure to family violence, including exposure to domestic violence, corporal punishment, and child abuse. Other family variables, such as parental monitoring and supervision, parenting styles, and family structure, also have been examined in relation to dating abuse perpetration.

EXPOSURE TO FAMILY VIOLENCE
Findings have not overwhelmingly supported the view that exposure to domestic violence increases the likelihood of adolescent dating abuse perpetration. Although several studies have found that witnessing parents hit one another was correlated with dating violence perpetration by adolescents (Chapple, 2003; Foshee, Bauman, &

Linder, 1999; Malik et al., 1997; O'Keefe, 1997; O'Keeffe et al., 1986), others found no association (Carlson, 1990; Gray & Foshee, 1997). Further, all six longitudinal studies that examined the effect of exposure to domestic violence on dating violence perpetration by adolescents found no association (Arriaga & Foshee, 2004; Capaldi & Clark, 1998; Foshee et al., 2001; Lavoie et al., 2002; McCloskey & Lichter, 2003; Simons et al., 1998).

More studies support the idea that exposure to corporal punishment, child abuse, and maltreatment are associated with dating abuse perpetration. Corporal punishment has been found to correlate with (Foshee et al., 1999) and predict (Simons et al., 1998) dating abuse perpetration. Some researchers have found that child abuse by parents was correlated with dating violence perpetration (Bank & Burraston, 2001; Smith & Williams, 1992), but others did not find an association (Gray & Foshee, 1997; Malik et al., 1997; O'Keefe, 1997; O'Keeffe et al., 1986). In a longitudinal study limited to boys, harsh parenting practices experienced when the boys were 10 to 12 years old predicted dating violence perpetration by the boys when they were 16 to 17 years old (Lavoie et al., 2002). Several studies have found that maltreatment, defined by a composite of a variety of family violence indicators such as exposure to domestic violence, corporal punishment, child abuse, and sexual abuse, is positively correlated with dating abuse perpetration (Schwartz et al., 1997; Wekerle et al., 2001; Wolfe et al., 1998, 2004; Wolfe, Scott, Wekerle, et al., 2001).

Although evidence shows that children who have been exposed to family violence are at greater risk of using violence against their dating partners, many children exposed to family violence do not use violence against their partners (O'Keefe, 1998; Smith & Williams, 1992). Studies identifying moderators of the family violence and dating violence relationships are beginning to explain this phenomenon. In the Safe Dates study, we found that associations between most of the family violence variables and dating abuse perpetra-

tion were moderated by groupings based on race, socioeconomic status, and family structure (Foshee, Ennett, et al., in 2005). For Black adolescents living in single-parent households, exposure to domestic violence predicted dating abuse perpetration, and for Black adolescents whose mothers did not graduate from high school, corporal punishment predicted dating abuse perpetration (Foshee, Ennett, et al., 2005). Attachment style also has been found to moderate the effect of maltreatment on dating abuse perpetration by males (Wekerle & Wolfe, 1998). Although not strictly a moderation analysis, O'Keefe (1998) found that, for boys exposed to domestic violence, lower socioeconomic status, exposure to school and community violence, acceptance of dating abuse, and lower self-esteem distinguished perpetrators of dating abuse from nonperpetrators. For girls exposed to domestic violence, exposure to school and community violence, poor school performance, and the experience of child abuse distinguished perpetrators of dating abuse from nonperpetrators (O'Keefe, 1998). Perhaps the main effect of family violence, especially domestic violence, on dating violence is being canceled in statistical models because the direction of the relationship varies by levels of moderator variables, which are rarely considered.

Several researchers have investigated the mechanisms or mediators that link exposure to family violence and dating abuse perpetration. Variables found to mediate the corporal punishment and perpetration relationship include variables derived from social learning theory, such as outcome expectations for using dating abuse, prescribed dating abuse norms, and aggressive conflict-response style (Foshee et al., 1999). Variables found to mediate the association between maltreatment and dating abuse perpetration by females include hostility (Wolfe et al., 1998) and trauma symptomatology (Wekerle et al., 2001). Unfortunately, none of these analyses could establish temporality of relationships due to cross-sectional designs. Mediation has been identified less often in longitudinal studies. For example, using longitudinal data, neither supportive parenting nor delinquent behavior mediated the corporal punishment and dating abuse perpetration relationship (Simons et al., 1998), and neither antisocial behavior nor parental monitoring mediated the association between harsh parenting and dating abuse perpetration (Lavoie et al., 2002). Wolfe et al. (2004), however, found that child maltreatment was correlated with trauma symptoms and that trauma symptoms predicted later perpetration of dating abuse. They concluded that trauma symptoms mediated the association between child maltreatment and dating abuse perpetration and that attitudes toward dating abuse, ability to emphasize with partners, and self-efficacy for handling sensitive and difficult issues with partners did not mediate that relationship (Wolfe et al., 2004). They did not, however, assess the main effect of child maltreatment on later dating abuse or the impact of trauma symptoms on that association. Studies that examine mediators and moderators of the family violence and dating abuse relationship can be very useful for guiding the development of interventions for children exposed to family violence.

OTHER FAMILY FACTORS

Four longitudinal studies have documented that parental supervision predicted dating abuse perpetration (Brendgen et al., 2001; Capaldi & Clark, 1998; Foshee et al., 2001; Lavoie et al., 2002), and in two of those studies, antisocial behavior mediated the association (Capaldi & Clark, 1998; Lavoie et al, 2002). In the Safe Dates study, we found that the association between parental supervision and dating abuse perpetration was no longer significant when controlling for having friends who were perpetrators, measures of normative beliefs, conflict resolution skills, weapon carrying, and race (Foshee et al., 2001). These results suggest that some family factors have indirect effects on subsequent dating abuse perpetration.

More comprehensive measures of parenting and family functioning also have been found to predict dating abuse perpetration. For example, supportive parenting (including warmth, adequate monitoring, consistent discipline, and inductive reasoning with the child) during early adolescence decreased the likelihood of dating violence perpetration by boys in late adolescence (Simons et al., 1998). As with parental supervision, that association was mediated by delinquent behavior by boys in middle adolescence (Simons et al., 1998). Another study showed that boys who perpetrated both street and dating violence could be distinguished from boys who did not perpetrate either type of violence based on family relationship characteristics, such as shared family beliefs, family cohesion, support, communication, and organization, and parenting practices, such as consistent discipline and monitoring (Gorman-Smith et al., 2001). Boys who perpetrated violence had lower scores on family functioning characteristics than those who did not (Gorman-Smith et al., 2001). Similarly, unskilled parental discipline practices when boys were in fourth to sixth grades predicted dating abuse perpetration by boys 10 years later (Bank & Burraston, 2001).

Some cross-sectional studies have failed to document a correlation between family structure and dating abuse perpetration (Malik et al., 1997; O'Keeffe et al., 1986), but we found that it correlated with dating abuse perpetration, such that adolescents living in single-parent households were more likely to abuse a date than were adolescents living in two-parent households (Foshee et al., 2001). In longitudinal analyses, family structure did not predict dating abuse perpetration (Foshee et al., 2001), however.

Summary of Etiological Findings

In summary, factors that predict dating abuse perpetration by females include trauma symptoms (especially anger), alcohol use, and having a friend involved in dating abuse. For some subgroups of Black females, exposure to domestic violence and corporal punishment predicted dating abuse perpetration (Foshee, Ennett et al., 2005). Factors found to predict perpetration of dating abuse by males include trauma symptoms, late childhood and early adolescent antisocial behavior, delinquency, substance abuse, attitudes that are accepting of dating abuse, exposure to harsh parenting practices, exposure to inconsistent discipline, and lack of parental supervision, monitoring, and warmth. For some subgroups of Black males, exposure to domestic violence and corporal punishment predicted dating abuse perpetration (Foshee, Ennett, et al., 2005). Reactive aggression in early adolescence predicted later dating abuse perpetration by males, but maternal warmth buffered those effects (Brendgen et al., 2001). The associations between parenting styles and supervision and dating abuse perpetration by males were mediated primarily by antisocial and delinquent behavior (Capaldi & Clark, 1998; Lavoie et al., 2002).

Many of the variables found to correlate with adolescent dating abuse perpetration in cross-sectional analyses were not predictors of dating abuse using longitudinal data, suggesting that much of the correlation is due to changes that occur after the abuse has happened. However, no studies have empirically examined the consequences of dating abuse perpetration. Targeting changes in factors that are consequences, not predictors of dating abuse, in prevention programs is unlikely to prevent dating abuse perpetration.

Program Evaluations

The prevalence and potential negative consequences of adolescent dating abuse and date rape have led to the design and implementation of numerous dating abuse prevention programs. Unfortunately, few of these programs have been evaluated, and evaluations of only 11 of these programs have been described in the literature (Avery-Leaf et al., 1997; Feltey, Ainslie, & Geib, 1991; Foshee et al., 1998, 2000; Foshee, Bauman et al., 2004; Foshee, Bauman, et al., 2005; Hilton, Harris, Rice, Krans, & Lavigne, 1998; Jaffe, Sudermann, Reitzel, & Killip, 1992; Jones, 1991; Krajewski, Rybarik, Dosch, & Gilmore, 1996; Lavoie, Vezina, Piche, & Boivin, 1995; Macgowan, 1997;

Weisz & Black, 2001; Wolfe, Wekerle et al., 2003). Only 3 of those 11 evaluations assessed program effects on dating abuse perpetration, and only 2 of those 3 used an experimental design. Seven measured the effects of the prevention program on attitudes about dating abuse, which may predict dating abuse perpetration. However, five of the seven used poor designs that did not control for common threats to internal validity. Here we briefly summarize the findings from the four experimental studies that examined the effects of a program on either attitudes about dating abuse or dating abuse perpetration.

Macgowan (1997) evaluated the Dating Violence Intervention and Prevention for Teenagers program developed by Kraizer and Larson (1993). Classrooms in a single, primarily African American, metropolitan school in Florida were matched by grade (six, seven, and eight) and level (regular or advanced), and then one of each matched pair was randomly allocated to the treatment condition. A pre-test, post-test, wait-list control group design was used to assess the effects of the program on a composite score reflecting knowledge about relationship violence, attitudes about dating abuse, and attitudes about seeking help for dating abuse. Findings showed a significant main effect of treatment condition on post-test scores, after adjusting for pre-test scores and other variables that were unbalanced across treatment and control groups at baseline. The treatment group showed significant improvement in scores from pre-test to post-test, whereas the control group did not. Male students with high academic ability showed the greatest and most significant gains. One limitation of this study was that substantial selection bias could have been introduced, because the analyses were limited to those who completed at least 19 of the 22 items used to measure the outcome and to those who were exposed to four of the five program sessions. Thus, although approximately 802 adolescents received the program at some point in time, only 440 were included in analyses of program effects. In addition, there was no attempt to control for clustering by classroom, and the post-test was given only 2 days after program completion.

Avery-Leaf et al. (1997) evaluated the effectiveness of their B.R.I.G.H.T. program. Health classes from one large New York City high school were randomly assigned to treatment and control conditions; 102 adolescents were in the treatment group and 90 in the control condition. Treatment group post-tests were administered immediately after program completion. Adolescents in the treatment group showed significant pre- to post-test changes on one of the two scales measuring justification of dating aggression, whereas the control group showed no significant change. No treatment effects were shown on justifications for dating jealousy or on the second scale measuring justification for dating abuse. However, the control group completed the pre-test and the post-test before the treatment group completed pre-tests. Thus, some of the threats to internal validity that are normally controlled with an experimental study (e.g., history) were not controlled. Also, as in the McGowan (1997) study, no attempt was made to control for clustering by classroom.

Wolfe et al. (2003) evaluated their program, titled the Youth Relationship Project (Wolfe et al., 1996), which has been the only non-school-based program to be evaluated. An experimental design was used in which 158 adolescents, 14 to 16 years old, with a history of maltreatment were randomly allocated to treatment ($n = 96$) and control conditions ($n = 62$). Data were collected at baseline and again 4 months later, after an intervention/control period, and then bimonthly for a total of seven waves of data. Approximately 60% of those eligible completed pre-tests; the 158 in the analyses constituted about 50% of those eligible. Treatment condition significantly predicted reductions over time in physical abuse perpetration, but did not predict changes in perpetration of emotional abuse or threatening behaviors. Wolfe et al. (2003) also examined the effects of the program on proposed "mediating" variables, but they did not do an empirical test to determine whether the mediators explained associations between treatment condition and outcomes. They found that treatment condition was associated with reductions in trauma symptoms over time, but had no effects on hostility or on communication and problem-solving skills.

We used an experimental design, described earlier in this review, to evaluate the effects of the Safe Dates program (Foshee & Langwick, 2004) on primary and secondary prevention of dating abuse victimization and perpetration (Foshee et al., 1998, 2000; Foshee, Bauman, et al., 2004; Foshee, Bauman, et al., 2005). The Safe Dates program was composed of a theater production performed by peers, a curriculum of 10 45-minute sessions, and a poster contest. Process evaluation data suggested high program fidelity in treatment schools (Foshee et al., 1998, 2000).

We used random coefficient models to examine the effects of Safe Dates over time in preventing or reducing psychological, moderate physical, severe physical, and sexual dating violence perpetration (Foshee, Bauman, et al., 2005). In the analyses we used four waves of follow-up data, with the fourth wave administered 3 years postintervention. We also examined (1) whether program effects were moderated by gender, race, or the adolescent's involvement in dating violence prior to the intervention; and (2) whether the relationships between treatment condition and dating violence perpetration at each wave were explained by theoretically based, time-dependent mediating variables that were the program focus.

We found that adolescents who were exposed to Safe Dates in the eighth or ninth grade reported less psychological, moderate physical, and sexual dating violence perpetration at all four follow-up periods than those adolescents who were not exposed to the program. In addition, adolescents exposed to Safe Dates who at baseline reported no or average prior involvement in severe physical perpetration reported less severe physical perpetration than controls at all four follow-up periods. Safe Dates had both primary and secondary prevention effects on all four of the outcomes examined, and the program was equally effective in preventing perpetration for males and females and for White and minority adolescents. Program effects were mediated primarily by changes in dating violence norms, gender-role norms, and awareness of community services. In other analyses, (Foshee, Bauman et al., 2004) we found that program effects on perpetration continued at the 4-year follow-up.

To summarize, evaluation results suggest that prevention programs have had some success in preventing dating abuse perpetration and in changing attitudes. One potential explanation for the favorable effects, which is not controlled with an experimental design, is that adolescents in treatment groups provided more socially desirable responses to the behavioral measures than controls. This is difficult to control for, because it is almost impossible to blind adolescents to treatment group status in evaluations of public health programs.

Directions for Future Research

Acts scales have been criticized for more than 20 years as inadequate for measuring partner violence perpetration; however, very little progress has been made in developing alternative measures. We need new and innovative ways of measuring dating abuse perpetration that capture the complexity of the phenomenon, while still lending themselves to quantitative analysis. One promising approach is to use qualitative and quantitative data on contextual aspects of perpetrated acts to develop typologies of acts or perpetrators, which then can become the dependent variables in etiological analyses. This approach is used extensively in domestic violence research (see Johnson & Ferraro, 2000, for a review), but rarely in adolescent dating abuse research.

Although there are many studies referenced in this review, it is important to note that many of the findings come from only

four studies: our Safe Dates Study in North Carolina, the Oregon Youth Study, Wolfe and colleagues' study with 10 high schools and Child Protective Services in Ontario, and O'Leary and colleagues' study in Long Island, New York. Thus, not all findings are independent assessments of relationships. Furthermore, these studies, as did all of the other studies referenced, used localized samples that in several cases were chosen based on very specific characteristics, such as having a history of maltreatment or being at high risk for aggression, which limits the generalizability of study findings. We need more nationally representative studies on adolescent dating abuse perpetration, including trend studies that would allow us to answer the commonly asked question that we cannot presently answer: "Is adolescent dating abuse more prevalent now than it was in the past?" Inclusion of dating abuse victimization questions on the Youth Risk Behavior Survey in the past few years is a step in the right direction.

Notably absent in the literature are studies that assess the prevalence and predictors of dating abuse perpetration by gay and lesbian adolescents. All of the adolescent dating abuse perpetration studies assume heterosexual relationships. Only three published adolescent dating abuse studies focus on gay and lesbian adolescents, and all of those studies assessed prevalence and predictors of dating abuse victimization but not perpetration (Freedner, Freed, Yang, & Austin, 2002; Halpern, Oslak, Young, Martin, & Kupper, 2001; Halpern, Young, Waller, Martin, & Kupper, 2004).

Obviously more etiological research, using longitudinal study designs, is needed, especially studies that include girls and that include multiple time points. Considerable evidence exists that significant numbers of female adolescents use violence against their dating partners and that some of that violence is purely offensive. Multi-wave longitudinal studies are expensive and take time, but those types of studies could help us learn more about how dating abuse develops over the course of adolescence and to determine if abuse during adolescence is in fact a predictor of abuse in adult relationships, as is often presumed.

More macro-level factors, including peer network characteristics, school characteristics and dating abuse policies, and neighborhood characteristics, need to be examined in etiological studies of dating abuse perpetration. Results from those types of studies can guide the development of interventions targeted at macro-level changes. We also need more longitudinal studies that assess theoretically based mediators and moderators of associations between predictor variables and dating abuse perpetration, because the results from those studies can add substantially to our understanding of the development of dating abuse perpetration and to the development of prevention programs. In addition, we need to broaden the focus of the longitudinal etiological research on dating abuse perpetration. The majority of the longitudinal studies focused either on the associations between other types of antisocial behavior and dating abuse perpetration or the association between maltreatment and dating abuse perpetration. Although the narrow focus allows for in-depth consideration of an issue, it also requires the researcher to neglect many factors that potentially influence the development of dating abuse perpetration. The amount of variance explained in dating abuse perpetration from the longitudinal studies ranges from 6% to 56%, suggesting that a substantial amount of variance is left unexplained.

Finally, we need more research that evaluates the effectiveness of dating abuse prevention programs. For the most part, the evaluations of dating abuse prevention programs have been hampered by (1) the use of poor designs that do not control for common threats to internal validity; (2) measurement of attitudes, knowledge, and intentions, rather than actual dating abuse behaviors; (3) lack of consistency between program goals and the constructs measured; (4) short follow-up periods; (5) substantial attrition; (6) inappropriate statistical applications; and (7) limited generalizability. In addition, theoretically or empirically based mediators of program effects, based on program goals, are rarely examined. Unfortunately, a theoretical base is notably absent in descriptions of most of the programs that have been evaluated. Program content primarily is guided by correlations found from cross-sectional studies and often by those found in studies with college student samples.

Given the short history of adolescent dating abuse perpetration research, we have learned quite a bit. As is evident from this review, however, we have a long way to go in understanding this phenomenon.

References

Archer, J. (2000). Sex differences in aggression between heterosexual partners: A meta-analytic review. *Psychological Bulletin*, *126*, 651–680.

Arriaga, X. B., & Foshee, V. A. (2004). Adolescent dating violence: Do adolescents follow their friends' or their parents' footsteps? *Journal of Interpersonal Violence*, *19*, 162–184.

Avery-Leaf, S., Cascardi, M., O'Leary, K. D., & Cano, A. (1997). Efficacy of a dating violence prevention program on attitudes justifying aggression. *Journal of Adolescent Health*, *21*, 11–17.

Bank, L., & Burraston, B. (2001). Abusive home environments as predictors of poor adjustment during adolescence and early childhood. *Journal of Community Psychology*, *29*, 195–217.

Bennett, L., & Fineran, S. (1998). Sexual and severe physical violence among high school students – power beliefs, gender, and relationship. *American Journal of Orthopsychology*, *68*, 645–652.

Berk, R. A., Berk, S. F., Loseke, D. R., & Rauma, D. (1983). Mutual combat and other family violence myths. In D. Finkelhor, R. J. Gelles, G. T. Hotaling, & M. A. Straus (Eds.), *The dark side of families: Current family violence research* (pp. 197–212). Beverly Hills, CA: Sage.

Bograd, M. (1990). Why we need gender to understand human violence. *Journal of Interpersonal Violence*, *5*, 132–135.

Breines, W., & Gordon, L. (1983). The new scholarship on family violence. *Signs: Journal of Women in Culture and Society*, *8*, 490–531.

Brendgen, M., Vitaro, F., Tremblay, R. E., & Lavoie, F. (2001). Reactive and proactive aggression: Predictions to physical violence in different contexts and moderating effects of parental monitoring and caregiving behavior. *Journal of Abnormal Child Psychology, 29,* 293–304.

Briere, J. (1987). Predicting self-reported likelihood of battering: Attitudes and childhood experiences. *Journal of Research in Personality, 21,* 61–69.

Bronfenbrenner, U. (1979). *The ecology of human development: Experiments by nature and design.* Cambridge, MA: Harvard University Press.

Burke, P. J., Stets, J. E., & Pirog-Good, M. A. (1988). Gender identity, self-esteem, and physical and sexual abuse in dating relationships. *Social Psychology Quarterly, 51,* 272–285.

Burt, M. R. (1980). Cultural myths and support for rape. *Personal Social Psychology, 38,* 217–230.

Cano, A., Avery-Leaf, S., Cascardi, M., & O'Leary, K. D. (1998). Dating violence in two high school samples: Discriminating variables. *Journal of Primary Prevention, 18,* 431–446.

Capaldi, D. M., & Clark, S. (1998). Prospective family predictors of aggression toward female partners for young at-risk males. *Developmental Psychology, 34,* 1175–1188.

Capaldi, D. M., & Crosby, L. (1997). Observed and reported psychological and physical aggression in young, at-risk couples. *Social Development, 6,* 184–206.

Capaldi, D. M., Dishion, T. J., Stoolmiller, M., & Yoerger, K. (2001). Aggression toward female partners by at-risk young men: The contribution of male adolescent friendships. *Developmental Psychology, 37,* 61–73.

Carlson, B. E. (1990). Adolescent observers of marital violence. *Journal of Family Violence, 5,* 285–299.

Carlson, C. L., Lahey, B. B., & Neeper, R. (1984). Peer assessment of the social behavior of accepted, rejected, and neglected children. *Journal of Abnormal Child Psychology, 12,* 187–198.

Cascardi, M., Avery-Leaf, S., O'Leary, K. D., & Slep, A. M. S. (1999). Factor structure and convergent validity of the Conflict Tactics Scale in high school students. *Psychological Assessment, 14,* 546–555.

Chapple, C. (2003). Examining intergenerational violence: Violent role modeling or weak parental controls? *Violence and Victims, 18,* 143–162.

Chase, K. A., Treboux, D., O'Leary, K. D., & Strassberg, Z. (1998). Specificity of dating aggression and its justification among high-risk adolescents. *Journal of Abnormal Child Psychology, 26,* 467–473.

Check, J. V. P., & Malamuth, N. M. (1983). Sex-role stereotyping and reactions to depictions of stranger versus acquaintance rape. *Journal of Personality and Social Psychology, 45,* 344–356.

Coker, A. L., McKeown, R. E., Sanderson, M., Davis, K. E., Valois, R. F., & Huebner, E. S. (2000). Severe dating violence and quality of life among South Carolina high school students. *American Journal of Preventive Medicine, 19,* 220–227.

Connolly, J., Pepler, D. J., Craig, W. M., & Taradash, A. (2000). Dating experiences of bullies in early adolescence. *Child Maltreatment, 5,* 299–310.

Dobash, R. E., & Dobash, R. P. (1979). *Violence against wives: A case against the patriarchy.* New York: Free Press.

Dobash, R. E., & Dobash, R. P. (1988). Research as social action: The struggle for battered women. In K. Yllö & M. Bograd (Eds.), *Feminist perspectives on wife abuse* (pp. 51–74). Newbury Park, CA: Sage.

Dobash, R. P., Dobash, R. E., Wilson, M., & Daly, M. (1992). The myth of sexual symmetry in marital violence. *Social Problems, 39,* 71–91.

Elliott, D. S., Huizinga, D., & Menard, S. (1989). *Multiple problem youth: Delinquency, substance use and mental health problems.* New York: Springer-Verlag.

Feltey, K. M., Ainslie, J. J., & Geib, A. (1991). Sexual coercion attitudes among high school students. *Youth and Society, 23,* 229–250.

Finn, J. (1986). The relationship between sex role attitudes and attitudes supporting marital violence. *Sex Roles, 14,* 235–244.

Foshee, V. A. (1996). Gender differences in adolescent dating abuse prevalence, types, and injuries. *Health Education Research, 11,* 275–286.

Foshee, V. A., Bauman, K. E., Arriaga, X. B., Helms, R. W., Koch, G. G., & Linder, G. F. (1998). An evaluation of Safe Dates, an adolescent dating violence prevention program. *American Journal of Public Health, 88,* 45–50.

Foshee, V. A., Bauman, K. E., Ennett, S. T., Linder, G. F., Benefield, T., & Suchindran, C. (2004). Assessing the long-term effects of the Safe Dates program and a booster in preventing and reducing adolescent dating violence victimization and perpetration. *American Journal of Public Health*, 94, 619–624.

Foshee, V. A., Bauman, K. E., Ennett, S. T., Suchindran, C., Benefield, T., & Linder, G. F. (2005). Assessing the effects of the dating violence prevention program "Safe Dates" using random coefficient regression modeling. *Prevention Science*, 6(3), 245–258.

Foshee, V. A., Bauman, K. E., Greene, W. F., Koch, G. G., Linder, G. F., & MacDougall, J. E. (2000). The Safe-Dates program: 1-year follow-up results. *American Journal of Public Health*, 90, 1619–1622.

Foshee, V. A., Bauman, K. E., & Linder, G. F. (1999). Family violence and the perpetration of adolescent dating violence: Examining social learning and social control processes. *Journal of Marriage and the Family*, 61, 331–342.

Foshee, V. A., Benefield, T. S., Ennett, S. T., Bauman, K. E., & Suchindran, C. (2004). Longitudinal predictors of serious physical and sexual dating violence victimization during adolescence. *Preventive Medicine*, 39, 1007–1016.

Foshee, V. A., Ennett, S. T., Bauman, K. E., Benefield, T. & Suchindran, C. (2005). The association between family violence and adolescent dating violence onset: Does it vary by race, socioeconomic status, and family structure? *Journal of Early Adolescence*, 25(3), 317–349.

Foshee, V., & Langwick, S. (2004). *Safe Dates: An adolescent dating abuse prevention curriculum.* [Program manual]. Center City, MN: Hazelden Publishing and Educational Services.

Foshee, V., Linder, F., Bauman, K., Rice, J., & Wilcher, R. (in press). Identifying male and female typologies of adolescent dating abuse perpetration. *Journal of Interpersonal Violence*.

Foshee, V. A., Linder, F., MacDougall, J. E., & Bangdiwala, S. (2001). Gender differences in the longitudinal predictors of adolescent dating violence. *Preventive Medicine*, 32, 128–141.

Freedner, N., Freed, L. H., Yang, Y. W., & Austin, S. B. (2002). Dating violence among gay, lesbian, and bisexual adolescents: Results from a community survey. *Journal of Adolescent Health*, 31, 469–474.

Gaertner, L., & Foshee, V. (1999). Commitment and the perpetration of relationship violence. *Personal Relationships*, 6, 227–239.

Gelles, R. J. (1974). *The violent home: A study of physical aggression between husbands and wives.* Newbury Park, CA: Sage.

Gorman-Smith, D., Tolan, P. H., Sheidow, A. J., & Henry, D. B. (2001). Partner violence and street violence among urban adolescents: Do the same family factors relate? *Journal of Research on Adolescence*, 11, 273–295.

Gray, H. M., & Foshee, V. (1997). Adolescent dating violence: Differences between one-sided and mutually violent profiles. *Journal of Interpersonal Violence*, 12, 126–141.

Halpern, C. T., Oslak, S. G., Young, M. L., Martin, S. L., & Kupper, L. L. (2001). Partner violence among adolescents in opposite-sex romantic relationships: Findings from the National Longitudinal Study of Adolescent Health. *American Journal of Public Health*, 91, 1679–1685.

Halpern, C. T., Young, M. L., Waller, M., Martin, S. L., & Kupper, L. (2004). Prevalence of partner violence in same-sex romantic and sexual relationships in a national sample of adolescents. *Journal of Adolescent Health*, 35, 124–131.

Henton J., Cate, R., Koval, J., Lloyd, S., & Christopher, S. (1983). Romance and violence in dating relationships. *Journal of Family Issues*, 4, 467–482.

Hilton, N. Z., Harris, G. T., Rice, M. E., Krans, T. S., & Lavigne, S. E. (1998). Antiviolence education in high schools: Implementation and evaluation. *Journal of Interpersonal Violence*, 13, 726–742.

Hird, M. J. (2000). An empirical study of adolescent dating aggression in the UK. *Journal of Adolescence*, 23, 69–78.

Jaffe, P. G., Sudermann, M., Reitzel, D., & Killip, S. M. (1992). An evaluation of a secondary school primary prevention program on violence in relationships. *Violence and Victims*, 7, 129–46.

Johnson, M. (1995). Patriarchal terrorism and common couple violence: Two forms of violence against women. *Journal of Marriage and Family*, 57, 283–294.

Johnson, M. P., & Ferraro, K. J. (2000). Research on domestic violence in the 1990s: Making distinctions. *Journal of Marriage and the Family*, 62, 948–963.

Johnson-Reid, M., & Bivens, L. (1999). Foster youth and dating violence. *Journal of Interpersonal Violence*, 14, 1249–1262.

Jones, L. E. (1991). The Minnesota School Curriculum Project: A statewide domestic violence prevention project in secondary schools. In B. Levy (Ed.), *Dating violence: Young women in danger* (pp. 258–266). Seattle, WA: Seal Press.

Koss, M., Leonard, H., Beazley, D., & Oros, C. (1985). Nonstranger sexual aggression: A discriminant analysis of the psychological characteristics of undetected offenders. *Sex Roles, 12*, 981–992.

Kraizer, S., & Larson, C. L. (1993). *Dating violence: Intervention and prevention for teenagers.* [Program manual]. Tulsa, OK: University of Oklahoma, College of Continuing Education, National Resource Center for Youth Services.

Krajewski, S. S., Rybarik, M. F., Dosch, M. F., & Gilmore, G. D. (1996). Results of a curriculum intervention with seventh graders regarding violence in relationships. *Journal of Family Violence, 11*, 93–112.

Lane, K., & Gwartney-Gibbs, P. (1985). Violence in the context of dating and sex. *Journal of Family Issues, 6*, 45–59.

Lavoie, F., Hebert, M., Tremblay, R., Vitaro, F., Vezina, L., & McDuff, P. (2002). History of family dysfunction and perpetration of dating violence by adolescent boys: A longitudinal study. *Journal of Adolescent Health, 30*, 375–383.

Lavoie, F., Vezina, L., Piche, C., & Boivin, M. (1995). Evaluation of a prevention program for violence in teen dating relationships. *Journal of Interpersonal Violence, 10*, 516–524.

Levy, B. (1990). Abusive teen dating relationships: An emerging issue for the 1990s. *Response, 13*, 3–12.

Levy, B. (1991). *Dating violence: Young women in danger.* Seattle, WA: Seal Press.

Macgowan, M. J. (1997). An evaluation of a dating violence prevention program for middle school students. *Violence and Victimization, 12*, 223–235.

Makepeace, J. M. (1986). Gender differences in courtship violence victimization. *Family Relations, 35*, 383–388.

Malik, S., Sorenson, S. B., & Aneshensel, C. S. (1997). Community and dating violence among adolescents: Perpetration and victimization. *Journal of Adolescent Health, 21*, 291–302.

McCloskey, L. A., & Lichter, E. L. (2003). The contribution of marital violence to adolescent aggression across different relationships. *Journal of Interpersonal Violence, 18*, 390–412.

McLeod, M. (1984). Women against men: An examination of domestic violence based on an analysis of official data and national victimization data. *Justice Quarterly, 1*, 171–193.

McLeroy, K. R., Bibeau, D., Steckler, A., & Glanz, K. (1988). An ecological perspective on health promotion programs. *Health Education Quarterly, 15*, 351–377.

Moffitt, T. E. (1993). Adolescence-limited and life-course persistent antisocial behavior: A developmental taxonomy. *Psychological Review, 100*, 674–701.

O'Keefe, M. (1997). Predictors of dating violence among high school students. *Journal of Interpersonal Violence, 12*, 546–568.

O'Keefe, M. (1998). Factors mediating the link between witnessing interparental violence and dating violence. *Journal of Family Violence, 13*, 39–57.

O'Keefe, M., & Treister, L. (1998). Victims of dating violence among high school students: Are predictors different for males and females? *Violence Against Women, 4*, 195–223.

O'Keeffe, N. K., Brockopp, K., & Chew, E. (1986). Teen dating violence. *Social Work, 31*, 465–468.

O'Leary, K. D. (1999). Developmental and affective issues in assessing and treating partner aggression. *Clinical Psychology: Science and Practice, 6*, 400–414.

O'Leary, K. D. (2000). Are women really more aggressive than men in intimate relationships? Comment on Archer (2000). *Psychological Bulletin, 126*, 685–689.

O'Leary, K. D., & Slep, A. S. (2003). A dyadic longitudinal model of adolescent dating aggression. *Journal of Child and Adolescent Psychology, 32*, 314–327.

Ozer, E. J., Tschann, J. M., Pasch, L. A., & Flores, E. (2004). Violence perpetration across peer and partner relationships: Co-occurrence and longitudinal patterns among adolescents. *Journal of Adolescent Health, 34*, 64–71.

Plass, M. S., & Gessner, J. C. (1983). Violence in courtship relations: A southern sample. *Free Inquiry into Creative Sociology, 11*, 198–202.

Poitras, M., & Lavoie, F. (1995). A study of the prevalence of sexual coercion in adolescent heterosexual dating relationships in a Quebec sample. *Violence and Victims, 10*, 299–313.

Richard, B. A., & Dodge, K. A. (1982). Social maladjustment and problem solving in school-aged children. *Journal of Consulting Clinical Psychology, 50*, 226–233.

Rubin, D. B. (1987). *Multiple imputation for nonresponse in surveys.* New York: Wiley.

Schwartz, M. D. (1987). Gender and injury in spousal assault. *Sociological Focus, 20*, 61–75.

Schwartz, M., O'Leary, S. G., & Kendziora, K. T. (1997). Dating aggression among high school students. *Violence and Victimization, 12*, 295–305.

Simons, R. L., Lin, K., & Gordon, L. C. (1998). Socialization in the family of origin and male dating violence: A prospective study. *Journal of Marriage and the Family, 60*, 467–478.

Slaby, R. G., & Guerra, N. G. (1988). Cognitive mediators of aggression in adolescent offenders: 1. Assessment. *Developmental Psychology, 24*, 580–588.

Slep, A. M., Cascardi, M. Avery-Leaf, S., & O'Leary, K. D. (2001). Two new measures of attitudes about the acceptability of teen dating aggression. *Psychological Assessment, 13*, 306–318.

Smith, J. P., & Williams, J. G. (1992). From abusive household to dating violence. *Journal of Family Violence, 7*, 153–165.

Stets, J. E., & Pirog-Good, M. A. (1987). Violence in dating relationships. *Social Psychology Quarterly, 50*, 237–246.

Straus, M. A. (1979). Measuring intrafamily conflict and violence: The Conflict Tactics Scales. *Journal of Marriage and the Family, 41*, 75–88.

Straus, M. A., Hamby, S. L., Boney-McCoy, S., & Sugarman, D. B. (1996). The revised Conflict Tactics Scales (CTS2): Development and preliminary psychometric data. *Journal of Family Issues, 17*, 283–316.

Symons, P. Y., Groër, M. W., Kepler-Youngblood, P., & Slater, V. (1994). Prevalence and predictors of adolescent dating violence. *Journal of Child and Adolescent Psychiatric Nursing, 7*, 14–23.

Walker, L. E. (1984). *The battered wife syndrome*. New York: Springer Publishing Co.

Weisz, A. N., & Black, B. M. (2001). Evaluating a sexual assault and dating violence prevention program for urban youth. *Social Work Research, 25*, 89–100.

Wekerle, C., & Wolfe, D. A. (1998). The role of child maltreatment and attachment style in adolescent relationship violence. *Development and Psychopathology, 10*, 571–586.

Wekerle, C., Wolfe, D. A., Hawkins, D. L., Pittman, A., Glickman, A., & Lovald, B. E. (2001). Child maltreatment, posttraumatic stress symptomatology and adolescent dating violence: Considering the value of adolescent perceptions of abuse and a trauma mediational model. *Development and Psychopathology, 13*, 847–871.

White, J. W., Smith, P. H., Koss, M. P., & Figueredo, A. J. (2000). Intimate partner aggression: What have we learned? Commentary on Archer's meta-analysis. *Psychological Bulletin, 126*, 690–696.

Wolfe, D. A., Scott, K., Reitzel-Jaffe, D., Wekerle, C., Grasley, C., & Straatman, A. L. (2001). Development and validation of the Conflict in Adolescent Dating Relationships Inventory. *Psychological Assessment, 13*, 277–293.

Wolfe, D. A., Scott, K., Wekerle, C., & Pittman, A. (2001). Child maltreatment: Risk of adjustment problems and dating violence in adolescence. *Journal of the American Academy of Child and Adolescent Psychiatry, 40*, 282–289.

Wolfe, D. A., Wekerle, C., Gough, R., Reitzel-Jaffe, D., Grasley, C., Pittman, A., et al. (1996). *The Youth Relationships Manual: A group approach with adolescents for the prevention of woman abuse and the promotion of healthy relationships*. Thousand Oaks, CA: Sage.

Wolfe, D. A., Wekerle, C., Reitzel-Jaffe, D., & Lefebvre L. (1998). Factors associated with abusive relationships among maltreated and nonmaltreated youth. *Developmental Psychopathology, 10*, 61–85.

Wolfe, D. A., Wekerle, C., Scott, K., Straatman, A. L., & Grasley, C. (2004). Predicting abuse in adolescent dating relationships over 1 year: The role of child maltreatment and trauma. *Journal of Abnormal Psychology, 113*, 406–415.

Wolfe, D. A., Wekerle, C., Scott, K., Straatman, A., Grasley, C., & Reitzel-Jaffe, D. (2003). Dating violence prevention with at-risk youth: A controlled outcome evaluation. *Journal of Consulting and Clinical Psychology, 71*, 279–291.

CHAPTER 22

Social Networks and Violent Behavior

Dorothy L. Espelage, Stanley Wasserman, and Mark Fleisher

Introduction

In an age in which many business and research communities are recognizing the importance of social networks in modern-day life, it is no surprise that researchers of violence have come to regard one's networks as important predictors of behavior. One could adopt the premise that, whenever social context matters, one needs to consider theoretically, take measurements on, and analyze social interactions.

Social network analysis (SNA) is a branch of social and behavioral science methodology that explicitly defines networks and their characteristics. SNA "re-frames" interpersonal and interorganizational phenomena in terms of the relationships among social entities. These entities might be people, businesses, cities, or countries, and the relationships might be defined by friendship, giving advice, control, or economic support, just to name a few possibilities. Wasserman and Faust (1994, p. 4), and Faber and Wasserman (2001), proposed four defining concepts in social network analysis:

1. Actors and their actions are viewed as interdependent.
2. Relational ties between actors are channels for transfer of resources.
3. Network models focusing on individuals view the network structural environment as providing opportunities for or constraints on individual action.
4. Network models conceptualize structure as lasting patterns of relations among actors.

Thus, SNA moves the focus from the level of a single actor (the common view in standard social and behavioral sciences) to collections of actors who are tied together by relationships through which socialization at some level occurs and resources flow.

Why use social networks to study violence? Good question. The answer focuses on the fact that SNA allows a researcher of violence to connect the micro- and macro-levels of research. Micro-situational studies show the context of violence; macro-level (mainly quantitative) studies show the nonrandom distribution of violence; and cultural studies describe norms, beliefs, and social rules of the culture of violence. How people in multiple contexts act in response to social structures, norms, and situations is the contribution of social network analysis. SNA helps us understand the actual types of relations that people have and how they make decisions and act.

Surveys, case studies, and ethnography; informal, semi-structured, and structured interviews; systematic qualitative data analysis; and formal quantitative models have yielded a holistic or multidimensional view of violence. Research studies of violence are found across many disciplines and include correlates and factors at multiple analytic levels (individual, family, peer group, school, and community). Case study researchers and ethnographers study violence and the results of violence most directly; sociologists, developmental psychologists, and other researchers explicate contextual influences of network members; psychologists and psychiatrists diagnose and treat the effects of exposure to violent environments; and emergency rooms patch and stitch the victims of violence. However, despite what is known from so many perspectives, few studies of violent behavior employ an analytic perspective of social network theory and method.

Indeed, violence research covers a broad range of methodological and theoretical approaches. There is no doubt that the manner in which violent behavior is studied and how it interacts within various contexts has a direct connection with the foci used to examine the etiology and correlates of violence. SNA has proven valuable in ethnographic and quantitative studies. Social network ethnography is the application of social network concepts and arguments to field research. In field research, observations of interactions among actors involves a focused and theoretical approach to studying the behavioral context of one or several actors among others, and more generally a to understanding that a social network has an influence on individual behavior is a simple but often overlooked approach to fieldwork research design.

Both violence and interactions within social networks persist across the lifespan, from childhood to adolescence, from schooling to gang membership to incarceration. In this chapter, the application of social network analysis to the study of violence is summarized along two lines of research. First, using a developmental framework, the research on social networks and aggression among school-aged children is presented. Theories are presented that highlight the strong empirical, quantitative research support for the socialization of aggression in peer groups and the benefits achieved from such aggressive acts. Second, these same social network influences are then discussed through ethnographic and quantitative investigations of gang membership patterns and how these relate to violence. Although these two areas of scholarship might appear very different at first glance, they both demonstrate the importance of examining violence within friendship and affiliation networks and the need to consider how these networks influence the perpetration of violence over time and how prevention and intervention need to affect these socializing agents.

Some Concepts

SNA involves a wide variety of methods, but often uses sets of measures to describe and quantify the ties that exist within a network. Such ties are usually dichotomous and can be either nondirectional, in which a tie does or does not exist between two actors, or directional, when ties are directed toward or away from an actor.

The network statistics that summarize these dichotomous relational ties quantify structural characteristics at several levels within the network. The *individual level* focuses on features of each actor within the network. For example, it might focus on the extent to which a person chooses others (*outdegree*) or is chosen by others (*indegree*) for a particular relation. The *dyadic level* of analysis describes relational ties between two actors. Measures at the dyadic level include *mutuality* indices that quantify how much two actors "extend" a certain type of relation to one another simultaneously. The *triadic level* considers relationships among three network actors and includes the measures of *structural balance, transitivity,* and *cyclicity.* These measures describe how resources are shared among three actors and can characterize the hierarchical relationships or "tightness" of relationships that exists within a network. *Subgroup analyses,* in general, focus on the existence of cohesive collections of actors who have many relational ties to one another. *Cliques* are one example of cohesive subgroups, but many others exist. At the highest level of analysis, *global measures* describe characteristics of the entire network. For example, network *centralization* reflects the overall variability or heterogeneity of actors' relational ties.

Network data are inherently multidimensional. Theoretically interesting and measured relations could be social support, economic exchange (food sharing), crime (mutual drug selling), and antagonism (jealousy over boyfriends). The concept of *embeddedness* is the "extent to which a dyad's mutual contacts are connected to one another" (Granovetter, 1992, p. 35). Embeddedness varies by the type, number, and intensity of relations shared among actors. For example, a gang member G may be partially embedded in a youth gang network if he shares with other actors a few hours of time per month on a street corner. If G's embeddedness is low, then G's influence on others (in specific types of interaction) might be low as well.

The activity of an actor in a network is called its *degree centrality.* Actors with a higher degree are more "central" in the overall network as they have the greatest number of direct ties linking them to other actors. Direct ties to and from an actor represent activity. Degree centrality is often associated with the prominence or prestige of an actor; for example, a greater number of ties make an actor particularly visible to other actors in the network. An actor with high centrality might have a higher prestige, such as a leader,

or be the most active in some particular gang behavior, such as drug dealing.

Betweenness centrality measures the ego's (e.g., actors, participants reporting on attributes) position in a social network through indirect ties, such that the shortest path between actor j to actor k is likely to have actor l as an intermediary (Wasserman & Faust, 1994, p. 190). This index signals how "between" each of the actors is. Actors high in this measure occupy positions "in between" different parts of the network. Actor betweenness centrality usually is viewed as an index of control.

Studies of social networks among children and adolescents include discussion of additional roles that can be found through SNA. Ennett and Bauman (1994, 1996) in their ground-breaking work on smoking among adolescents use nomination data to identify friendship groups. These authors make distinctions between *reciprocated friendships* as direct links between two individuals (or nodes) and *common friendships,* which refer to indirect links between two individuals via one or more other individuals. Ennett and Bauman have proposed the following criteria to identify peer groups: (1) at least 50% of a student's direct links (reciprocated friendships) must be in the peer group; (2) a direct or indirect link exists from each member to every other member of the peer group; and (3) indirect links must not exceed five links.

Based on these criteria, students can be described as one of the following: a clique member, loose group member, dyad member, isolate, or liaison. A *clique member* belongs to a group comprised of at least three individuals with direct links between all members, whereas a *loose group member* is assigned to a group of at least three individuals with varying degrees of direct and indirect links. Individuals assigned to a two-member group are considered *dyad members. Liaisons* are those individuals who interact with several groups, but are not clearly a member of one specific group. *Isolates* are those students who have no reciprocated friendships. Students with links to multiple groups are often assigned to the peer group with the greatest number of friendship links (assumed to be their primary peer group); however, if the links to the multiple groups are equivalent then the student is considered a liaison. Of note, criteria and classification vary depending on the objective of each study and statistical programs used.

Improving Violence Research with SNA

As mentioned earlier, the purpose of this chapter is to illustrate, using SNA, how research on violence can be improved. We focus on two particular research areas, youth aggression and gang membership, as we demonstrate the novel ways in which SNA has supported some long-standing developmental theories. Because these areas of investigation can be improved through a more widespread application of recent innovations in SNA techniques, thus, we suggest future areas of research.

Youth Aggression

The correlates and causes of adolescent aggression have been addressed in research for decades. Reasons why some children are aggressive have been identified in the literature as involving biological influences (Gottesman & Goldsmith, 1994; Miles & Carey, 1997), individual characteristics (Miles & Carey, 1997), peer influence (DeRosier, Cilessen, Coie, & Dodge, 1994; Espelage, Holt, & Henkel, 2003; Hudley, 1993), parental factors (Eron, Huesmann, & Zell, 1991), differences in emotional competence (Berkowitz, 1993), and deficits in social skills (Huesmann, 1998; Nelson & Crick, 1999). Studies have found verbal and physical forms of aggression during childhood to be relatively stable and often predictive of violence and criminal behavior during adolescence and adulthood (Olweus, 1978; Patterson, Reid, & Dishion, 1992; Zumkley, 1994). For example, in 1960, Eron and colleagues (1987) surveyed more than 800 third graders in the Midwest and found that children who bullied their peers at the age

of 8 were more likely to engage in similar behaviors as adults than students who did not bully at this age. In adulthood, these childhood bullies were more likely to commit serious crimes, abuse their wives physically, and raise children who were bullies. Furthermore, of the childhood bullies surveyed, one in four had a criminal record by the age of 30. This section of the chapter examines the evidence for peer involvement in youth aggression and bullying with a particular focus on how social network analysis has advanced our understanding in this area.

Importance of Peers on Shaping Social Behavior

Overview. Developmental psychologists and sociologists have long acknowledged the importance of the peer group during early adolescence in shaping and supporting the behavior of its members (Corsaro & Eder, 1990; Crockett, Losoff, & Peterson, 1984; Eder, 1985; Rubin, Bukowski, & Parker, 1988). Much of the research in this area has documented that peer experiences during early adolescence are qualitatively different from those of early childhood. For example, peer interactions become more frequent and less supervised. Concurrently, friendships increase in intensity and intimacy, with the same-sex clique emerging as a common social group (Brown, 1990; Rubin et al., 1988).

An extensive literature exists on the potent influence of social group participation on the development and maintenance of delinquency (Elliott, Huizinga, & Menard, 1989; Vitaro, Tremblay, Kerr, Pagani, & Bukowski, 1997). Although these studies did not employ social network analysis to investigate peer influences, their longitudinal nature provides support for peer group influence on delinquency. These studies have demonstrated that the majority of delinquent adolescents affiliate with deviant peers. However, many of these studies were limited by their assessment of peer delinquency; study participants were often asked to identify members of their primary social group and to report on their own delinquent behavior, as well as the behaviors of their friends (Elliott, Huizinga, & Ageton, 1985). Using this single informant approach has been criticized for its tendency to provide self-enhancing data and the high correlation between those characteristics reported for self and other (Cairns, Xie, & Leung, 1998).

These research investigations, along with much of the peer relations investigations of social behavior, have neglected to directly incorporate analyses of the broader social contexts, such as peer groups (Cairns et al., 1998). Cairns and colleagues (1998) asserted that "modern developmental research has typically reduced the study of social relationships to the individual or dyadic level by emphasizing such constructs as 'popularity' and 'friendship'" (p. 25). This trend is somewhat surprising given the plethora of theoretical and empirical writings (spanning the last century) that have emphasized group experiences as significant determinants of human nature (see Hartup, 1983, for a historical review).

Methods to assess peer networks. Cairns and colleagues (1988) therefore suggested an alternative procedure for determining peer networks – the social cognitive map approach (SCM). The SCM approach is based on Moreno's (1934) classic sociometric method. It uses a social-cognitive interview conducted with children and adolescents in which they are asked this question, "Are there some people who hang around together a lot?" (Cairns, Cairns, Neckerman, Gest, & Gariepy, 1988, p. 817), with interviewers prompting children to name as many groups/clusters as they could. In most cases, not all children in a class are interviewed because a subsample appears to yield reliable networks existing in the class. Followup questions provide additional information about the structure and makeup of peer clusters. These social-cognitive maps are then used to create a "co-nomination matrix," which summarizes the total number of times a given pair of children is named by peers as being in the same social group. This matrix is then analyzed to create discrete nonoverlapping social clusters using a variant of principal component analysis and cluster analysis (Cairns & Cairns, 1994; Cairns et al., 1988). Results from these investigations are summarized in the next section.

An alternative approach is one used by Ennett and Bauman (1994, 1996) that describes more completely the various social network roles that are characteristic of youth culture. In contrast to the method used by Cairns and colleagues, Ennett and Bauman assess social networks by asking students to identify and list those friends similar in age (but not their siblings) with whom they hang out with most often. Students are often restricted to naming friends who attend their same school, as prior studies indicate that 95% of adolescents named adolescents in the same school, even when they were allowed to list friends outside the school. Friendship data are then subjected to social network analysis in order to identify the variety of associations among students in peer networks, using a variety of statistical programs, including NEGOPY (Richards, 1995).

All of the published studies using this method in relation to youth aggression have discarded the liaisons and isolates. Instead they have focused on clique members and dyads to explore peer group influences. In some ways this is a disappointing practice because youth who are isolates (have no reciprocated or unreciprocated nominations) would be important to study in the area of school violence. These students might be victimized by their peers, placing them at additional risk for resorting to violence to seek revenge or manage their own victimization. Additionally, liaisons (students who are members of more than one peer group) might play an important role in diffusing aggression and violence, given their lack of investment in one specific peer group.

Theories of Peer Influence on Aggression

Given the social-ecological perspective that individual characteristics of adolescents interact with group-level factors, many scholars have turned their attention to how peers contribute to aggression, including verbal and physical forms (Espelage et al., 2003; Pellegrini & Long, 2002; Rodkin, Farmer, Pearl, & Van Acker, 2000). Several theories dominate the literature in this area, including the homophily hypothesis (Cairns & Cairns, 1994; Espelage et al., 2003), dominance theory (Pellegrini & Long, 2002), and attraction theory (Bukowski, Sippola, & Newcomb, 2000). Taken together, these theories present a complex picture of how social network characteristics of peer groups influence each other during early adolescence. Relative to other areas of youth aggression research, very few studies have tested these theories using social network analysis. Most of these studies have examined the homophily hypothesis, and a few recent papers use social network analysis to examine the dominance theory. Although we were unable to uncover a study that specifically used social network analysis to test attraction theory, we discuss that theory briefly as a guide to future social network studies on youth aggression.

Homophily hypothesis. Peer groups during late childhood and early adolescence form based on similarities in propinquity, sex, and race (Cairns & Cairns, 1994; Leung, 1994), and groups tend to be similar on behavioral dimensions, such as smoking behavior (Ennett & Bauman, 1994). This within-group similarity is called *homophily* (Berndt, 1982; Cohen, 1977; Kandel, 1978). Studies that have employed the social-cognitive mapping procedure report within-group similarity on aggression among peer social clusters (Gaines, Cairns, & Cairns, 1994; Leung, 1993; Neckerman, 1992; Xie, 1995). Other studies using this approach demonstrate support for aggressive behaviors within these social clusters (Cairns, Neckerman, & Cairns, 1989; Cairns et al., 1988; Rodkin et al., 2000). That is, aggressive participants are identified as nuclear members or are members with the highest centrality. These studies supported the homophily hypothesis for overt, physical aggression among elementary-school students (Cairns, Leung, & Cairns, 1995).

More recently, the hypothesis was evaluated separately for verbal and physical forms of aggression among middle-school students. Using Ennett and Bauman's approach, Espelage and colleagues (2003) used social network analysis (SNA) to identify peer cliques and dyads and employed hierarchical linear modeling (HLM) to determine the extent to which peers influenced each other in relation to changes in aggression. Overall, students tended to hang out with students who bullied at similar frequencies, and students who hung out with kids who bullied others increased in the amount of self-reported bullying over the school year. The effect was stronger for bullying than fighting, suggesting that peer influence plays a bigger role for low-level aggression than fighting. Although males in this sample reported slightly more bullying than females, this study demonstrates how an exclusive focus on individual mean level differences obscures mechanisms that influence aggression across sex. That is, the homophily hypothesis for bullying and fighting was supported for both male and female peer groups. These set of studies are important because they are the first to demonstrate that networks could be identified when grade (e.g., eighth grade) was the level of analysis, rather than a small classroom. This work has been instrumental in creating an international base of scholars using SNA to examine peer influences on aggression. For example, in a sample of Mainland Chinese children, SNA was used to replicate the homophily hypothesis (Xu, Farver, Schwartz, & Chang, 2004). Although these studies are encouraging, much more work needs to be conducted in this area.

Dominance and attraction theory. Early adolescence is also a time in which there is an increase in the amount of aggression (Pellegrini, 2002a; Pellegrini & Long, 2002; Smith, Madsen, & Moody, 1999). A potential explanation for this increase is dominance theory. Dominance is viewed as a relationship factor in which individuals are arranged in a hierarchy in terms of their access to resources (Dunbar, 1988). Pellegrini (2002b) argues that the transition to

middle school requires students to rene-
gotiate their dominance relationships, and
aggression (especially bullying) is thought to
be a deliberate strategy used to attain dominance in newly formed peer groups. In an
empirical test of the dominance theory of
aggression, Pellegrini and Long (2002) found
that bullying was used more frequently by
boys who targeted their aggression toward
other boys during this transition. Extending
this research to include a direct assessment
of social networks, Mouttapa, Valente, Gallaher, Rohrbach, and Unger (2004) argued
that social dominance was at work in their
sample of Latino and Asian sixth graders
($n = 1{,}368$). Friends' participation in
aggressive behaviors was found to be positively associated with being a bully or
an aggressive victim, and an interesting
finding was that female bullies received
fewer friendship nominations, but had the
highest proportion of reciprocated friendships. These findings not only support the
homophily and social dominance hypotheses but also highlight how research that
focuses on the simple count of friendship nominations, rather than exploring the
robustness of certain ties, might be misleading. Clearly, dominance theory is a great candidate for SNA, in which position within a
network can be used to demonstrate how
individuals differ in their ability to manipulate social behaviors of members over time.

Attraction theory posits that young adolescents, in their need to establish separation from their parents, become attracted
to other youth who possess characteristics
that reflect independence (e.g., delinquency,
aggression, disobedience) and are less
attracted to individuals who possess characteristics more descriptive of childhood (e.g.,
compliance, obedience; Bukowski et al.,
2000; Moffitt, 1993). These authors argue
that early adolescents manage the transition
from primary to secondary schools through
their attractions to peers who are aggressive.
In their study of 217 boys and girls during this transition, Bukowski and colleagues
(2000) found that girls' and boys' attraction
to aggressive peers increased on their entry
to middle school. This increase was larger

for girls, which is consistent with Pellegrini
and Bartini's (2001) finding that at the end
of middle school girls nominated "dominant
boys" as dates to a hypothetical party. This
theory has yet to be examined using SNA.

*Homophobic aggression – New application
of SNA.* An emerging area of interest in
adolescent research is the examination of
homophobia as conceptualized within the
context of the aggression literature (Kimmel & Mahler, 2003). Findings suggest that
homophobic aggression contributes to the
shaping of victimized gay, lesbian, and heterosexual students' negative perceptions of
the school climate and therefore is an important factor to be considered when examining
students' social experiences. Peer groups and
peer culture become increasingly influential
as individuals approach and develop through
adolescence, and a growing qualitative base
suggests that homophobic behavior occurs
frequently among peers (Plummer, 2001).

A recent investigation (Poteat, Espelage,
& Green, in press) expands on the extant
literature by looking beyond individual-
level analyses to incorporate the peer group
and social context in understanding and
predicting homophobic behavior. Participants included 213 high-school students
(108 females, 105 males) in grades 7
through 11. The sample was racially diverse
(approximately 40% racial minorities). Participants completed a self-report survey
including indicators of behavioral homophobia, dominance, and support for violence.
The included measures have demonstrated
consistently strong psychometric properties
in the literature. Students were also asked
to nominate up to eight students (male or
female) they considered as friends.

Friendship nominations were subjected to
SNA to identify peer groups using NEGOPY
(Richards, 1995). Sixteen cliques and two
dyads were identified and used in the subsequent analyses. Hierarchical linear modeling
was used to evaluate the influence of peer-
level support for violence and dominance
on individual-level homophobic behavior.
Because this study involves only one time
point at present, a level-two model was
interpreted in which individual homophobic

behavior was the outcome variable and predictor variables included support for violence and dominance aggregated for the individual's peer group. As hypothesized, support for violence ($\gamma = 0.33$, $p < 0.001$) and dominance ($\gamma = 0.21$, $p < 0.001$) at the peer level were predictive of greater individual homophobic behavior. These relations were not moderated by sex, suggesting that these predictors hold for both males and females. These findings suggest that students' own homophobic behaviors are influenced by attitudes toward violence and dominance within their primary peer group.

This investigation expanded on existing research by addressing the influence of the peer group on individuals' homophobic behavior, which has not been addressed in past research. Two peer-level social factors (support for violence and dominance) significantly predicted individual homophobic behavior. For intervention programs to decrease aggression (including homophobic aggression) more effectively among students, they must adequately address components of peer culture and students' social experiences, in addition to individual attitudes, motivations, and behaviors. These findings support the need for programs to specifically address how peers encourage homophobic behavior among group members. Future research should look to identify additional factors that contribute to decreased levels of homophobic behavior in some peer groups and factors that promote homophobic behavior in others.

Summary of Social Networks and Aggression

The introduction of SNA into the area of youth aggression has been slow, despite a long history of research on the saliency of peer relations on social behavior. It is our belief that the slowness of the infusion of social network studies into this area is primarily due to the complexity of social network methods. Despite this complexity, several researchers across this country and others have demonstrated the powerful impact of social networks on youth aggres-sion. When we closely examine the predominant theories on peer relations and aggression they beg for an approach like SNA to uncover how the social context affects individual decisions among children and adolescents.

We now turn our attention to an area in which a significant amount of progress has been made to explicate the extreme complexity of social networks on individual behaviors – gangs.

Social Networks and Gang Membership

Even an intuitive understanding of social network theory and method enables the application of more thorough reasoning to complex behavioral situations. However, an intuitive understanding applies background concepts but not necessarily the collection of social network data used in quantitative analysis. Fleisher (1995) used intuitive social network ethnographic reasoning to study patterns of homelessness and socioeconomic adaptation among former prison inmates in Seattle; he used a similar technique in Kansas City, Missouri, to study a coed, multiracial, multiethnic street gang (Fleisher, 1998). In Seattle, he used a key informant technique (a central actor who has substantial experience and knowledge of a subculture); Fleisher described patterns of social interaction among homeless men who customarily "reside" in widely separate areas of the city. By discovering specific bounded geographic areas of socioeconomic adaptation and the homeless men who are connected to one another, Fleisher created the social, geographic, and economic framework to understand broadly dispersed patterns of interaction. By accompanying his key informant "Popcorn," a gang member and cocaine seller, Fleisher determined the expansiveness of Popcorn's social links and how he used them for legal and illegal purposes.

The end product of more than 2 years of fieldwork was a narrative description of Popcorn's personal social network and how actors in his network link to actors across the city. "Successful" homelessness relies on a system of intersecting actors, each of whom open doors to particular types of resources, such as sleeping areas, profitable panhandling locations, sources of illegal drugs, best locations to sell drugs, and locations where a drug seller can safely hide from law enforcement.

Fleisher (2002) has combined an intuitive approach to fieldwork and a systematic approach to collecting quantifiable social network data (Fleisher, 2005a,b). Using techniques similar to those he used in Seattle, he spent 7 years in a gang neighborhood in Champaign, Illinois, studying patterns of social and economic adaptation among teenaged and adult women who claimed membership in street gangs. On-site observation and interviews gave information on who hung out with whom and reasons for their interaction and changes in interaction. He used SNA to illustrate the social structure that influenced interaction and how interaction influenced social structure.

A holistic description of gang social life and patterns of interaction among gang and nongang residents could have been accomplished with either an intuitive approach or a macro-level, quantitative approach. However, using one approach to the exclusion of the other would have meant a loss of explanatory power. Field observation showed that members of different gangs were friends, hung out together, sold drugs together, watched each other's children, and protected one another. This finding is contrary to the general assumption that gangs are bounded social groups whose members do not often interact. But Fleisher argued that membership in a gang is more symbolic than real, in the sense that membership constrained economic ties necessary to survival in a poor environment. Support for that argument can be offered by the concept of social embeddedness. This concept was used as an explanatory tool to understand the nature of social interaction among gang women.

Women gang members' social lives encompassed a complex array of friends, nonfriends, and enemies cross-cut by dozens of relations; Fleisher (2002) measured three dozen relations among and between same- and different-gang women. Fleisher gathered data sufficient to create a gang-women network. One can assume that women who do not know each other are not likely to protect each other; women who hate each other are not likely to engage in mutually productive crime. Women who are friends, however, are likely to have some types of exchange, depending on the degree of friendship.

Gang-women informants (referred to here as ego) were asked to list their friends, close friends, and best friends; from this information friendship-degree definitions were constructed. Components of the definitions revealed friendship-degree distinctions. A friend is someone ego knew, but did not hang out with. A close friend is a friend ego spent some time with and talked to, but not about personal issues. A best friend is a close friend with whom ego shared personal secrets. These definitions isolate traits of dyadic interaction of *social interaction* (frequency and duration of interaction), *personal interaction* (someone ego knows personally; someone ego would ride around town with), *affective interaction* (someone ego cares about and trusts; someone ego would ask to watch her children if she went out of town), and *gang interaction* (someone ego would ask to borrow a gun; someone ego would ask to participate in a high-profit illegal activity; someone whose home ego would use to hide out from police).

Gang affiliation might involve a few or many types of interaction among gang members. Relations were shared differentially; thus, behavior was conditioned on types of relations. Ego might sell cocaine with alter A, but not allow alter A to watch her children. These patterns of interaction illustrate that social networks have different combinations of relations, which lead to multiple types of interaction and behavioral characteristics.

As mentioned previously, embeddedness is a useful concept, especially in conducting youth gang research and in designing prevention and intervention initiatives. A common definition of a youth gang is a social group whose members commit crime. The Champaign gang-women analyses and other gang studies have exposed the multidimensionality of intra- and inter-gang interaction, and have shown that crime relations are unequally distributed among same-gang members; in fact, some gang members never commit crime with anyone, but do share other types of relational adaptations.

A real-world application of embeddedness has real-world applications in gang violence intervention and former inmate community re-entry. Well-embedded gang women, those who share multiple relations with alters, are going to be more difficult to extricate from gang networks than those who are poorly embedded. Violent well-embedded gang women will likely have a greater influence on others than a poorly embedded woman. Different types of violence might result from different patterns of embeddness and shared relations. Former inmates re-entering urban neighborhoods after prison terms of 10 to 15 years are unlikely to share relations with the same people or in some cases the relations after re-entry are strained. Research now shows that re-entering offenders are often rejected by their families and friends. The outcome is low embeddedness, which is likely to lead to engaging in a mechanism of self-survival (crime) and expressions of anger toward those who reject them. A common reason for former offender re-arrest is domestic violence.

Empirical Measures

Youth gangs have garnered our attention because they can act out violent behavior; however, a majority of gang violence is intra-gang violence. The application of SNA to gang data helps us resolve questions about violence, which other research techniques, including field observations and interviews, cannot answer. And SNA can help substantiate our observations and lend support to patterns in interview data. The analysis of violent behavior in social networks, such as the nature of the relation between an initia-

tor and victims and the links between them and bystanders, can be presented as a narrative description, but a more rigorous analysis requires ego-centric and socio-centric measures.

An ego-centric analysis might focus on how relations between and among members facilitate other group processes or behaviors. Do friendship networks mediate intergroup conflict? Are there cohesive subgroups within a larger gang? Who are the leaders and regular members versus periphery members? Which types of ties predict social status, power, or influence within the gang? How are particular types of relations translated into collective action? If data are gathered on contacts outside of the gang, such data might also guide our understanding of how gang members are integrated into the larger community and, for example, affect mechanisms of informal social control.

Several early gang studies focused on exactly these types of questions employing early network techniques and graphical representations. Papachristos (2006) applied social network techniques to data from Suttles' (1968) study of slums, which focused on patterns of cohesion.

Figure 22.1 graphically illustrates the multidimensionality among the Erls, one of 32 street corner groups. An analysis of the Erls on the relations "cool with," familial, and antagonistic shows that the gang lacked formal structure and that the social order was determined by each boy's frequency of interaction, type of relation to other members, commitment to "hanging out," fighting ability, and other interpersonal qualities. One boy was generally recognized as the "leader" (K-Man), even though the Erls did not use formal rank or titles.

Table 22.1 shows betweenness centrality scores calculated on "cool with" relations; each member had an average of 3.7 ties. K-Man was cited as most influential, but several others (Marty, Grug, and Troll) had degree centrality measures equal to K-Man's $(d(n_i) = 6)$. These three were also cool with the same number of alters on betweenness centrality as K-man had. Tatters, who was

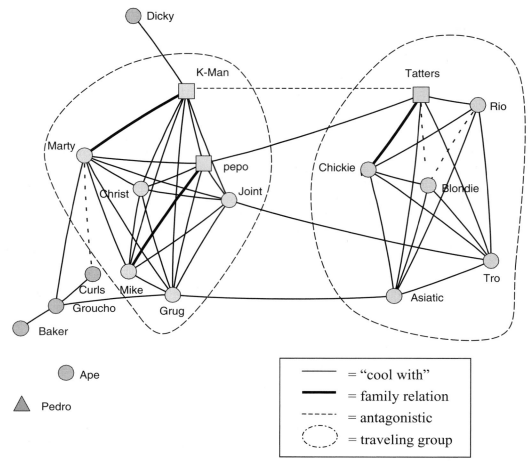

Figure 22.1. Patterns of relationships among the Erls, 1963. Source: Suttles (1968, p. 189, figure 1).

mentioned by the boys as another leader, was considerably lower on degree centrality.

The most central actor was a boy called Asiatic. Interestingly, he was not identified by gang boys as occupying an important position. Grug and Asiatic had scores more than double those of any other member and more than four times the network average of 10.8. These findings suggest that prominence is not the most important factor determining leadership, although in the case of K-Man it appears to be a contributing factor.

Summary of Social Networks and Gang Research

SNA is a testing platform for new observations and gang research findings made over decades. Here are three examples of common findings of gang research, which benefit by SN perspectives.

Gang members hang out in gangs on average for less than 2 years. That fact is interesting. However, SNA allows insightful discussion of social dynamics of social entry and exit. We can ask, How do youth acquire social affiliation through siblings, cousins, parents, friends, or acquaintances? Then, how does a point of initial affiliation influence the behavior of a new affiliate, knowing that adolescents will have greater or lesser propensity for violent crime? Perhaps we would find that more violent youth import more violent friends than regular members do. This hypothesis is testable via SNA, but would be terribly difficult to study with interviews and observations.

Table 22.1: Degree centrality and betweenness centrality among the Erls

	Degree Centrality	Betweenness
K-Man	6	20.333
Marty	6	15.833
Christ	5	3.317
Pepo	5	8.317
Mike	3	0.4
Joint	5	16.233
Grug	6	47.733
Dicky	1	0
Groucho	4	31
Curtis	1	0
Baker	1	0
Ape	0	0
Pedro	1	0
Asiatic	7	43
Troll	6	16.5
Chickie	4	0.333
Tatters	3	3
Rio	3	0
Blondie	3	0
Mean	*3.68*	*10.8*

Gang members have core, regular, and peripheral members. Gang research customarily applies structure-like labels to gang members. The terms *core* and *peripheral* infer a measurable social structural position, but gang research does not usually gather data needed to make even the simplest SN descriptions. Rather, in this case, gang social labels are defined by the amount of time youth spend on the street. However, time on the street has no necessary social implications. To make sense of structure-like gang labels we would need a great deal more fieldwork data about gang youth and their "hanging out" social context. Even with more field interviews and observations, we still lack structural position measures of youth gang members in the entire group. In the end, basic SNA allows us to describe personal network composition (e.g., core, regular, and peripheral members), members who commit violent crime, and members who commit no crime.

Gang members have friends who are not gang members. This observation infers that nongang friends do not participate in or influence the commission of crime by individual gang members, dyads, and large social units. Gang researchers have not gathered enough data on the functions of nongang members in gang members' everyday lives. Crime is the least time-consuming activity of youth gang members. Street research has shown that gang youth who have been on the street for months are episodically and in some cases literally homeless. Fleisher's 2002 Champaign research suggests that gang youth with a link to a permanent residence supervised by an adult do not commit violent crime as often as homeless youth.

Youth who do not get off the street are costly in social terms (a life lost to crime and prison) and financial terms (the criminal justice system is expensive). SNA lets us pursue new lines of research and add new perspectives to old lines of research. If we were able to combine qualitative analysis and select suitable SN methods, we might be more successful at understanding why youth gang intervention and prevention initiatives do not keep adolescents off the street.

Conclusion

As etiological models of violence become more complex, it is becoming increasingly obvious that individual behaviors, such as youth violence and gang involvement, are best explained through an examination of the larger social contexts. SNA offers concepts and techniques that provide social science answers to the questions about peer influence and interactions among network members, and it offers an in-depth examination of the complex world of networks and the various roles that persons take across peer groups and gangs. However, much more work needs to be conducted in these areas. In relation to youth aggression, studies need to be conducted on how social networks change in composition across the school years and how these network changes are predictive of subsequent developmental changes in types of aggression and violence. For example, there is some suggestion in recent longitudinal studies that students who are bullies during middle school are likely to become perpetrators of sexual harassment during high school and then are at further risk for becoming sexual assault perpetrators into adulthood. The next logical question would be to determine what roles these perpetrators held in their friendship networks or peer culture and how their roles might have promoted violence. More generally, SNA techniques need to combine basic descriptive analyses with more substantive areas of youth violence and gang research. Finally, simply thinking about the fundamentals of SN theory can assist gang field studies by stimulating research questions and theoretical perspectives, which fieldworkers and qualitative researchers might otherwise miss.

Acknowledgments

Research funding was provided by the University of Illinois Research Board and the Office of Naval Research to Indiana University. We thank Daniel Flannery for very helpful comments on this chapter.

References

Berkowitz, L. (1993). *Aggression: Its causes, consequences, and control*. New York: McGraw-Hill.

Berndt, T. J. (1982). The features and effects of friendship in early adolescence. *Child Development, 53,* 1447–1460.

Brown, B. B. (1990). Peer groups and peer culture. In S. S. Feldman & G. R. Elliott (Eds.), *At the threshold: The developing adolescent* (pp. 171–196). Cambridge, MA: Harvard University Press.

Bukowski, W. M., Sippola, L. K., & Newcomb, A. F. (2000). Variations in patterns of attraction to same- and other-sex peers during early adolescence. *Developmental Psychology, 36,* 147–154.

Cairns, R. B., & Cairns, B. D. (1994). *Lifelines and risks: Pathways of youth in our time*. Cambridge, UK: Cambridge University Press.

Cairns, R. B., Cairns, B. D., Neckerman, H. J., Gest, S. D., & Gariepy, J. L. (1988). Social networks and aggressive behavior. *Developmental Psychology, 25,* 320–330.

Cairns, R. B., Leung, M. C., & Cairns, B. D. (1995). Social networks over time and space in adolescence. In L. J. Crockett & A. C. Crouter (Eds.), *Pathways through adolescence: Individual development in relation to social contexts. The Penn State series on child and adolescent development* (pp. 35–56). Hillsdale, NJ: Lawrence Erlbaum.

Cairns, R. B., Neckerman, H. J., & Cairns, B. D. (1989). Social networks and shadows of synchrony. In G. R. Adams, R. Montemayor, & T. P. Gullota (Eds.), *Biology of adolescent behavior and development*. Thousand Oaks, CA: Sage.

Cairns, R. B., Xie, H., & Leung, M.-C. (1998). The popularity of friendship and the neglect of social networks: Toward a new balance. In W. M. Bukowski & A. H. Cillessen (Eds.), *Sociometry then and now: Building on six decades of measuring children's experiences with the peer group. New directions for child development, No. 80* (pp. 25–53). San Francisco: Jossey-Bass.

Cohen, J. M. (1977). Sources of peer group homogeneity. *Sociology of Education, 50,* 227–241.

Corsaro, W. A., & Eder, D. (1990). Children's peer cultures. *Annual Review of Sociology, 16,* 197–220.

Crockett, L. J., Losoff, M., & Petersen, A. C. (1984). Perceptions of the peer group and friendship in early adolescence. *Journal of Early Adolescence, 4,* 155–181.

DeRosier, M., Cillessen, A., Coie, J., & Dodge, K. (1994). Group social context and children's aggressive behavior. *Child Development, 65,* 1068–1079.

Dunbar, R. I. M. (1988). *Primate social systems*. Ithaca, NY: Cornell University Press.

Eder, D. (1985). The cycle of popularity: Interpersonal relations among female adolescents. *Sociology of Education, 58,* 154–165.

Elliott, D. S., Huizinga, D., & Ageton, S. S. (1985). *Explaining delinquency and drug use*. Newbury Park, CA: Sage.

Elliott, D. S., Huizinga, D., & Menard, S. (1989). *Multiple problem youth: Delinquency, substance use, and mental health problems*. New York: Springer-Verlag.

Ennett, S. T., & Bauman, K. E. (1994). The contribution of influence and selection to adolescent peer group homogeneity: The case of adolescent cigarette smoking. *Journal of Personality and Social Psychology, 67,* 653–663.

Ennett, S. T., & Bauman, K. E. (1996). Adolescent social networks: School, demographic, and longitudinal considerations. *Journal of Adolescent Research, 11*, 194–215.

Eron, L. D., Huesmann, L. R., Dubow, E., Romanoff, R., & Yarnel, P. W. (1987). Aggression and its correlates over 22 years. In D. H. Crowell & I. M. Evans (Eds.), *Childhood aggression and violence: Sources of influence, prevention, and control* (pp. 249–262). New York: Plenum Press.

Eron, L. D., Huesmann, L. R., & Zell, A. (1991). The role of parental variables in the learning of aggression. In D. J. Pepler & K. H. Rubin (Eds.), *The development and treatment of childhood aggression* (pp. 169–189). Hillsdale, NJ: Erlbaum.

Espelage, D. L., Holt, M. K., & Henkel, R. R. (2003). Examination of peer-group contextual effects on aggression during early adolescence. *Child Development, 74*(1), 205–220.

Faber, A., & Wasserman, S. (2001). Social support and social networks: Synthesis and review. In J. Levy & B. Pescosolido (Eds.), *Social networks and health. advances in medical sociology* (Vol. 8, pp. 29–72). Stamford, CT: JAI Press.

Fleisher, M. S. (1995). *Beggars and thieves: The lives of urban street criminals.* Madison, WI: University of Wisconsin Press.

Fleisher, M. S. (1998). *Dead end kids: Gang girls and the boys they know.* Madison, WI: University of Wisconsin Press.

Fleisher, M. S. (2002). *Women in gangs: A field research study.* Washington, DC: U.S. Department of Justice, Office of Juvenile Justice and Delinquency Prevention.

Fleisher, M. S. (2005a). Field research and social network analysis: Different methods creating complementary perspectives. *Journal of Contemporary Criminal Justice, 21*(2), 120–134.

Fleisher, M. S. (2005b). Degree centrality and youth gangs as an ecological adaptation. In J. Short & L. Hughes (Eds.), *Studying youth gangs.* Walnut Creek, CA: AltaMira Press.

Gaines, K. R. E., Cairns, R. B., & Cairns, B. D. (1994). *Social networks and risk for school dropout.* Paper presented at the Society for Research on Adolescence, San Diego.

Gottesman, I. I., & Goldsmith, H. H. (1994). Developmental psychopathology of antisocial behavior: Inserting genes into its ontogenesis and epigenesis. In C. A. Nelson (Ed.), *Threats to optimal development: Integrating biological, psychological, and social risk factors* (pp. 69–104). Hillsdale, NJ: Erlbaum.

Granovetter, M. (1992). Economic action and social structure: The problem of embeddedness. In M. Granovetter & R. Swedberg (Eds.), *The sociology of economic life.* Boulder, CO: Westview Press.

Hartup, W. W. (1983). Peer groups. In P. H. Mussen (Series Ed.) & E. M. Hetherington (Vol. Ed.), *Handbook of child psychology. Vol. 4: Socialization, personality, and social development* (4th ed.). New York: Wiley.

Hudley, C. (1993). Comparing teacher and peer perceptions of aggression: An ecological approach. *Journal of Educational Psychology, 85*, 377–384.

Huesmann, L. R. (1998). Social information processing. In R. Green & E. Donnerstein (Eds.), *Human aggression: Theories, research, and implications for social policy* (pp. 73–109). New York: Academic Press.

Kandel, D. B. (1978). Homophily, selection, and socialization in adolescent friendships. *American Journal of Sociology, 84*, 427–436.

Kimmel, M. S., & Mahler, M. (2003). Adolescent masculinity, homophobia, and violence. *American Behavioral Scientist, 465*, 1439–1458.

Leung, M.-C. (1993). *Social cognition and social networks of Chinese schoolchildren in Hong Kong.* Unpublished doctoral dissertation, University of North Carolina at Chapel Hill.

Leung, M. C. (1994). Social cognition and social networks of Chinese schoolchildren in Hong Kong. *Dissertation Abstracts International, 54* (12-B).

Miles, D., & Carey, G. (1997). Genetic and environmental architecture of human aggression. *Journal of Personality and Social Psychology, 72*, 207–217.

Moffitt, T. E. (1993). Adolescent-limited and life-course-persistent anti-social behavior: A developmental taxonomy. *Psychological Review, 100*, 674–701.

Moreno, J. L. (1934). *Who shall survive? A new approach to the problem of human interrelations.* Washington, DC: Nervous and Mental Disease Publishing Company.

Mouttapa, M., Valente, T., Gallaher, P., Rohrbach, L. A., & Unger, J. B. (2004). Social network predictors of bullying and victimization. *Source Adolescence, 39* (*154*), 315–335.

Neckerman, H. J. (1992). A longitudinal investigation of the stability and fluidity of social networks and peer relationships of children and adolescents. Unpublished doctoral dissertation, University of North Carolina at Chapel Hill.

Nelson, D. A., & Crick, N. R. (1999). Rose-colored glasses: Examining the social information-processing of prosocial young adolescents. *Journal of Adolescence, 19,* 17–38.

Olweus, D. (1978). *Aggression in the schools: Bullies and whipping boys.* Washington, DC: Hemisphere.

Papachristos, A. V. (2006). Social network analysis and gang research: Theory and methods. In J. Short & L. Hughes (Eds.), *Studying street gangs.* Walnut Creek, CA: AltaMira Press.

Patterson, G. R., Reid, J. B., & Dishion, T. J. (1992). *A social interactional approach. IV: Antisocial boys.* Eugene, OR: Castalia.

Pellegrini, A. D. (2002a). Bullying, victimization, and sexual harassment during the transition to middle school. *Educational Psychologist, 37,* 151–163.

Pellegrini, A. D. (2002b). Affiliative and aggressive dimensions of dominance and possible functions during early adolescence. *Aggression and Violent Behavior, 7*(1), 21–31.

Pellegrini, A. D., & Bartini, M. (2001). Dominance in early adolescent boys: Affiliative and aggressive dimensions and possible functions. *Merrill-Palmer Quarterly, 47,* 142–163.

Pellegrini, A. D., & Long, J. (2002). A longitudinal study of bullying, dominance, and victimization during the transition from primary to secondary school. *British Journal of Developmental Psychology, 20,* 259–280.

Plummer, D. C. (2001). The quest for modern manhood: Masculine stereotypes, peer culture and the social significance of homophobia. *Journal of Adolescence, 24,* 15–23.

Poteat, P., Espelage, D. L., & Green, H. (in press). Aggression, homophobia, and dominance among high school students. *Journal of Social and Personality Psychology.*

Richards, W. D. (1995). *NEGOPY 4.30 manual and user's guide.* Burnaby, British Columbia: School of Communication, Simon Fraser University.

Rodkin, P. C., Farmer, T. W., Pearl, R., & Van Acker, R. (2000). Heterogeneity of popular boys: Antisocial and prosocial configurations. *Developmental Psychology, 36,* 14–24.

Rubin, K. H., Bukowski, W., & Parker, J. G. (1988). Peer interactions, relationships, and groups. In W. Damon (Series Ed.) & N. Eisenberg (Vol. Ed.), *Handbook of child psychology. Vol 3: Social, emotional, and personality development* (5th ed.). New York: Wiley.

Smith, P. K., Madsen, K. C., & Moody, J. C. (1999). What causes the age decline in reports of being bullied at school? Toward a developmental analysis of risks of being bullied. *Educational Research, 41,* 267–285.

Suttles, G. (1968). *The social order of the slum.* Chicago: University of Chicago Press.

Vitaro, F., Tremblay, R. E., Kerr, M., Pagani, L., & Bukowski, W. M. (1997), Disruptiveness, friends' characteristics, and delinquency in early adolescence: A test of two competing models of development. *Child Development, 68,* 676–689.

Wasserman, S., & Faust, K. (1994). *Social network analysis.* New York: Cambridge University Press.

Xie, H. (1995). *Peer social networks of inner-city children and adolescents at school.* Paper presented at the biennial meeting of the Society for Research in Child Development, Indianapolis.

Xu, Y., Farver, J.-A. M., Schwartz, D., & Chang, L. (2004). Social networks and aggressive behaviour in Chinese children. *International Journal of Behavioral Development, 28,* 401–410.

Zumkley, H. (1994). The stability of aggressive behavior: A meta-analysis. *German Journal of Psychology, 18,* 273–281.

CHAPTER 23

Public Health and Violence: Moving Forward in a Global Context

Linda L. Dahlberg

National and cross-national data indicate that violence is an important public health problem throughout the world. Over 1.6 million people lose their lives to acts of violence each year (Krug, Dahlberg, Mercy, Zwi, & Lozano, 2002). Nearly half of these deaths are suicides, almost one third are homicides, and about one fifth are war-related. However, in all parts of the world, deaths represent only the tip of the iceberg. For everyone who dies as a result of violence, many more are victims of nonfatal violence and consequently suffer from a range of physical, sexual, reproductive, and mental health problems (Krug et al., 2002). Violence also places a massive burden on economies, costing billions in U.S. dollars each year in health care, legal costs, absenteeism from work, lost productivity, and strains on economic development (Waters et al., 2004).

Violence is often seen as an inevitable part of the human condition – a fact of life to respond to, rather than to prevent. The public health community challenged the notion that acts of violence are simply matters of family privacy, individual choice,

or inevitable facets of life more than two decades ago. In 1979, with the publication of the first report on health promotion and disease prevention, the Surgeon General of the United States stated that violence could be prevented and should not be ignored in the effort to improve the nation's health (U.S. Department of Health, Education, and Welfare, 1979). He stated further that, although violence is linked to factors not usually addressed by health programs, a strong effort must be made to test multifaceted community programs to reduce its individual and socially devastating effects. The issue was placed on the international agenda in 1996 when the World Health Assembly adopted a resolution (WHA49.25) declaring violence a leading worldwide public health problem, and more recently in the World Health Organization's *World Report on Violence and Health* – the first comprehensive examination of violence as a preventable global public health problem (Krug et al., 2002).

By any measure, violence is a major contributor to premature death, disability, injury, and a host of other health and social consequences. Making the case that violence is a preventable public health problem rests, in part, on demonstrating that violence is predictable, that the factors that make it more likely to occur are modifiable, and that violence prevention programs and policies can work.

The purpose of this chapter is three-fold: (1) to provide a public health framework for defining and understanding the nature, context, and forms of violence; (2) to briefly describe the magnitude and impact of violence on health and the contributions of public health to understanding and preventing violence; and (3) to highlight priorities for moving violence prevention efforts forward in a global context.

Public Health Approach to Violence

By definition, public health is not about individual patients. Its focus is on dealing with diseases and with conditions and with problems affecting health, and it aims to provide the maximum benefit for the largest number of people. This does not mean that public health ignores the care of individuals. Rather, its concern is to prevent health problems and to extend better care and safety to entire populations. It is also a multidisciplinary approach that draws on a wide range of professional expertise from medicine and epidemiology; to psychology, sociology, criminology, and other behavioral sciences; and to education and economics (Mercy, Rosenberg, Powell, Broome, & Roper, 1993). This broad approach has allowed the field of public health to be innovative and responsive to a wide range of public health problems around the world.

The public health approach also emphasizes collective action as opposed to individual action. Cooperative efforts from such diverse sectors as health, education, social services, justice, and policy are necessary to solve what are usually assumed to be purely "medical" problems or, in the case of violence, purely "social" problems. Each sector has an important role to play in addressing the problem of violence, and collectively, the approaches taken by each sector have the

potential to produce important reductions in violence.

The public health approach to violence is based on the rigorous requirements of the scientific method. In moving from problem to solution, it has four key steps (Mercy et al., 1993):

1. Uncovering as much basic knowledge as possible about all aspects of violence by systematically collecting data on the magnitude, scope, characteristics, and consequences of violence at local, national, and international levels.
2. Investigating why violence occurs – that is, conducting research to determine the causes and correlates of violence, the factors that increase or decrease the risk for violence, and the factors that might be modifiable through interventions.
3. Exploring ways to prevent violence, using the information from the first two steps, by designing, implementing, monitoring, and evaluating interventions.
4. Implementing, in a range of settings, interventions that appear promising, widely disseminating information, and determining the cost effectiveness of programs.

Public health is above all characterized by its emphasis on prevention. Rather than simply accepting or reacting to violence, its starting point is the strong conviction that violent behavior and its consequences can be prevented. It includes, yet moves beyond the identification of the problem, to finding ways to apply scientific knowledge and prevent violence from occurring in the first place or to lessen its consequences once it has already occurred.

Defining Violence

Any comprehensive framework for understanding violence should begin with a definition of violence so as to facilitate its scientific measurement. There are many possible ways to define violence – it is not an exact science. Notions of what is acceptable and unacceptable behavior, and what constitutes harm, are culturally influenced and constantly under review as values and social norms evolve. Public health, however, defines violence as it relates to the health of communities and populations as a whole. Accordingly, violence is defined as follows:

The intentional use of physical force or power, threatened or actual, against oneself, another person, or against a group or community, that either results in or has a high likelihood of resulting in injury, death, psychological harm, maldevelopment or deprivation.
(World Health Organization, 1996).

The definition associates intentionality with the committing of the act itself, irrespective of the outcome it produces. It encompasses interpersonal violence, as well as suicidal behavior and other collective forms of violence, such as armed conflict. It also covers a wide range of acts, going beyond physical acts to include threats and intimidation and those acts that result from a power relationship. The definition also includes a broad range of outcomes – including psychological harm, deprivation, and maldevelopment – reflecting a growing recognition among researchers and practitioners of the importance of including violence that does not necessarily result in injury or death, but nonetheless places a substantial burden on individuals, families, communities, and health care systems worldwide. Many forms of violence against women, children, and the elderly, for instance, can result in physical, psychological, and social problems that do not necessarily lead to injury or death. These consequences can be immediate, as well as latent, and can last for years after the initial victimization.

One of the more complex aspects of the definition is the matter of intentionality. Two important points about this aspect have been noted (Dahlberg & Krug, 2002). First, even though violence is distinguished from unintended events that result in injuries, the presence of an "intent to use force" does not necessarily mean that there was an "intent to cause damage." Indeed, there may be a considerable disparity between the intended

behavior and the intended consequence. A perpetrator may intentionally commit an act that, by objective standards, is judged to be dangerous and highly likely to result in adverse health effects, but the perpetrator may not perceive it as such.

As an example, a youth may be involved in a physical fight with another youth. The use of a fist against the head or the use of a weapon in the dispute certainly increases the risk of serious injury or death, though neither outcome may be intended. A parent may vigorously shake a crying infant with the intent to quiet the child. Such an action, however, may instead cause brain damage. Force was clearly used, but without the intention of causing an injury.

A second point related to intentionality lies in the distinction between the intent to injure and the intent to "use violence." Violence, according to Walters and Parke (1964), is culturally determined. Some people mean to harm others, but based on their cultural backgrounds and beliefs, do not perceive their acts as violent. The definition above, however, defines violence as it relates to health. Certain behaviors – such as hitting a spouse – may be regarded by some people as acceptable cultural practices, but are considered violent acts with important health implications.

Other aspects of violence, though not stated explicitly, are also included in the definition. For example, the definition implicitly includes all acts of violence, whether they are public or private; reactive (in response to previous events, such as provocation) or proactive (instrumental for or anticipating more self-serving outcomes; Dodge & Coie, 1987); criminal or noncriminal. Each of these aspects is important in understanding violence and in designing prevention programs.

Types and Contexts of Violence

There are many different types of violence, and they occur in a variety of contexts. They are also linked to each other in important ways, often sharing similar underlying risk factors. Various typologies of violence have been developed over the years, although none has been very comprehensive (Foege, Rosenberg, & Mercy, 1995; Powell, Mercy, Crosby, Dahlberg, & Simon, 1999). The typology proposed in the *World Report on Violence and Health* represents the first attempt to capture the many different types of violence as well as the nature of violent acts (Dahlberg & Krug, 2002).

The typology first divides violence into three broad categories according to the characteristics of those committing the violent act: self-directed violence, interpersonal violence, and collective violence. This initial categorization differentiates between violence a person inflicts upon him- or herself; violence inflicted by another individual or by a small group of individuals; and violence inflicted by larger groups, such as nation-states, organized political groups, militia groups, or terrorist organizations (see Figure 23.1).

These three broad categories are each divided further to reflect more specific types of violence. Self-directed violence is subdivided into suicidal behavior and self-abuse. The former includes suicidal thoughts, attempted suicides – also called "parasuicide" or "deliberate self-injury" in some countries – and completed suicides. Self-abuse, in contrast, includes acts such as self-mutilation. Interpersonal violence is divided into two subcategories: (1) family and intimate partner violence – that is, violence largely between family members and intimates and usually, though not exclusively, taking place in the home; and (2) community violence – violence between individuals who are unrelated and who may or may not know each other, generally taking place outside the home. The former group includes forms of violence, such as abuse and neglect by a parent, intimate partner violence, and elder abuse. The latter includes, for example, youth interpersonal violence, stranger rape and sexual assault, and violence in institutional settings, such as schools, workplaces, prisons, and nursing homes.

Collective violence is the instrumental use of violence by people who identify themselves as members of a group against another group or set of individuals, in order to achieve social, political or economic objectives. Unlike the other two broad categories, the subcategories of collective violence suggest possible motives for violence committed by larger groups of individuals and by nation-states. Economic violence, for instance, includes attacks carried out by larger groups motivated by economic gain – such as attacks carried out with the purpose of disrupting economic activity, denying access to essential services, or creating economic division and fragmentation. Clearly, however, acts committed by larger groups can have multiple motives. Collective violence can take a variety of forms, including armed conflicts within or between states, genocide, repression and other human rights abuses, terrorism, and organized violent crime.

The typology also illustrates the nature of violent acts, which can be physical, sexual, psychological, or involving deprivation or neglect. The horizontal axis in Figure 23.1 shows who is affected, and the vertical describes how they are affected. For instance, violence against children committed by a parent can include physical, sexual, and psychological abuse, as well as neglect. Community violence can include physical assaults between young people, sexual assaults in the workplace, and neglect of older people in long-term care facilities. Political violence can include such acts as rape during armed conflicts and physical and psychological warfare.

The typology, although far from being universally accepted and not perfect, provides a useful framework for understanding both the complex patterns of violence taking place around the world, as well as violence in the everyday lives of individuals, families, and communities. It also overcomes some of the limitations of other typologies by capturing the nature of violent acts, the relevance of setting, the relationship between perpetrator and victim, and – in the case of collective violence – possible motivations for the violence. However, in both research

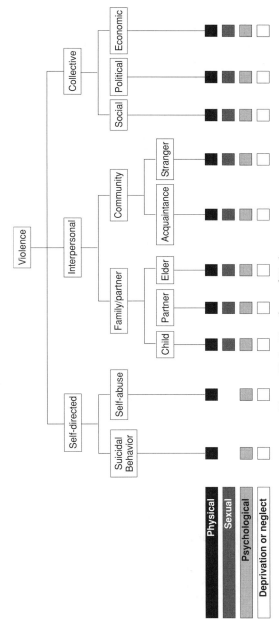

Figure 23.1. Topology of Violence.

and practice, it is important to note that the dividing lines among the different types of violence are not always so clear.

Magnitude and Impact of Violence

As stated earlier, violence is considered an important public health problem because it is a major contributor to death, disease, disability, and other health and social consequences. The full impact of violence and the burden it places on countries are not known, however, because countries are at different stages in the development of their data systems and there is also a great deal of variation in the completeness, quality, reliability, and usefulness of available information.

Fatal and Nonfatal Violence

Mortality data are the most widely collected and available of all sources of data. Many countries maintain death registries and keep basic counts of diseases, conditions, and external causes of death. Even so, only about half of the world's countries have data systems in place to capture information on violent deaths and report these deaths to the World Health Organization using the International Classification of Disease (ICD) codes. As a result, these data, as well as data from surveys, censuses, and epidemiological studies, are compiled by the World Health Organization to determine the global burden of disease and injury.

Like many other health problems in the world, violence is not distributed evenly among countries, regions, or sex and age groups. The highest rates of homicide in the world are found in Africa and the Americas, whereas the lowest rates are found in parts of Asia and in the Western Pacific (see Figure 23.2). In contrast, the highest rates of suicide are found in Europe and in the Western Pacific. Across the regions, the vast majority of violent deaths (whether from homicide, suicide, or operations of war) occur in low- to middle-income countries (over 90%), with a rate of violent death that is more than twice the rate of high-income countries (32.1 vs.

14.4 per 100,000 population; Dahlberg & Krug, 2002).

There are also wide variations among individual countries by income status. These differences are evident when examining homicide rates for young males in countries in which data are available (see Table 23.1). Rates of homicide among young males in the United States, for instance, exceed those of their counterparts in other high-income countries by several-fold. Among low- to middle-income nations, rates of homicide are highest in Latin American countries (for example, 207.1 per 100,000 in Colombia, 118.9 in El Salvador, and 101.6 in Venezuela), the Caribbean (for example, 74.6 in Puerto Rico), and the Russian Federation (48.9 per 100,000). Apart from the United States, in which the rate of homicide among males 15 to 34 years of age is 19.9 per 100,000, most countries with rates above 10.0 per 100,000 are either developing countries or those that have experienced rapid social, political, and economic change.

Almost everywhere, rates of violent death are lower among females than males – globally, a rate of about 4.0 per 100,000 across all age groups for homicide and 10.6 per 100,000 for suicide, with wide variations occurring among countries (Dahlberg & Krug, 2002). It is important to note, however, that violent deaths involving women, children, or the elderly are not always captured in mortality data. There can be significant levels of misclassification on death certificates. In some countries, for instance, official statistics show high rates of "accidental burns" for women, although public health officials suspect these are instances in which a woman was doused with kerosene during an instance of domestic violence, but was ruled to have died in a "kitchen accident." Many child and elderly deaths are also not routinely investigated or subject to postmortem examination, which makes it difficult to establish the precise numbers of fatalities from abuse.

For both males and females, nonfatal violence is much more common than fatal violence, which is why deaths are considered only the tip of the iceberg. Much of what

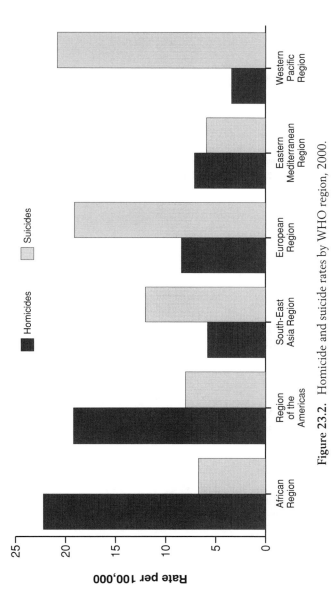

Figure 23.2. Homicide and suicide rates by WHO region, 2000.

Table 23.1: Homicide rates per 100,000 population among males by country – most recent year available[1]

Country	Year	Male homicide rate per 100,000			
		Total Number of Deaths	Rate All Ages	Total Number of Deaths	Rate 15–24 years
High Income					
Australia	2001	201	2.1	74	2.7
Austria	2002	29	0.7	7	–[2]
Belgium	1997	97	2.0	39	2.7
Canada	2000	337	2.2	150	3.4
Denmark	1999	30	1.1	16	–[2]
Finland	2002	89	3.5	30	4.5
France	2000	311	1.1	94	1.2
Germany	2001	325	0.8	84	0.8
Greece	2001	84	1.6	28	1.7
Ireland	2001	34	1.8	16	–[2]
Italy	2001	418	1.5	182	2.4
Japan	2002	445	0.7	88	0.5
The Netherlands	2002	134	1.7	55	2.5
New Zealand	2000	33	1.7	16	–[2]
Norway	2001	20	0.9	11	–[2]
Portugal	2002	125	2.5	58	3.8
Singapore	2001	14	0.8	5	–[2]
Spain	2001	322	1.6	140	2.2
Sweden	2001	57	1.3	17	–[2]
Switzerland	2000	25	0.7	11	–[2]
United Kingdom	2002	357	1.2	160	2.0
England and Wales	2002	239	0.9	104	1.5
Northern Ireland	2002	21	2.5	13	–[2]
Scotland	2002	97	4.0	43	6.6
United States of America	2002	13,640	9.3	8,143	19.9
Low and Middle Income					
Albania	2001	181	11.8	95	20.5
Argentina	2001	2,234	12.1	1 301	21.3
Armenia	2002	55	3.6	22	4.4
Azerbaijan	2002	176	4.4	85	6.1
Belarus	2001	735	15.7	229	15.4
Brazil	2000	41,570	49.0	28,644	91.9
Bulgaria	2002	175	4.6	53	4.6
Czech Republic	2002	80	1.6	22	1.4
Chile	2001	751	9.8	428	17.2
China (Hong Kong SAR)	2000	29	0.9	13	–[2]
Colombia	1999	23,926	117.0	15,267	207.1
Costa Rica	2002	205	9.8	96	13.1
Croatia	2002	38	1.8	9	–[2]
Cuba	2001	446	7.9	240	13.1
Ecuador	2000	1,922	30.8	1,140	49.9
Egypt	2000	39	0.1	26	0.2
El Salvador	1999	2,094	70.0	1,328	118.9
Estonia	2002	123	19.6	28	14.2
Guatemala	1999	1,800	32.1	1,039	54.2

Male homicide rate per 100,000

Country	Year	Total Number of Deaths	Rate All Ages	Total Number of Deaths	Rate 15–24 years
Hungary	2002	137	2.8	29	1.9
Kazakhstan	2002	1,432	20.0	574	22.6
Kyrgyzstan	2002	235	9.6	103	11.5
Latvia	2002	181	16.8	54	15.9
Lithuania	2002	189	11.7	59	11.7
Mexico	2001	8,885	18.0	4,591	25.4
Panama (excluding canal zone)	2000	260	17.5	182	34.3
Paraguay	2000	612	22.2	363	38.3
Philippines	1998	10,370	28.3	5,126	39.0
Poland	2002	486	2.6	130	2.2
Puerto Rico		608	33.2	432	74.6
Republic of Korea	2002	433	1.8	110	1.3
Republic of Moldova	2002	256	14.7	78	13.1
Romania	2002	553	5.2	151	4.2
Russian Federation	2002	33,536	50.2	10,709	48.9
Slovakia	2000	90	3.4	33	3.8
Slovenia	2002	19	1.9	7	—[2]
Thailand	2000	2,848	9.5	1,184	10.5
The Former Yugoslav Republic of Macedonia	2000	46	4.5	18	—[2]
Trinidad and Tobago	1998	84	13.2	44	19.2
Turkmenistan	1998	279	11.9	167	20.2
Ukraine	2002	3,961	17.8	1,212	17.1
Uruguay	2000	140	8.6	57	11.2
Uzbekistan	2000	540	4.4	254	5.8
Venezuela	2000	5,956	48.7	4,388	101.6

Data source: WHO mortality database.
[1] Most recent year available for countries with ≥1 million population.
[2] Fewer than 20 deaths reported; rate not calculated.

it known about nonfatal violence comes from hospital-based surveillance systems, population-based surveys, and special studies of different population groups. For example, data from the National Electronic Injury Surveillance System reveal that in 2003 there were more than 2 million violence-related injuries treated in emergency departments in the United States, including 576,000 assault-related injuries among youths 15 to 24 years of age (Centers for Disease Control and Prevention, 2005). Among countries with available data, there are at least 20 to 40 victims of nonfatal youth violence receiving medical treatment for every youth homicide (Mercy, Butchart,

Farrington, & Cerdá, 2002). In the United States, among youth 15 to 24 years of age, there are at least 100 violence-related assaults treated in emergency departments for every youth homicide.

As with deaths, many acts of violence against women, children, and the elderly are not fully captured in medical record data. For this reason, population-based surveys remain one of the most important mechanisms for ascertaining the incidence and prevalence of these types of violence, as well as information on risk behavior for these and other groups. Depending on the country and study, findings from national surveys reveal high rates of physical and sexual violence from intimate partners – on average, about one in three women worldwide report having been physically assaulted by an intimate partner in their lifetime and nearly one in four report sexual violence from a partner (Heise & Garcia-Moreno, 2002; Jewkes, Sen, & Garcia-Moreno, 2002). The mean lifetime prevalence rate of childhood sexual victimization reported in international studies is about 20% among women and between 5 and 10% among men (Finkelhor, 1994a,b), although these figures typically do not include sexual trafficking and other forms of forced sex involving children. Studies conducted in various regions also show high rates of harsh physical punishment of children. For example, in studies conducted in China, Egypt, Ethiopia, and the Republic of Korea, between one quarter and one half of children report severe and frequent physical abuse, including being beaten, kicked, or tied up by parents (Hahm & Guterman, 2001; Ketsela & Kedebe, 1997; Kim et al., 2000; Youssef, Attia, & Kamel, 1998).

Population-based surveys also reveal that weapon carrying, bullying, and involvement in physical fighting are common among young people in many parts of the world. In a study of health behavior among school-aged children in 27 countries, estimates of the prevalence of youth involved in bullying in the previous school term ranged from 11.9% in Sweden to 64.2% in Austria, with a median of 36.8% (Currie, 1998). In a nationally representative survey of students in grades 9 to 12 in the United States, 33% reported being involved in a physical fight one or more times in the year preceding the survey, and 17% reported carrying a weapon (e.g., gun, knife, or club) one or more days in the previous 30 days (Grunbaum et al., 2004).

Impact of Violence

In quantifying the impact of violence, it is important from the perspective of public health to consider both health and economic consequences. Ill health caused by violence forms a significant portion of the global bur-

den of disease. In addition to physical injury, violence has been linked to many immediate and long-term health outcomes. Intimate partner and sexual violence, for instance, are associated with gastrointestinal disorders, chronic pain syndromes, eating and sleep disorders, unwanted pregnancy, premature labor and birth, sexually transmitted diseases, and HIV/AIDS (Campbell, 2002; Coker et al., 2002; Jewkes et al., 2002). Experiences of abuse in childhood have been linked to cognitive impairment and developmental delays in children, poor school performance, alcohol and drug abuse, and other risk behaviors (Anteghini, Fonseca, Ireland, & Blum, 2001; Lau, Chan, Lam, Choi, & Lai, 2003), as well as several major forms of adult illness (Batten, Aslan, Maciejewski, & Mazure, 2004; Felitti et al., 1998). Victims of violence are also at higher risk of depression, anxiety, post-traumatic stress disorder, and suicidal behavior (Coker et al., 2002; Creamer, Burgess, & McFarlane, 2001; Fergusson, Horwood, & Lynskey, 1996; Jewkes et al., 2002).

The health and social consequences of violence exact an economic toll on nations as well, although the precise burden is unknown, particularly in developing countries in which economic losses and impact tend to be undervalued. For example, productivity losses associated with a single homicide are estimated to cost, on average, $15,319 in South Africa, $602,000 in Australia, $829,000 in New Zealand, and more than $2 million in the United States (Waters et al., 2004). The annual direct costs associated with medical care for victims of intimate partner violence (in 2001 U.S. dollars) are $454,000 in Jamaica and $1.1 billion in Canada (Waters et al., 2004). In general, there are widely varying estimates of the costs of violence because of differences in definitions, the types of costs included, and the methodologies used.

Despite variability in the figures themselves, findings related to the use of health services show that, on average, victims of abuse experience more operative surgeries, visits to doctors, and hospital stays throughout their lives than those without a history of abuse (Campbell, 2002; Heise & Garcia-Moreno, 2002). In the United States, these types of services – for intimate partner violence alone – result in an annual estimated cost of $4.1 billion (National Center for Injury Prevention and Control, 2003). Victims of violence are also more likely to experience spells of unemployment, absenteeism, and to suffer physical and mental health problems that affect job performance (Lloyd & Taluc, 1999). Findings from various cost studies also show that most countries expend a significant amount of resources as a result of violence on treatment, emergency response services, and law enforcement and judicial services; they also experience strains on economic development from damage to public property and infrastructure, disruptions in services, and disincentives to investment and tourism (Buvinic & Morrison, 1999; Waters et al., 2004).

Understanding How and Why Violence Occurs

Assessing and monitoring the magnitude and impact of violence constitute only the first step in addressing violence as a public health problem. Investigating why violence occurs, which factors increase or decrease

risk, and what can be done to prevent violence are the other important steps. Public health draws on various conceptual frameworks and models to describe violent events, identify risk and protective factors associated with violence, and suggest appropriate points of intervention. By virtue of its interdisciplinary nature, it also draws on many theories of behavior, social processes, and social organization to understand and prevent violence.

A classic model used in public health that has been adapted and applied to violence is the epidemiologic triangle (Powell et al., 1999). This model highlights the components of violent events, namely the *victim, perpetrator, weapon or method used, and environment* (see Figure 23.3). The model explores the characteristics of victims and perpetrators involved in violent events (e.g., in terms of their demographic and other characteristics); the important characteristics of weapons or methods used (e.g., type, owner, how the weapon came to be involved in the violent event); and the vast array of environmental factors, including those pertaining to the social environment, the immediate physical environment, and the historical environment. The factors can be considered individually or in combination. Preventive actions may address any of

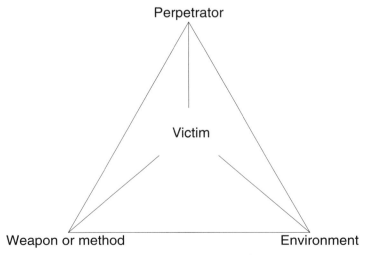

Figure 23.3. The epidemiologic triangle as applied to violent events.

the components. Because the model is conceptual rather than predictive, it presupposes no set relationships among the components (Powell et al., 1999). Although the model is useful in providing a description of violent events, it does not provide guidance about how the various factors interact to cause violence.

As other chapters in this volume illustrate, violence is the result of a complex interplay of biological, social, cultural, and environmental factors. Another model that has been applied to many public health issues and that may be useful to violence, given this interplay of factors, is the sufficient/component cause model (Powell et al., 1999). This particular model indicates that an event occurs when sufficient sets of component causes are present. Such factors as exposure to violence, poor parenting skills, concentrated disadvantage, and social norms are examples of component causes. A fundamental principle of the model is that no event has just one cause, but rather, events occur in response to a collection of component causes.

The model is sometimes referred to as the "causal pie" model because it is commonly described using slices of a pie to depict the component causes and whole pies to depict the sufficient causes (Powell et al., 1999). A violent event is said to occur when all slices (component causes) of a whole pie (sufficient causes) are present. Unfortunately, for complex events such as violence, complete knowledge of a sufficient cause is rare. Implicit in the model is also the possibility that a factor may be present in many violent events but a component cause in only some of them because component causes vary among individuals, communities, and nations (Powell et al., 1999). Therefore, the variability and dynamic nature of component causes also make it more difficult to determine sufficient causes. The strength of the model is that it helps conceptualize the complicated components and combinations of the causes of violence and provides guidance for its prevention. For example, it is not necessary to know all the components of a sufficient cause to take preventive action. It is only necessary to know one or some of the component causes that can be changed (Powell et al., 1999).

One model that is being increasingly used by public health researchers to illustrate the multifaceted and interactive nature between the individual and contextual factors of violence is the ecological model (see Figure 23.4). The model, itself, is not new and also has its limitations. First introduced in the late 1970s (Bronfenbrenner, 1979; Garbarino & Crouter, 1978,) the model was initially applied to child abuse and subsequently to youth violence (Tolan & Guerra, 1994). More recently, researchers have used it to understand intimate partner violence (Heise, 1998) and elder abuse (Schiamberg & Gans, 1999). The model is useful to the extent that it provides a

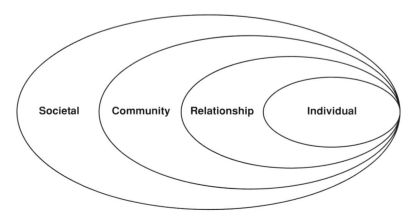

Figure 23.4. Ecological model for understanding and preventing violence.

conceptual framework for exploring and identifying some of the component and sufficient causes of violence. In this sense, it helps distinguish the myriad influences on violence while at the same time providing a framework for understanding how they might interact. It also helps convey the importance of a multilevel response for prevention.

The first level of the model seeks to identify the biological and personal history factors that influence how *individuals* behave and increase their likelihood of becoming a victim or perpetrator of violence. It includes biological and demographic factors, as well as such factors as impulsivity, low educational attainment, substance abuse, and a prior history of aggression and abuse.

The second level explores how proximal social *relationships* – for example, relations with peers, intimate partners, and family members – increase the risk for violent victimization and perpetration of violence. In the cases of partner violence and child maltreatment, for instance, interacting on an almost daily basis or sharing a common domicile with an abuser may increase the opportunity for violent encounters. Because individuals are bound together in a continuing relationship, it is likely in these cases that the offender will repeatedly abuse the victim.

The third level examines the *community* contexts in which social relationships are embedded – such as schools, workplaces, and neighborhoods – and seeks to identify the characteristics of these settings that are associated with violence. Drug trafficking, high levels of residential mobility, heterogeneity (with little of the social "glue" that binds communities together), and population density are examples of such characteristics. Areas of poverty or physical deterioration, where there are few institutional supports and widespread social isolation (for example, people not knowing their neighbors or having no involvement in the local community), are examples of other characteristics.

The fourth level of the ecological model looks at the broad *societal* factors that help create a climate in which violence is encouraged or inhibited, including the availability of weapons and social and cultural norms. Larger societal factors also include the health, education, economic, and social policies that maintain high levels of economic, gender, or social inequality between groups in society.

In addition to helping conceptualize the complex interactions between individual and contextual factors, the ecological model also suggests that in order to prevent violence it is necessary to address factors at all levels. This multilevel approach includes modifying individual behavior directly; modifying individual behavior by influencing close, interpersonal relationships and family environments; addressing the settings through which people move – for example, schools, workplaces, or neighborhoods; and making more societal, system-wide changes to improve, for example, educational or economic opportunities or change social and cultural norms.

Preventing Violence

One of the most important functions of public health is putting knowledge into practice – that is, using information about populations requiring preventive interventions and the factors that make violence more likely to design, implement, and evaluate interventions and to disseminate those with evidence of effectiveness more broadly. Putting knowledge into practice is one of the most challenging endeavors in public health. Prevention research is an iterative and continuous process. It involves continuous specifying and clarifying of risk and protective factors and finding ways to translate them into programs, extensive testing and refining of programs in different settings, and establishing how best to facilitate their diffusion.

Building the evidence base for violence prevention is important on several levels. First, it provides key insights into the types of programs that are likely to yield important reductions in violence. This type of information is particularly needed by others

Table 23.2: Examples of violence prevention approaches by ecological context[1]

Ecological Context	Intervention
Individual	Preventing unintended pregnancies
	Prenatal/postnatal care
	Preschool enrichment programs
	Academic enrichment programs
	Social development/life-skills training programs
	Counseling/therapeutic approaches
	Training for police, health care providers, employers
	Treatment programs
Relationship	Home visitation
	Parenting programs
	Family therapy
	Intensive family preservation services
	Mentoring
	Peer mediation
	Peer group norms
	Gang prevention programs
Community	Improving school settings
	Screening (IPV, SV, CM, EA)[2]
	Improving workplace, residential, primary care settings
	Public information campaigns
	Community coalitions
	Community policing
	Housing density/residential mobility programs
	Reducing availability of alcohol
	Increasing collective efficacy
Societal	Reducing access to means
	Legal remedies and judicial reforms
	Reforming educational systems
	National policies, programs, norms

[1] The approaches included in the table do not represent an exhaustive list, nor do they necessarily represent approaches that have proved effective.
[2] Intimate partner violence (IPV), sexual violence (SV), child maltreatment (CM), elderly abuse (EA).

trying to determine which strategies to adopt. Second, it forms an extremely useful part of advocacy, as it assures decision makers that something can be done. Even more importantly, it provides them with valuable guidance as to where investments should be made. In general, the science of violence prevention has made significant progress over the last two decades. Even so, much more progress needs to be made, particularly in building the evidence base across all levels of the ecological model and for all types of violence.

Approaches to Prevent Violence

A variety of approaches have been used to address the different types of violence. Table 23.2 includes examples of these approaches by ecological context. For instance, individual-level approaches are designed to change an individual's attitudes, beliefs, and behaviors directly and can be delivered in any setting. Some of the more common approaches at this level include preschool enrichment programs, social development programs, life-skills training, and programs designed to prevent unintended pregnancies and to encourage women to seek adequate prenatal and postnatal care. The latter types of approach, for instance, are believed to be key in ensuring better birth outcomes and reducing the risk for child maltreatment and the early developmental risk factors for youth violence (Williams, Guerra, & Elliott, 1997). There are also approaches aimed primarily at victims and perpetrators of violence and those at risk of harming themselves. Examples include counseling/therapeutic approaches; training of police, health care providers, and employers to make them better able to identify and respond to the different types of violence; and treatment programs for batterers, sex offenders, and those suffering from depression and psychiatric disorders.

Relationship-level interventions focus on changing behavior by influencing proximal interpersonal relationships and environments, such as the family environment. Family-based approaches provide education and training to parents with the goal of improving emotional bonds between parents and children and teaching participants how to effectively discipline, monitor, and supervise children. Some of these programs also try to improve the family environment by focusing on family relationships, communication, and problem solving. Others emphasize social support systems and try to provide families with skills to gain access to social support and resources to address external demands.

Other relationship approaches focus on mentoring and peers. Mentoring programs match a young person with a volunteer (a caring adult, a student, family member, or someone outside the family) who acts as a supportive role model. The objectives of such programs are to help young people develop skills and to provide a sustained relationship with someone who can provide guidance and support. The goal of many peer programs is to change negative peer influences into positive or prosocial peer influences (i.e., create a positive peer culture). Programs that attempt to redirect peer group activities or prevent associations with antisocial peers have also been tried, albeit with little success. Some have led to iatrogenic effects (i.e., unintended consequences or increases in violent behavior). One of the failed ingredients in these types of approach is the mixing of high-risk youth together, which has had the unintended consequence of increasing cohesiveness and facilitating delinquency (Dishion, McCord, & Poulin, 1999; Poulin, Dishion, & Barraston, 2001). Other peer interventions, such as peer mediation, use peers or age mates to resolve disputes.

Community-level interventions focus on modifying the characteristics of settings that promote violent behavior or create the conditions for violence to occur. Interventions at this level also focus on changes within institutional environments. There have been, for example, a number of efforts aimed at improving school settings with policies and programs that are designed to promote a prosocial environment in classrooms and throughout the school. Efforts to improve workplace, residential, and primary care environments have primarily focused on implementing appropriate policies, guidelines, and protocols for identifying and managing abuse.

Public information or prevention campaigns have been widely used to change community attitudes, beliefs, and norms surrounding violence. Multi-component prevention campaigns have been launched to address gang violence, bullying, child maltreatment, and domestic and sexual violence in many countries. Other types of community-level interventions include those that focus on community organizing, coordination of services, proactive policing, and increased cohesion among community residents, as well as those that address the density of housing and the availability of alcohol.

Societal interventions focus on the cultural, social, and economic factors related to violence, addressing such issues as access to means and gender, economic, or educational inequality. They emphasize changes in legislation, policies, and the larger social and cultural environment to reduce rates of violence. Measures for reducing access to means include restricting access to guns (e.g., bans on certain types of firearms, waiting periods, gun buy-backs, rules on licensing and registration, stricter policing of illegal possession and trafficking of guns, and rules for storing them safely). With suicide, it also includes fencing in high bridges, limiting access to roofs and high exteriors of tall buildings, automatic shut-off devices for motor vehicles, restricting access to pesticides and fertilizers, and measures to make prescription drugs safer (e.g., packaging and monitoring size and use).

Other societal-level interventions include measures to criminalize abuse by intimate partners, to broaden the definition of rape, to criminalize the harsh physical punishment of children in various settings, and to institute mandatory reporting laws for child and elderly abuse. There are also a number of other possible societal measures – for example, reforming educational systems, making policy changes to reduce poverty and inequality and improve support for families, as well as efforts to change social and cultural norms around issues of gender, racial, and ethnic discrimination and harmful traditional practices.

Determining Effective Responses

Comprehensive reviews on the effectiveness of violence prevention programs are available elsewhere (Howell & Hawkins, 1998; Krug et al., 2002; Lipsey & Wilson, 1998). However, it is worth noting that some of the strategies that offer the strongest evidence of effectiveness are family-based and interventions in early childhood (Bilukha et al., 2005; Henggeler, Clingempeel, Brondino, & Pickrel, 2002; Henggeler & Sheidow, 2003; Olds et al., 1997, 1998; Schweinhart, Barnes, & Weikart, 1993). The most successful programs address the internal dynamics of the family (e.g., cohesion, interaction style), the

family's capacity for dealing with external demands, parenting skills, and family management practices. The earlier these programs are delivered in the child's life, the greater the benefits, although significant benefits have also been demonstrated when delivered to high-risk populations (e.g., youths with substance abuse problems or who have already been arrested for violent or delinquent behavior; Henggeler & Sheidow, 2003; Lipsey & Wilson, 1998). In the case of home visitation, it is important to note that such factors as the timing of services, the nature and emphasis of the approach (e.g., service delivery vs. parent training and child development), the population served, and the person involved in the delivery of the program (e.g., nurse, case manager) seem to make a difference in producing and sustaining positive effects (Thornton, Craft, Dahlberg, Lynch, & Baer, 2000).

The evidence base for social development, therapeutic, and setting approaches is also growing. Studies have demonstrated positive effects, for example, with cognitive-behavioral and multisystemic therapy to prevent suicidal behavior (e.g., Huey et al., 2004; Linehan, Heard, & Armstrong, 1993); social development programs, especially those that are skill based and designed to build social, emotional, and behavioral competencies to reduce youth violence and dating violence (e.g., Farrell, Meyer, & White, 2001; Foshee et al., 2004; Hawkins et al., 1992; Wolfe et al., 2003); and environmental change programs in school settings that include elements of cooperative learning, social-competency training, parent involvement, and classroom management (e.g., Cook, Murphy, & Hunt, 2000; Flannery et al., 2003; Olweus, 1994).

At the community level, residential mobility programs – which are designed to decrease the concentration of poverty by providing housing vouchers or rent subsidies to low-income families – have demonstrated positive effects on school outcomes, problem behaviors, and mental and physical health and appear promising in preventing neighborhood crime, victimization, and social disorder (Anderson et al., 2002; Leventhal & Brooks-Gunn, 2003, 2004; Ludwig, Duncan, & Hirschfield, 2001). Public information campaigns, on the other hand, while showing changes in knowledge and attitudes have generally not led to measurable reductions in violent behavior.

With respect to societal-level measures, there is some evidence that restricting access to means is effective in reducing suicide and interpersonal violence (Bowles, 1995; Carrington & Moyer, 1994; Loftin, McDowall, Wiersema, & Cottey, 1991; Villaveces et al., 2000). However, a recent systematic review of all measures pertaining to firearms found insufficient evidence to conclude whether or not such measures are effective – citing inconsistencies in the findings and serious methodological flaws in the studies themselves (Hahn et al., 2005). Many of the other policy, legislative and judicial remedies across all types of violence have either not been evaluated or have demonstrated weak, negative, or no effects (Du Mont & Myhr, 2000; Feld, 1998; Garner, Fagan, & Maxwell, 1995; Heise & Garcia-Moreno, 2002).

In general, it is possible to identify some promising approaches, some effective approaches, and many more approaches that still require rigorous testing. The latter is especially true in the areas of intimate partner violence, sexual violence, elderly abuse, and child maltreatment. There is also a great need to rigorously evaluate violence prevention programs in developing countries. To date, much of the evidence base for violence prevention programs has come from developed countries. Whether such programs produce similar results in developing countries is a question that should be explored.

Moving Forward in a Global Context

Violence is an important global public health problem and one in which public health has a strong role to play in helping governments increase their knowledge of the problem and their confidence in workable solutions. Increasing their knowledge about the problem requires, first and foremost, good data.

Too many countries do not have systems in place to capture even the most basic data on violence. This failing should be remedied with data systems that are simple and cost effective to implement and that conform to both national and international standards. Efforts should also be made to facilitate the sharing of data among relevant authorities, such as those responsible for health, criminal justice, and social policy.

Confronting long-established attitudes and practices, particularly that nothing can be done about violence, with evidence is also vital so that decision makers can see that there are options other than attending to just policing and public security. In both developing and industrialized countries, this requires building the evidence base across all levels of the ecological model and for all types of violence. To date, there have been far more efforts aimed at changing individual and relationship factors than at changing some of the root causes of violence at the community or societal level. Priority has also been given to dealing with the immediate consequences of violence, providing support to victims and punishing offenders. Such responses, although important and in need of strengthening, should be accompanied by a greater investment in primary prevention – that is, measures to prevent violence from occurring in the first place. Primary prevention efforts, particularly those aimed at the root causes of violence, have the potential to prevent all forms of violence. Operating "upstream" of problems may also be more cost effective and beneficial over the longer term.

Finally, public health has an important role to play in facilitating partnerships of all kinds and at all levels – locally, nationally, and internationally. This effort involves promoting a greater exchange between researchers and practitioners working on different types of violence, who typically work in isolation of one another; among different sectors where much could be gained by sharing information and resources; and among different countries where important innovations and lessons learned could be shared and partnerships cultivated to achieve measurable reductions in violence. Violence is not inevitable. There is much that can be done to address and prevent it.

References

Anderson, L. M., Shinn, C., St. Charles, J., Fullilove, M. T., Scrimshaw, S. C., Fielding, J. E., et al. (2002). Community interventions to promote healthy social environments: Early childhood development and family housing. *MMWR Recommendations and Reports, 51*(RR-01), 1–8.

Anteghini, M., Fonseca, H., Ireland, M., & Blum, R. W. (2001). Health risk behaviors and associated risk and protective factors among Brazilian adolescents in Santos, Brazil. *Journal of Adolescent Health, 28,* 295–302.

Batten, S. V., Aslan, M., Maciejewski, P. K., & Mazure, C. M. (2004). Childhood maltreatment as a risk factor for adult cardiovascular disease and depression. *Journal of Clinical Psychiatry, 65,* 249–254.

Bilukha, O., Hahn, R. A., Crosby, A., Fullilove, M. T., Liberman, A., Moscicki, E., et al., & Task Force on Community Preventive Services (2005). The effectiveness of early childhood home visitation in preventing violence: A systematic review. *American Journal of Preventive Medicine, 28* (2 Suppl 1), 11–39.

Bowles, J. R. (1995). Suicide in Western Samoa: An example of a suicide prevention program in a developing country. In R. F. W. Diekstra, R. W. Gulbinat, D. DeLeo, & I. Kienhorst (Eds.), *Preventive strategies on suicide* (pp. 173–206). Leiden: Brill Publishers.

Bronfenbrenner, V. (1979). *The ecology of human development: Experiments by nature and design.* Cambridge, MA: Harvard University Press.

Buvinic, M., & Morrison, A. (1999). *Violence as an obstacle to development.* Technical Note 4: *Economic and social consequences of violence* (pp. 1–8). Washington, DC: Inter-American Development Bank.

Campbell, J. C. (2002). Health consequences of intimate partner violence. *Lancet, 359,* 1331–1336.

Carrington, P. J., & Moyer, M. A. (1994). Gun control and suicide in Ontario. *American Journal of Psychiatry, 151,* 606–608.

Centers for Disease Control and Prevention (2005). *Web-based Injury Statistics Query and Reporting System – WISQARS.* Retrieved June 25, 2005, from http://www.cdc.gov/ncipc/wisqars/default.htm.

Coker, A. L., Davis, K. E., Arias, I., Desai, S., Sanderson, M., Brandt, H. M., et al. (2002). Physical and mental effects of intimate partner violence for men and women. *American Journal of Preventive Medicine, 23,* 260–268.

Cook, T. D., Murphy, R. F., & Hunt, H. D. (2000). Comer's School Development Program in Chicago: A theory-based evaluation. *American Educational Research Journal, 37,* 535–597.

Creamer, M., Burgess, P., & McFarlane, A. C. (2001). Post-traumatic stress disorder: Findings from the Australian National Survey of Mental Health and Well-being. *Psychological Medicine, 31,* 1237–1247.

Currie, C. (Ed). (1998). *Health behaviour in school-aged children: A WHO cross-national study.* Bergen, Norway: University of Bergen.

Dahlberg, L. L., & Krug, E. G. (2002). Violence – a global public health problem. In E. G. Krug, L. L. Dahlberg, J. A. Mercy, A. B. Zwi, & R. Lozano (Eds.), *World report on violence and health* (pp. 1–21). Geneva, Switzerland: World Health Organization.

Dishion, T. J., McCord, J., & Poulin, F. (1999). When interventions harm: Peer groups and problem behavior. *American Psychologist, 54,* 755–764.

Dodge, K. A., & Coie, J. D. (1987). Social information processing factors in reactive and proactive aggression in children's peer groups. *Journal of Personality and Social Psychology, 53,* 1146–1158.

Du Mont, J., & Myhr, T. L. (2000). So few convictions: The role of client-related characteristics in the legal processing of sexual assaults. *Violence Against Women, 6,* 1109–1136.

Farrell, A. D., Meyer, A. L., & White, K. S. (2001). Evaluation of Responding in Peaceful and Positive Ways (RIPP): A school-based prevention program for reducing violence among urban adolescents. *Journal of Clinical and Child Psychology, 30,* 451–463.

Feld, B. C. (1998). Juvenile and criminal justice systems' responses to youth violence. In M. Tonry & M. H. Moore (Eds.), *Youth violence, crime and justice: A review of research* (Vol. 24, pp. 189–261). Chicago: University of Chicago Press.

Felitti, V. J., Anda, R. F., Nordenberg, D., Williamson, D. F., Spitz, A. M., Edwards, V., et al. (1998). Relationship of childhood abuse and household dysfunction to many of the leading causes of death in adults. The Adverse Childhood Experiences (ACE) Study. *American Journal of Preventive Medicine, 14*, 245–258.

Fergusson, D. M., Horwood, L. J., & Lynskey, M. T. (1996). Childhood sexual abuse and psychiatric disorder in young adulthood: II. Psychiatric outcomes of childhood sexual abuse. *Journal of the American Academy of Child and Adolescent Psychiatry, 35*, 1365–1374.

Finkelhor, D. (1994a). The international epidemiology of child sexual abuse. *Child Abuse and Neglect, 18*, 409–417.

Finkelhor, D. (1994b). Current information on the scope and nature of child sexual abuse. *The Future of Children, 4*, 31–53.

Flannery, D. J., Vazsonyi, A. T., Liau, A. K., Guo, S., Powell, K. E., Atha, H., et al. (2003). Initial behavior outcomes for the PeaceBuilders universal school-based violence prevention program. *Developmental Psychology, 39*, 292–308.

Foege, W. H., Rosenberg, M. L., & Mercy, J. A. (1995). Public health and violence prevention. *Current Issues in Public Health, 1*, 2–9.

Foshee, V. A., Bauman, K. E., Ennett, S. T., Linder, G. F., Benefield, T., & Suchindran, C. (2004). Assessing the long-term effects of the Safe Dates program and a booster in preventing and reducing adolescent dating violence victimization and perpetration. *American Journal of Public Health, 94*, 619–624.

Garbarino, J., & Crouter, A. (1978). Defining the community context for parent-child relations: The correlates of child maltreatment. *Child Development, 49*, 604–616.

Garner, J., Fagan, J., & Maxwell, C. (1995). Published findings from the spouse assault replication program: A critical review. *Journal of Quantitative Criminology, 11*, 3–28.

Grunbaum, J., Kann, L., Kinchen, S., Ross, J. G., Hawkins, J., Lowry, R., Harris et al. (2004). Youth risk behavior surveillance – United States, 2003. *Morbidity and Mortality Weekly Report, 53*(SS-2), 1–100.

Hahm, H., & Guterman, N. (2001). The emerging problem of physical child abuse in South Korea. *Child Maltreatment, 6*, 169–179.

Hahn, R. A., Bilukha, O., Crosby, A., Fullilove, M. T., Liberman, A., Moscicki, E., et al., & Task Force on Community Preventive Services (2005). Firearms laws and the reduction of violence: A systematic review. *American Journal of Preventive Medicine, 28*(2 Suppl 1), 1–92.

Hawkins, J. D., Catalano, R. F., Morrison, D., O'Donnell, J., Abbott, R., & Day, E. (1992). The Seattle Social Development Project: Effects of the first four years on protective factors and problem behaviors. In J. McCord & R. E. Tremblay (Eds.), *Preventing antisocial behavior: Interventions from birth through adolescence* (pp. 139–161). New York: Guilford Press.

Heise, L. (1998). Violence against women: An integrated, ecological framework. *Violence Against Women, 4*, 262–290.

Heise, L., & Garcia-Moreno, C. (2002). Violence by intimate partners. In E. G. Krug, L. L. Dahlberg, J. A. Mercy, A. B. Zwi, & R. Lozano (Eds.), *World report on violence and health* (pp. 87–121). Geneva, Switzerland: World Health Organization.

Henggeler, S. W., Clingempeel, W. G., Brondino, M. J., & Pickrel, S. G. (2002). Four-year follow-up of multisystemic therapy with substance-abusing and substance-dependent juvenile offenders. *Journal of the American Academy of Child and Adolescent Psychiatry, 41*, 868–874.

Henggeler, S. W., & Sheidow, A. J. (2003). Conduct disorder and delinquency. *Journal of Marital and Family Therapy, 29*, 505–522.

Howell, J. C., & Hawkins, J. D. (1998). Prevention of youth violence. In M. H. Moore & M. Tonry (Eds.), *Youth violence. Crime and justice: A review of research* (Vol. 24, pp. 263–315). Chicago: University of Chicago Press.

Huey, S. J, Jr., Henggeler, S. W., Rowland, M. D., Halliday-Boykins, C. A., Cunningham, P. B., Pickrel, S. G., et al. (2004). Multisystemic therapy effects on attempted suicide by youths presenting psychiatric emergencies. *Journal of the American Academy for Child and Adolescent Psychiatry, 43*, 183–190.

Jewkes, R., Sen, P., & Garcia-Moreno, C. (2002). Sexual violence. In E. G. Krug, L. L. Dahlberg, J. A. Mercy, A. B. Zwi, & R. Lozano (Eds.), *World report on violence and health* (pp. 147–181). Geneva, Switzerland: World Health Organization.

Ketsela, T., & Kedebe, D. (1997). Physical punishment of elementary school children in urban and rural communities in Ethiopia. *Ethiopian Medical Journal, 35*, 23–33.

Kim, D. H., Kim, P. I., Park, Y. C., Zhang, L. D., Lu, M. K., & Li, D. (2000). Children's experience of violence in China and Korea: A transcultural study. *Child Abuse and Neglect, 24*, 1163–1173.

Krug, E. G., Dahlberg, L. L., Mercy, J. A., Zwi, A. B., & Lozano R. (Eds.). (2002). *World report on violence and health*. Geneva, Switzerland: World Health Organization.

Lau, J. T., Chan, K. K., Lam, P. K., Choi, P. Y., & Lai, K. Y. (2003). Psychological correlates of physical abuse in Hong Kong Chinese adolescents. *Child Abuse and Neglect, 27*, 63–75.

Leventhal, T., & Brooks-Gunn, J. (2003). Moving to opportunity: An experimental study of neighborhood effects on mental health. *American Journal of Public Health, 93*, 1576–1582.

Leventhal, T., & Brooks-Gunn, J. (2004). A randomized study of neighborhood effects on low-income children's educational outcomes. *Developmental Psychology, 40*, 488–507.

Linehan, M. M., Heard, H. L., & Armstrong, H. E. (1993). Naturalistic follow-up of a behavioral treatment for chronically parasuicidal borderline patients. *Archives of General Psychiatry, 50*, 971–974.

Lipsey, M. W., & Wilson, D. B. (1998). Effective interventions for serious juvenile offenders: A synthesis of research. In R. Loeber & D. P. Farrington (Eds.), *Serious and violent juvenile offenders: Risk factors and successful interventions* (pp. 313–345). Thousand Oaks, CA: Sage.

Lloyd, S., & Taluc, N. (1999). The effects of male violence on female employment. *Violence Against Women, 5*, 370–392.

Loftin, C., McDowall, D., Wiersema, B., & Cottey, T. J. (1991). Effects of restrictive licensing of handguns on homicide and suicide in the District of Columbia. *New England Journal of Medicine, 325*, 1615–1620.

Ludwig, J., Duncan, G. J., & Hirschfield P., (2001). Urban poverty and juvenile crime: Evidence from a randomized housing-mobility experiment. *Quarterly Journal of Economics, 16*, 655–680.

Mercy, J. A., Butchart, A., Farrington, D., & Cerdá, M. (2002). Youth violence. In E. G. Krug, L. L. Dahlberg, J. A. Mercy, A. B. Zwi, & R. Lozano (Eds.), *World report on violence and health* (pp. 22–56). Geneva, Switzerland: World Health Organization.

Mercy, J. A., Rosenberg, M. L., Powell, K. E., Broome, C. V., & Roper, W. L. (1993). Public health policy for preventing violence. *Health Affairs, 12*, 7–29.

National Center for Injury Prevention and Control (2003). *Costs of intimate partner violence against women in the United States*. Atlanta: Centers for Disease Control and Prevention.

Olds, D. L., Eckenrode, J., Henderson, C. R., Jr., Kitzman, H., Powers, J., Cole, R., et al. (1997). Long-term effects of home visitation on maternal life course and child abuse and neglect: 15-year follow-up of a randomized trial. *Journal of the American Medical Association, 278*, 637–643.

Olds, D. L., Henderson, C. R. Jr., Cole, R., Eckenrode, J., Kitzman, H., Luckey, D., et al. (1998). Long-term effects of nurse home visitation on children's criminal and antisocial behavior: 15-year follow-up of a randomized controlled trial. *Journal of the American Medical Association, 280*, 1238–1244.

Olweus, D. (1994). Bullying at school: Basic facts and effects of a school-based intervention program. *Journal of Child Psychology and Psychiatry and Allied Disciplines, 35*, 1171–1190.

Poulin, F., Dishion, T. J., & Burraston, B. (2001). 3-year iatrogenic effects associated with aggregating high-risk adolescents in cognitive-behavioral preventive interventions. *Applied Development Science, 5*, 214–224.

Powell, K. E., Mercy, J. A., Crosby, A. E., Dahlberg, L. L., & Simon, T. R. (1999). Public health models of violence and violence prevention. In L. R. Kurtz (Ed.), *Encyclopedia of violence, peace, and conflict* (pp. 175–187). San Diego: Academic Press.

Schiamberg, L. B., & Gans, D. (1999). An ecological framework for contextual risk factors in elder abuse by adult children. *Journal of Elder Abuse and Neglect, 11*, 79–103.

Schweinhart, L. J., Barnes, H. V., & Weikart, D. P. (1993). *Significant benefits: the High/Scope Perry preschool project study through age 27*. Ypsilanti, MI: High/Scope Press.

Thornton, T. N., Craft, C. A., Dahlberg, L. L., Lynch, B. S., & Baer, K. (2000). *Best practices of youth violence prevention: A sourcebook for community action*. Atlanta: Centers for Disease Control and Prevention, National Center for Injury Prevention and Control.

Tolan, P. H., & Guerra, N. G. (1994). *What works in reducing adolescent violence: An empirical review of the field* (pp. 1–94). Boulder, CO: Center for the Study and Prevention of Violence, Institute for Behavioral Sciences, University of Colorado.

U.S. Department of Health, Education, and Welfare (1979). *Healthy people: The Surgeon General's report on health promotion and disease prevention* (Publication 79–55071). Washington, DC: Public Health Service, Office of the Assistant Secretary for Health and Surgeon General.

Villaveces, A., Cummings, P., Espitia, V. E., Koepsell, T. D., McKnight, B., & Kellermann, A. L. (2000). Effect of a ban on carrying firearms on homicide rates in two Colombian cities. *Journal of the American Medical Association, 283,* 1205–1209.

Walters, R. H., & Parke, R. D. (1964). Social motivation, dependency, and susceptibility to social influence. In L. Berkowitz (Ed.), *Advances in experimental social psychology* (Vol. 1, pp. 231–276). New York: Academic Press.

Waters, H., Hyder, A., Rajkotia, Y., Basu, S., Rehwinkel, J. A., & Butchart, A. (2004). *The economic dimensions of interpersonal violence.* Geneva, Switzerland: World Health Organization.

Williams, K. R., Guerra, N. G., & Elliott, D. S. (1997). *Human development and violence prevention: A focus on youth.* Boulder, CO: The Center for the Study and Prevention of Violence, Institute for Behavioral Science.

Wolfe, D. A., Wekerle, C., Scott, K., Straatman, A. L., Grasley, C., & Reitzel-Jaffe, D. (2003). Dating violence prevention with at-risk youth: A controlled outcome evaluation. *Journal of Consulting and Clinical Psychology, 71,* 279–291.

World Health Organization (1996). *Violence: A public health priority.* WHO Global Consultation on Violence and Health (Document WHO/EHA/SPI.POA.2). Geneva, Switzerland: World Health Organization.

Youssef, R. M., Attia, M. S., & Kamel, M. I. (1998). Children experiencing violence: Parental use of corporal punishment. *Child Abuse and Neglect, 22,* 959–973.

CHAPTER 24

Cross-National Research on Violent Victimization

Johan van Wilsem

Introduction

Cross-national studies of crime are an interesting line of research for several reasons. First, they offer an opportunity to assess the extent to which social, economic, and cultural differences among countries affect national crime rates. Second, and more specifically, the impact of varying socioeconomic and punitive policies across countries may be evaluated by comparing differences in crime outcomes. However, although cross-national crime data are attractive as a means to test hypotheses on a level that is highly relevant in terms of policy and theory, they also have a general reputation of poor comparability and limited availability (Neapolitan, 1997; van Wilsem, 2004). Furthermore, the absence of a wide number of comparable predictors across a large number of countries has restricted the ability to identify causes of crime at the level of countries.

As is evident in this chapter, this data problem has resulted in a research field that has traditionally been constrained by small samples of countries and an empirical focus on homicide, the single type of crime for which international data are considered to be suited for comparative purposes. Nevertheless, recent developments in the area of international data collection on crime victimization offer new possibilities to address neglected research questions, which are also outlined in this chapter. Individual-level data on crime targets, collected via the International Crime Victims Survey, offer the opportunity for micro- and macro-level research on nonhomicide crimes.

Official Crime Data

Traditionally, most cross-national crime research has been based on data from official sources, which provide macrolevel counts of crimes, suspects, or victims. The most widely used sources of comparative crime data are Interpol's *International Crime Statistics*, the United Nations' *UN Crime Survey*, and the World Health Organization's (WHO) *World Health Statistics Annual*. Both Interpol and the UN collect criminal justice data among member nations. The WHO provides national statistics on homicide by reporting on causes of death, for which one of the categories is "any act performed with the purpose of taking human life, in whatever circumstances." These data are collected from public health agencies and are based on death certificates. An additional and relatively new source of international crime data is the *European Sourcebook of Crime and Criminal Justice Statistics*. The second, most recent edition of this source provides police, court, and corrections data for 39 European countries for the years 1995–2000 (Council of Europe, 2003).[1]

Cross-national research on crime has been severely constrained by the flaws in the available data (Neapolitan, 1997). Because of inconsistencies in legal codes and differences in people's propensity to report crimes to the police – both across countries and over time – most cross-national studies on crime have focused on homicide (Gartner, 1990; Krahn, Hartnagel, & Gartrell, 1986; Messner, 1989; Neapolitan, 1998). Because of its fundamental nature, homicide is less sensitive than other offenses to definitional problems and reporting selectivity. National homicide rates are therefore considered to be the most reliable measure for cross-national studies of crime (Neapolitan, 1997). In contrast, definitions of theft (and other nonhomicide crimes) vary across countries, inconsistently excluding certain subcategories of theft (e.g., car theft) or even lacking detail on which subcategories make up the overall theft category. Also, the extent to which non-homicide crimes are reported to the police varies significantly across countries (Van Kesteren, Mayhew, & Nieuwbeerta, 2000). For the purpose of cross-national comparison, official data on nonhomicide crimes therefore seem to suffer from insurmountable quality deficiencies.

The available sources on homicide rates are also subject to quality differences. The WHO data are consistent in their exclusion of homicide attempts, unlike homicide data provided by the United Nations and Interpol. As a result, the volume of homicide can vary considerably according to the data source used, with UN and Interpol data sometimes offering substantially higher homicide rates than WHO data. Therefore, WHO data are generally considered the most valid source of cross-national comparative homicide data (Kalish, 1988; LaFree & Drass, 2002). As compared to Interpol data however, the WHO delivers data for a smaller number of countries. In a recent overview, WHO homicide data were available for 74 countries for the period 1990–2000 (Krug, Dahlberg, Mercy, Zwi, & Lozano, 2002), whereas Interpol have reported crime statistics for a total number of 154 countries (LaFree, 2003).

Cross-National Differences in the Volume and Trends of Homicide Victimization

Across countries, large differences in homicide rates have been documented. For instance, comparing WHO homicide rates for 70 countries in the period 1990–2000, LaFree (2003) found that six countries (Colombia, El Salvador, Brazil, Russian Federation, Albania, and Puerto Rico) had average homicide victimization rates over 20 per 100.000 population, whereas eight countries (Israel, Japan, United Kingdom, France, Spain, Ireland, Norway, and Germany) had rates under 1 per 100.000. In addition, there appears to be a strong relation between socioeconomic development and homicide. Nearly 83% of the 29 industrialized countries in this sample had homicide rates of 2 or less per 100.000.[2] In contrast, over 56% of the Latin American and Caribbean countries and nearly 32% of the Eastern European and Central Asian countries had homicide rates that exceeded 10 per 100.000 (LaFree, 2003).

Many studies have been concerned with cross-sectional differences in national homicide rates, but relatively little research has been conducted on the comparison of homicide trends over time (e.g., Eisner, 2001; Gurr, 1977). As one of the exceptions, LaFree and Drass (2002) conducted a systematic cross-national analysis of change and stability in homicide victimization over the period 1956–1998. Their results using WHO data show clear differences in the development of homicide, with some countries being characterized by stability or slow growth and others by radical changes in upward directions.[3] Of the 34 countries in this study, 12 were confronted with such "crime booms" – rapid accelerations in homicide for several consecutive years that were followed by stability at the higher homicide level. Interestingly, industrializing countries appeared to have higher incidence of crime booms (70%) compared to modern Western countries (21%).[4] These findings on homicide dynamics may be interpreted as supportive of modernization theory (LaFree & Drass, 2002). According to this perspective, the transition of countries from traditional to modern societies results in social and economic changes – industrialization, urbanization, and political reform – that disrupt established normative guidelines. In turn, such developments may weaken social control mechanisms and increase the potential for anomie, which ultimately lead to crime increases (Shelley, 1981).

Structural Correlates of Homicide Rates

In addition to examining the volume of national homicide rates, many researchers have studied their structural correlates. Before turning to a discussion of some of their major results, it is important to mention some of the difficulties facing cross-national comparative research, a field that is, by definition, constrained in its number of units of analysis. Furthermore, contrary to much individual-, neighborhood-, or city-level research, the units of analysis in cross-national research are not selected randomly, but rather on the basis of availability. This factor has had some important consequences for the results of multivariate analyses on international homicide patterns (LaFree, 2003; Neapolitan, 1997).

Because of the scarcity of both crime counts and explanatory variables, cross-national crime research has more commonly included Western, developed countries and has less commonly included developing countries. The overrepresentation of developed countries puts clear restrictions on the generalizability of empirical outcomes, because countries in other parts of the world (which are underrepresented) generally have a different economic and social context. Furthermore, the sample sizes analyzed in cross-national research are small and therefore offer limited statistical power. The results of some studies are dependent on only one or a few outliers. The small sample size also limits the use of statistical techniques, resulting in most cases in relatively straightforward direct effects models (but see Pampel & Gartner, 1995; Pratt & Godsey, 2003; Savolainen, 2000). To conclude, small sample sizes limit the range of variables that can be included in explanatory models to between 4 and 10 in most cross-national crime research, depending on sample size. To overcome this problem, in some studies, more than one observation per country was used by introducing year-specific values of crime and explanatory variables (e.g., Bennett, 1991; Gartner, 1990; Pampel & Gartner, 1995). This multiplies the number of observations by the number of years that are included for each country, therefore increasing statistical power.[5]

Despite these limitations, previous research has yielded a considerable list of predictors of national homicide rates. One of the most robust documented relations is the one between income inequality and homicide rates. Many studies have found that the higher the level of economic inequality, the higher the homicide rate (e.g., Gartner, 1990; Kick & LaFree, 1985; Krahn et al., 1986; Messner, 1982; Neapolitan, 1998). Other indicators of economic stress have also been found to be positively related to national homicide rates, such as economic discrimination (Messner, 1989), low governmental expenditures on social security[6] (Gartner, 1990; Savolainen, 2000), and measures of decommodification, which indicate the extent to which the state offers its citizens protection against economic market dynamics by offering them social rights and entitlements (Messner & Rosenfeld, 1997).

These findings are generally interpreted to be supportive of strain theory (Merton,

1957). According to this line of reasoning, inequality stimulates feelings of relative deprivation among the disadvantaged, while few institutional arrangements for basic income provision increase chances of absolute income deprivation. In turn, these factors may lead to greater probabilities of criminal activity, if delinquent actions are aimed at the reduction of deprivation by illegally obtaining material goods, or at the expression of frustration caused by the inaccessibility of material resources by committing violent crime. Interestingly, according to findings from two studies, social welfare arrangements moderate the effect of other economic stress indicators on crime. Savolainen (2000) found that the positive effect of income inequality on national homicide rates is limited to countries with weak collective institutions for social welfare. In addition, Pratt and Godsey (2003) conclude that income inequality has less serious consequences for homicide rates in countries with high government expenditures on health care. Both findings imply that crime-inducing effects of economic stress conditions may be limited to countries that fall short on providing institutional arrangements for economic or social support.[7]

National homicide rates have also been related to social indicators of disorganization, criminal opportunity, and cultural orientation. However, outcomes for these factors vary depending on the countries and time periods included in the samples used. For instance, divorce rates – indicating the possible effect of a lack of social integration – and homicide rates have been found to be positively associated in research on modern societies (Gartner, 1990; van Wilsem, 2004). However, analyses including countries with lower levels of development failed to show this association (Krahn et al., 1986). Similarly, some studies found higher levels of homicide in highly urbanized countries (Bennett, 1991; van Wilsem, 2004), whereas others did not (Kick & LaFree, 1985; Messner, 1989; Neapolitan, 1998). Routine activity theorists have argued that criminal opportunities increase crime rates, for instance through the exposure to offenders by high numbers of out-of-home populations (Cohen & Felson, 1979). As a proxy measure, the extent of female labor force participation has been used in cross-national homicide research. Gartner (1990) found higher levels of female and child homicide in countries with large proportions of female workers, whereas Bennett (1991) did not find such a relation for general homicide. Furthermore, although more potential offenders are expected among countries with large shares of youth populations (considering the strong relation between age and delinquency on the individual level; see, for example, Hirschi & Gottfredson, 1983; Sampson & Laub, 1993), cross-national research findings are quite consistent on their observed lack of association between the proportion of youths and homicides (Bennett, 1991; Gartner, 1990; Krahn et al., 1986; Messner, 1989; Neapolitan, 1998). However, a more detailed analysis by Pampel and Gartner (1995) supported the hypothesis that having a large proportion of youths only exerts crime-inducing effects if institutions for collective social protection are weak.

Differences among countries' cultural values regarding violence may also play a role in shaping homicide rates. For example, Gartner's (1990) results suggest a positive association between homicide and the involvement of countries in warfare. She also found higher homicide rates in countries that exercised capital punishment. The former finding possibly points to a habituation to violent acts for historical reasons, whereas the latter result may indicate a general tolerance to violence due to the existence of officially approved homicide (Gartner, 1990; Thomson, 1999).

Taking a broad overview of these results, it can be argued that the hypotheses of several criminological theories have been thoroughly tested with respect to their predictions on national homicide rates, albeit with the use of indirect indicators for theoretical concepts. At the same time, however, the empirical focus on homicide – caused by the quality restrictions on available data on other crimes – has narrowed the research field. It has resulted in a situation in which it is difficult to determine with official data if national homicide rates resemble the rates of other crimes. As a consequence, it remains unclear whether the structural correlates of national homicide rates relate to other types of crime. Thus, despite the merits of previous research, the body of knowledge on cross-national crime patterns therefore has considerable gaps.

However, there have been recent developments in the collection of internationally comparable victimization data, which offer the possibility of addressing some of the neglected research issues. The next section first discusses the advantages and limitations of these data and, subsequently, several results of research based on comparative survey data.

International Victim Survey Data on Violent and Property Crime

Several Western countries initiated victimization surveys in the late 1960s and 1970s (e.g., Ennis, 1967), partly because police-registered data were generally acknowledged to suffer from comparative problems. Although this first wave of victim surveys offered an alternative for estimates of national crime rates, they did not solve the problem of cross-national comparability. National surveys in different countries used differing research designs, fieldwork procedures, and interviewing questions, thereby limiting the comparability of victimization estimates across nations (Block, 1993). Furthermore, compared to official data, the number of countries that conducted such victimization surveys was very limited. To overcome these obstacles to cross-national comparison, the Dutch Ministry of Justice, along with the British Home Office, initiated the International Crime Victims Survey (ICVS) in 1989. In the ICVS, respondents are asked standardized questions on recent victimization experiences for various types of theft, violence, and vandalism. Victims are also asked about the circumstances of the offense and whether the police were involved. Questions also include the respondent's background and lifestyle characteristics.

The first ICVS wave in 1989 was conducted in 14 Western countries. Additional survey waves were conducted in 1992, 1996, and 2000 with the involvement of the UN Interregional Crime and Justice Institute (UNICRI). In these new waves, non-Western countries were also included. Currently, 27 countries have conducted ICVS surveys with samples for the general population aged 16 years or older. ICVS city surveys have also been conducted for an additional 45 countries, mainly developing ones. These surveys were restricted to the inhabitants of a large city in these countries. In 2004, a new wave of ICVS surveys has been conducted across a (provisional) total number of 32 countries.

Advantages of ICVS Data

Compared to official crime data, the ICVS data have three main advantages. First, through identical questionnaires the ICVS uses fully standardized victimization definitions. Second, it includes incidents not reported to the police by asking respondents to mention all victimizations they experienced in the past year. Consequently, the ICVS data mitigate the two main sources of measurement error across nations in cross-national police data: varying crime definitions and differences in rates of crimes not reported to the police (dark numbers). Third, as the ICVS data consist of survey answers of respondents, they can be disaggregated to the individual level for many individual characteristics, such as age, gender, educational level, and labor status. As such, they provide opportunities to calculate victimization risks for different social categories. Even more, with the use of multivariate techniques, it is possible to assess the generalizability of independent risk factors across countries. Because the ICVS contains questions on multiple types of victimization experiences, it has become an important data source for estimating country rates of (nonlethal) assault, car vandalism and several types of theft (Mayhew &

Van Dijk, 1997; Van Dijk & Mayhew, 1992; Van Dijk, Mayhew, & Kilias, 1990; Van Kesteren et al., 2000).

Limitations of ICVS Data

Although the use of victimization survey data offers new opportunities for cross-national comparison, the ICVS data also have several limitations, which must be carefully taken into account (Neapolitan, 1997). Six limitations most often mentioned with regard to ICVS data are discussed below, along with arguments on the extent to which each presents comparative problems. Some of these points have a bearing on general victimization, whereas others are especially relevant for the measurement of violent victimization.

First, the number of countries that have participated in the ICVS with nationwide samples is currently still small and selective. ICVS country estimates of property and nonlethal violent victimization are available for 27 countries, which are either highly industrialized or in Eastern Europe. Clearly, future efforts should be made to enlarge the ICVS country sample by including other countries with nationwide surveys, especially developing ones.

Second, data collection procedures are not identical for each country participating in the ICVS. In Western countries, surveys were conducted through telephone interviewing, whereas in developing countries, face-to-face interviews were held because of low levels of telephone ownership. This difference may bias results when survey data collected through varying modes are compared. Nevertheless, the comparability of results from surveys with different interview modes has been acknowledged (Dillman & Tarnai, 1989), especially when the same types of fieldwork are used, as is the case in the ICVS (Van Kesteren et al., 2000).

Third, unequal measurement error may be introduced by the differential response rates across nations, which vary from a minimum of 30% for the West German 1989 survey to a maximum of 86% for the 1992 and 1996 surveys of Finland. Evidence from previous research indicates that those who are victimized are most likely to respond (Block, 1993), which would result in an overestimation of crime rates in countries where response rates are low. On the other hand, low response rates may be associated with an underrepresentation of victims, because victims might be away from home more often than nonvictims. Van Kesteren et al. (2000) could not substantiate these claims with empirical evidence, as they found no relation between ICVS response rates and victimization rates. Similarly, van Wilsem (2003) also found no association between ICVS response rates and rates of violent and property victimization, after adjusting for other explanatory variables. Nevertheless, because of the small size of the current ICVS country sample, care is required in interpreting these results. Therefore, future analyses of larger ICVS country samples should continue to evaluate the effect of response rates on outcomes.

Fourth, ICVS sample sizes are relatively small, mostly between 1,000 and 2,000 respondents per survey. Considering that crime incidents – especially violent victimizations – are rare events, a small amount of sampling error can result in large effects on victimization rates. Several strategies can be undertaken to deal with this problem. The ICVS data can be weighted to ensure that the sample is representative of the population aged 16 or older, in terms of gender, age, household composition, and regional population distribution (Van Kesteren et al., 2000). In addition, in countries in which the ICVS has been conducted more than once, the data can be pooled to increase sample size and obtain more reliable victimization estimates (Lynch, 1993). Furthermore, country-level estimates can be obtained by employing multilevel models on cross-nationally pooled individual-level data (Snijders & Bosker, 1999). With this procedure, estimates of country victimization rates are treated as deviations from a "grand mean," which is the average risk across all countries. These deviations or, in multilevel terms, random intercepts are weighted as a function of the sample size. Thus, larger country samples have a greater influence on these estimates than the smaller samples. Finally, for crime types with similar properties, overarching categories can be constructed. By doing so, the proportion of people who experienced an incident within a category becomes larger, which makes the victimization estimate less sensitive to sampling errors. For example, a joint category for nonlethal violent victimization can be constructed by combining survey responses on assault and robbery.

Fifth, differences in the cultural interpretation of victimization experiences may affect the results. Thus, although survey questions may be identical, people from different cultures may define various types of victimization differently. Critics have argued that survey responses on violent and sexual victimization may especially be vulnerable to this type of inconsistency (Neapolitan, 1997). However, with respect to victimization experiences that are reported in the ICVS, Van Dijk and Van Kesteren (1996) showed that the perceived seriousness of victimization types is similar across cultures. In particular, for violent victimization they found no relation between GDP per capita and perceived seriousness of the incident across 51 countries, which offers some indication of the universality of meaning assigned to violent encounters by victims. Nevertheless, the empirical assessment of cross-national consistency in (violent) crime definitions among survey respondents remains a difficult issue.

In addition to defining victimization experiences differently, a sixth and final point is that particular crimes may be reported differently for *intentional* reasons because of respondents' refusal to answer questions. The ICVS, like many victimization surveys, seems susceptible to this criticism, especially with regard to domestic violence, sexual crimes, and other serious violent crimes. Obtaining accurate survey responses on these incidents is difficult in general (Mirrlees-Black, 1999), and seems especially hard in developing countries (Zvekic & Alvazzi Del Frate, 1995). Because

these crimes tend to be of a personal nature, victims may be reluctant to reveal them to interviewers, especially if cultural rules prohibit speaking about these matters at all. In general, self-completion formats of survey questions (via mail or computer assisted self interview) on serious victimization incidents are preferred as they emphasize anonymity and confidentiality (Mirrlees-Black, 1999). However, the ICVS uses either telephonic or regular face-to-face interviewing methods. It is therefore doubtful if the survey is suitable for appropriately estimating the national volume of domestic and sexual victimization.

Alternative strategies may be undertaken to achieve this goal. The first is to construct an index on serious violent victimization by combining data from various sources, such as a combination of official and survey data. Such a multisource approach has also been undertaken for the International Homicide Index (Haen & Block, 2004). A second means for estimating the incidence of domestic and sexual crime against women is offered by the recently initiated International Violence Against Women Survey (IVAWS). Data collection is currently in progress in 20 developing and modern countries. Of these, Australia and Switzerland were the first countries to finalize their fieldwork and did so in 2003. Mouzos and Makkai (2004) have reported the Australian findings of the IVAWS. Similarly to the ICVS, the Australian sweep of the IVAWS also uses a telephonic survey as the mode of interview, but differs on two main points: the sample population receives a pre-survey letter, and only female interviewers are used.

Tackling New Research Problems with ICVS Data

As the ICVS contains individual-level data on crime targets and victimization, it can address comparative research problems for both individual (micro-level) and country (macro-level) issues of victimization. For instance, it can be used to create estimates of national volumes of victimization that are not hampered by definitional inconsistency or reporting selectivity. On the individual level, one of the research possibilities is the comparison of characteristics of victims and nonvictims, which allows for the assessment of victimization risk factors. Furthermore, though on both levels of analysis separate cross-national research is possible, micro- and macro-level issues of victimization are to some extent intertwined. As such, they need to be integrated in empirical comparative research. To clarify, micro-level risk factors of victimization may have consequences for cross-national differences in crime rates if countries vary significantly in these individual traits. In reverse, macro-level conditions could relate to individual victimization (apart from individual, neighborhood, or other factors), if they independently influence the spatial and temporal convergence of targets and offenders. Therefore, in the next section, separate overviews of the macro- and micro-level results of ICVS analyses are followed by a discussion of empirical results on these micro-macro links.

Macro-Level ICVS Findings

As previously stated in this chapter, cross-national crime research has predominantly focused on homicide variation because of limitations on the quality of data on other crimes. Thus, although empirical tests of criminological theories have been performed at a cross-national level, few studies have examined country-to-country variation in crime rates for multiple types of offenses. Exceptions are studies performed by Bennett (1991), Kick and LaFree (1985), and LaFree and Kick (1986), which compared the determinants of theft and violence using a cross-national perspective. Their findings suggest that theft and violence have different structural correlates. For instance, Bennett (1991) found that theft rates are positively related to GDP per capita, whereas rates of violent crime are not.[8] Nevertheless, because of comparison problems associated with official police statistics on theft, it remains uncertain whether these results do point to different determinants for different

crime types or rather are due to systematic measurement errors.

To address this issue, van Wilsem (2004) related WHO homicide rates to national levels of nonviolent victimization and theft for those countries that participated in ICVS country-wide surveys. He also compared structural correlates for homicide with those for other crimes. The selection of 27 countries contained 20 Western countries, including the United States, Canada, and the United Kingdom; 6 East European countries; and Japan. For this sample, homicide rates tended to be positively related to rates of nonlethal violence and theft, indicating that the rate of the most frequently examined offense type in national profiles of crime is generally not atypical. Thus, countries with high homicide rates tend to have high levels of nonlethal assault and theft as well.

Furthermore, some overlap was found for the predictors of victimization rates across offense types. Having high proportions of large-city inhabitants (populations of more than 100,000) was related to high levels of homicide, theft, and nonlethal victimization.[9] Furthermore, high levels of these three crime types were generally found more often in countries with low levels of GDP per capita, indicating a negative relation between development and crime. Income inequality was positively related to rates of theft and nonlethal violence, but unexpectedly not to homicide for the selected countries.

In addition, because ICVS data offer information on whether the victimization incident was reported to the police, they enable comparisons to be made between national rates of *self-reported* victimization and *police-reported* victimization. In this respect, it is interesting to note that some of the relations between victimization and national context changed once the impact of the differential police-reporting behavior of crime victims was taken into account. For instance, although GDP per capita was negatively related to rates of self-reported victimization, no relation was found for rates of police-reported victimization. Thus, the fact

that victims of crime in developing countries report the incidents they experience
less often to the police leads to the erroneous suggestion that crime and socioeconomic development are not related if data
on police reports are used (van Wilsem,
2004).

Micro-Level ICVS Findings

On the individual level, the ICVS offers
possibilities to explore determinants of victimization across countries, and several
researchers have done so for violent victimization. In an analysis of ICVS 1992 data
for 15 Western and East European countries,
Lee (2000) found that community cohesion is a consistent predictor of low victimization risk for neighborhood assault and
neighborhood robbery. Combining insights
from opportunity and social disorganization
explanations of crime, Lee (2000) argues
that community cohesion offers guardianship to neighborhood inhabitants because
informal social control is realized more
effectively than in communities in which
social ties among inhabitants are absent
(see also Sampson, Raudenbush, & Earls,
1997). Additional analyses of ICVS city
data across 12 developing countries yielded
comparable findings, which lends support
to the assumption that community context is important in explaining victimization across different social contexts. As such,
Lee's (2000) findings underscore the generalizability of the relation between social disorganization and crime, which is a valuable
addition to the research field, as the available
empirical results of other studies have been
derived predominantly from the United
States (e.g., Bellair, 1997; Sampson et al.,
1997).

Focusing on another relation that has
been frequently documented in U.S. and
English research (e.g., Dodd, Nicholas,
Povey, & Walker, 2004; Hindelang, Gottfredson, & Garolalo, 1978; Tseloni, 2000),
Carcach (2002) argues that the inverse relation between age and victimization is found
in many countries, based on analyses of ICVS
data from 1989 to 2000. Although the age-

victimization curve is not totally equal across
countries, the basic pattern is the same. Similarly to life-course changes in delinquency
(Sampson & Laub, 1993), the risk of violent victimization seems to decline for young
males after marriage.

Van Wilsem, De Graaf, and Wittebrood
(2003) analyzed ICVS data for 18 Western and East European countries and distinguished between violent victimization
incidents that occurred inside and outside
the victim's neighborhood. Common determinants for both types of violence were
young age, being single, and living in a
large city. Furthermore, violent victimization within the victim's neighborhood was
more likely for people who do not perform
paid labor nor follow a fulltime education
(e.g. housewives, unemployed) and inhabitants of socially disorganized communities,
whereas violent victimization outside the
neighbourhood occurred more frequently
among paid workers and people with high
night-time activity.[10]

Linking Micro- and Macro-Perspectives of Victimization

For the explanation of cross-national crime
differences, contextual as well as compositional explanations can be used. Contextual explanations center on the idea that
aspects of the national social, economic,
or cultural structure determine the likelihood of crime (or victimization) in themselves. For instance, strain/anomie theorists
argue that inequalities in the distribution of
material resources induce offender motivation among the deprived. Therefore, crime
rates will be higher with increasing inequality (Blau & Blau, 1982; Merton, 1957).
In contrast, compositional explanations of
cross-national crime differences argue that
countries differ systematically with respect
to crime-related characteristics at within-
country levels of analysis, such as regions,
neighborhoods, or individuals. For instance,
some countries may have higher victimization rates than others, because at the
individual level they consist of more suitable targets (e.g., because of higher levels

of exposure through routine activities). As such, Cohen and Felson's (1979) routine activity theory offers an example of a compositional explanation for victimization. To explain temporal changes in U.S. crime rates since World War II, they argued that the displacement of daily activities from the home to the public domain (e.g., through women's increased participation in the labor force), combined with increased possession of portable luxury goods, led to increased criminal activity and victimization because of the greater criminal opportunities associated with these shifts. Thus, they used individual-level mechanisms to account for aggregate crime differences over time.

Although contextual and compositional explanations have been offered to account for cross-national differences in victimization (Gartner, 1990; Krahn et al., 1986; Messner & Rosenfeld, 1997; Neapolitan, 1998), a serious drawback is that the empirical tests performed have used country-level data because of the absence of comparable individual-level crime data across countries. Because it is problematic to infer micro-level mechanisms from macro-level findings (Robinson, 1950), it remains uncertain how to interpret the observed effects of population composition in these studies. In addition, it is questionable whether effects of national context on crime indicate the crime-inducing impact of social structure or whether they are the outcome of unmeasured, systematic lower level heterogeneity. For instance, does a relation between income inequality and homicide indicate that the country's material context stimulates the activity of offenders? Or, is the relation found because countries with high income inequality systematically have more people prone to victimization because of their characteristics as a target?

The sole availability of crime data at the macro-level has made it difficult to answer two basic, yet important questions for the cross-national study of victimization: (1) to what extent does cross-national variation in victimization result from compositional differences? and (2) to what extent

do country characteristics predict victimization rates, after compositional differences are taken into account? These two questions illustrate that micro-level and macro-level research questions on crime and victimization are interdependent. Therefore, a combination of micro-level and macro-level data on victimization, crime targets, subnational areas (e.g. cities), and country characteristics is required to address these questions properly.

Using such a combined set of ICVS data and country data from the World Bank and the International Labour Organization, Van Wilsem et al. (2003) show that national levels of income inequality remain related to the individual risk of both violent and theft victimization, after controlling for various individual, neighborhood, city, and region characteristics with the use of a multilevel model.[11] Although the country sample in this research was limited to 18 countries – mainly Western and some East European – the observed contextual effect of inequality on victimization was, for the first time, simultaneously adjusted for compositional heterogeneity between countries. As such, hypotheses from strain theory were subjected to stronger tests than previous cross-national studies, which were based on country-level data due to the lack of alternatives. However, replications of the analyses across a larger sample of countries are needed to evaluate the external validity of these findings.

In this study, the reverse link between micro- and macro-outcomes was also demonstrated because cross-national differences for violent victimization were reduced notably after controlling for compositional heterogeneity (van Wilsem et al., 2003). More specifically, the most relevant compositional factor was found to be the extent to which countries consisted of large-city residents, accounting for 10 to 15% of cross-national victimization differences. This finding supports the claim of compositional theories that cross-national variations in the distribution of lower level units (individuals, neighborhoods, cities) have consequences for macro-level crime outcomes.

Conclusions

Many cross-national analyses of crime have concentrated on homicide because of data restrictions associated with other crimes. Despite the fact that this is a fruitful line of research, which has offered much insight on differences in the volume, temporal development, and structural correlates of homicide, a great deal has remained unclear about cross-national variation in other crimes. For this reason, much is to be gained by furthering the analysis of international victimization survey data, as offered by the ICVS since 1989. Although this data source has limitations of its own, it also offers the possibility of giving estimates of nonhomicide crimes in a more reliable manner because it attenuates the two major problems of official crime data: varying rates of unreported crime (dark numbers) and different crime definitions. As a consequence of better data quality, multivariate analyses on ICVS data are also likely to yield more valid predictors of macro-level victimization rates as compared to Interpol and UN police registrations on nonhomicide crimes.

However, a serious current limitation to ICVS data is its availability for only a relatively small number of countries, mainly Western and several East European ones. Although ICVS data are also available for other countries, they are limited to the inhabitants of a major city and can therefore not be included in comparisons of national crime rates. Criminological hypotheses on cross-national crime differences have been tested across the current selection of countries participating in national samples of the ICVS (van Wilsem, 2004), but in the future they should also be done on larger country samples, especially including more non-Western countries. This will offer insights into whether the crime-inducing factors for Western countries can be generalized to other countries as well. ICVS findings on Japan's victimization rates suggest that this may not be the case. Despite its high level of urbanization, which is a crime-inducing factor in Western countries, Japan has very low levels of crime (van Wilsem, 2004).[12]

Furthermore, conducting more future ICVS waves for the current selection of participating countries enables researchers to identify temporal developments for non-homicide crimes. Such trend analyses have offered interesting results for homicide victimization, indicating that rapid increases of crime have been most prevalent in developing countries (LaFree & Drass, 2002). Despite shorter time series for a smaller (and more select) group of countries, ICVS analyses of sudden crime changes for non-homicide crimes are interesting to explore as well. Previous research by Lamon (2002) has shown that ICVS rates of property victimization and nonlethal violent victimization also follow varying trajectories of change and stability across countries. Moreover, it is interesting to compare these developments to national homicide changes in order to explore the generality of crime rate dynamics across offense types.

Methodological studies on the ICVS results are also needed. Especially if data are collected among developing countries, careful inspection is needed to evaluate (a) possible quality differences among national survey organizations (e.g., by continuing to explore the relation between response rates and victimization rates), and (b) the magnitude of interpretation and reporting differences for similar questions (e.g., on violent or sexual victimization). Furthermore, additional aspects of the survey should be reviewed for their effect on victimization-related survey answers and their potential consequences for national victimization estimates via compositional differences (Lynch, 2002). For example, if gender combinations of interviewer and respondent affect survey answers on victimization (e.g., victimization is reported more often when the interviewer is female) and these gender combinations vary across countries, they may have consequences for national victimization outcomes and should be taken into account.

On the micro-level, better measures of opportunity and social disorganization indicators offer another way to improve the prediction of victimization across countries. Direct indicators for the target's lifestyle and attractiveness and community cohesion are scarce in ICVS data collection, and measures on these topics are even absent for some countries. Inclusion and expansion of lifestyle and social disorganization indicators for every participating country in the ICVS will help systematize findings on predictors of victimization and allow for the improved disentangling of contextual and compositional effects (van Wilsem et al., 2003) across a larger sample of countries. Moreover, aggregation to the national level of individual survey answers from the ICVS on issues like out-of-home activities, community cohesion, and income dissatisfaction offers the opportunity to evaluate if these aggregated measures are related to often-used social and economic national indicators of criminal opportunity (e.g., female labor force participation), social disorganization (e.g., divorce rate), and strain (e.g., income inequality).

Finally, gaining knowledge on cross-national patterns of violent crime involves the analysis not only of national *volumes* of violence but also of the *nature* of violent incidents. The small amount of situational analyses on violent crime, especially in cross-national research (LaFree & Birkbeck, 1991), has left scholars with little knowledge on how violence is exercised across different contexts. However, an application of Black's (1976, 1983, 1993) theories of law, self-help, and partisanship to this matter would predict that violent crime in developing countries relatively more often involves multiple and unknown offenders as compared to violence in modern societies (Cooney, 2003). According to this line of reasoning, processes of individualization that accompany socioeconomic development increase social distance between citizens, which in turn decreases the chance that third parties will become involved in conflicts, as they are more often neutral to both sides involved. Thus, due to lower levels of partisanship, violent crimes are predicted to become less collective and more one-on-one. Furthermore, as development and individualization go together with decreased informal control and enhanced possibilities to set-

tle disputes by law, honor conflicts between strangers become less prominent, leaving residual violence to be of a more intimate nature. An interesting line of future research would therefore be to compare these characteristics of violent incidents across countries at different stages of social and economic development. Possibilities to do so exist by studying the context of violent victimizations that are reported by urban inhabitants in city samples of countries participating in the ICVS. This offers opportunities to explore and systemize the "neglected situation" (LaFree & Birkbeck, 1991) in cross-national crime research.

Notes

1. Additionally, Archer and Gartner's (1984) Comparative Crime Data File (CCDF) offers crime data for 110 countries and 44 cities, for the years between 1900 and 1970. However, these data have not been updated and are almost 30 years old. Furthermore, the CCDF does not use standardized definitions of homicide nor other types of crime, which reduces cross-national comparability.

2. The United States is one of the remaining industrialized countries with higher homicide rates, ranging between approximately 6 and 10 homicide victims per 100,000 population during this period.

3. As an exception, Japan was the only country that was characterized by a decline in homicide over this period. Roberts and LaFree (2004) relate this change to reductions in economic stress, declining youth populations, and the increasing certainty of punishment.

4. The United States and Canada were among the five modern countries that did experience crime booms.

5. In these cases, ordinary-least-squares regression models should be replaced by more appropriate methods (e.g., GLS or multilevel models), in order to adjust for dependency of errors in within-country time-series.

6. Including a variety of expenditures, such as on pensions, unemployment benefit, family allowance programs, and public health.

7. See Hannon and DeFronzo (1998) for a similar argument on the distribution of crime within a single country (i.e., the United States).

8. In addition, Bennett (1991) found a negative squared effect, which indicated that, at very high GDP levels, theft rates declined.

9. This relation was found after a dummy variable was introduced for Japan, because of its outlier position in the relation between urbanism and crime.

10. It may be hypothesized that individual risk factors, such as exposure of targets through nighttime outdoor activity, enhances victimization risk more strongly in countries with active and large offender populations. Interestingly however, no significant differences were found across countries in the effect sizes of various predictors of victimization (van Wilsem, 2003). For example, nighttime outdoor activity exerts consistent positive effects on violent victimization outside the neighborhood and thus appears to be equally important across countries in explaining victimization risk. Possibly, significant interaction results between ecological characteristics and behavior are found more often if spatial units are homogeneous (Smith, Frazee, & Davison, 2000), which is often not the case with countries in which there often is large within-unit variation.

11. The multilevel model takes account of the layered character of the data by separately employing submodels for each level distinguished (e.g. country, subnational region, and individual). It adjusts for the correlation between the error components of the separate levels that results from the hierarchical data structure (Snijders & Bosker, 1999). Furthermore, it corrects for the fact that, at higher levels of aggregation, fewer observations are available.

12. Previous work by Komiya (1999) and Roberts and LaFree (2004) offers more insight on Japan's low crime rate.

References

Archer, D., & Gartner, R. (1984). *Violence and crime in cross-national perspective*. New Haven, CT: Yale University Press.

Bellair, P. E. (1997). Social interaction and community crime: Examining the importance of neighbor networks. *Criminology, 35*, 677–703.

Bennett, R. R. (1991). Routine activities: A cross-national assessment of a criminological perspective. *Social Forces, 70*, 147–163.

Black, D. (1976). *The behavior of law*. New York: Academic Press.

Black, D. (1983). Crime as social control. *American Sociological Review, 48*, 34–45.

Black, D. (1993). *The social structure of right and wrong*. San Diego: Academic Press.

Blau, J. R., & Blau, P. M. (1982). The cost of inequality: Metropolitan structure and violent crime. *American Sociological Review, 47*, 114–129.

Block, R. (1993). A cross-national comparison of victims of crime: Victim surveys of twelve countries. *International Review of Victimology, 2*, 183–207.

Carcach, C. (2002). An empirical test of the life-course perspective to victimization. In P. Nieuwbeerta (Ed.), *Crime victimization in comparative perspective* (pp. 195–212). The Hague: Boom Juridische Uitgevers.

Cohen, L. E., & Felson, M. (1979). Social change and crime rate trends: A routine activity approach. *American Sociological Review, 44*, 588–608.

Cooney, M. (2003). The privatization of violence. *Criminology, 41*, 1377–1406.

Council of Europe (2003). *European sourcebook of crime and criminal justice statistics*. The Hague: WODC.

Dillman, D. A., & J. Tarnai. (1989). Administrative issues in mixed mode surveys. In R. M. Groves, P. P. Biemer, L. E. Lyberg, J. T. Massey, W. L. Nichols, & J. Waksberg (Eds.), *Telephone survey methodology* (pp. 509–528). New York: John Wiley & Sons.

Dodd, T., Nicholas, S., Povey, D., & Walker, A. (2004). *Crime in England and Wales, 2003/2004*. London: Home Office.

Eisner, M. (2001). Modernization, self control and lethal violence. *British Journal of Criminology, 41*, 618–638.

Ennis, P. (1967). *Criminal victimization in the United States: A report of a national survey*. Washington, DC: U.S. Government Printing Office.

Gartner, R. (1990). The victims of homicide: A temporal and cross-national comparison. *American Sociological Review, 55*, 92–106.

Gurr, T. (1977). Crime trends in modern democracies since 1945. *International Annals of Criminology, 16*, 41–85.

Haen Marshall, I., & Block, C. R. (2004). Maximizing the availability of cross-national data on homicide. *Homicide Studies, 8*, 267–310.

Hannon, L., & DeFronzo, J. (1998). The truly disadvantaged, public assistance, and crime. *Social Problems, 45*, 383–392.

Hindelang, M. S., Gottfredson, M., & Garofalo, J. (1978). *Victims of personal crime: An empirical foundation for a theory of personal victimization.* Cambridge, MA: Ballinger.

Hirschi, T., & Gottfredson, M. (1983). Age and the explanation of crime. *American Journal of Sociology, 89,* 552–584.

Kalish, C. (1988). *International crime rates.* Washington, DC: U.S. Department of Justice.

Kick, E. L., & LaFree, G. D. (1985). Development and the social context of murder and theft. *Comparative Social Research, 8,* 37–58.

Komiya, N. (1999). A cultural study of the low crime rate in Japan. *British Journal of Criminology, 39,* 369–390.

Krahn, H., Hartnagel, T. F., & Gartrell, J. W. (1986). Income inequality and homicide rates: Cross-national data and criminological theories. *Criminology, 24,* 269–295.

Krug, E. G., Dahlberg, L. L., Mercy, J. A., Zwi, A. B., & Lozano, R. (Eds.). (2002). *World report on violence and health.* Geneva: WHO.

LaFree, G. (2003). *International police and health statistics on homicide: Problems, prospects and post–World War II trends.* Retrieved May 3, 2005, from the Web site of the National Institute of Statistics, Rome: http://samoa.istat.it/Eventi/sicurezza/relazioni/LaFree_rel.pdf.

LaFree, G., & Birkbeck, B. (1991). The neglected situation: A cross-national study of the situational characteristics of crime. *Criminology, 29,* 73–98.

LaFree, G., & Drass, K. A. (2002). Counting crime booms among nations: Evidence for homicide victimization rates, 1956–1998. *Criminology, 40,* 769–800.

LaFree, G. D., & Kick, E. L. (1986). Cross-national effects of developmental, distributional and demographic variables on crime: A review and analysis. *International Annals of Criminology, 22,* 213–235.

Lamon, P. (2002). Crime trends in thirteen industrialized countries. In P. Nieuwbeerta (Ed.), *Crime victimization in comparative perspective* (pp. 29–52). The Hague: Boom Juridische Uitgevers.

Lee, M. R. (2000). Community cohesion and violent predatory victimization: A theoretical extension and cross-national test of opportunity theory. *Social Forces, 79,* 683–706.

Lynch, J. (1993). Secondary analysis of international crime survey data. In U. Zvekic, J. J. M. Van Dijk, & A. A. Del Frate (Eds.), *Understanding crime: Experiences of crime and crime control* (pp. 175–192). Rome: UNICRI.

Lynch, J. (2002). Effects of design differences on rate comparisons in the ICVS. In P. Nieuwbeerta (Ed.), *Crime victimization in comparative perspective* (pp. 431–457). The Hague: Boom Juridische Uitgevers.

Mayhew, P., & Van Dijk, J. J. M. (1997). *Criminal victimisation in eleven industrialised countries: Key findings from the 1996 International Crime Victims Survey.* The Hague: WODC.

Merton, R. K. (1957). *Social theory and social structure.* Glencoe, IL: The Free Press.

Messner, S. F. (1982). Societal development, social equality, and homicide: A cross-national test of a Durkheimian model. *Social Forces, 61,* 225–240.

Messner, S. F. (1989). Economic discrimination and societal homicide rates: Further evidence on the cost of inequality. *American Sociological Review, 54,* 597–611.

Messner, S. F., & Rosenfeld, R. (1997). Political restraint of the market and levels of criminal homicide: A cross-national application of institutional-anomie theory. *Social Forces, 75,* 1393–1416.

Mirrlees-Black, C. (1999). *Domestic violence: Findings from a new British crime survey self completion questionnaire.* London: Home Office.

Mouzos, J., & Makkai, T. (2004). *Women's experience of male violence: Findings from the Australian component of the International Violence Against Women Survey.* Canberra: Australian Institute of Criminology.

Neapolitan, J. L. (1997). *Cross-national crime: A research review and sourcebook.* Westport, CT: Greenwood Press.

Neapolitan, J. (1998). Cross-national variation in homicides: Is race a factor? *Criminology, 36,* 139–156.

Pampel, F. C., & Gartner, R. (1995). Age structure, socio-political institutions, and national homicide rates. *European Sociological Review, 11,* 243–260.

Pratt, T., & Godsey, T. W. (2003). Social support, inequality, and homicide: A cross-national test of an integrated theoretical model. *Criminology, 41,* 611–644.

Roberts, A., & LaFree, G. (2004). Explaining Japan's postwar violent crime trends. *Criminology, 42,* 179–210.

Robinson, W. S. (1950). Ecological correlations and the behavior of individuals. *American Sociological Review, 15,* 351–357.

Sampson, R. J., & Laub, J. H. (1993). *Crime in the making: Pathways and turning points through life*. Cambridge, MA: Harvard University Press.

Sampson, R. J., Raudenbush, S. W., & Earls, F. (1997). Neighborhoods and violent crime: A multilevel study of collective efficacy. *Science, 277*, 918–924.

Savolainen, J. (2000). Inequality, welfare state, and homicide: Further support for the institutional anomie theory. *Criminology, 38*, 1021–1042.

Shelley, L. I. (1981). *Crime and modernization: The impact of industrialization and urbanization on crime*. Carbondale, IL: Southern Illinois University Press.

Smith, W. R., Frazee, S. G., & Davison, E. L. (2000). Furthering the integration of routine activity and social disorganization theories: Small units of analysis and the study of street robbery as a diffusion process. *Criminology, 38*, 489–524.

Snijders, T., & Bosker, R. (1999). *Multilevel analysis. An introduction to basic and advanced multilevel modeling*. London: Sage.

Thomson, E. (1999). Effect of an execution on homicides in California. *Homicide Studies, 3*, 129–150.

Tseloni, A. (2000). Personal criminal victimization in the United States: Fixed and random effects of individual and household characteristics. *Journal of Quantitative Criminology, 16*, 415–442.

Van Dijk, J. J. M., & Mayhew, P. (1992). *Criminal victimisation in the industrialised world: Key findings from the 1989 and 1992 International Crime Surveys*. The Hague: Ministry of Justice.

Van Dijk, J. J. M., Mayhew, P., & Kilias, M. (1990). *Experiences of crime across the world*. Deventer: Kluwer Law and Taxation Publishers.

Van Dijk, J. J. M., & Van Kesteren, J. (1996). The prevalence and perceived seriousness of victimisations by crime: Some results of the International Crime Victims Survey. *European Journal of Crime, Criminal Policy and Criminal Justice, 4*, 48–71.

Van Kesteren, J., Mayhew, P., & Nieuwbeerta, P. (2000). *Criminal victimisation in seventeen industrialised countries: Key findings from the 2000 International Crime Victims Survey*. The Hague: WODC.

Van Wilsem, J. (2003). *Crime and context: The impact of individual, neighborhood, city and country characteristics on victimization*. Amsterdam: Thela Thesis.

Van Wilsem, J. (2004). Crime victimization in cross-national perspective: An analysis of rates of theft, violence and vandalism across 27 countries. *European Journal of Criminology, 1*, 89–109.

Van Wilsem, J., De Graaf, N. D., & Wittebrood, K. (2003). Cross-national differences in victimization: Disentangling the impact of composition and context. *European Sociological Review, 19*, 125–142.

Zvekic, U., & Alvazzi Del Frate, A. (1995). *Criminal victimisation in the developing world*. Rome: UNICRI.

CHAPTER 25

Violent Juvenile Delinquency: Changes, Consequences, and Implications

James C. Howell and Megan Q. Howell

Introduction

This chapter begins with an overview of juvenile violence trends during the past 20 years. Egregious myths and erroneous doomsday forecasts of a "coming wave" of juvenile violence are considered next. We then examine gang violence as a main component of youth violence. Transfers of juvenile offenders to criminal courts are highlighted as the most devastating consequence of a moral panic over delinquency. Lastly, we suggest program implications of these trends for public policy and programs.

Juvenile Violence Trends

A juvenile violence "epidemic" is said to have occurred during the late 1980s and early 1990s.[1] Three measures are used to gauge changes in serious and violent delinquency: official arrests, victimization surveys, and delinquency self-report surveys. Each of these measures can lead one to draw quite different conclusions regarding juvenile violence trends for this period (Howell, 2003b, pp. 3–11).

After years of little change, the violent juvenile delinquency arrest rate began to increase in the late 1980s and continued to climb each year thereafter, until it reached a peak in 1994. In the period from 1988 through 1994, the violent juvenile *arrest rate* increased 62% (Snyder & Sickmund, 1999). From 1984 through 1994, the *number* of juveniles arrested for homicide tripled (Snyder & Sickmund, 1995). A few researchers claimed that an "unprecedented epidemic" of youth violence occurred in the late 1980s and early 1990s (Blumstein, 1995a,b; Cook & Laub, 1998; Fox, 1996b). However, caution should be exercised in drawing such a broad conclusion, especially with respect to juveniles.

The "tyranny of small numbers" principle comes into play in analyses of juvenile violence, because of juveniles' very low base rates.[2] This principle refers to the fact that a slight increase in a small number will translate into a large percentage increase. Hence, the arrest rate and numeric changes shown above exaggerate the actual increase in the total volume of crimes for which juveniles were arrested.[3] This principle is

Table 25.1: Key juvenile delinquency trend data sources

Arrests	Victimizations	Self-Report Surveys
Uniform Crime Reports (UCR) – Federal Bureau of Investigation (FBI), U.S. Department of Justice	National Crime Victimization Survey (NCVS) – Bureau of Justice Statistics, U.S. Department of Justice	1) The National Youth Survey (NYS) – University of Colorado
Data source: Based on voluntary reports that thousands of law enforcement agencies across the United States make each year to the FBI	Data source: Annual interviews with persons age 12 or older, in a nationally representative sample of U.S. households	Data source: Interviews with a national probability sample of 1,725 youths ages 11–17 in 1976. The panel was interviewed annually from 1976 to 1980 and every 3 years thereafter
Key data: Annual number of arrests for specific offenses; also aggregated arrests for violent crimes (Violent Crime Index), serious property crimes (Property Crime Index)	Key data: Self-reported nonfatal crimes against persons, both reported and not reported to the police	Key data: A wide variety of self-reported delinquent behaviors and drug use 2) Monitoring the Future (MTF) study – University of Michigan Data source: Survey of a national sample of high-school seniors (eighth and tenth graders were added in 1991) Key data: Self-reported illicit drug use and violent acts

compounded in analyses that use the very lowest points in juvenile violence as the base year (e.g., Blumstein, 1995a,b; Fox, 1996b). Thus, the results can be very misleading.

These sources of distortion in presenting juvenile violence trends can be minimized by examining longer term data. Using Uniform Crime Report (UCR) data, Zimring (1998, pp. 31–47) examined violent arrests of 13- to 17-year-olds from 1980 through 1995. He found that two (robberies and rapes) of the four Violent Crime Index offenses[4] were essentially trendless over that 16-year period. Aggravated assault arrests increased 56% above the 1980 level, and a 34% gain was recorded for homicide. However, most of the increase in aggravated assault arrests occurred at the nonserious end of the seriousness scale. The 34% gain in homicide arrests contrasts sharply with the tripling in the number of juveniles arrested for homicide and the doubling of violent juvenile arrest rates in the shorter period of time cited above. Another long-term analysis of UCR data on crimes *cleared* by the arrest of juveniles for violent offenses from 1972 to 1992 showed little change (Howell, Krisberg, & Jones, 1995).

As a general observation, reliance on UCR arrest data to measure juvenile violence trends is very problematic.[5] Because juveniles tend to commit crimes in groups, several adolescents may be arrested for a crime that only one of them committed. In a test of this supposition, the UCR data exaggerated by about 40% the actual number of juveniles involved in a reported crime (McCord, Widom, & Crowell, 2001, pp. 27–28). It also is important to recognize that arrest data indicate society's *response* to juvenile delinquency, not the actual level of delinquency. Thus, one must examine data from more direct measures of delinquency to assess whether or not an "epidemic" has occurred. These data come from victimization surveys and delinquency self-report surveys, briefly described in Table 25.1.

Victimization data collected in the National Crime Victimization Survey (NCVS) show that violent juvenile victimizations increased during the late 1980s and early 1990s. In an analysis of NCVS data covering the period 1987–1992, the juvenile violent victimization rate increased 23% (Moone, 1994). Interestingly, this increase is only about one-third as large as the increase (62%) in the violent juvenile arrest rate between 1988 and 1994 shown above. Moreover, juvenile serious violent victimizations (rape, robbery, aggravated assault) did not increase significantly in this period, and most of the violent juvenile victimizations during this period were simple assaults that did not involve weapons and resulted in nothing more than minor injuries (Moone, 1994).

Data from self-report studies of juvenile violence refute the supposed sharp increase in the 1980s and early 1990s (other than for homicide). In the Monitoring the Future (MTF) national sample of high-school seniors, the prevalence of serious violence remained relatively stable for the period 1980–1998 (U.S. Department of Health and Human Services, 2001, p. 27). Self-report data from the National Youth Survey (NYS) and the Denver Youth Survey modeled after it suggest that there was a small increase (8–10%) in the proportion of adolescents involved in some type of serious violent offending in the late 1980s and early 1990s, but the frequency of offending remained about the same (Elliott, 1994; Huizinga, Weiher, Espiritu, & Esbenson, 2003).

What remains to be explained is the sharp increase in juvenile homicides from the mid-1980s to the early 1990s. Most of this increase involved firearms. From 1984 through 1993, the number of juveniles killed with firearms tripled, and the number of nonfirearm homicides remained relatively constant (Snyder & Sickmund, 1999). Despite the exaggeration for reasons noted above, it can properly be said that a gun homicide epidemic occurred in the late 1980s and the early 1990s, and juveniles were a part of it. However, the gun homicide epidemic was by no means limited to juveniles. Although adolescents showed the biggest proportional increase in homicide commission and victimization (due to the "tyranny of small numbers"), the biggest absolute change was for young adults aged 18–24 (Cook & Laub, 1998, p. 60).

It can also be said that a youth gun *suicide* epidemic occurred in the 1980s and early 1990s. The rate of youth (ages 0–19) suicides involving firearms increased 39% from 1980 through 1994, whereas the rate of suicides not involving firearms remained virtually unchanged during this period (Snyder & Sickmund, 1995, 1999). The concomitant change in gun homicides and suicides has not been explained, and the supposed crack cocaine epidemic (reviewed below) is not a plausible explanation for both phenomena.

Once multiple data sources are examined carefully, the conclusion that a general epidemic of juvenile violence occurred in the decade from the mid-1980s to the mid-1990s lacks empirical support. However, the sharp increase that occurred in both adolescent homicides and suicides by firearms during this period suggests that the common denominator in the growth of violent adolescent deaths in the 1980s and 1990s in the U.S. was the use of firearms, not an increase in interpersonal violent behaviors.

Explaining the Increase in Juvenile Homicides

The popular explanation offered by some criminologists for the growth in adolescent homicides cited above is the presumed "crack cocaine epidemic" of the late 1980s (Blumstein, 1995a,b; Cook & Laub, 1998; Fox, 1996b). However, the actual existence of a widespread crack cocaine epidemic has been seriously questioned (Hartman & Golub, 1999). It is interesting to note that in Canada youthful homicide rates also increased sharply in the mid- to late-1980s – without the presence of any crack cocaine epidemic (Hagan & Foster, 2000). This research suggests that the so-called crack cocaine epidemic is not a satisfactory explanation for the observed increase in juvenile homicide in the United States as a whole during this period. The growing availability of firearms and failures to secure them are, of course, associated with their use (Grossman et al., 2005). From 1973 through 1994, the number of guns in private ownership in the United States rose by 87 million (Malcolm, 2002) to an estimated 200 million (Reich, Culross, & Behrman, 2002), of which approximately 65 million are handguns (Ludwig, 2005). Not surprisingly, greater gun availability is associated with suicides and homicides (Cook & Ludwig, 2006).

Gangs and Guns

The growth in youth gangs[6] and the violence associated with them – particularly gun use – is the most overlooked factor in the increase in juvenile and young adult homicides in the late 1980s and the early 1990s. Rapid proliferation of youth gang problems in cities, towns, and rural areas across the United States occurred at the same time as the increase in youth homicides. More than half (57%) of the respondents (representatives of law enforcement agencies) to the National Youth Gang Survey said that their gang problems began in the early to mid-1990s (Howell, Egley, & Gleason, 2002). Nearly 9 out of 10 said that their gang problem began during the period 1986–1996. The mid-1990s was a peak period of reported gang activity across the country.

The use of firearms is a major feature of gang violence. Gang members are far more likely than other delinquents to carry guns and to use them. In a Rochester, New York study, the rate of gun carrying was about 10 times higher for gang members than it was for nongang juveniles (Thornberry, Krohn, Lizotte, Smith, & Tobin, 2003). Gang members who carried guns or who owned and carried guns also committed about 10 times more violent crimes than one would expect from their numbers in the sample population. Thornberry et al. (2003) state, "If illegal gun users have been characterized as the crime problem in the United States, then gang members with guns may be at the very core of the crime problem, especially the problem of youth violence" (p. 125).

Youth gang homicides increased at a faster pace than total homicides for the period between 1980 and 1995 (Howell, 1999), and the number of gang homicides reported by cities with populations of 100,000 or more increased 34% from 1999 to 2003 (Curry, 2004). Chicago and Los Angeles are now the youth gang homicide capitals,

and the number of gang homicides increased sharply during this period in both of these cities. The growth in youth gang homicides was driven mainly by increased access to and use of firearms, particularly more lethal weapons (automatic and semi-automatic firearms) (Howell, 1999). Partly because gang homicides have increased recently and did not decline as much as nongang homicides in the latter part of the 1990s and early into this century, more than half of all homicides in both Los Angeles and Chicago were reported to be gang related in 2001 (59% and 53%, respectively; Egley & Major, 2003).

Despite the fact that the period of rapid proliferation of youth gangs across the United States overlapped considerably with the time frame in which the so-called crack cocaine epidemic was presumed to have occurred (Egley, Howell, & Major, 2004), youth gangs were not actively involved, as organizations, in drug trafficking (Klein, 1995). It is a myth of epidemic proportion that youth gangs transformed themselves into entrepreneurial organizations and migrated all over the country setting up drug trafficking operations (Klein, 1995). To be sure, enormous gang growth occurred in the late 1980s and early 1990s, and gang homicides increased sharply during this period (Howell, 1999; Maxson, Curry, & Howell, 2002). However, relatively few gang homicides are directly related to drug trafficking (Braga, Kennedy, & Tita, 2002; Howell, 1999). Gang homicides typically stem from disputes within and between gangs, especially over turf issues, and conflicts between rival gang members. The drug wars of that era largely involved nongang entities, such as drug cartels and syndicates, and some adult groups that are called drug gangs, not youth gangs (Eddy, Sabogal, & Walden, 1988; Gugliotta & Leen, 1989). Ongoing gang wars, which most often stem from intergang and interpersonal disputes, sometimes last several years because of periodic episodes of retaliation and revenge. These events can produce large numbers of gang homicides, but few of these involve youth gangs (Block, Christakos, Jacob, & Przybylski, 1996). In sum, traditional patterns of gang-related homicides, coupled with the increased prevalence of guns, likely account for a large proportion of the increase in juvenile and young adult gun homicides in the late 1980s and early 1990s.

Serious, violent, and chronic juvenile offenders are often gang-involved youths (Howell, 2003b, pp. 83–84). This is mainly attributable to the fact that youth gang members are very high-rate offenders. Longitudinal studies in Denver, Colorado; Rochester, New York; and Seattle, Washington revealed that gang members, who make up a relatively small proportion (14%-31%) of these large adolescent samples, are responsible for about three fourths of all serious violent offenses self-reported by the entire samples (Thornberry, 1998). During periods of active gang membership, the Rochester gang members were responsible for, on average, four times as many offenses as their share of the total study population would suggest (Thornberry et al., 2003). Other research in these cities showed that gang member offense rates are up to seven times higher than the violent crime rates of adolescents who are not in gangs (Esbensen & Huizinga, 1993; Hill, Lui, & Hawkins, 2001; Thornberry, Krohn, Lizotte, & Chard-Wierschem, 1993). The gang context both facilitates and enhances delinquency involvement and violent behavior, but little of the gang violence is related to drug trafficking (Howell & Decker, 1999). Violence is a part of gang members' everyday lives, in their neighborhoods and families, apart from the gang (Decker, this volume, Chapter 18; Decker & Van Winkle, 1996). A great deal of gang violence also occurs within gangs, with members assaulting each other. It is imperative that community efforts to prevent and control serious and violent delinquency also address gang problems where they exist.

Myths and Doomsday Forecasts

In 1995, John DiIulio created and popularized the "super-predator" concept to describe high-rate juvenile offenders who supposedly had become more prevalent. He used the term to characterize them as a "new breed" of offenders, "kids that have absolutely no respect for human life and no sense of the future. . . . These are stone-cold predators!" (1995b, p. 23). Elsewhere, DiIulio and co-authors have described these young people as "fatherless, Godless, and jobless" and as "radically impulsive, brutally remorseless youngsters" (Bennett, DiIulio, & Walters, 1996, p. 27).

The super-predator myth got more media attention when it was linked to forecasts of increased levels of juvenile violence made by DiIulio (1995b) and James Q. Wilson (1995). They projected that 270,000 more juvenile super-predators would be filling the cities' streets by 2010, based on two factors. First, they assumed that the 6% of boys who were chronic offenders in the 1960s (in the Philadelphia Birth Cohort Study) would remain constant. Second, they factored this figure in with U.S. Bureau of the Census projections of juvenile population growth. According to these projections, the ages 0–17 population group in the United States was expected to grow by 4.5 million between 1996 and 2010. Therefore, using their method of reasoning, by 2010 the United States would have 270,000 (.06 × 4.5 million) more super-predators that would "come at us in waves over the next 20 years" (DiIulio, 1996, p. 25).

The illogical nature of the Wilson-DiIulio projection is readily apparent. They assumed that 6% of babies and children as well as juveniles would be chronic offenders. If we were to apply the 6% figure to the 1996 population under age 18, according to their analysis, there already were 1.9 million "super-predator" juvenile offenders in the United States. This number is nearly twice the total number of children and adolescents referred to juvenile courts each year.[7]

Nevertheless, speaking at a meeting of the American Association for the Advancement of Science, Fox warned of a "bloodbath" of teen violence (quoted in Associated Press, 1996). In a report to the U.S. Attorney General, Fox (1996b) wrote, "Our nation faces a future juvenile violence problem that may make today's epidemic pale in comparison" (p. 3). He called attention in particular to the projected growth in the black teenage (ages 14–17) population, which would increase 26% by 2005 (see also Blumstein, 1996).

At the time of this writing, two thirds of the 15-year period (1995–2010) covered in the doomsday projections of waves of juvenile violence have already passed, and juvenile violence has been decreasing year by year for a decade, not increasing. As it turns out, juvenile homicides had peaked in 1993, and juvenile violent crime arrests had peaked in 1994, just prior to publication of the doomsday forecasts. In 2003, for the ninth consecutive year, the rate of juvenile arrests for Violent Crime Index offenses declined, to a point lower than in any year since at least 1980 and 48% below the peak year of 1994.[8] The drop in the juvenile arrest rate for murder was even greater, having dropped 77% from its zenith in 1993 to 2003 to half of the 1980 rate.[9] Interestingly, the beginning of these decreases actually pre-dated the super-predator hype and doomsday projections.

Three key assumptions were tied to the super-predator myth: (1) that the relative proportion of serious and violent offenders; among all juvenile delinquents is growing, (2) that juvenile offenders are becoming younger and younger; and (3) that juveniles are committing more and more violent crimes. Neither the national Study Group on Serious and Violent Juvenile Offenders (Loeber & Farrington, 1998) nor the national Study Group on Very Young Offenders (Loeber & Farrington, 2001) found evidence to support these claims.

Moral Panic

Unfortunately, DiIulio's, Wilson's, and Fox's[10] doomsday forecasts were taken seriously for a number of years, and to this day legislatures act as if they were valid. The two compelling images, of "super-predators" and an eminent "crime bomb," were powerful, and they played well in the broadcast media and with politicians who wanted to draw public support by appearing tough on juvenile crime. Stories that played to readers' fears were common (Zimring, 1998). Fear of young people grew in the public's mind, and the majority of U.S. adults believed that the projected increases in juvenile crime were coming (Dorfman & Schiraldi, 2001). Legislators were quick to insert the pejorative images of the "new breed" of juvenile offenders and the potential juvenile crime explosion into their draconian proposals.[11] The inflammatory rhetoric fueled the seventh U.S. "moral panic"[12] over juvenile delinquency (Howell, 2003b, pp. 25–30), which was in full bloom by the late 1990s.[13] The conditions of a moral panic (Goode & Ben-Yehuda, 1994) had been met: (1) a consensus that the threat is real and serious, (2) a heightened level of concern, (3) concern that is disproportionate to the objective threat posed by the identified group, (4) hostility directed at those individuals engaged in the deviant behavior, and (5) volatile reactions.

Consequences of the Moral Panic

Punitive legislative changes designated larger proportions of juveniles as serious and violent offenders, resulting in the incarceration of more nondangerous juveniles, and extended periods of confinement in juvenile correctional facilities (Howell, 2003b, pp. 30–40). One comparison illustrates the overall trend. From 1990 through 1999, the total number of juvenile arrests for violent offenses *decreased* by 55%, and juvenile arrests for serious property offenses *decreased* by 23% (Snyder, 2000). Nevertheless, during approximately the same period, the total number of referrals to juvenile court *increased* by 44% (Stahl, 2001), creating burgeoning juvenile court intake and probation caseloads. Detention centers and juvenile reformatories have become and remain overcrowded, particularly with nonserious offenders. Conditions of confinement have also worsened, partly as a result of the overcrowding (Puritz & Scali, 1998).

Minority youth, particularly Black youngsters, are bearing the brunt of the punitive juvenile justice reforms that the panic over juvenile violence has wrought. Rehabilitation programs often were abandoned, whereas boot camps, "Scared Straight" programs, more detention centers, and more juvenile reformatories increasingly populated the nation's landscape (Howell, 2003b; Males, 1996; Roush & McMillen, 2000). In addition, growing numbers of juveniles were removed from the juvenile justice system altogether and transferred to the criminal justice system. We focus on this product of the most recent moral panic in this chapter, because of the disproportional relationship between research and transfer policies and practices.

Transfers of Juveniles to the Criminal Justice System

Over the past 20 years, every state has made it easier to transfer adolescents from the juvenile justice system to the criminal justice system (Howell, 2003b). As a result of the "get tough" movement, legislators enacted new laws that (1) expanded the list of crimes for which juveniles could be transferred while excluding certain offenses from juvenile court jurisdiction and (2) expanded the role of prosecutors in making the transfer decision. Many changes in the transfer of juveniles occurred in the 1990s when all but six states enacted or expanded transfer provisions – mainly lengthening the list of transferable offenses beyond serious violent crimes to include drug and property offenses and giving prosecutors more authority to make the transfer decision (Griffin, 2003). Ironically, these changes resulted in the transfer of more minor juvenile offenders in the last portion of the 20th century. In the late 1980s, the most common judicially waived case was a person-related offense (Puzzanchera, Stahl, Finnegan, Tierney, & Snyder, 2003). By 1998, property offense cases were more likely than person offense cases to be judicially waived. Working in the juvenile justice field in the current era has been described as being inside a walled village with a monster (the "get tough" move-

ment) just outside the gates. Fearful villagers attempt to satisfy the hunger of the monster, first throwing over the wall the most violent youths in the village, and then younger youths, then kids charged with less serious offenses, and so on (Butts, 1999). But the monster's hunger is never abated.[14]

The research base on transfers points us to several general conclusions (M. Q. Howell, 2004). First, there is a large amount of variation among the states in the use of transfer mechanisms, which is a reflection of their individual philosophies. Second, age is one of the most important factors in determining the likelihood for transfer. Third, for homicide offenders, the more risk factors youths have, the more likely they are to be transferred and to receiver longer sentences than if retained in juvenile court. Fourth, "juvenile status" is an extralegal factor that influences the length of sentence in adult court (Kurlychek & Johnson, 2004). This last observation calls into question the performance of the criminal justice system in transfer actions. We return to this matter shortly.

Knowing the method of transfer is a key stepping stone in determining the relational outcomes among transferred youth. Unfortunately, nonjudicial methods of transfer are seldom recorded in court records and thus are rarely studied (Mears, 2003). Although research on this matter is increasing, not much is known about the short- or long-term effects on youth who are transferred to criminal court. The few available comparative studies suggest that transferred juveniles are more likely to re-offend, to re-offend more quickly and at a higher rate, and perhaps to commit more serious offenses after they are released from prison than juveniles retained in the juvenile justice system (Bishop & Frazier, 2000; Fagan, 1995; Howell, 1996; Winner, Lanza-Kaduce, Bishop, & Frazier, 1997). In addition, juvenile transfers do not produce a general deterrent effect (Bishop & Frazier, 2000).

The Extent of Transfers

Incredibly, the number of juveniles transferred to the criminal justice system each year is unknown. Criminal justice system authorities prefer not to maintain these data, despite the fact that the United States is the only developed nation that often tries its youngest offenders in the adult criminal courts (Zimring, 2002). The black hole in the transfer picture has been expanded by two key actors, legislatures and prosecutors (Zimring, 1998). Official statistics do not cover their actions, creating a "dark figure of waiver" (Mears, 2003). Twenty-five years ago, juvenile court judges transferred most juveniles to criminal court; now, state legislatures and prosecutors are the leaders (Building Blocks for Youth, 2000). As of 2003, 45 states had long-standing judicial waiver provisions, 15 states had prosecutorial direct file laws, and 29 state legislatures had enacted statutory exclusion criteria (Griffin, 2003). However, prosecutors make most of the transfer decisions (45%), followed by state legislatures (40%; Building Blocks for Youth, 2000). Unfortunately, legislatures and prosecutors are least adept at selecting the most dangerous candidates for transfer (Howell, 1996).[15]

This problem is compounded by the fact that sentencing of juveniles versus adults in criminal courts is grossly disproportionate. Surprisingly, transferred juveniles convicted of felonies are handed prison sentences that are nearly twice as long as sentences that adults receive for comparable offenses (Brown & Langan, 1998). Worse yet, juveniles can be sentenced to life without parole (LWOP) in 41 states; 14 states allow a child of any age to be tried and punished as an adult and sentenced to life without parole; and three states (South Dakota, Vermont, and Wisconsin) allow children as young as age 10 to be tried and punished as an adult and sentenced to life without parole (American Civil Liberties Union of Michigan, 2004). Executions of juvenile offenders were permitted in the United States until this practice was finally prohibited in 2005 by the U.S. Supreme Court (*Roper v. Simmons*), thanks to the determined initiative of a large number of advocacy groups (Boyle, 2005). More juvenile offenders were executed in the United States in the 1990s than in all other countries combined. As of late, ours was the only country that claimed the legal authority to execute juvenile offenders.

Missing Research Support for Transfers

Research does not support the practice of transferring juveniles to criminal courts on any empirical criteria. The broad offense-based transfer criteria employed by legislatures do not capture the small subgroup of high-rate serious juvenile offenders who are most likely to re-offend (Howell, 1996). Even if this were the case, crime likely would not be reduced by incarcerating them in adult prisons. As seen earlier, research to date suggests that recidivism rates are lower when transfer candidates are handled in the juvenile justice system. Moreover, approximately two thirds of the inmates are rearrested within 3 years of release from adult prisons, and more than half of released prisoners are returned to prison (Langan & Levin, 2002). Adult probation is equally ineffective: about two thirds of adult probationers commit new crimes within 3 years of their sentences, and many of these crimes are serious (Manhattan Institute, 1999). In sum, the criminal justice system itself is a failure on many grounds (Howell, 2003b, pp. 156–172): it misuses legislative provisions, it is ineffective in rehabilitating offenders, it rarely uses research-based programs (particularly in prisons), and the prison system operates like a revolving door. It is no wonder that two highly respected criminologists have characterized the criminal justice system as having "lost its way" (Travis & Petersilia, 2001, p. 299). Ideally, all state policies that allow the transfer of juveniles to the criminal justice system for criminal conviction and adult punishment should be ended. The practice of exposing adolescents to adult courts and prisons is neither effective in reducing crime nor cost beneficial.

Implications for Prevention and Intervention

All of this research supports two important conclusions. First, the juvenile violence problem in the United States is not out of control, and we do not have a new breed of juvenile offenders who are beyond the capabilities of the juvenile justice system. Second, more attention needs to be given to gang-involved youths. Policymakers need to provide the resources that juvenile justice systems across the country need to operate in a more balanced, proactive, and cost-effective manner.

A Comprehensive Strategy

The Comprehensive Strategy (CS) for Serious, Violent, and Chronic Juvenile Offenders (Wilson & Howell, 1993; for updates see Howell, 2003a,b) appears to be a useful framework for guiding state and local system reforms to address juvenile delinquency in a cost-effective manner. The CS is a two-tiered system for responding proactively to juvenile delinquency. In the first tier, delinquency prevention, youth development, and early intervention programs are relied on to prevent delinquency and reduce the likelihood of delinquent career development among children who display problem behaviors. If these efforts fail, then the juvenile justice system, the second tier, needs to make proactive responses to juvenile delinquency by addressing the risk factors for recidivism and associated treatment needs of delinquents, particularly those with a high likelihood of becoming serious, violent, and chronic (SVC) offenders. A continuum of sanctions and services is needed for the juvenile justice system to reduce this likelihood while protecting the public. This continuum can be organized to prevent further development of offender careers toward SVC status.

The CS framework consists of six levels of program interventions and sanctions, moving from least to most restrictive:

1. prevention of delinquency by reducing risk and enhancing protection;
2. early intervention with pre-delinquent and child delinquents and their families;
3. immediate intervention for first-time delinquent offenders (misdemeanors

and nonviolent felonies) and nonserious repeat offenders;
4. intermediate sanctions for first-time serious or violent offenders, including intensive supervision for SVC offenders;
5. secure corrections for the most SVC offenders; and
6. post-release supervision.

Theoretical Support for the Comprehensive Strategy

The key question addressed here is this: How does the CS target SVC juvenile offenders, as its title suggests? Recent theoretical work on juvenile delinquency development demonstrates the value of focusing research and intervention efforts on these three offender career subtypes.

Current developmental theories of delinquency and crime have grown out of a unique sociological perspective for examining human experiences over time that is often referred to as the life-course perspective (Elder, 1997). Developmental criminology (Le Blanc & Loeber, 1998; Loeber & Le Blanc, 1990) has adopted the life-course perspective for the study of offender careers. As Le Blanc and Loeber (1998, p. 117) explain, developmental criminology is the study of within-individual changes in offending over time – characterized, for example, by initiation, escalation, and desistance in delinquent/criminal careers. The "developmental" perspective focuses studies in two areas: first, the age links to within-individual changes in offending, and second, risk or causal factors that explain changes in offending patterns over time.

Loeber and his colleagues (Loeber, Wei, Stouthamer-Loeber, Huizinga, & Thornberry, 1999) discovered an empirically based set of three main but overlapping pathways (offense patterns) in the development of delinquency from childhood to adolescence among boys: authority conflict (pre-delinquent offenses), the covert pathway (property offenses), and the overt pathway (violent offenses). Gang involvement (gang fighting) is an intermediate step in Loeber's overt pathway. The pathways are hierarchical in that those who have advanced to the most serious behavior in each of the pathways usually have displayed persistent problem behavior characteristics of the earlier stages in each pathway. This model has gained substantial empirical support; has been replicated in multiple data sets for White, Hispanic, and African American boys; and mostly fits the development of antisocial girls (Loeber, Slot, & Stouthamer-Loeber, 2007).

Thornberry's (2005) developmental interaction theory also has enormous practical value. This elegant theory specifies the relative influence of risk and protective factors that account for continuity and change in delinquency (and also prosocial careers) over the child and adolescent years. There are also other competing theories of juvenile delinquency that are not grounded explicitly in developmental theory. Farrington's (2003) Integrated Cognitive Antisocial Potential Theory integrates propositions from numerous other theories, including strain, control, learning, labeling, and rational choice. Farrington ingeniously integrates factors that account for both short- and long-term differences in offending, in an explicit set of testable propositions. Agnew's (2005; this volume, Chapter 26) general theory is another case in point. He brilliantly integrates the essential tenets from social learning, social control, strain, labeling, bio-psychological, and other theories into a single, unified theory that carries enormous plausibility. Each of these theoretical frameworks would have great utility in expanding the CS to encompass adult crime and the criminal justice system.

Loeber's explicit pathways model is particularly well suited for diffusion of research into practice within the juvenile justice system. As noted earlier, Loeber's covert and overt pathways correspond to the serious and violent offense categories, respectively. Taking into account offense progression in the three pathways over time, his theoretical model also accounts for chronic offending. These three offense categories are predominant in the statutory codes that juvenile court and correctional agencies

implement; that is, serious, violent, and chronic offenses. These agencies also use formal risk and needs assessment instruments to guide offender placements and develop comprehensive treatment plans that aim to forestall further progression in delinquent careers and promote desistance. These observations explain the enormous appeal that Loeber's three-pathway model has for juvenile justice officials and practitioners. The next step in the practical application of Loeber's model is to link predictors (risk factors) with offenders who advance in the covert (serious-chronic) and overt (violent-chronic) pathways, and this work is underway, under his direction.

Empirical Support for the Comprehensive Strategy

The Comprehensive Strategy guides jurisdictions in developing a continuum of responses that parallel offender careers, beginning with primary prevention and followed by early intervention and graduated sanctions linked with rehabilitative services. In the course of building such a continuum, a community can organize an array of programs that correspond with further development of offender careers over time. A continuum of programs aimed at different points along the offender pathways has a much better chance of succeeding than a single intervention. The Comprehensive Strategy has guided development of a continuum of effective delinquency prevention and reduction services and sanctions in several sites (Howell, 2003a; 2003b, pp. 293–300).

A plethora of evidence-based program services for reducing both general delinquency and serious and violent delinquency have been identified (Howell, 2003b; Howell & Lipsey, 2004; Lipsey, 1995; Lipsey & Wilson, 1998), refuting the myth promulgated in the literature that juvenile justice programs are ineffective (see Bilchik, 1998; Feld, 1998; Hsia & Beyer, 2000; Schwartz, Weiner, & Enosh, 1998).[16] Moreover, it may come as a surprise to some readers that juvenile delinquency treatment and rehabilitation programs are as effective – if not more so – with SVC offenders than with other less serious and violent youths (Lipsey & Wilson, 1998). A new method is available for strengthening programs across the entire continuum, Lipsey's Standardized Program Evaluation Protocol (see Howell & Lipsey, 2004). It contains program fidelity guidelines and scores programs in accordance with their correspondence to them, indicating areas that need improvement. This tool is based on Lipsey's meta-analyses of more than 500 well-evaluated juvenile justice programs across the entire continuum.[17]

In communities where gang problems exist, a continuum of gang programs and strategies should be an integral part of the community's strategy for preventing and reducing juvenile delinquency. Because youngsters involved in serious property crimes, violent delinquency, and gang involvement share common risk factors (cf. Howell & Egley, 2005 and Hawkins et al., 1998), this approach would increase localities' capacity to address multiple risk factors for delinquency and gang membership simultaneously. It would also increase their capacity to intervene at multiple points in individuals' criminal career progression – from minor misconduct to delinquency, to gang involvement, and to SVC offender careers. Gang members tend to evidence more risk factors and to demonstrate elevated risk in multiple domains (Howell & Egley, 2005). Gangs also support and reinforce criminal tendencies and norms. Thus, for optimal delinquency reduction, prevention programs should target youths at risk of delinquency and gang involvement; intervention programs should provide sanctions and needed services for delinquent youths and give priority attention to youngsters who are actively involved in gangs but not yet embedded in a criminal gang lifestyle to separate them from gangs; and law enforcement suppression strategies should target the most violent offenders, violent gangs and criminally active gang members.

A number of promising and evidence-based gang programs have been identified that provide more structured control and treatment settings for gang-involved youths along the entire continuum (Howell, 2000; 2003b, pp. 91–100).[18] Space limitations preclude extensive discussion of programs here. For illustrative purposes, we highlight four programs that can be arrayed along the juvenile justice continuum and address both delinquency and gang involvement.

The Montreal Preventive Treatment Program was designed to prevent antisocial behavior among boys (ages 7 to 9) of low socioeconomic status who had displayed disruptive problem behavior in kindergarten (Tremblay, Masse, Pagani, & Vitaro, 1996). This program demonstrated that a combination of parent training and childhood skills development can reduce delinquency and steer children away from gangs. An evaluation of the program showed both short- and long-term gains, including less substance use, less delinquency, and less gang involvement at age 15 (Tremblay et al., 1996).

The San Diego County Breaking Cycles program is a unique one that integrates the prevention and graduated sanctions components of the Comprehensive Strategy framework. The secondary prevention component targets youths who have not yet entered the juvenile justice system, but display problem behaviors (chronic disobedience to parents, curfew violations, repeated truancy, running away from home, drug and alcohol use, and other behavior problems). The graduated sanctions component assigns juvenile offenders to one of three graduated options (home placement, a community-based program, or a juvenile correctional institution) for variable lengths of time. A family-centered, strengths-based comprehensive treatment plan promotes accountability, rehabilitation, and community protection. The Breaking Cycles program effectively reduced delinquency among the overall group of high-risk youths, and the graduated sanctions component was effective in keeping offenders from progressing to more SVC delinquency (Burke & Pennell, 2001). Although gang members were included in the program, outcomes were not evaluated separately for them.

The Multidisciplinary Team Home Run (MDT) in San Bernardino County,

California, is an intermediate sanction and service program for both gang and nongang first-time offenders that is anchored in five multidisciplinary teams strategically located in separate cities. Each team consists of four professionals: a probation officer, a licensed therapist, a social worker, and a public health nurse. The high-risk youthful offenders and their families are referred by probation officers. Each team provides intensive and comprehensive wraparound services to high-risk youth offenders and their families for 6 months. An evaluation (Schram & Gaines, 2005) compared outcomes for randomly selected gang and nongang offenders. Both groups showed significant improvements on school measures (increased grade point average, lower number of school absences, and reduced number of suspensions); family functioning; alcohol and substance abuse; and reported arrests following the program.

One correctional post-release program has produced very worthwhile reductions in delinquency and gang involvement: the Lifeskills '95 program, which was implemented in California's San Bernardino and Riverside Counties (Josi & Sechrest, 1999). This program was designed for high-risk, chronic juvenile offenders released from the California Youth Authority. In addition to reintegrating these youths into communities, the Lifeskills '95 program aimed to reduce their need for gang participation and affiliation as a support mechanism. An evaluation of the program found that participating youths were far less likely to have frequent contacts with former gang associates than were members of the control group. In addition, youths assigned to the control group were about twice as likely as program participants to have been arrested, to be unemployed, and to have abused drugs and/or alcohol frequently since their release.

A Comprehensive Gang Model

A Comprehensive Gang Prevention, Intervention, and Suppression Model is available for communities' use in addressing gang problems (Spergel, 1995; Spergel & Curry,

1990, 1993). When it was well implemented in three sites (in Chicago; Mesa, Arizona, and Riverside, California), the Comprehensive Gang Model effectively guided these communities in developing services and strategies that contributed to reductions in gang violence and drug-related offenses[19] (Spergel, 2006; Spergel et al., 2003; Spergel, Wa, & Sosa, 2004). The combination of prevention, intervention, and suppression strategies and programs used in these sites proved effective; in contrast, the use of single strategies such as suppression tactics continue to show mixed results (Bynum & Varano, 2003; Decker, 2003). It is also important to recognize the limited applicability of suppression for adolescent gangs. "Communities will not support indiscriminate, highly aggressive, crackdowns that put nonviolent youth at risk of being swept into the criminal justice system" (Braga, 2004, p. 19).

An assessment protocol is available that any community can use to assess its gang problem and guide its development of a continuum of gang prevention, intervention, and suppression programs and strategies (National Youth Gang Center, 2002a). Resource materials that assist communities in developing an integrated action plan to implement the comprehensive gang model are also available (National Youth Gang Center, 2002b). For optimal effectiveness, gang programs and strategies need to be integrated with a community's Comprehensive Strategy for delinquency prevention and reduction.

Conclusion

Juvenile delinquency is not out of control. Juvenile justice systems are surprisingly effective in combating delinquency but there is much room for improvements. Building a continuum of effective juvenile justice programs requires a data-driven and research-based process. Community risk and resource assessments are needed to target the most prevalent risk factors with prevention programs. Juvenile justice system agencies must assess their delinquent populations for risk and treatment needs and strengths and classify and position offenders within a structured system of graduated sanctions that best protect the public and match offenders with programs that best address their treatment needs. Finally, evidence-based services must be used. User-friendly tools for achieving system-wide continuum building and research-based programming are now available.

Notes

1. Public health scientists use the word "epidemic" to refer to particular health problems that affect numbers of the population above expected levels, but they do not specify what constitutes an epidemic level.
2. Only one third of 1% of all juveniles are arrested for violent offenses (Snyder, 2000). Even at the height of the so-called juvenile crime wave (1993), only about 6% of all juvenile arrests were for violent crimes, and about two tenths of 1% were for homicide (McCord, Widom, & Crowell, 2001).
3. For example, adults were responsible for two thirds of the increase in murders and for three fourths of the increase in violent crimes from 1988 to 1992 (Snyder & Sickmund, 1995, p. 110).
4. Murder, forcible rape, robbery, and aggravated assault.
5. There are a number of important drawbacks to using UCR data as a measure of crime (McCord et al., 2001, pp. 26–29; Snyder, 2004). For one thing, arrest and clearance data give a very different picture of the juvenile contribution to crime. A crime is considered "cleared" if someone is formally charged with the crime. To use the UCR data properly, one must understand this difference (for an excellent illustration, see Snyder & Sickmund, 1999, pp. 113–114).
6. The age range of youth gang members is approximately 12 to 24.
7. See Howell, 2003b, pp. 15–19, and Zimring, 1998, for detailed critiques of DiIulio's super-predator myth and the doomsday projection. Blunstein, DiIulio, Fox, and Wilson each made the mistake of assuming a direct correlation between population size and crime rates. As Cook and Laub (1998) have shown, the size of the juvenile popu-

lation "is of little help in predicting violence rates" (p. 59).
8. Snyder, 2004; *OJJDP Statistical Briefing Book:* http://ojjdp.ncjrs.org/ojstatbb/crime/JAR_Display.asp?ID = qa0520120050228.
9. Harms & Snyder, 2004; *OJJDP Statistical Briefing Book:* http://ojjdp.ncjrs.org/ojstatbb/crime/JAR_Display.asp?ID = qa0520220050228.
10. DiIulio reportedly now regrets using the super-predator term, and Wilson has acknowledged that the forecast was erroneous.
11. House Committee on Economic and Educational Opportunities, Subcommittee on Early Childhood, Youth and Families, Hearings on the Juvenile Justice and Delinquency Prevention Act, Serial No. 104–68, 104th Cong., 2d sess, 1998, p. 90 (statement of Rep. Bill McCollum, Chairman, Subcommittee on Crime, House Judiciary Committee).
12. The term "moral panic" (Cohen, 1980) refers to circumstances in which the perceived threat from some group or situation is greatly exaggerated compared with the actual threat.
13. These moral panics have occurred regularly in the United States, about every 12 or 15 years, in what has been dubbed the "cycle of juvenile justice," the swinging of the pendulum between rehabilitation and punishment (Bernard, 1992).
14. Serious scholars have observed that beneath the traditional instrumental rationales for transfer lie ritualized sacrifice of children to the criminal courts and prisons to ensure the well-being of the state, a form of restorative justice at the community level (Titus, 2005).
15. Other issues have been raised concerning the role of prosecutors and legislatures. As Feld (1998) notes, "Prosecutorial waiver suffers from all of the vagaries of individualized discretion and without even the redeeming virtues of formal criteria, written reasons, an evidentiary record, or appellate review. Legislative offense exclusion suffers from rigidity, over-inclusiveness, and politicians' demagogic tendency to get tough" (p. 244). In addition, prosecutors' actions and the conduct of criminal courts are disturbing to many observers (Center for Public Integrity, 2003; Liebman, Fagan, & West, 2000; Zimring, 1998).
16. Some observers such as Feld and Schwartz have even suggested abolishing the juvenile

court, but it is widely accepted that this proposal amounts to nonsense (see Howell, 2003b, p. 162; Tanenhaus, 2004).

17. Papers about the meta-analysis work and related issues can be downloaded from www.vanderbilt.edu/cerm.

18. Others are available at the National Youth Gang Center Web site, www.iir/nygc.

19. Drug-related arrests of program clients were not reduced significantly in Riverside.

References

Agnew. R. (2005). *Why do criminals offend? A general theory of crime and delinquency*. Los Angeles: Roxbury Publishing Company.

American Civil Liberties Union of Michigan. (2004). *Second chances: Juveniles serving life without parole in Michigan*. Detroit, MI.

Associated Press. (1996, February 18). *Expert warns of U.S. "bloodbath"* (AP wire story).

Bennett, W. J., DiIulio, J. J., Jr., & Walters, J. P. (1996). *Body count: Moral poverty and how to win America's war against crime and drugs*. New York: Simon & Schuster.

Bernard, T. J. (1992). *The cycle of juvenile justice*. New York: Oxford University Press.

Bilchik, S. (1998). *A juvenile justice system for the 21st century* (Juvenile Justice Bulletin). Washington, DC: U.S. Department of Justice, Office of Juvenile Justice and Delinquency Prevention.

Bishop, D. M., & Frazier, C. E. (2000). Consequences of transfer. In J. Fagan & F. E. Zimring (Eds.), *The changing borders of juvenile justice: Transfer of adolescents to the criminal court* (pp. 227–276). Chicago: University of Chicago Press.

Block, C. R., Christakos, A., Jacob, A., & Przybylski, R. (1996). *Street gangs and crime: Patterns and trends in Chicago*. Chicago: Illinois Criminal Justice Information Authority.

Blumstein, A. (1995a, August). Violence by young people: Why the deadly nexus? *National Institute of Justice Journal, 229*, 1–9.

Blumstein, A. (1995b). Youth violence, guns, and the illicit-drug industry. *Journal of Criminal Law and Criminology, 86*, 10–36.

Blumstein, A. (1996). *Youth violence, guns, and the illicit drug markets* Research Preview. Washington, DC: U.S. Department of Justice, National Institute of Justice.

Boyle, P. (2005). Behind the death penalty ban. *Youth Today, 14*(4), 1, 36–38.

Braga. A. A. (2004). *Gun violence among serious young offenders* (Problem-Specific Guides Series no. 23). Washington, DC: Office of Community Oriented Policing Services.

Braga, A. A., Kennedy, D. M., & Tita, G. E. (2002). New approaches to the strategic prevention of gang and group-involved violence. In C. R. Huff (Ed.), *Gangs in America III* (pp. 271–285). Thousand Oaks, CA: Sage.

Brown, J., & Langan, P. (1998). *State court sentencing of convicted felons, 1994*. Washington, DC: U.S. Department of Justice, Bureau of Justice Statistics.

Building Blocks for Youth. (2000). *Youth crime/adult time: Is justice served?* Washington, DC.

Burke, C., & Pennell, S. (2001). *Breaking Cycles evaluation: A comprehensive approach to youthful offenders*. San Diego: San Diego Association of Governments.

Butts, J. A. (1999, May). Feeding kids to the monster. *Youth Today*, 23.

Bynum, T. S., & Varano, S. P. (2003). The anti-gang initiative in Detroit: An aggressive enforcement approach to gangs. In S. H. Decker (Ed.), *Policing gangs and youth violence* (pp. 214–238). Belmont, CA: Wadsworth/Thompson Learning.

Center for Public Integrity (2003). *Harmful error: Investigating America's local prosecutors*. Washington, DC.

Cohen, S. (1980). *Folk devils and moral panics: The creation of the mods and rockers*. New York: Basil Blackwell.

Cook, P. J., & Laub, J. H. (1998). The unprecedented epidemic of youth violence. In M. Tonry & M. H. Moore (Eds.), *Youth violence* (pp. 27–64). Chicago: University of Chicago Press.

Cook, P. J., & Ludwig. (2006). The social costs of gun ownership. *Journal of Public Economics, 90*(1–2), 379–391.

Curry, G. D. (2004). *Youth gang homicide trends in the National Youth Gang Survey*. Tallahassee, FL: National Youth Gang Center.

Decker, S. H. (Ed.). (2003). *Policing gangs and youth violence*. Belmont, CA: Wadsworth/Thompson Learning.

Decker, S. H., & Van Winkle, B. (1996). *Life in the gang: Family, friends, and violence*. New York: Cambridge University Press.

DiIulio, J. J., Jr. (1995a, November 27). The coming of the super-predators. *Weekly Standard*, p. 23.

DiIulio, J. J., Jr. (1995b). Arresting ideas. *Policy Review, 74*, 12–16.

DiIulio, J. J., Jr. (1996, Spring). They're coming: Florida's youth crime bomb. *Impact*, 25–27.

Dorfman, L., & Schiraldi, V. (2001). *Off balance: Youth, race, and crime in the news*. Washington, DC: Building Blocks for Youth.

Eddy, P., Sabogal, H., & Walden, S. (1988). *The cocaine wars*. New York: W.W. Norton.

Egley, A. E., Jr., Howell, J. C., & Major, A. K. (2004). Recent patterns of gang problems in the United States: Results from the 1996–2002 National Youth Gang Survey. In F. Esbensen, S. G. Tibbetts, & L. Gaines (Eds.), *American youth gangs at the millennium* (pp. 90–108). Long Grove, IL: Waveland Press.

Egley, A. Jr., & Major, A. K. (2003). *Highlights of the 2001 National Youth Gang Survey* (Fact Sheet # 2003–01). Washington, DC: U.S. Department of Justice, Office of Juvenile Justice and Delinquency Prevention.

Elder, G. H., Jr. (1997). The life course and human development. In R. M. Lerner (Ed.), *Handbook of child psychology. Volume 1: Theoretical models of human development* (pp. 939–991). New York: Wiley.

Elliott, D. S. (1994). *Youth violence: An overview*. Boulder, CO: Center for the Study and Prevention of Violence.

Esbensen, F., & Huizinga, D. (1993). Gangs, drugs, and delinquency in a survey of urban youth. *Criminology, 31*(4), 565–589.

Fagan, J. (1995). Separating the men from the boys: The comparative advantage of juvenile versus criminal court sanctions on recidivism among adolescent felony offenders. In J. C. Howell, B. Krisberg, J. D. Hawkins, & J. J. Wilson (Eds.), *Sourcebook on serious, violent and chronic juvenile offenders* (pp. 238–274). Thousand Oaks, CA: Sage.

Farrington, D. P. (2003). Developmental and life-course criminology: Key theoretical and empirical issues – The 2002 Sutherland Award Address. *Criminology, 41*(2), 221–255.

Feld, B. C. (1998). Juvenile and criminal justice systems' responses to youth. In M. Tonry & M. H. Moore (Eds.), *Youth violence* (pp. 189–262). Chicago: University of Chicago Press.

Fox, J. A. (1996a, October 10). The calm before the crime wave storm. *Los Angeles Times*, B9.

Fox, J. A. (1996b). *Trends in juvenile violence: A report to the United States Attorney General on current and future rates of juvenile offending*. Washington, DC: Bureau of Justice Statistics.

Goode, E., & Ben-Yehuda, N. (1994). *Moral panics: The social construction of deviance*. Cambridge, MA: Blackwell.

Grossman, D. C., Mueller, B. A., Riedy, C., Dowd, M. D., Villaveces, A., Prodzinski, J., et al. (2005). Gun storage practices and risk of youth suicide and unintentional firearm injuries. *Journal of the American Medical Association, 293*, 707–714.

Griffin, P. (2003). *Trying and sentencing juveniles as adults: An analysis of state transfer and blended sentencing laws* (Special Project Bulletin). Washington, DC: Office of Juvenile Justice and Delinquency Prevention.

Gugliotta, G., & Leen, J. (1989). *Kings of cocaine*. New York: Simon & Schuster.

Hagan, J., & Foster, H. (2000). Making corporate and criminal America less violent: Public norms and structural reforms. *Contemporary Sociology, 29*(1), 44–53.

Harms, P. D., & Snyder, H. N. (2004). *Trends in the murder of juveniles: 1980–2000* (Juvenile Justice Bulletin). Washington, DC: U.S. Department of Justice, Office of Juvenile Justice and Delinquency Prevention.

Hartman, D. A., & Golub, A. (1999). The social construction of the crack epidemic in the print media. *Journal of Psychoactive Drugs, 31*(4), 423–433.

Hawkins, J. D., Herrenkohl, T. I., Farrington, D. P., Brewer, D., Catalano, R. F., & Harachi, T. W. (1998). A review of predictors of youth violence. In R. Loeber & D. P. Farrington (Eds.), *Serious and violent juvenile offenders: Risk factors and successful interventions* (pp. 106–146). Thousand Oaks, CA: Sage.

Hill, K. G., Lui, C., & Hawkins, J. D. (2001). *Early precursors of gang membership: A study of Seattle youth* (Juvenile Justice Bulletin). Washington, DC: U.S. Department of Justice, Office of Juvenile Justice and Delinquency Prevention.

Howell, J. C. (1996). Juvenile transfers to the criminal justice system: State-of-the-art. *Law and Policy, 18*, 17–60.

Howell, J. C. (1999). Youth gang homicides: A literature review. *Crime and Delinquency, 45*(2), 208–241.

Howell, J. C. (2000). *Youth gang programs and strategies*. Washington, DC: U.S. Department of Justice, Office of Juvenile Justice and Delinquency Prevention.

Howell, J. C. (2003a). Diffusing research into practice using the Comprehensive Strategy for Serious, Violent, and Chronic Juvenile Offenders. *Youth Violence and Juvenile*

Justice: An Interdisciplinary Journal, 1(3), 219–245.

Howell, J. C. (2003b). *Preventing and reducing juvenile delinquency: A comprehensive framework.* Thousand Oaks, CA: Sage.

Howell, J. C., & Decker, S. H. (1999). *The youth gangs, drugs, and violence connection* (Juvenile Justice Bulletin, Youth Gang Series). Washington, DC: U.S. Department of Justice, Office of Juvenile Justice and Delinquency Prevention.

Howell, J. C., & Egley, A., Jr. (2005). Moving risk factors into developmental theories of gang membership. *Youth Violence and Juvenile Justice, 3*(4), 334–354.

Howell, J. C., Egley, A., Jr., & Gleason, D. K. (2002). *Modern day youth gangs.* (Juvenile Justice Bulletin, Youth Gang Series). Washington, DC: U.S. Department of Justice, Office of Juvenile Justice and Delinquency Prevention.

Howell, J. C., Krisberg, B., & Jones, M. (1995). Trends in juvenile crime and youth violence. In J. C. Howell, B. Krisberg, J. D. Hawkins, & J. J. Wilson (Eds.), *Sourcebook on serious, violent, and chronic juvenile offenders* (pp. 1–35). Newbury Park, CA: Sage.

Howell, J. C., & Lipsey, M. W. (2004). A practical approach to evaluating and improving juvenile justice programs. *Juvenile and Family Court Journal, 55*(1), 35–48.

Howell, M. Q. (2004). *A comparative analysis of judicial waiver trends: What can we learn from the states?* Unpublished master's thesis, University of South Carolina.

Hsia, H. M., & Beyer, M. (2000). *System change through state challenge activities: Approaches and products* (Juvenile Justice Bulletin). Washington, DC: U.S. Department of Justice, Office of Juvenile Justice and Delinquency Prevention.

Huizinga, D., Weiher, A. W., Espiritu, R., & Esbensen, F. (2003). Delinquency and crime: Some highlights from the Denver Youth Survey. In T. P. Thornberry & M. D. Krohn (Eds.), *Taking stock of delinquency: An overview of findings from contemporary longitudinal studies* (pp. 47–91). New York: Kluwer Academic/Plenum Publishers.

Josi, D., & Sechrest, D. K. (1999). A pragmatic approach to parole aftercare: Evaluation of a community reintegration program for high-risk youthful offenders. *Justice Quarterly, 16*(1), 51–80.

Klein, M. W. (1995). *The American street gang.* New York: Oxford University Press.

Kurlychek, M. C., & Johnson, B. D. (2004). The juvenile penalty: A comparison of juvenile and young adult sentencing outcomes in criminal court. *Criminology, 42*(2), 485–517.

Langan, P. A., & Levin, D. J. (2002). *Recidivism of prisoners released in 1994* (Special Report). Washington, DC: U.S. Department of Justice, Bureau of Justice Statistics.

Le Blanc, M., & Loeber, R. (1998). Developmental criminology updated. In M. Tonry (Ed.), *Crime and justice: A review of research* (pp. 115–198). Chicago: University of Chicago Press.

Liebman, J. S., Fagan, J., & West, V. (2000). *A broken system: Error rates in capital cases, 1973–1995.* New York: School of Law, Columbia University.

Lipsey, M. W. (1995). What do we learn from 400 research studies on the effectiveness of treatment with juvenile delinquents? In J. McGuire (Ed.), *What works? Reducing reoffending* (pp. 63–78). New York: John Wiley.

Lipsey, M. W., & Wilson, D. B. (1998). Effective interventions with serious juvenile offenders: A synthesis of research. In R. Loeber & D. P. Farrington (Eds.), *Serious and violent juvenile offenders: Risk factors and successful interventions* (pp. 313–345). Thousand Oaks, CA: Sage.

Loeber, R., & Farrington, D. P. (Eds.). (1998). *Serious and violent juvenile offenders: Risk factors and successful interventions.* Thousand Oaks, CA: Sage.

Loeber, R., & Farrington, D. P. (Eds.). (2001). *Child delinquents: Development, intervention, and service needs.* Thousand Oaks, CA: Sage.

Loeber, R., & Le Blanc, M. (1990). Toward a developmental criminology. In M. Tonry & N. Morris (Eds.), *Crime and justice: A review of research* (pp. 375–473). Chicago: University of Chicago Press.

Loeber, R., Slot, W., & Stouthamer-Loeber, M. (2007). A cumulative, three-dimensional, development model of serious delinquency. In P.-O. Wikstrom & R. Sampson (Eds.), *The explanation of crime: Context, mechanisms and development series* (pp. 153–194). Cambridge, UK: Cambridge University Press.

Loeber, R., Wei, E., Stouthamer-Loeber, M., Huizinga, D., & Thornberry, T. P. (1999). Behavioral antecedents to serious and violent offending: Joint analyses from the Denver Youth Survey, Pittsburgh Youth Study and the Rochester Youth Development Study.

Studies on Crime and Crime Prevention, 8(2), 245–263.

Ludwig, J. (2005). Better gun enforcement, less crime. *Criminology and Public Policy, 4*(4), 677–716.

Malcolm, J. L. (2002). *Guns and violence: The English experience.* Cambridge, MA: Harvard University Press.

Males, M. A. (1996). *The scapegoat generation: America's war on adolescents.* Monroe, ME: Common Courage Press.

Manhattan Institute, Center for Civic Innovation. (1999). Broken windows. In *Probation: The next step in fighting crime.* New York.

Maxson, C. L., Curry, G. D., & Howell, J. C. (2002). Youth gang homicides in the United States in the 1990s. In W. Reed & S. Decker (Eds.), *Responding to gangs: Evaluation and research* (pp. 107–137). Washington, DC: U.S. Department of Justice, National Institute of Justice.

Mears, D. P. (2003). Sentencing guidelines and the transformation of juvenile justice in the 21st century. In A. R. Roberts (Ed.), *Critical issues in criminal justice* (pp. 235–243). Thousand Oaks, CA: Sage.

McCord, J., Widom, C. S., & Crowell, N. A. (Eds.). (2001). *Juvenile crime, juvenile justice.* Washington, DC: National Academy Press.

Moone, J. (1994). *Juvenile victimization: 1987–1992* (Fact Sheet no. 17). Washington, DC: U.S. Department of Justice, Office of Juvenile Justice and Delinquency Prevention.

National Youth Gang Center. (2002a). *Assessing your community's youth gang problem.* Washington, DC: U.S. Department of Justice, Office of Juvenile Justice and Delinquency Prevention.

National Youth Gang Center. (2002b). *OJJDP comprehensive gang model: Planning for implementation.* Washington, DC: U.S. Department of Justice, Office of Juvenile Justice and Delinquency Prevention.

Puritz, P., & Scali, M. A. (1998). *Beyond the walls: Improving conditions of confinement for youth in custody.* Washington, DC: U.S. Department of Justice, Office of Juvenile Justice and Delinquency Prevention.

Puzzanchera, C., Stahl, A. L., Finnegan, T. A., Tierney, N., & Snyder, H. N. (2003). *Juvenile Court statistics: 1998.* Washington, DC: U.S. Department of Justice, Office of Juvenile Justice and Delinquency Prevention.

Reich, K., Culross, P. L., & Behrman, R. E. (2002). Children, youth and gun violence: Analysis and recommendations. *The Future of Children, 12*(2), 5–19.

Roush, D., & McMillen, M. (2000). *Construction, operations, and staff training for juvenile confinement facilities* (Juvenile Accountability Incentive Block Grants Program Bulletin). Washington, DC: U.S. Department of Justice, Office of Juvenile Justice and Delinquency Prevention.

Schram, P. J., & Gaines, L. K. (2005). Examining delinquent nongang members and delinquent gang members: A comparison of juvenile probationers at intake and outcomes. *Youth Violence and Juvenile Justice, 3*(2), 99–115.

Schwartz, I. M., Weiner, N. A., & Enosh, G. (1998). Nine lives and then some: Why the juvenile court will not roll over and die. *Wake Forest Law Review, 33*(3), 533–552.

Snyder, H. N. (2000). *Juvenile arrests 1999* (Juvenile Justice Bulletin). Washington, DC: U.S. Department of Justice, Office of Juvenile Justice and Delinquency Prevention.

Snyder, H. N. (2004). *Juvenile arrests 2002* (Juvenile Justice Bulletin). Washington, DC: U.S. Department of Justice, Office of Juvenile Justice and Delinquency Prevention.

Snyder, H. N., & Sickmund, M. (1995). *Juvenile offenders and victims: A national report.* Washington, DC: U.S. Department of Justice, Office of Juvenile Justice and Delinquency Prevention.

Snyder, H. N., & Sickmund, M. (1999). *Juvenile offenders and victims: 1999 national report.* Washington, DC: U.S. Department of Justice, Office of Juvenile Justice and Delinquency Prevention.

Spergel, I. A. (1995). *The youth gang problem.* New York: Oxford University Press.

Spergel, I. A. (2006). *Reducing youth gang violence: The Little Village Gang Project in Chicago.* Lanham, MD: AltaMira Press.

Spergel, I. A., & Curry, G. D. (1990). Strategies and perceived agency effectiveness in dealing with the youth gang problem. In C. R. Huff (Ed.), *Gangs in America* (pp. 288–309). Newbury Park, CA: Sage Publications.

Spergel, I. A., & Curry, G. D. (1993). The National Youth Gang Survey: A research and development process. In A. Goldstein & C. R. Huff (Eds.), *The gang intervention handbook* (pp. 359–400). Champaign, IL: Research Press.

Spergel, I. A., Wa, K. M., Choi, S., Grossman, S. F., Jacob, A., Spergel, A., et al. (2003).

Evaluation of the Gang Violence Reduction Project in Little Village: Final report summary. Chicago: School of Social Service Administration, University of Chicago.

Spergel, I. A., Wa, K. M., & Sosa, R. V. (2004). *The Comprehensive, Community-Wide Gang Program Model: Success and failure.* Chicago: School of Social Service Administration, University of Chicago.

Stahl, A. L. (2001). *Delinquency cases in juvenile court, 1998* (Fact Sheet no. 2001–31). Washington, DC: U.S. Department of Justice, Office of Juvenile Justice and Delinquency Prevention.

Tanenhaus, D. S. (2004). *Juvenile justice in the making.* New York: Oxford University Press.

Thornberry, T. P. (1998). Membership in youth gangs and involvement in serious and violent offending. In R. Loeber & D. P. Farrington (Eds.), *Serious and violent juvenile offenders: Risk factors and successful interventions* (pp. 147–166). Thousand Oaks, CA: Sage Publications.

Thornberry, T. P. (2005). Explaining multiple patterns of offending across the life course and across generations. *Annals of the American Academy of Political and Social Science, 602,* 156–195.

Thornberry, T. P., Krohn, M. D., Lizotte, A. J., & Chard-Wierschem, D. (1993). The role of juvenile gangs in facilitating delinquent behavior. *Journal of Research in Crime and Delinquency, 30*(1), 55–87.

Thornberry, T. P., Krohn, M. D., Lizotte, A. J., Smith, C. A., & Tobin, K. (2003). *Gangs and delinquency in developmental perspective.* New York: Cambridge University Press.

Titus, J. J. (2005). Juvenile transfers as ritual sacrifice: Legally constructing the child scapegoat. *Youth Violence and Juvenile Justice, 3*(2), 116–132.

Travis, J., & Petersilia, J. (2001). Reentry reconsidered: A new look at an old question. *Crime and Delinquency, 47,* 291–313.

Tremblay, R. E., Masse, L., Pagani, L., & Vitaro, F. (1996). From childhood physical aggression to adolescent maladjustment: The Montreal Prevention Experiment. In R. D. Peters & R. J. McMahon (Eds.), *Preventing childhood disorders, substance abuse, and delinquency* (pp. 268–298). Thousand Oaks, CA: Sage.

U.S. Department of Health and Human Services. (2001). *Youth violence: A report of the Surgeon General.* Rockville, MD: U.S. Department of Health and Human Services.

Wilson, J. J., & Howell, J. C. (1993). *A comprehensive strategy for serious, violent and chronic juvenile offenders.* Washington, DC: Office of Juvenile Justice and Delinquency Prevention.

Wilson, J. Q. (1995). Crime and public policy. In J. Q. Wilson & J. Petersilia (Eds.), *Crime* (pp. 489–507). San Francisco: ICS Press.

Winner, L., Lanza-Kaduce, L., Bishop, D. M., & Frazier, C. E. (1997). The transfer of juveniles to criminal court: Reexamining recidivism over the long term. *Crime and Delinquency, 43*(4), 548–563.

Zimring, F. E. (1998). *American youth violence.* New York: Oxford University Press.

Zimring, F. E. (2002). The common thread: Diversion in the jurisprudence of juvenile courts. In M. K. Rosenheim, F. E. Zimring, D. S. Tanenhaus, & B. Dohrn (Eds.), *A century of juvenile justice* (pp. 142–157). Chicago: University of Chicago Press.

CHAPTER 26

Strain Theory and Violent Behavior

Robert S. Agnew

Strain theories state that certain strains or stressors increase the likelihood of violence. These strains upset individuals, creating pressure for corrective action. Some individuals may respond in a violent manner, with violence being used to reduce the strain being experienced and/or obtain revenge against the source of the strain or related targets. For example, individuals may rob someone to get the money they desperately need or assault the person who has been harassing them. Whether individuals cope with strains through violence depends on their ability to engage in legal and violent coping, the costs of violence for them, and their disposition for violence. Violence is defined as the actual, attempted, or threatened use of physical force for the purpose of inflicting unwanted physical or nonphysical harm on another person(s).

These are several versions of strain theory, the most recent and comprehensive being Agnew's general strain theory (Agnew, 1992, 2006). General strain theory (GST) draws heavily on prior strain theories (e.g., Berkowitz, 1989; Cloward & Ohlin, 1960; Cohen, 1955; Elliott, Ageton, & Canter,

1979; Greenberg, 1977; Merton, 1938), as well as on the stress, justice, and emotions literatures. This article focuses on GST, examining (1) the types of strains most likely to lead to violence; (2) why certain strains lead to violence; (3) why some individuals are more likely than others to respond to strains with violence; and (4) how to explain group differences in violence, including age, gender, class, and race/ethnic differences.

The Types of Strains Most Likely to Lead to Violence

Strains refer to events and conditions that are disliked by the individual. There are three major types of strains. First, individuals may lose something they value; for example, their money or property may be stolen, a close friend or family member may die, or a romantic partner may break up with them. Second, individuals may be treated in an aversive or negative manner by others; for example, they may be sexually abused by family members or insulted by peers. Third, individuals may be unable to achieve their goals through legal channels; for example, they may be unable to obtain the money, status, or autonomy they want. Although GST focuses on the individual's personal experiences with strains, certain "vicarious" and "anticipated" strains may also contribute to violence (Agnew, 2002). Vicarious strains refer to strains experienced by others around the individual, like family members and close friends. Anticipated strains refer to the individual's expectation that his or her current strains will continue or that new strains will be experienced.

Many hundreds of specific strains fall into the three major categories of strains listed by GST. GST, however, states that only certain of these strains increase the likelihood of violence (Agnew, 2001). In particular, a strain is most likely to lead to violence when the following occur:

A. The strain is seen as severe or high in magnitude. Strains are more likely to be seen as severe when they are high in degree (e.g., much money is lost, there is much physical injury); they are frequent, recent, of long duration, and expected to continue; and they threaten the core needs, goals, values, activities, and/or identities of the individual.

B. The strain is seen as unjust. Strains are more likely to be seen as unjust when they involve the voluntary and intentional violation of a relevant justice norm.

C. The strain is associated with low social control. That is, the strain does *not* involve close supervision by conventional others, such as parents and teachers; close ties to conventional others; a strong investment in conventional institutions, such as school and work; or the acceptance of conventional beliefs and values. This is the case, for example, with parental rejection. Children who are rejected by their parents generally have weak ties to their parents and are poorly supervised by them. However, this is not the case with that type of strain experienced by professionals who work long hours. This strain is associated with a strong investment in conventional institutions and the acceptance of conventional values.

D. The strain creates some pressure or incentive for violent coping. Certain strains are resolved more easily through violence and resolved less easily through nonviolent channels than are other strains. For example, that type of strain involving a desperate need for money is resolved more easily through violence than is that type involving the inability to achieve educational success. Also, certain strains involve exposure to others who model violence, reinforce violence, or teach beliefs favorable to violence. For example, individuals who experience child abuse are exposed to violent models.

Drawing on these characteristics, Agnew (2001) lists several specific strains that should have a relatively strong effect on violence (and crime more generally). These strains include parental rejection; parental supervision that is erratic, excessive, and/or harsh; child abuse and neglect; negative secondary school experiences, including poor relations with teachers; abusive peer relations, including insults, ridicule, threats, attempts to coerce, and physical assaults; work in the secondary labor market (poorly paid jobs with unpleasant working conditions); chronic unemployment; marital problems, including frequent conflicts and verbal and physical abuse; criminal victimization; homelessness; experiences with race/ethnic and gender-based discrimination; and the inability to achieve certain goals – such as money and masculine status – through legal channels. Data suggest that these strains do increase the likelihood of crime and violence. In fact, certain of these strains – like criminal victimization – are emerging as the most important causes of violence (e.g., Agnew, 1990, 1992, 2001, 2002, 2006; Agnew & Brezina, 1997; Agnew & White, 1992; Aseltine, Gore, & Gordon, 2000; Baron, 2004; Colvin, 2000; Eitle,

2002; Eitle & Turner, 2002; Hagan & McCarthy, 1997; Simons, Chen, Stewart, & Brody, 2003).

Those strains that should have a relatively weak effect on violence include those that are *not* likely to be seen as unjust, such as strains that are the result of reasonable accident, natural causes, or the victim's own behavior; for example, strains that are part of many stressful life-event scales, such as accidents, serious illness, and family members leaving home for school. Still other strains should have a relatively weak effect on violence because they are associated with high social control or little pressure/incentive for violence. Such strains include the burdens associated with the care of conventional others, such as children and sick/disabled spouses (except for family violence); the excessive demands associated with conventional pursuits that provide rewards like high pay and prestige; unpopularity with peers, especially criminal peers; isolation from unsupervised peer activities; and the failure to achieve such goals as educational and occupational success (which imply some commitment to conventional values).

Why Certain Strains Increase the Likelihood of Violence

Certain strains increase the likelihood of violence because they reduce the individual's ability to cope in a legal manner, reduce the perceived costs of violence, and create a disposition for violence. This section first describes how the experience of these strains may lead to a particular incident of violence or a series of related incidents and then describes how the chronic or repeated experience of these strains may create a general predisposition or willingness to engage in violence if provoked or tempted.

Particular Incidents of Violence

The high magnitude of those strains conducive to violence reduces the ability of individuals to cope in a legal manner. It is generally more difficult to cope legally with large rather than small strains. For example, it is more difficult to obtain legally a large rather than small amount of money. Likewise, it is more difficult to ignore repeated abuse than a single, minor slight.

The unjust nature of those strains conducive to violence contributes to anger. This anger, in turn, increases the likelihood of violence. Anger reduces the ability to cope in a legal manner, making it more difficult for the individual to reason with others. Anger also reduces the individual's awareness of and concern for the costs of crime (individuals are "consumed with rage"). Further, anger creates a disposition for violence, fostering the belief that violence is justified (to "right a wrong") and creating a desire for revenge. Two recent studies of GST indicate that strains substantially increase the likelihood that individuals will become angry and that such anger explains much of the effect of strains on crime, including violent crime (Jang & Johnson, 2003; Mazerolle, Piquero, & Capowich, 2003). The larger literature on anger is compatible with these findings (e.g., Averill, 1982).

Strains conducive to violence may also temporarily reduce the individual's level of social control. For example, juveniles who are harshly punished by parents may come to dislike their parents for a brief period, or adults who are treated poorly at work may temporarily reduce their commitment to work. Finally, these strains may temporarily foster the social learning of crime. In particular, certain of these strains – like abuse and criminal victimization – involve exposure to others who model violence. Such exposure may lead individuals to (temporarily) conclude that violence is an appropriate or desirable coping mechanism.

A Predisposition for Violence

Chronic or repeated exposure to strains may create a predisposition for violence. Chronic or repeated strains reduce the ability of individuals to cope in a legal manner, because they tend to exhaust their coping resources and social supports. Chronic or repeated strains may also foster negative emotional *traits*, such as trait anger. Emotional traits are distinct from emotional states, with traits referring to the tendency to experience particular emotions. Someone high in trait anger, for example, tends to get angry a lot. They are upset by a broader range of factors than others and experience more intense anger when upset (Mazerolle et al., 2003). Chronic strains may lead to trait anger partly because they reduce the individual's ability to cope legally, so that new strains are more likely to overwhelm the individual and elicit strong emotional reactions. Several studies indicate that individuals who experience more strains are higher in trait anger and that such anger partly explains the effect of strains on violence (e.g., Agnew, 1985; Aseltine et al., 2000; Brezina, 1998; Mazerolle & Piquero, 1998).

Related to the above, chronic strains may foster personality traits conducive to crime, like low constraint and negative emotionality (Agnew, Brezina, Wright, & Cullen, 2002). Individuals subject to harsh, erratic treatment from parents, teachers, peers, and others may fail to develop self-restraint. In particular, data suggest that individuals develop self-restraint partly as a result of being consistently sanctioned in an appropriate manner when they misbehave (Colvin, 2000; Hay, 2003). Chronic mistreatment by others may also foster certain of the other traits that comprise low constraint and negative emotionality, including a tendency to attribute strains to the malicious behavior of others, little concern for the feelings or rights of others, and an antagonistic interactional style. These traits, in turn, reduce the ability to cope in a legal manner, reduce the awareness of and concern for the costs of violence, and create a predisposition for violence.

Further, chronic strains may reduce the individual's level of social control. Many of the above strains involve negative treatment by conventional others. This type of treatment includes abuse and harsh discipline by parents; demeaning treatment by teachers; conflict with spouses; unemployment; and work in poorly paid, unpleasant jobs. Such strains may reduce the individual's emo-

tional bond to conventional others. They may also reduce the individual's investment in conventional society, including his or her commitment to school and work. In addition, they may reduce the extent to which the individual is supervised and sanctioned by others because they may cause the individual to avoid or retreat from conventional others. These effects, in turn, may reduce the individual's acceptance of conventional values by weakening his or her ties to those who teach such values. Certain studies support these arguments, with data suggesting that chronic or repeated experiences with strains contribute to reductions in social control (Elliott, Huizinga, & Ageton, 1985; Hoffmann & Miller, 1998; Paternoster & Mazerolle, 1994).

In addition, chronic strains may foster the social learning of violence. In particular, the victims of chronic strains are more likely than others to associate with violent peers, who model violence, reinforce violence, and teach beliefs favorable to violence. Those experiencing chronic strains often view violent peers as a solution to their strains. For example, individuals who cannot achieve status through conventional channels may join violent groups like gangs because the gang makes them feel important and respected (see Cohen, 1955). Likewise, individuals who cannot achieve their monetary goals through conventional channels may join violent groups in an effort to better achieve such goals (e.g., through robbery, drug selling). Interviews with gang members support this argument, and quantitative studies indicate that juveniles experiencing more strains are more likely to join violent groups like gangs and delinquent peer groups (Agnew, 2005a; Eitle, Gunkel, & Van Gundy, 2004; Paternoster & Mazerolle, 1994).

Finally, chronic strains may directly foster the belief that violence is a desirable, justifiable, or excusable response to strains. Individuals experiencing chronic strains may believe that they have few legal options for dealing with such strains and that they are being unjustly treated by others. Further, their ties to conventional others and institutions may be weakened as a consequence of their strains. Such individuals may come to adopt beliefs favorable to violence. For example, Anderson (1994) states that many of the residents of poor, inner-city communities respond to the regular assaults on their status and physical safety by adopting the "code of the street," which justifies violent responses to even minor shows of disrespect.

Why Some Individuals Are More Likely to Respond to Strains With Violence

Although certain strains increase the likelihood of violence, most individuals do *not* respond to these strains with violence. Juveniles who are subject to peer abuse, for example, may ignore such abuse, redefine such abuse in a way that minimizes its negative impact, reason with the abusers in an effort to get them to stop, or notify the authorities. GST, therefore, lists those individual and environmental characteristics that increase the likelihood that strained individuals will engage in violence (Agnew, 1992, 2006). These characteristics influence the ability to engage in legal and violent coping, the costs of violence, and the individual's disposition for violence.

Individuals are said to be most likely to cope with strains through violence if the following occur:

A. They have limited skills and resources for legal coping. Among other things, they are low in intelligence, have personality traits like low constraint and negative emotionality (are quick to anger and disposed to aggressive responses), have poor social and problem-solving skills, are low in self-efficacy (believe they lack the ability to cope in a legal manner), and have low socioeconomic status.

B. They have abundant skills and resources for violent coping. Among other things, they have personality traits conducive to violence, like low constraint and negative emotionality. They are of large size,

are physically strong, and possess fighting skills. They have ready access to a gun, and they are high in "violent self-efficacy" (believe they have the ability to successfully engage in violence).

C. They have low levels of conventional social support. That is, others, such as parents, teachers, and employers, are unlikely to provide them with assistance in coping with strains, including information, material assistance, emotional support, and direct assistance.

D. They are low in social control. In particular, they are not closely supervised by others or consistently sanctioned for violence; they have weak ties to conventional others, they have little investment in conventional institutions; and they do not believe that violence is wrong. Those low in social control are more likely to perceive the costs of violence as low.

E. They associate with violent others. These others are more likely to model violence, reinforce violence, and teach beliefs favorable to violence, thereby influencing the individuals' disposition for violence. Others may also provide individuals with assistance in carrying out violent acts, thereby influencing their ability to engage in violence. Further, others may lower the perceived costs of violence, because they are seen engaging successfully in violence and there is strength in numbers.

F. They have beliefs favorable to violence. Although few individuals unconditionally approve of violence, some do believe that violence is desirable, justifiable, or excusable in certain situations. For example, they believe that violence is a justifiable response to a wide range of provocations, including what many would regard as mild insults.

G. They are in situations where the costs of violence are low and the benefits are high. The situational costs of violence are partly a function of the perceived ability of the target to resist violence and the likelihood that others will come to the aid of the target. In this area, Felson (1996) has found that small people seldom attack big people. The benefits of violence include the reduction of strain, as well as social approval from others, including audience members.

There has been some research on the extent to which certain of these factors influence or condition the effect of strains on crime, including violence. This research has produced mixed results (e.g., Agnew et al., 2002; Agnew & White, 1992; Aseltine et al., 2000; Baron, 2004; Mazerolle & Maahs, 2000; Paternoster & Mazerolle, 1994). For example, some studies suggest that strains are more likely to lead to crime and violence among those who associate with delinquent peers, whereas other studies do not. These mixed results may reflect the fact that it is difficult to detect conditioning effects using the survey research methods commonly employed by criminologists (McClelland & Judd, 1993).

Using GST to Explain Group Differences in Violence

Rates of criminal violence are higher among males; adolescents and young adults; lower class individuals; the residents of economically deprived communities; and the members of certain race and ethnic groups, such as African Americans (Agnew, 2005a). GST helps explain such differences by arguing that the members of these groups are more likely to experience strains conducive to violence and to cope with these strains through violence. GST can also help explain patterns of violent offending over the life course, including that "life-course persistent" pattern in which individuals commit relatively high rates of violence over much of their lives.

Gender Differences in Violence

Data suggest that females are as likely or more likely than males to experience strains or stressors. At the same time, there is reason to believe that males are more likely to experience many of those strains that are conducive to violence, including harsh parental discipline, abusive peer relations, criminal victimization, and the inability to achieve their monetary and masculine status goals (Agnew, 2006; Broidy & Agnew, 1997). Many of the strains more often experienced by females are not conducive to most forms of violence. This is particularly true of the burdens associated with caring for others, like children and sick or disabled spouses. These burdens tie females to the home, impose time-consuming obligations on them, and increase the costs of violence because violence may jeopardize their ability to care for others. These burdens, however, may be conducive to family violence, an area in which gender differences in offending are relatively small. At the same time, it is important to note that females are more likely to experience *certain* strains conducive to violence, such as sexual abuse and gender discrimination (Chesney-Lind, 1989; Eitle, 2002). In addition, the number of females experiencing monetary strain has increased dramatically in recent decades, largely because of an increase in the number of female-headed households. Sexual abuse by family members is a major source of serious female crime, with females often running away to escape from such abuse and engaging in a range of crimes to survive on the street. The increase in monetary strain has been used to explain the fact that females have come to commit a larger share of most crimes in recent years (Heimer, 2000). GST, however, argues that, overall, males are more likely to experiences those strains conducive to violence, and this partly explains their higher rates of violence.

GST also states that males are more likely than females to cope with strains through violence, although the data are somewhat mixed in this area (e.g., Broidy & Agnew, 1997; Hoffmann & Su, 1997; Mazerolle, 1998; Piquero & Sealock, 2004). There are several possible reasons why males may be more prone to violent coping. Males are more likely to experience moral outrage in response to strains, with such outrage being conducive to other-directed violence. Although females are as likely as males to get angry when they experience strains, the anger of females is more often accompanied by depression, guilt, anxiety, and shame. It is said that females more often blame themselves when experiencing strains, view their anger as inappropriate, and worry about hurting others and jeopardizing relationships. Males, however, are quicker to blame others for their strains, are less concerned about hurting others, and often view anger as an affirmation of their masculinity.

Gender differences in coping skills and resources may also explain why males may be more likely to engage in violent coping (Broidy & Agnew, 1997; Moffitt, Caspi, Rutter, & Silva, 2001; Steffensmeier & Allan, 1996). Among other things, males are more likely to be lower in constraint and higher in negative emotionality, lower in certain types of conventional social support, and larger and physically stronger than females. Further, males are lower in certain types of social control than females. In particular, males are less well supervised by parents, more weakly tied to school, and less likely to believe that violence is wrong. Finally, males are more likely to associate with violent others and hold beliefs favorable to violence.

Age Differences in Violence

Age, along with gender, is the strongest sociodemographic correlate of violence, with the rates of violence among adolescents and very young adults exceeding those of other age groups. GST argues that part of the reason for this is that adolescents/young adults are more likely to experience strains conducive to violence (Agnew, 1997). Such individuals, in particular, are no longer closely protected by parents, but they have not yet formed families of their own or developed careers. Further, they interact with a larger, more diverse group of people, including many people they do not know well. This reflects the fact that they frequently attend large, diverse schools and have more active social lives. These factors increase the likelihood that they will be in situations in which the risk of negative treatment is high; for example, they are more

likely to spend time with peers in unstructured, unsupervised activities (Osgood, Wilson, O'Malley, Bachman, & Johnston, 1996).

In addition, adolescents and young adults come to develop a strong desire for such goals as money, status, and autonomy from others; this desire reflects their biological maturity and changed social circumstances. But they often have trouble achieving such goals through legal channels. For example, teachers and others often treat them in a demeaning manner and their legal sources of income are limited, so they experience increased levels of goal blockage. Limited data provide some support for these arguments, suggesting that several types of strain are more common among adolescents and young adults, including criminal victimization (Agnew, 1997, 2003).

Unfortunately, adolescents/young adults are also more likely than children and adults to cope with the strains they experience in a violent manner. Unlike children, they cannot rely on parents to cope on their behalf or provide extensive social support. Unlike adults, they are often deficient in social and problem-solving skills and in coping resources like power and money. Adolescents/young adults, however, are at the peak of their physical condition, increasing their ability to engage in violent coping. They are also lower in several types of social control than children and/or adults, including supervision, ties to conventional others, investment in conventional activities, and beliefs condemning crime. Finally, adolescents/young adults are much more likely to associate with violent others and hold beliefs favorable to violence. Adolescents and young adults, then, experience more strains conducive to violence and are more likely to cope with such strains through violence.

Class Differences in Violence

GST argues that lower class individuals have higher rates of violence partly because they are more likely to experiences strains like family problems, including harsh discipline and abuse; school problems; peer abuse; criminal victimization; homelessness;

chronic unemployment; work in unpleasant jobs; and difficulty achieving monetary and status goals. In addition, lower class individuals are more likely to cope with strains in a violent manner. They lack certain legal coping skills and resources, most notably money. They are lower in many types of social control, such as their investment in conventional institutions. They are more likely to associate with violent others, partly because they more often live in communities where such others are common. Finally, they are more likely to hold beliefs favorable to violence (see Agnew, 2005b).

Community Differences in Violence

Rates of violence are much higher in some communities than others, with the highest rates in very poor communities with high rates of mobility and family disruption. Part of the reason for these high rates has to do with the characteristics of the people who live in these communities, but there is some reason to believe that the nature of the community itself exerts an independent effect on levels of violence.

Residence in a deprived community contributes to several strains conducive to violence. In particular, data suggest that, even after individual characteristics are taken into account, the residents of deprived communities have more trouble achieving their monetary and status goals. Among other things, the residents of deprived communities have less access to stable, well-paying jobs, which tend to be located outside the community, and to individuals with job connections. There are also fewer individuals in the community to teach and model those skills and attitudes necessary for successful job performance. The residents of such communities are also more likely to experience other strains, including family problems, such as abuse and harsh discipline; school problems; chronic unemployment; work in unpleasant jobs; peer abuse; criminal victimization; homelessness; and discrimination (Agnew, 1999, 2005a, 2006; Brezina, Piquero, & Mazerolle, 2001; Hoffmann, 2003; Warner & Fowler, 2003).

The residents of deprived communities are also more likely to respond to strains with violence. The residents of such communities are not only less able to legally cope as individuals but are also less able to cope as a community. That is, they are less able to unite with one another to solve community problems. High levels of poverty, family disruption, and mobility impede efforts at collective problem solving. In addition, levels of social control are lower in such communities, with residents being less likely to socialize young people in a conventional manner and intervene when violence occurs. Further, criminal groups are more common in such communities, and community residents – particularly young males – are more likely to develop values conducive to violence (Agnew, 1999, 2005a, 2006; Warner & Fowler, 2003).

Race/Ethnic Differences in Violence

Certain race and ethnic groups, such as African Americans and Latinos, have higher rates of violence than other groups (Hawkins, 2003). A substantial part of the reason for these higher rates is that the members of these groups are more likely to be poor and to live in high-poverty communities (although most African Americans are not poor). Poor African Americans, in particular, are several times more likely to live in high-poverty communities than poor Whites. As a consequence, African Americans are more likely to experience strains conducive to violence and react to these strains with violence for the reasons just indicated. In addition, African Americans are subject to a range of discriminatory treatment that results in additional strains beyond those associated with economic level. For example, evidence suggests that African Americans are more often subject to negative treatment by school officials and police. Further, African Americans may be more likely to attribute the strains they experience to unjust treatment (Kaufman, Rebellon, Thaxton, & Agnew, 2004).

Patterns of Violence Over the Life Course

Finally, GST can explain patterns of violence over the life course, including the "life-course persistent" pattern, in which individuals tend to commit relatively high rates of violence over much of their lives (Agnew, 1997, 2003; Moffitt, 1993). Although life-course persistent offenders make up a small portion of the population, they account for a large share of all violence, including a majority of serious violence.

GST argues that individuals engage in high rates of violence over their lives partly because they are more likely to experience strains conducive to violence and react to them with violence. This may occur because they develop the traits of low constraint and negative emotionality early in life. Individuals with these traits tend to provoke negative reactions from others. For example, they are more likely to antagonize parents, who may reject them or respond in a harsh manner. In addition, such individuals are more likely to select themselves into aversive environments, where they are treated in a negative manner by others. For example, they are more likely to be rejected by conventional peers and to associate with delinquent peers, end up in unpleasant jobs, and be unmarried or involved in "bad" marriages. Further, such individuals are more likely to interpret events and conditions in a negative manner. That is, they are more easily upset than others and quicker to blame their strains on the malicious behavior of others. The more frequent strains experienced by these individuals directly contributes to high levels of violence. Such strains also help maintain the traits of low constraint and negative emotionality, as indicated earlier. Finally, such individuals are more likely to cope with strains in a violent manner (see Agnew et al., 2002; Walsh, 2000).

Some individuals may also engage in high levels of violence over their lives because they are members of the urban underclass; that is, they are very poor individuals living in poor communities. As indicated above, such individuals are more likely to experience a range of strains conducive to violence, and they are more likely to cope with these strains through violence. The violence of these individuals, in turn, has consequences that increase the likelihood of further violence over the life course. Such violence, in particular, is likely to provoke negative treatment from others, thereby contributing to further strain. In addition, such violence reduces the likelihood of escape from the underclass, with violence impeding school performance and reducing prospects for decent work (De Li, 1999; Tanner, Davies, & O'Grady, 1999).

Summary

GST is based on a simple idea: if you treat people badly, they may respond with violence. GST, however, elaborates on this idea in several ways. In particular, GST describes those types of negative treatment most likely to increase violence, why such treatment increases violence, the characteristics of individuals most likely to engage in violent coping, and the effect of group characteristics on the experience of and reaction to strains. As is apparent from the above discussion, GST is compatible with other theories of violence, including bio-psychological, control, and social learning theories. Most notably, variables from these theories help explain why certain types of strain are more conducive to violence and why certain individuals are more likely to engage in violent coping. Further, the variables from these theories may mutually influence one another (e.g., personality traits like low constraint and negative emotionality contribute to strains while strains contribute to these traits). Nevertheless, GST is distinct from these theories, with GST focusing on the effect of disliked events and conditions on violence and explaining this effect partly through negative emotions like anger.

References

Agnew, R. (1985). A revised strain theory of delinquency. *Social Forces*, 64, 151–167.

Agnew, R. (1990). The origins of delinquent events: An examination of offender accounts. *Journal of Research in Crime and Delinquency*, 27, 267–294.

Agnew, R. (1992). Foundation for a general strain theory of crime and delinquency. *Criminology*, 30, 47–87.

Agnew, R. (1997). Stability and change in crime over the life course: A strain theory explanation. In T. P. Thornberry (Ed.), *Developmental theories of crime and delinquency: Advances in criminological theory* (Vol. 7, pp. 101–132). New Brunswick, NJ: Transaction.

Agnew, R. (1999). A general strain theory of community differences in crime rates. *Journal of Research in Crime and Delinquency*, 36, 123–155.

Agnew, R. (2001). Building on the foundation of general strain theory: Specifying the types of strain most likely to lead to crime and delinquency. *Journal of Research in Crime and Delinquency*, 38, 319–361.

Agnew, R. (2002). Experienced, vicarious, and anticipated strain: An exploratory study focusing on physical victimization and delinquency. *Justice Quarterly*, 19, 603–632.

Agnew, R. (2003). An integrated theory of the adolescent peak in offending. *Youth and Society*, 34, 263–299.

Agnew, R. (2005a). *Juvenile delinquency: Causes and control*. Los Angeles: Roxbury.

Agnew, R. (2005b). *Why do criminals offend? A general theory of crime and delinquency*. Los Angeles: Roxbury.

Agnew, R. (2006). *Pressured into crime: An overview of general strain theory*. Los Angeles: Roxbury.

Agnew, R., & Brezina, T. (1997). Relational problems with peers, gender, and delinquency. *Youth and Society*, 29, 84–111.

Agnew, R., Brezina, T., Wright, J. P., & Cullen, F. T. (2002). Strain, personality traits, and delinquency: Extending general strain theory. *Criminology*, 40, 43–72.

Agnew, R., & White, H. R. (1992). An empirical test of general strain theory. *Criminology*, 30, 475–499.

Anderson, E. (1994, May). The code of the streets. *Atlantic Monthly*, 273, 81–94.

Aseltine, R. H., Jr., Gore, S., & Gordon, J. (2000). Life stress, anger and anxiety, and delinquency: An empirical test of general strain theory. *Journal of Health and Social Behavior*, 41, 256–275.

Averill, J. R. (1982). *Anger and aggression: An essay on emotion*. New York: Springer-Verlag.

Baron, S. W. (2004). General strain, street youth and crime: A test of Agnew's revised theory. *Criminology*, 42, 457–483.

Berkowitz, L. (1989). The frustration-aggression hypothesis: An examination and reformulation. *American Psychologist*, 45, 494–503.

Brezina, T. (1998). Adolescent maltreatment and delinquency: The question of intervening processes. *Journal of Research in Crime and Delinquency*, 35, 71–99.

Brezina, T., Piquero, A. R., & Mazerolle, P. (2001). Student anger and aggressive behavior in school: An initial test of Agnew's macro-level strain theory. *Journal of Research in Crime and Delinquency*, 38, 362–386.

Broidy, L., & Agnew, R. (1997). Gender and crime: A general strain theory perspective. *Journal of Research in Crime and Delinquency*, 34, 275–306.

Chesney-Lind, M. (1989). Girls' crime and woman's place: Toward a feminist model of female delinquency. *Crime and Delinquency*, 35, 5–29.

Cloward, R., & Ohlin, L. (1960). *Delinquency and opportunity*. Glencoe, IL: Free Press.

Cohen, A. K. (1955). *Delinquent boys*. Glencoe, IL: Free Press.

Colvin, M. (2000). *Crime and coercion*. New York: St. Martin's Press.

De Li, S. (1999). Legal sanctions and youths' status achievement: A longitudinal study. *Justice Quarterly*, 16, 377–401.

Eitle, D. J. (2002). Exploring a source of deviance-producing strain for females: Perceived discrimination and general strain theory. *Journal of Criminal Justice*, 30, 429–442.

Eitle, D., Gunkel, S., & Van Gundy, K. (2004). Cumulative exposure to stressful life events and male gang membership. *Journal of Criminal Justice*, 32, 95–111.

Eitle, D., & Turner, R. J. (2002). Exposure to community violence and young adult crime: The effects of witnessing violence, traumatic victimization, and other stressful life events. *Journal of Research in Crime and Delinquency*, 39, 214–237.

Elliott, D. S., Ageton, S., & Canter, R. (1979). An integrated theoretical perspective on delinquent behavior. *Journal of Research in Crime and Delinquency*, 16, 3–27.

Elliott, D. S., Huizinga, D., & Ageton, S. S. (1985). *Explaining delinquency and drug use*. Beverly Hills, CA: Sage.

Felson, R. (1996). Big people hit little people: Sex differences in physical power and interpersonal violence. *Criminology, 34,* 433–452.

Greenberg, David F. (1977). Delinquency and the age structure of society. *Contemporary Crises, 1,* 189–223.

Hagan, J., & McCarthy, B. (1997). *Mean streets.* Cambridge, UK: Cambridge University Press.

Hawkins, D. F. (2003). *Violent crime: Assessing race and ethnic differences.* Cambridge, UK: Cambridge University Press.

Hay, C. (2003). Family strain, gender, and delinquency. *Sociological Perspectives, 46,* 107–136.

Heimer, K. (2000). Changes in the gender gap in crime and women's economic marginalization. In G. LaFree (Ed.), *The nature of crime: Continuity and change; Criminal justice 2000* (Vol. 1., pp. 427–483). Washington, DC: National Institute of Justice.

Hoffmann, J. (2003). A contextual analysis of differential association, social control, and strain theories of delinquency. *Social Forces, 81,* 753–786.

Hoffmann, J. P. & Miller, A. S. 1998. A latent variable analysis of general strain theory. *Journal of Quantitative Criminology, 14,* 83–110.

Hoffmann, J. P., & Su. S. S. (1997). The conditional effects of stress on delinquency and drug use: A strain theory assessment of sex differences. *Journal of Research in Crime and Delinquency, 34,* 46–78.

Jang, S. J., & Johnson, B. R. (2003). Strain, negative emotions, and deviant coping among African Americans: A test of general strain theory. *Journal of Quantitative Criminology, 19,* 79–105.

Kaufman, J., Rebellon, C. J., Thaxton, S., & Agnew, R. (2004). *A general strain theory of the race-crime relationship.* Unpublished manuscript.

Mazerolle, P. (1998). Gender, general strain, and delinquency: An empirical examination. *Justice Quarterly, 15,* 65–91.

Mazerolle, P., & Maahs, J. (2000). General strain and delinquency: An alternative examination of conditioning influences. *Justice Quarterly, 17,* 323–343.

Mazerolle, P., & Piquero, A. (1998). Linking exposure to strain with anger: An investigation of deviant adaptations. *Journal of Criminal Justice, 26,* 195–211.

Mazerolle, P., Piquero, A. R., & Capowich, G. F. (2003). Examining the links between strain, situational and dispositional anger, and crime. *Youth and Society, 35,* 131–157.

McClelland, G. H., & Judd, C. M. (1993). Statistical difficulties of detecting interactions and moderator effects. *Psychological Bulletin, 114,* 376–390.

Merton, R. K. (1938). Social structure and anomie. *American Sociological Review, 3,* 672–682.

Moffitt, T. E. (1993). Adolescence-limited and life-course persistent antisocial behavior: A developmental taxonomy. *Psychological Review, 100,* 674–701.

Moffitt, T. E., Caspi, A., Rutter, M., & Silva, P. A. (2001). *Sex differences in antisocial behaviour.* Cambridge, UK: Cambridge University Press.

Osgood, D. W., Wilson, J. K., O'Malley, P. M., Bachman, J. G., & Johnston, L. D. (1996). Routine activities and individual deviant behavior. *American Sociological Review, 1,* 635–655.

Paternoster, R., & Mazerolle, P. (1994). General Strain Theory and delinquency: A replication and extension. *Journal of Research in Crime and Delinquency, 31,* 235–263.

Piquero, N. L., & Sealock, M. D. (2004). Gender and general strain theory: A preliminary test of Broidy and Agnew's gender/GST hypotheses. *Justice Quarterly, 21,* 125–158.

Simons, R. L., Chen, Y., Stewart, E. A., & Brody, G. H. (2003). Incidents of discrimination and risk for delinquency: A longitudinal test of strain theory with an African American sample. *Justice Quarterly, 20,* 827–854.

Steffensmeier, D., & Allan, E. (1996). Gender and crime: Toward a gendered theory of female offending. *Annual Review of Sociology, 22,* 459–487.

Tanner, J., Davies, S., & O' Grady, B. (1999). Whatever happened to yesterday's rebels?: Longitudinal effects of youth delinquency on education and unemployment. *Social Problems, 46,* 250–274.

Walsh, A. (2000). Behavior genetics and anomie/strain theory. *Criminology, 38,* 1075–1108.

Warner, B. D., & Fowler, S. K. (2003). Strain and violence: Testing a general strain theory model of community violence. *Journal of Criminal Justice, 31,* 511–521.

Part V

CONTEXTUAL FACTORS
AND VIOLENT BEHAVIOR

CHAPTER 27

Self-Control Theory and Criminal Violence

Michael R. Gottfredson

Introduction

Self-control theory is a perspective in criminology that attempts to explain the distribution of crime and delinquency, including violence, among individuals, groups, and societies (Gottfredson & Hirschi, 1990). Unlike behavioral science theories that seek to discover what motivates people to steal and to be aggressive, control theories begin by assuming that the motives for crime and violence are similar to the motives for all other behavior. Beginning with the assumption that conforming behavior is problematic, control theories seek to understand the forces that compel most people, most of the time, to behave nonviolently and noncriminally. Self-control theory locates the basis for conforming behavior in the attachments formed early in life between parents or other caregivers and children. These attachments, or social bonds, develop into the tendency to regulate individual conduct by attending to the long-term consequences of actions (Gottfredson & Hirschi, 1990; Hirschi, 1969). Differences in parenting and

other early childhood experiences create differences among people in the ability to delay the gratification of near-term desires and needs and to avoid longer term negative consequences. These negative consequences include losing the respect and affection of others, low school achievement, and employment problems. Self-control theory has connections to theories of self-regulation (e.g., Baumeister & Heatherton, 1996) and problem behaviors (e.g., Donovan, Jessor, & Costa, 1991). Although Gottfredson and Hirschi (1990) focus attention on socialization in the creation of self-control (as does this chapter), other researchers (e.g., Moffitt, 1993) argue for a role for biology and for the interaction of biology and parenting in the lack of development of self-control (good reviews of possible biological sources are provided by Vold, Bernard, & Snipes, 2002, and Cullen & Agnew, 2003).

Control theory places much, but not all (as described below), violent behavior into the class of acts that the theory was designed to explain. As such, self-control theory is also a theory of violent behavior. Control theory owes much of its development to scientific studies of crime and delinquency. At the outset, it was designed to account for the major facts about individual differences in crime and delinquency as revealed in the empirical literature (Gottfredson, 2005). Because an appreciation of these facts is critical to an appreciation of the theory, some of the correlates of violence central to the development of self-control theory are outlined briefly. The chapter then addresses precisely what forms of violent behavior are included in the definition of violence specified by control theory, followed by a discussion of the contemporary research bearing on the validity of self-control theory.

Key Facts About Criminal Violence

Behavioral scientists interested in explaining violent behavior have at their disposal a considerable body of high-quality research studies that have produced a set of correlates that are impressively robust with respect to time and method of measurement. These correlates – or key facts about violence – are documented so strongly that explanatory schemes not attending to them or inconsistent with any of them cannot be said to be valid according to the best empirical science available. There are, to be sure, important uncertainties and arguments in the literature about some correlates of violent behavior, and there are many more arguments about the meaning of those correlates that are agreed on, but the foundational facts of a behavioral science of criminal violence surely must at least include the following:

1. There is a robust and substantial correlation between misconduct early in life and violence during adolescence and adulthood. The correlation between early childhood problem behaviors and crime (including violent behavior) later in life is reported regularly in longitudinal studies from a variety of disciplines (for summaries, see Gottfredson & Hirschi, 1990; Loeber & Dishion,

1983; Loeber & Stouthamer-Loeber, 1986). Studies documenting this effect are found in psychological research (e.g., Mischel, Shoda, & Peake, 1988), in basic criminology (e.g., Glueck & Glueck, 1950; Sampson & Laub, 1995), and in nearly all criminological recidivism studies (e.g., McCord & McCord, 1959).

2. There is a characteristic distribution of violent behavior over the life course, such that incidents of violence increase in frequency with age up to late adolescence or early adulthood and then rapidly and continuously decline throughout life. The general "age/crime" curve that has been studied for well over a century (Hirschi & Gottfredson, 1983) is generally applicable also to criminal violence. The peak age for some forms of criminal violence seems to be modestly older than for some forms of property offenses, but by and large the distributions are remarkably the same whatever the type of crime studied (Britt, 1994). The general distribution is illustrated in Figure 27.1, which depicts age-standardized offending rates from California in a recent year for homicide and for robbery (forcible taking of property from another), which are two prominent forms of criminal violence. For comparison purposes, Figure 27.2 shows the age-standardized rates for alcohol-impaired motor vehicle accidents and motor vehicle theft, offenses not generally considered falling within the concept of violence, but which have virtually identical relationships with age over the life course. The theoretical and practical importance of this fundamental relationship is considerable. Violent behavior, like most problem behaviors, is very disproportionately adolescent and young adult behavior. Rates of offending rise very sharply during the preteen years and decline rapidly after adolescence and then continuously throughout life, whatever the initial level of violence. Research has shown that these rates pertain to individuals, as well as to aggregates (Hirschi & Gottfredson,

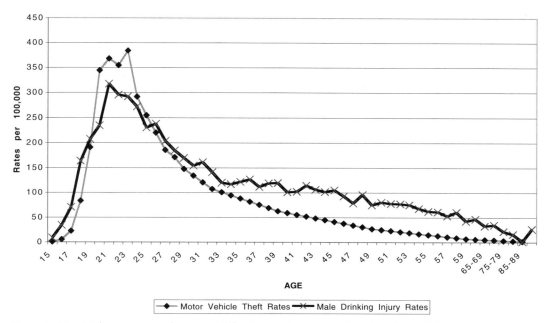

Figure 27.1. Male arrest rates by age, California 2000. Sources: Age data from California Department of Finance. www.dof.ca.gov/. Alcohol-involved accidents from California Highway Patrol, Annual Reporat SWITRS, 2000, table 5j.

1983; Sampson & Laub, 2003). Because this relationship is so ubiquitous, the initial level of activity greatly predicts the overall level of violence throughout life. Thus, violence, like other problem behaviors, must have important causes in the earliest years of life.

3. There is a substantial correlation between the amount of problem behaviors of parents and the level of violence of their children. Furthermore, there are strong correlations between the strength of attachment between children and their parents and the level of crime and violence. The effect of family on crime and violence has been a staple of empirical criminology for decades (Brannigan, Gemmell, Pevalin, & Wade, 2002; Glueck & Glueck, 1950; Gottfredson & Hirschi, 1990; Hirschi, 1969; Loeber & Dishion, 1983; Loeber & Stouthamer-Loeber, 1986; McCord & McCord, 1959).

4. There are substantial correlations for individuals between the level of violent behavior and the level of other forms of delinquency and criminal behavior; in addition, there are substantial correlations between violent behavior and other problem behaviors, such as drug use, accidents, illnesses, poor school performance, and unemployment. Offenders by and large do not specialize in either violent behavior or in nonviolent behavior, a fact validated in both self-report and in official statistics (Britt, 1994; Hindelang, Hirschi, & Weis, 1981; Osgood, Johnston, O'Malley, & Bachman, 1988; Sampson & Laub, 2003; Wolfgang, Figlio, & Sellin, 1972).

5. A derivative fact with considerable practical consequence is that there is significant, but only low-level, predictability for individuals for specific acts of violence. A related fact is that general measures of crime and delinquency, which include violence, are more reliable and have greater discriminant validity than do specific measures of crime and delinquency (Gottfredson & Hirschi, 1993; Hindelang et al., 1981). The fact that prediction of violence at the

Crime Rates By Age

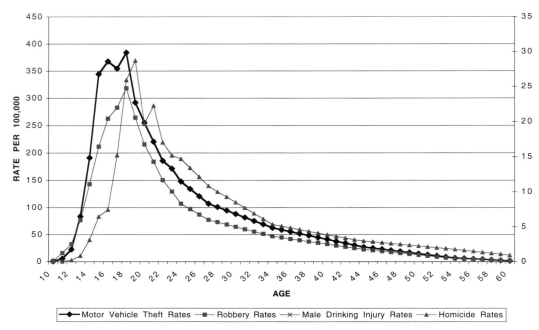

Figure 27.2. Motor vehicle theft arrest and motor vehicle alcohol involved injury rates, males, California, 2000.

individual level is problematic and that violence cannot be predicted as well as crime can suggests that violent or aggressive behavior belongs to the larger construct of problem behavior (Gottfredson & Hirschi, 1993).

6. Much, if not most, violent behavior is rather mundane, short-sighted, and seemingly adventitious. It produces little gain and engenders considerable long-term negative consequences for the actor. Violence tends not to be planned long in advance, but rather often seems nearly spontaneous (and, in hindsight even to the offender to be unaccountable). Quite frequently, alcohol or other drugs are involved (Boyum & Kleiman, 1995). In result, it can hardly be said to be utilitarian. There are, of course, exceptions, but studies of homicide, family violence, gang assaultive behavior, and other forms of interpersonal violence depict the nature of the acts as frequently unplanned, with alcohol involved, and without apparent gain to the offender (Gottfredson & Hirschi, 1990).

Self-Control Theory

These general correlates of crime and violence, and the nature of violence that they presume, helped shape the theory of self-control. Control theorists assume that all people are motivated to pursue self-interest and that individual behavior is motivated by the pursuit of pleasure and the avoidance of pain. There are, to be sure, countless constellations of pleasures and pains, from the physical to the emotional, from the near term to the long term. The unrestrained pursuit of these wants in everyday life inevitably leads to conflict with the wants and rights of others. Aggressive, bullying, and assaultive acts can result in the immediate satisfaction of wants, but only if the longer term costs are disregarded. Consequently, controls are established by social groups (including parents, communities, and states) to channel the pursuit of these wants in ways that minimize harm to others.

Sociologists have identified several forms of controls for violent behavior. Of course the legal system is the formal method, seeking to control crime and violence through fear of legal punishments. But many nonlegal mechanisms also help control unwanted behavior, such as the approval, respect, and affection of family, teachers, and friends. Because these controls are exerted at times and not exerted at times in the social environment, and because individuals experience different environments related to these controls, the extent to which individuals are "free to deviate" varies. When these controls need always to be present in the environment to be effective, they are often referred to as external or social controls. When the process of socialization during the early years of life establishes a tendency to be concerned about others and about the long-term costs of behaviors, this tendency is referred to as self-control. Self-control theory thus postulates important variation among people in their tendencies to subordinate momentary or immediate pleasure or satisfactions to the long term.

Put another way, self-control is the tendency to delay short-term personal gain for long-term personal and collective interests. Crime and delinquency can provide the satisfaction of universal human wants and desires, but only by risking longer term goals (the avoidance of punishment, the ability to achieve conventional accomplishments like education and employment, interpersonal relationships). Thus, those with lower levels of self-control are, all things equal, more likely than those with higher levels of self-control to behave violently, to commit crime, or to engage in delinquent acts. In addition, they tend to have relatively high rates of school and employment failure and difficulty forming lasting interpersonal relationships.

Self-control helps account for the fact that many delinquencies, crimes, and other problem behaviors seem to "go together" –

that interpersonal violence, stealing, drug use, accidents, and school misbehavior are commonly found in association. The acts associated with these problems all provide some immediate benefit for the actor (money, pleasure, the end of a troubling dispute), as do many other behaviors. But each also carries with it the possibility of harmful consequences to the actor or to others. What differentiates people is not that such acts may provide benefits, but that some routinely ignore the potential costs and do them anyway. Thus, self-control theory is sometimes called a "restraint" theory, a theory that focuses on why people do not engage in crime and delinquency, rather than why they do (Hirschi, 1969).

Self-control theory is influenced by the observation that differences among people in the tendency to ignore long-term costs appear to be established in childhood and, once established, tend to persist throughout life. Control theory assumes that human nature includes the general tendency to pursue the satisfaction of individual needs and desires. Left unregulated, the pursuit of this nature causes inevitable conflict with others and, because of that, potentially harmful consequences to the actor. As a result, those who care about the long-term interests of the child seek to train the child to restrict the pursuit of self-interest by attending to the needs and wants of others. For self-control theory, this process is what socialization entails.

As the child develops, caregivers (parents, other relatives, friends and neighbors, and schools) sanction selfish behavior. Children are taught to pay attention to the longer term consequences of their actions. When a caring adult is present in the developing child's environment and takes an active role in socialization, high levels of self-control are readily produced and appear to become a stable characteristic of the individual (Gottfredson & Hirschi, 1990). But sometimes such early caregiving is not present in the child's environment. Furthermore, there are differences among groups and even nations in the level and duration of this socialization process. These differences are thought to produce differences in the levels of crime, violence, and other problem behaviors among individuals, communities, and in different time periods. That is, it is the nature of early childhood socialization that produces differences in crime rates, not differences among people in their motivation to commit crimes or in values or cultural beliefs about crime. In this way, control theories can be distinguished from most other theories of crime and violence.

How socialization of young people generates self-control is described by Gottfredson and Hirschi (1990, 2004) as a sequence of steps: (1) Parental affection for the child establishes a long-term interest in the success of the child; (2) which enables a parenting style characterized by positive efforts to monitor conduct and appropriately sanction deviance; (3) which creates self-control; (4) which is expressed by affection from the child to the parent and, by logical extension, to other socializing institutions like schools and friends. This model implies that the social bonds among parents and children and self-control in the child will be very difficult to discriminate empirically and, under some circumstances, may amount to the same thing.

It is important to stress that in the creation of self-control, affection for the child is the key:

> A major premise of the model outlined is that the parent, caretaker, or guardian must care enough about the child or the child's behavior to devote the immense amounts of time and energy monitoring and discipline require... Interest in the outcome, whatever its source, tends to assure monitoring and discipline. It also severely limits the range of usable or acceptable sanctions.
> (Hirschi & Gottfredson, 2003, pp. 156–157)

Gibbs, Giever, and Martin (2003, p. 443) describe the theory well:

> For their children to develop high levels of self-control, parents must regularly monitor them, recognize deviant behavior when it occurs, and punish the behavior by noncor-

> poral means. Self-control is associated with the consistent application of these principles during the early development of the child. Investment in the child, which often takes the form of an emotional attachment, is pivotal. It is a necessary but insufficient condition for the implementation of child rearing practices that enhance self-control.

Considerable evidence suggests that parents or other early caregivers are crucial to the development of self-control. Wright and Cullen (2001; see also Burton et al., 1995) studied the connection between parenting behaviors and self-reported delinquency in the National Youth Survey data, documenting important effects for parenting:

> From these data, it appears that parents who are nurturing, reliable, and closely attached to their youths and who provide guidance in the form of rules and supervision reduce the delinquency of their adolescents, even when the effects of delinquent peers and sources of parental heterogeneity are controlled... Our empirical analysis found that delinquency was reduced by child-parent attachment, household rules, and parental supervision... Our research both reinforces and specifies the contention that control is central to the etiology of delinquent involvement. Parenting effects need not operate entirely through self-control, since supervision itself restricts the opportunity for some delinquency.
> (Wright & Cullen, 2001, pp. 693, 695; see also Feldman & Weinberger, 1994)

Some experimental evidence from planned interventions in parenting seems consistent with these expectations and thus provides empirical support for the theory. Clarke and Campbell (1998, p. 319) review these studies and conclude, "It is increasingly clear that the most effective approach to the prevention of chronic problem behaviors requires early intervention before these behaviors emerge in late childhood and early adolescence [citations omitted]." Eckenrode et al. (2001) report, "There are many forms of family support and parent education programs aimed at reducing child abuse and neglect, but the interventions that have received the greatest attention in recent years have involved home visitation services to new parents [citations omitted; p. 876]," and "These findings seem highly consistent with research suggesting that neglected children are as likely to be involved with antisocial behavior, even violent offenses, as are physically abused children [citations omitted, p. 886]." Olds et al. (1998, pp. 73–74) argue that parenting differences may account for the prevention effect discovered in their famous nurse visitation experiments.

Definition of Violence in Control Theory

Quite obviously, not all violent behavior, even criminal violence, fits the description of crime provided above. The intentional infliction of bodily harm, without excuse and not in defense, is the standard definition of criminal violence. In most instances of criminal violence, the violence permits the offender some momentary personal gain – the theft of property, the end of an argument, or even a sense of personal status. On the other hand, some criminal violence, such as some acts of terrorism, seems designed to satisfy collective rather than individual interests and long-term rather than short-term objectives. Some violence, such as child abuse, seems difficult to reconcile with either individual or collective advantage.

Should a behavioral theory of violence attempt to explain in the same way the wide variety of violent conduct, from schoolyard bullying, to homicides, to robberies, to spousal assaults, and to terrorism? Is criminal violence a category of conduct suitable for scientific explanation? Should we seek one causal explanation for violent crime and another for theft crimes, or one for domestic assault and a different one for street robbery? Should noncriminal violence be included or excluded? Certainly not all types of violent behavior are technically criminal; some "accidents" cause considerable damage to others, and there is much violent conduct in some sports. The threshold problem for the science of violent conduct is thus the problem of scope or definition.

Confronted with these issues (as all theories of violence surely are), control theorists reject a legal definition of violence and instead incorporate into the theory only those behaviors characterized as providing short-term benefit to the actor without regard to negative longer term consequences:

> *Violent and assaultive acts that produce immediate benefit at the same time they produce long term social costs are of interest to students of crime and deviance. Indeed, to the extent that aggressive acts share these defining characteristics of most forms of crime and deviance, they will easily fall within the scope of . . . control theory . . . Many violent acts can be understood in precisely this way . . . Much homicide, child abuse, spouse abuse, and violent robbery is undertaken to gain some momentary advantage without regard to long term social consequences. When a husband strikes his wife repeatedly as a way to end an argument; when a father physically assaults a child to end an annoyance of the moment; or, when a robber shoots a clerk because he is nervous about his escape, the advantage of the moment has outweighed consideration of distant costs.*
> (Gottfredson & Hirschi, 1993, p. 40)

Thus, a definition of violence for a theory of criminal violence does not include all conduct ordinarily classified as violence – not even according to criminal law. Many terrorist acts, involving homicide and assault, would not fall into the violence definition for control theory because these acts are undertaken precisely with the long term in view. Many are even very highly planned and difficult to execute. The individuals involved do not have extensive involvement with other problem behaviors; indeed some may be highly disciplined in other ways, having achieved higher education and substantial employment. Even though the legal system includes them as crimes, these acts are, in some ways, very different from the kinds of acts characterized by the kinds of behaviors included in control theories of violence. The theoretical strategy of defining the behavior to be explained in a way that is consistent with its underlying causes is controversial in criminology (but not so much in other sciences, such as the theory of natural selection in biology) because it seems to many to be merely tautological (cf. Akers, 1991; Hirschi & Gottfredson, 2000).

Other behavior that could be classified as violent, but not criminal, also does not belong in the definition used by control theorists. Some sports certainly involve aggression and interpersonal violence; violent behavior in military settings usually has long-term goals and, indeed, requires the subordination of individual self-interest to the collective interest. Sometimes, however, violence in military settings seems well within the intended scope of the theory, such as prisoner abuse or crimes committed during occupations.

Self-Control and Opportunity

Differences in self-control are not the only cause of delinquency and crime according to this theory, but they nearly always play an important role. Another feature of self-control theory is a focus on the concept of opportunity as an additional cause of crime. Self-control theory was influenced by developments in opportunity or routine activity theories that themselves focused attention on situational elements of crime as it typically occurs (Cohen & Felson, 1978; Hindelang et al., 1978). Self-control theory assumes that differences among people in self-control are also associated with the distribution of people in settings that vary in the opportunities for crime and delinquency. Thus, being among adolescent males in unsupervised settings, especially at night and in the presence of readily available drugs or alcohol, enhances opportunity for delinquency and is also a function of low self-control. Similarly, persistence in school and in the workforce is associated with higher levels of self-control and also with reduced opportunities for crime and violence. Throughout the life course, differences among people in self-control influence friend and family associations, employ-

ment patterns, and many other life experiences, which in turn affect the opportunities for violence (Tangney, Baumeister, & Boone, 2004).

Research on the Validity of Self-Control Theory

There are two broad classes of studies relevant to the question of the validity of self-control theory. The first pertains to the accuracy of the factual portrait of violence depicted earlier. The second pertains to studies that have tried to operationalize the concepts from the theory, especially that of self-control, and have applied the theory in a predictive fashion. Both bodies of research have strong implications for the utility of the theory.

Research on the "foundational facts" continues to support the claim that early childhood socialization, particularly parenting effects, is an important determinant of the level of aggressive or violent behavior (Brannigan et al., 2002; De Li, 2004; Eckenrode et al., 2001; Farrington, 2003; Gibbs et al., 1998; Maxfield & Widom, 1996; Olds et al., 1998; Perrone, Sullivan, Pratt, & Margaryan, 2004). In addition, it is clear that there is very considerable stability in individual differences in the tendency to engage in violence over the life course (see, e.g., the summaries in Baumeister & Heatherton, 1996; Farrington, 2003; Laub & Sampson, 2003; Zhang, Welte, & Wieczorek, 2002). The general age-violence distribution is replicated consistently (Laub & Sampson, 2003; for reviews, see Vold et al., 2002). The versatility effect, which implicates violent behavior in a complex of problem behaviors and which questions strongly those explanations for violence that take violence as a special or specific topic for study, continues to be reported; the overall finding is well described in Farrington's recent summary (2003, p. 224):

> *Offending is versatile rather than specialized ... The types of acts defined as offenses are elements of a larger syndrome of*

antisocial behavior, including heavy drinking, reckless driving, sexual promiscuity, bullying, and truancy. Offenders tend to be versatile not only in committing several types of crimes but also in committing several types of antisocial behavior.

With respect to the concept of self-control, a considerable body of contemporary research has found strong support for the validity of self-control theory (see, e.g., Lanier & Henry, 2004; Pratt & Cullen, 2000; Tittle, Ward, & Grasmick, 2003; Vold et al., 2002; Vazsonyi, Wittekind, Belliston, & Van Loh, 2004). Studies have found self-control effects for violence for males and females, for a variety of age groups, for offender samples, for several ethnicities, and in several countries (DeLisi, 2001a,b; Vazsonyi, Pickering, Junger, & Hesser, 2001; Vazsonyi et al., 2004). Baron (2003) found self-control effects for homeless youth for property crime, drug use, and violent crime. Studies have found that self-control predicts serious delinquency (Junger & Tremblay, 1999), intimate violence (Sellers, 1999), crime (Brownfield & Sorenson, 1993; Gibbs et al., 1998), a wide variety of delinquent acts and drug use in French-speaking Canadian samples (LeBlanc & Girard,1997), and general delinquency in a national probability sample of adolescents by De Li (2004). The list of empirical demonstrations of self-control effects in Tittle, Ward, and Grasmick (2004, p. 144) includes the following:

A relationship between low self-control and criminal or analogous behaviors has been documented for non-student adults [all citations omitted] . . . ; college students; youth; males as well as females; those with and without official criminal back grounds; and among people in various countries and place. In addition, many types of measures of self-control predict a variety of acts. At least some measures of self-control predict some misbehavior for cross- sectional and longitudinal samples as well as for experimental subjects.

The connection between self-control and a wide variety of acts analogous to violence has been documented by various researchers: cheating, drugs, accidents, and traffic risks (Perrone et al., 2004); accidents (Keane, Maxim, & Teevan, 1993); drinking, drug use, and delinquency among adolescents (Zhang et al., 2002); and attention-deficit hyperactivity disorder and bullying (Unnever & Cornell, 2003).

Control theories place considerable emphasis on the development of affectional bonds between children and parents in the creation of self-control (Hirschi & Gottfredson, 2003). Both overly harsh (including physically abusive) and overly neglectful parenting are associated with later problem behavior in children (Hirschi & Gottfredson, 2003). For example, Maxfield and Widom (1996) report that both abuse and neglect in early childhood later correlate with delinquency. Similar results are reported by Eckenrode et al. (2001, p. 877), who conclude, "Most of the maltreatment experienced by children in our study was neglect, and neglected children showed as many EO [early-onset problem behaviors] as children experiencing physical or sexual abuse."

Conclusion

In self-control theory, caring and attentive parents or other caregivers create the tendency in their children to subordinate their immediate desires to long-term interests. Self-control in children is created by establishing a reciprocal bond between parent and child. This bond inhibits the pursuit of short-term objectives unfettered by longer term concerns, such as parental and peer respect, interpersonal relations, and the development of social capital. Much violent criminal behavior jeopardizes these long-term interests and is thus generally prevented by high levels of self-control. The general characteristics of acts inhibited by high levels of self-control suggest a cause for the versatility effect routinely found in the literature, and the early development of self-control in childhood suggests a reason for the stability of individual differences in the tendency for problem behaviors to persist over the life course.

Acknowledgments

Age data from California Department of Finance. www.dof.ca.gov/.

Arrest data from California Department of Justice. //justice.hdcdojnet.state.ca.us/.

Alcohol-involved accident data from California Highway Patrol, Annual Report SWITRS, 2000, table 5j.

References

Akers, R. (1991). Self-control as a general theory of crime. *Journal of Quantitative Criminology* 7(2), 201–211.

Baron, S. (2003). Self-control, social consequences and criminal behavior: Street youth and the general theory of crime. *Journal of Research in Crime and Delinquency, 40*(4), 403–425.

Baumeister, R., & Heatherton, T. (1996). Self–regulation failure: An overview. *Psychological Inquiry, 7*(1), 1–15.

Boyum, D., & Kleiman, M. (1995). Alcohol and other drugs. In J. Wilson & J. Petersilia (Eds.), *Crime*. San Francisco: ICS Press.

Brannigan, A., Gemmell, W., Pevalin, D., & Wade, T. 2002. Self-control and social control in childhood misconduct and aggression: The role of family structure, hyperactivity, and hostile parenting. *Canadian Journal of Criminology*, 9–142.

Britt, C. (1994). Versatility. In T. Hirschi & M. Gottfredson (Eds.), *The generality of deviance*. New Brunswick, NJ: Transaction.

Brownfield, D., & Sorenson, S. (1993). Self-control and juvenile delinquency: Theoretical issues and empirical assessment of selected elements of a general theory of crime. *Deviant Behavior, 14*(243), 64.

Burton, V., Cullen, F., Evans, T., Dunaway, R., Kethineni, S., & Payne, G. (1995). The Impact of Parental Controls on Delinquency. *Journal of Criminal Justice, 23*, 111–126.

Burton, V., Evans, T., Cullen, F., Olivares, K., & Dunaway, R. (1999). Age, self-control, and adults' offending behaviors: A research note assessing *A general theory of crime. Journal of Criminal Justice, 27*(1), 45–54.

Clarke, S. & Campbell, F. (1998). Can intervention early prevent crime later? The abecedarian project compared with other programs. *Early Childhood Research Quarterly*, 319–343.

Cohen, L., & Felson, M. (1978). Social change and crime rate trends: A routine activities approach. *American Sociological Review, 44*, 588–608.

Cullen, F., & Agnew, R. (2003). *Criminological theory: Past to present* (2nd ed.). Los Angeles: Roxbury.

DeLisi, M. (2001a). Designed to fail: Self-control and involvement in the criminal justice system. *American Journal of Criminal Justice, 26*(1), 131–148.

DeLisi, M. (2001b). It's all in the record: Assessing self-control theory with an offender sample. *Criminal Justice Review, 26*(1), 116.

De Li, S. (2004). The impacts of self-control and social bonds on juvenile delinquency in a national sample of midadolescents. *Deviant Behavior, 25*, 351–373.

Donovan, J., Jessor, R., & Costa, F. (1991). Adolescent health behavior and conventionality–unconventionality: An extension of problem-behavior theory. *Health Psychology, 10*(1), 52–61.

Eckenrode, J., Zielinske, D., Smith, E., Marcynyszyn, L., Henderson, C. Jr., Kitzman, R., et al. (2001). Child maltreatment and the early onset of problem behaviors: Can a program of nurse home visitation break the link? *Development and Psychopathology, 13*, 873–890.

Farrington, D. (2003). Developmental and life–course criminology: Key theoretical and empirical issues – The 2002 Sutherland Award address. *Criminology, 41*(2), 221–255.

Feldman, S. & Weinberger, D. (1994). Self-Restraint as a Mediator of Family Influences on Boys' Delinquent Behavior: A Longitudinal Study. *Child Development 65*, 195–211.

Gibbs, J. Giever, D., & Martin, J. (1998). Parental management and self-control: An empirical test of Gottfredson and Hirschi's general theory. *Journal of Research in Crime and Delinquency, 35*, 42–72.

Glueck, S., & Glueck, E. (1950). *Unraveling juvenile delinquency*. Cambridge, MA: Harvard University Press.

Gottfredson, M. (2005). The empirical status of control theories in criminology. In Francis Cullen et al. (Eds.), *Taking stock: The empirical status of theory in criminology*. New Brunswick, NJ: Transaction.

Gottfredson, M. & Hirschi, T. (1994). The generality of deviance. New Brunswick, NJ: Transaction.

Gottfredson, M., & Hirschi, T. (1990). *A general theory of crime*. Palo Alto, CA: Stanford University Press.

Gottfredson, M., & Hirschi, T. (1993). A control theory interpretation of psychological research on aggression. In R. Felson & J. Tedeschi (Eds.), *Aggression and violence*. Washington, DC: American Psychological Association.

Hindelang, M., Gottfredson, M., & Garofalo, J. (1978). *Victims of personal crime: An empirical of personal victimization*. Cambridge, MA: Ballinger.

Hindelang, M., Hirschi, T., & Weis, J. (1981). *Measuring delinquency*. Beverly Hills, CA: Sage.

Hirschi, T. (1969). *Causes of delinquency*. Berkeley: University of California Press.

Hirschi, T., & Gottfredson, M. (1983). Age and the explanation of crime. *American Journal of Sociology, 89*, 552–584.

Hirschi, T. & Gottfredson, M. (2000). In Defense of Self-Control. *Theoretical Criminology. 4*(1), 55–69.

Hirschi, T., & Gottfredson, M. (2004). Punishment of children from the point of view of control theory. In C. Britt & M. Gottfredson (Eds.), *Advances in criminological theory. Vol. 12: Control theories of crime and delinquency*. New Brunswick, NJ: Transaction.

Junger, M., & Tremblay, R. (1999). Self-control, accidents and crime. *Criminal Justice and Behavior, 26*, 485–501.

Keane, C., Maxim, P., & Teevan, J. (1993). Drinking and driving, self control, and gender: Testing and general theory of crime. *Journal of Research in Crime and Delinquency, 30*, 30–46.

Laub, J., & Sampson, R. (2003). *Shared beginnings, divergent lives*. Cambridge, MA: Harvard University Press.

Lanier, M., & Henry, S. (2004). *Essential criminology*. Boulder, CO: Westview Press.

LeBlanc, M., & Girard, S. (1997). The generality of deviance: Replication over two decades with a Canadian sample of adjudicated boys. *Canadian Journal of Criminology*, 171–183.

Loeber, R., & Dishion, T. (1983). Early predictors of male delinquency: A review. *Psychological Bulletin, 94*, 68–99.

Loeber, R., & Stouthamer-Loeber, M. (1986). Family factors as correlates and predictors of juvenile conduct problems and delinquency. In M. Tonry & N. Morris (Eds.), *Crime and justice: An annual review of research* (Vol. 7,

pp. 29–149). Chicago: University of Chicago Press.

Maxfield, M., & Widom, C. (1996). The cycle of violence: Revisited 6 years later. *Archives of Pediatric and Adolescent Medicine, 150*, 390–395.

McCord, W., & McCord, J. (1959). *Origins of crime*. New York: Columbia University Press.

Mischel, W., Shoda, Y., & Peake, P. (1988). The nature of adolescent competencies predicted by preschool delay of gratification. *Journal of Personality and Social Psychology, 54*(4), 687–696.

Moffitt, T. E. (1993). Adolescence-limited and life-course persistent antisocial behavior: A developmental taxonomy. *Psychological Review, 100*, 674–701.

Olds, D., Pettitt, L., Robinson, J., Henderson, C., Eckenrode, J., Kitzman, H., et al. (1998). Reducing risks for antisocial behavior with a program of prenatal and early childhood home visitation. *Journal of Community Psychology, 26*(1), 65–83.

Osgood, D., Johnston, L., O'Malley, P., & Bachman, J. (1988). The generality of deviance in late adolescence and early adulthood. *American Sociological Review, 53*, 81–93.

Perrone, D., Sullivan, C., Pratt, T., & Margaryan, S. (2004). Parental efficacy, self-control, and delinquency: A test of a general theory of crime on a nationally representative sample of youth. *International Journal of Offender Therapy and Comparative Criminology, 48*(3), 298–312.

Pratt, T., & Cullen, F. (2000). The empirical status of Gottfredson and Hirschi's general theory of crime: A meta-analysis. *Criminology, 38*, 931–964.

Sampson, R., & Laub, J. (1995). *Crime in the making: Pathways and turning points through life*. Cambridge, MA: Harvard University Press.

Sampson, R., & Laub, J. (2003). Life–course desisters? Trajectories of crime among delinquent boys followed to age 70. *Criminology, 41*(3), 555–592.

Sellers, C. (1999). Self-control and intimate violence: An examination of the scope and specification of the general theory of crime. *Criminology, 37*, 375–404.

Tangney, J., Baumeister, R., & Boone, A. (2004). High self-control predicts good adjustment, less pathology, better grades, and interpersonal success. *Journal of Personality, 72*(2), 271–322.

Tittle, C., Ward, D., & Grasmick, H. (2003). Gender, age, and crime/deviance: A challenge to self-control theory. *Journal of Research in Crime and Delinquency, 40*(4), 426–453.

Tittle, C., Ward, D., & Grasmick, H. (2004). Capacity for self-control and individuals' interest in exercising self-control. *Journal of Quantitative Criminology, 20,* 143–172.

Unnever, J., & Cornell, D. (2003). Bullying, self-control and ADHD. *Journal of Interpersonal Violence, 18*(2), 129–147.

Vazsonyi, A., Pickering, L., M. Junger, M., & Hessing, D. (2001). An empirical test of a general theory of crime: A four-nation comparative study of self-control and the prediction of deviance. *Journal of Research in Crime and Delinquency, 38*(2), 91–131.

Vazsonyi, A., Wittekind, J., Belliston, L., & Van Loh, T. (2004). Extending the general theory of crime to "The East": Low self-control in Japanese late adolescents. *Journal of Quantitative Criminology, 20*(3), 189–216.

Vold, G., Bernard, T., & Snipes, J. (2002). *Theoretical criminology* (5th ed). Oxford: Oxford University Press.

Wolfgang, M., Figlio, R., & Sellin, T. (1972). *Delinquency in a birth cohort*. Chicago: University of Chicago Press.

Wright, J. and Cullen, F. (2001). Parental Efficacy and Delinquent Behavior: Do Control and Support Matter? *Criminology, 39,* 677–706.

Zhang, L., Welte, J. and Wieczorek, W. (2002). Underlying common factors of adolescent problem behaviors. *Criminal Justice and Behavior, 29*(2), 161–182.

CHAPTER 28

Why Observing Violence Increases the Risk of Violent Behavior by the Observer

L. Rowell Huesmann and Lucyna Kirwil

Overview

Severe violent behavior is almost always the product of predisposing individual differences and precipitating situational factors (Huesmann, 1998). One important environmental experience that contributes both to predisposing a person to behave more violently in the long run and to precipitating violent behavior in the short run is exposure to violence. Psychological theories that have emerged over the past few decades now explain the short-term precipitating effects mostly in terms of priming, simple imitation, and excitation transfer. However, the long-term predisposing effects involve more complex processes of observational learning of cognitions and of emotional desensitization.

In this chapter, these theories are elaborated, and the compelling empirical evidence in support of these theories from experiments and longitudinal field studies is reviewed. We explain why the processes operate equally well from exposure to real-life violence or exposure to dramatic violence in the mass media. We focus particu-

larly on the role of low emotional arousal and diminished emotional reactions to violence as consequences of exposure to violence and precursors of violent behavior. We argue that anticipated emotional responses play an important role in the cognitive processing that controls violent behavior. Abnormal violent behavior is not viewed as a consequence of "deficient" processing, but rather as a consequence of "different" processing.

Introduction

Sudden acts of individual violence have long fascinated Americans far out of proportion to the damage they cause. Whether it is "Lizzie Bordon taking an ax and giving her husband 40 whacks," Leopold and Loeb kidnapping and murdering a child for no apparent reason, Charles Manson and cronies killing Hollywood celebrities, or Dillon Klebold and Eric Harris murdering classmates in Columbine High School, the attention of the public becomes riveted on these events. We seek to understand what seems inexplicable, we seek to find the underlying cause that made these perpetrators do what they did, and we try to differentiate these perpetrators from the others around us who look no different on the surface.

In these environments there are many villains that are easy to blame, and usually they all receive some blame without any evidence to support the claim – poor parenting, defective genes, bad friends, easy availability of guns, and most recently media violence. Some people believe that the only reason some of these causes (e.g., gun availability and media violence) are blamed is that they are easy targets that deflect attention from the individual and from other more complex causes that society does not want to address. There may be some truth to this claim, but it does not relieve scholars of the responsibility of critically addressing each cause in a more dispassionate manner. Such scientific critical evaluation must involve two important linked components: (1) a theory that illuminates a psychological process by which the hypothesized cause produces the effect on violent behavior and (2) a body of empirical evidence that supports the theory.

In this chapter, we focus on this question: to what extent does individuals' exposure to violent behavior – in their personal world or in the larger world around them through the mass media – increase the risk for them behaving violently? The debate on this topic has long been passionate in the political and public arena probably because of the perceived threats to "free expression" and profits in the marketplace posed by finding media violence unquestionably guilty. However, the scientific debate has become more muted as evidence and theory have accumulated that exposure to violent behavior undoubtedly has an effect. The psychological processes through which exposure to violence in one's personal world or in one's media world engenders an increased risk of behaving violently are now understood, and the empirical evidence showing that exposure to violence increases risk has accumulated to the point of being indisputable. We review both these processes and the empirical evidence in this chapter. However, we must start by placing this chapter in

the framework of the other chapters in this book.

Despite the mass media's desire to pin violent acts on single underlying causes, violent behavior is almost never the result of a single cause. Violent behavior is usually the consequence of the convergence of multiple, longer term predisposing factors that have made an individual more receptive to violence and of multiple precipitating factors that have stimulated the individual to violence in the short run. Exposure to violence can play either role, we argue, but it is only one of many important factors as this book illustrates. Critics of the research (e.g., Freedman, 2002; Rhodes, 2000) often tear down the straw dog that media violence is the number one cause of violence in society. These are disingenuous exercises as no competent researcher considers the effects of exposure to violence (in the real world or in the mass media) to be anything more than one significant risk factor for violent behavior among many significant risk factors.

How Does Exposure to Violence Increase Risk for Violence

Although the underlying tenets of the current theories of media-violence effects were formulated decades ago (see Bandura, 1973; Bandura, Ross, & Ross, 1961, 1963a,b,c; Berkowitz, 1962; Eron, Walder, & Lefkowitz, 1971), researchers from a variety of disciplines, primarily psychology, communication, and sociology, have developed, tested, and refined ever-better theoretical models accounting for the consequences of exposure to media violence. The generally accepted theories that have evolved not only explain why exposure to media violence increases aggressive and violent behavior but also suggest numerous factors that might exacerbate or mitigate the effect. These models (e.g., Anderson & Bushman, 2001; Dodge, 1986; 1993; Huesmann, 1982a,b, 1988, 1997, 1998) generally fall under the rubric of social-cognitive information-processing models. Such models focus on how people perceive, think, learn, and come to behave in particular ways as a result of interactions with their social world, a world that includes observation of and participation in real social interactions (e.g., with parents and peers), as well as fictional social interactions (e.g., with various forms of media). These models explain how – within the overall structure of multiple predisposing individual-difference factors interacting with multiple precipitating situational factors to instigate violent behavior – observation of violence plays a role on both sides of the equation. It plays a role as something that predisposes individuals in the long run to be more likely to behave violently, and it plays a role as something that precipitates violent behavior in the short run.

The Social-Cognitive Information-Processing Model

Over the past three decades at least three similar information-processing models have been proposed to explain the psychological processing underlying social information processing (e.g., Anderson & Bushman, 2001; Dodge, 1986, 1993; Huesmann, 1982a, 1988, 1997, 1998). Although these models differ in their details, all view the social problem-solving process as one in which situational factors are evaluated, social scripts are retrieved, and these scripts are evaluated until one is selected to guide behavior. The latest revision of Huesmann's model is displayed in Figure 28.1 and is used below to describe the psychological processes through which exposure to violence exerts both short-term and long-term effects.

The model describes the information flow and decision processes that occur when an individual is faced with any social decision. The processes begin with evaluation of the social situation and end with the decision to behave in a certain way and then with the post-hoc self-evaluation of the consequences of behaving that way. The solid lines connecting the bold descriptions of processes in Figure 28.1 represent the flow of informa-

tion, whereas the dotted lines represent the causal influences of one factor on another.

Four cognitive/emotional factors play important roles in individual differences in social problem solving according to this model: *emotional predispositions, world schemas, social scripts,* and *normative beliefs*. Central to the model is the concept that social behavior is controlled to a great extent by social scripts. Scripts are sets of "production rules" representing sequences of expected behaviors and responses, and they describe how to deal with a variety of situations, including conflict (Abelson, 1981; Anderson & Huesmann, 2003; Huesmann, 1988, 1998; Huesmann & Miller, 1994). Scripts are stored in a person's memory and are used as guides for behavior and social problem solving. A script incorporates both procedural and declarative knowledge and suggests what events are to happen in the environment, how the person should behave in response to these events, and what the likely outcome of those behaviors would be. It is presumed that while scripts are first being established they influence the child's behavior through "controlled" mental processes (Schneider & Shriffrin, 1977; Shriffrin & Schneider, 1977), but these processes become "automatic" as the child matures. Correspondingly, scripts that persist in a child's repertoire, as they are rehearsed, enacted, and generate consequences, become increasingly more resistant to modification and change. A more violent person is generally a person whose repertoire of social scripts emphasizes violence.

World schemas are a second kind of cognition assumed to influence behaviors. Such schemas are the database that the individual employs to evaluate environmental cues and make attributions about others' intentions. These attributions in turn will influence the search for a script for behaving. An individual who believes the world is a mean place is more likely to make hostile attributions about others' intent and consequently more likely to retrieve a more aggressive script.

Normative beliefs are a third kind of cognitive schema hypothesized to play a central role in regulating aggressive behavior.

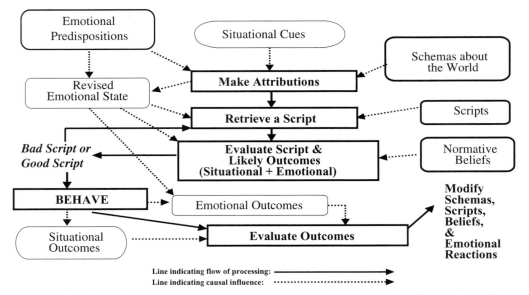

Figure 28.1. The information-processing social-cognitive model for social problem solving. The rounded boxes in bold represent enduring cognitive and emotional predispositions that differ across individuals. Flow of information processing is indicated by solid arrows, and causal influences are indicated by dotted arrows.

Normative beliefs are cognitions about the appropriateness of aggressive behavior. They are related to perceived social norms, but are different in that they concern what's "right for you." Normative beliefs are used to interpret other's behaviors, to guide the search for social scripts, and to filter out inappropriate scripts and behaviors. An individual who believes it is wrong for them to hit a female is likely to reject retrieved scripts that involved hitting females.

Finally, individual differences in emotional predispositions involve a variety of emotion-related tendencies, including a person's overall level of arousal, a person's propensity to become angered, a person's ability to regulate and control his or her emotions, and the associations between situations and emotions that an individual holds. In a social problem-solving situation a person's initial emotional state is modified by the situation and the person's attributions about the situation. The exact relation between propensities toward violence and emotional predispositions depends on the kind of aggressive and violent behavior (e.g., proactive or reactive). Those quick to

anger and poor at regulating their emotions are more likely to retrieve violent scripts and thus behave reactively violently. Those who are underaroused and do not experience intense emotions should not be particularly likely to retrieve violent scripts, but, if such a script meets the goals of the situation, they would also not be likely to reject it because of the negative emotional outcomes it might have. Whereas normal individuals may reject many scripts when they imagine the negative emotional consequences of the script during the script evaluation phase, underaroused individuals are less likely to feel any negative emotions during the evaluation phase.

In any given social setting, therefore, the characteristics of the situation interact with these four individual-difference factors to determine how the individual behaves. Imagine a teen-aged male suddenly discovering his girlfriend holding hands with another male. He makes attributions about what is happening on the basis of his current emotional state and his schemas about the world. Perhaps these lead to hostile attributions. His anger increases, and he is more likely to access a violent script for how to behave. If his repertoire of scripts is heavily loaded with aggressive scripts, accessing one becomes even more likely. He retrieves a script to hit his girlfriend. He evaluates the likely outcomes of the script and filters it through his normative beliefs. Does he feel any negative emotions as he imagines hitting the girl? Does he expect any negative consequences? Is hitting the girl consistent with his normative beliefs about what is OK for him to do? If all these tests are passed, he hits the girl. Finally, he may modify his schemas, scripts, normative beliefs, or emotional predispositions on the basis of the actual outcomes.

Short-Term Effects of Exposure to Violence

This model allows for three ways in which the exposure to violence can increase the risk of violent behavior in the observer in the short run: (1) the observed violent scene primes the retrieval of social scripts for violence that the observer has previously acquired; (2) the observer imitates immediately what he or she has just seen to solve another social problem; or (3) the observer becomes aroused by the violence he or she sees and that arousal increases the risk of behaving violently to solve a social problem.

Priming of Violent Scripts and Schemas

Neuroscientists and cognitive psychologists have discovered that the human mind often acts as an associative network in which ideas are partially activated (primed) by associated stimuli in the environment (Fiske & Taylor, 1984). An encounter with some event or stimulus can prime, or activate, related concepts and ideas in a person's memory even without the person being aware of this influence (Bargh & Pietromonaco, 1982). For example, exposure to violent scenes may activate a complex set of associations that are related to aggressive ideas or emotions, thereby temporarily increasing the accessibility of aggressive thoughts, feelings, and scripts (including aggressive action tendencies). In

other words, aggressive primes or cues make aggressive schemas more easily available for use in processing other incoming information, creating a temporary interpretational filter that biases subsequent perceptions. If these aggressive schemas are primed while certain events – such as ambiguous provocation – occur, the new events are more likely to be interpreted as involving aggression, thereby increasing the likelihood of an aggressive response. Priming effects related to aggression have been empirically demonstrated both for cues usually associated with violence, such as weapons (Anderson, Benjamin, & Bartholow, 1998; Bartholow, Anderson, Benjamin, & Carnagey, 2005; Berkowitz & LePage, 1967; Carlson, Marcus-Newhall, & Miller, 1990), and for initially neutral cues that have been observed repeatedly to be connected to violence, such as the color of a room in which violence is repeatedly observed (Leyens & Fraczek, 1983).

Priming effects are often seen as purely short-term influences. But, of course, the aggressive script or schema being primed may have been acquired long before the exposure to violence that primes its activation. In addition, research by cognitive and social-cognitive scientists has shown that repeated priming of certain scripts or schemas eventually makes them chronically accessible. In essence, frequently primed aggression-related thoughts, emotions, and behavioral scripts become automatically and chronically accessible. That is, they become part of the normal internal state of the individual, thereby increasing the likelihood that any social encounter will be interpreted in an aggression-biased way, and therefore increasing the likelihood of aggressive encounters throughout the individual's life (e.g., Anderson & Huesmann, 2003).

Mimicking Violent Scenes

In recent years indisputable evidence has accumulated that human and primate young have an innate tendency to mimic whomever they observe (Meltzoff, 2005; Meltzoff & Moore, 1977, 2000). They mimic expressions in early infancy and mimic behaviors by the time they can walk. Aggressive behaviors are no different from other observable motor behavior in this regard. Thus, the hitting, grabbing, pushing behaviors that young children see around them or in the mass media are generally immediately mimicked unless the child has been taught not to mimic them (Bandura, 1977; Bandura, Ross, & Ross, 1961, 1963a,b,c). Furthermore, there is good reason to believe that the automatic mimicking of expressions on others' faces also leads to the automatic activation of the emotion that the other was experiencing, as expressions are innately linked to emotions (Prinz, 2005: Zajonc, Murphy, & Inglehart, 1989).

This empirical evidence for automatic imitation in humans has been given added import by an explosion of neurophysiological findings (Iacoboni et al., 1999) and computational theorizing (Schaal, 1999) that explain how imitation works. The demonstration in the mid-1990s of the existence of "mirror neurons" that fire either when an action is observed or when it is executed (Gallese, Fadiga, Fogassi, & Rizzolatti, 1996; Rizzolatti, 2005) provided a strong basis for understanding the innate neurophysiological basis of imitation. Most recently this work has been connected directly with theorizing about social cognitions in adults and how they are acquired (Meltzoff & Decety, 2003). At the same time, the expanding work in artificial intelligence on learning by example (e.g., Dautenhahn & Nehaniv, 2002; Schaal, 1999) has stimulated some developmentalists to think more broadly about the role of imitation and observation in creating the schemas, scripts, beliefs, and emotional dispositions we call the self. The kind of imitation that is involved most often in very short-term effects of exposure to violence is a less complex kind of mimicry that does not involve the need to form a lasting or abstracted cognitive representation of the observed act, but only a "mirror" representation of it. However, that does not mean that the process of imitation in general is not a complex cognitive process. As Hurley and Chatter (2005, p. 1) recently wrote,

Imitation is often thought of as a low level, cognitively undemanding, even childish form of behavior. But recent work across a variety of sciences argues that imitation is a rare ability, fundamentally linked to characteristically human forms of intelligence, and in particular to language, culture, and the ability to understand other minds.

And from a generalists' point of view Brass & Heyes (2005, p. 1) add:

Imitation is based on the automatic activation of motor representations by movement observation. These externally triggered motor representations are then used to reproduce the observed behavior. This imitative capacity depends on learned perceptual-motor links. Finally, mechanisms distinguishing self from other are implicated in the inhibition of imitative behavior.

Arousal and Excitation Transfer

Observing violence is highly emotionally arousing (e.g., disturbing) for most people. That is, it increases heart rate, the skin's conductance of electricity, and other physiological indicators of arousal. There is evidence that this arousal can increase aggression in three different ways. First, the arousal that violence produces is experienced as unpleasant by most people. As such it can increase aggression inclinations just like any other unpleasant stimuli (e.g., loud noises, hot temperatures, foul odors, frustrations, provocations; Berkowitz, 1983). This would be particularly true if the arousal stimulated by the violence is "angry arousal." Second, arousal, regardless of the reason for it, can reach such a peak that performance on complex tasks declines, inhibition of inappropriate responses is diminished, and dominant scripts tend to be displayed in social problem solving. High arousal seems to energize or strengthen whatever an individual's dominant action tendency happens to be at the time. Consequently, if a person is provoked or otherwise instigated to aggress right after being aroused by a violent film, heightened aggression can result (e.g., Geen &

O'Neal, 1969). Third, if a person who is aroused by a violent film misattributes his or her arousal to a provocation by someone else, the propensity to behave aggressively in response to that annoyance is increased (e.g., Bryant & Zillmann, 1979; Zillmann, Bryant, Cominsky, & Medoff, 1981). Thus, people tend to react more violently to provocations immediately after watching exciting movies – violent, sexual, or otherwise exciting – than they do at other times. This kind of effect, called "excitation transfer," is usually short-lived, perhaps lasting only minutes.

Such arousal-transfer effects can occur with any kind of exciting activity, not just exciting movies, TV shows, music videos, or video games. For this reason, the arousal properties of violent media have not drawn as much attention as their other consequences. Nonetheless, it bears noting that frequent episodes in which exposure to violent media is followed by frustrating or provoking events could well lead to an increase in the viewers' aggressive social encounters, which in turn can affect their self-images and the aggressiveness of their social environment. Indeed, recent research shows that playing a violent video game for as little as 10 minutes increases the player's automatic association of "self" with aggressive actions and traits (Uhlmann & Swanson, 2004).

Long-Term Socializing Effects of Exposure to Violence

In addition to the short-term precipitating effects that exposure to violence has on violent behavior, exposure to violence also has long-term socializing effects that predispose those exposed to violence to be more at risk of behaving violently for a long time. These socialization processes alter the four enduring individual differences that affect social behavior according to the model in Figure 28.1: (1) world schemas, (2) social scripts, (3) normative beliefs, and (4) emotional predispositions. Of course, any of these individual differences can be altered through the enactive learning processes (classical and operant conditioning)

by which people learn on the basis of experience. However, repeated exposure to violence changes these individual differences through two other complex learning processes – (1) the observational learning of cognitions (world schemas, scripts, and normative beliefs) that make violent behavior more likely and (2) learned changes in emotional predispositions relevant to violence.

Observational Learning From Exposure to Violence

As described above, humans begin imitating other humans at a very early age, and the observation of others' behaviors is the likely source of many of a young child's motor and social skills (Bandura, 1977; Meltzoff & Moore, 1977). The innate neurophysiological processes that make imitation automatic (probably involving mirror neurons) allow the incorporation into the child's repertoire of simple social scripts at a very young age. Social interactions then hone these behaviors that children first acquire through observation of others, but observational learning remains a powerful mechanism for the acquisition of new social behaviors throughout childhood and maturity. As a child grows older, scripts are acquired instead of simple behaviors. Then, the acquired scripts become more abstract, and beliefs and attitudes are acquired from inferences made about observed social behaviors (Guerra, Huesmann, & Spindler, 2003). Theoretically, children can be expected to learn from whomever they observe – parents, siblings, peers, or media characters. Much of this learning takes place without an intention to learn and without an awareness that learning has occurred.

According to observational-learning theory, the likelihood that an individual will acquire an observed social script is increased when the model performing the script is similar to or attractive to the viewer, the viewer identifies with the model, the context is realistic, and the viewed behavior is followed by rewarding consequences (Bandura, 1977). The reinforcements a person receives when imitating a behavior are largely responsible for whether the behavior persists. For example, youngsters might be rewarded or punished by people in their social environment (parents, teachers, peers) for the actions they exhibit, or they might vicariously experience the rewards or punishments other persons obtain when these others imitate the portrayed behavior. Through imitation and reinforcement, children develop habitual modes of behavior (e.g., Bandura, 1977, 1986; Huesmann, 1997). Whether observational learning leads to long-term effects of media violence depends in part on the consequences that the imitated behaviors bring.

It is theorized that children learn not only specific behaviors from models but also more generalized, complex social scripts. Once learned, such scripts serve as cognitive guides for future behavior. For example, from observing violent people, children may learn that aggression can be used to try to solve interpersonal conflicts. As a result of mental rehearsal (e.g., imagining this kind of behavior) and repeated exposure, this approach to conflict resolution can become well established and easily retrieved from memory. Finally, through inferences they make from repeated observations, children also develop beliefs about the world in general (e.g., is it hostile or benign) and about what kind of behavior is acceptable.

Observational learning and imitation are often thought of as conscious processes, but that need not be the case. Recent theoretical and empirical work (e.g., Bargh & Chartrand, 1999; Neuman & Strack, 2000) suggests that some types of imitative behaviors are very automatic, nonconscious, and likely to be short-lived. It has been demonstrated that movements of human and robotic stimuli as well as their schematic visual presentations elicited automatic imitation in observers (Press, Bird, Flach, & Heyes, 2005). Fadiga, Craighero & Olivier (2005, p. 217) argue that

a large body of evidence supports the view that perception of others' actions is constantly accompanied by motor facilitation of the observer's CS system. This facilitation is not only present during action obser-vation but also while listening to action-related sounds and, more interestingly, while listening to speech.

The motor cortex dynamically replicates the observed actions, as if they were executed by the observer.

Similarly, observational learning of complex scripts and schemas (e.g., beliefs, attitudes, and other types of knowledge that guide perception, interpretation, and understanding) can also occur outside of awareness, even with no immediate imitation of behaviors. Theoretically, it should not matter much for the long-term consequences of observation of violent behavior whether or not the child is aware of its influence. Repeated observation of aggressive behavior should increase the likelihood that children will incorporate aggressive scripts into their repertoires of social scripts, particularly if their own use of those scripts is followed by reinforcement.

One facet of observational learning from exposure to violence is sometimes called *cognitive desensitization to violence*. More properly, desensitization is used to refer to emotional changes that occur with repeated exposures. However, when repeated exposures to violence are followed by changes in beliefs about violence – from the belief that violence and aggression are rare and unlikely behavior to the belief that violence is *common, mundane, and inevitable* – the process is sometimes called cognitive desensitization. Such cognitive desensitization results in more approving violence beliefs, in more positive moral evaluations of aggressive acts, and in more justification for inappropriate behavior inconsistent with social and an individual's moral norms. As a result, the individual may develop stronger pro-violence attitudes (i.e. attitudes approving violence as a means of regulating interpersonal contacts; Huesmann, 1998).

Changes in Emotions Associated With Violence and Provocation

In the earlier material on short-term effects, we discussed the role that heightened arousal from observing violence can play in increasing aggression in the short run. Increased arousal and particularly increased negative affect increase the risk for aggression. However, emotional arousal has a much more complex relation in the long run. Individual differences in the propensity to be aroused seem to interact with learning experiences to produce new individual differences in responsiveness to violence that have lasting effects on the risk for aggressive behavior. As a group these effects have come to be known in the literature as *sensitization effects* and *desensitization effects*. Sensitization refers to the process of becoming more likely to experience negative effect and arousal from scenes that are "provoking," whereas desensitization refers to the process of becoming less likely to experience negative effect and arousal from scenes that are very violent (see also our following section, "Emotional Desensitization to Violence").

The frequently observed short-term effects of arousal have led theorists to posit that some individual differences in the propensity to behave aggressively are related to individual differences in the propensity to become highly aroused and experience negative affect. Berkowitz (1993), Caprara (Caprara et al., 1985), Eisenberg (Eisenberg, Fabes, Nyman, Bernzweig, & Pinuelas, 1994), and Strelau (1982), among others, have suggested that individuals who are "quick to anger," "often in bad moods," and have difficulty "controlling their emotions" are more at risk for behaving aggressively. Implied but unsaid in a lot of this discussion has been the point that such individuals are more at risk particularly for hostile, emotional, reactive aggression, rather than for instrumental, proactive aggression. Significant empirical evidence has also accumulated that supports this individual-difference perspective on high reactivity or arousability (Berkowitz, 1993).

Individual-difference research has also revealed, however, what might at first seem to be a paradoxical finding about reactivity or arousability. Substantial evidence now exists that those males who are characteristically *lower* in baseline arousal are *more likely* to behave aggressively and antisocially over a period of time. For example, Raine and colleagues (Raine, Reynolds, Venables, & Mednick, 1997; Raine, Venables, & Williams, 1990) found in a longitudinal study of males from age 15 to 29 that those who at 15 had lower baseline heart rates, lower baseline skin conductance, and lower baseline EEG activation were significantly more likely to be arrested for a crime in the next 14 years. The psychological concept of psychopathy includes as a major element low reactivity (Hare, 1965, 1978), and psychopathy and low reactivity (particularly low electrodermal reactivity to aversive stimuli) have been shown to relate significantly to antisocial and aggressive behavior (Fowles, 1993; Lykken, 1995) though not particularly to violent behavior. The puzzle about these results, of course, is that no similar situational effects of lower emotional arousal causing increased aggression have been found in experimental studies.

A number of explanations have been offered to explain the relation between low arousal or reactivity and antisocial and aggressive tendencies. Three major hypotheses have been offered to explain why low reactivity might be related to antisocial and aggressive behavior. Perhaps the most widely cited have been the "poor conditioning" theories that have argued that low reactivity or arousability makes conditioning difficult and therefore makes appropriate socialization less likely (Eysenck, 1997). Another alternative has been the sensation-seeking theory that holds that individuals who are characteristically below their optimal level of arousal engage in antisocial and aggressive behavior for the "thrills" in order to raise their arousal level to a more "pleasant" place (Zuckermann, 1979). Still a third theoretical explanation is provided by the social-cognitive information-processing model described above (Huesmann, 1988, 1998). According to this model an individual's evaluation of a potential social script includes an evaluation of the emotions that are likely to result. Will it be an unpleasant experience or a pleasant experience? If a person experiences negative affect and arousal when thinking about the script and its outcome, its use will be inhibited. Consequently, those individuals who experience *less* "anxious arousal" at thoughts of aggression are *more* likely to use aggressive scripts to solve social problems.

This third theory differs from the other two in that it suggests that aggressive behavior is related not only to low reactivity or arousability in general but also specifically to low negative emotional reactivity to thinking about aggression. Lower baseline arousal is related to more aggression because lower baseline arousal translates into lower anxious arousal in response to thoughts of violence. However, individuals with average or even above-average baseline arousal who also experience lower anxious arousal to thoughts of aggression would also display more aggressive behavior according to this theory. This social information-processing theory also neatly explains how increased tendencies to become angered can result from repeated exposures to highly provoking scenes. The emotional reaction produced by attributions about the scene in the initial phase of information processing becomes associated with social and contextual cues present in the scene through classical conditioning. Subsequently the cues prime the reactions and probably the attributions as well, thereby making violence more likely.

Emotional Desensitization to Violence

Emotional desensitization is the name given to the habituation process through which repeated exposures to violence hypothetically cause a reduction in the observer's emotional reactions to violence. Desensitization to violence is seen as a natural, very subtle, and unconscious process, which occurs as an effect of repeated exposure to violent stimuli – real-life violence or filmed violence – and results from the habituation learning process. Habituation of neurophysiological responses over time is a well-established psychological phenomenon (though some responses resist habituation; for a review, see McSweeney & Swindell, 2002). Repeated presentation of the same stimulus usually results in smaller and smaller neurophysiological responses to that stimulus. Systematic desensitization procedures, based on this neurophysiological process, are highly successful in the treatment of strong unpleasant feelings typical of phobias (e.g., Bandura & Adams, 1977; Wolpe, 1958, 1982) and other anxiety or fear disorders (e.g., Pantalon & Motta, 1998). For example, systematically exposing someone with a snake phobia to snakes (initially under conditions designed to minimize anxiety and later under more anxiety-producing conditions) reduces the original anxiety reactions to such an extent that the person is no longer snake phobic. One feature of modern systematic desensitization treatments is to have the phobic person observe other people (live or filmed) successfully interacting with the feared stimulus (Bandura, Grusec, & Menlove, 1967; Bandura & Menlove, 1968). However, the term "desensitization" has been employed in so many different ways that the exact meaning of any particular usage can be quite unclear.

In our usage emotional desensitization to violence is understood as a decrease in both the physiological markers of the emotional arousal normally associated with fight/flight mobilization (e.g., decreases of electric skin conductance, heart rate and blood pressure) and a change in the cognitive interpretations of that arousal. The reactivity becomes gradually smaller with repeated exposures. This means that the organism is building up an emotional tolerance to violence in general or at least to an observed kind of violence. When this process being considered is a single response to a repeating single stimulus, the term "emotional habituation" is usually used. But when the process being considered is the emotional response to a repeating complex set of stimuli over a long run and in a broader context, the term "emotional desensitization" becomes more appropriate. Emotional desensitization thus refers to the joint processes of habituation of many characteristics of a complex stimuli that normally elicit strong emotional reactions.

In summary, we suggest that the label *emotional desensitization to violence* should be reserved to refer to a reduction in distress-related physiological reactivity to observations or thoughts of violence (Carnagey, Bushman, & Anderson, 2005). Emotional desensitization occurs when people who watch a lot of media violence no longer respond with as much unpleasant physiological arousal as they did initially. Because the unpleasant physiological arousal and negative emotional reactions normally associated with violence have an inhibitory influence on thinking about violence, condoning violence, or behaving violently, emotional desensitization – the diminution of the unpleasant arousal – can result in a heightened likelihood of violent thoughts and behaviors.

Empirical Evidence That Exposure to Violence Increases Risk for Violence

Having presented the underlying theory that explains the various psychological processes that explain why exposure to violence should increase violent behavior, let us now turn to a review of empirical evidence. As many fine recent reviews have covered the empirical evidence in great detail (Anderson et al., 2003; Anderson & Bushman, 2001; Huesmann, Moise, & Podolski, 1997; Paik & Comstock, 1994; Savage, 2004), we focus here only on a few classic studies and some more important recent studies.

It is also important to note again that we have defined violent behavior as serious physical aggression intended to harm someone. Such aggression might fit into a category of criminal behavior or it might not, and, if it did fit into a category it might be reflected in criminal statistics or it might not. In other words, the question of whether observation of violence increases the risk of criminally violent behavior is a related but different question that in many respects is more difficult to test because of the low frequency of arrests and convictions for criminally violent acts. For example, Savage (2004) concluded that the evidence to date has not proved that viewing violence causes criminal behavior. Although we do not agree with many ele-

ments of her review (which pays little attention to psychological theory), and although we believe that exposure to violence does cause increases in crime, the overall conclusion that it is unproven to date is probably fair. One can demonstrate that exposure to violence causes increased risk for aggression and increased risk for seriously violent behavior and still not be able to prove that it causes more crime.

Copycat Crimes, Imitation, and Priming

Jason V. Bautista, 20, and his 15-year-old half brother, Matthew Montejo, are accused of killing Jane M. Bautista, cutting off her head and hands and dumping her body along the Ortega Highway in Mexico. Jason Bautista told investigators he saw the same type of mutilation depicted in an episode of The Sopranos, *an HBO series about a Mafia family.*

As reported on the British TV show Panorama, *a Utah teenager kills his mother and half-sister in a fit of rage and then drives around with a friend talking about it and listening to the sound track from Oliver Stone's movie,* Natural Born Killers. *He has the video for the movie and has watched it over and over.*

In December 1997 Michael Carneal of Kentucky opened fire on classmates after a prayer meeting in his high-school lobby, killing three and wounding five. Carneal, later sentenced to life in prison, told detectives he was imitating a scene he believed to be in the film, The Basketball Diaries.

A teenager who is arrested for delinquency and taken to a police station suddenly grabs an officer's gun, shoots him, walks down the corridor of the station shooting others systematically, steals a police car, and races away. The scene closely mimics a scenario from the video game Grand Theft Auto, *which he has been playing over and over.*

A 7-year-old in Texas has been watching wrestling on television when he turns away from the TV and, mimicking a move he has just seen, runs at his 3-year-old brother with his arm extended, hits him in the neck, and kills him.

A gang of girls on a California beach, who have just seen the movie Born Innocent *in which a girl is raped with a broomstick, assault another girl they encounter on the beach and rape her in the same way.*

A young man robs a fast-food restaurant in Sault Lake City and forces the workers into a back room where he pours Drano down their throats just as a robber did in the Clint Eastwood movie he just saw.

In January 1998 in California Gina Castillo was stabbed 45 times by her son and another teenage boy. In court, a witness testified the boys were obsessed with Scream, *a film with a knife-wielding villain.*

These and other widely reported anecdotal stories of "copycat" crimes provide poor scientific evidence of any relation between exposure to media or game violence and violent behavior. For every copycat, there are large but unknown numbers of people who were exposed to the same crime or played the same game but did not then do anything similar. Nevertheless, these anecdotal cases make powerful, compelling, and suggestive examples. Furthermore, some systematic studies of criminal populations have indicated that significant numbers of criminals report that they got their ideas for violent crimes or were stimulated toward a crime by something they saw in the mass media. For example, Surette (2002) reports that among a sample of "serious and violent juvenile offenders" incarcerated as adults, somewhere between 25% and 33% reported that they have "tried the same crime they saw in the media," "gone out looking to get into a fight" after watching a particular program, or "wanted a gun after seeing a gun used" in a show. Similarly, systematic studies of media news reports of suicides have shown that there is a real "Marilyn Monroe" effect in which copycat suicides occur shortly after highly publicized suicides. Phillips (1979) in a statistical analysis of suicide and automobile accident rates showed that a likely copycat effect occurs after highly publicized suicides for perhaps 2 weeks. In addition, scholarly case studies of

individual violent offenders have often shown how observation of violent lifestyles in the movies or around them has provided the youth with validation for their own lifestyles (see, e.g., Coleman, 2002) and made continuation of their violence more likely.

But perhaps the most important role that such anecdotal instances can play is to illustrate some of the psychological processes described above that are involved in media effects but about which many criminologists and the general public are underinformed. Violent copycat crimes by definition occur "shortly" after the perpetrator sees a crime. Thus, it is the short-term psychological processes that are most relevant. Yes, there are certainly *predisposing* individual differences that make one person more likely to copy and carry out a crime than another, but the effect of witnessing a crime on committing a crime shortly afterward can best be viewed as a *precipitating* situational effect.

Priming and simple imitation are undoubtedly the major processes in this regard. The young boy watching wrestling simply immediately imitates what he sees on the closest target – his young brother. When the crime situation is more removed from the scene being copied, usually elements of the situation activate memories of the violent scene including scripts for behaving, and these memories and activated scripts guide the criminal's behaviors. Thus the boy robbing the fast-food store sees the can of Drano, which primes memories of the film seen and gives him the idea of poisoning the workers with it. The depressed individual has the idea of suicide primed by hearing about a recent suicide, and the method for doing it is primed by the same story. The youth who is filled with rage at his parents has ideas of killing them primed by seeing movies like *Natural Born Killers* and then imitates an activated script from that movie in carrying out the murder.

Should we say in such cases that seeing the film or video game "caused the crime?" Certainly seeing the film or video game was not a necessary or sufficient condition for the perpetrator committing the crime. Many others saw these films or played these games and did not commit crimes, and many others committed similar crimes without seeing similar films or playing similar games. Yet, it seems likely that seeing the film or video game was a precipitating factor for the particular perpetrators in question. Given our understanding of the social-cognitive psychological processes involved in social behavior, the most reasonable hypothesis would seem to be that an accumulation of predisposing factors in these individual perpetrators put them in a state in which the criminal behavior could be triggered by the exposure. Therefore, the exposure was one of the causes of the behavior for these individuals. However, a more general conclusion about the causal role of exposure to violence in promoting violent behavior must depend on more rigorous scientific studies, including experiments, one-shot observational studies, and longitudinal observational studies.

Experiments on Imitation and Priming

Ever since Bandura's classical early studies on imitation of film violence (Bandura, Ross, & Ross, 1961), experiments have played an important role in establishing that exposure to violence in the short run causes increases in immediate aggressive behavior. There can no longer be any dispute about this conclusion, and more recent studies than those of Bandura have dealt with more externally valid measures of serious aggressive or violent behavior.

Josephson (1987), for example, randomly assigned 396 7- to 9-year-old boys to watch either a violent or a nonviolent film before they played a game of floor hockey in school. Observers who did not know what movie any boy had seen recorded the number of times each boy physically attacked another boy during the game. Physical attack was defined to include hitting, elbowing, or shoving another player to the floor, as well as tripping, kneeing, pulling hair, and other assaultive behaviors that would be penalized in hockey (the only verbal act included in the measure was insulting another player

with an abusive name). One added element in this study was that a specific cue that had appeared in the violent film (a walkie-talkie) was carried by the hockey referees in some conditions. This particular cue presumably reminded the boys of the movie they had seen earlier. Josephson found that for aggressive boys (those who scored above average on a measure of aggressiveness), seeing a violent film prior to playing increased the likelihood of aggression, and the combination of seeing a violent film and seeing the movie-associated cue stimulated significantly more assaultive behavior than any other combination of film and cue. This is a classic confirmation of a priming effect coupled with an observational learning effect.

Two related randomized experiments demonstrated that exposure to violent media violence can lead to increased physical assaults by teenaged boys, at least in the short run. In a home for delinquent boys in Belgium, Leyens, Camino, Parke, and Berkowitz (1975) assigned boys in two cottages to see violent movies every night for 5 nights while boys in the other two cottages saw nonviolent films. The boys were observed interacting after the movies each evening and were rated for their frequency of hitting, choking, slapping, and kicking their cottage mates. Those boys who were exposed to the violent films engaged in significantly more physical assaults ($p < .025$) on their cottage mates during the week of viewing, most likely because aggressive ideas and scripts were *primed* by the films. Quite probably among these boys aggressive scripts were already well learned and were not "acquired" from the film. Rather these existing scripts were primed by the film and thus more readily employed when they felt provoked in some way.

Experiments on Emotional Desensitization

Some experiments have also provided support for more long-term processes. In particular several studies have shown how youth who watch violence become more tolerant of violence (*cognitive desensitization*) and experience less arousal to violence (*emotional desensitization*). For example, in studies with young children (Drabman & Thomas, 1974, 1975; Thomas & Drabman, 1975), both boys and girls who were shown a brief violent film clip were slower to call an adult to intervene when they saw two younger children fighting than were peers who had watched a neutral film. The single violent clip appeared to make the children more tolerant of aggression, at least temporarily. Furthermore, the children who saw the violent film showed less physiological reactivity to seeing children fighting (Molitor & Hirsch, 1994; Thomas, Horton, Lippincott, & Drabman, 1977). Similarly, Malamuth and Check (1981) found an increased acceptance of physical aggression toward women by college men several days after they had watched violent sex scenes. Linz (1988) and colleagues report similar findings of desensitization to violent "slasher" films.

Cross-Sectional Surveys Suggesting Observational Learning or Desensitization Effects

Although the experimental studies have shown unequivocally that exposure to media violence increases the risk for aggressive behavior in the short run, they have two major limitations. First, experiments cannot be used to investigate long-term effects very well. Second, the criterion measures of aggression in experiments have not been and cannot ethically be representative of the serious physical aggression that really harms the target of the aggression (i.e., violent aggression). However, both of these deficiencies have been remedied in recent years with the publication of a variety of cross-sectional surveys and longitudinal studies. The cross-sectional surveys add to the external validity of the laboratory experiments by investigating "real" violence. The longitudinal studies add to the external validity of experiments as well, but also extend the investigation to long-term effects of exposure to violence.

Cross-sectional surveys over the past 40 years have consistently provided evidence that the current physical aggression, verbal aggression, and aggressive thoughts of young people are correlated with the amount of television and film violence they regularly watch (see reviews by Chaffee, 1972; Comstock, 1980; Eysenck & Nias, 1978; and Huesmann & Miller, 1994). Moreover, the studies reporting significant correlations have used a variety of research methods and examined youngsters of different ages and from different cultures (e.g., Huesmann & Eron, 1986). In some studies, the aggression assessed has included physically aggressive acts serious enough to fit our definition of violence. For example, McLeod, Atkin, and Chaffee (1972) studied the correlations between "aggressive behavioral delinquency" (fighting, hitting, etc.) and TV violence viewing in samples of Wisconsin and Maryland high-school and junior-high-school students. They found significant correlations ranging from .17 ($p < .05$) to .28 ($p < .01$) for both males and females. In a study of English 12- to 17-year-old males, Belson (1978) reported 49% more violent acts in the past 6 months by heavy TV violence viewers than by light violence viewers.

Paik and Comstock's (1994) meta-analysis also examined cross-sectional surveys. For 410 tests of the hypothesis that viewing television violence is positively correlated with aggressive behavior, they reported an average r of .19. These authors identified 200 tests of the hypothesis in which the dependent measure of aggressive behavior was physical aggression against another person. The effect size was essentially the same for these studies as for all surveys combined (i.e., $r = .20$).

These cross-sectional surveys provide convincing evidence that frequent viewing of violence in the media is associated with comparatively high levels of aggressive behavior. The data from these surveys are consistent with the causal conclusions of experiments, though they do not really add to our certainty about the processes involved. The relations found in surveys cannot be due to simple short-term *imitation*, or *excitation transfer*, or *immediate priming* of aggressive thoughts and behaviors;

instead, they must be due to long-term processes, such as *complex observational learning* and *desensitization*. The best evidence these surveys have shown that is consistent with such hypothesized long-term processes is that aggressive cognitions, different emotional reactions to violence, and aggressive behavior have all been found to be more prevalent among those who are regularly exposed to more violence.

Longitudinal Studies, Observational Learning, Desensitization, and Justification

Now let us turn to the longitudinal studies that have directly investigated the long-term effects of media violence. Although these studies also cannot by themselves unequivocally demonstrate causation, they do provide more evidence than cross-sectional studies about the relative plausibility of several alternative causal models and processes.

A significant number of longitudinal studies now exist, and most have been reviewed in other places in more detail than we review them here (e.g., Anderson et al., 2003; Huesmann et al., 1997). Most of these studies focus on exposure to television and films, as few longitudinal studies on violent video games have yet been completed. These studies uniformly reveal longitudinal correlations between early habitual exposure to media violence and later aggressive and violent behavior. The one meta-analysis separating out longitudinal studies (Anderson & Bushman, 2001) found a statistically significant average effect size of .17 across 42 independent tests involving almost 5,000 participants.

In perhaps the first longitudinal study on this topic, initiated in 1960 in New York State, Eron, Huesmann, Lefkowitz, and Walder (1972) found that boys' early childhood viewing of violence on TV was statistically related to their aggressive and antisocial behavior 10 years later (after graduating from high school), even controlling for initial aggressiveness, social class, education, and other relevant variables (Lefkowitz, Eron, Walder, & Huesmann, 1977). On the other hand, behaving aggressively in middle childhood did not predict higher subsequent viewing of violence, making it implausible that the correlation was due to aggressive children turning to watching more violence. A 22-year follow-up of these same boys revealed that their early aggression predicted later criminality at age 30 and that early violence viewing also was independently but weakly related to their adult criminality (Huesmann, 1986, 1995, 2004). Even more recently, data collected when the participants were 48 years old have shown a correlation between TV violence exposure 40 years earlier at age 8 and aggression of several types at age 48 (Huesmann, 2004). None of these data provide any evidence that those boys who are more aggressive turn to watching more violence either because it justifies their behavior or for another reason.

Shortly after this first study was started, Milavsky, Kessler, Stipp, and Rubens (1982) conducted a longitudinal study (funded by NBC) of boys and girls aged 7 to 15 from two Midwestern cities. They examined the effects of television violence on aggression using measures that included serious physical aggression and delinquency. The youth were surveyed up to five times during a 3-year period (1970–1973). Cross-sectional correlations between viewing of TV violence and concurrent levels of aggression ranged from .13 to .23 for boys and .21 to .37 for girls. The investigators then examined the longitudinal regressions predicting aggressive behavior at one point in time from TV violence viewing at an earlier time, while statistically controlling for earlier aggression. They examined these regressions over 15 intervals ranging from 5 months to 3 years apart. For elementary-school boys, 12 of the 15 regression coefficients were positive, although only 2 were statistically significant. Ten of the 15 coefficients were positive for girls, although only 3 were statistically significant. A comparable analysis carried out in a subsample of teenaged boys showed a positive correlation in six of eight cases, but only one such "lag" yielded a significant effect. In all cases, adding SES as a covariate reduced the significant effects further. However, it

should be noted that these predictive analyses were based on subsamples from which
the research team had deleted the data of
many of the most aggressive children (25%
of boys and 16% of girls in the initial sample),
because they supposedly had not reported
their TV viewing accurately.

More recently Huesmann and colleagues
have completed a longitudinal study in
which serious physical aggression and violence in young adulthood were related to
habitual exposure to TV violence 15 years
earlier (Huesmann et al., 2003). Among
the sample of 329 young adults from the
Chicago area, the researchers found significant correlations between television violence viewing during childhood and physical, verbal, and indirect aggression during
young adulthood, for both men ($r = .21$,
$n = 153$, $p < .01$) and women ($r = .19$,
$n = 176$, $p < .01$). When the outcome
examined was restricted to physical aggression or violence (e.g., punch, beat, choke,
threaten, or attack with a knife or gun), the
correlations were still significant ($r s = .17$
and .15, respectively). Furthermore, when
the people who had watched violent programs frequently in childhood were compared with their counterparts who viewed
these programs much less often, it was found
that the former, as adults, committed significantly more acts of physical aggression,
such as having "pushed, grabbed, or shoved
their spouses" (p. 210; 42% vs. 22% in the
case of males) or "shoving, punching, beating or choking" (p. 210) someone who had
made them angry (17% vs. 4% for females).
Additionally, structural modeling analyses
showed that, although high aggressiveness
during childhood was related only slightly
and not significantly to viewing television
violence later in life, habitual exposure to
TV violence during childhood predicted significantly higher levels of serious aggressive
behavior even 15 years later. This longitudinal effect remained significant even when
the researchers controlled statistically for
parents' education, child-rearing behaviors,
aggression, and many other factors, as well as
the children's academic achievement. The
boys and girls who watched more TV vio-

lence consistently when they were between
6 and 10 years old grew up to be more seriously aggressive when they were 21 to 25
years old, *independently of how aggressive they
were initially*. In this study comparable data
were collected in three other countries –
Finland, Poland, and Israel. Although analyses of the data from the other countries are
not yet completed, preliminary results indicate that childhood exposure to media violence also predicts adult aggression in males
and females in Finland and in males in Israel,
but not in Poland, where the social transition of the 1980s seems to have changed
the relations (Huesmann, 2006; Huesmann
& Moise-Titus, 1999; Viemero, 2002).

One other very important finding from
this study was that adult normative beliefs
about the acceptability of aggression were
significantly related both to exposure to violence 15 years earlier and to concurrent adult
aggression (Huesmann, 2006; Huesmann &
Moise, 1999). In support of our conception that social cognitions such as normative beliefs are acquired though observational learning and mediate the long-term
effects of exposure to violence, it was shown
that the mediating effect of such normative
beliefs can explain a significant part (but not
all) of the long-term relation between childhood exposure and adult aggression.

Johnson and his colleagues (Johnson,
Cohen, Smailes, Kasen, & Brook, 2002) conducted another recent longitudinal study
that examined the effects of TV habits
in adolescence and early adulthood on
later violent behavior. They found that,
in their sample of over 700 youth, TV
exposure at age 14 significantly predicted
self-reported assault and fighting behavior
at 16 or 22 years of age (particularly for
males), even after controlling statistically for
family income, parental education, verbal
intelligence, childhood neglect, neighborhood characteristics, peer aggression, and
school violence. In addition, time spent on
TV viewing at age 22 was associated with
subsequent assaults or fights resulting in
injury in males and females and additionally
with subsequent aggressive behavior of any
kind and robbery, threats to injure, or use

of a weapon to commit a crime. Unfortunately, the only measure of media exposure was total viewing time, with no data being collected on the content viewed. Consequently, the mechanisms that might explain these results remain unclear. It is possible that those with greater overall exposure to the mass media also had greater exposure to violence in the mass media. However, it is also possible that the effects could be due to a "passive" process in which the time spent viewing the mass media detracts from better uses of time that promote nonaggressiveness.

An even larger longitudinal sample was surveyed recently by Slater and his colleagues (Slater, Henry, Swaim, & Anderson, 2003). They interviewed over 2,500 middle-school students over 2 years. Although their aggression measure did not assess particularly serious violence, they found compelling evidence of an effect of media violence on aggression. Using hierarchical linear growth curve modeling with imputations of missing data, they found a significant lagged effect of prior violence viewing on subsequent aggression, but no significant effect of prior aggression on subsequent violence viewing.

A very similar analysis technique was used by Guerra, Huesmann, and Spindler (2003) to demonstrate a longitudinal effect of exposure to neighborhood violence on serious aggressive behavior in children. As we said earlier in this chapter, the theory for how exposure to violence affects aggressive behavior does not distinguish between whether the violence is observed in the streets outside a child's house or on the TV. In this particular study over 4,000 children's exposure to neighborhood violence was assessed each year as they progressed from the first to sixth grade. The children all lived in high-violence neighborhoods in the Chicago area. The hierarchical linear growth curve model that fit the data showed that exposure to neighborhood violence in one year had a significant effect on the child's aggression in the next year, even after controlling for the prior level of aggression. However, the child's aggression did not affect how much violence they would see in the next year after one controlled for the vio-

lence they saw in the current year. There was no evidence at all of more aggressive children being more likely to be exposed to neighborhood violence.

Finally, in the one published longitudinal study on video games, Ihori, Sakamoto, Kobayashi, and Kimura (2003) studied Japanese fifth and sixth graders at two points in time separated by 4 to 5 months, measuring overall video game exposure rather than exposure to violent video games. They reported that the amount of exposure to video games was positively (and significantly) related to later levels of violent physical behavior after controlling for earlier violent behavior.

These longitudinal studies provide compelling evidence of a lasting effect of the regular observation of violence in childhood on serious aggressive behavior later in life. Furthermore, these studies contradict the theory that the correlation between exposure to violence and actual violent behavior is entirely due to more violent people liking to watch more violence. People indeed may justify their own behavior by turning to watching more violence in the media, but that effect cannot explain the data found in the several studies that have examined such a process (e.g., Guerra et al., 2003; Huesmann et al., 2003; Slater et al., 2003). When the longitudinal evidence is coupled with the experimental evidence presented earlier, the case for a lasting causal effect for exposure to violence on violent behavior seems more than just plausible. The long-term effect can be explained theoretically by the changes in cognitions and emotions that are engendered by exposure to violence and then persist for a long time. However, the amount of evidence demonstrating that such cognitive changes or emotional changes do indeed mediate the effect is still limited.

Moderators of the Long-Term Effects of Exposure to Violence

We did not devote much space above to a discussion of all the factors that moderate the long-term or short-term impact of observed violence on aggressive and violent behavior in the observer. Yet, the effects are clearly moderated by a very large number of factors, including characteristics of the viewer, the observed violence scene, and the setting in which the scene is viewed. For example, with regard to the person, genetic, personal, familial, community, and cultural factors all can moderate the effect. Not every child who is exposed to violence will behave noticeably more aggressively, even if they are affected to some extent. Most children are highly resilient, and it requires a convergence of many bad things to make them seriously "bad."

We began this analysis by noting in our theoretical model that observation of violence is just one factor among many predisposing and precipitating factors that combine to influence aggressive and violent behavior. These factors do not simply combine additively. They combine interactively. Thus, it is easier to talk about some of the factors that do not seem to play important moderating roles than to talk about factors that do play important roles. The most important moderating factors have been discussed in detail in several recent reviews (Anderson et al., 2003; Bushman & Huesmann, 2002; Huesmann, Moise, & Podolski, 1997), and we only summarize a few of their conclusions here. For example, identification with the aggressive perpetrator is a very important moderator of the effects, as are the extent to which the violence (1) seems true to life, (2) is portrayed as justified, and (3) is perceived as rewarded. Thus, one can expect first-person shooter games to have larger effects than third-person games, though this has yet to be confirmed. At the person level, the most aggressive behaviors will come from exposing already aggressive individuals to more violence, though exposure affects even nonaggressive individuals. Children experience more lasting effects than adults. Although children with lower IQs and lower SES are both exposed to more violence and behave more aggressively, exposure seems to affect children on all levels of these factors. Finally, the effects seem to be less for children whose

parents co-view with the child and discuss with the child what they are seeing (i.e., engage in parental mediation; Nathanson, 1999).

Empirical Data on Emotional Reactions to Violence

As outlined earlier in this chapter, the long-term effects of exposure to violence are viewed as due either to changes in cognitions, such as social scripts, world schemas, and normative beliefs, or to changes in emotional reactions to violence.

Of course, experiencing more anger in response to certain stimuli can increase the risk for aggressive behavior, so being sensitized to experience more anger should certainly increase the risk for aggression. In fact, some recent research has indicated that those who experience more anger when observing others being provoked are more at risk for reactive aggression (Huesmann, Moise, & Kirwil, 2004; Moise-Titus, 1999). However, there is little empirical research showing how repeated exposures to violence sensitize people to experience more anger, even though the theory is very plausible.

The other long-term emotional change that we linked theoretically above to increases in violent behavior is a decrease in negative emotional reactions to observing or thinking about violence. When there is little negative emotional reaction to thoughts of violence, the evaluation of violent outcomes looks more positive, and violent behavior becomes more likely. In this final section of the chapter we want to discuss some quasi-experimental studies that provide particular evidence consistent with the two parts of this theoretical proposition: (1) that negative emotional reactions to scenes or thoughts of violence diminish with repeated exposures to violence and (2) that diminished negative emotional reactions to violence increase the risk for violent behavior.

With regard to the first part of this proposition, research has indeed shown that violent scenes are less unpleasantly arousing to those who have observed more of them

(Cline, Croft, & Courrier, 1973; Oliver, 2004), and even relatively brief observations of media violence (or real-life violence) can reduce subsequent physiological reactions to the sight of real-world violence (Carnagey et al., 2005; Kirwil, 2002a; Moise-Titus, 1999; Molitor & Hirsch, 1994; Thomas et al., 1977). Such desensitization occurs for violent video games as well as films and can be detected in EEG changes as well as skin conductance (Bartholow et al., 2006). Desensitization occurs in children and adults, though the course of habituation for adult females may be slower (Kirwil, 2004a; Thomas et al., 1977). Emotional desensitization to observed aggression in children has also been related to more tolerance for aggression on children's parts (Thomas & Drabman, 1975). Viewing media violence can elicit strong emotions, such as fear or anger, but these emotions are usually temporary immediate reactions of relatively short duration and accompanied by increase in physiological arousal (Cantor, 2002; van der Voort, 1986). It has to be pointed out that emotional responses to such complex stimuli as filmed violence are composed of various basic emotions, usually negative in emotional tone, such as anxiety, distress, disgust, sadness, or empathy toward the victim or hate toward the perpetrator (Kirwil, 2002b). Emotional desensitization to observed violence takes place after repeated exposure to violence, when there is blunting of these emotional reactions to events or stimuli that normally elicit strong emotional responses in the observer. This means that frequent observers of violence became gradually less and less emotionally sensitive to acts of violence and they become less quickly frightened or angered or disgusted by violent scenes (Cantor, 2002, 2003; Kirwil, 2002b; Oliver, 2004).

Research has also shown that affective habituation may occur to subliminal exposure to extreme stimuli (violent stimuli are one of the kind of extreme negative stimuli) and that the size of the desensitization effect might be a direct function of how extreme the stimuli are (Dijksterhuis & Smith, 2002). The more intense the stimuli are, the more pronounced is the decrease in intensity of negative affective reactions toward violence. Consequently, the extreme negative violent stimuli became subjectively less extremely negative. As a result "initially strong excitatory reactions have become weak or have vanished entirely with repeated exposure to stimuli of a certain kind (very violent stimuli); and correspondingly, initially strong affective reactions have been blunted" (Zillmann, 1982, p. 61).

The second part of the proposition, that those who show diminished emotional reactions to violence behave more aggressively, has now also been confirmed with recent studies. In a quasi-experimental study Moise-Titus (1999) demonstrated that college males who displayed less anxious arousal (as measured by skin conductance and self-reports of emotions) when watching extremely violent and gory scenes of violence (e.g., scenes from *Reservoir Dogs*) had engaged in more physical aggression in the past and were more physically aggressive toward another student immediately after watching the film than were those who showed more anxious arousal to the violence. Kirwil and Huesmann followed this study with a series of studies that replicated and elaborated the results. They showed that more aggressive male college students show decreased arousal to repeated scenes of violence (i.e., they habituate faster physiologically to observed violence than do less aggressive male college students; Huesmann et al., 2004; Kirwil, 2002a, 2004a; Kirwil & Huesmann, 2003) and that this effect of faster diminishing physiological responses occurs in U.S. and Polish males (Kirwil, 2002a). However, similar to earlier findings reported by Thomas et al. (1977), Kirwil (2004a) found that these differences did not occur for females. Females, on the whole, showed much greater negative emotional reactions when observing males brutally attacking other males than did the males, and the most aggressive females (particularly reactively aggressive females) displayed more (not less) emotional arousal than other females when observing these scenes.

These results from the Kirwil (2004a) and Thomas et al. (1977) studies suggest that sensitization to provocation may be a more important emotional consequence of observing violence for females than is desensitization.

The desensitizing effects of exposure to violence on males and the relation of males' diminished reactions to violence to their aggressiveness appear to be fairly robust, however. For example, in addition to her findings with college males, Kirwil (2004b) also found a relation between diminished emotional reactions to observed violence and the extent to which policemen had been exposed to real-life violence. In particular, it was shown that Polish riot policemen, who are exposed to violence in their job, habituate physiologically to filmed violence faster than college students and show less arousal on the average. Furthermore, the magnitude of this decreased arousal in policemen depends on how long they have been policemen (Kirwil 2004b; Kirwil & Huesmann, 2003). Decreased emotional responses to observed violence have also been linked to more aggression in clinically aggressive boys. In a study comparing 59 boys diagnosed with Disruptive Behavior Disorder (DBD) with 44 normal boys, Grimes, Berger, Nochols, Vernberg, and Fonagy (2004) found almost identical results. When observing violent films clips, these DBD boys responded with significantly less physiological arousal (skin conductance level and vagal tone) than did the normal boys.

It seems clear, then, that decreased arousal in response to seeing or thinking about violence is a predictor or risk for behaving violently and that repeated exposure to violence decreases negative emotional (and cognitive) reactions to violence. However, three important related questions remain unanswered. First, is the relation between lack of a negative affective response to violence and risk for violent behavior simply an instance of a more general phenomenon that low arousal is a predictor of aggression? Or is the relation at least partially specific to exposure to violence? Second, is the lack of a negative emo-

tional response predictive of all kinds of violence or only of proactive, nonemotional, violent behavior? Third, are the individual differences in emotional reactions to violence that have been observed in empirical studies innate, are they acquired through repeated exposures to violence, or are they some combination of the two? Much empirical evidence has been collected to test the hypothesis that violent offenders are predisposed to manifest aggression because of extreme characteristics of their emotional reactivity (i.e., overreactivity in the case of impulsive reactive aggression or underreactivity in the case of premeditated proactive aggression; for a review, see Raine, 1993; Raine et al., 2006) or fear deficit (Lykken, 1995). However, there is not much research demonstrating what impact repeated exposure to filmed violence has on experienced intensity and valence of arousal, as well as real violent behavior in offenders. Does repeated exposure to violence make only the predisposed violent offender more emotionally desensitized and more cruel? Or does exposure to filmed violence gradually desensitize any individual and make him or her more inclined to be aggressive and to commit violent offences? Quite likely, the dynamics of physiological arousal and emotions experienced by violent offenders under impact of repeated exposure differs depending on the kind of violent crime they have committed.

Summary

Severe violent behavior is almost always the product of predisposing individual differences and precipitating situational factors (Huesmann, 1998). One important environmental experience that contributes both to predisposing a person to behave more violently in the long run and to precipitating violent behavior in the short run is exposure to violence. Psychological theories that have emerged over the past few decades now explain the short-term precipitating effects mostly in terms of priming, simple imitation, and excitation transfer. However, the long-term predisposing effects involve more complex processes of observational learning of cognitions and of emotional desensitization or sensitization. In particular, we argue that anticipated emotional responses play an important role in the cognitive processing that controls violent behavior. Abnormal violent behavior is not viewed as a consequence of "deficient" processing, but as a consequence of "different" processing.

In this chapter these theories were elaborated, and the compelling empirical evidence in support of these theories from experiments and longitudinal field studies is reviewed. The experimental studies have demonstrated causation unambiguously. Quasi-experimental studies have shown that desensitization does occur and that people with lower negative affective responses to observing violence are more at risk for behaving violently. The longitudinal and cross-sectional field studies have shown that children and young adults who regularly are exposed to more media violence or real-world violence around them behave more aggressively both immediately and many years later (see Anderson et al., 2003). The effect sizes typically are not large – ranging from .15 to .30 – but are highly replicable and obtain in many different cultures with different media systems (Anderson et al., 2003; Anderson & Bushman 2001; Huesmann, Moise, & Podolski, 1997; Paik & Comstock, 1994). They have been found for exposure to violent TV shows, for exposure to violent films, and for playing violent video games. Finally, they are as large as many other effect sizes that are considered to be public health threats.

Nevertheless, there are large holes in our knowledge of why and how exposure to violence stimulates violent behavior. The greatest need is for research that more specifically investigates links between media violence exposure and the more serious forms of aggression (e.g., criminally violent behavior), as well as links to theoretically relevant mediating variables. This need is best filled by research on high-risk populations, such as offender populations. This review also revealed a need for additional research on potential moderating factors (e.g., personal factors, family factors, and cultural factors) that determine who is more affected by observing violence. In sum, the proposed research is needed to provide a better estimate of the relative magnitude of media violence effects on serious violent and criminal behavior (relative to other risk factors), to identify populations most vulnerable to such media violence effects, and to provide a basis for sound public health policy regarding media violence.

References

Abelson, R. P. (1981). Psychological status of the script concept. *American Psychologist, 36,* 715–729.

Anderson, C. A., Benjamin, A. J., & Bartholow, B. D. (1998). Does the gun pull the trigger? Automatic priming effects of weapon pictures and weapon names. *Psychological Science, 9,* 308–314.

Anderson, C. A., Berkowitz, L., Donnerstein, E., Huesmann, L. R., Johnson, J., Linz, D., et al. (2003). The influence of media violence on youth. *Psychological Science in the Public Interest, 4*(3), 81–110.

Anderson, C. A., & Bushman, B. J. (2001). Effects of violent video games on aggressive behavior, aggressive cognition, aggressive affect, physiological arousal, and prosocial behavior: A meta-analytic review of the scientific literature. *Psychological Science, 12,* 353–359.

Anderson, C. A., & Huesmann, L. R. (2003). Human aggression: A social-cognitive view. In M. A. Hogg & J. Cooper (Eds.), *Handbook of social psychology* (pp. 296–323). London: Sage.

Bandura, A. (1973). *Aggression: A social learning theory analysis.* Englewood Cliffs, NJ: Prentice Hall.

Bandura, A. (1977). *Social learning theory.* Englewood Cliffs, NJ: Prentice Hall.

Bandura, A. (1986). *Social foundations of thought and action.* Englewood Cliffs, NJ: Prentice Hall.

Bandura, A., & Adams, N. E. (1977). Analysis of self-efficacy theory of behavioral change. *Cognitive Therapy and Research, 1,* 287–310.

Bandura, A., Grusec, J. E., & Menlove, F. L. (1967). Vicarious extinction of avoidance behavior. *Journal of Personality and Social Psychology, 5,* 16–23.

Bandura, A., & Menlove, F. L. (1968). Factors determining vicarious extinction of avoidance behavior through symbolic modeling. *Journal of Personality and Social Psychology, 8*, 99–108.

Bandura, A., Ross, D., & Ross, S. A. (1961). Transmission of aggression through imitation of aggressive models. *Journal of Abnormal and Social Psychology, 63*, 575–582.

Bandura, A., Ross, D., & Ross, S. A. (1963a). Imitation of film-mediated aggressive models. *Journal of Abnormal and Social Psychology, 66*, 3–11.

Bandura, A., Ross, D., & Ross, S. A. (1963b). A comparative test of the status envy, social power, and secondary reinforcement theories of identificatory learning. *Journal of Abnormal and Social Psychology, 67*, 527–534.

Bandura, A., Ross, D., & Ross, S. A. (1963c). Vicarious reinforcement and imitative learning. *Journal of Abnormal and Social Psychology, 67*, 601–607.

Bargh, J. A., & Chartrand, T. L. (1999). The unbearable automaticity of being. *American Psychologist, 54*, 462–479.

Bargh, J. A., & Pietromonaco, P. (1982). Automatic information processing and social perception: The influence of trait information presented outside of conscious awareness on impression formation. *Journal of Personality and Social Psychology, 43*, 437–449.

Bartholow, B. D., Bushman, B. J., & Sestir, M. A. (2006). Chronic violent video game exposure and desensitization to violence: Behavioral and event-related brain potential data. *Journal of Experimental Social Psychology, 42*(4), 532–539.

Bartholow, B. D., Anderson, C. A., & Carnagey, N. L. (2005). Interactive effects of life experience and situational cues on aggression: The weapons priming effect in hunters and non-hunters. *Journal of Experimental Social Psychology, 41*(1), 48–60.

Belson, W. A. (1978). *Television violence and the adolescent boy.* Hampshire, England: Saxon House, Teakfield.

Berkowitz, L. (1962). *Aggression: A social psychological analysis.* New York: McGraw-Hill.

Berkowitz, L. (1983). Aversively stimulated aggression: Some parallels and differences in research with animals and humans. *American Psychologist, 38*, 1135–1144.

Berkowitz, L. (1993). *Aggression: Its causes, consequences, and control.* New York: McGraw-Hill.

Berkowitz, L., & LePage, A. (1967). Weapons as aggression-eliciting stimuli. *Journal of Personality and Social Psychology, 7*, 202–207.

Brass, M., & Heyes, C. (in press). Imitation: is cognitive neuroscience solving the correspondence problem? *Trends in Cognitive Sciences, 9*(10), 489–495.

Bryant, J., & Zillmann, D. (1979). Effect of intensification of annoyance through unrelated residual excitation on substantially delayed hostile behavior. *Journal of Experimental Social Psychology, 15*, 470–480.

Bushman, B. J., & Huesmann, L. R. (2001). Effects of televised violence on aggression. In D. G. Singer & J. L. Singer (Eds.), *Handbook of children and the media* (pp. 223–254). Thousand Oaks, CA: Sage.

Cantor, J. (2002). The media and children's fears, anxieties, and perceptions of danger. In D. G. Singer & J. L. Singer (Eds.), *Handbook of children and the media* (pp. 207–21). Thousand Oaks: Sage.

Cantor, J. (2003). Media violence effects and interventions: The roles of communication and emotion. In J. Bryant, D. Roskos-Evoldsen, & J. Cantor (Eds.), *Communication and emotion* (pp. 197–219). Mahwah, NJ: Erlbaum.

Caprara, G. V., Cinanni, B., D'Imperio, G., Passerini, S., Renzi, P., & Travaglia, G. (1985). Indicators of impulsive aggression: Present status of research on irritability and emotional susceptibility scales. *Personality and Individual Differences, 6*, 665–674.

Carlson, M., Marcus-Newhall, A., & Miller, N. (1990). Effects of situational aggression cues: A quantitative review. *Journal of Personality and Social Psychology, 58*, 622–633.

Carnagey, N. L., Bushman, B. J., & Anderson, C. A. (2005). *Video game violence desensitizes players to real world violence.* Manuscript submitted for publication.

Chaffee, S. H. (1972). Television and adolescent aggressiveness (overview). In G. A. Comstock & E. A. Rubinstein (Eds.), *Television and social behavior: A technical report to the Surgeon General's Scientific Advisory Committee on Television and Social Behavior. Vol. 3: Television and adolescent aggressiveness* (DHEW Publication No. HSM 72–9058, pp. 1–34). Washington, DC: U.S. Government Printing Office.

Cline, V. B., Croft, R. G., & Courrier, S. (1973). Desensitization of children to television violence. *Journal of Personality and Social Psychology, 27*, 360–365.

Coleman, R. M. (2002). The *Menace II Society* copycat murder case and thug life: A reception study with a convicted criminal. In R. M.

Coleman (Ed.), *Say it loud! African-American audiences, media, and identity*. New York: Routledge.

Comstock, G. (1980). New emphases in research on the effects of television and film violence. In E. L. Palmer & A. Dorr (Eds.), *Children and the faces of television: Teaching, violence, selling* (pp. 129–148). New York: Academic Press.

Dautenhahn, K., & Nehaniv, C. (2002). *Imitation in animals and artifacts*. Cambridge, MA: MIT Press.

Dijksterhuis, A., & Smith, P. K. (2002). Affective habituation: Subliminal exposure to extreme stimuli decreases their extremity. *Emotion*, 2(3), 203–214.

Dodge, K. A. (1986). A social information processing model of social competence in children. In M. Perlmutter (Ed.), *The Minnesota symposium on child psychology* (Vol. 18, pp. 77–125). Hillsdale, NJ: Erlbaum.

Dodge, K. A. (1993). Social-cognitive mechanisms in the development of conduct disorder and depression. *Annual Review of Psychology*, 44, 559–584.

Drabman, R. S., & Thomas, M. H. (1974). Does media violence increase children's tolerance for real-life aggression? *Developmental Psychology*, 10, 418–421.

Drabman, R. S., & Thomas, M. H. (1975). Does TV violence breed indifference? *Journal of Communication*, 25, 86–89.

Eisenberg, N., Fabes, R. A., Nyman, M., Bernzweig, J., & Pinuelas, A. (1994). The relations of emotionality and regulation to children's anger-related reactions. *Child Development*, 65, 109–128.

Eron, L. D., Huesmann, L. R., Lefkowitz, M. M., & Walder, L. O. (1972). Does television violence cause aggression? *American Psychologist*, 27, 253–263.

Eron, L. D., Walder, L. O., & Lefkowitz, M. M. (1971). *The learning of aggression in children*. Boston: Little, Brown.

Eysenck, H. J. (1997). Personality and the bio-social model of anti-social and criminal behaviour. In A. Raine, D. P. Farrington, P. O. Brennen, & S. A. Mednick (Eds.), *The biosocial basis of violence* (pp. 21–37). New York: Plenum Press.

Eysenck, H. J., & Nias, D. K. B. (1978). *Sex, violence, and the media*. New York: Saint Martin's Press.

Fadiga, L., Craighero, L., & Olivier, E. (2005). Human motor cortex excitability during the perception of others' action. *Current Opinion in Neurobiology*, 15, 213–218.

Fiske, S. T., & Taylor, S. E. (1984). *Social cognition*. Reading, MA: Addison-Wesley.

Fowles, D. (1993). Electrodermal activity and antisocial behavior: Empirical findings and theoretical issues. In J.-C. Roy, W. Boucsein, D. Fowles, & J. Gruzelier (Eds.), *Progress in electrodermal research* (pp. 223–237). London: Plenum Press.

Fowles, J. (1999). *The case for television violence*. Thousand Oaks, CA: Sage.

Freedman, J. (2002). *Media violence and its effect on aggression*. Toronto: University of Toronto Press.

Gallese, V., Fadiga, L., Fogassi, L., & Rizzolatti, G. (1996). Action recognition in the premotor cortex. *Brain*, 119, 593–609.

Geen, R. G., & O'Neal, E. C. (1969). Activation of cue-elicited aggression by general arousal. *Journal of Personality and Social Psychology*, 11, 289–292.

Grimes, T., Berger, L., Nochols, K., Vernberg, E., & Fonagy, P. (2004). Is psychopathology the key to understanding why some children become aggressive when they are exposed to violent television programming? *Human Communication Research*, 30, 153–181.

Guerra, N. G., Huesmann, L. R., & Spindler, A. J. (2003). Community violence exposure, social cognition, and aggression among urban elementary-school children. *Child Development*, 74(5), 1507–1522.

Hare, R. D. (1965). A conflict and learning theory analysis of psychopathic behavior. *Journal of Research in Crime and Delinquency*, 12–19.

Hare, R. D. (1978). Electrodermal and cardiovascular correlates of psychopathy. In R. D. Hare & D. Schalling (Eds.), *Psychopathic behavior: Approaches to research* (pp. 107–144). New York: John Wiley & Sons.

Huesmann, L. R. (1982a). Information processing models of behavior. In N. Hirschberg & L. Humphreys (Eds.), *Multivariate applications in the social sciences* (pp. 261–288). Hillsdale, NJ: Erlbaum.

Huesmann, L. R. (1982b). Television violence and aggressive behavior. In D. Pearl, L. Bouthilet, & J. Lazar (Eds.), *Television and behavior: Ten years of scientific programs and implications for the 80s* (Vol. 2, pp. 126–137). Washington, DC: U.S. Government Printing Office.

Huesmann, L. R. (1986). Psychological processes promoting the relation between exposure to media violence and aggressive behavior by the viewer. *Journal of Social Issues*, 42(3), 125–139.

Huesmann, L. R. (1988). An information processing model for the development of aggression. *Aggressive Behavior, 14*, 13–24.

Huesmann, L. R. (1995). *Screen violence and real violence: Understanding the link* (Brochure). Auckland, NZ: Media Aware.

Huesmann, L. R. (1997). Observational learning of violent behavior: Social and biosocial processes. In A. Raine, D. P. Farrington, P. O. Brennen, & S. A. Mednick (Eds.), *The biosocial basis of violence* (pp. 69–88). New York: Plenum Press.

Huesmann, L. R. (1998). The role of social information processing and cognitive schema in the acquisition and maintenance of habitual aggressive behavior. In R. G. Geen & E. Donnerstein (Eds.), *Human aggression: Theories, research, and implications for social policy* (pp. 73–109). New York: Academic Press.

Huesmann, L. R. (2004). *Why those who observe violence behave more violently: Understanding the psychological process.* Paper presented at the meetings of the International Society for Research of Aggression, Santorini, Greece.

Huesmann, L. R. (2006). Long-Term Life-Span Effects and Medium-Term Childhood and Adulthood Effects of Media Violence on Aggression: Evidence from 3 Countries. *International Communication Association,* Dresden, Germany.

Huesmann, L. R., & Eron, L. D. (Eds.). (1986). *Television and the aggressive child: A cross-national comparison.* Hillsdale, NJ: Erlbaum.

Huesmann, L. R., & Miller, L. S. (1994). Long-term effects of repeated exposure to media violence in childhood. In L. R. Huesmann (Ed.), *Aggressive behavior: Current perspectives* (pp. 153–183). New York: Plenum Press.

Huesmann, L. R., & Moise-Titus, J. (1999). *The role of cognitions in mediating the effects of childhood exposure to violence on adult aggression: A 15-year comparison of youth in four countries.* Paper presented at the meeting of the European Society for Developmental Psychology, Spetses, Greece.

Huesmann, L. R., Moise, J. F., & Podolski, C. L. (1997). The effects of media violence on the development of antisocial behavior. In D. M. Stoff, J. Breiling, & J. D. Maser (Eds.), *Handbook of antisocial behavior* (pp. 181–193). New York: John Wiley & Sons.

Huesmann, L. R., Moise-Titus, J., & Kirwil, L. (2004, September). *The relation between negative emotional reactions to violence and aggression.* Paper presented at the XVI World Meeting of the International Society for Research in Aggression, Santorini, Greece.

Huesmann, L. R., Moise-Titus, J., Podolski, C. L., & Eron, L. (2003). Longitudinal relations between children's exposure to TV violence and their aggressive and violent behavior in young adulthood: 1977–1992. *Developmental Psychology, 39*, 201–221.

Hurley, S., & Chater, N. (2005). *Perspectives on imitation: From neuroscience to social science.* (Vols. 1 & 2). Cambridge, MA: MIT Press.

Iacoboni, M., Woods, R., Brass, M., Bekkering, H., Mazziotta, J., & Rizzolatti, G. (1999). Cortical mechanisms of human imitation. *Science, 286*, 2526–2528.

Ihori, N., Sakamoto, A., Kobayashi, K., & Kimura, F. (2003). Does video game use grow children's aggressiveness? Results from a panel study. In K. Arai (Ed.), *Social contributions and responsibilities of simulation and gaming* (pp. 221–230). Tokyo: Japan Association of Simulation and Gaming.

Johnson, J. G., Cohen, P., Smailes, E. M., Kasen, S., & Brook J. S. (2002, March 29). Television viewing and aggressive behavior during adolescence and adulthood. *Science, 295*, 2468–2471.

Josephson, W. L. (1987). Television violence and children's aggression: Testing the priming, social script, and disinhibition predictions. *Journal of Personality and Social Psychology, 53*, 882–890.

Kirwil, L. (2002a, July). *Negative emotional reactions to observed violence as an inhibitor of aggressive behavior: Gender differences.* Paper presented at the XV World Meeting of the International Society for Research on Aggression, Montreal, Canada.

Kirwil, L. (2002b). Reakcje emocjonalne kobiet na sceny przemocy ekranowej [Women's Emotional Responses to Screen Violence]. In W. Strykowski & W. Skrzydlewski (Eds.), *Media a edukacja w dobie integracji* (pp. 98–105). Pozna?: Wydawnictwo eMPi2.

Kirwil, L. (2004a, September). *Aggression and emotional arousal in response to violent stimuli: Gender differences.* Paper presented at the XVI World Meeting of the International Society for Research in Aggression, Santorini, Greece.

Kirwil, L. (2004b, September). *Emotional reactions to violence among police in Poland and Czech Republic.* Paper presented at the XVI World Meeting of the International Society for Research in Aggression, Santorini, Greece.

Kirwil, L., & Huesmann, L. R. (2003, May). *The relation between aggressiveness and emotional reactions to observed violence*. Paper presented at the Annual Meeting of Midwestern Psychological Association, Chicago.

Lefkowitz, M. M., Eron, L. D., Walder, L. O., & Huesmann, L. R. (1977). *Growing up to be violent: A longitudinal study of the development of aggression*. New York: Pergamon Press.

Leyens, J. P., Camino, L., Parke, R. D., & Berkowitz, L. (1975). Effects of movie violence on aggression in a field setting as a function of group dominance and cohesion. *Journal of Personality and Social Psychology, 32*, 346–360.

Leyens, J. P., & Fraczek, A. (1983). Aggression as an interpersonal phenomenon. In H. Tajfel (Ed.), *The social dimension* (Vol. 1., p. 192). Cambridge, UK: Cambridge University Press.

Linz, D. G., Donnerstein, E., & Penrod, S. (1988). Effects of long-term exposure to violent and sexually degrading depictions of women. *Journal of Personality and Social Psychology, 55*, 758–768.

Lykken, D. T. (1995). *The antisocial personalities*. Hillsdale, NJ: Erlbaum.

Malamuth, N. M., & Check, J. V. P. (1981). The effects of mass media exposure on acceptance of violence against women: A field experiment. *Journal of Research in Personality, 15*, 436–446.

McLeod, J. M., Atkin, C. K., & Chaffee, S. H. (1972). Adolescents, parents and television use: Adolescent self-report measures from Maryland and Wisconsin samples. In G. A. Comstock & E. A. Rubinstein (Eds.), *Television and social behavior: A technical report to the Surgeon General's Scientific Advisory Committee on Television and Social Behavior* (Vol. 3). Washington, DC: U.S. Government Printing Office.

McSweeney, F. K., & Swindell, S. (2002). Common processes may contribute to extinction and habituation. *Journal of General Psychology, 129*(4), 364–400.

Meltzoff, A. N. (2005). Imitation and other minds: The "Like Me" hypothesis. In S. Hurley & N. Chater (Eds.), *Perspectives on imitation: From mirror neurons to memes* (Vol. 2, pp. 55–78). Cambridge, MA: MIT Press.

Meltzoff, A. N., & Decety, J. (2003). *What imitation tells us about social cognition: A rapprochement between developmental psychology and cognitive neuroscience*. Retrieved from www.royalsoc.ac.uk.

Meltzoff, A. N., & Moore, K. M. (1977). Imitation of facial and manual gestures by human neonates. *Science, 109*, 77–78.

Meltzoff, A. N., & Moore, K. M. (2000). Resolving the debate about early imitation. In D. Muir (Ed.), *Infant development: The essential readings* (pp. 167–181). Malden, MA: Blackwell Publishers.

Milavsky, J. R., Kessler, R., Stipp, H., & Rubens, W. S. (1982). Television and aggression: Results of a panel study. In D. Pearl, L. Bouthilet, & J. Lazar (Eds.), *Television and behavior: Ten years of scientific progress and implications for the eighties. Vol. 2: Technical reviews* (DHHS Publication No. ADM 82–1196, pp. 138–157). Washington, DC: U.S. Government Printing Office.

Moise-Titus, J. (1999). *The role of negative emotions in the media violence-aggression relation*. Unpublished doctoral dissertation, University of Michigan, Ann Arbor.

Molitor, F., & Hirsch, K. W. (1994). Children's toleration of real aggression after exposure to media violence: A replication of the Drabman and Thomas studies. *Child Study Journal, 24*, 191–207.

Nathanson, A. (1999). Identifying and explaining the relationship between parental mediation and children's aggression. *Communication Research, 26*(2), 124–143.

Neuman, R., & Strack, F. (2000). "Mood contagion": The automatic transfer of mood between persons. *Journal of Personality and Social Psychology, 79*, 211–223.

Oliver, M. B. (2004). *Desensitization from long-term exposure to graphic violence*. Unpublished manuscript, Pennsylvania State University.

Paik, H., & Comstock, G. (1994). The effects of television violence on antisocial behavior: A meta-analysis. *Communication Research, 21*, 516–546.

Press, C., Bird, G., Flach, R., & Heyes, C. (2005). Robotic movements elicit automatic imitation. *Cognitive Brain Research, 25*, 632–640.

Pantalon, M. V., & Motta, R. W. (1998). Effectiveness of anxiety management training in the treatment of posttraumatic stress disorder: A preliminary report. *Journal of Behavior Therapy and Experimental Psychiatry, 29*, 21–29.

Phillips, D. P. (1979). Suicide, motor vehicle fatalities, and the mass media: Evidence toward a theory of suggestion. *American Journal of Sociology, 84*, 1150–1174.

Prinz, J. J. (2005). Imitation and moral development. In S. Hurley & N. Chater (Eds.), *Perspectives on imitation: From mirror neurons to memes* (Vol. 2, pp. 267–282). Cambridge, MA: MIT Press.

Raine, A. (1993). *The psychopathology of crime*. San Diego: Academic Press.

Raine, A., Dodge, K., Loeber, R., Gatzke-Kopp, L., Lynam, D., Reynolds, C., et al. (2006). Proactive and reactive aggression in adolescent boys. *Aggressive Behavior, 32*(2), 159–171.

Raine, A., Reynolds, C., Venables, P. H., & Mednick, S. A. (1997). Biosocial bases of aggressive behavior in childhood. In A. Raine, D. P. Farrington, P. O. Brennen, & S. A. Mednick (Eds.), *The biosocial basis of violence* (pp. 107–126). New York: Plenum Press.

Raine, A., Venables, P. H., & Williams, M. (1990). Relationships between CNS and ANS measures of arousal at age 15 and criminality at age 24. *Archives of General Psychiatry, 47*, 1003–1007.

Rhodes, R. (2000, September 17). Hollow claims about fantasy violence. *New York Times*, pp. 4–19.

Rizzolatti, G. (2005). The mirror neuron system and imitation. In S. Hurley & N. Chatter (Eds.), *Perspectives on imitation: From mirror neurons to memes.* (Vol. 1, pp. 55–76). Cambridge, MA: MIT Press.

Savage, J. (2004). Does viewing violent media really cause criminal violence? A methodological review. *Aggression and Violent Behavior, 10*, 99–128.

Schaal, S. (1999). Is imitation learning the route to humanoid robots? *Trends in Cognitive Science, 3*, 233–242.

Schneider, W., & Shiffrin, R. M. (1977). Controlled and automatic human information processing: I. Detection, search, and attention. *Psychological Review, 84*, 1–66.

Shiffrin, R. M., & Schneider, W. (1977). Controlled and automatic human information processing: II. Perceptual learning, automatic attending, and general theory. *Psychological Review, 84*, 127–190.

Slater, M. D., Henry, K. L., Swaim, R. C., & Anderson, L. L. (2003). Violent media content and aggressiveness in adolescents: A downward spiral model. *Communication Research, 30*, 713–736.

Strelau, J. (1982). Biologically determined dimensions of personality or temperament? *Personality and Individual Differences, 3*, 355–360.

Surette, R. (2002). Self-reported copycat crime among a population of serious and violent juvenile offenders. *Crime and Delinquency, 48*, 46–69.

Thomas, M. H., & Drabman, R. S. (1975). Toleration of real life aggression as a function of exposure to televised violence and age of subject. *Merrill-Palmer Quarterly, 21*, 227–232.

Thomas, M. H., Horton, R. W., Lippincott, E. C., & Drabman, R. S. (1977). Desensitization to portrayals of real-life aggression as a function of television violence. *Journal of Personality and Social Psychology, 35*, 450–458.

Uhlmann, E., & Swanson, J. (2004). Exposure to violent video games increases automatic aggressiveness. *Journal of Adolescence, 27*, 41–52.

van der Voort, T. H. A. (1986). *Television violence: A child's-eye view*. New York: Elsevier Science.

Viemero, V. (2002). Factors predicting aggression in early adulthood. *Psykologia, 37*(2), 138–144.

Wolpe, J. (1958). *Psychotherapy by reciprocal inhibition*. Stanford, CA: Stanford University Press.

Zajonc, R. B., Murphy, S. T., & Inglehart, M. (1989). Feeling and facial efference: Implications of vascular theory of emotions. *Psychological Review, 96*, 395–416.

Zillmann, D. (1982). Television viewing and arousal. In D. Pearl, L. Bouthilet, & J. Lazar (Eds.), *Television and behavior: Ten years of scientific progress and implications for the eighties. Vol. 2: Technical reviews* (DHHS Publication No. ADM 82–1196, pp. 53–67). Washington, DC: U.S. Government Printing Office.

Zillmann, D., Bryant, J., Cominsky, P. W., & Medoff, N. J. (1981). Excitation and hedonic valence in the effect of erotica on motivated intermale aggression. *European Journal of Social Psychology, 11*, 233–252

Zuckermann, M. (1979). *Sensation seeking: Beyond the optimal level of arousal*. Hillsdale, NJ: Erlbaum.

CHAPTER 29

Violence and Culture in the United States

Mark Warr

Americans are exposed to an unrelenting diet of images and messages about violence, messages that emanate from television, movies, newspapers, popular fiction, magazines, and other media. This state of affairs is no accident, nor is it an accurate reflection of the social world most Americans inhabit. Instead, it is the result of a confluence of forces – commercial, aesthetic, scientific, and social psychological – that emerged during the social and technological turmoil of 19th- and 20th-century America.

To be sure, violent events are intrinsically interesting events. As tense and sometimes dramatic episodes of human conflict, they raise profound questions about human motivation, the misfortune of innocents, the capacity of government to maintain order, and, ultimately, the presence of justice in human affairs. At an elemental level, they are also *frightening* events, and this feature, as we see later, is a key to understanding their peculiar force and appeal.

Still, what is so disturbing about the United States is how disproportionately *depictions* of violence in the mass media outnumber actual *incidents* of violence. That

disparity and its implications are two of the principal issues of this chapter.

The Mass Communication of Violence

The first truly mass medium to turn to crime for its subject matter was the newspaper. Crime stories have been a staple of many American newspapers since the early 19th-century "penny press." Capitalizing on rising literacy rates and technological improvements in mass printing, these largely working-class newspapers relied on police reports for an endless source of intrigue and scandal (Briggs & Burke, 2002); they were the forerunner of the "yellow journalism" that emerged later in the century (Surette, 1998). Even today, newspapers, which are read daily by about 4 out of 10 Americans (down from 7 out of 10 in 1972; see National Opinion Research Center, 2002), selectively cull police reports for the most "newsworthy" (meaning violent) crimes, which, as it happens, are also the least frequent crimes (see below). A similar process operates in the production of television newscasts, although visual interest and certain other criteria come into play (Ericson, Baranek, & Chan, 1987).

However selective they might be, news accounts of crime in newspapers, radio, and television are ostensibly aimed at recounting real events. These accounts pale in number, however, when compared with dramatic depictions of violent crimes in movies, literature, and television. An entire genre of literature (Mystery) continues to follow in the footsteps of Poe (its founder), Conan Doyle, and Christie and occupies a sizeable portion of most modern bookstores. Movies, which draw heavily from books, use violence to meet the perceived entertainment "needs" of audiences (including excitement and sadomasochism; see Jowett & Linton, 1989) and to maintain an advantage over their "free" but more closely regulated competitor, television. In fact, the advent of consumer television in the late 1940s nearly spelled the death of theatrical movies, not to mention radio. Thousands of theatres closed, and the number of theatergoers dropped by almost half (Biagi, 1990). Today, along with more graphic violence and sex, movies rely on the star system, spectaculars, special effects, and other devices to draw audiences away from their television sets and into the theater (Biagi, 1990; Jowett & Linton, 1989). The decades-old rivalry between movies and television resembles the contemporary struggle for viewers between cable television and the major broadcast networks.

The Television Age

Television is the dominant medium of our age, having largely replaced the written-word culture that flourished in early America and that began to decline with the introduction of telegraphy and photography (Postman, 1986). Fully 96% of Americans report that they average at least one hour of television viewing per day, with most watching a good deal more (National Opinion Research Center, 2002).

After experimenting with Broadway fare and live dramas, early television turned, iron-ically, to movies as a source of content, and networks bought up the holdings of major movie studios like Warner Brothers and Twentieth Century-Fox (Biagi, 1990). Along with comedies, soap operas, quiz and talk shows, dramas like *Dragnet* (1951), *Perry Mason* (1957), and *The Untouchables* (1959) established niches for police, courtroom, private detective, and other crime-theme shows that eventually blossomed into the seemingly ubiquitous and comparatively graphic fare of today.

Based on an historical analysis of network programming, Surette (1998, p. 36) has concluded that "the proportion of television time devoted to crime and violence makes crime the largest single subject matter on television." In its promotional material for the 2004/5 television season, for example, CBS emphasized its "Crimetime Saturday" line-up (despite the fact that crime shows also appear in prime time every other night of the week). In the week of June 21–27, 2004 (the week in which this chapter was undertaken), the five most-watched television shows in the United States according to the Nielsen ratings were *CSI: Crime Scene Investigation*, *Without a Trace*, *American Film Institute's 100 Years and 100 Songs*, *Law and Order*, and *CSI: Miami* (www.usatoday.com, June 30, 2004). Thus, four out of five of the top-rated television programs in the United States during that week focused on crime and criminal justice.

Obsession With Violence

Why such a preoccupation with crime and violence in the mass media? In addition to their dramatic value and intrinsic human interest, stories of crime – real or fictional – speak to citizens' sense of personal safety, and social psychological research suggests that "fear appeals increase attention. People are more likely to pay attention to messages that relate to their well-being" or that of "persons for whom they are responsible" (Heath & Bryant, 2000, p. 182). This phenomenon helps explain not only the ubiquity of violence in news and entertainment but also the prevalence of fear appeals in commercial advertising. Tacit or explicit threat messages are used to sell everything from life insurance to automobile options (remote ignitions, flat-less tires) to cellular phones (stay in contact at all times!) to airline travel insurance (terrorism) because people will often pause to pay attention to messages that "alert" them to risks and how they can be avoided.

Surette (1998, p. 25) has argued that "portrayals of crime also allow audiences voyeuristic glimpses of rare and bizarre acts – often coupled with lofty discussions of justice, morality, and society." Producers and writers of crime dramas claim access to insider information about the secret world of crime – information that, whatever its veracity, they offer to share with the viewer:

> Crime has been attractive to the entertainment media precisely because it is the preeminent backstage behavior. By nature and necessity, most crime is private, secretive, and hidden, surreptitiously committed and studiously concealed. To the degree that entertainment involves escapism and novelty, the backstage nature of crime inherently increases its entertainment value and popularity.
>
> (Surette, 1998, p. 25)

Who's Watching?

No abundance of messages about violence, of course, can affect the public if they do not receive or pay attention to those messages. Yet it is clear that most do both. In a study of residents of Chicago, Philadelphia, and San Francisco, Skogan and Maxfield (1981, p. 128) found that "more than three-quarters of the residents of these cities reported hearing about a crime story on television or reading about one in the newspapers on the previous day," and the authors describe their respondents as "hooked on the media" (1981, p. 140). When asked where they get their information about crime, members of the general public overwhelmingly cite the mass media (Graber, 1980; Roberts & Stalans, 1997; Skogan & Maxfield, 1981).

Mass media messages about violence clearly penetrate the information haze to reach the public, and that brings us again to a point raised earlier. Because violent crimes are statistically rare events, even in the United States (O'Brien, 2000), citizens are far more likely to hear about, read about, or watch violent events than to experience them. This fact has two immediate implications. First, the social consequences of violence cannot be understood by focusing exclusively on victims of violence. Without discounting the plight of victims, one must look beyond those who are directly victimized to those who suffer forms of "indirect victimization" (Conklin, 1975), the most pervasive of which is fear of crime. Second, media portrayals of violence are important not merely because they are ubiquitous, but because they are the only foundation (save for personal conversations about crime; see Skogan & Maxfield, 1981) on which most Americans can form their beliefs about violence. As we see later, that foundation is unreliable.

Fear of Crime in the United States

The most widely and carefully studied social consequence of violence in the United States has been public fear of crime. Some four decades ago, the President's Commission on Law Enforcement and Administration of Justice (1967, p. 3) offered this brief but trenchant observation: "The most damaging of the effects of violent crime is fear, and that fear must not be belittled." That statement prefigured a fundamental shift in the way that criminologists think about crime, drawing attention away from the causes of crime and criminal victimization toward an examination of indirect victims. The wisdom of this approach was quickly borne out by survey research demonstrating that fear of crime in the United States was far more common than actual victimization (often by orders of magnitude) and that Americans respond to this fear via a variety of precautionary behaviors so widespread and habitual that they form a defining element of

American culture (Warr, 1994). We return to those reactions shortly, after first exploring the nature of fear of crime.

The Nature of Fear

Fear is an emotion, a feeling of alarm or dread caused by an awareness or expectation of danger (see Sluckin, 1979). This affective state is ordinarily (though not invariably) associated with certain physiological changes, including increased heart rate, rapid breathing, sweating, decreased salivation, and increased galvanic skin response (Mayes, 1979; Thomson, 1979).

Fear may be aroused by an immediate danger, as when an individual is confronted by an armed attacker or is threatened verbally with harm. This type of intense, immediate experience appears to be what some have in mind when they speak of fear of crime. As sentient and symbolic beings, however, humans have the ability to anticipate or contemplate events that lie in the future or are not immediately apparent. Hence, people may experience fear merely in anticipation of possible threats or in reaction to environmental cues (e.g., darkness, litter, graffiti, loud voices) that seem to imply danger. Psychologists commonly use the terms "fear" and "anxiety" to differentiate reactions to immediate threats (fear) from reactions to future or past events (anxiety). Thus, an individual would fear an approaching assailant, but grow anxious when thinking about walking home late at night. This kind of clarity has not been consistently maintained in research on fear of crime, but it appears that most research has been designed to capture anxiety rather than fear of victimization.

By its very nature, the notion of fear seems to imply a deleterious emotional or psychological condition. Unlike love, pleasure, or happiness, fear is not a state that people ordinarily pursue. To assume that fear is therefore dysfunctional for an organism, however, is sorely inaccurate. Fear, in fact, is an essential survival mechanism. Without fear, prey animals would walk amid predators, and humans would stroll across busy freeways, knowingly eat toxic substances, or leave their infants unprotected. From an evolutionary point of view, organisms that lacked fear would be unlikely to live long enough to reproduce (Mayes, 1979; Russell, 1979). Fear, then, is not intrinsically bad. It is when fear is out of proportion to objective risk that it becomes dysfunctional for an organism or a society.

Survey Research on Fear of Crime

A bewildering variety of questions have been employed by investigators over the years to measure fear of crime (see DuBow, McCabe, & Kaplan, 1979; Ferraro, 1995; Ferraro & LaGrange, 1987). Much of this diversity stems from variation in the context stipulated in survey questions. Some ask about fear during the day; others ask about it at night. Some pertain to fear at home, others outside the dwelling. Still others ask respondents about their fear when alone or with others.

One item, however, has become something of a de facto standard for measuring fear of crime: "Is there anywhere near where you live – that is, within a mile – where you would be afraid to walk alone at night?" The item has become conventional not because it was chosen by social scientists but because it has been used by both the Gallup Organization and the National Opinion Research Center (NORC) to measure fear since the 1960s. During the past three decades, approximately 40 to 50% of Americans surveyed each year have responded affirmatively to this question (Maguire & Pastore, 2000; Warr, 1995).

The Gallup/NORC item has been criticized (e.g., Ferraro, 1995) on many grounds: it is hypothetical (how afraid *would* you be), is limited to nighttime, does not mention crime, and only crudely measures intensity. In fairness, the measured prevalence of fear obtained with this item is not radically different from that measured in other national surveys (see Warr, 1995), and the routine use of the item facilitates longitudinal comparisons of fear, if only in relative terms.

There is a more fundamental issue raised by questions of this kind, however. More than 20 years ago, Warr and Stafford (1983) asked residents of Seattle to report their everyday fear, not of crime in general, but of a variety of specific offenses ranging from violent crimes like homicide, rape, and robbery to various property and public order offenses. The rank order of offenses that emerged from their analysis remains surprising to many even today. Murder, for instance, fell low on the list of fears, whereas residential burglary outranked all other offenses on fear. Warr and Stafford showed that these findings were not anomalous or even counterintuitive. Fear, they demonstrated, is not determined solely by the perceived seriousness of offenses. Instead, the degree of fear attached to crimes is a multiplicative function of the perceived seriousness and the perceived risk (i.e., the subjective likelihood) of the offenses. To generate strong fear, an offense must be perceived to be both serious *and* likely to occur. Residential burglary, the most feared crime in the United States, holds that title because it is viewed as relatively serious and rather likely. Murder, on the other hand, is perceived to be very serious but very unlikely to occur.

Since the publication of Warr and Stafford's research, scattered offense-specific data on fear have been gathered (see Ferraro, 1995; Haghighi & Sorenson, 1996; Warr, 1995). These data generally corroborate the hierarchy of fear observed by Warr and Stafford (insofar as they use comparable offenses), but fear continues to be monitored primarily through generalized, omnibus measures of the sort used by Gallup and NORC. Such measures are not without value as an overall assessment of fear, but they offer an imperfect picture of fear.

Fear and Situational Cues to Danger

By their nature, surveys are better suited to measuring anxiety about crime rather than fear, strictly defined. In everyday life, fear of crime (in the strict sense) is likely to occur as people navigate their environment away from home – walking to school, or the grocery store, or a doctor's appointment, or traveling to work – and encounter signs of danger in their environment.

What exactly are these signs of danger? Using a factorial survey design, Warr (1991) identified several cues to danger that affect people in public places. One particularly potent cue is *darkness*; by its very nature, darkness obscures potential threats that may lurk in the vicinity. Another cue to danger (and not merely to humans; see Russell, 1979) is *novelty*; novel (unfamiliar) environments are more frightening than familiar ones. Still another cue is the *presence of bystanders or companions*. The presence of other people in the immediate vicinity ordinarily acts to alleviate the fear that individuals would otherwise feel if alone. This calming effect does not operate, however, if those "others" are themselves perceived to be dangerous persons. Warr (1991) found that young males are frightening to many individuals, and few cues are more alarming to the public than *a group* of young males.

In additional to these cues, a number of investigators have considered various "signs of incivility" that can provoke fear (cf. Ferraro, 1995). These include physical features of neighborhoods, such as graffiti, broken windows, trash and litter, stripped cars, or abandoned buildings, as well as social cues, such as beggars or homeless persons, raucous groups of young people, drug sellers and users, and prostitutes. Empirical evidence regarding the potency of such cues in producing fear is generally supportive (LaGrange, Ferraro, & Supancic, 1992), although it is largely indirect, and investigators rarely control for objective crime rates when examining the impact of incivilities.

Who Is Afraid?

One of the most distinctive features of fear of crime is that it is not uniformly distributed in the population. One of the largest differences is that between men and women. Women are more than twice as likely as men, for example, to report that they would be afraid to walk alone at night near their home (Maguire & Pastore, 1997).

At first glance, this pattern might seem to reflect the actual probability of victimization. That is, women might be more afraid than men simply because they are more likely to be victims of crime. In fact, exactly the opposite is true. Although they have the greatest fear, females are actually at substantially lower risk of victimization for most crimes than are males (see, e.g., Stafford & Galle, 1984).

How, then, can one explain the greater fear of women? One reason seems to be that women exhibit greater *sensitivity to risk*. That is, when exposed to the same risk of victimization, women are more afraid than men. Why? Apparently, women perceive crime in a way that differs significantly from men. Specifically, among most women, crimes are subjectively linked together in a way that is not true for men. For example, a substantial correlation exists between fear of burglary and fear of murder among women, suggesting that for women, murder is viewed as a likely outcome of burglary. Among men, however, the correlation is much lower, implying that the two crimes are not cognitively linked. In much the same way, a strong correlation exists between fear of "being approached by a beggar" and fear of robbery among women, but not men. These sorts of subjective linkages between different types of crimes (termed "perceptually contemporaneous offenses" by Warr, 1984) appear more frequently and more strongly among women than among men. The result is that many situations that appear relatively innocuous to men are likely to be viewed as more dangerous by women because of the offenses they portend (Warr, 1984).

One offense that looms large for women and for which they are *not* at lower risk, of course, is rape. According to one study of fear of rape (Warr, 1985; see also Ferraro, 1996), (1) rape is feared more than any other crime among young women; (2) rape is viewed as approximately equal in seriousness to murder by women; (3) the highest sensitivity displayed by any age or sex group to any crime is that of young women to rape; (4) fear of rape is closely associated with a variety of other offenses for which rape is a logical (though not necessary) outcome (for example, burglary, robbery, receiving an obscene phone call) or precursor (for example, homicide); and (5) fear of rape is strongly associated with certain lifestyle precautions (not going out alone, for example). Clearly, then, rape is central to the fears of many women.

Gender differences aside, fear of crime is often thought to be strongest among the elderly. There is in fact some evidence for this position, but age differences in fear occur only for some offenses and are generally not as large as sex differences in fear. Moreover, where age differences in fear do exist, fear is often strongest among middle-aged persons (i.e., those aged about 50–65) rather than among the truly elderly (Ferraro, 1995; LaGrange & Ferraro, 1989; Warr, 1984). The association between fear and age, then, is not as simple or straightforward as it is sometimes depicted.

Altruistic Fear

When individuals face an ostensibly dangerous environment, they may naturally fear for their own personal safety. At the same time, they may also fear for *other* persons (e.g., children, spouses, friends) whose safety they value. It is important, therefore, to distinguish *personal* fear – fear for oneself – from *altruistic* fear – or fear for others.

The prevalence and power of altruistic fear are illustrated by the enormous public reaction that often attends crimes committed against children (Polly Klaas, Jon Benet Ramsey). Such reactions surely reflect not only distress for the victim but also parents' profound concern for the safety of their own children. Using data from a survey of Texas residents, Warr and Ellison (2000) found that, within family households, altruistic fear is in fact more common and frequently more intense than personal fear. Husbands were more likely to worry about their wives than vice versa (especially at younger ages) and often exhibited greater concern for their wives than for themselves. Unlike personal fear, which is more common among women,

men were highly susceptible to altruistic fear, both for their wives and for their children. And unlike personal fear, altruistic fear generally declined through the life course. In fact, it appeared from these data that most individuals follow a life-course trajectory in which altruistic fear slowly gives way to personal fear as the dominant reaction to the threat of crime.

Another finding of Warr and Ellison was a pronounced and unmistakable concern directed toward one population group: young women. Why? The most likely explanation is that parents and husbands of young women are often acutely afraid for the safety of those women because they are potential victims of sexual assault. The analysis also indicated that what at first glance appear to be reactions to personal fear – installing home security devices, purchasing or carrying a weapon, participating in community crime watch programs – are often correlated more strongly with altruistic fear than with personal fear. These findings underscore the need to differentiate personal fear from altruistic fear in research on fear of crime.

Fear and the Mass Media

Do depictions of crime and violence in the mass media affect public fear of crime in the United States? To address that question, it is instructive to consider first how crime is depicted in the news media.

The mass media, as we saw earlier, are a powerful amplifying mechanism with respect to crime; information known only to a few can within hours or days become known to thousands or millions. But the information promulgated through the media is not a full accounting of crime nor even a representative sampling of crime events. On the contrary, a number of forms of distortion in news coverage of crime have been documented; these distortions tend to exaggerate the frequency and the seriousness of crime.

In the real world, for example, crimes occur in inverse proportion to their seriousness; the more serious the crime, the more

rarely it occurs (e.g., Erickson and Gibbs, 1979). Thus, in the United States, burglaries occur by the millions, robberies by the hundreds of thousands, and homicides by the thousands. In news coverage of crime, however, the emphasis is on newsworthiness, and a key element of newsworthiness is seriousness; the more serious a crime, the more likely it is to be reported. By using seriousness as a criterion, then, the media are most likely to report precisely those crimes that are least likely to occur to individuals (Roshier, 1973; Sheley & Ashkins, 1981; Sherizen, 1978; Skogan & Maxfield, 1981; Surette, 1998).

This mirror image of crime means that the media place extraordinary emphasis on violent crime. Skogan and Maxfield (1980) reported that homicides and attempted homicides constituted half of all newspaper crimes stories in the cities they examined, even though homicides are only a minute fraction of all criminal offenses. Furthermore, the number of homicide stories reported in city newspapers did not closely match the actual homicide rates of the cities examined, suggesting that the amount of space devoted to crime has more to do with the "news hole" allocated to crime by editors than with the true crime rate. Much like homicides, child abductions – though rarer still – can dominate the news for days at a time because, as newscasters understand, they speak to the primal fears of parents (Warr & Ellison, 2000).

News coverage of crime has been criticized on other grounds as well, including the practice of using crime news as "filler" when other news is slow, the use of crime news to attract larger audiences ("If it bleeds, it leads"), and a tendency to report trends in crime using numbers rather than rates, thereby ignoring changes in population (see Graber, 1980; Surette, 1998; Warr, 1980, 1995).

How do these forms of media distortion affect the public, if at all? The evidence on this question is indirect and limited, but it is highly suggestive. In the early 1980s, Warr (1980; see also Bordley, 1982) presented evidence that the objective and perceived incidence of offenses are related by a power function ($y = aX^b$). That is, people tend to systematically overestimate the frequency of rare offenses while underestimating the frequency of common ones. Public perceptions, to be sure, were remarkably accurate as to the relative frequencies of different crimes (people recognize that homicide is less common than burglary, for example), but considerably less accurate as to absolute frequencies.

As it happens, Warr's findings are corroborated by a small but persuasive body of research in cognitive psychology (see Lichtenstein, Slovic, Fischoff, Layman, & Combs, 1978; Slovic, Fischoff, & Lichtenstein, 1979, 1982), indicating that individuals tend to significantly exaggerate the risk of rare lethal events (that is, causes of death like tornadoes, homicide, floods, fire, accidents, or botulism) while underestimating the risk of common lethal events (e.g., deaths due to heart disease, diabetes, or cancer). Slovic, Fischoff, and Lichtenstein (1982) attribute this tendency to a common error of judgment arising from the *availability heuristic* (Tversky & Kahneman, 1982), or the tendency to judge the frequency of events by the ease with which they can be recalled or imagined.

But why would members of the public readily imagine or recollect what are actually rare causes of death? Slovic et al. (1979, 1982) cite evidence from Combs and Slovic (1979) showing that public perceptions of the frequency of various causes of death closely match the frequency with which those causes are reported in newspapers. Newspaper accounts, in turn, are glaringly at odds with reality:

> Many of the statistically frequent causes of death (e.g., diabetes, emphysema, various forms of cancer) were rarely reported by either paper during the period under study. In addition, violent, often catastrophic, events such as tornadoes, fires, drownings, homicides, motor vehicle accidents, and all accidents were reported much more frequently than less dramatic causes of death having similar (or even greater) statistical frequencies. For example, dis-

> eases take about 16 times as many lives as accidents, but there were more than 3 times as many articles about accidents, noting almost 7 times as many deaths. Among the more frequent events, homicides were the most heavily reported category in proportion to actual frequency. Although diseases claim almost 100 times as many lives as do homicides, there were about 3 times as many articles about homicides as about disease deaths. Furthermore, homicide articles tended to be more than twice as long as articles reporting disease and accident deaths.
>
> (Slovic, Fischoff, & Lichtenstein, 1982, p. 468)

These investigators do not insist on a causal connection between media reports and public perceptions, but they suggest that the pattern of errors in the two is much too similar to be coincidental.

In the end, the fact that the media present a distorted image of crime is no guarantee that the public believes or heeds what it sees, hears, and reads. Nevertheless, the evidence concerning public perceptions of crime and media distortion of crime news is strikingly corroborative, and it is difficult to believe that the media have little or no effect on perceptions, especially when the public cites the media as their primary source of information on crime and spends so much time attuned to them.

In the end, the causal influence of media crime coverage cannot be established without simultaneous measurements of (1) media content, (2) public exposure to that content, and (3) the postexposure effects of media communications. Such research is difficult to conduct in natural settings because of the enormous quantity and variety of media and interpersonal messages on crime to which the public is exposed (e.g., Graber, 1980). Still, the weight of existing evidence points toward a substantial media impact on public perceptions of crime.

The Consequences of Fear

What makes fear of crime so egregious as a social problem is the depth and breadth of its consequences for our society. Over the years, investigators have identified a large number of behavioral precautions that are associated with fear of crime. These range from relatively trivial and nearly universal behaviors (e.g., turning on lights and locking doors when leaving the home) to more personally and socially consequential actions (staying home at night or not going out alone; cf. Skogan & Maxfield, 1981; Warr, 1994, 2000).

According to survey data, the single most common reaction to fear of crime in the United States is *spatial avoidance*, or staying away from places that are perceived to be dangerous (Warr, 1994). In surveys of Seattle and Dallas residents, for example, Warr found that 63% and 77% of respondents, respectively, reported that they "avoided certain places in the city." More recently, 56% of respondents in a national Gallup survey answered affirmatively when asked whether they "avoid going to certain places or neighborhoods you might otherwise want to go" because of "concern over crime" (Maguire & Pastore, 2000). Along with spatial avoidance, fear of crime seems to affect the routes that people take, the forms of transportation they employ, and the times they choose to leave their residence (see DuBow, 1979; Warr, 1994). Not surprisingly, some precautionary behaviors are much more common among women than among men. Whereas 42% of women in a Seattle survey reported that they avoided going out alone, for example, only 8% of men reported the same precaution. And whereas 40% of women reported that they avoided going out at night, only 9% of men said the same (Warr, 1985).

Taken together, precautions like these suggest that fear of crime influences to a significant degree the ecology of American cities, including patterns of commerce, road use, leisure activities, tourism, and social interaction. Virtually all American cities have places or areas – parks, neighborhoods, beaches, parking garages – that are perceived to be dangerous places by residents, and it does not require a trained eye to discern the consequences of such a reputation. Retail businesses that are located in putatively dangerous areas, for instance, are likely to suf-fer a shortage of customers, and reputedly dangerous neighborhoods are likely to find themselves socially isolated (Conklin, 1975; Skogan, 1990).

Contemporary social commentators often assert that fear of crime has torn the very fabric of our society, making us afraid of one another as we go about our everyday business and rupturing the common trust that binds together communities. There may be some truth to this argument, but it is important to bear in mind that fear of crime also brings citizens *together*. As the sociologist Emile Durkheim noted long ago, crime integrates communities by drawing them together in the face of danger. Today, millions of Americans participate in community crime watch programs, cooperative police-community associations, "bring back the night" rallies and marches, and other forms of communal solidarity. Whether these two countervailing social forces – fear and community activism – ultimately cancel one another out is difficult to say, but fear is surely an integrative as well as a disintegrative force.

Conclusion

Crime and violence are integral elements of American culture. They pervade our news, our entertainment, and, at least vicariously, our lives. At the same time that they fear for their safety, however, many Americans remain fascinated by violent crime and romanticize criminals like Bonnie and Clyde, John Dillinger, the outlaws of the Old West (Jesse James, Butch Cassidy), and the gangsters of Prohibition (Al Capone). To others, criminals symbolize one of our most cherished values – rugged individualism – and thereby hold a rightful place in the iconography of American culture (see Surette, 1998).

The intense preoccupation of the mass media with crime and violence, on the other hand, is difficult to interpret as anything other than mercenary, and there are few signs of social responsibility among those who fill our television and movie screens and the racks at the local bookstore. The immense capacity of the media to deliver information and convey meaning could be used beneficially, of course, to provide citizens with objective information on crime risks and protective strategies, but that is unlikely to happen. Even government efforts to rein in violent content in movies and other entertainment media (such as video games) encounter obstacles like "ratings creep" or produce strangely incongruous results, as when television networks advertise the V-chip to block the very content they are continually promoting, or use the "viewer discretion advised" caution as an enticement rather than as a genuine warning.

For their part, most citizens have little scientific foundation for their beliefs about crime and violence. In their daily lives, they are constantly confronted with information from sources that may not appreciate nor care about the accuracy of that information and who may use violence to win votes, entertain, sell, advertise, or exploit. In the end, most citizens are left to reason as best they can about the risks of victimization. Because the consequences of victimization can be catastrophic for themselves and those they love, many are likely to err on the side of caution, worrying about and guarding against violence more than is necessary or defensible. The result is an unfortunate and needless constriction of freedom – the land of the free as the gated community.

Such a state of affairs would not be tolerated if the risk in question were, say, a communicable disease. The public would demand information on the associated risks, and public officials and government agencies would scramble to investigate and communicate any pertinent information. Yet violence is not like some virulent disease whose risks and epidemiology are poorly understood. The risks associated with most violent criminal offenses are understood with a degree of certitude that would startle many casual observers, and such information was developed largely at public expense. In an ideal world, the risks of violence would be communicated to the general public in a thoughtful, dispassionate, and scientifically defensible manner, in much the same

way that public campaigns about smoking and heart disease have been conducted successfully (National Research Council, 1989). Information could be disseminated through public schools, police departments (via public information officers), and the mass media themselves (for example, as public service announcements). In recent years an entirely new field known as risk communication has emerged in the sciences, one concerned with the problems, methods, and efficacy of communicating risk to the general public (National Research Council, 1989). This field has largely concentrated on new technological risks (recombinant DNA, nuclear power, pesticides, toxic waste disposal), medical/health risks (smoking, seatbelts, cholesterol, alcohol, cancer) and both natural and man-made disasters (hurricanes, floods, aircraft crashes, lightning, tornadoes, earthquakes), but the lessons of the field are directly applicable to violence. Many Americans might be surprised to learn, for example, that they are more likely to be a victim of suicide than of homicide, that automobiles kill more individuals than all violent crime, or that, as a group, children face greater danger from their parents than from strangers.

For the moment, however, it appears that violence is simply too entertaining and too lucrative to demystify, and Americans seem content to continue "amusing ourselves to death" (Postman, 1986). In an age with few standards of public morality, where celebrities and felons are often the same people, the glorification, commercialization, and normalization of violence proceed without serious opposition or public uproar. But they are not without consequence.

References

Biagi, S. (1990). *Media impact: An introduction to mass media.* Belmont, CA: Wadsworth.

Bordley, R. F. (1982). Public perceptions of crime: A derivation of Warr's power function from the Bayesian odds relations. *Social Forces, 61,* 134–143.

Briggs, A., & Burke, P. (2002). *A social history of the media: From Gutenberg to the Internet.* Malden, MA: Blackwell.

Combs, B., & Slovic, P. (1979). Newspaper coverage of causes of death. *Journalism Quarterly, 56,* 837–843.

Conklin, J. (1975). *The impact of crime.* New York: Macmillan.

DuBow, F., McCabe, E., & Kaplan, G. (1979). *Reactions to crime: A critical review of the literature.* Washington, DC: U.S. Government Printing Office.

Ericson, R. V., Baranek, P. M., & Chan, J. B. L. (1987). *Visualizing deviance: A study of news organization.* Toronto: University of Toronto Press.

Ferraro, K. F. (1995). *Fear of crime: Interpreting victimization risk.* Albany: State University of New York Press.

Ferraro, K. F. (1996). Women's fear of victimization: Shadow of sexual assault? *Social Forces, 75,* 667–690.

Ferraro, K. F., & LaGrange, R. (1987). The measurement of fear of crime. *Sociological Inquiry, 57,* 70–101.

Graber, D. A. (1980). *Crime news and the public.* New York: Praeger.

Haghighi, B., & Sorensen, J. (1996). America's fear of crime. In T. J. Flanagan, & D. R. Longmire, (Eds.), *Americans view crime and justice: A national public opinion survey* (pp. 16–30). Thousand Oaks, CA: Sage.

Heath, R. L., & Bryant, J. (2000). *Human communication theory and research* (2nd ed.). Mahwah, NJ: Erlbaum.

Jowett, G., & Linton, J. M. (1989). *Movies as mass communication* (2nd ed.). Newbury Park, CA: Sage.

LaGrange, R. L., & Ferraro, K. F. (1987). The elderly's fear of crime: A critical examination of the research. *Research on Aging, 9,* 372–391.

LaGrange, R. L., & Ferraro, K. F. (1989). Assessing age and gender differences in perceived risk and fear of crime. *Criminology, 27,* 697–719.

LaGrange, R. L., Ferraro, K. F., & Supancic, M. (1992). Perceived risk and fear of crime: Role of social and physical incivilities. *Journal of Research in Crime and Delinquency, 29,* 311–334.

Lichtenstein, S., Slovic, P., Fischoff, B., Layman, M., & Combs, B. (1978). Judged frequency of lethal events. *Journal of Experimental Psychology, 4,* 551–578.

Maguire, K., & Pastore, A. L. (2001). *Sourcebook of criminal justice statistics 2000* (U.S. Department of Justice, Bureau of Justice Statistics). Washington, DC: U.S. Government Printing Office.

Mayes, A. (1979). The physiology of fear and anxiety. In W. Sluckin, (Ed.), *Fear in animals and man* (pp. 24–55). New York: Van Nostrand Reinhold.

National Opinion Research Center. (2004). *General social survey codebook.* Retrieved July 13, 2004, from http://webapp.icpsr.umich.edu/GSS/.

O'Brien, R. M. (1995). Crime and victimization data. In J. Sheley, (Ed.), *Criminology: A contemporary handbook* (2nd ed., pp. 57–80). New York: Wadsworth.

Postman, N. (1986). *Amusing ourselves to death: Public discourse in the age of show business.* New York: Viking Penguin.

President's Commission on Law Enforcement and Administration of Justice. (1967). *The challenge of crime in a free society.* Washington, DC: U.S. Government Printing Office.

Roberts, J. V., & Stalans, L. J. (1997). *Public opinion, crime, and criminal justice.* Boulder, CO: Westview Press.

Roshier, B. (1973). The selection of crime news by the press. In S. Cohen & J. Young (Eds.), *The manufacture of news* (pp. 28–39). Beverly Hills: Sage.

Russell, P. A. (1979). Fear-evoking stimuli. In W. Sluckin (Ed.), *Fear in animals and man* (pp. 86–124). New York: Van Nostrand Reinhold.

Sheley, J. S., & Ashkins, C. D. (1981). Crime, crime news, and crime views. *Public Opinion Quarterly, 45,* 492–506.

Sherizen, S. (1978). Social creation of crime news: All the news fitted to print. In C. Winick, (Ed.), *Deviance and mass media* (pp. 203–224). Beverly Hills: Sage.

Skogan, W. G. (1990). *Disorder and decline: Crime and the spiral of decay in American neighborhoods.* New York: Free Press.

Skogan, W. G., & Maxfield, M. G. (1981). *Coping with crime: Individual and neighborhood reactions.* Beverly Hills, CA: Sage.

Slovic, P., Fischoff, B., & Lichtenstein, S. (1979). Rating the risks. *Environment, 21,* 14–20, 36–39.

Slovic, P., Fischoff, B., & Lichtenstein, S. (1980). Facts and fears: Understanding perceived risk. In R. C. Schwing & W. A. Albers, Jr. (Eds.), *Societal risk assessment: How safe is safe enough?* (pp. 181–214). New York: Plenum.

Slovic, P., Fischoff, B., & Lichtenstein, S. (1982). Facts versus fears: Understanding perceived risk. In D. Kahneman, P. Slovic, & A. Tversky, (Eds.), *Judgment under uncertainty: Heuristics and biases* (pp. 463–492). Cambridge, UK: Cambridge University Press.

Sluckin, W. (1979). *Fear in animals and man.* New York: Van Nostrand Reinhold.

Stafford, M. C., & Galle, O. R. (1984). Victimization rates, exposure to risk, and fear of crime. *Criminology, 22,* 173–185.

Surette, R. (1998). *Media, crime, and criminal justice: Images and realities* (2nd ed.). Belmont, CA: Wadsworth.

Thomson, R. (1979). The concept of fear. In W. Sluckin, (Ed.), *Fear in animals and man* (pp. 1–23). New York: Van Nostrand Reinhold.

Tversky, A., & Kahneman, D. (1982). Availability: A heuristic for judging frequency and probability. In D. Kahneman, P. Slovic, & A. Tversky, (Eds.), *Judgment under uncertainty: Heuristics and biases* (pp. 163–178). Cambridge, UK: Cambridge University Press.

Warr, M. (1980). The accuracy of public beliefs about crime. *Social Forces, 59,* 456–470.

Warr, M. (1984). Fear of victimization: Why are women and the elderly more afraid? *Social Science Quarterly, 65,* 681–702.

Warr, M. (1985). Fear of rape among urban women. *Social Problems, 32,* 238–250.

Warr, M. (1990). Dangerous situations: Social context and fear of victimization. *Social Forces, 68,* 891–907.

Warr, M. (1994). Public perceptions and reactions to violent offending and victimization. In A. J. Reiss, Jr. & J. A. Roth (Eds.), *Understanding and preventing violence. Consequences and control* (Vol. 4, pp. 1–66). Washington, DC: National Academy Press.

Warr, M. (1995). Public perceptions of crime and punishment. In J. F. Sheley (Ed.), *Criminology: A contemporary handbook* (2nd ed.) (pp. 15–30). New York: Wadsworth.

Warr, M. (1995). Poll trends: Public opinion on crime and punishment. *Public Opinion Quarterly, 59,* 296–310.

Warr, M. (2000). Fear of crime in the United States: Avenues for research and policy. In D. Duffee (Ed.), *Criminal justice 2000. Measurement and analysis of crime and justice* (Vol. 4, pp. 451–489). Washington, DC: U.S. Department of Justice, National Institute of Justice.

Warr, M., & Ellison, C. G. (2000). Rethinking social reactions to crime: Personal and altruistic fear in family households. *American Journal of Sociology, 108,* 551–578.

Warr, M., & Stafford, M. C. (1983). Fear of victimization: A look at the proximate causes. *Social Forces, 61,* 1033–1043.

CHAPTER 30

Terrorism as a Form of Violence

Kevin J. Strom and Cynthia Irvin

I'll wear no convict's uniform nor meekly serve my time that England might brand Ireland's fight 800 years of crime.

— Lyrics of popular song protesting removal of political prisoner status for IRA prisoners in 1976

Introduction

Acts of terrorism, whether bombings, assassinations, kidnappings, or other actions, are rooted in violent behavior. As observed by McCue (2005), "In many ways terrorism is violence with a larger agenda." Yet in contrast to most violent offenders, terrorists use violence to support the attainment of political, moral, or social goals (Hoffman, 1998; Jenkins, 1984; Laqueur, 1987; Rosenfeld, 2004). Violence (or the threat of violence) is used to send a message of intimidation beyond the immediate victims to a wider target group of secondary victims. By carrying out their crimes in a very public and deliberate manner, terrorists seek to carry out attacks that have lasting effects far beyond the immediate incident, including long-term psychological and economic repercussions.

Terrorism has become a considerable and constant threat in today's world. Large-scale attacks such as 9/11, the Madrid train bombings, and the London subway bombings, have demonstrated the increasing willingness of terrorists, mainly Islamic extremists, to engage in indiscriminate large-scale destruction and murder. Since 1968, 19,960 terrorist incidents have taken place worldwide, resulting in 66,757 injuries and 22,668 deaths (MIPT Terrorism Knowledge Database, 2005). Over this period, the number of international terrorist incidents has increased nearly 15-fold from 132 incidents in 1968 to 1,932 in 2004 (see Figure 30.1). As terrorist groups continue to diversify and proliferate, they represent an ever-growing threat for all countries including the United States. Today there are an estimated 71 active Islamic terrorist groups and 751 active domestic terrorist groups operating in America, each with its own particular mission and

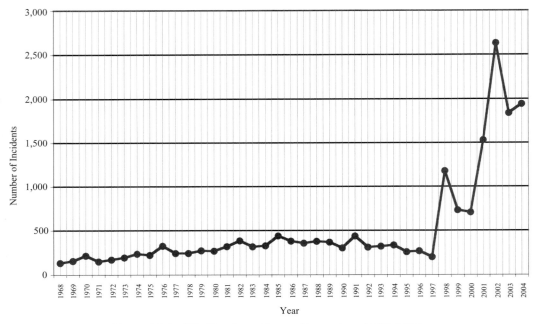

Figure 30.1. Worldwide incidents of terrorism, 1968–2004.

methods (Emerson, 2004; Southern Poverty Law Center, 2004).

One of the central questions for criminologists is how terrorism fits within the larger context of violence. Are there lessons learned from our understanding of other forms of violence that can be applied to terrorism, and can the analysis of terrorism enhance our understanding of violent crime? To better grasp these issues, this chapter compares and contrasts terrorism to more common forms of criminal violence, discussing conceptual similarities and differences in terms of the motivations, rationalization, and characteristics of offenders. It also outlines the major typologies of terrorism groups, including common motivations and belief structures.

Defining Terrorism

When discussing terrorism, one of the initial stumbling blocks is often the definitional complexities that arise when trying to explain exactly what terrorism refers to.

Although terrorism is a term that is used widely in modern vocabulary, there has been and continues to be much debate over how it should be defined (e.g., Hoffman, 1998; Rapoport, 1992; Schmid, 1998). For example, Schmid (1983) examined more than 100 existing definitions of terrorism and dedicated more than 100 pages to the discussion, but was still unable to make any reasonable progress toward a mutually acceptable definition. Interestingly, in his review he found that "violence" was by far the most common word used to define the concept of terrorism.

There are several factors that have complicated the development of a commonly accepted definition. For one, the term "terrorism" is fairly generic and is used by the media and others to refer to a tremendously wide range of acts, including assassinations, the distribution of chemicals such as anthrax through the mail, and insurgency efforts in countries such as Iraq. Another factor is that the label of terrorism is highly subjective; hence, the popular quote, "one man's terrorist is another man's freedom fighter." Brian

Jenkins (1980, p. 10) suggests that the "use of the term implies a moral judgment; and if one party can successfully attach the label of terrorist to its opponent, then it has indirectly persuaded others to adopt its moral viewpoint." Because of the moral repugnance that the term carries, terrorist organizations often try to distance themselves from the application of the term to their group and "deliberately cloak themselves in the terminology of military jargon" (Hoffman, 1998, p. 33). Another complicating issue is the fact that the term "terrorism" and what it represents have changed considerably over time. A related and significant difference is the extent to which contemporary organizations make use of public Web sites to provide information on their ideology and goals, to recruit, to garner public support, and possibly even to communicate with its members, in contrast to the relative secrecy sought by terrorist organizations in the past.

In some sense, terrorism can be seen as a method of struggle, rather than violence for violence's sake or for effect (Wilkinson, 1987). Jenkins (1980) described it as a "weapons-system" that can be used by a range of different actors, including governments, political factions, criminal gangs, and religious movements or cults. Hoffman (1998, p. 43) believes that "the terrorist is fundamentally a violent intellectual, prepared to use and indeed committed to using force in the attainment of his goals." He goes on to characterize terrorism as (a) political in aims and motives; (b) designed to have more widespread psychological effects beyond the immediate victims or targets; (c) carried out by a subnational group or nonstate entity; and (d) conducted by an organization with an identifiable chain of command or cell structure.

One could argue that the fundamental descriptions of terrorism that reference a strong collective element and allegiance to a particular organization are perhaps no longer accurate. In recent years, domestic terrorist groups as well as some Islamic fundamentalist groups have shifted from a cellular and hierarchical organizational model to a more uncoordinated, less structured system (Barkun, 1997; Jenkins, 2002). Indeed, a type of terrorism that has gained increasing attention since the 1990s is "leaderless resistance." The emergence of this new type has challenged the notion that organization and coordination are always necessary for terrorism to be effective (White, 2000). This new pattern has significant implications for law enforcement for, if there is no defined group, then collecting intelligence becomes extremely difficult from an investigative perspective. Furthermore, many terrorist groups are methodical and have long pre-operational planning cycles, attacking targets only after extensive surveillance.

Despite the rather extensive quantity and variety of the definitions of terrorism, models of terrorist behavior tend to fall into one of two paradigms: (1) the rational/strategic paradigm, which views terrorist behavior as a deliberate, calculated choice made by an organization as part of its overall strategy (Crenshaw, 1972, 1983, 1985; Hoffman, 1998; Sederberg, 1989; Wilkinson, 1982, 1986, 2000); and (2) the psychological paradigm, which argues that individuals who are drawn to and ultimately join terrorist organizations and commit violent acts are in some way psychologically damaged (Fields, 1978; Post, 1990, 2004; Rapoport, 1984, 1992). Although these two schools of thought remain dominant within the field, it is significant to note that, as the study of terrorism has expanded, most scholars acknowledge that multiple forces (i.e., social, psychological, political, economic, and cultural) contribute to an individual's decision to join a terrorist organization and to participate in the perpetration of terrorist acts. The recognition of these multiple areas of influence is critical if policymakers are to craft successful counter-terrorism strategies and to identify successful "exit strategies" for individuals, as well as terrorist organizations.

Characterizing Terrorism and Violence

Conceptually a greater understanding is needed of the congruence, or lack thereof, between terrorism and violent crime. Terrorists and organized criminal networks both use violence to achieve their goals, yet these groups have normally been seen as distinct threats. Yet, in recent years there is increasing evidence that criminal networks and terrorist organizations are working together with increasing regularity (Lal, 2005). As the threat of terrorism increases and as we continue to dedicate more resources toward preventing future attacks, it makes sense that we should benefit from our understanding of violent crime. A greater appreciation for the theoretical connections (and disconnections) between terrorism and "ordinary" violence could lead to the transfer of effective strategies used for analyzing and preventing violent crime (LaFree & Dugan, 2004). For instance, by identifying the areas of overlap, we can use advancements in the behavioral analysis of violent crime to improve our understanding and prediction of terrorist events (McCue, 2005). Furthermore, by identifying what it is about terrorism that makes it distinct from other forms of violence, we may expand our appreciation and theoretical framework for violence as a whole (Rosenfeld, 2002).

Terrorism is certainly more similar to some forms of violent crime, such as organized crime (Wardlaw, 1988), gang violence, and hate crimes, than such others as street robbery and domestic violence. Although some violent offenders tend to be impulsive and short-sighted and seek individual reward, others, such as serial murders, serial rapists, and some armed robbers, have different traits, including the ability to act collectively, plan over the long term, and selectively choose the victim and location (Douglas, Burgess, Burgess, & Ressler, 1992). These types of violent criminals may also stop from carrying out their intended crime if the circumstances do not meet their requirements. In the discussion that follows, it is important to recognize that these categorizations are generalities across the most common forms of behavior and are not unconditional.

Conceptual Differences

Terrorists Have Different Motivations for Using Violence

One of the key distinctions between terrorists and their criminal counterparts is motivation. Although terrorists engage in specific violent acts (e.g., homicide, assault, kidnapping), they are driven by political or moralistic goals against what they often perceive is some "chronic" grievance with a long history (e.g., political independence or return of a disputed land; Senechal de la Roche, 1996). Islamic fundamentalists, such as Osama bin Laden and his followers, are not motivated to attack America only because of recent acts committed by U.S. governments but by what they perceive are thousands of years of social injustice perpetuated by the West. In this sense, terrorists are altruistic and view their crimes as serving the greater good and supporting their constituency (Hoffman, 1998). Terrorists are highly motivated and loyal to a particular cause, and their actions have symbolic value and are meant to send a message to a wider audience (Paletz & Schmid, 1992). The immediate targets of violence, who are often innocent victims, are distinct from the targets of influence, which can represent an entire segment of society or the government decision makers representing them (Hoffman, 1998; Jenkins, 2002; Schmid, 1983). Unlike most criminals, terrorists often want their actions to be made public and to attach their group's identity to these crimes, as demonstrated by the recent use and distribution of videos of beheadings by a variety of Islamic groups (Clutterbuck, 1981; Crelinsten, 1990; Irvin, 1992; Schmid & Degraf, 1982). When captured and prosecuted, terrorists frequently seek to turn their trials into political theater (Hoffman, 1998).

In contrast to terrorists, who are motivated by ideology, religion, or a political cause, the typical offender engages in violent crime for personal gain (Douglas et al., 1992). For most offenders, violence is simply a method used for obtaining something desired by the individual, such as financial reward, drugs, revenge, or power. Criminal drug organizations use violence as a method of enforcement and to protect their business interests. An armed robber uses violence to accomplish the means of obtaining something of value, such as money or clothing, from a specific victim. With some notable exceptions, such as victims of hate crimes including racially motivated homicide and assassinations perhaps, the immediate victim of violence is not symbolic of a larger political or social agenda (Douglas et al., 1992).

Terrorists Seek Media Attention

Most criminals seek to commit their violent acts far from the media spotlight. There are exceptions to this rule, however, as some violent offenders appear to desire some recognition for their criminal "brilliance." For example, the "BTK" serial killer apprehended in 2005 in Wichita, Kansas, communicated with authorities and the news media through letters, postcards, and other means. Also, like many terrorists, serial killers, such as "BTK" and Jeffrey Dahmer, demonstrated an ability to evade detection over time.

Terrorist organizations usually seek maximum coverage of their actions and have gone so far as to coordinate their attacks with the timing of the major daily news broadcasts (Clutterbuck, 1981; Hoffman, 1998; Paletz & Schmid, 1992). Terrorism has, in general, proved remarkably ineffective as the major weapon for toppling governments and capturing political power (Wilkinson, 1982, 2000), although the recent Madrid train bombings illustrated they do have the potential for influencing elections. The violent acts orchestrated by terrorists have, however, been highly successful as a means of publicizing a political cause and relaying the terrorist threat to a wider audience, particularly in the open and pluralistic countries of the West. Through media coverage, these organizations hope to establish a *favorable understanding of their cause* in the mass public (Clutterbuck, 1981; Crelinsten, 1990; Paletz & Schmid, 1992; Schmid & Degraf, 1982). Good relationships with the press are important, and they are often cul-

tivated and nurtured over a period of years (Paletz & Schmid, 1992). Further, many terrorist movements are well aware that their cause can be damaged by unfavorable publicity and therefore develop highly sophisticated press offices to wage propaganda warfare directed both at domestic and international audiences (Crelinsten, 1990; Irvin, 1992; Paletz & Tawney, 1992).

Terrorists Are More Likely To Operate in Organized Structures

Terrorist organizations tend to be collectively focused and team oriented, with extremely strong devotion and unity from those who participate (Crenshaw, 1985; Hoffman, 1998; Senechal de la Roche, 1996). Most terrorist groups are organized with a multilevel command-and-control structure, which typically includes command (policy, planning, and general direction), the active cadre (operational arm), active supporters (field support and logistics), and passive supporters (e.g., financial supporters; Fraser & Fulton, 1984; White, 2003). Larger terrorist organizations generally create subunits called cells, which are capable of carrying out widespread operations on their own. Group members typically have close ties, a strong sense of camaraderie, and some shared sense of experience that have produced mutual hatred of their perceived enemies in "a highly moralistic, explosive, and lethal combination" (Black, 2004, p. 13; see also Black, 1998; Wievorka, 1993). Terrorism flourishes in small, socially isolated, homogeneous groups that exist within some higher level organization. As an example, suicide bombers in the Middle East very rarely operate as individuals. In many cases, these individuals are accompanied by preparation and support teams that serve critical roles in helping them carry out their missions (Taheri, 1987).

Most criminals tend to operate individually or perhaps in small groups. Even in a group context, the vast majority of criminals often look out for themselves first. It is widely known in law enforcement that one of the best methods for obtaining information is to turn one offender against another (Dyson, 2001). If apprehended, criminals generally deny their wrongdoing, or they may make a plea bargain and become informants against former partners. This being said, there are some criminal groups, such as international drug cartels and nationally syndicated street gangs, which operate in a structured and collective manner and are driven by a common cause. Street gangs can use violence against specific individuals to make statements against the larger community and rival gangs (e.g., witness intimidation; Klein, 1995; Riedel & Welsh, 2002). Although street gangs are rarely political or religious-based, an argument could be made that some larger and more organized gangs have certain political goals (e.g., neighborhood control).

Terrorist Organizations Rely to a Greater Extent on a Defined Leadership

Although many criminal groups certainly have a leadership hierarchy, terrorist leaders appear more important to their organizations than their criminal counterparts. The capture or death of a leader can cripple a terrorist group, as happened to the Sendero Luminoso (Shining Path) in Peru after the government apprehended Abimael Guzman Reynoso in September 1992 (Strong, 1993). Guzman was succeeded by Principal Regional Committee leader Oscar Alberto Ramirez Durand (alias "Feliciano") who, in turn, was captured by government forces in July 1999. Neither Durand nor his successor, Filomeno Cerron Cardoso (alias "Artemio"), has reversed the group's decline (Anderson, 2004).

In contrast, the death or capture of a criminal organization leader often has only a marginal impact. For example, Colombia remains the hub of narcotics activity; coca cultivation and leaf production have increased there every year since 1993 despite the arrests of seven leaders of the Cali crime syndicate and the death of Pablo Escobar, leader of the Medellin criminal organization (Anderson, 2004).

Terrorist Events Are Often Part of a Sustained Pattern of Symbolic Violence

Terrorists do not commit acts randomly or without purpose; instead they seek to maximize public attention for their acts and to intimidate the intended audience (Crenshaw, 1972, 1983, 1985; Hoffman, 1998; Irvin, 1999). Terrorist incidents always have a larger meaning and intended audience beyond the immediate incident and victims. As such, terrorist organizations are highly focused, and although they may select targets of opportunity, each target is selected because of its symbolic value (Bodrero, 2000). Because of these factors, predicting future terrorist attacks and creating effective prevention strategies can be more complex than traditional forms of crime prevention. It is also important to recognize that violent acts committed by terrorist organizations are generally carried out in accordance with the organization's strategic goals. As such, these actions represent only one tactic within a broader coercive strategy, which collectively constitutes a much broader political agenda (Sederberg, 1989).

Violent crime for the most part is opportunistic and in some cases impulsive (Douglas et al., 2002; Riedel & Welsh, 2002). In fact, impulsivity is one of the central concepts in several prominent criminological theories for criminal behavior (Gottfredson & Hirschi, 1990; Wilson & Herrnstein, 1985). Although there are certainly exceptions, most violent offenders do not plan their crimes extensively, but react when opportunities present themselves or when situational factors lead them to violence. For example, a felony murder refers to a homicide that is committed during the course of another crime, most commonly burglary or robbery. The vast majority of criminals are not committed to a cause and their primary objective is completing the crime without detection. Even for many career criminals such as professional burglars, crime is not a religion or ideology, but rather a means to an end.

Although most violent crime is unplanned, not connected to a larger cause, and not part of a more sustained pattern of violence there are certainly exceptions (e.g., serial murders and rapists; Ressler, Burgess, & Douglas, 1998). One notable exception is "criminal competition" homicides, which are carefully planned acts carried out by organized crime groups to send a message or make a statement (Douglas et al., 1992, p. 32). Another example is the serial rapist who can commit many crimes over time and develop a specific signature pattern with his victims.

The Types of Data Maintained on Crime Differ From Data Collected on Terrorism

Criminal justice data on violent crime generally come from three sources: (1) official sources, such as incident or arrest data reported by law enforcement agencies in the FBI's Uniform Crime Reports (2004); (2) victimization surveys that represent crime experiences of victims (e.g., National Crime Victimization Survey); or (3) self-report data from offenders. In contrast, until the 1990s, relatively few countries systematically reported statistics on official crimes of terrorism, and the majority of publicly accessible data sources on terrorism were derived from secondary sources, such as news wire services, academic reports, and Web sites (LaFree & Dugan, 2004). Controversies related to variations in official counts of terrorist events continue as evidenced by U.S. Secretary of State Colin Powell's public acknowledgment of the errors made regarding the terrorism statistics included in the State Department's annual Global Terrorism Reports. Future statistical reports on terrorism will now be published in the United States by the National Counterterrorism Center (Krueger & Laitin, 2004).

Conceptual Similarities

Terrorists and Violent Criminals Often Use Fear to Achieve Their Goals

Both terrorists and more ordinary violent offenders use fear as a means to achieve particular ends. A criminal who engages in an armed robbery can use fear to his or her advantage to ensure victim compliance by displaying a weapon and by using threatening speech. Hostage taking is a practice used by both violent criminal and terrorist groups as a mechanism for using fear to achieve some particular goal. In hostage situations, as well as other cases, terrorists use fear to their advantage, but seek to benefit from the use of terror among a wider, more general target far beyond those involved in the incident itself. As such, the goal-directed character of terrorist violence differentiates it from typical criminal violence. Nonpolitical violence also has goals; however these actions are very rarely motivated by a political agenda.

Terrorism and Violent Crime Are Both Disproportionally Committed by Young Males Alienated From Mainstream Society

Both terrorism and more common forms of violent crime are most likely to be committed by young males, typically individuals in their early to mid-twenties. One of the most consistent empirical findings in criminology is the age-crime curve (Gottfredson & Hirschi, 1990). On average, rates of offending increase through adolescence, peaking between ages 18 and 20 and then steadily declining thereafter. According to the FBI's Supplementary Homicide Reports (SHR), 91% of homicide offenders in 2002 were male, and the rate of offending for persons aged 18 to 24 was more than double that of any other age group (FBI, 2004). With regard to gender, although terrorism, like more traditional forms of violence, is mainly a male occupation, it is important to recognize that there is female participation in both. As an example, over the past several years, female suicide bombers from Chechnya, many of whose husbands were killed fighting Russian soldiers, have committed a series of attacks across Russia that have left hundreds of people dead (Zedalis, 2004).

Individuals who join terrorist organizations often are unemployed and have been marginalized by the dominant groups in society (Hoffman, 1998; Post, 1990,

2004; Shaw, 1986). However, in contrast to criminal offenders who tend to be socially alienated individuals, members of terrorist organizations tend to have strong social bonds within their communities (Clark, 1984; Irvin, 1999; Mishal & Sela, 2000). Those with little education may resort to crime or try to join a terrorist group out of boredom or a desire to have an action-packed adventure in pursuit of a cause they regard as just. Some individuals may be motivated mainly by a desire to use their special skills, such as bomb making. The more educated youths may be motivated more by genuine political or religious convictions. Often, violent encounters with police or other security forces motivate an already socially alienated individual to turn to violent crime or join a terrorist group. In her interviews with members of Sinn Fein and Herri Batasuna, Irvin (1999) found that the personal experience of violence, or the experience of violence by a family member at the hands of security forces, was the most significant factor in predicting support for violent actions by the IRA and ETA.

Terrorists and Criminals Have Both Proven to Be Adaptive and Learn From Past Behaviors

Organizational longevity is a function of adaptability. As stated by Jackson (2005), "If a terrorist group lacks the ability to learn, its effectiveness in achieving its goals will largely be determined by chance." In fact, the failure to adjust operationally and strategically has led to the demise of several terrorist groups, including Baader-Meinhoff and the Italian Red Brigades. The most durable terrorist groups are those that adjust both operationally and politically to changing circumstances, including new procedures and tactics used by intelligence and law enforcement agencies. When a terrorist group can learn and adapt it can improve many of its capabilities, including its ability to develop and employ new weapons or tactics and to collect and use intelligence necessary to carry out successful operations (Jackson, 2005).

For example, following the deaths of several IRA members at the hands of their own planted explosives, IRA bomb makers began creating means for detonating bombs at a distance by using radio controls from model aircraft. The IRA has proven to be adaptive politically as well, having successfully recast its image on numerous occasions (Irvin, 1992; Moloney, 2002). Similarly, Hezbollah now confronts the challenge of adaptation in southern Lebanon since Israel has withdrawn its forces from the buffer zone.

As with terrorist groups, many criminals and criminal organizations have proven themselves to be highly adaptable and modify their behaviors over time. For example, if a rapist has problems controlling a victim, he may adjust his modus operandi (MO) with subsequent victims by using duct tape or a weapon (Douglas et al., 2002; Ressler et al., 1988). Other examples of adaptation include the use of the Internet as a major source of fraud and theft and the use of new technologies, such as disposable cell phones by street-level drug dealers. There are also drug trafficking organizations in Latin American that have repeatedly demonstrated their ability to shift their transportation routes in response to shifting law enforcement strategies. For example, recently some Colombian narcotics traffickers have reduced their reliance on Mexican smuggling routes and returned to Caribbean ones popular in the 1980s.

Terrorist Group Typologies

In criminology, a convincing body of research has shown that all homicides are not alike and that disaggregating these events into meaningful subcategories is necessary to maximize the effectiveness of our analysis and interpretation of these diverse events (e.g., Block & Block, 1992; Wolfgang, 1958). Homicide classification systems are based on such factors as offender motivation, the relationship between the victim and offender, and the circumstances surrounding the incident. Similar to homicide, there is considerable variation in the motivations, ideology, and methods of different terrorists and terrorist groups.

This section categorizes terrorist groups into one of five typologies: religious fundamentalists, ethno-nationalists, right-wing extremism, left-wing extremism, and special interest groups. Table 30.1 describes the common objectives and motivations as well as examples of terrorist groups associated with these categories. However, the categories are not mutually exclusive as some groups can likely fit into multiple categories. Perhaps more importantly, as the nature and character of terrorism continue to evolve, clear distinctions between some of these classifications are becoming less clear.

Religious Extremism

What do the attacks on the World Trade Center in 1993 and 2001, the sarin nerve gas attacks on the Tokyo subway system, and the 1997 massacre of foreign tourists in an Egyptian temple have in common? These acts were all carried out by terrorist groups motivated by a sense of religious authority. Although a number of terrorism groups share common religious beliefs that unite their cause, the core motives and goals for religious fundamentalists revolve around their religious faith, rather than their political agendas. For example, a nationalist terrorist group such as the Irish Republican Army (IRA) is overwhelmingly Catholic. Yet, the primary objective for the IRA is the creation of a unified Ireland that is free of the rule of the British government. Likewise, the Palestinian Liberation Organization (PLO) is largely Muslim, but members unite first and foremost around their mission of creating a free Palestinian state. In contrast, for a religious extremist terrorist group such as Hezbollah, the principal motivations are to preserve and protect the religious sanctity of Islam by eliminating all enemies through large-scale violence. In the words of former Hezbollah leader Hussein Mussawi: "We are not fighting so that the enemy recognizes us and offers us something. We are fighting to wipe out the enemy" (Taheri, 1987). This is

not to say, however, that religious extremist groups do not have political goals. One clear example is the 2004 Madrid train bombings carried out by al Qaeda, which killed nearly 200 people and wounded thousands more. This highly coordinated attack occurred only 3 days before the Spanish national elections and in all likelihood greatly influenced the election, in which the ruling Conservative Party was defeated after holding a substantial lead in the polls only a few days earlier.

Terrorism is certainly not a phenomenon unique to modern times, as the ties between religion and terrorism have existed for thousands of years. According to Rapoport (1984), until the 19th century "holy terror" was the only true justification used for terrorism. One early example of religious terrorism is provided by the Jewish sect of Zealots, a name that has come to mean "fanatical enthusiast." In 66–73 A.D., this group fought against the Roman Empire's occupation of an area of land that is now called Israel (Hoffman, 1998; Rapoport, 1984). To convey a message of fear to a public audience, members of this group would routinely target certain Roman officials or Jewish sympathizers for assassination and, in a very public fashion, slit their throat for all to see. The goal of these acts was remarkably similar to the goals of modern terrorism, mainly to use violence for achieving a political or moralistic discourse. This group of "zealots" also engaged in one of the earliest known forms of chemical terrorism, poisoning Roman wells and the water supply of the larger Jerusalem area (Rapoport, 1984). Other examples of early religious terrorist groups include the Shia Muslim sect known as the Hashshashin, an organization that systematically assassinated persons in positions of leadership and influence during the 11th century. The English word "assassin" comes from the name Hashshashin.

Terrorism motivated by religious extremism represents one of the greatest terrorist threats in the world today (Hoffman, 1998; Post, 2004). According to the RAND-St. Andrews database, religious terrorist organizations carried out one quarter of reported attacks in 1995, yet these incidents

Table 30.1: Terrorist group typologies

Group typology	Characteristics	Group examples
Religious fundamentalism	• Have totalizing goals • Often personality driven • Supported by believers in the community • Prone to indiscriminant mass killings and destructive acts against a wide category of nonbelievers • Generally thought to be the most likely to use WMDs	• Al Qaeda • Hamas • Hezballah
Nationalist/separatists	• Goal is to increase national identify of group • Seek increased rights, autonomy, independence for segment of population that they represent • Target often restricted to specific rival or dominant ethno-nationalist group within the community or from foreign governments	• PLO • IRA • Tamil Tigers
Left-wing revolutionary	• Share Marxist-Leninist philosophy that is against the social and economic injustices found in many capitalistic, industrialized states • Seek destruction of existing political structures • Typically have support from some elements of society • Target government symbols of authority	• Red Brigade • Shining Path • FARC • Red Army Faction (RAF) • Second of June Movement
Right-wing revolutionary	• Politically reactionary • Seek destruction of existing political structure • Typically have sympathizers and support within existing political structure • Prone to indiscriminate attacks	• Combat 18 • Aryan Nation • Michigan Militia
Special interest	• Principal goal is to increase attention to a particular issue (e.g., abortion, animal rights, environment) • Target symbols of this issue (e.g., abortion clinics) • Typically have strong support from some elements of society • Often target property	• Liberation Front (ALF) • Earth Liberation Front (ELF)

accounted for nearly two thirds (58%) of all terrorism-related fatalities. Among acts that killed eight or more persons in that year, all were committed by religious terrorist groups (Hoffman, 1998). A major concern among governments around the world related to religious terrorist groups is their potential use of weapons of mass destruction (WMD), which can include nuclear, chemical and biological weapons. The goals of these groups are absolute, and they show no room for tolerance or negotiation. Furthermore, if these individuals were to die in the attack they are told that they will be rewarded in the afterlife. Hence, there are fewer moral and psychological obstacles that prohibit these groups from wiping out themselves and everyone else. Naturally, such an attack, if executed successfully, could have devastating consequences. Such groups as al Qaeda and the Japanese cult Aum Shrikio, among others, have shown a strong interest in the development and acquisition of WMDs, including chemical and biological agents (Central Intelligence Agency, 2003).

There are four major types of religious terrorist groups operating today: Islamic fundamentalists, Jewish extremist groups, Christian white supremacists, and religious cults (Hoffman, 1998). These terrorist groups, especially Islamic fundamentalists and religious cults, share a number of characteristics that make them an imminent threat and set them apart from other groups. One such defining characteristic is that they operate under different rules than other groups. Their principal goal is not to overthrow a social system or influence a political process. Rather, these groups seek either to convert the world to their religion or, if this fails, remove all nonbelievers from the face of the earth. Although other terrorist groups are driven by measurable objectives, such as media attention and government reaction, religious terrorists can justify even the most heinous violence crimes as sacramental acts. In other words, by carrying out acts of violence in "the name of God" or "Allah," their belief systems are used to legitimize and justify even the most egregious behaviors. Furthermore, the depiction of all non-

believers as "infidels" opens much of the Western world up as potential targets. This black-and-white level of distinction allows these groups to operate outside the bounds that can inhibit other politically motivated groups. For example, an organization such as Al Qaeda serves no direct constituency and therefore is not constrained by a large population from going too far with their campaign of terror. So, not only do terrorists motivated principally by religion have fewer constraints on the levels of violence they employ but they also have a larger range of targets from which to choose (Hoffman, 1998). In a sense, religious terrorist groups have no social limitations on the violence they commit. In their view, they are on a mission from God, and their violent behaviors are sanctified by divine blessing.

Ethno-Nationalism

Ethno-nationalist terrorists use violence in an attempt to forge national identity. Their primary purpose is to mobilize a community, and they do so by appealing to the nationalistic background of a particular ethnic group. Terrorist activity is used to make a statement about the group's identity as well as to secure resources for the organization. In some cases, groups strive for independence from the current state, as is the case with ETA in the Basque province of Spain (Irvin, 1999). Examples of ethnic-separatist terrorists include groups seeking independence from an occupying force, such as the Jewish Irgun in Palestine under the British Mandate and the IRA under British occupation.

The target selection for ethno-nationalist groups tends to be highly selective and discriminate, including symbolic targets they blame for economic or political repression, such as ambassadors, bankers, and dignitaries. These groups usually issue communiqués taking credit for, and explaining in great detail, their actions. Only rarely do such groups operate outside their home territory unless it is in their interest to do so or they claim to be representing the oppressed of the Third World or belong to some "diaspora."

When governments respond to terrorist actions with repression, it draws attention to the group and allows the terrorists to present themselves as victims and further strengthen group solidarity, often at the expense of moderates within the community. This repression increases public awareness and sometimes attracts finances and support. Terrorism also polarizes other ethnic groups and forces them to either ally with the terrorists or oppose them.

Ethnic terrorism is not an exclusively modern phenomenon. In the first century A.D., ethnic terrorism was used by two Jewish groups in Judea that sought to incite the local population to rise against the Roman occupiers. However, it was only in the colonial and neocolonial era (1950s, 1960s, and 1970s) that terrorism came to be associated with ethno-nationalist/separatist groups. During this period, terrorism was viewed as a successful strategy for nationalist groups in Israel, Cyprus, and Algeria. Beginning in the late 1960s, the Palestine Liberation Organization's (PLO) terrorist activism further demonstrated to other nationalist movements that internationalizing their cause could be beneficial. In 1968 when the PLO hijacked an Israeli El Al flight en route from Rome to Tel Aviv, it showed other nationalist groups that, if planned properly, these types of actions could bring worldwide attention to their cause.

An ethno-nationalist/separatist movement legitimizes itself, by relying "on the grievances of a collective memory to regain economic, political and cultural rights [and] by rejecting subordination and cultural assimilation" (Jalata, 2001). A small faction of that movement, if dissatisfied with the results of the political strategies pursued, may opt to resort to terrorism to enhance and secure their group identity through the acquisition of statehood or some other form of political autonomy. The victims of ethno-nationalist terrorist violence are most generally members of the security forces and of the dominant ethnic group, which is seen "as an occupying, opposing,

colonizing or foreign force" (Volkan, 1999, p. 157). It is important to note, however, that although the terrorist faction may have a high level of legitimacy among its members it does not necessarily follow that the terrorist group has the same degree of legitimacy in the eyes of the ethnic nationalists's public majority, who may reject violence for one reason or another at any given time (Irvin, 1999). Nonetheless, ethno-nationalist/separatist terrorist groups believe that terrorism is an effective means to get rid of the dominant ethnic group and/or to achieve the specific form of political autonomy they desire. To achieve repeated success these groups depend on the logistical assistance of governments, organizations, or individuals supporting their cause, as well as on the solidarity of their community (Irvin, 1999, 2000). A study of statements by known militants suggests that they idealize violence "to enhance self-esteem and as a defensive response to an individual's or group's sense of entitlement to revenge" (Volkan, 1999, p. 162). Terrorist organizations, to the extent that they provide a sense of belonging and substitute for a missing personal identity, face the "threat of success"; they must be successful enough to attract members and self-perpetuate, but not enough to no longer be needed and be in danger of dissolution.

Daniel Byman (1998), a RAND analyst, argues that ethnic nationalist terrorism has built-in advantages that make it *the most dangerous kind of terrorism* arguing that it (1) polarizes ethnic conflict and accentuates a primal fear of race war; (2) provokes government overreaction from those who see it as an insurgency problem; (3) frequently produces government concessions, which are seen as a sign of success; (4) often raises financial donations and public support quickly; and (5) involves a ready-made constituency.

Right-Wing Terrorism

During the last several decades, terrorism from racist and right-wing groups has emerged as an increasing threat. Right-wing extremist groups generally use violent acts to promote an anti-government or racist ideology, particularly in North America and Europe with the rise of white supremacy and neo-Nazi groups. Using U.S. federal prosecution data, Smith (1994) analyzed the common characteristics of American right-wing terrorists and found that they tended to be (1) based in rural areas, (2) anti-Marxist and often extremely religious, (3) supportive of the general economic system but not of the distribution of wealth, and (4) focused on attacks on symbols of government authority (e.g., Timothy McVeigh's attack on the Federal building in Oklahoma City). Examples of right-wing domestic terrorism in the United States include the April 1995 Oklahoma City bombing and the summer 1999 shooting sprees by lone gunmen targeting minorities in the Chicago and Los Angeles metropolitan areas, which left three people dead. In Europe, even normally peaceful countries such as Sweden have experienced their share of right-wing terrorism. During the late 1990s, neo-Nazis murdered two Swedish police officers, assassinated a labor union activist, bombed a journalist and his son in their car, and sent a letter-bomb to the Swedish Minister of Justice. Neo-fascists and neo-Nazi groups have also been active in such places as Canada, South Africa, Central and South America, and the former Soviet Union.

As seen by these examples, right-wing groups are prone to indiscriminate, sporadic attacks against particular types of targets (e.g., refugees, immigrants, ethnic groups). Violent acts are not random, but tend to be planned so as to appeal to their constituency. Although the Oklahoma City bombing was certainly an exception, groups typically do not want to solicit massive reaction by the government so they typically do not want to go overboard in their actions.

Terrorist acts by these groups have been motivated by opposition to federal taxation and regulation, international organizations such as the United Nations, and the U.S. government itself, as well as by a hatred of racial and religious minorities. Some of these forms of terrorism have long traditions. Violence against ethnic, racial, sexual, and political minorities has been going on for decades and even centuries in some countries. Lynchings of Blacks in the United States and violence against gypsies, refugees, and labor migrants in several European countries have a tragically long and established history. Yet, the U.S. general public was mentally unprepared for a *new* form of right-wing terrorism that virtually exploded with the truck bombing of the Federal office building in Oklahoma City in April 1995, killing 169 persons and wounding more than 400. FBI officials say right-wing militants – including skinheads, neo-Nazis, militia members, and the so-called Christian Patriot movement– now pose one of America's most serious domestic terrorist threats (FBI, 2004; Southern Policy Law Center, 2004). Many members of these organizations feel displaced by rapid changes in the U.S. culture and economy or are seeking some form of personal affirmation. As American society continues to change, the potential for hate crimes by extremist right-wing groups is of increasing concern.

In Europe, the problem of the resurgence of extreme right-wing violence has become a far more serious threat than the ideologically motivated left-wing violence that dominated in past decades. For example in Germany, the widespread disillusion with mainstream political parties, the strains of reunification on the economy, high levels of unemployment, and the arrival of hundreds of thousands of immigrants have created a climate in which violent right-wing extremism thrives. The German Interior Ministry estimates there are some 75 extreme right groups active in Germany with 65,000 activists, roughly 10% of whom have a record of violence. Between 1991 and 1993 the extreme right groups killed 30 people (Human Rights Watch, 1995). Most experts predict that violent attacks motivated by extreme right ideology are likely to increase over the next few years in many countries where conditions are conducive. However, extreme right-wing terrorism is likely to remain largely indigenous and shows no signs of developing a significant international dimension.

Special Interest Terrorism

Special interest terrorist groups represent one of the more dangerous and emerging terrorist threats, especially for governments in Europe and the United States (FBI, 2004; Smith, 1994; Smith & Damphousse, 1997). This form of terrorism differs from other types such as right-wing extremism in that special interest groups seek to address a particular social issue, rather than a comprehensive political agenda. Examples of special interest causes include ecological terrorism (i.e., environmental issues and animal rights); abortion, and anti-nuclear movements. These groups use violence to bring attention to their cause and to pressure both the public and representatives in government to enact legislation directly reflecting their particular concern. Their crimes, which are generally defined as acts of domestic terrorism, are intended to force segments of society to change attitudes about issues considered important to their cause. For example, extremists who oppose legalized abortion in the United States have attacked clinics and murdered doctors and other employees in hopes of denying women the right to abortion.

In the United States, ecological terrorists have demonstrated two major areas of interest: the first involves land-use issues and the second is concerned with animal rights, including cruelty toward animals by industry and by the scientific community through human experimentation (Smith, 1994; Smith & Damphousse, 1997). Guided by a philosophy that is still evolving and expanding, environmental and animal rights terrorists believe that only through terrorist acts can they convey their message and beliefs to others. More importantly, these groups exhibit a fatalistic view that, if left unchecked, humans will bring the world to a cataclysmic end. Although they rarely use violence, single-issue extremists, including those in the animal rights and environmental movements, have increasingly turned to vandalism and other terrorist activity to further their causes (FBI, 2004). Militant animal rights activists, for example, have used violence against scientists and laboratory technicians in their campaign to halt medical experimentation involving animals. Radical environmentalists, also referred to as eco-terrorists, have sabotaged logging operations and the construction of power grids to protest the spoiling of natural wilderness areas. They also tend to use arson and vandalism fairly frequently, including burning expensive homes and SUVs.

In the past decade, certain environmental and animal rights groups in the United States, such as the Animal Liberation Front (ALF) and its sister organization the Earth Liberation Front (ELF), have emerged as serious terrorist threats (FBI, 2004). The FBI estimates that the these two groups engaged in over 600 criminal acts between 1996 and 2001 alone, which resulted in over $43 million in damages. These groups are amorphous movements and have no organizational chart, which presents a particularly difficult situation for law enforcement. The Internet has served as a facilitating device, as propaganda and strategy disseminated via the Web can be used to encourage new believers to start their own violent cells or to join existing ones. Eco-terrorist groups such as the Earth Liberation Front (ELF) have carried out acts of destruction against housing developments and resorts that they feel threaten remaining natural habitats. Examples include the ELF arson fires at a ski resort in Vail, Colorado, in 1998 that caused $12 million in damages. In 2001, the FBI put the ELF on top of their list of the largest domestic terrorism threats.

Abortion is another issue that has incited the use of politically based violence, in many cases involving bombings of clinics or shooting of their staff by extremists who oppose legalized abortion. In the 1980s, there were nearly 40 bombings of abortion clinics across the United States, and during the 1990s these types of attacks spread to include shootings, arson, and targeted bombings of abortion supporters. Nice (1988) analyzed abortion bombings during the mid-1980s and found that these attacks tended to occur in urban areas that had experienced rapid population growth, that had high rates of abortions compared to live births, and that had more militant anti-abortion constituencies. When social controls declined in an area and when radical groups felt a greater urgency for political action, then politically oriented violence was often viewed as an appropriate form of response.

Although issue-group extremists aim at changing specific policies or practices rather than the whole socio-political system, their potential for endangering life and social and economic well-being should not be underestimated. The FBI reports that the violence and acts of destruction carried out by animal rights and environment terrorist groups have increased in frequency and intensity in recent years (FBI, 2004). As with other terrorist groups, these groups' ideology and operational tactics have become increasingly militant, including engaging in acts of product contamination and computer sabotage. Given this fact, we must continue to consider them a considerable risk to future domestic security.

Conclusion

In contrast to most offenders who engage in violence for personal motivations, such for financial gain or sexual gratification, terrorist violence is unique in that the act is used as a means of achieving social or political change. Perhaps one of the reasons that scholars and ordinary individuals have always stressed the differences between terrorism and other forms of violence is that the scale of carnage from acts of terrorism seem so unfathomable and so unexpected to so many of us. What is more, unlike a notorious serious killer such as Charles Manson, who is clearly pathological, many terrorists appear on the surface to be rational persons who are driven largely by revenge and hatred. But there are notable similarities between terrorism and other forms of violence, especially if we look deeper within certain forms of violent behavior. Similar to terrorists, some violent offenders such as serial murders and rapists have a longer range planning cycle and are selective in their target of choice

(Douglas et al., 2002; Ressler et al., 1998). There are also organized criminal groups that are highly structured and, in the case of some criminal organizations and street gangs, such as the two dominant Salvadoran gangs, *Mara Salvatrucha* and *18th Street*, driven by a common ideology (Riedel & Welsh, 2002).

One of the sources of confusion when contrasting terrorism with other forms of violence is that terrorism combines war-like objectives with criminally based predatory behaviors and methods. This unique interplay led Rosenfeld (2004, p. 22) to refer to terrorism as a form of "criminal warfare." But because terrorist groups do not have military forces or weaponry that is on equal footing to most conventional military forces, they use asymmetric means to affect our society. For this reason, terrorism is often referred to as an asymmetrical threat to the United States and our allies. Means of attack can range from the use of suicide bombers to improvised explosive devices (IEDs) to weapons of mass destruction. These methods of attack can have a dramatic impact on our society through the loss of human life as well as the disruption of critical infrastructures including power, transport, communications, and financial systems.

But why is it so important to discuss terrorism within the larger context of violence? For one, it could promote the transfer of effective criminal justice-based strategies for addressing violent crime to counterterrorism operations. As Lafree and Dugan (2004, p. 70) have argued, this expansion of the existing "knowledge-base of criminology" to terrorism research is not only helpful for conceptual reasons but can also lead to the transfer of effective data collection and research methods as well. Criminologists are well positioned to handle research on the links between terrorism and transnational organized crime, the modus operandi of terrorist groups, and to evaluate the effectiveness of various federal, state, and local criminal justice system responses to terrorist groups (Zahn & Strom, 2004). Criminal justice analytical strategies that emphasize the identification of behavior patterns

Table 30.2: Comparison between homicides and terrorism fatalities, 1998–2000[a]

	Number of deaths from:		Ratio (homicides to terrorism fatalities)
Country	Homicide	Terrorism	
India	113,631	224	507.3
Philippines	17,351	62	279.9
Colombia	73,983	364	203.3
Russian Federation	83,536	426	196.1
Indonesia	6,052	38	159.3
Northern Ireland (UK)	2,366	52	45.5
USA[b]	47,175	3,064	15.4
Pakistan	228	273	0.8
Israel[b]	123	127	1.0

[a] International homicide data are from the United Nations Surveys on Crime Trends; terrorism data are from the MIPT Terrorism Knowledge Database.
[b] Data are for the years 1999–2001.
[c] Data are for the years 1995–1997.

over time and place can also be extended to the area of terrorism research (McCue, 2005). This includes the analysis of behaviors that can be used to identify preplanning processes and surveillance activity by terrorist organizations of potential critical infrastructure targets. By clearly outlining why terrorist violence is distinct from many forms of ordinary criminal violence, we can also reassess existing theories of criminality to identify limitations in their applicability to all forms of violent behavior. This can lead to a more comprehensive understanding of the phenomenon of violence, including a wider range of motivations and causes for all forms of violent behavior. Ultimately, thinking about terrorism within the larger context of violence may help us better understand how we prevent these crimes.

Since 9/11, the nature and character of terrorism have continued to evolve, as has the nature of the threat to our society (Jenkins, 2002). Between 1968 and 1993, the targets of more than half of all terrorist attacks were either diplomatic (e.g., embassies or United Nation's property or personnel) or business-related targets (MIPT Terrorism Knowledge Database, 2005). Since 1994, the risk posed by terrorism to private citizens has increased substantially, as the most common target has become private citizens

and their property. Terrorist organizations are also becoming more amorphous and less hierarchical, creating additional challenges for law enforcement when attempting to track group activities and develop cases against group leaders.

Despite the risks posed by terrorism, including newly emerging threats and the increased targeting of private citizens, it is criminal violence that continues to effect a larger proportion of individuals in modern society. Most countries have homicide levels that far exceed terrorism-related fatalities (Table 30.2). Among countries with the highest incidence of terrorism activity, only Pakistan and Israel had terrorism and homicide levels that were comparable. All of the remaining countries, including the United States, had homicide death rates that far exceeded those from terrorism. Even if we examine the 3-year period from 2001 to 2003 that included the terrorism deaths from 9/11, the ratio of homicide to terrorism fatalities in the United States is still 16 to 1. Across U.S. cities, the discrepancy in risk between terrorism and homicide is also apparent, including for those places hit hardest by terrorism (Rosenfeld, 2004). These numbers demonstrate that as we continue to dedicate more resources toward the War on Terrorism, we should not lose sight of the fact that it is violent crime, not terrorism, that more immediately affects our daily lives. By thinking of terrorism and violence along the same continuum rather than as discrete categories of behavior, we can recognize that there are effective strategies that can address multiple forms of violence. As such, the allocation of resources to terrorism and violent crime does not have to be a zero-sum game.

Acknowledgments

We thank Colleen McCue and Margaret Zahn for their comments on earlier versions of this article.

References

Anderson, J. H. (2004). *International terrorism and crime: Trends and linkages*. Retrieved April 14, 2005, from http://www.jmu.edu/orgs/wrni/it2.html.

Barkun, M. (1997). *Religion and the racist Right: The origins of the Christian identity movement*. Chapel Hill, NC: University of North Carolina Press.

Black, D. (1998). *The social structure of right and wrong*. San Diego: Academic Press.

Black, D. (2004). Terrorism as social control. In M. DeFlem (Ed.), *Terrorism and counterterrorism: Criminological perspectives* (pp. 9–18). Oxford: Elsevier.

Block, R., & Block, C. R. (1992). Homicide syndromes and vulnerability: Violence in Chicago community areas over 25 years. *Studies on Crime & Crime Prevention, 1*, 61–87.

Bodrero, D. (2000). *State roles, community assessment, and personality profiles*. Tallahassee, FL: Institute for Intergovernmental Research.

Byman, D. (1998). The logic of ethnic terrorism. *Studies in Conflict and Terrorism, 21*, 149–169.

Central Intelligence Agency (2003). *Unclassified report to Congress on the acquisition of technology relating to weapons of mass destruction and advanced conventional munitions*. Retrieved March 14, 2005, from http://www.cia.gov/cia/reports/721_reports/july_dec2003.htm.

Clark, R. P. (1984). *The Basque insurgents: ETA, 1952–1980*. Madison, WI: University of Wisconsin Press.

Clutterbuck, R. (1981). *The media and political violence*. London: Macmillan.

Crelinsten, R. D. (1990). Images of terrorism in the media: 1966–1985. *Terrorism, 12*, 167–198.

Crenshaw, M. (1972). The concept of revolutionary terrorism. *Conflict Resolution, 16*, 383–396.

Crenshaw, M. (Ed.). (1983). *Terrorism, legitimacy, and power: The consequences of political violence*. Middletown, CT: Wesleyan University Press.

Crenshaw, M. (1985). An organizational approach to the analysis of political terrorism. *Orbis, 29*, 465–489.

Douglas, J., Burgess, A. W., Burgess, A. G., & Ressler, R. K. (1992). *Crime classification manual*. New York: Lexington Books.

Dyson, W. E. (2001). *Terrorism: An investigator's handbook*. Cincinnati, OH: Anderson Publishing.

Emerson, S. A. (1994). *American jihad: The terrorists living among us*. New York: Free Press.

Federal Bureau of Investigation. (2004). *Crime in the United States: Uniform crime reports*. Washington, DC: U.S. Government Printing Office.

Fields, R. (1978). *Society under siege: A psychology of Northern Ireland*. Philadelphia: Temple University Press.

Fraser, J., & Fulton, I. (1984). *Terrorism counteraction* (FC 100–37). Fort Leavenworth, KS: U.S. Army Command and General Staff College.

Gottfredson, M. R., & Hirschi, T. (1990). *A general theory of crime*. Palo Alto, CA: Stanford University Press.

Hoffman, B. (1998). *Inside terrorism*. New York: Columbia University Press.

Human Rights Watch (1995).

Irvin, C. (1992). Terrorists' perspectives: Interviews. In D. Paletz & A. C. Schmid, (Eds.), *Terrorism and the media*. London: Sage

Irvin, C. (1999). *Militant nationalism: Between movement and party in Ireland and the Basque country*. Minneapolis: University of Minnesota Press.

Irvin (2002).

Jackson, B. (2005). *Aptitude for destruction: Organizational learning in terrorist groups and its implications for combating terrorism* (MG-331). Santa Monica, CA: RAND.

Jalata, A. (2001). Ethno-nationalism and the global modernizing project. *Nations and Nationalism, 7*(3), 389.

Jenkins, B. M. (1980). *The study of terrorism: Definitional problems* (P-6563). Santa Monica, CA: RAND.

Jenkins, B. M. (1984). *The who, what, where, how, and why of terrorism*. Paper presented at the Detroit Police Department Conference, Urban Terrorism: Planning or Chaos?

Jenkins, B. M. (2002). *Countering Al Qaeda: An appreciation for the situation and suggestions for strategy*. Santa Monica, CA: RAND.

Klein, M. (1995). *The American street gang*. New York: Oxford University Press.

Kreuger & Caitin (2004).

LaFree, G., & Dugan, L. (2004). How does studying terrorism compare to studying crime? In M. DeFlem (Ed.), *Terrorism and counterterrorism: Criminological perspectives* (pp. 53–74). Oxford: Elsevier.

Lal, R. (2005). *Terrorists and organized crime join forces. International Herald Tribune*. Retrieved June 5, 2005, from http://www.iht.com.

Laqueur, W. (1987). *The age of terrorism*. Boston: Little, Brown.

McCue (1995).

MIPT Terrorism Knowledge Base (2005). *Incidents by region*. Retrieved March 15, 2005, from http://www.tkb.org/IncidentRegionModule.jsp.

Mishal, S., & Sela, A. (2000). *The Palestinian Hamas: Vision, violence, and coexistence*. New York: Columbia University Press.

Moloney (2002).

Nice, D. C. (1988). Abortion clinic bombings as political violence. *American Journal of Political Science, 32*, 178–195.

Paletz, D., & Schmid, A. P. (Eds.). (1992). *Terrorism and the media*. London: Sage

Paletz, D., & Tawney L. L. (1992). Broadcasting organizations' perspectives. In D. Paletz & A. P. Schmid (Eds.), *Terrorism and the media* (pp. 105–110). London: Sage

Post, J. M. (1990).Terrorist psycho-logic: Terrorist behavior as a product of psychological forces. In W. Reich (Ed.), *Origins of terrorism: Psychologies, ideologies, theologies, states of mind* (pp. 25–42) Cambridge, UK: Cambridge University Press.

Post, J. M. (2004). *Leaders and their followers in a dangerous world: The psychology of political behavior (Psychoanalysis and social theory)*. Ithaca, NY: Cornell University Press.

Rapoport, D. (1984). Fear and trembling: Terrorism in three religious traditions. *American Political Science Review, 78*(3).

Rapoport, D. (1992). Terrorism. In M. Hawkesworth & M. Kogan (Eds.), *Routledge encyclopedia of government and politics* (Vol. 2). London: Routledge.

Ressler, R. K., Burgess, A. W., & Douglas, J. E. (1988). *Sexual homicide: Patterns and motives*. New York: Lexington Books.

Riedel, M., & Welsh, W. (2002). *Criminal violence: Patterns, causes, and prevention*. Los Angeles: Roxbury.

Rosenfeld (2002).

Rosenfeld, R. (2004). Terrorism and criminology. In M. DeFlem (Ed.), *Terrorism and counterterrorism: Criminological perspectives* (pp. 19–32). Oxford: Elsevier.

Schmid, A. P. (1983). *Political terrorism: A research guide to concepts, theories, data bases, and literature*. Amsterdam: North Holland.

Schmid, A. P. (1989). Terrorism and the media: The ethics of publicity. *Journal of Terrorism and Political Violence, 1*(4), 539–565.

Schmid, A. P., & Degraf, J. F. A. (1982). *Violence as communication: Insurgent terrorism and the Western news media*. London: Sage

Schmid, A. P., & Jongman, A. J. (1988). *Political terrorism: A new guide to actors, authors, concepts, data bases, theories, and literature*. New Brunswick, NJ: Transaction Books.

Sederberg, P. (1989). *Terrorist myths: Illusion, rhetoric, and reality*. Englewood Cliffs, NJ: Prentice Hall.

Senechal de la Roche, R. (1996). Collective violence as social control. *Sociological Forum, 11*, 97–128.

Shaw (1986).

Silke, A. (2001). The devil you know: Continuing problems with research on terrorism. *Terrorism and Political Violence, 13*, 1–14.

Southern Poverty Law Center (2004). Active hate groups in the United States in the year 2003. *Intelligence Report, 113*.

Smith, B. L. (1994). *Terrorism in America: Pipe bombs and pipe dreams*. Albany: State University of New York Press.

Smith, B. L., & Damphousse, K. R. (1997). The American terrorist, 1998–2000: Characteristics, tactics, and prospects for the future. In H. Kushner (Ed.), *The future of terrorism* (pp. 132–154). Thousand Oaks, CA: Sage.

Strong, S. (1993). *Shining Path: The terror and revolution in Peru*. New York: Crown Publishers.

Taheri, A. (1987). *Holy terror: The inside story of Islamic terrorism*. London: Sphere.

Volkan (1999).

Wardlaw, G. (1988). Linkages between the illegal drugs traffic and terrorism. *Conflict Quarterly, 8*(3).

White, J. R. (2003). *Terrorism: An introduction*. Ontario: Thomson Wadworth.

Wieviorka, M. (1993). *The making of terrorism.* (D. G. White, Trans.). Chicago: University of Chicago Press.

Wilkinson, P. (1982). *British perspectives on terrorism.* New York: Unwin Hyman.

Wilkinson, P. (1986). Trends in international terrorism and the American response. In L. Freedman et al. (Eds.), *Terrorism and international order.* London: Routledge & Kegan Paul.

Wilkinson, P. (1987). *Terrorism and the liberal state* (2nd rev. ed.). New York: NYU Press.

Wilkinson, P. (2000). *Terrorism versus democracy: The liberal state response* (Cass Series on Political Violence, 9). London: Frank Cass Publishers.

Wilson, J. Q., & Herrnstein, R. J. (1985). *Crime and human nature.* New York: Simon and Shuster.

Wolfgang, M. E. (1958). *Patterns in criminal homicide.* Philadelphia: University of Philadelphia Press.

Zahn, M., & Strom, K. J. (2004). Terrorism and the federal social science research agenda. In M. DeFlem (Ed.), *Terrorism and counterterrorism: Criminological perspectives* (pp. 111–130). Oxford: Elsevier.

Zedalis (2004).

CHAPTER 31

Therapeutic Treatment Approaches to Violent Behavior

Richard E. Heyman and Amy M. Smith Slep

Introduction

Being asked to write a chapter on "Therapeutic Treatment Approaches to Violence" is a daunting and immensely humbling task. Don't believe us? Consider this. The history of benevolent control of aggression in human societies ranges from prohibitions in holy texts to formalized laws regarding rights to the building of redemptive "penitentiaries" to modern psychological and psychiatric interventions; typing "(aggression or violence) and (intervention or treatment)" into PsycINFO returns nearly 12,000 published articles or dissertations. Where to start? How does one boil down that much information into a short book chapter?

We made a few decisions that helped shape the imperfect summary you find before you. First, we decided to organize the chapter around specific *interventions* – rather than around presenting problems – and have grouped these interventions into general classes (e.g., behavioral, cognitive-behavioral, psychodynamic). Second, given the other chapters in this volume, we focused on psychological – as opposed to pharmacological or societal – interventions. Third, being asked to write a chapter on therapeutic treatments precluded a focus on exciting developments in the prevention of violence. Thus, we excluded interventions not specifically targeted at individuals identified as aggressive or angry (e.g., universal interventions for school-wide reductions in aggression; Embry, Flannery, Vazsonyi, Powell, & Atha, 1996); we even excluded prevention efforts that target individuals at higher risk for violence (e.g., youth with substance abuse problems). Fourth, developmental psychologists sometimes use a heuristic that places aggressive behavior on a mild-severe continuum, labeling the mild end "aggression" and the severe end "violence" (e.g., Anderson & Huesmann, 2003); however, there is no threshold distinguishing aggression from violence, and interventionists do not make this distinction in selecting participants or measuring outcomes. Therefore, we use the term "aggression" to mean behavior along the entire continuum (and specifically mean "physical aggression" when we refer to "aggression"). Finally, we make no claims about comprehensiveness. We have chosen to present, as succinctly as possible, the background and evidence for the predominant current approaches to therapies for violence. We conclude by summarizing the findings, drawing commonalities, and making a few comments about future directions.

Behavioral Interventions

Behavioral approaches rely on observable behavior (rather than on introspection), look for causes of behavior in the accumulated experience of environmental reward or punishment for behavior (rather than in internal processes), and emphasize small (rather than complex) phenomena for study/intervention (Domjan, 2003). This class of interventions ranges widely from (a) idiographic examinations/manipulations of the environmental response to aggression to (b) nomothetic treatments that presuppose the adaptive nature of nonaggressive competing responses.

All behavioral interventions are clinical implementations of one or more of the following basic learning principles: *positive reinforcement* (i.e., contingent application of a reward following nonaggressive behavior, increasing the likelihood that the nonaggressive behavior will be performed); *negative reinforcement* (i.e., contingent removal of an aversive stimulus following nonaggressive behavior, increasing the likelihood that the nonaggressive behavior will be performed); *punishment* (also known as "positive punishment;" i.e., contingent provision of an aversive consequence following aggressive behavior, decreasing the likelihood that the aggressive behavior will be performed); *omission* (also known as "negative punishment;" i.e., contingent removal of a reward following aggressive behavior, decreasing the likelihood that aggressive behavior will be performed); *extinction* (i.e., failure to reinforce a previously reinforced aggressive behavior, decreasing the likelihood that the aggressive behavior will be performed), or *stimulus control* (i.e., removing or changing antecedents or settings associated with aggressive behavior, decreasing the likelihood that the aggressive behavior will be performed).

Operant (Functional Analytic) Approaches

BACKGROUND

Operant approaches focus on the costs and rewards of aggressive behavior and attempt to modify the contingencies so that (a) aggressive behavior is either not reinforced or is punished, and (b) nonaggressive behavior is either reinforced or is not punished. Because of their specificity, operant approaches tend to be idiographic, and their effectiveness is often tested via single-subject experiments.

The hallmark of operant approaches is functional analysis, defined as "(1) The identification of important, controllable, causal functional relations applicable to specified behaviors for an individual . . . ; [and] (2) The experimental manipulation of hypothesized controlling variables as a method of determining functional relations" (Haynes & O'Brien, 2000, p. 302). Functional analysis is the practical application of behavioral theory, as it tries to (a) identify the antecedents, consequences, and settings that reward violent behavior and to (b) change these environmental factors so that nonaggression, rather than aggression, is rewarded.

Operant approaches have been used most frequently in treating aggression in people with developmental disabilities (DD) and in children. The popularity of these approaches with these subpopulations is likely due, at least in part, to their use in institutional settings where the intervener has great control over environmental responses to aggression.

EVIDENCE

Operant approaches comprise a variety of specific interventions, each of which will be described separately.

Differential Reinforcement Differential reinforcement of other behavior involves providing putative rewards following specified periods (e.g., 15 minutes) in which no aggressive acts are performed. Another form, the differential reinforcement of incompatible behavior, identifies a specific nonaggressive behavior to be reinforced, one that is physically incompatible with aggressive behavior (e.g., playing appropriately with a toy, touching a baby gently). Both interventions have a long history of support in reducing or eliminating aggression in single-subject designs (e.g., Egan, Zlomke, & Bush, 1993; Kahng, Abt, & Schonbachler, 2001).

Extinction. As defined above, extinction involves no longer reinforcing previously reinforced aggression. For example, Carr, Newsome, and Binkoff (1980) determined, via functional analysis, that a DD target child used aggression to escape from academic tasks; confining the child to a chair during the tasks produced profound drops in aggressive behavior. Interventionists using extinction must be prepared, however, for extinction bursts (i.e., increases in aggression after it is no longer rewarded; Domjan, 2003) and for other, potentially problematic, behaviors that may be evoked that serve the same function as aggression. For that reason, extinction is frequently paired with the teaching of functionally equivalent behaviors (see below).

Planned Ignoring. Planned ignoring involves the omission of attention following aggressive behavior. Haynes and O'Brien (2000) discriminate between extinction and planned ignoring; to be called "extinction," they argue, interventionists must conduct a careful functional analysis to establish independently that attention is a reward for aggression, something that rarely occurs in planned ignoring studies. Single-subject studies have demonstrated the effectiveness of planned ignoring (e.g., Martin & Foxx, 1973; Thompson, Fisher, Piazza, & Kuhn, 1998). Correct hypotheses about the function of aggression is critical; if the reward is something other than attention, ignoring can increase problem behaviors by increasing access to aggression-consequent rewards (see Solnick, Rincover, & Peterson, 1977). Further, as described in the extinction section above, the interventionist must be prepared for extinction bursts.

Teaching Functionally Equivalent Behaviors. A functional analysis is useful not only because it suggests what behaviors may be maintaining aggression but also because it allows the interventionist to hypothesize, teach, and reinforce behaviors that may serve the same function as aggression but are not harmful to others. For example, Thompson et al.'s (1998) assessments indicated that attention maintained a DD child's aggression. They combined extinction with functional communication training. There was a precipitous drop in the rate of aggression, accompanied by an increased rate of appropriate communication that matched the pretreatment rate of aggression.

Stimulus Control. If functional analysis reveals that certain stimuli are associated with aggression, then the interventionist can rearrange or remove the stimuli. For example, Touchette, MacDonald, and Langer's (1985) scatterplot analyses indicated aggression was more likely in the morning; they rescheduled morning activities to the afternoon and substantially decreased aggression.

Response Cost. Response cost is a form of negative punishment whereby specific rewards are removed contingent on aggressive behavior. "Timeout from positive reinforcement" is similar to response cost procedures, except it removes access to all rewards, not to specific rewards. A recent meta-analysis of single-subject designs found response cost and timeout procedures to be the most effective interventions with aggressive children and adolescents (Wellen, 1998).

Contingency Management. Carefully overseeing the rewards and punishments that the environment offers for aggressive acts is also the hallmark feature of a less idiographic class of interventions – *contingency-based interventions.* Because these approaches involve managing the environment, they are typically used with children. Contingency management typically includes response-cost procedures, token economy procedures (e.g., star charts), or both. These procedures can be a component in parent training, but are also often used as a stand-alone intervention in classroom settings. These approaches have been found to be very effective in reducing aggression in school-aged (e.g., Forman, 1980; Kellam, Ling, & Merisca, 1998) and preschool children (e.g., Goff & Demetral, 1983; Reynolds & Kelley, 1997).

Exposure and Response Prevention

Exposure and response prevention (ERP), a treatment of choice with anxiety disorders (Franklin, Abramowitz, Kozak, Leavitt, & Foa, 2000), has recently been used to intervene with people with anger control problems (some of whom are aggressive). ERP is believed to work both through habituation to the eliciting stimulus and through the prevention of negative reinforcement (i.e., preventing the escape from the aversive stimulus by performing some response – as in preventing the performance of anxiety-reducing compulsions in people with obsessive-compulsive disorder). Participants are exposed to provocations, but are prevented from responding with anger or aggression. Tafrate and Kassinove (1998) found that ERP resulted in moderate effect sizes for the reduction of anger, whereas ERP with coping self-statements resulted in large effect sizes. Because this study, the only empirical test of this approach, did not use a clinical population and did not measure aggression as an outcome, it is too early to know if this approach is an effective form of aggression treatment.

Social Skills Training

BACKGROUND

Social skills training (SST) is a treatment approach for aggressive children that focuses directly on the child, rather than on broader systems within which the child lives (as is the case with parent training and multisystemic therapy, discussed below). SST is built on a deficit model that presumes that aggression results from a lack of skill that would support an individual's ability to navigate conflict more adeptly (Nangle, Erdley, Carpenter, & Newman, 2002). SST generally refers to behaviorally oriented techniques that target a variety of interpersonal skills (e.g., com-

munication, conflict management) and are administered most often to children in group settings. Typically, instruction, modeling, in vivo and/or role-played practice, and feedback are included. SST can be brief (less than 2 hours total training) or more intensive, and it can be administered alone or in combination with cognitive interventions (e.g., problem-solving training; see Foster & Crain, 2002 for a review).

EVIDENCE

The literature evaluating SST is large and fairly heterogeneous. This is especially the case when trying to determine the effects of social skills training on children with particular problems, such as aggression (see Spence, 2003). Meta-analyses suggest that SST has a small to medium effect when used with aggressive children ($d = 0.13$; Kavale, Mauthur, Forness, Rutherford, & Quinn, 1997; $d = 0.37$; Schneider, 1992). It is important to note, however, that these effect sizes are on measures of social functioning, not specifically of aggression. Quinn, Kavale, Mauthur, Rutherford, and Forness (1999) and Taylor, Eddy, and Biglan (1999), in separate reviews, both concluded that the direct effect of social skills interventions on aggression is limited.

SST for young children has also been evaluated as an adjunct to parent training (described below) to reduce child behavior problems including aggression (Webster-Stratton & Hammond, 1997). Although combining social skills for the child with parent training for the parents did not result in significantly greater improvements in child behavior than parent training alone, additive effects were apparent in the areas of child social problem solving and conflict management.

Parent Training

BACKGROUND

Parent training approaches are designed to decrease children's aggression and other disruptive behaviors by teaching parents to use effective discipline techniques (i.e., consistently set limits, use firm but not harsh strategies) and encourage children's appropriate, prosocial behavior through praise and positive attention (e.g., Patterson & Gullion, 1968; Webster-Stratton, 1984; 1990; 1994; Webster-Stratton, Kolpacoff, & Hollinsworth, 1988). Thus, parent training approaches can be best thought of as behavioral in that the goal of the treatment is to have the parents change the contingencies for their children's behavior. As aggression is rewarded less and alternative behaviors are rewarded more, aggression decreases.

EVIDENCE

Arguably, parent training is the best researched and most supported intervention for children's aggression. Parent training interventions (Brestan & Eyberg, 1998) are the only ones to meet the stringent criteria for classification as an empirically supported treatment for conduct problem children (see Lonigan, Elbert, & Johnson, 1998). Furthermore, several of the treatments classified as probably efficacious are also parent training approaches. The efficacy and effectiveness of parent training have both been established, especially for children younger than 9 years old (Farmer, Compton, Burns, & Robertson, 2002), with meta-analyses suggesting medium to large effect sizes. Parent training approaches were developed for and appear to be most effective with younger children (through age 12; see Brestan & Eyberg, 1998; Farmer et al., 2002). This makes sense as parents structure, and are therefore are able to control, a greater proportion of the environments of younger children.

Typically, parent training targets children's physical aggression specifically and teaches parents to give children timeouts for aggression (e.g., Incredible Years BASIC; Webster-Stratton, 2001). When a child is physically aggressive, the parent is instructed to isolate the child immediately from potential rewards (e.g., attention, toys), restrict the child to this less rewarding environment for a few minutes, and formally release the child when the timeout is over. Thus, parents are taught to set consistent limits and manage contingencies for aggression specifically.

As noted earlier, a meta-analysis found that timeout is one of the most effective forms of intervention for aggressive children and adolescents (Wellen, 1998).

Interestingly, despite the wide range of target behaviors for both parents and children, parent training can be conducted very cost effectively. Webster-Stratton's program can be administered in groups using videotape vignettes and lay discussion leaders without a decrement in its effectiveness (Webster-Stratton, Hollinsworth, & Kolpacoff, 1989; Webster-Stratton, Kolpacoff, & Hollinsworth, 1988).

Parent training techniques are not only useful for reducing *children's* aggression but also have been shown to reduce physical discipline among mothers at risk for child abuse (Peterson, Tremblay, Ewigman, & Popkey, 2002). In this randomized trial, parent training augmented with anger management reduced physical punishment and increased the use of gentle discipline strategies. Additionally, spanking appears to be reduced by standard parent training packages (e.g., Webster-Stratton & Hammond, 1997). Parent training, combined with other cognitive behavioral elements including anger control and cognitive behavioral therapy for the child, was also found to be more effective than family therapy in reducing parents' physical discipline (Kolko, 1996).

Relaxation Training

BACKGROUND

Relaxation training attempts to boost participants' ability to induce, automatically or at will, parasympathetic bodily responses. Whereas the sympathetic nervous system is responsible for fight/flight responses, the parasympathetic nervous system is responsible for the opposite (e.g., muscle relaxation and decreases in heart rate and respiration). Relaxation training involves such activities as progressive muscle relaxation, diaphragmatic breathing, and relaxing imagery (e.g., Bernstein & Borkovec, 1973). As such, it employs the behavioral principles of reinforcement of incompatible behavior (i.e., rewarding calming responses), overlearning (i.e., practicing skills until previously effortful responses become automatic), and classical conditioning (i.e., extinguishing the automatic link between provocations and aggressive responses).

EVIDENCE

Relaxation training has been used with DD adults (McPahil & Chamove, 1989) and emotionally or behaviorally disordered elementary school children (Lopata, 2003), with moderate effects on aggression in the short-term but modest effects at follow-up.

Cognitive or Cognitive-Behavioral Interventions

Cognitive-behavioral therapeutic (CBT) approaches to aggression include an array of particular components, which can be combined in multiple ways. Unlike strictly behavioral approaches, cognitive-behavioral approaches focus specifically on how the individual perceives the world and thinks through responses to the environment. Components include cognitive restructuring of initial perceptions of the anger-provoking situation, problem-solving training (response generation, evaluation, and implementation), assertiveness training, and self-instruction.

Cognitive-Behavioral Treatment (CBT) of Child Aggression and Parent-Child Aggression

BACKGROUND

The general types of intervention components are described above. When targeting children's aggression, CBT, unlike parent training, intervenes directly with the aggressive child. Obviously, the interventions are tailored to the cognitive level of the child.

EVIDENCE

Recent meta-analyses suggest that CBT approaches for aggression have small to medium effects (i.e., weighted effect size of $d = 0.23$); effects appear to be stronger with older children and adolescents (see Bennett & Gibbons, 2000). This apparent greater impact on older children is a nice complement to parent training approaches, which are used most widely with younger children. One study has suggested that combining CBT for the aggressive child and parent training for the child's parents results in stronger effects (e.g., Kazdin, Siegel, & Bass, 1992).

CBT has also been applied successfully to parental aggression. For example, Kolko (1996) compared CBT to family therapy in treating physically abusive parents. CBT was more effective than family therapy in reducing the use of physical discipline.

Cognitive Appraisal

BACKGROUND

Social information-processing theory posits that people who frequently aggress make inferences (often incorrect) of hostile intent when others transgress (often unintentionally) against them (e.g., Dodge, 1993). Bugental et al. (2002) developed an intervention comprising (a) training in disputation of attributions of infants/young children's negative intent; and (b) problem-solving training.

EVIDENCE

Bugental et al. (2002) compared home visitation with and without the brief cognitive appraisal activities to a control condition in a sample of high-risk parents expecting or recently giving birth to a child; 97% of the sample was Latino. The control and home visitation without the cognitive appraisal activities had equivalent rates of child physical abuse (26% and 23%, respectively), whereas those who received the cognitive appraisal activities had far lower rates (4%).

Anger Management

BACKGROUND

Anger management, although not focused exclusively on aggressive individuals, is a frequent form of treatment for them. About half of the empirically tested programs can be described as cognitive-behavioral therapy (e.g., stress inoculation therapy, assertiveness training, social skills training, problem solving), with the remaining equally distributed among cognitive-only (e.g., cognitive restructuring, rational emotive therapy), relaxation training (including emotional education for children), and other programs (Del Vecchio & O'Leary, 2004, Sukhodolsky, Kassinove, & Gorman, 2004).

Probably the most influential program is that of Novaco (1975, 1983), who used a series of behavioral (e.g., stimulus control, extinction, differential reinforcement of incompatible behaviors) and cognitive techniques (e.g., modifying anger-eliciting appraisals and self-talk) to create a multi-intervention package, including the following:

> (a) self-monitoring anger frequency, intensity, and situational triggers; (b) devising a personal anger provocation hierarchy based on self-monitoring; (c) progressive muscle relaxation, breathing-focused relaxation, and guided imagery training to regulate physiological arousal; (d) cognitive restructuring of anger by altering attentional focus, modifying appraisals, and using self-instruction; (e) training behavioral coping, communication, and assertiveness skills through role play; and (f) practicing the new anger coping skills while visualizing and role-playing progressively intense anger-arousing scenes from their personal hierarchies.
>
> (Chemtob, Novaco, Hamada, & Gross, 1997, p. 186)

EVIDENCE

DiGuiseppe and Tafrate (2003) conducted a meta-analysis of 57 studies of adult anger management programs. They found a moderate effect size ($d = 0.71$) for treated participants across all dependent measures, albeit one that is lower than that typically found in treatments of depression or anxiety. Decreases in aggression demonstrated large effect sizes at post-treatment and follow-up, although the results at follow-up were about half the size of those at post-treatment.

The effect sizes for aggression were the largest for any dependent measure. However, a strong caveat applies: the vast majority of these studies were conducted with non-treatment-seeking college students (Del Vecchio & O'Leary, 2004).

Sukhodolsky et al. (2004) conducted a meta-analysis of 40 studies of child/adolescent cognitive-behavioral therapy anger management programs. Effect sizes were similar to those found for adults ($d = 0.67$). Skills training and multimodal treatments resulted in significantly greater reductions in aggression than did affective education and problem-solving treatments.

Self-Control Training: Self-Monitoring and Self-Instruction

BACKGROUND

Self-control training considers aggression (and other behavioral problems) as an outgrowth of insufficient or ineffective self-control. As such, children are taught strategies to improve their self-control of aggression. The approach involves teaching children to use verbal self-instruction, in combination with modeling and feedback, to help them change their behavior and maintain and generalize these changes. As children become more practiced with self-instruction, they are taught to use the techniques covertly by thinking to themselves, rather than speaking out loud (Robinson, Smith, Miller, & Brownell, 1999).

EVIDENCE

Self-control techniques have been demonstrated to be useful in reducing aggression, although effect sizes vary depending on the samples targeted. For example, Dush, Hirt, and Schroeder's meta-analysis (1989) found a relatively small effect when these techniques are used to treat aggression ($d = 0.18$), but many of the studies included extremely aggressive youth in a range of clinical settings. In contrast, Robinson et al.'s (1999) meta-analysis limited studies to those conducted in school settings with children and adolescents and found evidence for stronger effects ($d = 0.64$).

Problem-Solving Training

BACKGROUND
Social problem-solving training was developed to address cognitive processes thought to promote aggression (Spivack & Shure, 1974). Using a variety of techniques including role playing, children are taught to recognize problem situations, stop and think, generate alternative solutions, consider consequences, and match likely consequences with solutions (see Foster & Crain, 2002 for a review). Practice is required or encouraged to enhance generalization.

EVIDENCE
Interestingly, although problem-solving training has been shown to result in both cognitive and behavioral changes, cognitive change did not necessarily mediate behavioral outcomes (e.g., Rickel & Fields, 1983, Winer, 1982). In one evaluation of problem-solving training as a treatment specifically for aggression and antisocial behavior, Kazdin, Siegel, and Bass, 1992) found that it was effective in reducing aggression and other antisocial behaviors and was maintained through a 1-year follow-up, although these changes were more pronounced for children who received problem-solving training in conjunction with a parent's participation in parent training. Importantly, a no-treatment control group was not included in this study. Often problem-solving training is a component, along with social skills training, in more general cognitive-behavioral packages targeting child aggression.

Social Support Approaches

BACKGROUND
Social support-based treatments for physical aggression have primarily been evaluated as a treatment for child physical abuse. Research primarily on physically abusive mothers has found that abusive mothers have less access to social support and are more socially insulated than are nonabusive mothers (see Black, Heyman, & Slep, 2001; Wolfe, 1987, for reviews). Based on these findings, social support-based treatment approaches emerged (e.g., Parents Anonymous). Parents Anonymous consists of a network of weekly meetings that parents can attend. It is largely a self-help support group, but local professionals facilitate the groups and are available for consultation.

EVIDENCE
A national evaluation found that participating parents reported a reduction in their abusive behavior, although this finding is limited to parents' perceptions (Berkeley Planning Associates, 1980). A more rigorous effectiveness evaluation has not been conducted.

Psychoeducation

BACKGROUND
Psychoeducational approaches to the treatment of aggression rely on "teaching" participants about socially sanctioned beliefs and behaviors and how to enact them. The didactic emphasis in psychoeducation is far more pronounced than in other forms of therapeutic treatment.

Empirical evaluations of the psychoeducational treatment (not prevention) of aggression are almost exclusively found in the partner abuse literature. These programs tend to follow variants of a feminist/cognitive-behavioral approach, teaching men that they use aggression as a means of exerting male power and control over women and providing them a variety of cognitive restructuring, anger management, and communication skills (e.g., Pence & Paymar, 1997; also see Dutton & Sonkin, 2003 for chapters about myriad specific programs).

EVIDENCE
Babcock, Green, and Robie (2004) conducted a meta-analysis of 37 studies of psychoeducational groups for men who were physically aggressive toward their intimate

partners. They found that treatment, compared to nontreatment, had little effect on partner aggression ($d = 0.09$).

Insight/Psychoanalytic

Background

Aggression has been one of the hallmark interests of psychological treatment since the early days of psychoanalysis (e.g., Freud, 1930). It was, therefore, surprising that we located only one empirical study of the effectiveness of a psychoanalytic approach for the treatment of aggression. Saunders' program was "designed to end [men's partner] abusive behavior by (a) decreasing isolation and increasing emotional investment in others' welfare, (b) exploring the childhood roots of sex-role expectations and shame-based behaviors, and (c) increasing the capacity to express feelings directly and responsibly" (Browne, Saunders, & Staecker, 1997).

Evidence

Saunders (1996) found that, overall, men's psychodynamic and feminist-CBT groups had equivalent, modest effects on the cessation of partner aggression; there was no "no treatment" control group. As Saunders predicted, men with dependent personality traits responded better to the psychodynamic intervention, whereas those with antisocial traits responded better to the feminist cognitive-behavioral intervention.

Multicomponent Approaches

Multicomponent treatment approaches all use a wide variety of specific interventions, which may have demonstrated efficacy in their own right, to address aggression. Programs can either have a set content that all participants receive (e.g., Lutzker, Bigelow, Doctor, Gershater, & Greene, 1998), or can be extensively tailored to the individual, such that two clients may not have any treatment elements in common (e.g., Henggeler & Borduin, 1994). These approaches build

on the efficacy literature developed on more focused interventions and share the philosophy that aggression (and other related problems) may be too complex to be treated successfully with any one intervention, but may be treated successfully with a combination of interventions.

An example of a multicomponent approach for adult aggression that is focused on treating the aggressive individual can be found in the child abuse treatment literature. Although not individually tailored as some multicomponent interventions are, these comprehensive multicomponent treatment programs have also been found effective in reducing physical child abuse (see Lutzker, et al., 1998; Schellenbach, 1998). One extensive intervention, Project 12-Ways, includes parent training, social support, self-control training, assertiveness training, and stress management, as well as a broad array of less typical components including job placement, money management, and leisure counseling (Lutzker, 1994). These components are delivered at sites convenient for participants, primarily in the families' homes. Compared with a matched group of comparison mothers, mothers in Project 12-Ways had significantly lower recidivism rates (Lutzker & Rice, 1984). Interestingly, Lutzker and colleagues later developed a more streamlined treatment approach, including only parent training with an emphasis on promoting bonding, and skill building in the areas of child health care and home safety, as they felt these were the components of Project 12-Ways that were most essential in reducing risk for future child abuse (Lutzker et al., 1998). This reduced program, Project Safecare, was also effective in reducing recidivism among treated families as compared with matched comparison families (Gershater-Molko, Lutzker, & Wesch, 2003).

Family Therapy Approaches

Two approaches to family therapy appear to be effective in treating juvenile offenders (see Sexton & Alexander, 2002b). Both approaches, Multisystemic Therapy (MST) and Functional Family Therapy (FFT), are behaviorally based and grounded in systems theory.

Multisystemic Therapy

BACKGROUND

Multisystemic Therapy (MST; Henggeler & Borduin, 1994) is a manualized, empirically supported treatment for severely conduct-disordered youth. MST incorporates techniques from a number of theoretically oriented treatments. From a systems perspective, MST considers clients and their targeted problems (e.g., aggression) as embedded within multiple nested systems, each of which needs to be considered when formulating an intervention strategy. For example, if an aggressive child is not subject to consistent parental monitoring because of a parent's substance abuse, the parent's substance abuse becomes a target of intervention. From a behavioral perspective, MST explicitly considers stimuli that trigger and reward targeted behavior in the multiple systems and focuses on how to enhance the generalization of newly acquired behaviors. From a cognitive perspective, MST tailors intervention plans to address the individual needs of each child, often incorporating elements of more cognitive approaches to treating aggression.

EVIDENCE

This integration of multiple techniques into a single, flexible approach that is tailored to the needs and strengths of each family has led to impressive results. Initial trials of MST were with a population that had been previously considered nearly untreatable – juvenile offenders with long records of aggression and arrest. MST was effective in reducing aggression and producing a host of other laudable outcomes (Henggeler et al., 1986). It has also been more effective than parent training in changing the interaction patterns and other short-term outcomes of child-abusive parents (Brunk, Henggeler, & Whelen, 1987). Impressively,

MST has also been disseminated successfully to community mental health clinics, where it has been found to be as effective as in controlled efficacy trials (Borduin et al., 1995).

Functional Family Therapy

BACKGROUND

Functional Family Therapy (FFT; e.g., Alexander & Parsons, 1973; Sexton & Alexander, 2002a) is an approach to family therapy grounded in both systems and behavioral theory. The therapist works with the family to promote engagement and reduce negativity through such techniques as reframing, setting realistic goals that can be accomplished with a short-term course of therapy, changing relevant risk and protective factors by applying behavioral techniques (e.g., problem solving, parent training), and building toward generalization and relapse prevention. Similar to MST, the specific elements of FFT are tailored to the needs of each family.

EVIDENCE

In their recent review of family-based empirically supported interventions, Sexton and Alexander (2002b, p. 245) concluded that "the longest term, most systematic, and independently replicated series of family-based empirically-supported treatment research efforts has been with FFT." More than one dozen published clinical trials found that FFT, compared to no treatment and treatment-as-usual control groups, markedly reduces recidivism with offending and delinquent youth (a population with a high prevalence of aggression) within the juvenile justice system (Alexander, Pugh, Parsons, & Sexton, 2000). Longitudinal investigations including up to 5-year follow-ups suggest that effects are maintained. Interestingly, FFT also appears to reduce risk for younger siblings, who have been found to have fewer arrests than siblings of target adolescents receiving comparison treatments (see Sexton & Alexander, 2002b).

Conclusions

This overview of the current landscape of therapeutic treatments for aggression leaves us with six predominant reactions.

1. Labeling Aggression as "Dysfunctional" Is a Trap

It is convenient to argue (or even "psychoeducate") that aggression is a dysfunctional response in nearly every context. We make the meta-argument that that position is literally dysfunctional – "dys" (i.e., bad) both in terms of being bad functionalism and in terms of setting up therapy to fail in many contexts.

The dysfunctional stance is bad functionalism for several reasons. First, and most obviously, a functional approach looks at reinforcement and punishment of behavior. By not examining, or at least hypothesizing about, the client's natural environment, interventionists put themselves at a disadvantage in targeting incompatible behaviors to reinforce. Second, the assumption that aggression is always dysfunctional is belied by Little, Brauner, Jones, Nock, and Hawley's (2003) recent study examining reactive and proactive aggression, which found that adolescents who were the lowest on both instrumental and reactive physical and/or verbal aggression had consistently poor academic, emotional, and social markers, whereas those high on instrumental aggression or average on both reactive and proactive aggression had the best markers. Thus, a monolithic "aggression is bad" stance may inhibit understanding the role that aggression may play in healthy development. This is not to say that less hurtful behaviors should not be promoted, but it does argue for understanding the function that aggression plays. Third, although nonaggressive behavior may be rewarded in many contexts (e.g., teacher-student, college student-stranger interactions), many situations (e.g., angry families, prisons, or peers) either do not reward nonaggressive behavior or punish it. Interventionists who expect that an individual's will and self-control will perpetually triumph over environmental contingencies are both overly optimistic and almost certainly likely to be disappointed.

2. Assumptions From One Context or Successful Treatment Might Not Transfer to Another Context

Some contexts (e.g., schools and institutions) allow the interventionist to have strong control over environmental contingencies. In these contexts, a therapeutic focus on the individual may succeed brilliantly. These contexts also allow for more careful, formal functional analyses, as the interventionist manipulates the environment. Other contexts (e.g., families, peers) not only allow for very little environmental manipulation but also involve interlocking emotional and behavioral systems among the interactants, each of whom may be both perpetrator and victim of aggression (e.g., Patterson, 1982). In these contexts, a therapeutic focus solely on the individual is unlikely to succeed. Thus, the conditional nature of efficacy and effectiveness data on aggression interventions must be carefully considered.

3. Multiple Pathways for Aggression Give Multiple Points of Intervention

Aggression is likely multidetermined by biological, psychological, and social factors. This is probably why many classes of intervention work and why, in the most difficult cases, multiple types of intervention at multiple levels will likely be necessary (e.g., MST).

4. "First, Do No Harm."

Recent work by Dishion and colleagues (e.g., Dishion, McCord, & Poulin, 1999; Poulin, Dishion, & Burraston, 2001) indicates that group interventions for high-risk adolescents actually increase, rather than reduce, delinquent behavior. These studies, and similar findings from other labs, should give interventionists pause before conducting group interventions for aggressive people. Proponents believe groups to be cost effective and provide opportunities for group process. However, Dishion's work indicates that peers reinforce each other's deviant behavior. Such reinforcement undercuts the intended intervention. Worse still, because the interventionist set up the group, the increased symptoms are iatrogenic. Thus, the most popular format for treatment of aggressive adolescents and adults – group treatments – should be reconsidered, as the format itself may be problematic.

5. There's No Such Thing as Unlearning

Converging neurobiological and behavioral research indicates that there is no such thing as "unlearning;" instead, extinction involves new learning that coexists with the previously reinforced pairing (Bouton, 2002). The longer and stronger a pattern (such as aggression) is reinforced, the harder it is to permanently eliminate its performance. This may be why many interventions for family aggression (including child maltreatment, partner abuse, and elder abuse) find decrements in, but not permanent cessation of, aggression. Further, the intertwined developmental trajectories of ongoing aggression and increasing social and environmental stressors (e.g., Patterson, Reid, & Dishion, 1994) create a seemingly intractable cycle of aggression potentiation.

Thus, prevention – from home visitation programs with a cognitive appraisal component to parent training to school-based interventions reinforcing prosocial behavior (e.g., Flannery et al., 2003) to early relationship skills training (e.g., Markman, Renick, Floyd, Stanley, & Clements, 1993) – likely will be far more cost effective and health promoting than countering adults' established aggression learning histories.

6. A Plea for Translational Research

Despite the notable successes of a variety of interventions for a very stubborn, difficult phenomenon, the effective therapeutic treatment of aggression for many people under many contexts still has a long way to go. We believe that several bur-

geoning fields of basic research – including emotion regulation, neurobiology, and the etiology of aggression – can provide important findings that can be translated into improved clinical interventions. Further, clinical and prevention scientists can provide important phenomena or contexts to improve the exportability of basic science research questions. Both types of translational research will likely be the source of future breakthroughs and are the type of research currently being encouraged by the National Institute of Mental Health. The current state of the art in therapeutic intervention offers both reason for optimism and a mandate for making drastic improvements to our clinical science.

Acknowledgment

Preparation of this chapter was supported by the National Institute of Child Health and Human Development (Grant R01 HD046901).

References

Alexander, J. F., & Parsons, B. V. (1973). Short-term behavioral intervention with delinquent families: Impact on family process and recidivism. *Journal of Abnormal Psychology, 81,* 219–225.

Alexander, J. F., Pugh, C., Parsons, B., & Sexton, T. L. (2000). Functional family therapy. In D. Elliott (Series Ed.), *Book three: Blueprints for violence prevention* (2nd ed.). Golden, CO: Venture.

Anderson, C. A., & Huesmann, L. R. (2003). Human aggression: A social-cognitive view. In M. A. Hogg & J. Cooper (Eds.), *The Sage handbook of social psychology.* Thousand Oaks, CA: Sage.

Babcock, J. C., Green, C. E., & Robie, C. (2004). Does batterers' treatment work? A meta-analytic review of domestic violence treatment. *Clinical Psychology Review, 23,* 1023–1053.

Bennett, D. S., & Gibbons, T. A. (2000). Efficacy of child cognitive-behavioral interventions for antisocial behavior: A meta-analysis. *Child and Family Behavior Therapy, 22,* 1–15.

Berkeley Planning Associates. (1980). *Child abuse and neglect treatment programs: Final report and summary of the National Demonstration Program in Child Abuse and Neglect.* Berkeley, CA: Office of Child Development.

Bernstein, D. A., & Borkovec, T. D. (1973). *Progressive relaxation training.* Champaign, IL: Research Press.

Black, D. A., Heyman, R. E., & Slep, A. M. S. (2001). Risk factors for child physical abuse. *Aggression and Violent Behavior, 6,* 121–188.

Borduin, C. M., Mann, B. J., Cone, L. T., Henggeler, S. W., Fucci, B. R., Blaske, D. M., et al. (1995). Multisystemic treatment of serious juvenile offenders: Long-term prevention of criminality and violence. *Journal of Consulting and Clinical Psychology, 63,* 569–578.

Bouton, M. E. (2002). Context, ambiguity, and unlearning: Sources of relapse after behavioral extinction. *Biological Psychiatry, 52,* 976–986.

Brestan, E. V., & Eyberg, S. M. (1998). Effective psychosocial treatments of conduct-disordered children and adolescents: 29 years, 82 studies, and 5,272 kids. *Journal of Clinical Child Psychology, 27,* 180–189.

Browne, K. O., Saunders, D. G., & Staecker, K. M. (1997). Process-psychodynamic groups for men who batter: A brief treatment model. *Families in Society, 78,* 265–271.

Brunk, M., Henggeler, S. W., & Whelen, J. P. (1987). Comparison of multisystemic therapy and parent training in the brief treatment of child abuse and neglect. *Journal of Consulting and Clinical Psychology, 55,* 171–178.

Bugental, D. B., Ellerson, P. C., Lin, E. K., Rainey, B., Kokotovic, A., & O'Hara, N. (2002). A cognitive approach to child abuse prevention. *Journal of Family Psychology, 16,* 243–258.

Carr, E. G., Newsome, C. D., & Binkoff, J. A. (1980). Escape as a factor in the aggressive behavior of two retarded children. *Journal of Applied Behavior Analysis, 13,* 101–117.

Chemtob, C. M., Novaco, R. W., Hamada, R. S., & Gross, D. M. (1997). Cognitive-behavioral treatment for severe anger in posttraumatic stress disorder. *Journal of Consulting and Clinical Psychology, 65,* 184–189.

Del Vecchio, T., & O'Leary, K. D. (2004). Effectiveness of anger treatments for specific anger problems: A meta-analytic review. *Clinical Psychology Review, 24,* 15–34

DiGuiseppe, R., & Tafrate, R. C. (2003). Anger treatment for adults: A meta-analytic review. *Clinical Psychology: Science and Practice, 10,* 70–84.

Dishion, T. J., McCord, J., & Poulin, F. (1999). When interventions harm: Peer groups and problem behavior. *American Psychologist, 54,* 755–764.

Dodge, K. A. (1993). Social-cognitive mechanisms in the development of conduct disorder and depression. *Annual Review of Psychology, 44,* 559–584.

Domjan, M. (2003). *The principles of learning and behavior* (5th ed). Belmont, CA: Thomson/Wadsworth.

Dush, D. M., Hirt, M. L., & Schroeder, H. E. (1989). Self-statement modification in the treatment of child behavior disorders: A meta-analysis. *Psychological Bulletin, 106,* 97–106.

Dutton, D. G., & Sonkin, D. J. (Eds.). (2003) *Intimate violence: Contemporary treatment innovations.* Binghamton, NY: Haworth Press.

Egan, P. J., Zlomke, L. C., & Bush, B. R. (1993). Utilizing functional assessment, behavioral consultation and videotape review of treatment to reduce aggression: A case study. *Special Services in the Schools, 7,* 27–37.

Embry, D. D., Flannery, D. J., Vazsonyi, A. T., Powell, K. E., & Atha, H. (1996). PeaceBuilders: A theoretically driven, school-based model for early violence prevention. *American Journal of Preventive Medicine, 5,* 91–100.

Farmer, E. M., Compton, S. N., Burns, B. J., & Robertson, E. (2002). Review of the evidence base for treatment of childhood psychopathology: Externalizing disorders. *Journal of Consulting and Clinical Psychology, 70,* 1267–1302.

Flannery, D. J., Vazsonyi, A. T., Liau, A. K., Guo, S., Powell, K. E., Atha, H., et al. (2003). Initial behavior outcomes for the PeaceBuilders universal school-based violence prevention program. *Developmental Psychology, 39,* 292–308.

Forman, S. G. (1980). A comparison of cognitive training and response cost procedures in modifying aggressive behavior of elementary school children. *Behavior Therapy, 11,* 594–600.

Foster, S. L., & Crain, M. M. (2002). Social skills and problem-solving training. In F. Kaslow & T. Patterson (Eds.), *Comprehensive handbook of psychotherapy,* (Vol. 2, pp. 31–50). New York: John Wiley & Sons.

Franklin, M. E., Abramowitz, J. S., Kozak, M. J., Levitt, J. T., & Foa, E. B. (2000). Effectiveness of exposure and ritual prevention for obsessive-compulsive disorder: Randomized compared with nonrandomized samples.

Journal of Consulting and Clinical Psychology, 68, 594–602.

Freud, S. (1930). *Civilization and its discontents* (J. Riviere, Trans.). London: Hogarth Press.

Gershater-Molko, R. M., Lutzker, J. R., & Wesch, D. (2003). Project SafeCare: Improving health, safety, and parenting skills in families reported for, and at-risk for child maltreatment. *Journal of Family Violence, 18,* 377–386.

Goff, G. A., & Demetral, G. D. (1983). A home-based program to eliminate aggression in the classroom. *Social Work in Education, 6,* 5–14.

Haynes, S. N., & O'Brien, W. H. (2000). *Principles and practice of behavioral assessment.* New York, NY: Kluwer.

Henggeler, S. W., & Borduin, C. M. (1990). A multisystemic approach to the treatment of serious delinquent behavior. In R. J. McMahon & R. D. Peters (Eds.), *Behavior disorders of adolescence: Research, intervention, and policy in clinical and school settings,* (pp. 63–80). New York: Plenum Press.

Henggeler, S. W., Rodick, J. D., Borduin, C. M., Hanson, C. L., Watson, S. M., & Urey, J. R. (1986). Multisystemic treatment of juvenile offenders: Effects on adolescent behavior and family interaction. *Developmental Psychology, 22,* 132–141.

Jacobson, E. (1938). *Progressive relaxation.* Chicago: University of Chicago Press.

Kahng, S., Abt, K. A., & Schonbachler, H. E. (2001). Assessment and treatment of low-rate high-intensity problem behavior. *Journal of Applied Behavior Analysis, 34,* 225–228

Kavale, K. A., Mauthur, S. R., Forness, S. R., Rutherford, R. B., & Quinn, M. M. (1997). Effectiveness of social skills training for students with behavior disorders: A meta-analysis. In T. E. Scruggs & M. A. Mastropieri (Eds.), *Advances in learning and behavioral disabilities* (Vol. 11, pp. 1–26). Greenwich, CT: JAI.

Kazdin, A. E., Siegel, T. C., & Bass, D. (1992). Cognitive problem-solving skills training and parent management training in the treatment of antisocial behavior in children. *Journal of Consulting and Clinical Psychology, 60,* 733–747.

Kellam, S. G., Ling, X., & Merisca, R. (1998). The effect of the level of aggression in the first grade classroom on the course and malleability of aggressive behavior into middle school. *Development and Psychopathology, 10,* 165–185.

Kolko, D. J. (1996). Clinical monitoring of treatment course in child physical abuse: Psychometric characteristics and treatment comparisons. *Child Abuse and Neglect, 20,* 23–43.

Little, T. D., Brauner, J., Jones, S. M., Nock, M. K., & Hawley, P. H. (2003). Rethinking aggression: A typological examination of the functions of aggression. *Merrill-Palmer Quarterly, 49,* 343–369.

Lonigan, C. J., Elbert, J. C., & Johnson, S. B. (1998). Empirically supported psychosocial interventions for children: An overview. *Journal of Clinical Child Psychology, 27,* 138–145.

Lopata, C. (2003). Progressive muscle relaxation and aggression among elementary students with emotional or behavioral disorders. *Behavioral Disorders, 28,* 162–72

Lutzker, J. R. (1994). Project 12-Ways: Treating child abuse and neglect from an ecobehavioral perspective. In R. F. Dangel & R. A. Polster (Eds.), *Parent training: Foundations of research and practice* (pp. 260–279). New York: Guilford Press.

Lutzker, J. R., Bigelow, K. M., Doctor, R. M., Gershater, R. M., & Greene, B. F. (1998). An ecobehavioral model for the prevention and treatment of child abuse and neglect: History and applications. In J. Lutzker (Ed.), *Handbook of child abuse research and treatment* (pp. 239–266). New York: Plenum Press.

Lutzker, J. R., & Rice, J. M. (1987). Using recidivism data to evaluate Project 12-Ways: An ecobehavioral approach to the treatment and prevention of child abuse and neglect. *Journal of Family Violence, 2,* 283–289.

Markman, H. J., Renick, M. J., Floyd, F. J., Stanley, S. M., & Clements, M. (1993). Preventing marital distress through communication and conflict management training: A 4- and 5-year follow-up. *Journal of Consulting and Clinical Psychology, 61,* 70–77.

Martin, P. L., & Foxx, R. M. (1973). Victim control of the aggression of an institutionalized retardate. *Journal of Behavior Therapy and Experimental Psychiatry, 4,* 161–165.

McPhail, C. H., Chamove, A. S. (1989). Relaxation reduces disruption in mentally handicapped adults. *Journal of Mental Deficiency Research, 33,* 399–406.

Nangle, D. W., Erdley, C. A., Carpenter, E. M., & Newman, J. E. (2002). Social skills training as a treatment for aggressive children and adolescents: A developmental-clinical integration. *Aggression and Violent Behavior, 7,* 169–199.

Novaco, R. W. (1975). *Anger control: The development and evaluation of an experimental treatment.* Lexington, MA: D.C. Heath.

Novaco, R. W. (1983). *Stress inoculation therapy for anger control: A manual for therapists.* Unpublished manuscript, University of California, Irvine.

Patterson, G. R. (1982). *Coercive family processes.* Eugene, OR: Castalia Press.

Patterson, G. R., & Gullion, M. E. (1968). *Living with children: New methods for parents and teachers.* Champaign, IL: Research Press.

Patterson, G. R. Reid, J. B., & Dishion, T. J. (1992). *Antisocial boys.* Eugene, OR: Castalia Press.

Pence, E., & Paymar, M. (1997). *Education groups for men who batter: The Duluth model.* New York: Springer.

Peterson, L., Tremblay, G., Ewigman, B., & Popkey, C. (2002). The parental daily diary: A sensitive measure of the process of change in a child maltreatment prevention program. *Behavior Modification, 26,* 627–647.

Poulin, F., Dishion, T. J., & Burraston, B. (2001). 3-year iatrogenic effects associated with aggregating high-risk adolescents in cognitive-behavioral preventive interventions. *Applied Developmental Science, 5,* 214–224.

Quinn, M. M., Kavale, K. A., Mauthur, S. R., Rutherford, Jr., R. B., & Forness, S. R. (1999). A meta-analysis of social skill interventions for students with emotional or behavioral disorders. *Journal of Emotional and Behavioral Disorders, 7,* 1063–4266.

Reynolds, L. K., & Kelley, M. L. (1997). The efficacy of a response cost-based treatment package for managing aggressive behavior in preschoolers. *Behavior Modification, 21,* 216–230.

Rickel, A. U., & Fields, R. B. (1983). Storybook models and achievement behavior of preschool children. *Psychology in the Schools, 20,* 105–113.

Robinson, T. R., Smith, S. W., Miller, M. D., & Brownwell, M. T. (1999). Cognitive behavior modification of hyperactivity-impulsivity and aggression: A meta-analysis of school-based studies. *Journal of Educational Psychology, 91,* 195–203.

Saunders, D. G. (1996). Feminist-cognitive-behavioral and process-psychodynamic treatments for men who batter: Interaction of abuser traits and treatment models. *Violence and Victims, 11,* 393–414.

Schellenbach, C. J. (1998). Child maltreatment: A critical review of research on treatment for physically abusive parents. In P. Trickett & C. Schellenbach (Eds.), *Violence against children in the family and the community* (pp. 251–268). Washington, DC: American Psychological Association.

Schneider, B. H. (1992). Didactic methods for enhancing children's peer relations: A quantitative review. *Clinical Psychology Review, 12,* 363–382.

Sexton, T. L., & Alexander, J. F. (2002a). Functional family therapy for at-risk adolescents and their families. In F. Kaslow & T. Patterson (Eds.), *Comprehensive handbook of psychotherapy* (Vol. 2, pp. 117–140). New York: John Wiley & Sons.

Sexton, T. L., & Alexander, J. F. (2002b). Family-based empirically supported interventions. *The Counseling Psychologist, 30,* 238–261.

Solnick, J. V., Rincover, A., & Peterson, C. R. (1977). Some determinants of the reinforcing and punishing effects of timeout. *Journal of Applied Behavioral Analysis, 10,* 415–424.

Spence, S. H. (2003). Social skills training with children and young people: Theory, evidence, and practice. *Child and Adolescent Mental Health, 8,* 84–96.

Spivack, G., & Shure, M. B. (1974). *Social adjustment of young children: A cognitive approach to solving real-life problems.* Oxford: Jossey-Bass.

Sukhodolsky, D. G., Kassinove, H., & Gorman, B. S. (2004). Cognitive-behavioral therapy for anger in children and adolescents: A meta-analysis. *Aggression and Violent Behavior, 9,* 247–269.

Tafrate, R., & Kassinove, H. (1998). Anger control in men: Barb exposure with rational, irrational, and irrelevant self-statements. *Journal of Cognitive Psychotherapy, 12,* 187–211.

Taylor, T. K., Eddy, J. M., & Biglan, A. (1999). Interpersonal skills training to reduce aggressive and delinquent behavior: Limited evidence and the need for an evidence-based system of care. *Clinical Child and Family Psychology Review, 2,* 169–182.

Thompson, R. H., Fisher, W. W., Piazza, C. C., & Kuhn, D. E. (1998). The evaluation and treatment of aggression maintained by attention and automatic reinforcement. *Journal of Applied Behavioral Analysis, 31,* 103–116.

Touchette, P. E., MacDonald, R. F., & Langer, S. N. (1985). A scatter plot for identifying stimulus control of problem behavior. *Journal of Applied Behavioral Analysis, 18,* 343–351.

Webster-Stratton, C. (1984). Randomized trial of two parent-training programs for families with conduct-disordered children. *Journal of Consulting and Clinical Psychology, 52,* 666–678.

Webster-Stratton, C. (1990). Enhancing the effectiveness of self-administered videotape parent training for families with conduct-problem children. *Journal of Abnormal Child Psychology, 18,* 479–492.

Webster-Stratton, C. (1994). Advancing videotape parent training: A comparison study. *Journal of Consulting and Clinical Psychology, 62,* 583–593.

Webster-Stratton, C. (2001). The incredible years: Parents, teachers, and children training series. *Residential Treatment for Children and Youth, 18,* 31–45.

Webster-Stratton, C., & Hammond, M. (1997). Treating children with early-onset conduct problems: A comparison of child and parent training interventions. *Journal of Consulting and Clinical Psychology, 65,* 93–109.

Webster-Stratton, C., Hollinsworth, T., & Kolpacoff, M. (1989). The long-term effectiveness and clinical significance of three cost-effective training programs for families with conduct-problem children. *Journal of Consulting and Clinical Psychology, 57,* 550–553.

Webster-Stratton, C., Kolpacoff, M., & Hollinsworth, T. (1988). Self-administered videotape therapy for families with conduct-problem children: Comparison with two cost-effective treatments and a control group. *Journal of Consulting and Clinical Psychology, 56,* 558–566.

Wellen, D. G. (1998). A meta-analysis of single-subject studies of therapies for children and adolescents with aggression. *Dissertation Abstracts International, 59*(1-B), 431. (UMI No. AAG9820707)

Winer, J. I. (1982). The evaluation of a kindergarten social problem-solving program. *Journal of Primary Prevention, 2,* 205–216.

Wolfe, D. A. (1987). *Child abuse: Implications for child development and psychopathology.* San Diego: Sage.

CHAPTER 32

Psychopharmacology of Violence

Markus J. P. Kruesi

This chapter reviews known information about the psychopharmacology of violence. Psychopharmacology offers both an approach for attempting to alter pathophysiology that underlies some violence and a set of tools for understanding that neurobiology.

This chapter selects as its focus pharmacological agents, currently used by humans, which have been shown either to increase or decrease violence. This chapter addresses the psychopharmacology of aggression – particularly nonpredatory aggression directed at other humans or mammals – by examining whether a class of agents has been demonstrated to decrease or increase aggression. The chapter gives selective weight to agents whose properties have been demonstrated in one or more double-blind controlled trials.

Mechanisms of action receive more limited attention in this chapter. Although preclinical and animal investigations of pharmacological mechanisms related to violence have progressed, methodological limitations and questions about cross-species generalizations call for caution in the specificity of attributions. Accordingly, this chapter seeks to point out what might be considered broad

or consistent clues about mechanisms. The neurotransmitter serotonin is discussed as an example of the state of progress in our pharmacological understanding of mechanisms of violence. One might wonder why we do not know more.

Violence is a logical target for pharmacological therapy because it can result in the loss of human life or liberty. Consequently, one might expect violence to be a high-priority area in the investigation and development of psychopharmacological agents. However, despite the salience of violence and the suffering it causes, there is comparatively limited investigation. Inquiry has often been stalled by political concerns and limited by a dearth of financial support (Enserink, 2000). Development of psychopharmacological agents using animal models of aggression has evoked a lack of enthusiasm from both the National Institutes of Health and the pharmaceutical industry, major sources of research funding. Obstacles delaying approval by the U.S. Food and Drug Administration of medication for aggression led to the scuttling of the only industry program thus far aimed at developing a class of aggression-reducing drugs (Enserink, 2000).

Definitions of Violence and the Description of Aggression

Definitions are critical to understanding studies of the psychopharmacology of violence. Our examination of the psychopharmacology of violence focuses largely on nonpredatory aggression. This definition implies that violence is aggression out of control or out of proportion to the circumstances. This chapter focuses on, but is not entirely limited to, this relatively narrow definition because, at this point in time, this is the type of violence for which psychopharmacological treatment may have the greatest relevance.

The term "aggression" encompasses a wide range of behaviors. Some of this diversity can be parsed by description of the aggression. Attempts to collapse global ratings across diverse descriptors like frequency, severity, and/or target are recognized as sources of confusion within aggression research (Kruesi & Gray, 2006). The Child Behavior Checklist (CBCL) is the most frequently used measure to evaluate the level of childhood and adolescent aggression in genetic studies (Achenbach & Edelbrock, 1983). However, only two items on the CBCL aggressive subscale refer to physical aggressiveness. In a study of disruptive and aggressive children, CBCL aggressive scale scores did not correlate significantly with the severity of physical aggressiveness (Kruesi et al., 1994).

The legal system has long distinguished between premeditated or predatory aggression versus nonpredatory or impulsive violence. Predatory murders have been termed "cold blooded" in contrast to crimes of passion whose affective nature was described as "hot blooded." Synonyms for predatory include instrumental, goal directed, offensive, and premeditated, whereas affective aggression is often described as impulsive, reactive, or defensive. Predatory aggression is seen as linked to parasympathetic activity and affective aggression to sympathetic

Table 32.1: DSM-IV disorders with aggression

As a Diagnostic Feature	As an Associated Feature
Antisocial Personality	ADHD
Borderline Personality	Bipolar Affective Disorder
Conduct Disorder	Mental Retardation
Intermittent Explosive Disorder	Psychoactive Substance Abuse Psychotic Disorder

activity – as evidenced by the need for lowered heart rate during some hunting activity in contrast to the rage and sympathetic discharge that accompany affective aggression (Moyer, 1968). Studies of youth and of adults indicate that impulsive and premeditated forms of aggression are independent constructs (Barratt, Stanford, Dowdy, Liebman, & Kent, 1999; Dodge & Coie 1987; Vitiello, Behar, Hunt, Stoff, & Ricciuti, 1990).

Often affective aggression is an associated feature or symptom of a psychiatric disorder. Table 32.1 shows a list of DSM-IV (American Psychiatric Association, 1994) disorders in which aggression is a criterion symptom or an associated feature.

Differentiating among types of aggression can be pertinent to psychopharmacological trials. For example, a study of a variety of medications in adults with borderline personality disorder noted that carbamazepine was efficacious in decreasing the number of episodes of major dyscontrol (which often included physical injury or abuse), but did not alter day-to-day verbal aggression (Gardner & Cowdry, 1986). Animal studies also demonstrate that the pharmacological responsiveness of aggression paradigms may differ. Chronic inhibition of monoamine oxidase or 5-HT uptake with antidepressant treatment is recognized as reliably facilitating defensive aggression, but not attack behavior in rodents (for review, see Miczek, Haney, Tidey, Vivian, & Weerts, 1994). Thus, at least in animal studies, affective and predatory forms of aggression differ in their psychopharmacological response. As noted below, some evidence exists that predatory and affective aggression in humans may not have the same psychopharmacological responsiveness.

The Complexity of Neurobiological Mechanisms of Aggression Using Serotonin as an Example

In the preceding two decades the measurement of the concentration of serotonin or a metabolite or its amino acid precursor (tryptophan) in body fluids has been central to the search to understand the neurobiology of aggression (Kruesi & Jacobsen, 1997). The seminal study in 1976 (Asberg, Thoren, & Traskman, 1976) linking low cerebrospinal fluid (CSF) concentrations of the serotonin metabolite 5-hydroxyindoleacetic acid (5-HIAA) with violent suicide attempts inaugurated a focus on serotonergic mechanisms of aggression. Subsequent studies demonstrated that other-directed violence in adults (Brown, Goodwin, Ballenger, Goyer, & Major, 1979) and youth (Kruesi et al., 1990, 1992) was associated with low concentrations of CSF 5-HIAA. Further studies clarified that impulsive/affective violence and not predatory aggression was related to low concentrations of 5-HIAA (Linnoila et al., 1983; Virkkunnen, Eggert, Rawlings, & Linnoila, 1989). Meta-analyses of multiple studies confirm the relationships between low CSF 5-HIAA and suicide (Lester, 1995) and between low CSF 5-HIAA and aggression (Moore, Scarpa, & Raine, 2002). One possible conclusion from this data was overly simplistic: lower serotonin levels equal increased violence. Recognition of a range of environmental and contextual variables as a part of the low 5-HIAA-aggression relationship suggested the complexity of the neurobiology of violence (Kruesi & Jacobsen, 1997). For example, in crayfish the modulatory effect of serotonin on aggressive behavior depended not only on the crayfish's current social status but also on its *prior* status (Yeh, Fricke, & Edwards, 1996).

More recently, indices of the genes encoding for receptor or transporter proteins or synthetic enzymes have become a research focus (Lesch & Merschdorf, 2000). The recognition of seven different families of serotonin receptors with several subtypes as well as transporter sites, each encoded by an identified gene, has brought about manifold possibilities for receptor-selective intervention (Olivier, Mohs, Van Oorschot, & Hen, 1995).

Another set of confounds concerns the specificity of psychopharmacological response both in terms of behavior and biological target. Risperidone serves as an example: it decreases aggression in animals, but only at doses that also slow locomotor activity (Rodriguez-Arias, Minarro, Aguilar, Pinazo, & Simon, 1998). In addition, risperidone acts as an antagonist at dopamine D2 receptors as well as at 5-HT2A serotonin receptors (Schotte et al., 1996). Most psychopharmacological agents available for human use do not have singular pure biological properties that act at only one specific chemical target. Rather, most agents act on multiple systems.

Psychopharmacological Agents That Decrease Aggression

Neuroleptics

Neuroleptics refer to a general class of psychopharmacological agents that are recognized for the treatment of psychosis. Historically, a common property shared by most neuroleptic compounds is dopamine receptor blocking. The first generation or "typical" neuroleptics targeted dopamine D2 receptors and were the drugs of choice for treatment of aggression in schizophrenics (Yudofsky, Silver, & Schneider, 1987). This property has been thought to explain at least part of the antiaggressive properties of neuroleptics. All three major brain dopamine (DA) systems (nigrostriatal, mesocortical, and mesolimbic) have been implicated as involved in aggression in animal studies (Miczek, Fish, De Bold, & De Almeida, 2002; Miczek et al., 1994). Brain DA systems appear involved in (1) the rewarding

Table 32.2: Psychiatric groups in which neuroleptics have demonstrated efficacy for aggression

Conduct Disorder
Borderline Personality Disorder
Dementia
Schizophrenia
Post-Traumatic Stress Disorder
Developmental Disabilities
Sub-average IQ
Autism
Agitated/aggressive psychiatric emergency room patients

or reinforcing aspects of aggression possibly via mesolimbic and mesocortical DA systems and (2) the initiation, execution, and termination of aggressive behavior patterns possibly via the nigrostriatal and mesolimbic DA systems. However, it needs to be noted that most neuroleptics have a wide variety of pharmacological effects other than those at D2 receptors. For some neuroleptics, it is possible that properties other than blocking dopamine receptors may be relevant to their antiaggressive actions.

Neuroleptics have demonstrated efficacy against aggression in a wide variety of individuals, as suggested in Table 32.2. Children, adults, and the elderly have all been shown to respond to neuroleptics. The range of diagnoses – from autism and disruptive behavior disorders in childhood to post-traumatic stress disorder in adults to schizophrenia and other psychoses as well as dementia – in which aggression has been reduced increases confidence that its efficacy is not a chance finding.

Mentally retarded and developmentally disabled individuals, as well as individuals with psychosis, warrant particular attention in any review of the psychopharmacology of violence. Most persons with mental retardation are not violent, but there is an increased risk of inappropriate aggression among individuals with psychiatric diagnoses in general including mental retardation (Kruesi, Keller, & Wagner, 2003). Individuals with cognitive impairment (Borderline Intelligence or mental retardation) living in residential facilities had a prevalence rate of aggression rang-

ing from 16 to 30% (Harris, 1995). A state-wide prevalence survey of institutionalized mentally retarded individuals found 13.6% engaged in self injurious behavior (Griffin, Williams, Stark, Altmeyer, & Mason, 1986), with over half engaging in such behavior daily.

Because psychosis is a risk factor for violence, the effects of neuroleptics on violence are particularly relevant. A study using large Danish birth cohorts ($N > 324{,}000$) found individuals hospitalized with schizophrenia and men with organic psychosis had the highest rate of arrest for violence (Brennan, Mednick, & Hodgins, 2000).

Although the older generation of so-called typical neuroleptics have efficacy against aggression, some of the newer generation neuroleptics, which are referred to as atypical neuroleptics, appear advantageous. Atypical neuroleptics, by definition, differ from typical antipsychotic agents in producing significantly fewer extrapyramidal symptoms and having a lower risk of tardive dyskinesia in vulnerable clinical populations at doses that produce comparable control of psychosis (Meltzer 2004). The atypical drugs differ from the typical ones in their mechanism of action, but not all share the same mechanism. Many, but not all, atypicals have been found to improve cognitive function, which could confer an advantage. Clozapine, the prototype of these atypicals, has been found to improve delusions and hallucinations in patients who fail to respond to other antipsychotic drugs and to reduce the risk of suicide (Meltzer et al., 2003). These agents have been found to increase cortical dopamine and acetylcholine release, as well as have a variety of effects on the glutamatergic system that are not shared by the typical agents (Meltzer, 2004). A recent study of 157 treatment-resistant inpatients with chronic schizophrenia or schizoaffective disorder randomly assigned those patients to treatment with an atypical neuroleptic (clozapine, olanzapine, or risperidone) or with a typical neuroleptic (haloperidol) in a 14-week, double-blind trial (Volavka et al., 2004). Clozapine was significantly better than haloperidol in decreasing aggressive events.

However, because clozapine has a risk of agranulocytosis, a potentially fatal condition, it is not a first-line treatment. Recent investigation of risperidone, an atypical neuroleptic, in conduct disorder (Buitelaar, van de Gaag, Cohen-Kettenis, & Melman, 2001; Ercan et al., 2003; Findling et al., 2000), autism (McCracken et al., 2002), youth with subaverage intelligence (Aman et al., 2002; Snyder et al., 2002; Zarcone et al., 2001), adults with post-traumatic stress disorder (Monnelly, Ciraulo, Knapp, & Keane, 2003), and dementia (Brodaty et al., 2003) all have yielded positive results.

Stimulants

Over 200 studies have demonstrated the efficacy of stimulants for the core symptoms of attention deficit/hyperactivity disorder (ADHD; Spencer et al., 2000). However, comparatively few studies have examined stimulant effects on aggression in ADHD. A recent meta-analysis examined effect size for stimulants on overt (28 studies) and covert (7 studies) aggression-related behaviors in children with ADHD, separately from stimulant effects on the core symptoms of ADHD (Connor, Barkley, & Davis, 2000). Overt aggression-related behaviors were defined as aggression resulting in a direct confrontation with the environment (Frick et al., 1993; Loeber & Schmaling, 1985). Overt behaviors in the Connor et al. (2000) meta-analysis included physical assault, verbal threats, oppositional and defiant behavior, noncompliance, malicious teasing of others, conduct problems, explosive outbursts of property destruction, temper tantrums, rage attacks, hostility, and/or irritability. Covert aggression-related behaviors were defined as aggression that is furtive and hidden from the environment. These included cheating, lying, stealing, delinquency, vandalism, and fire-setting. However, the overt versus covert categorization is not equivalent to the predatory vs. affective distinction. For example, fire-setting can be predatory or affective/impulsive (Virkunnen, Eggert, Rawlings, & LInnoila, 1989). The overall weighted mean effect size was 0.84 for overt and 0.69 for covert aggression related behaviors in ADHD. No gender effects were discerned. Comorbid conduct disorder was associated with diminishing stimulant effect size for overt aggression. This result and the detailed findings of the controlled trial of methylphenidate for conduct disorder (Klein et al., 1997) are consistent with the clinical impression that it is affective aggression, rather than predatory aggression, that responds to currently available human psychopharmacological intervention. Methylphenidate decreased many conduct disorder behaviors, with the exception of socialized aggression (gang-type delinquency that likely reflects predatory acts) in a controlled trial (Klein et al., 1997). There is evidence, however, for possible developmental differences: in adults there are studies suggesting that stimulants such as amphetamine can increase aggression (Cherek, 1986; Eichelman, 1987).

Anti-Hypertensive Agents

Anti-hypertensive agents form a broad grouping of pharmacological agents that lower blood pressure, including beta-blockers, such as propranolol, pindolol, and nadalol, and alpha agonists, such as clonidine and guanfacine. Beta-blockers have been reported to reduce aggression across a range of psychiatric patients, including schizophrenics (Caspi et al., 2001), patients with dementia (Yudofsky et al., 1981), and youth (Mattes, 1990). In contrast, reports of alpha agonist benefit for aggression appear confined to pediatric patients (e.g., Connor et al., 2000; Hazell & Stuart, 2003). Evidence for the effect of anti-hypertensive agents in reducing aggression is less compelling than that seen for neuroleptics.

Lithium, Anti-Convulsants, and Benzodiazepines

Lithium and anti-convulsants are used as mood stabilizers for persons with manic-depressive disorder. Benzodiazepines are used as anti-anxiety agents, sedatives, and as anti-convulsants. For the purposes of this chapter, benzodiazepines are grouped with the range of anti-convulsants used as aggression reduction agents both because some benzodiazepines are used in treating seizures and because action at gamma butyric acid (GABA) receptors is a pharmacological action that is common to many anti-convulsants including benzodiazepines. Benzodiazepines and anti-convulsants are used both as sole agents and as adjuncts to other pharmacological treatments.

GABA is an inhibitory neurotransmitter with widespread distribution in the brain. Post-mortem GABA levels are inversely correlated with aggression in animal studies (see Miczek et al., 2002, for review). Low plasma GABA concentrations were associated with high aggressivity in a human study (Bjork et al., 2001).

At least four anti-convulsants have demonstrated some efficacy in reducing aggression in humans: carbamazepine (Groh, 1976; Puente, 1976; Tariot et al., 1998, phenytoin (Barratt, Stanford, Felthous, & Kent, 1997; Stanford et al., 2001), topiramate (Nickel et al., 2004) and valproate. Valproate has been found useful for aggression reduction in controlled trials of youth with conduct disorder and/or explosive aggression (Donovan et al., 2000; Steiner, Petersen, Saxena, Ford, & Matthews, 2003), adults with schizophrenia already receiving atypical neuroleptics (Citrome et al., 2004), and individuals with dementia (Sival, Haffmans, Jansen, Duursm, & Eikelenbloom, 2002) and borderline personality disorder (Hollander et al., 2003). However, not all individuals or all trials for patient groups with problematic aggression show aggression reduction (Cueva et al., 1976; Hollander et al., 2003).

Benzodiazepines are useful for the rapid reduction of aggression in such settings as emergency room psychiatric services (TREC Collaborative Group, 2003). A recent trial compared intramuscular injection of midazolam with an injection of a typical neuroleptic, haloperidol (plus promethzine – a sedative antihistamine) in 301 agitated/aggressive psychiatric emergency room patients. The primary outcome measure was the percentage of patients tranquil or asleep 20 minutes after injection. Results favored midazolam: 89% versus 67% tranquil or asleep (relative risk 1.32, 95% confidence interval 1.16–1.49). A separate study comparing (1) lorazepam with haloperidol with (2) the combination of both the benzodiazepine and neuroleptic for rapid tranquilization of psychotic individuals found the combination was quicker than either agent alone (Battaglia et al., 1997).

Lithium has proven efficacy in reducing aggression in placebo-controlled trials in youth with conduct disorder or explosive aggression, mentally handicapped adults, and adult prison inmates (Campbell et al., 1995; Craft et al., 1987; Malone et al., 2000; Sheard et al., 1976). Not every trial (Rifkin et al., 1997) nor all individuals within the other trials experienced decreased aggression with lithium. One clue to lithium responsiveness is aggression in children that fails to respond to the structured milieu of an inpatient unit (Malone et al., 1997). In other words, change of environment and context did not decrease the aggression. Moreover, the aggression that responds is generally described as explosive or affective and not predatory. The mechanism of lithium's anti-aggressive action is unclear, but it likely includes enhancement of serotonergic function (Coccaro & Siever, 2002).

Anti-Depressants

Serotonin reuptake inhibitors (SSRIs) are currently the most commonly prescribed class of anti-depressant compounds. They also see extensive clinical use as anti-anxiety agents. Fluoxetine was the first selective SSRI marketed in the United States and for this chapter serves as an exemplar of the SSRI class. Fluoxetine decreased impulsive aggression in individuals with personality disorders in a well-controlled trial (Coccaro & Kavoussi, 1997), but verbal rather than physical aggression was what showed benefit. In addition, a controlled trial in schizophrenic patients of citalopram, an SSRI added to the patients' usual neuroleptic regimen, found that it reduced aggression.

However, questions have been raised whether SSRIs can increase aggression or suicide. A recent review of 702 placebo-controlled trials found an increase in the risk of suicide attempts with SSRIs compared to placebo (odds ratio, 2.28; 95% confidence, 1.14–4.55; number needed to treat to harm, 684; Fergusson et al., 2005). Thus, there appears to be a subtle increase in the risk of suicide attempt when taking SSRIs versus placebo, at least among participants in controlled drug trials. Examination of pharmaco-epidemiological data suggests caution before generalizing this risk to the population at large who are exposed to these drugs. An examination of the association between anti-depressant medication prescription and suicide rate at the county level across the United States found increases in prescriptions for SSRIs and other new-generation non-SSRIs are associated with lower suicide rates both between and within counties over time; this finding may reflect anti-depressant efficacy, compliance, a better quality of mental health care, and low toxicity in the event of a suicide attempt by overdose (Gibbons et al., 2005). Another study, using multinational data of variation across countries over time in SSRI sales and suicide, found that an increase of one pill per capita (a 13% increase over 1999 levels) is associated with a 2.5% reduction in suicide rates (Ludwig & Marcotte, 2005). Once again there are suggestions of individual variability in response, as the relationship they found is more pronounced for adults than for children. It should be kept in mind that the aggregate nature of observational data in the two pharmaco-epidemiological studies preclude a direct causal interpretation of the results.

Psychopharmacological agents That Enhance Aggression

Most, but not all, of the agents thought to enhance aggression are potential substances of abuse. The notion that some pharmacological agents can increase aggression seems more than plausible to anyone who has seen a combative drunk. This kind of case report has produced a reputation for certain drugs of abuse as promoters of aggression (e.g., phencyclidine; Hoaken & Stewart, 2003). However, empirical evidence to support the aggressive reputation of various substances of abuse is often discrepant. Intoxication, a direct pharmacological effect, is the more commonly recognized mechanism promoting aggression. However, prolonged use of a drug raises the possibility of either neurotoxicity or withdrawal on abstinence as other mechanisms of enhanced aggression.

Alcohol

Alcohol is the prototypical substance of abuse for investigating relationships between pharmacological agents and aggression. Ethyl or "beverage" alcohol is the exception to the rule that evidence does not support conventional wisdom. Studies of crime consistently implicate ethanol intoxication as related to violent behavior. Review of 26 studies across 11 countries found that 62% of offenders had consumed alcohol shortly before committing a violent crime (Murdoch, Pihl, & Ross, 1990). Alcohol was twice as likely to be associated with violent as compared with nonviolent crimes. The crime studies, however, represent correlations between alcohol and aggression, rather than a clear cause and effect.

Controlled laboratory studies have repeatedly confirmed an etiologic role for alcohol in aggressive behavior (Ito, Miller, & Pollock, 1996). Each of several meta-analyses of experimental studies has concluded that even moderate doses of alcohol increase the probability of acting aggressively (for a review, see Hoaken & Stewart, 2003). Although there exists overwhelming evidence that alcohol and aggression are related, the mechanism or mechanisms operating are less clear. A frequent question is why some individuals respond aggressively after consuming alcohol, whereas others do not. Contextual, situational, and pharmacological variables have been demonstrated to be involved, but may not account for as much of the variance in responding as differences between individuals (Pihl, Asaad, & Hoaken, 2003). In everyday vernacular, there really are some individuals who are "mean drunks," whereas under the same set of conditions, in the same setting, with the same blood alcohol concentration other individuals do not behave aggressively.

There are four mechanisms by which alcohol is thought to exert its pro-aggressive effects: (1) reward properties, (2) anxiolytic properties, (3) cognitive interference, and (4) analgesic properties. Reward properties are evident during the ascending limb of the blood-alcohol concentration curve – while the drink is being absorbed (Pihl & Peterson, 1995). The reward properties appear to be mediated by dopamine and are thus analogous to the rewarding properties of stimulants, such as cocaine (Boileau et al., 2003). The alterations in reward accompanied by psychomotor stimulation may lead to increased provocative and confrontational behavior, which then leads to aggression. Alcohol's anxiolytic action is thought to be mediated by increased firing of GABA neurons in prefrontal/limbic regions that mediate threat perception (Gray, 1987). Impairment of threat appraisal is thought to be responsible for the pro-aggressive effects of alcohol and other anxiolytics, such as benzodiazepines or barbiturates. Impairments of cognitive functions are consistent with PET scan studies demonstrating that acute alcohol intoxication reduces prefrontal glucose metabolism (Volkow, Wang, & Doria, 1995). Analgesic properties of ethanol are well known, and alcohol has even been used as an anesthetic for surgery (Mullin & Luckhardt, 1934). However, the relationship among alcohol, pain, and aggression is not one of simple numbing leading to more aggression. Pain sensitivity increases when blood alcohol concentrations are increasing (Gustafson, 1985). Thus, alcohol may promote aggression by increasing reactivity to pain at least during part of a drinking session.

Benzodiazepines and Barbiturates

Benzodiazepines and barbiturates have each been used as anti-convulsants, sedatives, anxiolytics, and drugs of abuse. Benzodiazepines are a class of drug exemplified by diazepam (Valium). By contrast, barbiturates have lower prescription rates in more recent practice. Both benzodiazepines (Cowdry & Gardner, 1988; Dietch & Jennings, 1988) and barbiturates have been shown to increase aggressive responding (Cherek et al., 1989). Experimental evidence in humans as well as animals suggests that the amount of violence produced by benzodiazepines pales in comparison to that produced by alcohol (see Hoaken & Stewart, 2003, for review). A recent study found that, analogous to the situation with alcohol, considerable individual variation exists across humans in their response to benzodiazepines. A recent study of aggressive responding to 10 mg of diazepam found it was those men with the greatest hostility prior to the drug challenge who were most susceptible to the aggression-enhancement effect of the benzodiazepine (Ben-Porath & Taylor, 2002). As noted earlier, there are also studies supporting the use of some benzodiazepines to reduce aggression acutely, although this appears to require sedative doses.

Cholesterol-Lowering Agents

A landmark controlled trial of pharmacological lowering of serum cholesterol in humans, with gemfibrizol was associated with an increase in violent deaths (including suicide) in those men (Wysowski et al., 1990). Correlations between lower cholesterol and aggressive behavior were reported in other samples (Muldoon et al., 1993; New et al., 1999). Monkeys randomized to a low-cholesterol and low-fat diet were less prosocial and more aggressive than peers fed a high-cholesterol diet (Kaplan et al., 1994). However, a meta-analysis of controlled trials of the more recent statin class of cholesterol-lowering agents did not reveal any evidence of a suicide-promotion effect

(Yang, Jick, & Jick, 2003), but a trend toward increased deaths from suicide and violence was observed in trials of dietary interventions and non-statin drugs (odds ratio, 1.32; 95% confidence interval, 0.98 to 1.77; $p = 0.06$; Muldoon et al., 2001).

Cocaine and Psychostimulants

There has been a popular belief that cocaine, if not all stimulants, is associated with aggression (for review see Taylor & Hulsizer, 1998). Earlier reports in the scientific literature also suggested that psychostimulants, such as amphetamines, as well as cocaine are associated with increased violence in adults (Brody, 1990; Eichelman, 1987; Ellinwood, 1971). However, only one experimental study has found cocaine to increase aggression and then only at the higher of two doses (Licata, Taylor, Berman, & Cranston, 1993). In contrast, studies contrary to the belief that stimulants increase aggression do exist. A study of 311 psychiatric emergency department patients (Dhossche, 1999) found that patients whose toxicology screens were positive for cocaine were less likely to be aggressive than those negative for cocaine. As discussed under agents reducing aggression, methylphenidate and amphetamine have been shown to reduce aggression in multiple controlled trials for children with ADHD.

The divergence between popular perception and more recent scientific studies is likely explained, at least in part, by individual differences. Cocaine-dependent individuals without comorbid antisocial personality disorder (ASP) were not more aggressive than controls (Moeller et al., 2002). However, cocaine-dependent individuals with ASP were more aggressive. A study of individuals hospitalized for treatment of cocaine dependence found that previous aggressive behavior predicted level of aggressivity, whereas cocaine craving, withdrawal symptoms, and amount of previous usage did not (Moeller et al., 1997). Both studies suggest it was not the cocaine per se that related to aggression, but rather characteristics of the individual – their antisocial personality – that related to their aggression.

Opiates

Confusion exists about the ability of opiates to provoke aggression in humans. Controlled trials of the opiates, morphine and codeine, have reported increased aggression in humans during laboratory aggression paradigms (Berman et al., 1993; Spiga et al., 1990). However, other lines of evidence suggest a complex picture involving the duration and course of drug exposure in combination with characteristics of the individual. Opiate withdrawal, induced by abstinence after chronic usage consistently leads to heightened aggressivity in animals (Tidey & Miczek, 1992). In contrast, acute opiate administration in animals temporarily reduces aggressivity (Espert et al., 1993). The aggression reduction diminishes as tolerance to the drug develops (Rodriguez-Arias et al., 2001). Although exogenous opiates are not uncommon in drug screens of criminal populations (Fraser, Zamecnik, Keravel, McGrath, & Wells, 2001) and opiates such as heroin are associated with crime, the pharmacological effects of opiates on human aggression are not clear cut. On a laboratory measure of aggression, heroin-individuals maintained on methadone, another opiate, were more aggressive than controls (Gerra et al., 2001). But, it is unclear whether that increased aggressivity represents a characteristic of individuals with opiate dependence or the opiate they were chronically receiving. In a separate study, arrestees who were heroin abusers were found less likely to commit violent offenses than arrestees without a substance abuse diagnosis (Morentin et al., 1998).

Phencyclidine (PCP)

Phencyclidine (PCP) or "angel dust" is a Schedule II controlled substance by FDA regulations and has a reputation as a dangerous drug (see Murray, 2002, for review).

Abusers usually smoke the drug mixed with marijuana, parsley, or cocaine. In healthy volunteers, PCP can induce symptoms that mimic those of schizophrenia, lasting from a few days to more than a week. The neurotransmitter glutamate and N-methyl-D-aspartate (NMDA) appear to play a role in the mechanisms by which PCP induces schizophrenic symptoms and cognitive defects (Javitt & Zukin, 1991; Lahti, Koffel, LaPorte, & Tamminga, 1995; Robbins 1990). Because serious psychiatric illness, including psychosis, is associated with increased risk of aggression (Brennan et al., 2000), it seems plausible that a drug that can induce psychotic symptoms could increase aggression. However, the absence of controlled experiments limits any conclusions (Gillet, Polard, Mauduit, & Allain, 2001; Kinlock, 1991). As with other drugs of abuse, observations suggest that there are significant individual differences in response. Personality characteristics were found predictive of aggressivity among individuals reporting PCP use as an intoxicant (McCardle & Fishbein, 1989). Gender differences in pharmacodynamic response were reported in one study: males reported being aggressive while PCP intoxicated, whereas female PCP users reported aggression in between intoxication episodes (Fishbein, 1996).

Androgens and Anabolic Steroids

In most species, androgens appear to exert a significant influence on the form and degree of aggressive behavior (Rubinow & Schmidt, 1996). Steroid hormones are thought to play two distinct roles in modulating behavior: an organizational and an activational role. Gonadal steroids act around the time of birth to organize which brain and other tissues will be steroid responsive. Later, the hormone activates behavioral patterns such as mating behavior.

Non-medicinal use of these compounds, often by young males, athletes, or body builders, has been linked to aggression in retrospective reports (Choi et al., 1990; Pope & Katz 1994; Yates, Perry, & Murray, 1992).

However, controlled trials of testosterone have shown considerable individual variability in response. One recent controlled trial of 8 weekly testosterone injections in 30 eugonadal men found no increase in aggression over placebo injections (O'Connor, Archer, Hair, & Wu, 2002), whereas another controlled trial of 6 weeks of testosterone administered to normal adult males found a significant increase in aggressive responses on a laboratory measure (Pope, Kouri, & Hudson, 2000). The later trial noted significant interindividual variability in response to testosterone. A trial of testosterone or estrogen replacement in hypogonadal male and female adolescents, respectively, found a significant increase in physical aggressiveness, but not verbal aggressiveness, with the hormonal replacement therapy (Finkelstein et al., 1997).

Cannabis

Cannabis sativa or marijuana received popular press in the 1920s as a drug that elicited aggression and violent crime (see Julien, 1992, for review). Urine toxicology screens at correctional institutions find cannabis is the most prevalent drug in prisoners' urine (Fraser et al., 2001). Urine drug screens by social service agencies concerned with child abuse and neglect also find cannabis to be the most prevalent substance (Fraser, 1998). However, controlled experiments find that tetrahydrocannabinol, the major psychoactive compound in cannabis, in moderate to higher doses suppresses aggression (Myerscough & Taylor 1986; Taylor et al., 1976). Animal studies also demonstrated an anti-aggressive effect (Miczek, 1978).

A possible pro-aggressive relationship for cannabis may exist during withdrawal. Cannabis withdrawal is described as characterized by anorexia, insomnia, irritability, and restlessness that can last a week to 10 days (Budney, Hughes, Moore, & Novy, 2001; Budney, Novy, & Hughes, 1999). In a laboratory setting, long-term cannabis users were significantly more aggressive on Day 3 and Day 7 of abstinence than controls or than their own behavior prior to abstinence or on Day 28 of abstinence (Kouri, Pope, & Lukas, 1999).

Summary and Prospects for the Integration of Environmental and Pharmacological Interventions

Violence can be reduced by psychopharmacological agents both acutely and over time. Neuroleptics, lithium, and anti-convulsants have the most evidence in support of their use, with generally lesser support for anti-hypertensives, such as beta-blockers and alpha agonists. Benzodiazepines, when used in truly sedating doses, do reduce aggression acutely. Neurotransmitter systems that are most consistently implicated in aggression reduction are serotonin, dopamine, and GABA (see Miczek et al., 2002).

Psychopharmacological increases in aggression can and do occur, but not across all individuals. Evidence is strongest for alcohol as such an agent. The importance of individual sensitivity, as well as environmental contextual variables, lends considerable credence to the concept of environmental interventions. Alcohol serves as an example.

Given the violence-promoting properties of alcohol, bars would appear a logical site for integrating environmental interventions. The Safer Bars Programme (Graham et al., 2004) succeeded in attaining significant reductions in notable violence (hitting, kicking, shoving and grappling) within Toronto bars. A total of 734 pre- and post-intervention observations were conducted by trained observers on Friday and Saturday nights between midnight and 2 A.M. in 18 large capacity (> 300) Toronto bars and clubs assigned randomly to receive the intervention (69% participation rate of the 26 assigned) and 12 control bars. As part of the intervention, owners/managers completed the risk assessment workbook to identify ways of reducing environmental risks, and 373 staff and owners/managers (84% participation rate) attended a 3-hour training session focused on preventing the escalation of aggression, working as a team, and resolving problem situations safely. The program was designed to help the bar owner or manager evaluate and address potential environmental risk factors that increase the likelihood of aggression without reducing the patronage and profitability of the business. This program suggested that overall alcohol consumption, as reflected by profitability, would not decrease with these risk reduction measures.

Another environmental manipulation that can be integrated with pharmacology to reduce violence is means restriction. Limiting access to lethal or injurious means is an environmental manipulation with a rationale familiar to those working in a psychiatric hospital or jail. The means restriction concept has been successfully extended to other encounters – parents of youth at risk of suicide or homicide during emergency room visits have been given injury prevention education about limiting access to firearms (Kruesi et al., 1995, 1999). Because firearms are the major method of death (Kellermann et al., 1992, 1993) and the means of suicide with the lowest survival rate, limiting access will increase the odds of survival. Analogous to firearms as lethal means, it is recognized that glassware is a potential hazard in drinking establishments. Bar glassware is responsible for about 10% of assault injuries that present to emergency units in the United Kingdom (Shepherd et al., 1990). Accordingly, there is a suggestion that increasing the impact resistance of bar glassware may decrease injuries (Warburton & Shepherd, 2000). Limiting access to agents that increase aggression is also an environmental intervention. The aim of limiting access to alcohol by youth at times of suicide risk parallels the aim of limiting access to lethal means. Alcohol is recognized to facilitate youth suicide (Brent, Perper, & Allman, 1987).

In summary, there are pharmacological agents that decrease and increase aggression risk. There is also research to suggest that considerable individual and contextual variability in pharmacological response exists, but future studies are needed to better understand the role of these influences on aggressive responses to pharmacological agents.

References

Achenbach, T. M., & Edelbrock, C. S. (1983). *Manual for the Child Behavior Checklist and Revised Child Behavior Profile*. Burlington, VT: Department of Psychiatry, University of Vermont.

Aman, M. G., De Smedt, G., Derivan, A., et al. (2002). Double-blind, placebo-controlled study of risperidone for the treatment of disruptive behaviors in children with subaverage intelligence. *American Journal of Psychiatry*, 159, 1337–1346.

Asberg, M., Thoren, L., & Traskman, P. (1976). Serotonin depression: A biochemical subgroup within affective disorders. *Science, 191*, 478–480.

Asberg, M., Traskman, L., & Thoren, P. (1976). 5-HIAA in the cerebrospinal fluid: A biochemical suicide predictor? *Archives of General Psychiatry, 33*, 1193–1197.

Barratt, E. S., Stanford, M. S., Dowdy, L., Liebman, M. J., & Kent, T. A. (1999). Impulsive and premeditated aggression: A factor analysis of self-reported acts. *Psychiatry Research, 86*(2), 163–173.

Barratt, E. S., Stanford, M. S., Felthous, A. R., & Kent, T. A. (1997). The effects of phenytoin on impulsive and premeditated aggression: A controlled study. *Journal of Clinical Psychopharmacology, 17*, 341–349.

Battaglia, J., Moss, S., Rush, J. Kang, J., Mendoza, R., Leedom, L. Dubin, W., McGlynn, C., Goodman, L. (1997). Haloperidol, lorazepam, or both for psychotic agitation? A multicenter, prospective, double-blind, emergency department study. *American Journal of Emergency Medicine, 15*(4), 335–340.

Ben-Porath, D. D., & Taylor, S. P. (2002). The effects of diazepam (valium) and aggressive disposition on human aggression: An experimental investigation. *Addictive Behaviors, 27*, 167–177.

Berman, M., Taylor, S., & Marged, B. (1993). Morphine and human aggression. *Addictive Behaviors, 18*(3), 263–268.

Bjork, J. M., Moeller, F. G., Kramer, G. L., Dram, M., Suris, A., Rush, A. J., Petty, F. (2001). Plasma GABA levels correlate with aggressiveness in relatives of patients with unipolar depressive disorder. *Psychiatry Research, 101*(2), 131–136.

Boileau, I., Assaad, J. M., Pihl, R. O., Benkelfat, C., Leyton, M., Diksic, M., et al. (2003). Alcohol promotes dopamine release in the human nucleus accumbens. *Synapse, 49*, 226–231.

Brennan, P., Mednick, S., & Hodgins, S. (2000). Major mental disorders and criminal violence in a Danish birth cohort. *Archives of General Psychiatry, 57*, 494–500.

Brent, D. A., Perper, J. A., & Allman, C. J. (1987). Alcohol, firearms and suicide among youth. *Journal of the American Medical Association, 257*, 3369–3372.

Brodaty, H., Ames, D., Snowdon, J., Woodward, M., Kirwan, J., Clarnette, R., et al. (2003). A randomized placebo-controlled trial of risperidone for the treatment of aggression, agitation, and psychosis of dementia. *Journal of Clinical Psychiatry, 64*(2), 134–143.

Brody, S. L. (1990). Violence associated with acute cocaine use in patients admitted to a medical emergency department. *National Institute on Drug Abuse Research Monograph Series, 103*, 44–59.

Brown, G. L., Goodwin, F. K., Ballenger, J. C., Goyer, P. F., & Major, L. F. (1979). Aggression in humans correlates with cerebrospinal fluid amine metabolites. *Psychiatry Research, 1*, 131–139.

Budney, A. J., Hughes, J. R., Moore, B. A., & Novy, P. L. (2001). Marijuana abstinence effects in marijuana smokers maintained in their home environment. *Archives of General Psychiatry, 58*, 917–924.

Budney, A. J., Novy, P. O., & Hughes, J. R. (1999). Marijuana withdrawal among adults seeking treatment for marijuana dependence. *Addiction, 94*, 1311–1322.

Buitelaar, J. K., van der Gaag, R. J., Cohen-Kettenis, P., & Melman, C. T. M. (2001). A randomized controlled trial of risperidone in the treatment of aggression in hospitalized adolescents with subaverage cognitive abilities. *Journal of Clinical Psychiatry, 62*, 239–248.

Campbell, M., Adams, P. B., Small, A. M., Kafantaris, V., Silva, R. R., Shell, J., et al. (1995). Lithium in hospitalized aggressive children with conduct disorder: A double blind and placebo-controlled study. *Journal of the American Academy of Child and Adolescent Psychiatry, 24*, 445–453.

Caspi, N., Modai, I., Barak, P., Waisbourd, A., Zbarsky, H., Hirschmann, S., et al.

(2001). Pindolol augmentation in aggressive schizophrenic patients: A double-blind crossover randomized study. *International Clinical Psychopharmacology, 16,* 111–115.

Cherek, D. R., Kelly, T. H., & Steinberg, J. L. (1986). Behavior contingencies and d-amphetamine effects on human aggressive and non-aggressive responding. *National Institute on Drug Abuse Research Monograph Series, 67,* 184–189.

Cherek, D. R., Spiga, R., Steinberg, J. L. (1989). Effects of secobarbital on human aggressive and non-aggressive responding. *Drug and Alcohol Dependence, 24*(1), 21–29.

Choi, P. Y., Parrott, A. C., & Cowan, D. (1990). High-Dose anabolic steroids in strength athletes: Effects upon hostility and aggression. *Human Psychopharmacology, 5,* 349–356.

Citrome, L., Casey, D. E., Daniel, D. G., Wozniak, P., Kochan, L. D., & Tracy, K. A. (2004). Adjunctive divalproex and hostility among patients with schizophrenia receiving olanzapine or risperidone. *Psychiatric Services, 55*(3), 290–294.

Coccaro, E. F., & Kavoussi, R. J. (1997). Fluoxetine and impulsive aggressive behavior in personality-disordered subjects. *Archives of General Psychiatry, 54*(12), 1081–1088.

Coccaro, E., & Siever, L. (2002). *Pathophysiology and treatment of aggression in neuropsychopharmacology: The fifth generation of progress.*

Connor, D. F., Barkley, R. A., & Davis, H. T. (2000). A pilot study of methylphenidate, clonidine, or the combination in ADHD comorbid with aggressive oppositional defiant or conduct disorder. *Clinical Pediatrics (Phila.), 39*(1), 15–25.

Cowdry, R. W., & Gardner, D. L. (1988). Pharmacotherapy of borderline personality disorder. Alprazolam, carbamazepine, trifluoperazine, and tranylcypromine. *Archives of General Psychiatry, 45*(2), 111–119.

Craft, M., Ismail, I. A., Krishnamurti, D., Mathews, J. Regan, A., Seth, R. V., North, P. M. (1987). Lithium in the treatment of aggression in mentally handicapped patients. A double-blind trial. *British Journal of Psychiatry, 150,* 685–689.

Cuva, J. E., Overall, J. E., Small, A. M. et al. (1996). Carbamazepine in aggressive children with conduct disorder: A double-blind and placebo-controlled study. *Journal of the American Academy of Child and Adolescent Psychiatry, 35,* 480–490.

Dhossche, D. M. (1999). Aggression and recent substance abuse: Absence of association in psychiatric emergency room patients. *Comprehensive Psychiatry, 40,* 343–346.

Dietch, J., & Jennings, R. (1988). Aggressive dyscontrol in patients treated with benzodiazepines. *Journal of Clinical Psychiatry, 48,* 184–188.

Dodge, K. A., & Coie, J. D. (1987). Social information processing factors in reactive and proactive aggression in children's peer groups. *Journal of Personality and Social Psychology, 53*(6), 1146–1158.

Donovan, S. J., Stewart, J. W., Nunes, E. V., Quitkin, P. M., Parides, M., Daniel, W., et al. (2000). Divalproex treatment for youth with explosive temper and mood lability: A double-blind, placebo-controlled crossover design. *American Journal of Psychiatry, 157,* 818–820.

Eichelman, B., (1987). Neurochemical and psychopharmacological aspects of aggressive behavior. In H. Y. Meltzer (Ed.), *Psychopharmacology: The Third Generation of Progress* (pp. 697–704). New York, Raven Press.

Ellinwood, E. H. (1971). Assault and homicide associated with amphetamine abuse. *American Journal of Psychiatry, 127,* 1170–1175.

Enserink, M. (2000). Searching for the mark of Cain. *Science, 289,* 575–579.

Ercan, E. S., Kutlu, A., Cikoglu, S., et al. (2003). Risperidone in children and adolescents with conduct disorder: a single-center, open-label study. *Current Therapeutic Research, 64*(1), 55–64.

Espert, R., Navarro, J. F., Salvador, A., & Simon, V. M. (1993). Effects of morphine hydrochloride on social encounters between male mice. *Aggressive Behavior, 19*(5), 377–383.

Findling, R. L., McNamara, N. K., Branicky, L. A., Schuluchter, M. D., Lemon, E., & Blumer, J. L. (2000). A double blind pilot study of risperidone in the treatment of conduct disorder. *Journal of the American Academy of Child and Adolescent Psychiatry, 39,* 509–561.

Fergusson, D., Doucette, S., Glass, K. C., Shapiro, S., Healy, D. Hebert, P., Hutton, B. (2005). Association between suicide attempts and selective serotonin reuptake inhibitors: Systematic review of randomized controlled trials. *British Medical Journal, 330*(7488), 396.

Finkelstein, J. W., Susman, E. J., Chinchilli, V. M., Kunselman, S. J., D'Arcangelo, M. R., Schwab, J., et al. (1997). Estrogen or testosterone increases self-reported aggressive behaviors in hypogonadal adolescents. *Journal of Clinical Endocrinology and Metabolism, 82*(8), 2433–2438.

Finley, G. A., Buffett-Jerrott, S., Stewart, S. H., & Millington, D. (2002). Effects of midazolam on preoperative anxiety in children. *Canadian Journal of Anesthesia, 49,* A11.

Fishbein, D. H. (1996). Dangerously aggressive behavior as a side effect of alprazolam. *American Journal of Psychiatry, 146,* 276.

Fraser, A. D. (1998). Urine drug testing for social service agencies in Nova Scotia, Canada. *Journal of Forensic Science, 43*(1), 194–196.

Fraser, A. D., Zamecnik, J., Keravel, J., McGrath, L., & Wells, J. (2001). Experience with urine drug testing by the Correctional Service of Canada. *Forensic Science International, 121* (1–2), 16–22.

Frick, P., Lahey, B., Loebert, R., Tannenbaum, L., et al. (1993). Oppositional defiant disorder and conduct disorder: A meta-analytic review of factor analyses and cross-validation in a clinic sample. *Clinical Psychology Review, 13*(4), 319–340.

Gardner, D. L., & Cowdry, R. W. (1986). Positive effects of carbamazepine on behavioral dyscontrol in borderline personality disorder. *American Journal of Psychiatry, 143*(4), 519–522.

Gerra, G., Zaimovic, A., Ampollini,, R., Giusti, F., Delsignore, R., Raggi, M. A., Laviola, G., Macchia, T., & Brambilla, F. (2001). Experimentally induced aggressive behavior in subjects with 3,4-methylenedioxy-methamphetamine ("ecstasy") use history: Psychobiological correlates. *Journal of Substance Abuse, 13,* 471–491.

Gibbons, R. D., Hur, K., Bhaumik, D. K., Mann, J. J. (2005). The relationship between antidepressant medication use and rate of suicide. *American Journal of Psychiatry, 163*(11), 1861–1863.

Gillet, C., Polard, E., Mauduit, N., & Allain, H. (2001). Acting out and psychoactive substances: Alcohol, drugs, illicit substances. *Encephale, 27,* 351–359.

Graham, K., Osgood, D. W., Zibrowski, E., Purcell, J., Gliksman, L., Leonard, K., et al. (2004). The effect of the Safer Bars programme on physical aggression in bars: Results of a randomized controlled trial. *Drug and Alcohol Review, 23,* 31–41.

Gray, J. A. (1987). *The psychology of fear and stress* (2nd ed). New York: Cambridge University Press.

Griffin, J. C., Williams, D. E., Stark, M. T., Altmeyer, H. K., & Mason, M. (1986). Self-injurious behavior: A state-wide prevalence survey of the extent and circumstances. *Applied Research in Mental Retardation, 7*(1), 105–116.

Groh, C. (1976). The psychotropic effect of Tegretol in non-epileptic children, with particular reference to the drug's indications. In W. Birkmayer (Ed.), *Epileptic Seizures-Behavior-Pain* (pp. 259–263). Switzerland, Hans. Huber.

Gustafson, R. (1985). Alcohol-related aggression: a further study of the important of frustration. *Psychological Reports, 57*(3 Pt 1), 683–697.

Harris, J. C. (1995). *Developmental neuropsychiatry: Assessment, diagnosis, and treatment of developmental disorder.* Oxford: Oxford University Press.

Hazell, P. L., & Stuart, J. E. (2003). A randomized controlled trial of clonidine added to psychostimulant medication for hyperactive and aggressive children. *Journal of the American Academy of Child and Adolescent Psychiatry, 42*(8), 886–894.

Hoaken, P. N. S., & Stewart S. H. (2003). Drugs of abuse and the elicitation of human aggressive behavior. *Addictive Behaviors, 28,* 1533–1554.

Hollander, E., Tracy, K. A., Swann, A. C., Coccaro, E. F., McElroy, S. L., Wozniak, P., et al. (2003). Divalproex in the treatment of impulsive aggression: Efficacy in cluster B personality disorders. *Neuropsychopharmacology, 28*(6), 1186–1197.

Ito, T. A., Miller, N., & Pollock, V. E. (1996). Alcohol and aggression: A meta-analysis on the moderating effects of inhibitory cues, triggering events, and self-focused attention. *Psychology Bulletin, 120*(1), 60–82.

Julien, R. M. (1991). *A primer of drug action.* New York: Freeman.

Kellermann, A. L., Hackman, B. B., Fligner, C., et al. (1992). Suicide in the home in relation to gun ownership. *New England Journal of Medicine, 327,* 467–472.

Kellermann, A. L., Rivara, F. P., Rushforth, N. B., et al. (1993). Gun ownership as a risk factor for homicide in the home. *New England Journal of Medicine, 329,* 1084–1091.

Kinlock, T. W. (1991). Does phencyclidine (PCP) use increase violent crime? *Journal of Drug Issues, 21,* 795–816.

Klein, R. G., Abikoff, H., Klass, E., et al. (1997). Clinical efficacy of methylphenidate in conduct disorder with and without attention deficit hyperactivity disorder. *Archives of General Psychiatry, 54*(12), 1073–1080.

Kouri, E. M., Pope, H. G., & Lukas, S. E. (1999). Changes in aggressive behavior during withdrawal from long-term marijuana use. *Psychopharmacology, 143,* 302–308.

Kruesi, M. J. P., & Gray, K. (2006). Conduct disorder/sociopathy. In C. E. Coffey & R. Brumback (Eds.), *Textbook of pediatric neuropsychiatry* (2nd ed.). Washington, DC: American Psychiatric Press.

Kruesi, M. J. P., Grossman, J., & Hirsch, J. (1995). *Five minutes of your time may mean a lifetime to a suicidal adolescent.* Chicago: Ronald McDonald House Charities, University of Illinois-Chicago.

Kruesi, M. J. P., Grossman, J., Pennington, J. M., Woodward, J. P., Duda, D., & Hirsch, J. G. (1999). Parent education in the emergency department for suicide and violence prevention. *Journal of the American Academy of Child and Adolescent Psychiatry, 38,* 250–255.

Kruesi, M. J. P., Hibbs, E. D., Hamburger, S. D., Rapoport, J. L., Keysor, C. S., & Elia, J. (1994). Measurement of aggression in children with disruptive behavior disorders. *Journal of Offender Rehabilitation, 21,* 159–172.

Kruesi, M. J. P., Hibbs, E. D., Zahn, T. P., Keysor, C. S., Hamburger, S. D., Bartko, J. J., et al. (1992). A 2-year prospective follow-up study of children and adolescents with disruptive behavior disorders: Prediction by cerebrospinal fluid 5-hydroxyindoleacetic acid, homovanillic acid, and autonomic measures. *Archives of General Psychiatry, 49,* 429–435.

Kruesi, M. J. P., & Jacobsen, T. (1997). Serotonin and human violence: Do environmental mediators exist? In A. Raine, D. Farrington, P. Brennan, & S. A. Mednick (Eds.), *Biosocial bases of violence* (pp. 189–205). New York: Plenum.

Kruesi, M. J. P., Keller, S., & Wagner, M. W. (2003). Neurobiology of aggression. In M. A. Scahill, D. S. Charney, & J. F. Leckman (Eds.), *Pediatric psychopharmacology: Principles and practice* (pp. 210–223). New York: Oxford University Press.

Kruesi, M. J. P., Rapoport, J. L., Hamburger, S., Hibbs, E., Potter, W. Z., Lenane, M., et al. (1990). Cerebrospinal fluid monoamine metabolites, aggression, and impulsivity in disruptive behavior disorders of children and adolescents. *Archives of General Psychiatry, 47,* 419–426.

Lahti, A. C., Koffel, B., LaPorte, D., Tamminga, C. A. (1995). Subanesthetic doses of ketamine stimulate psychosis in schizophrenia. *Neuropsychopharmacology, 13*(1), 9–19.

Lesch, K. P., & Merschdorf, U. (2000). Impulsivity, aggression, and serotonin: A molecular psychobiological perspective. *Behavioral Science and the Law, 18*(5), 581–604.

Lester, D. (1995). The concentration of neurotransmitter metabolites in the cerebrospinal fluid of suicidal individuals: A meta-analysis. *Pharmacopsychiatry, 28*(2), 45–50.

Licata, A., Taylor, S., Berman, M., & Cranston, J. (1993). Effects of cocaine on human aggression. *Pharmacology, Biochemistry and Behavior, 45*(3), 549–552.

Linnoila, M., Virkkunen, M., Scheinin, M., Nuutila, A., Rimon, R., & Goodwin, F. K. (1983). Low cerebrospinal fluid 5-hydroxyindoleacetic acid concentration differentiates impulsive from nonimpulsive violent behavior. *Life Sciences, 33,* 2609–2614.

Loeber, R., Schmaling, K. B. (1985). Empirical evidence for overt and covert patterns of antisocial conduct problems: a metaanalysis. *Journal of Abnormal Child Psychology, 13*(2), 337–353.

Ludwig, J., Marcotte, D. E. (2005). Antidepressants, suicide, and drug regulation. *Journal of Policy Analysis Management, 24*(2), 249–272.

Malone, R. P., Delaney, M. A., Luebbert, J. F., Cater, J., & Campbell, M. (2000). A double blind placebo-controlled study of lithium in hospitalized aggressive children and adolescent with conduct disorder. *Archives of General Psychiatry, 57,* 649–654.

Malone, R. P., Luebbert, J. F., Delaney, M. A., Biesecker, K. A., Blaney, B. L., Rowan, A. B., et al. (1997). Nonpharmacological response in hospitalized children with conduct disorder. *Journal of the American Academy of Child and Adolescent Psychiatry, 36*(2), 242–247.

Mattes, J. A. (1990). Comparative effectiveness of carbamazepine and propranolol for rage outbursts. *Journal of Neuropsychiatry and Clinical Neuroscience, 2*(2), 159–64.

McCardle, L., & Fishbein, D. H. (1989). The self-reported effects of PCP on human aggression. *Addictive Behaviors, 14*, 465–472.

McCracken, J. T., McGough, J., Shah, B., Cronin, P., Hong, D., Aman, M. G., et al., with Research Units on Pediatric Psychopharmacology Autism Network. (2002). Risperidone in children with autism and serious behavioral problems. *New England Journal of Medicine, 347*(5), 314–321.

Meltzer, H. Y. (2004). What's atypical about atypical antipsychotic drugs? *Current Opinion in Pharmacology, 4*(1), 53–57.

Meltzer, H. Y., Alphs, L., Green, A. I., Altamura, A. C., Anand, R., Bertoldi, A., et al., with the International Suicide Prevention Trial Study Group. (2003). Clozapine treatment for suicidality in schizophrenia: International Suicide Prevention Trial (InterSePT). *Archives of General Psychiatry, 60*(1), 82–91.

Miczek, K. A. (1978). D-sup-tetrahydrocannibinol: Antiaggressive effects in mice, rats, and squirrel monkeys. *Science, 199*(4336), 1459–1461.

Miczek, K. A., Fish, E. W., De Bold, J. F., & De Almeida, R. M. (2002). Social and neural determinants of aggressive behavior: Pharmacotherapeutic targets at serotonin, dopamine and gamma-aminobutyric acid systems. *Psychopharmacology (Berl), 163*(3–4), 434–458.

Miczek, K., Haney, M., Tidey, J., Vivian, J., & Weerts, E. (1994). *Neurochemistry and pharmacotherapeutic management of aggression and violence. Understanding and preventing violence* (Vol. 2, pp. 245–514). Washington, DC: National Academy Press.

Moeller, F. G., Dougherty, D. M., Rustin, T., Swann, A. C., Allen, T. J., Shah, N., et al. (1997). Antisocial personality disorder and aggression in recently abstinent cocaine dependent subjects. *Drug and Alcohol Dependence, 44*, 175–182.

Moeller, F. G., Dougherty, Barratt, E. S., Oderomde. V., Mathias, C. W., Harper, R. A., Swann, A. C. (2002). Increased impulsivity in cocaine dependent subjects independent of antisocial personality disorder and aggression. *Drug and Alcohol Dependence, 68*(1), 105–111.

Monnelly, E. P., Ciraulo, D. A., Knapp, C., & Keane, T. (2003). Low-dose risperidone as adjunctive therapy for irritable aggression in posttraumatic stress disorder. *Journal of Clinical Psychopharmacology, 23*(2), 193–196.

Moore, T. M., Scarpa, A., & Raine, A. (2002). A meta-analysis of serotonin metabolite 5-HIAA and antisocial behavior. *Aggressive Behavior, 28*, 299–316.

Morentin, B., Calladod, F. F., & Meana, J. J. (1998). Differences in criminal activity between heroin abusers and subjects without psychiatric disorders: Analysis of 578 detainees in Bilbao, Spain. *Journal of Forensic Sciences, 43*, 993–999.

Moyer, K. E. (1968). Kinds of aggression and their physiological basis. *Communication in Behavioral Biology, 2*, 65–87.

Morentin, B., Calladod, F. F., & Meana, J. J. (1998). Differences in criminal activity between heroin abusers and subjects without psychiatric disorders: Analysis of 578 detainees in Bilbao, Spain. *Journal of Forensic Sciences, 43*, 993–999.

Muldoon, M. F., Manuck, S. B., Mendelsohn, A. B., Kaplan, J. R., & Belle, S. H. (2001). Cholesterol reduction and non-illness mortality: Meta-analysis of randomised clinical trials. *British Medical Journal, 322*(7277), 11–15.

Mullen, F. J., & Luckhardt, A. B. (1934). The effect of alcohol on cutaneous tactile and pain sensitivity. *American Journal of Physiology, 109*, 7–78.

Murdoch, D., Pihl, R. O., & Ross, D. (1990). Alcohol and crimes of violence: Present issues. *International Journal of the Addictions, 25*, 1065–1081.

Murray, J. B. (2002). Phencyclidine (PCP): A dangerous drug, but useful in schizophrenia research. *Journal of Psychology, 136*(3), 319–327.

Myerscough, R., & Taylor, S. P. (1986). The effects of marijuana on human physical aggression. *Journal of Personality and Social Psychology, 49*(6), 1541–1546.

New, A. S., Sevin, E. M., Mitropoulou, V., Reynolds, D., Novotny, S. L., Callahan, A., Trestman, R. L., Siever, L. J. (1999). Serum cholesterol and impulsivity in personality disorders. *Psychiatry Research, 85*(2), 145–150.

Nickel, M. K., Nickel, C., Mitterlehner, F. O., Tritt, K., Lahmann, C., Leiberich, P. K., et al. (2004). Topiramate treatment of aggression in female borderline personality disorder patients: A double-blind, placebo-controlled study. *Journal of Clinical Psychiatry, 65*(11), 1515–1519.

O'Connor, D. B., Archer, J., Hair, W. M., & Wu, F. C. (2002). Exogenous testosterone, aggression, and mood in eugonadal and hypogonadal men. *Physiology and Behavior, 75*(4), 557–566.

Olivier, B., Mohs, J., Van Oorschot, R., & Hen, R. (1995). Serotonin receptors and animal models of aggressive behavior. *Pharmacopsychiatry, 28*, 80–90.

Pihl, R. O., Assaad, J. M., & Hoaken, P. N. S. (2003). The alcohol-aggression relationship and differential sensitivity to alcohol. *Aggressive Behavior, 29*, 302–315.

Pihl, R. O., & Peterson, J. B. (1995). Drugs and aggression: Correlations, crime and human manipulative studies and some proposed mechanisms. *Journal of Psychiatry and Neuroscience, 20*(2), 141–149.

Pope, H. G., & Katz, D. L. (1994). Psychiatric and medical effects of anabolic-androgenic steroid use: A controlled study of 160 athletes. *Archives of General Psychiatry, 51*(5), 375–382.

Pope, H. G., Kouri, E. M., & Hudson, J. I. (2000). Effects of supraphysiologic doses of testosterone on mood and aggression in normal men: A randomized controlled trial. *Archives of General Psychiatry, 57*(2), 133–140.

Puente, R. (1976). The use of carbamazepine in the treatment of behavioral disorders in children. In W. Birkmayer (Ed.), *Epileptic seizures-behavior-pain* (pp. 244–247). Bern, Switzerland: Hans Huber.

Rifkin, A., Karajgi, B., Dicker, R., et al. (1997). Lithium treatment of conduct disorders in adolescents. *American Journal of Psychiatry, 154*(4), 554–555.

Rodriguez-Arias, M., Minarro, J., Aguilar, M. A., Pinazo, J., & Simon, V. M. (1998). Effects of risperidone and SCH 23390 on isolation-induced aggression in male mice. *European Neuropsychopharmacology, 8*(2), 95–103.

Rodriguez-Arias, M., Minarro, J., & Simon, V. M. (2001). Development of tolerance to the anti-aggressive effects of morphine. *Behavioral Pharmacology, 12*, 221–224.

Robbins, T. W. (1990). The case of frontostriatal dysfunction in schizophrenia. *Schizophrenia Bulletin, 16*(3), 391–402.

Rubinow, D. R., & Schmidt, P. J. (1996). Androgens, brain and behavior. *American Journal of Psychiatry, 153*(8), 974–984.

Schotte, A., Janssen, P. F., Gommeren, W., Luyten, W. H., Van Gompel, P., Lesage, A. S., et al. (1996). Risperidone compared with new and reference antipsychotic drugs: In vitro and in vivo receptor binding. *Psychopharmacology (Berl.), 124*(1–2), 57–73.

Sheard, M. H., Marini, J. L., Bridges, C. I., Wagner, E. (1976). The effect of lithium on impulsive aggressive behavior in man. *American Journal of Psychiatry, 13*(12), 1409–1413.

Shepherd, J. P., Shapland, M., Pearce, N. X., et al. (1990). Pattern, severity, and aetiology of injuries in victims of assault. *Journal of the Royal Society of Medicine, 83*, 75–78.

Sival, R. C., Haffmans, P. M., Jansen, P. A., Duursma, S. A., & Eikelenboom, P. (2002). Sodium valproate in the treatment of aggressive behavior in patients with dementia – A randomized placebo controlled clinical trial. *International Journal of Geriatric Psychiatry, 17*(6), 579–585.

Snyder, R., Turgay, A., Aman, M., et al. (2002). Effects of risperidone on conduct and disruptive behavior disorders in children with subaverage IQs. *Journal of the American Academy of Child and Adolescent Psychiatry, 9*(41), 1026–1036.

Spencer, T., Biederman, J. Wilens, T. (2000). Pharmacotherapy of attention deficit hyperactivity disorder. *Child and Adolescent Psychiatric Clinics of North America, 1*(9) 77–97.

Spiga, R., Cherek, D. R., Roache, J. D., & Cowan, K. A. (1990). The effects of codeine on human aggressive responding. *International Clinical Psychopharmacology, 5*(3), 195–204.

Stanford, M. S., Houston, R. J., Mathias, C. W., Greve, K. W., Villemarette-Pittman, N. R., Adams, D. (2001). A double-blind placebo-controlled crossover study of phenytoin in individuals with impulsive aggression. *Psychiatry Research, 103*(2–3), 193–203.

Steiner, H., Petersen, M. L., Saxena, K., Ford, S., & Matthews, Z. (2003) Ivalproex sodium for the treatment of conduct disorder: A randomized controlled clinical trial. *Journal of Clinical Psychiatry, 64*(10), 1183–1191.

Tariot, P. M., Erb, R., Podgorski, C. A., Cox, C., Patel, S., Jakimovich, L., Irvine, C. (1998). Efficacy and tolerability of carbamazepine for agitation and aggression in dementia. *American Journal of Psychiatry, 155*(1), 54–61.

Taylor, S. P., & Hulsizer, M. R. (1998). Psychoactive drugs and human aggression, In R. G. Geen, & E. Donnerstein (Eds.), *Human aggression*: Theories, research, and implications for social policy (pp. 139–165). San Diego, CA: California Press.

Taylor, S., Vardaris, R., Rawich, A., Gammon, C., Cranston, J., & Lubetkin, A. I. (1976). The effects of alcohol and delta-9-tetrahydrocannabinol on human physical aggression. *Aggressive Behavior, 2*, 153–161.

Tidey, J. W., & Miczek, K. A. (1992). Heightened aggressive behavior during morphine withdrawal: Effects of d-amphetamine. *Psychopharmacology, 107*, 297–302.

TREC Collaborative Group. (2003). Rapid tranquillization for agitated patients in emergency psychiatric rooms: A randomized trial of midazolam versus haloperidol plus promethazine. *British Medical Journal, 327*, 708–714.

Virkkunen, M., Eggert, M., Rawlings, R., & Linnoila, M. (1989). A prospective follow-up study of alcoholic violent offenders and fire setters. *Archives of General Psychiatry, 53*(6):523–529.

Vitiello, B., Behar, D., Hunt, J., Stoff, D., & Ricciuti, A. (1990). Subtyping aggression in children and adolescents. *Journal of Neuropsychiatry and Clinical Neurosciences, 2*, 189–192.

Volavka, J., Czobor, P., Nolan, K., Sheitman, B., Lindenmayer, J. P., Citrome, L., et al. (2004). Overt aggression and psychotic symptoms in patients with schizophrenia treated with clozapine, olanzapine, risperidone, or haloperidol. *Journal of Clinical Psychopharmacology, 24*(2), 225–228.

Volkow, N. D., Wang, G., & Doria, J. (1995). Monitoring the brain's response to alcohol with positron emission tomography. *Alcohol Health and Research World, 19*, 296–299.

Warburton, A. L., & Shepherd, J. P. (2000). Effectiveness of toughened glassware in terms of reducing injury in bars: A randomised controlled trial. *Injury Prevention, 6*, 36–40.

Wysowski, D. K., Gross, T. P. (1990). Deaths due to accidents and violence in two recent trials of cholesterol-lowering drugs. *Archives of Internal Medicine. 150*(10), 2169–2172.

Yang, C. C., Jick, S. S., & Jick, H. (2003). Lipid-lowering drugs and the risk of depression and suicidal behavior. *Archives of Internal Medicine, 163*(16), 1926–1932.

Yates, W. R., Perry, P., & Murray, S. (1992). Aggression and hostility in anabolic steroid users. *Biological Psychiatry, 31*, 1232–1234.

Yeh, S., Fricke, R. A., & Edwards, D. H. (1996). The effect of social experience on serotonergic modulation of the escape circuit of crayfish. *Science, 271*, 366–369.

Yudofsky, S., Silver, J. M. and Schneider, S. E. (1987). Pharmacologic treatment of aggression. *Psychiatric Annals, 17*, 397.

Yudofsky, S., Williams, D., Gorman, J. (1981). Propranolol in the treatment of rate and violent behavior in patients with chronic brain syndromes. *American Journal of Psychiatry, (138*(2), 218–220.

Zarcone, J. R., Hellings, J. A., Crandall, K., Reese, R. M., Marquis, J., Fleming, K., et al. (2001). Effects of risperidone on aberrant behavior of persons with developmental disabilities: I. A double-blind crossover study using multiple measures. *American Journal of Mental Retardation, 106*(6), 525–538.

CHAPTER 33

Social Learning and Violent Behavior

Gary F. Jensen

On April 20th, 1999, two students at Columbine High School in Littleton, Colorado, snuck into the school heavily armed, dressed in black trench coats with black masks. They opened fire on their classmates and teachers, killing 12 students and a teacher and wounding 23 others. The two boys ended the attack by killing themselves. This alarming episode was the most dramatic of a number of attacks on schoolmates and teachers that captured headlines between 1996 and 1999. One of the most recent attacks took place on an Indian reservation in Minnesota, with nine killed in a shooting involving many of the same features as Columbine, including suicide by the teenage assailant.

Whenever such horrible events occur, media pundits, politicians, and criminologists are asked "Why?" and a variety of distinct "causes" are proposed. Some of the "usual suspects," such as urban decay, drug trafficking, and economic inequality, could not be raised for Columbine because the youth involved were suburban teens with middle-class backgrounds. Old clichés, such as increasing the threat of the death penalty,

did not make sense because the youth executed themselves. In contrast, any search of news and editorials on this rash of unusual violence, as well as violence in general, is virtually certain to find one particular "cause" highlighted: media violence. Indeed, the day after Columbine, an editorial in *USA Today* proposed that "violence" in the media was to blame (Meyer, 1999), citing research by psychologists on imitation and desensitization. Such explanations have been endorsed and incorporated into the official advice of the American Medical Association and other professional associations.

Any search of the Internet under the terms "media violence," "violence," "school shootings," or "media effects" will find reference to one particular perspective linked to such topics, a theoretical perspective on human behavior commonly referred to as social learning theory. In fact, the link is so common that many people attempting to understand violence might conclude that media effects are the central focus of that theory. Concepts, such as desensitization, imitation, and modeling, are so central to discussions of media effects that it is easy to overlook the fact that social learning theory is a general theory of human behavior that would persist as a viable perspective even if it were found that the media play a minor role in the explanation of violence. Indeed, the social learning perspective applies to more features of such episodes at the spatial, temporal, group, and individual level than any other perspective on violent behavior.

This chapter addresses the relevance of that general perspective to the explanation of variations in violence over time and among people, settings, and societies. The first task is to summarize the development of that perspective and the distinct academic traditions that have addressed social learning mechanisms. Second, the features of that perspective that distinguish it from other theories of violence are outlined. The theory has been misrepresented terribly by prominent advocates of alternative sociological theories, and those misrepresentations have been reified in much of the criminological literature. Third, research relevant to its comparative explanatory power when properly represented is considered. Fourth, research on media effects is considered critically in the context of other social learning processes that are more important for understanding violence. Finally, key areas for further research and theoretical development of social learning theory are proposed to serve as a guide for the 21st century.

Theoretical Convergence of Two Traditions

Two academic traditions in the United States have been central to the development of social learning theory: psychology and sociology. Credit for the name should go to Neal E. Miller and John Dollard at Yale University who published *Social Learning and Imitation* (1941) in which they proposed to "apply training in two different fields – psychology and social science – to the solution of social problems." The book is dedicated to a psychologist, Clark Leonard Hall, who was interested in imitation, and to a sociologist, William Fielding Ogburn, who was

interested in diffusion, contagion, and the transmission of cultural innovations. Unfortunately, these links are not well known to contemporary critics of the theory in criminology. As is proposed later in this chapter, such links should be re-examined to provide the foundation for applying the theory to variations in violence over time and space.

Miller and Dollard begin their work with this simple, but profound, statement: "Human behavior is learned; precisely that behavior which is widely felt to characterize man as a rational being, or as a member of a particular nation or social class, is acquired rather than innate" (1941, p. 1). They identified their learning theory as "social learning" theory because they applied principles of learning to understand "social" behavior and the "conditions imposed by society in which a particular individual lives" (pp. 2–3). They were interested in "the mechanisms by which culture is transmitted from one generation to another" and the stability of cultural patterns, once they are acquired" (p. 5). Another profound claim was that "the transmission of culture must follow the laws of learning" (p. 4).

Although the label "social learning" was not invoked in the early development of sociological perspectives in American academia, many of the same principles identified by psychologists were reflected in the emergence of sociological perspectives at the University of Chicago in the 1920s and 1930s. The emerging perspective was quite radical because the central, underlying theses were that criminal behavior is learned in the same manner as other forms of behavior and that support for such a view could be found in both ecological patterns of crime and delinquency and in case studies of individuals and groups. Shaw, Zorbaugh, McKay, and Contrell (1929) observed that certain areas of Chicago tended to keep high rates of delinquency despite successive changes in the ethnic groups residing in them. They suggested that those problems were (a) generated by the social conditions experienced by these groups rather than by any genetic or biological predisposition and/or (b) by "traditions of crime and delinquency" that develop and are perpetuated through interaction among new and established residents of social areas.

In addition to analysis of the distribution of problems among social areas, scholars and researchers at the University of Chicago systematically documented the activities, culture, and organization of distinct groups of people in the city of Chicago, ranging from *The Polish Peasant in Europe and America* (Thomas & Znanieki, 1927) and *The Ghetto* (Wirth, 1928) to *The Hobo* (Andersen, 1923), *The Taxi-Dance Hall* (Cressey, 1932), and *The Gang* (Thrasher, 1927). In his research on gangs Frederick Thrasher identified regularities in the emergence of gangs that still hold true today.

The reputed "father" of scientific criminology in the United States, Edwin Sutherland, was trained at the University of Chicago and was the first scholar to expound a systematized sociological explanation of crime and criminality. His *Principles of Criminology* was first published in 1924, and by 1939 was organized into a set of propositions that emphasized the role played by "conflicting definitions" of appropriate and inappropriate conduct in a complex society and "differential association" with people communicating conflicting definitions. Sutherland's systematic elaboration of a theory of both crime and criminality in a set of nine fundamental propositions earned him honors as the most influential theoretical criminologist of the 20th century. Applied to delinquency, the central proposition of differential association was simply that "a person becomes delinquent because of an excess of definitions favorable to violation of law over definitions unfavorable to violation of law (Sutherland, 1947, p. 7)." Definitions were the symbolic messages communicated in everyday interaction with significant others, such as parents, peers, and teachers.

The two traditions – psychological development of a social learning theory of human behavior and sociological development of criminological theories emphasizing normal learning processes – proceeded rather independently until the mid-1960s. Ronald Akers, a sociological criminologist, teamed with Robert Burgess, a sociologist trained in operant theory, to modify Sutherland's principles using the terminology and principles of modern behaviorism (Burgess and Akers, 1966). This "differential-association-reinforcement" theory of criminal behavior became the foundation for a perspective in criminology that Akers later elaborated as a "social learning theory" of deviant behavior (1973). Since the first test of his theory conducted more than 25 years ago (Akers, Krohn, Lanza-Kaduce, & Radosevich, 1979), social learning theory has been subjected to more empirical inquiry in relation to a wider range of forms of deviance and in a wider range of settings and samples than any other criminological theory in history.

In the development and application of the theory, Akers drew not only on Skinnerian principles of operant theory but he also drew extensively on the work of psychologists working in the tradition established by Miller and Dollard, especially Albert Bandura. Bandura extended the study of modeling and vicarious learning mechanisms to adolescent aggression in 1959 and published *Aggression: A Social Learning Approach* in 1973. The focus on aggression facilitated Akers' integration of social learning mechanisms identified by psychologists with mechanisms of symbolic learning and differential social interaction as key features of a social learning theory of deviance and crime. Psychologists integrated sociological ideas with learning mechanisms to develop social learning theory in the 1940s, and Akers integrated psychological theory and research with sociological theories of deviance and crime 30 years later. Because this volume focuses on theories of violence, this chapter's discussion of specific properties of a social learning theory of violence draws on Akers' version of the theory, acknowledging the indebtedness of that theory to works by psychologists.

Properties of Social Learning Theory

The central principle of a social learning approach to any form of crime is the restatement of Miller and Dollard's claim that "human behavior is learned." Simply stated, law-breaking behavior is best understood if it is approached as *learned*, rather than biologically determined, behavior. Moreover, following Sutherland, the learning mechanisms involved are the same for law-breaking as for law-abiding conduct. These principles are closely linked to another principle. As learned behavior, law-breaking and law-abiding conduct are not totally random or unpredictable, but are instead more common in some circumstances than in others. What those exact circumstances are varies from one theory to another, but all sociology theories share the view that it is dimensions of the *social environment* that explain the distribution of different types of conduct and variations in the probability that individuals will learn different forms of conduct. Important aspects of the social environment are its *values, norms, beliefs, and technical knowledge* (i.e., how to do things, including crime); the nature and operations of such *socializing forces* as the family, school, church, community, and peer groups; and the *structure of opportunities* for engaging in law-breaking and law-abiding conduct.

Akers proposes four distinct concepts or variables as the central features of social learning processes: (1) differential association, (2) definitions, (3) differential reinforcement, and (4) imitation. Because no distinct formal definitions of concepts are presented, there is considerable ambiguity in the specific meaning of the first concept, differential association. Akers states that it involves interaction and normative dimensions, as well as modeling and identification with reference groups. However, because normative learning is encompassed under "definitions" and "modeling" can be encompassed under imitation, the concepts need to be differentiated more precisely. There is no ambiguity or overlap if differential association is defined as time spent interacting or observing other people distinguishable in their physical and verbal behavior. Moreover, as stated by Sutherland, "differential associations may vary in frequency, duration, priority, and intensity (Sutherland, 1947, p. 7)." These are all dimensions of the inter-

actional relationship between an individual and associates.

How do such interactional relationships get translated into law-abiding or law-breaking conduct? The other three concepts in Akers' social learning theory encompass the major processes through which people affect one another. The dimension of social learning referred to as definitions encompasses phenomena referred to in sociological discussions of socialization. When interaction involves attempts to teach or convey the attitudes, values, norms, and beliefs appropriate for a particular social role, that type of interaction can be called socialization and it encompasses the "definitional" learning distinguished by Akers.

Another social learning mechanism is imitation. When a person copies a behavior because it has yielded rewarding outcomes or prevented negative outcomes for someone else, this type of observational learning can be called vicarious reinforcement, modeling, or imitation. In fact, whenever parents say "Do as I say, not as I do," they are acknowledging imitative learning processes and are assuming that socialization (i.e., teaching norms about good behavior among children ["as I say"] can overcome such vicarious processes ["as I do"]). Differential associations can affect behavior through such observational processes independent of how socialization processes affect internalized "definitions." Imitation was central to Miller and Dollard's attempt to integrate sociology and psychology and is one of the mechanisms in Bandura's theory and research. It is a key mediating mechanism in media effects research.

Akers and his colleagues (Akers et al., 1979) report that, as measured in their research on drug use, imitation made a trivial contribution to explained variance when other learning processes are controlled. However, the variable they measured was the *opportunity* for imitation processes to occur, as indicated by the "number of admired persons who use drugs." Whether subjects imitate such behavior can only be inferred from the correlation of that measure with drug use. Moreover, as measured, *imitation* and *differential association* are neither distinct theoretically nor operationally in that one of the measures of differential association is friends who use drugs, and the measure of imitation is based on the number of admired peers and others who use drugs. A more appropriate measure of imitation would require observational methods in the laboratory and or natural settings.

The third mechanism through which associations affect behavior is differential reinforcement, defined by Akers and Sellers (2004, p. 87) as "the balance of anticipated or actual rewards and punishments that follow or are consequences of the behavior." In its original formulation, differential association-reinforcement theory included both social and nonsocial reinforcers because some consequences that may reinforce or inhibit further behavior are physiological. However, when incorporated into social learning theory, the emphasis is on rewards and punishments controlled by other people. Moreover, differential social reinforcement refers to the actual responses of one party to another's physical and verbal behavior as distinct from imitation. Such responses may be accompanied by attempts to convey messages about proper attitudes, values, norms, and beliefs, but differential reinforcement is conceptually distinct from such socialization processes.

Research on Social Learning and Violent Behavior

By the turn of the 21st century there had been more than 100 empirical tests of Akers' specific version of the theory (see Sellers, Pratt, Winfree, & Cullen, 2000), and if tests of closely related theories were added, there would be hundreds of studies relevant to one or another feature of that perspective. The number of relevant studies could easily exceed a thousand when considering investigations of (1) continuity in violence across settings attributed to imitation, socialization, and differential reinforcement; (2) the influence of distinctive variations in values,

norms, and beliefs in the generation and perpetuation of violence; (3) the effects of shifts in social interaction and relationships over the life course; (4) specific learning mechanisms, such as imitation and modeling; and (5) the separable mediating effect of peer group interaction when other variables are controlled.

Studies of several different forms of violence have supported the social learning hypothesis that witnessing violence by others increases the odds that observers will engage in similar behavior in similar circumstances either immediately or in the future. This hypothesis has been central not only to research on televised violence and aggression, which is discussed separately, but also to research on the generation of violence across settings and time. For example, children's' experiences of violence in the family increase the odds of violence in outside settings or in subsequent intimate relationships. Violence between parents or parental violence toward children increases the odds that children will engage in violence within the family, in other contexts, and at other stages of the life course (Gelles, 1987). This reproduction of violence also applies to corporal punishment by parents, in that children who have been physically disciplined are more likely to be violent toward siblings when in the family of origin, toward others outside the family, and toward spouses when they create their own families (Straus & Donnelly, 1994). As stated by Wiesner, Capaldi, and Patterson (2004, p. 318), the "coercive interaction styles and anti social behavior learned through interactions with family members are generalized into new settings." The fact that experimental interventions affecting parental disciplinary styles have subsequent effects on children's antisocial behavior has supported a social learning model over any theory attributing continuities to shared genetic traits (Patterson, Bank, & Reid 1987).

Social learning processes have been discerned in research on sexual aggression and rape as well. Straus's study of corporal punishment found that a "fusion of sex and violence" with masochistic sexual fantasies and behavior, including rape fantasies, positively correlated with spanking as a child (Straus & Donnelly, 1994, pp. 121–136). In a direct test of Akers' social learning theory, Sellers, Cochran, and Winfree (2003) found that 33% of variation in "courtship violence" against a dating partner was explained by associations with peers who had used physical violence with partners, the perceived costs of such violence, and the perception of admired role models who had used violence against a spouse or partner. Moreover, "rape myths" (Burt, 1980), "machoism," and other sets of beliefs (Poppen & Segal, 1988) that are commonly cited as conducive to sexual aggression can be subsumed under the normative learning mechanisms emphasized in social learning theory.

Peer group relationships have always been a central and distinguishing feature of differential association theory, and most tests of that theory have focused on associations with delinquent peers. However, the key variable in both differential association and social learning theory is "differential" association, and the number of delinquent or criminal friends or associates is only one characteristic of those associations. As expressed by Sutherland, the key process was variations in relationships with people espousing a variety of "definitions favorable and unfavorable to the violation of law." Social learning theory does not limit the impact of relationships with others to such normative processes of socialization; rather, the behavior engaged in by others, as well as their responses to a youth's behavior, have consequences separable from the values, norms, and beliefs that may be conveyed. Recognizing that association with delinquent peers is only one way that differential associations can affect behavior, it can be observed that it is one of the most enduring and substantial correlates found in research (Warr, 2002). Moreover, that correlation has been found for violent behavior, as well as for less serious offenses (Gordon et al., 2004).

There are four distinct ways in which normative learning has entered into attempts to explain criminal behavior: "attenuated culture (Warner, 2003)," "oppositional contra-cultures" (Anderson, 1999), "subterranean" culture (Matza & Sykes, 1961), and enduring "subcultures" linked to race, class, region, and/or gender (e.g., Wolfgang & Ferracuti, 1967). The notion of attenuated culture encompasses the variable internalization of dominant, conventional cultural standards that accord respect to law-abiding conduct and the pursuit of approved values. When such standards are not taught or are not learned, the odds of the illegal use of force and fraud are increased relative to those who have internalized conventional cultural standards. Oppositional subcultures or contracultures are best illustrated by Anderson's "code of the streets" (1999), which reverses the standards for obtaining honor and respect, according admiration to "being bad" and aggressively defending self-images of "toughness." Such oppositional standards are especially likely to be created and sustained among minority male youth. The concept of subterranean values reflects a conception of shared culture as "layered," with some infracultural standards conflicting with more abstract standards stigmatizing crime. Such conflicts are epitomized in the admiration of entrepreneurs who skirt the law, the endorsement of aggressive responses to insults, and definitions of appropriate "male" behavior and attitudes. Theorists emphasizing such conflicts do not limit such "criminogenic codes" to "the street," but view them as extensions of definitions variably taught and learned in a variety of quite "conventional" contexts. Finally, the original emphasis in Sutherland's theory was on cultural conflict in society as a whole, with some forms of criminal behavior merely attempts to abide by enduring subcultural traditions. This conception was the foundation for the conception of Sutherland's theory as a "cultural deviance" theory. Variations in crime were products of normal learning processes, but the content of that learning differed.

Despite the importance of cultural concepts in all sociological perspectives, including social learning theory, there is very little research relevant to the empirical merits of these disparate views of the manner in which culture affects violence. Criminological research is unequivocal in its empirical delineation of the importance of learned definitions and attitudes in the explanation of crime and violence, but that research does not allow a determination of the validity of these distinct views. Research designed to measure the "code of the streets" includes questions and items thought to capture an oppositional value system and finds embracement of the code is a positive correlate of violence. Whether that code originated in the streets or is an extension of subterranean values that are more pervasive in society is never addressed. Research examining attenuated culture supports the argument that young people who do not embrace dominant cultural values are more likely to break laws, but no attempt is made to simultaneously consider whether oppositional codes are also relevant. In short, it is well established that variation in normative learning is an important source of variation in violent behavior, but the structural and historical foundation and the specific cultural form of those influences are totally undetermined at present.

Another type of research relevant to the validity of social learning theory focuses on the role of imitation, differential reinforcement, normative learning, and differential association as mediating mechanisms explaining variations in violence among categories of people. A powerful theory should be able to make sense of the biggest difference in violence among sociodemographic categories – the gender difference. The gender difference in violence and other forms of delinquency and crime has received considerable attention over the last two decades, and such research has shown that gender itself has no separable impact on self-reported violence when social learning mechanisms are introduced into multivariate analysis. Whether using police measures of offending or self-reports, the gender gap can be explained by variations in general normative learning, gender-based variations in attitudes and self-images, and variations

in interaction and identification with peer groups and parents (Jensen, 2003).

Mass Media and Violence

The most common culprit introduced in media discussions of upward trends or surges in violence is exposure of people, especially children and youth, to the violent content of many forms of mass media. Scholarly input to such discussions is typically solicited from psychologists who have identified several distinct learning mechanisms through which media content could contribute to violent behavior, including imitation, desensitization, normative socialization, and vicarious reinforcement. In fact, the general public is more likely to encounter references to such learning mechanisms in media treatments of violence than from any other source.

Such theoretical notions have garnered some support through research on televised violence and aggression. In 1972, L. D. Eron and his colleagues (Eron, Huesmann, Lefkowitz, & Walder, 1972) claimed to have "demonstrated that there is a probable causative influence of watching violent television programs in early formative years on later aggression" A 3-year research project by the Surgeon General's Scientific Advisory Committee on Television and Social Behavior (1971) concluded that violence on television can induce mimicking in children shortly after exposure and that *under certain circumstances* television violence can lead to an increase in aggressive acts. Another government overview a decade later (Pearl, Bouthilet, & Lazar, 1982) concluded that the studies strongly suggest that viewing violent television programs contributes to aggressive behavior.

Dorr (1986) has reviewed research on the impact of television on children, including panel studies carried out in 1972 and 1982. The 1972 study found a small relationship between mother's reports of third graders' viewing habits and peer ratings of how aggressive a youth was. There was a relationship between violence of a child's favorite show based on mother's report and peer ratings of aggression at subsequent points in time among boys, but not among girls. The 1982 study focused on peer nominations as aggressive, as well as reports of violent behavior and viewing habits, based on both the subject's and the mother's reports of favorite shows. However, when race and socioeconomic status were controlled, they found little or no relationship between exposure to television violence and aggression. Dorr concludes that the studies of television and aggression "suggest that the effects of exposure to television violence are attenuated in everyday life as compared to the laboratory" and that effects on the individual over time "are particularly weak or even nonexistent (1986, p. 78)."

Paik and Comstock (Comstock & Paik, 1991; Paik & Comstock, 1994) reach a somewhat different conclusion in more recent meta-analyses of the effects of television violence on antisocial behavior. They note that findings of small relationships are sufficiently common across several types of studies to conclude that there is a small and statistically significant relationship between television violence and antisocial behavior, but that the relationship is more prominent for aggression toward objects than people and is weakest for actual criminal violence. Felson (1996) reaches a similar conclusion based on a review of available research.

When accorded careful attention, there are serious problems with arguments that attribute either upward trends or surges in violence to violent television content. For one, Americans were as prone to murder on the average when their exposure to media violence was limited to dime novels, comic books, radio, and the movies than after the invention of television. Few people are aware of the fact that the homicide rate was higher in the first half of the 20th century than in the second half. Claims that the upward trend in murder after World War II were products of the spread of television (see Centerwall, 1992) have been challenged by research showing that the relationship disappears when family breakdown and alcohol abuse are taken into account (Jensen, 2001). Such research has supported Suther-

land's original contention that variations in primary group relationships are more consequential for understanding criminal or delinquent behavior than the content of mass media. Social learning theory can be invoked to explain media effects when found, but also implies that relationships with parents, peers, and other people are more consequential for explaining violence than media content.

As noted by the National Academy of Science (Moore, Petrie, Braga, & McLaughlin, 2002), violence can occur in waves, with highly publicized crimes copied by others. The social learning processes reflected in such contagious episodes include imitation and vicarious reinforcement. Not only are techniques used in one instance copied in other instances but the attention accorded the crime can also become part of the motivation for copying it. However, waves of violence can reflect other processes encompassed by social learning theory as well. For example, violence is one means of gaining and maintaining control over illicit markets. Such escalations can reflect disruptions in the organization of markets, leading to competition for control by new groups or competition for control of new products that can be produced and supplied outside of existing markets. Moreover, Blumstein (1995) argues that violence associated with attempts to gain control over illicit drug markets or violence associated with gang conflicts can lead other youths to arm themselves for self-protection. Thus, the proliferation of weapons and the escalation of fear can lead to further escalation of violence.

Of course, a wave or a surge in violence is a product of both an escalation and a de-escalation, and social learning processes apply to both. De-escalation can reflect triumph among contenders, an exhaustion of willing participants, the escalating costs of violent tactics relative to potential gains, and/or increases in law enforcement and communal efforts at control. As Akers proposes, changes in crime can reflect changes in "reinforcement schedules." Contagious crimes occur in short bursts because they are self-exhausting and/or because control agents take preventive action. None of the alternative sociological theories of violence can address such complexities.

Directions for the 21st Century

With a huge variety of tests of the basic social learning model and features of that model, a call for more tests is not likely to excite scholars interested in violent behavior. Rather, the focus in extending research on social learning theory and violent behavior should be on those topics on which little research has been conducted. It is time to return to the integration of sociological and psychological perspectives that was central to the original advocacy of the theory in the 1940s and Akers' reformulation in the 1970s. The key emphasis in the theoretical and empirical development of social learning theory should be on micro–macro transitions and the perplexing complexities involved in linking ideas about social structure and culture to the theory.

Social learning theory incorporates normative learning mechanisms and has been linked in the past to Sutherland's conception of the role of culture in the explanation of crime. However, it is clear that other types of cultural influences seem to fit just as well. A priority in future research should be an assessment of the applicability of the distinct conceptions of culture to the explanation of violence and the development of a micro-macro model that can predict or explain the form of cultural influences.

Akers' attempt to expand social learning theory into a social structure-social learning (SSSL) theory that can explain variations among sociodemographic categories has been quite fruitful and needs to be applied to a fuller range of variations (Akers, 1998; Akers and Jensen, 2003). Social learning theory has been found to explain gender variations quite well, but no comparable attempt has been made to explain racial/ethnic variations. African American youth tend to have high rates of interpersonal violence relative to White youth, but

the specific sources of that variation have received little attention among social learning theorists or researchers testing other theories. It is easy to forget that the most quoted research monograph in criminology in the 20th century was based on White male youth alone (Hirschi, 1969).

In addition to extending the SSSL model, variations in the relative importance and form of learning mechanisms in distinct categories of people need to be explored. For example, it has been demonstrated that the relatively small association of measures of social class or social status with delinquency can reflect "countervailing mechanisms" (Wright, Caspi, Mottitt, Miech, & Silva, 1999). Privilege can help advantaged youth avoid formal sanctions, and family income can facilitate involvement in approved activities that actually provide the freedom and opportunity for crime. At the same time, commitments to long-term goals and other constraints imposed by social advantage can inhibit involvement in crime. Social learning theory encourages not only an examination of potentially countervailing learning mechanisms but also a thorough consideration of the balance of complex contingencies of reward and cost when attempting to explain variations among groups. No other verified theoretical framework in criminology encourages the consideration of as many intricacies as social learning theory.

References

Akers, R. L. (1973). *Deviant behavior: A social learning approach*. Belmont, CA: Wadsworth.

Akers, R. L. (1998). *Social learning and social structure: A general theory of crime and deviance*. Boston: Northeastern University Press.

Akers, R. L., & Jensen, G. F. (2003). *Advances in criminological theory. Vol. 11: Social learning theory and the explanation of crime: A guide for the new century*. New Brunswick, NJ: Transaction Books.

Akers. R. L., Krohn, M., Lanza-Kaduce, L., & Radosevich, M. (1979). Social learning and deviant behavior: A specific test of a general theory. *American Sociological Review, 44,* 636–655.

Akers, R. L., & Sellers, C. S. (2004). *Criminological theories: Introduction, evaluation, and application.* Los Angeles: Roxbury.

Anderson, E. (1999), *Code of the street: Decency, violence, and the moral life of the inner city.* New York: W.W. Norton.

Anderson, N. (1923). *The hobo.* Chicago: University of Chicago Press.

Bandura, A. (1973). *Aggression: Social learning analysis.* Englewood Cliffs, NJ: Prentice-Hall.

Bandura, A., & Walters, R. H. (1959). *Adolescent aggression.* New York: Ronald Press.

Blumstein, A. (1995). Youth violence, guns and the illicit-drug industry. *Journal of Criminal Law and Criminology, 86,* 10–36.

Burgess, R. L., & Akers, R. L. (1966). A differential association-reinforcement theory of criminal behavior. *Social Problems, 14,* 363–383.

Burt, M. R. (1980). Cultural myths and supports for rape. *Journal of Personality and Social Psychology, 38,* 217–230.

Centerwall, B. S. (1992). Television and violence: The scale of the problem and where to go from here. *Journal of the American Medical Association, 267,* 3059–3063.

Comstock, G., & Paik, H. (1991). *Television and the American child.* San Diego: Academic Press.

Cressey, P. G. (1932). *The taxi-dance hall: A sociological study in commercialized recreation and city life.* Chicago: University of Chicago Press.

Dorr, A. (1986). *Television and children.* Beverly Hills, CA: Sage.

Eron, L. D., Huesmann, L. R., Lefkowitz, M. M., & Walder, L. O. (1972). Does television violence cause aggression? *American Psychologist, 27,* 253–263.

Felson, R. B. (1996). Mass media effects on violent behavior. *Annual Review of Sociology, 22,* 103–128.

Gelles, R. J. (1987). *The violent home.* Newbury Park, CA: Sage.

Gordon, R. A., Lahey, B. B., Kawai, E., Loeber, R., Stouthamer-Loeber, M., & Frrington, D. (2004). Anti-social behavior and youth gang membership: Selection and socialization. *Criminology, 42,* 55–87.

Hirschi, T. (1969). *Causes of delinquency.* Berkeley, CA: University of California Press.

Jensen, G. F. (2001). The invention of television as a cause of homicide: The reification of a spu-

rious relationship. *Homicide Studies, 5,* 114–130.

Jensen, G. F. (2003). Gender variations in delinquency: Self-images, beliefs and peers as mediating mechanisms. In R. L. Akers & G. F. Jensen (Eds.), *Social learning and the explanation of crime: New directions for a new century* (pp. 151–177). New Brunswick, NJ: Transaction.

Matza, D., & Sykes, G. M. (1961). Juvenile delinquency and subterranean values. *American Sociological Review, 26,* 712–717.

Meyer, P. (1999, April 22). Believe it: TV violence stalks streets of Littleton – and your town. *USA Today,* p. 15A.

Miller, N. J., & Dollard, J. (1941). *Social learning and imitation.* New Haven: Yale University Press.

Moore, M. H., Petrie, C. V., Braga, A. A., & McLaughlin, B. L. (2002). *Deadly lessons: Understanding lethal school violence.* Washington, DC: National Academies Press.

Paik, H., & Comstock, G. (1994). The effects of television violence on anti-social behavior: A meta-analysis. *Communication Research, 21,* 516–546.

Patterson, G., Bank, L., & Reid, J. B. (1987). Delinquency prevention through training parents in family management. *Behavior-Analyst, 10,* 75–82.

Pearl, D., Bouthilet, L., & Lazar, J. (1982). *Television and behavior.* Rockville, MD: National Institute of Mental Health.

Poppen, P. J., & Segal, N. J. (1988). The influence of sex and sex role orientation on sexual coercion. *Sex Roles, 19,* 689–701.

Sellers, C. S., Cochran, J. K., & Winfree, L. T., Jr. (2003). Social learning and courtship violence: An empirical test. In R. L. Akers & G. F. Jensen (Eds.), *Social learning and the explanation of crime: New directions for a new century* (pp. 109–127). New Brunswick, NJ: Transaction.

Sellers, C. S., Pratt, T. C., Winfree Jr,. L. T., & Cullen, F. T. (2000). *The empirical status of social learning theory: A meta-analysis.* Paper presented at the Annual Meeting of the American Society of Criminology, San Francisco.

Shaw, C. F., Zorbaugh, F., McKay, H. D., & Contrell, L. S. (1929). *Delinquency areas.* Chicago: University of Chicago Press.

Straus M. A., & Donnelly, D. A. (1994). *Beating the devil out of them: Corporal punishment in American families.* New York: Lexington Books.

Sutherland, E. H. (1947). *Principles of criminology*. Philadelphia: J.B. Lippincott.

Surgeon General's Scientific Advisory Committee on Television and Social Behavior. (1971). *Television and growing up: The impact of televised violence*. Washington, DC: National Institute of Mental Health.

Thomas, W. I., & Znaniecki, F. (1927). *The Polish peasant in Europe and America* New York: Alfred A. Knopf.

Thrasher, F. M. (1927). *The gang*. Chicago: University of Chicago Press.

Warner, B. D. (2003). The role of attenuated culture in social disorganization theory. *Criminology, 41*, 73–98.

Warr, M. (2002). *Companions in crime: The social aspects of criminal conduct*. Cambridge, UK: Cambridge University Press.

Wiesner, M., Capaldi, D. M., & Paterson, G. (2003). Development of anti-social behavior and crime across the life-span from a social interactionist perspective: The coercion model. In R. L. Akers & G. F. Jensen (Eds.), *Social learning and the explanation of crime: New directions for a new century* (pp. 317–337). New Brunswick, NJ: Transaction.

Wirth, L. (1928). *The ghetto*. Chicago: University of Chicago Press.

Wolfgang, M., & Ferracuti, F. (1967). *The subculture of violence*. London: Tavistock.

Wright, B. E., Caspi, A., Moffitt, T. E., Miech, R. A., & Silva, P. A., (1999). Reconsidering the relationship between SES and delinquency: Causation but not correlation. *Criminology, 37*, 175–194.

CHAPTER 34

Substance Use and Violent Behavior

Jeff M. Kretschmar and Daniel J. Flannery

Introduction

This chapter provides a general overview of the literature on the association between substance use and aggressive and violent behavior. Understanding this link is important because many types of interpersonal violence, especially domestic violence, often occur when one or both partners are under the influence of alcohol or drugs. For the purposes of this chapter, aggressive and violent behavior are defined as acts of interpersonal violence, which include acts of physical aggression that results in harm toward another person or persons. This is inclusive of such behavior as hitting, fighting, and other acts of aggression in its milder forms and of assault, assault resulting in physical injury, and homicide in its most severe forms. The chapter does not review studies on the relationship between intrapersonal violence and substance use, nor do we focus on other specific types of violence, such as rape or sexual victimization. How-ever, we do focus in the latter part of the chapter on domestic and family violence as a particular form of violence that has been studied quite extensively regarding its association with substance use. When we review the results of a particular study or body of work, we try to retain whatever term was used by the researchers to describe the particular form of aggressive or violent behavior being examined (e.g., aggression, interpersonal violence, assault, violent behavior, homicide, intimate partner violence).

This review begins with a description of substance use prevalence rates, general trends in use, and demographic characteristics of users. We then examine research that specifically addresses the connections between substance use and interpersonal violence, including a focus on intimate partner aggression. We conclude the review by summarizing several of the proposed empirical and theoretical explanations for the relationship between substance use and violent behavior.

Prevalence Rates of Substance Use

Alcohol

According to a 2003 report by the Substance Abuse and Mental Health Services Administration (SAMHSA), 7.6% of Americans aged 12 and older are dependent on or abuse alcohol (SAMHSA, 2003). The highest rate of dependence or abuse occurs among individuals between the ages of 18 and 25 (17.4%). In 2004, 50.3% of Americans over the age of 12 were current drinkers of alcohol, whereas 22.8% of those surveyed admitted to binge drinking (i.e., consuming five or more alcoholic beverages on the same occasion) in the past 30 days. Nearly 7% of Americans reported being heavy drinkers, defined as binge drinking at least five times in the past month (SAMHSA, 2005). Most binge and heavy drinking occurs between the ages of 18 to 25, with a peak at age 21 (SAMHSA, 2005). A consistent finding is that alcohol use decreases with age. In 2004, 69.8% of 21-year-olds reported current alcohol use, in contrast to 35.3% of those 65 and older. Binge and heavy drinking rates also decrease with age (SAMSHA, 2005; Winger, Woods, & Hofmann, 2004).

Despite declines in alcohol use with age, underage drinking continues to be a problem. Results from the 2004 National Survey on Drug Use and Health (NSDUH) indicate that 28.7%, or 10.8 million people between the ages of 12 and 20 reported drinking at least one alcoholic beverage in the prior month. Of people over the age of 12, males (56.9%) were more likely to report past-month alcohol use than females (44.0%). There were also ethnic group differences in use. For example, Whites were more likely to report current alcohol use (55.2%) than Hispanics (40.2%), Asians (37.4%), or African Americans (37.1%). Of the 16.7 million heavy drinkers over 12 years old, 32.2% were also using illicit drugs (SAMHSA, 2005). This finding highlights the importance of studying alcohol; as it often serves as a gateway drug to illicit substance use and abuse.

Marijuana

More Americans use marijuana than any other illicit drug (Gold & Tullis, 1999). In 2004, 14.6 million individuals in the United States aged 12 and older admitted to using marijuana in the past month, whereas 25.5 million Americans reported using marijuana in the past year (SAMHSA, 2005). In the same year, 2.1 million people reported using marijuana for the first time. The average age of first-time users was 18, but the majority (63.8%) of first-time users were younger than age 18. Current marijuana use declined for the third straight year among youth between the ages of 12 and 17, falling from 8.2% in 2002 to 7.9% in 2003 and 7.6% in 2004. Most of the decline appears to be accounted for by a drop in use among young males. For instance, since 2002, past-month marijuana use for males between the ages of 12 and 17 has declined, whereas the rate for females has remained constant. The current marijuana use rate for adults aged 26 and older was 4.1%. Males (8.0%) were nearly twice as likely to report current marijuana use as females (4.3%; SAMHSA, 2005).

Cocaine and Crack

In 2004, there were two million current cocaine users. Of those two million users, 467,000 used crack, which is a form of cocaine base. These numbers were down slightly from 2003, when an estimated 2.3 million persons reported current cocaine use (5.9 million reported the annual use of cocaine), 604,000 of whom used crack. Less than 1% of youth between the ages of 12 and 17 reported using cocaine within the past 30 days (0.5%). For people aged 18 to 25, however, this number increases to 2.1%, but then drops to less than 1% for adults over age 26. In 2004, approximately one million people were first-time cocaine users, and a majority of those people (65.8%) were 18 years of age or older. On average, first-time cocaine users were 20 years old (SAMHSA, 2005).

According to a 2005 report, 3.2% of males and 1.6% of females have used cocaine in the past year (SAMHSA, 2005). Between the ages of 12–17, 1.7% of males and 1.5% of females reported past year cocaine use. The most significant gender difference in past year cocaine use occurs between the ages of 18–25: 8.5% of males report previous year use while 4.7% of females report similar use. This gap once again narrows when examining males and females over 26 years of age, as 2.4% of males and 1.1% of females admit to past year use.

Heroin

The 2004 National Survey on Drug Use and Health (SAMHSA, 2005) reported that 3.1 million Americans over the age of 12 reported lifetime heroin use (used at least once), whereas 166,000 people reported current heroin use, which is an increase over 2003 estimates of 119,000 current users. There were 118,000 first-time heroin users in 2004 with an average age for first-time users of 24.4 years. Results from the 2005 Monitoring the Future study indicate that 1.5% of 8th, 10th, and 12th graders reported lifetime heroin use (Johnston, O'Malley, Bachman, & Schulenberg, 2006).

Amphetamines

MDMA (ECSTASY)
There were a reported 470,000 current Ecstasy users in 2003. That number fell slightly in 2004 to 450,000 (SAMHSA, 2005). However, these figures are both significant decreases from 2002, when 676,000 Americans admitted to current use. According to the 2003 Monitoring the Future survey, ecstasy use by 8th, 10th, and 12th graders decreased by 53% from 2001. Only 1% of 10th and 12th graders and 0.6% of 8th graders reported using Ecstasy in the past 30 days. In 2005, the lifetime use for 8th, 10th, and 12th graders was 2.8%, 4.0%, and 5.4%, respectively (Johnston et al., 2006). There were 607,000 first-time Ecstasy users in 2004, with a first-time user averaging 19.5 years of age.

METHAMPHETAMINES
An estimated 583,000 Americans are current methamphetamine users. For youth between the ages of 12 and 17, annual methamphetamine use fell from 0.9% in 2002 to 0.7% in 2003 (SAMHSA, 2005). There were an estimated 318,000 first-time users of methamphetamines in 2004. The average age of a new user was 22.1 years, compared with 18.9 years in 2002 and 20.4 years in 2003. Although the lifetime use of methamphetamines for youth in 8th, 10th, and 12th grades was 3.1%, 4.1%, and 4.5%, respectively, current use, measured by use in the past 30 days, was 0.7%, 1.1%, and 0.9%, respectively (Johnston et al., 2006).

LSD
According to the 2004 NSDUH, there were 141,000 current LSD users, whereas 23.4 million Americans reported using LSD in their lifetime. The number of first-time LSD users rose slightly from 2003, from 200,000 to 235,000. In 2002, there were 338,000 first-time users. The 2005 Monitoring the Future study reports that the annual use of LSD is below 2% for 8th, 10th, and 12th graders, whereas 30-day rates are less than 1% for each grade.

Substance Use and Violent Behavior

Alcohol

By far the greatest support for a link between substance use and violent behavior involves alcohol. Of course, alcohol does not always produce violence, because the majority of people who drink do not become violent (Pihl, Assaad, & Hoaken, 2003). However, there exists overwhelming evidence that implicates alcohol in the expression of violence. Although rates vary, Murdoch, Pihl, and Ross (1990) estimate that, in over 50% of crimes, assailants have been using alcohol prior to the offense. There is a long history of research on the association among alcohol use, crime, and aggressive or violent behavior. In one early study, Mayfield (1976) examined the connection among alcohol, homicides, and felony assaults in a North Carolina sample. He found that 57% of the offenders and 40% of the victims were drinking at the time of the crime. Pittman and Handy (1964) reported that 31% of assault cases involved alcohol. Although offender-only drinking was present in 21% of the cases, 55% of the cases involved drinking by both the offender and victim.

Several classic studies have examined the alcohol-homicide link. Wolfgang (1958) examined homicides over a 4-year period in Philadelphia. He found that the victim or offender had been drinking alcohol in 64% of the cases and specifically that both had been drinking in 44% of the incidents. Eronen, Hakola, and Tiihonen (1996) investigated 693 homicide offenders in Finland. In their study the majority of offenders were intoxicated during the perpetration of the homicide, and 39% of the offenders met criteria for a diagnosis of alcoholism. Similarly, in a sample of 71 homicide cases, Lindqvist (1986) found that both the offender and the victim were drinking in 44% of the cases. Of this sample, 100% of the homicides resulting from an argument were committed by intoxicated individuals.

Numerous laboratory investigations into the alcohol-violence relationship have also been conducted. Bailey and Taylor (1991) report that, for individuals with aggressive personalities, consumption of alcohol amplifies these aggressive tendencies. Taylor, Schmutte, Leonard, and Cranston (1979) found that intoxicated subjects responded more aggressively to a confederate whom they thought would harm them than did nonintoxicated subjects. Taylor and Sears (1988) found that intoxicated participants were significantly more susceptible to socially pressured aggression than nonintoxicated participants. As a result of the numerous investigations of this nature, several reviews and meta-analyses have been conducted (Bushman, 1997; Bushman & Cooper, 1990; Collins, 1981; Ito, Miller, & Pollock, 1996; Miczek et al., 1994; Parker & Auerhahn, 1998). One finding is consistent across all of these investigations: *alcohol, even in very low doses, increases the likeli-hood that an individual will display aggressive behavior.*

Marijuana

There are conflicting reports on the association between marijuana and violence (see Moore & Stuart, 2005, for a more detailed review). Reiss and Roth (1993) report that marijuana actually reduces violence in both humans and animals. In animals, acute amounts of tetrahydrocannabinol (THC), the main psychoactive ingredient in marijuana, increases submissive behavior and reduces aggressive attacks (Olivier, van Aken, Jaarsma, van Oorschot, Zethof, & Bradford, 1984; Reiss & Roth, 1993; Sieber, 1982). Miczek and colleagues (1994) provide a comprehensive review of the effects of marijuana on many animal species, and the overarching finding is that marijuana is not related to increased animal aggression. However, when marijuana is introduced with other environmental stressors, such as foot shock or sleep deprivation, rodents have shown signs of increased aggression (Miczek et al., 1994). Wei, Loeber and White (2004) found that the relationship between marijuana use and violence was eliminated when controlling for common risk factors, such as race and additional hard drug use. Taylor et al. (1976) found that high doses of THC actually suppressed aggressive behavior in response to provocation. In a follow-up study, Myerscough and Taylor (1985) found that participants in a low-dose THC condition responded more aggressively to provocation than participants in either the moderate- or high- dose groups.

Other research has illustrated a link between marijuana use and increased violence. Controlling for alcohol and cocaine use, an investigation by Harrison and Gfroerer (1992) found that marijuana use was positively related to involvement in property and violent crime. In an examination of drug use and violent behavior in an African American sample, marijuana was found to be positively related to attempted homicide, reckless endangerment, and weapon use (Friedman, Glassman, & Terras,

2001). Dawson (1997) found that, for women, the use of marijuana alone was related to higher rates of fighting than the combined use of marijuana and alcohol. Among men who only used marijuana, fighting behaviors increased only for those men who never became intoxicated. Murphy, O'Farrell, Fals-Stewart, and Feehan (2001) found that, after controlling for other drug use, alcoholic men who perpetrated domestic violence reported greater marijuana use than nonviolent alcoholic men.

Cocaine and Crack

Several research studies have found a link between cocaine use and the perpetration of violence and aggression. Licata, Taylor, Berman, and Cranston (1993) gave participants a placebo, a low dose, or a high dose of orally administered cocaine. Participants who were given the high dose (2 mg/g) behaved more aggressively on a competitive reaction-time task than the placebo group at all provocation levels. Goldstein and Bellucci (1991) found that, for men, the volume of cocaine use was positively associated with a greater probability of being a perpetrator of violence. The authors suggest that this violence may be a function of their living environment and not necessarily related to direct cocaine use. Manschreck and colleagues (1988) examined cocaine users admitted to a hospital in the Bahamas. Results indicated that over half (55%) of the psychotic patients and 36% of the nonpsychotic patients presented with violent behaviors. Other researchers confirm the finding of increased violent behaviors from cocaine users in hospital and treatment facilities (Brody, 1991; Mendoza & Miller, 1992). White and Hansell (1998) concluded that cocaine use was significantly related to later violent behavior in their sample. Dawson (1997) found that cocaine use increased fighting behaviors associated with the use of the drug. Cocaine use has also been shown to be a significant predictor of male-to-female intimate partner violence (Fals-Stewart, Golden, & Schumacher, 2003).

However, not all researchers find support for the cocaine-violence relationship. Collins, Powers, and Craddock (1989) used urinalysis to identify recent cocaine users from a group of newly arrested individuals. They determined that recent cocaine users were actually less likely to have been arrested for a violent crime than nonusers. Using medical chart review, Dhossche (1999) showed that cocaine users were less likely to be violent compared to those who did not use cocaine. Swett (1985) reported that, among inmates admitted to a prison hospital, cocaine users engaged in similar amounts of violent behavior as those who were not cocaine users. In an examination of cocaine users admitted for treatment, Moeller, Dougherty, Rustin et al. (1997) found that only previous violent behavior (unrelated to cocaine use) predicted the current level of violence. Moeller and colleagues submit that the link between cocaine and violence may also be mediated by the presence of an antisocial personality disorder, such that violence occurs under the influence of cocaine only for individuals with antisocial personality disorder. In their study, cocaine users who did not demonstrate antisocial personality disorder were more impulsive, but not more violent than controls (Moeller et al., 2002).

Heroin and Opioids

Virtually no evidence exists to support a link between the use of opioids and violence. Examples of opioids include heroin, morphine, and hydrocodone. Opioids produce altered moods that often resemble euphoria and decreased anxiety (Jaffe & Jaffe, 1999). The vast majority of studies have found that opioids have either no effect or actually decrease aggression in many types of animals, including mice, rats, squirrel monkeys, cats, and fish (Avis & Peeke, 1975; Emley & Hutchinson, 1983; Kinsley & Bridges, 1986; Krstic, Stefanovic-Denic, & Beleslin, 1982; Yen, Katz, & Krop, 1970). And although an experimental investigation by Berman, Taylor, and Marged (1993) did find that participants who had been given morphine behaved more aggressively than controls, other investigations involving humans echo results of animal studies and conclude that opioids do not increase violent behavior (Mirin & Meyer, 1979; Woody, Persky, McLellan, O'Brien, & Arndt, 1983).

Recent reports from the National Drug Intelligence Center (2001, 2002) found that, although heroin users may commit crimes in order to obtain the drug, there was little to no evidence of a heroin-violence connection. Ball (1991) investigated heroin addicts in three Eastern metropolitan cities and concluded that the effects of heroin on *violent* crime were minimal at best. Although there is little evidence to suggest that heroin use increases violent behavior, heroin *withdrawal* has been linked to increases in violence (Gellert & Sparber, 1979; Jaffe & Jaffe, 1999; Kantak & Miczek, 1986, 1988; Roth, 1994).

Amphetamines and Methamphetamines

Amphetamines can cause altered moods, hyperawareness, increased irritability, hallucinations, and psychosis (Kosten & Singha, 1999; Volavka & Tardiff, 1999). Miczek et al., (1994) report that dose and chronicity of exposure are important variables in the amphetamine-violence link. Experimental investigations involving animals have uncovered a possible connection between low doses of amphetamines and increased aggressive behavior (for a thorough review, see Miczek et al., 1994). In humans, Cherek and colleagues (Cherek, Spiga, & Steinberg, 1989; Cherek, Steinberg, Kelly, & Robinson, 1986) found similar results for dosage in that low doses of amphetamines increased aggressive responding, whereas high doses actually decreased aggression toward a confederate. In higher doses, offensive aggression does not increase, whereas defensive reactions may become more aggressive and violent. Initially, repeated exposure to amphetamines increased fighting behavior and other forms of aggression in laboratory mice. Chronic amphetamine use resulted in decreases in these behaviors.

Although amphetamine use can produce psychosis and thus increases in aggressiveness, this relationship is likely mediated by previous mental health conditions (Roth, 1994). In his study of 13 murderers who were heavy amphetamine users, Ellinwood (1971) concluded that amphetamine use created paranoid delusions and/or other emotional reactions that led directly to the perpetration of a homicide. Further, although amphetamine use is associated with psychosis, the prevalence rates of amphetamine users who develop psychosis remain unclear. Several researchers conclude that the key factor in the amphetamine-violence connection is the production of psychosis, which then leads to aggressive behavior (Allen, Safer, & Covi, 1975; Miczek & Tidey, 1989; Moss, Salloum, & Fisher, 1994). Finally, it should be noted that amphetamines have been successful in *reducing* aggression in hyperactive children (Connor & Steingard, 1996).

Family Violence and Substance Use

The National Center for Victims of Crime (NCVD) defines domestic violence as "the willful intimidation, assault, battery, sexual assault or other abusive behavior perpetrated by one family member, household member, or intimate partner against another" (NCVD, 1999). In the United States, estimates of domestic violence incidents range from 960,000 incidents to nearly four million incidents per year (Commonwealth Fund, 1999; Henise, Ellsberg, & Geottemoeller, 1999; National Institute of Justice, 1997). According to a 1998 report released by the Bureau of Justice Statistics (BJS), females were the victims in approximately 85% of all intimate partner violence victimizations (BJS, 1998).

The role of substance abuse in domestic violence incidents has been studied widely, and convergent evidence from most studies indicates that substance use increases the likelihood of an individual becoming a victim of domestic violence (Kantor, 1993; Leonard, 2001; Leonard & Blane, 1992;

Moore & Stuart, 2004; Murphy & O'Farrell, 1994). A 1997 report from the National Institute of Justice (NIJ) summarized data from a study on domestic violence in Memphis, Tennessee. According to family members, 92% of those accused of domestic violence had used either drugs or alcohol earlier that day and 45% of assailants were described as daily alcohol or drug users (National Institute of Justice, 1997).

Leonard and Blane (1992) examined 320 married and co-habitating young men who participated in an alcohol consumption survey. These men completed surveys designed to assess hostility, marital satisfaction, and alcohol dependence and answered two specific questions related to domestic violence. Results indicated that a positive relationship between alcohol and aggression existed even after controlling for the effects of demographics, trait hostility, and marital satisfaction.

Murphy and O'Farrell (1994) examined both aggressive and nonaggressive alcoholic men. Binge drinkers were overrepresented in the aggressive alcoholic group, and men who engaged in partner violence had an earlier onset of problem drinking and a richer family history of alcoholism among male relatives. Kantor (1993) also found support for the link between binge drinking and domestic violence.

O'Leary and Schumacher (2003) examined the association between intimate partner violence (IPV) and alcohol consumption. Using data from the National Family Violence Survey and the National Survey of Families and Households, the researchers confirmed a slight linear trend between alcohol consumption and IPV, with greater alcohol use related to increased risk of IPV, although the effect sizes were modest. In addition to this association, there was also a threshold effect. In this case, a threshold effect refers to the notion that one must consume a certain amount of alcohol before there is a significant risk of IPV. Binge and heavy drinkers seemed to be driving much of the association between alcohol consumption and IPV. The authors conclude that the differences in the pattern of drinking may

be a better indicator of potential IPV than differences in overall alcohol consumption.

Although most investigations of domestic violence focus on male assailants, females also engage in partner abuse. In one study, researchers examined 35 females who were arrested for domestic violence (Stuart, Moore, Ramsey, & Kahler, 2003). The women completed multiple measures of substance abuse and marital aggression. Women were divided into hazardous drinkers (HD) and nonhazardous drinkers (NHD). Nearly half of the study participants were categorized as hazardous drinkers, and over 50% of the sample had partners who were hazardous drinkers. Women categorized as HD reported engaging in more marital aggression and general violence than NHD women. There was little support for a link between HD and victimization, although both groups of women reported high rates of victimization. Although many studies report a positive connection between a woman's drinking and her experiences of domestic violence, some studies fail to find such a connection (Hotaling & Sugarman, 1990; Testa, Livingston, & Leonard, 2003).

Although the effects of alcohol on IPV have been reported widely, less is known about the effects of other substances on domestic violence. In one study examining illicit substance use, Moore and Stuart (2004) found that, even after controlling for the effects of alcohol, men who admitted to using at least one illicit substance engaged in more partner violence than men who reported no illicit drug use. The authors also found that the type of illicit substance use had no effect on the likelihood of partner abuse perpetration. Interestingly, results showed greater illicit substance use not only for perpetrators of partner violence but also for victims of partner violence.

Cocaine use has also been linked to domestic abuse. Chermack, Fuller, and Blow (2000) found that cocaine use was more frequent in individuals who engaged in partner violence than in those who did not. Logan and colleagues (Logan, Walker, Staton, & Leukfeld, 2001) found that, among incarcerated men, a positive relationship existed between cocaine use and the commission of domestic violence. Bennett, Tolman, Rogalski, and Srinivasaraghavan (1994) examined residents in an inpatient substance abuse treatment facility. Cocaine use was found to be positively related to both physical and psychological partner abuse. In a sample of 151 men who had been court ordered to a batterer intervention program, Moore and Stuart (2004) found that nearly 24% had used cocaine in the past year and 10% had used in the past month.

Several researchers have turned their attention to the cocaine-alcohol-violence relationship. A 1997 NIJ report indicated that 67% of a sample of domestic violence perpetrators had used both alcohol and cocaine the day of the assault. The combination of cocaine and alcohol creates a substance called cocaethylene, which intensifies the effects associated with cocaine use and increases the risk for aggression and violence. Hutchinson (2003), in an examination of domestic violence incidents reported to the police, discovered that 36% of the perpetrators had used both alcohol and cocaine in the past 6 months. Of the cocaine users, 40% used cocaine three times a week in the month prior to the domestic violence incident. In a study of 20 domestic violence homicides, 20% of the perpetrators used a combination of alcohol and cocaine (Slade, Daniel, & Heisler, 1991).

Explaining the Connection Between Substance Use and Violent Behavior

There is far greater support for the relationship between alcohol and violent behavior than there is for the relationship between illicit substance use and violent behavior. Therefore, the following section, which highlights some of the possible explanations for these relationships, focuses more on alcohol than other drugs. Although the majority of research supports the connection between alcohol and violence, what is less understood are the mechanisms through which alcohol produces these effects. Below we review

the psychopharmacological effects of alcohol and identify several possible theories that account for the connection between substance use and violent behavior.

Pharmacological Effects of Alcohol

One of the most compelling theories explaining the relationship between alcohol and violence involves the pharmacological effects of alcohol and how these changes can directly produce violent behavior. The precise pharmacological effects of alcohol remain unknown; however much of the research focuses on neurotransmitters, such as gamma-aminobutyric acid (GABA), dopamine, and serotonin (Acquas, 2000; Brown, 1999).

GABA is the primary inhibitory neurotransmitter in the brain, and the effects of alcohol are seen at the GABA receptor. Alcohol alters neural activity by binding GABA to its receptor and allowing an increased amount of chloride ions to enter the post-synaptic neuron, much like barbiturates and benzodiazepines (Winger, Woods, & Hofmann, 2004). This creates increased inhibition and effectively decreases neural activity, which leads to decreased coordination and the typical lethargy that often follow drinking alcohol. However, this effect also hinders the ability of the post-synaptic neuron to create an action potential that can delay or impede a response to a stimulus. For example, low levels of GABA have been implicated in increased aggression (Guillot & Chapouthier, 1996; Miczek, DeBold, Van Erp, & Tornatzky, 1997: Miczek & Fish, 2006). Alcohol is an allosteric modulator of the GABA (subA) receptors and in low doses increases aggressive behavior (Miczek & Fish, 2006). Rouhani et al. (1992, p. 401) report "that alcohol may potentiate shock-induced aggressive responses by decreasing GABA signaling, perhaps through the GABA(subA) receptor."

Alcohol and cocaine are also associated with increases in the accumulation of the neurotransmitter dopamine (also referred to as a neuro-mediator). Unlike

GABA, dopamine is an excitatory neuro-transmitter that can affect emotional reactions and motor functioning (e.g., Flannery, 2006). The release of additional dopamine serves to increase the positive, rewarding feelings that accompany alcohol consumption (Di Chiara, 1997). Monoamine oxidase is responsible for breaking down dopamine, and alcohol has been implicated in interfering with that breakdown. Several researchers have reported on the possible connections between inflated dopamine levels and increased aggression (or suppressed dopamine levels and decreased aggression), specifically in animals (Geyer & Segal, 1974; Hadfield, 1983; Lammers & Van Rossum, 1968; Miczek, 1981). Although the exact connection is far from clear, Miczek, Fish, Almeida, Faccidomo, and DeBold (2004) report that excessive dopamine, specifically in the ventral tegmental area (VTA) of the brain, can be a requirement for increased aggression.

Alcohol and cocaine use also increase the levels of the neurotransmitter serotonin (5-hydroxytryptamine [5-HT]). Serotonin is associated with emotional regulation, impulse control, and motivation (e.g. Flannery, 2006; Lovinger, 1997). Although low levels of alcohol consumption may increase serotonin levels, chronic consumption serves to decrease serotonin levels in the brain (Pihl & LeMarquand, 1998). Lovinger (1999) reviews additional research that connects alcohol abuse and abnormally low serotonin levels. Low levels of serotonin are also widely implicated in the development of depression (Baldessarini, 1996; Caspi et al., 2003; Owens & Nemeroff, 1994). Saudou and colleagues (1994) discovered that mice that were intentionally bred to have low serotonin levels responded more aggressively to provocation than mice with normal serotonin levels. Other researchers have found that low levels of serotonin were also associated with spontaneous aggression in primates (Doudet et al., 1995; Higley et al., 1992; Higley, Suomi, & Linnoila, 1996). Correlational and experimental studies report similar results for humans (see Pihl & LeMarquand, 1998, for a thorough review).

Brain Systems and Alcohol

Pihl and Peterson (1995) contend that people respond differently to the effects of alcohol, and that these differences may be related to various brain systems: "Just as individual variability exists in how alcohol affects these systems, individual differences in these systems also impacts on alcohol's effects, reflecting a bidirectional relationship" (Pihl et al., 2003; pp. 302–303). Pihl et al. (2003) review three possible systems that may produce aggression following alcohol consumption: the cue for reinforcement system, the threat system, and the executive control system. The cue for reinforcement system is associated with impulsivity and excitement and can produce asocial behavior. The system is thought to be mediated by the neurotransmitter dopamine, which is affected by alcohol. Alcohol may also produce its effects by acting on the body's threat system, which interferes with the development and maintenance of inhibitions and disrupts emotional balance. Individuals under the influence of alcohol may be disinhibited and experience a reduced sensitivity to threat: "It is as if situations which would normally produce fear and caution no longer elicit concern when intoxicated" (p. 305). Finally, alcohol may be working on the executive control system, which is responsible for executive cognitive functions (ECF). ECFs are implicated in "the ability to plan, initiate, and maintain or alter some form of goal-directed behavior" (p. 306). ECFs involve the prefrontal cortex, which has also been implicated in aggression (Harmon-Jones & Sigelman, 2001; McAllister & Price, 1987; Peterson, Rothfieisch, Zelazo, & Pihl, 1990; Soderstrom et al., 2000).

Disinhibition Hypothesis

The consumption of alcohol has been associated with a loss of inhibitions and resulting behavior that, under normal circumstances, would not occur (Collins, 1982; Pihl & Peterson, 1993; Taylor & Chermack, 1993; Taylor & Leonard, 1983). One of the most commonly held assumptions is that alcohol consumption leads to disinhibited behavior. Alcohol may interfere with the brain's ability to suppress violent behavior (Bushman, 1997). This explanation is analogous to Pihl et al.'s (2003) "threat system" model of alcohol effects. Alcohol affects the neurotransmitter GABA, which is the brain's main inhibitory neurotransmitter. For sober individuals, when environmental cues produce high levels of anxiety, aggression is often inhibited. Alcohol has anxiety-reducing, or anxiolytic properties, which interfere with an appropriate appraisal of a situation. Because fear is diminished, stressful or anxiety-producing situations become much more tolerable. As a result, aggressive behavior may increase (Hoaken & Stewart, 2003). Parker and Rebhun (1995) refined this theory with their selective disinhibition theory. According to the selective disinhibition theory, alcohol can lead to disinhibition under certain social, psychological, or environmental conditions, which vary depending on the individual. Parker and Auerhahn (1998, p. 301) contend that "the selective nature of alcohol-related homicide is dependent upon the interaction of an impaired rationality and the nature of the social situation."

Inhibition Conflict

Closely related to disinhibition theory are the notions of alcohol myopia and inhibition conflict (Steele & Josephs, 1990; Steele & Southwick, 1985). Alcohol myopia involves a reduction in a person's ability to cognitively process the entirety of a situation and the consequences that may occur from action. In this state, highly salient cues guide action, and more peripheral cues often fail to have the impact they would normally have if the person was not under the influence of alcohol. Inhibition conflict occurs when the strength of the cues that work to cause a response is similar to the strength of the cues working to inhibit such action. If a sober person is provoked by another, the desire to retaliate violently may be tempered by the fear of the consequences associated with such a response. However, if this same person is intoxicated, immediate retaliation is more salient and requires less cognitive processing than understanding and appreciating the situation and the potential costs of the violent behavior. The conflict that the sober person experienced is now reduced or eliminated altogether. Conversely, if there is not a strong conflict between instigatory and inhibitory cues, it is unlikely that alcohol will produce such behavior. If a nonviolent individual is provoked, it is unlikely that this individual, even when intoxicated, will respond violently.

Goldstein's Tripartite Model

According to Goldstein (1985), substance abuse and violence are related in three important ways: psychopharmacologically, economically, and systemically. Psychopharmacological violence describes the effects of the drug itself. Alcohol consumption affects brain neurotransmitters, which in turn have a direct effect on violence. As we have seen, alcohol disrupts the normal flow of such neurotransmitters as serotonin and dopamine. This disruption may play a direct role in the production of violence. Essentially, any substance that disturbs neurotransmitters can potentially lead to violence.

Economic violence is associated with crimes committed in order to secure the substance. For example, an individual may commit an armed robbery in order to obtain money with which to purchase drugs. Because of their highly addictive properties and high costs, Goldstein (1985) reports that economic violence is associated most closely with cocaine and heroin use.

Systemic violence refers to the violence associated with the subculture of substance use and distribution. A drug dealer may use violence as a means to intimidate other dealers from encroaching on his or her territory or to make an example out of a customer who fails to pay a debt incurred from drug use. Because of the illegal nature of these substances, turning to the police for conflict resolution is not an option. Goldstein (1985) submits that simply being involved in the drug business increases the likelihood of becoming a victim or perpetrator of violence.

In support of this model, Goldstein, Brownstein, Ryan, and Belluci (1989) reported that nearly 90% of the drug-related homicides in New York City involved either crack (65%) or cocaine (22%), with the vast majority of these murders categorized as systemic. After a thorough review of the literature, Fagan and Chin (1990) contended that crack dealers were typically more violent and were involved in more serious and violent crimes than dealers of other drugs. The authors add that "factors unique to crack distribution apparently contribute to the increased violence" (Fagan & Chin, 1990, p. 37).

Howell and Decker (1999) examined the connection among youth gangs, drugs, and violence. The authors summarize findings from several studies that connect the rise in cocaine and crack use in the United States during the mid-1980s to increases in gang activity and violent crime. Inciardi (1990) found that the homicide rate in New York City increased 34.4% from 1985 (the year prior to the widespread crack epidemic) to 1988. Homicide rates in Atlanta during that same time period increased 46.7%. However, not all major cities experienced such dramatic increases in homicides.

There are many other explanations for the effects of alcohol on violence that are not covered in detail here. For example, MacAndrews and Edgerton (1969) highlight the importance of cultural expectations concerning the relationship between alcohol and violence. Collins and Messerschmidt (1993) suggest that individual expectancies about appropriate behaviors while intoxicated are equally important in understanding alcohol's differential effects. Coggans and McKellar (1995) suggest that children learn about the connections between alcohol and violence in the home, similar to a social learning model of alcohol and violence. Although theories abound, to date there exists no single theory that fully explains the connection between alcohol and violence.

Another topic not covered here is the growing problem of prescription drug dependence and abuse. According to a recent report, 9.3% of 12th graders used Vicodin without a prescription, whereas 5% used oxycontin (Johnston et al., 2006). Johnston et al., (2006) reports that the most commonly abused classes of drugs are opioids, central nervous system depressants such as anti-anxiety medication, and stimulants, such as attention-deficit hyperactivity disorder drugs. Growing interest in these areas may provide insight into any type of connection between prescription drugs and violent behavior. Further, although we briefly discussed the alcohol-cocaine-violence connection in relation to domestic violence, this chapter does not cover other polydrug use and violence.

Conclusion

The purpose of this chapter was to summarize a growing body of literature surrounding the relationship between substance use and violence. It is clear that alcohol and drug use continue to be a major problem, particularly early-onset use and experimentation with illicit drugs. Although recent empirical evidence has called into question the strength of the relationship between illicit substance use and violent behavior, there exists overwhelming evidence in support of a link between alcohol use and violent behavior.

Future research on the relationship between substance use and violent behavior should provide a more complete understanding of the mechanisms through which this link operates. For example, new breakthroughs in the area of behavior genetics and brain functioning may provide additional support for a direct connection between substance use and violence. Advances in technology (e.g., functional magnetic resonance imaging [MRI], computer-aided tomography [CAT] scans) have allowed researchers to gain a better understanding of brain structure and functioning, particularly how environmental stimuli and stressors affect brain chemistry and function. As this technology evolves, so too should our understanding of processes underlying the link between substance use and violence and how this association may change over time.

Researchers may also find additional support for a sociocultural model, highlighting the issues that drive increased accessibility and use, such as economic or political factors. As we have seen, drugs such as cocaine and heroin have been shown to be related to violence, but for very different reasons and ones that are not always related to the physical or emotional effects of the drug on the individual user.

As long as substance use rates remain high, age of first onset continues to decline, and experimentation with natural and synthetic illicit drugs persist, we need to continue our efforts to understand how substance use and abuse are related to the perpetration of aggression and violence in all its forms, across all contexts and settings.

References

Acquas, E. (2000). Molecular pharmacology and neuroanatomy. In G. Zernig, A. Saria, M. Kurz, & S. S. O'Malley (Eds.), *Handbook of alcoholism*. Boca Raton, FL: CRC Press.

Allen, R. P., Safer, D., & Covi, L. (1975). Effects of psychostimulants on aggression. *Journal of Nervous and Mental Diseases, 160,* 138–145.

Avis, H. H., & Peeke, H. V. S. (1975). Differentiation by morphine of two types of aggressive behavior in the convict cichlid (Cichlasoma nigrofasciatum). *Psychopharmacolgia, 43,* 287–288.

Bailey, A., & Taylor, S. (1991). Effects of alcohol and aggressive disposition on human physical aggression. *Journal of Research on Personality, 25,* 334–342.

Baldessarini, R. J. (1996). Drugs and the treatment of psychiatric disorders: Depression and mania. In J. G. Hardman, L. E. Limbird, P. B. Molinoff, R. W. Ruddon, & A. G. Gilman

(Eds.), *Goodman and Gilman's The pharmacological basis of therapeutics* (9th ed.) (pp. 431–460). New York: McGraw-Hill.

Ball, J. C. (1991). The similarity of crime rates among male heroin addicts in New York City, Philadelphia, Baltimore. *Journal of Drug Issues, 21,* 413–427.

Bennett, L. W., Tolman, R. M., Rogalski, C. J., & Srinivasaraghavan, J. (1994). Domestic abuse by male alcoholic and drug addicts. *Violence and Victims, 9,* 359–367.

Berman, M., Taylor, S., & Marged, B. (1993). Morphine and human aggression. *Addictive Behaviors, 18,* 263–268.

Brody, S. L. (1990). Violence associated with acute cocaine use in patients admitted to a medical emergency department. *National Institute on Drug Abuse Research Monograph Series, 103,* 44–59.

Brown, S. (1999). Neurotransmitters and violence. In K. Tardiff (Ed.), *Medical management of the violent patient: Clinical assessment and therapy* (pp. 59–86). New York; Basel.

Bureau of Justice Statistics (1998). *Violence by intimates: Analysis of data on crimes by current or former spouses, boyfriends, or girlfriends* (U.S. Department of Justice, Office of Justice Programs. NCJ-167273). Washington DC.

Bushman, B. J. (1997). Effects of alcohol on human aggression: Validity of proposed explanations. In D. Fuller, R. Dietrich, & E. Gottheil (Eds.), *Recent developments in alcoholism: Alcohol and violence* (pp. 227–243). New York: Plenum Press.

Bushman, B. J., & Cooper, H. M. (1990). Effects of alcohol on human aggression: An integrative research review. *Psychological Bulletin, 107,* 341–354.

Caspi, A., Sugden, K., Moffitt, T. E., Taylor, A., Craig, I., Harrington, H. L., et al. (2003). Influence of life stress on depression: Moderation by a polymorphism in the 5-HTT gene. *Science, 301,* 386–389.

Cherek, D. R., Spiga, R., & Steinberg, J. L. (1989). Effects of secobarbital on human aggression and non-aggressive responding. *Drug and Alcohol Dependence, 24,* 21–29.

Cherek, D. R., Steinberg, J. L., Kelly, T. H., & Robinson, D. E. (1986). Effects of d-amphetamine on human aggressive behavior. *Psychopharmacology, 88,* 381–386.

Chermack, S. T., Fuller, B. E., & Blow, F. C. (2000). Predictors of expressed partner and non-partner violence among patients in substance abuse treatment. *Drug and Alcohol Dependence, 58*, 43–54.

Coggans, N., & McKellar, S. (1995). *The facts about alcohol, aggression, and adolescence.* London; Cassell.

Collins, J. J. (1981). Alcohol use and criminal behavior: An empirical, theoretical, methodological overview. In J. J. Collins (Ed.), *Drinking and crime: Perspectives on the relationship between alcohol consumption and criminal behavior.* New York: Guilford.

Collins, J. J. (1982). Alcohol careers and criminal careers. In J. J. Collins (Ed.), *Drinking and crime: Perspectives on the relationship between alcohol consumption and criminal behavior.* London: Tavistock.

Collins, J. J., & Messerschmidt, P. M. (1993). Epidemiology of alcohol-related violence. *Alcohol, Health, and Research World, 17*, 93–99.

Collins, J., Powers, L. L., & Craddock, A. (1989). *Recent drug use and violent arrest charges in three cities.* Research Triangle Park, NC: Research Triangle Institute.

Commonwealth Fund. (May 1999). *Health concerns across a woman's lifespan: 1998 survey of women's health.* New York.

Connor, D. F., & Steingard, R. J. (1996). A clinical approach to the pharmacotherapy of aggression in children and adolescents. *Annals of the New York Academy of Sciences, 794*, 290–307.

Dawson, D. A. (1997). Alcohol, drugs, fighting, and suicide attempt/Ideation. *Addiction Research, 5*, 451–473.

Dhossche, D. M. (1999). Aggression and recent substance abuse: Absence of association in psychiatric emergency room patients. *Comprehensive Psychiatry, 40*, 343–346.

Di Chiara, G. (1997). Alcohol and dopamine. *Alcohol Health and Research World, 21*, 108–114.

Doudet, D., Hommer, D., Higley, J. D., Andreason, P. J., Moneman, R., Suomi, S. J., et al. (1995). Cerebral glucose metabolism, CSF 5-HIAA levels, and aggressive behavior in rhesus monkeys. *American Journal of Psychiatry, 152*, 1782–1787.

Ellinwood, E. H. (1971). Assault and homicide associated with amphetamine abuse. *American Journal of Psychiatry, 127*, 1170–1175.

Emley, G. S., & Hutchinson, R. R. (1983). Unique influences of ten drugs upon post-shock biting attack and pre-shock manual recording. *Pharmacology, Biochemistry, and Behavior, 19*, 5–12.

Eronen, M., Hakola, P., & Tiihonen, J. (1996). Mental disorders and homicidal behavior in Finland. *Archives of General Psychiatry, 53*, 497–501.

Fagan, J. A., & Chin, K. L. (1990). Violence as a regulation and social control in the distribution of crack. In M. De la Rosa, E. Y. Lambert, & B. Gropper (Eds.), *Drugs and violence: Causes, correlates, and consequences* (Vol. 103, pp. 8–43). Rockville, MD: National Institute on Drug Abuse.

Fals-Stewart, W., Golden, J., & Schumacher, J. A. (2003). Intimate partner violence and substance abuse: A longitudinal day-to-day examination. *Addictive Behaviors, 28*, 1555–1574.

Flannery, D. F. (2006). *Violence and mental health in everyday life: Prevention and intervention strategies for children and adolescents.* Lanham, MD: AltaMira Press.

Friedman, A. S., Glassman, K., & Terras, A. (2001). Violent behavior as related to use of marijuana and other drugs. *Journal of Addictive Diseases, 20*, 49–72.

Gellert, V. F., & Sparber, S. B. (1979). Effects of morphine withdrawal on food competition hierarchies and fighting behavior in rats. *Psychopharmacology, 60*, 165–172.

Geyer, M. A., & Segal, D. S. (1974). Shock-induced aggression: Opposite effects of intraventricularly infused dopamine and norepinephrine. *Behavioral Biology, 10*, 99–104

Gold, M. S., & Tullis, M. (1999). Cannabis. In M. Galanter & H. D. Kleber (Eds.), *Textbook of substance abuse treatment* (2nd ed.) (pp. 165–181). Washington, DC: American Psychiatric Press.

Goldstein, P. J. (1985). The drugs/violence nexus: A tripartite conceptual framework. *Journal of Drug Issues, 15*, 493–506.

Goldstein, P. J., & Bellucci, P. A. (1991). Volume of cocaine use and violence: A comparison between men and women. *Journal of Drug Issues, 21*, 345–367.

Goldstein, P., Brownstein, H. H., Ryan, P. J., & Belluci, P. A. (1989, Winter). Crack and homicide in New York City 1988: A conceptually based event analysis. *Contemporary Drug Problems*, 651–687.

Guillot, P. V., & Chapouthier, G. (1996). Intermale aggression and dark preference in ten inbred mouse strains. *Behavioural Brain Research, 77*, 211–213.

Hadfield, M. G. (1983). Dopamine: Mesocortical versus nigrostriatal uptake in isolated fighting mice and controls. *Behavioral Brain Research, 7*, 269–281.

Harmon-Jones, E., & Sigelman, J. (2001). State anger and prefrontal brain activity: Evidence that insult-related relative left-prefrontal activation is associated with experienced anger and aggression. *Journal of Personality and Social Psychology, 80,* 797–803.

Harrison, L., & Gfroerer, J. (1992). The intersection of drug use and criminal behavior: Results from the national household survey on drug abuse. *Crime and Delinquency, 38,* 422–443.

Henise, L., Ellsberg, M., & Geottemoeller, M. (1999, December). Ending violence against women. *Population Reports* (Series L #11).

Higley, J. D., Mehlman, P. T., Taub, D. M., Higley, S. B., Suomi, S. J., & Vickers, J. H. (1992). Cerebrospinal fluid monoamine and adrenal correlates of aggression in free-ranging rhesus monkeys. *Archives of General Psychiatry, 49,* 436–441.

Higley, J. D., Suomi, S. J., & Linnoila, M. (1996). A nonhuman primate model of type II excessive alcohol consumption? Part 2. Diminished social competence and excessive aggression correlates with low cerebrospinal fluid 5-hydroxzindoleacetic acid concentrations. *Alcoholism: Clinical and Experimental Research, 20,* 643–650.

Hoaken, P. S., & Stewart, S. H. (2003). Drugs of abuse and the elicitation of human aggressive behavior. *Addictive Behaviors, 28,* 1533–1554.

Hotaling, G. T., & Sugarman, D. B. (1990). An analysis of risk markers in husband to wife violence: The current state of knowledge. *Violence and Victims, 2,* 101–124.

Howell, J. C., & Decker, S. H. 1999. *The youth gangs, drugs, and violence connection* (Bulletin, Youth Gang Series). Washington, DC: U.S. Department of Justice, Office of Juvenile Justice and Delinquency Prevention.

Hutchinson, I. W. (2003). Substance use and abused women's utilization of the police. *Journal of Family Violence, 18,* 93–106.

Inciardi,, J. A. (1990). The crack-violence connection within a population of hardcore adolescent offenders. *National Institute on Drug Abuse Research Monograph Series, 103,* 92–111.

Ito, T. A., Miller, N., & Pollock, V. E. (1996). Alcohol and aggression: A meta-analysis on the moderating effects of inhibitory cues, triggering events, and self-focused attention. *Psychological Bulletin, 120,* 60–82.

Jaffe, H. J., & Jaffe, A. B. (1999). Neurobiology of opiates and opioids. In M. Galanter & H. D. Kleber (Eds.), *Textbook of substance abuse treatment* (2nd ed.) (pp. 11–19). Washington, DC: American Psychiatric Press.

Johnston, L. D., O'Malley, P. M., Bachman, J. G., & Schulenberg, J. E. (2006). *Monitoring the future: National results on adolescent drug use: Overview of key findings, 2005* (NIH Publication No. 06–5882). Bethesda, MD: National Institute on Drug Abuse.

Kantak, K., & Miczek, K. A. (1986). Aggression during morphine withdrawal: Effects of method of withdrawal, fighting experience and social role. *Psychopharmacology, 90,* 451–456.

Kantak, K., & Miczek, K. A. (1988). Social, motor, and automatic signs of morphine withdrawal: Differential sensitivities to catecholaminergic drugs in mice. *Psychopharmacology, 96,* 468–476.

Kantor, G. K. (1993). Refining the brushstrokes in portraits of alcohol and wife assaults. In S. Martin (Ed.), *Alcohol and interpersonal violence: Fostering multidisciplinary perspectives* (pp. 281–290; NIAAA Research Monograph 24). Rockville MD: National Institutes of Health.

Kinsley, C. H., & Bridges, R. S. (1986). Opiate involvement in postpartum aggression in rats. *Pharmacology, Biochemistry, and Behavior, 25,* 1007–1011.

Kosten, T. R., & Singha, A. K. (1999). Stimulants. In M. Galanter & H. D. Kleber (Eds.), *Textbook of substance abuse treatment* (2nd ed., pp. 183–193). Washington, DC: American Psychiatric Press.

Krstic, M., Stefanovic-Denic, K., & Beleslin, D. B. (1982). Effect of morphine and morphine-like drugs on carbachol-induced fighting in cats. *Pharmacology, Biochemistry, and Behavior, 17,* 371–373.

Lammers, A. J. J. C., & Van Rossum, J. (1968). Bizarre social behaviour in rats induced by a combination of a peripheral decarboxylase inhibitor and DOPA. *European Journal of Pharmacology, 5,* 103–106.

Leonard, K. E. (2001). Domestic violence and alcohol: What is known and what do we need to know to encourage environmental interventions? *Journal of Substance Use, 6,* 235–245.

Leonard, K. E., & Blane, H. T. (1992). Alcohol and marital aggression in a national sample of young men. *Journal of Interpersonal Violence, 7,* 19–30.

Licata, A., Taylor, S., Berman, M., & Cranston, J. (1993). Effects of cocaine on human aggression. *Pharmacology, Biochemistry, and Behavior, 45,* 549–552.

Lindqvist, P. (1986). Criminal homicide in northern Sweden 1970–1981: Alcohol intoxication, alcohol abuse, and mental disease. *International Journal of Law and Psychiatry, 8,* 19–37.

Logan, T. K., Walker, R., Staton, M., & Leukfeld, C. (2001). Substance use and intimate violence among incarcerated males. *Journal of Family Violence, 16,* 93–114.

Lovinger, D. M. (1997). Serotonin's role in alcohol's effects on the brain. *Alcohol Health and Research World, 21,* 114–120.

Lovinger, D. M. (1999). The role of serotonin in alcohol's effects on the brain. *Current Separations, 18,* 23–28.

MacAndrew, C., & Edgerton, R. B. (1969). *Drunken comportment: A social explanation.* Chicago: Aldine.

Manschreck, T. C., Laughery, J. A., Weinstein, C. C., Allen, D., Humblestone, B., Neville, M., et al. (1988). Characteristics of freebase cocaine psychosis. *Yale Journal of Biology and Medicine, 61,* 115–122.

Mayfield, D. (1976). Alcoholism, alcohol intoxication, and assaultive behavior. *Diseases of the Nervous System, 37,* 288–291.

McAllister, T., & Price, T. (1987). Aspects of the behavior of psychiatric inpatients with frontal lobe damage: Some implications for diagnosis and treatment. *Comprehensive Psychiatry, 28,* 14–21.

Mendoza, R., & Miller, B. L. (1992). Neuropsychiatric disorders associated with cocaine use. *Hospital and Community Psychiatry, 43,* 677–680.

Miczek, K. A. (1981). Differential antagonism of d-amphetamine effects on motor activity and agnostic behavior in mice. *Neuroscience Abstracts, 7,* 343.

Miczek, K. A., DeBold, J. F., Haney, M., Tidey, J., Vivian, J., & Weerts, E. M. (1994). Alcohol, drugs of abuse, aggression, and violence. In A. J. Reiss & J. A. Roth (Eds.), *Understanding and preventing violence. Vol. 3: Social influences* (pp. 377–468). Washington, DC: National Academy Press.

Miczek, K. A., DeBold, J. F., Van Erp, A. M. M., & Tornatzky, W. (1997). Alcohol, GABAA-benzodiazepine receptor complex, and aggression. In M. Galanter (Ed.), *Alcoholism and violence: Recent developments in alcoholism* (pp. 139–171). New York: Plenum Press.

Miczek, K. A., & Fish, E. W. (2006). Monoamines, GABA, glutamate, and aggression. In R. J. Nelson (Ed.), *Biology of aggression* (pp. 114–149). New York: Oxford University Press.

Miczek, K. A., Fish, E. W., de Almeida, R. M. M., Faccidomo, S., & DeBold, J. F. (2004). Role of alcohol consumption in escalations to violence. *Annals of New York Academy of Sciences, 1036,* 278–289.

Miczek, K. A., & Tidey, J. W. (1989). Amphetamines: Aggressive and social behavior. *NIDA Research Monograph, 94,* 68–100.

Mirin, S. M., & Meyer, R. E. (1979). Psychpathology and mood during heroin use. In R. E. Meyer & S. M. Mirin (Eds.), *The Heroin Stimulus: Implications for a theory of addiction* (pp. 93–118). New York: Plenum Medical Book Company.

Moore, T. M., & Stuart, G. L. (2004). Illicit substance use and intimate partner violence among men in batterers' intervention. *Psychology of Addictive Behaviors, 18,* 385–389.

Moore, T. M., & Stuart, G. L. (2005). A review of the literature on marijuana and interpersonal violence. *Aggression and Violent Behavior, 10,* 171–192.

Moeller, G. F., Dougherty, D. M., Barratt, E. S., Oderinde, V., Mathias, C. W., Harper, R. A., et al. (2002). Increased impulsivity in cocaine dependent subjects independent of antisocial personality disorder and aggression. *Drug and Alcohol Dependence, 68,* 105–111.

Moeller, G. F., Dougherty, D. M., Rustin, T., Swann, A. C., Allen, T. J., Shah, N., et al. (1997). Antisocial personality disorder and aggression in recently abstinent cocaine dependent subjects. *Drug and Alcohol Dependence, 44,* 175–182.

Moss, H. B., Salloum, I. M., & Fisher, B. (1994). Psychoactive substance abuse. In M. Hershen, R. T. Ammerman, & L. A. Sisson (Eds.), *Handbook of aggressive and destructive behavior in psychiatric patients* (pp. 175–201). New York: Plenum Press.

Murdoch, D., Pihl, R. O., & Ross, D. (1990). Alcohol and crimes of violence: Present issues. *International of Journal of the Addictions, 25,* 1065–1081.

Murphy, C. M., & O'Farrell. (1994). Factors associated with marital aggression in male alcoholics. *Journal of Family Psychology, 8,* 321–335.

Murphy, C. M., O'Farrell, T. J., Fals-Stewart, W., & Feehan, M. (2001). Correlates of intimate partner violence among male alcoholic patients. *Journal of Consulting and Clinical Psychology, 69,* 528–540.

Myerscough, R., & Taylor, S. (1985). The effects of marijuana on human physical aggression. *Journal of Personality and Social Psychology, 49,* 1541–1546.

National Center for Victims of Crime. (1999). *Domestic violence.* Washington DC.

National Drug Intelligence Center (2001). *South Carolina Drug Threat Assessment.* Washington, DC: U.S. Department of Justice, Office of Justice Programs.

National Drug Intelligence Center (2002). *Tennessee Drug Threat Assessment.* Washington, DC: U.S. Department of Justice, Office of Justice Programs.

National Institute of Justice (1997). *Drugs, alcohol, and domestic violence in Memphis.* Washington, DC: U.S. Department of Justice, Office of Justice Programs.

National Institute on Drug Abuse. (2004). *Marijuana.* Bethesda, MD: National Institute of Health, U.S. Department of Health and Human Services.

O'Leary, K. D., & Schumacher, J. A. (2003). The association between alcohol use and intimate partner violence: Linear effect, threshold effect, or both? *Addictive Behaviors, 28,* 1575–1585.

Olivier, B., van Aken, H., Jaarsma, I., van Oorschot, R., Zethof, T., & Bradford, D. (1984). Behavioural effects of psychoactive drugs on agonistic behaviour of male territorial rats (resident-intruder model). *Progress in Clinical and Biological Research, 167,* 137–156.

Owens, M. J., & Nemeroff, C. B. (1994). Role of serotonin in the pathophysiology of depression: Focus on the serotonin transporter. *Advances in Clinical Chemistry, 40,* 288–295.

Parker, R. N., & Auerhahn, K. (1998). Alcohol, drugs, and violence. *Annual Review of Sociology, 24,* 291–311.

Parker, R. N., & Rebhun, L. (1995). *Alcohol and homicide: A deadly combination of two American traditions.* Albany, NY: State University Press.

Peterson, J. B., Rothfleisch, J., Zelano, P. D., & Pihl, R. O. (1990). Acute alcohol intoxication and cognitive functioning. *Journal of Studies on Alcohol, 51,* 114–122.

Pihl, R. O., Assaad, J. M., & Hoaken, P. N. S. (2003). The alcohol-aggression relationship and differential sensitivity to alcohol. *Aggressive Behavior, 29,* 302–315.

Pihl, R. O., & Lemarquand, D. (1998). Serotonin and aggression and the alcohol-aggression relationship. *Alcohol and Alcoholism, 33,* 55–65.

Pihl, R. O., & Peterson, J. (1993). Alcohol/drug use and aggressive behavior. In S. Hodgins (Ed.), *Mental disorder and crime* (pp. 263–283). Newbury Park, CA: Sage.

Phil, R. O., & Peterson, J. (1995). Drugs and aggression: Correlations, crime and human manipulative studies and some proposed mechanisms. *Journal of Psychiatry and Neuroscience, 20,* 141–149.

Pittman, D. J., & Handy, W. (1964). Patterns in criminal aggravated assault. *Journal of Criminal Law, Criminology, and Police Science, 55,* 462–470.

Reiss, A. J., & Roth, J. A. (1993). Alcohol, other psychoactive drugs, and violence. In A. J. Reiss & J. A. Roth (Eds.), *Understanding and preventing violence. Volume 3: Social influences* (pp. 182–220). Washington, DC: National Academy Press.

Roth, J. A. (1994, February). *Psychoactive substances and violence.* Washington, DC: National Institute of Justice, Office of Justice Programs.

Rouhani, S., Emmanouilidis, E., Payan, C., Tran, G., Castresana, A., Soulairac, A., et al. (1992). Effects of alcohol dependence on shock-induced fighting: Action of muscimol and homotaurine. *Phamacology, Biochemistry, and Behavior, 41,* 49–51.

Saudou, F., Amara, D. A., Dierich, A. Lemeur, M., Ramboz, S., Segu, L., et al. (1994). Enhanced aggressive behavior in mice lacking 5-HT1B receptor. *Science, 265,* 1875–1878.

Sieber, B. (1982). Influence of hashish extract on the social behavior of encountering male baboons. *Pharmacology Biochemistry and Behavior, 17,* 209–216.

Slade, M., Daniel, L. J., & Heisler, C. J. (1991). Application of forensic toxicology to the problem of domestic violence. *Journal of Forensic Sciences, 36,* 708–713

Soderstrom, H., Tullberg, M., Wikkelso, C., Ekholm, S. & Forsman, A. (2000). Reduced regional cerebral blood flow in non-psychotic violent offenders. *Psychiatry Research, 98,* 29–41.

Steele, C. M., & Josephs, R. A. (1990). Alcohol myopia: Its prized and dangerous effects. *American Psychologist, 45,* 921–933.

Steele, C. M., & Southwick, L. (1985). Alcohol and social behavior I: The psychology of drunken excess. *Journal of Personality and Social Psychology, 48,* 18–34.

Stuart, G. L., Moore, T. M., Ramsey, S. E., & Kahler, C. W. (2003). Relationship of aggression and substance use among women court-referred to domestic violence intervention programs. *Addictive Behaviors, 28,* 1603–1610.

Substance Abuse and Mental Health Services Administration. (2003). *Results from the 2002 national survey on drug use and health: National findings* (Office of Applied Studies, NHSDA Series H-22, DHHS Publication No. SMA 03–3836). Rockville, MD.

Substance Abuse and Mental Health Services Administration. (2005). *Results from the 2004 national survey on drug use and health: National findings* (Office of Applied Studies, NSDUH Series H-28, DHHS Publication No. SMA 05–4062). Rockville, MD.

Swett, C. (1985). History of street drug use: Relationship to diagnosis and violent behavior among admissions to a prison hospital. *Journal of Prison and Jail Health, 5,* 94–101.

Taylor, S. P., & Chermack, S. T. (1993). Alcohol, drugs, and human physical aggression. *Journal of Studies on Alcohol, 11,* 78–88.

Taylor, S. P., & Leonard, K. E. (1983). Alcohol and human physical aggression. In R. G. Geen & E. I. Donnersein (Eds.), *Aggression: Theoretical review. Vol. 2: Issues in research* (pp. 77–101). New York: Academic Press.

Taylor, S. P., Schmutte, G. T., Leonard, K. E., & Cranston, J. W. (1979). The effects of alcohol and extreme provocation on the use of a highly noxious electric shock. *Motivation and Emotion, 3,* 73–81.

Taylor, S. P., & Sears, J. D. (1988). The effects of alcohol and persuasive social pressure on human physical aggression. *Aggressive Behavior, 14,* 237–243.

Taylor, S., Vardaris, R., Rawich, A., Gammon, C., Cranston, J., & Lubetkin, A. I. (1976). The effects of alcohol and delta-9-tetrahydrocannabinol on human physical aggression. *Aggressive Behavior, 2,* 153–161.

Testa, M., Livingston, J. A., & Leonard, K. E. (2003). Women's substance use and experiences of intimate partner violence: A longitudinal investigation among a community sample. *Addictive Behaviors, 28,* 1649–1664.

Volavka, J., & Tardiff, K. (1999). Substance abuse and violence. In K. Tardiff (Ed.), *Medical management of the violent patient: Clinical assessment and therapy* (pp. 153–172). New York: Basel.

Wei, E. H., Loeber, R., & White, H. R. (2004). Teasing apart the developmental associations between alcohol and marijuana use and violence. *Journal of Contemporary Criminal Justice, 20,* 166–183.

White, H. R., & Hansell, S. (1998). Acute and long-term effects of drug use on aggression from adolescence into adulthood. *Journal of Drug Issues, 28,* 837–858.

Winger, G., Woods, J. H., & Hofmann, F. G. (2004). *A handbook on drug and alcohol abuse.* Oxford: Oxford University Press.

Wolfgang, M. E. (1958). *Patterns in criminal homicide.* London: Oxford University Press.

Woody, G. E., Persky, H., McLellan, A. T., O'Brien, C. P., & Arndt, I. (1983). Psychoendocrine correlates of hostility and anxiety in addicts. In E. Gottheil, K. A. Druley, T. E. Skoloda, & H. M. Waxman (Eds.), *Alcohol, drug abuse and aggression.* Springfield, IL: Charles C. Thomas.

Yen, H. C. Y., Katz, M. H., & Krop, S. (1970). Effects of various drugs on 3,4-dihydroxyphenylalanine (*DL*-DOPA)-induced excitation (aggressive behavior) in mice. *Toxicology and Applied Pharmacology, 17,* 597–604.

CHAPTER 35

Poverty/Socioeconomic Status and Exposure to Violence in the Lives of Children and Adolescents

Holly Foster, Jeanne Brooks-Gunn, and Anne Martin

Introduction

Poverty and socioeconomic disadvantages in the neighborhood and family environments are associated with children's behavioral and emotional problems (Brooks-Gunn & Duncan, 1997; Brooks-Gunn, Duncan, & Aber, 1997; Brooks-Gunn, Duncan, Klebanov, & Sealand, 1993; Duncan & Brooks-Gunn, 1997; Duncan, Yeung, Brooks-Gunn, & Smith, 1998; Evans, 2004; Leventhal & Brooks-Gunn, 2000; McLeod & Shanahan, 1993). Poverty and socioeconomic status (SES) are also associated with exposure to violence (ETV) in the lives of children and youth, which in turn has pervasive short- and long-term effects on children's behavior problems and well-being (Buka, Stichick, Birdthistle, & Earls, 2001; Fantuzzo & Mohr, 1999; Hagan & Foster, 2001; Lynch & Cicchetti, 1998; Margolin & Gordis, 2000; Osofsky, 1999; Overstreet, 2000). Although poverty has been systematically reviewed in relation to violent behaviors (e.g., Crutchfield & Wadsworth, 2003), less systematic attention has yet been given to the association between exposure to violence and SES. Even though recent comprehensive reviews of children's exposure to violence include poverty and SES within the literature on the broad range of risk factors for ETV involving individual child, family, and community levels of analysis (e.g., Buka et al., 2001; Garbarino & Bradshaw, 2003), a more systematic review of the causal direction and research implications between poverty/SES and ETV in children's lives has not yet been conducted.

In this chapter we consider the evidence for and research implications of the direction of influence between socioeconomic disadvantage and exposure to violence. We draw on social causation and social selection perspectives on the inverse associations between SES and mental health problems to generate research hypotheses on the connections among SES, exposure to violence, and children's emotional and behavioral problems and well-being over the life course (e.g., Dohrenwend et al., 1992; McLeod & Kaiser, 2004).

Social Causation and Social Selection Perspectives

Social causation and social selection perspectives on the associations between SES and mental health problems involve different causal processes. In general, social causation perspectives hold that observed associations between SES and mental health problems occur because lower SES elevates levels of mental health problems (McLeod & Kaiser, 2004). In addition to this direct effect, theoretical explanations of social causation also posit an indirect effect in which the inverse association between SES and mental health problems is attributed to the "adversity and stress associated with low social statuses" (Dohrenwend et al., 1992, p. 946). Social selection perspectives, in contrast, posit the reverse direction of causality: those with more mental health problems will have more difficulties in school or eventually in employment, which will decrease socioeconomic attainments (McLeod & Kaiser, 2004). In the social selection perspective then, mental health problems lead to lower SES.

Further research indicates that the associations between mental health disorders and educational attainment in the transition to adulthood vary by the type of mental disorder considered (Miech, Caspi, Moffitt, Wright, & Silva, 1999). Using prospective longitudinal data from the Dunedin Multidisciplinary Health and Development study on a birth cohort sample, Miech et al. (1999) found that social causation was better supported as the causal process connecting low SES to the internalizing mental health problems of depression and anxiety. However, social selection processes were better supported for conduct disorder and attention deficit disorder, given that these externalizing problems in adolescence were found to impair educational attainment in the transition to adulthood (Miech et al., 1999). This study also found that social causation processes were further involved in externalizing disorders in that lower early adulthood educational attainments were found to

increase antisocial behaviors at age 21. These results indicate that both selection and causation processes are operative with antisocial behavior problems and SES attainments (Miech et al., 1999).

We elaborate social causation and social selection models of SES and mental health problems by examining the role of violence exposure as a mediating mechanism in the lives of children and youth. Although a comprehensive test of the associations between exposure to violence and SES (and their connections to children's emotional and behavioral problems) would necessarily control for co-variates and examine a range of mediating and moderating effects, we simplify our causal models to three main variables for clarity of discussion in this chapter. These causal models build on social causation and social selection perspectives and are presented in Figure 35.1.

The social causation perspective is presented in Model A of Figure 35.1, and the social selection perspective is presented in Model B. In both models, there is a direct effect hypothesized between SES and child emotional and behavioral problems and an indirect effect hypothesized to work through the mediating variable of exposure to violence. SES in these models may not only refer to the children's family of origin SES but also to early adulthood educational attainments. Children's emotional and behavioral problems may include both continuous and categorical or clinically significant measures of the internalizing problems of depression and anxiety and of externalizing problems, including delinquency and aggression. We operationalize stress exposure in terms of exposure to violence as a pervasive and significant form of stress in the lives of children and youth. We include four types of exposure to violence in our model: parent-to-child maltreatment, exposure to interparental violence on adult intimate partner (IPV) adolescent intimate partner violence, and community victimization and witnessing of violence.

The social causation model involves both direct and indirect effects of SES on mental

A. Social Causation Model

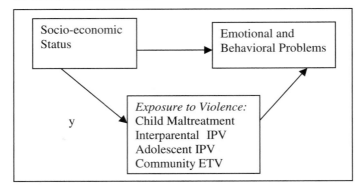

B. Social Selection Model

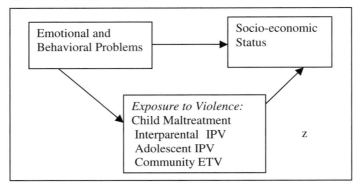

Figure 35.1. Social causation and social selection models of exposure to violence, SES, and children's emotional and behavioral problems. A. Social causation model. B. Social selection model.

health problems. The indirect effect of SES on mental health problems is rooted in social structural perspectives on stress exposure, which hold that those in more disadvantaged social locations should have higher levels of stress exposure and, in our model, exposure to violence (Aneshensel, 1992; McLeod & Kaiser, 2004, p. 637; Mirowsky & Ross, 2003; Pearlin, 1989; Turner, Wheaton, & Lloyd, 1995). Higher levels of violence exposure will in turn increase children's emotional and behavioral problems. The causal pathway from SES to ETV (indexed by path y) is also consistent with ecological perspectives on child maltreatment and social disorganization perspectives on violence in criminology (Garbarino & Sherman, 1980; Sampson, 1997; Sampson, Raudenbush, & Earls, 1997).

In contrast, social selection perspectives involve both direct and indirect effects of emotional and behavioral problems on concurrent or later SES. The direct effect implies that mental health problems in youth and childhood may impair one's own educational levels and occupational attainments as indicators of SES (e.g., McLeod & Kaiser, 2004). An indirect effect from children's emotional and behavioral problems may also work through exposure to violence, as in the model in Panel B. For example, among youth aged 9 to 24, violent offenders have higher mean levels of past-year and lifetime total exposure to violence (including witnessing and victimization) in the community (Selner-O'Hagan, Kindlon, Buka, Raudenbush, & Earls, 1998). There is also precedent for this type of effect in the child maltreatment literature, which has reported that children with developmental disabilities are at greater risk for being victimized (Garbarino & Bradshaw, 2003; Kotch, Muller, & Blakely, 1999), and very young female children with difficult temperaments were found to receive greater maternal harsh discipline, although this finding was not found with male children (Smith & Brooks-Gunn, 1997, p. 783).

The causation and selection models as specified in Figure 35.1 are also consistent with ecological-transactional perspectives on child maltreatment (Lynch & Cicchetti, 1998). Ecological-transactional models draw on ecological perspectives on child development (e.g., Bronfenbrenner, 1986) and differentiate levels of analysis in children's environments, including the "exosystem" involving neighborhood contexts and the "microsystem" involving family contexts. The ecological-transactional model also attends to the individual child and his or her level of "ontogenetic adaptation" or adaptation to the environment. The last component emphasizes the transactional nature of the model, in which individuals are conceptualized as actively shaping environments, and also examines how environments affect children. Neighborhood and family contexts and children's emotional and behavioral problems are seen as mutually influencing one another (Lynch & Cicchetti, 1998, p. 236). A longitudinal test of the transactional model found that substantiated occurrences of child maltreatment (physical abuse, sexual abuse, physical neglect, and emotional maltreatment) increased children's externalizing problems, a finding consistent with social causation premises. Conversely, children with higher externalizing behavior problems at time 1 were found to have higher levels of witnessing violence and becoming victimized by violence in the community one year later (time 2), which is consistent with social selection premises (Lynch & Cicchetti, 1998). These exposures to violence may in turn decrease SES in later life as indicated in path z of Figure 35.1B, and serve to worsen social inequalities over the life course (Macmillan, 2001).

In this chapter, however, we focus less on the overall social selection model and instead specifically examine the evidence for and implications of path z in Figure 35.1B, or the causal chain from violence exposure in the lives of children and youth and their current and subsequent personal or familial socioeconomic attainments. The indirect effect then posits that children's emotional and behavior problems, including delinquency for example, may lead to more involvement in contexts in which they are more exposed to violence, including witnessing and victimization. Higher levels of ETV in turn decrease youth income and educational outcomes in early adulthood (Macmillan, 2001; Macmillan & Hagan, 2004). Although research has shown that direct victimization reduces SES, little research has been conducted on witnessing ETV and children's immediate and long-term socioeconomic circumstances.

When viewed from an ecological-transactional perspective on individual development over the life course, the social causation and social selection models are not necessarily incompatible. For example, early childhood socioeconomic family status may affect children's exposure to violence, which in turn affects their externalizing mental health problems, and those mental health problems may impair subsequent educational attainments. It is likely that both social causation and social selection processes are at work over the life course, during which different processes may be at work at different stages (McLeod & Kaiser, 2004; Miech et al., 1999).

In the following sections, we detail national estimates of exposure to the four main types of violence in the lives of children and youth: witnessing interparental violence, parent-to-child maltreatment, adolescent intimate partner violence, and community violence exposure. We then detail the range of indices available to measure family and community SES. In four subsequent sections, we consider the evidence in extant research on the associations between family and neighborhood SES and each of the four types ETV, as expressed in paths y and z of Figure 35.1. These models generate different hypotheses depending on the type of violence considered. Future empirical tests of the research hypotheses generated from our review will advance research on the connections among violence exposure, social inequality, and children's well-being over the life course and may inform avenues for prevention and intervention.

Estimates of Children's Exposure to Violence

The Developmental Victimization Survey (DVS) is a recent national study obtained through random digit dialing and includes children (aged 2–17) and their parents (Finkelhor, Ormrod, Turner, & Hamby, 2005). This study provides 1-year incidence estimates of rates of exposure to violence among children, including child maltreatment, witnessing domestic violence, broader victimization, and witnessing or indirect victimization in the community (Finkelhor et al., 2005). According to this study, more than half or approximately 530/1,000 youth in the United States experienced a physical assault, which includes 12 forms of assaults against the child perpetrated by siblings, multiple perpetrators, or any assault against the person with or without a weapon, and with or without injury. This definition of physical assault excludes bullying or teasing during the year of the study. Included in this estimate are assaults from dating partners, with or without injury, estimated at a rate of 19/1,000 or 1 in 53 youth. Child maltreatment (including physical, sexual, and emotional abuse and neglect) was experienced by 1 in 7 children nationally or 138/1000. One third of the national sample or 357/1,000 children in the United States had witnessed the victimization of another person or had indirect exposure to violence. Included in this estimate are children who witnessed domestic violence, estimated at 35/1,000 children or 1 in 29 (Finkelhor et al., 2005).

Estimates of parent-to-child physical aggression (PCPA) from the Project for Human Development in Chicago Neighborhoods (PHDCN) data yield comparable estimates to national child maltreatment data. Approximately 69.9% of children aged 3 to 15 had experienced minor PCPA, which includes being slapped/spanked or pushed/grabbed/shoved, or having had their parent throw something at them); 32% had experienced severe PCPA (includes hit/tried to hit with object, beaten up, kicked/bit/hit with fist, or burned/scalded); and 5.5% had experienced very severe PCPA (same as severe PCPA, but excludes hit/ tried to hit with object Molnar, Buka, Brennan, Holton, & Earls, 2003, p. 90). Analyses of a sample of youth from the PHDCN (aged 9 to 24) also indicated that considerable percentages of youth witness and are victimized by community violence (Selner-O'Hagan et al., 1998, p. 218). Finally, analyses of the National Longitudinal Study of Adolescent Health provide estimates of adolescent intimate partner violence. About 20% of heterosexual youth (aged 12 to 21) experienced psychological violence, whereas 12% experienced physical violence or physical and psychological violence (Halpern, Oslak, Young, Martin, & Kupper, 2001). About a quarter (24.3%) of homosexual youth in this study experienced some form of intimate partner violence, with 17% experiencing psychological abuse and 15% experiencing physical violence or physical and psychological violence (Halpern, Young, Waller, Martin, & Kupper, 2004, p. 128).

Measurement of SES/Poverty

Measures of socioeconomic disadvantages in children's lives range from those of separate dimensions of resource deprivation, including total family or household income, parental education, parental unemployment, and welfare receipt, up to composite indices involving education, occupational prestige, and income. Income-based measures range from continuous dollar amounts through indicators of poverty status and income-to-needs ratios. Family poverty status is measured using poverty thresholds that take household size into account and are adjusted each year for cost of living using the consumer price index. Categorical measures of poverty status for any given year may be derived from use of the poverty thresholds, in which families with incomes above the threshold are considered "not poor," whereas those below the threshold are considered "poor" (Brooks-Gunn, Duncan, & Maritato, 1997, p. 3).

Income-to-needs or income-to-poverty ratios are size-adjusted measures of family income that are obtained by dividing total household income by the official U.S. poverty threshold corresponding to the size of the given household (Duncan et al., 1998, p. 412; U.S. Census Bureau, 2005). Income-to-needs ratios may also be used to form categorical measures distinguishing among income groups. More finely grained distinctions are possible through this form of measurement in which, for example, ratios of less than 1 may be used to distinguish those living in poverty (income-to-needs ratios of 0.5 to 1.0) from those in deep poverty (income-to-needs ratios of 0.5 or less). Income-to-needs ratios greater than 1 may be used to distinguish among those living in near poverty (income-to-needs ratios of 1.0 to 1.5), low income (income-to-needs ratios of 1.5 to 2.0), middle income (income-to-needs ratios of 2.0 to 3.0), as well as in affluent families (income-to-needs ratios of 3.0 or higher; (Brooks-Gunn, Duncan, & Rebello Britto, 1999). Measures involving income have also been used to capture dynamics in family economic status over time (e.g., Duncan & Moscow, 1997). These measures include information on poverty dynamics gained by examining children's duration of exposure, distinguishing children living in persistent poverty conditions from those experiencing transitory poverty (McLeod & Shanahan, 1993), and the timing of exposure to poverty in the child's life (Duncan et al., 1998).

An inclusive definition of SES measures includes those indexing the "relative position of an individual or family on a hierarchical social structure, based on their access to or control over wealth, prestige, and power" (Willms, 2002, p. 71). Other measures of SES status use composite indices involving occupational prestige scales, parental educa-

tion, and household income (e.g., Hauser & Warren, 1997). Some of the research on children's exposure to violence uses the Hollingshead two-factor index, a composite measure of SES based on education and occupation of parents (e.g., Dodge, Pettit, & Bates, 1994; O'Keefe & Sela-Amit, 1997). Other definitions of relative SES in the ETV literature involve the relative standing of partners in couples. Research on adult intimate partner violence in particular shows that the *relative* levels of SES within couples are also influential. Relative measures are used in this context to measure power differentials reflected in relative socioeconomic positions of partners that may threaten traditional gender roles and elevate the risk of this type of ETV.

Finally, measures of SES status have also been formed for neighborhood contexts, consistent with ecological perspectives on child development (Bronfenbrenner, 1986; Earls & Carlson, 2001; Garbarino, 1977; Leventhal & Brooks-Gunn, 2000). Neighborhood-level measures of SES of geographical areas include continuous factor-analyzed scores based on census data, as well as categorical indices classifying neighborhoods as poor (e.g., the proportion of families in a census tract with incomes under $10,000 or another meaningful level) and affluent (the fraction of families in a census tract with incomes over $30,000 or another meaningful level; Brooks-Gunn et al., 1993; Duncan & Aber, 1997). A measure of neighborhood concentrated disadvantage may also be formed by taking neighborhood poverty into account, along with other geographic factors highly associated with neighborhood poverty. For example, a scale of neighborhood concentrated disadvantage was formed from 1990 Census data and was used in analyses with the Project for Human Development in Chicago neighborhoods study involving poverty, public assistance, percent of female-headed families, percent unemployed, the density of children (younger than 18), and the percentage of Black residents (Sampson et al., 1997). Research on children's ETV, including parent-to-child maltreatment, has also incorporated concentrated disadvantage at the neighborhood level into analyses (Molnar et al., 2003). Even broader macro-level economic indicators may also be included in research on ETV, as in a recent study examining the influence of welfare reform policies on child maltreatment (Paxson & Waldfogel, 2003).

SES/Poverty and Exposure to Violence Associations

In this section, we review the evidence for associations between SES and four major forms of violence in the lives of children and youth: parent-to-child maltreatment, interparental or adult intimate partner violence, adolescent intimate partner violence, and witnessing of and/or victimization by violence in the community. We conclude each subsection with recommendations for future research in the form of hypotheses suggested by the social causation and social selection perspectives for the observed associations.

Parent-to-Child Maltreatment

Reviews of poverty and child maltreatment as measured by official data tend to indicate a consistent positive association between these two variables (Gelles, 1992). However, more disadvantaged families may be monitored more easily by social control agents, for example, through contacts with public agencies. Labeling biases are therefore likely in associations found between poverty and child abuse in official data (Gelles, 1992, p. 258). Self-reported survey data also indicate associations between family and community economic disadvantages and child maltreatment, in which the consistency of the pattern depends on the measurement of child maltreatment used and several other modifiers considered below.

FAMILY SES/POVERTY
Economic deprivation indicated by income-based poverty measures is associated with various indicators of child maltreatment in survey data. Studies of harsh parenting practices clarify these associations with poverty.

Although family poverty is associated with harsher parenting as measured by the number of times the parent spanked the child (4 to 8 years of age), these effects are further distinguished by the duration of poverty exposure (McLeod & Shanahan, 1993). Persistent poverty over time is negatively associated with the number of times the child was spanked, whereas an indicator of the family being currently poor was positively associated with the number of times spanked. These findings indicate that parenting is taxed by *recent* poverty in particular (McLeod & Shanahan, 1993). Second, an analyses of the antecedents of physical punishment in a sample of low-birthweight infants found that household income effects on very young children (age 3) differed by the child's gender (Smith & Brooks-Gunn, 1997). Males in poor and near poor households were more likely than those in affluent families to be at an elevated risk for maternal hitting and maternal self-reported use of more than one physical punishment per week. In contrast, female children in all household income levels were not at an elevated risk of harsh maternal punishment (Smith & Brooks-Gunn, 1997).

Another set of studies found associations between a range of child maltreatment outcomes and family poverty and socioeconomic disadvantages. Comparisons of the percent of youth ever victimized across five types of violence in a national survey of 2,000 10- to 16-year-olds in the United States finds that two of these types of violence varied significantly with family income levels (Finkelhor & Dziuba-Leatherman, 1994, p. 417). A higher percentage of victimized youth were found among families with very low incomes (<20K) compared to those in households with incomes above this amount for both family assault and genital violence. The family assault item includes perpetration by siblings and/or caregivers, and the genital violence item includes any occurrence. These findings therefore indicate a variation in family assault against children by SES, but it is not clear whether the patterns specifically pertain to violence by parents as perpetrators against their children or to violence from another source instead (e.g., siblings or related adults).

A more recent national study by Finkelhor and colleagues (2005) of children aged 2 to 17 years of age further examined a broad range of violence exposures in association with household income and race/ethnicity. Physical abuse, sexual assault by a known adult, and child neglect were *not* associated with household income in this study. However, youth in families with incomes of $20,000 or lower had higher rates of psychological and emotional abuse than did youth in families with higher incomes (Finkelhor et al., 2005). A national study of 12- to 17-year-olds shows more complex patterning of SES with different forms of violence exposure, contingent on race/ethnicity (Crouch, Hanson, Saunders, Kilpatrick, & Resnick, 2000). The lifetime prevalence of physically abusive punishment by a parent or someone in charge of the child was found to have an inverse relationship by household income for White youth, but not for African American or Hispanic youth (Crouch et al., 2000, p. 633).

Another group of studies focus on child maltreatment specifically, rather than a range of violence exposures. Two of these studies use national survey data, conducted in 1979 and 1985, respectively, finding that families with poverty-level income or below reported higher percentages of *severe and very severe* physical violence (measured by the Conflict Tactics Scales or CTS [Straus, 1979]) against children than did families with higher incomes (Gelles, 1992, p. 264). The poverty-child maltreatment association varied by the type of violence (severe vs. overall) and was stronger among younger children, those living with younger parents, and in single-parent families (Gelles, 1992).

Further research shows consistency in poverty-maltreatment associations when the severity of violence is considered. For example, maternal education ranks among the strongest risk factors for infant homicide: less than or equal to 11 years of maternal education increases the relative risk of infant homicide (during the first year of life) by eight times in the United States (Overpeck, Brenner, Trumble, Trifiletti, & Berendes, 1998). In bivariate analyses, higher levels of maternal education are also protective against inflicted traumatic brain injury in children during the first 2 years of life (Keenan et al., 2003). Results from a large cohort study of infants born in 1996 in Florida found that higher risks of substantiated cases of infant maltreatment (age 0 to 3 years) were associated with lower maternal education (Wu et al., 2004). In sum, greater levels of socioeconomic disadvantage are associated with higher levels of child maltreatment, both in self-report data and official data. However, this association varies by the type of maltreatment considered and is modified by the age and gender of children, among other factors.

NEIGHBORHOOD SES/POVERTY

Although family economic disadvantages are associated with child maltreatment, fewer studies have examined neighborhood SES. A recent article links low neighborhood SES to situations conducive to children's firearms injuries and deaths through risky firearms storage practices in the household (e.g., keeping the gun loaded; Vacha & McLaughlin, 2004). Criminological research indicates that the presence of firearms increases the likelihood of a crime being completed (Wintemute, 2000, p. 47). Therefore the situational factor of the accessibility of firearms in lower income communities may also increase the potential *lethality* to children of exposure to violence in and beyond the household.

Two recent multileveled studies are consistent with ecological perspectives on child maltreatment in linking neighborhood SES to child maltreatment more directly. One of these studies examined the child maltreatment potential of caregivers with a child under age 18 in the home, which is a measure of risk for maltreatment, rather than actual acts of maltreatment. This study found that 5% of the variance in this outcome was attributable to between-neighborhood variation, whereas 2% of the variance in actual physical abuse was due to between-neighborhood variance (Coulton, Korbin, &

Su, 1999). Molnar et al. (2003) also partitioned the variance in parent-to-child physical aggression (PCPA; as measured by the CTS) reported at Wave 1 of the Project for Human Development in Chicago Neighborhoods and similarly found that 2% of the variance in PCPA was due to between-neighborhood variation. These findings concur with ecological perspectives by indicating that neighborhood-level factors are associated with child maltreatment.

More detailed analyses of neighborhood effects on child maltreatment specify how neighborhoods affect children's PCPA. Hierarchical linear models indicate that concentrated neighborhood disadvantage increases PCPA, net of children's age and gender (Molnar et al., 2003). This association is fully mediated when family factors are added to the model. Net of individual and neighborhood characteristics, robust effects are found for higher family SES on decreasing PCPA, whereas parental unemployment increases PCPA (Molnar et al., 2003).

Another multileveled study found cross-level interactions between family risk and protective factors and neighborhood characteristics. The study showed that violence in the family of origin was a weaker predictor of child maltreatment in more impoverished areas and that parental educational attainment was only protective against child maltreatment under neighborhood conditions of low child care burden (Coulton et al., 1999). Although only marginally significant, these findings are nonetheless suggestive of future research directions addressing how family and neighborhood factors combine to affect child maltreatment and children's exposure to violence more generally (e.g., Sheidow, Gorman-Smith, Tolan, & Henry, 2001).

The findings on child maltreatment tend to be consistent with social causation perspectives, indicated by path y in Model A of Figure 35.1, by which low SES in the family and communities leads to financial strains, and elevate more severe forms of child maltreatment, which in turn elevates children's behavior problems. A social selection perspective as outlined in path z of Model B of Figure 35.1 implies that youth experiencing

maltreatment in the home will be less able to engage in school-related activities, leading to the child's lowered socioeconomic attainments in later life. It is less likely that parent-child maltreatment would affect household SES in children's immediate circumstances. These paths may also be intertwined over the life course by which early social causation then leads to long-term disadvantages in the labor market as per the social selection model.

Children's Exposure to Adult Intimate Partner Violence

Children's witnessing of or indirect exposure to adult-to-adult physical partner violence includes viewing and hearing it, as well as experiencing the aftermath of violence (Edleson, 1999, p. 844). Other definitions include emotional and sexual forms of interadult abuse in the home (Fantuzzo & Mohr, 1999), and sometimes they include children's direct involvement in violent incidents (Edleson, 1999, p. 844). In this section, we draw on research on risk factors for adult intimate partner violence more generally. The likelihood of children's violence exposure increases with partner violence in the home, given the overlap among forms of violence and empirical linkages found among marital aggression and child abuse potential and its actual occurrence (Dong et al., 2004; Finkelhor & Dziuba-Leatherman, 1994; Margolin & Gordis, 2003).

FAMILY SES/POVERTY
Several studies indicate an inverse association between family SES and children's witnessing of violence among adults in the household. Results from a national survey of children (aged 2 to 17 years) and their parents indicated that children in households with lower levels of household income (<$20,000) have higher rates of witnessing domestic violence than do children living in families with higher incomes (Finkelhor et al., 2005, p. 16). The rate among children in lower income families is estimated at 109/1,000 children; this rate is significantly different from the rate in middle-income

families ($20,000 to $50,000), which is estimated at a rate of 32/1,000 children, and the rate in high-income families (>$50,000) with 20/1,000 children exposed to domestic violence. A study of young children (preschoolers to grade 3) also found that low SES, as measured by the Hollingshead index, is associated with higher exposure to violence, including parental dyad violence (Dodge et al., 1994). These findings are consistent with results from a longitudinal study of a cohort of children in New Zealand using information gathered retrospectively at age 18 on respondents' childhood exposure to interparental violence, as measured by the Conflict Tactics Scales (Fergusson & Horwood, 1998). The latter study found that low SES was consistently associated with higher levels of exposure to interparental violence across four measures of family socioeconomic background: maternal educational qualifications at birth, family living standards from ages 0 to 10, family income from ages 0 to 10, and an SES index based on occupation (Fergusson & Horwood, 1998, p. 149).

The inverse pattern of associations found in surveys is consistent with the results of a study using substantiated cases of adult female abuse from the Spousal Assault Replication Program (SARP). This data set includes information from five U.S. cities on misdemeanor domestic violence cases, including such details as who was present in the home at the time of the incident (Fantuzzo, Boruch, Beriama, Atkins, & Marcus, 1997). Analyses comparing the characteristics of these households to city census data in each of the research sites found that poverty and low education were more likely to be present in homes where domestic violence occurred, although these data are indeterminate of whether children themselves were exposed to the violence reported in the household (Fantuzzo & Mohr, 1999).

Literature on adult intimate partner violence more generally finds that, although intimate partner violence (IPV) occurs in all social classes, evidence consistently indicates an association between low SES and higher IPV exposure (Cunradi, Cateano, &

Schafer, 2002, p. 378; Rennison & Planty, 2003; Van Wyck, Benson, Fox, & DeMaris, 2003, pp. 417–418). For example, results from a national study of physical domestic violence by adult males and females in married or co-habiting households showed that controlling for race/ethnicity, family poverty was a risk factor (Benson, Fox, DeMaris, & Van Wyck, 2000, p. 103). Similarly, when controlling for race/ethnicity, the inverse SES-IPV association was also found using a measure of family income in the National Crime Victimization Survey data (Rennison & Planty, 2003). Furthermore, analyses of a national sample of married and cohabiting couples found that annual household income was associated more strongly with IPV, as measured by the Conflict Tactics Scales, than were other indicators of SES, including unemployment and education (Cunradi et al., 2002). In analyses of a national sample family income was also consistently associated with the cessation of wife assaults, indexed by the CTS (Aldarondo & Kaufman Kantor, 1997). Finally, a large national study examined bivariate predictors of both minor and severe domestic violence among co-habiting and married respondents, also using the Conflict Tactics Scales, and further provided support for the pattern that lower income and low education elevate both types of exposure (Kessler, Molnar, Feurer, & Appelbaum, 2001). However, the patterns in the latter study vary by the gender of the reporter and tend to be stronger for female reports of either female victimization or male victimization, whereas SES effects were not found for male reports of female victimization of minor violence. The authors note that the differing patterns of association by gender may be related to a differential willingness to admit exposure to violence, rather than actual differences in these associations (Kessler et al., 2001, p. 500).

The inverse SES-IPV association is also found in the results of studies of pregnant samples of women. One of these studies uses the Pregnancy Risk Assessment Monitoring System in North Carolina (NC-PRAMS) data, which is a population-based survey of women who have recently given birth, as indicated by the state's birth certificate files (Martin, Mackie, Kupper, Buescher, & Moracco, 2001). This study found that poverty status and an education level of less than high school graduation significantly differentiated the risk of any physical abuse of women occurring 12 months before pregnancy, during pregnancy, or after delivery, compared to those with no experience of abuse in any of these three periods (Martin et al., 2001, p. 1582). Another study draws on data from the Pregnancy Risk Assessment Monitoring System in South Carolina (SC-PRAMS), again based on state birth certificates, and found that income-based poverty but not education level was associated with higher risks of physical intimate partner violence (Cokkinides & Coker, 1998).

BETWEEN-PARTNER RELATIVE SES

The set of studies reviewed in this section highlight the contributions of relative partner SES in the etiology of adult intimate partner violence, as detailed in status inconsistency or incompatibility perspectives. These studies examine potential power differences between adult partners in the home that occur when women have more economic status in the household than men, potentially threatening their masculinity and traditional gender role norms. Violence and abuse toward women may be a means by which males reassert control in these circumstances (Johnson, 1995). This perspective has social policy implications for the prevention of children's exposure to interadult violence in the home by drawing attention to the role of relative spousal SES as a risk factor in addition to absolute family socioeconomic disadvantages.

Empirical evidence in support of the influence of relative spousal differences in SES on IPV has been found across Canadian, American, and Chinese studies. Results from a large national sample of women 18 years of age and older in Canada found that the SES-IPV association (using an adapted version of the Conflict Tactics Scales) was contingent on the SES of the women's partner. The results indicated that female employment

increases her risks of IPV, but only when her male partner is unemployed. When both the female and her spouse are employed, her risk for severe "systematic" physical abuse decreased (Macmillan & Gartner, 1999, p. 955). A recent study of a different Canadian sample of over 25,000 men and women also found support for the relative socioeconomic positions of partners in the etiology of IPV as measured by the Conflict Tactics Scales (Kaukinen, 2004). This study found that educational differences favoring women rather than relative partner employment status increased the risk of physical violence against women. This study furthers extended the status incompatibility perspective to emotional abuse. SES disparities in couples favoring women in terms of higher education, personal income, and relative employment status (where the woman was employed and her partner was unemployed) were associated with higher probabilities of male-to-female partner emotional abuse (Kaukinen, 2004, pp. 464–465).

These relative spousal SES differences involved in IPV are also found in studies in the United States. A longitudinal study tracked women at three intervals during pregnancy and then 6 months after giving birth. This study found in multivariate analyses that higher levels of women's education were associated strongly with an increased risk of moderate or severe partner-perpetrated violence (Gielen, O'Campo, Faden, Kass, & Xue, 1994, p. 785). This finding regarding women's higher education as a risk factor was also supported in a second analyses of these data incorporating neighborhood disadvantage, but it was less statistically significant in the second study (O'Campo et al., 1995, p. 1095). Another American study examined female-to-male partner violence (FMPV) and found contingencies by race/ethnicity in which the risk of FMPV was elevated by male unemployment among Whites, but not among Blacks or Hispanics (Cunradi, Caetano, Clark, & Schafer, 2000).

Further support for the status inconsistency perspective was found in a recent study of 600 women randomly selected from an outpatient gynecological clinic in China (Xu et al., 2005). This study found that spousal educational differences favoring the respondent compared to her spouse were associated with higher lifetime levels of intimate partner physical and sexual abuse (p. 81). However, these results were not replicated across SES indicators in this study, with no significant associations found for relative spousal measures of income or job status. In multivariate analyses, the same study found evidence that spousal economic control (e.g., partner refuses to give respondent money) elevates the risk of lifetime IPV occurrence by an odds ratio of 5 times (Xu et al., 2005, p. 83).

Consistent with social causation perspectives, these findings emphasize the importance of economic circumstances as risks for IPV exposure. Studies of adult partners consistently find inverse associations between low family income and IPV. Studies of adult intimate partner violence also find that relative SES differences between partners in education levels and employment status were influential. Although some research supports absolute deprivation as a risk factor, additional research points to the importance of examining role strains (i.e., status incompatibility) in families in the etiology of IPV and possibly for children's exposure to violence. A social selection hypothesis generated from these results concerns the pathway from intimate partner violence in the household to household SES. Abuse between parents may lead to lowered overall household economic attainments.

NEIGHBORHOOD SES/POVERTY

Social disorganization perspectives on violence have found positive associations with neighborhood levels of concentrated disadvantage that are in turn mediated by the community-level process of collective efficacy (Sampson et al., 1997). This perspective has been extended to the study of intimate partner violence (IPV), where Browning (2002) merged data sources from Chicago and similarly found that the positive association between community disadvantage and IPV as reported by individuals was mediated by the community-level process of collective efficacy. Multivariate analyses of aggregate-level data also found a positive association between resource deprivation (neighborhood poverty and income inequality) and higher rates of IPV in census tracts in Florida (Miles-Doan, 1998). Another study in the social disorganization perspective further analyzed the National Survey of Families & Households data in the United States (Van Wyck et al., 2003). This study found a cross-level interaction effect between neighborhood disadvantage and the respondent's levels of social support, in which neighborhood disadvantage increased women's physical violence in heterosexual relationships when she also had low social support (Van Wyck et al., 2003).

Further evidence of neighborhood socioeconomic influences on intimate partner violence was found in a study of women in their child-bearing year studied prospectively in Baltimore (O'Campo et al., 1995). Residence in impoverished neighborhoods and in neighborhoods with high unemployment rates strongly increase the risk of partner-perpetrated violence, as measured by the Conflict Tactics Scales, net of women's family SES and partner characteristics including drug use (O'Campo et al., 1995). Analyses of a national survey conducted in 1995 (the National Alcohol Survey) also incorporated both neighborhood and family factors on the risk for individual's IPV, using a modified version of the Conflict Tactics Scales, as perpetrated by both females and males (Cunradi et al., 2000). The latter study found contingencies in neighborhood effects by race/ethnicity, in which neighborhood poverty was found to elevate the odds of male-to-female partner violence by three times among Black couples, but not among Hispanics or Whites (Cunradi et al., 2000, p. 304). This study further found that neighborhood poverty increased female-to-male partner violence among Whites and Blacks, but not among Hispanics (Cunradi et al., 2000, p. 304). Together, these studies consistently indicate that disadvantaged community contexts elevate the risk of intimate partner violence. Children in disadvantaged contexts may therefore be more at risk for witnessing IPV than children living in more affluent communities. Research on children's exposure to interparental violence should be multileveled to incorporate both family and community SES risks.

These neighborhood level findings are consistent with social causation perspectives as per path y of Model A of Figure 35.1. Low SES in the community is positively associated with adult intimate partner violence. Children in communities with low SES then may be more likely to witness IPV in their families, which will in turn elevate youth's emotional and behavioral problems. Social selection perspectives expressed in path z of Figure 35.1, Model B would add to current research by drawing attention to the research implication that interparental violence in the household should have deleterious effects on short- and long-term family SES. The occurrence of IPV among adults may attenuate the earnings of either partner and especially the victim of IPV, predicting a decrease in children's current household SES, which may further lead to residence in lower SES neighborhoods. Although research to date is clearly in support of the social causation model, the financial implications of violence against women and adult partners, in terms of the financial consequences for adults who have experienced IPV and their children, should be considered further.

Adolescent Intimate Partner Violence Exposure

In contrast to the fairly consistent patterns of associations found between SES and child maltreatment and between SES and interparental or adult intimate partner violence, the evidence between SES and adolescent intimate partner violence (IPV) is far less consistent. As reviewed below, the associations between adolescent IPV and their family's SES status are mixed, with some contingencies found by the gender of the adolescent. More consistent patterns are found in studies of young adults and IPV when their personal SES indicators are measured in early adulthood.

FAMILY SES/POVERTY

Several studies have found no significant associations between parental SES and adolescent intimate partner violence. A recent national survey on children's violence exposure among 2- to 17-year-olds also included questions on dating violence, which were administered to children aged 12 and over. The results showed no association between dating violence (e.g., being slapped or hit, with or without injury) and family income (Finkelhor et al., 2005). Similarly, a study of high-school students aged 14 to 17 from a city in Los Angeles County also indicated no association between parental education and dating violence victimization using questions based on the physical violence subscale of the Conflict Tactics Scales (Malik, Sorenson, & Aneshensel, 1997, p. 298). Another study analyzed data on a subsample of homosexual youth from the first two waves (1995–1996) of the National Longitudinal Study of Adolescent Health (Add Health), in which intimate partner violence among adolescents was measured by five items from the Conflict Tactics Scales (Halpern et al., 2004). This study also found no significant association between parental education and adolescent IPV exposure (Halpern et al., 2004).

Another group of studies found significant associations between SES and IPV, but the patterns varied by adolescent gender. One of these studies examined predictors of intimate partner violence (as measured by five items from the Conflict Tactics Scales) among heterosexual adolescents in romantic relationships over the first two waves of the Add Health study (Halpern et al., 2001). This study found that parental education at the college level and above as compared to less than high-school education decreased males' exposure to psychological IPV. However, the results for females indicated that when the highest level of parental education in the household was high-school graduation, as compared to less than high-school graduation, the odds ratio for females' psychological abuse increased. Higher levels of parental education beyond high school did not significantly differentiate the risk of

IPV exposure for females from those whose parents had less than a high-school education (Halpern et al., 2001, p. 1683).

In contrast, another study used three waves (1995–2002) of data on females in the Add Health study with an ordinal measure of parental education and found a protective effect on IPV exposure (Foster, Hagan, & Brooks-Gunn, 2004). In operationalizing exposure to IPV, this study used responses to questions asked of those in both romantic relationships as well as in nonromantic sexual relationships. This study of females found that parental education had no significant impact on verbal abuse, but decreased the odds of exposure to a combined measure of verbal and physical intimate partner violence exposure (Foster et al., 2004). Protective SES effects were similarly found in analyses of females from the National Crime Victimization Survey of the general U.S. population of households of persons aged 12 or older over the period of 1993–1999. Rates of physical intimate partner violence among females aged 16 to 19 were higher among those with annual household incomes of less than $7,500, and IPV rates decreased as household income increased (Rennison, 2001, p. 5).

Although family of origin SES effects are mixed in relation to adolescent's IPV exposure as shown in the studies reviewed above, the patterns of association between indicators of older adolescents' and early adults' own SES tend to be more consistently associated with their experiences of intimate partner violence. A study of males and females (aged 18 to 30) found that the respondent's SES as measured by their occupational status was differentially related to different types of intimate partner violence victimization as measured by the Conflict Tactics Scales. Lower SES elevated the risk of receiving minor physical IPV, but no associations were found by respondent's SES with verbal or severe physical violence (Stets & Henderson, 1991, p. 33).

Furthermore, studies of young adults also indicated some gender-contingent patterns of associations between SES and IPV. For example, a longitudinal study found that unemployment and lower levels of education among early adults (aged 21) were associated with severe physical violence victimization as measured by the Conflict Tactics Scales, but the patterns depended on the gender of the respondent (Magdol, Moffitt, Caspi, Newman, Fagan, & Silva, 1997, p. 74). The findings indicate that unemployment is significantly higher and education level is significantly lower among males experiencing severe physical violent victimization compared to males who have not. However, females experiencing severe physical violent victimization by their partners were not distinguishable from those not experiencing partner violence on SES factors (Magdol et al., 1997). Multivariate analyses of another prospective general community sample of males and females aged 16 to 21 in New Jersey counties also found gender-specific associations with IPV (Chen & Raskin-White, 2004). A protective effect among females was found in this study for higher levels of respondent's own education on decreasing physical intimate partner violent victimization using questions based on the CTS. Education level was not significantly associated with intimate partner violent victimization among males. These studies together indicate that future research and theory on adolescent IPV should attend to gender contingencies between SES and IPV to further illuminate the social processes involved.

NEIGHBORHOOD SES/POVERTY

Fewer studies to date have analyzed neighborhood contexts in relation to adolescent IPV. However, the results of at least one study indicate an association between community context and adolescent IPV exposure (Bergman, 1992). This study of female adolescents found an association between community status and severe sexual and physical violence in their dating relationships, but the form of the relationship is unclear. The community patterns indicate that females residing in suburban contexts had the highest levels of IPV, those living in the inner city had lower levels, and those residing in rural communities had the lowest levels of all (Bergman, 1992, p. 24). Further research is required on which aspects of the community or more immediate neighborhood context affect adolescent IPV.

At present, the evidence is inconsistent regarding SES and adolescent's risk for IPV exposure. The associations that have been found between low family SES and higher levels of IPV in adolescence are in support of the social causation model, or path y of Model A of Figure 35.1. Future research on social causation would further test this model to discern the direct connections between SES and emotional and behavioral problems and to determine to what extent this pathway is mediated by adolescent IPV exposure. Building on the findings of Miech et al. (1999), future research on adolescents and social causation and social selection processes would need to differentiate between types of internalizing and externalizing disorders. Further research on pathway z in the social selection model (Model B of Figure 35.1) is also required. This model predicts that experiencing intimate partner violence in adolescence will lead to compromised school performance in the short term and compromised socioeconomic attainments in the long term. Prior research provides some support for this prediction in that youth who experienced intimate partner violence in adolescence were more likely to drop out of school (Hagan & Foster, 2001), and youth who experience other forms of violent victimization in adolescence experience socioeconomic disadvantages in the transition to adulthood (Macmillan, 2001; Macmillan & Hagan, 2004).

Children's Exposure to Community Violence

The salience of family and community SES as risk factors for exposure to violence is most consistent in the context of community violence. In this section, we examine the associations between SES and children's exposure to violence in the community, including their witnessing and direct victimization, as found in empirical studies and recent comprehensive reviews (Buka

et al., 2001; Sheidow et al., 2001). SES tends to be measured at the familial level of analysis in extant research on children's exposure to violence, but several studies are more recently inclusive of community SES. These findings point to the pervasiveness and severity of community violence exposure in the lives of disadvantaged adolescents. Fewer of these studies to date have examined younger children's exposure to community violence.

FAMILY SES/POVERTY

Results from a recent national survey of children (aged 2 to 17) and their parents showed inverse associations between family income and rates of community violence exposure (Finkelhor et al., 2005). Children and youth with lower household incomes had higher levels of direct physical victimization than those with higher family incomes (e.g., assault with a weapon and multiple perpetrator assault). Children and youth residing in households with lower incomes also had higher rates of witnessing or indirect exposure to community violence – in the forms of witnessing assault with a weapon, exposure to shooting, bombs, and riots, and having someone close murdered – than those with higher incomes (Finkelhor et al. 2005, p. 16). The exception to the inverse association between income and ETV in this national study was for being victimized by bullying, in which youth living in families with higher incomes (i.e., >$50,000) reported higher levels than youth with lower SES. Together, these findings indicate that youth living in families with lower incomes are at risk of more severe types of violence exposures and higher levels of overall violence exposure, including both direct and indirect exposure in their communities.

Prior studies on community ETV in the lives of children and youth involved highly disadvantaged samples that further indicated inverse associations between SES and community ETV. Richters and Martinez (1993) found that, among younger children (aged 6 to 10) in a highly disadvantaged sample (i.e., one quarter received public assistance and the majority of parents had not completed high school), there was a trend in the findings toward decreased parental education and the type of violence exposure. Decreased parental education was associated with ETV involving a person familiar to the child, but not to ETV involving a stranger. A second study involved a sample of highly disadvantaged youth with 2,000 students in grades 6, 8, and 10, of whom approximately half received a free lunch (Schwab-Stone et al., 1995). This study found that receipt of a school lunch was significantly associated with more frequent exposure to *severe* violence as measured by the self-reported frequency of having seen someone shot or stabbed in the past year.

Other studies with broader samples find mixed effects of SES on children's exposure to violence. Multivariate analyses of a sample of adolescents drawn from a range of schools (i.e., inner-city and other schools) in Los Angeles County found no significant associations between parental education and adolescent victimization in the community (Malik et al., 1997). In contrast, multivariate analyses with national data indicate an inverse effect of family SES, using the Hollingshead scale based on parental occupation and education, in which higher family SES was protective and was associated with lower adolescent physical victimization risk over the ages of 13 to 17 (Macmillan & Hagan, 2004, p. 142). Analyses of a Los Angeles sample of approximately 1,000 high-school students showed a similar pattern in descriptive results, in which higher levels of ETV were found at lower levels of SES, also using the Hollingshead scale (O'Keefe & Sela-Amit, 1997). However, in the latter study, the initial descriptive pattern did not hold in multivariate analyses in that SES was no longer a significant predictor of ETV. This study further found that race/ethnicity effects held net of SES: Blacks, Latinos, and Asians were more exposed to violence than Whites (O'Keefe & Sela-Amit, 1997).

Another set of studies on family SES and community ETV found that the inverse association was further modified by the adolescent's race/ethnicity. A study of a national probability sample of over 3,000 adolescents (aged 12 to 17) examined their direct violent victimization (physical and sexual) and their indirect exposure, including witnessing violence (Crouch et al., 2000). This study further supported the patterns found in other studies in that lower household income was associated with higher levels of witnessing violence and exposure to physical and sexual assault. However, when race/ethnicity of adolescents was taken into account, more complex patterns emerged. The inverse association between lower income and higher witnessing of violence held among White youth, but this pattern was not supported among African American and Hispanic youth (Crouch et al., 2000). Furthermore, within each SES level, race/ethnicity differentiated risk for ETV, in which minority youth had consistently higher risks of exposure to violence than White youth. These findings again suggest the importance of attending to other aspects of the social contexts in which youth live to better differentiate risk for violence exposure, as has been noted in other work on violence (Sampson & Wilson, 1995). Further research on associations between family SES and exposure to community violence is needed on ethnically and socioeconomically diverse samples and on younger children in addition to studies of adolescents.

NEIGHBORHOOD SES/POVERTY
One of the early studies of exposure to violence among adolescents (aged 11 to 24) compared levels among youth who attended medical clinics across two locales (Gladstein, Rusonis, & Heald, 1992). One of the clinics was situated in an inner-city environment comprised of predominantly African American youth, and the other involved predominantly White adolescents in a resort community. Comparisons between youth in the two locales were conducted in which community location was used to index the respondent's SES. The comparative results clearly indicated that more youth in lower SES circumstances had been victims, or had witnessed violence, or knew the victim of the violence personally. Types of violent victimization

that were higher among low-SES youth included very severe violent acts, in which the respondent was robbed with a weapon, assaulted with a weapon, raped without a weapon, shot, knifed, or had their life threatened. Differences between the samples were also found on indirect exposure to the more severe items in terms of incidents in which they had known the victim personally, with the exception of no group differences in robbery or assault without a weapon. However, statistically significant differences were shown for higher levels of witnessing violence among low-SES youth on all types of violence (Gladstein et al., 1992). These results support the consistent pattern shown in other studies of more severe violence exposure in disadvantaged samples.

More recent literature incorporates contextual neighborhood conditions, including community SES, in examining children's violence exposure risks (Sampson, 1997). In their review of the literature on children's exposure to community violence, Buka and colleagues (2001) found evidence across at least six studies that ETV was highest among those in poorer communities (p. 301). Their review further indicates that differences in the type or severity of violence exposure varied across neighborhood contexts, with more severe exposure occurring in urban rather than suburban areas (Buka et al., 2001, p. 302; Fitzpatrick & Boldizar, 1993). Results from the Project for Human Development in Chicago Neighborhoods indicate that the severity of violence exposure among youth (aged 9 to 24) varies with neighborhood conditions (Selner-O'Hagan et al., 1998). Past-year exposure to violence was greater in high- and medium-crime neighborhoods than in low-crime neighborhoods (Selner-O'Hagan et al., 1998).

Further research on SES and children's exposure to community violence may expand on two directions found in recent literature. One of these is the elaboration of findings indicating more complex interactive effects between neighborhood type and family processes in influencing exposure to violence among youth from highly disadvan-

taged circumstances (Sheidow et al., 2001). Second, a recent article found that more time in risky contexts (i.e., unstructured and unsupervised time) increased youth's levels of exposure to violence, whereas more time in protective contexts (i.e., more structured activities and time with family) decreased these levels (Richards et al., 2004). Future research would build on these findings by investigating poverty dynamics by taking into account the length of exposure (e.g., chronic vs. intermittent) to neighborhood and family socioeconomic disadvantages and risk for community ETV.

The findings on SES and community ETV are consistent in their support of social causation perspectives predicting that children living in socioeconomically disadvantaged families and communities are more likely to have higher levels of exposure to violence in the community, which in turn will elevate their emotional and behavioral problems. However, research on path z of the social selection model, from higher levels of community violence to lower SES, is also required to determine which forms and combinations of violence exposure have immediate and lasting impacts on children's educational attainments, early adult income levels, and potentially on residence in more disadvantaged community contexts. By using longitudinal designs, the interplay between social causation and selection pathways can best be modeled over the life course (e.g., Wheaton, 1978).

Conclusions

This chapter found that children in more socioeconomically disadvantaged household and community circumstances are at risk for elevated total levels of violence exposure and more severe types of exposure to violence. However, there is some variation in the consistency of associations between SES and specific forms of violence in children's lives. Consistent evidence was found for inverse associations among family SES and parent-to-child maltreatment and community ETV. Lower SES was also associated consistently with higher levels of children's witnessing of interparental or domestic violence among adults. Finally, less consistent associations were found between family SES and adolescent's victimization by their intimate partners. When inverse associations were found between familial SES and adolescent IPV, they tended to be contingent on gender. However, associations between early adult's own SES levels and IPV were more consistently inverse.

Although research on witnessing interparental violence shows that socioeconomic disadvantage is a risk factor, we also drew on a broader literature on adult intimate partner violence and noted the findings that relative spousal SES favoring women compared to men may reflect power differentials and was also influential on adult partner abuse. We suggest that research on risk factors for children's exposure to intimate partner violence among adults in the household should further measure relative spousal SES, in addition to more absolute forms of deprivation, including income-based poverty measures. Measurement of relative and absolute SES as risk factors for children's exposure to adult intimate partner or domestic violence would most fully guide prevention and intervention initiatives.

These findings on SES and the four forms of violence considered in this chapter are predominantly in support of social causation models as per Model A in Figure 35.1. These patterns indicate that lower SES is a risk factor for parent-child maltreatment, witnessing adult intimate partner violence, and witnessing and direct victimization by community violence. These violence exposures in turn have deleterious effects on children's emotional and behavioral problems (e.g., Margolin & Gordis, 2000). We have noted throughout our review that consistent with social selection pathways (e.g., path z of Model B of Figure 35.1) violence exposure in childhood and adolescence has implications for current educational functioning and later-life accrual of education and job experience, and therefore

status attainments (e.g., Macmillan, 2001). Further research is required on the interplay between social causation and social selection processes over the life course (e.g., Miech et al., 1999). For example, recent research finds that low familial SES in early adolescence increases physical violent victimization in adolescence, but violent victimization in turn has pervasive effects on educational and occupational attainments in early adulthood (e.g., Macmillan & Hagan, 2004). Further research incorporating witnessing violence in the home and in the community alongside children's direct victimization would expand these findings on SES as both a cause and consequence of exposure to violence over the life course. The interplay between selection and causation processes is also consistent with more elaborate and longitudinal ecological-transactional theoretical models of child maltreatment involving SES, violence exposure, and children's emotional and behavioral problems (e.g., Cicchetti & Lynch, 1993). Further research may facilitate a fuller integration of this group of theoretical perspectives.

Another area of future research guided by ecological-transactional perspectives on child maltreatment would involve examining interconnections among forms and levels of violence exposure (Lynch & Cicchetti, 1998; Margolin & Gordis, 2004). For example, research testing the ecological-transactional model indicates that residence in a community with higher levels of violence (i.e., exosystem) is positively associated with physical abuse in children in families (i.e., microsystem; Lynch & Cicchetti, 1998, p. 245). A further systematic investigation of interconnections among risk of exposure to different forms of violence (e.g., interparental abuse and child maltreatment, or community violence and adolescent intimate partner violence) is needed to better understand the etiology of children's exposure to violence. One particularly salient research direction involves examining how children in disadvantaged families and neighborhoods may be at risk for multiple ETV exposures at any one point in time, as well as cumulatively over their life course, further elaborating theoretical research on stress accumulation and cumulative disadvantage (Lynch & Cicchetti, 1998; Margolin & Gordis, 2003; Rutter, 1989; Sampson & Laub, 1993; Wheaton, 1995). Promising data sets for future research involve prospective and multileveled designs with comprehensive measures of types, levels, and degrees of ETV, alongside multiple and dynamic measures of family and community SES, including the Project for Human Development in Chicago Neighborhoods (Buka et al., 2001; Finkelhor et al., 2005; Kindlon, Wright, Raudenbush, & Earls, 1996; Molnar et al., 2003; Sampson et al., 1997; Selner-O'Hagan et al., 1998).

Further research on SES and ETV in children's lives would also involve more complex models with a fuller consideration of mediating and moderating factors. For example, financial strain was found to moderate the association between marital aggression and parental child maltreatment potential (Margolin & Gordis, 2003), indicating a condition under which this association was strengthened. Cross-level interactions between community and family contexts also require further examination across different samples and age groups, in which preliminary support has been found between neighborhood type and family functioning in influencing children's levels of community ETV (e.g., Sheidow et al., 2001). Other studies found SES and ETV associations were further modified by race/ethnicity and gender. Investigation of the conditions under which SES is connected to ETV would better inform its prevention and intervention. Future research should also explore the dynamics of risk factors, as indicated by a recent study indicating that more time spent in risky contexts is linked to higher adolescent ETV in the community (Richards et al., 2004). In most of the studies reviewed on children's exposure to violence, SES was often measured at only one time point and needs further exploration in terms of the dynamics of poverty exposure, including its duration and tim-

ing (e.g., Brooks-Gunn & Duncan, 1997; Duncan et al., 1998; McLeod & Shanahan, 1993). Finally, research on SES and children's exposure to violence in the American context must further attend to race and ethnicity, given ample evidence of the disproportionate location of African Americans and other minorities in highly disadvantaged contexts and with longer duration of exposure to impoverished conditions (Benson et al., 2000; Brooks-Gunn et al., 1997; Van Wyck et al., 2003).

Acknowledgments

We gratefully acknowledge the support provided for this research by the National Institute of Child Health and Human Development (Grant #R01 HD049796–01), the MacArthur Foundation, and the Marx Family Foundation.

References

Aldarondo, E. & Kaufman Kantor, G. (1997). Social Predictors of Wife Assault Cessation. In G. Kaufman Kantor & J. L. Jasinski (Eds.), *Out of the darkness: Contemporary perspectives on family violence* (pp. 183–193). Thousand Oaks, CA: Sage Publications.

Aneshensel, C. S. (1992). Social stress: Theory and research. *Annual Review of Sociology, 18,* 15–38.

Benson, M. L., Fox, G. L., DeMaris, A., & Van Wyck, J. (2000). Violence in families: The intersection of race, poverty, and community context. In G. L. Fox & M. L. Benson (Eds.), *Families, crime, and criminal justice* (pp. 91–109). New York: JAI Press.

Bergman, L. (1992). Dating violence among high school students. *Social Work, 37,* 21–27.

Bronfenbrenner, U. (1986). Ecology of the family as a context for human development: Research perspectives. *Developmental Psychology, 22,* 723–742.

Brooks-Gunn, J., & Duncan, G. J. (1997). The effects of poverty on children. *Future of Children, 7*(2), 55–71.

Brooks-Gunn, J., Duncan, G., & Aber, J. L. (Eds.). (1997). *Neighborhood poverty: Context and consequences for children* (Vol. 1). New York: Russell Sage Foundation.

Brooks-Gunn, J., Duncan, G. J., Klebanov, P. K., & Sealand, N. (1993). Do neighborhoods influence child and adolescent development? *American Journal of Sociology, 99,* 353–395.

Brooks-Gunn, J., Duncan, G. J., & Maritato, N. (1997). Poor families, poor outcomes: The well-being of children and youth. In G. J. Duncan & J. Brooks-Gunn (Eds.), *Consequences of growing up poor* (pp. 1–17). New York: Russell Sage Foundation.

Brooks-Gunn, J., Duncan, G. J., & Rebello Britto, P. (1999). Are socioeconomic gradients for children similar to those for adults? Achievement and health of children in the United States. In D. P. Keating & C. Hertzman (Eds.), *Developmental health and the wealth of nations: Social, biological, and educational dynamics* (pp. 94–124). New York: Guilford Press.

Browning, C. (2002). The span of collective efficacy: Extending social disorganization theory to partner violence. *Journal of Marriage and the Family, 64,* 833–850.

Buka, S. L., Stichick, T. L., Birdthistle, I., & Earls, F. (2001). Youth exposure to violence: Prevalence, risks, and consequences. *American Journal of Orthopsychiatry, 71,* 298–310.

Chen, P., & Raskin-White, H. (2004). Gender differences in adolescent and young adult predictors of later intimate partner violence. *Violence Against Women, 10,* 1283–1301.

Cicchetti, D., & Lynch, M. (1993). Toward an ecological/transactional model of community violence and child maltreatment: Consequences for children's development. *Psychiatry, 56,* 96–118.

Cokkinides, V. E., & Coker, A. L. (1998). Experiencing physical violence during pregnancy: Prevalence and correlates. *Family and Community Health, 20,* 19–38.

Coulton, C. J., Korbin, J. E., & Su, M. (1999). Neighborhoods and child maltreatment: A multi-level study. *Child Abuse and Neglect, 23,* 1019–1040.

Crouch, J. L., Hanson, R. F., Saunders, B. E., Kilpatrick, D. G., & Resnick, H. S. (2000). Income, race/ethnicity, and exposure to violence in youth: Results from the National Survey of Adolescents. *Journal of Community Psychology, 28,* 625–641.

Crutchfield, R. D., & Wadsworth, T. (2003). Poverty and violence. In W. Heitmeyer & J. Hagan (Eds.), *International handbook of violence research* (pp. 67–82). Dordrecht, The Netherlands: Kluwer Academic.

Cunradi, C. B., Caetano, R., Clark, C., & Schafer, J. (2000). Neighborhood poverty as a predictor of intimate partner violence among white, black, and Hispanic couples in the United States: A multilevel analysis. *Annals of Epidemiology, 10,* 297–308.

Cunradi, C. B., Caetano, R., & Schafer, J. (2002). Socio-economic predictors of intimate partner violence among white, black, and Hispanic couples in the United States. *Journal of Family Violence, 17,* 377–389.

Dodge, K. A., Petit, G. S., & Bates, J. E. (1994). Socialization mediators of the relation between socioeconomic status and child conduct problems. *Child Development, 65,* 649–665.

Dohrenwend, B. P., Levav, I., Shrout, P. E., Schwartz, S., Naveh, G., Link, B. G., et al. (1992). Socio-economic status and psychiatric disorders: The causation-selection issue. *Science, 255,* 946–952.

Dong, M., Anda, R. F., Felitti, V. J., Dube, S. R., Williamson, D. F., Thompson, T. J., et al. (2004). The interrelatedness of multiple forms of childhood abuse, neglect, and household dysfunction. *Child Abuse and Neglect, 28,* 771–784.

Duncan, G. J., & Aber, J. L. (1997). Neighborhood models and measures. In J. Brooks-Gunn, G. J. Duncan, & J. L. Aber (Eds.), *Neighborhood poverty. Volume I: Context and consequences for children* (pp. 62–78). New York: Russell Sage Foundation.

Duncan, G. J., & Brooks-Gunn, J. (1997). *Consequences of growing up poor.* New York: Russell Sage Foundation.

Duncan, G. J., & Moscow, L. (1997). Longitudinal indicators of children's poverty and dependence. In R. M. Hauser, B. V. Brown, & W. R. Prosser (Eds.), *Indicators of children's well-being* (pp. 258–278). New York: Russell Sage Foundation.

Duncan, G. J., Yeung, W. J., Brooks-Gunn, J., & Smith, J. R. (1998). How much does childhood poverty affect the life chances of children? *American Sociological Review, 63,* 406–423.

Earls, F., & M. Carlson. (2001). The social ecology of child health and well-being. *Annual Review of Public Health, 22,* 143–166.

Edleson, J. L. (1999). Children's witnessing of adult domestic violence. *Journal of Interpersonal Violence, 14,* 839–870.

Evans, G. W. (2004). The environment of child-hood poverty. *American Psychologist*, 59, 77–92.

Fantuzzo, J., Boruch, R., Beriama, A., Atkins, M., & Marcus, S. (1997). Domestic violence and children: Prevalence and risk in five major U. S. cities. *Journal of the American Academy of Child and Adolescent Psychiatry*, 36, 116–122.

Fantuzzo, J. W., & Mohr, W. K. (1999). Prevalence and effects of child exposure to domestic violence. *Future of Children: Domestic Violence and Children*, 9(3), 21–32.

Fergusson, D. M., & Horwood, L. J. (1998). Exposure to interparental violence in childhood and psychosocial adjustment in young adulthood. *Child Abuse and Neglect*, 22, 339–357.

Finkelhor, D., & Dziuba-Leatherman, J. (1994). Children as victims of violence: A national survey. *Pediatrics*, 94, 413–420.

Finkelhor, D., Ormrod, R., Turner, H., & Hamby, S. L. (2005). The victimization of children and youth: A comprehensive, national survey. *Child Maltreatment*, 10, 5–25.

Fitzpatrick, K. M., & Boldizar, J. P. (1993). The prevalence and consequences of exposure to violence among African American youth. *Journal of the American Academy of Adolescent Psychiatry*, 32, 424–430.

Foster, H., Hagan, J., & Brooks-Gunn, J. (2004). Age, puberty, and exposure to intimate partner violence in adolescence. *Annals of the New York Academy of Sciences*, 1036, 151–166.

Garbarino, J. (1977). The human ecology of child maltreatment: A conceptual model for research. *Journal of Marriage and the Family*, 39, 721–735.

Garbarino, J., & C. Bradshaw. (2003). Violence against children. In W. Heitmeyer & J. Hagan (Eds.), *International handbook of violence research* (pp. 719–735). Dordrecht, The Netherlands: Kluwer Academic.

Garbarino, J., & Sherman, D. (1980). High-risk neighborhoods and high-risk families: The human ecology of child maltreatment. *Child Development*, 51, 188–198.

Gelles, R. J. (1992). Poverty and violence toward children. *American Behavioral Scientist*, 35, 258–274.

Gladstein, J., Rusonis, E. J. S., & Heald, F. P. (1992). A comparison of inner-city and upper-middle class youths' exposure to violence. *Journal of Adolescent Health*, 13, 275–280.

Gielen, A. C., O'Campo, P. J., Faden, R. R., Kass, N. E., & Xue, X. (1994). Interpersonal conflict and physical violence during the child-bearing year. *Social Science and Medicine*, 39, 781–787.

Hagan, J., & Foster, H. (2001). Youth violence and the end of adolescence. *American Sociological Review*, 66, 874–899.

Halpern, C. T., Oslak S. G., Young, M. L., Martin, S. L., & Kupper, L. L. (2001). Partner violence among adolescents in opposite-sex romantic relationships: Findings from the National Longitudinal Study of Adolescent Health. *American Journal of Public Health*, 91, 1679–85.

Halpern, C. T., Young, M. L., Waller M. A., Martin, S. L., & Kupper L. L. (2004). Prevalence of partner violence in same-sex romantic and sexual relationships in a national sample of adolescents. *Journal of Adolescent Health*, 35, 124–131.

Hauser, R. M., & J. R. Warren. (1997). Socioeconomic indexes for occupations: A review, update and critique. *Sociological Methodology*, 27, 177–298.

Johnson, M. P. (1995). Patriarchal terrorism and common couple violence: Two forms of violence against women. *Journal of Marriage and the Family*, 57, 283–294.

Kaukinen, C. (2004). Status compatibility, physical violence, and emotional abuse in intimate relationships. *Journal of Marriage and the Family*, 66, 452–472.

Keenan, H. T., Runyan, D. K., Marshall, S. W., Nocera, M. A., Merten, D. F., & Sinal, S. H. (2003). A population-based study of inflicted traumatic brain injury in young children. *Journal of the American Medical Association*, 290, 621–626.

Kessler, R. C., Molnar, B. E., Feurer, I. D., & Appelbaum, M. (2001). Patterns and mental health predictors of domestic violence in the United States: Results from the National Comorbidity Study. *International Journal of Law and Psychiatry*, 24, 487–508.

Kindlon, D. J., Wright, B. D., Raudenbush, S. W., & Earls, F. (1996). The measurement of children's exposure to violence: A Rasch analysis. *International Journal of Methods in Psychiatric Research*, 6, 187–194.

Kotch, J. B., Muller, G. O., & Blakely, C. H. (1999). Understanding the origins and incidence of child maltreatment. In A. A. Fagan (Ed.), *Violence in homes and communities: Prevention, intervention, and treatment* (pp. 1–38). London: Sage.

Leventhal, T., & Brooks-Gunn, J. (2000). The neighborhoods they live in: The effects of neighborhood residence on child and adolescent outcomes. *Psychological Bulletin*, *126*, 309–337.

Lynch, M., & Cicchetti, D. (1998). An ecological-transactional analysis of children and contexts: The longitudinal interplay among child maltreatment, community violence, and children's symptomatology. *Development and Psychopathology*, *10*, 235–257.

MacMillan, R. (2001). Violence and the life course: The consequences of victimization for personal and social development. *Annual Review of Sociology*, 27, 1–22.

MacMillan, R., & Gartner, R. (1999). When she brings home the bacon: Labor force participation and the risk of spousal violence against women. *Journal of Marriage and the Family*, *61*, 947–58.

MacMillan, R., & Hagan, J. (2004). Violence in the transition to adulthood: Adolescent victimization, education, and socioeconomic attainment in later life. *Journal of Research on Adolescence*, *14*, 127–158.

Magdol, L., Moffitt, T. E., Caspi, A., Newman, D. L., Fagan, J., & Silva, P. A. (1997). Gender differences in partner violence in a birth cohort of 21 year-olds: Bridging the gap between clinical and epidemiological approaches. *Journal of Consulting and Clinical Psychology*, *65*, 68–78.

Malik, S., Sorenson, S. B., & Aneshensel, C. S. (1997). Community and dating violence among adolescents: Perpetration and victimization. *Journal of Adolescent Health*, *21*, 291–302.

Margolin, G., & Gordis, E. B. (2000). The effects of family and community violence on children. *Annual Review of Psychology*, *51*, 445–479.

Margolin, G., & Gordis, E. B. (2003). Co-occurrence between marital aggression and parents' child abuse potential: The impact of cumulative stress. *Violence and Victims*, *18*, 243–258.

Margolin, G., & Gordis, E. B. (2004). Children's exposure to violence in the family and community. *Current Directions in Psychological Science*, *13*, 152–155.

Martin, S. L., Mackie, L., Kupper, L. L., Buescher, P. A., & Moracco, K. E. (2001). Physical abuse of women before, during, and after pregnancy. *Journal of the American Medical Association*, *285*, 1581–1584.

McLeod, J. D., & Kaiser, K. (2004). Childhood emotional and behavioral problems and educational attainment. *American Sociological Review*, 69, 636–658.

McLeod, J. D., & Shanahan, M. J. (1993). Poverty, parenting, and children's mental health. *American Sociological Review*, 58, 351–366.

Miech, R. A., Caspi, A., Moffitt, T. E., Wright, B. R. E., & Silva, P. A. (1999). Low socioeconomic status and mental disorders: A longitudinal study of selection and causation during young adulthood. *American Journal of Sociology*, *104*, 1096–1131.

Miles-Doan, R. (1998). Violence between spouses and intimates: Does neighborhood context matter? *Social Forces*, *77*, 623–645.

Mirowsky, J., & Ross, C. E. (2003a). *Education, social status, and health*. New York: Aldine De Gruyter.

Mirowsky, J., & Ross, C. E. (2003b). *Social causes of psychological distress* (2nd ed.). New York: Aldine De Gruyter.

Molnar, B. E., Buka, S. L., Brennan, R. T., Holton, J. K., & Earls, F. (2003). A multilevel study of neighborhoods and parent-to-child physical aggression: Results from the Project for Human Development in Chicago neighborhoods. *Child Maltreatment*, *8*, 84–97.

O'Campo, P., Gielen, A. C., Faden, R. R., Xue, X., Kass, N., & Wang, M. C. (1995). Violence by male partners against women during the childbearing year: A contextual analysis. *American Journal of Public Health*, *85*, 1092–1097.

O'Keefe, M., & Sela-Amit, M. (1997). An examination of the effects of race/ethnicity and social class on adolescents' exposure to violence. *Journal of Social Services Research*, *22*, 53–71.

Osofsky, J. D. (1999). The impact of violence on children. *Future of Children*, *9*(3), 33–49.

Overpeck, M. D., Brenner, R. A., Trumble, A. C., Trifiletti, L. B., & Berendes, H. W. (1998). Risk factors for infant homicide in the United States. *New England Journal of Medicine*, *339*, 1211–1216.

Overstreet, S. (2000). Exposure to community violence: Defining the problem and understanding the consequences. *Journal of Child and Family Studies*, *9*, 7–25.

Paxson, C., & Waldfogel, J. (2003). Welfare reforms, family resources, and child maltreatment. *Journal of Policy Analysis and Management*, *22*, 85–113.

Pearlin, L. I. (1989). The sociological study of stress. *Journal of Health and Social Behavior*, *30*, 241–256.

Pearlin, L. I., Leiberman, M. A., Menaghan, E. G., & Mullan, J. T. (1981). The stress process. *Journal of Health and Social Behavior, 22,* 337–356.

Rennison, C. M. (2001). *Intimate partner violence and age of victim, 1993–99* (#NCJ 187635). Washington, DC: U. S. Department of Justice, Office of Justice Programs.

Rennison, C., & Planty, M. (2003). Nonlethal intimate partner violence: Examining race, gender, and income patterns. *Violence and Victims, 18,* 433–443.

Richards, M. H., Larson, R., Miller B. V., Luo, Z., Sims, B., Parrella, D. P., et al. (2004). Risky and protective contexts and exposure to violence in urban African American young adolescents. *Journal of Clinical Child and Adolescent Psychology, 33,* 138–148.

Richters, J., & Martinez, P. (1993). The NIMH community violence project: Children as victims of and witnesses to violence. *Psychiatry, 56,* 7–21.

Rutter, M. (1989). Pathways from childhood to adult life. *Journal of Child Psychology and Psychiatry, 30,* 23–51.

Sampson, R. J. (1997). The embeddedness of child and adolescent development: A community-level perspective on urban violence. In J. McCord (Ed.), *Violence in childhood in the inner city* (pp. 31–77). New York: Cambridge University Press.

Sampson, R. J. & Laub, J. H. 1993. *Crime in the making: Pathways and turning points through life.* Cambridge, MA: Harvard University Press.

Sampson, R. J., Raudenbush, S. W., & Earls, F. (1997). Neighborhoods and violent crime: A multilevel study of collective efficacy. *Science, 277,* 918–924.

Sampson, R. J., & Wilson, W. J. (1995). Toward a theory of race, crime, and urban inequality. In J. Hagan & R. Peterson (Eds.), *Crime and inequality* (pp. 37–56). Palo Alto, CA: Stanford University Press.

Schwab-Stone, M. D., Ayers, T. S., Kasprow, W., Voyce, C., Barone, C., Shriver, T., et al. (1995). No safe haven: A study of violence exposure in an urban community. *Journal of the American Academy of Child and Adolescent Psychiatry, 34,* 1343–1352.

Selner-O'Hagan, M. B., Kindlon, D. J., Buka, S. L., Raudenbush, S. W., & Earls, F. J. (1998). Assessing exposure to violence in urban youth. *Journal of Child Psychology and Psychiatry, 39,* 215–224.

Sheidow, A. J., Gorman-Smith, D., Tolan, P. H., & Henry, D. B. (2001). Family and community characteristics: Risk factors for violence exposure in inner-city youth. *Journal of Community Psychology, 29,* 345–360.

Smith, J. R., & Brooks-Gunn, J. (1997). Correlates and consequences of harsh discipline for young children. *Archives of Pediatrics and Adolescent Medicine, 151,* 777–786.

Stets, J. E., & Henderson, D. A. (1991). Contextual factors surrounding conflict resolution while dating: Results from a national study. *Family Relations, 1991,* 40, 29–36.

Straus, M. A. (1979). Measuring intrafamily conflict and violence: The Conflict Tactics (CT) Scales. *Journal of Marriage and the Family, 41,* 75–88.

Turner, R. J., Wheaton, B., & Lloyd, D. A. (1995). The epidemiology of social stress. *American Sociological Review, 60,* 104–125.

U.S. Census Bureau. (2005). *How the Census Bureau measures poverty.* Retrieved April 29, 2005, from http://www.census.gov/hhes/poverty/povdef.html.

Vacha, E. F., & McLaughlin, T. F. (2004). Risky firearms behavior in low-income families of elementary school children: The impact of poverty, fear of crime, and crime victimization in keeping and storing firearms. *Journal of Family Violence, 19,* 175–184.

Van Wsyck, J. A., Benson, M., Fox, G. L., & DeMaris, A. (2003). Detangling individual-, partner-, and community-level correlates of partner violence. *Crime and Delinquency, 49,* 412–438.

Wheaton, B. (1978). The sociogenesis of psychological disorder: Reexamining the causal issues with longitudinal data. *American Sociological Review, 43,* 383–403.

Wheaton, B. (1995). Sampling the stress universe. In W. R. Avison & I. H. Gotlib (Eds.), *Stress and mental health: Contemporary issues and prospects for the future* (pp. 77–114). New York: Plenum Press.

Willms, J. D. (2002). Socioeconomic gradients for childhood vulnerability. In J. D. Willms (Ed.), *Vulnerable children: Findings from Canada's National Longitudinal Survey of Children and Youth* (pp. 71–102). Edmonton, Alberta: University of Alberta Press.

Wintemute, G. (2000). Guns and gun violence. In A. Blumstein & J. Wallman (Eds.), *The crime drop in America* (pp. 45–96). Cambridge, UK: Cambridge University Press.

Wu, S. S., Ma, C. X., Carter, R. L., Ariet, M., Feaver, E. A., Resnick, M. B., et al. (2003). Risk factors for infant maltreatment: A population-based study. *Child Abuse and Neglect, 28,* 1253–1264.

Xu, X., Zhu, F., O'Campo, P., Koenig, M. A., Mock, V., & Campbell, J. (2005). Prevalence and risk factors for intimate partner violence in China. *American Journal of Public Health, 95,* 78–85.

CHAPTER 36

Social Contagion of Violence

Jeffrey Fagan, Deanna L. Wilkinson, and Garth Davies

Introduction

Like many large American cities, New York City experienced a sudden and dramatic increase in homicides beginning in 1985. The homicide run-up was highest for adolescents, but rates increased quickly for older persons as well (Fsagan, Zimring, & Kim, 1998). Unlike many other cities, in which homicides declined gradually over the next decade yet remained above their pre-1985 levels, the increase in New York was followed by an even larger decline over the next 5 years. By 1995, homicide in New York City had dropped below its 1985 level; by 1996, it was lower than the 1985 rates; by 1998, homicide rates were 25% lower than the 1985 levels; and by 1998, homicide rates were lower than three decades earlier. The drop in crime generally, and not just homicide, was an order of magnitude greater than any observed in large American cities since the 1950s (Zimring, 2007).

Explanations of this roller-coaster pattern of violence beginning in the 1960s have tended to partition the periods of increase and decline as distinct phenomena with unique causes. Moreover, these causes are typically regarded as exogenous to the people or areas affected. For example, the onset and severity of the homicide trend were attributed to the sudden emergence of unstable street-level crack markets, with high levels of violence between sellers (Baumer, 1994; Baumer, Lauritsen, Rosenfeld, & Wright, 1998; Fagan & Chin, 1991; Fryer, Heaton, Levitt, & Murphy, 2005; Grogger & Willis, 2000). Others suggested that drug markets created a demand for guns that in turn trickled down from drug sellers into the hands of adolescents (Blumstein, 1995; Fagan, 1992). Structural theorists implicated race-specific economic deficits in inner cities (Krivo & Peterson, 2000; Peterson & Krivo, 1993) or racial residential segregation (Massey, 1995). There have been many claims regarding the sources of the decline, including changes in police strategy (Kelling & Cole, 1996), demographic changes (Cook & Laub, 1998; Eckberg, 1995), incarceration (Blumstein & Beck, 1999), and lower demand for illegal drugs (Curtis, 1998).

None of the popular explanations of either the increase or the decline is fully satisfying. Moreover, the gap between the scale of demographic and policy changes and the scale of the crime decline suggests that there are processes at work other than these usual suspects. Some have used the term "epidemic" metaphorically to describe the homicide run-up and decline, but with little precision and often conflating several features of epidemics, such as social concentration, spatial diffusion, and temporal spikes (see, for example, Bailey, 1975).

Epidemic is a term used widely in the popular and scientific literature to describe two quite separate components of a phenomenon: an elevated incidence of the phenomena and its rapid spread via a contagious process within a population in a short period of time. For example, Gladwell (2000) describes how the incidence of an ordinary and stable phenomenon such as a seasonal flu can become epidemic when its incidence increases in a very short time from a predictable base rate to an elevated rate of infections. Moreover, epidemics need not be contagious. Consider an outbreak of food poisoning from contaminated materials or a cancer cluster near a polluted water supply. These medical problems may occur at a rate well above an expected base rate, but are not spread from person to person through physical contact or an infectious process. In contrast, an outbreak of influenza, the adaptation of cultural fads, medical or industrial innovation, or changes in the rates of antisocial behavior all reflect spread through interpersonal exposure to an "infectious" agent.

Although disease spreads through a host and agent (Robertson, 1990; Rothman, 1986), social contagion involves the mutual influence of individuals within social networks who turn to each other for cues and behavioral tools that reflect the contingencies of specific situations (Bailey, 1967; Burt, 1987; Coleman, Katz, & Menzel, 1966). The contagious dimension is especially salient during the upswing of an epidemic, when physical or social contact is critical to spread pursuant to exposure. But epidemics also end, as the rate of new incidence of the phenomenon declines. This decline may occur because the density of contacts may decrease or because some form of resistance develops that reduces the odds of transmission from one person to the next, even in the presence of exogenous contributing factors (Bailey, 1967; Burt, 1992).

In this chapter, we assess whether the roller-coaster pattern of homicides in New York City beginning in 1985 fits a contagion model and identify mechanisms of social contagion that predict its spread across social and physical space. This framework for interpreting the homicide trends as an epidemic includes two perspectives. First, the sharp rise and fall are indicative of a nonlinear pattern in which the phenomenon spreads at a rate far beyond what would be predicted by exposure to some external factor and declines in a similar pattern in which the reduction from year to year exceeds what might be expected by linear regression trends. This leads to the second perspective: the factors leading to its spread are not exogenous factors, as in the case of contamination or disaster. Instead, the nonlinear increase and decline suggest that the phenomenon is endemic to the people and places where its occurrence is highest and that this behavior may be effectively passed from one person to another through some process of contact or interaction.

We assess the validity of these assumptions in three ways. In the section "Violence as Social Contagion," we introduce a framework of social contagion that informs this analysis. The diffusion and spread of social behaviors are recurring themes in both the scientific and popular literatures. But there has been little theorizing on the mechanisms of social diffusion generally and specifically on the social interactions that may qualify as a contagious process. This section reviews the literature generally on social contagion and then constructs an analytic framework to explain the spread of youth violence over time and space. In the section "The Epidemiology of Youth Homicide in New York City," we analyze Vital Statistics data from the New York City Department of Health and Mental Hygiene to construct simple time series data that characterize the increase and decline in homicides from 1985–2000. We concentrate on homicides involving adolescents and young adults, populations who experienced the sharpest rise and decline in homicide, both in New York and nationally (Cook & Laub, 1998; Fagan & Davies, 2004; Fagan et al., 1998).

In the section "Neighborhood Effects on Social Contagion of Youth Homicide," we estimate models to identify the spatial and social trends in youth homicide. Using growth curve or hierarchical models, we disaggregate homicide and nonlethal injury data by neighborhoods over the 11-year period and fit models to demonstrate the spatial diffusion of youth homicide from one neighborhood to the next across New York City. By co-varying neighborhood social and economic characteristics with temporal homicide trends, we are able to show that the diffusion of homicide in this era was specific to the most socially isolated areas of the city. We isolate gun homicides as the contagious agent, showing that it is gun homicides that diffused across New York City neighborhoods and that gun homicides retreated just as quickly.

In the section "Violent Events, Social Networks, and Social Contagion," we present data from interviews with young males active in gun violence during this time. Their reports of the role of guns in violent events further specify how diffusion may in fact be the result of a dynamic process of social contagion. We conclude the chapter by integrating these perspectives into a unifying framework that links elements of models of infectious disease with social interactionist perspectives to explain the social contagion that contributed to New York City's homicide epidemic, which remains today as the source of contentious debates in public policy and social science.

Violence As Social Contagion

Background

There are many examples of social contagion that inform the development of

this research, especially among adolescents: trends in fashion and art (Gladwell, 2000), as well as problematic social behaviors, such as alcohol and drug use (Rowe & Rodgers, 1994), smoking (Rowe & Rodgers, 1991), teenage pregnancy (Crane, 1991), suicide (Berman, 1995; Gould, Wallenstein, & Kleinman, 1990; Gould, Wallenstein, Kleinman, O'Carroll, & Mercy, 1990), and delinquency (Jones, 1997). Common to each of these examples is the social structure of transmission. Thus, the fundamental *social* causes of disease – primarily social structural or social interactionist in nature – can be seen as pathways along which more micro-level causes can exert their effect (Farmer, 1999; Gostin, Burris, & Lazzarini, 1999, p. 74; Lynch et al., 1998; Tolnay & Beck, 1995; Tolnay, Deane, & Beck, 1996; Wilkinson & Fagan, 1996).

The spread of ideas, behaviors, and practices is contingent on the way in which social structure brings people together in close physical proximity within dense social networks (Burt, 1987, p. 1288). For example, Rowe and Rodgers (1994) show that that an epidemic model combining social contagion through social contacts among adolescents within a narrow age band explains the onset and desistance of adolescent sexual behavior (see also Rodgers & Rowe, 1993). HIV transmission also has been modeled as a contagious epidemic (May, Anderson, & Blower, 1990). Through a process of mutual influence involving contact, communication, and competition, adoption of behaviors occurs when information about behaviors is transmitted in a way that communicates the substance of an innovation and the consequences of its adoption. The consequences can be socially rewarding or intrinsically pleasurable and may be reinforced through the benefits of a vicarious experience or a trial use. In addition, these behaviors acquire social meaning that is communicated through repeated interactions within social networks (Kahan, 1997; Lessig, 1995, p. 1947).

Contagious epidemics involve the transmission of an agent via a host through susceptible organisms whose resilience is weakened by other conditions or factors (Bailey, 1967). Susceptibility is critical to the ability of an agent to exert its process on a host. This medical rendering of contagion can be analogized to social contagion (Jones & Jones, 1994, 1995). Thus, the fundamental social causes of disease – primarily social structural, or ecological – can be seen as pathways along which more micro-level causes can exert their effect (Gostin et al., 1999, p. 74). According to Gostin and colleagues (1999), these fundamental social causes reflect inequalities that work in two ways. First, these conditions increase exposure to the more proximal causes, whether microbic or behavioral. Second, they compromise the resistance or resilience of social groups to these proximal causes. That is, their exposure and their behavior in those structural circumstances both have social roots.

Memetics provides a complementary framework for understanding how beliefs, ideas, and behaviors spread throughout society. Memes are singular ideas that evolve through a process of natural selection not unlike the evolution of genes in evolutionary biology (Balkin, 1998; Lynch, 1996). The principal law governing the birth and spread of memes is that of the "fittest ideas," defined as those ideas that are the best at self-replication rather than those that may be truest or have the greatest utilitarian value (Lynch, 1996). In the present analysis, violence may be the "fittest" behavior, even when it contradicts more socially useful normative values imported from the dominant society. Memes achieve high-level contagion through a variety of social interactions across social units, such as families and social networks, and each mode increases the "host" population for that meme. The meme is then reproduced within networks and transmitted across interstitial network boundaries.

Replicated memes become what Balkin (1998, pp. 42–57) refers to as "cultural software" that is expressed in language, behavior, and normative beliefs, creating a set of normative expectations or behavioral "scripts." (Abelson, 1976, 1981; Fagan, 1999). According to Abelson, the script

framework is an event schema used to organize information about how people learn to understand and enact commonplace behavioral patterns. A "script" is a cognitive structure or framework that organizes a person's understanding of typical situations, allowing the person to have expectations and to make conclusions about the potential result of a set of events. Script theory has been used widely in social psychology to identify patterns of decision making and social interactions that persist among persons within social networks. Script theory can explain contagion in several ways: (1) Scripts are ways of organizing knowledge and behavioral choices; (2) individuals learn behavioral repertoires for different situations; (3) these repertoires are stored in memory as scripts and are elicited when cues are sensed in the environment; (4) the choice of scripts varies among individuals, and some individuals will have limited choices; (5) individuals are more likely to repeat scripted behaviors when the previous experience was considered successful; (6) scripted behavior may become "automatic" without much thought or weighing of consequences; and (7) scripts are acquired through social interactions among social network members (Abelson, 1976, 1981).

Accordingly, social contagion is the convergence of transmission of behaviors and of beliefs that motivate or sustain them. Social contagion arises from people in proximate social structures using one another to manage uncertainty of behavior (Burt, 1987; Gostin, 1991; Rodgers & Rowe, 1993; Rowe & Rodgers 1991, 1994). It requires an interaction in which information, behavioral innovation, belief, or meme is transmitted across a social synapse. At its core, contagion occurs when two people interact where one has adopted a construct and the other has not. Contact, communication, and imitation are influential processes that make transmission possible (Burt, 1987, pp. 1288–1289). Synapses themselves are situated within social networks, and the adoption of an innovation or a meme triggers the adoption by another person. Burt (1987) suggests that adoption has less to do with the cohesion of people within social structures or networks and more to do with the structural equivalence – the social homogeneity – of the network. That is, transmission is more likely to occur between similarly situated persons – siblings, fellow graduate students, street corner boys – than persons simply because they are closely bonded (Burt, 1987, p. 1291).

Within structurally equivalent networks, similarly situated people are likely to influence or adopt behaviors from one another that can make that person more attractive as a source of further relations. The importance of structural equivalence – or placement within a socially homogeneous interpersonal network – is that it fosters interconnected patterns of relationships that make contagion efficient.

In the remainder of this section, we show how transmission of violence occurs across neighborhoods whose social structures of densely packed networks are vulnerable to rapid contagion. Our previous work on urban youth violence has shown how the memes of toughness and the valued status from violence are the object of transmission and exchange among similarly situated male youth (Fagan & Wilkinson, 1998a,b; Wilkinson, 2003). The implications for a social influence model of contagion are discussed in the concluding section.

Guns and Social Contagion

Several processes have contributed to the epidemic of lethal violence. The growth in illegal markets heightens the demand for guns as basic tools that are associated with routine business activity in illegal markets (Blumstein, 1995; Johnson, Williams, Dei, & Sanabria, 1990). In turn, the increased presence of weapons and their diffusion into the general population change normative perceptions of the danger and lethality associated with everyday interpersonal disputes, giving rise to an "ecology of danger" (Fagan & Wilkinson, 1998a). Thus, we hypothesize that guns were initially an exogenous factor in launching an epidemic of gun homicide, but became endogenous to socially

isolated neighborhoods and came to dominate social interactions (Wilkinson & Fagan, 1996). Everyday disputes, whether personal insults or retributional violence, in turn are more likely to be settled with potentially lethal violence (Fagan & Wilkinson, 1998a; Wilkinson, 2003).

Whether viewed in social, medical, or memetic frameworks, guns can be constructed as a primary agent of violence contagion over the most recent epidemic cycle. Guns are a form of social toxin (Delgado, 1985; Fagan & Wilkinson, 1998b) in everyday social interactions, altering the outcome of disputes and changing the developmental trajectories of young males whose adolescent development took place in the contexts of high rates of gun use and widely perceived danger, contributing to an ecology of danger that had profound developmental impacts on adolescents growing up in these settings (Bingenheimer, Brennan, & Earls, 2005; Fagan, 1999).

The development of such an *ecology of danger* reflects the confluence and interaction of several sources of contagion. First is the contagion of fear. Weapons serve as an environmental cue that in turn may increase aggressiveness (Slaby & Roedell, 1982). Adolescents presume that their counterparts are armed and, if not, could easily become armed. They also assume that other adolescents are willing to use guns, often at a low threshold of provocation.

The second source is the contagion of gun behaviors themselves. The use of guns has instrumental value that is communicated not only through urban "myths" but also through the incorporation of gun violence into the social discourse of everyday life among pre-adolescents and adolescents. Guns are widely available to adolescents (Cook & Ludwig, 2004), and when carried by adolescents, they are frequently displayed (Harcourt, 2006; Wilkinson, 2003).[1] They are salient symbols of power and status and strategic means of gaining status, domination, or material goods (Wilkinson, 2003). Wilkinson's interviews with adolescents and young adults in two New York City neighborhoods during the mid-1990s show that guns are used in a myriad of different ways and for different purposes; some uses are seemingly more mild and symbolic than others, but may be the first steps or building blocks for later more serious use. For example, very first steps might be simply seeing someone or knowing someone who has a gun, then looking for a gun in one's own house, then maybe trying to get one, then just flashing one when trying to threaten/scare an opponent, then using the gun for pistol whipping, then firing the gun to scare someone but not aiming to hit them, then actually firing toward someone, then firing to injure but not kill, and then firing to kill. The socialization process into the urban youth gun world begins at a young age, with influences coming from family and peer networks (Wilkinson, 2003; Wilkinson & Fagan, 2001a). How these processes unfold at the event level is explored in Part IV of this chapter.

Third is the contagion of violent identities and the consequent eclipsing or devaluation of other identities in increasingly socially isolated neighborhoods. These identities reinforce the dominance hierarchy built on "toughness" and violence, and its salience devalues other identities. Those unwilling to adopt at least some dimensions of this identity are vulnerable to physical attack. Accordingly, violent identities are not simply affective styles and social choices, but instead are strategic necessities to navigate through everyday dangers (Wilkinson, 2003).[2]

Finally, when the group nature of youth violence is examined, diffusion and contagion of attitudes, scripts, and behaviors are clearly visible. The proximal link between one violent conflict and the next is startling. In addition, the social meanings of violent events reach a broader audience than those immediately present in a situation. Each violent event or potentially violent interaction provides a lesson for the participants, first-hand observers, vicarious observers, and others influenced by the communication of stories about the situation that may follow. Expectations, a violent status hierarchy, and norms of interpersonal conduct

among groups of socially isolated young men work to hinder nonviolent conflict resolution. Conflict handling among youth who are affiliated with other youth at least in part to enhance their personal safety in a dangerous environment acts to increase the amount of violence that youth experience, rather than decrease it. We examine these issues empirically at the neighborhood level as well as at the micro-translational level in New York City.

The Micro-Processes of Social Contagion: Social Identity and Violence

Previously, Wilkinson (2003) and Fagan and Wilkinson (1998a) identified several processes operating at the event level that illustrate the spread of violence within social structures and that exert a contracting influence on social networks of adolescents: (1) Achieving a highly valued social identity; occurs through extreme displays of violence, (2) achieving a "safe" social identity may also require the use of extreme forms of violence, (3) the ready availability of guns clearly increases the stakes of how one achieves status; (4) much behavior is motivated by avoiding being a punk or "herb" (sucker or weakling); (5) identities can change from being a punk or herb into a more positive status such as "hold your own"; (6) guns equalize the odds for some smaller young men through the process of "showing nerve"; (7) one can feel like a punk for a specific situation but not take on a punk identity; and (8) one can feel like a "crazy" killer in a specific situation but not take on a "crazy" or killer identity. If "compulsive masculinity" or Anderson's (1994, 1999) "street orientation" is dominant in public spaces and personal safety as our data suggest, then those who do not conform will be victimized.

The maintenance and reinforcement of identities supportive of violence are made possible by an effective sociocultural dynamic that sets forth an age-grading pathway to manhood that includes both behaviors and the means of resolving violations of respect. Wilkinson (2003) described the strong influence of street codes similar to the codes identified by Anderson (1999) or the code of honor described by Toch (1969), over the behaviors of young children, adolescents, and young adults. The absence of alternative means of attaining valued masculine identities further compounds the problem. The transmission of these social processes occurs on both the micro- and macro-levels. Children growing up in this environment learn these codes, or behavioral-affective systems, by navigating their way through interpersonal situations that often involve violent encounters.

The Epidemiology of Youth Homicide in New York City

Historical and Current Homicide Trends

The epidemic of youth violence in New York City since the mid-1980s is best understood in a social and historical context that spans nearly 35 years. Like the nation's largest cities, New York experienced a sharp increase in homicide and other violence rates beginning in the mid-1960s. The homicide rate rose from 4.7 per 100,000 population in

1960 to 31.0 in 1995. By 1996, the rate had receded to 13.9 per 100,000, a level unseen since 1968. Figure 36.1 shows the gun and nongun homicide rates for 1968–2000.

From 1900 through the beginning of the run-up in homicide in the mid-1960s, and with one exceptional era following the passage of the Volstead Act in 1919, homicide rates in New York City varied narrowly between 3.8 and 5.8 per 100,000 population (Monkonnen, 2001).[3] From 1965 to 1970, the average annual homicide rate rose from 7.6 to 12.6 and rose again to 21.7 by 1975. Thus, homicide in New York nearly tripled within a decade. The rates remained elevated above the 1968 rates until 1998. Accordingly, Figure 36.1 suggests that, for three decades, homicides in New York were normalized at an elevated rate and were for a long time characteristic of the city's social landscape. Thus, the escalation in killings until the 1990s was cumulative, with each new peak building on the elevation of the base rate established in the previous peak. One interpretation of the recent decline may simply be the recession of this longer-term social and historical trend.

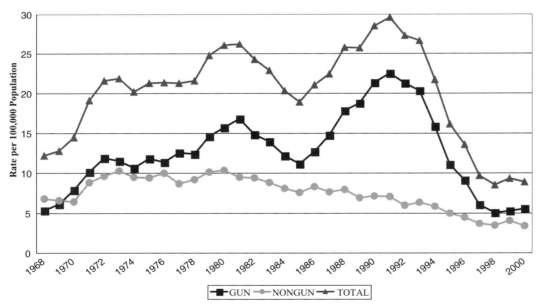

Figure 36.1. Gun and nongun homicide rates per 100,000 persons, 1968–2000, New York City. Source: Office of Vital Statistics and Epidemiology, New York City Department of Health and Mental Hygiene, various years.

Figure 36.1 also shows that this long-term trend involves three sub-epidemics. The first of these peaked in 1972, the second in 1981, and the third in 1991. Each coincided temporally with drug epidemics and the growth of retail drug markets: heroin in the early 1970s (Agar & Reisinger, 2002; Egan & Robinson, 1979; Hunt & Chambers, 1976; Inciardi, 1979), the emergence of urban street drug markets in the late 1970s where powdered cocaine was openly sold (Johnson et al., 1990; Johnston, 1987; Williams, 1989; Zimmer, 1987, 1990), and crack beginning in 1985 (Johnson et al., 1990). The successive epidemics were cumulative in their trends, not distinct. To re-introduce an idea from Part I, the pattern of killings in particular resembles a roller coaster, with an ascent through the late 1970s to a relatively low peak, a return to near the previous low point, and a sharp increase to a high peak in 1990 followed by a sharp drop.

Figure 36.1 shows the growing importance of guns in homicides in each of the three peaks. Increases in both gun and nongun homicides contributed to the tripling of homicide rates through 1972. In 1972, the ratio of gun to nongun homicides was 1.23. By the next peak in 1981, the 1,187 gun deaths were nearly 1.76 times greater than the 673 nongun homicides. In 1991, the modern peak, the 1,644 gun homicides were 3.16 times greater than the 519 nongun homicides. In addition to sharp increases in the number of gun homicides, the gun:nongun ratio also rose sharply because of a long-term decline in the number of nongun homicides. Since 1980, the number and rate of nongun homicides have declined by nearly 50%, from 735 to 335 nongun killings in 1996. There are thus two dynamic and different patterns in the data on homicide by weapon. Gun killings follow the roller-coaster pattern of steadily increasing peaks beginning in 1972. Nongun killings trend down from 1980 to rates unseen since 1960. This long-term secular trend in nongun killings is substantial, but it has not previously been noticed.

Figure 36.1 also shows that the recent cycle beginning in 1985 was qualitatively different from the preceding peaks in five important ways: (1) Its starting point was lower than the starting point for the previous (1981) peak, (2) its peak was about 15% higher than the preceding peak, (3) it had a far greater share of gun killings, (4) its decline was far steeper than any previous decline, and (5) homicides have remained at their low point far longer than in any of the previous three epidemics.

To illustrate the extent of the differences between the 1985–2000 cycle and its predecessors, Figure 36.2 presents the data from Figure 36.1 normed to the 1985 base.[4] Gun killings accounted for all of the increase in homicides since 1985 and most of the decline. Although the declines after 1992 in nongun killings are a continuation of the 8 years of previous decreases, the increase and decline in gun killings are evidence of a homicide spike that is unique from its predecessors. Nongun killings declined steadily since 1986 and by 1996 were about half the 1985 rate, suggesting a secular decline in nongun homicide that may be independent of the gun homicide epidemic.

The epidemic pattern was well-observed through homicide data, but public health data on nonlethal violence in part tell the same story. Data from the City's Injury Surveillance System provide information on hospitalizations for intentional injuries (NYC Department of Health and Mental Hygiene, 1997, and various years). Figure 36.3 shows that the decline in homicides was accompanied by a general decline in nonfatal assaults. These data were available for analysis beginning in 1990, about the same time that the homicide epidemic reached its peak. Figure 36.3 shows that, beginning in 1990, nearly all the decline in nonfatal assaults were declines in gun assaults; assaults by other means, such as blunt instruments or cutting instruments (e.g., knives), declined at a much lower rate. So, the rise and fall in homicides did not necessarily reflect changes either in the lethality of gun violence or a change in the case-fatality rate. Rather, gun violence declined generally over time following increases that also were almost exclusively the result of gun violence.

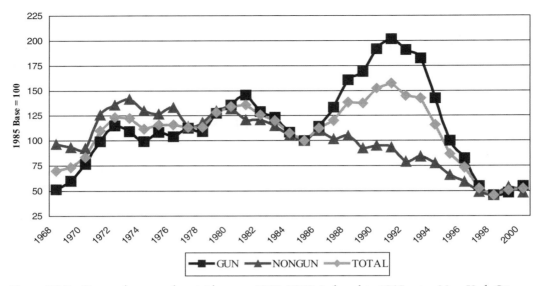

Figure 36.2. Gun and nongun homicide rates, 1968–2002, indexed to 1985 rates, New York City. Source: Office of Vital Statistics and Epidemiology, New York City Department of Health and Mental Hygiene, various years.

The importance of the most recent era of homicide rise and decline, not only in its epidemiological pattern but also in its influence on law and policy (Feld, 1999; Stuntz, 2001; Zimring, 1999), leads us to focus the analysis in the next part and also in the section titled "The Epidemiology of Youth Homicide in New York City" on the patterns of homicide and violence in this era, and especially on the period from 1985–1996, when the rise and fall in homicide were the most dramatic and acute.

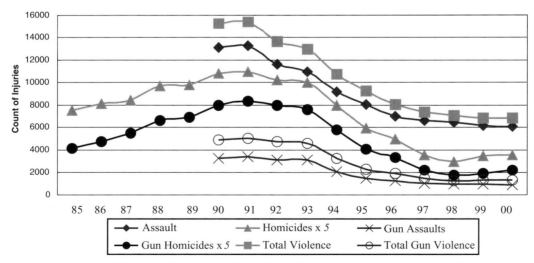

Figure 36.3. Gun and nongun homicide and assault by firearm, 1985–2000. Source: Office of Vital Statistics and Epidemiology, New York City Department of Health and Mental Hygiene, various years; Injury Prevention Bureau, New York City Department of Health and Mental Hygiene, various years.

The Social Structure of Homicide

The demographic patterns of gun and nongun homicide victimization during this period tell a series of interesting stories, some predictable and others surprising. First, the homicide trends for women differ from the patterns for men. Any benefits of the end of the violence epidemic accrued to men; women's risk of violent victimization remained stable at a level far lower than that of men. Second, changes in adolescent homicide rates were accompanied by parallel but less dramatic changes among older populations. This trend varies from the national picture of steadily declining rates among older groups. Third, as we saw earlier, the homicide run-up and decline were concentrated in gun killings. Fourth, the homicide epidemic was concentrated among non-Whites. We observed these trends for both homicide victims and offenders, which are discussed below. The data are available at: http://www2.law.columbia.edu/fagan/researchdata/contagion.

GENDER

Nearly all the increase and decline in killings from 1985–1995 were gun homicides of males. The rate of gun killings among males doubled from 21.8 per 100,000 in 1985 to 44.5 in 1991. Nongun killings of males declined steadily throughout this period and by 1995 were less than half the 1985 rate. Killings of males were increasingly gun events: the ratio of gun to nongun homicide victimizations of males increased from about 1.5:1 in 1985 to 3.23:1 in 1995.

The temporal patterns were similar for females. The rate of gun homicides of females peaked in 1991, the same year as males, and sustained their peak rate for approximately 3 years before dropping sharply in 1994. By 1995, gun homicides for females had dropped 5% below their 1985 levels. Nongun homicides of women declined steadily throughout this period, from 4.7 per 100,000 in 1985 to 3.8 per 100,000 in 1995. But unlike males, the rates of nongun homicides of females were higher than the rates of gun homicides. Throughout the period, the changes in rates for females were quite small, and not far from the expected rates historically. The same is true of male nongun killings. Accordingly, this epidemic is confined to gun killings among males.

AGE

Much of public and scholarly attention on violence in the past decade has focused on the increase in gun homicides by adolescents (Blumstein, 1995; Cook & Laub, 1998). Trends nationwide show that gun homicide rates for adolescents increased during this period while gun homicide rates for persons over 25 years of age were declining. In New York City, homicides were not confined to younger age groups, but were a serious problem across a wide age range from 15 to 34 years of age. Table 36.1 shows that gun homicide rates were higher than nongun rates for all age groups. For each year, gun homicide rates were highest for persons aged 20 to 24 in all years. Gun homicides by adolescents aged 15 to 19 rose more sharply over this period than other older population groups. Nevertheless, although adolescent participation in gun homicide rose sharply from 1985–1991, rates for other age groups also continued to rise during this period.

Gun homicide rates declined sharply for all three age groups from 1992–1995, to about 50% of their peak rates in 1991, and were about the same as their 1985 rates. Although the post-1991 decline was precipitous for adolescents aged 15 to 19, their 1995 gun homicide rates remained 25% above their 1985 base rate. Table 36.1 also shows that nongun homicide rates declined steadily for all age groups and by 1995 were 50% or more lower than their 1985 rates (NYC Department of Health and Mental Hygiene, 1997). Similar to gun homicide rates, the nongun homicide rates were highest for persons aged 20 to 24.

RACE

Nationally, virtually all increases in homicide rates from 1985 to 1990 among people 10 to

Table 36.1: Adolescent gun and nongun homicide rates by age, New York City, 1985–1995

Year	<15	15–19	20–24	25–34	≥35
Gun Homicides					
1985	0.6	20.8	34.1	21.1	7.1
1986	1.1	19.9	44.1	25.6	6.9
1987	1.2	33.1	50.6	25.3	8.5
1988	1.5	45.5	56.8	33.5	9.2
1989	1.3	43.1	60.0	37.9	9.0
1990	2.2	50.9	66.3	42.2	10.8
1991	1.0	57.4	66.3	42.2	12.6
1992	1.3	48.3	68.1	42.8	11.0
1993	1.6	48.5	63.8	37.5	11.7
1994	0.7	39.6	47.5	30.0	8.3
1995	0.8	26.0	34.7	18.1	6.9
Nongun Homicides					
1985	2.9	10.4	15.7	12.2	9.4
1986	3.4	8.0	17.7	14.1	8.4
1987	1.8	6.3	14.1	12.7	7.8
1988	3.0	6.1	14.6	12.3	7.9
1989	2.6	6.5	12.3	13.4	7.0
1990	3.4	12.8	15.5	14.7	7.4
1991	3.1	8.0	11.1	10.9	6.5
1992	2.4	6.9	8.6	7.9	6.2
1993	4.1	3.9	7.0	8.9	6.5
1994	3.1	6.1	7.0	8.8	5.7
1995	2.6	5.2	6.8	6.6	5.1

Table 36.2: Gun and nongun homicide rates per 100,000 persons by race, 1985–1995

Year	Gun		Nongun	
	White	Non-White	White	Non-White
1985	10.1	12.8	8.0	10.6
1986	10.9	15.2	7.3	11.3
1987	9.8	20.7	6.1	10.1
1988	13.2	23.6	6.4	10.1
1989	15.1	23.2	6.7	8.9
1990	18.8	25.1	8.9	9.0
1991	19.4	26.6	6.4	7.8
1992	19.3	24.3	6.0	6.0
1993	17.2	24.5	5.5	7.2
1994	12.8	18.9	5.7	5.8
1995	9.5	12.8	4.5	5.5

34 years of age were due to deaths of African American males. Most of these were firearm fatalities that were overwhelmingly concentrated demographically and spatially among African American males in urban areas (Fingerhut, Ingram, & Feldman, 1992a,b.) Table 36.2 shows that the trends in New York mirror these national trends. Unfortunately, none of the data sources permitted detailed disaggregation of the homicide trends by ethnicity over the entire 1985–1995 period. Detailed data were available only for African Americans; Whites and Hispanics were not distinguished in the police or Vital Statistics data until after 1990. Therefore, our analysis is limited to comparisons between whites and non-Whites; non-Whites are primarily persons of African descent, including some Hispanics.

The within-race ratio of gun to nongun homicide rates for each year in the 1985–1995 period illustrates the concentration of the homicide epidemic in gun homicides among non-Whites. For Whites, the ratio rises from 1.26:1 in 1985 to a peak of 3.23:1 in 1992, before receding to 2.1:1 in 1995. For non-Whites, the ratio rises from 1.20:1 in 1985 to a peak of 4.05:1 in 1992 and recedes to 2.32:1 in 1995. However, the narrow difference between Whites and non-Whites may reflect the inclusion of Hispanics among the Whites in the population and homicide counts. The extent of this bias can be seen in 1993 data from the New York City Department of Health injury surveillance system. The mortality and morbidity rates of gunshot wounds for Hispanics are 228 per 100,000 persons, compared to 302 for African Americans and 60 for Whites in that period (NYC Department of Health and Mental Hygiene, 1992; New York State Department of Health, 1994).

VICTIM-OFFENDER HOMOGENEITY

Most homicides are within-group events, especially with respect to gender, race, and ethnicity (Cook & Laub, 1998; Sampson & Lauritsen, 1994).[5] We analyzed data from police reports on the within-age distribution of homicide events for each year in the recent homicide cycle to estimate the proportion of homicides in which victims and offenders both came from their own age group. From 1985–1995, we observed within-group homogeneity with respect to our limited categories of race, a trend evident also in national data (Cook & Laub, 1998). Age homogeneity was more varied and depended on the method of homicide. Age homogeneity for gun homicides was highest for homicide offenders aged 25 to 34 and lowest for 20- to 24- year-olds. The low rates for the group aged 20 to 24 reflects their age status between the two other groups and the higher likelihood of cross-age interactions.

Age differences widened during the homicide cycle beginning in 1985. At the outset of the homicide run-up in 1985, age homogeneity for gun and nongun homicides was low: about one gun homicide in four involved persons within the same age categories. For adults aged 25 to 34, about 4 in 10 gun homicides were within-age killings. A year later, both age homogeneity and homicide rates increased. Within-age gun homicides for young adults aged 20 to 24 rose from 22.9% of gun homicides in 1985 to 35.8% in 1990; for offenders aged 25 to 34 years, within-age group homicides rose from 38.5% in 1985 to 54.9% in 1989. Even with these increases, however, the majority of gun killings involved persons from different age groups. During the same period, within-age nongun homicide rates varied from year to year in an inconsistent pattern.

The results are not surprising: age stratification of peer groups has traditionally created age-specific social networks. Age grading is a hallmark of street gangs (Klein, 1995) and adolescent cliques (Schwendinger & Schwendinger, 1985). These rigid age boundaries offered few opportunities for cross-age social interactions among delinquent groups. But contextual changes in street corner life in inner cities, where homicides were concentrated throughout this period, contributed to a breakdown of traditional age grading. The emergence of street drug markets and dense street corner groups of males not in the workforce contributed to a mixing of the ages on the street. Among adolescents and young adults, competition

for street status through violence contributes to a process of "status forcing" that promotes cross-age interactions (Wilkinson, 2003).

CONTEXTUAL EFFECTS

Both popular and social science explanations of the homicide epidemic in New York and elsewhere have focused on social trends, particularly changes in drug markets (Baumer, 1994; Baumer et al., 1998; Blumstein, 1995; Cork, 1999; Grogger & Willis, 2000). Fagan et al. (1998) discuss the appeal of these explanations. First, homicide and drug epidemics have been closely phased, both temporally and spatially, in New York and nationwide, for nearly 30 years (Fagan, 1990; Fagan & Wilkinson, 1997). Homicide peaks in 1972, 1979, and 1991 mirror three drug epidemics: heroin, cocaine hydrochloride (powder), and crack cocaine. These long-term trends predict that trends in drug use would occur contemporaneously with trends in homicide. Second, the emergence of volatile crack markets in 1985 is cited as one of the primary contextual factors that have driven up homicide rates in New York (Bourgois, 1995; Goldstein, Brownstein, Ryan, & Bellucci, 1989; Johnson et al., 1990). Competition between sellers, conflicts between buyers and sellers, and intraorganizational conflict were all contributors to lethal violence within crack markets (Fagan & Chin, 1989, 1991; Hamid, 1990). Crack also is implicated in the decline of homicide since 1991 (Curtis, 1998).

Figure 36.4 compares trends in gun homicides for three age groups with trends in drug overdose deaths. Drug overdose deaths follow a pattern of short cycles, with relatively brief periods of increase and decline. The rates increase from 1986 to 1988, decline through 1990, and increase again for 3 years before leveling off. The run-up of gun homicide rates in 1985 to 1988 matches an increase in drug overdose deaths, but homicides continued to increase even as drug overdose deaths declined. Drug overdose death rates increase from 1992 to 1994, even as gun homicide rates decline. Accordingly, there appears to be little mutual influence of drug overdose deaths and gun

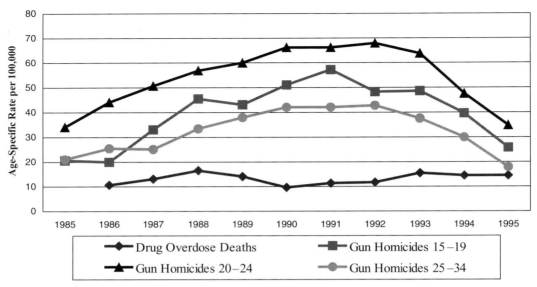

Figure 36.4. Drug overdose death and age-specific gun homicide victimization rate, 1985–1995. Source: Office of Vital Statistics and Epidemiology, New York City Department of Health and Mental Hygiene, various years.

homicide trends for any of the three age groups.[6] Changes in drug use patterns may explain this disjuncture, with drugs such as heroin returning as the favored street drug and displacing crack and crack markets (Curtis, 1998). These drugs are more likely to cause overdose deaths.

An alternative indicator of drug market activity is drug arrests. The size, location, and intensity of drug markets can be approximated by drug arrest rates (Cork, 1999; Rosenfeld & Decker, 1999). Accordingly, drug arrests reflect both strategic decisions by police and drug market characteristics. In conjunction with other indicators, arrests are a useful marker of drug trends. However, the trend lines in Figure 36.5 for age-specific homicide victimization rates and felony drug arrest rates show little relationship between gun homicides and drug arrests. Both drug arrests and gun homicide rates increase from 1986 through 1989, but the trend lines move in different directions after that. Homicides increase through 1991 for adolescents and 1992 for young adults. Drug arrests decline from 1990 through 1993 and begin to rise again in 1994. Most of these felony drug arrests were for sale or

possession with intent to sell, and most were either crack or cocaine arrests, the two drugs that were traded most actively in street markets. The portion of felony drug arrests that involved crack or cocaine rose from 57% in 1986 to 64% in 1988 and declined steadily to 48% in 1995.

These figures show that neither drug selling activity nor increases in problematic drug consumption adequately explain the run-up and decline in gun homicides. Violence associated with drug use remained relatively infrequent during the onset of the crack crisis (Fagan, 1992; Fagan & Chin, 1989, 1991). Moreover, the share of homicides due to drug selling did not rise during the homicide run-up (Goldstein et al., 1989). Drug selling accounts for an unknown proportion of homicides, with estimates ranging from about 10% nationwide in the FBI's Supplemental Homicide Reports (FBI, various years) to 50% in local studies in New York (Goldstein et al., 1989) or Los Angeles (Klein, Maxson, & Cunningham, 1991). Thus, a decline in street-level drug selling activity may have reduced, to some unknown extent, the types of social interactions that lead to gun killings. But drug

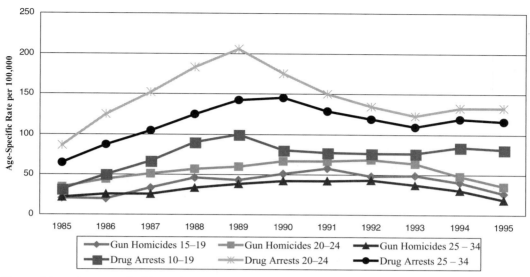

Figure 36.5. Age-specific felony drug arrest rates and gun homicide victimization rates, 1985–1995. Source: Office of Vital Statistics and Epidemiology, New York City Department of Health and Mental Hygiene, various years; New York City Police Department, various years.

selling alone is unlikely to have produced the unprecedented run-up or decline in gun killings so consistently across time, social groups, and areas.

Finally, demographic changes also offer limited explanations for either the homicide increase or decline. The population for the highest risk groups, non-White males aged 15 to 29, declined by about 10% from 1985–1995 (Fagan et al., 1998), a far smaller scale of change than the change that could produce the observed declines in gun homicides. Although it is tempting to dismiss demography as a correlate of the homicide decline, the relationship of population to a changing behavioral pattern may be nonlinear (Gladwell, 2000). In other words, did the population decline reach a threshold where it could lead to a decline in the incidence of gun homicides? According to Burt (1987), network density promotes social contagion by increasing exponentially the extent of contact between persons within groups is nonlinear. Perhaps population density among the highest risk groups rose during the run-up in violence and reached a threshold or tipping point at which behavioral change accelerated and spread through a popula-

tion before beginning its process of decline (see, for example, Crane, 1991; Gladwell, 2000). As the population declined, so too did the rate of contacts. This is a plausible but unlikely explanation. First, the age decline was small: less than 10% in the highest risk groups. Second, the breakdown in age grading of violence during this period may have mitigated cohort effects and diffused behaviors broadly across age groups. Like the effects of declining drug markets, the contraction in the highest risk population is a potentially important influence in the decline in firearm homicides from 1992–1996, one that may contain the mechanisms of decline. We turn to these mechanisms in the next sections.

Neighborhood Effects on Social Contagion of Youth Homicide

We begin with a set of analyses that estimate the probabilities of the diffusion of behaviors across social areas or neighborhoods. We use the census tract as the boundary for "neighborhood," based on the size (area) of tracts in New York and their isomorphism with important social units, such as public housing developments and feeder school patterns. Tracts are commonly used to represent neighborhoods in sociological research because of their size and robustness in predicting variation in a variety of social interactions (see, for example, Land, McCall, & Cohen, 1990). Other studies have estimated diffusion across similarly small areas comprised of a few tracts that represent neighborhoods with meaningful social boundaries (e.g., Crane, 1991; Fagan, West, & Holland, 2003; Morenoff, Sampson, & Raudenbush, 2001). These analyses set the stage for the analysis in Part V of microsocial interactions in which social interactions animate dynamics of social contagion that diffuse violence across groups and places.

Susceptibility: Neighborhood Risk

We draw on the literature of neighborhoods and violence to construct a framework of structural risk that simultaneously compromises resilience against transmission while increasing susceptibility. Both theory and empirical research suggest that neighborhoods are susceptible to the spread of violence when structurally weakened (Massey, 1995; Patterson, 1991; Roncek & Maier, 1991; Rose & McClain, 1990; Taylor & Covington, 1988). For example, recent studies suggest that violence shares several explanatory variables with concentrated poverty (Sampson & Lauritsen, 1994; Wilson, 1987, 1991), resource deprivation (Land et al., 1990; Williams & Flewelling, 1988), and inequality (Messner & Tardiff, 1986; Morenoff & Tienda, 1997; Sampson, 1987; Shihadeh & Steffensmeier, 1994). These constructs describe the lack of sufficient means, including income poverty and inequality, to sustain informal social control (Sampson, 1993; Sampson & Wilson, 1995).

Wilson (1987) argues that there has been both an economic and a social transformation of the inner city, in which the exodus of manufacturing jobs beginning in the 1970's has changed the social and economic composition of inner cities, leading to a concentration of resource deprivation. He suggests that the concentration of resource deprivation in specific areas led to dynamic changes in the processes of socialization and social control in those areas. As middle- and working class African American families moved away from the inner cities when their jobs left, there remained behind a disproportionate concentration of the most disadvantaged segments of the urban populations: poor female-headed households with children and chronically unemployed males with low job skills. The secondary effects of this exodus created conditions that were conducive to rising teenage violence: the weakness of mediating social institutions (e.g., churches, schools), and the absence of informal social controls to supervise and mentor youths.[7] Wilson (1987) refers to these conditions of weak social control as social isolation.

The concept of social isolation suggests an ecological dynamic in which the components of poverty and structural disadvantage are interconnected with the dynamics of social control and opportunity structures. The decline of manufacturing jobs increased unemployment among adult males, primarily African Americans, whose lack of technical skills and deep human capital limited them to low-wage and short-term unskilled labor positions. Other economic transformations, including the rise of service and technical jobs outside central cities, motivated the exodus of middle-class families to the outer rings and suburbs surrounding the inner cities. Remaining within the abandoned central cities were unskilled males whose "marriage capital" was low, giving rise to an increasing divorce rate and declining marriage rate.

Changes in the composition of central city neighborhoods also weakened the social institutions that were critical to the informal social control and collective supervision of youths. The weakening of social controls had their strongest effects in transactional settings of neighborhoods and in places like schools and church where adolescent development takes place. And, the exodus of middle-class families from inner cities weakened the political strength of the remaining families, leading to physical deterioration

(Wallace, 1991), lower housing values, and in turn increased residential (spatial) segregation (Massey & Denton, 1993).

In turn, the social isolation of people and families was extended to institutions (Wacquant & Wilson, 1989). The rise in poverty and weakening of social institutions also undermined the presence of and institutional support for conventional behaviors. As a result, conventional values and behaviors were attenuated because they were not salient and had little payoff for one's survival or status (Elliott et al., 1996; Tienda, 1991; Wilson, 1987). These dynamics in turn attenuated neighborhood social organization, increasing the likelihood that illegitimate opportunity structures would emerge: illegal economies including drug distribution or extortion, gangs (Fagan, 1989, 1993; Brotherton et al., 2004), and social networks to support them. These structures competed with declining legal work opportunities both as income sources and as sources for social status. As these networks flourished, the systems of peer and deviant social control replaced the controls of social institutions and conventional peer networks (Fagan, 1992, 1993).

Accordingly, violence and homicide are more likely to occur in an ecological context of weak social control, poorly supervised adolescent networks, widespread perceptions of danger and the demand for lethal weapons, and the attenuation of outlets to resolve disputes without violence. It is in this ecology of danger that violence becomes transmittable through weapons and their impact on perception and decision making in social interactions.

Analytic Models: Diffusion and Contagion

We estimated models of contagion of gun violence (homicide and assault) and its diffusion across New York City neighborhoods from 1985–2000. Although the sharpest changes in violence rates occurred from 1991–1995, we took advantage of data through 2000 to chart the continuing pattern of decline over the succeeding 5 years. We tested two distinct conceptual models

for the spread of gun violence from one neighborhood to the next. An outward contagion model posits that adolescent violence spreads out from a central census tract (T) or the immediate neighborhood to adjacent census tracts (X, Y, and Z) or the surrounding community. In this model, the incidence and prevalence of adolescent homicide or assault violence in a given neighborhood exert a significant influence over the incidence and prevalence of adolescent violence rates in the adjacent community.

This influence is hypothesized to operate in at least two different ways. First, a threshold effect is expected concerning adolescent homicide counts, such that the presence of at least one adolescent homicide in a given neighborhood will substantially increase the probability of experiencing at least one adolescent homicide in the surrounding community. Second, with respect to adolescent homicide rates more precisely, positive covariation is anticipated whereby increases or decreases in the adolescent homicide rate of violence in a neighborhood are reflected in concomitant increases or decreases in the surrounding community's adolescent homicide violence rate.

It is also possible that the contagion effect of adolescent violence is reversed. Accordingly, the inward contagion model asserts that the level of adolescent violence in an immediate neighborhood is at least partially contingent on the level of adolescent violence in its broader community. Again, the two distinct relationship forms (threshold effect and positive co-variation) are possible. By considering the simultaneous influence of adjacent spaces, we address the problem of spatial autocorrelation by effectively controlling for mutual influences within and over time.

In addition to corresponding adolescent violence rates, both the outward and inward contagion models incorporate relevant structural and demographic features of neighborhoods and communities as key explanatory constructs. Thus, for the full outward contagion model, the presence and rate of the adolescent homicide rate or assault rate in the surrounding community are a function of the relevant characteristics of the community, as well as the presence or rate of adolescent homicide violence in the neighborhood. In contrast, the full inward contagion model suggests that both relevant neighborhood features and the presence or rate of adolescent homicide in the community predict the presence or rate of adolescent violence in the neighborhood. Although these factors are presumed to play a significant, independent role in the prediction of adolescent violence rates, it is nonetheless hypothesized that effects of homicide violence rates as independent variables will remain substantial, even once controls for relevant neighborhood and community characteristics have been introduced.

Models were estimated using mixed effects regression models. Mixed effects regression models can be used to approximate multilevel models in which data are hierarchically organized. For example, this class of models is useful in such cases as estimating the simultaneous effects of school climate and individual student family background on standardized test scores, or neighborhood characteristics and household composition on crime rates (Bryk & Raudenbush, 1992; Singer & Willett, 2003; Snijders & Bosker, 1994). Mixed effects models also are useful in estimating individual growth curves or within-subject change over time. In these examples, we might specify the ecological effects of school or neighborhood as fixed effects and individual household or family influences as random effects. This specification approximates the presumed hierarchy of influences. One may reverse the specification as well, comparing estimates to assess reciprocal effects between the two sets of predictors. Mixed effects models simulate the hierarchy of effects by estimating the differences in error-co-variance matrix structures for each set of effects (Singer & Willett, 2003).[8]

In this analysis, the contagion models are specified using both fixed and random effects. The fixed effects of the neighborhood (outward model) and adjacent community (inward model) structural characteristics and violence rates are interpreted as standard regression coefficients. But the analytic strategy also assumes that neighborhoods and communities have varying mean violence levels and that they exhibit distinct trajectories of violence over time. We account for the variance in average levels of violence by specifying random intercepts in our models. To estimate changes over time, we use a repeated measures design in which year is included as a random effect that approximates a developmental growth curve (Goldstein, 2003). We also estimate an autoregressive co-variance structure to account for the strong correlations of homicide and violence rates through time in census tracts and their surrounding neighborhoods.

We use the Poisson form of the model to estimate counts of both gun and nongun homicides and assaults. Poisson techniques are appropriate to identify factors that predict the number of occurrences of an event within a specific observation period (Gardner, Mulvey, & Shaw, 1995; Land, McCall, & Nagin, 1996). Such "count" models are appropriate, given the relatively low number of homicides in most tracts in most years and the sharp right-hand skew in the distribution of both homicides and assaults. To estimate the adolescent component of the total violence rate, including both homicides and assaults, we included co-variates that estimate the age composition of neighborhoods including the ratio of youths aged 15–24 to persons over age 50 in each tract. Because homicide and assault victimization during this period was disproportionately due to gun violence and also concentrated among African Americans, we estimate separate models for total homicide or assault, gun homicide or violence, and gun victimization for African Americans.

Data

DEPENDENT VARIABLES
The dependent variables include counts of homicides, gun homicides, injury assaults that lead to hospitalization, and gun injury assaults. We also estimate specific counts of these variables for African American victims. These data were obtained from the

Table 36.3: Means and standard deviations for census tracts, New York City, 1990

Variable	N	Mean	Standard Deviation
% Households with Public Assistance Income	2,157	13.81	13.28
Gini for Total Household Income	2,157	0.37	0.09
% Households Under Poverty Level	2,157	18.10	15.06
% High-School Graduates – Total – 25+	2,174	66.33	16.34
% Employed in Managerial, Professional, or Technical Jobs	2,162	29.69	15.17
Employment Rate	2,164	90.27	7.08
Labor Force Participation Rate	2,175	60.64	11.55
% Non-White	2,175	54.86	36.17
Racial Fragmentation Index	2,175	0.38	0.19
% Female Headed Households with Children <18	2,157	10.09	10.43
Supervision Ratio (25–64 by 5–24)	2,162	2.42	2.08
% Youth Population (5–15)	2,175	14.69	6.74
Residential Mobility – Same House as 1985	2,175	62.93	11.84
Population – 1990	2,216	3,304.41	2,465.07
Foreign Born	2,175	27.32	15.13
Linguistic Isolation	2,175	10.95	10.13
Vacancy Rate	2,160	5.53	5.93
% Occupied Units That Are Rentals	2,157	65.10	25.89
Density – Mean Persons Per Occupied Room	2,157	0.67	0.61

Source: U.S. Census Bureau, 1990 Census of Population and Housing, Summary File STF 3 AFile.

Injury Surveillance System of the New York City Department of Health and Mental Hygiene. The Injury Surveillance System collates information from the New York City Department of Health (DOH) to form a database of injury and fatality locations for cases involving violence victims. All weapon assault injuries, fatal and nonfatal, are generated through this archive. The data come from two public health data sources: Vital Statistics (mortality records) and the New York State hospital admissions database, SPARCS, for hospitalized assault injuries. The latter data were compiled from the hospital patient discharge summaries, with ICD-9 E-Codes (injury codes) for the supplementary classification of external causes of injury. The data are hierarchically organized to avoid duplications for persons who were initially hospitalized but then died.[9] Unfortunately, nonlethal injury data were unavailable until 1990, and so the time series begins at the point when the trends already had begun their decline.

INDEPENDENT VARIABLES

Independent variables operationalize the model of neighborhood risk or susceptibility described earlier. Data reflecting the structural and demographic composition of neighborhoods and communities are predictors in the contagion models. Following Land et al. (1990), we selected 19 tract-level variables from the 1990 Census (STF3A and 3B files) to characterize social areas. Means and variances for the 19 initial variables are presented in Table 36.3. Principal components analysis was used to eliminate autocorrelation among the 14 variables and identify 3 orthogonal and conceptually distinct factors. Table 36.4 shows that neighborhoods and communities are characterized along three dimensions: deprivation, population characteristics, and social control. Because communities are actually composites of census tracts, their factor scores are actually weighted factor score composites. Estimates were weighted by the 1990 tract population.

Table 36.4: Factor composition, New York City census tracts, 1990

Factor	Rotated Factor Score	Eigenvalue	% Variance Explained
Poverty/Inequality		2.54	84.73
% Households Under Poverty Level	0.96		
% Households with Public Assistance Income	0.93		
Gini for Total Household Income	0.87		
Labor Market/Human Capital		2.60	65.03
% High-School Graduates – Total – 25+	0.91		
% Managerial, Professional, or Technical Jobs	0.84		
Employment Rate	0.74		
Labor Force Participation Rate	0.72		
Segregation		1.31	65.27
Racial Fragmentation Index	0.81		
% Non-White	0.81		
Social Control #1 – Supervision		1.97	65.56
% Youth Population (5–15)	0.92		
% Female Headed Households w/Children <18	0.80		
Supervision Ratio (25–64 by 5–24)	−0.70		
Social Control #2 – Anonymity		1.02	50.78
Population – 1990	0.71		
Residential Mobility – Same House as 1985	0.71		
Immigration		1.52	76.25
Linguistic Isolation	0.87		
Foreign Born	0.87		
Housing Structure		1.24	41.48
% Occupied Units That Are Rentals	0.76		
Density – Persons Per Occupied Room	0.55		
Vacancy Rate	0.60		

CONTAGION EFFECTS

The "contagion effect" of adolescent homicide is not expected to be immediate. Similar to the concept of incubation, it is more reasonable to assume that some period of time must elapse between the occurrence of an adolescent homicide (threshold effect) or change in the adolescent homicide rate (positive co-variation) and the realization of a related occurrence or rate change. For this study, the time elapsed is estimated to be 1 year. For example, with the outward contagion model, the adolescent homicide rate in a neighborhood for 1990 is used to predict the rate in the surrounding community for 1991. Conversely, the adolescent rate for a neighborhood in 1993 under the inward contagion model is estimated using the community adolescent homicide rate from 1992. However, models with 2-year time lags produced results very similar to those reported here. Thus the results as reported do not appear to be an artifact of the lag time chosen.

Results

On a preliminary note, we remind readers that the critical parameter in this class of models is the interaction of the time by contagion measures. The parameter estimate for the interaction indicates whether the rate of change in the parameter is a significant predictor of the rate of change of the dependent variable. The main effects can be interpreted as explanations for differences in the average rates over the entire duration of the panel. The results in Tables 36.5 and 36.6 show parameter estimates for the factors of interest in the contagion story, including spatial autocorrelation. All models are controlled statistically for the neighborhood susceptibility factors discussed earlier. We use a quadratic form of the time parameter to reflect the nonlinear distribution of the homicide and injury rates over time.

There is evidence of both inward and outward contagion for homicide and injury assault, but the patterns vary by type of violence, means of violence, and race of the victims. For total homicide, including gun and nongun homicides, Table 36.5, Panel A shows results of three outward contagion models. Neither total homicides nor gun homicides are statistically significant. The parameter estimate for the interaction of time by homicide in the surrounding tracts is significant only in the model for gun homicide victimization of African Americans, and the direction is negative. The interpretation for the coefficient is somewhat counterintuitive – it does not imply that there are fewer homicides in the surrounding tracts over time. Instead, as the overall homicide trend declines, a negative coefficient suggests that this factor is opposing that trend in the dependent variable. In this case, then, the negative coefficient for the time by homicide interaction indicates that the rate of homicide victimization of African Americans in the surrounding neighborhoods is increasing, controlling for the rates in the surrounded neighborhood in the previous year. The exponentiated coefficient is 0.989, suggesting that an increase of one homicide in a neighborhood in T_0 predicts an increase of 1.1% in the number of homicides in any of the surrounding areas.

Panel B in Table 36.5 presents consistent evidence of homicide contagion. The estimates for time by contagion are significant and negative in all three models. The exponentiated coefficient for total homicide is 0.992, suggesting that an increase of one homicide in the surrounding tracts in T_0 predicts an increase of 0.8% in the number of

homicides in the surrounded tracts in T_1. For the other models in Panel B, the effects also are significant and are larger: an increase of 1.0% for gun homicides for an increment of one homicide in the surrounding tracts, and 2.0 for gun homicide victimizations of African Americans.

The results for contagion of injury assault suggest that there are contagion effects. All the models in both panels of Table 36.6 are significant, but the effects seem at first glance to be small. The exponentiated coefficients suggest that assaults increase by less than 1% for each increment in assaults in the surrounding tracts for outward contagion or in the surrounded tracts for inward contagion. Contagion is evident both for gun violence and nongun violence in these models, suggesting a more ambiguous role of guns. Although there may be a cross-over contagion effect of gun violence to nongun violence in the surrounding areas, it is unlikely conceptually and empirically to be any larger than these observed effects for within-type contagion.

Several features of this analysis merit further note. First, the coefficients for outward homicide contagion parameters are relatively small and significant only for the model for African American gun homicide victimization. This is not surprising, given that homicides are comparatively rare events. But the primary tale in Table 36.5 is one of inward contagion. Consider first the sheer magnitude of the estimates for spatial lag in the outward models, and second the large and significant coefficients for the inward contagion parameters. Taken together, these findings confirm that the inward contagion of homicide is more potent than outward contagion, that a neighborhood is affected more by its adjacent community than it affects that same community.

Though not as dramatic, the same pattern is evident in Table 36.6. Here, there is evidence of both outward and inward contagion of nonlethal assaults. The coefficients for the outward contagion of assault are not large, but they are consistently significant. In relative terms, however, the coefficients

Table 36.5: Poisson regression results for models of inward and outward contagion of homicide, New York City census tracts, 1985–2000 (coefficient, *t* statistic, statistical significance of predictor, exponentiated coefficient)

A. Outward Contagion

Predictor	Total Homicides				Gun Homicides				African American Gun Homicides			
	B	Exp (B)	t	p(t)	B	Exp (B)	t	p(t)	B	Exp (B)	t	p(t)
Intercept	−0.069	0.942	−3.35	b	−0.4919	0.611	−26.00	c	−2.169	0.114	−63.32	c
Time	0.112	1.127	26.56	c	0.149	1.160	28.94	c	0.155	1.167	20.35	c
Homicide Contagion	0.003	1.003	1.01	ns	0.008	1.008	2.22	a	0.040	1.041	4.34	c
% African American Population	0.010	1.010	22.54	c	0.012	1.012	24.20	c	0.030	1.030	35.14	c
Homicide Spatial Lag	0.888	2.429	119.73	c	1.169	3.219	117.99	c	1.425	4.157	100.77	c
Time *Homicide Contagion	−0.0009	0.999	−0.84	ns	−0.002	0.990	−1.30	ns	−0.011	0.989	−2.73	c
Time *Homicide Spatial Lag	−0.072	0.931	−20.88	c	−0.098	0.906	−19.88	c	−0.085	0.918	−9.11	c

B. Inward Contagion

Predictor	Total Homicides				Gun Homicides				African American Gun Homicides			
	B	Exp (B)	t	p(t)	B	Exp (B)	t	p(t)	B	Exp (B)	t	p(t)
Intercept	−1.743	0.175	−70.27	c	−2.204	0.110	−77.92	c	−2.176	0.113	−58.44	c
Time	0.156	1.168	14.80	c	0.1888	1.207	15.56	c	0.173	1.189	11.28	c
Homicide Contagion	0.050	1.052	26.61	c	0.066	1.069	25.88	c	0.078	1.081	10.18	c
% African American Population	0.012	1.102	23.52	c	0.014	1.014	23.97	c	−0.016	0.984	−13.66	c
Time *Homicide Contagion	−0.008	0.992	7.47	c	−0.010	0.990	−8.02	c	−0.020	0.980	−5.30	c

p(t): a < 0.05; b < 0.01; c < 0.001; ns = not significant.
1. All models were estimated using mixed effects Poisson regression models with autoregressive co-variance structures.
2. Outward contagion models include adjustment for spatial autocorrelation of homicides in the surrounding census tracts.
3. All model results were adjusted for effects of tract social and economic factors: percent of persons below poverty, percent in labor market, ratio of adults to juveniles, percent population living in tract 5 years or less, percent population not born in U.S., percent of households in public housing, and total population.
4. All models were estimated with time as quadratic (nonlinear) predictor.

Table 36.6: Poisson regression results for models of inward and outward contagion of assault, New York City census tracts, 1990–2000 (coefficient, t statistic, statistical significance of predictor, exponentiated coefficient)

A. Outward Contagion

Predictor	Total Assaults				Gun Assaults				African American Gun Assaults			
	B	Exp (B)	t	p(t)	B	Exp (B)	t	p(t)	B	Exp (B)	t	p(t)
Intercept	2.226	9.263	120.58	c	0.086	2.356	37.04	c	−0.338	0.713	−9.98	c
Time	−0.004	0.996	−42.87	c	−0.008	0.992	−46.81	c	−0.008	0.992	−31.33	c
Assault Contagion	0.0002	1.002	3.45	c	0.008	1.008	2.33	c	0.004	1.004	0.81	ns
% African American Population	0.008	1.008	17.31	c	0.012	1.012	21.41	c	0.026	1.025	30.70	c
Assault Spatial Lag	0.100	1.105	67.64	c	0.283	1.328	33.88	c	0.303	1.354	24.70	c
Time*Assault Contagion	−0.0001	0.999	−2.45	c	−0.0002	0.998	−3.57	c	−0.0002	0.998	−2.19	a
Time*Assault Spatial Lag	0.001	1.001	44.94	c	0.004	1.004	31.17	c	0.005	1.005	26.18	c

B. Inward Contagion

Predictor	Total Assaults				Gun Assaults				African American Gun Assaults			
	B	Exp (B)	t	p(t)	B	Exp (B)	t	p(t)	B	Exp (B)	t	p(t)
Intercept	0.506	1.659	22.13	c	−1.113	0.328	−36.43	c	−2.64	0.071	−58.43	c
Time	−0.007	0.993	−11.99	c	−0.021	0.979	−18.27	c	−0.023	0.978	−12.89	c
Assault Contagion	0.005	1.005	15.66	c	0.020	1.020	13.91	c	0.021	1.021	10.87	c
% African American Population	0.011	1.01	21.37	c	0.016	1.016	24.47	c	0.031	1.032	34.65	c
Time*Assault Contagion	−0.0001	0.999	−3.59	c	−0.001	0.999	−9.06	c	−0.001	0.999	−7.99	c

$p(t)$: a < 0.05; b < 0.01; c < 0.001.
1. All models were estimated using mixed effects Poisson regression models with autoregressive co-variance structures.
2. Outward contagion models include adjustment for spatial autocorrelation of homicides in the surrounding census tracts.
3. All model results were adjusted for effects of tract social and economic factors: percent of persons below poverty, percent in labor market, ratio of adults to juveniles, percent population living in tract 5 years or less, percent population not born in U.S., percent of households in public housing, and total population.
4. All models were estimated with time as quadratic (nonlinear) predictor.

for the inward contagion assault model again indicate that neighborhoods exert less of an influence over their surrounding communities and instead are more susceptible to events in those communities.

The presence of gun contagion of both gun homicides and gun assaults underscores the importance of guns in the dynamics of social contagion at the population level. In an earlier article, Fagan and Davies (2004) showed that the neighborhoods with the highest homicide, injury, and gun violence rates are New York City's poorest neighborhoods. Those finding were confirmed in these models in the significant contribution of the co-variates that express the susceptibility of the poorest neighborhoods to contagion (data available from authors). Accordingly, the corollary finding of socioeconomic risk as a contributor to the spread of violence captures both the significance of susceptibility and the importance of structural equivalence in shaping the trajectory of diffusion. That is, the adoption at the population level of gun violence as a means of social control and exchange was facilitated by the social concentration of poverty and of the close social synapses intrinsic to poor neighborhoods. Accordingly, the social and spatial clustering of homicide suggests that it is concentrated within overlapping social networks in small areas (Fagan & Wilkinson, 1998b).

Social contagion theory suggests that individuals are likely to mutually influence the behaviors of others with whom they are in frequent and redundant contact (Bovasso, 1996, p. 1421; Burt, 1987). The social interactions underlying assaultive violence suggest its spread by social contact (Loftin, 1986), and, as we show below and in other articles, by specific forms of social interaction (Wilkinson, 2003). We explore these themes next.

Violent Events, Social Networks, and Social Contagion

We turn next to an analysis of the individual- and group-level processes of social conta-gion. We identify dynamic social processes that fuel the social contagion of youth violence. At the heart of this process are the interactions of individuals within and across social networks. Violence plays a central role in the maintenance of organizational boundaries, norms, and cohesion. Two elements in the contagion of youth violence are conflict between networks of youths and the role of violence in resolving conflicts. The violent events in which these processes unfold and change over time represent opportunities to build or maintain status within networks; in some events, violence is an imperative with costs when it is not invoked (Wilkinson, 2003). Third parties are especially important in the spread of violence between networks; third parties can animate or intensify violence once a conflict begins, or they can help mediate and suppress it. They also convey the outcomes of violent events to others in the larger social worlds that surround these social networks, helping sustain norms and provide context for the next conflicts that may arise. The strategic role of guns in these processes intensifies the dynamics that fuel the epidemic. In some instances, the presence of guns in events links together persons and events across time and sustains the processes of social contagion.

This section unfolds in three parts. First, we discuss the mechanisms through which violence may spread between social groups or networks and show how these mechanisms are best understood through the analysis of specific events. Next, the chapter focuses on the importance of third parties in violent events. The third section presents three scenarios that illustrate the intersection of these themes that produce violent events and often set the stage for future ones.

Violent Events

For any attitude, expectation, behavior, or virus to be "spread" from person to person or group to group, interpersonal contact is typically required. Exposure can be direct or indirect. Direct exposure to gun use and violent behaviors among similarly situated networks of young men would likely increase the risk of transmission. Observations of young men's decision-making processes in violence use and avoidance provide a window into the processes that shape interpersonal transmission. Studying violence from an event perspective combines the study of offenders, victims, and social context to yield a more complete picture of its etiology (Meier, Kennedy, & Sacco, 2001). The event perspective considers the co-production by victim(s), offender(s), and others of a violence experience. It emphasizes event precursors; the event as it unfolds; and the aftermath, including reporting, harm, and redress. The event perspective integrates concepts from symbolic and situational interactionism, routine activity, and rational choice theories. The social geometry of violent conflict provides clues to understanding what distinguishes one conflict situation from another or more precisely what distinguishes a nonviolent conflict from a violent conflict (Phillips & Cooney, 2005).

Several investigators have found evidence that the interplay between the primary actors determines, in part, the outcome. For example, Felson and Steadman (1983) found that violent incidents usually began with identity attacks, were followed by attempts and failures to influence the opponent, then included verbal threats, and finally, ended in physical attack. In a study of ex-offenders, ex-mental patients, and a sample drawn from the general population, Felson (1982, 1984) found a similar pattern. Hughes and Short (2005) confirmed Felson's earlier findings with a sample of gang-involved youth.

Similarly, Oliver (1994) used detailed narratives of violent confrontations between Black males in bars and bar settings. Oliver employed both participant observation and interview methods over a 5-year period (1983–1987) to "systematically examine the social functions of the black bar and how black males interacted with each other and with females in this setting." The sample consisted of 41 Black men 28 to 45 years old who frequented the research locations.

Oliver examined violent behaviors to identify the "rules of engagement" and situational causes of violence in the bar setting. He observed a five-stage sequence of events similar to Felson and Steadman's previous classification. His work added insights about violent events from a sample of African American men, especially with regard to understanding event closure and the aftermath of violent events. In all of these studies, victim actions, including retaliation, denial of claims, and aggressiveness, were found to be important factors.

A focus on violent events demonstrates that most violence is a process of social interactions with identifiable rules and contingencies (Campbell, 1986; Felson, 1982; Felson & Steadman, 1983; Luckenbill, 1977; Luckenbill & Doyle, 1989; Oliver, 1994; Polk, 1994; Sommers & Baskin, 1993; Wilkinson, 2003). Contrary to common wisdom, violent acts can be understood as rational or purposive behavior. Most experts agree that rationality is "bounded"; that is, individuals rarely have all of the information necessary to make a truly "rational" decision. The likelihood of violence reflects the progression of decisions across a series of identifiable stages. Much of this research concludes that there are contingencies in each stage, shaped by external influences and social interactions of the actors. Yet the data have generally not been available to answer more useful questions, such as what the contingencies are, how actors take them into account, and how they vary as an event progresses through these stages. Although prior studies provide generalized classifications of violent event stages, a finer-tuned assessment of the actions and reactions of actors in violent encounters than is possible from detailed event narratives will shed new light on the micro-decisions and contextual influences across a range of types of violent encounters. Previous studies have generally ignored information about precipitating actions, as well as the aftermath of violent events. The analysis of event stages must also take into account the heterogeneity of violent events by examining a wide range of violent acts.

Studies of Third Parties in Violent Events

Third parties witness or somehow become involved in an estimated two thirds of acts of interpersonal violence in the United States (Planty, 2002). The percentage is even greater (approximately 73%) for violence among young people. Despite the common nature of third-party presence, researchers know little about the specific contributions that third parties make in promoting or preventing the escalation of interpersonal conflict to violence. Previous research concludes that bystanders and third parties contribute significantly to the outcome of violent encounters (see Black, 1993; Cooney, 1998; Decker, 1995; Felson, 1982; Felson, Ribner, & Siegel, 1984; Oliver, 1994; Phillips & Cooney, 2005; Wilkinson, 2003). For example, Felson (1982, 1993) found that, when a dispute occurred between parties of the same sex, the presence of third parties increased the likelihood that a verbal disagreement would turn into a physical fight. Third parties may be viewed both as part of the sociocultural context and as participants in the co-production of violent events. Largely due to the work of Donald Black and his followers, theory in the area of third parties has evolved while empirical studies of third-party roles in violence remain rare and unfocused within criminology.

Black's (1993) theoretical work on the social structure of conflict includes a typology of third parties with specification across two domains: the *nature* and *degree* of the intervention. He identified 12 third-party roles, "including five support roles (informer, adviser, advocate, ally, and surrogate) and five settlement roles (friendly peacemaker, mediator, arbitrator, judge, and repressive peacemaker)." Two other roles that do not fit within either category are the "negotiator" whose partisanship cross-cuts both sides and the "healer." The types are rank ordered in terms of degree of intervention, with supporting roles organized by the extent of partisanship and settlement roles by the authoritative status of the third parties. Settlement roles come into play when, according to Black (1993, p. 108), "third parties intervene without taking sides."

As Black explains, the role of third parties often depends on personal allegiance (or lack of it) to the main actors. He argues that audience members allied with either the protagonist or the antagonist may contribute to the escalation or de-escalation of a dispute through verbal statements, body language, cheering, nonverbal social pressure, or physical acts of violence. *Partisanship* and *solidarity* are key features of Black's thesis. Cooney (1998) elaborated Black's theory to include variables on group membership status and articulated hypotheses for four configurations of third-party social locations in determining their influence over the principals in a conflict situation. They specified the predictive power of third parties with close and distant ties to individuals, close and distant ties to groups, cross-cutting ties, and no ties. Using interviews with 100 incarcerated offenders of assault or homicide, Phillips and Cooney (2005) found moderate support for these hypotheses in the first empirical test to date.

Wilkinson (2007) examined the role of network peers and third parties as potential agents of social control in 237 violent events reported by 159 urban youth. The study classified third parties by their relational ties to the focal respondent and his opponent(s). The study showed that third parties who were closely tied to the primary participants were mostly likely to *join in* the violence, rather than doing anything to stop it (55% of the respondent's associates actively used violence, whereas 42% of the opponent's associates did). Bystanders who were neutral parties toward either side rarely became involved in the violence itself, although they actively engaged in some type of social control action in about 20% of events. Bystander actions typically involved yelling to try to stop the violence (8%), actions to break up the conflict (10%), and coming to the aid of participants nonviolently (3%). From the respondents' perspective, bystanders very rarely called the police. Third-party presence seems to coincide with police becoming involved in both serious and nonserious events. Events that occurred at night and without neutral bystanders present were less likely to come to the attention to police (at least from the respondents' experience).

Three Scenarios

Moving beyond these descriptive findings, in the remainder of this section we examine *how* third-party involvement relates to social contagion in 782 violent events. An event-level analysis is the best way to examine how violence "flows" as a process from individual to individual, as well as from group to group. By focusing specifically on the dynamics of gun violent events reported by 418 New York City male youth aged 16 to 24, we identify dynamic social processes that fuel the social contagion of youth violence. Peer network involvement in violent acts takes several forms. First, and most common, is co-participation or co-offending. The decision to co-participate happens at any stage as violent conflicts unfold. These processes are evident in analyses of the action by actor sequences of violent events. Peer network members become actively involved in conflicts that lead to violence through several avenues: (1) Their involvement in the violent event is strategic and anticipated from the outset; (2) they come to the aid of an associate who is losing in the battle; (3) they are threatened/offended/disrespected at some point during the course of observing a dispute unfold; (4) they use violence either in the moment or after the fact to obtain justice or right some wrong that was perpetrated against a group member; or (5) they are influenced by gossip about the performance and reputation of violence participants and take up conflicts to restore the reputation of group members. Peer network members who are present during disputes that escalate into violence play different roles depending on the relationship among the combatants, weapon type, and injury outcomes. Three scenarios of violence are presented that illustrate the nuances of how violence is diffused across peer networks.

SCENARIO 1: STREET CORNER STORE AND RESIDENTIAL NEIGHBORHOOD

In this scenario, let's call the respondent (Aron) and the opponent (Bruce). Aron argues with Bruce at a neighborhood corner store over cutting in line. They step outside and begin to fight. None of the witnesses in the setting were closely tied to either party, but they did know both youths by face and reputation. After about 5 minutes of fighting with fists, Bruce pulls out a razor on Aron and uses it to slice him across his arm that Aron had extended to protect his face. Someone in the audience yells at the youth to stop before the police are called. Both youth flee. Aron goes back to his block and recounts the story to his associates. He rallies their support for a counterattack by highlighting the ways that his opponent was trying to destroy his attractiveness by scarring his face and how he disrespected him. After a few days pass and the group was fueled by visions of revenge, Aron and four of his associates armed themselves with handguns and went to Bruce's block. Aron's group finds Bruce, two guys, and one girl sitting on the front steps of a neighborhood building. Without verbal warning, Aron pulls his 9 mm from his waist and starts shooting in the direction of Bruce's group. Bruce was caught off guard as he was not expecting conflict that day. One of Bruce's companions pulls out his gun and returns fire. After a few brief minutes the shooting stops. Two people are shot – one relatively minor wound to the leg on Aron's side and one serious injury to Bruce's friend. According to the respondent, the beef or conflict remains ongoing. Aron is anticipating a retaliatory attack to avenge the injury to Bruce's friend and because he escalated the beef to a "life and death" issue.

SCENARIO 2: A CLUB AT 2 A.M.

Here, Rich, Mike, and four of his associates go to a club to party and socialize with females. In the club, Mike sees a girl named Becky with whom he has a casual relationship. She came to the club with six of her girlfriends to dance and have fun. Rich sees Becky dancing and joins her. Rich rubs his body up against Becky. Mike observes the violation directly. Mike informs Rich of his wrongdoing and asks for an account. Rich denies wrongdoing, states claim to the girl, and places blame on Mike. Mike pulls the girl away from Rich and returns to his group. Mike's boys comment on the violation. Mike watches Rich, thinks about the violation, and is angry. Mike's boys report back information about Rich and his boys. Mike returns to his prior activity. Mike's girl goes back to dancing.

The girl's friends compliment her on being desired by two guys. Rich talks with his buddies about the girl and Mike's capabilities. Both parties wait to see what the other will do. After some time passes, Rich begins dancing provocatively with Mike's "girl" again. Mike is not watching, but hears about it from his man. Rich's friends watch to see if Rich gets the girl. Mike walks up to Rich and punches him in the face. Rich hits Mike back. Both sets of friends watch initially. Rich lands some good punches. Mike's first friend jumps on Rich. Club security breaks up the fight, issuing warnings. The youths go back to drinking and partying.

Mike discusses ways of punishing Rich. Both sides watch the other. The status of who "gets" the girl remains open. Both sides plan to attack at the end of the night. Mike believed that Rich must have called some of his friends for additional reinforcements and to make sure that when Rich got outside he would have a gun available. Mike and his boys essentially make the same type of preparations. As soon as Mike moved toward exiting the club, Rich's group was preparing for a gun battle. Mike recalls that his side had three guns that they retrieved from nearby stashes, whereas it seemed like the other side had five or more guns. With more than 20 shots fired, injuries were sustained on both sides. The police came to the scene, but no one was arrested.

The injured were transported to the hospital, and one youth from Rich's side died at the hospital as a result of this gun event. Mike heard rumors that Rich had been seen with Becky following the shoot-out, which fueled his anger and, in his mind, justified

his need for revenge on Rich. Mike's boy suffered serious damage to his knee, which angered Mike as well. Rumors of revenge for the death of Rich's associate were spreading around. Both sides were on guard and looking for strategic advantage for the next violent event. Mike anticipated that more violence would follow from this event.

SCENARIO 3: A DRUG STASH HOUSE NEAR A STREET DRUG SPOT

Pete and his two associates planned a robbery of a drug stash house manned by a Dominican crew. Pete got information about the best day and time to rob the house, what types of weapons would be used to defend the stash house, and so on. However, his information was incomplete. When he and his associates made their armed robbery attempt, they were confronted by additional armed drug dealers who were protecting the drug stash. Pete's group exchanged fire with the drug dealers as they fled the building following a failed robbery attempt. Pete's friend Franky almost got shot. Franky was recognized by the Dominican drug crew. They came to Pete's neighborhood to find and shoot him as revenge for the attempted robbery incident. Pete describes the situation to our interviewer:

(Pete): They recognized him and shit. So it was some Dominican kids. They went to our block and we seen like this blue Lincoln Towne or Escort or some shit. We seen this coming around and coming around. And we was like, 'yo Franky, I was like you know them niggas right there man?' He was like, 'nah, I was like the niggas got something with us, either they scheming at us or the niggas ready to hit somebody else.' Niggas is sitting up in there either waiting for somebody or waiting for us to make a move. He gave a peek and as soon as he looked, Franky told me, 'yo Pete that's one of them nigga from that stash house. My hands got real sweaty, we didn't have our ghats on us, My hands got real sweaty. And it's like I could front it off and I call you from across the way, hey 'yo what's up come here.' You know what I'm saying by that time, Franky tells me yo Pete just run your way and I ran inside the building. And I said alright I'm going to run to this Alicia's house right there where the gate is at. You know what I'm saying the car all of the sudden just right down the block see but we didn't want to run as soon as that shit come. You know what I'm saying as soon as that car come down slowly, it didn't do nothing. The Dominican kid didn't do nothing, he just looked at us. And went right around the block. We was like that ain't them, that ain't them. Give it like two to three minutes they came walking, walking, it was like a good little 50 yards. And I said, 'yo, Franky that's them right there.' He was like, 'where I don't see the car.' I said, 'nah they on foot right there.' And Franky said, 'oh shit, that's them.' When me and Franky look at them they looked at us and I see them real quick running to pull out they ghat. And....they just started busting. Blah, blah, blah and I caught my reaction I ran where I said I was going to run. Franky ran in there but niggas was just kept blah, blah, blah and they went after Franky more than me. They kept just shooting blah, blah, blah and they ran in the building. That was like oh shit, I jumped over the gate and I was oh shit. I didn't have my ghat or nothing. I was damn Franky, Franky.

Interviewer: What happened?

(Pete): Really they didn't caught Franky, You know what I'm saying they didn't get him. But the next day they caught, they shot him up.

(Interviewer): So they came back the next day?

(Pete): Early in the morning cause Franky was out there pitching, early in the morning. They came back the next day and they were shooting at him and he didn't feel it while he was running but it cause the bullet went in and out. I was like you know, everybody was yo what happen why they niggas shot up Franky and shit. We didn't want to tell nobody that we went to stash house to hit. It was like, 'nah we had beef with these kids and they came around and shit like.'

(Interviewer): Why didn't you want to tell?

(Pete): Because if he tell niggas that we hitting other peoples stash houses they going to probably. God forbid they hit up the stash house in our block they the first thing they going to say is 'yo I think it was Pete and Franky and Zee 'cause niggas like hitting stash houses. Everybody in my block think shysty-ness, so the first nigga they will probably will is to us and they will probably try to smoke us and it ain't us. You know what I'm saying.

The event process can be dissected into specific stages: anticipatory stage, opening moves, countermoves and brewing period, persistence stage, intensification stage, early violence stage, stewing period, assessment stage, the casting/recasting stage, and the retaliatory stage. The examples above demonstrate that network peers play important roles at almost every stage of a conflict that escalates into violence. The communication of normative expectations, violence scripts, and violence strategies filters through direct observation, word of mouth via rumors, and telling of "war stories."

Social Contagion and Social Norms

The dynamics of social contagion can be accommodated within concepts of social influence and social norms. The social influence concept of behavior borrows from both economics and sociology (Harcourt, 1998; Lessig, 1995). Its economic component suggests that people will act to maximize their utility, whereas its sociological dimension suggests that conduct is shaped through direct and vicarious social interactions. A simple version of this nexus suggests that the choice of conduct is influenced by observation and practice of the most effective options. Choices are contextualized as well, reflecting both the range of available options and the specific contingencies in which they are applied (Fagan, 1999).

In the contagious dynamics of violence, the social meaning of violence is constructed through the interrelationship of its action and its context. The social meaning in this case involves actions (violence) that have both returns (identity, status, avoidance of attack) and expectations that, within tightly packed networks, are unquestioned or normative. Conduct impregnated with social meaning has influence on the behaviors of others in immediate proximity. The social meaning of violence influences the adaptation of behavioral norms, expected responses (scripts), and even beliefs (memes) about systems of behavior. Social norms are the product of repeated events that demonstrate the meaning and utility of specific forms of conduct. Social influence thus has a dynamic and reciprocal effect on social norms (Harcourt, 1998; Lessig, 1995). In poor neighborhoods, social interactions are dominated by street codes, or local systems of justice, that reward displays of physical domination and offer social approval for antisocial behavior.

The endogeneity of social contagion to networks and neighborhoods illustrates the differences in the two types of epidemics. The origins of a contagious epidemic that travels through a population become distal influences on the pathway and dynamics of transmission through populations over time. The setting or context of contagion reflects the susceptibility of populations to the transmission of a socially meaningful behavior, as well as its exposure to the behavior that has acquired meaning (Fullilove et al., 1998). This can be true both for fashion and art (Gladwell, 1997; Servin, 1999) and for problematic social behaviors, such as drug use (Rowe & Rodgers, 1991), teenage sexual activity (Rodgers & Rowe, 1993), teenage pregnancy (Crane, 1991), child maltreatment (Coultin, Korbin, Su, & Chow, 1995), and violence (Anderson, 1999; Cork, 1999; Fagan, 1999; Loftin, 1986).

Recent applications of social influence models to crime control emphasize the seminal role of the exogenous influence of "disorder," in which minor crimes signal to would-be criminals that crimes in that area will be tolerated and not reported (Kelling & Cole, 1996; Wilson & Kelling, 1982). At first glance, "Broken Windows" suggests that there is a spread of norms supporting crime that overwhelm norms of orderliness. The spread comes from the continuing signals from disorder. Withdrawal of the signs of disorder will change social norms by allowing the social influence of orderliness to flourish. Apart from the problematic nature of this dichotomous categorization of persons (Harcourt, 1998), Broken Windows medicalizes the conditions of disorder and criminality. It assumes that exposure to the disorder is a constant and recurring process that signals to the motivated offender that crime can succeed. Removing the signs of disorder will change social norms by allowing the social influence of orderliness to flourish. But this theory is limited by focusing only on the introduction of the original cues or sources of crime and relying on the causal effects of these exogenous factors. This is analogous to the food poisoning model of epidemics. Moreover, a literal reading of Broken Windows theory would invite problematic legal policy responses, such as "social quarantine," which have limited efficacy and raise moral quandaries (Markovits, 2005).

The dynamics of social contagion instead suggest an endogenous process, in which the spread of social norms occurs through the everyday interactions of individuals within networks that are structurally equivalent and closely packed. Here, the ill grows and spreads from the inside, often long after the origins have subsided. This is analogous to influenza contagion or to the spread of cultural or political thought (Cavalli-Sproza & Feldman, 1981).

The concept of contagion neutralizes the categorizations of disorder and order that theoretically inform the new path of deterrence. A literal translation of contagion would emphasize guns as a recurring source of violence and as an agent in the transmission of violence norms. Because the recent epidemic cycle of violence was in reality a gun homicide epidemic, the case for gun-oriented policing strategies (Fagan, 2002; Fagan, et al., 1998) is much stronger than practices based on the more diffuse and unsupported theory of disorder control and order-maintenance strategies. Although disorder opposes orderliness, cleanliness, and sobriety (Harcourt, 2001), violence appears to travel on vectors quite unrelated to that particular set of social norms.

Acknowledgments

An earlier version of this paper was presented at the Urban Seminar Series on Children's Health and Safety, John F. Kennedy School of Government, Harvard University, in May 2000. Members of the Kennedy School Urban Seminar Series, Columbia Law School, and the Columbia Center for Youth Violence Prevention provided valuable comments on earlier versions of the chapter. This research was supported by grants from the Centers for Disease Control, the National Institute of Justice, and the Robert Wood Johnson Foundation, in addition to support from the Sloan Working Group on Social Contagion of Youth Violence. All opinions and errors are those of the authors. We thank Assistant Commissioner Susan A. Wilt, former director of the Injury Prevention Program of the New York City Department of Health and Mental Hygiene, for generously sharing data on homicide and injury assault characteristics and locations. Frank Zimring provided excellent comments during the course of the project. Workshop participants at the Sloan Working Group on Contagion on Social Contagion, Columbia Law School, the Mailman School of Public Health at Columbia University, the Urban Health Seminar at the John F. Kennedy School at Harvard University, and the Fortunoff Colloquium at the New York University School of Law all provided helpful comments on earlier drafts. Jay Galluzzo, Tamara Dumanovsky, Marlene Pantin, and Carolyn Pinedo provided excellent research assistance. Thanks also to interviewers Richard McClain, David Tufino, Davon Battee, Jason Mercado, and Whetsel Wade for creating a unique and rich source of data on street corner life in New York City.

Notes

1. Cook and Ludwig (2004) developed estimates of the effects of gun availability, controlling for any effects due to reverse causation in which the demand for guns among teenagers may affect prevalence.

2. One important development is a breakdown in the age grading of behaviors, in which the traditional segmentation of younger adolescents from older ones, and behavioral transitions from one developmental stage to the next, are short-circuited by the strategic presence of weapons. Mixed-age interactions play an important role in this process. Older adolescents and young adults provide modeling influences as well as more direct effects. We found that they exert downward pressure on others their own age and younger through identity challenges that, in part, shape the social identities for both parties. At younger ages, boys are pushing upward for status by challenging boys a few years older.

3. With the exception of the decade influenced by both the passage of the Volstead Act and the social and economic instability of the Great Depression, homicide rates in New York City varied little. In its 1996 report, the Office of Vital Statistics and Epidemiology reports homicide rates prior to 1985 in 5-year intervals. Homicide rates rose from an average of 4.9 in 1916–1920 to 7.6 in 1931–1935, and declined to 4.5 by 1936–1940 (NYC Department of Health and Mental Hygiene, 1997).

4. The 1990 spike for male nongun homicides most likely reflects the 90 arson homicide deaths in the Happyland Social Club fire. We could not adjust the age-, race-, or gender-specific rates for these homicide deaths since data were not available on their characteristics. The nongun total for 1990 has been adjusted by deleting 89 of the 90 killings from the Happyland Social Club fire, in effect counting that episode as one homicide.

5. Exceptions include domestic homicides, and homicides that follow rape (see Dugan, Nagin, and Rosenfeld, 1999).

6. Other indicators, such as drug use among arrestees recorded in the Drug Use Forecasting System (DUF), also show little relationship with trends in gun homicide rates. Fagan et al. (1998) show that the incidence of drug-positive arrestees remained unchanged throughout the period, and was unrelated to both firearm and nonfirearm homicide trends.

7. The male divorce rate also is a consistent predictor of violence and homicide rates, and effects are greater for juveniles than for adults. For example, Messner and Sampson (1991) showed that Black family disruption was substantially related to rates of murder and robbery involving Blacks. These findings are consistent with the consistent findings in the delinquency literature on the effects of broken homes on social control and guardianship. The effects of male divorce can be interpreted either as a consequence and correlate of the rise of female-headed households, or as an indicator of weak social control of children who then are raised primarily by women. Whatever its meaning, the male divorce rate has positive, clear cut effects on robbery, assault, rape and homicide (Sampson and Lauritsen, 1994).

8. A second advantage of the mixed models approach is that it allows for greater flexibility in specifying the covariance structure of the data. Specifically, mixed models allow for the analysis of data where the requisite assumptions of Ordinary Least Squares regression concerning error term independence are violated. This is particularly important in research involving aggregate units. Because the neighborhoods and communities are comprised of geographically contiguous census tracts, autocorrelation is inherent in the data structure and it would be inappropriate to assume a simple covariance structure for these analyses. All of the models are instead analyzed with an autoregressive covariance structure.

9. Additional records are available on deaths from other means (accidents, disease classifications, self-inflicted violence) to estimate overall mortality rates by area and by cause. Accordingly, the database has the capacity for spatial, temporal, and demographic disaggregation and analysis of several dimensions of mortality.

References

Abelson, R. P. (1976). Script processing in attitude formation and decision-making. In J. S. Carroll & J. W. Payne (Eds.), *Cognition and social behavior*. Hillsdale, NJ: Erlbaum.

Abelson, R. P. (1981). Psychological status of the script concept. *American Psychologist, 36,* 715–729.

Agar, M., & Reisinger, H. S. (2002). A heroin epidemic at the intersection of histories: The 1960s epidemic among African Americans in Baltimore. *Medical Anthropology, 21*(2), 115–156.

Anderson, E. (1994, May). The code of the streets. *Atlantic Monthly*, 81–94.

Anderson, E. (1999). *Code of the street: Decency, violence, and the moral life of the inner city*. New York: W. W. Norton.

Bailey, N. T. (1967). *Mathematical approach to biology and medicine*. New York: Wiley.

Bailey, N. T. (1975). *The mathematical theory of infectious diseases and its applications*. London: Griffin.

Balkin, J. M. (1998). *Cultural software: A theory of ideology*. Danbury, CT: Yale University Press.

Baumer, E. (1994). Poverty, crack, and crime: A cross-city analysis. *Journal of Research in Crime and Delinquency, 31*(3), 311–327.

Baumer, E., Lauritsen, J. L., Rosenfeld, R., & Wright, R. (1998). The influence of crack cocaine on robbery, burglary, and homicide rates: A cross-city, longitudinal analysis. *Journal of Research in Crime and Delinquency, 35*(3), 316–340.

Berman, A. L. (1995). Suicide prevention: Clusters and contagion. In A. L. Berman (Ed.), *Suicide prevention: Case consultations* (pp. 25–55). New York: Springer.

Bingenheimer, J. B., Brennan, R. T., & Earls, F. J. (2005). Firearm violence exposure and serious violent behavior. *Science, 308,* 1323–1326.

Black, D. (1993). *The social structure of right and wrong*. New York: Cambridge University Press.

Blumstein, A. (1995). Youth violence, guns, and the illicit-drug industry. *Journal of Criminal Law and Criminology, 86*(1), 10–36.

Blumstein, A., & Beck, A. J. (1999). Population growth in U.S. prisons, 1980–1996. In M. Tonry & J. Petersilia (Eds.), *Prisons* (Vol. 26, pp. 17–62). Chicago: University of Chicago Press.

Bourgois, P. (1995). *In search of respect: Selling crack in El Barrio*. New York: Cambridge University Press.

Bovasso, G. (1996). A network analysis of social contagion processes in an organizational intervention. *Human Relations, 49*(11), 1419–1435.

Brotherton, D., & Barrios, L. (2004). *The almighty Latin king and queen nation: Street politics and the transformation of a New York City gang*. New York: Columbia University Press.

Bryk, A. S., & Raudenbush, S. W. (1992). *Hierarchical linear models: Applications and data analysis methods*. Newbury Park, CA: Sage.

Burt, R. S. (1987). Social contagion and innovation: Cohesion versus structural equivalence. *American Journal of Sociology, 92*(6), 1287–1335.

Burt, R. S. (1992). *Structural holes: The social structure of competition*. Cambridge, MA: Harvard University Press.

Campbell, A. (1986). The streets and violence. In A. Campbell & J. Gibbs (Eds.), *Violent transactions: The limits of personality*. New York: Blackwell.

Cavalli-Sproza, L. L., & Feldman, M. W. (1981). *Cultural transmission and evolution: A quantitative approach*. Princeton NJ: Princeton University Press.

Chin, K. (1996). *Chinatown gangs: Extortion, enterprise, and ethnicity*. New York: Oxford University Press.

Coleman, J. S., Katz, E., & Menzel, H. (1966). *Medical innovation; A diffusion study*. Indianapolis: Bobbs-Merrill Co.

Cook, P. J., & Laub, J. H. (1998). The unprecedented epidemic in youth violence. *Crime and Justice, 24*, 27–64.

Cook, P. J., & Ludwig, J. (2004). Does gun prevalence affect teen gun carrying after all? *Criminology, 42*, 27–54.

Cooney, M. (1998). *Warriors and peacemakers: How third parties shape violence*. New York. New York University Press.

Cork, D. (1999). Examining space-time interaction in city-level homicide data: Crack markets and the diffusion of guns among youth. *Journal of Quantitative Criminology, 15*(4), 379–406.

Coulton, C. J., Korbin, J. E., Su, M., & Chow, J. (1995). Community-level factors and child maltreatment rates. *Child Development, 66*, 1262–1276.

Crane, J. (1991). The epidemic theory of ghettos and neighborhood effects on dropping out and teenage childbearing. *American Journal of Sociology, 96*(5), 1226–1259.

Curtis, R. (1998). The improbable transformation of inner-city neighborhoods: Crime, violence, drugs, and youth in the 1990s. *Journal of Criminal Law and Criminology, 88*, 1233–1276.

Decker, S. H. (1995). Reconstructing homicide events: The role of witnesses in fatal encounters. *Journal of Criminal Justice, 23*(5), 439–450.

Delgado, R. (1985). "Rotten social background": Should the criminal law recognize a defense of severe environmental deprivation? *Law and Inequality, 3*, 9–90.

Eckberg, D. L. (1995). Estimates of early twentieth-century U.S. homicide rates: An econometric forecasting approach. *Demography, 32*(1), 1–16.

Egan, D. J., & Robinson, D. O. (1979). Models of a heroin epidemic. *American Journal of Psychiatry, 136*, 1162–1167.

Elliott, D. S., Wilson, W. J., Huizinga, D., Sampson, R. J., Elliott, A., & Rankin, B. (1996). The effects of neighborhood disadvantage on adolescent development. *Journal of Crime and Delinquency, 33*, 389–426.

Fagan, J. (1989). The social organization of drug use and drug dealing among urban gangs. *Criminology, 27*(4), 501–536.

Fagan, J. (1990). Intoxication and aggression. *Drugs and Crime – Crime and Justice: An Annual Review of Research, 13*, 241–320.

Fagan, J. (1992). Drug selling and licit income in distressed neighborhoods: The economic lives of street level drug users and dealers. In A. Harrel & G. Peterson (Eds.), *Drugs, crime, and social isolation* (pp. 99–146). Washington, DC: Urban Institute Press.

Fagan, J. (1993). The political economy of drug dealing among urban gangs. In R. Davis, A. Lurigio, & D. P. Rosenbaum (Eds.), *Drugs and community*. Springfield, IL: Charles Thomas.

Fagan, J. (1999). Context and culpability of adolescent violence. *Virginia Review of Social Policy and Law, 6*(3), 101–174.

Fagan, J. (2002). Policing guns and youth violence. *Future of Children, 12*(2), 133–151.

Fagan, J., & Chin, K. (1989). Initiation into crack and powdered cocaine: A tale of two epidemics. *Contemporary Drug Problems, 16*(4), 579–617.

Fagan, J., & Chin, K. (1991). Social processes of initiation into crack cocaine. *Journal of Drug Issues, 21*, 432–466.

Fagan, J., & Davies, G. (2004). Natural history of neighborhood violence. *Journal of Contemporary Criminal Justice, 20*(2), 127–147.

Fagan, J., & Wilkinson, D. L. (1997). Firearms and youth violence. In D. Stoff, J. Brieling, & J. D. Maser (Eds.), *Handbook of antisocial behavior.* New York: Wiley.

Fagan, J., & Wilkinson, D. L. (1998a). Guns, youth violence, and social identity in inner cities. *Crime and Justice, 24*, 105–188.

Fagan, J., & Wilkinson, D. L. (1998b). Situational contexts of adolescent violence. *Revue Europenéenne des Migrations Internationales, 14*, 63–76.

Fagan, J., Zimring, F. E., & Kim, J. (1998). Declining homicide in New York City: A tale of two trends. *Journal of Criminal Law and Criminology, 88*(4), 1277–1324.

Fagan, J., West, V., and Holland, J. (2003). "Reciprocal Effects of Crime and Incarceration in New York City Neighborhoods." *Fordham Urban Law Journal (30)*, 1551–1602.

Farmer, P. (1999). *Infections and inequalities: The modern plagues.* Berkeley, CA: University of California Press.

Federal Bureau of Investigation. (various years). *Uniform crime reports [United States]: Supplementary homicide reports, 1976–2003* (ICPSR Study No. 4351, 2005). Retrieved from http://webapp.icpsr.umich.edu/cocoon/ICPSRSTUDY/04351.xml.

Feld, B. C. (1999). *Bad kids: Race and the transformation of the juvenile court.* New York: Oxford University Press.

Felson, R. B. (1982). Impression management and the escalation of aggression and violence. *Social Psychology Quarterly, 45*(4), 245–254.

Felson, R. B. (1993). Predatory and dispute-related violence: A social interactionist approach. In R. V. Clarke & M. Felson (Eds.), *Routine activity and rational choice: Advances in criminological theory* (Vol. 5, pp. 103–126). New Brunswick, NJ: Transaction Press.

Felson, R. B. (1984). Patterns of aggressive social interaction. In A. Mummendey (Ed.), *Social psychology of aggression: From individual behavior to social interaction* (pp. 107–126). New York: Springer-Verlag.

Felson, R. B., Ribner, S. A., & Siegel, M. S. (1984). Age and the effect of third parties during criminal violence. *Sociology and Social Research, 68*(4), 452–462.

Felson, R. B., & Steadman, H. J. (1983). Situational factors in disputes leading to criminal violence. *Criminology, 21*(1), 59–74.

Fingerhut, L. A., Ingram, D. D., & Feldman, J. J. (1992a). Firearm and nonfirearm homicide among persons 15 through 19 years of age. Differences by level of urbanization, United States, 1979 through 1989. *Journal of the American Medical Association, 267*(22), 3048–3053.

Fingerhut, L. A., Ingram, D. D., & Feldman, J. J. (1992b). Firearm homicide among black teenage males in metropolitan counties. Comparison of death rates in two periods, 1983 through 1985 and 1987 through 1989. *Journal of the American Medical Association, 267*(22), 3054–3058.

Fryer, R. G., Jr., Heaton, P., Levitt, S. D., & Murphy, K. M. (2005). *Measuring the impact of crack cocaine* (No. 11318). Washington, DC: NBER Working Papers.

Fullilove, M. T., Heon, V., Jimenez, W., Parsons, C., Green, L. L., & Fullilove, R. E. (1998). Injury and anomie: Effects of violence on an inner-city community. *American Journal of Public Health, 88* (6), 924–927.

Gardner, W., Mulvey, E. P., & Shaw, E. C. (1995). Regression analyses of counts and rates: Poisson, overdispersed poisson, and negative binomial models. *Psychological Bulletin, 118*(3), 392–404.

Gladwell, M. (1997, March 17). Annals of style: The coolhunt. *The New Yorker.*

Gladwell, M. (2000). *The tipping point: How little things can make a big difference.* Boston: Little Brown.

Goldstein, H. (2003). *Multilevel statistical models* (Vol. 3). London: Edward Arnold.

Goldstein, P., Brownstein, H. H., Ryan, P. J., & Bellucci, P. A. (1989). Crack and homicide in New York City, 1988: A conceptually based event analysis. *Contemporary Drug Problems, 16*, 651–687.

Gostin, L. O. (1991). The interconnected epidemics of drug dependency and AIDS. *Harvard Civil Liberties-Civil Rights Law Review, 26*, 114–184.

Gostin, L. O., Burris, S., & Lazzarini, Z. (1999). The law and the public's health: A study of infectious disease law in the United States. *Columbia Law Review, 99*(1), 74.

Gould, M. S., Wallenstein, S., & Kleinman, M. (1990). Time-space clustering of teenage suicide. *American Journal of Epidemiology, 131*(1), 71–78.

Gould, M. S., Wallenstein, S., Kleinman, M., O'Carroll, P., & Mercy, J. (1990). Suicide clusters: An examination of age-specific effects. *American Journal of Public Health, 80*(2), 211–212.

Grogger, J., & Willis, M. (2000). The emergence of crack cocaine and the rise in urban crime rates. *Review of Economics and Statistics, 82*(4), 519–529.

Hamid, A. (1990). The political economy of crack-related violence. *Contemporary Drug Problems, 17,* 31–78.

Harcourt, B. E. (1998). Reflecting on the subject: A critique of the social influence conception of deterrence, the broken windows theory, and order-maintenance policing New York style. *Michigan Law Review, 97*(2), 291.

Harcourt, B. E. (2001). *Illusion of order: The false promise of broken windows policing.* Cambridge, MA: Harvard University Press.

Harcourt, B. E. (2006). *Language of the gun: Youth, crime, and public policy.* Chicago: University of Chicago Press.

Hughes, L., & Short, J. (2005). Disputes involving youth street gang members: Micro-social contexts. *Criminology, 43*(1), 43–76.

Hunt, L. G., & Chambers, C. D. (1976). *The heroin epidemics.* New York: Spectrum Publications.

Inciardi, J. A. (1979). Heroin use and street crime. *Crime and Delinquency, 25,* 335–346.

Johnson, B. D., Williams, T., Dei, K. A., & Sanabria, H. (1990). Drug use in the inner city: Impact on hard-drug users and the community. *Crime and Justice: An Annual Review (Drugs and Crime), 13,* 9–67.

Johnston, L. D. (1987). *National trends in drug use and related factors among American high school students and young adults, 1975–1986* (No. ED288142, DHS ADM 87–1535). Ann Arbor, MI: University of Michigan.

Jones, D. R., & Jones, M. B. (1994). Testing for behavioral contagion in a case-control design. *Journal of Psychiatric Research, 28,* 149–164.

Jones, D. R., & Jones, M. B. (1995). Preferred pathways of behavioral contagion. *Journal of Psychiatric Research, 29,* 193–209.

Jones, M. B. (1997). Behavioral contagion and official delinquency: Epidemic course in adolescence. *Social Biology, 45*(1–2), 134–142.

Kahan, D. M. (1997). Social influence, social meaning, and deterrence. *Virginia Law Review, 83,* 367–373.

Kelling, G., & Cole, C. (1996). *Fixing broken windows.* New York: Free Press.

Klein, M. W. (1995). *The American street gang: Its nature, prevalence, and control.* New York: Oxford University Press.

Klein, M. W., Maxson, C., & Cunningham, L. (1991). Crack, street gangs, and violence. *Criminology, 29*(4), 623–650.

Krivo, L. J., & Peterson, R. D. (2000). The structural context of homicide: Accounting for racial differences in process. *American Sociological Review, 65*(4), 547–559.

Land, K., McCall, P., & Cohen, L. (1990). Structural covariates of homicide rates: Are there any invariances across time and space? *American Journal of Sociology, 95*(4), 922–963.

Land, K., McCall, P., & Nagin, D. S. (1996). A comparison of poisson, negative binomial and semiparametric mixed poisson regression models with empirical applications to criminal careers data. *Sociological Methods and Research, 24*(4), 387–442.

Lessig, L. (1995). The regulation of social meaning. *University of Chicago Law Review, 62,* 943–1046.

Loftin, C. (1986). Assaultive violence as a contagious process. *Bulletin of the New York Academy of Medicine, 62*(5), 550–555.

Luckenbill, D. F. (1977). Homicide as a situated transaction. *Social Problems, 25,* 176–186.

Luckenbill, D. F., & Doyle, D. P. (1989). Structural position and violence: Developing a cultural explanation. *Criminology, 27*(3), 419–436.

Lynch, A. (1996). *Thought contagion: How belief spreads through society.* New York: Basic Books.

Lynch, J. W., Kaplan, G. A., Pamuk, E. R., Cohen, R. D., Heck, K. E., Balfour, J. H., et al. (1998). Income inequality and mortality in metropolitan areas of the United States. *American Journal of Public Health, 88*(7), 1074–1080.

Markovits, D. (2005). Quarantines and distributive justice. *Journal of Law, Medicine, and Ethics, 33*(2), 323–344.

Massey, D. (1995). The new immigration and ethnicity in the United States. *Population and Development Review, 21*(3), 631–652.

Massey, D., & Denton, N. (1993). *American apartheid.* Cambridge, MA: Harvard University Press.

May, R. M., Anderson, R. M., & Blower, S. M. (1990). The epidemiology and transmission dynamics of HIV-AIDS. In S. R. Graubard (Ed.), *Living with AIDS.* Cambridge, MA: MIT Press.

Meier, R. F., Kennedy, L. M., & Sacco, V. F. (Eds.). (2001). *Advances in criminological theory.*

Vol. 9: The process and structure of crime: Criminal events and crime analysis. New Brunswick, NJ: Transaction.

Messner, S., & Tardiff, K. (1986). Economic inequality and levels of homicide: An analysis of urban neighborhoods. *Criminology, 24,* 297–318.

Monkkonen, E. H. (2001). *Murder in New York City.* Berkeley, CA: University of California Press.

Morenoff, J., Sampson, R. J., & Raudenbush, S. (2001). Neighborhood inequality, collective efficacy, and the spatial dynamics of urban violence. *Criminology, 39,* 517–560.

Morenoff, J. D., & Tienda. M. (1997). Underclass neighborhoods in temporal and ecological perspective. *Annals of the American Association of Political and Social Science, 551,* 59–72.

New York City Department of Health and Mental Hygiene. (1992). *Injury mortality in New York City, 1980–1990.* New York: Office of Vital Statistics and Epidemiology.

New York City Department of Health and Mental Hygiene. (1997). *Summary of vital statistics, 1996.* New York: Office of Vital Statistics and Epidemiology.

New York State Department of Health. (1994). *Injury facts for New York State.* Albany, NY.

Oliver, W. (1994). *The violent social world of black men.* New York: Lexington Books.

Patterson, E. B. (1991). Poverty, income inequality, and community crime rates. *Criminology, 29*(4), 755–776.

Peterson, R. D., & Krivo, L. J. (1993). Racial segregation and urban Black homicide. *Social Forces, 71,* 1001–1026.

Phillips, S., & Cooney, M. (2005). Aiding peace, abetting violence: Third parties and the management of conflict. *American Sociological Review, 70*(2), 334–354.

Planty, M. (2002). *Third-party involvement in violent crime, 1993–1999.* Washington, DC: Bureau of Justice Statistics Special Report.

Polk, K. (1994). *When men kill: Scenarios of masculine violence.* New York: Cambridge University Press.

Robertson, L. S. (1992). *Injury epidemiology.* New York: Oxford University Press.

Rodgers, J., & Rowe, D. C. (1993). Social contagion and sexual behavior: A developmental EMOSA model. *Psychological Review, 100,* 479–510.

Roncek, D., & Maier, P. A. (1991). Bars, blocks, and crimes revisited: Linking the theory of

routine activities to the empiricism of hot spots. *Criminology, 29,* 725–754.

Rose, H., & McClain, P. (1990). *Race, place, and risk: Black homicide in urban America.* Albany NY: SUNY Press.

Rosenfeld, R., & Decker, S. H. (1999). Are arrest statistics a valid measure of illicit drug use? The relationship between criminal justice and public health indicators of cocaine, heroin, and marijuana use. *Justice Quarterly, 16,* 685.

Rothman, K. (1986). *Modern epidemiology.* Boston: Little Brown.

Rowe, D. C., & Rodgers, J. (1991). Adolescent smoking and drinking: Are they "epidemics"? *Journal of Studies on Alcohol, 52,* 110–117.

Rowe, D. C., & Rodgers, J. (1994). A social contagion model of adolescent sexual behavior: Explaining race differences. *Social Biology, 41,* 1–18.

Sampson, R. J. (1987). Urban Black violence: The effect of male joblessness and family disruption. *American Journal of Sociology, 93,* 348–382.

Sampson, R. J. (1993). Linking time and place: Dynamic contextualism and the future of criminological inquiry. *Journal of Research in Crime and Delinquency, 30*(4), 426–444.

Sampson, R. J., & Lauritsen, J. L. (1994). Violent victimization and offending: Individual, situational, and community-level risk factors. In A. J. Reiss Jr. & J. Roth (Eds.), *Understanding and preventing violence: Social influences* (Vol. 3, pp. 1–114). Washington, DC: National Academy Press.

Sampson, R. J., Raudenbush, S. W., & Earls, F. J. (1997). Neighborhoods and violent crime: A multilevel study of collective efficacy. *Science, 277,* 918–924.

Sampson, R. J., & Wilson, W. J. (1995). Toward a theory of race, crime, and urban inequality. In J. Hagan & R. D. Peterson (Eds.), *Crime and inequality* (pp. 37–54). Palo Alto, CA: Stanford University Press.

Schwendinger, H., & Schwendinger, J. S. (1985). *Adolescent subcultures and delinquency.* New York: Praeger.

Servin, J. (1999, February). Cool hunting with Jane. *Harpers Bazaar,* 90.

Shihadeh, E. S., & Steffensmeier, D. J. (1994). Economic inequality, family disruption, and urban Black violence: Cities as units of stratification and social control. *Social Forces, 73,* 729–751.

Singer, J., & Willett, J. B. (2003). *Applied longitudinal data analysis: Modeling change and event occurrence*. New York: Oxford University Press.

Slaby, R. G., & Roedell, W. C. (1982). Development and regulation of aggression. In J. Worell (Ed.), *Psychological development in the elementary years* (pp. 97–149). New York: Academic Press.

Snijders, T., & Bosker, R. (1994). Modeled variance in two-level models. *Sociological Methods and Research, 22,* 342–363.

Sommers, I., & Baskin, D. (1993). The situational context of violent female offending. *Journal of Research in Crime and Delinquency, 30,* 136–162.

Stuntz, W. J. (2001). The pathological politics of criminal law. *Michigan Law Review, 100*(3), 505–600.

Sullivan, M. (1989). *Getting paid: Youth crime and work in the inner city.* Ithaca, NY: Cornell University Press.

Taylor, R. B., & Covington, J. (1988). Neighborhood changes in ecology and violence. *Criminology, 26*(4), 553–590.

Tienda, M. (1991). Poor people in poor places: Deciphering neighborhood effects on behavioral outcomes. In J. Huber (Ed.), *Macro-micro linkages in sociology* (pp. 244–262). Newbury Park, CA: Sage.

Toch, H. (1969). *Violent men: An inquiry into the psychology of violence.* Chicago: Aldine.

Tolnay, S. E., & Beck, E. M. (1995) *A festival of violence: An analysis of lynchings, 1882–1930.* Urbana, IL: University of Illinois Press.

Tolnay, S. E., Deane, G., & Beck, E. M. (1996). Vicarious violence: Spatial effects on Southern lynchings, 1890–1919. *American Journal of Sociology, 12,* 788–815.

Wacquant, L. D., & Wilson, W. J. (1989). The costs of racial and class exclusion in the inner city. *Annals of the American Association of Political and Social Sciences, 501,* 8–25.

Wallace, R. (1991). Expanding coupled shock fronts of urban decay and criminal behavior: How U.S. cities are becoming "hollowed out." *Journal of Quantitative Criminology, 7,* 333–356.

Wilkinson, D. L. (2003). *Guns, violence and identity among African-American And Latino youth.* New York: LFB Scholarly Publishing.

Wilkinson, D. L. (2007). Local social ties and willingness to intervene: Textured views among violent urban youth of neighborhood social control dynamics and situations. *Justice Quarterly* (forthcoming).

Wilkinson, D. L., & Fagan, J. (1996). Understanding the role of firearms in violence "scripts": The dynamics of gun events among adolescent males. *Law and Contemporary Problems, 59* (1), 55–90.

Wilkinson, D. L., & Fagan, J. (2001a). A theory of violent events. In R. F. Meier, L. W. Kennedy, & V. F. Sacco (Eds.), *Advances in criminological theory. Vol. 9: The process and structure of crime: Criminal events and crime analysis* (pp. 169–196). New Brunswick, NJ: Transaction.

Wilkinson, D. L., & Fagan, J. (2001b). What we know about gun use among adolescents. *Clinical Child and Family Psychology Review, 4*(2), 109–132.

Wilkinson, R. G. (1996). *Unhealthy societies: The afflictions of inequalities.* London: Routledge.

Williams, K. R., & Flewelling, R. L. (1988). The social production of criminal homicide: A comparative study of disaggregated rates in American cities. *American Sociological Review, 53,* 421–431.

Williams, T. (1989). *The cocaine kids: The inside story of a teenage drug ring.* Reading, MA: Addison-Wesley.

Wilson, J. Q., & Kelling, G. L. (1982). Broken windows. *Atlantic Monthly, 249*(3), 29–36, 38.

Wilson, W. J. (1987). *The truly disadvantaged.* Chicago: University of Chicago Press.

Wilson, W. J. (1991). Studying inner-city social dislocations: The challenge of public agenda research. *American Sociological Review, 56,* 1–14.

Zimmer, L. (1987). *Operation pressure point: The disruption of street-level trade on New York's Lower East Side.* New York: New York Research Center in Crime and Justice, New York University School of Law.

Zimmer, L. (1990). Proactive policing against street-level drug trafficking. *American Journal of Police, 9,* 43–74.

Zimring, F. E. (1999). *American youth violence.* New York: Oxford University Press.

Zimring, F. E. (2006). *The great American crime decline.* New York: Oxford University Press.

Part VI

METHODS FOR STUDYING VIOLENT BEHAVIOR

CHAPTER 37

Studying Aggression With Structural Equation Modeling

Noel A. Card and Todd D. Little

Introduction

Structural equation modeling (SEM) is one of the most powerful and flexible analytic tools for studying aggression and violent behavior. To illustrate its flexibility, we briefly describe four applications of SEM that are particularly effective in the study of aggression: (1) modeling means, variances, and correlations in a single group; (2) examining group differences in means, variances, and correlations; (3) decomposing the multidimensionality of aggression; and (4) modeling the interdependent nature of aggression. Although this list of topics is not exhaustive, it represents core uses that are relevant to the study of aggressive behavior. In addition, although we use examples from childhood and adolescence, the approaches we discuss are readily applicable to the study of violent behavior throughout the life span.

SEM is a latent variable technique. As such, one of its primary advantages is that constructs are represented without the presence of measurement error. In the social and behavioral sciences, manifest variable techniques, such as ANOVA or regression, are conducted in the presence of some degree of measurement error (unreliability). As a consequence, any estimates of effect size, be they differences in means or the degree of an association, are underestimated and are prone to bias because of sampling variability. As we describe, SEM is not limited to adjusting covariance relationships for unreliability, but is also able to adjust mean-level estimates for measurement error. In addition to the error corrections of SEM, it also allows for nearly any system of linear equations to be simultaneously estimated, meaning that direct, indirect, mediated, and moderated relationships can be directly specified and estimated (Little, Card, Bovaird, Preacher, & Crandall, 2007).

In the process of specifying SEM models, the key is to measure multiple indicators for a given construct. In this chapter, we first discuss some of the choices that a researcher can make in estimating latent constructs with multiple indicators, and then we discuss the various steps and procedures that are used in testing for similarities and differences in latent constructs.

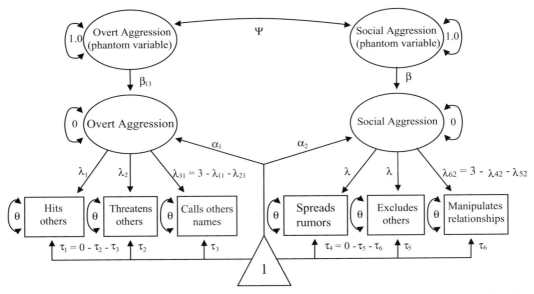

Figure 37.1. Hypothetical example of modeling overt and social aggression in SEM. Note: In SEM manifest (i.e., measured) variables are represented as rectangles and latent variables are represented as ovals. Nondirectional paths (i.e., correlations, often indicated as θ_{xy} when between manifest variables and as ψ_{xy} when between latent variables) are represented as curved double-headed arrows between two variables. Double-headed arrows starting and ending at the same indicator variable, θ_{xx}, represent the residual variance of the indicator, and those starting and ending at the same latent variable, ψ_{xx}, represent the variance of the latent variable. Directional paths (i.e., directional regression paths), either from latent variables to manifest indicators of that variable (factor loadings, often indicated as λ_{xy}) or between latent variables (structural paths, often indicated as β_{xy}), are represented as single-headed arrows (with the arrow on the presumed dependent variable). Mean levels are indicated by the paths from the constant 1 (represented as a triangle) to the indicators (these paths are often referenced as τ) and latent variables (often referenced as α).

Modeling Means, Variances, and Correlations in the Study of Aggression

As mentioned, the analysis of latent variables with SEM offers several advantages over the analysis of manifest variables using such traditional techniques as analysis of variance or regression. Advantages include a greater ability to model complex multivariate relations (e.g., multiple dependent variables, indirect or mediated processes, interactive processes), estimating disattenuated parameter estimates (i.e., correcting for measurement error), and obtaining fit indices for these complex models (which allows for rigorous tests of competing models and specific hypotheses; see, e.g., Kline, 2005; Little, Card, Slegers, & Ledford, 2007).

Consider the hypothetical example depicted in Figure 37.1. The latent overt aggression construct is operationalized by three measured indicators (i.e., hits others, threatens others, and calls others nasty names), and the social aggression construct is operationalized by three measures (i.e., spreads rumors about others, excludes others from activities, and hurtfully manipulates relationships). Although constructs can be represented by as few as two indicators (i.e., measures representing a construct), there are numerous advantages to having three indicators for each construct. Most notable among these advantages is that the measurement of a given construct is locally "just identified." That is, once a scaling parameter has been fixed, the number of parameters needed to estimate the variance, loadings, and residuals associated with a given construct is equal to the number of unique variances and covariances among the indicators used to define the construct. With two indicators, the constructs parameters are not locally identified, which can lead to model identification problems unless additional constraints are placed on the estimates (e.g., a common constraint is to make the loadings of the two indicators be equal in magnitude; see Little, Lindenberger, & Nesselroade, 1999). If a researcher has four or more indicators of a construct, issues of identification are not in play, but the estimation of such constructs can be problematic as the number of indicators increases. On the other hand, if a researcher has a sufficient number of homogeneous indicators (items, scales, or measures) of a construct, combining indicators through parceling techniques can used to represent constructs in a valid and unbiased manner (see Little, Cunningham, Shahar, & Widaman, 2002).

To model latent variables, it is necessary to set the scale of each latent variable in a model. In setting the scale of the variance/covariance structure, two common approaches are to fix the variances of the latent variables at 1.0 or to fix the loading of one arbitrarily selected indicator of each latent variable at 1.0. Both of these approaches provide a sufficient condition to estimate the parameters of a given model, but the estimates are all in a metric that is generally arbitrary. An alternative approach that provides a less arbitrary metric is to constrain the factor loadings of the indicators to average 1.0 (for details, see Little, Slegers, & Card, 2006). Because of its less arbitrary metric, we view this latter approach as a particularly informative and useful method of setting the scale of the latent variables.

When modeling means (i.e., mean and covariance structures [MACS] analysis, see Little, 1997; Little, Card, Slegers, & Ledford, 2007), the approaches to scale setting and identification of mean structures parallel those for scale setting on the variance/covariance parameters (and the method chosen to identify the mean structure should be the same as that chosen for the variance/covariance structure). Perhaps the most common approach is to fix all latent means in a reference group and estimate the latent means as relative differences across groups (an approach that is only useful in multigroup analyses; see next section). A second approach is to arbitrarily choose an indicator intercept to fix at zero. Both these methods also lead to an arbitrary metric for the mean structures of a model (see Little, Slegers, & Card, 2006, for details). An alternative approach that yields less arbitrary estimates (which parallels the constraining method described above) is simply to constrain the means of all indicators of a given construct to average zero (see Little, Slegers, & Card, 2006, for sample syntax and a comparison of the various methods).

The constraining method (also call effects-coded method; Little, Slegers, & Card, 2006) of scale setting has two critical advantages. A first advantage of this approach is that the latent means (i.e., α's) are estimated on the same metric as the manifest indicators. This property thereby allows comparisons of mean levels across constructs, not just across groups, and allows one to interpret the corresponding scale values (e.g., a latent mean of 4 where the indicators are all measured on a 1 to 7 scale means that respondents, on average, are at the midpoint of the scale). A second advantage of this method is that it allows one to examine the patterns of indicator means to determine which indicators have higher mean levels than others (e.g., in Figure 37.1, name calling may be more common than hitting others).

Returning to the hypothetical aggression example of Figure 37.1, our recommended approach to setting the latent scales would involve constraining the loadings (λ) of the hitting, threatening, and name calling indicators on overt aggression to average 1.0 and placing a similar constraint on the loadings of the three social aggression indicators. Assuming that all indicators are on a common metric (e.g., a 1 to 7 self-report scale, or percentages of peers nominating the individual), the latent construct metric would now be on this same metric. Then, if the intercepts (i.e., means) of these indicators are constrained such that the estimates sum to zero, the latent mean (α) of the constructs is estimated on the same scale as its indicators (see Little, Slegers & Card, 2006).

It is only with this constraining (effects-coded) approach that the means or the variances can be readily compared across these two forms of aggression (as well as across time or groups, as described below). To test whether the latent means or variances between overt and relational aggression differ, one would perform a nested-model comparison of (1) an unrestricted model in which all latent means and variances are freely estimated with (2) a restricted model in which the two means or the two variances are equated. Such nested-model comparisons use the resulting change in χ^2 between the unrestricted and restricted models ($\Delta\chi^2 = \chi^2_{\text{restricted}} - \chi^2_{\text{unrestricted}}$, with $df = df_{\text{restricted}} - df_{\text{unrestricted}}$) to test the cross-construct differences in the means or variances. If the change is significant, then the equality constraint is not tenable, and the means or variances in overt and social aggression are different from one another.

As mentioned, comparisons of means in SEM are more powerful than such comparisons with manifest variables (i.e., traditional t-tests or analysis of variance) because the latent means are not attenuated by measurement error. Further, the resulting effect sizes will be disattenuated from the measurement error inherent in manifest variable analyses, such as t-tests. Considering the example of overt and social aggression, the latent, disattenuated effect size for differences in the levels of these forms of aggression could be indexed by Cohen's $d = (\alpha_{\text{overt}} - \alpha_{\text{social}})/\sqrt{(^1/_2(\psi_{\text{overt}} + \psi_{\text{social}}))}$. Note that the latent variances are represented in Figure 37.1 as the paths to the phantom variables, as described below; thus $\psi = \beta^2$.

In addition, although comparisons of variances are not commonly performed in aggression research, SEM makes the decision to evaluate these differences explicit. Such comparisons are an important step in

aggression research because they have the potential to reveal the degree of individual differences in aggressive behavior within a population. This consideration becomes especially important when comparing across different types of aggression, comparing different groups, and in longitudinal studies of aggression.

Finally, SEM represents a powerful approach to examining associations, whether directional (i.e., regression paths) or nondirectional (i.e., correlations), between variables. Because associations between latent variables are generally computed as co-variances, they are dependent both on the degree of association between variables and the variability of the two variables. To model associations in a common metric, however, we suggest using phantom variables. Even though SEM programs can output standardized estimates (i.e., correlations), such estimates cannot be directly tested for differences. The method of using phantom variables is valuable because it allows comparison of latent associations between different variables, across groups, or across time that are estimated in a common standardized metric.

Phantom variables are a second set of latent variables paralleling those already in the model; for example, Figure 37.1 displays a set of phantom variables that are linked to their respective latent variables. To achieve the standardization process, the variances of these phantom variables are fixed at 1.0, and the variances of the latent variables to which they are linked are fixed at 0. Information regarding latent variance is not lost, however, because this information is now represented as the regression coefficient (β) of the path between the phantom and original latent variables (with the latent variance equal to the square of this coefficient, β^2). The estimated covariance between the phantom variables of the constructs is now interpreted as a latent correlation (similar interpretations can be made of directional paths), and meaningful comparisons between different correlations in a model (e.g., comparing correlations between overt and social aggression assessed via self versus peer reports) can now be made using nested-model comparisons.

The latent correlations obtained in SEM are larger in magnitude than those obtained through correlating manifest variables because latent correlations are disattenuated (i.e., correlations between manifest variables underestimate true associations because each measure contains random measurement error). Latent correlations, however, represent the most accurate estimate of the true relation between two constructs. Moreover, significance testing of whether these correlations differ from some value (e.g., 0) will typically be more powerful when performed with latent rather than manifest variables.

In this section, we have highlighted the advantages of using latent variable SEM over traditional approaches to analyzing manifest variables when studying aggression and have demonstrated the flexibility of SEM in estimating and comparing means, variances, and correlations among latent variables. In the next section, we build on these ideas in discussing the ability of SEM to compare these parameter estimates across different groups of individuals.

Group Differences in Aggression

Differences between males and females, across age groups, and across cultural settings in the mean levels, variances, and intercorrelations of aggressive behavior represent important foci of study. Most SEM packages have multiple-group options that allow these parameters to be compared across two or more groups. In addition to correcting all latent estimates across all groups for any degree of unreliability, SEM methods can be used to ensure comparability in the measurement of constructs across groups. This comparability is referred to as *measurement invariance* (for an excellent example of establishing measurement invariance of aggression constructs across gender, age, and cohorts, see Vaillancourt, Brendgen, Boivin, & Tremblay, 2003).

Three conditions are necessary to establish measurement invariance of constructs across groups (see Card & Little, 2006; Little & Slegers, 2005; Meredith, 1993). First, one must ensure that the basic structure of the model is equivalent across groups (known as configural invariance). Here, one simply ensures that the measurement structure is equivalent across groups by fitting a model within each group in which the indicators are specified to load on the same constructs across groups. Consider a situation in which a researcher wishes to fit the model depicted in Figure 37.1 to a sample of boys and a sample of girls. Configural invariance would be established if the same indicators load on overt aggression, but not on social aggression, among both boys and girls. When establishing this and other levels of measurement invariance across groups, one generally does not place any constraints on the latent parameters in the model (i.e., the latent means, variances, and covariances are freely estimated) – these parameter estimates can be meaningfully compared across groups only after measurement invariance is established.

The second step in establishing measurement invariance is to equate the magnitudes of the indicator loadings across groups, a condition known as weak factorial invariance. Here, the loading of each indicator on its respective latent construct (e.g., the loading of "hits others" on overt aggression) is constrained to be proportionally equal in magnitude across groups (i.e., the loadings are weighted by the common factor variance, which is allowed to vary across groups). This constraint ensures that variances in the indicators translate into variance in the latent constructs in a proportionally equivalent manner across groups. Weak invariance would be established in our hypothetical model of Figure 37.1 if all six loadings (λ) could be reasonably equated across boys and girls.

The third and final step[1] in establishing measurement invariance across groups is to equate the means of the manifest indicators (τ), a condition known as strong invariance (see Little, 1997; Meredith, 1993).

Considering again our hypothetical example, this step involves equating the mean of each corresponding indicator (i.e., the paths from the constant to the manifest indicators) across groups. This constraint does not imply that the mean levels of the construct are constrained to be equal across groups; instead, any group differences in aggression are examined as differences in latent means (α). Equating the indicator means ensures that those aspects of a construct that are relatively common in one group are also relatively common in other groups. For example, if "calling others names" was more common than "hitting others" among boys, it is necessary that "calling others names" is also more common than "hitting others" among girls in order to ensure the equivalent measurement of overt aggression across gender.

Before concluding our discussion of establishing measurement invariance across groups, two issues merit mention. First, establishing measurement equivalence is an issue of plausibility, rather than one of formal significance testing. Given that SEM is a statistically powerful technique often used with large samples, even substantively trivial differences in measurement across groups will often emerge as statistically significant. Therefore, we recommend progressing through the three steps outlined above primarily in order to detect if substantial differences in measurement are evident between groups; however, for most applications in the social and behavioral sciences, the final evaluation of whether measurement invariance is tenable should be made based on the fit of the model after implementing the three sets of equalities describe above. If the model with strong metric invariance across groups shows adequate model fit (e.g., RMSEA <.08, CFI and similar indices >.90; see Hu & Bentler, 1995) then measurement invariance can be concluded. Second, there exist several strategies for proceeding if strong metric invariance is not plausible (see Card & Little, 2006; Little & Slegers, 2005; Millsap & Kwok, 2004). These strategies include removing constructs from the model for which measurement invariance is not tenable, relaxing the offending cross-group constraints and analyzing models under partial invariance, or choosing not to make cross-group comparisons. If measurement equivalence can be established across groups, however, one can compare latent means, variances, and correlations across groups using nested-model comparisons (described above).

Thus far, we have described SEM methods of modeling means, variances, and correlations among aggression constructs that are commonly used in the study of one or more groups of individuals, albeit with attention to some recent innovations in these techniques. In the next two sections, we describe more advanced applications of SEM in the study of aggression. First, we describe an approach similar to multi-trait multi-method decompositions that can be used to disentangle the multidimensionality of aggression. Then we provide recommendations for studying the interdependent nature of aggression.

The Multidimensional Nature of Aggression

Aggression is a multidimensional phenomenon, with distinctions commonly made in terms of the forms and the functions of aggressive behavior. The forms of aggression refer to the specific behavior enacted and are often distinguished into those that are overt in nature (e.g., hitting, pushing, teasing, direct name calling) versus those that are more covert or indirect (e.g., excluding one from the group, spreading rumors, manipulating interpersonal relationships; e.g., Crick, 1996; Lagerspetz, Björkqvist, & Peltonen, 1988). Another distinction that has often been made refers to the function that the aggression serves and is commonly separated into that which is driven by instrumental motives (e.g., aggression to obtain social status or to receive tangible rewards) versus that which is reactive in nature (e.g., an angry aggressive response to a perceived threat or mistreatment; e.g., Dodge & Coie, 1987). In this section, we briefly review problems in distinguishing these forms and functions

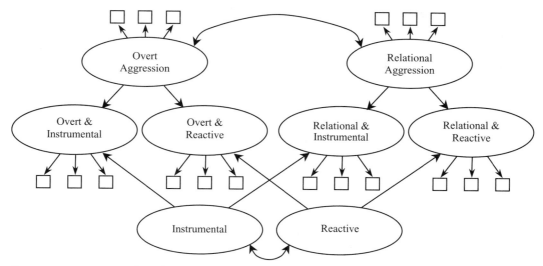

Figure 37.2. Disentangling the forms and functions of aggression using SEM (from Little et al., 2003).

using traditional analytic techniques and present results of a study showing how they can be better disentangled through modified measures and SEM.

Traditional measures of aggression often yield extremely high interrelations between the different forms (typically ranging from $r = .50$ to .80; Card, Stucky, Sawalani, & Little, 2007) and functions (e.g., average $r = .68$; see Card & Little, 2006) of aggression. Although exploratory factor analyses have provided support for these distinctions based on form (e.g., Crick, 1996; Vaillancourt et al., 2003) and function (e.g., Day, Bream, & Pal, 1992; Poulin & Boivin, 2000), these high interrelations leave unanswered questions regarding the extent to which distinct correlates of different forms and functions of aggression can be detected.

Part of the reason for these high correlations may be due to the fact that traditional measurement procedures have confounded the discrete forms and functions of aggression. For example, typical items assessing different functions of aggression often share a form component (e.g., "I hit others to get what I want"; "I hit others if they make my mad or upset"), which artificially inflates observed correlations. To remedy this problem, Little, Jones, Henrich, and Hawley (2003) developed a measurement

strategy to disentangle the forms and functions of aggression. As shown in Figure 37.2, one can measure overt and relational forms of aggression by using items that are descriptive only of the behavior without reference to the function that the aggression may serve (e.g., "I'm the kind of person who hits, kicks, or punches others"; "I'm the kind of person who says mean things about others"). Then, one can use items that deliberately combine forms and functions of aggression to assess overt-instrumental (e.g., "I often threaten others to get what I want"), overt-reactive (e.g., "If others have angered me, I often hit, kick, or punch them"), relational-instrument (e.g., "To get what I want, I often gossip or spread rumors about others"), and relational-reactive aggression (e.g., "If others upset or hurt me, I often tell my friends to stop liking them"). Finally, as shown in Figure 37.2, SEM can be used to extract the latent form variance from these four latent form-function combinations, and the remaining functional information can be used to create latent variables representing the pure assessment of the instrumental and reactive functions of aggression.

Using this approach with a large sample of German adolescents, Little et al. (2003) found that overt and relational forms of aggression remained highly intercorrelated (disattenuated $r = .83$), but the instrumental and reactive functions of aggression were essentially orthogonal (disattenuated $r = -.10$). Further analyses of these pure forms and functions of aggression demonstrated important validity relationships that would not have been possible to detect with traditional approaches to measurement and analysis. For example, they showed that when the form of aggression is removed the pure information about reactive aggression is very highly related to both hostility and ease of frustration, but that instrumental aggression is not. They also showed that instrumental aggression is significantly more highly related with deliberate coercive strategies of influence than is reactive aggression (see Little et al., 2003, for details). These correlations with the mixed form-function measures of instrumental and reactive aggression would have been contaminated and confounded by the form information (i.e., the overt vs. relational form of aggression) had SEM not been used to separate the sources of variability in the measures. Moreover, follow-up work showed that youth who are primarily instrumental in their aggressive behavior do not suffer the typical ill consequences of being aggressive relative to youth who are primarily reactively aggressive (see Little, Brauner, Jones, Nock, & Hawley, 2003). The primary point here is that SEM procedures, in combination with carefully crafted measures, can be used to disentangle the many sources of variability that are common to most measures of aggressive and violent behavior and provide a critical analytic tool to test complex hypotheses about the nature of aggressive and violent behavior.

Modeling the Interdependency of Aggression

An emerging body of research suggests that aggression can be better understood by looking not only at the aggressors or the victims in isolation but also by considering the interpersonal relations between aggressors and victims (e.g., Pierce & Cohen, 1995). Adapting such a perspective has much to offer in understanding aggression, but is complicated by violations of assumptions of independence found in traditional analytic approaches (including traditional approaches in SEM). Fortunately, several approaches to managing the nonindependence in interdependent data exist (for further discussion of modeling interdependent data using SEM, see Little & Card, 2005).

Before describing these approaches, two distinctions need to be made before deciding on an approach. First, one must determine whether the level of analysis is on dyads or dependencies within groups. Dyadic analysis is more appropriate when one wishes to focus on pairs of individuals (e.g., aggressor-victim dyads; Card & Hodges, 2005), whereas group-based methods are more appropriate when one wishes to model groups of three or more interacting individuals (e.g., play groups in which observations of interpersonal aggression are conducted; Coie et al., 1999). Second, one must determine whether it is more appropriate to consider individuals as exchangeable or distinguishable cases. Distinguishable cases are those in which each individual can be considered to have a distinct role, such as the aggressor in a unidirectional aggressor-victim relationship, whereas exchangeable cases are those in which there is no meaningful basis to assign individuals to certain roles (e.g., a child in a mutually aggressive dyad).

Dyads that consist of distinguishable members include non-twin siblings (in which siblings are distinguished by age), cross-sex friendships or romantic relationships (in which individuals are distinguished by sex), and aggressor-victim relationships (in which individuals are distinguished by their role as aggressor or victim). These situations can be analyzed using the Actor-Partner Interdependence Model (APIM; see Cook & Kenny, 2005), in which each dyad is considered a case, and the characteristics of the aggressors and their victims are represented as separate variables. In the APIM, relations among variables of one individual

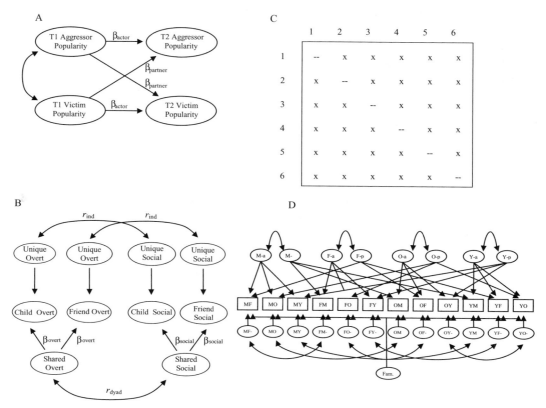

Figure 37.3. Modeling interdependency in studying aggression. A. Actor-partner interdependence model. B. Exchangeable case correlation approach. C. Basic round robin design. D. Social relations model represented as SEM.

are considered actor effects, whereas relations among variables across individuals are partner effects.

Figure 37.3a shows a hypothetical example of relations among aggressors' and their victims' popularity at two time points. The relations of each individual's popularity across time are considered actor effects; hence the stability of aggressors' popularity and of victims' popularity are considered actor effects.[2] In contrast, the relation between aggressors' popularity with the later popularity of their victims is considered a partner effect (e.g., a negative relation might be expected, such that being victimized by popular aggressors predicts decreases in victims' popularity), as would the relation between victims' popularity with the later popularity of those aggressing against them (e.g., this relation might also

be expected to be negative, because aggressing against unpopular targets might be reinforced, whereas aggressing against popular targets might bring negative social ramifications). The most accurate estimates of these paths are obtained when SEM is applied so that these relations are not attenuated by measurement error. To our knowledge, no published studies have applied the APIM to aggressor-victim dyads, but we believe that this approach has considerable potential.

Examples in which dyads should be considered exchangeable include same-sex friendships, identical or same-sex fraternal twins, and mutually aggressive dyads in which there is no meaningful way to consistently distinguish dyad members. Here, the APIM is not appropriate because there is no nonarbitrary means to place one member of the dyad in one position versus the other. For these exchangeable case dyads, an alternative approach is the double-entry (intra-class) correlational approach of Griffin and Gonzalez (1995). This approach requires that each dyad be entered as two cases, alternating the order in which individuals in the dyad are entered. Figure 37.3b depicts a hypothetical example of same-sex (exchangeable) friends' levels of overt and social aggression, in which each child's and his or her friend's overt and social aggression are measured with three indicators (not portrayed for simplicity). In this model, r_{ind} represents the disattenuated correlation between individuals' overt and social aggression (corrected for dyadic dependency), and r_{dyad} represents the association between pairs of friends' overt and social aggression. In this setup, similarity between friends' levels of overt aggression is represented as the square of the equated paths β_{overt}, and similarity in friends' social aggression as the square of β_{social}. Standard errors (and resulting significance tests or confidence intervals) are based on a modified N depending on the degrees of dependencies among dyads (see Griffin & Gonzalez, 1995).

These two approaches to analyzing dyadic data can be adapted to handle either type of situation. In the distinguishable case, one can double-enter the data, but include a dummy-coded covariate that distinguishes the meaningful ordering of the dyad members (e.g., a dummy code of 0 when aggressors are entered before their victims and 1 when victims are entered before their aggressors; Gonzalez & Griffin, 1999). Similarly, the APIM can be adapted for the exchangeable case through a method of analyzing means and difference scores of the dyads (see Kenny, 1996).

Interdependencies occurring in small groups are commonly analyzed using the Social Relations Model (SRM; see Kenny, 1994). Although variations in group designs that can be analyzed exist, the most common is the round robin design depicted in Figure 37.3c. For example, Cillessen (see Coie et al., 1999; Lashley & Bond, 1997) observed interpersonal aggression in artifi-

cial play groups consisting of six boys each. Over the course of several play group sessions, observations were made of the number of aggressive acts that each child made toward each peer. These values would be represented as xs in Figure 37.3c. Note that the number of times Child 1 was aggressive against Child 2 is not necessarily identical to the number of times that Child 2 was aggressive against Child 1; hence, this matrix is nonsymmetric. The values on the major diagonal are missing because it is not expected that a child is aggressive against her or himself (and if he or she was, it would likely represent a qualitatively different phenomenon).

When considering interdependent group data, it is also necessary to decide whether individuals are distinguishable or exchangeable. For example, if observations of aggression are made in children's play groups, there is no readily apparent distinguishing factor among the individuals, and they would generally be considered exchangeable. The SRM is an effective method of analyzing these data, and programs to perform such analyses are readily available from Kenny (http://davidakenny.net/kenny.htm). A current limitation of the SRM with exchangeable case data is the inability to model parameters in latent space, so we do not discuss it further here.

Groups can also be considered in terms of distinguishable roles. For example, Cook and Kenny (2004) examined patterns of perceived negativity within four-person families. Because each family member can be identified as having a distinct role (father, mother, older adolescent, and younger adolescent), these data are considered distinguishable cases. This type of SRM can be modeled as a latent variable SEM, as shown in Figure 37.3d. In this setup, it is possible to estimate means and variances at the level of the family (the degree of negativity across families), actor effects for each family member (e.g., older adolescents seeing others as negative), and partner effects for each family member (e.g., fathers being seen as negative), as well as generalized reciprocities for each family member (e.g., are mothers who perceive others as negative also perceived as negative?) and dyadic reciprocities for each dyad (are older adolescents who perceive their younger siblings as negative also perceived this way by their siblings?).

Conclusions

We first described basic techniques of analyzing means, variances, and correlations in one or more groups of individuals using SEM and then described more advanced applications of decomposing the multidimensional nature of aggression and modeling interdependencies inherent in the study of aggression. In doing so, we have offered some future directions for improving analytic techniques in the study of aggression. The topics we have discussed are only a small portion of those that could be considered when using SEM in research on aggression and violence (see Chapter 38, this volume). Nevertheless, we hope that the brief introduction provided in this chapter illustrates to aggression researchers the power and flexibility of SEM in addressing a wide range of research questions.

Acknowledgments

This work was supported in part by grants from the NIH to the University of Kansas through the Mental Retardation and Developmental Disabilities Research Center (5 P30 HD002528), the Center for Biobehavioral Neurosciences in Communication Disorders (5 P30 DC005803), a NRSA fellowship to the first author (1 F32 MH072005), and an NFGRF grant (2301779) from the University of Kansas to the second author.

Notes

1. A fourth step is possible but is not necessary for measurement invariance to hold. Namely, the residual variances of the indicators can also be tested for equality across groups. This condition is called strict invariance (see Meredith, 1993). This condition, however, is overly restrictive for comparing latent construct information and should not be enforced because it forces all potential sources of measurement bias into the latent parameter space (see Little, 1997).

2. Other within-individual effects would be considered actor effects, for example, if we looked at the concurrent or longitudinal relation of aggressors' prosocial behavior on their popularity.

References

Card, N. A., & Hodges, E. V. E. (2005, April). Power differential in aggressor-victim relationships. In N. A. Card & E. V. E. Hodges (Chairs), *Aggressor-victim relationships: Toward a dyadic perspective*. Paper presented at the biennial meeting of the Society for Research in Child Development, Atlanta, GA.

Card, N. A., & Little, T. D. (2006). Proactive and reactive aggression in childhood and adolescence: A meta-analysis of differential relations with psychosocial adjustment. *International Journal of Behavioral Development, 30*, 466–480.

Card, N. A., & Little, T. D. (2006). Analytic considerations in cross-cultural research on peer relations. In X. Chen, D. C. French, & B. Schneider (Eds.), *Peer relations in cultural context*. New York: Cambridge University Press.

Card, N. A., Stucky, B. D., Sawalani, G., & Little, T. D. (2007). *Overt and relational forms of aggression: A meta-analytic review of intercorrelations, gender differences, and relations to maladjustment*. Manuscript under review.

Coie, J. D., Cillessen, A. H. N., Dodge, K. A., Hubbard, J. A., Schwartz, D., Lemerise, E. A., et al. (1999). It takes two to fight: A test of relational factors and a method for assessing aggressive dyads. *Developmental Psychology, 35*, 1179–1188.

Cook, W. L., & Kenny, D. A. (2004). Application of the social relations model to family assessment. *Journal of Family Psychology, 18*, 361–371.

Cook, W. L., & Kenny, D. A. (2005). The actor-partner interdependence model: A model of bidirectional effects in developmental studies.

International Journal of Behavioral Development, 29, 101–109.

Crick, N. R. (1996). The role of overt aggression, relational aggression, and prosocial behavior in the prediction of children's future social adjustment. *Child Development, 67,* 2317–2327.

Day, D. M., Bream, L. A., & Pal, A. (1992). Instrumental and reactive aggression: An analysis of subtypes based on teacher perceptions. *Journal of Clinical Child Psychology, 21,* 210–217.

Dodge, K. A., & Coie, J. D. (1987). Social information-processing factors in reactive and instrumental aggression in children's playgroups. *Journal of Personality and Social Psychology, 53,* 1146–1158.

Gonzalez, R., & Griffin, D. (1999). The correlational analysis of dyad-level data in the distinguishable case. *Personal Relationships, 6,* 449–469.

Griffin, D., & Gonzalez, R. (1995). Correlational analysis of dyad-level data in the exchangeable case. *Psychological Bulletin, 118,* 430–439.

Hu, L.-T., & Bentler, P. M. (1995). Evaluating model fit. In R. H. Hoyle (Ed.), *Structural equation modeling: Concepts, issues, and applications.* Thousand Oaks, CA: Sage.

Kenny, D. A. (1994). *Interpersonal perception: A social relations analysis.* New York: Guilford.

Kenny, D. A. (1996). Models of non-independence in dyadic research. *Journal of Social and Personal Relationships, 13,* 279–294.

Kline, R. B. (2005). *Principles and practice of structural equation modeling* (2nd ed.). New York: Guilford.

Lagerspetz, K. M. J., Björkqvist, K., & Peltonen, T. (1988). Is indirect aggression typical of females? Gender differences in aggressiveness in 11- to 12-year-old children. *Aggressive Behavior, 14,* 403–414.

Lashley, B. R., & Bond, C. F., Jr. (1997). Significance testing for round robin data. *Psychological Methods, 2,* 278–291.

Little, T. D. (1997). Means and covariance structures (MACS) analyses of cross-cultural data: Practical and theoretical issues. *Multivariate Behavioral Research, 32,* 53–76.

Little, T. D., Brauner, J., Jones, S. M., Nock, M. K., & Hawley,, P. H. (2003). Rethinking aggression: A typological examination of the functions of aggression. *Merrill-Palmer Quarterly, 49,* 343–369.

Little, T. D., & Card, N. A. (2005). On the use of the social relations and actor-partner inter-dependence models in developmental research. *International Journal of Behavioral Development, 29,* 173–179.

Little, T. D., Card, N. A., Bovaird, J. A., Preacher, K. J. & Crandall, C. S. (2007). Representing mediation and moderation with contextual factors in SEM. In T. D. Little, J. A. Bovaird, & N. A. Card (Eds.), *Modeling ecological and contextual effects in longitudinal studies of human development.* Mahwah, NJ: Erlbaum.

Little, T. D., Card, N. A., Slegers, D. W. & Ledford, E. C. (2007). Modeling contextual effects in multiple-group MACS models. In T. D. Little, J. A. Bovaird, & N. A. Card (Eds.), *Modeling ecological and contextual effects in longitudinal studies of human development.* Mahwah, NJ: Erlbaum.

Little, T. D., Cunningham, W. A., Shahar, G., & Widaman, K. F. (2002). To parcel or not to parcel: Exploring the questions, weighing the merits. *Structural Equation Modeling, 9,* 151–173.

Little, T. D., Jones, S. M., Henrich, C. C., & Hawley, P. H. (2003). Disentangling the "whys" from the "whats" of aggressive behaviour. *International Journal of Behavioral Development, 27,* 122–133.

Little, T. D., Lindenberger, U., & Nesselroade, J. R. (1999). On selecting indicators for multivariate measurement and modeling with latent variables: When "good" indicators are bad and "bad" indicators are good. *Psychological Methods, 4,* 192–211.

Little, T. D., & Slegers, D. W. (2005). Factor analysis: Multiple groups with means. In B. Everitt & D. Howell (Eds.) & D. Rindskopf (Section Ed.), *Encyclopedia of statistics in behavioral science* (Vol. 2, pp. 617–623). Chichester, UK: Wiley.

Little, T. D., Slegers, D. W., & Card, N. A. (2006). An alternative method of identifying and scaling latent variables in SEM and MACS models. *Structural Equation Modeling, 130,* 59–72.

Meredith, W. (1993). Measurement invariance, factor analysis and factorial invariance. *Psychometrika, 58,* 525–543.

Millsap, R. E., & Kwok, O. M. (2004). Evaluating the impact of partial factorial invariance on selection in two populations. *Psychological Methods, 9,* 93–115.

Pierce, K. A., & Cohen, R. (1995). Aggressors and their victims: Toward a contextual framework for understanding aggressor-victim relationships. *Developmental Review, 15,* 292–310.

Poulin, F., & Boivin, M. (2000). Reactive and instrumental aggression: Evidence of a two-factor model. *Psychological Assessment, 12,* 115–122.

Vaillancourt, T., Brendgen, M., Boivin, M., & Tremblay, R. E. (2003). A longitudinal confirmatory factor analysis of indirect and physical aggression: Evidence of two factors over time? *Child Development, 74,* 1628–1638.

CHAPTER 38

Overview of a Semi-Parametric, Group-Based Approach for Analyzing Trajectories of Development

Daniel S. Nagin

Introduction

In this chapter I provide a brief, nontechnical overview of my decade-long research program aimed at developing a group-based method for analyzing developmental trajectories. This work is described more fully, including technical details, in Nagin (1999) and Nagin and Tremblay (2001a). A comprehensive book length treatment is provided in Nagin (2005) In addition, a SAS-based procedure with the capability for supporting all of the analysis described in this overview is also available free of charge from the Web site, www.andrew.cmu.edu/user/bjones/index.htm. Documentation is also available at the site. For an overview of the software see Jones, Nagin, and Roeder (2001) and Jones and Nagin (forthcoming).

Longitudinal data provide the empirical foundation for research on wide-ranging topics in the social and behavioral sciences and in medicine. Consider these few examples: psychologists and psychiatrists use longitudinal data to study the developmental course of psychopathologies, criminologists use longitudinal data to analyze the progression of delinquency and criminality over life stages, economists use longitudinal data to estimate models of income dynamics, sociologists use longitudinal data to study the evolution of the socioeconomic status of communities, and medical researchers use longitudinal data to study the progress of diseases and physiological processes.

The common statistical objective across these diverse application domains is modeling the progression of a phenomenon as it evolves over age or time. Over the past quarter-century, two main branches of methodology have evolved for the statistical analysis of growth processes: hierarchical modeling (Bryk & Raudenbush, 1987, 1992; Goldstein, 1995), and latent curve analysis (McArdle & Epstein, 1987; Meredith & Tisak, 1990; Muthen, 1989; Willett & Sayer, 1994). Although these two classes of models differ in important respects, they also have important commonalities (MacCallum, Kim, Malarkey, & Kiecolt-Glaser, 1997; Raudenbush, 2001; Willett & Sayer, 1994). For the purposes of this chapter, one commonality is key: both model the unconditional and conditional population

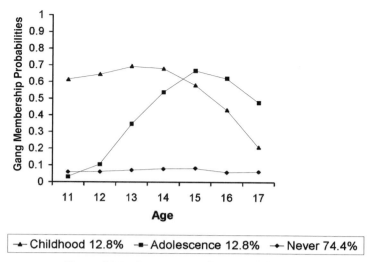

Figure 38.1. Trajectories of gang membership.

distribution of growth curves based on *continuous* distribution functions. Unconditional models estimate two key features of the population distribution of growth curve parameters – their mean and co-variance structure. The former defines average growth within the population, and the latter calibrates the variances of growth throughout the population. The conditional models are designed to explain this variability by relating growth parameters to one or more explanatory variables.

In this overview I describe a distinct semi-parametric, group-based approach for modeling developmental trajectories. As described in Nagin (1999; 2005) and Nagin and Tremblay (2001), the method is based on finite mixture modeling. Its application to a Montreal-based data set is illustrated in Figure 38.1. Specifically, this data are a product of a study that tracked 1,037 White males of French ancestry. Subjects were selected in 1984 from kindergarten classes in low socioeconomic Montreal neighborhoods. After an assessment at age 6, the boys and other informants were interviewed annually from ages 10 to 17. Assessments were made on a wide range of factors. Among these were self-reports by the boy of whether or not he had been involved with a delinquent gang in the past year.

As reported in Lacourse, Nagin, Vitaro, Claes, and Tremblay (2003), application of the group-based method to this gang involvement data identified the three highly distinct groups shown in Figure 38.1. The trajectory for each group is described by the probability of gang membership at each age. One was a large group, estimated to comprise 74.4% of the population, whose probability of gang membership was very small over all ages. The second group, called the childhood-onset group, started with a high probability of gang membership at age 11 that rose modestly until age 14 and then declined thereafter. The third group, called the adolescent-onset group, started off with a near-zero probability of gang membership at age 11, but thereafter rose to a rate that actually exceeded that of the childhood-onset group. The method estimates that the latter two groups each constitute 13.4% of the sampled population.

The essence of the motivation for the group-based method is captured in a late 19th-century temperance print. The left side of the print depicts a socially and personally productive life course. The first panel shows an earnest boy, book in hand, walking to school. In the second panel, the boy is now a young man with his wife and child lovingly looking on as he is hard at work. In the third panel, the focal character is now an old man sitting in a garden with the family of his grown child. In contrast, the right side depicts a socially counterproductive and personally destructive life course. In the first panel, the boy is drinking and carousing with his mates; in the second, he is abusing his wife in a drunken rage; and in the final panel, he is working at hard labor in prison. Minus the Victorian moral undertones of this print, the group-based method is designed to identify such distinctive life trajectories and provide a statistical basis for uncovering the forces that propel people down these very different life paths.

Raudenbush (2001, p. 59) describes the group-based approach as a "multinomial" modeling strategy and offers valuable insight into an important class of problems for which a group-based approach is particularly appropriate. For some developmental problems it is reasonable to assume that all individuals either increase or decrease according to a common growth process. He offers language acquisition as a quintessential example. Another good example is time spent with peers from childhood through adolescence (Warr, 2001). Conventional growth curve methods are well suited for analyzing such developmental phenomena. However, there are large classes of problems for which growth curve models do not naturally fit. Raudenbush uses depression as an example. He observes, "It makes no sense to assume that everyone is increasing (or decreasing) in depression. . . . Many persons will never be high in depression, others will always be high, while others will become increasingly depressed." For this class of problems he recommends the group-based approach that is the subject of this chapter.

The basis for Raudenbush's distinction between the developmental processes underlying language acquisition and depression is fundamental. Because the vocabularies of all young children from normal populations increase with age, it is sensible to ask the following questions: What is the average growth curve of children' vocabulary over a specified age range? How large is the variation across children in their individual-level language acquisition growth curves? How do such between-person variations relate to factors, such as the child's cognitive functioning and parental education? How are within-person changes in acquisition related to changes in interactions with primary caregivers caused, for example, by parental conflict?

These questions are framed in the language of analysis of variance as reflected in the use of such terms as "within-person changes" and "between-person change." Using this language is only natural because conventional growth curve analysis has its roots in analysis of variance. Like analysis of variance, growth curve analysis is designed to sort out factors accounting for variation about a population mean. It also adopts the normality assumption, which is the cornerstone of analysis of variance. Specifically, growth curve analysis assumes that individual-level growth parameters are normally distributed in the population.

Framing a statistical analysis of a time-varying process in the conceptual apparatus of analysis of variance requires that it be sensible to characterize population differences in a phenomenon in terms of variation about its mean time trend. For processes like language acquisition the mean trend is, in fact, a sensible statistical anchor for describing individual variability. However, for many processes evolving over time or age, it is not. Returning to the depression example, it makes no sense to frame a statistical analysis of population differences in the developmental progression of depression in terms of variation about a mean "trajectory of depression." Other examples of evolving behavioral phenomena that are not properly described in terms of variation about a population mean are most forms of psychopathology, smoking, drinking, and illicit drug use. More generally a group-based approach to analyzing repeated measure data is usefully applied to phenomena in which there may be qualitatively different trajectories of change over age or time across subpopulations that are not identifiable ex ante based on some measured characteristic, such gender or race.

Other Rationales for a Group-Based Statistical Model

There is a long tradition in developmental psychology of group-based theorizing about both normal and pathological development. Examples include theories of personality development (Caspi, 1998), drug use (Kandel, 1975), learning (Holyoak & Spellman, 1993), language and conceptual development (Markman, 1989), depression (Kasen et al., 2001), eating disorders (Tyrka et al., 2000), anxiety (Cloninger, 1986), and the development of prosocial behaviors such as conscience (Kochanska, Murray, & Coy, 1997) and of antisocial behaviors such as delinquency (Loeber, 1991; Moffitt, 1993; Patterson, DeBaryshe, & Ramsey, 1989).

Because conventional growth curve modeling methods are ill suited to their needs, developmental researchers have commonly resorted to using assignment rules based on subjective categorization criteria to construct categories of developmental trajectories. For example, Haapasalo and Tremblay (1994) propose a taxonomy comprised of five groups—stable high fighter, desisting high fighters, late-onset high fighters, variable high fighters, and nonfighters. The groups were created based on assessments of physical aggression spanning a period from age 6 to 12 in the previously described Montreal-based longitudinal study. In this study, subjects were scored each assessment period on a three-item scale of physical aggression: kicking, biting, and hitting other children; fighting with other children; and bullying and intimidating children.

Haapasalo and Tremblay labeled boys who scored high on this scale for any given period as a "high fighters" for that period. They then defined rules for assigning individuals into the five-group taxonomy. These rules were based on the frequency and trend of each boy's classification as a high fighter. For example, desisting high fighters were boys who were high fighters in kindergarten but who were classified as high fighters in no more than one of the ensuring assessment periods. See Tremblay, Desmarais-Gervais,

Gagnon, and Charlebois (1987) for further details on this study.

Moffitt's (1993) well-known taxonomy is more parsimonious. She posits only two distinct developmental trajectories of problem behavior. One group follows what she calls a life-course persistent (LCP) trajectory of antisocial behavior, and the other group is posited to follow an adolescent-limited (AL) trajectory. In empirical tests of her theory (e.g., Moffitt, Caspi, Dickson, Silva and Stanton 1996) she uses classification rules that are conceptually similar to those used by Haapasalo and Tremblay (1994). LCPs are defined as individuals who score one or more standard deviation above the mean in three of four assessments of a conduct disorder index between ages 5 and 11 and who also score at least one standard deviation above the mean in self-reported delinquency at least once at either age 15 or 18. The ALs are defined as individuals who do not meet the LCP criterion for childhood conduct problems, but who do achieve the LCP threshold for adolescent delinquency.

Although such assignment rules are generally reasonable, there are limitations and pitfalls attendant to their use. One is that the existence of distinct developmental trajectories must be assumed a priori. Thus, the analysis cannot test for their presence, a fundamental shortcoming. A second and related pitfall is the risk of simultaneously "over- and under-fitting" the data by creating trajectory groups that reflect only random variation and failing to identify unusual but still real developmental patterns. Third, ex ante specified rules provide no basis for calibrating the precision of individual classifications to the various groups that comprise the taxonomy. That is, the uncertainty about an individual's group membership cannot be quantified in the form of probabilities with associated confidence intervals.

To illustrate these limitations, consider the Haapasalo and Tremblay (1994) study. Figure 38.2 displays the results of an application of the group-based method to the same Montreal-based data set used in that analysis. Specifically, the method was applied to annual assessments of physical aggression

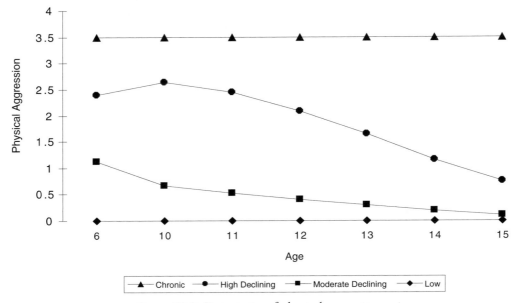

Figure 38.2. Trajectories of physical aggression.

made at age 6 and again at age 10 to 15. The application, which was first reported in Nagin and Tremblay (1999), found that a four-group model best fitted the data. A group called "lows" is made up of individuals who display little or no physically aggressive behavior. This group is estimated to comprise about 15% of the sample population. A second group, which comprises about 50% of the population, is best labeled "moderate decliners." At age 6, boys in this group displayed modest levels of physical aggression, but by age 10 they had largely desisted. A third group, comprising about 30% of the population, is labeled "high-level decliners." This group starts off scoring high on physical aggression at age 6, but scores far lower by age 15. Notwithstanding this marked decline, at age 15 they continue to display a modest level of physical aggression. Finally, there is a small group of "chronics," comprising about 5% of the population, who display high levels of physical aggression throughout the observation period.

The Nagin and Tremblay analysis provides formal statistical support for the presence of three of the groups hypothesized in the Haapasalo and Tremblay taxonomy: the

stable high fighters who correspond to the chronic trajectory group, the desisting high fighters who correspond to the high declining trajectory group, and the lows, who correspond to the nonfighters. However, there is no evidence of a trajectory corresponding to the late-onset high fighter group or of a variable high fighter group. These are examples of classifications that are likely over-fitting the data by creating groups that are confounding random variation with real structural differences. There also seems to be evidence of the under-fitting problem. The taxonomy fails to identify the moderate declining trajectory group. In Nagin and Tremblay (1999) and Nagin, Pagani, Tremblay, and Vitaro (2003), the moderate declining group is found to be distinctive in some respects from the low physical aggression trajectory group.

Two other examples of the utility of the formal group-based trajectory method compared to ad hoc classification procedures are studies by Nagin, Farrington, and Moffitt (1995) and Lacourse et al. (2003). The former application was intended to test several predictions of Moffitt's taxonomic theory. One was to test for the very presence

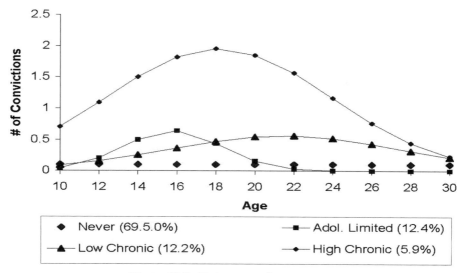

Figure 38.3. Trajectories of convictions.

of the trajectories predicted by the taxonomy. Based on an analysis of data convictions from age 10 to 32 in a sample of 403 males from a poor neighborhood in London, England, three offending trajectories were found. The trajectories are shown in Figure 38.3. One trajectory, which peaks sharply in late adolescence, closely matches the adolescent-limited group predicted by the theory. The high hump-shaped trajectory is similar in some respects to Moffitt's life course persistent group. The group is already actively engaged in delinquency at age 10. However, their frequency of antisocial behavior, at least as measured by conviction, is very age dependent – a pattern that is not anticipated by Moffitt's theory. It rises until about age 18 and then begins a steady decline. By age 30 the frequency of antisocial behavior has dropped below its starting point at age 10 and is about equal to the rate of a third group called low- rate chronic offenders. This final group was not included in Moffitt's taxonomy. Thus, this application of the group-based method provided basic confirmation of the presence of the AL and LCP trajectories that Moffitt predicts in her taxonomy, but also suggests that the LCP trajectory may be more age dependent than

anticipated by the theory. Further, the taxonomy did not predict the low-rate chronic trajectory.

The Lacourse et al. (2003) analysis reported in Figure 38.1 illustrates two other valuable properties of the group-based modeling approach compared to the use of classification rules. One is the capacity to identify qualitatively distinct developmental progressions that are not readily identifiable using ad hoc, ex ante classification rules. In principle the childhood-onset and adolescent-onset groups are identifiable ex ante, but given their specific developmental courses it would be very difficult to distinguish them from chance variation without a formal statistical methodology. A second closely related advantage stems from the use of a statistical structure. It is because of this structure that the methodology has the capacity to distinguish chance variation across individuals from real differences and to calibrate whether within-individual change is real or only random variation. Because the child- and adolescent-onset trajectories are the product of a formal statistical model, there is a firmer basis for their reality than if they had been constructed based on subjective classification rules.

Table 38.1: Physical aggression group profiles

| Variables | Group | | | |
	Never	Low Desister	High Desister	Chronic
Years of School – Mother	11.1	10.8	9.8	8.4
Years of School – Father	11.5	10.7	9.8	9.1
Low IQ (%)	21.6	26.8	44.5	46.4
Completed 8th Grade on Time (%)	80.3	64.6	31.8	6.5
Juvenile Record (%)	0.0	2.0	6.0	13.3
# of Sexual Partners at Age 17 (Past Year)	1.2	1.7	2.2	3.5

The group-based methodology is also responsive to appeals for the development of "person-based" approaches to analyzing development (Bergman, 1998; Magnusson, 1998). Such appeals are motivated by a desire for methods that can provide a statistical snapshot of the distinguishing characteristics and behaviors of individuals following distinctive developmental pathways. The group-based method lends itself to creating such profiles.

This capacity is illustrated by the summary statistics reported in Table 38.1 that profile the characteristics of individuals following the four physical aggression trajectories shown in Figure 38.2. After the trajectories are estimated, the model's parameter estimates can be used to calculate the probability of an individual belonging to each of the trajectory groups. To create the profiles reported in Table 38.1, individuals were assigned to the trajectory group in which they mostly likely belonged based on their measured history of physical aggression. The summary statistics reported in the table are simply the product of cross-tabulations of group membership so defined with the various individual characteristics and outcomes reported in the table.

The profiles conform to long-standing findings on the predictors and consequences of problem behaviors, such as physical aggression. The chronics have the least educated parents and most frequently score in the lowest quartile of the sample's IQ distribution. By contrast, the nevers are least likely to suffer from these risk factors. Fur-

ther, 90% of the chronics fail to reach the eighth grade on schedule, and 13% have a juvenile record by age 18. In comparison, only 19% of the nevers have fallen behind by the eighth grade, and none has a juvenile record. In between are the low-level and high-level decliners.

Table 38.1 demonstrates that trajectory group membership varied systematically with individual characteristics as well as circumstances, such as parental education that predate the measurement series. An important generalization of the base model allows for joint estimation of both the shapes of the trajectory groups and also the impact of various psychosocial characteristics on the probability of trajectory group membership. This extension, which is described in Nagin (1999; 2005) and Roeder, Lynch, and Nagin (1999), provides the capability for identifying and testing early predictors of long-run patterns of behavior. For example, such an analysis shows that the probability of trajectory group membership is significantly predicted by low IQ, low paternal education, and being born to a mother who began child bearing as a teenager (Nagin & Tremblay, 2001b).

Two other important extensions of the basic model are important to note. One, which is elaborated in Nagin et al. (2003 in press), provides the capacity for obtaining *trajectory group-specific estimates* of whether and to what degree a turning-point event, such as being held back in school, an intervention like counseling, or an ecological factor such as changing neighborhood poverty,

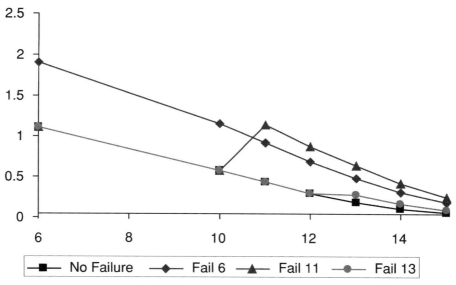

Figure 38.4. School failure impacts: Moderate decliner trajectory.

alters the developmental course of the behavior under investigation. Figure 38.4 illustrates this extension. It is the product of a statistical analysis reported in Nagin et al. (2003) that examines the influence of grade retention on physical aggression for each of the trajectory groups depicted in Figure 38.2. Statistically significant impacts were found only for the two middle groups. Figure 38.4 depicts the results of the model for the moderate declining trajectory group. The results show that the impact of grade retention seems to depend on age: retention at ages 6 to 10 has approximately the same aggravating influence on physical aggression as retention at ages 11 to 12, whereas retention from age 13 to 15 seemingly has no material influence.

The second major extension involves the capacity for estimating joint trajectory models. Two prominent themes in developmental psychology, developmental psychopathology, and developmental criminology are comorbidity and heterotypic continuity. Comorbidity refers to the contemporaneous occurrence of two or more undesirable conditions, such as conduct disorder and hyperactivity during childhood or anxiety and depression in adulthood. Heterotypic continuity is the manifestation over

time of a latent individual trait in different but analogous behaviors.

Comorbidity and heterotypic continuity are typically represented by a single summary statistic, usually a correlation or odds ratio, that either measures the co-occurrence of the two behaviors or symptoms of interest (e.g., hyperactivity and conduct disorder at age 6) or, alternatively, relates the two distinct behaviors measured at different life stages (e.g., physical aggression at age 5 and violent delinquency at age 15). Nagin and Tremblay (2001a) develop and demonstrate an extension of the group-based model that relates the entire longitudinal course of the two behaviors of interest. The generalization provides the capacity for the joint estimation of trajectory models for two distinct, but theoretically related, measurement series. Three key outputs of the model are (1) the form of the trajectory of distinctive subpopulations for both measurement series, (2) the probability of membership in each such trajectory group, and (3) the joint probability of membership in trajectory groups across behaviors. This final output is the key advance of the joint model, which offers two novel features. First, the joint probabilities can characterize the linkage in the developmental course of distinct but related behaviors. Second, the joint probabilities can measure differences within the population in the form of this linkage.

The aim of this chapter was to provide a nontechnical overview of my work program on group-based trajectory modeling. Much work remains to be done. Perhaps the most important is to provide the capacity for taking account of the possibility that turning-point events, such as school failure, or treatments, such as counseling, may be both a cause and effect of the behavior under study. Still another important issue is developing firm guidelines for making well-informed judgments on the optimal number of groups to create. Although much more work is required to develop the method to its fullest potential, I now feel confident in judging it a valuable addition to the statistical tools available for the study of trajectories of development.

Acknowledgment

This chapter was originally prepared for the 10th Anniversary Conference of The Netherlands Institute for the Study of Crime and Law Enforcement.

References

Bergman, L. R. (1998). A pattern-oriented approach to studying indivdual development: Snapshots and processes. In R. B. Cairns, L. R. Bergman, & J. Kagan (Eds.), *Methods and models for studying the individual* (pp. 83–122). Thousand Oaks, CA: Sage.

Bryk, A. S., & Raudenbush, S. W. (1987). Application of hierarchical linear models to assessing change. *Psychology Bulletin, 101*, 147–158.

Bryk, A. S., & Raudenbush, S. W. (1992). *Hierarchical linear models for social and behavioral research: Application and data analysis methods*. Newbury Park, CA: Sage.

Caspi, A. (1998). Personality development across the life course. In N. Eisenberg (Ed.) & W. Daom (Series Ed.), *Handbook of child psychology. Vol. 3: Social, emotional, and personality development* (5th ed.) (pp. 311–388). New York: Wiley.

Cloninger, R. C. (1986). A unified biosocial theory of personality and its role in the development of anxiety states. *Psychiatric Developments, 3*, 167–225.

Cloninger, R. C. (1987). A systematic method for clinical description and classification of personality variants. *Archives of General Psychiatry, 44*, 573–588.

Goldstein, H. (1995). *Multilevel statistical models* (2nd ed.). London: Edward Arnold.

Haapasalo, J., & Tremblay, R. E. (1994). Physically aggressive boys from ages 6 to 12: Family background, parenting behavior, and prediction of delinquency. *Journal of Consulting and Clinical Psychology, 62*(5), 1044–1052.

Heckman, J., & Robb, R. (1985). Alternative methods for evaluating the impact of interventions. In J. Heckman & B. Singer (Eds.), *Longitudinal analysis of labor market data* (pp. 156–245). New York: Cambridge University Press.

Holyoak, K., and B. Spellman. (1993). "Thinking." *Annual Review of Psychology, 4*: 265–315.

Jones, B. L., Nagin, D., & Roeder, K. (2001). A SAS procedure based on mixture models for estimating developmental trajectories. *Sociological Research and Methods, 29*, 374–393.

Jones, B. L., and Nagin, D. S. (Forthcoming). "Advances in Group-based Trajectory Modeling and a SAS Procedure for Estimating Them." *Sociological Methods and Research.*

Kandel, D. B. (1975). Stages in adolescent involvement in drug use. *Science, 190*, 912–914.

Kasen S., Cohen, P., Skodol, A. E., Johnson, J. G., Smailes, E., & Brook, J. S. (2001). Childhood depression and adult personality disorder – Alternative pathways of continuity. *Archives of General Psychiatry, 58*, 231–236.

Kochanska, G., Murray, K., & Coy, K. C. (1997). Inhibitory control as a contributor to conscience in childhood: From toddler to early school age. *Child Development, 68*, 263–277.

Lacourse, E., Nagin, D., Vitaro, F., Claes, M., & Tremblay, R. E. (2003). Developmental trajectories of boys' delinquent group membership and facilitation of violent behaviors during adolescence. *Development and Psychopathology, 15*(1):183–197.

Loeber, R. (1991). Questions and advances in the study of developmental pathways. In D. Cicchetti & S. Toth (Eds.), *Models and integrations. Rochester Symposium on Developmental*

Psychopathology (Vol. 3, pp. 97–115). Rochester: University of Rochester Press.

MacCallum, R. C., Kim, C., Malarkey, W. B., & Kiecolt-Glaser, J. K. (1997). Studying multivariate change using multilevel models and latent curve models. *Multivariate Behavioral Research, 32,* 215–253.

Maddala, G. S. (1983). *Limited-dependent and qualitative variables in econometrics.* New York: Cambridge University Press.

Magnusson, D. (1998). The logic and implications of a person-oriented approach. In R. B. Cairns, L. R. Bergman, & J. Kagan (Eds.), *Methods and models for studying the individual* (pp. 33–64). Thousand Oaks, CA: Sage.

Markman, E. M. (1989). *Categorization and naming in children: Problems of induction.* Cambridge, MA: MIT Press.

McArdle, J. J., & Epstein, D. (1997). Latent growth curves within developmental structural equation models. *Child Development, 58,* 110–133.

Meredith, W., & Tisak, J. (1990). Latent curve analysis. *Psychometrika, 55*(1), 107–122.

Moffitt, T. E. (1993). Adolescence-limited and life-course persistent antisocial behavior: A developmental taxonomy. *Psychological Review, 100*(4), 674–701.

Moffitt, T. E., A. Caspi, N. Dickson, P. Silva, and W. Stanton. (1996). "Childhood-Onset Versus Adolescent-Onset Antisocial Conduct Problems in Males: Natural History from Ages 3 to 18." *Development and Psychopathology, 8,* 399–424.

Muthen, B. O. (1989). Latent variable modeling in heterogeneous populations. *Psychometrika, 54*(4), 557–585.

Nagin, D. (1999). Analyzing developmental trajectories: Semi-parametric, group-based approach. *Psychological Method, 4,* 139–177.

Nagin, D. S. (2005). *Group-based Modeling of Development.* Cambridge, MA: Harvard University Press.

Nagin, D., Farrington, D., & Moffitt, T. (1995). Life-course trajectories of different types of offenders. *Criminology, 33,* 111–139.

Nagin, D. S., & Land, K. C. (1993). Age, criminal careers, and population heterogeneity: Specification and estimation of a nonparametric, mixed Poisson model. *Criminology, 31,* 327–362.

Nagin, D., Pagani, L., Tremblay, R., & Vitaro, F. (2003). Life course turning points: A case study of the effect of grade retention on interpersonal violence. *Development and Psychopathology,* 15: 343–36.

Nagin, D. S., & Tremblay, R. E. (1999). Trajectories of boys' physical aggression, opposition, and hyperactivity on the path to physically violent and nonviolent juvenile delinquency. *Child Development, 70,* 1181–1196.

Nagin, D. S., & Tremblay, R. E. (2001a). Analyzing developmental trajectories of distinct but related behaviors: A group-based method. *Psychological Methods, 6,* 18, 34.

Nagin, D. S., & Tremblay, R. E. (2001b). Parental and early childhood predictors of persistent physical aggression in boys from kindergarten to high school. *Archives of General Psychiatry, 58,* 389–394.

Patterson, G. R., DeBaryshe, B. D., & Ramsey, E. (1989). A developmental perspective on antisocial behavior. *American Psychologist, 44,* 329–335.

Raudenbush, S. W. (2001). Comparing personal trajectories and drawing causal inferences from longitudinal data, *Annual Review of Psychology, 52,* 501–525.

Roeder, K., Lynch, K., & Nagin, D. (1999). Modeling uncertainty in latent class membership: A case study in criminology. *Journal of the American Statistical Association, 94,* 766–776.

Tremblay, R. E., Desmarais-Gervais, L., Gagnon, C., & Charlebois, P. (1987). The preschool behavior questionnaire: Stability of its factor structure between culture, sexes, ages and socioeconomic classes. *International Journal of Behavioral Development, 10,* 467–484.

Tyrka, A. R., J. A. Graber, and J. Brooks-Gunn. (2000). "The Development of Disordered Eating." In J. A. Sameroff, M. Lewis, and S. M. Miller (eds.), *Handbook of Developmental Psychopathology,* 2nd ed. New York: Kluwer Academic/Plenum Publisher.

Warr, M. (2002). *Companions in Crime: The Social Aspects of Criminal Conduct.* New York: Cambridge University Press.

Willett, J. B., & Sayer, A. G. (1994). Using covariance structure analysis to detect correlates and predictors of individual change over time. *Psychological Bulletin, 116*(2), 363–381.

CHAPTER 39

Relocating Violence: Practice and Power in an Emerging Field of Qualitative Research

Bowen Paulle

Violence has been a central force in human history. Qualitative researchers have shown themselves to be uniquely situated to investigate both the objective mechanisms of violent behavior *and* the subjective meanings and motives of participants immersed in violent social action. I argue here that we do not have to relinquish scientific rigor to gain subjective meaning. Indeed this chapter argues that the meticulous social scientific study of violent behavior goes hand in hand with sensitivity to practical meanings, situational conditions, and affectivity. The papers I chose to review in this chapter illustrate, furthermore, that methodology, theory, and interpretation are inextricably woven in qualitative studies of violence.

In this chapter, I compare four pairs of studies of violence. First, I compare the research of Primo Levi and Jack Katz. Levi's writings have a wide audience. Levi wrote on human extermination, survival, and moral ambiguity in Auschwitz. The focus here is on *The Drowned and the Saved* (1988). A sociologist by training, Katz became prominent among criminologists as well as among social scientists more generally with *The Seductions*

of Crime (1988). In their own ways, Levi and Katz argue that methods used to study violence must focus specially on violence to identify the power of contextual settings.

The second pair of studies was generated by Nancy Scheper-Hughes (1992) and Arthur Kleinman (2000). Although their anthropological fieldwork was done in highly divergent settings and structured according to quite divergent methodological precepts, both of these studies ask similar questions about the dynamics of everyday violence. Their research generates provocative questions about the dynamics of violence that are outside of actors' (and very often researchers') view in part because, in numerous instances, they emerge as natural parts of daily life.

The third pair of violence studies is based on immersion in epidemics of impoverishment. Bourgois's 1995 study *In Search of Respect* explores the details of daily life among Puerto Rican crack dealers in Spanish Harlem. It is used here to illustrate how a fieldworker's approaches to violence can shift as a result of the power of direct observations. Paul Farmer's 2003 study *Pathologies of Power* shows us how cultural details can be used in convincing ways to link violence to macro-level political-economic and historical forces. Bourgois and Farmer argue for a wider conceptualization of violence from local derivation to structural forces beyond the reach of oppressed people.

The fourth pair of studies examines culturally defined sexualities and the complexities of gendered violence. Mark Fleisher's influential ethnography opened up the worlds of urban gangs and correctional facilities. Fleisher's 2006 research on rape and expressions of sexuality in American prisons illustrates the multiplicity of cultural definitions of sexual violence and consensual sexual behavior in a sociocultural environment largely unknown to most social scientists and community members. Fleisher's research moves to Pierre Bourdieu's *Masculine Domination* (2001), a seminal investigation of symbolic violence. Taken together, these studies force us to ponder sexualities generated in specific sociocultural realms and the meaning of gendered violence within these spaces.

Locating Violence

Studying violence remains a tricky business. Let's briefly consider domestic violence. We know that abusers often were victims of childhood abuse and that effects of domestic and childhood abuse spill outside families. Whether a scholar is an historical comparative sociologist studying violence in processes of state formation or an ethnographer trying to understand the dynamics of violence behind the closed doors of a single family's dwelling, the same fundamental question arises: how can we best *locate* violence in the milieu of culture and social life?

As the case of domestic violence makes clear, focusing strictly on either quantitative or qualitative methods makes it difficult to adequately engage such a cultural phenomenon. Not surprisingly then, and at least since the work of Mills (1959/2000), some of our most important scholars have been skeptical about the utility of our deeply entrenched qualitative (quantitative dichotomy. Reiterating Mills's early warnings and perhaps overstating their case a bit, Bourdieu and de Saint Martin (in Bourdieu & Wacquant, 1992, pp. 27–28, italics in original) urged "qualitative" and "quantitative" scholars to think relationally and dynamically about what they do:

> *How artificial the ordinary oppositions between theory and research, between quantitative and qualitative methods, between statistical recording and ethnographic observation, between the grasping of structures and the construction of individuals can be. These alternatives have no function other than to provide a justification for the vacuous and resounding abstractions of theoreticism and for the falsely rigorous observations of positivism, or, as the divisions between economists, anthropologists, historians, and sociologists, to legitimize the limits of* competency: this is to say that they function in the manner of a *social censorship, liable to forbid us to grasp the truth which resides in the* relations *between realms of practice thus arbitrarily separated.*

I am sympathetic to these types of concerns. However, most of the qualitative researchers whose work is examined below make explicit use of statistical findings. It is important to recognize that qualitative researchers do not deliberately exclude research tools, such as statistical methods. Today's best ethnographers are also good social scientists. Qualitative researchers might be said to *think statistically* when they calculate, for example, how representative a given situational condition or a given element of an informant's discourse is. In other words, what looks like an investigation of a qualitative researcher necessarily includes, I would argue, mixed methods.

It follows from these opening comments that the studies of violence in this chapter should be approached as *dynamic wholes* – that is, research methods and theories of violence will be conceptualized not as separate things, but as interdependent aspects of unfolding social processes. Indeed I argue that, in the study of violence, there is an element of danger in severing research methods and theories. Doing so can lead us to mis-locate violence and to overlook centrally important aspects of violence that have received too little prior consideration.

Comparative Approaches to Violence

Studying Transformative Environments: Visions of Violence in Levi and Katz

PRIMO LEVI SURVIVES THE "GRAY ZONE" Primo Levi, an Italian Jewish chemist, found the courage to write details about his experiences in Auschwitz. Although a horrendous tragedy on the scale of the Holocaust might seem inappropriate for a commentary of scientific research and violence, I have chosen to examine Levi for a number of reasons.[1]

The Drowned and the Saved (1988) was finished just before Levi committed suicide in 1987. In it Levi meticulously described the inner workings of Auschwitz, the world's most infamous death camp, as a morally ambiguous "gray zone." Survival, Levi argued, required him to become a "privileged prisoner," which in turn led him to intense feelings of personal guilt and grief. Levi describes how a European, middle-class scientist was quickly transformed into someone capable of "collaborating," he said, in the systemic slaughter of innocents.

We see through Levi's eyes the generative power of social relations, situations, and social positions within totalitarian institutions. Levi's writing enlivens the conceptualization that social structures, or zones of human interdependence and practice, are at least as real as the people who comprise them. Levi teaches us that the conceptualization of violence unifies a focus on individual-based research and on critical forces operating on individuals' behavior. And Levi's work therefore leads to a decision point, especially for researchers of the Holocaust. Should we focus our energy on (the grand schemes of) Nazis and their transformation within broad social-political contexts? Or should we seek to conceptualize the transformative nature of the here-and-now, the microstructures and

social processes that inevitably create once-unthinkable people?

Students of violence cannot avoid asking other questions as well. The ways we study violent contexts and the contexts themselves influence, to some degree, emotions and feelings, which in turn influence perceptions, interpretations, and analysis. How can we be reasonably sure our data (observations and interview narratives) are sufficiently neutral? How can we be sure, that is, that the data are not overly subject to researcher affect and that our contributions can enable the development of violence interventions because they address aspects of violence without an overly biased personal interpretation?

Clearly, Levi influenced and was influenced by his context. And yet, independent of methodological rigor and challenges to research validity, Levi gave us a first-hand view of an infamous Nazi death camp. Levi's work on this most powerful of zones satisfies a core requirement of fieldwork: convince the reader that you were there.

KATZ'S VIOLENT SEDUCTIONS: THE POWER OF THE HERE-AND-NOW

That which intoxicates, the sensually ecstatic, the sudden surprise, the urge to be profoundly stirred at any price – dreadful tendencies!

– Nietzsche

In Seductions of Crime: The Moral and Sensual Attractions of Doing Evil (1988), Jack Katz questions the ways that social scientists use poverty and its consequences as a near-universal motivation to commit deviant acts. In the traditions of phenomenological thought, ethnomethodology, symbolic interactionism, and social psychology, Katz supported his arguments by closely interrogating gruesome crimes committed often by the truly destitute. Bypassing unequal opportunity structures and disadvantaged backgrounds, Katz argues that the motivation to commit crime is not located in opportunity structures but rather in the transformative power of the here-and-now.

Katz's (1988) challenge to mainstream criminology drew almost entirely on detailed analyses of qualitative materials.[2] Using a wide range of secondary sources, Katz takes us as close as possible to a litany of crimes from a man who slaughtered half his family in a small village in France to extremely violent scenes dominated by "hard men" in American ghettos. Katz's point seems clear: to capture a systemic, descriptively rich understanding of "evil" practices we must begin our study with the nature of the primeval seductions of violence itself. The morality and emotion-altering social processes, so powerful in the seduction to crime in the here-and-now, is where Katz locates what he calls the magic of motivation. "Watch their stuttering street display," Katz (p. 312) maintains,

> and you will be struck by the awesome fascination that symbols of evil hold for young men who are linked to the groups we often call gangs. . . . And if we examine the lived sensuality behind events of cold-blooded 'senseless' murder, we are compelled to acknowledge the power that may be still created in the modern world through the sensualities of defilement, spiritual chaos, and the apprehension of vengeance.[3]

Katz's research delved into the minutia of experiential details of crime and, in doing so, got close to the central nature of immediate experiences.[4]

In sum we can say that, despite their divergent content areas, Levi and Katz emphasize the transformative potential of violence-inducing social settings. These scholars tell us that we can very quickly lose our grip on and underestimate the power of contextual experiences, and if we are to understand violence in context there is no substitute for getting as close as possible to the social realms of violence.

Scheper-Hughes and Kleinman: Understanding the Violence of Everyday Life

> What puzzled me was the seeming 'indifference' of Alto women to the deaths of their babies and their willingness to attribute to their own offspring an 'aversion' to life that

> made their deaths seem wholly natural, indeed all but expected.
> (Scheper-Hughes 1992, p. 270)

From mass annihilation in the work of Levi we move to the other end of the "continuum of violence" (Scheper-Hughes & Bourgois, 2004, p. 21): the *violence of everyday life* (Kleinman, 2000; Scheper-Hughes, 1992).

Scheper-Hughes's 1992 book, *Death without Weeping*, makes a striking observation: unthinkable violence can become part of natural everyday life. Scheper-Hughes set out to study mother-child relations against the backdrop of high-infant mortality rates in an impoverished region of Northeast Brazil. Living among local people, Scheper-Hughes reports on a woman whose three small children died within a few months. She found that other women had lost even more children over longer periods of time. Although the government was officially reporting high rates of infant mortality, Scheper-Hughes's door-to-door investigations documented that, in particular years and in some neighborhoods, roughly 30% of child deaths were not registered. She then went on to discover why the official accounts typically were wrong. Dead children were buried in cardboard coffins distributed by civil servants who "processed" each child in "two or three minutes" (1992, p. 295).

Scheper-Hughes documented that violence was part and parcel of local culture, that infant death and violence among desperately poor mothers was "naturalized." She described how victimized mothers acquired a very specific type of second nature and how infant mortality was normalized as part of the daily routine. Everyday violence drives the normalization of violence. The web of normal practices, everyday discourses, and ordinary developments in this region of Northeastern Brazil provided the ironic context that generated high infant mortality rates.

An example of everyday violence occurs when doctors provide tranquilizers to anxious, malnourished children. In her treatment of *nervoso*, Scheper-Hughes explains where she located the violence (1992, p. 174):

> *There was a time not long ago when people of the Alto understood nervousness (and rage) as a primary symptom of hunger, as the* delirio de fome. *Today hunger (like racism) is a disallowed discourse in the shantytowns of Bom Jesus da Mata, and the rage and the dangerous madness of hunger have been metaphorized. . . . The transition from a popular discourse on hunger to one on sickness is subtle but essential in the perception of the body and its needs. A hungry body needs food. A sick and 'nervous' body needs medications. A hungry body exists as a potent critique of the society in which it exists. A sick body implicates no one.*

The motives of clinic doctors lead to an interesting conceptual issue: if clinic doctors' actions did not have a deliberate intention of harming children, should social scientists refrain from using the term "violence" to describe their actions in everyday life? Scheper-Hughes's answer to this question is more or less the *raison d'etre* for her entire *oeuvre*. Without deliberately trying to harm the children in their clinics and by simply doing what naturally came to them, the doctors' actions fueled everyday relational dynamics that were leading to the deaths of hundreds of young children and, concomitantly, to indifference about these fatalities.

KLEINMAN ON BOURGEOIS VARIETIES OF
VIOLENT LIFE IN AMERICAN SUBURBS
The violence of everyday life in *Bom Jesus da Mata* takes us to another, perhaps far more exotic setting: middle-class America. In his analysis of "bourgeois varieties" of "violences of everyday life," Kleinman (2000, pp. 228–231) introduces us to Jane Huffberg. Huffberg is a 42-year-old guidance counselor who lives in a suburb and works in an inner-city school. Kleinman came into contact with her while taking part in a research project on chronic pain. Repeated visits and ongoing conversations revealed that she had been in therapy and had tried medications for years before she met

Kleinman. Her list of unceasing physical ailments, her depressive disorder, and her anxiety disorder all seemed impervious to her medical psychological care.

Jane is always on the run and perpetually exhausted. In addition to being ideologically devoted to her work, Jane feels compelled to do what is necessary to "succeed." Her painful memories of growing up in poverty drive her actions. Her daughters seem to be forever angry at her, largely because she spends little time with them. Jane complains about her abusive, alcoholic ex-husband and the incompetent supervisors at her school. Indeed, in laymen's terms, Jane suffers stress, which threatens her health. Huffberg conceptualized her situation this way:

> *You know, it's strange to say, but in a way, I think my problem is violence too, just like the violence these kids I work with have to go through. I'm not talking about street violence. You know, they are the victims of a violence our society does to them, and so really am I. Only a different kind really. . . . Sometimes, you know, I think . . . I mean life is violence. It does violence, kind of. You know, family, work, things you got to live with, yourself really. I'm not talking big stuff, but that too; I mean the whole damn thing. All the things! I've got two teenage girls; you really, you know, you can't say to them. They couldn't get it, you know. . . . But that's how I feel it is, you know: violent.*
>
> (Kleinman, 2000, p. 229)

Kleinman forces readers to ask questions: which of us would dare to tell Jane Huffberg that, except for the physical abuse inflicted by her ex-husband, what she is discussing does not really relate to violence? Or, if it is violence, how do we collect data on everyday violence in settings, such as our own schools, offices, and (gated) communities?

Ethnography and Epidemics: The Cultural Details and What Lies Beneath

Anthropologists Philippe Bourgois (1995) and Paul Farmer (2003) spent years immersed in a range of distressed settings around the world. Their use of field-based research had a specific purpose: to generate close-up, detailed observational data. But, in their own ways, they also aimed to link the cultural details they documented to broader structures of domination. The methods we use to study violence, they argue, determine to a large degree how we construct, conceptualize, and measure violence using observational and interview data.

BOURGOIS IN EL BARRIO

Bourgois began his book by noting that he was "forced into crack against [his] will (1995, p. 1)." And indeed, when Bourgois moved in the spring of 1985 into a tenement in El Barrio, New York's "Spanish" or East Harlem, he could not have known that his neighborhood would become an epicenter of a drug epidemic. What is more, he did not initially aim to pay special attention to "interpersonal 'delinquent violence,' including self-destructive substance abuse ... brutality in the family and ... adolescent gang rape" (Scheper-Hughes & Bourgois, 2004, p. 3).

Paul Willis (1981) influenced Bourgois's scholarship. In other words, Willis's strongly class-based framework and his writings on *consciously rebellious* "lads" and the ascription of "agency" to their working-class adolescent peer-group culture served as Bourgois's analytic point of departure (see Paulle, 2003, pp. 548–549). The focus was, initially, on the interface of broader political economic forces and what a student of Willis might see on the street: cultural resistance and agency, oppositional styles, and, in the end, rebellious yet self-destructive practices.

However, his sustained period of immersion in El Barrio forced Bourgois to rethink his initial theoretical perspectives and compelled him to generate a different argument on poverty, drugs, ethnicity, and violence. Bourgois's *Search of Respect (1995)* shows how ethnographic immersion can influence theory-refining processes and fundamentally alter an ethnographer's politics of cultural representation.

What Bourgois heard about and witnessed – from baseball-bat wielding crack dealers cracking open the skulls of "crack heads" to rituals of boasting about participation in roof-top gang rapes to re-enactments of the ways mentally handicapped pupils were beaten in local schools – led him to see the fusion of young peoples with their intensely violent environments. Bourgois's fieldwork dispelled politically influenced interpretations of drug dealing and violence based on the "street culture of resistance." The actions of the youthful dealers (and their family members or friends) were not being guided by consciously held (oppositional) ideologies. Instead of framing his informants as rebels with an ideological cause – or, for example, as rational actors who used conscious violent outbursts to guarantee revenue and respect – the dealers were, in the final analysis, depicted as victims of a ruthless capitalist system caught up in frenzies of anger, shame, substance abuse, and belligerence.

Reflecting on his drug dealers' experiences in school, Bourgois argued as follows:

> In or outside of schools it is easy to glorify inner-city violence as a "culture of resistance." This is certainly a way to sanitize the hideous everyday destructiveness of violence and drugs. What is so amazing is that the direct administrators of social suffering are not the school teachers or the parole officers, the police officers and the welfare officers – but rather the crack dealer; the rapist; the violent uncle and the gang. That is what the child comes into contact with and is terrified of. And this is what the child adapts to, tries to out-smart, but too often becomes a part of.
>
> (cited in Paulle, 2003, p. 604)

FARMER'S PATHOLOGIES OF POWER

Farmer's (2003) accounts of epidemics were based on sustained first-hand observations and direct participation in establishing health care clinics in some of the most impoverished places around the world. He aimed to fuse fieldwork and medical practice as well as to connect heart-wrenching details of medical emergencies to macrostructural forces. Farmer ties the dynamics of what seem to be locally derived and ephemeral tragedies to less ethnographically observable and longer term processes of economic restructuring and transnational political conflicts. Farmer argues that making the right connections is a political necessity:

> When we study the social impact of a hydroelectric dam, of terrorism, or of a new epidemic, we run a great eliding risk. Erasures, in these instances, prove expedient to the powerful. . . . Without a historically deep and geographically broad analysis, one that takes into account political economy, we risk seeing only the residue of meaning. We see the puddles, perhaps, but not the rainstorms and certainly not the gathering thunderclouds.
> (Farmer, 2004, p. 309)

Farmer's *Pathologies of Power* (2003, p. 31) begins with the story of a Haitian woman, Acéphie Joseph, who is terminally ill and utterly powerless. Acéphie was not the victim of direct physical violence. Farmer nevertheless conceptualizes her premature death from AIDS and the death of her child soon after birth as a result of "structural violence."

Farmer starts to locate violence in the state's decision, made well before Acéphie was born, to transform a once-fertile valley into a reservoir required for a dam project. Although Haiti received aid from the United States during the years of the Duvalier dictatorships, the Haitian government provided neither significant compensation nor emergency assistance to the people who were displaced by the flood. This U.S.-sponsored macro-economic-political strategy, which was officially aimed at generating aggregate growth, led Acéphie's reasonably well-to-do peasant family into desperate poverty.

Acephie was forced to go to work, bringing her family's now meager agricultural goods to a local market, before she could graduate from primary school. Like other female "water refugees," Acéphie came into regular contact with soldiers who occupied positions on the road leading to the market. Despite levying made-up taxes on the women heading to the market, soldiers were the only salaried men in the area and were highly respected. Unlike the members of

Acéphie's family, soldiers were never malnourished.

Acéphie slept with the married military man, Captain Honorat. Although she knew he had other sexual partners, Acéphie sensed the real possibility that her association with him might be an extended one. This, however, was not to be, and after a stint in the city, the disease she picked up from her brief affair with Honorat forced Acéphie's return to her family's village. There she was denied medical care and left to die a painful death. Farmer summarizes Acéphie's story to "[bring] into relief many of the forces restricting not only her options, but those of most Haitian women" (2003, p. 39). After years of thinking about whether or not stories such as Acéphie's were about violence, Farmer came to the conclusion that violence killed her just as surely as it kills people in wars, drive-by shootings, or ethnic cleansings: "I have grappled, as have many others, with conditions that could only be described as violent – at least to those who must endure them. Since the misery in question need not involve bullets, knives, or impairments of torture, this misery has often eluded those seeking to identify violence and its victims" (Farmer, 2003, p. 8).

Farmer argues that HIV and tuberculosis epidemics and other human rights abuses are caused first and foremost by structural violence. Although we experience a degree of agency in this woman's life story, it illustrates how the impoverished world suffers an inability to alter macro- and micro-level forces of structural violence. Bourgois and Farmer argue that we should get a close-up look at violence to understand its dynamics. However, in their own ways, they both add that we should remember to connect microcontents to broader structures of oppression.

Violence, Domination, and Sex

> Exterminate all the brutes!
> –Kurtz in Joseph Conrad's Heart of Darkness

We look now at studies that examine the interface among violence, domination, and sexuality. We first examine Mark Fleisher's (2006) qualitative study of socio-sexual relations and sexual violence in women's and men's prisons in American. Then we examine Bourdieu's *Masculine Domination* (2001), a study based on his ethnographic work in Kabylia, a mountain area in northeastern Algeria; research conducted in his native provincial town in Southwestern France; and his ethnographic experiences on the Parisian Left Bank, where he reigned over a generation as the dominant male intellectual force. These two studies generate insights into methodological and theoretical approaches to gender-related violence.

FLEISHER: SOCIALIZED SEXUALITIES AND SITUATED NOTIONS OF VIOLENCE

Predators are sneaky and dangerous. He'll just get it [sex]. They're outside the program, meaning that they do not follow conventional rules of the socio-sexual system. (Quote from an inmate and Fleisher's comments, 2005)

When prison populations were in decline during the 1950s and 1960s, there was a strong and thriving tradition of prison ethnographies in the United States. Curiously, during the unprecedented incarceration boom of the past three decades there has been a remarkable decline in the number of close-up, detailed accounts of life behind bars in America (Wacquant, 2002). One cultural anthropologist and criminal ethnographer who has been trying "to turn the stick the other way" is Mark Fleisher. Fleisher has done meticulous research on the interfaces of gender, thug life, and adolescents in ultra-violent urban slums (Fleisher, 1998).

The U.S. House of Representatives' Prison Rape Elimination Act of 2003 (PREA; H.R. 1707) supported national research on rape (and other forms of sex-related violence) in American prisons. Fleisher was funded by the National Institute of Justice to conduct a national study of the culture of prison rape and sexuality in men's and women's prisons with attention focused on highsecurity adult correctional institutions.

The study sought to identify and clarify definitions of various types of sexual violence in prison with the goal of helping policymakers, practitioners, and politicians understand the ways in which male and female inmates draw distinctions between consensual and coercive sex. Prison rape and sexuality studied from the perspective of inmate culture or, for that matter, from any other culture-based perspective, had not previously been conducted on a national scale; thus there were no precedents for research design and analysis.

Fleisher's interview guide was developed and tested in the field. Research findings are based on replicable inmate-selection procedures as well as an explicit and replicable inductive analysis procedure using a coding scheme based on Fleisher's in-depth knowledge of the key terms and concepts needed to clarify the complexities of American prisons. He and his team conducted 564 interviews, amassing more than 6,000 pages of interview narratives gathered in major geographic regions of the United States.

Time wears you out, and you give in to [sexual] temptation.

Fleisher shared with me in pre-published form a variety of findings. First, in free-flowing narratives inmates do not talk about sex as being either "consensual" or "coercive." These terms are neither part of the individual inmates' lexicon or their sociocultural universe. The unambiguous legal terminology and definitions found in PREA have little to do with the microsocial dynamics and semantically messy yet nuanced meanings reported by the prisoners. In other words, the outsider-theoretical and insider-practical definitions of sex and sexual violence do not correspond to each other.

Second, Fleisher notes that where PREA definitions might lead one to talk about rape, inmates might see "helping a man come to terms with his own sexuality." This quote points out the gap between insider and outsider perceptions and semantic schemes. On the inside, the question is often not "are you gay or straight?" Rather, the question is "are you celibate by choice?" and "for how long and under what conditions will you remain celibate?" Inmates' choice to have sex, they say, expresses their need for emotional support more than giving in, or being taken by, the sensual pleasures of physical sex.

Fleisher's findings are, one might say, about the "coming out" of socially produced, culturally situated sexualities. An inmate does not distinguish among a range of objectively possible sexual roles available. Rather, situational sex roles emerge and re-emerge in different contexts. Resources sent to an inmate from home might result in the adoption of a particular sex role, such as "stud" in a women's prison, whose aggressive style may lead to exploiting a less aggressive inmate's canteen item purchased with her newly received resources. Embeddedness in a gang may require men inmates to play out sex roles on the "down low."

Gender questions are, of course, especially interesting here. On the one hand, Fleisher found that cultures of inmate sexuality are similar across gender; that is, in men's and women's prisons. On the other hand, gendered terms are used in men's prisons to label more and less dominant sexual roles ("daddy" or "bitch" and "husband" or "wife"). As one might expect the overt appearance of so-called female tendencies, such as displaying body movements that inmates say are like women's, increases an inmate's chance of sexual involvement.

Perhaps the most interesting and profound findings relate to the effects of prisons on the creation of context-specific sexual adaptations and institutionally shaped notions of violent and nonviolent behavior. Indeed, within the bounded reality of prison, this study finds that outsider distinctions between sexual and nonsexual, violent and nonviolent, physical and emotional, victims and victimizers, "bootie bandits" and "hoes," economic exploiters and thieves are anything but hard and fast. Apparently, that which we often think of as most primordial, private, and constant – our sexual drives, orientations, and notions of violence – are reshaped by collective adaptive practices.

BOURDIEU ON GENDER DOMINATION AND SYMBOLIC VIOLENCE

> [G]ender domination... seems to me to be the paradigmatic form of symbolic violence.... The case of gender domination shows better than any other that symbolic violence accomplishes itself through an act of cognition and of misrecognition that lies beyond – or beneath – the controls of consciousness and will, *in the obscurities of the schemata of habitus [e.g., in the obscurities of the socialized second nature] that are at once gendered and gendering.*
>
> *Bourdieu & Wacquant, 1992, pp. 170–172)*

Wacquant (Bourdieu & Wacquant, 1992, pp. 14–15) pointed out that "the whole of Bourdieu's work may be interpreted as a materialist anthropology of the specific contribution that various forms of symbolic violence make to the reproduction and transformation of structures of domination." The opening quote illustrates that Bourdieu maintained that gender domination, rather than class domination, for example, most clearly revealed how "symbolic violence" operates.

This section aims to shed light on how Bourdieu's reliance on ground-breaking qualitative research techniques, based on direct observations in a number of fields, led him to his influential notion of symbolic violence. In the case of Bourdieu's investigations, yet again, it becomes clear that research methods and theories of violence are best conceptualized in "dynamic, continuous, and processual terms" (Emirbayer, 1997, p. 281).

The Disguised Dynamics of Masculine Domination. Let's look at Bourdieu's understanding of the term "symbolic violence" and how this term relates to masculinity, femininity, and gender domination. What follows is a brief sketch of a few aspects of the domination concept as it was applied in *Masculine Domination* (2001).

Bourdieu understood that sexualities and forms of gender domination differ across time and space. He saw before his death in 2001 that in France and throughout the Western world there are virtually no "games" – structured fields of social practice – that are still *formally* reserved exclusively for men. The days of legal exclusion and domination of women within educational, economic, and other domains have ended. On the other hand, women in societies, such as contemporary France, continue to be excluded from or subordinated within a number of fields. Women tend to be less well paid for the exact same positions as their male counterparts, even when they hold exactly the same credentials and have similar amounts of experience. Most obviously, women are underrepresented in the most dominant positions of the most powerful institutions, such as military, political, economic, and academic institutions. Just as in the regions of Algeria and provincial France where Bourdieu had conducted ethnographic research, women were effectively dominated, and men apparently had the urge to dominate "their women" in Paris during the 1980s and 1990s.

Something seemingly as eternal as male domination was being successfully reproduced even as superficial analyses seemed to indicate that everything had changed. Western women in post-1970s feminist-movement eras did not report feeling that they were being dominated, yet domination persisted through subtly disguised dynamics. Clearly, adequate explanations for this context demand careful historical analysis, comparative assessments, and analyses able to dip beneath the level of discourse and consciousness.

Dipping Beneath the Level of Consciousness in Masculine Domination. Bourdieu attempts to solve the riddle of why gender domination continues through the ages and throughout various areas of the world. Bourdieu makes the case that, at the most fundamental level, unconscious acts of collective collusion and "misrecognition" are responsible for reproduction and transformation of sexual orders on opposite sides of the Mediterranean and, by extension, far beyond.

The argument boils down to the claim that as dominators and the dominated in modern Western societies and in developing Northern African societies, we are *Strangers to Ourselves* (Wilson, 2002). We unconsciously learn how to be a typically more dominant man or typically more dominated women. However, we do not understand that the hidden curriculum consists of the everyday practices, positions, and power ratios that make up the social worlds we inhabit. The result of our "embodiment" – that is, the unintended internalization of the-taken-for-granted inequalities and classifications inherent in various fields, such as private firms and public educational systems – leaves little room for consciousness raising.

> *Symbolic violence is the coercion which is set up only through the consent that the dominated cannot fail to give to the dominator (and therefore to the domination). . . . The effect of symbolic domination (sexual, cultural, linguistic, etc.) is exerted not in the pure logic of knowing consciousness but in the obscurity of the dispositions of habitus, in which are embedded the schemes of perception and appreciation which, below the level of the decisions of the conscious mind, and the controls of the will, are the basis of a relationship of practical knowledge and recognition that is profoundly obscure to itself.*
> *(Bourdieu, 2000, pp. 170–171)*

The hidden causes of gender domination may operate beneath the level of consciousness to a large degree and may involve symbols and struggles over schemes of classification. However, we still have to wonder if we are dealing with violence.

Bourdieu anticipated such questions about symbolic violence. Forms of symbolic violence that underpin masculine domination extend, he claims, to more than struggles resolved in a symbolic realm. Bourdieu's concept of symbolic violence relates directly to the desires, passions, and adaptations that manifest in, for example, gang rape and war (Bourdieu, 2001, pp. 51–75). Here we enter the terrain that most would have no problem associating with "real" violence. Bourdieu's answers continue in *Masculine Domination* (2001, p. 34):

> *Understanding 'symbolic' as the opposite of 'real, actual', people suppose that symbolic violence is purely 'spiritual' violence which ultimately has no real effects. It is this naive*

distinction, characteristic of crude materialism, that the materialist theory of the economy of symbolic goods, which I have been trying to build up over many years, seeks to destroy, by giving its proper place in theory to the objectivity of subjective experience of relations of domination.

The Interdependence of Method and Theory. Bourdieu's use of qualitative methods was as responsible for generating his mature notions of masculine domination and symbolic violence as were his years of training to become a philosopher and decades spent on crafting concepts. His early multisite ethnographic investigations and his immersion in two different worlds, each characterized by taken-for-granted forms of masculine domination and social suffering, set him up, as it were, for studies of objectively structured subjective beliefs and adaptive "strategies" that required no calculating "strategists."

His jolting experiences in disconnected fields were the basis of Bourdieu's gradual emergence as an "ethno-sociologist" who was interested in an empirically rooted total science of the human condition. A lifetime of ethnographic experiences and a continuous search for ever more revealing concepts led Bourdieu to the discovery of the need to radically transform the social conditions reproducing the interwoven *desire for the dominant (libido dominantis)* and *the desire to dominate (libido dominandi).* Only historical accounts of the ways in which libidinal impulses and unconscious drives related to domination and have been socialized in specific fields can adequately explain the "extraordinary autonomy of sexual structures relative to economic structures" (p. 81).

In summary, Fleisher's interview-based study points up the ways in which shifting sexualities are culturally constructed and socially structured. Bourdieu's feminist classic illustrates the need to radically reorganize the conditions leading men to be dominated by their own domination and leading women and men to be held hostage by the "violent games" that men, fearing the female in themselves, feel they have to "play."

Conclusion

Today the main danger we face is the growing split between theory and research that can be observed everywhere, and which fuels the concurrent growth of methodological perversion and theoretical speculation. [The goal is] a new form of scientific practice founded at once upon greater theoretical exigency and increased empirical rigor. (Bourdieu quoted in Bourdieu and Wacquant, 1992, pp. 174–175, italics in original)

The goal of this chapter was to make two main points. First, some genuinely new ideas about how and where violence should be located are coming out of what can be treated as an emerging field of (mostly) qualitative research. Second, the empirical rigor and theoretical exigency associated with the ongoing process of (re-)locating violence are best conceptualized as mutually constitutive elements, rather than as self-enclosed substances that, like billiard balls, can exist before they begin interacting and somehow retain their separate essences once they begin transacting. In making these points, the chapter illustrated that qualitative and quantitative research approaches are on par with each other; they are equally significant in the contribution to the study of violent behavior in cultural context. This chapter has illustrated that qualitative approaches are complements to quantitative approaches, that they can supplement statistical analyses, and that they can add rich narrative depth and first-hand observations. The following summation focuses on what this treatment of *interdependent methods, theories,* and *empirical objects* has taught us about redefining the contours and re-examining the dynamics of violence.

Clearly, Levi (1988) taught us a great deal about the inner workings of the most violent institution in recorded history. Most importantly, for our purposes, is the way in which Levi located violence less in the minds of monolithic agents or deranged political regimes than in the morally ambiguous "gray zone." The violence was situated in overpowering social realms and processes in which victims become victimizers. Levi's unique and (in this field of research at least) influential theory of violence has usefulness because it was the product of his forced confrontation with a new empirical object. What can be treated as his immersion and quest for survival-based methods, rather than any pure confrontation with other theories, led to his distinctive conceptual approach to mass violence as well as to his own.

Katz's study of more and less violent crimes in a range of settings (1988) illustrates the transformative power of the here-and-now. But in Katz's study even more strongly than in Levi's, the triggers of various forms of "evil" are located in the foreground more so than they are in the background (Katz, 1988, p. 4). The key methodological point here is clear: when it comes to studying violent encounters and the transformative processes associated with them, being there – or getting as close as possible – is crucial. When violent actions in overwhelming social settings are seen as catalysts rather than as results, the goal must be to get a lived sense of the here-and-now. Data obtained in the heat of the moment should be, from this perspective, crucial for advanced scientific understandings of various forms of human belligerence and the ways in which people are gradually or quickly altered by exposure to the seductions and horrors of violence.

Scheper-Hughes (1992) and Kleinman (2000) attempt to locate various forms and dynamics of violence in the ostensibly "normal" proceedings of everyday life. In Weberian terms we might say that their anthropological projects are based on the de-naturalization – that is, the discovery and reconceptualizing – of forms of legitimate violence. In the seemingly neutral protocols of doctors and nurses treating "nervous" babies in impoverished Northeastern Brazil and in the socialization leading to the indifference of mothers who do not weep when their babies die, Scheper-Hughes reveals nothing less than the dynamics generating and maintaining small-scale genocide. Behind the apparently routine experiences of a middle-class American suburbanite,

Kleinman urges readers to see the wear and tear of "bourgeois varieties of violence." In seemingly ordinary trajectories, circumstances, and organizations he locates the violence leading to the breakdown of one woman's immune system.

Bourgois's *In Search of Respect* (1995) ended up being a study similar to Levi's work on the gray zone. The economically marginal people in Bourgois's book seemed, in the final analysis, to be drowning in relentless waves of gendered violence and mutual self-destruction. First and foremost they were overwhelmed, not oppositional. The implicit theory of violence that Bourgois (1995) described was not the one he initially set out to refine and empirically validate. *In Search of Respect* was treated here, therefore, as an illustration of the power of ethnographic methods.

Even more relentlessly than Bourgois, Farmer (2003) challenges his readers to link the cultural details one can observe at the epicenter of an epidemic with the violent political-economic structures and historical forces that undergird them. In Farmer's work, what might appear prima facie as locally determined causes of mass suffering in places like provincial Haiti are located squarely in the generations of decisions made in pathological centers of political and economic power. His technique is to link the external to the local and to work for change on both fronts.

Fleisher (2006) and Bourdieu (2001) relocate various forms of violent forces and show us we must reconsider what we thought we knew about gender domination and sex. Fleisher discovered that a prison culture exists and that this culture reshapes the ways in which sexualities and notions of violence are constructed. Sexual and other types of violence do take place in Fleisher's total institutions where inmates' experience of violence overlaps with ours, such that prison violence has interpersonal and materialistic motives. In this sense the insiders' and outsiders' understandings seem to overlap. But to be adequately understood from the insiders' perspective, sexualities and (non-) violence must also be located within the constraints and possibilities inherent in the enduring culture of American prison.

The proof of this statement resides in the fact that much of what outsiders would rush to associate with the violence of rape and physical urges takes on culture-specific meanings: what we see as violent sex inmates interpret as an inmate helping another to ease into his or her new sexuality. That which many people assume to be the most private and stable aspects of themselves as human sexual beings proves, once again, under extreme circumstances, to be social and transient. People sentenced to confinement in American prisons are forced into worlds so culturally as well as emotionally and structurally distant from most intellectuals and policymakers that no sense can be made of our and their understandings of terms like violence, forced sex, and consensual sex without the simultaneous empirical and theoretical work of highly skilled researchers who understand the cultural world of the outside and inside translators.

Symbolic violence, the discovery that arose out of Bourdieu's relentless empirical research and decades of theoretical fine-tuning, is the most complex and perhaps the most useful concept discussed in this chapter. He shows that the underlying "order of things" in specific social contexts (France in the 1990s, Algeria during the war of independence) produces second natures that in turn *predispose* people to perceive and feel toward and respond within these social arenas in ways that conserve male domination. This perpetuation of domination arises through the active complicity of both the dominated (women) and the dominant (men) who turn out, ironically, to be dominated by their domination.

To look for or focus on the intentional use of power misses the subtlety and value of Bourdieu's understanding of domination. The interests, desires, and schemes of perception and appreciation that reproduce gender domination are, on one hand, embodied in the habitus; that is, the feel for the game, the internal steering mechanism that operates largely beneath the level of consciousness or discourse. On the other hand, they are embedded in the structure of the game. Elaborating on the effects of the field, Bourdieu (2001, p. 1) argues that it is the "established order, with its relations of domination, its rights and prerogatives, privileges and injustices [that explains why masculine domination] ultimately perpetuates itself so easily and [why] the most intolerable conditions of existence can so easily be perceived as acceptable and even natural."

Bourdieu's socio-analytic investigation raises a key question: in the interest of the dominant and the dominated, how can the fit between habitus and field be broken? How can we be freed from the shackles of dehistorization? How can dynamics at once as invisible, omni-present, self-evident, natural, and automatically legitimate as those associated with the symbolic violence leading to gender domination be challenged successfully? Social relations and processes generating the habitus, he argues, remain complicit with its own domination. Consciousness raising will not alter such a situation. If he is correct, then the violence producing gender domination, which Bourdieu associates with, for example, lower pay for the same work, gang rape, and war, must be located in the everyday socialization processes generative of our unconscious minds.

Acknowledgments

This chapter was originally prepared for the 10th Anniversary Conference of the Netherlands Institute for the Study of Crime and Law Enforcement. I thank Joop Goudsblom for his comments on an early version of this paper and I thank Mark Fleischer for sharing with me some of his pre-published data as well as a lot of his time.

Notes

1. I am sympathetic to the idea that the violence of the Holocaust should not be associated with, or (implicitly) compared with, non-Holocaust related violence. However, Levi's writing had a major influence on the scholarly

research discussed here (see Das et al., 2000, p. 17; Scheper-Hughes & Bourgois, 2004, pp. 10–12; Bourgois, 2005).

2. The diversity of materials included, in Katz's (1988, p. 11) own words,[0] "the ethnographies and life histories produced by professional social scientists, reconstructions of situated criminality by the police and by academics using police records, autobiographies by self-professed ex-criminals, best-selling biographies of criminals written by professional journalists, and an occasional instance of *cinema verité* or participant observation ('new') journalism."

3. A phrase like "the power that may...be created" is reminiscent of Durkheim's ritual theory – the theory of collective effervescence and group beliefs that Durkheim based on ethnographic studies of Australian natives. Similarly, Katz points us in the direction of Goffman's *Interaction Rituals* (1967, p. 3), in which the emphasis is shifted from "men and their moments" to "moments and their men." Not the evildoer's socioeconomic background, not his ethnicity or gender, but the transformative powers of the situation and the largely unconscious "moral emotions" experienced by beings-in-the-world – this is the primary focus for Katz. In a more recent study, with a more explicit focus on the centrality of what Merleau-Ponty (1962) called the lived body, Katz (1999) used ethnographic methods to further examine the emotional processes that "seduce" people to act. In *How Emotions Work* he reveals, for example, how road rage wells up from below when we are "cut off" by another car. In such cases, the drivers' bodies never actually touch, and even the cars rarely make any contact. As Katz points out, however, from inside the situated, living, car-operator's body, it feels as if something has been penetrated or even severed. For those few seconds, many of us are led to do things that we would never under normal conditions find ourselves doing – like stepping on the gas and giving a stranger the finger.

4. I am arguing, in effect, that there is reason to resist the temptation to conclude that Katz had a theoretical agenda and simply twisted his use of methods and sources to fit it. In Katz's own words: "Because the search for evidence and the development of theory proceed in mutually altering steps, the analytic results do not emerge from a straight-forward, deductive, hard or inflexible application of theory to fact. Rather, the methodological quality increases the more the theory is pushed around and beaten into shape by frustrated applications" (1988, p. 11).

References

Bourdieu, P. (2000). *Pascalian meditations*. Palo Alto, CA: Stanford University Press.

Bourdieu, P. (2001). *Masculine domination*. Cambridge, UK: Polity Press.

Bourdieu, P., & Wacquant, L. (1992). *An invitation to reflexive sociology*. Cambridge, UK: Polity Press.

Bourgois, P. (1995). *In search of respect: Selling crack in El Barrio*. Cambridge, UK: Cambridge University Press.

Bourgois, P. (2005). Missing the Holocaust: My father's account of Auschwitz from August 1943 to June 1944. *Anthropological Quarterly, 78*(1), 89–123.

Das, V., Kleinman, A., Ramphele, M., & Reynolds, P. (Eds.). (2000). *Violence and subjectivity*. Berkeley: University of California Press.

Emirbayer, M. (1997). Manifesto for a relational sociology. *American Journal of Sociology, 103*, 281.

Farmer, P. (2003). *Pathologies of power: Health, human rights and the new war on the poor*. Berkeley: University of California Press.

Farmer, P. (2004). An anthropology of structural violence. *Current Anthropology, 45*, 305–325.

Fleisher, M. (1998). *Dead end kids: Gang girls and the boys they know*. Madison, WI: University of Wisconsin Press.

Fleisher, M. (2006). *The culture of prison rape*. Unpublished manuscript, Case Western Reserve University, Cleveland.

Goffman, E. (1967). *Interaction rituals: Essays in face-to-face behavior*. Chicago: Aldine.

Katz, J. (1988). *Seductions of crime: Moral and sensual attractions in doing evil*. New York: Basic Books.

Katz, J. (1999). *How emotions work*. Chicago: University of Chicago Press.

Kleinman, A. (2000). The violences of everyday life: The multiple forms and dynamics of social violence. In V. Das, et al. (Eds.), *Violence and subjectivity*. Berkeley, CA: University of California Press.

Levi, P. (1988). *The drowned and the saved*. New York: Summit Books.

Merleau-Ponty, M. (1962). *The phenomenology of perception*. London: RKP. (Originally published in 1945.)

Mills, C. (2000). *The sociological imagination*. New York: Oxford University Press. Work originally published in 1959.

Paulle, B. (2003). Philippe Bourgois in Amsterdam: An interview. *Amsterdams Sociologisch Tijdschrift*, 30, 544–574.

Scheper-Hughes, N. (1992). *Death without weeping: The violence of everyday life in Brazil*. Berkeley, CA: University of California Press.

Scheper-Hughes, N., & Bourgois, P. (Eds.). (2004). *Violence in war and peace: An anthology*. Malden, MA: Blackwell.

Wacquant, L. (2002). The curious eclipse of prison ethnography in the age of mass incarceration. *Ethnography*, 3(4), 371–397.

Willis, P. E. (1981). *Learning to labor: How working class kids get working class jobs*. New York: Columbia University Press.

Wilson, T. (2002). *Strangers to ourselves: Discovering the adaptive unconscious*. Cambridge, MA: Harvard University Press.

Part VII

LOOKING TOWARD THE FUTURE

CHAPTER 40

Violent Behavior and the Science of Prevention

Albert D. Farrell and Monique Vulin-Reynolds

Introduction

Efforts to address violence through prevention have received increasing attention in recent years. Within the United States, federal agencies have mounted major efforts to identify effective prevention strategies (e.g., Thornton, Craft, Dahlberg, Lynch, & Baer, 2000, U.S. Department of Health and Human Services [USDHHS], 2001), and implementation of violence prevention programs has been incorporated into the national goals (USDHHS, 2000). At the international level, the World Health Organization's *World Report on Violence and Health* (Krug, Dahlberg, Mercy, Zwi, & Lozano, 2002) called on countries to develop, implement, and monitor a national plan for violence prevention. Other specific recommendations called for the promotion of primary prevention efforts and increasing collaboration and international exchange of information on violence prevention. Within 18 months of the report's release its recommendations were adopted by the World Health Assembly, the African Union, and the Human Rights Commission (Butchart,

Phinney, Check, & Villaveces, 2004). Violence prevention has also received increasing attention within the scientific community as reflected in the growing literature evaluating the effectiveness of various approaches to prevention (e.g., Lipsey & Derzon, 1998; USDHHS, 2001).

A major focus of violence prevention efforts has been on reducing violence among young people. Dramatic increases in arrest rates for violent crimes among youth between the ages of 10 and 17 that occurred in the United States between 1983 and 1993 (USDHHS, 2001) led to intensified efforts to develop and implement youth violence prevention strategies. Schools have implemented a diverse array of approaches to prevention (Farrell & Camou, 2005). These have included numerous programs designed to teach students such specific skills as problem solving and conflict resolution, peer mediation programs, "bully" prevention programs directed at students and teachers, interventions that enhance teachers' classroom management skills, attempts to change the social climate of schools, revisions in disciplinary strategies, and environmental interventions such as the installation of metal detectors and security cameras (Howard, Flora, & Griffin, 1999). Youth violence prevention programs have not been limited to school settings. A variety of interventions have been implemented in other settings, including family-focused interventions and interventions implemented at the community and neighborhood levels (USDHHS, 2001).

During the 1990s, researchers attempting to develop effective strategies for addressing youth violence began increasingly to rely on a public health approach to guide their efforts (Hammond & Yung, 1993; Mercy, Rosenberg, Powell, Broome, & Roper, 1993). The public health approach to prevention involves four distinct steps: (1) defining the problem through collection of data on such factors as prevalence rates among specific groups of individuals; (2) identification of causes, including factors that place an individual or group at greater risk for a disorder; (3) development and evaluation of interventions designed to address the disorder; and (4) dissemination and more widespread implementation of interventions found to be effective (Mercy et al., 1993). This process is often cyclical wherein information at later stages informs earlier stages (Mrazek & Haggerty, 1994). Researchers have begun to appreciate the complexity of developing effective methods of addressing problems such as youth violence. The application of a public health approach to address youth violence represents a larger trend toward the development of a discipline of prevention science that seeks to develop effective prevention strategies for a wide array of mental health problems (Coie et al., 1993).

This chapter provides an overview of the field of youth violence prevention. It begins by discussing several themes that appear key to developing effective prevention programs (Coie et al., 1993; Farrell & Camou, 2005, Tolan & Guerra, 1994). These themes include clarifying the goals of prevention, specifying the intended population, identifying and addressing relevant risk and protective factors, and establishing procedures for implementation and dissemination. This is followed by an overview of current youth violence prevention strategies and a general discussion of their effectiveness. The chapter concludes with recommendations for future work in this area.

Considerations in Developing Effective Prevention Strategies

The Focus of Prevention Efforts

A critical first step in the development of a prevention program is to define its goals. These goals may include reducing a particular type of violence, preventing a constellation of problem behaviors, and broader efforts to promote positive development (Farrell & Camou, 2005). Clarifying the focus of a prevention program is the first step toward determining the specific risk and protective factors it should target, its intended population, and the most appropriate mechanism for its delivery.

Researchers in the area of youth violence have noted important distinctions among different forms of violence and aggression. Moffitt (see Chapter 3, this volume), for example, has articulated a taxonomic theory that differentiates between two distinct prototypes for the development of antisocial behavior – a life-course persistent pattern that begins early in life and continues into adulthood and an adolescent-limited pattern that emerges during puberty and does not persist into adulthood. Tolan and Guerra (1994) differentiated among four types of violence: situational violence, relationship or interpersonal violence, predatory violence, and psychopathological violence. Dodge (1991) described two forms of aggression with distinct trajectories, reactive and proactive aggression. Because these types of violence differ in their risk and protective factors and their age of onset, they are likely to require different prevention strategies, and the optimal time to intervene may differ across types. Prevention efforts have also been developed to address specific behaviors, such as verbal and physical confrontations that may escalate to violence, relational aggression (see Chapter 11 by Crick, Ostrov, & Kawabata, this volume), and dating violence (see Chapter 21 by Foshee & Matthew, this volume).

Although some interventions have focused specifically on youth violence prevention, interrelations among a broader constellation of problem behaviors and their shared risk and protective factors suggest that prevention efforts could be focused more broadly (Weissberg, Kumpfer, & Seligman, 2003). For example, risk factors that have been implicated in the development of interpersonal aggression, such as impulse control, peer deviancy, attitudes supporting deviance, poor parenting, and lack of attachment to conventional institutions, have also been found to be associated with drug use and the broader category of conduct disorder and antisocial behavior (Gottfredson, 2001).

Not surprisingly, many programs designed to reduce youth violence focus on some of the same elements as programs designed to address other problem behaviors. This is reflected in the number of drug prevention programs that have been identified as effective for violent behavior (e.g., USDHHS, 2001). Efforts to clarify risk factors that are shared by different problem behaviors and those that are specific to a particular problem behavior could do much to improve the efficiency of prevention programming. These efforts could result in broadly focused prevention programs, rather than separate programs that focus on specific problem areas. Such programs might address common risk and protective factors, but could also include strategies that focus on factors specific to a given problem area (Nation et al., 2003; Weissberg et al., 2003).

Some prevention scientists have moved away from a definition of prevention that focuses solely on the prevention of disorders to a broader focus on promoting positive development (Coie et al., 1993). Proponents of this perspective argue that producing positive outcomes is not simply a matter of preventing problem behaviors. In contrast, they maintain that efforts that produce positive outcomes through promoting the development of social, emotional, cognitive, and behavioral skills may be the most effective approach to reducing problem behaviors (e.g., Greenberg et al., 2003). Weissberg et al. (2003) underscored the need for such interventions, arguing that relatively low percentages of youth acquire the skills, values, attitudes, and environmental support needed to protect them from high-risk behaviors and promote their positive development.

Clarifying the goals of a prevention effort is critical to developing effective strategies. Implementing focused interventions aimed at promoting positive development may be effective in reducing specific forms of violence to the extent that they address the relevant risk and protective factors for a given population. Such programs may not, however, include risk and protective factors relevant to particular forms of violence, such as instrumental aggression or psychopathological violence. The specific objectives of a prevention effort must be defined so that the appropriate risk and protective factors can be identified and effective strategies developed to address them.

The Intended Population

The development of effective prevention programs requires careful consideration of the specific population being targeted. Important characteristics include the degree of risk, developmental stage, and cultural and contextual factors. Prevention programs have been categorized into three different types depending on the degree of risk evident in the target population (Mrazek & Haggerty, 1994). *Universal* interventions are designed to address an entire population irrespective of risk. For example, a school-based universal intervention program might be implemented on a school-wide basis with all students and teachers participating. *Selective* interventions are designed for individuals or subgroups with risk factors that place them at above average risk. For example, given the connection between environmental risk factors and violence, programs might be developed specifically for youth in neighborhoods with high rates of poverty and crime. Finally, *indicated* programs are designed for individuals who have already begun to exhibit aggressive behaviors, but who have not yet exhibited more extreme levels of aggression or violence. These three prevention approaches are likely to result in rather different interventions because children at different levels of risk may benefit from interventions that vary in their focus and intensity (Prinz, 2000).

Prevention efforts are not, of course, limited to choosing only one approach. In recent years there has been a trend toward combining universal with selective or indicated interventions. For example, the Fast Track intervention combined a universal school-based intervention with a more intensive selective intervention directed at higher risk students (Conduct Problems Prevention Research Group [CPPRG], 1999). Part of the rationale for this combination was that reducing the disruptive impact of higher risk students would make it easier for other students to respond to a universal intervention.

To be effective, prevention programs must address risk factors before they become stable and less responsive to intervention (Coie et al., 1993). Violence prevention strategies thus differ across developmental stages because risk and protective factors play a different role at each stage (Dahlberg & Potter, 2001; Samples & Aber, 1998). Interventions directed at different age groups may also reflect differences in the critical skills required at different stages of development. For example, an important focus for elementary-school programs is on self-control and emotional awareness (Samples & Aber, 1998). Middle-school interventions, in contrast, are more likely to focus on developing problem-solving skills for nonviolent conflict resolution and managing peer relations (e.g., Meyer, Farrell, Northup, Kung, & Plybon, 2000). It is important to note that arguments for early intervention (e.g., Dahlberg & Potter, 2001) do not imply that interventions should be restricted to early stages of development. Intervention should begin early, but is most likely to be effective if it includes a series of coordinated programs designed for each specific stage of development (Weissberg et al., 2003). For example, the social-contextual model indicates that parenting behaviors will affect children when they are young, but will also influence the kinds of peer relationships children develop in early and middle adolescence (Scaramella, Conger, Spoth, & Simons, 2002). Thus, the influence of parenting does not cease in adolescence; rather the emerging influence of peers allows an additional and developmentally relevant point of intervention. As Guerra (1998) noted, further work is needed to establish the optimum age for specific types of interventions and for booster sessions to support these interventions.

Prevention programs must also pay careful attention to issues related to culture and context (Nation et al., 2003; Weissberg et al., 2003). Individuals are influenced by multiple forces that include historical time and lived experience; their internal world; and interactions with family, peer, school, and neighborhood/community networks (Bronfenbrenner, 1979). Programs are more likely to be successful if they optimize the fit between persons and environments (Coie et al., 1993). Such programming requires a clear understanding of the specific manner in which risk and protective factors occur in specific environments and the strategies that are most likely to be effective for a particular subgroup. For example, violence prevention programs that focus on teaching adolescents skills to address problem situations must be informed by research that illuminates the types of problematic situations they are most likely to encounter, available resources, and strategies that are most likely to be effective in addressing those situations (Farrell et al., in press). Potentially relevant characteristics of the population include the community setting (e.g., urban, suburban, or rural), neighborhood characteristics, and ethnic composition (Ollendick, 1996). Such factors determine not only the focus of the program but also influence specific elements, such as the use of ethnically congruent role models, language, and materials (e.g., Yung & Hammond, 1998). The development of effective interventions also requires a clear understanding of gender differences (see Chapter 11 in this volume). The failure to address gender differences in aggression may be partly responsible for the relatively poor response of girls to earlier violence prevention efforts (Farrell & Meyer, 1997).

Risk and Protective Factors

The goal of prevention is to develop effective strategies for eliminating or reducing risk factors and enhancing protective factors related to the development of a specific disorder. One of the key implications of this goal is that prevention efforts can only be successful to the extent that (1) researchers have been able to identify the risk and protective factors most salient for the development of a particular problem within a specific subgroup and that (2) program developers are able to develop effective methods of modifying these risk and protective factors (Coie et al., 1993; Kellam, Koretz, & Moscicki, 1999).

As the preceding chapters illustrate, substantial progress has been made in identifying the diverse array of risk factors associated with youth violence (for reviews also see Dahlberg & Potter, 2001; Hawkins, Herrenkohl, et al., 1998; Lipsey & Derzon, 1998; USDHHS, 2001). At the individual or child level, examples include temperament, impulse control, low self-regulation, low IQ, poor prenatal health, involvement in other problem behaviors, antisocial attitudes and beliefs, and deficits in social information-processing skills. Examples of family risk factors include poverty, parental mental health problems, single parenthood, young motherhood, poor parent-child relations, poor parenting skills, older siblings with antisocial behavior, and low family cohesion. Peers have also been found to exert a strong influence on violence through such risk factors as peer models, peer deviancy, and peer norms. Factors within the school environment include teacher-child conflict, school norms promoting violence, and poor classroom management. Community-level factors include neighborhood crime, neighbor-

hood disorganization, exposure to violence, access to weapons, poverty, unemployment, dense housing, drug distribution, and limited positive opportunities for youth and adults. Finally, risk factors at the more macro level include rapid demographic and social changes, income inequality, political structures, and cultural influences (e.g., media exposure). Research on risk and protective factors has become increasingly refined and has begun to examine the extent to which different factors are associated with specific developmental trajectories and the stage of development at which these factors exert their influence (e.g., Chapters 3 and 10, this volume). Such a research base is critical to the development of more effective prevention programs.

Effective prevention strategies depend not only on identifying relevant risk and protective factors but also on developing effective methods to alter these factors. Although numerous protective and risk factors have been identified, strategies that alter these processes and subsequent developmental pathways are much less clear. For example, it is not sufficient to know that certain deficits in social information processing are associated with aggression (e.g., Crick & Dodge, 1994). Additional information is needed to determine what strategies might be used to effectively prevent the development of these deficits. The fact that risk and protective factors are often present in multiple contexts makes it likely that comprehensive efforts will be needed (Elliott, Hamburg, & Williams, 1998; Gottfredson, 2001; Prinz, 2000). As Weissberg et al. (2003) noted, "Young people grow up in families, schools, and neighborhoods, not in programs" (p. 429). Changes at the individual level are not likely to persist if they are not supported within the environment (Elliott & Tolan, 1999).

Overview of Youth Violence Prevention Programs

This section provides a broad overview of the variety of prevention strategies that have been developed to address youth violence. The diverse array of available programs precludes a more detailed analysis of these programs and their effectiveness (for detailed reviews, see Gottfredson, 2001; Hawkins, Farrington, & Catalano, 1998; Lipsey & Derzon, 1998; Samples & Aber, 1998; USD-HHS, 2001). This discussion is not intended to be exhaustive. Programs are organized in terms of their primary focus within an ecological model.

School-Based Programs

Schools are the most common setting in which youth violence prevention programs have been implemented (Farrell, Meyer, Kung, & Sullivan, 2001). The majority of such programs have had a universal focus (e.g., Aber, Jones, Brown, Chaudry, & Samples, 1998; McMahon & Washburn, 2003; Wilson, Lipsey, & Derzon, 2003), although others have combined universal and selective programs (e.g., CPPRG, 2004; Metropolitan Area Child Study Research Group, 2002). Both universal and selective programs tend to focus on addressing skills at the individual child level, although some include additional components that target parenting skills. For example, programs such as Fast Track (CPPRG, 1999), Responding in Peaceful and Positive Ways (RIPP; Meyer et al., 2000), and Second Step (Orpinas, Basen-Engquist, Grunbaum, & Parcel, 1995) have focused on teaching emotion understanding and communication, self-regulation skills, social problem-solving skills, and prosocial friendship skills.

The Fast-Track – Universal Intervention (CPPRG, 2004) is curriculum based and teaches social-cognitive skills to students in grades one through five. Teachers implement this universal program approximately two to three times per week. The universal program is paired with a selective intervention for high-risk youth. Youth in the selective program receive the curriculum-based intervention as well as additional social skills training and academic tutoring. In the selective intervention, parents are also offered group and individual sessions focused on positive parenting skills and improving coping and problem-solving behaviors.

RIPP is a universal school-based prevention program developed for use in middle schools or junior high schools based on a health promotion model that emphasizes the development of social-cognitive skills (Meyer & Farrell, 1998). It uses an adult role model to teach knowledge, attitudes, and skills that promote nonviolence and a peer-mediation program to promote school-level change. Participants are instructed in the use of a social-cognitive problem-solving model and specific skills for violence prevention through experiential and didactic activities. Each component addresses critical developmental issues at specific grades. The 25-session sixth-grade curriculum focuses on violence prevention broadly, the 12-session seventh-grade curriculum focuses on conflict-resolution skills in friendships, and the 12-session eighth-grade curriculum focuses on making a successful transition to high school (Meyer et al., 2000).

Other school-based programs have focused on changing school climate and peer influences. For example, the PeaceBuilders program (Embry, Flannery, Vazsonyi, Powell, & Atha, 1996; Flannery et al., 2003) attempts to change the climate of the school by teaching prosocial skills, reinforcing positive behavior, and providing adult models of prosocial behaviors. PeaceBuilders is a school-wide program for elementary schools (grades K-5) based on the theory that violent children and youth show cognitive, social, and imitative differences from their peers. Thus, the entire school (e.g., students, teachers, and staff) is taught a common language and rules associated with peace building. Tactics, such as cues and symbols for peace-building behavior, prompts to generalize skills across people and situations, and innovative techniques for times when peace building may break down, are used to help students learn and apply their new skills. The program also includes components that may be implemented by the schools to address the broader context in which problem behavior develops. These components include parent education, marketing to families, collateral training for community volunteers, and mass media tie-ins.

Several school-based programs have targeted adults and focus on restructuring the youth's social environment. For example, the Bully Prevention Program (Kallestad & Olweus, 2003; Olweus, 1994) was developed to reduce bullying, prevent the development of new bully/victim problems, and achieve better peer relations and school conditions. The program helps teachers and school personnel reduce bullying by enforcing classroom and school rules against bullying and by holding interventions with bullies, victims, and their parents. This program attempts to use adults in the children's environment to provide consistent expectations and consequences regarding bullying.

Family-Focused Interventions

Another common focus has been on family interventions (Mihalic, Irwin, Elliott, Fagan, & Hansen, 2001; Serketich & Dumas, 1996). Some programs, such as Incredible Years (Reid, Webster-Stratton, & Baydar, 2004), have focused on specific parenting skills, including selective reinforcement, nonviolent discipline strategies, setting consequences, and problem-solving strategies. This selective program targets parents with children between the ages of 2 and 8 who are considered at risk for conduct problems. The Incredible Years series also includes optional components to address family-level risk factors, the child's school performance, teacher training, and child training for those children already exhibiting conduct problems. Targeting the development of positive parenting skills has been found to be most effective with young children (MacKenzie & Hilgedick, 1999; Serketich & Dumas, 1996).

Other programs, such as Nurse Home Visitations (Olds et al., 1998), begin early with prenatal home visits to at-risk mothers. This program targets three main aspects of maternal functioning: positive health-related behaviors through the child's early years, competent parenting skills, and maternal personal development. As part of accomplishing their goals for maternal functioning, nurses link families with other needed services and attempt to include other members of the family and the larger extended family and community. As part of the Nurse Home Visitation Program, nurse visits are conducted every 1 to 2 weeks for the first 2 years of the child's life.

Most family-focused programs are selective interventions (Lochman & Wells, 2004), although a few universal interventions have been developed (e.g., Dishion, Kavanagh, Schneiger, Nelson, & Kaufman, 2002). The Coping Power Program (Lochman & Wells, 2004) includes a selective family intervention that targets preadolescent aggressive children in the fourth and fifth grades. The child component features group sessions to teach skills, such as goal setting, self-regulation, coping, anger management, social information-processing skills, and social problem-solving skills. The parent component also features group sessions and focuses on parenting techniques, such as identifying antecedents to prosocial and antisocial behavior, giving rewards and consequences, setting rules, and giving effective instructions. Parents learn to support the skills that the children are learning and to improve family functioning in general through weekly family meetings.

Some family programs have been combined with school-based efforts. For example, the Adolescent Transitions Program is a multilevel family intervention delivered within a middle-school setting (Dishion et al., 2002). Components include a Family Resource Center (universal intervention), Family Checkup (selective intervention), and Family Intervention (indicated intervention). The Family Resource Center involves a classroom-based curriculum for students to address norms for prosocial behavior, parent-child interaction homework, and a family newsletter to facilitate dissemination of the information taught to the students. The Family Checkup consists of an assessment followed by a brief family intervention to build parental motivation and engage families in the most appropriate family intervention for their needs. The family then selects one or more intervention options from the family interventions menu. Finally, the Family Intervention Menu addresses existing problem behaviors. It focuses on using incentives to promote positive behavior, limit setting and monitoring, and family communication and problem solving. The program is thus designed for flexible implementation to meet the family's needs and motivations.

Community Interventions

Although community factors, such as neighborhood crime, neighborhood disorganization, exposure to violence, access to weapons, and social isolation, have been found to play a significant role in the development of aggression, relatively few community-based programs have been developed and evaluated (Sampson, 2002). One such program is the Violence Intervention Program (VIP) for Children and Families, which attempts to attenuate the effects of exposure to violence on children and families (Osofsky et al., 2004). Components include police training to raise awareness about the effects of violence exposure and increase referrals to VIP counseling following a crisis. Thus, the program attempts to build community partners to ensure that children receive necessary mental health services following violence exposure. VIP staff also offer services to police officers following violent experiences.

Other programs include community-building components as part of larger intervention programs. The Better Beginnings, Better Futures Project (Peters, Petrunka, & Arnold, 2003) includes community cohesion activities, such as community gardens and community kitchens. As part of the project, the communities aim to develop local organizations to implement programs for children and families, establish and maintain resident involvement in the commu-

nity, and develop partnerships with other agencies. This community-level intervention is paired with other levels of intervention, including school-based enrichment programs, free breakfast programs, social skills training, after-school programs, and parent relief and child drop-in programs. Another program included community service as a supplement to a classroom curriculum (ODonnell et al., 1999). Under teacher guidance, youth spent several hours each week providing services in local health care agencies, such as nursing homes. Results indicated not only reductions in violence after the intervention program but also the formation of positive relationships between the youth and the elderly patients in the nursing home.

Macro-System Interventions

Few programs have been developed to address youth violence within the context of more macro-level factors, such as media influence and poverty. Some community-level interventions address distal risk factors, such as employment, housing, and neighborhood drug availability, in an effort to improve the well-being of urban minority youth (Black & Krishnakumar, 1998). Such programs do not, however, include violence prevention as a specific goal or focus, and their impact on such outcomes remains to be determined. Other programs attempt to reach the larger macro-level factors by using media to promote prosocial norms and behavior. One such program is the APA-MTV "Warning Signs" program (Peterson & Newman, 2000). This program aims at educating youth to recognize warning signs of violence in oneself or others, to seek help when problems arise, and to stop a violent act before it occurs. The program consists of a documentary on teens and violent behavior, a guide to educate youth about violence and indicators of violence, and community outreach through classroom, school, or community-youth forums. Although there is some evidence that such programs may be effective in increasing knowledge and awareness of the problem of youth violence, there has been little research on their impact.

Moving Beyond Current Prevention Efforts

Although a variety of prevention programs have been developed and implemented, numerous reviews (e.g., Gottfredson, 2001; Howard et al., 1999; USDHHS, 2001) have noted that the majority have either not been evaluated or have been evaluated using weak research designs that make it difficult to draw clear conclusions about their effectiveness. For example, although schools have been the most frequent setting for youth violence programs, Howard et al. (1999), in their review of school-based violence prevention programs published between 1993 and 1997, were able to identify only 44 school-based evaluation studies. Of these, only 13 met a minimum standard that involved either having a control group or including pre- and post- measures of the same individuals. More recent reviews have identified a relatively small number of youth violence prevention programs that have been designated as "Model" or "Effective" based on research evaluating their impact (Catalano, Berglund, Ryan, Lonczak, & Hawkins, 2002; Mihalic et al., 2001; USDHHS, 2001). For example, the Blueprints Violence Prevention Initiative (Mihalic et al., 2001) reviewed over 500 programs, of which only 11 were designated Model Programs.

Even those programs considered promising typically produce modest effects that are often of limited duration (Farrell & Camou, 2005; Gottfredson, 2001). Many of the positive effects reported in evaluation studies reflect changes in knowledge, attitudes, and responses to hypothetical situations, rather than in actual behavior (Howard et al., 1999). Effects are often gender-specific (e.g., Farrell & Meyer, 1997), are limited to subgroups of participants (e.g., Farrell, Meyer, & White, 2001; Tolan & Gorman-Smith, 2002), or occur in applications where

fidelity or dosage is particularly strong (e.g., Aber et al., 1998). Such effects are evident even among programs designated as model or exemplary. The extent to which these programs can produce significant effects in the real world has yet to be established.

Although important progress has been made in youth violence prevention, it is clear that a considerable effort is needed to improve the effectiveness of current programs (USDHHS, 2001). The development of effective youth violence prevention programs involves an iterative process in which intervention development is informed by more basic research on youth violence, and our understanding of youth violence is informed by evaluations of intervention efforts (Coie et al., 1993). Advances in basic research on youth violence and emerging trends in prevention science have important implications for improving the effectiveness of prevention efforts. In particular, there is a need for prevention programs guided by recent research findings that document the complexity of risk and protective factors associated with various forms of violence, as well as for further work to identify the most effective methods to address these factors. This section discusses several specific recommendations for improving the effectiveness of these efforts.

We Need Prevention Programs That Reflect the Complex Nature of Youth Violence

Research on the nature of violence and its associated risk and protective factors provides the basis for developing effective prevention programs (Coie et al., 1993; Mrazek & Haggerty, 1994). Developing and evaluating interventions is a lengthy process. This is particularly true for prevention programs whose ultimate impact may not be evident until several years after their implementation. One consequence of this process is that interventions described in even the most recently published reviews were typically developed based on research that is more than 10 years old. The preceding chapters in this volume detail the numerous advances that have been made in the study of youth violence. These advances include a clearer explanation of the different forms or subtypes of violent behavior and differences in the risk and protective factors associated with each subtype. These findings have important implications for developers of prevention programs.

Research attempting to identify risk and protective factors associated with youth violence has highlighted the complex nature of this phenomenon and indicated that there is no single common pathway. There are different forms of violence that differ in their associated risk and protective factors and developmental trajectories. For this reason, developers of prevention programs must specify the type of violence they are attempting to address and design a strategy to address the specific risk and protective factors related to that type (Tolan & Guerra, 1994).

For example, the evidence supporting two distinct trajectories for the development of antisocial behavior reviewed by Moffitt (see Chapter 3) suggests that interventions designed for each approach should be very different. Moffitt described a life-course persistent pattern of antisocial behavior that begins in childhood and progresses to a pattern of physical aggression and antisocial behavior that continues into adulthood. Research suggests that this pattern is caused by early neurodevelopmental deficits combined with a high-risk environment (e.g., poor parenting, disrupted family bonds, and poverty). In contrast, adolescent-limited antisocial behavior is a more common pattern that begins during adolescence and does not persist into adulthood. The development of the adolescent-limited pattern is believed to be influenced by social processes. In particular, Moffitt suggested that adolescents who experience a gap between their level of biological maturity and their access to the privileges and rights of adults may resort to delinquent behavior to demonstrate their autonomy and gain social status with their peers. She noted that many of these individuals will adopt a more conventional lifestyle

as adults, unless caught in a "snare," such as drug or alcohol dependency or the juvenile justice system. The life-course persistent pattern occurs much less frequently than the adolescent-limited pattern, but is responsible for a disproportionately higher number of violent offenses. For example, Moffitt described a 32-year longitudinal study of 1000 New Zealanders in which the life-course persistent offenders represented 10% of the sample, but accounted for over half of the sample's self-reported violent offenses at age 26. In contrast, the adolescent-limited sample represented 26% of the sample and accounted for 29% of the violent offenses. However, adolescent-limited aggression cannot be considered to be benign. Such youth are not only aggressive but are also more likely to endorse high levels of internalizing symptoms and life stress (Aguilar, Sroufe, Egeland, & Carlson, 2000). Differences in the trajectories and risk factors associated with these two patterns of antisocial behavior have important implications for the development of effective violence prevention programs. Programs designed to address the life-course persistent pattern should begin early in life, perhaps even during prenatal development, and include a component designed to address family risk factors. In contrast, violence prevention programs directed at an adolescent-limited pattern should begin during early adolescence and might include efforts to provide youth with alternative methods of obtaining autonomy and peer status.

This is but one example of how prevention programs that differ in focus require different strategies and of the important role of basic research in intervention development. Researchers have drawn distinctions between a variety of different forms of youth violence and related adjustment problems. Prevention programs designed to address different forms of aggression will likely differ in the specific risk and protective patterns on which they focus, their timing and intensity, and the specific strategies they employ. Ideally they will be guided by the most recently available research on risk and protective factors associated with the specific pattern they are attempting to prevent. The general lesson is the need to move away from generic violence prevention programs toward programs more specific in their focus.

We Need a Stronger Research Base to Guide the Development of Prevention Efforts

Although we have made considerable advances in our understanding of youth violence, there are also critical gaps in our current knowledge base. A clearer understanding of the risk and protective factors related to specific forms of violent behavior for particular subgroups of youth could promote the development of more effective prevention programs.

For example, efforts to develop more effective universal programs for addressing individual-level risk factors could be facilitated by a clearer understanding of the factors associated with violent behavior in specific subgroups of adolescents. A common focus of many such interventions has been to teach participants various skills related to information processing, social skills, social problem solving, and conflict resolution (Pepler & Slaby, 1994; Tolan & Guerra, 1994). Such programs are based on research indicating that aggressive adolescents often lack critical skills needed to deal effectively with interpersonal situations (e.g., Crick & Dodge, 1994). Much of our knowledge of social-cognitive deficits has been based on studies of developmental trajectories of boys with severe behavior problems and those in correctional or other institutional settings (e.g., Guerra & Slaby, 1990; Kazdin, Bass, Siegel, & Thomas, 1989; Pardini, Lochman, & Frick, 2003; Sarason & Ganzer, 1973). Studies of social-cognitive deficits conducted with normative populations have primarily focused on aggression in early or middle childhood (Dodge, Laird, Lochman, Zelli, & CPPRG, 2002; Huesmann & Guerra, 1997; Rudolph & Heller, 1997; Zelli et al., 1999). These deficits might therefore be more evident among adolescents displaying a life-course persistent pattern of antisocial behavior. Programs that

focus on these skills may be effective for individuals fitting this particular pattern, but may prove less effective for others. Further work is needed to determine the extent to which social-cognitive deficits play a role in the violent behavior of more general populations of male and female adolescents and to identify the role played by other factors. For example, research identifying factors related to violence among youth fitting the adolescent-limited pattern of antisocial behavior (see Chapter 3, this volume), dating violence (see Chapter 21, this volume), and aggression among females (see Chapter 11, this volume), would provide a stronger base for developing more effective interventions for these particular subgroups.

Although information about characteristics that differentiate aggressive youth from their peers might be valuable, prevention programs might also benefit from research identifying factors that predict prosocial behavior. Not all adolescents growing up in high-risk environments develop adjustment problems. One promising strategy is to identify the social, cognitive, and emotional skills used by adolescents who have developed effective nonviolent strategies for dealing with problem situations and other factors that support their use (Coie et al., 1993; Durant, Cadenhead, Pendergrast, Slavens, & Linder, 1994; Masten & Coatsworth, 1998). A better understanding of these factors could facilitate the development of interventions by providing effective alternatives to aggression. As Catalano et al. noted, "A successful transition to adulthood requires more than avoiding drugs, violence, or precocious sexual activity" (2002, p. 9).

There is a clear need to help youth develop the specific skills necessary to address the particular demands of their environments (Coie et al., 1993). Low-income African American youth in particular tend to be overrepresented as both victims and perpetrators of violence (Guerra, Huesmann, Tolan, Van Acker, & Eron, 1995; Hammond & Yung, 1993). Interpersonal homicide and violence are especially widespread in poor inner-city neighborhoods and public housing projects (Garbarino, Dubrow,

Kostelny, & Pardo, 1992; Tolan & Gorman-Smith, 2002). Because youth growing up in poor urban areas face unique challenges (e.g., Allison et al. 1999; Black & Krishnakumar, 1998; Evans, 2004), prevention programs are not likely to be effective unless they are preceded by efforts to improve our understanding of the particular risk factors associated with this environment and factors that buffer youth from its negative impact.

We recently completed a series of studies to guide our efforts to develop a universal middle-school violence prevention program for students in an urban public school system that serves a high percentage of African American students from low-income families. This project illustrates the type of research that can inform the development of prevention programs. The first step was to conduct interviews with adolescents, their parents, and other adults (e.g., school and community center staff) in their environment to identify problem situations encountered by these adolescents (Farrell et al., in press). These interviews identified a variety of problem situations at the individual, peer, family, school, and neighborhood level. The relevance of these problem situations was confirmed by asking a larger sample of 171 students from the same school system to indicate how frequently they encountered these situations and how difficult they were to handle (Farrell, Sullivan, et al., 2006).

Once relevant problem situations were identified, we conducted interviews with adolescents to identify different strategies that adolescents would use to handle specific situations that were found to be particularly prevalent and difficult. The effectiveness of these strategies was then rated by a separate sample of adolescents and adults from the community. These data were used to identify strategies that both adolescents and the adults considered effective for addressing each situation. The final step in this process was to interview another sample of adolescents who were read descriptions of situations and strategies for handling them and asked whether they would use that strategy in that situation. They were also asked to identify factors that would make it eas-

ier and factors that would make it more difficult for them to use that strategy in that situation. This process was used to identify barriers and supports for prosocial responses that had been rated effective. We also asked adolescents to identify factors that impeded and supported aggressive responses to specific situations. Qualitative coding of these interviews provided a rich source of information about the factors that inhibit and support prosocial behavior and aggression within this population (Farrell, Erwin et al., 2006). This model will next be validated in a study designed to examine relations among exposure to high- risk situations, effective problem-solving skills, barriers and supports for using these skills, and violent behavior and victimization. The final step will be to use the information to inform our efforts to improve the relevance and ecological validity of prevention programs for this population.

We Need to Determine if Prevention Strategies Produce Their Intended Effects

Once relevant risk and protective factors have been identified, further effort is needed to determine the most effective approaches for altering these processes (Farrell, Meyer, Kung, & Sullivan, 2001; Gottfredson, 2001). Although evaluations of youth violence prevention programs typically assess their impact on primary outcomes such as violent behaviors, few studies include a full assessment of the risk and protective factors targeted by the intervention. For example, although some studies assess the degree to which students have learned the skills taught in the intervention (e.g., Aber et al., 1998; Farrell, Meyer, & White, 2003; Grossman et al., 1997; Skroban, Gottfredson, & Gottfredson, 1999), few studies provide evidence of the use of these skills in real-life situations. As Coie et al. (1993) noted, well-designed prevention studies enhance our understanding of risk and protective factors by providing experimental tests of these models. Studies that only address primary outcomes do not provide a basis for determining the extent to which a prevention program successfully affected the specific risk and protective factors it targeted and the extent to which changes in these factors were responsible for producing changes in aggression (Kellam et al., 1999; Tolan & Gorman-Smith, 2002).

There are multiple reasons why an intervention may produce limited effects on aggression. One possibility is that it did not successfully alter the specific risk or protective factors it targeted. In such circumstances logical next steps would be to consider whether the dosage was adequate, whether the intervention was implemented successfully, whether an alternative strategy is needed, or whether other factors may be reducing the intervention's impact. Interventions do not always produce their desired effects (e.g, Dishion & Andrews, 1995). We need to build an empirical basis for identifying the most effective methods to reduce the impact of specific risk factors and support protective factors for specific subgroups. A careful analysis of different mechanisms for implementing interventions can identify approaches that are not effective and those that produce adverse effects (cf. Dishion, McCord, & Poulin, 1999). What works in one setting may not work in others. In particular, an organization's capacity to implement the intervention, including school and individual staff commitment, effective training, and establishing a shared vision, is critical to the fidelity and sustainability of an intervention (Meyer et al., 2000). Many inner-city schools and neighborhoods already face extreme economic and social strain and may lack the capacity to fully implement an intervention. For example, the Metropolitan Area Child Study Research Group (2002) reported that an early intervention program for high-risk students was associated with a decrease in aggression for students in schools in a poor, urban (but not inner city) school, but an increase for students in an inner-city community. Thus, interventions must not only address the needs of the youth in the schools but also fit within the resources of the community.

In some cases, an intervention may successfully alter the risk and protective factors it targets but not produce the desired changes in the primary outcome. This pattern of findings might raise questions about the relevance of the specific risk and protective factors or could imply that other risk factors need to be addressed concurrently. For example, participants in an intervention designed to teach effective social problem-solving skills may learn these skills, but choose to fight when confronted with a problem situation in order to maintain or achieve social status with their peers. In this case learning skills may be a necessary, but not sufficient condition for reducing aggression. The failure to test the intervention's underlying model of change makes it extremely difficult to interpret negative outcomes. As Prinz noted, the failure to incorporate theory into the development and evaluation of prevention programs seriously impedes progress in this area: "scientists and evaluators do not want to bounce randomly from one unsuccessful program to another, hoping to discover the right one" (2000, p. 25).

Evaluating the extent to which an intervention produces its intended effect on risk and protective factors may require the development of innovative research designs. In contrast to the typical pre–post design, more frequent assessments of risk and protective factors may be needed to determine the point at which the intervention produces changes in these factors. Many of the processes targeted by current interventions, such as emotional processing and problem-solving skills, may require more innovative approaches to assessment than commonly used procedures, such as paper-and-pencil measures. Qualitative methods may be particularly useful for evaluating the relevance of a prevention program for a particular population. For example, for an intervention that focuses on teaching specific skills, such as problem solving or conflict resolution, to be effective, the skills taught by these interventions must be relevant to the types of problem situations typically faced by the target population, successfully mastered by participants in the program, actually used outside of the intervention setting, and found to be effective when used. Some insight into the extent to which these objectives are achieved could be obtained by procedures such as interviews with participants. This information could then be used to increase the relevance of intervention efforts and to ensure that they address any obstacles that reduce their potential impact.

Putting the Pieces Together

A comprehensive review of violence prevention efforts by the U.S. Surgeon General concluded that we have moved beyond the prevailing view from 10 years ago that nothing works for preventing and reducing youth violence (USDHHS, 2001). Although we have begun to build the scientific base needed to address this problem, considerable work is needed to move to the point where effective programs are implemented on a wide-scale basis. Developing effective programs to reduce youth violence is a challenging task that will require a focused and persistent effort (Mercy & Potter, 1996). Advances in our understanding of the complex nature of youth violence make it clear that no single program will address this problem adequately. There are different types of youth violence, and we have yet to understand fully the similarities and differences in the risk and protective factors associated with each. Even within types, it cannot be assumed that specific risk and protective factors will play the same role with different groups of individuals. We are just beginning to identify effective strategies for influencing factors associated with the development of violent behavior.

A central theme of this chapter is that developing an effective prevention program requires specifying the type of aggression or pattern of problem behavior to be addressed, identifying the intended population, identifying the risk and protective factors relevant to that specific behavior for the intended population, and identifying effective methods of addressing those factors. The field has clearly reached the point where questions about whether or not an intervention

works must be replaced by questions about whether a specific strategy is effective for addressing a particular form of violence with a particular group of youth and determining the circumstances under which it is most likely to be effective. Researchers in the field of youth violence prevention would do well to heed the advice given to psychotherapy researchers by Kiesler (1966) and Paul (1969) nearly 40 years ago urging them to move beyond questions such as "does psychotherapy work" to address more complex issues: "What treatment, by whom, is most effective for this individual with that specific problem, under which set of circumstances, and how does it come about?" (Paul, 1969, p. 44). In some respects the challenges faced by prevention researchers are more daunting, in that the focus is not on addressing the problems of individuals, but on a larger social problem that occurs at multiple levels.

Because risk and protective factors occur in multiple contexts and play different roles at different developmental stages, it is likely that comprehensive efforts that involve interventions at multiple levels across different stages of development are needed to address this problem (Nation et al., 2003; Tolan, Guerra, & Kendall, 1995; USDHHS, 2001). Developing and evaluating comprehensive programs that represent a sustained effort across multiple contexts, including larger social systems such as schools and neighborhoods, is a serious challenge that will take considerable resources and time and will likely involve teams of researchers (e.g., CPPRG, 2004; Multi-Site Violence Prevention Project, 2004). Comprehensive efforts will only be successful to the extent that each component accomplishes its objective. The time and expense involved in evaluating such efforts suggest that much might be gained by starting with smaller scale studies to develop and evaluate individual components. Separate work might be conducted to determine the most effective approaches to addressing the specific individual, family, and school risk and protective factors that emerge at a specific age for a particular form of violence. Once these components have been developed they could be incorporated into a larger program that might address multiple developmental stages. One drawback to this approach is that individual components are likely to produce only limited effects on primary outcomes until they are implemented as part of a larger effort. Such components will need to be judged more on the basis of the extent to which they successfully address the specific risk and protective factors they target. Some effort will therefore need to be made to determine how narrowly to focus such efforts – programs too narrowly focused may not produce any measurable effect.

Building a comprehensive program will require an organizational framework to identify the components most likely to be effective. Some years ago Kiesler (1969) proposed a grid model to pinpoint progress in the field of psychotherapy research. A similar approach might be used to organize our efforts at violence prevention. Relevant dimensions within the grid might include the goals of the program; participant (e.g., level or risk, stage of development) and setting (e.g., neighborhood risk level) characteristics; and the level of social system it attempts to change (e.g., individual, close interpersonal, macrosystem; Farrell & Camou, 2005; Prinz, 2000; Tolan & Guerra, 1994). This approach would also clarify the theory of change inherent in a given program by articulating the risk factors that each component of the intervention is designed to address. Such a framework would go beyond current reviews that focus more generally on classifying programs and strategies according to whether or not they appear effective (Krug et al., 2002; Thornton et al., 2000) and would point out those areas in most need of further development.

The development of effective programs is an important step, but such programs will have little impact if they are not implemented widely (Pentz, 2004). Considerable work is needed to move to the point at which effective programs are implemented on a wide-scale basis (USDHHS, 2001). Because of the difficulty and cost of implementing science-based prevention programs, many communities develop or adapt their own programs that achieve marginal effects (Nation et al., 2003). A 1998 survey of 886 middle- and high-school principals indicated that although schools used a median of 14 specific prevention activities to address problem behavior, the quality of many of these activities was questionable, and research evidence was among the least frequently used sources of information for selecting activities (Crosse, Burr, Cantor, Hagen, & Hantman, 2001). Gottfredson (2001) observed that there have been no systematic studies examining the quality of prevention programs as they are typically implemented in schools. Indeed, it has been argued that few schools are likely to have the resources or technical expertise to implement most currently available programs (Samples & Aber, 1998). This is particularly true of programs that have not accounted for school and neighborhood capacity in their design. Similarly, little is known about what is needed to maintain a program's effectiveness when it is implemented on a wide scale (USDHHS, 2001). We hope that increasing advocacy for research-based prevention practices coupled with efforts to disseminate these practices will lead to the development of appropriate standards and the more widespread use of effective programs (Biglan, Mrazek, Carnine, & Flay, 2003).

Acknowledgments

This work was supported by grant #1 R21 HD40041 from the National Institute of Child Health and Human Development (NICHD) and #1U49CE000730 from the Centers for Disease Control and Prevention (CDC). The research and interpretations reported are the sole responsibility of the authors and are not necessarily endorsed by NICHD or CDC or represent the views, opinions, or policies of their staff.

References

Aber, J. L, Jones, S. M, Brown, J. L., Chaudry, N., & Samples, F. (1998). Resolving Conflict

Creatively: Evaluating the developmental effects of a school-based violence prevention program in neighborhood and classroom context. *Development and Psychopathology, 10,* 187–213.

Aguilar, B., Sroufe, L. A., Egeland, B., & Carlson, E. (2000). Distinguishing the early-onset/persistent and adolescence-limited antisocial behavior types: From birth to 16 years. *Development and Psychopathology, 12,* 109–132.

Allison, K. A., Burton, L., Marshall, S., Perez-Febles, A., Yarrington, J., Kirsh, L. B., et al. (1999). Life experiences among urban adolescents: Examining the role of context. *Child Development, 70,* 1017–1029.

Biglan, A., Mrazek, P. J., Carnine, D., & Flay, B. R. (2003). The integration of research and practice in the prevention of youth problem behaviors. *American Psychologist, 58,* 433–440.

Black, M., & Krishnakumar, A. (1998). Children in low-income urban settings: Interventions to promote mental health and well-being. *American Psychologist, 53,* 635–646.

Bronfenbrenner, U. (1979). Contexts of child rearing: Problems and prospects. *American Psychologist, 34,* 844–850.

Butchart, A., Phinney, A., Check, P., & Villaveces, A. (2004). *Preventing violence: A guide to implementing the recommendations of the World Report on Violence and Health.* Geneva: Department of Injuries and Violence Prevention, World Health Organization.

Catalano, R. F., Berglund, M. L., Ryan, J. A. M., Lonczak, H. S., & Hawkins, J. D. (2002). Positive youth development in the United States. Research findings on evaluations of the Positive Youth Development Programs. *Prevention and Treatment, 6,* Article 15. Retrieved August 12, 2002, from http://journals.apa.org/prevention/volume5/pre0050015a.html.

Coie, J. D., Watt, N. F., West, S. G., Hawkins, J. D., Asarnow, J. R., Markman, H. J., et al. (1993). The science of prevention: A conceptual framework and some directions for a national research program. *American Psychologist, 48,* 1013–1022.

Conduct Problems Prevention Research Group (1999). Initial impact of the Fast Track prevention trial for conduct problems: II. Classroom effects. *Journal of Consulting and Clinical Psychology, 67,* 648–657.

Conduct Problems Prevention Research Group. (2004). The effects of the Fast Track program on serious problem outcomes at the end of elementary school. *Journal of Clinical Child and Adolescent Psychology, 33,* 650–661.

Crick, N. R., & Dodge, K. A. (1994). A review and reformulation of social information-processing mechanisms in children's social adjustment. *Psychological Bulletin, 115,* 74–101.

Crosse, S., Burr, M., Cantor, D., Hagen C. A., & Hantman, I. (2002). *Wide scope, questionable quality: Drug and violence prevention efforts in American schools.* Washington, DC: U.S. Department of Education, Planning and Evaluation Service.

Dahlberg, L. L., & Potter, L. B. (2001). Youth violence: Developmental pathways and prevention challenges. *American Journal of Preventive Medicine, 20* (Suppl. 1), 3–30.

Dishion, T. J., & Andrews, D. W. (1995). Preventing escalation in problem behaviors with high-risk young adolescents: Immediate and 1-year outcomes. *Journal of Consulting and Clinical Psychology, 63,* 538–548.

Dishion, T., Kavanagh, K., Schneiger, A. K. J., Nelson, S., & Kaufman, N. (2002). Preventing early adolescent substance use: A family centered strategy for the public middle school. *Prevention Science, 3,* 191–202.

Dishion, T. J., McCord, J., & Poulin, F. (1999). When interventions harm: Peer groups and problem behavior. *American Psychologist, 54,* 755–764.

Dodge, K. A. (1991). The structure and function of reactive and proactive aggression. In D. J. Pepler & K. H. Rubin (Eds.), *The development and treatment of childhood aggression* (pp. 201–218). Hillsdale, NJ: Erlbaum.

Dodge, K. A., Laird, R., Lochman, J. E., Zelli, A., & Conduct Problems Prevention Research Group (2002). Multidimensional latent-construct analysis of children's social information processing patterns: Correlations with aggressive behavior problems. *Psychological Assessment, 14,* 60–73.

Durant, R. H., Cadenhead, C., Pendergrast, R. A., Slavens, G., & Linder, C. W. (1994). Factors associated with the use of violence among urban adolescents. *American Journal of Public Health, 84,* 612–617.

Elliott, D., Hamburg, B., & Williams, K. (Eds). (1998). *Violence in American schools: New perspectives and solutions.* New York: Cambridge University Press.

Elliott, D. S., & Tolan, P. H. (1999). Youth violence prevention, intervention, and social policy: An overview. In D. J. Flannery & C. R.

Huff (Eds.), *Youth violence prevention, intervention, and social policy* (pp. 3–46). Washington, DC: American Psychiatric Press.

Embry, D. D., Flannery, D. J., Vazsonyi, A. T., Powell, K. E., & Atha, H. (1996). Peacebuilders: A theoretically driven, school-based model for early violence prevention. *American Journal of Preventive Medicine, 12,* 91–100.

Evans, G. W. (2004). The environment of childhood poverty. *American Psychologist, 59,* 77–92.

Farrell, A. D., & Camou, S. (2005). School-based interventions for youth violence prevention. In J. Lutzker (Ed.), *Preventing violence: Research and evidence-based intervention strategies.* Washington DC: American Psychological Association.

Farrell, A. D., Erwin, E. H., Allison, K., Meyer, A. L., Sullivan, T. N., Camou, S., et al. (in press). Problematic situations in the lives of urban African American middle school students: A qualitative study. *Journal of Research on Adolescence.*

Farrell, A. D., Erwin, E. H., Bettencourt, A., Mays, S., Vulin-Reynolds, M., Sullivan, T. N., et al. (2006). *Barriers and supports for prosocial behavior versus fighting: A qualitative study with urban African American adolescent.* Manuscript submitted for publication.

Farrell, A. D., & Meyer, A. L. (1997). The effectiveness of a school-based curriculum for reducing violence among urban sixth-grade students. *American Journal of Public Health, 87,* 979–984.

Farrell, A. D., Meyer, A. L., Kung, E. M., & Sullivan, T. N. (2001). Development and evaluation of school-based violence prevention programs. *Journal of Clinical Child Psychology, 30,* 207–220.

Farrell, A. D., Meyer, A. L., & White, K. S. (2001). Evaluation of Responding in Peaceful and Positive Ways (RIPP): A school-based prevention program for reducing violence among urban adolescents. *Journal of Clinical Child Psychology, 30,* 451–463.

Farrell, A. D., Sullivan, T. N., Kliewer, W., Allison, K. W., Erwin, E. H., Meyer, A. L., et al. (2006). Peer and school problems in the lives of urban adolescents: Frequency, difficulty, and relation to adjustment. *Journal of School Psychology, 44,* 169–190.

Flannery, D. J., Vazsonyi, A., Liau, A., Guo, S., Powell, K., Atha, H., et al. (2003). Initial behavior outcomes for the Peacebuilders universal school-based violence prevention program. *Developmental Psychology, 39,* 292–308.

Garbarino, J., Dubrow, N., Kostelny, K., & Pardo, C. (1992). *Children in danger: Coping with the consequences of community violence.* San Francisco: Jossey-Bass.

Gottfredson, D. C. (2001). *Schools and delinquency.* New York: Cambridge University Press.

Greenberg, M. T., Weissberg, R. P., O'Brien, M. U., Zins, J. E., Fredericks, L., Resnik, H., et al. (2003). Enhancing school-based prevention and youth development through coordinated social, emotional, and academic learning. *American Psychologist, 58,* 466–474.

Grossman, D., Neckerman, H., Koepsell T., Liu, P., Asher, K., Beland, K., et al. (1997). Effectiveness of a violence prevention curriculum among children in elementary school. *Journal of the American Medical Association, 277,* 1605–1611.

Guerra, N. G. (1998). Serious and violent juvenile offenders: Gaps in knowledge and research priorities. In R. Loeber & D. P. Farrington (Eds.), *Serious and violent juvenile offenders: Risk factors and successful interventions* (pp. 389–404). Thousand Oaks, CA: Sage.

Guerra, N. G., Huesmann, L. R., Tolan, P. H., Van Acker, R., & Eron, L. D. (1995). Stressful events and individual beliefs as correlates of economic disadvantage and aggression among urban children. *Journal of Consulting and Clinical Psychology, 63,* 518–528.

Guerra, N. G., & Slaby, R. G. (1990). Cognitive mediators of aggression in adolescent offenders: 2. Intervention. *Developmental Psychology, 26,* 269–277.

Hammond, W. R., & Yung, B. (1993). Psychology's role in the public health response to assaultive violence among young African-American men. *American Psychologist, 48,* 142–154.

Hawkins, J. D., Farrington, D. P., & Catalano, R. F. (1998). Reducing violence through the schools. In D. S. Elliott, B. A. Hamburg, & K. R. Williams (Eds.), *Violence in American schools: A new perspective* (pp. 188–216). New York: Cambridge University Press.

Hawkins, J. D., Herrenkohl, T., Farrington, D., Brewer, D., Catalano, R., & Harachi, T. (1998). A review of predictors of youth violence. In R. Loeber & D. P. Farrington (Eds.), *Serious and violent juvenile offenders: Risk factors and successful interventions* (pp. 106–146). Thousand Oaks, CA: Sage.

Howard, K. A., Flora, J., & Griffin, M. (1999). Violence prevention programs in schools: State of the science and implications for future research. *Applied and Preventative Psychology, 8*, 197–215.

Huesmann, L. R., & Guerra, N. G. (1997). Children's normative beliefs about aggression and aggressive behavior. *Journal of Personality and Social Psychology, 72*, 408–419.

Kallestad, J. H., & Olweus, D. (2003). Predicting teachers' and schools' implementation of the Olweus Bullying Prevention program: A multilevel study. *Prevention and Treatment, 6*, Article 21. Retrieved August 31, 2005, from http://www.journals.apa.org/prevention/volume6/pre0060021a.html.

Kazdin, A. E., Bass, D., Siegel, T., & Thomas, C. (1989). Cognitive-behavioral therapy and relationship therapy in the treatment of children referred for antisocial behavior. *Journal of Consulting and Clinical Psychology, 57*, 522–535.

Kellam, S. G., Koretz, D., & Moscicki, E. K. (1999). Core elements of developmental epidemiologically based prevention research. *American Journal of Community Psychology, 27*, 463–482.

Kiesler, D. J. (1966). Some myths of psychotherapy research and the search for a paradigm. *Psychological Bulletin, 65*, 110–136.

Kiesler, D. J. (1969). A grid model for theory and research in the psychotherapies. In L. D. Eron & R. Callahan (Eds.), *The relation of theory and practice in psychotherapy*. Chicago: Aldine.

Krug, E. G., Dahlberg, L. L., Mercy, J. A., Zwi, A. B., & Lozano, R. (Eds.). (2002). *World report on violence and health*. Geneva, Switzerland: World Health Organization.

Lipsey, M. W., & Derzon, J. H. (1998). Predictors of violent or serious delinquency in adolescence and early adulthood: A synthesis of longitudinal research. In R. Loeber & D. P. Farrington (Eds.), *Serious and violent juvenile offenders: Risk factors and successful interventions* (pp. 86–105). Thousand Oaks, CA: Sage.

Lochman, J. E., & Wells, K. C. (2004). The Coping Power Program for preadolescent aggressive boys and their parents: Outcome effects at the 1-year follow-up. *Journal of Consulting and Clinical Psychology, 72*, 571–578.

MacKenzie, E. P., & Hilgedick, J. M. (1999). The Computer-Assisted Parenting Program (CAPP): The use of a computerized behavioral parent training program as an educational tool. *Child and Family Behavior Therapy, 21*, 23–43.

Masten, A. S., & Coatsworth, J. D. (1998). The development of competence in favorable and unfavorable environments: Lessons from research on successful children. *American Psychologist, 53*, 205–220.

McMahon, S. D., & Washburn, J. J. (2003). Violence prevention: An evaluation of program effects with urban African American students. *Journal of Primary Prevention, 24*, 43–62.

Mercy, J. A., & Potter, L. B. (1996). Combining analysis and action to solve the problem of youth violence. *American Journal of Preventive Medicine, 12* (suppl.), 1–2.

Mercy, J. A., Rosenberg, M. L., Powell, K. E., Broome, C. V., & Roper, W. L. (1993, Winter). Public health policy for preventing violence. *Health Affairs*, 7–29.

Metropolitan Area Child Study Research Group (2002). A cognitive-ecological approach to preventing aggression in urban settings: Initial outcomes for high risk children. *Journal of Consulting and Clinical Psychology, 70*, 179–194.

Meyer, A. L., & Farrell, A. D. (1998). Social skills training to promote resilience and reduce violence in African American middle school students. *Education and Treatment of Children, 21*, 461–488.

Meyer, A. L., Farrell, A D., Northup, W., Kung, E. M., & Plybon, L. (2000). *Promoting nonviolence in early adolescence: Responding in Peaceful and Positive Ways*. New York: Kluwer.

Mihalic, S., Irwin, K., Elliott, D., Fagan, A., & Hansen, D. (2001, July). *Blueprints for violence prevention* (Juvenile Justice Bulletin). Washington, DC: U.S. Department of Justice.

Mrazek, P. J., & Haggerty, R. J. (Eds.). (1994). *Reducing risks for mental disorders: Frontiers for preventive intervention research*. Washington, DC: National Academy Press.

The Multi-Site Violence Prevention Project. (2004). The Multi-Site Violence Prevention Project: Background and overview. *American Journal of Preventive Medicine, 26*(1S), 3–11.

Nation, M., Crusto, C., Kumpfer, K., Wandersman, A., Seybolt, D., Morrissey-Kane, E., et al. (2003). What works in prevention: The characteristics of effective prevention programs. *American Psychologist, 58*, 449–456.

O'Donnell, L., Stueve, A., San Doval, A., Duran, R., Haber, D., Atnafou, R., et al. (1999).

Violence prevention and young adolescents' participation in community youth service. *American Journal of Public Health*, 89, 176–181.

Olds, D. L., Henderson, C. R., Cole, R., Eckenrode, J., Kitzman, H., Luckey, D., et al. (1998). Long-term effects of nurse home visitation on children's criminal and antisocial behavior: 15 year follow-up of a randomized control trial. *Journal of the American Medical Association*, 280, 1238–1244.

Ollendick, T. H. (1996). Violence in youth: Where do we go from here? Behavior therapy's response. *Behavior Therapy*, 27, 485–514.

Olweus, D. (1994). Annotation: Bullying at school: Basic facts and effects of a school-based intervention program. *Journal of Child Psychology and Psychiatry*, 35, 1171–1190.

Orpinas, P. K., Basen-Engquist, K., Grunbaum, J. A., & Parcel, G. S. (1995). The comorbidity of violence-related behaviors with health-risk behaviors in a population of high school students. *Adolescent Health*, 16, 216–225.

Osofsky, J. D., Rovaris, M., Hammer, J. H., Dickson, A., Freeman, N., & Aucoin, K. (2004). Working with police to help children exposed to violence. *Journal of Community Psychology*, 32, 593–606.

Pardini, D. A., Lochman, J. E., & Frick P. J. (2003). Callous/unemotional traits and social-cognitive processes in adjudicated youths. *Journal of the American Academy of Child and Adolescent Psychiatry*, 42, 364–371.

Paul, G. L. (1969). Behavior modification research: Design and tactics. In C. M. Franks (Ed.), *Behavior therapy: Appraisal and status* (pp. 29–62). New York: McGraw-Hill.

Pentz, M. A. (2004). Form follows function: Designs for prevention effectiveness and diffusion research. *Prevention Science*, 5, 23–29.

Pepler, D. J., & Slaby, R. G. (1994). Theoretical and developmental perspectives on youth and violence. In L. D. Eron, J. H. Gentry, & P. Schlegel (Eds.), *Reason to hope: A psychosocial perspective on violence and youth* (pp. 27–58). Washington, DC: American Psychological Association.

Peters, R. D., Petrunka, K., & Arnold, R. (2003). The Better Beginnings, Better Futures Project: A universal, comprehensive, community-based prevention approach for primary school children and their families. *Journal of Clinical Child and Adolescent Psychology*, 32(2), 215–227.

Peterson, J. L., & Newman, R. (2000). Helping to curb youth violence: The APA-MTV "Warning Signs" initiative. *Professional Psychology: Research and Practice*, 31, 509–514.

Prinz, R. (2000). Research-based prevention of school violence and youth antisocial behavior: A developmental and educational perspective. *National Institute of Justice Research Forum* (NCJ 180972), 23–36.

Reid, M. J., Webster-Stratton, C., & Baydar, N. (2004). Halting the development of conduct problems in Head Start children: The effects of parent training. *Journal of Clinical Child and Adolescent Psychology*, 33, 279–291.

Rudolph, K. D., & Heller, T. L. (1997). Interpersonal problem solving, externalizing behavior, and social competence in preschoolers: A knowledge-performance discrepancy? *Journal of Applied Developmental Psychology*, 18, 107–118.

Samples, F., & Aber, L. (1998). Evaluations of school-based violence prevention programs. In D. Elliott, B. Hamburg, & K. Williams (Eds.), *Violence in American schools* (pp. 217–252). New York: Cambridge University Press.

Sampson, R. J. (2002). Transcending tradition: new directions in community research, Chicago style. *Criminology*, 40, 13–230.

Sarason, I. G., & Ganzer, V. (1973). Modeling and group discussion in the rehabilitation of juvenile delinquents. *Journal of Counseling Psychology*, 20, 442–449.

Scaramella, L. V., Conger, R. D., Spoth, R., & Simons, R. L. (2002). Evaluation of a social contextual model of delinquency: A cross-study replication. *Child Development*, 73, 175–195.

Serketich, W. J., & Dumas, J. E. (1996). The effectiveness of behavioral parent training to modify antisocial behavior in children: A meta-analysis. *Behavior Therapy*, 27, 17 1–186.

Skroban, S., Gottfredson, D., & Gottfredson, G. (1999). A school-based social competency promotion demonstration. *Evaluation Review*, 23, 3–27.

Thornton, T. N., Craft, C. A., Dahlberg, L. L., Lynch, B. S., & Baer, K. (2000). *Best practices of youth violence prevention: A sourcebook for community action*. Atlanta: Centers for Disease Control and Prevention, National Center for Injury Prevention and Control.

Tolan, P., & Gorman-Smith, D. (2002). What violence prevention research can tell us about developmental psychopathology. *Development and Psychopathology*, 14, 713–729.

Tolan, P., & Guerra, N. (1994). *What works in reducing adolescent violence: An empirical review of the field*. Boulder, CO: The Center for the Study and Prevention of Violence.

Tolan, P. H., Guerra, N. G., & Kendall, P. (1995). A developmental-ecological perspective on antisocial behavior in children and adolescents: Toward a unified risk and intervention framework. *Journal of Consulting and Clinical Psychology, 63*, 579–584.

U.S. Department of Health and Human Services. (2000). *Healthy people 2010: Understanding and improving health*. Washington, DC: U.S. Government Printing Office.

U.S. Department of Health and Human Services (2001). *Youth violence: A report of the Surgeon General*. Washington, DC: U.S. Department of Justice.

Weissberg, R. P., Kumpfer, K. L., & Seligman, M. E. P. (2003). Prevention that works for children and youth. *American Psychologist, 58*, 425–432.

Wilson, S. J., Lipsey, M. W., & Derzon, J. H. (2003). The effects of school-based intervention programs on aggressive behavior: A meta-analysis. *Journal of Consulting and Clinical Psychology, 71*, 136–149.

Yung, B. R., & Hammond, W. R. (1998). Breaking the cycle: A culturally sensitive violence prevention program for African American children and adolescents. In J. Lutzker (Ed.), *Handbook of child abuse research and treatment* (pp. 319–340). New York: Plenum.

Zelli, A. Dodge, K. A., Lochman, J. E., Laird, R. D., & Conduct Problems Prevention Research Group (1999). The distinction between beliefs legitimizing aggression and deviant processing of social cues: Testing measurement validity and the hypothesis that biased processing mediates the effects of beliefs on aggression. *Journal of Personality and Social Psychology, 77*, 150–166.

CHAPTER 41

New Directions in Research on Violence: Bridging Science, Practice, and Policy

*Daniel J. Flannery, Alexander T. Vazsonyi,
and Irwin D. Waldman*

This volume on violent behavior addresses multiple issues from a variety of perspectives and disciplines. The chapters clearly illustrate that violence is a complex behavior and phenomenon that demands a multifaceted approach not only to understanding it but also to prevention, intervention, and policy. Understanding violence means that we know how to define violent behavior and the theoretical underpinnings of why and how it occurs. Several chapters address theoretical models of violent behavior, and others address potential causal mechanisms of violent behavior. Those causal mechanisms range from personality and biological factors to interpersonal influences to sociocultural influences. The treatment of violent behavior was not a focal point of this volume; rather most chapters address the etiology, developmental course, related risk factors, and impact of violence (as victim or perpetrator) on behavior and mental health.

It is noteworthy that a number of authors also discuss theory and research related to aggression. This makes sense because many theories and etiological approaches to violence consider aggressive behavior to be a developmental precursor to violent behavior. Because so many authors felt the need to include a discussion of aggression in their chapter, or in fact focused on aggressive behavior, we ended up adding the word "Aggression" to the title of the *Handbook*. As many chapters illustrate, even though the focus of the handbook is on violent behavior it remains essential to recognize the important role of aggression in any consideration of violence or violent behavior. Last, although this volume covers many topics related to aggression and aggressive behavior, there is also much research on aggression that is not covered here.

Despite the different disciplines and perspectives represented in this volume, it is reassuring that many consistent themes emerged throughout the chapters. There is simply no way to capture all of the important topics covered, but several core ideas and themes stand out for us regarding the current state of scholarship on violent behavior:

1. How one defines violence has significant implications across all other domains, including theory, prevention, intervention,

and policy. Violence occurs at many levels (e.g., individual, family and peers, community, cultural systems, and across nations). Defining the outcome clearly is the first step to effective prevention and intervention. We need a shared understanding of what constitutes violence and violent behavior across these levels, political ideologies, and over time. There are important distinctions being made between violence that is self-directed versus interpersonal violence and collective or cultural violence.

2. Violent behavior must be understood as a lifelong, developmental phenomenon. For most individuals, violence appears to be a learned behavior – depending on the theoretical orientation, one that is either taught or one that is prevented through teaching and socialization processes. For the most violent individuals, conversely, behavior-genetic studies indicate a substantial heritability of violence and violent crime. But most of us, from a very early age, are socialized how to handle our emotions, how to self-regulate, and how to interact and problem solve (resolve conflicts) with others. These social experiences interact with our physical makeup, our brain development, and our personalities to determine who we are and how we will act as we mature. Barring significant physical injury, environmental insult, or emotional upset, most individuals do not suddenly become violent. Typically, aggression precedes violence, and for those most at risk of becoming violent, aggressive behavior will gradually increase in severity and complexity over time without appropriate intervention.

3. The next great frontier of research on understanding the causes and consequences of violence appears to be in functional brain mapping and molecular genetic studies of the role of genes on the expression of behaviors and traits related to violence, such as temperament, impulse control, and aggression. Studies of brain structure and function have provided significant insight into how environmental exposures, insults, and influences affect brain development and into the neurochemistry and neurocircuitry of the brain, which affect behavior, emotions, and self-regulation. For example, neurochemical markers in the brain have helped us identify different types of violence, differentiate among developmental pathways to aggression and violence, and further clarify risk assessment. However, predicting who will act in a violent way is still a very shaky venture, given all of the complicating factors that come into play, and we still have more false positives than false negatives. We will probably never reach completely accurate prediction of such a complex phenomena, but we can get better at identifying those most at risk (for perpetration and victimization) and those most amenable to treatment and rehabilitation.

4. Violence is a problem across different ethnic and racial groups, across cultures, and across nations. More cross-cultural and cross-national comparative research is needed to further understand how best to prevent violence and intervene successfully in particular groups or regions of the world. There is new evidence of past and of ongoing genocides caused by perceived differences in appearance, history, or beliefs. Terrorist acts also occur at times because of perceived differences among groups. At the same time, it is clear that we must differentiate ritualized acts of violence between groups, on a large scale, from acts of violence committed by individuals.

5. Of recent concern is the increased rate of violence perpetration and victimization among females. Historically, most of the long-term developmental studies of etiology and trajectory have been conducted on males, but this is beginning to change. Because of this emphasis, most current preventive-intervention programs are based on what we know about aggression and violence among males. Findings from prevention science inform us, however, that some programs that are effective for one gender are not as effective for the other. Therefore, we need to continue to pay attention to gender differences in the etiology of violence and its prevention and effective treatment.

6. Rates of witnessing violence and victimization are high, even among nonclinical

community samples. Do these high rates reflect increasing levels of exposure to violence or just an increasing awareness of the problem? Probably a little bit of both. Young people are exposed more immediately and more intensely to all forms of violence in their communities via the media, the Internet, and the various forms of entertainment marketed to young people. We do not yet know the full effect of this more immediate, intense, and frequent exposure on brain development, socialization, self-regulation, and mental health. What we do know is that young people in community samples report very high rates of exposure to violence and comorbid mental health issues, such as post-traumatic stress disorder symptoms. Studies of juvenile violent offenders also report high rates of comorbid substance use and mental health problems, such as anxiety, depression, anger, and suicidal ideation. The effects of chronic exposure to violence in community settings on physiology, overall physical health, and well-being are not yet fully understood.

7. Violence prevention and intervention will advance only if we continue to emphasize the use of science-based principles and practices. These principles and practices should be regularly informed by current science and new, emerging methodologies and technologies. The field cannot wait several years to learn about new thinking and new findings. Applied community-based evaluation studies that provide immediate feedback for practice and policy should complement more rigorous, long-term efforts that examine violent behavior.

8. To understand violence, both qualitative and quantitative methods are valuable and need to be used in an integrative fashion. Quantitative methods can provide us with systematic, reliable information about violent behavior that can be compared across samples and over time and be compared to other behavior due to standardization. On the other hand, qualitative methods provide a richness of observation and explanation that quantitative data and numbers just cannot represent. Observations, individual stories (narratives), and emotional experience

are what give the numbers meaning and substance.

9. Longitudinal studies are critical to our understanding of violence. Knowing about developmental trajectories can inform prevention, early identification, critical periods, and appropriate treatment modalities. We won't know what is psychopathological unless we first understand what is normative and expectable at any given age or developmental stage.

In addition to the issues mentioned above, several integrative themes emerged across several of the authors' chapters, particularly in the context of directions for future research on violence. These integrative themes include the following:

1. A focus on gene-environment interactions as they contribute to aggression and violence: This issue arose in the context of both animal studies (e.g., in mice) and in human studies of aggression, violence, and other antisocial behaviors in children, adolescents, and adults. There has been a strong resurgence in researchers' interest in gene-environment interactions of late throughout the fields of psychiatric genetics and developmental psychopathology, in large part because of the studies published by Caspi, Moffitt, and their colleagues in *Science* in 2002 and 2003 (cited in various chapters herein). Nonetheless, it is important to acknowledge that studies of aggression in mice suggest that gene- gene interactions (i.e., epistasis) may be just as important and that many issues remain to be settled in gaining a comprehensive understanding of gene-environment interactions for aggression and violence in humans. These issues include the form and replicability of such interactions, the specific biological and psychological mechanisms that underlie them, and the extent to which they pertain equivalently or to different degrees to aggression, violence, and other forms of antisocial behavior. It also is worth noting that gene-environment interactions are only one important source of heterogeneity that is germane for understanding the etiology and development of violence

and aggression. These investigations may be especially pertinent, given that recent meta-analyses suggest that aggression, violence, and other forms of antisocial behavior represent particularly sensitive phenotypes in terms of differences in their etiology across different situations and environmental contexts.

2. A focus on gender differences in violence and aggression: Several authors suggested that there are important gender differences not only in the manifestation of violence and aggression but they also raised the possibility of different developmental trajectories and etiologies for males and females. Included within this suggestion is the notion that at least some of the mechanisms underlying aggression and violence might also differ by gender. As such, gender differences in violence and aggression may represent an issue that bears more than a passing similarity to gene-environment interactions and may be studied in a similar manner using similar study designs.

3. Role of shared or familial environmental influences and socialization effects on violence and aggression: Hypotheses on these effects are suitable for testing in rigorous behavior-genetic designs (e.g., twin and adoption studies) in which the nature of the parent-offspring transmission or sibling influences can truly be distinguished rather than presumed. Fortunately, there is a growing convergence between (a) studies of substantive topics, theories, and methodological approaches that historically reside within the sociological tradition and (b) sophisticated behavior-genetic designs and analyses that permit such shared or familial influences and socialization effects to be properly disentangled from genetic influences. Genetic effects often represent an alternative explanation for observed relations among family members for relevant variables. We predict that there will be greater collaboration among investigators from such disparate research traditions in future research on the etiology and development of aggression and violence.

4. Underlying mechanisms important to the etiology of violence and aggression across disparate theoretical approaches: As one example, authors from several perspectives emphasized the importance of responses to perceived threat to the self as a mechanism underlying the development of aggression and violence. These multiple theoretical perspectives included structural models of personality and its emphasis on the trait of Alienation, a social information-processing perspective and its emphasis on hostile attributional biases, and psychophysiological approaches that have found that relations between trait hostility/aggressiveness and cardiovascular functioning appear only to be present or strong in the presence of interpersonal threats. Such an emphasis on a particular psychological trait or cognitive/neuropsychological mechanism across disparate theoretical perspectives underscores the potential importance of that variable to the etiology of aggression and violence.

5. The reciprocal relation between brain regions and circuits thought to be important to aggression and violence and the selection of candidate genes and environments important to etiology: On the one hand, hypotheses suggesting or empirical findings demonstrating that certain brain regions or aspects of nervous system functioning are related to aggression and violence further suggest that the genes and/or environments that underlie such functions are good candidates for involvement in the etiology of aggression and violence. On the other hand, several researchers have emphasized the importance of endophenotypes for finding genes and/or environments that underlie aggression and violence and for better understanding their effects. Endophenotypes refer to biological, neurological, or psychological constructs that are thought to underlie traits (e.g., violence or aggression) or disorders (e.g., Conduct Disorder or Antisocial Personality Disorder) and to be influenced more directly by the relevant genes than are the manifest symptoms of the disorder or trait. As such, they are considered closer to the immediate products of such genes (i.e., the proteins they code for) and are thought to be influenced more strongly

and directly by the genes that underlie them than the manifest trait or symptoms of disorder that they in turn undergird. Endophenotypes also are thought to be "genetically simpler" in their etiology than are complex traits, such as manifest disorders or their symptom dimensions, suggesting that the underlying structure of genetic influences on endophenotypes is simpler than that of complex disorders and traits in that there are fewer individual genes (or sets thereof) that contribute to their etiology. Several authors emphasized the importance of endophenotypes that reflect cognitive, psychophysiological, or neurological function in increasing our understanding of the etiology of aggression and violence in future research.

Subject Index

Author Index is available for downloading at www.cambridge.org/9780521845670.